The **Rough Guide** to the

Pacific Northwest

written and researched by

JD Dickey, Tim Jepson, and Philip C Lee

NEW YORK • LONDON • DELHI

www.roughguides.com

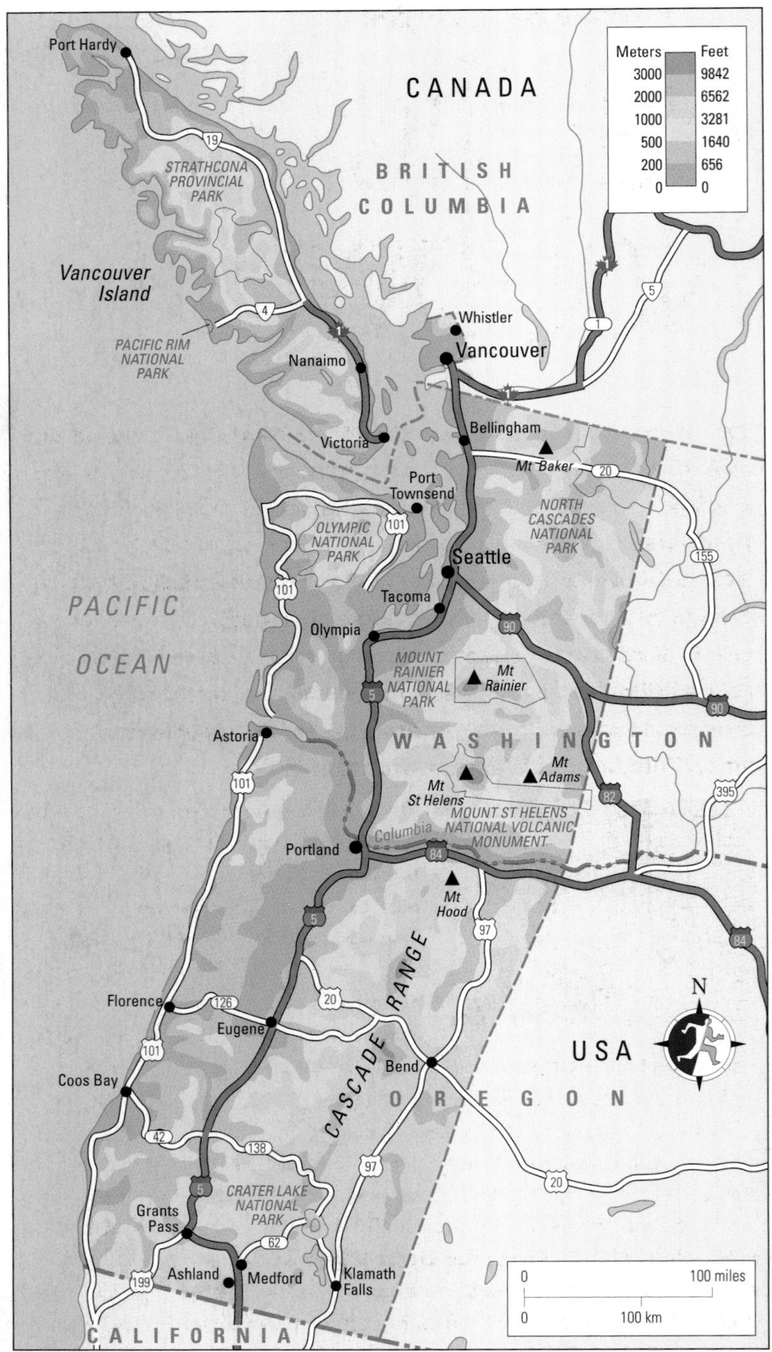
Meters
Feet
3000
9842
2000
6562
1000
3281
500
1640
200
656
0
0
CANADA
BRITISH COLUMBIA
Port Hardy
STRATHCONA PROVINCIAL PARK
Vancouver Island
PACIFIC RIM NATIONAL PARK
Nanaimo
Victoria
Whistler
Vancouver
Bellingham
Mt Baker
NORTH CASCADES NATIONAL PARK
Port Townsend
OLYMPIC NATIONAL PARK
Seattle
Tacoma
Olympia
PACIFIC OCEAN
MOUNT RAINIER NATIONAL PARK
Mt Rainier
WASHINGTON
Astoria
Mt St Helens
Mt Adams
MOUNT ST HELENS NATIONAL VOLCANIC MONUMENT
Columbia
Portland
Mt Hood
CASCADE RANGE
Florence
Eugene
Bend
Coos Bay
USA
OREGON
CRATER LAKE NATIONAL PARK
Grants Pass
Ashland
Medford
Klamath Falls
CALIFORNIA
N
0
100 miles
0
100 km
19
4
1
5
20
101
155
90
82
395
84
97
126
42
138
62
199

Introduction to the

Pacific Northwest

The stunningly verdant terrain of the Pacific Northwest is one of North America's scenic gems, a highly varied realm of striking forests, beaches, and mountains, where the outdoors in all its rugged glory is always close at hand. Nestled between the Pacific Ocean and a lengthy spine of craggy peaks, the region's isolated geography preserves within it abundant fauna and flora – from wolves to whales and wildflowers to Western hemlocks – and a formidable landscape of active volcanoes, sheer cliffs, towering waterfalls, and untouched wilderness.

It's also a place of historical riches, from Native American and pioneer heritage and legend, to elegantly preserved Victorian buildings and abandoned military forts. Beyond the compelling displays of nature and history, though, the region hums with contemporary activity, with excellent seafood and Northwest cuisine, state-of-the-art museums, and some of the continent's most urbane and civilized cities and charming small towns.

Up until the turn of the twentieth century, the Pacific Northwest was really the **Last Frontier**, a very distant land accessible to the wealthy by steamer, but for most people reachable only over a network of stark, rutted wagon trails. Most of these trails were carved in the middle of the nineteenth century during the **Great Migration**, the massive exodus of farmers and prospective settlers from the Midwest to the edge of the continent – an unprecedented immigration encouraged by the promise

Fact file

- Seattle is the 24th largest city in the US and Portland the 28th, while Vancouver is the third biggest in Canada. All three cities have 530–570,000 people in their city limits, though the metro regions of Seattle and Vancouver are about twice as large as that of Portland.
- Ethnically, Oregon and Washington are about 80 percent Anglo, 12 percent Latino, 4–5 percent Asian, 2–3 percent black, and less than 2 percent Native American. British Columbia is 78 percent Anglo, but 15 percent Asian, and 4 percent Native American.
- Mount Rainier is the region's tallest, at 14,411 feet; Crater Lake is the deepest in North America, at 1932 feet at its lowest point; and the Columbia River, at 1214 miles, is the second longest in the Western Hemisphere, flowing into the Pacific Ocean.
- The name Oregon was derived either from the French word for hurricane, *ouragan*, or from a cartographical error. Although Vancouver is now only rarely referred to as Terminal City, Seattle is widely known as the Emerald City, and Portland is variously called the Rose City, PDX, or Stumptown.
- Vancouver hosted the World's Fair in 1986, while Seattle did so in 1962, calling it the "Century 21 Exposition."
- Quillayute, Washington, is the rainiest place in the Pacific Northwest, getting 105 inches per year on the coast of Olympic National Park. Oregon's leader, Astoria, is a distant second, receiving 66 inches at the mouth of the Columbia River.

of cheap land, good soil, and a fresh start. Since those hallowed days – partly enshrined in myth, but partly genuine – the region has grown in fits and starts, boosted by a gold rush here or bountiful fishing there, but all too susceptible to the boom-and-bust cycles of resource-based economies: by decimating the fisheries, clear-cutting the timber, or scouring the gold, eventually the natural supply disappears – and disappear it has on several occasions. **Seattle**, Washington, is in many ways emblematic of the Northwest's continuing cycle of **economic rise and fall**: starting as a mill town, the city burgeoned as a trading post for the Alaska Gold Rush, hit an economic downturn before being revived by the defense industries of World War II, declined in the 1970s before exploding as a high-tech center in the 1990s – only to crash again when the technology bubble burst. The same pattern is true for **Portland**, Oregon, and, to an even greater degree, the smaller towns that sit at the edge of forests, rivers, or the ocean.

Just over the border, the cosmopolitan city of **Vancouver** and **Vancouver Island** in British Columbia have charted their own, somewhat different course, still dependent in part on the resource economy, but also branching out to embrace Asia in a way that Anglo-dominated Washington and Oregon could only dream of. By opening its doors to myriad immigrants from Hong Kong and other cities in China and elsewhere, Vancouver has truly become an international cultural city, with tolerant liberal social policies that draw more than a few Americans up here for work, or exile. The two Pacific Northwest US states of Washington and Oregon are visually similar in some ways to British Columbia – boasting stately forests, striking parks, and shorelines, and well-designed cities – but differ in their attitudes toward **change** and **development**. With the notable exception of Seattle, the major cities and towns of **Washington** are more relaxed and unassuming, from pleasant mountain hamlets like Winthrop to quirky burgs like Oysterville. The more conservative of the two states, Washington heartily embraces the defense establishment, resulting in a slew of military bases and defense contractors such as

Volcanoes

The Cascades comprise the only active **volcano chain** in the contiguous United States, and run from southern British Columbia to Northern California, but are most visible as the mountainous spine that crosses central Oregon and Washington. Although the geologic history of these mountains is impressive enough (see box, p.217), what really grabs you about traveling through this alpine landscape is what a varied terrain it is – though one continually shaped and violently rearranged by geothermal and climatic forces. Encompassing chilly lava-tube caves, great expanses of rocky basalt, majestic icy summits, assorted hot springs and waterfalls, cinder-cone buttes, blown-out craters, and huge hills of black volcanic glass, the Cascades provide vivid testimony to the power of the earth's dynamic forces. There are countless opportunities to go wandering through this volcanic land as well, whether trekking through it on skis or a snowboard, plunging down its river canyons on a kayak, using crampons to climb up glaciers, or simply hiking around in a sturdy pair of boots. For some journeys you may need a detailed forest map, especially if exploring an official wilderness area, but for most trips the major highways should suffice. In fact, just off the road you may find some of the region's best settings, paths, and views of this scenic topography, without having to resort to an endless slog through the outback.

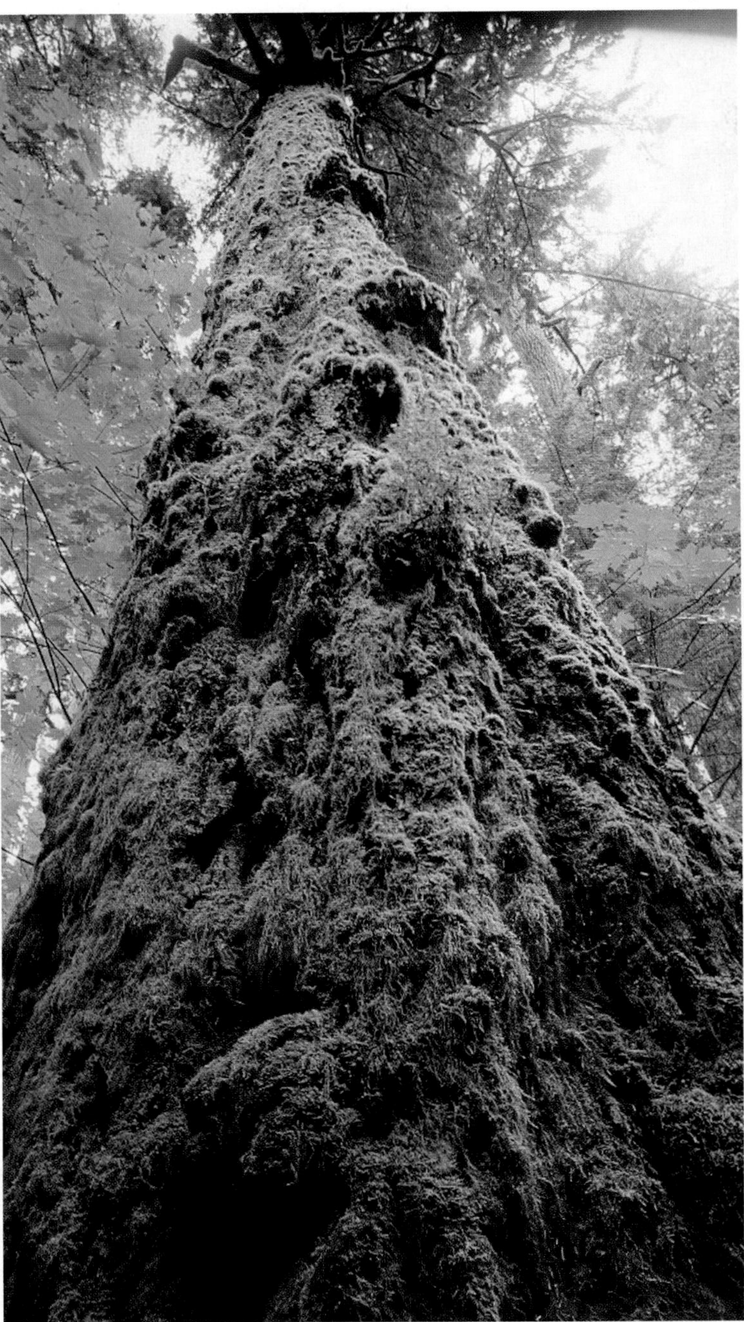

△ Western hemlock

Boeing, and has few concerns about business development and "progress" as the proper ways to advance civic goals. In these ways and others, **Oregon** couldn't be more different. Perhaps the most proudly provincial place in the country, the state is well-known for its hostile attitudes toward unencumbered development and paving over the past to ensure future profits. For that, it has suffered economically, with major corporations pulling up stakes left and right, but this small-town attitude – fairly unusual in modern America – has also helped it preserve its heritage, as well as countless parks and natural reserves.

△ Hood River

Where to go

Of the Pacific Northwest's three major cities, **Vancouver** in British Columbia is by far the most cosmopolitan, sitting in a beautiful mountain-and-seafront setting that provides countless opportunities for adventures from skiing and hiking to sailing and kayaking, as well as world-class theater and plenty of good bars and clubs. In its own range of outdoor pursuits, **Seattle**, as frenetic and freewheeling a place as you're likely to find on the West Coast outside California, is also packed with scenic hills and winding streets, with an appealing array of public artworks and outdoor markets. South in Oregon, straddling the Willamette River, **Portland** is the region's third major city – with no intention of getting bigger – but still boasting excellent bars, clubs, and restaurants, and featuring some of the best parks, gardens, and wilderness you'll find in any urban area. Portland is a national leader in that elusive element known as "**quality of life**," wherein providing clean air, preserving rustic parks, and promoting slow growth get more attention than building casinos, freeways, and gated communities. Of the Northwest's smaller cities, **Victoria**, on Vancouver Island, offers an ersatz taste of Merry Olde England and some of the region's best museums, while Washington's second city of **Tacoma** is an increasingly popular spot for viewing contemporary art and historic preservation.

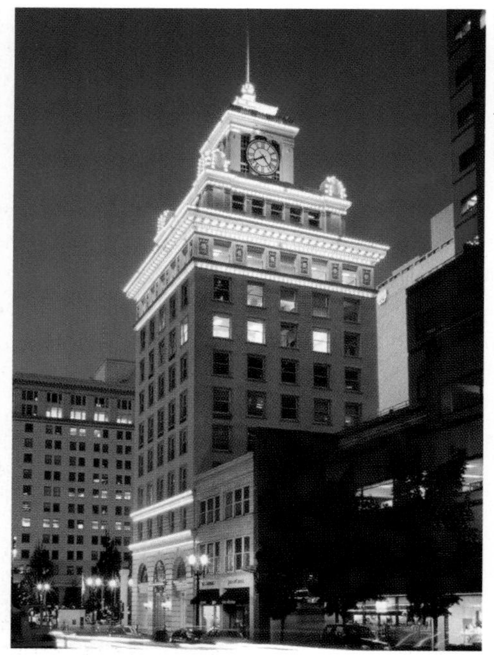
▽ Jackson Tower, Portland

Beyond these cities, though, there can be no mistaking the Pacific Northwest's real attraction: its eye-popping array of gorgeous **land and seascapes**, brimming with majestic peaks that soar over wooded valleys, expansive glaciers resting on the sides of volcanoes, stark lava fields and craters, thundering whitewater rivers, colossal sand dunes, brightly colored fossil beds, sun-dappled rainforests, and serpentine beaches peppered with giant rocky seastacks. Much of this remains **wild**, empty, and fairly untouched by modern hands, yet at the same time rendered accessible by a network of superbly run national, state, and provincial parks.

A trip through the Northwest is best organized by topography, starting east of Portland with the massive, geological oddity of the **Columbia River Gorge**, where historic roads pass by high waterfalls, charming burgs like Hood River, great imposing structures such as the Bonneville Dam, and some of the best windsurfing spots in the country. West of Portland, the beautiful **Oregon Coast** is a well-protected strip of beaches, sand dunes, and rocky cliffs punctuated by excellent state parks and hiking trails, and a few interesting towns like the old redoubt of Astoria and the pleasant port and aquarium of Newport. South of Portland, I-5 leads you through the **Willamette and Rogue River valleys**, which preserve much of Oregon's trailblazing history in state park designation and management, pioneer and religious enclaves, and old-time country lanes and covered bridges. In the Willamette Valley, the state capital of Salem is mildly interesting for its museums and architecture, but less enticing than the thumping college town of Eugene and its funky bars and clubs and a few good eateries as well. The Rogue River Valley is mainly worthwhile for the historic preserve of Jacksonville and the Shakespeare center of Ashland. Due east of the valleys, the great volcanic spine of the **Oregon Cascades** holds some of the region's most dramatic landscapes, good for exploring craggy peaks and lava fields, or hidden caves and hot springs, on winding mountain drives past blooming wildflowers, looming glaciers, and glittering lakes and rivers. The area's scenic focal point, however, is the dazzling blue oasis of **Crater Lake**, the nation's deepest, occupying the bowl of an ancient volcano, while the mid-sized towns of Bend and Klamath Falls are good bases for trips into the great outdoors.

Great cruises

To access many parts of the Pacific Northwest, you may need to ride a **ferry**, either traveling on foot or with a bike, or hauling your car along as well. Luckily, this is one of the best ways really to experience the region in all its glittering natural beauty, as you cruise past rocky beaches, sea cliffs, forested hills, and charming little ports. Traveling from Vancouver to Vancouver Island is the most obvious reason to hop on a ferry – and crossing the striking Georgia Strait is an appealing trip by itself – but you can also get to the island from various points around Washington, including towns such as Port Angeles, Seattle, and Friday Harbor. The islands off Puget Sound are also accessible by scenic ferry rides (see p.320), and, in Oregon, you can still cross the winding Willamette River at three points between Portland and Salem. The most appealing of these is at Willamette Mission State Park, where a little car ferry can help you float over the river in the same way that covered wagons or stagecoaches might have done in the nineteenth century.

▽ John Day Fossil Beds

Washington's landscapes are a bit less varied than Oregon's, though no less appealing. Branching out from the Emerald City, **Puget Sound** is for many the recreational focus of the state, a huge inlet bounded by engaging cities such as Bellingham and Olympia at either end, but best for its collection of sparkling islands and fetching waterside scenery, where hamlets like Port Gamble preserve the splendor of the past while bastions like Fort Ebey and the American and English camps are historically evocative treasures. Indeed, for many visitors, the highlight of the Sound is a trip to the **San Juan Islands**, isolated locales of rustic beauty and small-town quaintness on the ferry route to Canada. Continuing west from Puget Sound, the **Olympic Peninsula** is notable for the nineteenth-century Victoriana of Port Townsend and the native culture of Neah Bay, but is most importantly the site of the huge **Olympic National Park**, an eclectic wonderland of glacial peaks, winding trails, temperate rainforests, towering ridges, and remote beaches, crowned by the dramatic presence of **Mount Olympus** in the center. South of the peninsula, Southwest Washington has few sights except for the rugged headlands of Cape Disappointment State Park and the historical site of Fort Vancouver. East from here, the **Washington Cascades** stretch north-south along the center of the state, separating its wet western half from its drier eastern counterpart. The explosive giant of **Mount St Helens** is the most famous member of this lengthy mountain range, but other major peaks include scenic **Mount Rainier** – the tallest of the Cascades – and the winter playground of **Mount Baker**. The best driving concourse in these mountains, and perhaps in the entire region, is the massive circuit of the **Cascade Loop**, which navigates the high slopes of North Cascades National Park and passes such compelling sights as the thin finger of Lake

Chelan and oddball theme towns encompassing the Wild West of Winthop and the Bavaria of Leavenworth.

Finally, north of the border, across the Georgia Strait from Vancouver, lies Vancouver Island, whose major city is Victoria. The island's real highlights, though, are the rich mountain landscapes of **Strathcona Provincial Park**, the tremendous seascapes of **Pacific Rim National Park**, and the snowcapped peaks, rippling hillsides, and eye-catching coastline.

Scenic drives

In visiting the Pacific Northwest, you may find the best way of experiencing the region is to take a **scenic drive** on any of several unmissable routes. In southern British Columbia, the main choice is Highway 19 (see p.505) on the eastern side of Vancouver Island, but Washington has several compelling choices. The most prominent of these is the huge Cascade Loop (see p.378) through the north-central part of the state, a 350-mile circuit leading over mountain slopes and valleys and past quirky small towns and attractive waterfalls. Also worthwhile is the section of US-101 around Olympic National Park (see p.361), bringing you close to the park's various beaches, rainforests, canyons, and mountain peaks. The section of this highway in Oregon is perhaps even better, lining the Oregon Coast and its eye-catching ports, beaches, sand dunes, and lighthouses – most of them linked by an interconnected string of state parks. The most well-known of the state's various scenic drives, though, is the Historic Columbia River Highway (see p.123), an early auto route from the 1910s that leads past some of the gorge's most stunning scenery – waterfalls, rocky cliffs, and wildflower meadows – and has been converted in some places to a hiking and biking zone. Finally, Oregon's main section of the Cascades has many excellent drives, the finest of which may be the seasonally open Highway 242 (see p.239), which passes volcanic peaks, beautiful alpine lakes, and a massive lava field crowned by a jagged stone observatory.

When to go

Although wary attitudes toward the larger world are most apparent in Oregon, they're not absent from the rest of the region, either. One handy way of keeping out interlopers, and thereby managing growth, is to encourage the most exaggerated stories of the area's overcast **weather** and **rainy spells**. Instead of downplaying the wet weather – or mentioning that the region is far from a national precipitation leader, and it's only in **winter** that storms are constant – Northwesterners enjoy frightening outsiders by tales of gale-force winds, unending weeks of rain, permanently gloomy skies, and occasional bouts of punishing hail and snow. Of course, you can get quite drenched here from November to March, but the **summers** are typically lovely and free of storm clouds, and most residents have long since learned to deal with the elements by bundling up and wearing stocking caps – umbrellas are a rare sight, held only by newcomers and tourists. Keep in mind that during the **spring** and **fall**, the weather can get quite **erratic**, and no one day may be purely sunny, rainy, or windy – indeed, sometimes the climate can turn from chilly and rainy to bright and sunny within a single hour or less. It's not unheard of, either, to go sunbathing just a short time after it's been hailing. While such fickle weather drives some visitors to distraction (particularly in dressing properly), many locals consider it a quirky hallmark of the region, just one more way the Pacific Northwest has its own identity separate from the rest of America and Canada.

In planning your trip, keep in mind that **midsummer** may be the most crowded time of the year, but it's also undeniably the most enjoyable, both for the good weather and the numerous festivals in the large and small towns. **Accommodation** can get scarce, especially on the Oregon Coast and the Puget Sound islands, but with enough advance planning you should be fine. If you want a bit more elbow room, **May**, **June**, and **September** are all recommended, although the weather won't be quite as warm, or as dry. Outside these parameters, you risk getting caught in one of the region's wet spells – though even in **winter** there's still plenty going on to keep you occupied, especially throughout the Cascades, where the ski resorts and lodges are a huge draw. With this in mind, you should reserve well in advance.

Average temperatures and rainfall

	Jan	Feb	Mar	Apr	May	Jun	Jul	Aug	Sep	Oct	Nov	Dec
Portland												
Av High °F	46	50	56	61	67	73	79	79	74	63	51	46
Av Low °F	37	39	41	44	49	53	57	58	55	48	42	37
Rainfall (in)	6.2	5.0	4.5	3.1	2.5	1.6	0.7	1.0	1.9	3.4	6.4	6.8
Seattle												
Av High °F	46	50	53	58	64	70	75	76	70	60	51	46
Av Low °F	36	37	39	42	47	52	55	56	52	46	40	36
Rainfall (in)	5.1	4.1	3.8	2.6	1.8	1.5	0.8	1.0	1.6	3.2	5.9	5.6
Vancouver												
Av High °F	42	47	50	56	61	67	69	69	66	57	48	42
Av Low °F	33	35	39	42	49	54	57	57	52	45	39	34
Rainfall (in)	5.7	4.8	4.0	2.7	2.2	1.9	1.2	1.46	2.3	4.6	6.1	6.8

To convert Fahrenheit to Celsius (°C), subtract 32 and multiply by 5/9.

To convert inches to millimeters (mm), multiply by 25.4

28 things not to miss

It's not possible to see everything that the Pacific Northwest has to offer in one trip – and we don't suggest you try. What follows is a selective taste of the region's highlights: hip cafés, breathtaking outdoor scenery, charming towns, enchanting festivals, and more. They're arranged in five color-coded categories, which you can browse through to find the very best to see and experience. All highlights have a page reference to take you straight into the Guide, where you can find out more.

01 **Oregon beaches** Page **170** • Beautiful, interconnected strips of sandy beaches and dunes, rocky shores, and basalt cliffs that can be crossed by bicycle or on foot (as well as Highway 101), and which have been almost completely preserved as state parks and wildlife refuges.

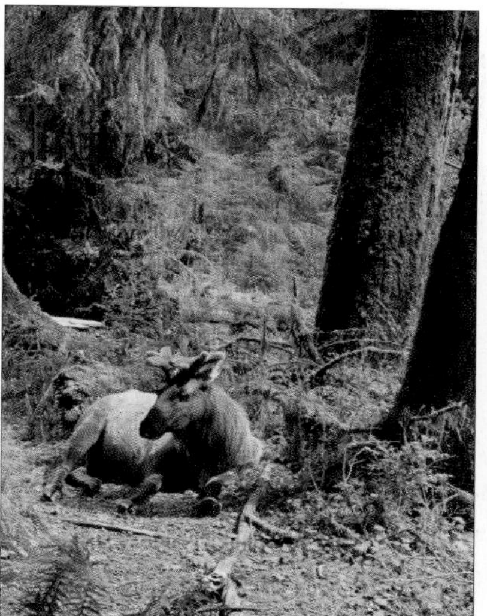

02 Olympic National Park Page 360 • A wonderfully varied natural treasure occupying much of the Olympic Peninsula, where you can expect to wander through rainforests, cross deserted beaches, and rise up to high mountain ridges and looming glaciers.

03 Multnomah Falls Page 126 • Always a favorite attraction for Portland visitors, a tower of water that plunges 612ft into two pools and is spanned by a pleasant little old-fashioned bridge.

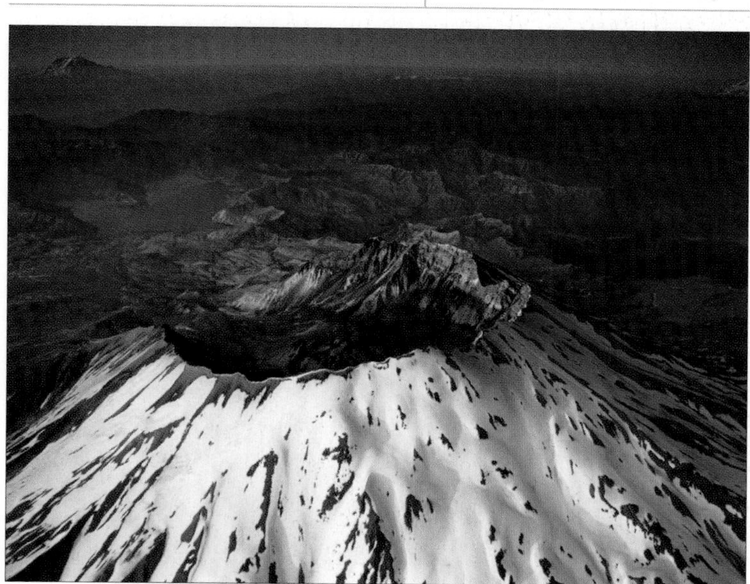

04 Mount St Helens Page 400 • The thermoblasted ruin of what was once a quaint snowy peak, now transformed into a colossal emblem of volcanic fury and natural destruction – and not surprisingly, one of the region's chief tourist draws.

05 Butchart Gardens Page **486** • Over a million plants and 700 different species are spread across British Columbia's most celebrated gardens.

06 Crater Lake Page **227** • Oregon's only national park, and one of the region's top sights, a huge, dark blue expanse of fresh water covering the pit of the blown-out volcano Mount Mazama, which has since become the country's deepest lake.

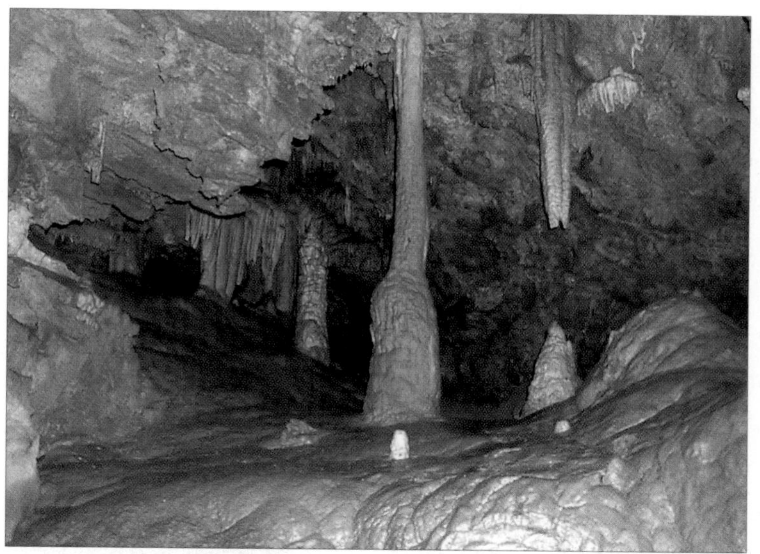

07 Oregon Caves Page **160** • Strange and elaborate limestone formations, echoing dark caverns, and narrowly winding rock passages, together preserved in a national monument not far from the California border.

08 Seafood Page **45** • Salmon, tuna, bass, and sturgeon are but a few of the fishy delights that appeal to the Northwest palate, much of it freshly caught by local trawlers. Beyond the ocean, the freshwater trout plucked from mountain streams are also delicious.

09 Wonderland Trail Page **398** • Essential hiking for any hardy visitor to the Northwest, a memorable 93-mile loop around Mount Rainier, showcasing pristine lakes, glacier-fed rivers, old-growth forests, and some of the best views of the entire region.

10 Mount Constitution Page **334** • The highest and most scenic point on Orcas Island in the San Juans, featuring a steep trail overlooking idyllic creeks and pastures, and leading up to a rugged tower resembling a medieval fortress.

11 Rose Festival Page **100** • Portland's one big yearly shindig, a flower fête celebrated with two parades across town, an explosion of blooms in the Rose Test Garden, the arrival of giant warships on the river, and a chaotic "Fun Center" on Waterfront Park.

12 Whale watching Page **487** • The coastal waters of the Pacific Northwest teem with whales, easily visible either on tours or kayaking.

13 Historic Columbia River Highway Page **123** • An official national treasure built in the 1910s, this evocative driving route travels over narrrow bridges past canyons, parks, and waysides.

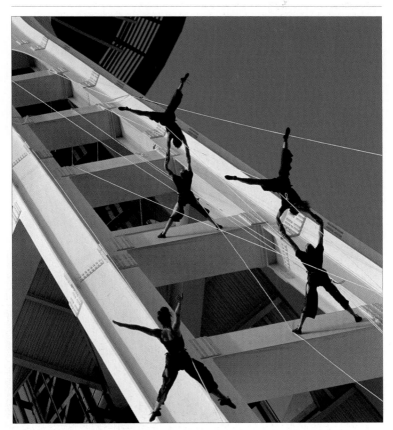

14 Bumbershoot Page **299** • Seattle's most freewheeling festival, encompassing music, food, theater, dance, and countless other things, all taking place at venues across the city but with their focus at Seattle Center.

15 Snoqualmie Falls Page **389** • Familiar from the TV show *Twin Peaks*, a 270-foot waterfall that flows from the heights of a solid bedrock gorge, and located near the grand wooden Salish Lodge, another favorite for David Lynch fans.

16 Museum of Anthropology Page **437** • Bill Reid's *The Raven and the First Men* is one of countless outstanding pieces of aboriginal art in Vancouver's most compelling museum.

17 Lake Chelan Page **382** • Nestled snugly between forested hills and mountains, serpentine Lake Chelan is a glacially carved gem, with countless fine hiking trails striking out from its shores.

18 Seattle café culture Page **290** • Not only places to sip a latte, but also bonafide bastions of high and low culture where you can check out homegrown art, listen to a music jam or poetry slam, access the Internet, or order a pastrami sandwich.

19 Pike Place Market Page **259** • Seattle's best contribution to American urban culture, a frenetic scene loaded with fish vendors, produce stalls, fancy restaurants, underground book and record stores, and just about anything else you can think of.

20 Windsurfing Page **129** • Cruising over white-caps and troughs, windsurfers can find plenty of good places to ride the waves in Oregon, from the beautiful Columbia River Gorge near Hood River to the remote beaches and seastacks of Pistol River State Park.

21 Whistler Page **464** • Whistler is best known for its skiing, snowboarding, and other winter activities, but there is plenty to do in the summer too.

22 Port Townsend Page **350** • On the Olympic Peninsula, a nicely preserved Victorian hamlet from the late nineteenth century, loaded with elegant mansions and quaint restaurants and boutiques.

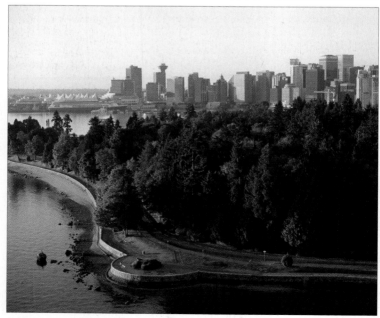

23 Stanley Park, Vancouver Page **431** • North America's largest urban park is a green oasis of woodland, ancient forest, marshes, beaches, and peaceful trails.

24 **Wine tours** Page 394 • Whether you're exploring the vintages of the Yakima Valley, the Columbia River Gorge, or the upper Willamette Valley, there are plenty of good opportunities to sample the region's increasingly popular wines – highlighted by cabernet and pinot noir.

25 **Oregon Shakespeare Festival** Page 211 • An unexpected treat in the little southern Oregon town of Ashland, where three stages play host to the work of the Bard and other playwrights from February to October.

26 Fremont public art Page **275** • A handful of Seattle's most colorful and bizarre public artworks, scattered around one of its most bohemian and free-spirited districts, highlighted by a menacing troll under the Aurora Bridge.

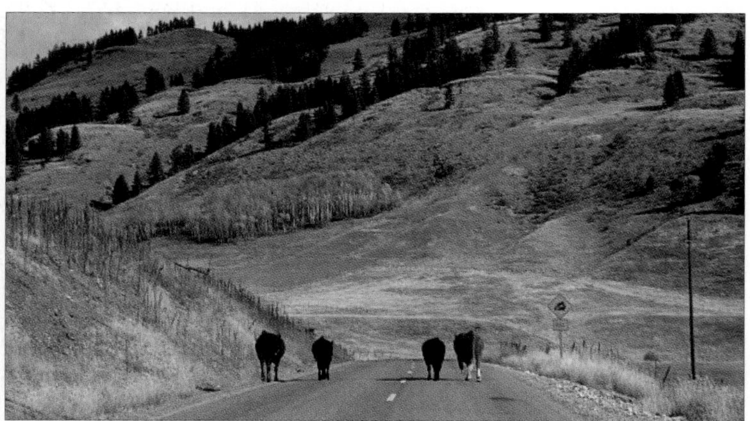

27 The Cascade Loop Page **378** • Washington's premier driving concourse, a 350-mile loop through the North Cascades, taking you past grand peaks and glaciers and several quirky small towns, and the gorgeous and narrow Lake Chelan.

28 The Underground Tour Page **264** • A fun, fascinating, and lengthy trip into the netherworld of Seattle's Pioneer Square, where you can hear all about the history and legends of the area before it was buried under 10ft of earthen fill at the turn of the nineteenth century.

Contents

Using this Rough Guide

We've tried to make this Rough Guide a good read and easy to use. The book is divided into five main sections, and you should be able to find whatever you want in one of them.

Color section

The front color section offers a quick survey of the Pacific Northwest. The **introduction** aims to give you a feel for the region, with suggestions on where to go. We also tell you what the weather is like and include a basic regional fact file. Next, our authors round up their favorite aspects of the Pacific Northwest in the **things not to miss** section – whether it's a Cascades hike, savory cuisine, or a spirited festival. Right after this comes a full **contents** list.

Basics

The Basics section covers all the **pre-departure** nitty-gritty to help you plan your trip. This is where to find out which airlines fly to your destination, what paperwork you'll need, what to do about money and insurance, Internet access, food, public transport, car rental – in fact just about every piece of **general practical information** you might need.

Guide

This is the heart of the Rough Guide, divided into user-friendly chapters, each of which covers a major city or a general region. Every chapter starts with a list of **highlights,** a practical **map**, and an **introduction** that helps you to decide where to go. Chapters then move on to **detailed coverage** of your destination. Introductions to the various cities, towns, and smaller regions within each chapter should help you plan your itinerary. We start most **town accounts** with information on arrival and accommodation, followed by a tour of the sights, and finally reviews of places to eat and drink, and details of nightlife. Longer accounts also have a directory of practical listings.

Contexts

Read Contexts to get a deeper understanding of what makes the Pacific Northwest tick. We include a brief **history** of the region and an overview of its **wildlife**, together with detailed sections that review dozens of **films** and **books** relating to the Northwest.

Index + small print

Apart from a **full index**, which includes maps as well as places, this section covers publishing information, credits, and acknowledgments, and also has our contact details in case you want to send in updates and corrections to the book – or suggestions as to how we might improve it.

Chapter list and map

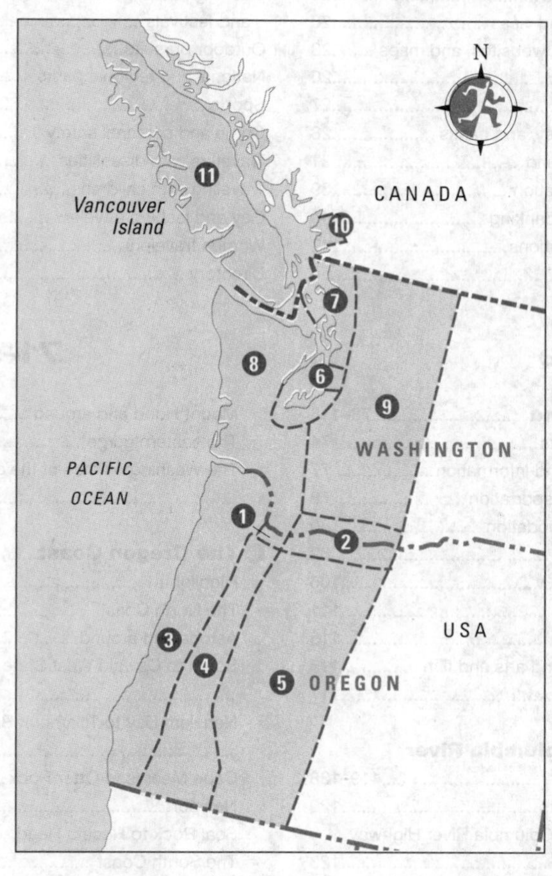

Contents

Color section i–xxiv

Basics 7–70

Guide 71–534

CONTENTS

Contexts 535–567

Index + small print 579–592

Basics

Basics

Getting there

Unless you live on the West Coast, the quickest and easiest way of getting to the Pacific Northwest is to fly. While alternatives exist – there are some excellent train and road routes – most people's first view of the region will come from the air. Approaches by rail are possible in both Canada and the US, but the most cost-effective way to the region is by bus - though you'll pay a heavy price in terms of comfort and the time involved in traveling. Coming here by car may also take time, but will allow you to be far more flexible once you arrive.

Airfares always depend on the season, with the highest fares being charged from around June to the end of August and over the Christmas period; you'll get the best prices during the **low season**, which is generally mid-January to the end of February, and from October to the end of November, excluding the days around Christmas and New Year's Day, when prices are hiked and seats are at a premium; **shoulder seasons**, where prices hover between the low- and high-season averages, cover the rest of the year.

While it's worth calling airlines directly to inquire about their fares, you'll save yourself a lot of time, and often cut costs, by going through a **specialist flight agent** – either a **consolidator**, who buys up blocks of tickets from the airlines and sells them at a discount, or a **discount agent**, who in addition to dealing with discounted flights may also offer special student and youth fares (see p.11 for listings of these). A variety of **package deals** to the Pacific Northwest are also available, but few include international flights (see p.14 for lisitngs).

Booking flights online

Many airlines and discount travel websites offer you the opportunity to book your tickets online, cutting the costs of agents and middlemen. Good deals can often be found through discount or auction sites, as well as through the airlines' own websites.

Online booking agents and travel sites

Ⓦ **www.cheapflights.com** Flight deals, travel agents, plus links to other travel sites.

Ⓦ **www.cheaptickets.com** Discount flight specialists (US only).

Ⓦ **www.etn.nl/discount** A hub of consolidator and discount agent Web links, maintained by the nonprofit European Travel Network.

Ⓦ **www.expedia.com** Discount airfares, all-airline search engine, and daily deals.

Ⓦ **www.flyaow.com** Online air travel info and reservations site.

Ⓦ **www.gaytravel.com** Gay-oriented online travel agent, offering accommodation, cruises, tours, and more.

Ⓦ **www.geocities.com/thavery2000** Extensive list of airline toll-free numbers (from the US) and websites.

Ⓦ **www.hotwire.com** Bookings from the US only. Last-minute savings of up to forty percent on regular published fares. Travelers must be at least 18 and there are no refunds, transfers, or changes allowed.

Ⓦ **www.lastminute.com** Offers good last-minute packages and flight-only deals.

Ⓦ **www.priceline.com** Name-your-own-price website that has deals at around forty percent off standard fares. You cannot specify flight times (although you do specify dates) and the tickets are non-refundable, non-transferable, and non-changeable.

Ⓦ **www.skyauction.com** Bookings from the US only. Auctions tickets and travel packages using a "second bid" scheme. The best strategy is to bid the maximum you're willing to pay, since if you win you'll pay just enough to beat the runner-up regardless of your maximum bid.

Ⓦ **www.travelocity.com** Destination guides, hot web fares, and best deals for car hire, accommodation, and lodging as well as fares. Provides access to the travel agent system SABRE, the most comprehensive central reservations system in the US.

Ⓦ **www.travelshop.com.au** Australian site offering discounted flights, packages, insurance, and bookings.

www.travel.yahoo.com Incorporates a lot of Rough Guides material in its coverage of destination countries and cities across the world, with information about places to eat, sleep, and so on.

From elsewhere in North America

The best means of getting to the Pacific Northwest from most places in North America is to **fly**, as many airlines offer daily services – both nonstop and connecting – from points across the US and Canada to the region's key hubs in Seattle, Portland, and Vancouver. Another plus is that if you book your ticket in advance, flying is often not much more expensive than **rail** or **bus**.

By plane

The principal **airports** in the Pacific Northwest are those in **Seattle**, **Portland**, and **Vancouver**. Major US air carriers such as American Airlines, Delta, United, Continental, and Northwest regularly fly to these cities from other places in the region, though services to Seattle tend to be both more direct and more frequent. Air Canada should be your first choice for frequent service from major cities in Canada.

As airlines tend to match each other's prices, there's little difference in their quoted fares. However, with many companies experiencing economic troubles in recent years, week-to-week prices can vary dramatically, with some financially strapped airlines reducing their flight schedules and range of bargains, and tacking on stiff fees for meal service and nonstop routes.

What makes more difference than your choice of carrier are the conditions governing the ticket: whether it is fully refundable, the time and day, and, most importantly, the time of year you travel. Least expensive is a low-season midweek flight with a weekend stay-over, booked and purchased at least three weeks in advance. Booked by many discount travel agents (see opposite), one of the best value tickets is the **APEX** (Advanced Purchase Excursion Fare) ticket, which has to be purchased between 7 and 21 days ahead of your departure date and requires a Saturday night stay-over. Some no-frills carriers can often provide good value as well, notably Southwest Airlines, Jet Blue, and Frontier and Air Canada's two recent subsidiaries, Air Canada Jazz and Air Canada Tango.

For Portland and Seattle, the cheapest round-trip prices generally start at around $250 from New York, $170 from Chicago, $300 from Miami, $210 from LA, $150 from Vancouver, BC, and $420–440 from Toronto or Montréal. Air Canada flights operate several times daily from Toronto and other

Airlines in the US and Canada

Air Canada ⓣ1-800/247-2262, ⓦwww.aircanada.ca
Air Canada Jazz ⓣ1-888/247-2262, ⓦwww.flyjazz.ca
Air Canada Tango ⓣ1-888/247-2262, ⓦwww.flytango.com
Alaska Air ⓣ1-800/426-0333, ⓦwww.alaska-air.com
America West ⓣ1-800/235-9292, ⓦwww.americawest.com
American Airlines ⓣ1-800/433-7300, ⓦwww.aa.com
Continental domestic ⓣ1-800/525-0280, international ⓣ1-800/231-0856, ⓦwww.continental.com
Delta domestic ⓣ1-800/221-1212, international ⓣ1-800/241-4141, ⓦwww.delta.com
Frontier ⓣ1-888/241-7821, ⓦwww.frontierairlines.com
Horizon ⓣ1-800/547-9308, ⓦwww.horizonair.com
JetBlue ⓣ1-800/JETBLUE, ⓦwww.jetblue.com
Northwest/KLM domestic ⓣ1-800/225-2525, international ⓣ1-800/447-4747, ⓦwww.nwa.com or www.klm.com
Reno Air ⓣ1-800/433-7300, ⓦwww.aa.com. Part of American Airlines.
Southwest ⓣ1-800/435-9792, ⓦwww.iflyswa.com
United domestic ⓣ1-800/241-6522, international ⓣ1-800/538-2929, ⓦwww.ual.com
US Airways domestic ⓣ1-800/428-4322, international ⓣ1-800/622-1015, ⓦwww.usair.com

major Canadian cities to Vancouver: there are also some direct flights to Victoria, but most flights to the latter city involve a connection in Vancouver. The lowest round-trip APEX fares from Toronto to Vancouver are approximately Can$450/575, but less expensive deals are often available.

Discount travel agents

Air Brokers International ⓣ1-800/883-3273, ⓦwww.airbrokers.com. Consolidator and specialist in round-the-world tickets.
Airtreks.com ⓣ1-877/AIRTREKS, ⓦwww.airtreks.com. Features an interactive database that lets you build and price your own round-the-world itinerary.
Council Travel ⓣ1-800/2COUNCIL, ⓦwww.counciltravel.com. Nationwide organization that mostly specializes in student/budget travel. Flights from the US only. Owned by STA Travel.
Educational Travel Center ⓣ1-800/747-5551, ⓦwww.edtrav.com. Student/youth discount agent.
Skylink US ⓣ1-800/247-6659, Canada ⓣ1-800/759-5465, ⓦwww.skylinkus.com. Consolidator.
STA Travel ⓣ1-800/781-4040, ⓦwww.sta-travel.com. Worldwide specialists in independent travel; also student IDs, travel insurance, car rental, rail passes, etc.
TFI Tours ⓣ1-800/745-8000, ⓦwww.lowestairprice.com. Consolidator.
Travac ⓣ1-800/TRAV-800, ⓦwww.thetravelsite.com. Consolidator and charter broker.
Travel Avenue ⓣ1-800/333-3335, ⓦwww.travelavenue.com. Full-service travel agent that offers discounts in the form of rebates.
Travel Cuts Canada ⓣ1-800/667-2887, US ⓣ1-866/246-9762, ⓦwww.travelcuts.com. Canadian student-travel organization.
Travelers Advantage ⓣ1-877/259-2691, ⓦwww.travelersadvantage.com. Discount travel club; annual membership fee required ($1 for 3 months' trial).
Worldtek Travel ⓣ1-800/243-1723, ⓦwww.worldtek.com. Discount travel agency for worldwide travel.

By train

The only reason to consider traveling to the Pacific Northwest **by train** from farther-flung parts of North America is if you think of the rail journey in itself as an enjoyable part of your vacation. The most tempting trip is on the trans-Canadian VIA Rail route through the Rockies. However, services are not as frequent as they used to be, and fares are not necessarily any cheaper than flying.

Across the US

The national passenger rail line – **Amtrak** (ⓣ1-800/USA-RAIL, ⓦwww.amtrak.com) – is a leisurely but expensive option. Although financially precarious for years, the company has managed to keep running, though rarely ever on time. The trains themselves vary in style, amenities, and speed, so it's worth checking ahead to see what type of train services your route.

Amtrak's **Cascades** line runs four times per day north to Seattle from Eugene, Oregon, and the daily **Empire Builder** travels west from Chicago. The most memorable route, however, is the **Coast Starlight**, which runs between San Diego and Seattle, passing by some of the most appealing scenery anywhere, from coastal whale-watching between San Luis Obispo and Santa Barbara to an evening trip around Mt Shasta or a journey through the wooded terrain of the Cascade Mountains.

One-way cross-country fares can be as low as $175 during the offseason, or as high as twice that much during peak periods. And, while Amtrak's basic fares are good value, the cost rises quickly if you want to travel more comfortably: sleeping compartments, which include small toilets and showers, start at around $100 for one or two people, but can climb as high as $400, depending on the class of compartment, number of nights, season, and so on. These options include three meals per day, making up somewhat for the high price.

Amtrak also offers package deals combining hotels, rental cars, and other services for American travelers, as well as rail passes. The **North America Rail Pass** 30-day rail pass includes Canadian routes on VIA Rail (see overleaf) and costs $699 for summer travel and $495 during the off-season.

Overseas travelers can choose from four **rail passes** that include the Pacific Northwest, each valid for fifteen or thirty days. The most useful of these are the 30-day **Coastal Pass** ($285 peak, $235

Amtrak rail passes

	15-day (June–Aug)	15-day (Sept–May)	30-day (June–Aug)	30-day (Sept–May)
Far West	$245	$190	$320	$250
West	$325	$200	$405	$270
Coastal	–	–	$285	$235
National	$440	$295	$550	$385

Outside the US, Amtrak rail passes are available at the following locations:

Australia Asia Pacific Travel Marketing, St David's Hall, 17 Arthur St, Surry Hills, Sydney ⓣ612/9319 6624, ⓦwww.aptms.com.au

Ireland USIT, 19/21 Aston Quay, O'Connell Bridge, Dublin ⓣ01/602-1600, ⓦwww.usitworld.com

New Zealand Walshes World, Ding Wall Building, 87 Queen St, Auckland ⓣ09/379-3708, or from almost any travel agent

UK Destination Group, 14 Greville Street, London EC1N 8SB ⓣ020/7400 7045, ⓦwww.destination-group.com

offseason), permitting unlimited rail travel on the East and West coasts – but not in between the two. Passes must be purchased before your trip at travel agents, or at Amtrak stations in the US, on production of a passport issued outside the US or Canada.

Across Canada

The railroad may have created modern **Canada**, but passenger services are now few and far between – at the beginning of 1990 over half the services of **VIA Rail Canada** (ⓣ1-888/842-7245, ⓦwww.viarail.ca) were eliminated at a stroke, and fares increased dramatically. Like Amtrak, Via Rail trains can be slow, and delays are common as passenger services give way to freight; however, rail travel can still be highly rewarding, especially on trains with special "dome cars" that allow an uninterrupted rooftop view of the countryside. Such services operate from the east to Vancouver via Edmonton and Jasper, with fares varying widely according to time of year and seat/sleeper arrangements.

For further details, VIA has an international network of ticket agents: in the UK and Ireland, First Rail, Trafford House, 11 Floor, Chester Rd, Old Trafford, Manchester M32 ORS (ⓣ0845 644 3553, ⓦwww.firstrail.co.uk); in Australia, Asia Pacific Travel (ⓣ0061 2 9319 6624, ⓦwww.aptms.com.au); and in New Zealand, Discover Holidays (ⓣ0064 9 529 4796, ⓦwww.discoverholidays.com).

By bus

Bus travel is a slow, often agonizing way to get to the Pacific Northwest, and in the end you won't really save that much money. Still, if your budget's rather tight, it's an option worth considering.

Across the US

Greyhound (ⓣ1-800/231-2222, ⓦwww.greyhound.com), is the sole long-distance operator servicing Seattle and Portland, and will cost you at least $200 round-trip, paid at least seven days in advance, from major cities like New York, Chicago, and Miami. The main reason to take Greyhound is if you're planning to visit other places en route; the company's **Ameripass** is good for unlimited travel within a set time; 7 days of travel costs $183; 15 days, $279; 30 days, $367; and 60 days, $519; passes for overseas travelers run about ten percent less. Passes are valid from the date of purchase, so it's a bad idea to buy them in advance; overseas visitors, however, can buy Ameripasses before leaving home, and passes will be validated at the start of the trip.

Ameripass outlets outside the US

Australia STA Travel, 79 Oxford St, Darlinghurst, Sydney ⓣ02/9361 4966

Ireland DUST, Students Union House 6, Trinity College, Dublin ⓣ01/677 5076

New Zealand Greyhound International, 1 Montrose Terrace, Suite 5A, Mairangi Bay, Auckland ⓣ09/479 6555

UK STA Travel, 85 Shaftesbury Ave, Soho, London ⓣ020/7432 7474, ⓦwww.sta-travel.com

Across Canada

Bus travel in Canada is much the same as in the US: there's only one national bus line and it is operated by Greyhound. **Greyhound Canada** (1-800-661-TRIP, ⓦwww.greyhound.ca) offers major long-distance routes to Vancouver from such easterly cities as Toronto and Montréal as well as many cities in between.

If you're intending to explore parts of the Canadian PNW and beyond by bus, you can save a lot of money by buying a **pass** before leaving home. In general, Canadian and US travelers must purchase a pass at least 14 days in advance, international travelers at least 21 days ahead. Prices quoted below (which exclude tax) are for adults; students and seniors get discounted rates.

The **Canada Pass** – for Canadians and non-Canadians – covers travel around the country, as well as buses from New York, Detroit, and Buffalo to Toronto, New York to Montréal and Seattle to Vancouver, and also VIA Rail trains between Toronto, Ottawa, and Montréal. The pass is valid for 7, 10, 15, 21, 30, 45, or 60 days. Sample prices are Can$255 for seven days, Can$375 for fifteen days, up to Can$575 for sixty days.

Other options – which all include travel in both the US and Canada, and so are more expensive – are split between passes for Canadian and US travelers, and everyone else. For the former, the best options for PNW travelers is the **Domestic Westcoast CanAm Pass**, available in ten-day (US$265) and 21-day (US$345) versions. The Westcoast pass covers travel in BC and Alberta as far north as Whitehorse, YK, as well as Washington State and the western US down to Tijuana.

For non-US and non-Canadian citizens, the equivalent is the **International Westcoast CanAm Pass**, available in the same configurations as above, for the same prices. Note that you can't buy these at Greyhound stations in the US (although if you're not a US or Canadian citizen you can still get a domestic pass over the counter). In Canada, if you're not a US or Canadian citizen, you can buy these passes at international rates at the gateway cities of Vancouver, Calgary, Edmonton, Ottawa, and Toronto.

By car

Road links to the Pacific Northwest make access by car convenient for those who live within reasonable striking distance of the region. The freeway choices are straightforward: from the east, I-90 in Washington or I-84 in Oregon; and I-5 from the south or north. In recent months, however, connecting to the southbound I-5 from Canada has become a rather tedious process, often resulting in hours of waiting time at the border while drivers are grilled about drugs, weapons, and the like.

Driving your own car (or renting one) may maximize your freedom and flexibility, but if you're traveling cross-country you'll need to allow plenty of time. If you do use your own car, make sure your insurance is up to date and that you are completely covered. In Canada and the US, automobile insurance is mandatory; the Canadian Non-Resident Inter-Provincial Motor Vehicle Liability Insurance Card, available from any US insurance company, is accepted as evidence of financial responsibility in Canada. General advice and help with route planning can be had from either the American Automobile Association (AAA), which has offices in most US cities (ⓣAAA-HELP or 1-800/222-4357 for roadside help; ⓣ212/757-2000 for general information; ⓦwww.aaa.com), or the Canadian Automobile Association (CAA) at Suite 200, 1145 Hunt Club Rd, Ottawa, ON KIV 0Y3 (Mon–Fri 8.30am–4.30pm; ⓣ1-800/267-8713, ⓦwww.caa.ca).

If you don't have a car or don't trust the one you have, one option worth considering is a **driveaway**. Certain automobile-transit companies, operating in most major cities, are paid to find drivers to take a customer's car from one place to another. The company will normally pay for your insurance and one tank of gas; after that, you'll be expected to drive along the most direct route and to average 400 miles a day. Companies are keen to hire overseas travelers, but you'll need to be at least 21 and be willing to put down a $350 deposit, which you can get back once you've returned the car in good condition. Look under "Automobile transporters and driveaways" in the *Yellow Pages* for more information, or contact Auto Driveaway, with offices throughout the US and Canada (ⓣ1-800/346-2277, ⓦwww .autodriveaway.com).

Other options include **renting a car** (see box for major companies) or taking a **fly-drive deal**, which offers bargain-rate and sometimes free car rental with purchase of airline ticket. They usually work out to be less than renting on the spot and are especially good value if you intend to do a lot of driving.

Car rental companies

Advantage ⓣ1-800/777-5500, ⓦwww.arac.com
Alamo ⓣ1-800/462-5266, ⓦwww.goalamo.com
Avis ⓣ1-800/331-1212, ⓦwww.avis.com
Budget ⓣ1-800/527-0700, ⓦwww.budgetrentacar.com
Dollar ⓣ1-800/800-4000, ⓦwww.dollar.com
Enterprise ⓣ1-800/325-8007, ⓦwww.enterprise.com
Hertz ⓣ1-800/654-3131, in Canada ⓣ1-800/263-0600, ⓦwww.hertz.com
National ⓣ1-800/328-4567, ⓦwww.nationalcar.com
Payless ⓣ1-800/729-5377, ⓦwww.paylesscarrental.com
Thrifty ⓣ1-800/847-4389 , ⓦwww.thrifty.com

Package tours

If you're happy to have everything planned for you, including transportation, a **package tour** can make your vacation much easier; if you don't yet know what you want to do, they're worth checking out for ideas. Also, free-spirited, adventuresome types may appreciate the convenience of the "independent packages" put together by the airlines' tour departments.

Tour operators

AmeriCan Adventures/TrekAmerica ⓣ1-800/873-5872, ⓦwww.americanadventures .com. Seven- to 25-day sports and sightseeing trips along the West Coast, from $500 to $1200.
American Airlines Vacations ⓣ1-800/321-2121, ⓦwww.aavacations.com. Multi-day packages to Vancouver and Seattle.
American Express Vacations ⓣ1-800/241-1700, ⓦwww.americanexpress.com/travel. Flights, hotels, last-minute specials, and specialty tours.
Amtrak Vacations ⓣ1-800/321-8684, ⓦwww.amtrakvacations.com. Rail/hotel customized packages to Seattle and Portland.
Backroads ⓣ1-800/GO-ACTIVE or 462-2848, ⓦwww.backroads.com. A mix of cycling/walking and hiking/multisport packages, including trips to national parks and stays in luxury accommodation.
Collette Vacations ⓣ1-800/340-5158, ⓦwww.collettevacations.com. Anything from short jaunts ($150–200) to 13-day trips up and down the West Coast ($2300).
Contiki Holidays ⓣ1-888/CONTIKI, ⓦwww .contiki.com. Youth-oriented sightseeing and national parks trips.
Cosmos/Globus Gateway ⓣ1-800/556-5454, ⓦwww.globusandcosmos.com. A variety of coach tours bookable through travel agents.
Elderhostel ⓣ617/426-8056, ⓦwww.elderhostel.org. Specialists in educational and activity programs and cruises for senior travelers (companions may be younger).
Globus Journeys ⓣ1-866/755-8581, ⓦwww.globusjourneys.com. Multi-day treks to national parks and West Coast cities.
Gray Line of Seattle ⓣ1-800/426-7505, ⓦwww.graylineofseattle.com. Extensive range of

day-tours, overnight packages, and longer trips in the region.

Maupintour ⓣ1-800/255-4266 or 913/843-1211, ⓦwww.maupintour.com. Multi-day land trips of the region, as well as other international destinations.

Suntrek ⓣ1-800/SUNTREK, ⓦwww.suntrek.com. One- to thirteen-week journeys around the West Coast and the rest of the US, from $400 to $5400.

Trek America ⓣ1-800/221-0596, ⓦwww.trekamerica.com. Multi-activity camping/adventure tours.

United Vacations ⓣ1-888/854-3899, ⓦwww.unitedvacations.com. Chain and boutique hotel accommodation, car rental, and other options.

From the UK and Ireland

Flying **from the UK** to the Pacific Northwest, you'll most likely have to stop over in one of the major hubs – Chicago, New York, or Atlanta – and expect about 14–16hrs of travel time. Seattle and Vancouver are, however, accessible by a few nonstop flights (see below), taking between nine and eleven hours for the trip. Because of the time difference between Britain and the West Coast (eight hours most of the year), flights usually leave the UK mid-morning and arrive in the Northwest in the late afternoon or early evening of the same day. Note that you will often obtain much better deals to Vancouver by flying via a US hub or Toronto – flying to Seattle and taking the bus or train can save money.

There are no nonstop direct flights **from Ireland** to Seattle or Portland, but two airlines do operate nonstop scheduled services to other parts of the US. From both Dublin and Shannon airports, Aer Lingus flies to New York, Chicago, Los Angeles, and Boston, while Delta flies to New York and Atlanta. Both can arrange onward flights to Seattle and Portland, and often offer good-value special deals.

Fares, routes, and agents

Britain is one of the best places in Europe to obtain bargain flights, though **fares** vary widely according to season, availability, and the current level of inter-airline competition. Although each **airline** decides the exact dates of its seasons, low season generally runs April 11–30, Nov 1–Dec 14 and Dec 25–March 28; shoulder season March 29–April 10, May 1–June 30 and Sept 1–Oct 31; and high season July 1–Aug 31 and Dec 15–Dec 24. Return tickets start at £260 in low season and £425 in high. Prices are for departures from London and Manchester and do not include a UK airport tax of £40–50. The travel ads in the weekend papers, on the holiday pages of ITV's *Teletext* give an idea of what's available; in London, scour *Time Out* and the *Evening Standard*. Giveaway magazines aimed at young travelers, like *TNT*, are also useful resources.

British Airways and Aer Lingus offer service from Dublin (12–15hrs), usually with a stopover in London and possibly another in the US, for £330 in low season and £440 in high season. KLM/Northwest offers similarly priced service, with at least one stopover in Amsterdam and possibly another in the US. In addition, other airlines – primarily British Airways and Air Canada – can quote you through-fares from Dublin to Seattle and Portland via major gateway cities. Otherwise, the cheapest flights to North America – if you are under 26 or a student – are available from UsitNOW (see overleaf).

For an overview of the various offers and unofficially discounted tickets from the UK and Ireland, go straight to agents specializing in low-cost flights. Especially if you're under 26 or a student, they may be able to knock up to thirty percent off the regular Apex fares. The same agents also offer cut-price seats on **charter flights**. These are

Nonstop flights from the UK to the Pacific Northwest

Air Canada ⓣ0870/524-7226, ⓦwww.aircanada.ca. Heathrow to Vancouver (1–3 daily).

British Airways ⓣ0870/850-9850, ⓦwww.ba.com. Heathrow to Vancouver (1–2 daily) and Seattle (one daily).

particularly good value if you're traveling from a UK city other than London, although they tend to be limited to the summer season and restricted to so-called "holiday destinations," with fixed departure and return dates. Brochures are available in most high-street travel agents; otherwise, contact the specialists direct.

The conditions on **Apex tickets** are pretty standard whoever you fly with – seats must be purchased seven days or more in advance, and you must stay for at least one Saturday night; tickets are normally valid for up to six months. Some airlines also offer less expensive **Super-Apex** tickets of two types: the first is around £150 cheaper than an ordinary Apex but must be bought 21 days in advance and requires a minimum stay of seven days and a maximum of one month; the second costs about £100 less than an Apex, must be purchased fourteen days in advance and requires a minimum stay of a week and a maximum of two months – such tickets are usually non-refundable or -changeable.

Airlines

Aer Lingus ⓣ01/886 8844, ⓦwww.aerlingus.ie
American Airlines ⓣ0845/778 9789 or 020/8572 5555, ⓦwww.aa.com
British Airways ⓣ0845/773 3377, ⓦwww.ba.com
Continental ⓣ0800/776 464, ⓦwww.flycontinental.com
Delta ⓣ0800/414 767, ⓦwww.delta.com
KLM/Northwest ⓣ0870/507 4074, ⓦwww.klmuk.com
United Airlines ⓣ0845/844 4777, ⓦwww.unitedairlines.co.uk
Virgin Atlantic ⓣ0870/380 2007, ⓦwww.virgin-atlantic.com

Travel agents

Bridge the World UK ⓣ0870/444 7474, ⓦwww.bridgetheworld.com. Specializing in round-the-world tickets, with good deals aimed at backpackers.
Flightbookers UK ⓣ0870/010 7000, ⓦwww.ebookers.com. Low fares on an extensive selection of scheduled flights.
Flynow UK ⓣ0870/444 0045, ⓦwww.flynow.com. Large range of discounted tickets.
North South Travel UK ⓣ01245/608 291, ⓦwww.northsouthtravel.co.uk. Friendly, competitive travel agency, offering discounted fares worldwide. Profits are used to support projects in the developing world, especially the promotion of sustainable tourism.
Premier Travel Northern Ireland ⓣ028/7126 3333, ⓦwww.premiertravel.uk.com. Discount flight specialists.
STA Travel UK ⓣ0870/1600 599, ⓦwww.statravel.co.uk. Worldwide specialists in low-cost flights and tours for students and those under 26, though other customers welcome.
Top Deck UK ⓣ020/7244 8000, ⓦwww.topdecktravel.co.uk. Long-established agent dealing in discount flights.
Trailfinders UK ⓣ020/7628 7628, ⓦwww.trailfinders.co.uk, Republic of Ireland ⓣ01/677 7888, ⓦwww.trailfinders.ie. One of the best-informed and most efficient agents for independent travelers. Produces a very useful quarterly magazine worth scrutinizing for round-the-world routes.
Travel Bag UK ⓣ0870/890 1456, ⓦwww.travelbag.co.uk. Discount flights to the US.
Travel Cuts UK ⓣ020/7255 2082 or 7255 1944, ⓦwww.travelcuts.co.uk. Canadian company specializing in budget, student and youth travel and round-the-world tickets.
UsitNOW Republic of Ireland ⓣ01/602 1600, Northern Ireland ⓣ028/9032 7111, ⓦwww.usitnow.ie. Student and youth specialists for flights and trains.

Tour operators

Airtours UK ⓣ0870/238 7788, ⓦwww.uk.mytravel.com. Large tour company offering trips worldwide.
AmeriCan Adventures UK ⓣ01295/756 200, ⓦwww.americanadventures.com. Small-group camping adventure trips throughout the US and Canada.
American Holidays Belfast ⓣ028/9023 8762, Dublin ⓣ01/433 1009, ⓦwww.american-holidays.com. Specialists in travel to the US and Canada.
Bales Worldwide UK ⓣ0870/241 3208, ⓦwww.balesworldwide.com. Family-owned company offering high-quality escorted tours, as well as tailor-made itineraries.
British Airways Holidays ⓣ0870/442 3820, ⓦwww.baholidays.co.uk. A tour outfit mainly using British Airways and offering an exhaustive range of package and tailor-made vacations around the world.

Discover the World UK ⓣ01737/218 800, ⓦwww.discover-the-world.co.uk. Well-established wildlife vacation specialist, with groups led by naturalists to Europe, the Americas, Africa, and Asia. Popular whale- and dolphin-watching vacations. Fly-drives available.

Europa Travel ⓣ044/2890 623211, ⓦwww.europatravel.com. Belfast-based operator for sports and leisure packages.

Martin Randall Travel UK ⓣ020/8742 3355, ⓦwww.martinrandall.com. Small-group cultural tours: experts on art, archeology, or music lead travelers in USA, as well as the Middle East and North Africa.

North America Travel Service UK ⓣ0207/938 3737, ⓦwww.americatravelservice.com. Tailor-made flights, accommodation, car hire as well as other services. Branches in London, Nottingham, Manchester, and North and South Yorkshire.

Premier Holidays UK ⓣ0870/889 0850, ⓦwww.premierholidays.co.uk. Flight-plus-accommodation deals.

Thomas Cook UK ⓣ0870/5666 222, ⓦwww.thomascook.co.uk. Long established one-stop 24-hour travel agency for packages or scheduled flights, with bureaux de change issuing Thomas Cook travelers' checks, travel insurance, and car rental.

Top Deck Travel UK ⓣ020/7244 8000, ⓦwww.topdecktravel.co.uk. Agents for numerous adventure-touring specialists.

Travelpack UK ⓣ08705/747101, ⓦwww.travelpack.co.uk. Escorted tours and tailor-made vacations.

Trek America UK ⓣ01295/256777, ⓦwww.trekamerica.com. Touring-adventure packages.

United Vacations UK ⓣ0870/606 2222, ⓦwww.unitedvacations.co.uk. City breaks, custom-made trips, and fly-drives.

Up & Away UK ⓣ020/8289 5050. Tailor-made packages and fly-drive options.

Virgin Holidays UK ⓣ0870/220 2788, ⓦwww.virginholidays.co.uk. Packages to a wide range of destinations, mostly using Virgin Atlantic as well as partner airlines.

Packages

Packages – fly-drive, flight/accommodation deals, and guided tours (or a combination of all three) – can work out cheaper than arranging the same trip yourself, especially for a short stay. The obvious drawbacks are the loss of flexibility and the fact that most operators use hotels in the mid-range bracket, but there is a wide variety of options to choose from.

Fly-drive deals, which give cut-rate (sometimes free) car rental when buying a transatlantic ticket, always work out cheaper than renting on the spot and give especially great value if you intend to do a lot of driving. On the other hand, you'll probably have to pay more for the flight than if you booked it through a discount agent. Competition between airlines and tour operators means that it's well worth phoning to check on special promotions. Watch out for hidden extras, such as local taxes and **"drop-off"** charges, which can be as much as a week's rental, and Collision Damage Waiver insurance. Remember, too, that while you can drive in the States with a British license, there can be problems renting vehicles if you're under 25. For more car-rental and drive-away details, see p.37.

There are plenty of specialist **touring and adventure packages** that include transportation, accommodation, food, and a guide. Some of the more adventurous carry small groups around on minibuses and use a combination of budget hotels and campgrounds (equipment, except a sleeping bag, is provided). Most also have a food kitty of around £25 per week, with many meals cooked and eaten communally, although there's plenty of time to leave the group and explore your own interests.

From Australia and New Zealand

From Australia and New Zealand most flights to Pacific Northwest destinations either land in Vancouver or are routed through LA. Airfares are seasonal, and the differences can add up to as much as Aus$465/NZ$500. **Travel agents** offer the best deals on fares and have the latest information on limited special offers, such as free stopovers and fly-drive-accommodation packages. Flight Centre and STA Travel (which offer fare reductions for ISIC cardholders and under 26s) generally offer the lowest fares. Seat availability on most international flights out of Australia and New Zealand is often limited, so it's best to book at least several weeks ahead.

The total travel time between Auckland or Sydney and Seattle or Portland is 17–22 hours. **From Australia**, there are daily flights from Sydney to LA on United Airlines and Qantas for around Aus$1955 in low season, with many options for connecting flights on to Seattle, for around Aus$326 in low season; the total price (around Aus$2280) is about the same when traveling on Air Canada to Vancouver. For high-season rates, add around Aus$260–390 to the above costs. Qantas offer the most direct through-service to destinations via Vancouver – around Aus$1950 in low season.

From New Zealand, the best deals are out of Auckland on Qantas, Alaska Airlines, United, or Air New Zealand, with low-season deals around NZ$2240–2390, both with stopovers in LA; add about NZ$120–240 for Christchurch and Wellington departures. Air New Zealand flies either via Honolulu or direct to Vancouver, or Qantas via either Sydney or Honolulu and United Airlines via LA to Vancouver, all from around NZ$1950 low season to NZ$2500 high season.

If you intend to do a fair amount of flying around, you might be better off taking advantage of some of the **coupon deals** that can be bought with your international ticket and cost US$100–300 each, depending on the distance involved. For example, American Airlines' Coupon Pass costs US$350 for the first three coupons, and between US$60 and $100 for each additional one (maximum of ten total). If you prefer to travel overland, Amtrak and Greyhound **Ameripasses** offer myriad routes and destinations throughout the country (see p.33).

Airlines

Air New Zealand Australia ⓣ13 24 76, New Zealand ⓣ09/357 3000, ⓦwww.airnz.com
Air Pacific Australia ⓣ1800/230 150, New Zealand ⓣ0800/800 178, ⓦwww.airpacific.com
America West Airlines Australia ⓣ02/9267 2138 or 1300/364 757, New Zealand ⓣ0800/866 000, ⓦwww.americawest.com
American Airlines Australia ⓣ1300/650 747, New Zealand ⓣ09/309 9159, ⓦwww.aa.com.
Cathay Pacific Australia ⓣ13 17 47 or 1300/653 077, New Zealand ⓣ09/379 0861 or 0508/800 454, ⓦwww.cathaypacific.com
Continental Australia ⓣ1300/361 400, New Zealand ⓣ09/308 3350, ⓦwww.flycontinental.com
Delta Australia ⓣ02/9251 3211 or 1800/500 992, New Zealand ⓣ09/379 3370, ⓦwww.delta-airlines.com
Japan Airlines Australia ⓣ02/9272 1111, New Zealand ⓣ09/379 9906, ⓦwww.japanair.com
KLM/Northwest Australia ⓣ1300/303 747, ⓦwww.klm.com/au_en, New Zealand ⓣ09/309 1782, ⓦwww.klm.com/nz_en
Korean Air Australia ⓣ02/9262 6000, New Zealand ⓣ09/914 2000, ⓦwww.koreanair.com.au
Qantas Australia ⓣ13 13 13, ⓦwww.qantas.com.au, New Zealand ⓣ09/357 8900, ⓦwww.qantas.co.nz

Round-the-world and air passes

If you plan to visit the Pacific Northwest as part of a world trip, a **round-the-world** (**RTW**) ticket offers the best value for the money. The most US-oriented are the fourteen airlines (among them Air New Zealand and Lufthansa) making up the "Star Alliance" network; for more details, call through individual carriers or visit ⓦwww.star-alliance.com. The Star Alliance deals offer a minimum of three up to a maximum of fifteen stopovers worldwide, with a total trip length from ten days to a year. An alternative option includes the eight carriers of the "One World Alliance" (such as Qantas, American Airlines, and British Airways; ⓦwww.oneworldalliance.com), which bases its rates on travel to and within the six populated continents, allowing two to six possible stopovers in each. Costs for both plans can be as low as US$80, Can$110, UK£50, €75, Aus/NZ$150 per segment, with the total cost for low-season fares around US$1500, Can$2000, UK£950, €1350, Aus$2400/NZ$2700 and high-season rates at US$2100, Can$2800, UK£1300, €1900, Aus$3400/NZ$3800.

Singapore Airlines Australia ⓣ13 10 11, New Zealand ⓣ09/303 2129, ⓦwww.singaporeair.com
United Australia ⓣ13 17 77, ⓦwww.unitedairlines.com.au, New Zealand ⓣ09/379 3800 or 0800/508 648, ⓦwww.unitedairlines.co.nz
Virgin Atlantic Australia ⓣ02/9244 2747, New Zealand ⓣ09/308 3377, ⓦwww.virgin-atlantic.com

Travel agents

Anywhere Travel Australia ⓣ02/9663 0411, ⓦwww.anywheretravel.com.au
Budget Travel New Zealand ⓣ0800/808 480, ⓦwww.budgettravel.co.nz
Flight Centre Australia ⓣ13 31 33 or 02/9235 3522, ⓦwww.flightcentre.com.au, New Zealand ⓣ0800 243 544 or 09/358 4310, ⓦwww.flightcentre.co.nz
New Zealand Destinations Unlimited New Zealand ⓣ09/414 1685 ⓦwww.holiday.co.nz
Northern Gateway Australia ⓣ1800/174 800, ⓦwww.northerngateway.com.au
STA Travel Australia ⓣ1300/733 035, ⓦwww.statravel.com.au, New Zealand ⓣ0508/782 872, ⓦwww.statravel.co.nz
Student Uni Travel Australia ⓣ02/9232 8444, ⓦwww.sut.com.au, New Zealand ⓣ09/300 8266, ⓦwww.sut.co.nz
Thomas Cook Australia: Sydney ⓣ02/9231 2877, Melbourne ⓣ03/9282 0222; New Zealand ⓣ09/307 0555, ⓦwww.thomascook.com
Trailfinders Australia ⓣ02/9247 7666, ⓦwww.trailfinders.com.au
Travel.com.au Australia ⓣ02/9249 5444 or 1300/130 482, ⓦwww.travel.com.au
YHA Travel Australia: Sydney ⓣ02/9261 1111, Melbourne ⓣ03/9670 9611, Brisbane ⓣ07/3236 1680, ⓦwww.yha.com.au

Tour operators

Adventure World Australia ⓣ02/8913 0755, ⓦwww.adventureworld.com.au, New Zealand ⓣ09/524 5118, ⓦwww.adventureworld.co.nz. Agents for a vast array of international adventure travel companies that operate trips to every continent.
Canada & America Travel Specialists Australia ⓣ02/9922 4600, ⓦwww.canada-americatravel.com.au. Wholesalers of Greyhound Ameripasses, plus flights and accommodation in North America.
Silke's Travel Australia ⓣ1800/807 860 or 02/8347 2000, ⓦwww.silkes.com.au. Gay and lesbian specialist travel agent, helping provide US accommodation and air transit.
Surf Travel Co Australia ⓣ02/9527 4722 or 1800/687 873, New Zealand ⓣ09/473 8388, ⓦwww.surftravel.com.au. Packages and advice for catching waves or snow through the whole Pacific region.
Sydney International Travel Centre ⓣ02/9299 8000 or 1800/251 911, ⓦwww.sydneytravel.com.au. US flights, accommodation, city stays, and car rental.
Viatour Australia ⓣ02/8219 5400, ⓦwww.viator.com. Bookings for hundreds of travel suppliers worldwide.

Red tape and visas

By design, entry requirements into the US and Canada can vary dramatically, depending on your resident country, overall length of stay, and purpose while in the Pacific Northwest. For a brief excursion into the US, Canadian citizens do not necessarily need even a passport – just some form of ID, but considering the current state of security in the US, you should really have a passport with you, too, and if you plan to stay for more than ninety days you'll need a visa, which you can apply for by mail through the US embassy or nearest US consulate. Bear in mind that if you cross into the US in your car, trunks and passenger compartments are subject to spot searches by US Customs personnel. Remember too, that without the proper paperwork, Canadians are legally barred from seeking employment in the US.

Furthermore, most if not all airlines and the major bus companies will now insist on both photo identification and proof of citizenship before accepting you as a passenger. In all cases, it's certainly recommended to take your passport and, if you plan to stay for more than ninety days, you'll need it along with a visa.

Visitors entering Canada from the US should be ready to declare their citizenship, place of residence, and proposed length of stay. You should also have photo identification – a passport is always the best bet. If you are arriving by car, then vehicle insurance, with minimum liability coverage of US$200,000, is compulsory. You should also bring all relevant documents pertaining to proof of insurance cover, vehicle ownership, and driving license.

United States

Under the **Visa Waiver Program** (Ⓦwww.travel.state.gov/vwp), designed to speed up lengthy entry requirements, citizens of the UK, Ireland, Australia, New Zealand, and 23 other countries (most of them in Western Europe) who visit the United States for a period of less than ninety days only need an onward or return ticket, a full passport, and a visa waiver form.

The visa waiver form will be provided by your travel agency or by the airline during check-in or on the plane, and must be presented to immigration on arrival in the US. The same form covers entry across the land borders with Canada and Mexico. For visitors from the **UK**, "British Citizen" must be listed on the passport, otherwise the program does not apply. If visitors for whom the program applies intend to work, study, or stay in the country for more than ninety days, they must apply for a regular visa through their local US embassy or consulate. In the UK, you must apply in person at the US Embassy in London (see below), under rules adopted in 2003.

If you're an **Australian** or **New Zealand** passport holder and you plan to stay longer than 90 days, US multiple entry visas cost the local equivalent of US$50. You'll need an application form, available from the US visa information service (Ⓣ1902/262 682), one signed passport photo and your passport; you can either send the completed form, photo, and your passport by post or personally lodge it at one of the American embassies or consulates. For postal applications in Australia, payment for the visa can be made at any post office; you'll also need to include the receipt of payment and a self-addressed, stamped envelope. Processing takes about ten working days for postal applications; personal lodgements usually take two days – check with the consulate first.

Citizens of all other countries should contact their local US embassy or consulate for details of current entry requirements, as they are often required to have both a valid passport and a **non-immigrant visitor's**

visa. To obtain a visa, fill in the application form available at most travel agents, as well as at dozens of sites on the Internet, and send it with the appropriate fee, two photographs, and a passport – valid for at least six months from the end of your planned stay – to the nearest US embassy or consulate. Visas are not issued to convicted criminals. You may also experience difficulties if you admit to being HIV positive or having TB, hepatitis, or other major communicable diseases. Furthermore, in January 2004 the US government began **fingerprinting** all visitors to the US from countries not covered by the Visa Waiver Program, and doing spot background checks looking for evidence of past criminal or terrorist connections.

For details on extensions, special work or study visas, and all other specific exceptions to these general rules, contact the US State Department website (ⓦwww.travel.state.gov). In light of real and perceived threats to national security, many of these particular requirements have been changing rapidly in recent months, so make sure to check for updates before planning your trip.

US embassies and consulates abroad

For a more complete list around the world, check ⓦusembassy.state.gov.

Australia

Canberra Moonbah Place, Yarralumla, Canberra, ACT ⓣ02/6214 5600, ⓦusembassy-australia.state.gov/embassy
Perth 553 St Kilda Rd, Melbourne ⓣ03/9526 5900; 16 St George's Terrace, 13th Floor, Perth ⓣ08/9231 9400 or 08/9202 1224
Sydney MLC Centre, Level 59, 19–29 Martin Place, Sydney ⓣ02/9373 9200

Canada

Ottawa 490 Sussex Drive, Ottawa, ON K1P 5T1 ⓣ613/238-5335, ⓦwww.usembassycanada.gov
Calgary 615 Macleod Trail SE, Room 1000, Calgary, AB T2G 4T8 ⓣ900/451-2778
Halifax Suite 904, Purdy's Wharf Tower II, 1969 Upper Water St, Halifax, NS B3J 3R7 ⓣ902/429-2485
Montréal 1155 St Alexandre St, Montréal, PQ H2Z 1Z2 ⓣ514/398-9695
Québec City 2 Place Terrasse Dufferin, CP 939, Québec City, PQ G1R 4T9 ⓣ418/692-2095
Toronto 360 University Ave, Toronto, ON M5G 1S4 ⓣ416/595-1700, ⓦwww.usconsulatetoronto.ca
Vancouver 1095 W Pender St, Vancouver, BC V6E 2M6 ⓣ604/685-4311

Ireland

Dublin 42 Elgin Rd, Ballsbridge, Dublin 4 ⓣ01/668-7122, ⓦwww.usembassy.ie

New Zealand

Auckland 3rd Floor, Citibank Building, 23 Customs St, Auckland ⓣ09/303 2724 or non-immigrant visas, Private Bag 92022, Auckland 1
Wellington 29 Fitzherbert Terrace, Thorndon, Wellington ⓣ04/462 6000, ⓦwww.usembassy.org.nz

United Kingdom

Belfast Queens House, 14 Queen St, Belfast BT1 6EQ ⓣ028/9032 8239
Edinburgh 3 Regent Terrace, Edinburgh EH7 5BW ⓣ0131/556 8315
London 24 Grosvenor Square, London W1A 1AE ⓣ020/7499 9000, visa hotline ⓣ09068/200290, ⓦwww.usembassy.org.uk

Embassies and consulates in Oregon and Washington

Australia

Seattle 401 Andover Park East, Seattle, WA ⓣ206/575-7446

Canada

Seattle 600 Stewart St #412, Seattle, WA ⓣ206/443-1777

New Zealand

Seattle 6810 51st Ave NE, Seattle, WA ⓣ206/525-0271

United Kingdom

Portland (phone only) ⓣ503/227-5669
Seattle 900 Fourth Ave, Seattle, WA ⓣ206/622-9255

Canada

British citizens, as well as citizens of the European Union (EU), Scandinavia, and most British Commonwealth countries do not need an entry visa to visit **Canada**: all that is required is a full valid passport. In addition, all visitors to Canada have to complete a **customs/registration form**, which is handed out on incoming planes, on ferries, and at border crossing points (with the US). The completed forms are processed during immigration control at your initial point of arrival on Canadian soil. The form requires details of where you are staying on your first night and the date you intend to leave Canada. Recently, visitors have also been obliged to complete forms relating to possible previous exposure to SARS. Admission is normally granted for a period of up to ninety days and you may be asked to demonstrate that you have enough money to pay for your stay – Can$400 per week in cash or a credit card should be sufficient. If you plan a longer trip, Canadian immigration officials may permit stays of up to a maximum of six months: check with the Canadian High Commission for details before you leave.

Canadian embassies and consulates abroad

Australia

Canberra Commonwealth Ave, Canberra, ACT 2600 ⓣ02/6270 4000
Perth 267 St George's Terrace, Third Floor, Perth, Western Australia 6000 ⓣ08 9322 7930
Sydney Level 5, Quay West Building, 111 Harrington St, Sydney, NSW 2000 ⓣ02/9364 3000

Ireland

Dublin 65 St Stephen's Green, Dublin 2 ⓣ01/417 4100

New Zealand

Auckland 9th Floor, Jetset Centre, 44–48 Emily Place, Auckland 1 ⓣ09/309 3690, ⓦwww.Auckland.gc.ca
Wellington PO Box 12049, Thorndon, Wellington ⓣ04/471-2082, ⓦwww.wellington.gc.ca

UK

London Macdonald House, 1 Grosvenor Square, London W1K 0AB ⓣ020/7258 6600
There are consular representatives in Belfast, Birmingham, Cardiff, and Edinburgh.

United States

Chicago Suite 2400, 2 Prudential Plaza, 180 N Stetson Ave, Chicago, IL 60601 ⓣ312/616-1860
Los Angeles 9th Floor, 550 S Hope St, Los Angeles, CA 90071-2627 ⓣ213/346-2700, ⓦwww.losangeles.gc.ca
New York 16th Floor, Exxon Building, 1251 Avenue of the Americas, New York, NY 10020-1175 ⓣ212/596-1628
Seattle 412 Plaza 600, Sixth and Stewart, Seattle, WA, 98101-1286 ⓣ206/443-9662, ⓦwww.can-am.gc.ca/seattle
Washington, DC 501 Pennsylvania Ave NW, Washington, DC 20001 ⓣ202/682-1740

Embassies and consulates in Canada

Australia

Vancouver Suite 1225-888 Dunsmuir St, Vancouver BC V6C 3K4 ⓣ604/684-1177

Ireland

Vancouver Honorary Consul, 401-1385 West 8th Ave, Vancouver BC V6H 3V9 ⓣ604/683-9233

United States

Vancouver 1095 W Pender St, Vancouver, BC V6E 2M6 ⓣ604/685-4311

US and Canadian customs

Customs officers in both Canada and the US will relieve you of your customs declaration form, which you receive with your waiver form when it is handed out on incoming planes, on ferries, and at border crossing points. It asks if you're carrying any fresh foods and if you've visited a farm in the last month.

As well as food and anything agricultural, in the US it's prohibited to carry into the country any articles from such places as North Korea, Iran, Syria, Libya, or Cuba, while both countries draw the line at things like protected wildlife species and ancient artifacts. Anyone caught sneaking drugs into either country will not only face prosecution but be entered in the records as an undesirable and probably denied entry for all time. For **duty-free allowances** and other information regarding customs, in the US call ⓣ202/354-1000 or visit ⓦwww.customs.gov; for Canada call ⓣ1-800/461-9999 within Canada or 204/983-3500 or 506/636-5064 from outside Canada, ⓦwww.ccra-adrc.gc.ca.

Information, websites, and maps

The most useful source of information on the Pacific Northwest is the enormous range of free maps, leaflets, and brochures distributed by national tourist offices in the UK, US, or elsewhere, and each of the various state and provincial tourist offices. Write well in advance of your departure, and be as specific as possible about your interests – or just print the stuff off from their websites.

There are also various **state and provincial tourist offices** in the Northwest, which offer a vast array of free brochures and other material. They are particularly helpful if you're able to specify a particular interest – fishing in BC or skiing in the Cascades, for example – in which case they'll be able to save you huge amounts of time and trouble by sending you the latest rules, regulations, equipment rental shops, tour operators, and so forth regarding your request.

Visitor centers go under a variety of names throughout the Northwest, but they all provide detailed information about the local area. Typically they're open Mon–Fri 9am–5pm, Sat 9am–1pm, except in summer, when they may be open seven days a week from 8am or 9am until 6pm or later. In smaller towns many offices will close for the winter from about mid-September to mid-May. In the US, visitor centers are often known as the "Convention and Visitors Bureau" (CVB), while in smaller towns in both Canada and the US many operate under the auspices of the **Chamber of Commerce**, who promote local business interests. Most large communities also have free **newspapers** carrying entertainment listings. You'll also find small visitor centers in the arrival halls of the region's airports and there's usually a free phone system connecting to leading local hotels, too.

Park visitor centers (again, the name varies) should invariably be your first destination in any national, state, or provincial park. Staff are usually outdoors experts, and can offer invaluable advice on trails, current conditions, and the full range of outfitting or adventure specialists. These are also the places to go to obtain national park permits and, where applicable, permits for fishing or backcountry camping.

State and provincial tourist offices

British Columbia Tourism British Columbia, Parliament Buildings, Victoria, BC V8V 1X4 ⓣ604/603-6000, toll-free within Canada and mainland US ⓣ1-800/663-6000, ⓦwww.hellobc.com

Oregon Oregon Tourism Commission 775 Summer St NE, Salem, OR 97310 toll-free within Canada and mainland US ⓣ1-800/547-7842 ⓦwww.traveloregon.com; Central Oregon Visitors Association, 63085 N Hwy 97, Suite 107, Bend, OR ⓣ541/389-8799 or 1-800/800-8334, ⓦwww.covisitors.com; Southern Oregon Visitors Association, PO Box 1645, Medford, OR ⓣ541/779-4691 or 1-800/448-4856, ⓦwww.sova.org

Washington Washington State Tourism Development Division 101 General Administration Building, PO Box 42500, Olympia, WA 98504-2500 toll-free within Canada and mainland US ⓣ1-800/544-1800, ⓦwww.experiencewashington.com; Northwest Washington Tourism Association, ⓣ1-800/382-5417, ⓦwww.travel-in-wa.com

Tourist offices in the UK

British Columbia British Columbia House 1 Regent St, London SW1Y 4NS ⓣ020/7930 6857, ⓦwww.hellobc.com

Canada Visit Canada Centre, 62–65 Trafalgar Square, London WC2N 5DT ⓣ0906/871 5000, ⓦwww.travelcanada.ca. Open weekdays 9am–5.30pm. Call for brochures and general information.

USTTA The United States Travel and Tourism Administration USTTA (ⓦwww.tinet.ita.doc.gov), has offices all over the world, usually in US embassies and consulates. In the UK, they have a premium-rated number for ordering brochures and obtaining general information (ⓣ0906/550 8972).

The Internet

You can obtain plenty of information about the Pacific Northwest, whether you're planning your trip or you're already here and checking to see what's going on, from the Internet. The various sites include information on the area's history, lore, and quirks, and offer information on city hotels, restaurants, and clubs, along with pages devoted to art and architecture and the like. Some of these sites are listed below, but don't forget to visit our own site at ⓦtravel.roughguides.com for other suggestions for the Northwest and beyond.

Oregon

Oregon State Parks and Recreation ⓦ**www.prd.state.or.us.** Official state website, and surprisingly easy to use, detailing regional parks and campgrounds, and allowing reservations for all manner of facilities.
Palahniuk.com ⓦ**www.chuckpalahniuk.com.** Personal blog and website for the cult author and local oddball, best known for penning *Fight Club*.
PDX History ⓦ**pdxhistory.com.** Cluttered but fascinating pages displaying the glory of old-time Portland in photographs, postcards, and general lore.
Portland Visitors Association ⓦ**www.travelportland.com.** Official city tourism website with a lengthy, if typical, array of hotel, restaurant, and shopping listings.
Willamette Week ⓦ**www.willametteweek.com.** Portland's alternative-weekly site showcasing music reviews, cultural listings, and intrepid muckraking.

Washington

Bumbershoot ⓦ**www.bumbershoot.org.** Outlines the popular Seattle arts festival and offers online ticket sales.
City of Seattle ⓦ**www.cityofseattle.net.** The official tourist guide to Seattle, loaded with information on everything from local politics to sightseeing and entertainment to road conditions.
HistoryLink ⓦ**www.historylink.org.** Encyclopedia of Seattle and King County history, with more than 1500 searchable essays, cybertours of historic areas, copious links, and many fascinating old photos and documents.
Seattle Parks and Recreation ⓦ**www.ci.seattle.wa.us/parks.** Info on all of the city's parks, as well as the events, amenities, athletic, and recreational activities they offer.
Washington State Parks and Recreation Commission ⓦ**www.parks.wa.gov.** Maps and descriptions of state parks throughout Washington, including many in the Puget Sound region.

British Columbia

Hotel reservations ⓦ**www.Vancouver.com.** A central reservations service with occasional good room deals.
Tourism Vancouver ⓦ**www.tourismvancouver.com.** Comprehensive city guide offering accommodation options and an events guide that's updated daily.
Tourism Victoria ⓦ**www.tourismvictoria.com.** Official site of Victoria's visitor center.
Vancouver Aquarium ⓦ**www.vanaqua.org.** An detailed collection of online exhibits and worthy features on various aspects of marine biology. The Orca ("Killer Whale") pages contain helpful advice on whale watching in the area.
Vancouver events and listings ⓦ**www.straight.com.** Website for the excellent and long-established *Georgia Straight* listings magazine.

General outdoors

Backcountry Resource Center ⓦ**www.pweb.jps.net/~prichins/backcountry_resource_center.** Superb non-commercial site laden with valuable information on backcountry skiing, climbing, and general outdoor interests.
Meteorological Service of Canada ⓦ**www.weatheroffice.ec.gc.ca.** The official Canadian government weather site.
Great Outdoor Recreation Page ⓦ**www.gorp.com.** Covers outdoor pursuits throughout the world, but best on North America. Particularly strong on hiking advice and locations.
Ski Maps ⓦ**www.skimaps.com.** The latest snowfall reports, plus the snow-base depth and trail maps for all the major skiing and snowboarding resorts in the region.

Maps

The free maps issued by each state, provincial, or local tourist office are usually fine for general driving and route planning and can be used in conjunction with the maps provided in this guide. To get hold of tourist office maps, either write to the office directly or stop by any visitor center.

Cities with confusing layouts, such as Seattle's, can make detailed maps highly advisable if you're venturing into the more remote edges of town. If you're a member, you can get free maps from the local office of the **American Automobile Association**, near Seattle Center at 330 Sixth Avenue N (Mon–Fri 8.30am–5.30pm; ⓣ206/448-5353, ⓦwww.aaawa.com), or in Portland at 600 SW Market St (Mon–Fri 9am–5pm; ⓣ503/222-6767). An even better choice may be to invest in an all-inclusive map-book like the excellent *2004 Thomas Guide to King and Snohomish County Streets* ($31.95), or the same company's *Metropolitan Puget Sound* guide ($41.95) and *2004 Portland Metropolitan Guide* ($29.95). Specialized **hiking** and **trail** guides, very useful in the mountainous and scenic Puget Sound region, are carried by most bookstores and camping/outdoors shops as well.

The well-equipped bookstores that you'll find in Seattle, Vancouver, and Portland – as well as camping shops, and park ranger or warden stations in national parks, state and provincial parks and wilderness areas – will all sell good-quality local **hiking maps** for a few dollars. If you want to be absolutely sure of getting the maps you need for independent wilderness travel in Canada, contact the Canada Map Office, 130 Bentley Ave, Ottawa, ON K1A OE9 (ⓣ613/952-7000). It supplies map indexes, which will identify the map you need; it also produces two useful brochures entitled *How to Use a Map* and *Maps and Wilderness Canoeing*, and publishes two main series of maps, at 1:250,000 and 1:50,000 scale.

Map outlets

In the US and Canada

ADC Map & Travel Center 1636 I Street NW, Washington, DC 20006 ⓣ1-800/544-2659, ⓦwww.adcmap.com

Adventurous Traveler.com US ⓣ1-800/282-3963, ⓦwww.adventuroustraveler.com

Book Passage 51 Tamal Vista Blvd, Corte Madera, CA 94925 ⓣ415/999-7909; ⓦwww.bookpassage.com

Complete Traveler 199 Madison Ave, New York, NY 10016 ⓣ212/685-9007; 3207 Fillmore St, San Francisco, CA 92123 ⓣ415/923-1511

Distant Lands 56 S Raymond Ave, Pasadena, CA 91105 ⓣ626/449-3220, ⓦwww.distantlands.com

Globe Corner Bookstore 28 Church St, Cambridge, MA 02138 ⓣ1-800/358-6013, ⓦwww.globercorner.com

International Travel Maps and Books 530 W Broadway, Vancouver BC V5Y 1P8 ⓣ604/879-3621, ⓦwww.itmb.com

Map Link 30 S La Petera Lane #5, Santa Barbara, CA 93117 ⓣ805/692-6777, ⓦwww.maplink.com

Open Air Books and Maps 25 Toronto St, Toronto ONT M5C 2R1 ⓣ416/363-0719

Phileas Fogg's Books & Maps #87 Stanford Shopping Center, Palo Alto, CA 94304, ⓣ1-800/533-FOGG

Powells Travel Books 701 SW Sixth Ave, Portland, OR 97204 ⓣ503/228-1108, ⓦwww.powells.com

Rand McNally US ⓣ1-800/333-0136, ⓦwww.randmcnally.com. Around thirty stores across the US; dial ext 2111 or check the website for the nearest location.

Savvy Traveler 301 S Michigan Ave, Chicago, IL 60604 ⓣ312/913-9800, ⓦwww.thesavvytraveller.com

Sierra Club Bookstore 6014 College Ave, Oakland, CA 94618 ⓣ510/658-7470, ⓦwww.sanfranciscobay.sierraclub.org

Travel Books & Language Center 4337 Wisconsin Ave NW, Washington, DC 20814 ⓣ1-800/220-2665 ⓦwww.ambook.org/bookstore/travelbks

Travel Bug Bookstore 2667 W Broadway, Vancouver, BC V6K 2G2 ⓣ604/737-1122, ⓦwww.swifty.com/tbug

Ulysses Travel Bookshop 101 Yorkville Ave, Toronto M5R 1C1 ⓣ1-800/268-4395

World of Maps 1235 Wellington St, Ottawa, Ontario K1Y 3A3 ⓣ1-800/214-8524, ⓦwww.worldofmaps.com

In the UK and Ireland

Blackwell's Map and Travel Shop 53 Broad St, Oxford OX1 3BQ ⓣ01865/792792; 100 Charing Cross Rd, London WC2H 0JG ⓣ020/7292 5100, ⓦbookshop.blackwell.co.uk

Daunt Books 83 Marylebone High St, London W1M 3DE ⓣ020/7224 2295; 193 Haverstock Hill, NW3 4QL ⓣ020/7794 4006

Easons Bookshop 40 O'Connell St, Dublin 1 ⓣ01/858 3881, ⓦwww.eason.ie

Heffers Map Centre 20 Trinity St, Cambridge CB2 1TJ ⓣ01865/333 536, ⓦwww.heffers.co.uk

Hereford Map Centre 24–25 Church St, Hereford HR1 2LR ⓣ01432/266322, ⓦwww.users.globalnet.co.uk/~mapped
Hodges Figgis Bookshop 56–58 Dawson St, Dublin 2 ⓣ01/677 4754
James Thin Ltd 53–62 South Bridge, Edinburgh EH1 1YS ⓣ0131/622 8222
John Smith and Sons 57–61 St Vincent St, Glasgow G2 5TB ⓣ0141/221 7472, ⓦwww.johnsmith.co.uk
The Map Shop 30a Belvoir St, Leicester LE1 6QH ⓣ0116/247 1400, ⓦwww.mapshopleicester.co.uk
National Map Centre 20–22 Caxton St, Westminster, London SW1H 0QU ⓣ020/7222 2466, ⓦwww.mapstore.co.uk
Newcastle Map Centre 55 Grey St, Newcastle-upon-Tyne NE1 6EF ⓣ0191/261 5622
Ordnance Survey Ireland Phoenix Park, Dublin 8 ⓣ01/802 5300, ⓦwww.osi.ie
Ordnance Survey of Northern Ireland Colby House, Stranmillis Court, Belfast BT9 5BJ ⓣ028/9025 5755, ⓦwww.osni.gov.uk
Stanfords 12–14 Long Acre, London WC2E 9LP ⓣ020/7836 1321; 29 Corn St, Bristol BS1 1HT ⓣ0117/929 9966, ⓦwww.stanfords.co.uk
The Travel Bookshop 13–15 Blenheim Crescent, London W11 2EE ⓣ020/7229 5260, ⓦwww.thetravelbookshop.co.uk
Waterstone's Queens Bldg, 8 Royal Ave, Belfast BT1 1DA ⓣ028/9024 7355; 69 Patrick St, Cork ⓣ021/276522, ⓦwww.waterstones.co.uk

In Australia and New Zealand

Auckland Map Centre 1A Wyndham St, Auckland ⓣ09/309 7725
Hema Maps in Australia at 25 McKechnie Drive, Eight Mile Plains, Queensland 4113 ⓣ07/3340 0000; in New Zealand at Unit D 24, Ra Ora Drive, East Tamaki, Auckland ⓣ09/273 6459, ⓦwww.hemamaps.com
Map Land 372 Little Bourke St, Melbourne, Victoria 3000 ⓣ03/9670 4383, ⓦwww.mapland.com.au
Map World 371 Pitt St, Sydney, NSW 2000 ⓣ02/9261 3601, ⓦwww.mapworld.net.au
Mapworks 184 Keilor Rd, North Essendon, Victoria 3041 ⓣ03/9379 7533, ⓦwww.mapworks.com.au
Melbourne Map Centre 259 High St, Kew, Victoria 3101 ⓣ03/9853 3526, ⓦwww.melbmap.com.au
Specialty Maps 58 Albert St, Auckland ⓣ09/307 2217
Travel Bookshop Shop 3, 175 Liverpool St, Sydney, NSW 2000 ⓣ02/9261 8200
World Wide Maps & Guides 187 George St, Brisbane, Queensland 4001 ⓣ07/3221 4330, ⓦwww.worldwidemaps.com.au

Insurance

Although not compulsory, travelers from abroad should really have some form of travel insurance: the US has no national health system, and it can cost an arm and a leg (so to speak) having even minor medical treatment. Before paying for a new policy, however, it's worth checking whether you are already covered; this is recommended for US residents as well. Canada has an excellent national health service, but non-residents have to pay substantially to use it. There is no free treatment, and in some Canadian provinces doctors and hospitals actually add a surcharge to treatment meted out to foreigners.

Beyond this, provincial health plans usually provide partial cover for medical mishaps while outside the country. In addition, holders of official student/teacher/youth cards in Canada and the US are entitled to meager accident coverage and hospital in-patient benefits. Students will often find that their student health coverage extends during the vacations and for one term beyond the date of last enrollment.

Rough Guides travel insurance

Rough Guides Ltd offers a low-cost travel insurance policy, especially customized for our statistically low-risk readers by a leading British broker, provided by the American International Group (AIG) and registered with the British regulatory body, GISC (the General Insurance Standards Council). There are five main Rough Guides insurance plans: **No Frills** for the bare minimum for secure travel; **Essential**, which provides decent all-round cover; **Premier** for comprehensive cover with a wide range of benefits; **Extended Stay** for cover lasting four months to a year; and **Annual Multi-Trip**, a cost-effective way of getting Premier cover if you travel more than once a year. Premier, Annual Multi-Trip, and Extended Stay policies can be supplemented by a "Hazardous Pursuits Extension" if you plan to indulge in sports considered dangerous, such as skiing or trekking. For a policy quote, call the Rough Guide Insurance Line: toll-free in the UK ⓣ0800/015 09 06 or ⓣ+44 1392 314 665 from elsewhere. Alternatively, get an online quote at ⓦwww.roughguides.com/insurance.

After exhausting the possibilities above, you might want to contact a **specialist travel insurance** company, or consider the travel insurance deal we offer (see box). A typical travel insurance policy usually provides cover for the loss of baggage, tickets, and – up to a certain limit – cash or checks, as well as cancellation or curtailment of your journey. Most of them exclude so-called dangerous sports unless an extra premium is paid: in the US, this can mean rock-climbing, whitewater rafting, and windsurfing, though probably not kayaking or hiking. Many policies can be changed to exclude coverage you don't need – for example, sickness and accident benefits can often be excluded or included at will. If you do take medical coverage, ascertain whether benefits will be paid as treatment proceeds or only after your return home, and whether there is a 24-hour medical emergency number. When securing baggage cover, make sure that the per-article limit – typically under £500/$US780 – will cover your most valuable possession. If you need to make a claim, you should keep receipts for medicines and medical treatment, and in the event you have anything stolen, you must obtain an official statement from the police.

Health

If you have a serious accident while in the US or Canada, emergency medical services will get to you quickly and charge you later. For emergencies or ambulances in both countries, dial ⓣ911 (or whatever variant may be on the information plate of the pay phone). If you have medical or dental problems that don't require an ambulance, most hospitals will have a walk-in emergency room: for your nearest hospital, check with your hotel or dial ⓣ411. The same is true for dental work.

Should you need to see a **doctor**, lists can be found in the *Yellow Pages* under "Clinics" or "Physicians and Surgeons." A basic consultation fee is around $60–100, payable in advance. Medications aren't cheap either – keep all your receipts for later claims on your insurance policy.

Many minor ailments can be remedied using the fabulous array of potions and lotions available in **drugstores**. Foreign visitors should bear in mind that many pills available over the counter at home need a prescription in the US and Canada, and that local brand names can be confusing; ask for advice at the pharmacy in any drugstore. **US residents** on the hunt for cheap drugs in Canada will find some prescription-only medications in America available here without a prescription (such as codeine-based painkillers). As for official regulations, if you're coming back with a considerable amount of prescription drugs, and they are discovered at the border, you could be detained by a US Customs agent and asked all manner of probing, hostile questions and subjected to other official browbeating. To save the trouble, follow the official rules and bring back no more than a three-month supply.

Travelers from Europe do not require **inoculations** to enter the US or Canada.

Costs, money, and banks

Even more than in most other parts of the country, the Pacific Northwest's economy has been mired in stagnation, if not outright recession, since the turn of the twenty-first century, due largely to the bursting of the high-tech bubble. Although this isn't good for local businesses, it's not so bad for visitors, who can find numerous options for cheap amenities and amusements, along with many bargains and affordable costs for goods and services. Beyond this, even when the exchange rate is at its least advantageous, most Western European visitors find virtually everything – accommodation, food, gas, cameras, clothes, and more – to be better value in the US, and to a lesser extent Canada, than it is at home.

Costs

Generally, if you're sticking to a very tight **budget** – camping and buying groceries from shops – you could squeeze by on US$20–35 per person a day. You're not going to last long living like this, though, and a more comfortable average daily budget, covering a motel room, bus travel, a museum or two, and a restaurant meal would work out at around US$75–85. Naturally, once you upgrade your accommodation, eat out two or three times a day, and take in the city nightlife, this figure can easily double.

Accommodation is likely to be your biggest single expense. Few hotel or motel rooms in the cities of either country cost under US$40/Can$45, and even a marginally decent room will run anywhere from US$50–90, with fancier hotels costing much, much more – upwards of US$300 in

Prices

Prices are given in either US or Canadian dollars as appropriate, with a label – US$ or Can$ – where confusion may arise. The two currencies do not have a one-for-one exchange rate, though Canadian shops and hotels are often prepared to accept US dollars, but note this arrangement is not reciprocated in the US.

Unless otherwise stated, the hotel price codes (see p.39) are for the cheapest double room in high season, exclusive of any local taxes and special deals. For museums and similar attractions, the prices we quote are for adults; young children and seniors usually get in half-price or free.

some cases. **Hostels** offering dorm beds – usually for US$15–20 – are one alternative (with private rooms US$40–45), and camping is also cheap, ranging from free to US$21/Can$27 per night. Accommodation prices may often be higher from June to early September, and throughout the more remote areas of the region.

Unlike accommodation, prices for good **food** range widely, from espresso carts to chic restaurants. You could get by on as little as US$15 a day, but realistically you should aim for around US$40 – and remember, too, that the area has plenty of great spots for a splurge.

Traveling around on buses and trains is reasonably economic, too – in cash terms if not in time, whilst a group of two or more, renting a car, at around US$150 a week, can be a very good investment, not least because it will enable you to stay in the ubiquitous budget motels along the interstates. Finally, you should figure in costs for **tipping** into your travel budget. Expect to tip about 15 percent of the bill before tax to waiters in most restaurants (unless the service is truly wretched), and 20 percent in upscale establishments. In the US, this is where most of a waiter's income comes from, and not leaving a fair amount is seen as a big faux pas. About 15 percent should also be added to taxi fares; afterwards, round up to the nearest 50¢ or dollar, as well. A hotel porter should get $1 per bag; chambermaids $1–2 a day; and valet attendants $1.

Taxes

In almost every state and province, **sales tax**, at varying rates up to fifteen percent in Canada and 8.8 percent in Washington, is added to virtually everything you buy in shops – except in Oregon, where there is none. The shock is strongest when it comes to accommodation, where certain regions, including Oregon, levy a **hotel room tax** on top of provincial, state, or federal sales taxes. In British Columbia the room tax is between five and ten percent, in Washington 16 percent, and in Oregon 12–14 percent.

All of Canada, though, levies the seven-percent **Goods and Services Tax** (GST). However, note that a GST rebate is available to visitors for certain goods and accommodation expenditure over Can$200 during a maximum period of one month. This can add up to a significant amount, so take the trouble to pick up claim forms, available from many shops and hotels or from any Canadian embassy. Return them, with all receipts, to Visitor Rebate Program, Canada Customs and Revenue Agency, Summerside Tax Centre, 275 Pope Rd, Suite 104, Summerside, PE C1N 6C6. For more information call ⓣ902/432-5608 (outside

Money: a note for foreign travelers

US and Canadian currency come in bills of $1, $5, $10, $20, $50, and $100, plus various larger (and rarer) denominations in Canada. In the United States, confusingly, all are the same size and same greenish color (with a splash of pastel recently introduced into the $20), making it necessary to check each bill carefully. In Canada the notes all have different colors and designs, while the country's $1 bill has been replaced by a gold-colored coin known as a "**loonie**" (after the bird on one face). No one's really come up with a decent name for the $2 coin, though "twoonie" has been tried.

The dollar in both Canada and the US is made up of 100 cents in coins with the same names in both countries: 1 cent (penny), 5 cents (nickel), 10 cents (dime) and 25 cents (quarter). In the US, look out for the **state quarter** designs being introduced one month at a time until 2008, and also the golden "**Sacajawea**" dollar coin, named after the Native American women who assisted Lewis and Clark on their expeditions through the uncharted West, and recently discontinued. Very occasionally in the US, you might come across the JFK half-dollars (50¢), Susan B. Anthony dollar coins, or Thomas Jefferson two-dollar bills. Change (quarters are the most useful) is needed for buses, parking meters, vending machines, and telephones, so always carry plenty.

Canada) or ⓣ1-800/668-4748, ⓦwww.ccra-adrc.gc.ca/visitors; further information is also available at ⓦwww.canadatourism.com.

Travelers' checks

US or Canadian dollar **travelers' checks** are the best way to carry money for both North American and foreign visitors, and offer the security of knowing that lost or stolen checks will be replaced. In most cases they can also be widely used as cash if they're made out in the currency in which you're spending them. Only if you're restricting your travels to Canada is it worth opting specifically for Canadian-dollar checks. In neither country are you likely to have any problems using checks in shops, restaurants, and gas stations, but it's definitely worth investing in one or other of the two best-known types – American Express or Visa. Be sure to have plenty of the $10 and $20 denominations for everyday transactions.

Travelers' checks can be cashed at most banks, though the commission charged (which usually incorporates both a flat fee and a one-to-two percent levy) varies substantially. In general, you would do better to change large amounts occasionally than small amounts frequently. Checks made out in Canadian dollars can often be used as cash for many transactions. For converting **foreign currency** in either country, exchange bureaux such as Thomas Cook or American Express, always found at airports, tend to charge less commission. Rarely do hotels change foreign currency.

For proper **security** in all cases, keep the purchase agreement and a record of check serial numbers safe and separate from the checks themselves. In the event that checks are lost or stolen, the issuing company will expect you to report the loss immediately (see p.62 for emergency numbers). Most companies claim to replace lost or stolen checks within 24 hours.

Credit and ATM cards

For many services, it's simply taken for granted that you'll be paying with plastic. You'll be asked to show a credit card when renting a car, bike, or other such item, or to start a "tab" at hotels for incidental charges; in any case, you can always pay the bill in cash when you return the item or check out of your room. Visa, MasterCard, Diners Club, Discover, and American Express are the most widely used (see p.62 for emergency numbers).

With MasterCard or Visa it is also possible to **withdraw cash** at any bank displaying relevant stickers, or from appropriate automatic teller machines (**ATMs**). Make sure you have a **personal identification number**, or PIN, that's designed to work overseas. Credit-card cash advances are treated as loans, with interest accruing daily from the date of withdrawal (there may be a transaction fee on top of this), and with substantially higher interest rates for such cash advances than for regular purchases. Diners Club cards can be used to cash personal checks at Citibank branches. American Express cards can only get cash, or buy travelers checks, at American Express offices (check the *Yellow Pages*) or from the travelers'-check dispensers at most major airports. Most Canadian credit cards issued by hometown banks will be honored in the US and vice versa. To find the nearest ATM, call Amex ⓣ1-800/CASH-NOW; Cirrus ⓣ1-800/4-CIRRUS; The Exchange ⓣ1-800/237-ATMS; or Plus ⓣ1-800/843-7587.

Most cash-dispensing cards issued by **foreign banks** are accepted in the US and Canada, as long as they are linked to the international networks above – check before you set off. Overseas visitors should also bear in mind that fluctuating exchange rates may result in spending more (or less) than expected when the item eventually shows up on a statement.

Financial emergencies

If you run out of money abroad, or there is some kind of **emergency**, the quickest way to get money sent out is to contact your bank at home and have them wire the cash to the nearest bank. Having money **wired** from home is never convenient or cheap, and should be considered a last resort. If you must, the quickest way to do it is to have someone take cash to the nearest **American Express Moneygram** office (ⓣ1-800/543-4080, also available at participating Thomas Cook branches) and have it instantaneously wired to you, minus a ten-percent commission that varies according to the amount sent – the entire process should take no longer than ten minutes. For similar, if slightly pricier, services, **Western Union** has offices in major cities (information at ⓣ1-800/325-6000 in the US, ⓣ1-800/235-0000 in Canada, ⓣ0800/833833 in the UK, and ⓣ1800/649 565 in Australia, ⓦwww.westernunion.com), with credit-card payments subject to an additional $10 fee.

It's a bit less expensive to get a bank to transfer cash by cable, while if you have a few days' leeway, sending a postal money order through the mail, which is exchangeable at any post office, is cheaper still. The equivalent for foreign travelers is the **international money order**, for which you need to allow up to seven days in the international air mail before arrival. An ordinary check sent from overseas takes two to three weeks to clear.

Foreigners in difficulties have the final option of throwing themselves on the mercy of their nearest national **consulate** (see pp.21–22), which will – in worst cases only – repatriate you, but will never, under any circumstances, lend you money.

Getting around

The days when you could explore the Pacific Northwest by train are long gone, and Amtrak in the US and VIA Rail in Canada now only provide a skeletal service, though they do link the major cities and have several particularly scenic routes. In both countries, Greyhound buses offer a more extensive network of services, while local bus companies supplement Greyhound's coverage, more so in Canada than in the US. Along the coast, the boats of BC Ferries and Washington State Ferries are frequent, fast, and efficient. Flying is a key way – sometimes the only way – of reaching some destinations in the Northwest, but it is more expensive, though competition in the skies can lead to some decent bargains.

On most forms of public transport there are **discounted fares** for children under 12, youths between 13 and 21, and seniors. Nevertheless, things are always easier if you have a **car**. Many of the most spectacular and memorable destinations in the Pacific Northwest are far removed from the cities and unreachable by public transport. Even if a bus or train could take you to the vicinity of a national park, it would prove impossible to explore the interior without your own vehicle.

By train

Neither the American Amtrak nor the Canadian VIA Rail networks serve many centers anymore, and services are generally restricted to one or two trains a day, sometimes on only a few days each week. That said, train travel is by far the most comfortable – and often the most scenic – way to go, and long-distance rides especially can be a great opportunity to meet people.

Amtrak

Details of the **Amtrak** (ⓣ1-800/USA-RAIL, ⓦwww.amtrak.com) routes that connect the states of Washington and Oregon with the rest of the United States, together with information on Amtrak's pricing and reservation policies, can be found on p.11. Within the Pacific Northwest, the most appealing of these routes is the **Coast Starlight**, which meanders up the coast from Los Angeles and Oakland (for bus connections from San Francisco) to cross the Oregon border near Klamath Falls, then links to the Willamette Valley before traveling to Seattle and connecting with buses going on to Vancouver. The other major regional trains include the **Empire Builder**, which originates in Chicago and crosses eastern Washington to terminate in either Portland or Seattle, and the **Cascades**, a shorter route linking Eugene with Seattle. In 2003 Amtrak also began offering a summertime **Lewis and Clark** line between Portland and Astoria, Oregon, though whether this becomes a permanent seasonal route is uncertain.

Always **reserve** as far in advance as possible; all passengers must have seats, and some trains, especially between major cities, are booked solid. Supplements are also payable for **sleeping compartments** (around $100 extra per night for one or two people, including three full meals). However, even standard Amtrak carriages are surprisingly spacious, and there are additional dining cars and lounge cars, some with full bars and glass-domed 360° viewing compartments.

For any one specific journey, the train can be more expensive than taking a Greyhound or even a plane, though special deals, especially in the off-peak season (Sept–May), bring the costs down considerably. Visitors can further reduce costs by buying an Amtrak rail pass (see p.11): the **North America Rail Pass** is issued in conjunction with VIA Rail and is valid for 30 consecutive days of travel up to one year from the date of purchase, and you may travel up to four times, one-way, over any given route segment. The pass is valid for coach (second-class) travel, but can be upgraded for an additional charge. Many trains fill quickly, so it's worth making reservations.

Canadian rail services

Details of **VIA Rail** services from the rest of Canada to the Northwest – insofar as they still exist – and of the company's transcontinental pricing and reservation policies are covered on p.12. From Vancouver, you can travel with VIA Rail to Kamloops, Jasper, Edmonton, and points east and south to Seattle by both Amtrak train and bus. The other VIA Rail service in British Columbia links Victoria with Nanaimo and Courtenay on Vancouver Island.

By bus

Buses are by far the least expensive way to get around. The main long-distance service is **Greyhound** in both the US and Canada, though separate companies run the two national schedules. Greyhound buses link all major cities and many smaller towns in the Northwest, though you will have little call to use Greyhound's Canadian coverage unless you are heading beyond the areas covered in this guide.

Out in the countryside and in the smaller towns, buses are fairly scarce, sometimes appearing only once a day, and here you'll need to plot your route with care. But along the **main highways**, buses run around the clock to a fairly full timetable, stopping only for meal breaks (almost always fast-food dives) and driver changeovers. Nearly all Greyhounds are non-smoking, have toilets, and are less uncomfortable than you might expect. It's feasible to save on a night's accommodation by traveling overnight and sleeping on the bus – though you may not feel up to much the next day. To avoid possible hassle, lone female travelers in particular should take care to sit as near to the driver as possible, and to arrive during daylight hours, since bus stations are often in fairly dodgy areas. Don't assume any given bus stop to be anywhere near the town center.

Seats can be **reserved** either in person at a bus station or on the toll-free number, but this is rarely necessary and only recommended on the busy, medium-haul intercity services like that between Seattle and Portland or services out of Vancouver to BC destinations. Even if you arrive to find a bus full, another bus will be employed to take on overflow passengers.

Fares are relatively inexpensive, but over long distances soon add up – for example, it costs around US$25 from Portland to Seattle, and Can$130 between Vancouver and Calgary (though if you buy in advance you can bring costs down: one-day advance purchase on this route, for example, costs $70 and a seven-day advance purchase is

Major Pacific Northwest bus companies

Clallam Transit ⓣ360/452-4511 or 1-800/858-3747, ⓦwww.clallamtransit.com. Washington's Olympic Peninsula.
Greyhound America ⓣ1-800/231-2222, ⓦwww.greyhound.com. Washington, Oregon, and the rest of the US.
Greyhound Canada ⓣ1-800/661-8747, ⓦwww.greyhound.ca. Long-distance across western Canada.
Jefferson Transit ⓣ360/385-4777, ⓦwww.jeffersontransit.com. Washington's Olympic Peninsula.
Laidlaw ⓣ250/385-4411, ⓦwww.grayline.ca/victoria. Vancouver Island.
Malaspina Coach Lines ⓣ1-877/227-8287. The Sunshine Coast, Powell River, Whistler, Pemberton, and Nanaimo on Vancouver Island.
Pacific Coach Lines ⓣ604/662-8074, 250/385-4411 or 1-800/661-1725, ⓦwww.pacificcoach.com. Vancouver, Vancouver Island, and the Sunshine Coast.
Perimeter ⓣ604/266-5386 or 905-0041, ⓦwww.perimeterbus.com. From Vancouver and Vancouver airport to Squamish and Whistler.
Quick Shuttle ⓣ604/940-4428 or 1-800/665-2122, ⓦwww.quickcoach.com. Sea-Tac Airport, Seattle, Bellingham, Vancouver, and Vancouver airport.

$62). For long trips the bus costs a little less than the train in both countries, though considering the time involved on some journeys, it's not always that much cheaper than flying. However, the bus is the best deal if you plan to visit a lot of places: in the US, the domestic **Ameripass** is good for unlimited travel nationwide, from a week to two months (see p.12). Discounts are available for children under 12, seniors over 62, and students enrolled in a college or university. To buy online, you must purchase your pass no fewer than 14 days prior to the start of travel. Otherwise you can purchase a pass at any participating Greyhound terminal or agency. Note that the Ameripass is not valid for travel in Canada, except for the Seattle to Vancouver route.

Greyhound Canada's **Canada Pass** works in a similar way, but is not a good value unless you intend to travel a fair amount beyond Vancouver and Vancouver Island. More extensive intercity bus services are offered by smaller, local companies such as Pacific Coach Lines and Laidlaw (see box, above).

International passes

International travelers intending to explore the US Northwest by bus can save a lot of money by purchasing a bus pass before they reach North America. The international **Ameripass** for non-US citizens works in similar fashion, offering visitors bound for Oregon and Washington (and the rest of the US) unlimited travel within a set time limit. **Rates** in US dollars for online booking range all the way from 4 days for $128 to 15 days for $269 to 60 days for $479; for the full schedule of options and fares, check ⓦwww.greyhound.com. If you wish to purchase online, then you must buy the pass no fewer than 21 days before the start of travel. International Ameripasses are not available from Greyhound terminals, but international passengers can purchase the domestic pass once they're in the US at the standard domestic rates. No daily extensions are available on either the Canadian or US pass. For a list of selected Ameripass vendors outside the US, see box on p.13.

By plane

Taking a **plane** is easily the quickest way to get about the Pacific Northwest. Across the region, the big international airlines compete with a plethora of smaller, regional companies. One appealing alternative, **Kenmore Air** schedules five **seaplane** flights daily from downtown Seattle on Lake Union to Victoria ($116 one-way, $177–198 round-trip; ⓣ1-800/543-9595; ⓦwww.kenmoreair.com), as well as six flights to the San Juan Islands ($98 one-way, $163–194 round-trip).

If you're planning to zip around the Northwest by plane, then you might consider purchasing an **airpass**, which all the main US and Canadian airlines (and British Airways in conjunction with various carriers) offer. Conditions vary from airline to airline, but all share the same basic principles, notably that passes must be bought before you travel, with the proviso that you cross the Atlantic with the given airline. All the deals are broadly similar, whether you are flying with US or Canadian carriers, and involve the purchase of between a minimum of three and maximum of ten flight **coupons**. Air Canada, for example, offers between three and eight coupons for travel in the US and Canada or from the UK, and offers best rates on the pass if you cross the Atlantic with Air Canada or United. Rates are higher for other transatlantic carriers, but these carriers can only be a non-North American airline such as British Airways. For the North America Airpass for flights in the US and Canada, three coupons with Air Canada-United cost US$529 in high season (mid-June-Aug) and $469 low season and US$729/669 for five coupons. Rates are similar for coupons bought in the UK. Coupons can be used for any routing, but **conditions** apply. These are similar across most airlines: in the case of Air Canada you must specify a routing (but not necessarily precise dates and flights) for all coupons at the time of purchase.

By ferry

Ferries play an important role in transportation in the Pacific Northwest – indeed, some of the islands that dot the region's long and fretted coastline can only be reached by boat. Around Seattle and Vancouver ferries transport thousands of commuters a day to and from work, but for visitors, they're a novelty: an exhilarating way to experience the scenic splendor of the area. Ferry travel can be expensive, however, when you bring a car along.

BC Ferries

BC Ferries (☎1-888-223-3779 from anywhere in BC; otherwise 604/444-2890 or 250/386-3431 in Vancouver, Victoria, or outside BC, Ⓦwww.bcferries.com), also known as the "Friendship Fleet", operate some forty ships to serve more than forty ports of call along the coast of British Columbia, from tiny two-minute lake crossings in the interior to the endless shuttles that ply back and forth across the Georgia Strait between Vancouver and Vancouver Island. Numerous ferries also crisscross between the Gulf Islands that lie scattered between Vancouver Island and the BC mainland. See box, p.491 for more information.

Washington State Ferries

Washington State Ferries (☎206/464-6400 or 1-800/84-FERRY; Ⓦwww.wsdot.wa.gov/ferries), with a commuter-oriented fleet of some twenty-five ferries, handles more than 23 million passengers per year. They run between Anacortes, Washington, and Sidney, BC (for Victoria and Vancouver Island); from Anacortes to the San Juan Islands; from Port Townsend to Keystone on Whidbey Island; and between Seattle and points on the Kitsap Peninsula and Vashon and Bainbridge islands. Reservations are not accepted – except on cross-border services – and you should try to avoid peak commuter travel times. **Tickets** are available from Pier 52, Colman Dock, in Seattle and schedules are available on the piers and at many places throughout town, usually at the same locations that carry racks of bus schedules. Timetables and fares vary by season, and sailing times vary between weekdays and weekends, so it's best to pick up sailing/fare schedules before making plans. See box, p.320 for more information.

Other regional ferries

Other ferry companies in the region include **Black Ball Transport** (☎360/457-4491, Ⓦwww.cohoferry.com), which runs routes from Port Angeles, Washington, to Victoria in Canada (2–4 daily, except in Feb) for $9 walk-on one-way fare and $33.50 for a car, with a crossing time of ninety minutes and no reservations; **Victoria Express** (☎360/452-8088 or 1-800/633-1589, Ⓦwww.victoriaexpress.com), operating a faster, one-hour trip on the same route, for passengers only (2–3 daily; $25 round-trip);

and the high-speed, passenger-only **Victoria Clipper** jet catamarans (summer four daily, winter one daily; $59–79 one-way, $99–142 round-trip; ⓣ206/448-5000, ⓦwww.victoriaclipper.com), from Seattle's Pier 69 to Victoria, BC, in two to three hours. Two increasingly popular boats provide unforgettable trips off Vancouver Island: the MV *Lady Rose* from Port Alberni, which runs through the gorgeous seascapes of the Pacific Rim National Park (see box, p.509), and the *Uchuck III*, a World War II minesweeper-turned-ferry, which patrols the villages of the island's northwest coast (see p.528).

By car

Although the weather may not always be ideal and parking in Seattle and Vancouver can be a pain, traveling **by car** is easily the best way to experience the whole of the Pacific Northwest. Apart from anything else, a car makes it possible to choose your own itinerary and to explore the wide-open landscapes that may well provide your most enduring memories of the region.

The Northwest holds some of the continent's greatest **highways**, notably Washington's North Cascades Loop, penetrating the glaciated heart of the spectacular Cascade Mountains, to Oregon's dramatic bluffs and waterfalls along the Historic Columbia River Highway and the diverse beauty of the state's coastal route. For more practical concerns, many Northwestern towns sprawl for so many miles in all directions that your hotel may be miles from the sights you came to see, or perhaps simply on the other side of a freeway that provides no pedestrian crossing. Even in smaller places the motels may be six miles or more out along the highway, and the restaurants in a shopping mall on the far side of town.

In both Canada and the US, most vehicles – and almost every rental car – run on unleaded gas, which is sold by the liter in Canada and by the gallon in the US; prices vary and have been rising in recent years, but are generally around Can75–85¢ per liter, US$1.50-2.20 per gallon. **Fuel** is readily available, though gas stations thin out markedly in the more remote regions.

The main **border crossing** between the US and Canada, by car, is on Interstate 5 (I-5) at Blaine, Washington, 30 miles south of Vancouver. In recent years, in light of heightened security concerns, crossing the boundary has become a rather tedious process, often resulting in hours of waiting time while drivers are grilled about drugs, weapons, and the like. At other, more obscure entry points the duty officers can be even more rigid, so don't be amazed if you're considerably delayed.

Backcountry driving

The Northwest possesses an extraordinarily extensive and well-maintained network of **roads**, especially considering that the mountains which cross the region experience the fiercest of winters. Every major and almost all minor towns and villages are reachable on a paved road, but for some of the scenic highlights you're likely to have to use rougher **forest roads** and **logging routes** – marked

Driving distances through the Pacific Northwest

Driving distances in kilometres and miles (km/miles)

	Eugene	Portland	Seattle	Vancouver	Victoria
Eugene	–				
Portland	142/88	–			
Seattle	416/258	274/170	–		
Vancouver	644/400	504/313	228/142	–	
Victoria	732/455	592/368	316/197	88/55	–

Victoria: assumes journey via Vancouver/ferry connections

by a number, if at all – and even gravel and dirt roads. These gravel-topped roads are often in poor condition and can be treacherous when wet. Dust and flying stones represent major **hazards**, as does subsidence caused by ice and the thundering "big rig" trucks that use such routes with little regard for automobiles. **Weather** is another potential danger, with severe snow falls possible in some areas even in summer, and dense fog plaguing the coast of Washington and Oregon. If you're planning to do a significant amount of driving along these gravel and dirt roads, then radiators and headlights should be protected from stones and insects with a wire screen and headlight covers. Always carry a spare tire and fan belt, gas can (preferably full), fill up at every opportunity, and check where the next gas station is available (on remote stretches, it could be literally hundreds of miles away). It goes without saying your car should be in excellent shape: it's also a good idea to carry flares, tire jacks, and a set of tools and wrenches. If you're planning a lot of dirt-road driving, you'd be well-advised to rent a four-wheel-drive or perhaps a pick-up.

Roads, rules, and regulations

The best **roads** for covering long distances quickly are the straight and fast multi-lane highways that radiate out from major cities. These are a maximum of six lanes divided by a central causeway and are marked on maps with thick lines and shields that contain the highway or US interstate number. Outside populated areas and off the principal arteries, highways go down to one lane each way and, though paved, the hard shoulder consists of gravel. Up in the north and off the beaten track, forest roads and other byways may be gravel-topped. In Washington and Oregon, the principal highways are the **interstates**. Across the region, lesser roads go by a variety of names – county roads, provincial routes, rural roads, or forest roads – but for the most part we've used the general "highway" designation in the guide unless a road's rough condition or other special feature demands otherwise.

Americans and Canadians drive on the **right-hand** side of the road, and in most urban areas streets are on a **grid system**, often with octagonal "Stop" signs at all four corners of junctions: priority is given to the first car to arrive, and to the car on the right if two or more cars arrive at the same time. Traffic in both directions must stop if a yellow school bus is stationary with its flashing lights on, as this means children are getting on or off. Although sizable cities such as Vancouver and Seattle present few driving hazards you haven't experienced elsewhere in North America, beware of the special, unexpected demands of cruising through the streets of Portland, Oregon, including aggressive bicyclists, narrow lanes, and ubiquitous jaywalking (see box, p.83).

Out of town, exits on multi-lane highways are numbered by the distance from the beginning of the highway, as opposed to sequentially – thus exit 55 is 10 miles (or km in Canada) after exit 45. Junctions close together may carry the same number supplemented by "A" or "B," etc. Rural **hazards** include bears, moose, and other large animals lumbering onto the road – particularly in the summer, and at dawn and dusk, when the beasts crash through the undergrowth onto the highway to escape flies, and in spring, when they are attracted to the salt on the roads. Warning signs are posted in the more hazardous areas. Headlights can dazzle wild animals and render them temporarily immobile.

The uniform maximum **speed limit** on major highways is 100kph in Canada or 65-70mph in the USA. Americans and Canadians have a justifiable paranoia about speed traps and the traffic-control planes that hover over major highways to catch offenders. On-the-spot **fines** are standard for speeding violations, for failing to carry your license with you, and for having anyone on board who isn't wearing a seat belt. Needless to say, **drunk driving** is punished severely; keep any alcohol in the trunk of the car. On the road, spot checks are frequently carried out, and the police only need a thin excuse to stop you.

If you're using your own vehicle – or borrowing a friend's – get the appropriate insurance and make sure you're covered for free **breakdown service**. Your home motoring organization – in the UK, the RAC and

AA – will issue an appropriate insurance and breakdown policy with all the appropriate documentation. The Canadian Automobile Association (Ⓣ613/247-0117, Ⓦwww.caa.ca), is the biggest recovery and repair company in Canada, and has offices in most major cities. The US equivalent is the **AAA** (Ⓣ1-800/AAA-HELP or 1-800/222-4357, Ⓦwww.aaa.com), also with offices in most major cities.

Car rental

Conditions for **renting a car** – including the names of the rental companies – are virtually identical in both Canada and the US (see box in "Getting there," p.14, for the major firms). Any US, Canadian, and UK national over 21 with a driving license is allowed to drive in the Northwest, though rental companies may refuse to rent to a driver who has held a license for less than one year, and under-25s will get lumbered with a higher insurance premium. Car-rental companies will also expect you to have a credit card; if you don't have one they may let you leave a hefty **deposit** (at least $300), but don't count on it. The driving licenses of other countries are recognized throughout the Pacific Northwest too – check with your home motoring organization. Many companies prohibit travel on dirt or gravel roads or other potentially hazardous terrain; as an alternative, you may be able to sign a damage waiver, pay an additional premium, or rent a pick-up or four-wheel-drive vehicle more suitable for such travel. If you're renting a car in winter, check where and if chains and other equipment are required or advised.

Often the least expensive way to rent a car is either to take a **fly-drive package** (see p.14) or book in advance with a major rental company. If you take a transatlantic flight, check to see if your airline offers discounted car rental for its passengers. At the height of the season in the more popular tourist areas, it's by no means uncommon to find that you can't locate an available vehicle for love nor money – another reason to book ahead. By contrast, **special deals** are more commonplace in the shoulder and low season, though rates are consistently higher on the islands and in the wilderness north than they are in the city. At a bare minimum it will likely **cost** you Can$200/US$150 to rent a basic subcompact for a week with unlimited mileage, with greater charges for larger vehicles with more features. **Taxes** are extra, but the biggest hidden surcharge is often the drop-off charge, levied when you intend to leave your car in a different place from where you picked it up. This is usually equivalent to a full week's or more rental, and can go as high as Can$500/US$350.

As for **driving insurance**, if you aren't already covered by your own policy. a **Loss Damage Waiver** – sometimes called a Collision Damage Waiver (CDW) – may be well worth the expense. At around Can$16/US$12 a day, it can add substantially to the total cost, but without it you're liable for every scratch to the car, even if it wasn't your fault.

For **breakdown** problems, an emergency number may be attached to the dashboard or stored in the glove compartment. If you're stranded on a main road, sit tight and wait for the police. An extra safety option is to rent a **mobile phone** from the car rental agency – you often only have to pay a nominal amount unless you actually use it. Finally, if you take a rental car **across the US–Canada border**, be sure to keep a copy of the contract with you. It should bear an endorsement stating that the vehicle is permitted entry into the respective country. For information on using a **driveaway**, a variation on standard car rental, see "Getting there," p.14.

RV rental

Recreational vehicles (RVs) can be rented through most travel agents specializing in US and Canadian holidays. It's best to arrange rental before getting to the Pacific Northwest, as RV rental outlets are not too common there (most people who drive them, own them), and foreign travel agents will often give cheap rates if you book a flight through them as well. You can rent a huge variety of RVs, right up to giant mobile homes with two bedrooms, showers, and fully fitted kitchens. A price of around US$900/Can$1200 in low and

US$1400/Can$1900 in high season for a five-berth van for one week is fairly typical, and you also have to take into account the cost of fuel (many RVs do less than 15mi per liter/12mi per gallon), drop-off charges, and the cost of spending the night at designated trailer parks. Regulations for dumping and overnighting are especially strict in all national, state, and provincial parks. Canada and the US also have strict but different regulations on the size of vehicle allowed: if you're planning to venture into both countries, check the regulations with your travel agent. The best UK-based rental company is Hemmingways Ltd, 56 Middle St, Brockham, Surrey RH3 7HW (ⓣ01737/842735, ⓦwww.hemmingways.co.uk), with various packages and pick-up points in the US.

By bicycle

Cycling is an affordable and healthy way to get around the Pacific Northwest, whether it's in the parks – you'll find that most have rental outlets and designated mountain-bike trails – or in the big **cities**, all three of which have cycle lanes, and in the case of Portland, a great many. In **country areas**, roads are usually well maintained and many have wide shoulders. For casual riding, bikes can be **rented** by the hour, half-day, full day, or, sometimes, by the week. Rates vary considerably depending on the type of bike you rent: reckon on US$15–35 per day. Outlets are usually found close to beaches, parks, university campuses, or simply in areas that are good for cycling. If you're taking a bike around with you, Greyhound will take bikes (so long as they're in a box), and VIA Rail and Amtrak make small charges for their transportation. Carriage charges on ferries are reasonable too, but the terms of transportation and costs do vary considerably – check with individual companies (see "By ferry," p.34). A number of companies across the region organize multi-day cycle tours, either camping out or staying in country inns, and we've mentioned local firms where appropriate. Oregon, in particular, excels with its cycling routes, and boasts the outstandingly scenic and well-maintained **Oregon Coast Bike Route**, which runs right along the state's 360-mile shoreline; a detailed brochure is available from the Oregon tourist office. All the region's state and provincial tourist offices provide general cycling information as well.

The only other non-motorized alternative for traveling the region's roads, **hitchhiking**, is almost always a bad idea – both dangerous and illegal.

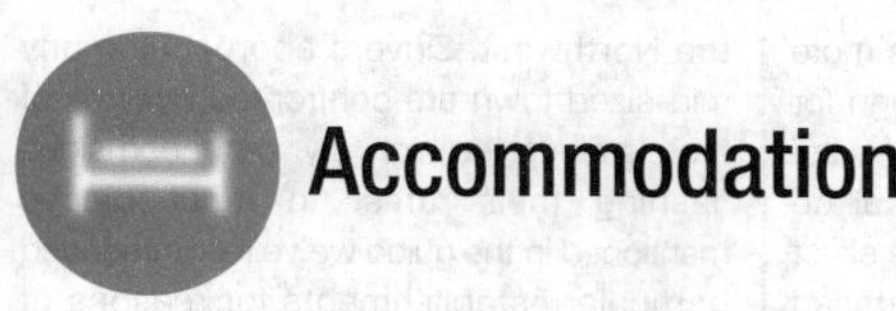

Accommodation

The standard of accommodation in the Pacific Northwest is high and related costs invariably form a significant proportion of the expenses for any traveler exploring the region. At the bottom of the accommodation price heap are campsites and hostel dormitory beds, though be warned that both are heavily used in the Northwest's major cities and resorts, especially in this current era of severe economic doldrums – you may need to reserve months in advance for the more popular spots. Campsite rates range from free to around $30 in both countries, and typically $15-21 in the state parks. Beds in a hostel in the US or Canada usually cost between US$10–25 (typically $16–25 for non-members), with private rooms for $35–50. Many hotels will set up a third single bed for around US$10 on top of the regular price, reducing costs for three people sharing.

Since inexpensive beds in tourist areas tend to be taken up quickly, always **reserve in advance** and look out for prominent local events and festivals, when beds will be even harder to find at such times. If you get stuck try **visitor centers**, which offer free advice and will either book accommodation for you or perhaps provide a "courtesy phone" to call round after vacancies.

Reservations can be made over the phone by credit card; wherever possible take advantage of **toll-free numbers**, but note that almost all are accessible only in a single province or state, and if you call them from abroad you'll either pay international call rates or find the number unavailable. Reservations are only held until 5pm or 6pm unless you've informed the hotel you'll be arriving late.

It can also be worth confirming check-in/check-out times, particularly in busy areas, where your room may not be available until late afternoon. Check-out times are generally between 11am and 1pm. Most places have a 24-hour notice **cancellation** policy, though in a few big resorts it can be 48 hours or so.

Wherever you stay, you'll be expected to **pay in advance**, at least for the first night, particularly if it's high season and the hotel's expecting to be busy. Payment can be in

Accommodation price codes

All the **accommodation** listed in this book been graded with the **price codes** below, according to the cost of the least expensive double room. However, with the exception of the budget motels and lowliest hotels, there's rarely such a thing as a set rate for a room. A basic motel in a seaside or mountain resort may double its prices according to the season, while a big-city hotel that charges $250 per room during the week will often slash its rate at the weekend when its business clientele have gone home. As the high and low seasons for tourists vary widely across the region, astute planning can save a lot of money. Remember, too, that a third person in a double room usually costs only a few dollars more.

Only where noted do these room rates include local taxes.

Code	US	Canada
1	up to US$30	up to Can$40
2	US$30–45	Can$40–60
3	US$45–60	Can$60–80
4	US$60–80	Can$80–100
5	US$80–100	Can$100–125
6	US$100–130	Can$125–175
7	US$130–165	Can$175–210
8	US$165–200	Can$210–250
9	US$200+	Can$250+

cash or travelers' checks, though it's more common to use a credit card and sign for everything when you leave. Virtually every state and province has a **room tax**: all go under different names, but all have the effect of adding a few dollars to the advertised price of a room.

For the benefit of overseas travelers, many of the higher-rung hotel chains offer prepaid **discount vouchers**, which in theory save you money if you're prepared to pay in advance. To take advantage of such schemes, British travelers must purchase the vouchers in the UK, at a usual cost of between £30–60 per night for a minimum of two people sharing. However, the money you may save is counterbalanced by a loss in flexibility and the dullness in staying with the same hotel chain wherever you go.

Hotels

In Canada and the United States **hotels** tend to fall into three categories: high-class establishments and major resorts, mid-range chains, and grim, shambling dives, often above a downtown bar or diner.

Upper-end hotels can be very grand indeed, catering to a mix of rich tourists and business travelers, with high-season rooms anywhere from US$150–500 – though $250 will get you a first-class double anywhere in the Northwest. It's always worth inquiring about midweek reductions and out-of-season discounts, as these can reduce rates to as low as $100 per night. **Mid-range** hotels usually belong to one of the big chains, and offer standard-issue modern facilities, often in a downtown location. High-season doubles in this price bracket go for around US$85/Can$80–150. **Bottom-end** hotels, costing US$25–40, are mostly holdovers from the days when liquor laws made it difficult to run a bar without an adjoining restaurant or hotel. Needless to say, for their battered units with little more than a basic bed, washroom, and TV, they're among the last options you should choose. For the same money, it's better to seek out a cheap motel or hostel, if possible.

Motels

As with the rest of the country, it is consistently easy to find a basic **motel** in most of the Northwest. Drivers approaching any mid-sized town are confronted by lines of motels along the highway, with neon signs flashing their rates. In most places mentioned in the guide we've recommended particular establishments for reasons of value or uniqueness, but there are often many more choices around that are clean, cheap, and fairly spartan – check the *Yellow Pages* for the full gamut. The cheapest properties tend to be family-run, independent businesses, with the national chains costing $10–15 more for similar facilities.

Whether called inns, lodges, or motor hotels, most of these establishments amount to much the same thing; prices across the board are generally a few dollars higher in Canada than the US. The **budget** ones are usually pretty barebones, mostly doubles with bathroom, TV, and phone. For more than US$60 or Can$75, the rooms get a bit bigger and better, and may even offer a swimming pool and in-room coffeemaker, iron and ironing board, and complimentary newspaper.

During **off-peak periods** (usually Oct–April) many motels struggle to fill their rooms; staying in the same place for more than one night may bring further reductions. Some places have cheap triple- or quadruple-berth rooms, and most are fairly relaxed about introducing an extra bed into a double. Many places also offer a **Family Plan**, whereby kids sharing their parents' room stay free. Prices tend to drop in the larger towns and cities the further you move from downtown, and in the more remote areas, many places are likely to close in the offseason.

Bed-and-breakfasts

Increasingly, **bed-and-breakfasts** have become popular options for travel, as comfortable and usually less expensive alternatives to conventional hotels. Sometimes B&Bs – also known as **guesthouses** and **inns** – are just a couple of furnished rooms in someone's home, and even the larger establishments tend to have no more than ten units, often laden with flowers, stuffed cushions, and the occasional atmosphere of contrived quaintness. The range of quality is considerable, from restored Belle Epoque "heritage houses" of great charm, to postwar ranch houses mocked up in chintz and ersatz Victoriana.

Prices also vary, from $50 to more than $150 in both Canada and the US, and may include a huge and wholesome breakfast, though the trend is increasingly to provide only a skimpy "continental" meal (toast, coffee, and perhaps cereal). The other cost factor is whether each room has an en-suite bathroom; those that do tend to charge $20–30 more per unit. Another issue to consider is whether the establishment has a private **guest entrance**, useful if you're likely to be staggering in late or simply don't want to mix with your hosts. Avoid those places that have an implicit **curfew** for their guests – as in "all doors bolted at 10pm" – often a red flag for rigid, pedantic innkeepers. Also take careful note of an establishment's **location**: in cities and larger towns they may be out in the suburbs and inconvenient for transport and downtown sights, though some hosts will pick you up from the airport or bus station on your arrival. The top neighborhoods for B&Bs are typically Capitol Hill in Seattle, Northwest Portland, and the leafy suburbs of North and West Vancouver in Vancouver.

Youth hostels

Although **youth hostels** are not as plentiful in the US and Canada as in Europe, provision for backpackers and low-budget travelers is good in the hiking and outdoors areas of the Northwest. Unless you're alone, though, most hostels work out little cheaper than motels, so there's only any real point using them if you prefer their youthful ambience and sociability.

Most of the region's hostels are affiliated to either the Canadian Hostelling Assocation or the American Youth Hostel (AYH) networks, organizations which are, in turn, affiliated to Hostelling International (see box for information). There are also privately run hostels in the Northwest, and additionally there are YMCAs and YWCAs (often known as "Ys") that sometimes offer dormitories or, in a few cases, women-only accommodation, and which increasingly have rooms, facilities, and reservations to match those of mid-range hotels.

To stay in a hostel in either country, you're supposed to be, in theory, a **HI member**, but in practice you can join the HI on the spot, or pay a slightly higher charge for non-members. Be warned that members are usually given priority when it comes to booking, which is an important consideration in some of the more popular locations. Most places offer communal recreational and cooking facilities, plus pillows and blankets, though in simpler places you're expected to provide your own sleeping bag and towels. Especially in high season, it's advisable to **reserve ahead**, in writing, or by credit card over the phone, either to the relevant hostel or via a central reservation number. Some hostels will allow you to use a **sleeping bag** as well.

Youth hostel organizations

Australia Australian Youth Hostels Association, 422 Kent St, Sydney ⓣ02/9261 1111, ⓦwww.yha.com.au

Canada Hostelling International-Canada, Room 400, 205 Catherine St, Ottawa, ON K2P 1C3 ⓣ613/237-7884 or 1-800/663-5777, ⓦwww.hihostels.ca

England Youth Hostel Association (YHA), Trevelyan House, 8 St Stephen's Hill, St Alban's, Herts AL1 2DY ⓣ0870/870 8808, ⓦwww.yha.org.uk

Ireland An Oige, 61 Mountjoy St, Dublin 7 ⓣ01/830 4555, ⓦwww.irelandyha.org

New Zealand New Zealand Youth Hostels Association, 173 Gloucester St, Christchurch ⓣ0800/278 299, ⓦwww.yha.co.nz

Northern Ireland Hostelling International Northern Ireland, 2232 Donegall Rd, Belfast BT12 5JN ⓣ028/9032 4733, ⓦwww.hini.org.uk

Scotland Scottish Youth Hostel Association, 7 Glebe Crescent, Stirling FK8 2JA ⓣ0870/155 3255, ⓦwww.syha.org.uk

USA Hostelling International American Youth Hostels (HI-AYH), 733 15th St NW, Suite 840, Washington, DC 20005 ⓣ202/783-6161, ⓦwww.hiayh.org

The invaluable *International Handbook* covers the Americas, Africa, and the Pacific; the *Hostelling Handbook for the USA and Canada*, produced each May, lists more than four hundred HI and private hostels, and is available for $5 by writing to Hostel Handbook, Dept. HHB, 722 St Nicholas Ave, New York, NY, 10031(Ⓣ212/926-7030), or viewable online at Ⓦwww.hostelhandbook.com.

Canadian hostels

British Columbia has 15 HI-affiliated hostels, including three in Vancouver and one in each of Victoria and Whistler. Additionally there are a growing number of unaffiliated hostels which may feature in HI-C literature and are often aspiring to full hostel status.

HI hostels are graded in four categories (basic, simple, standard, and superior), and accommodation is mostly in single-sex dorms that cost about $10–25 for members ($12–28 for non-members), depending on category and location, though family and private double rooms are becoming more prevalent. Most hostels offer communal recreation areas and all have cooking facilities, plus pillows and blankets, though you're expected to provide, or rent, your own sheet sleeping bag and towels – normal sleeping bags are generally not allowed.

Most hostels are open from 8–9am to 8–9pm (or 24 hours) and lockouts during the day are now rare. Curfews, or "quiet times" (typically 11pm–7am) are, however, usually imposed and so is a three-day limit on stays. Many hostels have been renovated in the past few years and often have cafeterias and recreation areas.

A computerized booking scheme, means you can book into most hostels in BC up to six months ahead. These major hostels accept credit-card and fax bookings, although you still might have to send a deposit for the first night's stay. You may also use a HI Advance Booking Voucher, available from any HI office or specialist travel agents – though check that the hostel you're after accepts them. The larger hostels also act as booking agents for a number of smaller hostels around the region (see entries in the main text for details). Details of private hostels are included in the Guide.

US hostels

In **Washington** and **Oregon**, hostels are fewer and further between than in Canada, with most located either in cities or in coastal towns, though a smattering can be found in good hiking country. In both states, hostels may still observe the old hosteling niceties – a limited check-in time (usually 5–8pm) and strict daytime lockouts (9.30am–5pm). Rates range between about $10 and $25 per night, depending on grade and location, and non-members pay a few dollars extra.

YMCAs and YWCAs

Both the **YMCA** and **YWCA** – known as "Ys" – have establishments in most of the Pacific Northwest's big cities. The quality of accommodation is usually excellent, invariably exceeding that of most other hostels, with cafeterias, sports facilities, gyms, and swimming pools for guest use. Though you can sometimes find bunks in shared dorms from $20, the trend is for single, double, and family units (with optional private bathrooms) to range from $30–70. In cities Ys are usually in downtown locations, and in Vancouver they can offer the best-value rooms around.

Credit-card **reservations** in advance are virtually essential to secure private singles and doubles in the high season. Most places keep a number of rooms and dorm bunks available each day for walk-in customers as well. The old demarcation of the sexes is breaking down somewhat, though many YWCAs will only accept men if they're in a mixed-sex couple. Some YWCAs accept women with children, others only in emergencies.

Camping

Few areas of North America offer as much scope for **camping** as the Pacific Northwest, and all national parks and many state and provincial parks have outstanding government-run sites. In many wilderness areas you can camp pretty much anywhere you want (but ask permission and get a permit if necessary).

If you're with a tent it's vital to check a campsite's details for the number of unserviced (tent) sites, as many places cater chiefly for **recreational vehicles** (RVs), providing them with full or partial hook-ups for water and electricity (or "serviced sites"). If you want peace and quiet, it might be worth checking the number of tent sites available: there's a big difference between a cozy 20-pitch site and a 500-site tent village. Province- and statewide campsite details are available from the major tourist offices and the tourist boards listed on p.23.

Take special care plotting your route if you're camping during **public holidays** or the high season (June–Aug), or hoping to stay at some of the big campsites near lake or river resorts, or in any of the national parks. Either aim to arrive early in the morning or book ahead. **Reservations** can be made at private campsites and at many national and provincial/state parks, though in the parks, most sites are available on a first-come, first-served basis. US national forest sites are almost entirely non-reservable.

Oregon and Washington state parks share the same campsite reservation line, Reserve America (Ⓣ1-800/452-5687, Ⓦwww.reserveamerica.com), while Discover Camping (Ⓣ1-800/689-9025, Ⓦwww.discovercamping.ca) handles reservations For British Columbia's provincial parks. Finally, check that your chosen site is open – many campsites only open seasonally, usually from May to October.

Campsite types

At the bottom of the pile are **municipal campsites**, usually basic affairs with few facilities, which are either free or cost only a few dollars – typically $5 per tent, $10 per RV. **Private campsites** run the gamut from basic facilities to huge outdoor complexes with shops, restaurants, laundries, swimming pools, tennis courts, even saunas, and Jacuzzis. Best-known among the latter is the familiar Kampgrounds of America (KOA) network, with campsites across the Northwest (information at Ⓣ406/248-7444, Ⓦwww.koa.com). Some private campsites **charge** by the vehicle, others per couple, comparatively few on a tent or per person basis. Two people sharing a tent might pay anything between $2.50 and $25 each, though an average price would be nearer $7–11. Where we've given a price it's invariably for two people sharing a tent. There's often no need to **reserve** outside busy areas as most businesses are obliged to keep a certain number of pitches available on a first-come, first-served basis.

National park campsites are generally run by Parks Canada and the National Park Service in the US: individual provincial and state parks are run by state and provincial governments. All are immaculately turned out and in practice most are available year-round, though key facilities are offered and fees collected only in the summer: off-season you may be expected to leave fees in a box. You'll usually find at least one site serviced for winter camping in the bigger national parks. **Prices** vary from about $8.50 to $19 per tent, depending on location, services, and the time of year – prices may be higher during June and August.

Sites in the major parks, especially close to towns, usually offer a full range of **amenities** for both tents and RVs, and often have separate sites for each. As a rule, though, provincial sites and more remote national park campsites tend to favor tents and offer only water, stores of firewood (for an additional charge), and pit toilets. Hot showers, in particular, are rare. Alternatively, a number of Oregon state parks offer novel accommodation in the form of **cabins** and **yurts** – Mongolian-style domed circular tents – both of which may have wooden floors, electricity, and lockable doors, as well as bunk beds and a futon (yurts $27 per night, cabins $35; Ⓣ1-800/452-5687, Ⓦwww.oregonstateparks.org). See the website for the range of choices – some of the units can get rather elaborate.

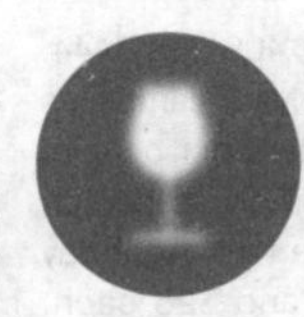

Eating and drinking

Of the various restaurants, bars, and cafés in the Pacific Northwest, for the most part there's little to distinguish the mainstream urban cuisines of the region's towns and cities: shopping malls, main streets, and highways are lined with American chains, each trying to outdo the other with bargains and special offers. However, this overall uniformity is leavened in the bigger cities by a plethora of ethnic restaurants, and places that specialize in seafood and "Northwest Cuisine," a variant of California Cuisine that employs fresh, locally available ingredients and novel combinations with a nod to nouvelle French dining. Even out in the country – the domain of often grim family-run diners – you'll find the odd ethnic or seafood restaurant to save the day. Also not to be missed are the region's excellent wineries and microbreweries, which are justly becoming nationally renowned for their artisan techniques and generally fine quality. Of the wines, Pinot Noir is among the best choices, while favored beers include hand-crafted ales, stouts, and porters.

Breakfast

Breakfast is taken very seriously all over the region, and with prices averaging between US$5–10 (Can$6–11) it can be very good value. Whether you go to a café, coffee shop, or hotel snack bar, the breakfast menu, on offer until around 11am, is fairly standard. **Eggs** are the staple ingredient: "sunny side up" is fried on one side, leaving a runny yolk; "over easy" is flipped for a few seconds to give a hint of solidity; and "over hard" is more or less fried to a thick, rubbery texture. Scrambled and poached eggs and omelettes are popular, too. The usual meat is **ham** or **bacon**, streaky and fried to a crisp, or skinless and bland **sausages**. Whatever you order, you nearly always seem to receive a dollop of **fried potatoes**, called hashbrowns or sometimes home fries. Other favorite breakfast options include English muffins, pancakes, waffles, and healthier fare like bran muffins.

Whatever you eat, you can wash it down with as much **coffee** as you can stomach: for the price of a cup, waiters will provide free refills until you beg them to stop. Diner coffee is fairly dismal, the type of "mud" you drink only to keep awake, while the better coffeehouses create their complex brews from a wide mix of savory beans. **Tea**, with either lemon or milk, is also drunk at breakfast, and some places emphasize the English connection by using imported brands, or local varieties such as Tazo. **Chai** is an increasingly popular Indian-derived brew made from black tea, milk, and spices, served hot or cold.

Lunch and snacks

Between around 11.30am to 2 or 3pm many big-city restaurants offer **lunch specials** that are generally excellent value. In Chinese and Vietnamese establishments, for example, you'll frequently find rice and noodles, or dim sum feasts for US$5–8, and many Japanese restaurants give you a chance to eat sushi for under $10, far cheaper than usual. **Pizza** is also widely available, from larger chains to family-owned restaurants and pavement stalls. Some **cafés** feature whole- and vegetarian foods, though few are nutritionally dogmatic, serving traditional seafood and meat dishes and sandwiches too; most have an excellent selection of daily lunch specials for around US$8–10.

For quick **snacks** many **delis** do ready-cooked meals from US$5, as well as a range of sandwiches and bagels. Regional snacks are all things nautical – from salmon and halibut to clams and shrimp, all of them potentially delicious. By contrast, the fare at shopping-mall **food courts** and **fast-food**

Vegetarian and vegan options

In the big cities of the Northwest, being a **vegetarian** presents few problems. Cholesterol-fearing North Americans are increasingly turning to healthfood, and most towns of any size boast a vegetarian café, while selected Mexican restaurants tend to include at least one vegetarian item on their menus. However, don't be too surprised in rural areas if you find yourself restricted to a diet of eggs, sandwiches, salads, and cheese pizza. Keep in mind that some apparently "safe" foods such as baked beans, and the nutritious-sounding red beans and rice, often contain bits of diced pork, and even french fries may be cooked in beef fat. **Vegans** will find it even tougher going, with just a few dedicated cafés in places like Portland and Seattle, many of them holding somewhat militant attitudes that may prohibit anything from leavened bread to sugar and gluten. Not surprisingly, many travelers may find the idea of confining their diets to soy brownies and wheatgrass smoothies somewhat unpalatable.

joints is highly caloric and best avoided unless you're near-starving.

Some city **bars** are used as much by diners as drinkers, who turn up in droves to gorge on the free **bar food** laid out between 5 and 7pm weekdays in an attempt to grab commuters. For the price of a drink you can stuff yourself with the likes of chicken wings, mozzarella sticks, burgers, and deep-fried shrimp. That apart, the old-style urban dive bar is on the defensive here – as in other parts of North America – replaced by the **café-bar**, many of which serve up regional and European wines and bistro-style food influenced by Italian and French cuisine.

Dinner and specialities

While the predictable burgers, piles of ribs, or rotisserie chickens, served up with salads, vegetables, and bread, are found everywhere, you should aim to explore the diverse regional cuisines of the Pacific Northwest when it comes to eating **dinner**. As you'd expect, **fish** and **shellfish** – anything from salmon and lobster to king crab, oysters, and shrimp – dominate the menus of just about all the coastal areas. **Salmon**, especially, is predominant, either served straight or stuffed, or sometimes in pasta – though you're increasingly likely to be served the blander farm-raised rather than the sharper wild variety. Of the shellfish, the more notable are **clams** and **oysters** (taken from places like Willapa Bay and, yes, Oysterville), Washington's highly rated **Dungeness crab** – smoother and creamier than the average kind – and, most strikingly, Puget Sound **geoduck** (pronounced "gooeyduck"), huge mollusks of intensely phallic appearance that are often served coyly chopped up.

Ethnic variations are endless, especially in the major cities. Chinese food is everywhere, and can be among the cheapest available. Japanese is not far behind, with an array of options from high-priced yuppie enclaves to cheap and tasty **sushi bars**. As Pacific Rim immigration gathers pace, other **East Asian** imports are making much headway, such as Thai, Indonesian, and, especially, Vietnamese cuisine. **Italian** food is popular in excess of the number of quality establishments serving it, but can be cheap and good – with the Northern Italian variety typically being pricier and tastier. **French** food, too, is available, though always pricey, and **Northwest Cuisine** employs many of the same techniques – exotic ingredients, unusual combinations, and artful designs. **Mexican** food is one of the cheapest types of food to eat, and even a full dinner with a drink will rarely be over $10 – though the cuisine is closer to Tex-Mex than authentic south-of-the-border dining. Other interesting, and occasionally worthwhile, ethnic fare includes **Indian**, with predictably variable results; **Mediterranean**, best for its Arabic and Lebanese eateries, and somewhat weaker for Greek diners; **German**, delivered with a heavy, gut-busting punch in a few places; and, best of all, Spanish **tapas bars**, which have become all the rage in recent years, with moderate to

Tipping

Almost everywhere you eat or drink, the service will be fast and friendly – thanks to the institution of **tipping**. Waiters and bartenders depend on tips for the bulk of their earnings and, unless the service is dreadful, you should top up your bill by at least fifteen percent. A refusal to tip is considered rude and mean in equal measure. If you're paying by credit card, there's a space on the payment slip where you can add the appropriate tip – though most servers prefer to be tipped in cash, with the implicit reason that it's easier to hide such gratuities from the watchful eye of the taxman.

expensive prices. Finally, however tempting, imitation **British pubs** – notably in Victoria, BC and Ashland, Oregon – are usually best avoided, their bangers and mash and fish 'n' chips only a pale imitation of the real thing.

Drinking

Canadian and American **bars** are mostly long and dimly lit counters with a few souls perched on stools, and the rest of the clientele occupying the surrounding tables and booths. Yet, despite the similarity of layout, bars vary enormously, from the male-dominated, rough-edged drinking holes concentrated in the blue-collar parts of the cities, to the far more fashionable city establishments that provide food, live entertainment, and an inspiring range of cocktails. Indeed, it's often impossible to separate cafés from bars.

To **buy** and consume alcohol in almost every US state, you must be 21, and you may be asked for ID even if you look 30 or older. The legal drinking age is 19 in British Columbia, and it's rare to be asked for **ID**, except at government-run liquor shops, which hold a virtual monopoly on the sale of alcoholic beverages direct to the public. Buying is easier in Washington and Oregon, where laws are more relaxed, and wine and beer are sold by most supermarkets and groceries. Hard liquor, however, attracts tighter regulation, and in both Washington and Oregon it can only be purchased from a state liquor store. Across the Pacific Northwest, bars usually stay open until 2am.

Microbreweries

Although most American **beer** tends to be limited to fizzy and insipid national brands, in the last two decades countless **microbreweries** and **brewpubs** have sprung up all over the Northwest, making the region the undisputed king of "craft brewing" in the nation. They are usually friendly and welcoming places too, and almost all serve a wide range of good-value, hearty **food** to help soak up the drink. Brands to look out for in particular include ESB and Red Hook Ale in Seattle; Black Butte Porter in Bend, Oregon; Rogue Ales in Newport; Full Sail Ale in Hood River; and, the most famous, Widmer Hefeweizen in Portland – though you can find such brews in any decent grocery and the list of tangy concoctions is almost endless. True microbrew fanatics can hunt down their favorite local and international suds in specialized **beer stores** with racks of fancy bottles and oddball draughts arrayed on the walls; the names to watch for are **Bottleworks**, 1710 N 45th St #3, in Seattle's Wallingford district (Ⓣ206/633-BIER, Ⓦwww.bottleworks.com), with more than four hundred brews from twenty different countries, and **Liquid Solutions**, in the Portland suburb of Tigard, 12162 SW Scholls Ferry Rd (Ⓣ503/524-9722, Ⓦwww.liquidsolutions.ws), offering about as many choices, along with potent drinks like hard cider and mead.

Drinking bottled beer in a bar works out a good deal more expensive than the draught, which is usually served by the 170ml glass or by the pint; even cheaper is a **pitcher**, which contains six to seven glasses, or four pints.

Wine and spirits

Both Washington and Oregon produce large quantities of **wine** and have done so since the 1960s. In Washington, the main wine-producing area is along the Yakima Valley in central Washington, though there are also vineyards on Puget Sound and in the Columbia River Gorge area; in Oregon, the vineyards are concentrated in the Willamette Valley. Both states have their own appellations, and the quality of production is closely regulated. Largely as a result, the general standard is high, with the best vintages receiving international plaudits. In Canada, parts of British Columbia's Okanagan produce increasingly good wines, many of which can be found in Vancouver, Victoria and other restaurants.

Local wines are readily available in the region's cafés, restaurants, and bars, and it's well worth experimenting. Wines are sold by grape type as much as by vineyard, and some of the best-known and –regarded kinds include rich, complex varieties of **pinot noir**, **pinot gris**, and **cabernet sauvignon**. Prominent vintner names include Columbia Winery, Archery Summit, and Rex Hill, among many others. Needless to say, the industry takes itself very seriously and free **tours** and **tastings** of the region's wineries (and sometimes vineyards) are commonplace. Every local visitor center can provide opening times and directions. For an overview – and a glossy brochure – contact the **Washington Wine Commission**, 93 Pike St, Suite 315, Seattle, WA (Ⓣ206/667-9463, Ⓦwww.washingtonwine.org), or the **Oregon Wine Advisory Board**, 1200 NW Naito Parkway, Suite 400, Portland, OR, 97209 (Ⓣ1-800/242-2363, Ⓦwww.oregonwine.org). For more on Okanagan wines, visit Ⓦwww.owfs.com or www.okanaganwine.ca.

Wine may have made some inroads, but Northwest bars really excel with their **spirits**. Even in run-of-the-mill places there are startling arrays of gins, rums, and vodkas, as well as a good selection of whiskeys featuring both imported and domestic brands. Also worth looking for is Portland's own **Clear Creek Brandy**, whose genuine fruit brandy (also known as *eau de vie*) uses locally grown apples, pears, and other fruits – be warned, though, that this innocuous-looking clear liquid is one of the most potent drinks made in the region. Finally, in the smarter bars, you can experiment with all sorts of **cocktails**, anything from a dry martini and creamy Brandy Alexander to a sweet Singapore Sling or the dreaded Pink Squirrel.

Communications

Even more than most parts of North America, the Pacific Northwest has an excellent communications infrastructure, with all manner of high-tech links to the rest of the world. Not surprisingly for such a well-connected spot, there are good options for telephone service and email, with much network support for fiber-optic cable and the Internet having been created in the last ten years. These advantages do not, however, apply to the US mail, which is predictably slow and prone to misplacing letters and packages. Canada Post, by contrast, has a good reputation.

Telephones

Public telephones in the US and Canada invariably work, and in cities, at any rate can be found everywhere – on street corners, in railway and bus stations, hotel lobbies, bars, and restaurants. They take 25¢, 10¢, and 5¢ coins. The cost of a **local call** from a public phone (within a limited radius, rather than the entire area covered by any one code) is 50¢. States and provinces within the

Pacific Northwest telephone area codes

206 Seattle
250 British Columbia, excluding Vancouver
253 Tacoma, south Seattle
360 Western Washington, excluding Seattle region and Tacoma
425 Eastside Seattle suburbs
503 Portland, Salem, north coast
541 Oregon, excluding Portland, Salem, and north coast
604 Vancouver

Northwest have different **area codes** – three-digit numbers that must precede the seven-figure number if you're calling from abroad or from a region with a different code. In this book, we've highlighted the local area codes per each region in the text, and they're also listed in the box. Outside the immediate calling zone, you'll have to dial a 1, plus the area code, then the telephone number, and you'll be charged a bit more than local calls, depending on where you're calling from and dialing to. For detailed information about calls, area codes, and rates, consult the front of the telephone directory (*White Pages*).

It is worth noting that it can be surprisingly difficult to make long-distance calls via the operator with a **credit card**. Canada has an increasing number of public phones that accept credit cards directly (as well as cash), but these are still scarce in much of the US.

In general, calling from your **hotel room** will cost considerably more than if you use a pay phone; hotels often charge a connection fee of at least $1 for all calls, even if they're local or toll-free, and international calls will cost a small fortune. **Long-distance** and **international calls** dialed direct are most expensive during daylight hours (7am–6pm), with evening charges slightly reduced (6–11pm) and early morning hours cheapest of all (11pm–7am).

Many major hotels, government agencies, and car rental firms have **toll-free numbers** that are recognizable by their ⓣ1-800 or ⓣ1-888 prefixes. Some of these numbers are meant to be accessed nationally, others only within a given state – dialing is the only way to find out. Numbers with a ⓣ1-900 prefix are **toll calls**, typically sports information lines, psychic hotlines, and phone-sex centers, and will cost you a variable, though consistently high, fee for just a few minutes of use. Even worse, swiping a regular **credit card** at a public phone at, say, the airport can incur astronomical charges for long-distance service, including a mysteriously high "connection fee" – with the total amount as much as $7 a minute.

Telephone charge cards

In the **US** and **Canada**, AT&T, MCI, Sprint, Canada Direct, and other North American long-distance companies all enable their customers to make calling-card calls while away from home, billed to your home number. Call your company's customer service line to find out if they provide this service, and if so, what the toll-free access code is.

In **the UK** and **Ireland,** it's possible to obtain a free BT Chargecard (ⓣ0800/800838), from which all calls made while overseas can be charged to your quarterly domestic account. AT&T (dial ⓣ0800/890 011, then 1-888/641-6123 when you hear the AT&T prompt to be transferred to the Florida Call Center, free, 24hrs/day) has the Global Calling Card, a charge card that can be used in more than 200 countries, while the Mercury Calling Card (ⓣ0500/100 505) can be used in more than sixty countries abroad, including the US, though the fees cannot be charged to a normal phone bill.

To call **Australia** or **New Zealand** from overseas, telephone charge cards such as Telstra Telecard or Optus Calling Card in Australia and Telecom NZ's Calling Card can be used to make calls while abroad, which are charged back to a domestic account or credit card. Apply to Telstra (ⓣ1800/038 000), Optus (ⓣ1300/300 937), or Telecom NZ (ⓣ04/801 9000).

Mail

Post offices in the US and Canada are usually open Monday to Friday from 9am

Useful Numbers

Directory information ☎411
Directory inquiries for toll-free numbers ☎1-800/555-1212
Emergencies ☎911; ask for the appropriate emergency service: fire, police, or ambulance
International operator ☎00
Long-distance directory information ☎1- (area code/province code)/555-1212
Operator ☎0

Calling the Northwest from abroad

Calling US/Canada from the UK 001 + province code
Canada from the US 1 + province code
US from Canada 1 + area code
US/Canada from Australia 0011 + country code
US/Canada from New Zealand 00 + country code

Calling home from the Northwest

Australia 00 + 61 + city code
New Zealand 00 + 64 + city code
Republic of Ireland 00 + 353 + city code
UK and Northern Ireland 00 + 44 + city code

until 5pm, and Saturday from 9am to noon or 1pm. Stamps can also be bought from automatic vending machines, the lobbies of larger hotels, airports, train stations, bus terminals, and many retail outlets and newsstands. Mailboxes are blue in the US, red in Canada. Ordinary mail sent within the US costs 37¢ (at press time) for letters weighing up to an ounce, while standard postcards cost 23¢. For anywhere outside the US, airmail letters weighing up to an ounce cost 80¢; postcards and aerogrammes 70¢. **Air mail** between the US and Europe generally takes about a week. There is no separate air mail rate in Canada for mail sent abroad: **aerogrammes** can only be mailed to destinations within Canada.

The last line of the address is made up of an abbreviation denoting the state or province (Washington is "WA," Oregon "OR," and British Columbia "BC") and a multi-digit number – the **zip code** (US) or **postal code** (Canada) – denoting the local post office (codes in Canada have a mix of numbers and letters). Addresses must include the zip, or postal code, as well as the sender's address on the envelope. Letters which don't carry a code are liable to get lost or at least delayed; if you don't know it, phone books carry a list for their service area, and post offices – even in Europe – have directories.

Letters can be sent c/o **General Delivery** in both the US and Canada (what's known elsewhere as **poste restante**) to the one relevant post office in each town or city, but must include the zip code and will usually only be held for thirty days (fifteen in Canada) before being returned to sender – so make sure there's a return address on the envelope. If you're receiving mail at someone else's address, it should include "c/o" and the regular occupant's name otherwise it, too, is likely to be returned. In Seattle, letters will end up at the main post office downtown at 301 Union St, zip code 98101 (Mon–Fri 7.30am–5.30pm; ☎206/748-5417 or 1-800/275-8777), and in Portland at 715 NW Hoyt St, 97208 (Mon–Fri 8am–6.30pm, Sat 9am–5pm; ☎1-800/275-8777). Letters will also be held at **hotels** – mark such mail "Guest Mail, Hold For Arrival" but ensure you place a date for collection.

If you want to send **packages** overseas, check the front of telephone directories for packaging requirements. Bear in mind that you'll need to fill in a green **customs declaration form**, which is available from post offices. International parcel **rates** for items weighing less than a pound run from $5 to $16, depending on the package's size and destination, and how quickly you want it to arrive.

Email

Email is often the cheapest and most convenient way to keep in touch. **Cybercafés** are found throughout major cities in the Pacific Northwest (and especially in Seattle and Vancouver), either as a part of a regular café or as a place specifically devoted to coffee drinking and computer access, often for around $6 per hour. Additionally, many public libraries have computers that provide free Internet access, usually for Web surfing or for accessing the library database.

If neither of these options fit the bill, or if you just need a fast machine with assorted peripherals, then find a commercial photocopying and printing shop (look under "Copying" in the *Yellow Pages*). They'll charge around 25¢ a minute for use of their computers, but you're guaranteed fast access. Most upscale hotels also offer email and Internet access – though at a steep price. By far the easiest way to collect and send email on the road is to sign up with one of the advertisement-funded **free email** accounts – such as yahoo.com and hotmail.com – which can be accessed from any Net-linked computer.

The media

In terms of the media, the Pacific Northwest is not much different from anywhere else in Canada and the US for mass culture: corporate control predominates in a slew of TV and radio stations owned by the goliath Clear Channel and Infinity networks, among a few other national heavyweights. This hegemony is only limited by Canada's state-subsidized TV stations and film productions, and by the independent newspapers and cultural entities found in the major urban areas of Washington and Oregon.

Newspapers

In the US, some of the more familiar national **newspapers** include the *New York Times*, *Wall Street Journal*, *Washington Post*, and *USA Today*. The most-prominent papers in the region are the *Seattle Post-Intelligencer* (Ⓦ seattlepi.nwsource.com), simply called "the *P-I*" by locals, the *Seattle Times* (Ⓦ seattletimes.nwsource.com), and Portland's *Oregonian* (Ⓦ www.oregonian.com); all are published in the mornings. Canada's national paper is the *National Post* and more staid, Ontario-based *Globe and Mail*, published in a western edition and available everywhere in British Columbia. Every large town, state, or province has at least one morning and/or evening paper, generally excellent or at least adequate at covering its own area, but relying on agencies for foreign – and even national – reports.

Every community of any size has at least one **free newspaper**, found in street distribution bins or in shops and cafés. Like town, city, and provincial papers these can be handy sources for bar, restaurant, nightlife, and other listings, and we've mentioned the most useful titles in the relevant cities.

Television

Except for local stations, the Canadian Broadcasting Corporation (CBC) and one or two public broadcasting channels in Canada, the **television** of the Pacific Northwest is effectively the TV of mainstream America. As an alternative, Seattle's KCTS (channel 9; Ⓦ www.kcts.org) and Portland's OPB (channel 10; Ⓦ www.opb.org) are **public broadcasting** affiliates that provide in-depth political and social documentaries, assorted nature and science programming, and a smattering of light history along the lines of Ken Burns miniseries.

Most motel and hotel rooms are hooked up to some form of **cable TV**, though the number of channels available to guests depends on where you stay. See the daily papers for channels, schedules, and times. Most cable stations are actually no better than the big broadcast networks, though some of the specialized channels are interesting: CNN and CNN Headline News both have round-the-clock news, with Fox News providing a right-wing slant on the day's events. ESPN is your best bet for all kinds of sports, MTV for youth-oriented music videos and programming, and VH-1 for easy listening and adult contemporary. HBO and Showtime present big-budget Hollywood flicks and excellent shows such as *The Sopranos*, while American Movie Classics (AMC) and the far superior Turner Classic Movies take their programming from the Golden Age of cinema.

Many major **sporting events** are transmitted on a pay-per-view basis, and watching an event like a heavyweight boxing match will set you back at least $50, billed directly to your motel room. Most hotels and motels also offer a choice of **recent movies** that have just finished their theatrical runs, at around $8–10 per film.

Radio

Radio stations are even more abundant than TV channels, but most are even more rigidly programmed, owned by a handful of mega-companies that care little about the needs or interests of their local listeners. Except for news and chat, stations on the AM band are best avoided in favor of FM, in particular the nationally funded **public** and **college stations** found between 88 and 95 FM. These provide diverse and listenable programming, be it bizarre underground rock or obscure theatre, and they're also good sources for local nightlife news. Seattle's top choices are KUOW (94.9 FM; ⓦwww.kuow.washington.edu), the local National Public Radio affiliate, for its excellent public affairs and news programming; KPLU (88.5 FM; ⓦwww.kplu.org), which is strong on news, jazz, and blues; KEXP (90.3 FM; ⓦwww.kexp.org), for all sorts of alternative and independent sounds; and KBCS (91.3 FM; ⓦkbcs.fm), best for its jazz and folk, as well as some blues and world music. The choices are slimmer in Portland, basically a pair of inspired NPR affiliates next to each other on the dial: the solidly liberal KOPB (91.5 FM; ⓦwww.opb.org), and more leftist and alternative KBOO (90.7 FM; ⓦwww.kboo.fm).

Beyond the larger cities, you're out of luck – except for the lone public-broadcasting affiliate in each town – and will probably have to resort to aimlessly scanning the frequencies, between rerun soft-rock "classics," modern country-and-western crooners, fire-and-brimstone Bible thumpers, and various crazed phone-in shows.

Opening hours, public holidays, and festivals

No matter how carefully you've planned your trip to the Pacific Northwest, you may find the gates of your favorite park or museum closed if you don't check in advance about the various public holidays and festivals taking place throughout the year, which may shut down certain businesses altogether and otherwise throw a spanner into your well-laid plans. Beyond this, regular opening hours are more predictable, and though listed per each attraction in the guide, most operate according to the same general schedule.

Opening hours

As a general rule, most **museums** are open Tuesday through Saturday (occasionally Sunday, too), from 10am until 5 or 6pm, with somewhat shorter hours on the weekends. Many museums will also stay open late one evening a week – usually Thursday, when ticket prices are sometimes reduced. Government **offices**, including post offices, are open during regular business hours, typically 8 or 9am until 5pm, Monday through Friday (though some post offices are open Saturday morning until noon or so). Most stores are open daily from 10am and close at 5 or 6pm, while specialty stores can be more erratic, usually opening and closing later in the day, from noon to 2pm until 8 to 10pm, and remaining shuttered for two days of the week. **Malls** tend to be open from 10am until 7 or 8pm daily, though individual stores may close before the mall does.

While some diners stay open 24hrs, the more typical **restaurants** open daily around 11am or noon for lunch and close at 9 or 10pm. Places that serve breakfast usually open early, between 6 to 8am, serve lunch later, and close in the early or mid-afternoon. Dance and live-music **clubs** often won't open until 9 or 10pm, and many will serve liquor until 2am and then either close for the night or stay open until dawn without serving booze. **Bars** that close at 2am may re-open as early as 6am to grab bleary-eyed regulars in need of a liquid breakfast.

Public holidays

The biggest and most all-American of the US **public holidays** is **Independence Day**, on the fourth of July. **Canada Day** three days earlier is similar, but accompanied by less nationalistic fervor. **Halloween** (Oct 31) is not a public holiday, despite being one of the most popular yearly flings. More sedate is **Thanksgiving**, on the last Thursday in November in the US, the second Monday in October in Canada.

Of the **national holidays** listed in the accompanying box, banks, government

National holidays

Each holiday is **officially celebrated** in both Canada and the US, unless otherwise noted.

New Year's Day Jan 1
Martin Luther King's Birthday US; third Mon in Jan
President's Day US; third Mon in Feb
Good Friday Canada; varies (late March to mid-April)
Easter Monday Canada; varies (usually early April)
Victoria Day Canada; Mon before May 25
Memorial Day US; last Mon in May
Canada Day Canada; July 1
Independence Day US; July 4
Labor Day first Mon in Sept
Columbus Day US; second Mon in Oct
Veterans' Day/Remembrance Day Nov 11
Thanksgiving US; fourth Thurs in Nov
Christmas Dec 25
Boxing Day Canada; Dec 26

offices, and many museums are liable to be closed all day. Small stores, as well as some restaurants and clubs, are usually closed as well, but shopping malls, supermarkets, and department and chain stores increasingly remain open, regardless of the holiday. Most parks, beaches, and cemeteries stay open during holidays, too. The traditional season for **tourism** runs from Memorial Day in the US, Victoria Day in Canada to Labor Day (around Sept 5 in both), and some tourist attractions, information centers, motels, and campsites are only open during that period.

Festivals

Someone is always celebrating something in the USA or Canada, though few **festivals** are shared throughout the respective countries. Instead, there is a disparate multitude of local events: art and craft shows, county fairs, ethnic celebrations, music festivals, rodeos, sandcastle-building competitions, and many others of almost every variety. For further details of the selected festivals and events listed below see the relevant page of the guide, or contact the local tourist authorities direct. The provincial state tourist boards listed on p.23 can provide free calendars as well.

January

Polar Bear Swim Vancouver, BC. A New Year's Day dip in the freezing waters of English Bay Beach – said to bring good luck for the year.

February

Oregon Shakespeare Festival Ashland, OR. Premier Bard-fest from mid-Feb to Oct in a cute small town.

March

Pacific Rim Whale Festival Vancouver Island, BC. Celebrating the spring migration of grey whales with lots of whale-spotting expeditions, as well as music and dance events.

Irish Week Seattle, WA. A salute to the Emerald Isle with food, drink, and dance, centered around St Patrick's Day, celebrated almost as colorfully – if only for one night – in Portland, OR.

April

TerrifVic Jazz Party Victoria, BC. Dixieland, and other jazz bands, from around the globe.

Seattle Poetry Festival Seattle WA. A week of poetry readings at various venues throughout the city, culminating in the Seattle Grand Slam, the ultimate poetry competition. Held late in the month.

May

Northwest Folklife Festival Seattle, WA. Well-regarded folk-fest with many American and international artists; held on Memorial Day weekend.

Sandcastle competition Cannon Beach, OR. An annual summertime eruption of seaside sculpture and local color, held on Memorial Day weekend.

Seattle Maritime Festival Seattle, WA. In the middle of the month, featuring port tours, tugboat races, a boat-building competition, and a chowder cook-off.

Maifest Leavenworth, WA. Community parades and marching bands, and the odd drink here and there.

June

Portland Rose Festival Portland, OR. A grand Sunday parade and copious displays of roses, highlighted by an evening procession, The Starlight Parade, and a raucous waterfront "Fun Center." Early to mid-June.

Fremont Fair & Solstice Parade Seattle, WA. Held in late-month in that colorfully artsy district, a cavalcade of odd art displays, weird costumes, and energetically manic locals.

Pride Parade and Freedom Rally Occurring in the major cities in the region at the end of the month, a celebration of tolerance and diversity, with zany costumes, outlandish floats, and various musical acts.

July

Festival of American Fiddlers Port Townsend, WA. Second weekend in July. Big and prestigious folk music event.

Oregon Country Fair Veneta, OR. First weekend after Fourth of July. Huge fair and live-music shindig.

Pow-wows Traditional Native Canadian celebrations that take place on reserves in July and Aug.

August

Seafair Seattle, WA. Early in the month, an intermittent three-week celebration of Northwest maritime culture, held at various locations in town.

Chief Seattle Days Suquamish, WA. Just over the bridge from Bainbridge Island, the Suquamish tribe celebrates this mid-month weekend festival with Native American food, culture, and canoe races.

September

Bumbershoot Seattle, WA. Massive art, music, and literature festival held at many venues, including the Seattle Center, with hundreds of artists and performers. Labor Day weekend.

Puyallup Fair Puyallup, WA. Throughout the month, western Washington's biggest country fair, with livestock and home-made craft displays sharing space with a rodeo, rides, food, and mainstream country music.

October

Vancouver International Film Festival BC. A highly rated Canadian film festival.

November

Cultural Crossroads Bellevue, WA. Three-day multicultural music, food, and crafts fair, representing more than one hundred ethnic groups. Early in the month.

December

Winter Worldfest Seattle, WA. Early in the month, a weekend of crafts, food, and music from around the world, with an ice rink and dance lessons, too. The kickoff of the Seattle Center's month-long Winterfest.

Coral Ships Vancouver, BC. Coral singers sail around Vancouver Harbor in sparkly boats.

Outdoor pursuits

The Pacific Northwest is scattered with fabulous backcountry and wilderness areas, swathed in dense forests, scoured by mighty whitewater rivers, and capped by majestic mountains and vast glaciers. Opportunities for outdoor pursuits are almost limitless, and the facilities to indulge them some of the best on the continent.

The most popular activities are hiking, skiing, and fishing; other activities such as whale watching, horseback riding, and rafting are covered where appropriate in the main guide. Once you're in the Northwest you can rely on finding outfitters, equipment rental, charters, tours, and guides to help you in most areas: tourist offices invariably carry full details or contact numbers. Most local bookstores also have a separate outdoor pursuits section with a wide variety of specialist guides.

Hiking

The Pacific Northwest boasts some of North America's finest **hiking**, and whatever your abilities you'll find a walk to suit you almost anywhere in the region; you don't need wilderness training or hiking experience to tackle most trails. All major parks have well-marked and -maintained trails, and a visit to any park center or local tourist office will furnish you with adequate **maps**. If you're entering into the backcountry, try to obtain the appropriately detailed maps (see p.25). Be sure to consult park staff on the better walks, or to pick up the **trail guides** that are widely available in local bookshops for most of the region's prime walking areas.

Some of the best-known and most well-developed hiking areas are in the national parks of Washington, most dramatically among the glacial summits of the **North Cascades** and around high peaks like **Mount Rainier** and the scorched earth around **Mount St Helens**. In Oregon **Crater Lake** presents some of the region's most stunning scenery, **Mount Hood** is a favorite for glacial climbers, and the other, smaller peaks in the **Oregon Cascades** have their own charm. In lower British Columbia the top choices are **Garibaldi**, north of Vancouver, and **Strathcona**, on Vancouver Island. Excellent **long-distance** trails include the **West Coast Trail** (see p.521), which runs for 80km along the edge of Vancouver Island's Pacific Rim National

Outdoor health tips

When it comes to protecting your **health** in the wilderness, camping or hiking at lower elevations should present few problems, though the thick swarms of **insects** you may encounter near any body of water can drive you crazy; **mosquitoes**, in particular, are out in force from July until October. Some studies recommend megadoses of Vitamin B to cut down on insect bites, though a good old-fashioned repellent may be an easier alternative. **Candles** with allethrin or citronella can also help deter the little beasts.

If you develop a large rash and flu-like symptoms in the backcountry, you may have been bitten by a **tick** carrying **lyme disease**, which is prevalent in wooded country. The condition is easily curable, but if left untreated can lead to nasty complications. Get advice from a park ranger or warden if you've been bitten; otherwise buy a strong tick repellent and wear long socks, trousers, and sleeved shirts when walking.

One very serious backcountry problem is **Giardia,** water-borne bacteria causing an intestinal disease, whose symptoms are chronic diarrhea, abdominal cramps, fatigue, and weight loss. To prevent it, never drink from rivers, streams, or glaciers, however clear and inviting they may look, boil water that doesn't come from a tap for at least ten minutes, and filter it with an iodine-based or Giardia-rated filter, available from any camping or sports store. Neither ordinary filters nor standard water-purification tablets will remove the bacteria.

Beware, too, of **poison oak**, which grows all over the region, usually among oak trees. Its leaves come in groups of three and are distinguished by prominent veins and shiny surfaces (waxy green in spring, rich red and orange in autumn). It causes open blisters and lumpy sores up to ten days after contact. If you come into contact with it, wash your skin and clothes as soon as possible, and don't scratch: the only way to ease the itching is to smother yourself in calamine lotion or to take regular dips in the sea. In serious cases, hospital emergency rooms can give antihistamine or adrenaline jabs.

There's also a danger of being bitten or stung by various **poisonous creatures**. Current medical practice rejects the idea of cutting yourself open and attempting to suck out the venom; instead, apply a cold compress to the wound, constrict the area with a tourniquet to prevent the spread of venom, drink lots of water, and bring your temperature down by resting in a shady area. Stay as calm as possible and seek medical help immediately.

Hiking at higher elevations demands special care: late snows are common, even into July, and in spring there's a real danger of **avalanches**, not to mention meltwater making otherwise simple stream crossings hazardous. **Altitude sickness**, brought on by the depletion of oxygen in the atmosphere, can affect even the fittest of athletes. Take it easy for the first few days you go above seven thousand feet, drink lots of water, avoid alcohol, eat plenty of carbohydrates, and protect yourself from the increased radiation of the sun. Watch out for signs of **exposure** – mild delirium, exhaustion, an inability to get warm, – and in the snow or high country during the summer take a good sun block.

Park; the **Oregon Coast Trail**, hugging the 360 miles of coastline from the Columbia River to the Californian border; and the **Pacific Crest Trail** (Ⓦwww.pcta.org), an epic 2650-mile path from Mexico to the Canadian border.

Wherever you go, and at whatever altitude, make sure you're **properly prepared** and **equipped**: good boots, waterproof jacket, warm clothing, and spare food and drink to cover emergencies are all essential. On longer walks be sure to tell the park center of your intentions, so if something goes wrong there's a chance someone will come and hunt for you. Be prepared for sudden changes of weather, ready for encounters with wildlife of all kinds, and aware of the potential dangers to your health (see box above). Outdoor clothing can be bought easily in most towns, and in most mountain areas there's a good chance of being able to rent tents and specialized cold-weather gear.

Skiing

Wherever there's hiking in the Northwest, there's also usually **skiing**. Washington has sixteen ski areas, mostly in the **Cascades**, and many within easy striking distance of Seattle. Oregon boasts **Mount Bachelor** (see p.224), offering some of North America's finest skiing, and **Mount Hood** (see p.132), where you can ski throughout the summer. Vancouver has world-class skiing at **Whistler**, two hours' drive north of the city, plus excellent skiing in the small parks of North Vancouver just minutes from the city center. Despite the expense involved, **heli-skiing** is also taking off, a sport that involves a helicopter drop deep into the backcountry (or to the actual summits of mountains) followed by some of the wildest and most exhilarating skiing you're ever likely to experience; contact visitor centers for details of packages and outfitters. For many locals, though, **night skiing** is the most invigorating option, tooling down an ice field in the evening, illuminated only by distant floodlights or moonlight. Even better, lift tickets cost half that of regular day fees in most resorts.

US and Canadian **ski packages** are available from most foreign travel agents, while companies and hotels in many Northwest cities organize their own mini-packages to nearby resorts. It is, however, perfectly feasible to organize your own trips, but be sure to book well ahead if you're hoping to stay in some of the better-known resorts. Visitor centers in ski areas open up in the winter to help with practicalities, and most towns have ski shops to buy or rent equipment. **Costs** for food, accommodation, and ski passes, in Canada at least, are still fairly modest by US and European standards (see box for cost-cutting tips). Generally you can rent equipment from about Can$15 per day, and expect to pay perhaps another Can$40 per day for lift tickets. The American price for lift tickets averages $40–45, and equipment may cost another $20–30 more, but can be much cheaper if included in a **package deal** with a lift ticket. A cheaper option is **cross-country skiing**, or ski-touring. Backcountry ski lodges dot mountainous areas, offering rustic accommodation, equipment rental, and lessons, from as little as Can$10 a day for skis, boots, and poles, up to about Can$100, for an all-inclusive weekend tour.

Truly gung-ho skiers may wish to opt for a combination **hike-and-ski** trek, carrying their equipment as they ascend a peak such as Mount Adams, then schussing down or across the slopes in a burst of winter glory – only to trudge back up the mountain once more. Although you'll obviously save money on lift tickets this way (and such peaks as Adams are not equipped with chairlifts in any case), this rather extreme approach to skiing

Saving money on the slopes

The Pacific Northwest features some of the best ski terrain in the world, but without careful planning a **ski vacation** can be horribly **expensive**. In addition to the tips listed below, phone (toll-free) or write in advance to resorts for brochures, and when you get there, scan local newspapers for money-saving offers.

- Visit during early or late season to take advantage of lower accommodation and lift ticket rates.
- The more people in your party, the more money you save on lodgings. For groups of four to six, a condo rental unit costs much less than a motel.
- Before setting a date, ask the resort about package deals with flights, rooms, and lift tickets. This can be a very economical way to book a ski vacation.
- Shop around for the best boot and ski rentals – prices can vary significantly.
- If you have to buy lift tickets at the resort, save money by purchasing multi-day tickets.
- If you're a novice, look out for resorts that offer free beginners' lessons with the purchase of a lift ticket.
- Finish your day's skiing in time to take advantage of happy hours and dining specials, which usually last from 4 to 7pm.

should only be considered by the most vigorous athletes and hardcore outdoor enthusiasts.

Fishing

The Pacific Northwest is nirvana for **fishing**. While each area has its dream catches, such as the Pacific salmon of Washington and British Columbia, excellent fishing can be found in most of the region's abundant lakes, rivers, and coastal waters. Most towns have a fishing shop for equipment, and any spot with fishing possibilities is likely to have companies running boats and charters. As with every other type of outdoor activity, states and provinces publish detailed booklets on outfitters and everything that swims within the area of their jurisdiction.

Fishing in Canada and the US is governed by a medley of **regulations** that vary from state to state, and province to province. These are baffling at first glance, but usually boil down to the need for a non-resident permit for freshwater fishing, and another for saltwater. These are obtainable from most local fishing or sports shops for about US$45 (Can$30) and are valid for a year. Short-term (one- or six-day) licenses are also available in some areas. In a few places you may have to pay a premium to go after particular fish, and in Canadian national parks you need a special additional permit. There may also be quotas or a closed season on certain fish. Shops and visitor centers always have the most current regulations and fishing conditions.

National and regional parks

Protected backcountry areas in the Northwest include national parks, large federally controlled areas of great natural beauty or historical significance; Canada's provincial parks and the US's state parks, which are often of similar size and splendor, but run by local or regional governments; national monuments in the States and national historic sites in Canada offer outstanding geological or historical features covering smaller areas than national parks; national seashores, lakeshores, and so on that protect a specific type of geography; and national forests, which often surround national parks and are also federally administered, but usually much less protected, allowing some logging and industries such as ski resorts and mining operations. Regulations common to all parks may include prohibitions against firearms, hunting, snowmobiles, or off-road vehicles, the feeding of wildlife, and the removal or damaging of any natural objects or features.

National parks are usually supervised locally by a ranger (US) or warden (Canada) based at a park office or a park **information center**, which can provide the lowdown on hiking and activities such as fishing, camping, or rock-climbing – pursuits which often require a **permit** (see below). Most centers have information and audiovisual displays on flora, fauna, and outdoor activities, and virtually all employ highly experienced staff who can provide firsthand advice on your chosen trail or pursuit. It's unusual, though, for state and provincial parks to have dedicated visitor centers, though tourist offices or chambers of commerce may carry background material.

For up-to-the-minute **online information** on the US national park system, access the official website at ⓦwww.nps.gov, which features full details of the main attractions of the national parks, plus opening hours, the best times to visit, admission fees, hiking trails, and visitor facilities. In Canada the equivalent Parks Canada website can be found at Ⓦparkscanada.pch.gc.ca.

Keep in mind that in many remote areas, proper **planning** is essential, even if it's just making sure you have enough fuel in the tank to get you to the next gas station. Weather can also turn, even in summer, and knowing the lay of the land can be important if you wish to avoid getting lost, being trapped in an isolated site after dark, or stumbling into a mountain lion's den.

Entrance fees

In **Canadian national parks,** all individuals and motor vehicles, including motorbikes, must have a **Park Permit**, obtainable from park visitor centers, certain stores, automated machines (in a few cases), or a roadside booth at the point where the road crosses the park boundary. Permits cost around Can$5 per day, or Can$35 annually, and are valid for all parks. There are exemptions for vehicles passing straight through certain parks without stopping overnight. Annual and group permits are also available; see p.513 for precise details of the national park permit required for entry to the Pacific Rim National Park, the one Canadian national park covered in the Guide. Provincial parks are usually free, though day-use parking fees of a few dollars are being introduced at a handful of the busiest parks.

Comparable arrangements exist in the **United States**, though here fees range from US$5–20, which covers a vehicle and all its occupants. Fees are always collected at roadside entrance kiosks. If you plan to visit more than a couple of **national parks**, buy a Golden Eagle passport (US$50), which gives unlimited access to a named driver and all passengers in the same vehicle to (almost) any national park or national monument. Special discounts or free passes are available for travelers with disabilities (see p.65), and for seniors, who only have to pay US$10 to get a lifetime pass. On top of the Golden Eagle itself, truly gung-ho park lovers can pay an additional US$15 to receive passage to similar federal parks managed by the US Fish and Wildlife Service, Forest Service, and Bureau of Land Management. As for US **state parks**, the days when most were free have unfortunately passed, due to budget cuts, but the most you'll be charged for vehicle entry will be $5, or $3 for pedestrians and bicyclists.

Camping in the parks

If your time and money are limited, but you want to get a feel for the wilderness, one of the best options is **camping** out at night and cooking your own meals on a portable stove (if local regulations allow). If you don't fancy roughing it this way, there is usually also a wide array of public and commercially run campsites: **primitive**, a flat piece of ground that may or may not have a water tap, and which may be free; **semi-primitive**, usually providing wood, water, and pit toilets, where "self-registration" is the norm and a small fee ($5–15) is left in a box provided; and **full**, offering a broader mix of amenities, sometimes with shops, restaurants, and washing facilities, for $12–25. An additional fee of $3–5 may be charged if you want to buy and use firewood.

Campsites in **national and provincial parks** are bound by special rules, and in both Canada and the US are always federally controlled. Some are for tents, some for RVs only, and most have at least one site that remains open for basic **winter camping** (check opening times carefully: most sites operate only in the summer). **Fees** depend on facilities, and currently run from US$5 (Can$7) per tent (semi-primitive) to US$15 (Can$25) for those with electricity, sewage, water, and showers. Most campsites are operated on a first-come, first-served basis, but advance **reservations** are accepted at an increasing number of parks.

Primitive camping

Official permission and registration is required in both countries' parks for **backcountry camping**, whether you're rough camping or using designated primitive or semi-primitive sites. This enables the authorities to keep a check on people's whereabouts and to know your itinerary and planned return time.

To camp in the backcountry in Canadian parks you must obtain an **overnight** or

wilderness permit from a park center or the park office. These are either free or cost a few dollars, in addition to any campsite fees you may also have to pay. Increasingly, quota systems are in operation, and you may need to book campsites and/or the trails required to reach them: details are given under individual park entries.

Note, however, that while registration and permits are obligatory, other regulations for rough camping vary enormously. Some parks allow backcountry camping only in tightly defined sites; others have a special **primitive wildland** zone where you can pitch a tent within a designated distance of the nearest road or trailhead. Throughout the US and Canadian national parks, though, a quota system operates in the more popular areas: no permits will be issued once a set number have been allocated for a particular trail or backcountry campsite.

When camping in the outback – particularly in the dry tinder lands of central and southern Oregon – check that **fires** are permitted before you start one; even if they are, try to use a camp stove – in some places firewood is scarce, although you may be allowed to use deadwood. In wilderness areas, try to camp on **previously used** sites. Where there are no toilets, bury human waste at least eight inches into the ground and two hundred feet from the nearest water supply and campsite. Never wash directly into rivers and lakes – use a container at least fifty feet from either, and try to use a biodegradable soap. It is unacceptable to burn any rubbish; the preferred practice is to **pack out**, or carry away all garbage, the ideal being to leave no trace of your presence whatsoever.

Sports

Few occasions provide better opportunities for mixing with the locals than catching a baseball game on a summer afternoon or joining in with the screaming throngs at a football or ice hockey game. Professional sports teams almost always put on the most spectacular shows, but big games between college rivals and minor-league baseball games provide an easy and enjoyable way to get on closer terms with a place.

Baseball

Because its teams play so many games – 162 in all, usually five a week throughout the summer – **baseball** is probably the easiest sport to catch when in the United States, and it's also among the cheapest sports to watch (at around $10 a seat), with a season running from April to October.

In the early 1970s the **Seattle Mariners** arrived and faced many years of hardship on the field, with success finally coming in the mid- to late 1990s. Even though the franchise set an all-time record for American League wins in 2001, it's still failed to get to the World Series, much less win a championship. Nonetheless, the team's success enabled it to gain the public funds for an open-air stadium, Safeco Field (see p.300). **Tickets** are $6 for the cheapest seats, in the centerfield bleachers, and $45 for the most expensive, in the lower box section; there's a whole range of prices and seats in between (call ⓣ206/622-HITS or visit ⓦseattle.mariners.mlb.com to purchase tickets). To get tickets in person, without dealing with TicketMaster (linked by the team's website), drop by the Safeco Field box office or visit one of the Mariners team shops in Westlake Center or Bellevue Square.

Minor league baseball can be found elsewhere in the region: in Washington, Tacoma's triple-A-level **Rainiers** play at Cheney Stadium (April–Sept; ⓣ253/752-7700 or 1-800/281-3834, ⓦwww.tacomarainiers.com), while Everett's single-A **Aquasox** play at Everett Memorial Stadium (June–Sept; ⓣ206/258-3673, ⓦwww.aquasox.com); tickets run $5–12 at both stadiums. In Vancouver, the **Canadians** (ⓣ604/872-5232, ⓦwww.canadiansbaseball.com) are in the Northwest League and play their games at the charming Nat Bailey stadium: tickets start at just Can$7.50. Finally, Oregon's **Portland Beavers** (April–Sept; $6–25; ⓣ503/553-5555, ⓦwww.pgepark.com/beavers) are a somewhat woeful franchise best known for their overpriced stadium, PGE Park, and indifferent fan base. This hasn't stopped the city from attempting to acquire a major-league team, though, most likely by stealing one from another city, such as Montréal.

Football

Pro football can be quite the opposite of baseball – tickets are expensive and difficult to get, particularly if the team is successful, which the **Seattle Seahawks** have been as of late. Additional interest in the team stems from their new home, Seahawks stadium (see p.266) which opened in 2002 near Safeco Field. As you might expect, **tickets** are far from cheap, ranging from $20 to $280 (Sept–Jan; call ⓣ1-888/NFL-HAWK or visit ⓦwww.seahawks.com to purchase). In Vancouver, the British Columbia Lions (ⓣ604/589-ROAR, ⓦwww.bclions.com) play in the far less exalted Canadian Football League, one of the most impressive things about the team being its stadium – the vast BC Place. Tickets are inexpensive (from Can$20) and easily obtained.

Not surprisingly, with the success of three of its four PAC-10 league teams, **college football** has become much bigger in the Northwest than the pro leagues; the season runs from September to December or early January, if one of the teams is in a big bowl game. The most longstanding powerhouse, UW's football team, the **Huskies**, usually ranks among the nation's top twenty college squads, and plays at the 72,000-seat Husky Stadium on the edge of the campus, near Lake Washington. **Tickets** are $16–18 for general admission to the bleachers, and $32–36 for reserved seats (call ⓣ206/543-2200 or visit ⓦwww.gohuskies.com). In the last decade, however, the "Dawgs" have sometimes been overshadowed by two more rural rivals: the much-hated Washington State **Cougars**, from the sticks of Pullman, in Eastern Washington ($15–27; ⓣ1-800/462-6847, ⓦwsucougars.ocsn.com), who typically roll into town to ruin the Huskies' chance at playing in the Rose Bowl; and the Oregon **Ducks**, based out of Eugene ($13–35; ⓣ1-800/WEBFOOT, ⓦwww.goducks.com), known for their garish yellow outfits and expensive renovated stadium with $3-million locker rooms. The fourth PAC-10 team, the Oregon State **Beavers** ($12–33; ⓣ541/737-4455, ⓦosubeavers.ocsn.com) are a favorite in the burg of Corvallis, but only provide rooting interest on rare occasions.

Basketball

Now that the Vancouver Grizzlies have been shipped off to Memphis, Tennessee, there are only two **pro basketball** teams in the Northwest, both having achieved about the same level of success since their inception in the 1970s – one championship, a few more attempts at a title, and a short-lived presence in the playoffs in recent years. That said, the **Portland Trailblazers**, who play at the Rose Garden on the Eastside (Nov–June; ⓣ503/234-9291, ⓦwww.nba.com/blazers), have by far the worst reputation, widely known as the "Jail Blazers" for their public violation of drug laws and assorted acts of violence. By contrast, the **Seattle Supersonics**, based at Key Arena in the Seattle Center (ⓣ206/283-DUNK, ⓦwww.nba.com/sonics), are a bit less exciting all around, with more solid citizens and a less eventful style of play. Tickets to either of these teams will set you back anywhere from $15 to more than $300, with the best decent seats around $40. **Women's basketball** has experienced more difficulties in getting off the ground than the men's league, with teams often changing pricing plans, schedules, and marketing efforts season to season, leaving potential fans bewildered; the local representative in the WNBA, the **Seattle Storm** ($8–60; ⓣ206/217-WNBA, ⓦwww.wnba.com), plays at Key Arena along with the Supersonics.

Other spectator sports

Although **ice hockey** ignites the passions of virtually all Canadians, and many Americans as well, there is only one major-league pro team in the Northwest, the **Vancouver Canucks** (ⓣ604/280-4400 or 1-800/663-9311, ⓦwww.canucks.com), who in recent years have not always hit the heights of rivals the Edmonton Oilers and Calgary Flames. The team plays at General Motors Place and tickets start from Can$35.

With players hurtling around at 50kph, and the puck clocking speeds of 160kph, ice hockey is a tremendous sport to watch live, the adrenaline rush increased by the relaxed attitude to physical contact on the rink. Teams play around ninety games over a season that runs from October to May. Tickets for all but the biggest games are usually available, though it's always an idea to try and obtain seats in advance: prices start at around $10–15. In the lesser Western Hockey League, the **Seattle Thunderbirds** (ⓣ206/448-PUCK, ⓦwww.seattle-thunderbirds.com) play in Key Arena, while the **Portland Winter Hawks** (ⓣ503/224-4400, ⓦwww.winterhawks.com) provide competition at the Rose Garden; tickets for both run $10–25.

Soccer enthusiasts can watch local squads in the A-League, the highest US pro soccer level other than major league soccer. The **Sounders** play at Memorial Stadium in the Seattle Center ($12–22; ⓣ206/622-3415 or 1-800/796-KICK, ⓦwww.seattlesounders.net), while the **Timbers** can be seen at Portland's PGE Park ($8–20; ⓣ503/553-5555, ⓦwww.pgepark.com/timbers).

Finally, **horse racing** is held at **Emerald Downs**, in the Tacoma suburb of Auburn (ⓣ253/288-7000, ⓦwww.emdowns.com), and **Portland Meadows**, just off I-5 north of downtown (ⓣ503/285-9144, ⓦwww.portlandmeadows.com). The racing season runs from mid-April through mid-September, Thursdays to Sundays (Wed–Sun from mid-July through August).

Crime and personal safety

Although the Pacific Northwest is hardly free of crime, it is a much safer region than other urban parts of North America, and in Canada street violence is often unusual. Away from the major centers, crime is low-key but for the odd bar brawl in a rough-and-ready small town. Even the lawless reputation of larger American cities tends to be exaggerated, and most parts of these cities, by day at least, are fairly safe; at night, though, a few areas should be avoided. By being careful, planning ahead, and taking good care of your possessions, you should, generally speaking, have few real problems.

Foreign visitors tend to report that the police are helpful and obliging when things go wrong, although they'll be less sympathetic if they think you brought the trouble on yourself through carelessness.

Mugging and theft

If you're unlucky enough to get **mugged**, just hand over your money; resistance is generally not a good idea. After the crime occurs, immediately report it to the police so you can later attempt to recover your loss from an insurance provider – unlikely, but worth a try. Also, keep **emergency numbers** for credit cards and travelers' checks handy, so they can be canceled after

Emergency numbers for lost cards and checks

American Express cards ⓣ1-800/528-4800, ⓦwww.americanexpress.com
American Express checks ⓣ1-800/221-7282
Citicorp checks ⓣ1-800/645-6556, ⓦwww.citicorp.com
Diners Club ⓣ1-800/234-6377, ⓦwww.dinersclub.com
Discover ⓣ1-800/DISCOVER, ⓦwww.discovercard.com
MasterCard ⓣ1-800/826-2181, ⓦwww.mastercard.com
Thomas Cook/MasterCard checks ⓣ1-800/223-9920, ⓦwww.travelex.com or ⓦwww.thomascook.co.uk
Visa cards ⓣ1-800/847-2911, ⓦwww.visa.com
Visa checks ⓣ1-800/227-6811

the crime occurs (see below). One prime spot to be mugged is at an **ATM** outside the tourist areas, where you're likely to be told to make the maximum withdrawal and hand it over. Needless to say, you should treat ATM use with the strictest caution and not worry about looking paranoid.

If your passport is stolen (or if you lose it), call your country's consulate (see list on pp.21–22), and pick up or have sent to you an application form, which you must submit with a notarized photocopy of your ID and a reissuing fee, often around $30. Because the process of issuing a new passport can take up to six weeks, you should also spend an extra $10 or so to have the consulate fax record departments back home.

To avoid being the victim of a **hotel room theft** – a more frequent problem for lower-end establishments, though even the elite hotels are not immune from it – lock your valuables in the room **safe** when you leave, and always keep doors locked when you're in the room. Don't open the door to suspicious individuals, and if a questionable visitor claims to be a hotel representative, phone the front desk to make sure of it.

Finally, a few **simple rules** to keep yourself safe are worth remembering: don't flash money around, don't leave your wallet open or count money in public, and don't look panicked, even if you are.

Breaking the law

Whether intentionally or not, foreign visitors may find themselves **breaking the law** on occasion. Aside from **speeding** or **parking violations**, one of the most common ways visitors bring trouble on themselves is through **jaywalking**, or crossing the road against red lights or away from intersections. Fines can be stiff, and the police will most assuredly not take sympathy on you if you mumble that you "didn't think it was illegal." This is particularly true in Seattle, which has a reputation for cracking down hard on such pedestrian scofflaws, though not so applicable in Portland, where jaywalking is rampant downtown.

Alcohol laws provide another source of irritation to visitors, particularly as the law prohibits drinking liquor, wine, or beer in most public spaces like parks and beaches, and, most frustrating of all to European tourists, liquor is officially off-limits to anyone under 21. Some try to get around this with a phony driver's license, even though getting caught with a **fake ID** will put you in considerable jeopardy if you're from out of the country. The same is true for misdemeanor **marijuana possession**, which locals sometimes chance for amounts under an ounce, and which may get foreign visitors thrown out of the country – or into jail for larger amounts. Other infringements include **insulting a police officer** (ie, arguing with one), and **riding a bicycle at night** without proper lights and reflectors.

Car crime and safety

Crimes committed against tourists driving **rental cars** have made headlines in the last decade, but there are certain precautions you can take to keep yourself safe. In major urban areas, any car you rent should have nothing on it – such as a special license plate – to distinguish it as a rental car. When driving, under no circumstances should you immediately stop if you are "accidentally" rammed by the driver behind you; instead, drive on to the nearest well-lit and busy spot and phone the police at ⓣ911. Keep doors locked and hide valuables out of sight, either in the trunk or the glove compartment, and leave any valuables you don't need for you journey back in your hotel safe. Should a relatively uncommon "**carjacking**" occur, in which you're told to hand over your car at gunpoint, you should flee the vehicle as quickly as possible, get away from the scene, and then call the police. There is absolutely no reason why you should die for the sake of an automobile.

If your car **breaks down** at night while on a major street, activate the emergency flashers to signal a police officer for assistance, or, if possible during the day, find the nearest phone book and call for a tow truck. Should you be forced to stop your car on a **freeway**, pull over to the right shoulder of the highway – never the left – and activate your flashers. Wait for assistance either in your vehicle while strapped in by a seat belt or on a safe embankment nearby. If you need to do "on the spot" repair work to your vehicle beside the highway, be careful: numerous would-be mechanics have been killed while adjusting engines, fixing headlights, and changing flat tires.

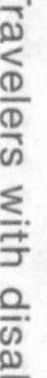

Travelers with disabilities

The US and Canada are extremely accommodating for travelers with mobility problems or other physical disabilities. All public buildings have to be wheelchair accessible and provide suitable toilet facilities, almost all street corners have dropped curbs, public telephones are specially equipped for hearing-aid users, and most public transport systems have such facilities as subways with elevators, and buses that "kneel" to let riders board. Even movie theaters – that last holdout for equal access – have been forced by courts in recent years to allow people in wheelchairs to have a reasonable, unimpeded view of the screen.

Information

Most states and provinces provide **information** for disabled travelers – contact the tourism departments on p.16. In **Canada** the Canadian Paraplegic Association (see box, p.65) can provide a wealth of information on traveling in specific provinces, and most of its regional offices produce a free guide on the most easily accessed sights. Provincial tourist offices are also excellent sources of information on accessible hotels, motels, and sights: some also supply special free guides. You may also want to get in touch with Kéroul in Montréal, an organization that specializes in travel for mobility-impaired people, and publishes the bilingual guide *Accès Tourisme* (Can$15 plus $3 postage).

In **Vancouver** itself there are various organizations that can provide help and assistance for those with disabilities. The BC Paraplegic Association, 780 South West Marine Drive (ⓣ604/324-3611, ⓦwww.canparaplegic.org), has lift-equipped vans for rent in and around the city, BC Disability Sports in Vancouver (ⓣ604/737-3039, ⓦwww.disabilitysport.org) has details of competitive and recreational sports and facilities in the city (including riding, sailing, climbing, and track and field events), while the BC Mobility Opportunities Society (ⓣ604/688-6464, ⓦwww.disabilityfoundation.org) also offers sailing and other recreational activities. There is also a help centre at the city's university, the UBC Disability

Resource Centre ⓣ604/822-5844 or 604/822-9049 (TDD), ⓦwww.student-services.ubc.ca/drc/. Note, too, that if you are camping, the BC Parks Disabled Access Pass (call ⓣ250/356-8794 for details) offers free camping in all BC's provincial parks. If you want help on the city's transit, make use of the TransLink HandyDART, a specially adapted bus service (further information ⓣ604/453-4634).

Among major organizations in the **United States** are SATH and Mobility International (see box for both), and the Washington Coalition of Citizens with Disabilities, 4649 Sunnyside Ave N, Suite 100, Seattle, WA, 98103 (ⓣ206/461-4550, ⓦwww.wccd.org), a prominent group offering useful information and services to the disabled. *Easy Access to National Parks*, by Wendy Roth and Michael Tompane, explores every national park from the point of view of people with disabilities, senior citizens, and families with children, and *Disabled Outdoors* is a quarterly magazine specializing in facilities for disabled travelers who wish to get into the countryside.

Accommodation

The major hotel and motel chains are your best bet for accessible **accommodation**. At the higher end of the scale, Embassy Suites has been working to comply with new standards of access that meet or, in some cases, exceed ADA requirements, involving building new facilities, retrofitting older hotels and providing special training to all employees. To a somewhat lesser degree, the same is true of Hyatt Hotels and the other big

Contacts for travelers with disabilities

Australia and New Zealand

Australian Council for Rehabilitation of the Disabled (ACROD), PO Box 60, Curtin, ACT 2605 ⓣ02/6282 4333, ⓦwww.acrod.org.au. Provides lists of travel agencies and tour operators for people with disabilities.

Barrier-Free Travel 36 Wheatley St, North Bellingen, NSW 2454 ⓣ02/6655 1733. Fee-based service providing disabled travel-access information.

Disabled Persons Assembly Level 4, Wellington Trade Centre, 173–175 Victoria St, Wellington ⓣ04/801 9100, ⓦwww.dpa.org.nz. Resource center with lists of travel agencies and tour operators.

Britain and Ireland

Access Travel 6, The Hillock, Astley, Lancashire M29 7GW ⓣ01942/888844, ⓕ01942/891811, ⓦwww.access-travel.co.uk. A range of services, from consumer protection to car hire and adapted vehicles.

Holiday Care 7th floor Sunley House, 4 Bedford Park, Croydon, Surrey CR0 2AP ⓣ0845/124 9971, ⓕ0845/124 9972, Minicom ⓣ0845/124 9976, ⓦwww.holidaycare.org.uk. Offers free lists of accessible accommodation in the US and other destinations. Information on financial help for holidays available.

Irish Wheelchair Association Blackheath Drive, Clontarf, Dublin 3 ⓣ01/818 6400, ⓦwww.iwa.ie. Regards traveling abroad with a wheelchair.

Mencap Holiday Services Optium House, Clippers Quay, Salford Quays, Manchester M52 2XP ⓣ0161/888 1200, ⓦwww.mencap.org.uk. Provides information on holiday travel for the disabled, including an annual guide.

Tripscope The Vassall Centre, Gill Ave, Bristol BS16 2QQ ⓣ08457/58 56 41, ⓕ0117/939 7736, ⓦwww.tripscope.org.uk. Registered charity providing a national telephone information service offering free advice on UK and international transport for those with mobility problems.

Canada

Canadian National Institute for the Blind (CNIB) ⓣ604/431-2121, ⓦwww.cnib.ca. Assistance and information for the visually impaired.

chains such as Red Roof, Best Western, Radisson, and Journey's End.

The great outdoors

The **Golden Access Passport**, issued free to US citizens with permanent disabilities, (ⓦwww.nps.gov/fees_passes), is a lifetime pass to federally operated parks, monuments, historic sites, and recreation areas that charge admission fees. The pass must be picked up in person, from the sites described, and it also provides a fifty percent discount on fees charged at facilities for camping, boat-launching, and parking. Furthermore, the Washington State Parks and Recreation Commission offers a free annual **Disability Pass** that allows for half-priced camping and boat-launching fees (ⓦwww.parks.wa.gov/ada-rec).

Transportation

Major **car rental** firms can provide vehicles with hand controls for drivers with leg or spinal disabilities, though these are typically available only on the pricier models. **Parking regulations** for disabled motorists are now uniform: license plates for the disabled must carry a three-inch-square international access symbol, and a placard bearing this symbol must be hung from the car's rearview mirror. A good resource, the *Handicapped Driver's Mobility Guide*, is published by the American Automobile Association (ⓣ206/448-5353, ⓦwww.aaawa.com).

In order to obtain a Canadian **parking privilege permit**, drivers with disabilities must complete the appropriate form from the province in question. Contact addresses

Canadian Paraplegic Association. Main office at Suite 230, 1101 Prince of Wales Drive, Ottawa, Ontario K2C 3W7 ⓣ613/723-1033, ⓦwww.canparaplegic.org. They also have offices in every province – details from the website or from ⓣ1-800/720-4933. Provides a wealth of information on traveling in specific provinces, and most of its regional offices produce a free guide on the most easily accessed sights.

BC Coalition of People with Disabilities 204-456 West Broadway, Vancouver V5Y 1R3 ⓣ604/875-0188 or 604/875-8835 (TDD). Advocacy Access ⓣ604/872-1278. Offers advice and assistance for travelers in BC.

VIA Rail ⓣ1-888/842 7245 ⓦwww.viarail.ca. VIA Rail operates most of Canada's train network. Their website has a specific section devoted to travelers with disabilities ("Special needs") and there's a speech- and/or hearing-impaired helpline on ⓣ1-800/268-9503.

United States

Access-Able PO Box 1796, Wheat Ridge, CO, 80034 ⓣ303/232-2979, ⓦwww.access-able.com. Information service and network that assists travelers with disabilities by putting them in contact with other people with similar conditions.

Easy Access Travel 5386 Arlington Ave, Riverside, CA, 92504 ⓣ1-800/920-8989. Travel consulting services with comprehensive tour packages.

Mobility International USA PO Box 10767, Eugene, OR 97440 ⓣ541/343-1284, ⓦwww.miusa.org. Answers travel questions and operates an exchange program for the disabled. Annual membership ($35) includes quarterly newsletter.

Society for Accessible Travel and Hospitality (SATH) 347 Fifth Ave, #610, New York, NY, 10016 ⓣ212/447-7284, ⓦwww.sath.org. Nonprofit travel-industry entity that includes travel agents, tour operators, hotel and airline management, and those with disabilities.

Wheels Up! ⓣ1-888/38-WHEELS, ⓦwww.wheelsup.com. Online service that provides discounted airfares, tour, and cruise prices for disabled travelers; publishes a free monthly letter as well. chains such as Red Roof, Best Western, Radisson, and Journey's End.

and organizations vary from province to province, though the permit, once obtained from one province, is valid across Canada. Contact provincial tourist offices for details. In British Columbia you should contact the Social Planning and Research Council of British Columbia, 201-221 E Tenth Avenue, Vancouver BC V5T 4V3 (ⓣ604/718-7744, ⓦwww.sparc.bc.ca). Its conditions are typical: enclose a letter with name, address, phone number, and date of birth, the medical name of the disabling condition, a letter from a doctor with original signature (not a photocopy) stating the disability that makes it difficult for a person to walk more than 100m, and whether the prognosis is temporary or permanent. You should also include date of arrival and departure in Canada, a contact address if known, a mailing address for the permit to be sent to, date and signature, and a check or money order (call for latest charge) to cover processing. Note that the application form can be downloaded from the website.

American **airlines** must by law accommodate those with disabilities, and some even allow attendants of those with serious conditions to accompany them on the trip for a reduced fare. With many of the same requirements in Canada, the best-equipped carrier north of the border is Air Canada. Almost every **Amtrak train** includes one or more cars with accommodation for disabled passengers, along with wheelchair assistance at train platforms, adapted on-board seating, free travel for guide dogs, and fifteen-percent discounts on fares, with 24 hours' advance notice. Passengers with hearing impairment can get information by calling ⓣ1-800/523-6590 or checking out ⓦwww.amtrak.com. By contrast, traveling by **Greyhound** and **Amtrak Thruway** bus connections is often problematic. Buses are not equipped with platforms for wheelchairs, though intercity carriers are required by law to provide assistance with boarding, and disabled passengers may be able to get priority seating. Those unable to travel alone, and in possession of a doctor's certificate, may receive two-for-one fares to bring a companion along. Call Greyhound's ADA customer assistance line for more information (ⓣ1-800/752-4841, ⓦwww.greyhound .com).

Both BC Ferries and the Alaska Marine Highway offer discount cards to disabled travelers on their **ferries**; for a few dollars the latter also offers a two-year pass good for free stand-by travel on all boats from October to April, and on some boats from May to September. BC Ferries allow a companion to travel free unless the disabled passenger is taking a car onto the ferry. For full details contact the companies directly (see p.34). Passengers with disabilities can travel on Washington State Ferries for half the regular fare by presenting a Regional Reduced Fare Permit or other proof of disability.

Traveling with children

Traveling with children in the more populous parts of the Pacific Northwest is relatively problem-free, children are readily accepted in public places across the region, most state and national parks organize children's activities, and virtually every town or city has clean and safe playgrounds.

Restaurants often try hard to lure parents in with their kids. Most of the national chains offer highchairs and a special menu, packed with huge, excellent-value (if not necessarily healthy) meals. Virtually all **museums** and tourist attractions offer reduced rates for kids, and most large cities have natural-history museums or aquariums, and quite a few have hands-on children's museums and, in the case of Seattle, even a children's theater (see p.299). State, city, or provincial tourist offices can provide specific information and ideas on activities or sights that are likely to appeal to children; a huge range of books and guides is also available on the subject.

Transportation

Children under 2 **fly free** on domestic routes, and usually for ten percent of the adult fare on international flights – though that doesn't mean they necessarily get a seat. Kids aged from 2 to 12 are usually entitled to half-price tickets, though recent airline-industry economic troubles have reduced perks like these in some measure.

Traveling **by bus** may be the cheapest way to go, but it's also the most uncomfortable for kids. Babies and toddlers can travel (on your lap) for free, whereas youths aged 2 to 4 are usually charged ten percent of the adult fare, as are any toddlers who take up a seat. Children under 12 are charged half the standard fare.

Even if you discount the romance of the rails, **train travel** is by far the best option for long journeys – not only does everyone get to enjoy the scenery, but you can get up and walk around, relieving pent-up energy. Most cross-country trains have sleeping compartments, which may be quite expensive but are a great adventure. Children's discounts are much the same as for bus or plane travel.

Most families choose to travel **by car**, but if you're hoping to enjoy a driving holiday with your kids, it's essential to plan ahead. Don't set yourself unrealistic targets, pack plenty of sensible snacks and drinks, plan to stop (don't make your kids make you stop) every couple of hours, arrive at your destination well before sunset, and avoid traveling through big cities during rush hour. If you're taking a fly-drive vacation, note that when **renting a car** the company is legally obliged to provide free car seats for kids.

Recreational vehicles (RVs) are also a good option for family travel, successfully combining the convenience of built-in kitchens and bedrooms with the freedom of the road (see p.37).

Gay and lesbian travelers

The big cities of the Pacific Northwest are progressive bastions for gays and lesbians, with many having moved to the region from other parts of the US and Canada due to the area's liberalism and increasingly cosmopolitan character. Although mostly integrated into their respective cities, gays and lesbians are most prominent in Seattle at Capitol Hill, in Vancouver around Denham and Davie, and in Portland in Eastside districts like Hawthorne and Irvington. Most hotels will provide at least the appearance of tolerance, and it's only when you get away from the urban areas that finding gay-friendly lodging becomes more of a problem. In the same way, most restaurants cater to gay customers without issue.

By marked contrast, however, and not surprisingly, **rural areas** of the Northwest can still be rather unwelcoming, with residents at best shunning open displays of same-sex affection and at worst reacting with violence. There are notable exceptions, however: in Washington, Olympia has a well-regarded progressive and alternative scene welcoming to gays and lesbians, as do Tacoma and Bellingham to a lesser degree; in Oregon progressive smaller towns include Eugene, Corvallis, and Ashland – all having passed anti-discriminatory municipal policies in recent years. Regardless of the place, throughout the guide gay and lesbian **social centers**, **bars,** and **clubs** are listed for the more welcoming cities.

On the last Sunday in June, Seattle's gay and lesbian **Pride Parade and Freedom Rally** – one of several such events annually held in the major towns – takes place over a dozen blocks on Capitol Hill's main strip, Broadway; it's one of the area's most exuberant events, drawing some 75,000 participants and spectators.

Information

One good source for **information** is the **International Gay & Lesbian Travel Association**, 4331 N Federal Hwy, Suite 304, Fort Lauderdale, FL, 33308 (ⓣ1-800/448-8550, ⓦwww.iglta.com), a trade group providing lists of gay-owned or gay-friendly travel agents, accommodations, and other travel businesses.

Publications specific to the region include the biannual *Lesbian & Gay Pink Pages Northwest* (free; ⓦwww.lesgaypinkpages.com), available at various cafes and shops throughout the area, which lists companies supportive of the gay and lesbian community and includes a comprehensive resource directory. **Beyond the Closet**, 518 E Pike St, Seattle, WA (ⓣ206/322-4609, ⓦwww.beyondthecloset.com), is the best-stocked gay & lesbian bookstore in the Pacific Northwest; it's also a good source of information for local and regional events and news. Finally, in progressive coffeehouses and other businesses you'll find numerous free **magazines** detailing weekly listings for gay-oriented bars, clubs, and cultural venues.

For detailed information on **gay and lesbian** events in and around Vancouver and Victoria, check out *X-xtra* (ⓣ604/684-XTRA, ⓦwww.xtra.ca) a regular free magazine aimed specifically at the gay and lesbian community, which is available at clubs, bookshops, and many stands around Vancouver. Also useful is the monthly *Outlooks* (ⓦwww.outlooks.ca) magazine. Other general contacts include the **Gay & Lesbian Centre Help Line** (ⓣ604/684-6869) and the **Gay & Lesbian Business Association** (ⓣ604/253-4307 or 739-4522), the latter being a source for gay- and lesbian-friendly businesses in Vancouver.

Women travelers

Located in one of the more socially liberal and progressive corners of North America, the Pacific Northwest has a good amount of women's resources, especially in the major cities. Practically speaking, a woman traveling alone in the Northwest, especially in places like Portland, Seattle, and Vancouver, is not usually made to feel conspicuous, or likely to attract unwelcome attention.

Information

There are multiple sources of **information** in both the US and Canada for women. In the US the **National Organization for Women** (NOW) has done much to effect positive legislation, and its branches, listed in local phone directories, can provide referrals for rape crisis centers and counseling services, feminist bookstores and lesbian and women-friendly bars. **Call of the Wild**, 2519 Cedar St, Berkeley, CA, 94708 (ⓣ510/849-9292, ⓦwww.callwild.com), is a tour operator offering hiking adventures for women of all ages and abilities, whose trips include visits to aboriginal ruins, backpacking in national parks, cross-country skiing, dog-sledding, and jaunts to Hawaii. **Womanship**, 410 Severn Ave, Annapolis, MD, 21403 (Ⓣ410/267-6661, Ⓦwww.womanship.com), provides live-aboard, learn-to-sail cruises for women of all ages. Destinations include idyllic spots in the Pacific Northwest and elsewhere, and a choice of 3- 5- or 7-day trips.

National information can also be found in *Women's Travel in Your Pocket*, Ferrari Publications, PO Box 37887, Phoenix, AZ 85069 (Ⓣ602/863-2408), an annual guide for women traveling to the US, Canada, Mexico, and the Caribbean.

Safety matters

Generally throughout the Northwest, going into **bars** and **clubs** should pose no problems, as women's privacy is often respected, especially in dance and rock clubs. However, sexual harassment is more common for single women in country-and-western clubs, and in working-class taverns and rural bars. If in doubt, gay and lesbian bars are generally trouble-free alternatives.

By contrast, **small towns** and mining and lumber centers in the region may not have the same liberal attitudes toward lone women travelers. If your vehicle **breaks down** in a country area, walk to the nearest house or town for help, on interstate highways or heavily traveled roads, wait in the car for a police or highway patrol car to arrive. One option is to rent a portable telephone with your car, for a small additional charge – a potential lifesaver. On **Greyhound** buses, sit as near to the front – and the driver – as possible (new booking schemes make it possible to select seats in such positions in advance, see "By bus" p.32). Should disaster strike, all big cities and the larger towns have some kind of rape counseling service; if not, the local RCMP or sheriff's office should arrange for you to get help and counseling, and, if necessary, transport home.

As a rule, women (or men, for that matter) should **never hitchhike** anywhere in the city alone. This mode of travel leaves you open to every thug and would-be rapist motoring down the highway; if you're driving, avoid hitchhikers just as steadfastly. Also on the danger list is **walking** through desolate, unlit streets at night; you're better off taking cabs to your destination, if even for just a few blocks. If you don't appear confused, scared, or drunk, and project a serious or wary countenance instead, your chances of attack may be lessened.

One option for women travelers to the US that's unavailable in most European countries and Canada is **pepper spray** or **mace**, which comes in a small canister that you can carry in a purse or pocket. Upon contact with an attacker's eyes, the spray causes terrible, temporary pain – giving you the opportunity to flee the scene and alert the police. You should never enter an airport with the spray, and always get rid of it before you return home.

Directory

Addresses Roads in built-up areas are typically laid out in a grid, creating "blocks" of buildings. The first one or two digits of a specific address refer to the block, which will be numbered in sequence from a central point, usually downtown, for example, 620 S Cedar Avenue will be six blocks south of downtown. It is crucial, therefore, to take note of components such as "NW" or "SE" in addresses, 3620 SW Washington Blvd will be a very long way indeed from 3620 NE Washington Blvd. Seattle's grid coordinates can be especially confusing (see p.258).

Airport tax Invariably included in the price of your ticket, though certain departure taxes may not be. At Vancouver an "Airport Improvement Fee" (see p.413) is levied on all departing passengers taking both internal and international flights. Pay with cash or credit card.

Dates In the North American style, the date 1.8.04 means not August 1 but January 8, 2004.

Drugs Varying, often stringent, penalties for most narcotics possession, with harsher sentences for sales or distribution. Marijuana possession under one ounce is treated as a misdemeanor ($200–500 fine), though foreigners may find themselves thrown out of the country as well.

DUI Driving Under the Influence, or drunken driving. Aggressively punished throughout the region, with loss of license, fines, and potential jail time for those caught breaking the law with a police-enforced "Breathalyzer" test. The current limit is a blood-alcohol level of .08, or three drinks within a single hour for a 150-pound person.

Electricity 110V AC in both the US and Canada. Many plugs are still two-pronged and rather flimsy. Some European-made travel plug adapters don't fit American sockets.

Floors The first floor in the US and Canada is what would be the ground floor in Britain, the second floor would be the first floor, and so on.

ID Should be carried at all times. Two pieces should suffice, one of which should have a photo: a passport and credit card(s) are your best bets, though some longer-term travelers may need a visa.

Measurements and sizes The US has not gone metric, so measurements are in inches, feet, yards, and miles, weight in ounces, pounds, and tons. American pints and gallons are about four-fifths of imperial ones. Clothing sizes are always two figures less what they would be in Britain – a British women's size 12 is a US size 10 – while British shoe sizes are 1 1/2 below American ones. Canada officially uses the metric system (though many people still use the old imperial system): distances are in kilometers, temperatures in Celsius, and food, fuel, and drink are sold in grams, kilograms, and liters.

Smoking Severely frowned upon in the vast majority of public places. Most cinemas are non-smoking, restaurants are usually divided into non-smoking and smoking sections, and smoking is universally forbidden on public transport – including all domestic airline flights. Work places, too, tend to be smoke-free zones, so employees are reduced to smoking on the street outside.

Tax Except for Oregon's lack of a sales tax, federal and/or state and provincial sales or services taxes are added to virtually every goods or services purchased in both the US and Canada, but aren't generally part of the marked price. The actual rate varies from place to place. Hotel tax will add 5 to 15 percent to most bills. See also p.29.

Temperatures Given in degrees Fahrenheit in the US, Celsius in Canada.

Time zones The Pacific Standard Time zone includes Oregon, Washington, and British Columbia, and is three hours behind New York, eight hours behind the UK.

Tipping In bars or restaurants 15–20 percent; about the same amount should be added to taxi fares. Hotel porters receive $3–5. See also box, p.46.

Videos and DVDs The standard format of VHS cassettes in North America is different from that in Britain, and you cannot buy videos in the US or Canada compatible with a video camera bought in Britain. The same is true for locally bought DVDs, which will only work in North American players, marked "Region 1."

Guide

Guide

Portland

N
Vancouver Island
CANADA
PACIFIC OCEAN
WASHINGTON
USA
OREGON
1 2 3 4 5 6 7 8 9 10 11

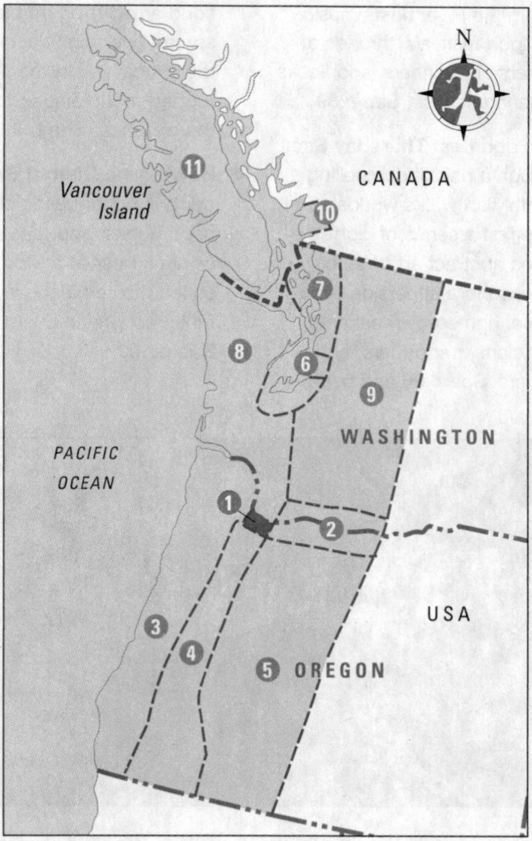

CHAPTER 1

Highlights

* **Pioneer Courthouse Square** Portland's indisputable core built around a set of concentric brick terraces, and home to the full spectrum of city life. See p.84

* **Tom McCall Waterfront Park** This elegant grassy concourse on the west bank of the Willamette River hosts music and food festivals, throngs of walkers and runners, and flocks of Canada geese. See p.89

* **First and Last Thursday** Stroll through a pair of compelling monthly art walks worlds apart – the first a series of high-priced abstract art galleries, the second a streetside explosion of homegrown painters, musicians, performers, and partiers. See p.96 and p.105

* **Forest Park** A huge natural preserve with countless hiking paths and striking views, and a thickly wooded topography that seems remote from the urban bustle. See p.98

* **Rose Test Garden** In addition to the Rose Parade in June, the "City of Roses," offers this florid array of bright blooms spread over many acres, with the evocative skyline and rugged mountains visible in the distance. See p.99

* **Hawthorne District** Browse in oddball boutiques, pick up used books, and take in a film or drink beer at a Moorish-styled movie palace in this funky bohemian Eastside strip. See p.103

△ Pioneer Square

Portland

Portlanders understand and appreciate how differently beautiful it is in this part of the world – the white city against the deep evergreen of the hills, the snow mountains to the east, the everchanging river and its boat life – and the grays, blues and greens, the smoke dimmed sunsets and pearly hazes of August, so characteristic of the Pacific Northwest.

John Reed

Having been spared Seattle's aggressive, remorseless development, **PORTLAND** retains a pleasant, small-city feel, both for its well-preserved Beaux Arts architecture and walkable urban core, as well as its easygoing atmosphere. Indeed, most of the city's handful of major attractions are located within close walking distance of each other on the short city blocks – half the size of most American cities. While Portland's unpretentious bohemian flavor may be lost on more gung-ho travelers, the city remains an excellent spot for casual visitors to while away weeks at a time, with a wealth of good diners, microbreweries, clubs, bookstores, and coffeehouses to keep you occupied and intrigued.

Sometimes called the most "unchurched" city in the nation, with fewer adherents to mainstream religion than practically anywhere else in the US, Portland prides itself on having a certain free-thinking, freewheeling character, with all kinds of liberal policies – a relaxed attitude toward marijuana, almost blanket protection for free speech (including pornography), and a generally hostile climate toward big business and over-development. That said, co-existing with the city's leftist element is a strong libertarian bent, wary of taxes and government programs – to the degree that in early 2003 the city garnered national headlines for leaving its school system dangerously underfunded and many social programs on the verge of collapse. While the city has inched away from that precipice, it continues to exhibit an often erratic character, unsure if it would like to bask in its reputation, fostered throughout the 1990s, as a highly livable place with model "slow-growth" urban policies, or would rather be rid of the attention entirely.

Some history

The city was founded in 1843 and named after Portland, Maine, following a coin toss between its two East Coast founders in 1845 ("Boston" was the other option). It was then no more than a clearing in the woods, but its location on a deep part of the Willamette River, near the Columbia River just eighty-odd miles from the Pacific, and surrounded by fertile valleys, made it a perfect trading port. It grew rapidly, supplying lumber to San Francisco and the Californian gold fields. As the money poured in, Portland's elite built themselves elegant

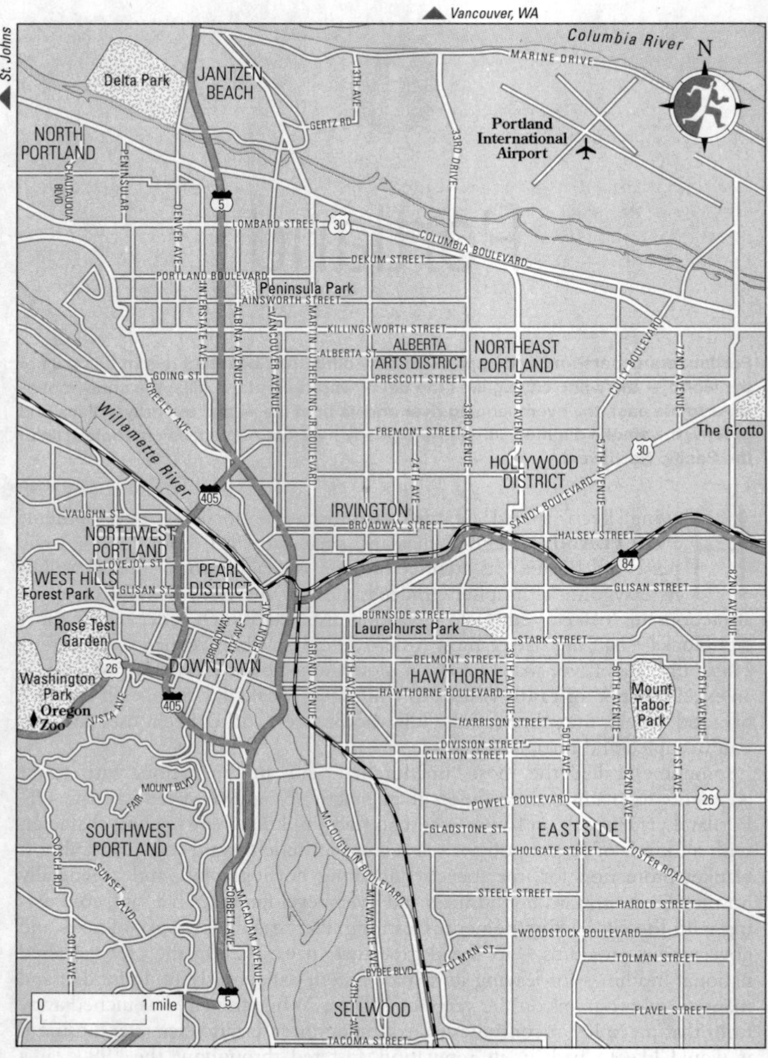

mansions and a suitably opulent business district, replacing the initial clapboard buildings with impressive Neo-Gothic, Florentine, and Second Empire edifices.

Not everyone benefited from the boom. Away from the richer parts of town lurked the seamier side of Portland – the "North End" (along the waterfront north of Burnside Street), a violent, bawdy district, notorious for gambling, liquor, prostitution, and opium dens. At its peak, towards the end of the nineteenth century, the North End's vice industry was so well entrenched, and the police so heavily bribed, that its ringleaders were even able to run a large-scale shanghaiing operation (see box, p.93), with scores of unwitting men drugged, drunk, or beaten unconscious to wake up as members of a ship's crew out on the Pacific. Local debauchery was dire enough that Simon Benson, one of the area's timber magnates, even paid for the creation of numerous "**Benson Bubblers**" around town to encourage local laborers to guzzle a liquid other than alcohol. If this plan had any effect is doubtful, but these constantly flowing, four-headed drinking fountains are still one of the prime fixtures on Downtown streets – just lean over for a gulp.

In the 1920s, with the regional ascendancy of the new ports of Puget Sound – principally Seattle – Portland declined, leaving behind huge swaths of derelict riverside warehouses and rail yards. As a consequence of this and a later decline in the lumber industry, city planners in the 1970s faced a downtown in tatters, its historic buildings decayed or sacrificed to parking lots and expressways. Under the helm of pioneering mayor **Neil Goldschmidt**, Portland salvaged what was left of its past while risking the odd splash of postmodernist architectural color, and even removed a riverside highway to convert it into Tom McCall Waterfront Park. In the last few decades, it has continued to replace concrete with red brick, introducing folksy statues and murals and a number of innovative mass-transit programs.

While the city's rehabilitation, along with its "**urban growth boundary**" to limit development, has done much for its image nationwide, more recently it's also achieved an unfortunate reputation as financial ground zero. Portland now faces the nation's worst unemployment rates, school-funding crises, and economic conditions, all brought on by the **bust in the high-tech sector**, which was as devastated here as anywhere in the US. Unlike residents of most other cities, though, when faced with such an economic disaster, Portlanders didn't move out in droves, but have tried to make the best of a dismal situation, whether this means college graduates manning espresso stands or computer geeks reduced to selling hot dogs. Surprisingly enough, the grim times haven't kept new arrivals away, so the city continues to grow even in the midst of a regional depression – with everyone from Seattle indie-rock refugees to former underground LA filmmakers finding the gloomy climate much to their liking.

Arrival and information

Strangely enough, **PDX**, the name for **Portland International Airport**, is also shorthand for the city itself – so don't get confused if you hear a local praising "the great club scene in PDX." The airport proper is located twelve miles northeast of Downtown, beside the Columbia River. From Terminal C, the **MAX Red Line** light rail (3–5 hourly, 4am–11pm; $1.60) shuttles passengers on a forty-minute journey along interstates 205 and 84 before heading downtown, traveling along SW First Avenue and SW Morrison Street (for more details of MAX, see "City transportation" below). Since the light rail has superseded airport bus service, the one motorized alternative is the **Gray Line Airport Express** shuttle (every 45min 5am–midnight; $15 one-way, $22

The area code for Portland is ⓣ503.

round-trip; ⓣ1-888/684-3322, ⓦwww.grayline.com), which drops off at major Downtown hotels. A **taxi** from the airport into town costs $25–30.

In Downtown Portland, the Greyhound **bus station** is at 550 NW Sixth Ave at Glisan (ⓣ503/243-2357 or 1-800/231-2222, ⓦwww.greyhound.com). The Amtrak **train station** is adjacent at Union Station, 800 NW Sixth Ave (ⓣ503/273-4865 or 1-800/872-7245, ⓦwww.amtrak.com). From here, it's about a ten-minute walk south to the city center, but if you arrive at either terminal at night take a taxi – this part of town is not safe after dark. If you are arriving by **car**, I-5 will bring you into the city from the north or south: heading south, take the City Center/Morrison Bridge exit 300B (with a fork right after the exit); northbound use the Naito Parkway/Front Avenue exit 299B. Approaching from the east, I-84 joins I-5 just east of Downtown – and exit 300B. Arriving from the west via Highway 26 (Sunset Hwy), or if coming from the coast, the road splits into three exits after the West Hills tunnel. The left exit leads to Northwest Portland and the Pearl District, the center goes Downtown, and the right connects to I-5 southbound to Salem.

Portland's **visitor center** is located Downtown, in Pioneer Square at 701 SW Sixth Ave (Mon–Fri 8.30am–5.30pm, Sat 10am–4pm, Sun 10am–2pm, ⓣ503/275-8355 or 1-877/678-5263, ⓦwww.pova.org). They issue free city maps, bus timetables, and a glossy city brochure, which includes accommodation listings. They also have plenty of information on the rest of the state, with details on everything from state parks, cycle routes, and bus services to lists of forthcoming events. For more information, contact **Oregon Tourism** (ⓣ1-800/547-7842, ⓦwww.traveloregon.com).

City transportation

There are many options for **transportation** in Portland, and the city's network of buses, streetcars, and lightrail lines provides a large part of its national renown as a center of thoughtful urban planning and mass-transit solutions. Like all reputations, this one is somewhat overblown – according to a 2003 study, the city has the eighth-worst traffic in the US, largely in the suburbs – but there are still plenty of choices if you're not bringing a car with you into town. Indeed, practically all major city sights are within easy access of bus or lightrail stops.

Buses

Portland's comprehensive **bus service** is operated by **Tri-Met**. Each bus shelter is labeled with a colored symbol – brown beaver, purple rain, blue snowflake, etc. – which serves as a code for a route in a particular area of the city. Although designed for simplicity, the system can still be pretty confusing, with different lines often sharing the same number: visit the **Tri-Met Customer Assistance Office** in Pioneer Courthouse Square (Mon–Fri 8.30am–5.30pm; ⓣ503/238-7433, for disabled customers ⓣ503/238-4952, ⓦwww.trimet.org) to get a free transit map and route-planning advice. They also sell all-zone day tickets ($4), "Quik Tik" six-hour passes ($3), books of ten tickets ($12.50), and monthly passes ($47) with special disabled rates ($34).

Major bus routes

From Downtown transit mall
#4 Division St, eastside
#6 Northeast Portland via Grand and MLK avenues
#9 Broadway, east and westside; Powell Blvd, eastside; Alberta St, eastside
#10 Clinton St, eastside
#12 Sandy Blvd, eastside
#14 Hawthorne Blvd, eastside
#15 Northwest Portland via 23rd Ave, Belmont District
#17 Northwest Portland via 21st Ave, St. Johns, Sauvie Island
#18 Forest Park
#19 Sellwood, Burnside St, eastside
#20 Burnside St, east and west
#32, #33 Oregon City
#63 Washington Park
#77 Troutdale
#83 OMSI

Major Eastside routes
#70 Sellwood to Lloyd District
#72 82nd Avenue
#75 Southeast to Northeast Portland via 39th Avenue

Buses and MAX trains are **free** in the Downtown zone – "**Fareless Square**" – edged by the Willamette to the east, Irving Street to the north, and I-405 to the south and west, with a narrow extension across the river to the Lloyd Center mall. Outside this area, the basic fare is $1.30, with another 30¢ for trips to the suburbs, airport, and Washington Park.

MAX light rail

Also operated by Tri-Met, **MAX** (Metropolitan Area Express), Portland's **light rail**, takes passengers around Downtown, traveling east along SW Yamhill Street and west along SW Morrison Street, between SW 18th and SW First avenues. On SW First Avenue, MAX travels in both directions, its **Red Line** passing through Old Town on its way to the Steel Bridge over to the northeast quadrant and the airport, with another line to the eastern suburbs. West from SW 18th Avenue, MAX **Blue Line** tunnels under Washington Park (and the zoo) bound for the western suburbs. The MAX fee is the same as the bus, but tickets must be purchased before you start your journey. There are ticket machines at every stop, and these both issue new tickets and validate unused ones purchased ahead of time. Further extensions to the transit system are planned, namely a **Yellow Line** extension from Downtown to the Expo Center along Interstate Avenue (following I-5 a few blocks east), scheduled to open by summer 2004.

Other transportation options

Vintage **trolley cars**, aimed at the tourist trade, also use the more central of the MAX lines, heading along SW Morrison Street, SW Yamhill Street, and SW First Avenue as far as Burnside Street. As an alternative, the brightly colored cars of the **Portland Streetcar** (Ⓦwww.portlandstreetcar.org) line ply a separate, equally tourist-oriented route between Portland State University, the Pearl District, and Northwest Portland, covering most Downtown sights on NW and SW 10th and 11th streets. Fares are free inside Fareless Square, otherwise $1.30. Portland's **taxis** don't stop in the street; you'll have to either get one at a hotel or call Broadway Cab (Ⓣ503/227-1234) or Portland Taxi Co (Ⓣ503/256-5400). Finally, to **rent a car** there are countless citywide firms (see "Listings," p.118), and you can also pick one up at the airport from the major chains, which are based on the ground level of the parking structure, across the concourse from the hotel-van and bus-transit pickup zones.

Cruises

Few would claim Portland's slice of the Willamette River is much to look at, but **Portland Spirit River Cruises** gamely offers **dinner cruises** (ⓣ503/224-3900 or 1-800/224-3901, ⓦwww.portlandspirit.com; nightly 7–9.30pm; $56 per person) and **two-hour sightseeing trips** (April–Oct 1–2 daily; $16), departing from the jetty at the foot of Salmon Street. A replica stern-wheeler, the **Columbia Gorge** (ⓣ541/374-8427, ⓣ1-800/643-1354, ⓦwww.sternwheeler.com), offers a similar service with two-hour sightseeing trips (Oct–June Sat & Sun 2 daily; $15), and three-hour dinner cruises (Oct–June 1 weekly; $49.50). Departures are from Tom McCall Waterfront Park, just north of the Morrison Bridge at the foot of Stark Street. Another prominent cruiser you'll see prominently along the river is **Willamette Jetboats**, 1945 SE Water Ave (ⓣ503/231-1532 or 1-888/538-2628, ⓦwww.jetboatpdx.com), which runs small, open-top blue vehicles on short, tourist-oriented routes during the summer. The two main options include a basic one-hour city tour, as seen from the river (July–Aug 1 daily; $17), and a two-hour jaunt that takes you down to Oregon City and back (May–Sept 2 daily; $27). Both trips depart from the *Blueback* submarine site at OMSI (see p.102).

Accommodation

Dozens of inexpensive **motels** line the main roads into Portland, but for most visitors the **Downtown** area provides more than enough choices for mid- to upper-end lodging, from refurbished classic **hotels** to stylish modern high-rises, all in a laid-back, amiable atmosphere – all with a uniform hotel tax in the neighborhood of 11.5 percent. Other than a few reasonable chain motels, you won't find much in the way of budget rooms here (unless you want to settle for one of the frightful fleabags around Old Town), so you may have to venture further afield. Other than the suburbs – too far away from the main action and too uninteresting, as well – there are only two decent choices outside Downtown: **Northwest Portland**, for a **B&B** here and a hotel there, and the **Eastside**, which has a range of appealing choices (mostly in the McMenamins brewpub-hotel chain) scattered across its main boulevards – though it's best to avoid seedy motel corridors like Sandy Boulevard and 82nd Avenue. The city also has two reputable **hostels** – one each in the southeast and northwest quadrants, and both a quick bus ride from Downtown.

Hotels, motels, and bed-and-breakfasts

Downtown

Benson Hotel 309 SW Broadway ⓣ503/228-2000 or 1-888/523-6766, ⓦwww.bensonhotel.com. The usual spot for visiting dignitaries and celebs, this classy hotel has a superb walnut-paneled 1912 lobby, swank bedrooms with modern appointments, suites, and even penthouses. Facilities include a health club and two restaurants. ❽

Days Inn City Center 1414 SW 6th Ave at Clay St ⓣ503/221-1611 or 1-800/899-0248, ⓦwww.daysinn.com. Great Downtown location and good value with well-tended, motel-style rooms. ❸

Embassy Suites 319 SW Pine St ⓣ503/279-9000, ⓦwww.embassyportland.com. Grand, renovated complex spread out over a full city block just north of the main Downtown sights (and a few blocks from Old Town), the *Embassy* boasts spacious suites, an indoor pool and fitness center, and a fine restaurant and bar, *Portland Steak and Chophouse*, on the ground floor. ❼

Four Points Downtown Sheraton 50 SW Morrison St at Naito Pkwy Ⓣ503/221-0711 or 1-800/899-0247, Ⓦwww.fourpointsportland.com. This modern hotel has a great location across Front Avenue from the Willamette River, and right by the MAX light rail. The front rooms overlook the river, but they don't have balconies, whereas those at the side do. The rooms themselves are somewhat large and comfortable with modern furnishings. ❻

Governor 611 SW 10th Ave at Alder Ⓣ503/224-3400 or 1-800/554-3456, Ⓦwww.govhotel.com. What some claim to be Portland's best hotel, the *Governor* has elegant rooms and suites with fireplaces, spas, plush sofas, and stylish decor (including carved woodwork), plus an onsite pool and fitness center. Mostly housed in an imaginatively styled Italian Renaissance 1923 office building, the lobby holds a striking sepia-toned mural inspired by the Lewis and Clark expedition. Centrally located a block from MAX and streetcar lines. ❼

Heathman 1001 SW Broadway at Salmon St Ⓣ503/241-4100 or 1-800/551-0011, Ⓦwww.heathmanhotel.com. Occupies a finely restored Neoclassical building, with an elegant, teak-paneled interior and much marble and brass. Splendid rooms and suites, excellent restaurant, and popular lobby-lounge where you can swill among the swells. Substantial discounts are frequently offered on the weekend. ❼

Hotel Lucía 400 SW Broadway Ⓣ503/225-1717, Ⓦwww.hotellucia.com. Minimalist, Asian-influenced lobby, arty B&W photos in the hallways, and chic decor throughout make this one of the city's more prominent boutique hotels – though the rooms can be quite cramped. ❻

Mallory 729 SW 15th Ave at Yamhill Ⓣ503/223-6311 or 1-800/228-8657, Ⓦwww.malloryhotel.com. On the edge of Downtown by the light rail tracks, a longstanding hotel with a handsome facade of sandy-colored brick decorated with geometric and herringbone patterns. The lobby is similarly stylish, with grand wooden fittings, chandeliers, and a coffered ceiling, but the rooms beyond are much plainer. ❺

Mark Spencer 409 SW 11th Ave at Stark Ⓣ503/224-3293 or 1-800/548-3934, Ⓦwww.markspencer.com. Large, modern, and fairly comfortable rooms with kitchenettes, but located in a loud, relatively dodgy Downtown location. ❺

Paramount 808 SW Taylor at Park Ave Ⓣ503/223-9900 or 1-800/426-0670, Ⓦwww.portlandparamount.com. Neo-Art Deco high-rise in a central location, boasting more than a hundred and fifty rooms, each tastefully decorated in modern style. The hotel has a fitness center, and some rooms have balconies. Most popular for its ground-floor *Dragonfish* pan-Asian bar and eatery (see p.107). ❻

Vintage Plaza 422 SW Broadway at Washington Ⓣ503/228-1212 or 1-800/243-0555, Ⓦwww.vintageplaza.com. An intimate boutique hotel in a handsome old building complete with imaginative settings and decor, with oversized rooms and a calm, relaxed atmosphere. Wine is offered in the afternoons in the lobby. One of the city's few dog-friendly hotels. ❻

Westin Portland 750 SW Alder St at Park Ave Ⓣ503/294-9000, Ⓦwww.westin.com. Recently built, top-notch luxury hotel a block from Broadway. Chic and modern, the spacious rooms and suites are replete with full amenities, and the onsite restaurant and fitness center make this a favorite for business travelers. The only downside is the drab, uninspired postmodern facade. ❽

Northwest Portland

Heron Haus 2545 NW Westover Rd Ⓣ503/274-1846, Ⓦwww.heronhaus.com. Stylish 1904 Tudor B&B, with some large suites featuring fireplaces, spas, and cozy sitting areas. Excellent continental breakfast and close hiking access to Portland's expansive Forest Park. ❻

Inn at Northrup Station 2025 NW Northrup St Ⓣ503/224-0543, Ⓦwww.northrupstation.com. Poised right on the streetcar line (thus the name) in Northwest Portland and offering a range of colorful suites with splashy retro designs, and some with kitchens, patios, and wet bars. ❺

MacMaster House 1041 SW Vista Ave Ⓣ503/223-7362 or 1-800/774-9523, Ⓦwww.macmaster.com. Grand, opulent 1895 mansion sporting a mix of Queen Anne and Colonial Revival styles, with five rooms and suites arrayed over three levels. Decor is tasteful retro-Victorian, and the striking location – perched on King's Hill overlooking the city – is minutes from the main action on NW 23rd Avenue. ❻

Silver Cloud Inn 2426 NW Vaughan St at NW 25th Ave Ⓣ503/242-2400 or 1-800/205-6939, Ⓦwww.silvercloud.com. Smart, well-kept motel with eighty rooms on the edge of Northwest Portland by the 405 freeway. ❹

Eastside

Edgefield 2126 SW Halsey St Ⓣ503/669-8610 or 1-800/669-8610,

Ⓦwww.mcmenamins.com/edge. Fifteen minutes east of the airport in the drab suburb of Troutdale (take bus #77), this unique brewery-resort features restaurants, bars, winery, and tasting room, distillery, movie theater, gardens, and an 18-hole golf course. Also with its own hostel, at $20 per dorm bed. With plenty of onsite drinking, the facility can get pretty loud at night, especially on weekends. Rooms ❹

Kennedy School 5736 NE 33rd Ave Ⓣ503/249-3983 or 1-888/249-3983, Ⓦwww.mcmenamins.com/kennedy. Thirty-five B&B rooms, in a refurbished schoolhouse with chalkboards and cloakrooms, plus modern conveniences. Excellent breakfast, multiple brewpubs, movie theater, outdoor bathing pool, and "detention bar." ❺

Lion & the Rose 1810 NE 15th Ave Ⓣ503/287-9245 or 1-800/955-1647, Ⓦwww.lionrose.com. Six rooms in a late-Victorian 1906 mansion near the Irvington neighborhood. Offers spacious beds, private baths, some units with Jacuzzis, and fairly precious period decor. ❻

White Eagle 836 N Russell St Ⓣ503/282-6810, Ⓦwww.mcmenamins.com/eagle. Hands-down Portland's best bargain, a refurbished old hotel now boasting a hip brewpub in an industrial-bohemian neighborhood. Rooms are clean and simple, and surprisingly cheap, with shared baths. Live music nightly. ❷

Hostels

HI-Portland Hawthorne 3031 SE Hawthorne Blvd Ⓣ503/236-3380 or 1-866/447-3031, Ⓦwww.portlandhostel.com. Hostel facilities in a cheery Victorian house, well located on the western edge of the Hawthorne District. Also offers Internet access, van tours of local sights, barbecues, and occasional live music performances. $19 dorms, $48 private rooms. Take bus #14 (brown color) from the transit mall on SW 5th Avenue. Reservations recommended.

HI-Portland Northwest 1818 NW Glisan Ⓣ503/241-2783, Ⓦwww.2oregonhostels.com. Located in a nineteenth-century home in Northwest Portland, near the popular *Mission Theatre & Brewpub* and just east of the main action on 21st and 23rd streets. Contains an espresso bar and family rooms. $21 dorms, doubles with private bathrooms $52. Take bus #17 (purple color) from the 6th Avenue transit mall.

The City

Portland has an appealingly straightforward layout, with the **Willamette** ("wah-LAM-it") **River** dividing the city into its east and west sides and **Burnside Street** delineating the north from the south; each street address describes its relation to these dividers – NE, SE, NW, and SW. The **Downtown** core lies between the river's west bank and the I-405 freeway, in the city's southwest quadrant. Engagingly laid-back, the area boasts a harmonious mix of old and new architectural styles, where fading plasterwork and terracotta reliefs face seamless steel and glass, all punctuated by small grassy parks and whimsical street sculptures.

Downtown's pleasant air fades a bit, however, as it stretches north into **Old Town**, along West Burnside Street from Eighth Avenue to the river. Where the city's first merchants and loggers set up shop, today restored nineteenth-century buildings are occupied by busy restaurants and bars – in unhappy contrast to the dejected street people crowded around the Salvation Army mission at SW Ankeny and Second Avenue. Just a few blocks north and west, though, beyond small **Chinatown** and its handful of authentic blocks, the rising condos of the **Pearl District** have become the city's unquestioned economic bright spot recently – and an undeniable yuppie magnet, filled with pricey boutiques and chic restaurants. Much of the same is found further west, in **Northwest Portland** along 21st and 23rd avenues, with the added benefit of surviving Victorian architecture and a more relaxed, semi-bohemian air in places. Beyond this, the pick of the outlying attractions are amongst the **West Hills** – notably the ornate **Pittock Mansion**, the leafy trails and formal gardens of sprawling **Washington Park**, and the hiking paradise of **Forest Park**.

For many visitors, the **Eastside** across the river is unknown territory – though it shouldn't be. Along major routes such as **Hawthorne Boulevard**, **Belmont Street**, and **Broadway**, you can find a number of excellent vintage clothiers, novelty shops, fine ethnic diners, and all kinds of eccentric, only-in-Portland boutiques. From the antique dealers of **Sellwood** in the south up to the rough-and-ready bars of **St. Johns** in the north, the Eastside has plenty of districts with their own quirky character, though some are a bit more charming than others. The further east you go, the more uninviting the territory becomes, though the ethereal shrine of **The Grotto**, located off a dismal stretch of Sandy Boulevard, can make for an enjoyable pilgrimage for the faithful.

Downtown

In true West Coast style, you can mill about the **Downtown** core for hours, sipping lattes and listening to street musicians, wandering into vintage boutiques, or browsing in book- and record stores. The unquestioned center is **Pioneer Courthouse Square**, from where cultural life in the city spills out in all directions, particularly along the splashy stretch of **Broadway**, home to many of the city's leading stores, restaurants, and theaters. Further west, the

The perils of Portland driving

If you're used to the wide-open thoroughfares of other West Coast cities like LA and Seattle, **driving in Portland** will doubtless be one of the most unnerving experiences you're likely to have. This is especially true Downtown, where the blocks are half the size of most US cities, novice drivers run red lights or drive against one-way traffic, and there are all manner of other distractions. To prepare yourself, maintain extra following distance behind the car in front of you, go 5-10 mph slower than you would in other cities, and pay special attention to maps, which can help you navigate the thorniest parts of town – the spaghetti-like chaos of asphalt at the west end of the Ross Island Bridge, the looping and circuitous roads of the West Hills, and the difficulty of accessing the I-5 freeway from Downtown.

Also bear in mind the special, **non-automotive hazards** of city driving. Foremost are the aggressive cyclists who take advantage of the local bike-friendly climate to run red lights and stop signs, dart in between cars, and verbally (and sometimes physically) challenge drivers who don't offer them enough space. Also unsettling is Portland's widespread **jaywalking**, an infraction rarely enforced by police except on major boulevards, and resulting in swarms of people scurrying – and sometimes sauntering – across the roadway directly in front of vehicles, confident that most city drivers will indulge their lawbreaking. Luckily, however, Portland drivers are much less prone to speeding and tailgating, at least Downtown, than those of other major cities, and chronic horn-honking is generally not a problem in such a laid-back place. Indeed, more than other drivers, your biggest dangers may be from the street layout and the secondary distractions – making the alternative of **taking a bus**, like countless city residents, that much more desirable.

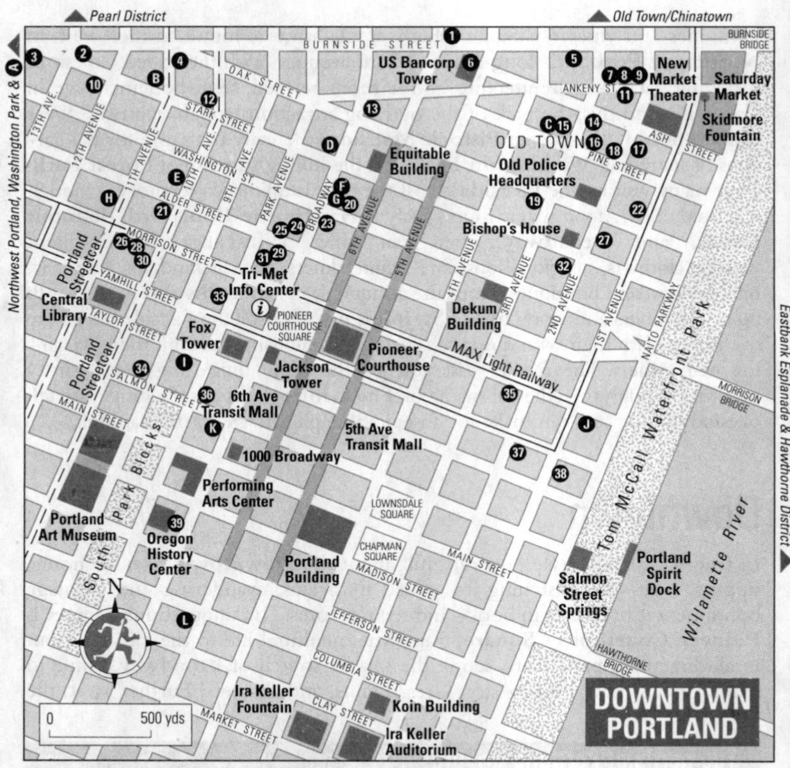

ACCOMMODATION		RESTAURANTS, BARS AND CLUBS					
Benson	D	Abou Karim	18	Higgins	39	Portland City Grill	6
Days Inn City Center	L	Ash Street Saloon	8	Huber's	32	Portland Steak and Chophouse	15
Embassy Suites	C	Berbati's Pan	7	Hunan	24	Red Sea	27
Four Points Sheraton	J	Bijou Café	16	India House	26	Ringlers Annex	2
Governor	E	Brasserie Montmatre	31	Jake's Famous Crawfish	10	Rock Bottom Brewery	35
Heathman	K	Coffee People	36	Jake's Grill	21	Roseland Theater	1
Hotel Lucia	F	Crystal Ballroom	3	Kell's	17	Ruth's Chris Steak House	19
Mallory	A	Dan and Louis Oyster Bar	11	Maya's Tacqueria	30	Saucebox	13
Mark Spencer	B	Dante's	5	McCormick and Schmick's	22	Shanghai Tunnel	9
Paramount	I	Fernando's Hideaway	38	New York City Sub Shop	25	South Park	34
Vintage Plaza	G	Fez Ballroom	4	Panorama	12	Stumptown Roasters	14
Westin	H	Good Dog Bad Dog	29	Pazzo	20	Virginia Café	33
		Great Harvest Bread Company	37	Peet's Coffee and Tea	23		
				Persian House	28		

linear green strip of the **South Park Blocks** hosts several decent museums, while to the east the riverside stretch of **Tom McCall Waterfront Park** is rivaled only by Pioneer Courthouse Square for cultural activity. As you head north and get closer to Old Town, Downtown's main highlights are mostly architectural – highly ornamented old office blocks that easily put the city's postmodern colossus, the **Portland Building**, to shame.

Pioneer Courthouse Square and around

Sitting in a space once occupied by the legendary *Portland Hotel* – until it was unceremoniously razed in the 1950s to make way for a department-store parking lot – **Pioneer Courthouse Square** more than lives up to its historic predecessor as a true urban hub of social and cultural activity, and even boasts a few of the hotel's original wrought-iron gates and fixtures at its margins. Hosting a broad range of types – everyone from pinstriped bankers to pierced-and-tattooed street kids – the square and its red-bricked, curving terraces and modest waterfalls are wedged directly between the eastbound and westbound light rail tracks, and adjacent to Downtown's main strip of Broadway.

Activity in the square largely depends on the season, with lunchtime rock concerts and fashion shows held during the summer, periodic book and antique sales throughout the year, and a sizable Christmas tree during the holiday season. Near the southwest corner, a folksy, life-size bronze of a man with an open umbrella (*Allow Me*, by Seward Johnson) personifies the area's easygoing character. Equally iconic, the stylish **weathervane**, in the center of the square, supposedly predicts the climate on any given day: on warm days a churlish sun appears, on dark stormy days a growling dragon, and during plain old wet, overcast weather, a placid blue heron – naturally, the most common omen of all.

While major department stores (Nordstorm and Meier and Frank) dot the square to the west and northeast, one shop with a proud local feel and well worth a visit is Powell's Travel Store (ⓣ503/228-1108, ⓦwww.powells.com), on a lower level under the square's southeast corner. One of seven Portland-area Powell bookstores, here you can quite enjoyably pass an afternoon browsing a good selection of maps and travel guides (including copious Rough Guides), sipping a coffee, or stocking up on tourist brochures and bus schedules from the visitor center underneath the waterfalls.

Across the square, at the corner of Yamhill Street, is **Jackson Tower**, one of Portland's many historic terracotta office blocks built in the early twentieth century, a splendid 1912 concoction faced with white-glazed panels and crowned with a looming clock. To the east, and completed in 1868, lies the **Pioneer Courthouse**, the first major federal building constructed in the Pacific Northwest. The style is a local take on Renaissance Revival, accentuated by a modest dome. Although there used to be a post office here, it's now mainly known as the Portland quarters for the US Ninth Circuit Court of Appeals, when it occasionally hears cases outside of its San Francisco base.

From the square, you can take a two-and-a-half hour **walking tour** of the city's highlights (Fri–Sun 10.30am; $15; ⓦwww.portlandwalkingtours.com), a good introduction to Portland for first-time visitors.

SW Broadway

Serving as the square's western border, **SW Broadway** is where Portland's combination of old grandeur and contemporary style most successfully coalesces. A brief stroll north along Broadway from the square takes you past a sequence of handsome office blocks, hotels, and banks, the pick of which date from the twentieth century's inaugural decades. Particularly fine buildings include the exuberantly Neoclassical **US National Bank** at Broadway and Stark Street, and just opposite, the imposing red-brick-and-stone symmetries of the **Benson Hotel** (see "Accommodation," p.80). A few blocks east are a pair of notable modern high-rises, the first being the **US Bancorp Tower**. Better known as **Big Pink**, at Fifth Avenue and Pine Street, this magenta-colored block has a mirrored-glass top that seems to change color – from red to orange – depending on the time of the day. Two blocks south, the 1948 **Equitable Building** (now the "Commonwealth"), clad in aluminum and glass, was the first truly modern office building built west of the Mississippi River, and designed by Pietro Belluschi, better known for creating the Portland Art Museum (see opposite).

South of Pioneer Courthouse Square on Broadway are several of Portland's more contemporary structures, which like other public buildings, must by law host a certain amount of **retail space** on their ground levels; usually this means movie theaters, clothing chains, fast-food franchises, and assorted boutiques. Thus, the human traffic is much busier along here on weekends than you'd find if these buildings were relegated to being mere corporate fortresses, as in the downtown cores of most other major cities. Some of the more prominent edifices that host such businesses include the **Fox Tower**, cater-corner to the southwest of Pioneer Courthouse Square, and **1000 Broadway**, two blocks further south. Both have replaced a pair of classic movie palaces with their glossy, modern designs: the former topped with a convex glass curtain-wall and the latter a shiny pink dome – leading some to derisively compare it to a roll-on deodorant stick.

Across the street, at Broadway and Main Street, and more appealing is the striking **Portland Center for the Performing Arts**, 1111 SW Broadway (ⓣ503/248-4335 or 224-4000, ⓦwww.pcpa.com), with two main buildings – the **Arlene Schnitzer Concert Hall** and the **New Theater Building**, containing the Dolores Winningstad Theater and Newmark Theater. The "Schnitz" is a sumptuously restored 1928 vaudeville and moviehouse that presents big musical extravaganzas, dance, and theater, while the latter is a flashy construction of brick and dark glass, whose cherry wood-paneled lobby is topped with a spectral light dome that changes color with the light of the sky. Further south, Broadway leads on to the campus of Portland State University and the entry ramps for the southbound I-5 freeway.

The South Park Blocks and around

Immediately west of the Center for the Performing Arts, the **South Park Blocks**, a block-wide strip of elm-shaded park, stretches eleven blocks from the university campus up to Main Street. This green belt is another favorite urbanite hangout, where retirees commingle with teen slackers and the homeless, and the Portland Streetcar (see p.79) ambles through to its southern turnabout. On the lawn are several notable **statues**, including two bronzes from the 1920s near the art museum (see opposite), the first of which features a gloomy-looking **Abraham Lincoln** with his head lowered in quiet anguish – an image so dour, in fact, that the city almost sent it back to the sculptor. However, unlike many more typically heroic statues – such as the second bronze nearby, a militaristic **Theodore Roosevelt** shown as a "Rough Rider" from his days as a cavalry leader in the Spanish-American War of 1898 – the Lincoln sculpture is one of the city's most affecting and thoughtful public artworks.

Close by the statues, on the south side of the blocks, rises the top-heavy tower of the **First Congregational Church** (1126 SW Broadway), an ungainly pile allegedly in the Venetian Gothic style and dating to 1896. This church is only one of several historic structures in the area, which were built for various denominations in different styles – from Carpenter Gothic to Neoclassical – and date from the late-Victorian period.

Further south, around the university campus, the park hosts a very popular, seasonal **farmers market** (May–Oct Wed 10am–2pm, May–Nov Sat 8.30am–2pm; ⓦwww.portlandfarmersmarket.org) that draws fruit and vegetable growers from around the region, and other local vendors of bread, pastries, beeswax candles, and handicrafts. On Saturdays, you might also take in a cooking demonstration, hear music from live bands – anything from rock to folk to polka – and encounter a bevy of petitioners, supporting a range of liberal causes from equal rights to veganism.

Looming near the market is the marvelously refurbished **Simon Benson House**, adjacent to the park at Montgomery Street (Mon–Fri 11am–5pm; donation; ⓦwww.alumni.pdx.edu/benson). Once sitting on a nearby block, it decayed almost to the point of collapse until the university physically moved the house onto its campus and turned it into an alumni center. As the former home of one of the city's most famous timber barons, responsible for the eponymous hotel and the constantly flowing "Benson Bubblers" on street corners, the Queen Anne mansion features rooms paneled in different types of regional wood, graceful moon windows and horseshoe arches, and a lovely wraparound veranda.

Oregon Historical Society

Also adjacent to the Park Blocks, the newly renovated **Oregon Historical Society**, 1200 SW Park Ave (Tues–Sat 10am–5pm, Sun noon–5pm; $6; ⓦwww.ohs.org), is primarily a research facility, but has some imaginative exhibits exploring different facets of the state's history. It also puts on temporary shows displaying famous regional and national documents – in one recent case, a 1776 copy of the Declaration of Independence. The society's collections focus on different aspects of the area's heritage, encompassing photographs, artifacts, and mementos from a span of hundreds of years. These include art and craftwork of native tribes, early coins minted before Oregon became a state, an early version of a streetcar, then-and-now photos of notable city boulevards, and assorted twentieth-century trinkets and souvenirs. Among the highlights of the latter are vintage matchbooks from forgotten hotels, cheeky advertising for state products, and campaign buttons for local politicians like Wayne Morse – one of only two US senators to vote against the Gulf of Tonkin resolution, which paved the way for the Vietnam War.

The society is also well known for its towering Richard Haas murals, which grace the south and west walls of the center in *trompe l'oeil* form, with curving walls and Neoclassical columns that seem to open out toward the viewer. The **south mural**, a vision of the Oregon Trail crawling up the building, more resembles a pioneer pyramid than a trek to the horizon, while the **west mural** showcases the Lewis and Clark expedition, its members wedged uncomfortably into the complex painted architecture. In autumn 2005, the latter mural will be augmented by the society's bicentennial commemoration of that famous journey, complete with a huge array of artifacts, documents, and other items relating to the expedition and to early American history.

Portland Art Museum

Across the Park Blocks from the Historical Society lies the long, low facade of early-modernist architect Pietro Belluschi's **Portland Art Museum** (Tues, Wed & Sat 10am–5pm, Thurs & Fri 10am–8pm, Sun noon–5pm; $10; ⓦwww.pam.org), which incorporates the adjacent, somewhat ponderous, old Masonic Temple. The museum prides itself on its temporary exhibitions, but it also possesses a large permanent collection – too large, in fact, to show at any one time, which means that exhibits are regularly rotated. The collection is spread over three floors, with the ground floor featuring two main sections. One is devoted to contemporary, mostly American artists, with the varied collection of arch-modernist critic **Clement Greenberg** – responsible for elevating the likes of Jackson Pollock and David Smith, among others – occasionally on display, but with fewer big names than you might expect. The other, the **Asian Art Galleries**, has one room each for Korean, Japanese, and Chinese pieces. The basement holds prints, photographs, and a modest sample of African applied art – masks, figurines, and so forth.

Rather more interesting – and on the top floor – are the European Galleries, which trace the evolution of European fine art, beginning with medieval painted wooden panels and Italian Renaissance paintings and running through to modernism. The strongest feature here is devoted to the **Impressionists** and **post-Impressionists**, with minor examples of the work of Cézanne, Monet, Pissarro, Renoir, and Degas. On the same floor, there is a room of finely crafted English silverware and a separate section for the museum's Native American collection, with the emphasis on the Pacific Northwest.

Continuing on from the European Galleries, the Hirsch Wing focuses on American painters from the eighteenth century to modern times. Amongst the early works, look out for a couple of routine portraits by Gilbert Stuart (1755–1828), the artist responsible for the portrait of George Washington that graces the one-dollar bill. Stuart painted his first Washington in 1796, and it proved so popular that he went on to produce no fewer than seventy copies. The Hirsch Wing also contains a good sample of nineteenth-century landscape painters who frequently visited or moved to the Pacific Northwest. In particular look out for **Cleveland Rockwell** (1836–1907), a New Yorker who came to Oregon in 1868 to survey the coast for the US government and painted soft and warmly hued land- and seascapes in his spare time. Of the later artists on display, two of the more impressive are the Fauvist-influenced **Milton Avery** (1877–1965) and **Julian Alden Weir** (1852–1919), a local painter whose tense realism is well illustrated by his *Ice Cutters* of 1898.

The Portland Building and around

A couple of minutes' walk east, at the junction of Madison and Fifth, is Portland's one sight of national, if not world, renown – architect Michael Graves's **Portland Building**, a boxy concoction of concrete and glass, adorned with dark-red and blue-green tiling with pale-blue ribbons to match. Despite its adornments, it's quite possible to walk straight past without realizing this is anything special, but on closer examination there's little doubt it's an eclectic structure. An uninhibited (some say flippant) reworking of classical and other motifs, it was one of the most talked-about US buildings of the 1980s, establishing the public face of the postmodern style, for better or worse. Portland positively relished the controversy, and, in a burst of civic zeal, hoisted the colossal copper figure of *Portlandia* on to the porch above the main entrance – where she kneels, one hand clutching a trident, the other reaching down towards Fifth Avenue. The sculpture is popular enough that mayor Vera Katz once even threatened to level the building and move *Portlandia* onto the west bank of the Willamette River – surely one of the most bizarre images ever put forward by a public official. Like Katz, local residents are ambivalent about the worth of the building and city workers working there generally despise it – the tiny windows are about half the size of those in most office buildings, and the interior has been compared to a tomb.

To the east, at Main Street and Third Avenue, in pleasant little **Lownsdale Square**, the **Soldiers' Monument** commemorates those Oregon volunteers who died in the Spanish-American War of 1898. Unfortunately, though, neighboring **Chapman Square** has been recently marred by a kitsch sculpture of an Oregon Trail family, gazing west with apple-cheeked, po-faced expressions.

Between the squares, and smack in the middle of Main Street, is a **bronze elk**, which was one of the city's earliest street sculptures, plonked in 1900 on top of the granite horse trough that still sits beneath it. It's not a very successful piece – the poor animal looks strangely lopsided – but it did prompt major municipal rows on several occasions when plans were announced to move it to speed traffic.

Along with hosting various sculptures, Lownsdale and Chapman squares are also some of Portland's earliest green spaces, and while nothing much happens there on most days, they're occasionally the sites of fervent political protests, rallies by national politicians, and the start and finish line for the Portland Marathon.

Tom McCall Waterfront Park

A short walk to the east from the squares lies the **riverfront**, which has been rescued from more than a century of burial beneath wharves, warehouses, and, in the 1970s, an express highway. Now the mile-long grassy strip along the west bank of the Willamette, reborn as **Tom McCall Waterfront Park**, accommodates a popular walking and cycling path and offers excellent views of the city's stylish old bridges, while in the distance you can spot the triangular, snow-capped hump of Mount Hood (see p.132). The park is named after liberal Republican governor McCall, a key figure in the late 1960s and 1970s movement to improve the state and the prime mover behind dozens of environmental measures (see box).

Oregon's proud provincialism

Oregon, and Portland in particular, is nationally renowned as a leader in "**smart growth**" policies, embracing urban-growth boundaries, stringent land-use rules, re-use of historic structures, and red tape to control billboards and other visual blight. All of this is meant to keep fervent development at bay, the atmosphere pleasant and low-key, and the mountains and forests visible in the distance – without being blocked by scores of high-rises. Moreover, in few other places in the US do you find the same degree of antipathy for population growth; if anything, exaggerated stories of constant rainfall and gray skies are viewed as appropriate tools to keep sun-worshipping interlopers away – preferably to much-derided places like Phoenix and Los Angeles. And while outsiders might view Seattle as a place that shares much in common with Portland, albeit on a larger scale, Oregonians often invoke their neighbor as a textbook example of the dangers of unrestrained urban growth, huge corporate tax breaks to companies like Boeing, and the looming menace of Microsoft and Starbucks.

Some claim this tradition of proud **provincialism** dates back to the days of the Oregon Trail, though pioneering governor Oswald West really set the tone by helping protect most of the state's beaches from development in the 1910s. The most prominent exponent of the tradition, though, was governor **Tom McCall**, responsible in the 1960s and 70s for groundbreaking environmental laws and a host of anti-sprawl regulations. A larger-than-life figure, McCall even placed signs at the border stating, "You are welcome to visit Oregon, but please don't stay," though he was not, as is commonly thought, responsible for the celebrated phrase "Don't Californicate Oregon," meaning not to overdevelop it. Even today McCall's legacy looms large over the state among partisans of all political stripes, and Oregon politicians are as loath to criticize the legendary governor as Bible Belt pols would be to denounce religion. And even in the midst of a deep regional recession, the state has avoided embracing a corporate-friendly slogan like "Open for business" – its current official mantra is the much more relaxed and nebulous "We love dreamers."

Waterfront Park runs south from the Burnside Bridge to the marina at the foot of Clay Street. In early June's **Rose Festival** (see p.100), the northern part of the park features the presence of all manner of colossal US Navy destroyers and cruisers docked alongside, which sometimes allow tours, depending on the national level of terrorism fears. In the middle of the park, opposite Salmon Street, you'll find the Portland Spirit River Cruises jetty (see p.80 for cruise details) and the playful, gushing fountains of **Salmon Street Springs**, which spurt forth from ground level and attract children and the odd adult to caper around in their waters. The southern end of the park has the most expansive greenery, and hosts countless summertime festivals and concerts – with the **Waterfront Blues Festival** (Ⓦwww.waterfrontbluefest.com) being one of the highlights. Around the marina, though, the visual interest peters out in a rather antiseptic, waterside strip mall with high prices and several vacant storefronts.

Ira Keller Auditorium and Fountain

Three blocks inland from the park, Downtown's last major sights of note can be found at SW Third and Clay, where the **Ira Keller Auditorium** (Ⓣ503/274-6560) is home to traveling musicals, occasional rock shows, and the **Portland Opera** (Ⓣ503/241-1407, Ⓦwww.portlandopera.org). More eye-catching, though, is the **Ira Keller Fountain** across the street, one of the rare successful examples of modernist fountain design. This array of concrete blocks, staircases, alcoves, and troughs provides countless locals with an outlet for wading and splashing throughout the year. While some prefer to take it easy on the terraced concrete slabs away from the water, others perch perilously – and get soaked – atop the sheer walls above, where the torrents flow in a thick mist. A favorite gathering place for residents, the fountain is designed in a much more appealing style than its surrounding counterparts – huge, lifeless office blocks, enlivened only by the presence of the **KOIN Building**, cater-corner at Third and Clay. This 1980s curiosity, looking like a brick-red rocket, was home to a decent second-floor theater; the building is best known as an essential part of a picture-postcard view of Portland's cityscape.

Old Town

From the Willamette River to Sixth Avenue, between the Morrison and Burnside bridges, **Old Town** was the site where Portland was founded in 1843, and throughout the rest of the century and up until the 1920s, was the focus of the city's business as a thriving port. The warehouses and docks were once numerous and ungainly along the river shoreline, with hulking wooden shells on the banks and jagged arrays of pilings in the water, though the addition of a sea wall by the 1930s put an end to the crusty, old-fashioned nautical atmosphere.

Visually the area is still distinctive, though. By the 1850s, wealthy Portlanders were edging the streets with grand, cast-iron frame buildings for their businesses, less expensive and faster to build than their stone and brick predecessors. They also had the added advantage of extra strength – supporting piers could be much narrower than before, which, in turn, let in more light. The popularity of the material was, however, short-lived. In 1889 it was abruptly replaced by steel, mostly with terracotta embellishments, a fashion that lasted until the 1930s. But long before this, Old Town had fallen into decline: the area tended to flood, and when the railroad came in 1883 the town center started to shift away from the river, a gradual process that eventually pushed Old Town

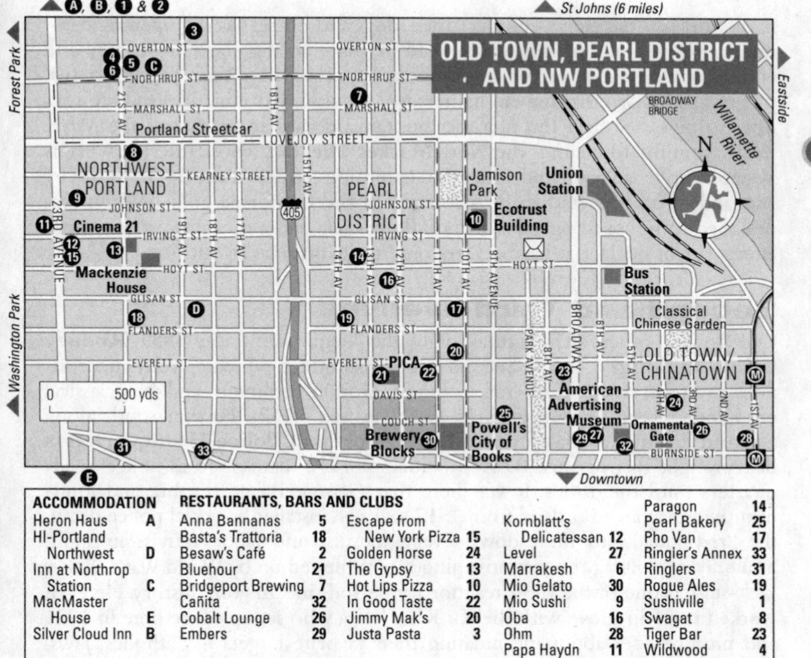

right down the social scale. "Improvement" schemes in the 1950s almost finished the district off, and gaps still show where buildings were pulled down to make way for parking lots.

Recent attempts at **rejuvenation** have been more respectful, though, and the area now holds an attractive patchwork of restored old buildings, many of which house bistros and boutiques. That said, Old Town is a dicey area after dark: the poverty of Burnside Street is too close for comfort and, particularly around the Salvation Army mission at Ankeny Street and SW 2nd Avenue, the well-heeled and the down-and-out eye each other dubiously in a division that is – for Oregon at least – uncomfortably sharp. Nevertheless, if you're a club-goer, you won't be able to escape the area, for the stretch around Third Avenue (north and south) and Burnside is home to the city's most exciting and frenetic concert halls and dance clubs (see p.114).

Skidmore Fountain and New Market Theater

One of the best excuses for a visit to Old Town, the **Saturday Market** (March–Dec Sat 10am–5pm, Sun 11am–4.30pm; Ⓦwww.portlandsaturdaymarket.com) packs the area south of, and under, the Burnside Bridge with arts and crafts stalls, eclectic street musicians, spicy foods, and lively crowds, all crammed cheek-to-jowl by the MAX tracks.

In the middle of the market area, at First Avenue and Ankeny Street, stands the **Skidmore Fountain**, a bronze basin raised by caryatids above a granite pool, designed to provide European elegance for the citizens – and water for hard-worked nineteenth-century "men, dogs and horses" as the opening ceremony had it. The fountain was opened in 1888 to the cheers of a large and enthusiastic crowd, though many of them might not have been so appreciative if they had known that the city fathers had previously declined a local brewer's offer to pipe free beer through the fountain on its first day. Across the MAX tracks from the fountain is the **New Market Theater**, whose interior, with its Venetian-style arcades and cast-iron trimmings, dates from 1872. Built by Alexander Ankeny, who made a fortune in the California gold fields, it was designed to house a vegetable market downstairs and a theater upstairs – and, after years of neglect, it has been restored to its original layout.

Second and Third avenues

Old Town's other architectural highlights begin with the 1889 **Rodney Glisan Building**, 112 SW Second Ave at Ash Street, which cleverly incorporates several styles, its cast-iron columns, Gothic pediment, and Neoclassical entrance presently home to *Kells Irish Pub* (see p.112). Further south along **Second Avenue** at Oak Street is the old **Portland Police Headquarters**, a heavyweight Renaissance Revival edifice of 1912 that served as police headquarters until the 1980s. It was here that George Baker, the big and loud-mouthed mayor of Portland from 1917 to 1924, installed a special police detail, the "red squad," to hunt down every socialist and labor activist in sight. Skillfully exploiting the primitive jingoism whipped up by World War I, Baker kick-started one of the most reactionary periods in Oregon's history. He even worked hand-in-glove with the Ku Klux Klan, who set up office here in 1921 and promptly set about intimidating their favorite targets – Catholics, Jews, Asians, and, most viciously of all, the Wobblies (see box, p.544) – and posed for ominous group photographs with area politicians (images sometimes on display at the Oregon Historical Society; see p.87). This sordid chapter in the city's history is avoided at the **Portland Police Historical Museum**, further south at the Justice Center, 1111 2nd Ave, 16th floor (Mon–Thurs 10am–3pm; free), which features antique uniforms, badges, and weapons, including the types of old-time guns and knives popular with local miscreants.

Back along Second Avenue in Old Town, the 1891 **Concord Building**, no. 208 at Stark Street, features elegant brick and sandstone-trimmed lines that mark an early departure from the more ornate buildings that went before. Opposite, and in striking contrast, is the Gothic Revival **Bishop's House**, a brick, cast-iron, and stucco structure built in 1879 for the city's Catholic archbishop and subsequently used as a Prohibition speakeasy and now a Lebanese restaurant. Around the corner, at Third Avenue and Washington, are two of the city's finest buildings, the **Postal Building** of 1900, whose Renaissance Revival order is adorned by frilly terracotta panels and a delightfully intricate cornice, and opposite, the slightly earlier **Dekum Building**, created for the confectioner Frank Dekum in 1892, with the word "Dekum" spelled out in rough, stylized letters. Here, the brick and terracotta upper levels perch on rough-hewn red sandstone in an outstanding example of the Romanesque Revival, representing an influential departure from the daintier preoccupations of the 1880s.

Chinatown

North of West Burnside from Old Town, the several blocks immediately adjacent were in the nineteenth century known as the North End, where all kinds

Shanghaiing

Until the end of the nineteenth century, international trade depended on wooden sailing ships, requiring large, docile **crews** and sailing times that varied enormously depending on the weather. The result was that ships could lie empty in harbor for weeks, if not months and, to keep costs down, captains habitually dismissed most of the ship's crew when they reached their destination, but this created difficulties when they were ready to leave – low wages and poor conditions never attracted enough volunteers. Into the breach stepped dozens of waterfront hoodlums, or **crimps**, who were hired to supply the crews with no questions asked. **Shanghaiing**, as it became known in the US (as China was the principal destination), was big business, nowhere more so than in Portland, where thugs like Joseph "Bunco" Kelly and Jim Turk – whom contemporaries described as "225 pounds of florid-faced, beef-fed Britisher" – worked the scam, owning boardinghouses from whose residents they could select their victims with all the violent aplomb of a press gang. And if this failed, they simply roamed the waterfront brothels and bars, descending on their victims when their pants or inhibitions were down.

Although it was the steamship rather than the law that polished off Portland's crimps, this grim period in city history lives on in the **Shanghai Tunnels Tours** ($11, by reservation only at ⓣ503/622-4798), which depart on periodic evenings from *Hobo's* bar in Old Town at 120 NW Third Ave. While these are as much about cheesy ghost stories as they are about authentic history, they do take you on an eye-opening 90min journey through the corridors and cellars beneath the streets, where shanghaiing victims were supposedly held in tiny, dank cells and would-be rebels were "managed" with a clunk to the skull with a brick or blackjack. While you should take much of the tour's running commentary with a grain of salt – the likes of haunted rooms and pop-up mannequins only confusing, not illuminating, matters – it can be quite unsettling to prowl around in these darkened spaces, imagining the horrors that ordinary men were forced to undergo with the connivance of both criminals and the law.

of vice and sordid doings flourished – often making Old Town pale by comparison – and the Portland bourgeoisie worked in vain to try to impose a solution to the problems. Writer Dean Collins described the conflict as "the Puritan soldiers of the Lord vs. the Adversary Satan's City," a battle won by the latter, as the commerce generated from the shipping trade made the vice lords – who ran the flophouses and bordellos, controlled the underworld, and operated shanghaiing schemes – too formidable to control.

Around the same time, beginning in the 1860s, the **Chinese** population of the area began to grow, from a mere two hundred at the end of the Civil War to almost eight thousand by the turn of the century. Most were concentrated in **Chinatown**, which in the late nineteenth century was the second-largest such community on the West Coast, after San Francisco. Today the **ornamental gate** at Fourth Avenue marks the neighborhood, which is an unfortunate shadow of its former self, due to mass racial violence unleashed by the "Chinese Must Go" campaigns of the era (which were somewhat less intense here than in other West Coast cities like Seattle and Los Angeles). Still, there's enough of a community here to support a range of cheap ethnic restaurants, antique stores, and dive bars, along with a smattering of fun dance clubs and rock venues.

As far as conventional sights go, Chinatown's main attraction is the **Classical Chinese Garden**, NW Third Avenue at Everett (daily April–Oct 9am–6pm; Nov–March 10am–5pm; $7; Ⓦwww.portlandchinesegarden.org), a

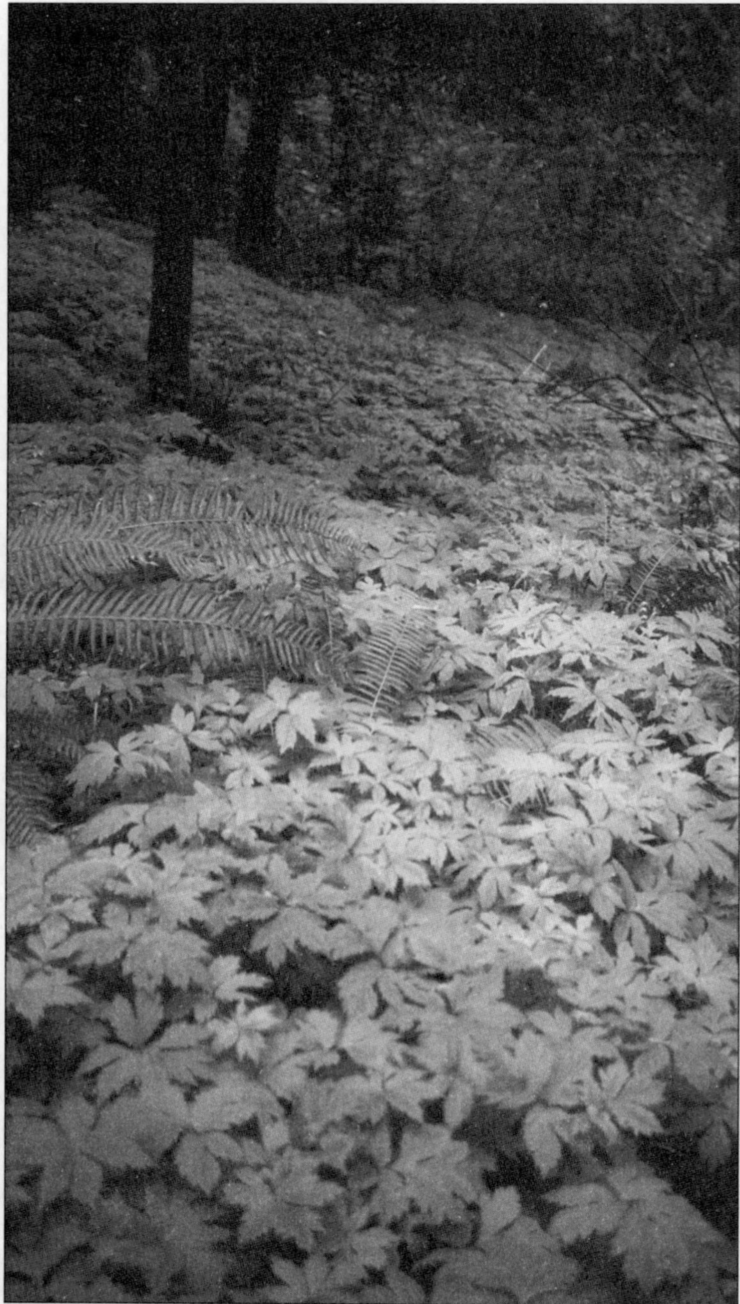

△ Forest Park

Suzhou-styled garden with traditional vegetation, ponds, and walkways. A recent creation quite lovely in places, it leaves you hungry to discover more about the history and culture of the local community but, at present, there's no Chinese-American Museum, so if you're interested in the region's ethnic heritage, you'll have to find out more through the Oregon Historical Society (see p.87).

The other major sight in the area, the **American Advertising Museum**, 211 NW Fifth Ave (Wed–Sun noon–5pm; $5; ⓦwww.admuseum.org), has nothing to do with the community, but does give a fascinating account of the rise of advertising, from posters to tapes of old radio and TV ads. For a detailed look at the district, including Old Town, Portland Walking Tours hosts "**A Walk Through Time**" (Fri–Sun 3pm; $15; reserve at ⓣ503/275-8352, ⓦwww.portlandwalkingtours.com), giving the full picture of the architectural and cultural background of the area.

The Pearl District

The rise of the **Pearl District**, due north and west of Chinatown, is a recent phenomenon. Much like Seattle's Belltown, this was for many decades considered an irredeemable dead zone by politicians and developers, known throughout most of its history as **Slabtown**, and home to automotive garages, industrial facilities, grim warehouses, and a few artists' lofts. The district's proximity to Downtown, however, proved just too enticing to ignore. To kick-start the makeover, the area was given a fanciful name in the 1980s, and in the last five years it has experienced some rather dramatic changes. In the former burned-out shells of flophouses, high-rise condominiums sell for $1 million per unit; where greasy spoons once drew a loyal working-class clientele, stylish bistros and smart cafés (see p.110) now draw the swells; and where rutted pavement and crumbling architecture once littered the streets, snappy public art and the sleek Portland Streetcar now mark a new "urban village" – at least according to city planners. In truth, there's a bit less here than meets the eye, and while you can have a fine time strolling the district's narrow streets, shopping for baubles, and dining at swanky restaurants, the place has little in the way of green spaces or quirky small businesses - which are legion in the rest of the city.

Loosely bounded by NW Broadway, Naito Parkway, and the I-405 freeway, "the Pearl," as all residents call it, has a rather amorphous shape, but seems always to be growing in new directions. Where maps only a year or two old show railroad tracks, there are likely now condos or office towers. Centered around **NW 10th Avenue** and **Lovejoy Street**, the district's new development means the cranes are in constant motion, as new chain retailers, a rash of swanky galleries, and the usual rash of *Starbucks* coffeehouses take root. A handful of sights stand out for your attention.

The Ecotrust Building and around

The **Ecotrust Building**, at NW Tenth and Johnson (ⓦwww.ecotrust.org/ncc), is a good starting point to an excursion into the Pearl District, providing a sharp contrast between the new and the old. An 1895 brick-and-timber warehouse now remodeled into a sleek new facility, it hosts a range of environmental organizations, along with what is arguably the city's best pizza joint, *Hot Lips* (see p.109). Across Tenth Avenue is another neighborhood bright spot, **Jamison Park**, which offers a scattered amount of paltry trees and benches, but is best for its delightfully terraced **fountain**. It is popular with countless children, who frolic and leap in the puddled water below while adult visitors sit and sunbathe or read books on the stone slabs above them.

Lining the west side of the park is the **Portland Streetcar** line (see p.79), which connects west to Northwest Portland and south to Downtown. The bright colors and stylish silhouettes of the cars themselves are much more appealing than the "whimsical" public art nearby – a procession of madly grinning, cartoonish totem poles. Plans are afoot to add a second square just to the north. This proposed **Neighborhood Square** will go well beyond Jamison Park, and feature a built-up western wall and sloping turf that will allow water to funnel and eddy through the park down to a grate on the east side, with a marshy, wetland-style terrain and low greenery throughout.

PICA and First Thursday

The Pearl District is well known for its **gallery** scene, and the main institution in the area is **PICA** (Ⓦwww.pica.org), which used to operate its own gallery but now focuses on periodic festivals, theatrical performances, and film screenings, all of them with a heavy experimental and conceptual bent, but still quite popular. The biggest such event is **Time Based Art**, a ten-day September event with theater, film, and multimedia presentations at different venues in the Pearl (tickets $15 per show; blanket admission $150); the 2003 festival was an unexpected citywide hit, and in an area starved for actual high-culture, future years promise more of the same.

Elsewhere in the district, the quality of the art is much more variable, and while there are countless galleries here, many of them serve as mere excuses for wine bars and boutiques. Indeed, at their worst some of these facilities present the likes of imitation Andrew Wyeth farmscapes and plump marble seagulls, which undoubtedly look better after a few glasses of overpriced vino. That said, there are a few decent art galleries in the neighborhood, and most of them are covered in the district's renowned **First Thursday** art walk (6–9pm; free; Ⓦwww.firstthursday.org), which follows no linear path but is simply a collection of upper-end establishments that keep their doors open late on the initial Thursday of each month. The walk draws yuppies, tourists, and serious art-lovers alike for its mostly abstract or conceptual paintings and drawings, with a sprinkling of Pop Art and mixed-media thrown in.

Powell's City of Books and the Brewery Blocks

From PICA it's a short walk east to **Powell's City of Books**, W Burnside Street and 10th Avenue (daily 9am–11pm; Ⓣ503/228-4651, Ⓦwww.powells.com), which claims to be the largest bookstore in America and is clearly one of the city's major tourist attractions. The "City" occupies an entire block and spreads over four floors, issuing free maps so customers can find their way around. It's particularly gratifying to find a wide selection of used, out-of-print, and discounted titles here and there's a coffee shop where you can browse before you buy. The rooms are **color-coded** by topic, with most of the new books and magazines at the entrance on Burnside. An alternate entrance, at 11th Avenue and Couch Street, provides access to the discounted volumes, and sits directly across from the high-rise behemoth known as the **Brewery Blocks** (Ⓦwww.breweryblocks.com). Occupying the site (and in one case, the actual facility) of the former Blitz-Weinhard Brewery, the Blocks are the most visible example of the changes sweeping through the Pearl in the last few years.

No longer an industrial facility connected by rail to the trainyards, the five-block Brewery site has become home to coffee shops, organic groceries, condos, and the best *gelateria* in the Pacific Northwest, *Mio Gelato* (see p.111). Indeed, with towering residential piles sprouting all around it, Powell's Books looks almost small by comparison – a heretical thought to most Portlanders.

Northwest Portland

Due west of the Pearl District, across the recessed channel of the I-405 freeway, lies the district most residents call **Northwest Portland** (even though the Pearl District and Chinatown also sport NW prefixes to their streets). The neighborhood, however, was originally known, and still is in many tourist brochures, as **Nob Hill** – its name borrowed from San Francisco, imported by a grocer who hoped the area would become as fashionable as the one back home. The district does, like its counterpart, feature a number of beautifully refurbished Victorian townhouses and mansions, along with a charming number of renovated churches, historic-revival buildings, the city's main Jewish temple, and, along **21st and 23rd avenues**, some of the city's smarter boutiques and restaurants. One of the key architectural highlights – of which there are many – is the **Mackenzie House**, 615 NW 20th Ave, looking like a medieval-Norman hunting lodge with a prominent cast-iron stag's head, rough stone arches and a fortress-like design. Beyond this, if you want to explore further, take a walking **tour**, such as the one offered online by Timber Press (Ⓦ www.timberpress.com/houses).

NW 21st and 23rd avenues

Despite the quality of its historic architecture, Northwest Portland is best known to locals for its two main strips of NW 21st and 23rd avenues, which together feature many of the city's best restaurants, coffeehouses, and boutiques. The more modest of the two, **NW 21st Avenue**, is at its liveliest around NW Hoyt Street, where **Cinema 21** (Ⓣ 503/223-4515, Ⓦ www.cinema21.com) draws the crowds for its steady diet of art films and independent releases. In the same area, there are a number of old-time bars and clubs that attract a loyal crowd, but further north around Overton Street are some of Portland's swankiest restaurants, with *Wildwood* the highlight among them (see p.109). Although these eateries offer valet parking, if you want to visit the less expensive diners or other establishments in the area, you'll be forced to contend with what some call the **worst parking** in the Pacific Northwest, with residents and visitors battling it out for every inch of pavement, and drivers often forced to hunt for twenty minutes or more to find a space. To escape the congestion, take a bus here (#15 and #17 lines), or better yet, hop on the **Portland Streetcar** (see p.79) from Downtown, which runs through Northwest Portland along Lovejoy and Northrup streets.

Two blocks west, **NW 23rd Avenue** is much more chic and upscale, with snooty attitudes and well-heeled shoppers to match. Decades ago, the road used to be one of the neighborhood's grungier stretches, where grim diners and shambling flophouses attracted only the down-and-out and a few bohemian interlopers. Like the Pearl District, though, this area's seedy past has since been sanitized by a welter of fancy new clothing boutiques and pricey restaurants. Here, though, the process has been going on for twenty years – not five – and the renovated blocks stretch all the way from Burnside to Vaughn streets: almost the full gamut of the district's alphabetically ordered east-west roads. There's no real center along the 23rd axis, so you'll have to wander along like the rest of the visitors, window-shopping from one business to the next.

From Vaughn Street, you can immediately access the I-5 and 405 freeways to the east, or if you head west along Thurman, can enter into the vast urban greenery of Forest Park (see below).

The West Hills

The long line of wooded bluffs that make up the **West Hills** has long restricted Portland's capacity to expand westward. Although a good slice now accommodates the homes of the wealthy, there remain large chunks of dark and dense forest, which far-sighted city planners and conservationists have long fought to keep free of development. Because of this, the road connections to the west are quite limited and circuitous, and include the winding slope of **West Burnside** as it rises over the crest of the hills, and the hairpin turns and tunnels of **Cornell Road**, which links to Lovejoy Street in Northwest Portland. Despite the hills being relatively undeveloped, though, the terrain is still home to several of the city's top attractions, from museums and zoos to nature preserves.

Forest Park

Forest Park (#18 bus from Downtown) is one of the best – and largest – nature preserves contained within the boundaries of any US city. A colossal acreage that sprawls many miles to the northwest from Portland's west side, Forest Park has a myriad points of entry and possibilities for hiking, biking, and exploring. You're best off focusing on one of two main routes into the park, both accessible from Northwest Portland (with less inviting spots off of Cornell Road). The first, the thirty-mile route of the **Wildwood Trail**, can be accessed around NW 31st Avenue and Upshur Street, and is best for casual walkers and hikers who really want to explore the scenery and get a feel for the plants and topography of the park. It's not necessary to travel the full distance, of course, but unless you have a trail **map** (available from entry kiosks or from Ⓦwww.friendsofforestpark.org), you may well get lost unless you retrace your steps back to the beginning.

The second route, **Leif Erickson Drive**, accessible from where NW Thurman Street comes to a dead end, is a very different approach into Forest Park. As the name suggests, it's a graveled, partially paved concourse that wends some fifteen miles into the park, and attracts some of the city's more gung-ho mountain bikers and long-distance runners. With that in mind, stay alert and steer well clear of the cyclists, who have been known to tumble downhill around the sharp graveled curves and take out a few unwitting hikers as they go – a daunting thought considering the wooded precipices at the edge of the trail.

Pittock Mansion

Justifiably one of the first sights mentioned in any tourist brochure to Portland, the **Pittock Mansion**, 3229 NW Pittock Drive (daily noon–4pm, summer 11am–4pm, closed Jan; $5.50; Ⓣ503/823-3624; Ⓦwww.pittockmansion.com), is a luxurious estate located off – and up in the hills from – West Burnside

Street, a couple of miles from Downtown. Perched on a ridge with great views of the city, the mansion was built for Henry Pittock, who came to Portland in 1853 as a sixteen-year-old printer's helper. Eight years later, he founded *The Oregonian*, still the state's most influential newspaper, and his publication rapidly became the flagship of the political Right under the formidable editorship of the long-serving, walrus-moustached Harvey W. Scott. Scott was a tub-thumping reactionary who took few prisoners – he labeled the editor of a rival rag a "pimp generalissimo of a small, cheap paper" – but he wasn't the only member of his family to master the biting phrase. When Harvey's editorials declared against women's suffrage in 1900, his sister Abigail wrote to him "the cheap male sycophants who suck their sustenance from your editorial seats have flattered you until you are insane on the sex question."

Completed in 1914, it took five years to build Pittock Mansion in a broadly French Renaissance-style, and its 22 rooms are a perfect illustration of the energetic, ostentatious character of the American tycoon. The house is stuffed with antique furnishings and fittings, and there's a mind-boggling mix of styles: the library is English Jacobean, the smoking room Turkish, and the drawing room Renaissance Revival. Neither did the tycoon neglect the latest inventions, installing a room-to-room telephone system, showers with multiple showerheads, and an ambitious central vacuum-cleaning system. It's a delightful mishmash in any case, and when you've finished looking round, you can stroll the carefully manicured gardens and check out some of the city's best views from the expansive front lawn – which has the added benefit of free access, without requiring admission.

To get to Pittock Mansion by **bus** from Downtown, take orange-coded bus #20 west along W Burnside Street and you'll be dropped at the start of the steep, signed, half-mile side road that winds up to the entrance.

Washington Park

Cutting through the West Hills from the south side of downtown Portland (via Clay Stret), Hwy 26 serves as the main approach to **Washington Park**, a green and hilly expanse that holds many of the city's biggest-name attractions. The most popular is the **Oregon Zoo** (daily April–Sept 9am–6pm; Oct–March 9am–4pm; $8; Ⓣ503/226-1561, Ⓦwww.zooregon.org), on the park's southern perimeter. The zoo's star turn is its set of Asian elephants, now a sizable breeding herd that in 1962 produced the first birth of an Asian elephant in the Western Hemisphere. Perhaps its most unusual feature is the Elephant Museum, detailing the biological and cultural history of pachyderms – and decorated with a giant mastodon skeleton. The zoo puts on a program of live music throughout the summer, and shows are free with the price of admission; call Ⓣ503/226-1561 for details.

Back at the zoo entrance, it's a couple of minutes' walk over to the **World Forestry Center** (daily 10am–5pm; $4.50; Ⓣ503/228-1367, Ⓦwww.worldforestry.org), which largely celebrates the glories of the timber industry using lots of interactive exhibits. Among several displays, the push-button reconstruction of the "Tillamook Burn," a colossal fire that ravaged a vast stretch of the state's coastal forests in the 1930s, is the most diverting.

A miniature train connects the zoo and the forestry center with two formal gardens further north in the park. The first, the five-acre **Washington Park International Rose Test Garden** (daily 7am–9pm; free), is justifiably one of the city's highlights, an explosion of enticing colors set on a hillside overlooking the fetching cityscape. The garden is at its best between May and August, when eight thousand rose bushes cover layered terraces with a gaudy range of blooms, which are labeled by each bush's year of vintage – some date back almost to the nineteenth century. Billing itself as America's "oldest official, continuously operated public rose test garden," the place earns its name by testing new varieties of rose sent here by growers, which are checked for two years and are judged on their color, fragrance, and form. Also look out for the **Royal Rosarian** and **Shakespearean gardens**, the former home to some stately, old-fashioned blooms with historic pedigrees, and the latter a display of the roses mentioned in the works of the Bard, including the sprightly Angel's Trumpet – mentioned in three separate tragedies.

On the hill above the roses, the **Japanese Garden** (daily April–Sept 10am–7pm, Oct–March 10am–4pm; $6.50; Ⓦwww.japanesegarden.com) is actually a collection of five traditional gardens with ponds, bridges, foliage, and sand designs. It's a tranquil spot, with cool, green shrubs reflected in pools, and abstract sand-and-stone patterns making minimal use of color. Finally, a bit further west in the park, **Hoyt Arboretum**, 4000 Fairview Blvd (daily 6am–10pm; free; Ⓦwww.hoytarboretum.org), is well worth a leisurely walk for its collection of ten thousand trees and plants from throughout the region and

Seeing roses in the City of Roses

The Rose Test Garden is the obvious first stop if you're interested in discovering why Portland lays claim to the title "**City of Roses**," as does viewing the crowded and colorful **Rose Festival** (Ⓦwww.rosefestival.org) held in early June. For the event, a rose festival **Queen** and **Court** are selected from local high-school girls, and thousands flock to Burnside Street, among other routes, to watch a massive parade with multicolored floats, marching bands, and the whole works. Although not quite the national spectacle as Pasadena's Rose Parade, it's a bit less stodgy, and involves more than just a parade (or a football game). The weekend **Starlight Parade**, for one, takes a Downtown route to showcase bands, local bigwigs, and other marchers, while the ongoing **Fun Center** spreads out along Waterfront Park to offer a blinding array of carnival rides, fast-food stands, and crushing crowds packed with families and youthful hedonists. Looming above the Center are the silhouettes of US Navy warships, who make this their port of call for a week or two, but no longer allow public tours in the wake of terrorism fears.

If you have no interest in parades, but still want to sample the city's fine blooms, there are a few places around town that are good choices during the growing season. Well off the beaten track, one such place is **Peninsula Park**, in Northeast Portland three blocks east of the Portland Boulevard exit on I-5. Spread over eight blocks, the park presents a wide array of blossoms amid a tranquil setting with copious paths and trees. Only the neighborhood's inflated reputation for crime keeps more people from coming here, but you should have few problems unless you want to poke around after dark. The Eastside's other top area for roses is **Ladd's Addition**, north of Division Street and south of Hawthorne Boulevard, between 12th and 20th avenues. Here, the only thing keeping outsiders from seeing the tremendous blooms is the bizarre street pattern. Instead of the usual grid, the roads and alleys – built in the 1890s – are laid out in an **axial form**, meaning they radiate out from a central circle and lead in all kinds of odd directions. However, it's well worth plunging into this maze to see the four striking rose gardens here, which have many of the same classic blooms as the Rose Test Garden, with only a fraction of the crowds. Surrounded by stately architecture (especially the Neoclassical mansion at Maple and Poplar avenues), this neighborhood is one of Portland's great little treasures – just be sure to bring a map.

the world. Other sites worth a look include two very different memorials: on the park's southern side, the first honors local soldiers who died in the **Vietnam War** with a chronological procession of names listed on a winding hillside concourse, while on the northeast side, influential local Communist **John Reed** is remembered with a commemorative bench and plaque – though he's actually buried inside the Kremlin walls.

In terms of access, side roads weave through Washington Park connecting all of its (clearly signposted) attractions. Most sights have convenient access to MAX **light rail** ($1.60 from Downtown), whose station is buried deep underground and accessible only by elevator. Once you get here, you can hop on a summertime **shuttle** (every 15min June–Sept 10am–7pm; $1.25) and access all the park's attractions on a cheap day pass. To go straight to the Japanese Gardens or the International Rose Test Garden from Downtown, take the orange-coded elk **bus** #63 (hourly) from the Sixth Avenue transit mall at Main Street.

The Eastside

While the west side of the Willamette River provided an agreeably deep port, the east side was too shallow for shipping and the area remained undeveloped for the first fifty years of Portland's life. Even before the Hawthorne, Steel, and Broadway bridges crept across the river in the early nineteenth century, residential neighborhoods were rapidly spreading east, stretching out towards the forested foothills that approach Mount Hood (see p.132). These extensive former suburbs – **the Eastside**, for short – now accommodate most of Greater Portland's population of 1.8 million, and you can find a number of stretches here popular with young hipsters and aging bohemians, and good for their cheap ethnic diners, quirky boutiques, and vintage clothiers. In most cases, worthwhile neighborhoods like Sellwood and Laurelhurst are built around a historic neighborhood movie theater from the early twentieth century, such structures surviving here long after the grand cinema palaces downtown were demolished.

Keep in mind, however, that the Eastside's **main drags** – Sandy and Powell boulevards and 82nd and Grand avenues – are uniformly unappealing, and have largely given the area a bad name, even among locals, for their rank motels and grungy strip clubs. It's easy enough to stay clear of these dismal concourses, though, and explore the area's interesting districts on less traveled side streets.

The east bank of the Willamette

While the **east bank of the Willamette** is still filled with plenty of gritty stretches – storage facilities, grim warehouses, and looming overhead freeways – it has in the last few years experienced a bit of an upswing, made most apparent by the completion of the **Eastbank Esplanade**. A $30-million concourse that runs across floating walkways and cantilevered footpaths, it offers striking views of Downtown and close-up perspectives on the city's industrial zone amid the roar of I-5. As a three-mile loop that connects to Waterfront Park on the river's west side (see p.89), the Esplanade is hardly the kind of quaint little footpath you would expect from that name. Nonetheless, it attracts a good number of runners, strollers, and cyclists, even on rainy days, and provides views of the cityscape you simply won't find elsewhere in town.

From the giant red-and-green towers of the 1910 **Hawthorne Bridge** (the city's oldest), the pathway leads under the deafening traffic of the less

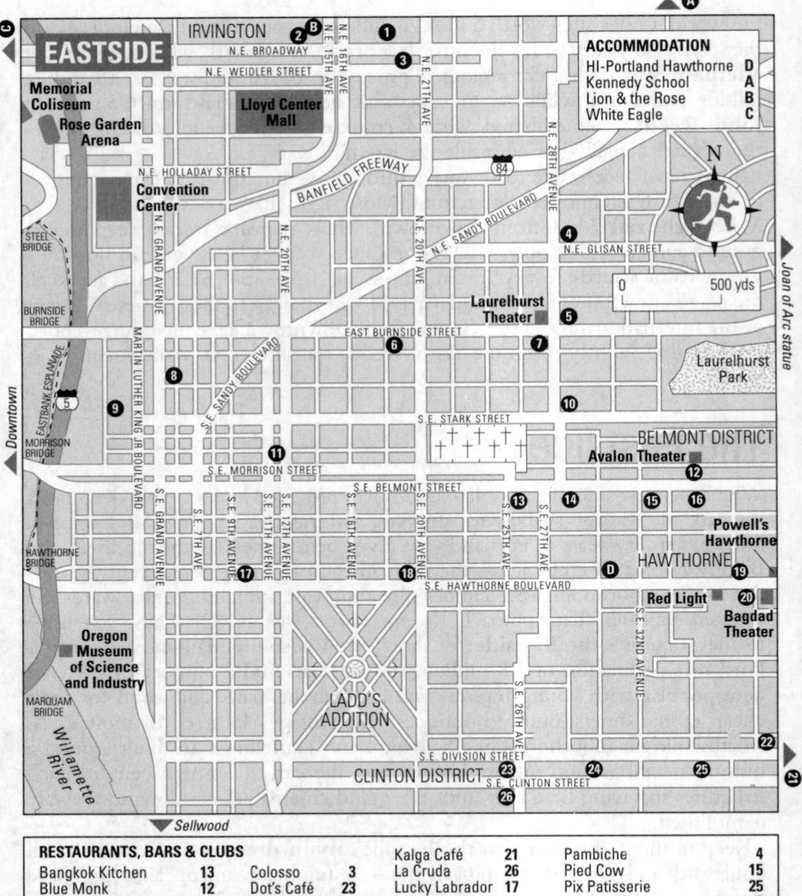

appealing Morrison and Burnside bridges, drops down to river level on bobbing concrete slabs, then crosses under stunning, sky-high freeway off-ramps to cross the double-decked **Steel Bridge**, itself almost as old as the Hawthorne. This last section before the river's west bank is indeed the highlight, as you pass over the black, ancient-looking Industrial Age icon, where sparkling waterside views spread out below you and, on occasion, Amtrak and commercial trains roar by just a few feet away.

On the opposite end of the Esplanade, at 1945 SE Water and Clay, the large and lavish **Oregon Museum of Science and Industry**, best known as **OMSI** (June–Aug daily 9.30am–7pm, Sept–May Tues–Sun 9.30am–5.30pm; $8.50; Ⓦwww.omsi.edu), offers splashy exhibits primarily geared toward children, with hundreds of interactive booths, toys, and kiosks aimed at those with only a sketchy knowledge of science. In the Space Science hall, for example, you can check your weight on Mars and clamber into a space capsule. In addition, there's an OMNIMAX theater (an extra $8.50, $6.50 for seniors and kids 3–13 years old), a planetarium ($5 extra), and the USS *Blueback* submarine (daily 10am–4.30pm; $5 extra) docked in the Willamette River. To save costs, OMSI does a full museum package covering all its attractions for $18 ($14 for seniors and kids). Bus #83 (hourly) serves the site from the Downtown transit mall at Fifth Avenue and Salmon Street.

Sellwood

Going south to north, the first Eastside district of any consequence is **Sellwood**, which was an independent city until Portland annexed it about a century ago, and which still sports pleasant, slightly shambling architecture. It's not exactly close to the rest of the city, though, and to get there you'll have to take a lengthy **bus ride** (#19 line) – which is no problem if you're hunting for affordable **antiques**. Indeed, while the district's commercial center is at SE 17th Avenue and Bybee Boulevard – where you can find a number of decent coffeehouses, fancy eateries, and the area's signature Moreland moviehouse – its hub for "antiquing" is a little over a mile away, at SE 13th Avenue north of Tacoma Street. This popular strip hosts numerous sellers of all kinds of castoffs, from authentic nineteenth-century furniture to Pop Art novelties to worthless junk that both looks and smells bad. Although most of the dealers here are no suckers, willing to part with a dusty copy of the US Constitution or a Beatles "butcher cover" LP for chump change, if you're lucky you may find, wedged into some alcove or stuck in a mezzanine, that essential black-velvet painting or pair of 1960s go-go boots you've been trying to find for several decades.

Clinton Street and the Hawthorne District

Several miles north of Sellwood, past the cheerless traffic corridors of McLoughlin and Powell boulevards, at the intersection of SE 26th Avenue sits the one really appealing section of **Clinton Street**. This two-block-long array of businesses features coffeehouses and ethnic diners (Mexican to Hawaiian), vintage clothing stores (including one of the city's best, Xtabay, at no. 2515), and hipster bars and clubs – foremost being the ever-popular *Dot's Café*, no. 2521 (see p.113) – along with a few alternative galleries. You can easily explore the area in an hour or so, and if you're still hungry for a taste of local bohemian culture, drift a little over a half-mile north to the **Hawthorne District**, a half-mile along the eponymous boulevard, which has become *the* alternative shopping district for Portland, and still attracts a wide array of visitors. You won't find *McDonald's* here, though, after district residents waged a tenacious campaign to keep the hamburger giant out of the neighborhood – so in its place, at 34th Avenue, there now sits a formidable set of high-priced steel-and-glass condos with ground-level retail.

"Hawthorne," as it is known, is thick with groceries, antique dealers, music- and bookstores, and novelty shops. The highly visible center of the district is the neon spectacle of the historic **Bagdad Theater**, at SE 37th Avenue (Ⓣ503/225-5555, ext. 8830; Ⓦwww.mcmenamins.com), a second-run moviehouse and brewpub in the local McMenamins chain, which includes a stunning 1927 Moorish Revival interior, complete with ornamental columns and dark mood lighting. Across the street you can find a good, sizable branch of **Powell's Books** (Ⓣ503/238-1668, Ⓦwww.powells.com), while further west clubkids and costume-partygoers won't be able to resist a stop at **Red Light**, 3590 Hawthorne Blvd (Ⓣ503/963-8888), a secondhand clothing merchant that's best for its bizarre, irreverent **window displays** – anything from Dick and Jane dissecting a corpse to a drag-king Elvis shooting out a TV screen.

As you continue on Hawthorne further east, you rise up the slopes of **Mount Tabor**, the only (dormant) volcano contained within the bounds of a major US city. Attracting a constant flow of hikers and dog-walkers, the small mountain makes for a good, robust morning trek, when the Downtown towers are visible three miles away, and the city's more fervent exercisers are going through their paces. Enter by foot on SE Salmon Street east of 60th Avenue, or take the #15 bus (or the #14 on Hawthorne, with a half-mile extra walk from SE 50th Avenue).

Belmont Street to 28th Avenue

Six and fifteen blocks north of Hawthorne are a pair of districts that have only taken off in the last five years, when the Eastside has drawn increasing attention in general. The first, **Belmont Street** (#15 bus line), sits in a truly old part of town whose most vibrant section lies from SE 30th to 37th avenues. Here you can see the type of early-twentieth-century storefronts (almost flush with the road) and neon signs that have long since disappeared from other neighborhoods. However, the district itself is far from shambling, and boasts all manner of chic, up-to-date businesses in these historic digs, from swanky café-clubs like the *Blue Monk*, no. 3341 (see p.113) to elegant teahouses like the *Tao of Tea*, no. 3430 (see p.111), to offbeat novelty stores like Spoink!, at SE 30th Avenue. As with so many other Eastside districts, this one too is built around a classic theater, the **Avalon**, no 3451 (☎503/238-1617), which still shows movies and offers a video arcade to boot.

A few blocks north, **Laurelhurst Park** is one of the city's most attractive green spaces, a sloping concourse of hills built around a small lake, which draws myriad dog-owners as well as children. The park itself is quite lovely, one of the urban green spaces designed by the **Olmsted brothers** (sons of Frederick Law Olmsted, the landscaper of New York's Central Park), and occasionally home on summer evenings to "**bike-ins**," increasingly popular evening movie showings aimed at cyclists. Five blocks north along SE 39th Avenue, another unmissable sight sits in the middle of a giant, European-style traffic circle – the stalwart figure of **Joan of Arc** riding her horse, carrying a banner, and emblazoned in eye-blinding gold leaf.

Finally, the second rejuvenated district in the area, **28th Avenue**, has only emerged as a destination in the last few years, when a sudden group of swanky restaurants, clothing boutiques, and salons set up shop here, north and south of East Burnside Street (the only appealing section of this otherwise dreary route). Sure enough, this district has an anchor theater, too, the **Laurelhurst**, 2735 E Burnside St (☎503/232-5511), a remodeled mid-century gem showing second-run movies and selling beer and pizza.

Northeast Portland

Historically, the sections of east Portland north of Burnside Street have been home to a more racially mixed population than the rest of this mostly white city. In **Northeast Portland**, along what is now Martin King Jr Boulevard and further east, African Americans were redlined into living in segregated districts isolated from the rest of the city by geographic and social boundaries. These days, many of the barriers have fallen, but life hasn't gotten easier for the residents, who face a new threat from the evils of **gentrification**. Nowhere is this process more evident than on the east-west corridor of **Alberta Street**, paralleling East Burnside about two and a half miles north.

Now rechristened the **Alberta Arts District**, running from NE 15th to 30th avenues, the strip is both visually fascinating and socially unsettling for the manner in which funky new galleries and shops stand adjacent to black storefront churches and neighborhood diners and barbershops. In many ways, it could well be the most heterogeneous such area in Portland, and you're bound to find an interesting mix of classes and cultures here – along with some fairly good bargains in the cut-rate antique stores, junk emporia, and trinket shops. Although it can get a bit dicey at night, you definitely shouldn't miss the district's exciting, eye-opening gallery walk known as **Last Thursday** – a reaction to the Pearl District's stodgier First Thursday event (see p.96) – which takes place the last such day of every month from about 6–10pm, and really draws a crowd of all stripes, especially during the summer. Completely unlike almost every other regular event in the city, Last Thursday is a fervent bustle of noise, color, and chaos, in which self-taught painters and sculptors sprawl their work across the pavement, wild rock bands and hip-hop DJs play at every other corner, oddball galleries display all kinds of bizarre curiosities, and a thick mass of people mill about dancing, eating, and staring with eyes agape at the whole spectacle. This loud and crazy scene is not for the easily intimidated, but it does serve as a good disclaimer to Portland's reputation as a quiet, laid-back kind of place. To get here from Downtown, take the #9 Broadway bus line and get off when it crosses Alberta.

Further south and west, and closer to the I-84 freeway, the other main attraction of northeast Portland is the section of **NE Broadway** that runs through the charming old precinct of **Irvington**, from NE 20th to 12th avenues, which itself has been gentrifying rapidly in the last decade, with tasteful bistros and boutiques, a number of decent breakfast spots, and stately homes – from Colonial Revival to Craftsman – dating from the early twentieth century (mostly located on the several blocks north of Broadway). Unlike the Eastside's other worthwhile districts, though, there's no classic moviehouse here, only big-name chain theaters based around the **Lloyd Center** mall (Ⓦwww.lloydcenter.com), two blocks south of Broadway, which offers the usual rash of chain stores, with the added draw of an ice rink. You can take the #6 or #9 bus lines to get here, or hop on the MAX light rail – the mall zone itself is considered a part of **Fareless Square**, and thus free for all riders from Downtown.

Finally, only sports fans and conventioneers should bother to visit the nearby, overly hyped **Rose Quarter** (Ⓦwww.rosequarter.com), where a green-spired convention center and basketball stadium are the only points of interest amid a clutch of overpriced restaurants and dreary chain motels.

North Portland

There aren't too many reasons to travel any more than a few miles beyond Downtown to reach **North Portland**, primarily residential and industrial turf roughly west of the northern section of I-5, but if you're willing, there are a few areas of note here and there. The first, **Jantzen Beach**, lies almost exactly between the downtown zones of Portland and Vancouver, Washington, on the south bank of the Columbia River off of I-5.

Named after the clothing giant, Jantzen Beach is one of the districts near the front of any tourist brochure. However, unless you plan to spend a lot of time shopping at big-box chain retailers, there's not a lot to do here. Even the mainstream hotels are fairly staid and colorless, and too far away from the main city action to be of any use.

Several miles west of Jantzen Beach off of Columbia Boulevard (or Lombard Street directly west from I-5) sits another of Portland's small historic neighborhoods that were once independent cities, **St. Johns**. As with Sellwood, this is fairly far from the central city, but does boast a historic, working-class (former) Downtown on **North Lombard Street** and some handsome old architecture. Further west, the Willamette River is crossed by what is easily the city's most beautiful span, the **St. Johns Bridge**, a towering green structure with lofty spires and Gothic Revival arches underneath, best viewed from below in the pleasant confines of **Cathedral Park**, off N Edison Street. Finally, from downtown St. Johns you can hop on the #17 bus line (from Downtown) and head north to **Sauvie Island**, many residents' favorite weekend getaway. Almost completely undeveloped, the island features a pleasant, if chilly, beach on its eastern side and many miles of country lanes, seasonal fruit sellers, and evocative riverside views. It's also great for jogging and cycling, and has its own simple B&B, *River's Edge*, on the island's east side at 22502 NW Gillihan Rd (Ⓣ503/621-9856, Ⓦwww.riversedge-bb.com; ❺), with a pleasant location and a pair of basic rooms.

The Grotto

Further out in Northeast Portland is the Roman Catholic complex of **The Grotto** (daily 9am–5.30pm; free; Ⓣ503/254-7371, Ⓦwww.thegrotto.org), located in its own wooded setting and isolated from a truly dismal stretch of NE Sandy Boulevard. Nevertheless, you'll have to take a Sandy bus to get here (#12, stopping around 82nd Avenue and following the signs), and ride through some of the city's more depressing sections (a route highlighted only by the flamboyant Baroque facade of the Hollywood Theatre, an art cinema at Sandy and 42nd Avenue; Ⓦwww.hollywoodtheatre.org).

The Grotto itself is a strange and quiet spot, spread out over some twenty square blocks or sixty acres, officially known as the **National Sanctuary of Our Sorrowful Mother** – though a bit less depressing in practice. As a religious shrine and sanctuary first established by the Servite order of monks some eighty years ago, the Grotto offers a serene, contemplative environment, and not just for Catholics. Although there are the traditional altars and statuary around, the real highlights include the **Moyer Meditation Chapel**, whose curving steel-and-glass wall perches out over a heart-stopping rock cliff, several pleasant gardens with symbolic foliage and statues, and a series of carved wooden panels depicting the Stations of the Cross. If you're not feeling overly pious, the whole effect can get a bit much, but for the spiritually inclined the Grotto is one of Portland's more notable, if anomalous, attractions.

Eating

Friendly and unpretentious, Portland features great **cafés** and **restaurants**, especially as intense competition almost invariably keeps prices down to reasonable levels. In terms of food style, your best bet may be to sample the city's **Northwest Cuisine** (see p.44), which, as in Seattle, is a mix of international cooking and fresh regional produce, offering many excellent options for all palates and pocketbooks. **Seafood**, too, features prominently, with salmon a particular favorite, either grilled, seared, or broiled, or used in more elaborate pastas and stews. For more traditional cuisines – **Italian**, **French**, etc. – you may have to look a little harder for truly inspired fare, but you can still find it at a handful of establishments. All-American food like **burgers** and **steaks** is ubiquitous, but not especially tempting, except in a few specialized burger joints and nationally known steakhouses. **Pan-Asian** cooking, though, can be an excellent choice, from the affordable sushi bars popping up almost everywhere, to the Vietnamese bistros that serve up cheap and delicious meals, to the good assortment of Thai and Chinese restaurants found in most parts of the city. **Indian**, **Middle Eastern**, and **Caribbean** cuisines are a bit thinner on the ground, but do have serviceable eateries if you know where to look. Lastly, **vegetarian** and **vegan** cooking is becoming increasingly popular, especially when mixed with various international cuisines (Mexican to Middle Eastern), with the best being a delicious takeoff on Northwest Cuisine and the worst being the sort of flavorless sprouts-on-spelt sandwiches and tofu casseroles that make carnivores cringe.

Cafés and coffeehouses

Local **cafés** are a good bet for noshing at all hours, often serving up food similar to their restaurant rivals but at cheaper prices. Coffee, too, is a predictably big deal in Portland, and has given rise to specialist **coffeehouses**, which mostly take the form of a takeaway bar with a few stools where a bewildering variety of coffees are on offer together with cakes and snacks. Cafés and coffeehouses are scattered all over the city, but are at their quirkiest and most inventive on the **Eastside**, and include the most familiar chain java merchants to the quirkiest holes-in-the-wall.

Downtown

Bijou Café 132 SW 3rd Ave ☎503/222-3187. Laid-back Downtown café that uses local, organic ingredients in its wide-ranging menu. Lunches are especially good with meat and fish dishes as well as vegetarian-friendly offerings like quesadillas and tofu.

Coffee People 737 SW Salmon St ☎503/227-1794. Although the original "coffee people" associated with this homegrown chain have long since been bought out, the company still doles out solid espressos, mochas, sweets, and the like from a number of citywide locations. This one is the closest to the main Downtown action.

Great Harvest Bread Company 810 SW 2nd Ave at Yamhill ☎503/224-8583. Sells a wonderful range of breads with different types featured every day, including a free taster. Elephantine cinnamon buns and the city's best muffins, too.

Maya's Tacqueria 1000 SW Morrison at 10th Ave ☎503/226-1946. Bright and breezy Mexican café with all the favorites – enchiladas, burritos, and so forth – at inexpensive prices. Right off the light rail tracks.

Peet's Coffee & Tea 508 SW Broadway ☎503/973-5540. Rather smarter than many of its corporate rivals, this cheerfully decorated coffeehouse offers teas as an added bonus. Just north of Pioneer Courthouse Square.

Stumptown Roasters 128 SW 3rd Ave ☎503/295-6144. Easily the best coffee in town, perhaps in the entire region. A very serious java-brewer that uses seven different beans in its "Hair Bender" espresso blend, and attracts a fervent crowd of coffee fanatics for its various gourmet drinks. Two other citywide branches.

Virginia Café 725 SW Park Ave ☎503/227-0033. The shopworn wooden booths get crowded in this popular Downtown café as it serves up choice budget food all day. New Age clientele mixed with slackers, yuppies, and tourists.

Pearl District

In Good Taste 231 NW 11th Ave ⓣ503/248-2015. A combination cooking school, kitchen-utensil store, and lunchtime café that has the best food you're ever likely to get for $5–10, mainly because the budding chefs here are in training, though they rarely make mistakes with their tasty salads, pastas, and desserts.
Mio Gelato 25 NW 11th Ave ⓣ503/226-8002. Easily the best *gelato* in the Pacific Northwest, located in one of the Brewery Blocks. Fruit flavors like lime, grapefruit, and kiwi are enough to make your taste buds tremble with delight. Also serves scrumptious sandwiches, soups, espresso, and gourmet coffee drinks.
Pearl Bakery 102 NW 9th Ave ⓣ503/827-0910. Appropriately located in the Pearl District, a favorite lunchtime hangout for its French breads, sweet rolls, desserts, and sandwiches. Due to an inexplicable lack of tables and chairs – in an otherwise sizable space – you may have to eat standing up.

Northwest Portland

Anna Bannanas 1214 NW 21st Ave ⓣ503/274-2559. The type of place that never makes the tourist brochures but that locals adore. A very laid-back coffeehouse serving inventive java concoctions, with a popular deck and overstuffed chairs for inspired slacking.
Besaw's Café 2301 NW Savier St at 23rd Ave ⓣ503/228-2619. Old-fashioned bar and grill, one of the most longstanding cafés in Portland, dating back about a century. Good-sized burgers, steaks, and sandwiches, plus solid, inexpensive breakfasts.
Kornblatt's Delicatessen and Bagel Bakery 628 NW 23rd Ave ⓣ503/242-0055. Portland's most authentic East Coast deli – mouthwatering bagels, breads, and lots of smoked meats. Unmissable if you're cruising the boutiques on 23rd.

Eastside

Bread and Ink Café 3610 SE Hawthorne Blvd ⓣ503/239-4756. Busy, spacious café on the Eastside that puts together a varied menu of bagels, burritos, and Mediterranean food; come on Sunday for the special Yiddish brunch.
Cadillac Café 1801 NE Broadway ⓣ503/287-4750. Great, popular place for breakfast and lunch, with "French custard waffles" (encrusted with crumbled hazelnuts) that are among the best in the city. Its name comes from a pink Cadillac on view inside behind glass.
Kalga Café 4147 SE Division St ⓣ503/236-4770. Dark, mysterious Indian-vegetarian hangout where you can munch on green curry, potato pastries, and assorted finger foods while listening to the eerie sound of Bhangra DJs on weekend nights.
Milo's City Café 1325 NE Broadway ⓣ503/288-6456. Easily one of the city's most crowded and tempting spots for breakfast. Nothing too fancy here, just straightforward waffles, eggs, and omelettes served in a variety of ways.
Pied Cow 3244 SE Belmont Ave ⓣ503/230-4866. Longstanding favorite for coffee, tea, and dessert in a stately Victorian house, with late-night hours, lush garden seating, and the option to puff fruit-flavored tobacco from a hookah pipe ($10).
Pix Patisserie 3402 SE Division ⓣ503/232-4407. Popular hot spot with a colorful range of inventive French desserts prepared by a Parisian-trained chef known as the "Pixie." The café's bright red walls are unmistakable on an otherwise bleak stretch of the Eastside.
Rimsky-Korsakoffee House 707 SE 12th Ave ⓣ503/232-2640. Despite having an awful name and possibly the city's worst service, an excellent place to linger for hours on end over dessert and coffee. Immensely popular with bohemians and slackers.
Tao of Tea 3430 SE Belmont St ⓣ503/736-0119. More than 120 different kinds of teas are served in an exquisite room with Zen-like decor and a somewhat pretentious air, in the heart of the Belmont scene.

Restaurants

If you're looking for a particular type of **restaurant**, Downtown, the Pearl District, and Northwest Portland offer a lively mix of bistros, bakeries, and Pacific-fusion and vegetarian restaurants, while the Eastside has the best cheap grub and ethnic diners. Downtown also has numerous **food carts** that dole out Mexican food, Italian panini, Indian cuisine, and rice-bowl bentos – concentrated in parking lots at SW 5th and Oak, and SW 9th and Alder.

Downtown

Brasserie Montmartre 626 SW Park Ave ☎503/224-5552. The city's most popular bistro and the favorite lunching spot for shoppers at nearby Nordstrom, serving delicious French and Italian dishes, with freshly made pasta and boasting free live jazz on most evenings. Main courses around $15.

Dragonfish 909 SW Park Ave ☎503/243-5991. Decent pan-Asian restaurant on the ground floor of the *Paramount* hotel (see p.81), with dishes such as grilled-chicken yakisoba noodles marinated in a spicy Korean red-bean paste, and sugar-snap peas stir-fried with shiitake mushrooms. Adjoining bar is a definite scene for the black-clad hipster crowd.

Good Dog Bad Dog 708 SW Alder St ☎503/222-3410. The city's one essential gourmet hot-dog spot. Doling out delicious franks and sausages made from local ingredients – with names like Oregon Smokey and Magma Dog – this diner is the epitome of delicious, gut-busting cuisine. Wear drawstring pants if you have to, but make sure to power down some baked beans and chili, too.

Heathman 1009 SW Broadway ☎503/241-4100. One of the ritziest restaurants in town, offering outstanding Northwest Cuisine for dinner and extravagant teas in the afternoon. The seared salmon is especially delicious. After your meal head to the swank lobby-lounge for light jazz, desserts, and spirits.

Higgins 1239 SW Broadway at Jefferson ☎503/222-9070. Nationally recognized Northwest Cuisine restaurant, where fresh local ingredients and scrumptious desserts are served in cozy quarters just south of the city's main attractions. The shellfish in particular is worth a taste. By Portland standards, it's a formal kind of place – but reasonably priced with main courses around $20.

Hunan Morgan's Alley, 515 SW Broadway ☎503/224-8063. Well-established Chinese restaurant on the mezzanine level of a tiny shopping precinct leading off Broadway. Courteous service with all the frills. The dim sum is recommended.

India House 1038 SW Morrison at 11th Ave ☎503/274-1017. Reliable East Asian restaurant serving all the classics plus a few more at inexpensive prices. The premises are modern and plain, but the food more than compensates. The curries and the *khormas* are tops.

Jake's Famous Crawfish 401 SW 12th Ave ☎503/226-1419. A landmark restaurant for more than a hundred years, with a staggering choice of fresh fish like Columbia River Sturgeon, Depot Bay Dungeness Crab, and spicy crawfish cakes. The innocuous-sounding "Bag of Chocolate" is a famously delicious, belt-unbuckling dessert. Lunch specials from $5.

Jake's Grill 611 SW 10th Ave at Alder ☎503/220-1850. A superb restaurant, sister to *Jake's Famous Crawfish*, that occupies a tastefully converted 1910s building, complete with mosaic floors, glass domes, and thick wooden paneling. The savory menu is strong on meat and seafood with dishes finely presented; desserts are gorgeous, too. Busy bar section attracts a yuppie-leaning crowd.

New York City Sub Shop 725 SE Alder St ☎503/525-4414. Usually having a name like this outside Manhattan is a bad sign, but this sandwich joint is an exception. Hot, deliciously greasy subs, packed crowds at lunchtime, and curt, finger-snapping service give this place an air of the Big Apple.

Pazzo 627 SW Washington St, in the *Hotel Vintage Plaza* ☎503/228-1515. One of the city's better Italian restaurants, known for its traditional pastas, pancetta, and veal and salmon dishes. Just as popular is the bar, a hot spot for networking and carousing for the Downtown elite.

Persian House 1026 SW Morrison St ☎503/243-1430. Cozy and low-key Persian restaurant serving tasty, traditional dishes such as lamb kabobs and fessenjan – chicken in pomegranate sauce – at inexpensive prices. Main courses average about $10.

Portland Steak and Chophouse 121 SW 3rd Ave, in the *Embassy Suites* hotel ☎503/223-6200. Located off the hotel's chic lobby, a swanky spot with expensive steak and seafood entrees, which are delicious if unsurprising. There's much cheaper, but still excellent, food in the bar such as pizzas, burgers, and salads – and especially affordable during happy hour.

Ruth's Chris Steak House 309 SW 3rd Ave at Oak ☎503/221-4518. Fine chain steakhouse providing juicy steaks in a cheerfully upscale atmosphere. A quality range of Northwest wines and microbrews are also on offer.

South Park Seafood Grill 901 SW Salmon St at 9th Ave ☎503/326-1300. Bistro-style restaurant specializing in seafood, of which it offers a wide variety, washed down by a good range of beers and wines. It's a popular spot, appropriately looking toward the South Park Blocks. Main courses around $18.

Old Town and Chinatown

Abou Karim 221 SW Pine St ☎503/223-5058. The pick of Old Town's Lebanese restaurants, quite fine for its roasted lamb, traditional stews, and *baba ganoush*. Lunch is what really draws people here, when prices are $5–10 cheaper than the still-affordable dinner fare.

Cañita 503 W Burnside St ⓣ503/274-4050. Well worth braving a rather dicey area to sample the restaurant's savory Cuban entrees – delicious, very affordable choices from *vaca frita* to fried plantains and yucca root to sizable steaks and black beans. Don't leave without trying the tasty, traditional cakes and pies or potent cocktails like margaritas and mojitos.

Dan and Louis Oyster Bar 208 SW Ankeny St ⓣ503/227-5906. Decorated in a kitschy nautical theme and located off of an alley, this might not seem like one of the city's longstanding classic eateries, but it has been for about a century. Clam chowder and oysters on the half shell are the highlights, though the breaded shellfish is less appealing.

Golden Horse 238 NW 4th Ave ⓣ503/228-1688. Most of the top Chinese eateries in Chinatown are located within three blocks north of Burnside on NW 4th and 5th avenues, and this is one of the finest. Salt-and-pepper shrimp, fresh crab, and wontons are but a few of the highlights, and most of the prices are nice and cheap.

McCormick and Schmick's 235 SW 1st Ave at Oak ⓣ503/224-7522. The first location of what's become a national chain of fine seafood restaurants, offering fresh nightly specials and a lively oyster bar with a happening singles scene. Entrees around $15. Located right off the light rail tracks.

Pearl District

Bluehour 250 NW 13th Ave ⓣ503/226-3394. If you can handle all the pretension, uptight attitudes, and "conceptual" decor (minimalist light screens and white walls) here, you'll find the Northwest Cuisine fare to be some of the city's best – gnocchi with truffles, seared salmon, and the like. Still, pretty pompous by Portland standards.

Hot Lips Pizza 721 NW 10th Ave ⓣ503/595-2342. Located inside the Ecotrust Building (see p.95), a pizza joint serving what some claim to be the city's best pies – complex, delicious concoctions that use organic, locally grown ingredients.

Oba 555 NW 12th Ave ⓣ503/228-6161. Flashy, Nuevo Latino eatery that fuses flavors from all over Latin America to create food you won't find anywhere else in town – especially during happy hour in the bar, when the tasty entrees, including coconut shrimp and *queso fundido* dip, are $3–4.

Paragon 605 NW 13th Ave ⓣ503/833-5060. A mix of all-American and Northwest Cuisine at this ever-popular staple – savory pot roast flavored with fancy herbs, well-cooked salmon and trout entrees, plus inventive desserts – though the place has been cruising on its somewhat inflated reputation of late.

Pho Van 1012 NW Glisan St ⓣ503/248-2172. Quite possibly the best restaurant in the Pearl, as long as you like Vietnamese cuisine prepared with a French twist. The savory fried crepes, big bowls of *pho* soup, and braised chicken and duck are all top-notch. In the $10–15 range for entrees, the prices are cheaper than you might expect from the condo-heavy location, too.

Northwest Portland

Basta's Trattoria 410 NW 21st Ave ⓣ503/274-1572. Informal Italian restaurant with an imaginative menu – ranging from basic pizzas and pastas to more original Northwest Cuisine dishes – that still manages to keep its rural, North Italian heart.

Escape from New York Pizza 622 NW 23rd Ave ⓣ503/227-5423. While the service is erratic and the attitudes are just this side of scornful, this pizza joint lives up to its name with hot, flat pies that might just past muster in the Big Apple.

Justa Pasta 1326 NW 19th Ave ⓣ503/243-2249. Despite the uninspired name, this hole-in-the-wall serves some of the city's best and least expensive Italian fare, including savory soups, delicious pastas, and locally grown Painted Hills Beef. The coconut cake and assorted ice creams are also a treat.

Marrakesh 1201 NW 21st Ave ⓣ503/248-9442. Plop down on the ground or into an overstuffed cushion, watch belly dancers gyrate, and partake of some truly tempting Moroccan cuisine, such as traditional stews, pitas, and desserts.

Mio Sushi 2271 NW Johnson St ⓣ503/221-1469. Fine sushi, sashimi, and combo meals, plus solid and inexpensive *bentos* (rice and meat in a bowl). Another good branch at 3962 SE Hawthorne Blvd, on the Eastside ⓣ503/230-6981.

Papa Haydn 701 NW 23rd Ave ⓣ503/223-7317. Expect at least a half-hour wait for a table at this upscale eatery on weekend nights – worth it for a taste of the fifty-odd desserts on the menu, with the best on view behind glass. Always a popular gathering place for both urban- and suburbanites.

Sushiville 1514 NW 23rd Ave ⓣ503/226-4710. Bright, modern, somewhat plastic-looking place, where you grab plates of ultra-cheap sushi and combo rolls off of a two-way conveyor belt moving through the restaurant. It's all a bit goofy, but the food is good and fairly authentic, and the place is always packed during peak hours.

Swagat 2074 NW Lovejoy St ⓣ503/227-4300. Nothing fancy here, just cheap and straightfoward

Indian fare – the usual vindaloos, tandooris, and curries – prepared with just the right spiciness and served in heaping portions.

Wildwood 1221 NW 21st Ave at Overton ⓣ503/248-9663. Young, hip Northwest Cuisine restaurant with a warm interior, friendly staff, and imaginative food like bacon-wrapped pork loin and oyster-and-pancetta salad. Fresh local ingredients are the rule, served up by perennial big-name chef Corey Schreiber. The best in a cluster of pricey eateries, though the service can be erratic.

Eastside

Bangkok Kitchen 2534 SE Belmont St ⓣ503/236-7349. Forget the higher-priced joints Downtown (1.5 miles west): this dreary-looking spot has Portland's best – and cheapest – Thai food. And if you don't like the ugly red-vinyl booths or kitschy decor, just order take-out.

Bombay Cricket Club 1925 Hawthorne Blvd ⓣ503/231-0740. Excellent restaurant with arguably the town's best Indian food – and its most aggravating service. Try to ignore the snooty attitudes and dive into the delicious vindaloos and tandooris. A mile west of the main Hawthorne scene.

Clay's Smokehouse Grill 2932 SE Division St ⓣ503/235-4755. Among the top barbecue houses in town, serving up rich and hearty fare like ribs and pork sandwiches, as well as super-sweet, old-fashioned desserts like pineapple upside-down cake.

Colosso 1932 NE Broadway ⓣ503/288-3333. Dark, brooding design and low lighting give this tapas joint big hipster credentials, and the food's not bad, either. A variety of rotating, Spanish-inspired "little plates" and a smoky bar that really brings out the black-clad crowd.

Esparza's 2725 SE Ankeny St ⓣ503/234-7909. The height of Tex-Mex in the Pacific Northwest, a cheery place loaded with kitsch dolls, antique posters, and jaw-dropping bric-a-brac, and offering big plates of traditional fare like burritos with lamb or pork, as well as unconventional entrees like ostrich and alligator.

Genoa 2832 SE Belmont St 503/238-1464. Frequent candidate for top restaurant in Portland, some might even say the entire region. Ultra-expensive Northern Italian food that changes by the month, often including a fixed-price menu with seven courses. Formal, but not pretentious, despite the average $100 cost per person – not including wine.

La Cruda 2500 SE Clinton St ⓣ503/233-0745. Frenetic hangout for the slacker and bohemian crowd, and worthwhile for its huge plates of tasty burritos, tamales, and the like – not to mention the kick-ass jukebox and margaritas poured from a Slurpee machine.

Navarre 10 NE 28th Ave ⓣ503/232-3555. The best of a recent wave of moderately priced Northwest Cuisine eateries scattered around the Eastside. This one has tapas with local ingredients, along with some Italian and French cuisine, as well as good home-made bread and desserts.

Pambiche 2811 NE Glisan St ⓣ503/233-0511. Cuban and Caribbean food served up for surprisingly low prices, including excellent plantains, shredded beef and pork, and very fine desserts. The big downside is the lack of space and cramped setting – forget about having a private conversation here.

Toney Bento 1423 SE 37th Ave ⓣ503/234-4441. A lively Hawthorne spot with giant bowls of tasty, inexpensive noodle concoctions, and delicious sushi – made by a master first-generation chef.

Nightlife

Portland has a surprising number of offerings for **nightlife** for a city its size – far more solid choices, in fact, than can be listed below – and like Seattle, draws drinkers, dancers, and hedonists from up and down the West Coast, and sometimes farther afield. The comprehensive *Willamette Week* (ⓦwww.wweek.com) and the slimmer *Portland Mercury* (ⓦwww.portlandmercury.com) carry up-to-the-minute weekly **listings** and reviews of what's on and where. They're available free in the self-service stands on many street corners and at leading bookshops. The Friday edition of *The Oregonian* (35¢), the main local newspaper, has a useful listings section too, called *A&E*.

Bars and microbreweries

The city's many **microbreweries** are proof of the resurgence of the Northwest's proud brewing traditions, making porters, ales, and stouts on the premises and usually offering bar food, sometimes of a high standard. The local **McMenamins** chain operates many such places, often in combination with hotels and theaters, which is where they're listed in the guide (or see Ⓦ www.mcmenamins.com for the full list). Many of Portland's **bars** operate till two in the morning, and open up again as early as 7am. You're apt to find almost anything in them, from the most obscure oatmeal-chocolate porter to big-name industrial brews like Pabst Blue Ribbon, supposedly more popular here than anywhere else in the US – locals just call it by its acronym, PBR.

Downtown

Goose Hollow Inn and Tavern 1927 SW Jefferson St Ⓣ503/228-7010. Great microbrews, the city's best Reuben sandwich, and a convenient location near the MAX tracks, a mile west of Downtown. Watch for owner Bud Clark, the colorful city mayor in the 1980s, known for his signature slogan, "Whoop whoop!"

Huber's 411 SW 3rd Ave Ⓣ503/228-5686. Hands-down the most historic bar around, an 1879 marvel with a stained-glass skylight, classic brass fixtures, terrazzo flooring, and mahogany paneling. Also famed for its roast-turkey sandwiches and Spanish coffee – hot or iced – and a fine array of beers, wines, and cocktails.

Portland City Grill 111 SW 5th Ave, 30th floor of the US Bancorp Tower Ⓣ503/450-0030. Skip this restaurant's pricey meals and head straight for happy hour in the lounge, which not only offers tasty booze and delicious and cheap appetizers, but also one of the best views of the city. If you get here much past 6pm, though, you won't find a place to sit, and will have to contend with a meatmarket scene that only gets more lascivious by the hour.

Rock Bottom Brewery 206 SW Morrison at 2nd Ave Ⓣ503/796-2739. Fairly conventional, but popular, chain microbrewery. The bar food here is filling and tasty, but it's probably best to stick to the more straightforward dishes. Burger and fries cost around $10. Housed in an attractive old building with lots of space.

Old Town and Chinatown

Kells 112 SW 2nd Ave Ⓣ503/227-4057. Longstanding favorite Irish bar, with fine authentic cuisine (Irish stews, soda bread) and a range of microbrews, imported beers, and of course, Irish (and Scotch) whiskey.

Shanghai Tunnel 211 SW Ankeny St Ⓣ503/220-4001. Located just off Burnside Street, a subterranean bar popular with hipsters and offering Asian-style soul food.

Tiger Bar 317 NW Broadway Ⓣ503/222-7297. Uber-hip lounge with a tiger-striped bar and long banquettes. Dark, sultry, and smoke-friendly, with late-night food.

Pearl District

Bridgeport Brewing, 1313 NW Marshall St Ⓣ503/241-3621. Huge late-Victorian, ivy-covered warehouse that's now home to Oregon's oldest microbrewery (1984) and one of the city's largest and liveliest beer bars, pouring pints of home-brewed Bridgeport Ale. Tasty pizzas and bar food make for good ballast.

Ringlers Annex 1223 SW Stark St Ⓣ503/525-0520. Great people watching in the sizable basement of the ornate wedge-shaped 1917 Flatiron Building. Companion bar, *Ringlers*, is two blocks away at 1332 W Burnside St (Ⓣ503/225-0627).

Rogue Ales Public House 1339 NW Flanders St Ⓣ503/222-5910. One of the top choices for microbrew-guzzling in the Pearl District, with an eye-popping range of brews – from Yellow Snow Ale to a jalapeño beer – but best for its scrumptious Chocolate Porter. Also has solid burgers and BBQ fare.

Northwest Portland

The Gypsy 625 NW 21st Ave Ⓣ503/796-1859. Purple-colored joint located across from the Cinema 21 theater, broken up into two rooms: a dark back room with music and the usual libertine atmosphere, and a brighter front room with a friendlier crowd and rollicking Thursday night karaoke.

Portland Brewing 2730 NW 31st Ave Ⓣ503/226-7623. The various beers and ales on tap have made this one of the city's more renowned microbreweries. The menu features

Northwest and traditional German food, either indoors or on the outdoor patio.

Eastside

The Alibi 4024 N Interstate Ave ⓣ503/287-5335. The pinnacle of Polynesian Tiki bars in the region, a fun and somewhat divey joint in a grim North Portland neighborhood, which nonetheless has cheap, powerful drinks, a spirited atmosphere, and a Thurs–Sun karaoke scene that's among the city's best.

Dot's Café 2521 SE Clinton St ⓣ503/235-0203. In the center of the small-but-hip Clinton district, a cheap, if grungy, late-night spot with a good variety of stiff booze and music. Decked out in garage-sale decor, it also offers a classic bacon cheeseburger, vegan burritos, and the best grilled-cheese sandwich in Portland.

Lucky Labrador 915 SE Hawthorne Blvd ⓣ503/236-3555. Just across the river from Downtown, or a mile and a half west of the main Hawthorne action, this unpretentious brewpub occupies a large warehouse space with an outdoor patio. Fresh ales, great sandwiches, BBQ specials, and a delicious peanut-curry bento.

Produce Row 204 SE Oak St ⓣ503/232-8355. Be one of the rare tourists at this local favorite, stuck in an unglamorous location by the railroad tracks, but an unexpected paradise for beer lovers, with nearly thirty taps and countless bottled brews. Also with a nice range of live music from country to rock, and a colorful clientele of hard-bitten regulars and even a few newbies.

Live music venues

For **live music**, Portland is a small but vital presence on the national map, with countless alternative and punk bands relocating here in the last few years. To get a sense of the scene, the coolest venues are located around east and west Burnside. In addition, there is a reasonable range of folk, rock, jazz, and blues spots. Except for big-name bands, cover charges – where they exist at all – are minimal.

Rock and pop

Ash Street Saloon 225 SW Ash St ⓣ503/226-0430. Popular Old Town club featuring a wide range of bands, many of them playing blues, rock, or metal. A place to spot up-and-coming local talent, with solid microbrews on tap.

Berbati's Pan 10 SW 3rd Ave ⓣ503/248-4579. Features a reconstructed nineteenth-century European bar in back and nightly selection of eclectic bands – local to international – usually for no more than $10 cover.

Crystal Ballroom 1332 W Burnside St ⓣ503/778-5625. Just above the *Ringlers* bar (see opposite), a nineteenth-century dance hall with a "floating" floor on springs. Bands range from hippie to hip-hop and feature good DJs in "Lola's Room" upstairs. The place oozes history – Glenn Miller played here and so did the likes of Marvin Gaye, Tina Turner, and James Brown.

Dante's 1 SW 3rd Ave ⓣ503/226-6630. Perhaps the city's hippest night spot. Cabaret acts and live music mix with the club's signature "Sinferno" Sunday strip shows, "Karaoke from Hell" Mondays, and the disturbing lounge-punk stylings of "Storm and the Balls" Wednesdays.

Keller Auditorium SW 3rd Ave and Clay St ⓣ503/274-6560. Although a decent venue for opera and musicals, this isn't so great for mid-level rockers – though for some acts you may have no choice. Instead of dancing, moshing, or head-banging, you'll be forced to sit dutifully in your chair.

Roseland Theater 8 NW 6th Ave ⓣ503/224-2038. Located in one of the city's dicier corners, but a top spot for rock and alternative acts – often the last affordable venue for fans before the groups start touring the bigger concert halls with higher-priced tickets.

Jazz and blues

Benson Hotel 309 SW Broadway ⓣ503/228-2000. Live jazz in one of the city's smartest Downtown hotels. Mostly local acts, but occasional touring stars too.

Blue Monk 3341 SE Belmont St ⓣ503/595-0575.A hip little spot along a rejuvenated Eastside stretch, where you can devour serviceable Italian food upstairs and hear the mainstream sounds of local jazz performers downstairs. Music Tues & Thurs–Sat only.

Brasserie Montmartre 626 SW Park Ave ⓣ503/224-5552. Live jazz for the price of a dinner or a drink (see "Restaurants," p.107).
Green Room 2280 NW Thurman St ⓣ503/228-6178. An unassuming, tiny club on the northern edge of Northwest Portland that offers some of the better folk, blues, and soul acts in town.
Jimmy Mak's 300 NW 10th St at Everett ⓣ503/295-6542. Now that the famed Jazz de Opus has closed, this is Northwest Portland's last serviceable jazz joint, with swinging live tunes on the second floor, a bar in the basement, and seasonal outdoor seating, with Greek and American food on offer as well.

All ages

Meow Meow 527 SE Pine St ⓣ503/230-2111. The crowd can sometimes get a little too young at this all-ages joint, and of course there's no booze available, but for pulse-pounding alternative rock and punk, this is one of Portland's better choices.
Nocturnal 1800 E Broadway ⓣ503/239-5900. Increasingly popular and crowded night spot, with a subterranean bar attracting young adults who look like teenagers, and a ground-level, all-ages concert space attracting real teenagers. Expect a heavy focus on indie rock and punk for the latter.
Rose Garden Arena 1401 N Wheeler Ave ⓣ503/224-4400. Where the big touring rock and pop acts appear. On the east side of the Willamette River, just north of Downtown, the arena seats 21,000 and is part of a large, bland shopping complex.

Clubs

The **clubs** in town often feature a revolving cast of DJs and musical styles, though some present dance music in the salsa and reggae vein. **Gay**-oriented clubs are generally located around SW Stark Street, off West Burnside a block south, from 10th to 13th avenues.

Cobalt Lounge 32 NW 3rd Ave ⓣ503/225-1003. A fun club in Old Town with stiff drinks and a party crowd, where DJs mix new house sounds with retro favorites on rotating evenings. Come on Saturdays for "Flux" to mix it up with a spooky-looking Goth and industrial crowd.
Embers 11 NW Broadway ⓣ503/222-3082. An often-crowded club with drag shows in the gay-oriented front room and high-energy dancing and a pair of go-go cages in the straight-leaning room in back.
Fernando's Hideaway 824 SW 1st Ave at Yamhill ⓣ503/248-4709. Popular Spanish place in a handsome old building with a restaurant and bar serving wonderful and authentic tapas, with 2-for-1 deals on Mondays. Also offers Thurs–Sat night salsa lessons, and thumping salsa music.
Fez Ballroom 316 SW 11th Ave, 3rd floor ⓣ503/226-4171. Presents irregular, but often interesting shows with a variety of DJs and live-music acts – rock, folk, electronica, and hip-hop, among other styles – plus occasional theme nights and costume parties.
Goodfoot 2845 SE Stark St ⓣ503/239-9292. Frenetic underground live-music joint and dance club decorated in mildly retro-70s decor, and always sweaty, smoky, and packed on weekends – but still worth it to hear top-notch DJs spinning and scratching the lights out.
Level 13 NW 6th Ave ⓣ503/228-8888. Awfully posy for Portland, with an upscale dress code and quite a bit of attitude, but it's still one of the few multi-level dance clubs in town. Has a loyal following and is almost unavoidable for some club-hoppers, especially suburbanites in silk shirts and leather pants.
Ohm 31 NW 1st Ave ⓣ503/223-9919. Located near Saturday market by the light rail tracks, a top spot for electronica and hip-hop music, with both live acts and DJs. Weekends are packed and stuffy, so come during midweek for a more relaxed environment.
Panorama 341 SW 10th Ave ⓣ503/221-7262. Frenetic gay-and-straight scene with wild dancing spread over several dark rooms, with occasional theme nights – drag, goth, fetish – and foam parties to make your head spin. Open until 4am weekends.
Red Sea 318 SW 3rd Ave ⓣ503/241-5450. Dine on African/Middle Eastern cuisine while you groove to reggae and African tunes on weekends. Also offers the occasional belly dancer.
Saucebox 214 SW Broadway ⓣ503/241-3393. Easily missable spot – identified by a sign with an ice cube – features great pan-Asian cuisine, colorful cocktails, and eclectic nightly music that attracts black-clad poseurs and serious hipsters.

Sports

When it comes to **sports** of the spectator variety, Portland has nothing on Seattle, and can only boast a handful of minor-league squads and one perpetually troubled major-league one. The latter is, of course, basketball's **Portland Trail Blazers** (Nov–June; tickets $10–150; ⓣ503/234-9291, ⓦwww.nba.com/blazers), whose once-rabid fans have largely deserted the team in recent years due to a rash of player drug busts, poor community relations, and various run-ins with police and other authorities – making the team one of the most notorious in all of professional sports, and inspiring its "Jail Blazers" nickname. Still, the squad can be counted on to offer an entertaining display, especially when playing big-name teams like the Los Angeles Lakers – who despite being perennial champions only rarely scratch out wins in the Blazers' Rose Garden Arena.

For less eventful spectator sports, the **Portland Beavers** (April–Sept; $6–25; ⓣ503/553-5555, ⓦwww.pgepark.com/beavers) play minor-league AAA baseball in PGE Park, but their play is uneven at best and the park is best known for being a multimillion-dollar white elephant. It's also home to the **Timbers** ($8–20; ⓣ503/553-5555, ⓦwww.pgepark.com/timbers) who play in soccer's A league (the highest level below the majors), but are still fairly unknown to most residents. Another minor-league franchise, the Western Hockey League's **Winter Hawks** (Oct–May; $10–25; ⓣ503/224-4400, ⓦwww.winterhawks.com) hit the puck at the Rose Garden, and are now more locally esteemed than their basketball counterparts who share the same arena. Finally, horse racing fans can place bets at **Portland Meadows**, just off I-5 north of Downtown (ⓣ503/285-9144, ⓦwww.portlandmeadows.com), from mid-April through mid-September, Thursdays to Sundays (Wed–Sun from mid-July through August).

Performing arts and film

Portland's **performing arts** scene revolves, logically enough, around the Portland Center for the Performing Arts (PCPA) at 1111 SW Broadway (ⓣ503/248-4335 or 224-4000, ⓦwww.pcpa.com; see overleaf) – though confusingly the term "PCPA" often includes the Keller Auditorium on SW 3rd Avenue and Clay Street, too (ⓣ503/274-6560; see overleaf). Broadway's PCPA is where you'll find much of the city's best **theater**, though several good-quality companies perform elsewhere in smaller digs. The complex also incorporates the Arlene Schnitzer Concert Hall, the place to go for **classical music** and home to the prestigious Oregon Symphony Orchestra. During the summer, **free concerts** are held at Pioneer Courthouse Square, Tom McCall Waterfront Park, the zoo, and the amphitheater at the International Rose Test Garden. For arts listings, try the *Oregonian*'s Friday *A&E* section or the alternative *Willamette Week*, available free from street racks every Wednesday.

Tickets can be purchased direct or from **Ticket Central**, inside Portland's visitor center, at 701 SW Sixth Ave (May–Oct daily 9am–5pm; Nov–April Mon–Fri 9am–5pm & Sat 10am–2pm; ⓣ503/224-4400). This is a walk-in service, but there is a day-of-show information line (ⓣ503/275-8358).

Classical music, dance, and opera

In 2003 Portland's high-culture scene saw a dramatic change as most of its major figures from the last five to ten years departed, making way for a trio of newcomers directing and programming the various arts. Although the future is unsettled, and local critics predict a return to provincial conservatism, you're well advised to take in a performance as Portland generally offers better-quality productions that you might expect from a city its size. **Classical music** and **opera** are predictably the most cautious in their programming, generally focusing on light pops fare and the traditional war-horses of the canon, though the **dance** scene has been a bit more risk-taking in recent years. As for venues, these can vary widely between major institutions, churches, and college settings, with **prices** depending largely on the prominence of the institution – anywhere from $5 for an alternative dance show in an art gallery to $100 for prime tickets at one of the major venues. As always, check arts listings (see above) for the best options.

Chamber Music Northwest ⓣ503/294-6400, ⓦwww.cmnw.org. Presents affordable chamber music in rotating venues around town (often old-time churches), and are appreciated for their wide sweep of composers presented – from the spiritual odes of Palestrina to the modern modes of Ned Rorem, with plenty of Bach and Haydn in between.

Keller Auditorium SW 3rd Ave and Clay St ⓣ503/274-6560. Large venue for concerts, operas, and big touring theatrical productions – typically familiar musicals.

Oregon Ballet Theater 1120 SW 10th Ave ⓣ503/222-5538, ⓦwww.obt.org. Oregon's premier ballet company has a core repertoire of the classics, but they do modern and experimental pieces, too. The company offers performances at the Broadway PCPA's Schnitzer Concert Hall.

Oregon Symphony Orchestra 921 SW Washington St ⓣ503/228-1353, ⓦwww.orsymphony.org. A first-rate orchestra that performs at the Schnitzer Concert Hall between September and May. The orchestra's program, led by Carlos Kalmar, is beefed up with special events and guest performers.

PICA or the Portland Institute for Contemporary Art, 219 NW 12th Ave ⓣ503/242-1419, ⓦwww.pica.org. Almost impossible to classify in any one area, but mixes art, music, dance, and even opera into a variety of performances, often in festivals, throughout the year. One of the prime performance-art entities in the city.

Portland Center for the Performing Arts (PCPA) 1111 SW Broadway at Main ⓣ503/248-4335 or 224-4000, ⓦwww.pcpa.com. Offers a varied program of performing arts from theater through chamber music, opera, and ballet. Comprises the Arlene Schnitzer Concert Hall and the New Theater Building, which is itself divided into the Dolores Winningstad Theater and the Newmark Theater.

Portland Opera 1515 SW Morrison St ⓣ503/241-1407, ⓦwww.portlandopera.org. Puts on five annual productions, mixing the usual operatic warhorses with a sprinkling of more modern works. Their season runs from September to July and performances are at the Keller Auditorium (see above).

Theater

Theater in Portland has many devoted local adherents, and you're apt to see almost anything on its variety of stages, from canonical works by Shakespeare, Ibsen, and Shaw, to quirky alternative fare, to shows that straddle the border between drama and performance art. The PCPA is the centerpiece of the major venues (and usually draws the tourists and suburbanites), but is far from the only worthwhile facility. Smaller venues can be found throughout the Pearl District and the Eastside, usually for much cheaper **prices** – around $5–15, compared to $20 or more at the PCPA. The selection below is only meant to provide an initial taste of the dramatic scene, and if you have further interest in it you're well advised to scour the weekly arts listings for the full range of shows and venues.

Artists Repertory Theater 1516 SW Alder St ⓣ503/241-1278, ⓦwww.artistsrep.org. The emphasis here is on modern plays, with imaginative scripts, striking settings, and strong acting.

Back Door Theater 4319 SE Hawthorne Blvd ⓣ503/993-9062. A good spot to catch modern plays – both avant-garde and modern classics – performed by some of the city's most talented theater groups.

Imago 17 SE 8th Ave ⓣ503/231-9581, ⓦwww.imagotheatre.com. Portland's one essential theater troupe, and its only nationally known ensemble. An inventive, often bizarre group putting on shows mixing different acting styles, creative staging and lighting, and puppets and multimedia to create an inexplicable, wonderful result.

Liminal 403 NW 5th Ave ⓣ503/890-2993, ⓦwww.liminalgroup.org. Anything conceptual, minimal, and experimental is on display for this daring company, willing to tinker with time, space, and audience endurance in pursuit of artistic perfection. Expect to see and hear the work of John Cage, Samuel Beckett, and even Yoko Ono.

Portland Center Stage at the Portland Center for the Performing Arts, 1111 SW Broadway at Main ⓣ503/248-6309, ⓦwww.pcs.org. Portland's premier professional theater troupe offers contemporary and classical works. The specialty is Shakespeare and the troupe has links with Ashland's Shakespeare Festival (see p.53). May be relocating to the Brewery Blocks (see p.96) in the Pearl District, starting in the 2005 season.

Stark Raving Theatre 2257 NW Raleigh St ⓣ503/232-7072, ⓦstarkravingtheatre.org. Gripping dramas, topical issue-oriented plays, and disturbing and experimental new works are but a few of the highlights at this risk-taking theater.

Theater! Theatre! 3430 SE Belmont St ⓣ503/239-5919, ⓦwww.tripro.org. Quirky, comic, sometimes melodramatic plays that dig up some of the city's more unheralded thespians and present compelling, entertaining work.

Film

If you're interested in watching a **film**, the monolithic Regal chain owns most of the town's theaters. Decent alternatives include Cinema 21, 616 NW 21st Ave (ⓣ503/223-4515, ⓦwww.cinema21.com), for foreign and independent movies; the Guild, 879 SW Ninth Ave (ⓣ503/221-1156), for classics and retrospectives; and the grand Hollywood, 4122 NE Sandy Blvd (ⓣ503/281-4215, ⓦwww.hollywoodtheatre.org), for all of the above. The **Northwest Film Center**, at the Portland Art Museum, 1219 SW Park Ave (ⓣ503/221-1156, ⓦwww.nwfilm.org), shows art-house, foreign-language, and classic movies. The selection is adventurous and often obscure, and be sure to look out for the themed evenings and frequent festivals. There are also many good historic neighborhood **moviehouses** on the Eastside that show art films, second runs, and classics; these are listed in the respective section on each district.

Listings

Airlines Air Canada ⓣ1-800/247-2262, ⓦwww.aircanada.ca; Alaska Air ⓣ1-800/426-0333, ⓦwww.alaska-air.com; American ⓣ1-800/433-7300, ⓦwww.aa.com; Continental, domestic ⓣ1-800/525-0280, international ⓣ1-800/231-0856, ⓦwww.continental.com; Delta, domestic ⓣ1-800/221-1212, international ⓣ1-800/241-4141, ⓦwww.delta.com; Frontier ⓣ1-888/241-7821, ⓦwww.frontierairlines.com; Horizon ⓣ1-800/547-9308, ⓦwww.horizonair.com; Lufthansa ⓣ1-800/645-3880, ⓦwww.lufthansa.com; Northwest/KLM, domestic ⓣ1-800/225-2525, international ⓣ1-800/447-4747, ⓦwww.nwa.com or ⓦwww.klm.com; Reno Air (part of American Airlines) ⓣ1-800/433-7300, ⓦwww.aa.com; United, domestic ⓣ1-800/241-6522, international ⓣ1-800/538-2929, ⓦwww.ual.com.

American Express Travel service with poste restante, 1100 SW 6th St ⓣ503/226-2961, ⓦwww.americanexpress.com.

Banks Major branches Downtown include Bank of America, 1001 SW 5th Ave (ⓣ503/275-2222); Wells Fargo, 1300 SW 5th Ave (ⓣ503/886-3340), and US Bank, 1200 SW Morrison Ave (ⓣ503/275-6911) and 1340 SW 2nd Ave (ⓣ503/275-6692). ATMs are located at the airport and across town.

Bike rental Bike Central, 732 SW 1st Ave ⓣ503/227-4439; Citybikes, 734 SE Ankeny St ⓣ503/239-6951; Fat Tire Farm, 2714 NW Thurman St ⓣ503/222-3276.

Bookshops Powell's City of Books, 1005 W Burnside St (daily 9am–11pm; ⓣ503/228-4651, ⓦwww.powells.com; see p.96), is a huge labyrinth of new and secondhand books. Other good branches include Powell's Travel Store, in Pioneer Courthouse Square (ⓣ503/228-1108); Powell's Hawthorne, 3723 SE Hawthorne Blvd (ⓣ503/238-1668); and Powell's PDX, inside the airport (ⓣ503/249-1950).

Car rental Alamo, at the airport (ⓣ503/252-7039); Avis, 330 SW Washington St (ⓣ503/227-0220), at the airport (ⓣ503/249-4950 or 1-800/831-2847); Dollar, 132 NW Broadway (ⓣ503/228-3540), at the airport (ⓣ503/249-4792 or 1-800/800-4000); Enterprise, 445 SW Pine St (ⓣ503/275-5359), at the airport (ⓣ503/252-1500); Hertz, 330 SW Pine St (ⓣ503/249-5727), at the airport (ⓣ503/249-8216 or 1-800/654-3131); Thrifty, at the airport (ⓣ503/254-2277).

Consulates The UK consulate (ⓣ503/227-5669) exists only as an answerphone; try the one in Seattle at 900 Fourth Ave ⓣ206/622-9255.

Emergencies Police and medical emergencies ⓣ911.

Gay and lesbian *Just Out* (ⓦwww.justout.com), a free, twice-monthly newssheet, has articles on gay issues and provides cultural and social listings. The best place to pick it up is at Powell's City of Books, 1005 W Burnside St (see above). There's a gay and lesbian counseling center at 522 SW 5th Ave (ⓣ503/223-8299). Most of Portland's clubs are gay- and lesbian-friendly. Otherwise, many gay-male bars and clubs can be found on SW Stark Street between 10th and 13th avenues; the main, perhaps the only, lesbian bar is the Egyptian, 3701 SE Division St (ⓣ503/236-8689).

Hospital Legacy Good Samaritan Hospital and Medical Center, 1015 NW 22nd Ave ⓣ503/413-7711, ⓦwww.legacyhealth.org.

Internet access Downtown at Kinko's (24hr), 221 SW Alder St (ⓣ503/224-6550); many free terminals at the Downtown library, with a short waiting time.

Library Downtown's grand Central Library 801 SW 10th Ave (ⓣ503/988-5123, ⓦwww.multcolib.org), is a renovated, Renaissance Revival jewel with a sizable collection spread over three floors and a reading room for books and magazines. Annual circulation is 16 million, making for an average of 24 books checked out per year for each county resident.

Parks Oregon State Parks' office is south of Downtown near the Marquam Bridge at 2501 SW 1st Ave, Suite 100 (Mon–Fri 8am–5pm; ⓣ503/731-3293 or 1-800/551-6949, ⓦwww.prd.state.or.us); they have brochures and information on almost all of Oregon's parks. Camping reservations for Oregon and Washington state parks can be made by phone or online (ⓣ1-800/452-5687, ⓦwww.reserveamerica.com). Information on Portland city parks at 1120 SW Fifth Ave, Suite 1302 (ⓣ503/823-PLAY, ⓦwww.parks.ci.portland.or.us).

Police Central Precinct, 1111 SW 2nd Ave ⓣ503/823-0097.

Post office The main city post office, and by far the best, is in the Pearl District, 715 NW Hoyt St, zip code 97208 (Mon–Fri 8am–6.30pm, Sat 9am–5pm; ⓣ1-800/275-8777). Letters can be sent c/o General Delivery and picked up during public hours; if you're receiving mail at someone else's address, it should include "c/o" and the regular occupant's name.

Road conditions ⓣ503/222-6721.

Tax Oregon has no sales tax, but hotel taxes in the city are currently 11.5 percent.

Tours Gray Line, PO Box 17306 (ⓣ503/285-9845 or 1-800/422-7042, ⓦwww.grayline.com), operates a range of summer bus tours visiting spots throughout Oregon. Examples are tours of the city itself (Feb–Dec 1 daily; 3hr; $30); Mount Hood/Columbia Gorge (April–Oct 3 weekly; 8hr 30min; $52); and the North Oregon coast (mid-May to mid-Oct 3 weekly; 9hr; $52).

Weather ⓣ503/261-9246, ⓦwww.wrh.noaa.gov/Portland.

Women's Crisis and Rape Hotline ⓣ503/235-5333.

2

The Columbia River Gorge

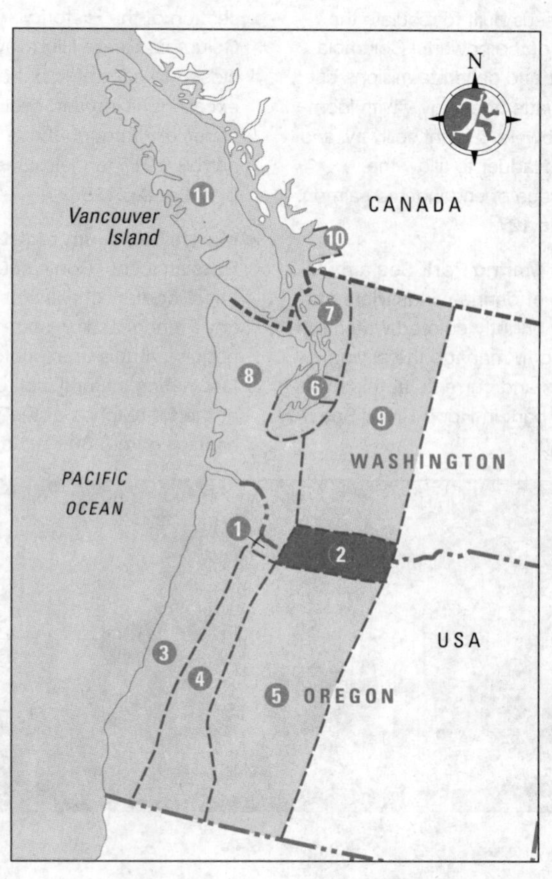

CHAPTER 2 Highlights

* **Multnomah Falls** One of the most popular of Oregon's many scenic attractions, this thin torrent of water topples over a high basaltic ledge and crashes down dramatically into two pools surrounded by thick forest. See p.126

* **Bonneville Dam** New Deal colossus built to regulate the flow of the powerful Columbia River and generate millions of kilowatts of energy – with looming towers, a giant spillway, and a fish ladder to allow the passage of endangered salmon. See p.127

* **Port Marina Park** See a multitude of daring windsurfers and their brightly colored watercraft trying to manage the strong gales and currents at this riverside park in Hood River. See p.130

* **Timberline Lodge** The epitome of a classic mountain lodge – a rough-hewn stone-and-timber edifice sitting on an upper slope of Mount Hood, with a classic 1930s design and a forbidding, rugged presence in The Shining. See p.133

* **The Twin Tunnels** An eastern section of the Historic Columbia Gorge Highway, now closed to car traffic but offering excellent hiking and cycling, especially through these stark, narrow 1917 tunnels. See p.134 and p.129

* **Maryhill Museum of Art** Savor Russian icons, Rodin sculptures, oddball chess sets, and tiny French fashion mannequins at this unexpectedly fascinating cultural institution at the far reaches of the eastern gorge. See p.136

△ Crown Point Vista House

2

The Columbia River Gorge

The mighty **Columbia River** rises in Canada's Rocky Mountains and takes a sloping, circuitous path through Washington before the last leg of its journey to the Pacific, defining much of the border between Washington and Oregon along the way. As it was for the Oregon Trail pioneers (see box, p.186) and the Native Americans before them, the last portion of the Columbia River Valley is the quickest and most obvious route between the wet, wooded valleys of western Oregon and the arid plains of the east. Interstate 84 runs along the river's Oregon side from Portland to Boardman, and along the way passes through the most scenic part of the river valley, the 80-mile **Columbia River Gorge**. Carved by the Columbia as it powered through the topsoil and hillsides on its way to the sea, the gorge stretches eighty miles from Corbett – 22 miles east of Portland – to Maryhill in Washington.

With its western reaches covered with green fir and maple trees, which turn fabulous shades of gold and red in the fall, the gorge's thin white waterfalls cascade down its sides over mossy fern-covered rocks – fine scenery that's at its best along the delightful **Historic Columbia River Highway**, roughly paralleling the freeway to the south. Perhaps the two biggest sights within easy reach of Portland are **Multnomah Falls**, a strikingly beautiful tower of mist that was long the state's top attraction, and **Bonneville Dam**, that New Deal colossus immortalized by Woody Guthrie, and one of many such titans that now controls the river's flow. Further east, roughly halfway along the gorge, pocket-sized **Hood River** is a lively little town, a popular windsurfing center with several good places to stay. It's easily the most appealing settlement hereabouts and is also an important crossroads. To the south are the forested slopes of **Mount Hood**, where skiing is a big wintertime draw (just 55 miles from Portland), as well as the central Oregon sports hub of Bend (see p.220). To the northeast, in Washington, the verdant forests are left behind for bare, sweeping steppes, where you can find the art collection of the eccentric tycoon Sam Hill, displayed in the singular **Maryhill Museum of Art**, and the workaday town of **The Dalles**. Along the way are some unexpectedly good places to hike, including the restored, and recently reopened for foot traffic, **Twin Tunnels**, offering a taste of the great early-twentieth-century age of motor transport.

Apart from hiking, the best way to see the gorge is by **car** – there's no public transit along the Historic Columbia River Highway, though Greyhound **buses** do stop at Hood River and Biggs, near Maryhill, as they whiz along I-84 to and from Portland. Another alternative is Gray Line (ⓣ503/285-9845 or 1-800/422-7042, ⓦwww.grayline.com), which operates **day tours** (April–Oct 3 weekly; 8hr 30min; $38.50) of the gorge from Portland, but don't really allow you time to do the scenery justice – it's frustrating not to have time to take a

The Bretz Floods

Despite a sequence of dams that have turned what was once a raging torrent into a comparatively docile current, the **Columbia River**'s width and majesty still impresses. Although the river once fed more directly into the Pacific across central Washington, massive **lava flows** some 15 million years ago altered its course into the current, more southerly route. The resultant river valley then assumed a fairly conventional, gently sloping V-shape, which it maintained until fairly recently in geologic time. This changed after a mind-bending sequence of events near the end of the last **Ice Age**.

Oddly enough, the current topography of the gorge owes much to the existence of an ancient lake in western Montana. Hemmed in by an advancing ice sheet some 18,000 years ago, **Glacial Lake Missoula** once held around five hundred cubic miles of water – more than lakes Erie and Ontario combined – and was kept in its icy lair only by a single dam around what is now Pend Oreille, Idaho. Although two thousand feet high, this giant **ice dam** failed and unleashed an almost unbelievable catastrophe, draining the entire lake in as little as 48 hours. A gargantuan wall of water thousands of feet tall broke through the chasm and rushed into eastern Washington with ten times the force of all of today's rivers put together – tearing loose trees, stripping away the topsoil, and uncovering the earth down to the level of basalt from the ancient lava flows. Indeed, the current moniker of the **Channeled Scablands** for the desolate stretches of rock in that region is highly accurate. The glacial flood created a colossal trail of destruction as its channels surged and crossed in huge flows and tributaries, creating monstrous **waterfalls** – seen in desiccated form today in places like Dry Falls and Upper Coulee – hundreds of feet high and many miles across. Even worse, the flood channeled into the Columbia River Valley at the narrow constriction of **Wallula Gap**, only making the current pick up more speed and cause greater damage.

By the time the torrent reached the river valley, it was a murky, dark brown stew of topsoil, tree limbs, boulders, and icebergs, demolishing anything in its path at a speed of up to 200mph. Naturally, the valley's thin ground cover and sloping scenery couldn't fight such a flow for very long, and the flood eventually tore away the river bottom and hillsides entirely, exposing the stark, jagged columns of basalt that are now visible throughout the area. Moreover, the flood turned what was a sylvan, V-shaped valley into a sprawling, **U-shaped gorge**, its sides miles apart in places and its slopes made into high precipices where waterfalls – formerly gentle streams and tributaries – tumbled down from the edges of gaping cliffs. The water reached its final destinations at both the mouth of the Columbia River, near present-day Astoria, and in the Willamette Valley, where the rich farmland is even today built upon the transplanted soil and rocks of eastern Washington.

Perhaps the most amazing thing about this geologic spectacle is not that it happened at all, but that it occurred repeatedly (perhaps fifty or more times) over the course of thousands of years as the lake kept refilling behind new ice dams and breaking through when the dams failed – dramatic events that may have occurred as recently as twelve thousand years ago, when native tribes were probably living in the region. Only the end of the Ice Age, and the retreat of North American ice sheets, put a halt to these **Bretz Floods** – named after their University of Washington discoverer – but by that time the damage of millennia of glacial turmoil had permanently altered the landscape, from western Montana all the way to the Pacific Ocean.

hike. Indeed, it's only when you get out on one of the many short trails dotted along the historic highway that the real charm of this lushly forested ravine becomes apparent – which means it's a good idea to spend the night locally, preferably at Hood River.

Some history

Native tribes such as the Yakima and Klickitat had fished and transported goods along the Columbia River for centuries by the time the exhausted pair of Meriwether Lewis and William Clark reached **"The Great River of the West,"** as it came to be known, in 1806. Less than forty years after their 28-month trek across the continent, the gorge was the site of the perilous final leg of the **Oregon Trail** (see p.186), negotiated by pioneer families on precarious rafts, which were known to buckle and capsize in the tumultuous currents of the fast-flowing water. Although this remained a rather grim memory for many, years later when **gold** was discovered in eastern Oregon in 1861, the river turned into a lifeline for pioneering miners and farmers, and a prime target for a lucrative transportation monopoly. A Portland-based company saw the opportunity and put **steamboats** on the river, and soon raked in the profits from the dependent (and bitter) residents of the arid east. By the 1880s, the steamboats were already carrying tourists, too, and because of their size were managing the sharp currents much better than the flimsy rafts of decades earlier.

By the twentieth century, aside from the creation of a historic highway alongside it, the biggest events in the Columbia Gorge have been the construction of a series of massive hydroelectric **dams**, such as Bonneville (see p.127), starting in the 1930s but continuing apace until the 1960s. Not only generating energy for a wide swath of the West in today's world, these dams (along with Washington's Grand Coulee and Nevada's Hoover) played a large role in creating the hydropower necessary for the energy- and water-intensive **aluminum** industry, which reached its peak during World War II in the creation of military supplies and war material. Indeed, if not for the use of such colossal industrial works, it's doubtful the US could ever have become the **"Arsenal of Democracy,"** as FDR termed it, and thereby won the war. In the end, it's a touch ironic, but not surprising, that the gorge, borne out of geological calamity (see opposite), would have a significant role in ending the biggest human catastrophe in world history.

Historic Columbia River Highway

The advent of automotive tourism in the early twentieth century prompted the construction in 1915 of what's now known as the **HISTORIC COLUMBIA RIVER HIGHWAY**. Although this 22-mile stretch of road, now bypassed by I-84, offers the area's prettiest views and most striking landscapes, it was not always regarded so fondly. With its narrow lanes and hairpin curves, the road could be a nightmare to travel, especially when the weather got bad; in later decades the rise of big-rig trucking not only threatened commuter traffic, it also put into question the entire viability of the route. Not surprisingly, the construction of I-84 in the 1960s relieved much of the strain, and gave the highway a historic, rosy glow that it never quite attained in its heyday. Keep in mind that, being a most popular day-tripper's road from Portland, the highway can still be very busy on weekends, when a few of its old problems – lane size, tight curves, etc. – can cause inconveniences once more. Most people come

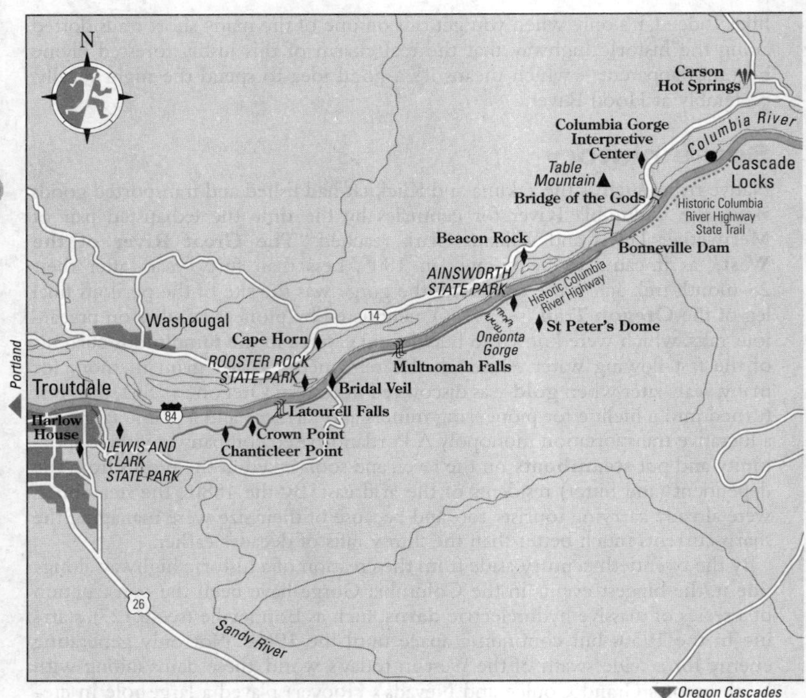

from Portland via I-84, getting off at Corbett (Exit 22), but there are several other access points, including one at Multnomah Falls (Exit 31).

If you're interested in taking the route for its entirety, you'll have to poke through the stretches of Portland's eastern suburbs, namely the uneventful burg of **Troutdale**. Here there are but two attractions: the fun brewpub-hotel, and former mental asylum and old folks' home, now known as the **Edgefield**, 2126 SW Halsey St (see "Accommodation," p.81), and the stately **Harlow House**, 726 E Columbia River Hwy (June–Sept Wed–Sat 10am–4pm, Sun 1–4pm; Oct–May Sat & Sun 1–4pm; donation), a 1900 structure that was the home of the city's founder, a former sea captain, and displays Victorian-era relics and acts as the town's historical society. Both sites are accessible off I-84, exits 17 or 18, and can provide further information on the historic highway and Columbia Gorge in general.

Lewis and Clark State Park to Latourell Falls

A few miles east of Troutdale, the first major sight along the highway, **LEWIS AND CLARK STATE PARK** (dawn–dusk; free; ☎1-800/551-6949), marks the spot where the explorers set up camp on their westward journey in November 1805. Somewhat famous as the site of the **Sandy River**, where Clark tried to wade but feared its bottom was quicksand, the park offers a decent, easy hiking trail or two, but mainly acts as the gateway to the **Columbia River Gorge National Scenic Area**. In this federally protected

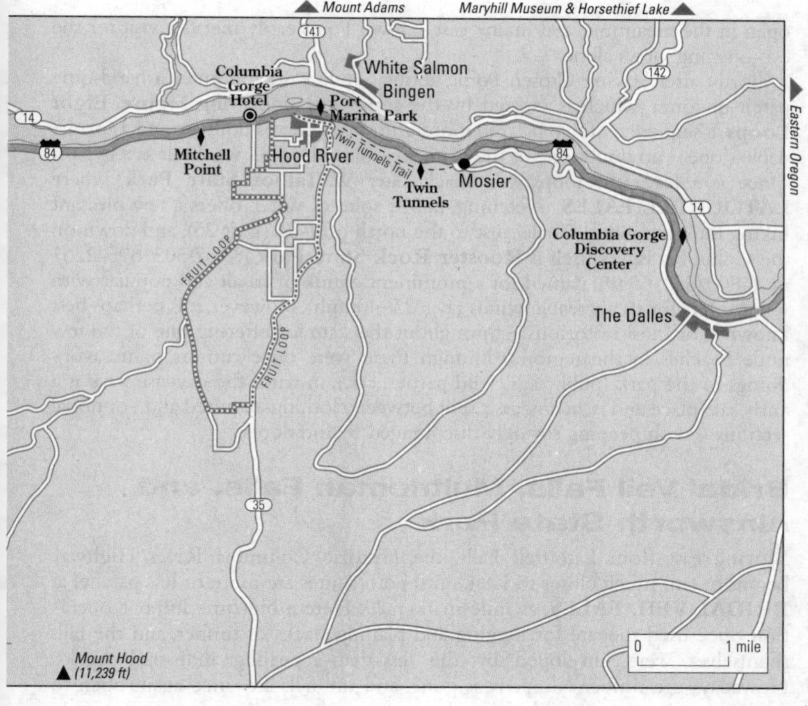

zone of more than a quarter-million acres, development is strictly controlled and there are numerous state parks along the way (check out Ⓦwww.oregonstateparks.org for full descriptions). One of these is named for the **Portland Women's Forum**, nine miles further east, and marks the spot of **Chanticleer Point**, site of an old inn where the highway's developers first met in 1913 to plot the course of the road. You can see how easily they were inspired: the views from here are some of the best in the gorge, with sweeping vistas over the basalt cliffs to the winding river on the horizon. If you get here at the right time in the spring or fall, the sight can be awe-inspiring, with the sun breaking through thick clouds and morning mist to illuminate a rugged river valley – almost beyond description in evocative beauty.

One of the major sights visible from Chanticleer Point is the striking promontory of **Crown Point**. Located at milepost 24 and reachable from I-84 at Exit 22, its sheer dark walls – resulting from countless layers of soil being stripped away from the hillside – offer dramatic testimony to the power of the Bretz Floods. Despite this, the point is best known for its octagonal, copper-domed **Vista House**, to many the essential image of the Columbia Gorge. This stone-faced 1918 concrete structure was designed by one of the historic road's builders to provide views in which "the Columbia could be viewed in silent communication with the infinite." Unfortunately, decades of visiting tourists and crushing gorge winds (up to 110mph, by some estimates) have combined to severely damage the site, which now requires extensive renovation. The project is still ongoing with no completion date, but a **visitors center** (hours vary, generally Fri–Sun 9am–6pm; donation suggested; Ⓦwww.vistahouse.com) with information and displays is open in the meantime, and in any case Crown Point easily merits a visit for the eye-opening views alone.

Shortly after leaving Crown Point, about a mile east, you enter a handsome patch of forest which is crossed by the somewhat unnerving **Figure Eight Loops**, a sequence of five hairpin loops with tight curves built around a formidable slope – no doubt one of the prime reasons why I-84 was built as a bypass. Once you leave the loops, you reach **Guy W. Talbot State Park**, where **LATOURELL FALLS**, a fetching, 250-ft spire of water, offers a few pleasant hiking trails around it. Finally, just to the north off I-84 (Exit 25), and down on the Columbia River itself is **Rooster Rock State Park** ($3; ⓣ503/695-2261 or 1-800/551-6949), named for a prominent chunk of basalt and popular with windsurfers for its agreeable winds (avg. 25–40mph). However, it is perhaps best known – or most notorious – throughout the state for offering one of the few nude beaches in the region. Although there were once rumors of unsavory doings in the park (public sex, wild parties, etc.), in truth the day-use park is a fairly safe place and is, in any case, split between clothing-required and –optional sections – with peeping strongly discouraged by interlopers.

Bridal Veil Falls, Multnomah Falls, and Ainsworth State Park

Moving east from Latourell Falls, the Historic Columbia River Highway begins to run much closer to I-84, until both routes are more or less parallel at **BRIDAL VEIL FALLS**, at mile marker 29. Here a big-time lumber operation once used the site for logging and planing stacks of timber, and the falls themselves were enveloped by the less-than-appealing industrial works. Nowadays the timber company is gone, and the falls are once again open to public view in a state park bearing the name of the cascading waters (free; ⓣ1-800/551-6949). A lower-level trail offers a good taste of the site, and wends around the base of the falls, but the upper-level trail is more appealing, taking you to the precipice over which the waters plunge. The upper hike also features some splendid gorge flora and a close view of the **Pillars of Hercules**, a massive, 120-ft basalt column left exposed by the Bretz Floods, and a predictably popular spot for rock climbers in training.

Beyond Bridal Veil the highway reaches the 242-ft **Wahkeena Falls**, the starting point for a number of trails into the backcountry of the **Mount Hood National Forest**. In particular, the two-mile **Perdition Trail** is a stiff hike that takes you high above Wahkeena through thick groves of cottonwood and maple. At the end of Perdition Trail is the junction with Larch Mountain Trail, which you can follow for the mile-long descent to the tallest and most famous of the gorge's waterfalls, and the only one that most day-trippers visit, the two-tiered **MULTNOMAH FALLS** (reachable off I-84 via a sudden left-lane exit, in both directions). This dramatic waterfall plummets 542ft down a mossy rockface, collects in a pool, then tumbles another 70ft and collects in another. Folklore has it that when a sickness threatened the Multnomah tribe, the chief's daughter threw herself over the falls to appease the Great Spirit. You're supposed to be able to see her face in the mist – the quaint **Benson Bridge**, spanning the rocks above the lower waterfall, was partly built with this in mind. At the foot of the falls, the appealing rustic stone and timber *Multnomah Falls Lodge* (daily 8am–9pm; ⓦwww.multnomahfallslodge.com) has been catering to tourists since 1925. The food is inexpensive, but pretty standard tourist fare – stick to the home-made bread and soups. The **visitor center** (daily 9am–5pm; ⓣ503/695-2372) next door issues free maps of the historic highway's hiking routes – though for the longer routes you'll need to buy one of their more detailed maps.

Multnomah Falls can get jam-packed, but within easy striking distance to the east is **AINSWORTH STATE PARK**, milepost 35, where the much less visited and equally impressive **Horsetail Falls** is a powerful torrent that comes crashing down close to the road. From here, the Horsetail Falls Trail climbs the short distance to the quieter **Ponytail Falls** before pushing on to the **Oneonta Falls**, just over a mile from the trailhead. It's a lovely hike and rather than returning the way you came, you can scramble back to the road just west of Horsetail Falls beside the **Oneonta Gorge**, an starkly evocative site with towering rock walls, and alive with countless floral treasures in its own botanical reserve, among them endemic trees, flowers, and shrubs. Also looming near the park site is the massive **St Peter's Dome**, a huge, rounded basalt tower that is, at 2000ft, every bit the geological equivalent of its architectural namesake. The state park also offers seasonal **campgrounds** (March–Nov; $12–16; ⓣ503/695-2301 or 1-800/551-6949), making it one of the best places to rough it before you reach Hood River.

Bonneville Dam

At the east end of the motorized section of the historic highway, across I-84, it's a few minutes' drive to **BONNEVILLE DAM** (daily 9am–5pm; free; ⓣ541/374-8820), named after Benjamin Bonneville, the mid-nineteenth-century commander of Fort Vancouver (see p.371), who later became a general in the Union Army. As the first in a chain of WPA dams that made the Columbia River the biggest producer of hydroelectric power in the world, this dam and the others were immortalized by Woody Guthrie's lyrical paean, "Roll on, Columbia," in which the folk poet sang, "your power is turning our darkness to dawn, so roll on Columbia, roll on." Doubtless, the 1937 structure is an engineering marvel deserving of Guthrie's praise, but ironically it also did much to erase the history and lore of this part of the Columbia River. Here native tribes once fished in abundance at various river falls along the way and explorers like Lewis and Clark and pioneers on the Oregon Trail experienced a white-knuckle ride down a series of plunging flumes – harrowing but necessary to go any further west. However, these and countless other natural attractions were summarily buried underwater with the construction of the dam, which also had the effect of backing up the river for many miles eastward and turning its once-fearsome stretches into little more than a placid, slow-moving lake.

Designed to process more than 700 million gallons of water per minute through its huge turbines, the dam is built over one of the river's steepest stretches to generate such a colossal amount of energy, which it sends throughout the region and even down to power-hungry California. While it's been great for churning out hydroelectricity, the dam, like countless others in the region, has had a dismal effect on native salmon, which used to swim in abundance upstream. Nowadays, their markedly reduced flow up the dam's **fish ladders** is visible through viewing windows in the visitor center – something of a depressing scene when you consider what came before. Indeed, it's no surprise that most salmon from Washington and Oregon are now raised in aquacultural farms, rather than being caught directly out of the river.

If you're mainly interested in the still-impressive architecture of the dam, you can drive along its western wall and over its giant spillway to reach the **visitor center**. Inside, there are a few interpretative displays that mostly soft-pedal the dam's environmental impact, and nothing to keep you for more than a half-hour. For the most part, the best thing about coming out here is to see this titanic monolith up close, with its looming transmission towers, grand navigation locks, and imposing presence across the equally impressive Columbia River.

Historic Columbia River Highway State Trail

Beyond the turnoff for Bonneville Dam, most drivers heading east abandon the historic highway and rejoin I-84 at exit 40. However, the route actually continues as a pedestrianized section known as the **HISTORIC COLUMBIA RIVER HIGHWAY STATE TRAIL**. As one part of a compelling trail laid out in two sections (the other around the Twin Tunnels; see p.134), the old highway here has been converted to use by cyclists and hikers, who can now, without fear of being run over, check out the road's commanding views of the gorge and its lovely bridges, narrow tunnels, and decorative railings. Running a little over five miles until its junction with Cascade Locks, the non-motorized highway begins from the west at **Tooth Rock**, where a parking lot allows you to deposit your automobile during daylight hours. The first major sight, beyond the stunning array of natural scenery, is the **Eagle Creek Bridge**, designed in 1915 to look much older than its year of completion. Although built solidly of concrete, its rough-hewn stone facing, low arch, and rustic guardrails are supposed to call to mind the sturdy bridges of old Europe. Just beyond in the vicinity of Eagle Creek State Park you'll have access to the 25-mile route of the **Gorge Trail** – a striking overview of the area's scenery that leads back to Bridal Veil – and a short trail to the **Punchbowl**, a low basaltic chamber into which a short waterfall drops – a good spot for lounging in crisp, bubbling pools amid verdant scenery in the summer months. Finally, closer to the state trail's eastern end, near Exit 44 on I-84, the area around **Ruckel Creek** offers a steeply sloping trail along the gorge's high rock walls and past fetching collections of native trees and flowers.

Cascade Locks and the Bridge of the Gods

At the practical end of this section of historic highway (motorized or not), you cross over I-84 at Exit 44 to reach what is now the uneventful burg of **CASCADE LOCKS**, which was once yet another harrowing spot on the pioneer river route, where the water level dropped twenty feet in the space of 1200ft – a daunting prospect for wagons traveling on flimsy rafts, which often had to be portaged around the riparian hazard. The site gets its present name from the 1896 locks that were built here to protect river traffic from the dangerous rapids, though the backwaters of Bonneville Dam covered these by the end of the 1930s. Around the old spot where the locks operated, a **historical museum** (May–Sept noon–5pm; free) gives details on the perils of navigating this stretch of the river, along with assorted pioneer and native relics. You can also **stay** in Cascade Locks in a few chain motels, though you're better off pushing on to Hood River or camping in one of the nearby state parks. While visiting, keep in mind that the little town around the locks narrowly escaped devastation in the summer of 2003, when firefighters thwarted a fast-moving wildfire in the gorge at the last minute, but not before it had burned to the ground a bed-and-breakfast in its way.

Toward the west end of town, a toll bridge marks the fabled site of the Native Americans' **BRIDGE OF THE GODS**. Legend has it that a natural stone bridge once crossed the water here, but the sons of the Great Spirit, who had been sent to earth as snow mountains, quarreled and belched out so much fire, ash, and stone that the sun was hidden and the bridge was destroyed. There's some truth in the story: about a thousand years ago, a gigantic landslide blocked the river here, creating an inland sea that eventually tunneled through the barrier, leaving a natural stone bridge suspended above. Although you'll see no trace of any such span today, you can't miss the colossal 1925 **steel bridge** named after the native legend, which crosses over to Washington south of the town of Stevenson, and itself had to be hoisted by forty feet in the 1930s to avoid being drenched by the backed-up waters formed by Bonneville Dam.

Further east along I-84, there are some good, if minor, state parks on the way to Hood River, with an assortment of agreeable hiking trails and a few campgrounds. Most, however, are secondary attractions compared to those arrayed to the west around the Historic Columbia Gorge Highway, which is here crumbling and mostly inaccessible south of the freeway, though you can spot a few enticing, off-limits features of the old roadway at certain spots. The highlight is a grand rock outcropping, before mile 58 on I-84, where the historic road once wended along a steep hillside through the **Mitchell Point Tunnel**, whose five "windows" gave passing motorists tremendous views of the gorge. Unfortunately, the tunnel was deemed structurally unworthy of car traffic in the 1950s and destroyed a decade later. While you can't miss the tower of basalt rising from the south side of the freeway, you'll sadly have to imagine the rest of this once-picturesque scene.

Hood River

Just five miles east of Mitchell Point, the charming town of **HOOD RIVER** (I-84, Exit 63) is one of the most popular **mountain biking** and **windsurfing** centers in the Pacific Northwest. Windsurfers are especially drawn by an unusual but relatively reliable phenomenon: in summertime the heat of the eastern steppes draws cooler air in from the west at a rate too great to be smoothly absorbed within the narrows of the Columbia Gorge. By around noon, the pressure has built up to such an extent that it has to be released – in great gusts of air that rip along the gorge, with the windsurfers ready and waiting to "catch the blow." Since they appeared on the scene in the early 1980s, the windsurfers have effectively reinvented Hood River, turning what was once a workaday agricultural burg into a quaint hillside community complete with laid-back cafés and restaurants and all manner of outdoor-sports equipment stores.

Arrival and information

Long-distance Greyhound **buses** from Portland in the west and points east pull in at 600 E Marina Way (Ⓣ541/386-1212, Ⓦwww.greyhound.com), in Port Marina Park, near I-84's Exit 64. From here, it's a five- to ten-minute walk southwest to the town center, on the other side of the interstate. There are no Amtrak trains. The **visitor center** (Ⓣ541/386-2000 or 1-800/366-3530, Ⓦwww.hoodriver.org) is located down by the river off I-84 (Exit 63), a good ten-minute walk from the town center. The visitor center has free maps, accommodation listings, and details of recommended sports outfitters. Some of these include **bike rental** companies like Discover Bicycles, 205 Oak St (Ⓣ541/386-4820, Ⓦwww.discoverbicycles.com), which has a good selection of mountain bikes and recommends cycling trails; you can rent **windsurfers**

($35 per half-day) from the well-established Rhonda Smith Windsurfing Center, 100 Port Marina Way (daily mid-May to early Sept; T541/386-9463 or 1-800/241-2430, Wwww.hoodriverwaterplay.com), which also provides lessons and even rents out kites and kayaks.

Accommodation

The town has a reasonable supply of motels, hotels, and B&Bs, but finding a **place to stay** can still get a little difficult in the summer, when advance reservations are advised and prices jump by about $20 per night. A handful of medium-priced **B&Bs** sit west of the town center, while sitting a few blocks south is the *Inn at the Gorge*, 1113 Eugene St (T541/386-4429, Wwww.innatthegorge.com; ④), a stately 1908 Colonial Revival home that has been transformed into a tasteful, elegant B&B with minimal Victorian kitsch. Rooms and suites are well decorated, and the house features a wraparound veranda and pleasant rear terrace. Also centrally located, *Love's Riverview Lodge*, 1505 Oak St (T541/386-8719 or 1-800/789-9568, Wwww.riverviewforyou.com; ③) is a basic but clean motel within walking distance of the center. The *Columbia Gorge Hotel*, 4000 Westcliff Drive, a mile west of town, at Exit 62 on I-84 (T541/386-5566 or 1-800/345-1921, Wwww.columbiagorgehotel.com; ⑧), is perched on a clifftop right above the gorge. Created for the lumber king Simon Benson in 1921, the hotel's exquisite gardens even have their own waterfalls, and the rooms are lavish and relaxing. The Sunday tea service ($22 per person) is a pricey, but savory, indulgence. Less expensive hotel accommodation can be found at *Hood River Hotel*, 102 Oak St (T541/386-1900 or 1-800/386-1859, Wwww.hoodriverhotel.com; ④). Built in 1913 and featuring a serviceable Italian restaurant, this pleasantly renovated establishment offers simple, tasteful rooms to more elaborate suites with river views.

The Town

The small-scale and period architecture of Hood River, combined with its leisure pursuits and homegrown industries (gourmet jellies, beeswax candles) almost give it the feel of a **boutique town** – a place where serious business is conducted somewhere else, and the prominent attractions are geared primarily to the tourist trade. Even the setting itself – perched quaintly on a hillside above a gorge landscape of undeniable beauty – makes it seem like no one here does anything but shop for kites, eat bistro food, drink microbrews, and go windsurfing. This impression is, of course, something of a put-on, but few small towns in Oregon have such a relaxed, engaging atmosphere, despite the relative paucity of conventional attractions.

Port Marina Park

The first stop is obvious: **Port Marina Park**, immediately north of I-84 at Exit 64, the main windsurfers' hot spot, which sits amid a wide landscape of sweeping riverside scenery and stark, rocky vistas – the whole of it enlivened by strong gorge winds and dappled sunlight in the summer. Take a seat on the sloping grass or the gravelly shore, with a fleet of brightly colored watercraft lying around you, and watch the seasoned windsurfers go through their paces, managing the whitecapped currents, finessing the gales, and dodging novices who can barely stay upright. Other than the visitor center (see above), there's little else to do here and hardly anything in the way of food or facilities, but the park nonetheless offers a good introduction to the town – and a ready explanation for its rising popularity.

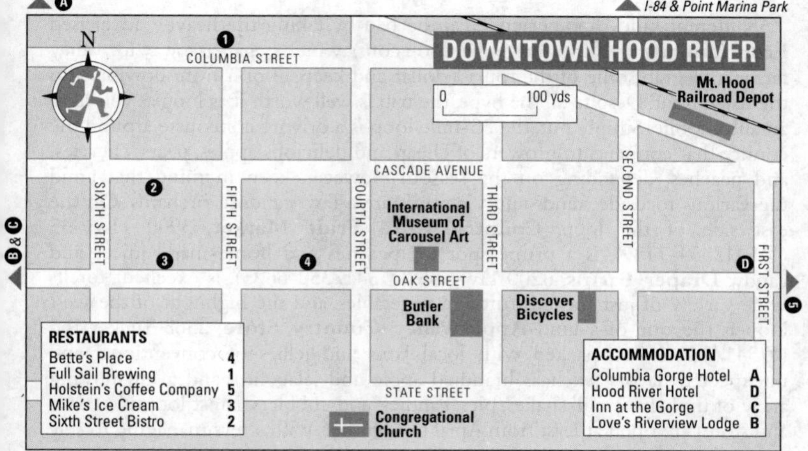

Downtown

From the park, make your way back over the freeway to ascend the slope on which **downtown** sits. Arrayed from First to Sixth streets, there are in theory three main drags in town – Cascade Avenue and Oak and State streets – though you can easily see most of the historic highlights with a simple stroll on Oak. From First Street, climb the hill past some of Hood River's more stately architectural gems, passing grand hotels such as the *Hood River* (see opposite) and various eateries along the way. The old **Butler Bank**, Third and Oak streets, is worth a look for its spartan design and Egyptian Revival columns, while a two blocks away at Fifth and State, the former **Congregational Church** is a massive 1912 stone pile that dominates the streets below it. Just about every other building in this stretch has one or another historic aspect to it, which you can read about on the copious plaques attached to the structures. Beyond the architecture itself, it's hard to say that there are any truly essential sights downtown, amid all the diners, windsurfer dealers, and antique stores. One exception may be the incongruous **International Museum of Carousel Art**, across from the bank (daily 11am–3pm; $5), basically an excuse to display around 150 quaint old carousel horses from old-time carnivals – a visual treat for fans of the ornamental wooden creatures.

The Mount Hood Railroad and the Fruit Loop

Between downtown and the I-84 freeway, hop on the charming **Mount Hood Railroad** (Ⓣ541/386-3556 or 1-800/872-4661, Ⓦwww.mthoodrr.com), for a twenty-mile sightseeing trip down along the Hood River Valley south of town. The railroad was originally built in 1906 to service the valley's agricultural communities, but today the four-hour-and-fifteen-minute ride is just a tourist junket – the antique blue-and-red trains, with their dining cars and old-fashioned appointments, are the obvious highlight. Trains depart from the old railway station at 110 Railroad Ave, just off Second Street (April–Dec 2–6 weekly; $23; departures at 10am and/or 3pm). The railroad also offers alternate trips throughout the year on the same route, focusing on brunch ($57), dinner ($70), or holiday ($76) excursions, or special "murder mystery" trains ($80) – basically dinner theater on rails.

A different kind of experience can be had by taking the heavily advertised **Fruit Loop** (Ⓦwww.hoodriverfruitloop.com), which began as a way for valley farmers to grab some of the tourist dollar and keep all of it from flowing into the town itself. Despite all the hype, the trip is well worth it as long as you have an automobile. Simply put, the 35-mile loop is a driving concourse around the county that connects to growers of cheap and delicious apples, pears, cherries, and peaches, depending on the season. However, keep in mind that amid the various roadside stands and vineyards are a few standout orchards. On the east side of the loop, **Country Faire Fruit Market**, 3900 Hwy-35 (Ⓣ541/354-1189), is a prime spot for peaches and home-made juices and candy; **Draper Farms**, 6200 Hwy-35 (Ⓣ541/352-6625), is excellent for its wide variety of just-picked fruit and vegetables; and the highlight of the west loop is the one-of-a-kind **Apple Valley Country Store**, 2363 Tucker Rd (Ⓣ541/386-1971), packed with local jams and jellies of conventional and unexpected flavors (such as brandied apple and jalapeño), and a gut-busting array of fresh-fruit milkshakes, pies, candies, and cobblers. Most loopside farms and stores are open at least from April to October, with a few managing to stay open all year round.

Eating and drinking

Good places to **eat** downtown include the easygoing and popular *Holstein's Coffee Company*, 12 Oak St (Ⓣ541/386-4115), which serves up tasty light meals, great coffees, and sandwiches, and the more traditional burgers and soups of *Bette's Place*, at the Oak Mall, 416 Oak St (Ⓣ541/386-1880). Alternatively, the *Sixth Street Bistro & Loft*, at Cascade Avenue (Ⓣ541/386-5737), has microbrews, seafood, and pasta at affordable prices. The busiest **bar** in town is the *Full Sail Brewing Company*, 506 Columbia St (Ⓣ541/386-2281), a fine microbrewery that also offers limited free tours of its facility. To cool down, *Mike's Ice Cream*, 504 Oak St (Ⓣ541/386-6260), sells a great range of ice creams, highlighted by its legendary huckleberry milkshakes.

Moving on from Hood River

Along with being a pleasant and attractive little place, Hood River is also something of a **crossroads** for the Columbia Gorge. Although most of the scenic riverside attractions lie to the west along the Historic Columbia River Highway (see above, p.123), there are many worthwhile sights in the other directions. To the **south**, and unmistakable as it looms over the Hood River Valley, **Mount Hood** is a top-notch spot for skiing, hiking, and hanging out in mountainside lodges; to the **east**, the remaining section of the historic highway is now a striking **scenic trail**, while The Dalles is altogether bigger and blander than Hood River; and to the **north**, the attractions on the Washington side of the gorge are fewer and farther between, though the **Maryhill Museum of Art** has considerable appeal, and Mount Adams (see p.404), due north of Hood River, is another excellent spot for outdoor activities.

Mount Hood and around

From Hood River, Hwy-35 heads south towards the snowcapped monolith of **MOUNT HOOD**. At 11,235ft, the peak is the tallest of the Oregon Cascades; while it's about three thousand feet shorter than Washington's biggest, Mount

Rainier (see p.396), it dominates the surrounding landscape just as much. The road begins by running through the Hood River Valley (the eastern side of the Fruit Loop; see above), before climbing to skirt the mountain's heavily forested southern flank. Eventually, after about forty miles, the road reaches its highest point, **Barlow Pass**.

Beyond Barlow Pass, Hwy-35 meets Hwy-26, which leads either west to Portland (where it becomes SE Powell Boulevard) or southeast to Madras and Bend (see p.220). Note, however, that the section of US-26 just south of the mountain is one of the state's most dangerous stretches, where blinding late-afternoon sunshine causes several fatal wrecks every year. It's about a mile from the crossroads to the signposted, six-mile-long turnoff that weaves up the mountainside to **Timberline Lodge** (Ⓣ503/272-3311 or 1-800/547-1406, Ⓦwww.timberlinelodge.com; ❺), rightfully one of Oregon's most celebrated hotels. Constructed in the 1930s as part of a New Deal job-creation program, the hotel is a grand and handsome affair, solidly built in rough-hewn stone and timber with an interior loaded with Arts and Crafts-style wooden furniture and antique fittings. Note the main staircase, which is decorated with finely carved animals, the rooms with wooden bedframes and paneled walls, and the expansive atrium with wooden galleries and a huge, stone fireplace. Appealing though all this may be, the hotel is much too popular for its own good, and the assembled hordes rob it of much atmosphere. Most people know the lodge as the exterior location for Stanley Kubrick's *The Shining* – through the film's interiors were shot in a British soundstage and the grounds, unfortunately, lack that movie's fiendish hedge maze.

At 6000 feet, *Timberline* is also at the center of a busy, year-round **ski resort** (Ⓣ503/219-3192; lift tickets $39) – one of three (and undoubtedly the best) on the mountain – with six chair lifts and 35 runs to suit all abilities, though the majority are aimed at experienced skiers and snowboarders. The highest chair lift, **Palmer**, climbs to 8540ft, with an average snowfall of 350 inches per year. The adjacent, ugly Wy'east Day Lodge is the place to **rent ski equipment** (skis, boots, and poles $22 per day; snowboards and boots $33) and learn how to ski (Ⓣ503/231-5402). Along with Timberline, two other downhill ski areas – Mount Hood Meadows (Ⓦwww.skihood.com; $44) and Mount Hood SkiBowl (Ⓦwww.skibowl.com; $39) – offer nighttime **skiing** from November

The Barlow Road

Since the Columbia River Gorge was impassable by wagon, when the early pioneers reached The Dalles, they were forced to change means of transport, which meant floating precariously down the river on rafts. Knowing how much the pioneers dreaded battling the turbulent waters, **Samuel Barlow**, a wagon-train leader who managed to blaze a new final leg to the Oregon Trail, led a party off to forge a second route around the south side of Mount Hood in 1845. Unfortunately, they were trapped by snow while chopping their way through the thick forests and had to leave their wagons behind in the struggle to reach the Willamette Valley, for fear that they would otherwise starve or freeze to death. Barlow returned a year later, however, and this time he completed the **Barlow Road** (the upper reaches of which are still followed by highways 35 and 26). Not surprisingly, many migrants chose to brave its steep ridges – where wagons frequently skidded out of control and had to be lowered by ropes in places – rather than face the wrathful Columbia. To the irritation of many pioneers, Barlow grew rich on his endeavors, charging them a crunching $5-per-wagon fee to use his road, while his partner completed the rip-off at the end of the trail by opening the one and only general store in the area.

to April (around $20). There are also many miles of cross-country skiing trails and summer hiking trails throughout the **Mount Hood National Forest**. For more information on mountain activities, contact the Mount Hood Information Center (Ⓣ503/622-4822 or 1-888-622-4822, Ⓦwww.mthood.info). To check **snow conditions**, call Ⓣ503/222-2211 or 1-877/754-6734; also check if tire-chains are required for the last leg of the journey up to the lodge – they are often necessary until well into summer.

Finally, if you're up for **climbing** the mountain, check the Information Center, which can put you in touch with outfitters, guides, and other essentials for ascending to the summit. Keep in mind, though, that despite its popularity, climbing the mountain is not for novices, and you can expect to face numerous hazards including sudden blizzards and whiteouts, deep and hard-to-spot ravines, and the looming threat of avalanches. Every year at least one climbing party gets trapped on the mountain and has to be airlifted out, or sometimes even faces the death or disappearance of some of its members.

The eastern gorge

Heading east from Hood River along I-84, you begin to enter the strikingly different terrain of the **eastern gorge** – instead of verdant forests and mossy glades, there are bare cliffs and rocky shelves; instead of damp forest trails home to countless wildflowers and native plants, it's mostly dusty scrubland and parched earth; and instead of beautiful vistas clouded with mist and fog, there are bleak Wild West horizons on the edge of the unforgiving desert. Still, if you prefer the arid landscape of eastern Oregon there's much to be said for the area, although in few other places is the landscape devastated by the Bretz Floods quite so desolate or wind-blasted. Even the gorge itself less resembles a deep emerald ravine than it does a gaping brown chasm.

The Twin Tunnels

Despite the rather bleak landscape, the eastern gorge can be quite evocative in places, and nowhere more so than along the hiking route of the **TWIN TUNNELS** between Hood River and the small burg of Mosier. This five-mile, pedestrianized route is actually the course of the old **Historic Columbia Gorge Highway** (see p.129), which, east of Cascade Locks, only exists in fragments. Here it's a well-preserved delight, a restored stretch of roadway that state engineers labored over for many years. The centerpiece is, of course, the pair of classic old tunnels on the eastern approach to the trail, which were finished around 1919 but had to be closed decades later because of falling rocks. After that they were summarily filled in and practically ruined until the state undertook the laborious process of unsealing them, reinforcing their failing structure, and opening them once more to traffic – this time strictly limited to walkers and cyclists.

To access the route you can either approach from the west at the **Hatfield Trailhead**, where Hwy-30 ends motorized access east of Hwy-35, or from the east at **Rock Creek Road** in Mosier, Exit 69 off I-84. The day-use **fee** is $3 (information at Ⓣ1-800/551-6949), and unless someone's willing to pick you up, you'll have to make a ten-mile round-trip if you want to see the whole route. Still, for those with the stamina, it's a great hike, full of stunning vistas of the arid gorge, towering basalt monoliths, and the historic highway's restored fixtures and passages. Inside the narrow, somewhat eerie tunnels themselves, it's hard to imagine how mid-twentieth-century traffic could have ever fit through; decades before this, drivers could even become snowbound within the dark chambers if the weather suddenly turned bad – which explains the stray pieces of graffiti here and there on the walls, some of which date back to the 1920s.

The Dalles

Thirteen miles east of Mosier on I-84 is the other prominent site in the eastern gorge, the ugly industrial township of **THE DALLES**, an old military outpost and halting point on the Oregon Trail. It was here that many of the pioneers transferred to rafts and bateaux for the perilous journey down the last stretch of the Columbia River. Before then, this spot had been a meeting place for French-speaking Canadian trappers, who named it after the basaltic rocks that lined this stretch of the river, looking – so they thought – like flagstones (*les dalles*). Just a mile or two upstream, but now flooded by **The Dalles Dam**, the Columbia once tumbled over a series of rocky shelves called **Celilo Falls**, long used by Native Americans as fishing grounds and the source of much folklore – "the great fishing place of the Columbia" echoed Washington Irving. The dam was completed in 1957, in typical disregard of native traditions, and the waters drowned what could have been a compelling attraction in a more environmentally conscious age. As it is, though, the dam is a bland mechanical facility (much less inviting than Bonneville Dam), and the town is resolutely unenticing – not even remotely as interesting as Hood River. That said, there are some classic old buildings in town dating from the late nineteenth century, but to reach them you'll have to trudge by a slew of chain motels, thrift stores, supermarkets, and gas stations. Perhaps more than any other place in Oregon, The Dalles has completely failed to capitalize on the striking scenery surrounding it.

The one sight in the vicinity that is worth seeing, though, is the **Columbia Gorge Discovery Center** (daily 10am–6pm; $6.50; ⓦ www.gorgediscovery.org), on the riverbank at the western edge of The Dalles, at 5000 Discovery Drive (Exit 82 on I-84). If you're interested in a broad but informative overview of the history of the region – from ancient lava flows and Ice Age floods to nineteenth-century explorers to more contemporary pursuits like hydroelectricity and windsurfing – this is a fine place to start, with antique relics from early state history, assorted rocks and geologic specimens, and various dioramas and walk-through exhibits. One of these, a small-town street from over a century ago, is a bit on the romantic side, but nonetheless more enticing than the dour modern cityscape beyond the museum.

Beyond The Dalles I-84 leaves the official Columbia Gorge National Scenic Area and continues on into the desert heart of eastern Oregon, while heading south US-97 skirts the eastern side of the Oregon Cascades on the way down to Madras and Bend (see p.220). North on 197, you cross over into Washington and toward the more isolated, but still worthwhile, sites on that side of the gorge.

The Washington side of the gorge

Traditionally, the **Washington side** of the Columbia River Gorge is less visited by travelers, viewed as altogether starker and less interesting than the Oregon side and its many attractions. This is understandable to a large degree

– Washington Highway 14, the main riverside route, has nothing on the Historic Columbia River Highway – but there are a handful of sights that merit a stop (reviewed here from east to west). However, the most interesting – the Maryhill Museum of Art – lies another twenty miles east of the bridge from the Oregon side, out in the middle of bleak and remote nowhere.

Maryhill Museum of Art

In an austere region where the trees thin out and fade away to be replaced by barren gulches and sagebrush plateaus, sits the extraordinary **MARYHILL MUSEUM OF ART** (mid-March to mid-Nov daily 9am–5pm; $7; ⓦwww.maryhillmuseum.org), the singular creation of idiosyncratic tycoon **Samuel Hill**, who was born into a Quaker family in North Carolina in 1857. Nothing if not ambitious, Hill moved to Seattle in the early 1900s and married the daughter of a railroad owner before skillfully amassing a fortune by manipulating the stock market. With money matters out of the way, he threw himself into all manner of projects – some, like his championing of road construction, eminently sensible, others downright nutty.

In the latter category came his plan for "Maryhill" – named after his wife and daughter – which he declared a "Garden of Eden" and where in 1907 he planned to establish a Quaker farmers' colony. But the Quakers he brought over took one look at the parched slopes of the Columbia Gorge and opted out, so he concentrated on the house instead, building a three-story, concrete-and-steel extravagance in a vaguely penitentiary style. Not content with this, Hill turned to his trusty concrete again and built a miniature copy of **Stonehenge** (daily 7am–10pm; free) on a hill overlooking the Columbia, four miles upstream from his mansion. In its "unruined," idealized form, it's a pacifist's tribute to those who died in World War I, for Hill believed Stonehenge to be a sacrificial site, its faithful reproduction appropriate as "humanity is still being sacrificed to the god of war."

Despite Hill's best endeavors, however, no one, and least of all his family, showed the slightest interest in living at Maryhill and the house stood neglected for years. Then in the 1920s – in another strange twist – two of Hill's European chums, **Queen Marie of Romania** and the well-connected Folies-Bergere dancer and Auguste Rodin model **Loie Fuller**, saved the whole enterprise. First, they persuaded Hill to turn the house into an art museum and then helped by donating a generous sample of fine and applied art. Their gifts remain the kernel of the collection, which is displayed over the mansion's three floors. On the entry level are the assorted baubles and trinkets given by Queen Marie, including a small but delightful collection of Russian icons, Marie's Fabergé coronation crown, and an imposing corner throne carved in Byzantine style in 1908. Also on this floor, the **Theatre de la Mode**, presents a small selection of 1940s French wire-frame mannequins clothed by some of the leading fashion houses of the day. There was a desperate shortage of fabric in postwar Europe and these miniatures were an ingenious way around the problem of how to advertise new designs. Downstairs, there's a fine sample of the sculptures of **Rodin**, the gift of Fuller, and a bizarre collection of **chess sets** – including a Nixon vs McGovern edition. There's also a Native American gallery, at its best in the sections devoted to the bands of the Columbia River Valley and its environs – with everything from small totemic figures and arrow straighteners through to petroglyphs and pile drivers. The museum's only real downside is its spotty collection of European artworks and a rather kitschy array of American "classical realism" pieces – apparently meaning garishly painted saints, grotesque crucifixions, and the like. There's a **café** on this floor, too (10am–4pm), while the uppermost floor is largely given over to temporary exhibitions.

Along Washington Highway 14

WASHINGTON HIGHWAY 14, which loosely parallels I-84 on the north side of the Columbia, is a slower route than the freeway, but about as scenic. Driving from the east back toward Vancouver, Washington, there are quite a few rocky buttes, pleasant parks, and arduous hikes along the way (see ⓦwww.parks.wa.gov for more information), though if you have limited time, it's better spent on the Oregon side of the river. Still, if headed this way, or if you've just returned from the Maryhill Museum, it's worth stopping at **Horsethief Lake**, off Hwy-14 a few miles east of the US-197 junction. As a 90-acre body of freshwater, the lake was created during the backfill of The Dalles Dam; it's serviceable enough for day use and has agreeable basaltic scenery and first-come-first-served **camping** ($15–21), but it's mostly notable as the site for preserved native **petroglyphs**. These mysterious-looking designs, from jagged and angular icons to more rounded, anthropomorphic forms, were created many centuries ago, and are strange and compelling even if you know little about the subject. Tours run seasonally and must be reserved well in advance (April–Oct Fri & Sat 10am; free; ⓣ509/767-1159). Further west, Highway 14 plows through long reaches of parched gorge landscapes and past rugged cliffs and lava towers, skirting the little towns of **Bingen** and **White Salmon** and offering northbound access to Mount Adams (see p.404) on Highway 141. Throughout this dry, seemingly inhospitable terrain, the Washington side of the gorge has a handful of decent **wineries** that, while not quite on the level with those further north around Yakima (see p.393), nonetheless are beginning to make a name for themselves. Contact the **Klickitat Wine Alliance** (ⓣ1-800/785-1718, ⓦwww.gorgewine.org) for details on locations, tastings, and tours.

Twenty miles west of White Salmon, century-old **Carson Hot Springs**, 372 St Martin Rd (ⓣ1-800/607-3678), a small-time resort that operates a basic hotel (❸), golf course, and a few bubbling tubs ($12 a dip), is a favorite destination of mineral bathers. Beyond this, the next ten miles west on Hwy-14 offer an up-close view of the **landslide** that inundated this part of the Columbia River a thousand years ago, shifting the river's course and creating the short-lived, stone Bridge of the Gods (see p.128), replaced in the modern era with a steel version that crosses from south of Stevenson over to Cascade Locks. In Stevenson itself, true gorge enthusiasts can check out the **Columbia Gorge Interpretive Center**, 990 SW Rock Creek Drive (daily 10am–5pm; $6; ⓦwww.columbiagorge.org), which isn't quite as involved or as interesting as its counterpart in The Dalles, though it does sport a number of mildly diverting antiques and relics, including an old sawmill's steam engine, Native American fishing gear and more modern "fishwheels" for harvesting salmon, and assorted photographs and artifacts from human and geologic history. Around the site the largest peak is the 600-ft **Table Mountain**, north of Hwy-14 and Bonneville Dam, whose spikier higher levels feature basaltic columns of the region's lava flows from fifteen million years ago. Nowadays the blockier terrain around the mountain – the accumulated debris of that colossal landslide – can make hiking a bit of a challenge, but the views can be quite striking with their eye-opening mix of thick forest, sheer cliff walls, and rocky spires.

A few miles to the west is the last major sight worth seeking out on the Washington side of the gorge, the 900ft-tall monolith of **Beacon Rock**, sitting in its own state park (☎509/427-8265) just off the highway, which was once a simple tall plug of volcanic rock surrounded by looser sedimentary soils. These were, of course, summarily wiped out when the Bretz Floods charged through the river, and only this oddly shaped haystack of basalt remains. On a mile-long trail full of catwalks and switchbacks, you can hike up to the summit of the rock and peer down at fine views of the river and the gorge. If sufficiently inspired, you can even **camp** here (first-come-first-served; $15–21) – though note that the rock is only about a half-hour drive from Vancouver, Washington, and can be a popular retreat for horseback-riders and mountain cyclists during the summer months.

Finally, when making your way back to Vancouver or Portland, less than five miles to the west Highway 14 curves towards the south and then takes a sharp bend back to the west along the promontory of **Cape Horn**. Appropriately named after that hazardous South American point, this cape is one of the best places to catch a fleeting view of the gorge in all its glory – and also one of the most perilous, with oncoming traffic and narrow shoulders as sightseeing hazards and gales infamous for pounding the hillsides at more than 110mph during windstorms.

3

The Oregon Coast

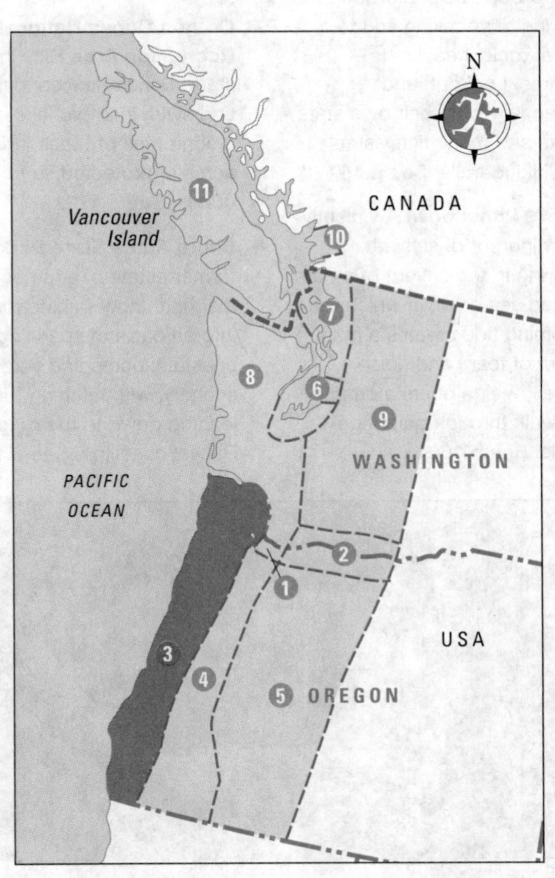

CHAPTER 3

Highlights

* **Astoria Column** Look out over the stunning vastness of the Columbia River as it merges with the Pacific Ocean from this towering pillar painted with a winding mural of pioneer history. See p.147

* **Three Capes Scenic Loop** A striking drive taking you to a trio of rocky headlands – Meares, Lookout, and Kiwanda – with their own state parks and many fine vistas and hiking trails. See p.157

* **Devil's Punchbowl** A violently churning pot of saltwater brewing in the cavern of a collapsed sea cave, in which the incoming tide creates a maelstrom of foam and noise – while low tide offers a charming walk through quiet tidepools. See p.160

* **Cape Perpetua** One of the more colossal promontories on the coast, a great mound of rock and forest you can hike up on the challenging St Perpetua Trail, full of switchbacks and excellent views of distant ocean shores. See p.166

* **Oregon Dunes National Recreation Area** Hike in stark, Sahara-like conditions and swim in idyllic lakes among tens of thousands of acres of protected sand dunes. See p.170

* **Shore Acres State Park** A former estate of a lumber magnate, now transformed into an oasis of sparkling coastal blooms and verdant scenery, with fetching trails leading down to the rugged Pacific coastline. See p.172

△ Pistol River State Park

3

The Oregon Coast

A ninety-minute drive west from Portland and the Willamette Valley, the **OREGON COAST** is a magnificent, 350-mile stretch of undeveloped beaches and parks, scenic hills and forests, and rugged coves and cliffs. Amid this sparkling terrain are also more unexpected sights like craggy headlands jutting out at strange angles, Sahara-like sand dunes, and mysterious-looking sea stacks. On a sunny day the trip along the coast is wonderfully exhilarating, though some claim stormy days are even better. This superb scenery is often best appreciated from the string of state parks – and their campgrounds – that have been preserved in what amounts to a linear oceanside parkway covering the length of the state. However, several of the coast's towns are appealing too, including the diverse charms of **Newport**, the grand old mansions of **Astoria**, and the subtle beauty of **Bandon**. Each of these makes for a lovely one- or two-night stay, and most towns along the shoreline have evaded the crass development that has engulfed small sections here and there, the worst examples being at **Lincoln City** and **Seaside**. Overall, the **North Coast** is a bit more commercialized and much more tourist-oriented than the **South Coast**, which is best known for its largely unspoiled views and remote, evocative landscapes.

The coast's high degree of protection results largely from the pioneering work of citizen-activists over the decades like **William Tugman** and **Samuel Boardman** (both of whom have excellent parks named after them; see p.172 and p.178), and the conservationist governor **Oswald West**, who was only in office for four short years in the 1910s but managed to politically engineer much of this preservation. As a prime example of that long-forgotten breed of environmentalist Republicans, West's name and reputation are enshrined in several places around the state, but particularly at the state park named after him (see p.154) – appropriately, and intentionally, a rugged stretch of coastal hills and lowlands with few facilities.

The North Coast

While the Oregon coast is as beautiful as any stretch of American coastline, for much of the year California's sun lures the tan-seeking hordes, leaving Oregonians and their visitors to wander the elongated shoreline with barely a

Exploring the Oregon Coast

If you're looking for the best way to explore the coast, the main route of **Highway 101** is the obvious means – a winding roadway that closely follows the contours of the seaboard and takes you past many eye-opening vistas, including clifftop perches, deep ravines, and expansive tidal flats. The road was completed in the 1930s under a Work Projects Administration program orchestrated by inventive engineer **Conde McCullough**, who was responsible for the string of beautifully designed **bridges** that remain a highlight of the coastal drive.

If you're planning to travel by **bus**, one of Greyhound's (ⓣ1-800/229-9424, ⓦwww.greyound.com) Portland–San Francisco services is routed along the coast between Lincoln City and Brookings. Don't expect Greyhound to drop you in the middle of town – you're just as likely to be left beside the main road, a long haul from the center. North of Lincoln City, you're dependent on intermittent local buses, the most significant of which is the **Sunset Empire** service ($1–2; ⓣ503/325-0563, ⓦwww.ridethebus.org), linking Astoria, Cannon Beach, and Seaside.

The popular **Oregon Coast Bike Route** follows, for the most part, reasonably wide, cyclist-only shoulder lanes (about 3ft wide) on either side of the highway, though small sections do travel quiet country roads. You have to be fairly fit to manage the hills, and the occasional logging truck may put the wind up you, but for the most part it's a delightful and comparatively straightforward bike ride that takes six to eight days to complete. It's best attempted between May and October when the prevailing winds pretty much dictate a north–south itinerary. Oregon Tourism produces a detailed brochure (ⓣ1-800/547-7842, ⓦwww.traveloregon.com) on the route.

Most **hikers** are more than satisfied with the hundreds of walking trails that criss-cross the coast's forests and wilderness areas – anything from short afternoon strolls to full-scale expeditions. One such long-distance hiking route, the **Oregon Coast Trail**, weaves through some of Oregon's finest coastal landscapes and is aimed at outdoor adventurers. Information is available from Oregon State Parks, 1115 Commercial St NE, Salem, OR 97301-1002 (ⓣ503/378-4168, ⓦwww.oregonstateparks.com).

crowd in sight. Nonetheless, when summer comes tourists arrive en masse, and the prime destination for many is the **North Coast**, roughly from Astoria to Heceta Head, which is home to the more developed towns and the coast's handful of tourist traps. Once outside such places, extensive and sometimes isolated beaches offer many free activities throughout the year, ranging from beach-combing to shell-fishing, whale watching or, in winter, stormwatching – but rarely swimming: the currents are too strong and dangerous and floating logs too common a hazard to make this practicable. That said, some adventurers do surf amid the potential hazards, but you'll need a wetsuit at a minimum and may not be able to stand the icy currents even then.

Despite its scenic splendor and many legal protections, the North Coast has not escaped commercialism and sports a series of conspicuous resorts for golf, tennis, and the like. Luckily, most of these are not garish, high-rise atrocities that litter Southern California, so the broad sweep of oceanside beauty remains inviolate. From the northern edge of the Oregon Coast and heading south, the first prominent town is **Astoria**, a stately old industrial burg trying to reinvent itself as a boutique community, located a few miles inland near the mouth of the Columbia River. Starting south on **Highway 101**, the touristy confines of **Cannon Beach** and **Seaside** are often the first, though rarely the best, choices for coastal visitors, while places like **Manzanita** and **Tillamook** are known for vacationing urbanites in rented condos and tourable cheese companies,

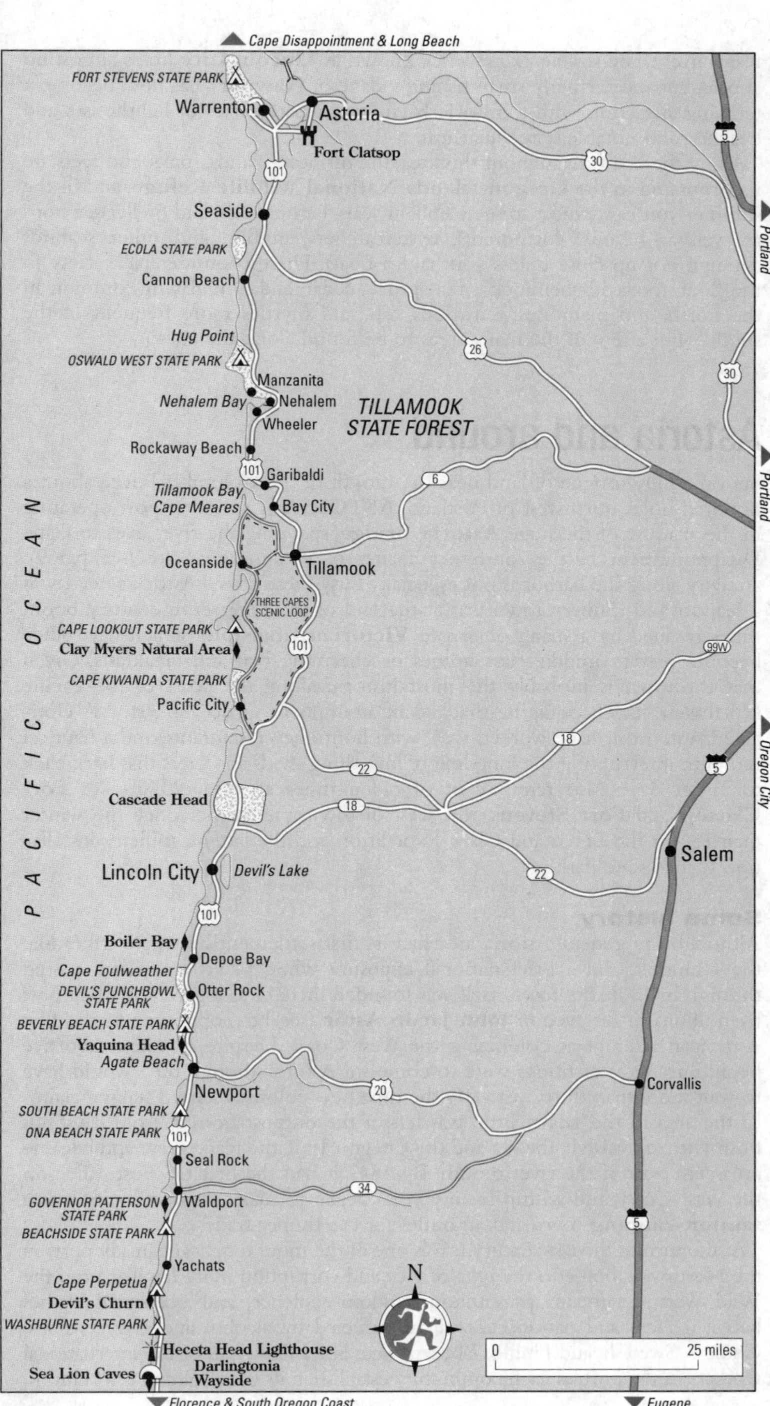
Cape Disappointment & Long Beach
FORT STEVENS STATE PARK
Warrenton
Astoria
Fort Clatsop
101
30
5
Seaside
Portland
ECOLA STATE PARK
Cannon Beach
Hug Point
OSWALD WEST STATE PARK
26
30
Manzanita
Nehalem Bay
Nehalem
Wheeler
TILLAMOOK STATE FOREST
Rockaway Beach
Portland
101
Garibaldi
Tillamook Bay
Cape Meares
6
Bay City
Oceanside
Tillamook
THREE CAPES SCENIC LOOP
CAPE LOOKOUT STATE PARK
Clay Myers Natural Area
101
99W
CAPE KIWANDA STATE PARK
Pacific City
PACIFIC OCEAN
Oregon City
18
5
22
Cascade Head
18
Salem
Lincoln City
Devil's Lake
22
101
Boiler Bay
Depoe Bay
Cape Foulweather
DEVIL'S PUNCHBOWL STATE PARK
Otter Rock
BEVERLY BEACH STATE PARK
Yaquina Head
Agate Beach
Newport
20
Corvallis
SOUTH BEACH STATE PARK
ONA BEACH STATE PARK
101
Seal Rock
34
GOVERNOR PATTERSON STATE PARK
Waldport
5
BEACHSIDE STATE PARK
Yachats
N
Cape Perpetua
Devil's Churn
WASHBURNE STATE PARK
0
25 miles
Heceta Head Lighthouse
Darlingtonia Wayside
Sea Lion Caves
Florence & South Oregon Coast
Eugene

respectively. The sizable excrescence known as **Lincoln City** holds almost no appeal, but the formerly small fishing village of **Newport** has now become a fetching attraction with a historic bayfront, pleasant series of lighthouses and beaches, and notable state aquarium.

Along the coast throughout this area, the offshore islands, rocks, and reefs are incorporated in the **Oregon Islands National Wildlife Refuge**, and in the summer you can expect to see elephant seals, harbor seals, and Steller sea lions as well as herons, cormorants, oystercatchers, puffins, and other seabirds (though not up close unless you have a boat). There's considerable variety in the flora, too, with hemlock, sitka spruce, cedar, and Douglas fir common in the north, and madrones, redwoods, ash, and myrtles more frequent in the south – but a few of the many trees to be found along the coast.

Astoria and around

Set on a hilly tongue of land near the mouth of the Columbia River, about a hundred miles northwest of Portland, **ASTORIA** is a modest port operating in the shadow of the huge **Astoria Bridge**, spanning the river over to Cape Disappointment in the southwest corner of Washington State (see p.369). Activity along the harbor is not especially busy these days – Astoria's heyday as a seaport and cannery town was at the end of the nineteenth century, boom times recalled by a string of ornate **Victorian mansions** which have since become private middle-class homes or charming bed-and-breakfasts. Given that the town is probably the most historic along the coast of the Pacific Northwest, it's encouraging that recent attempts to spruce up Astoria's elongated waterfront have worked well, with boutiques, restaurants, and a nautical museum interrupting the long line of low-slung sheds and piers that hark back to busier days. Also reminiscent of olden times are the old sites of **Fort Clatsop** and **Fort Stevens**, just west of town, the former once the winter quarters for the Lewis and Clark Expedition and the latter a military installation turned state park.

Some history

Although the general Astoria area had its first settlement by native tribes like the Chinook, and a brief national exposure when Lewis and Clark passed through in 1806, the town itself was founded in 1811 as a private trading post by millionaire fur tycoon **John Jacob Astor** (see box, opposite), as the first American attempt at colonizing the West Coast. Despite its rather abortive beginnings, greater things were to come for Astoria, though they would have to wait more than thirty years. By the time new colonists started staking claims to the area in the 1840s, little was left of the outpost from the old days, but flush with arrivals via the sea and the Oregon Trail, the place grew and became a nascent port at the river mouth. By 1847 it had the first US post office on the West Coast, and within twenty years began to make a name for itself as a **salmon-canning** town and an outlet for the timber trade.

At the turn of the last century it was one of the more rough-and-ready ports in the Northwest, home to the type of vice and corruption more familiar from the Wild West – rampant prostitution, random violence, and occasional clashes between races and nationalities, all of it fueled by alcohol and class tensions. Chinese, Swedish, and Finnish laborers were but a few types of the international workers in the port, as each community established its own cultural celebrations, rituals, and meeting halls. Almost inevitably, Astoria became notorious for **shanghaiing** (see box, p.93), whereby drunken revelers had more than a passing chance of waking up halfway across the Pacific, sold to complement an unscrupulous captain's crew. Indeed, the situation got so bad at one point that workers at quayside canneries carried guns to get themselves safely to the night shift.

In 1920 much of the town burned down in a cataclysmic **fire** that engulfed the port's shambling old wooden-frame buildings, and before it had a chance to fully rebuild, another fire hit two years later. More catastrophic, perhaps, were the structural **economic changes** over the next fifty years, which led to the demise of many cannery businesses and a depression in the wood-products industry – a double blow for the resource-based local economy. Only by the 1980s, and after the commercial disuse of the local rail line, did residents see that

The price of fur

In 1779, exhausted British sailors, after failing in their search of the fabled Northwest Passage during Captain Cook's long final voyage, docked in Canton. There they discovered, quite by accident, that the sea otter pelts they had traded for baubles in the Northwest were worth a fortune. The intelligence reached **John Jacob Astor** back in America and prompted the fur tycoon's decision to establish a **Pacific Coast trading post** called Astoria. Though it was a bold gamble in the teeth of stiff competition from the Canada-based North West Company, Astor's idea behind founding his namesake was simple enough: gather furs here from all over the Northwest and then export them to Asia, where demand verged on the feverish. It was not, however, quite so simple.

Almost as soon as his plans – comprising both overland and seafaring parties – began to take shape, Astor's whole enterprise turned into a fiasco. The first problems arose with the *Tonquin*, the ship Astor commissioned to establish the trading post – or more exactly with its captain, a certain **Jonathan Thorn**, who cuts something of a Captain Bligh figure: an excellent seaman with a bad temper and few leadership skills. The ship left New York in September 1810, and trouble broke out in the Falklands when Thorn intemperately set sail without his landing party, abandoned just because they were late. Thorn was only persuaded to go back for the men when one of the fur traders held a pistol to his temple – and, as you might expect, relations remained strained thereafter. Indeed, when the **Tonquin** reached the mouth of the Columbia River, Thorn dumped the fur traders off as quickly as possible and sailed north – to his death at the hands of the Nootka of British Columbia, one of whose chieftains he unwisely rubbed in the face with a fur.

Meanwhile, Astor's **overland party**, which had left St Louis in March 1811, was in trouble too. First there were endless delays and then the party argued so bitterly that it broke up into separate groups, each of which endured extraordinary hardships in the struggle to press on west in the depths of winter. Perhaps no one endured quite as much as **John Day**, who caught fever and lay at death's door for weeks; got hopelessly lost in the mountains; lived for days by eating moccasins, beaver skins, and roots; and finally, just when he began to get his bearings, was robbed and stripped by hostile natives on the banks of the Columbia River, forcing him to wander around naked before friendlier natives took pity on him. Day's sufferings, including his own severe bouts of dementia, soon acquired almost mythical status and a string of towns and a valley in eastern Oregon now bear his name. Remarkably, most of Astor's overland party managed to dribble into "Fort Astoria" early in 1812, but, exhausted and sick, they were more of a liability than a reinforcement, and the dispirited Americans were only too willing to sell out to the Canadians at the onset of the War of 1812. Washington Irving made the best of the saga in his chunky novel *Astoria*, published just twenty years later.

a change was necessary, so like just about every place else along the coast, Astoria has tried to embrace **tourism**. It's worked, at least to some degree, but if you talk long enough to grizzled old-timers it's obvious what they really think: they would much rather be dependent on their own logging and canning labors, no matter how difficult, than tied to the endless pursuit of tourist dollars.

Arrival and information

The Greyhound station is at 95 W Marine Drive. Local **bus** service is provided by Sunset Limited ($1; ⓣ503/325-0563, ⓦwww.ridethebus.org), which principally runs along Marine Drive but can also connect you with the center of town (route #10), within range of forts Stevens and Clatsop (#15), and further south on to Seaside and Cannon Beach (#101 express; $2). On the seasonal **train** line from Portland, Amtrak provides once-a-day summer service (June–Sept Fri–Mon 7.30am; 4hr; $40) along the waterfront. Astoria's clearly signposted and well-stocked **visitor center**, 111 W Marine Drive (summer daily 8am–6pm; winter Mon–Fri 9am–5pm, Sat & Sun 10am–2pm; ⓣ503/325-6311, ⓦwww.oldoregon.com), is located near the base of the massive US-101 bridge over the Columbia River. They issue a free and extremely detailed brochure on the town and its surroundings and also sell a detailed *Walking Tour* leaflet ($3) guiding visitors to the town's historic homes. To make a leisurely trip along the waterfront, hop aboard the **Astoria Trolley** (summer Mon–Thurs 3–9pm, Fri–Sun noon–9pm; rest of year Sat & Sun noon–6pm; $2), historic rail cars that ply a tourist-oriented route.

Accommodation

Astoria prides itself on its B&Bs, mostly housed in the splendid old mansions uptown. If you're on a tighter budget, there are a number of more routine modern motels on Marine Drive. You can also camp – in yurts or traditional campsites – in the vicinity at Fort Stevens State Park (sites $18–20, yurts $27–35; ⓣ1-800/452-5687; see p.149).

Astoria Inn 3391 Irving Ave ⓣ503/325-8153 or 1-800/718-8153. An 1890s farmhouse-turned-B&B offering sweeping views across the Columbia from its location high up on the bluff, a mile or so east of the town center. Four guest rooms are nice, if unsurprising. ❹

Clementine's 847 Exchange St ⓣ503/325-2005 or 1-800/521-6801, ⓦwww.clementines-bb.com. Five pleasant bedrooms in a handsome 1888 villa, which provides delicious breakfasts and has agreeable period decor. Unexpectedly, the B&B also operates two suites in an adjoining former "Moose Lodge" with more modern furnishings and not so much chintz. Rooms ❹, suites ❻

Crest 5366 Leif Erickson Drive ⓣ503/325-3141 or 1-800/421-3141, ⓦwww.crest-motel.com. Immaculately maintained motel perched on a wooded ridge two and a half miles east of the center along US-30. Large modern rooms are pleasantly decorated with kitchenettes, microwaves, and balconies with fine riverside views. ❹

Elliott 357 12th St ⓣ1-877/EST-1924, ⓦwww.hotelelliott.com. Simply put, the only decent hotel in town, a historic 1924 charmer that's recently been refurbished in grand style. Located in the heart of downtown, this chic affair offers upscale amenities in its rooms and suites, some with fireplaces and Jacuzzis, and all with tasteful modern furnishings. The rooms are cheapest in winter; add about $30 per unit in the summer high season. ❻

Franklin St Station 1140 Franklin St ⓣ503/325-4314 or 1-800/448-1098, ⓦwww.franklin-st-station-bb.com. Comfortable spot built by a local shipbuilder for his son at the end of the nineteenth century, with eleven en-suite rooms and a potpourri of period furnishings. ❺

Lamplighter 131 W Marine Drive ⓣ503/325-4051 or 1-800/845-8847. An unsurprising but reasonable motel yards from the visitor center. ❷

Rose River Inn 1510 Franklin Ave ⓣ503/325-7175 or 1-888/876-0028, ⓦwww.roseriverinn.com. Not quite as precious as the average B&B, but still with tasteful decor and a solid breakfast.

The highlights, though, are the use of the inn's sauna and a massage by the Finnish owner. ❺

Rosebriar 636 14th St ⓣ503/325-7427 or 1-800/487-0224, ⓦwww.astoria-usa.com/rosebriar. Larger and less personal than some B&Bs, but still a good choice for its imposing setting on a hillside – the place was built as a convent in 1902 – and rooms with tasteful furnishings. ❹

The Town

Arriving from Portland on US-30, the main road into Astoria, **Marine Drive**, runs parallel with the **waterfront**, whose assorted piers and sheds give little indication of the Victorian-era debauchery that once spawned dozens of harborside saloons and brothels. Today, they are long gone, and the waterfront is the town's cultural and historic centerpiece, and Marine Drive is the axis for most activity. **Downtown** lies a few blocks inland, and although the rest of Astoria stretches some distance further south along a peninsula, the only major highlight therein is the **Astoria Column**, on the highest hill in the center of town.

The Columbia River Maritime Museum

The waterfront's prime attraction is the expansive **Columbia River Maritime Museum**, 1792 Marine Drive at 17th Street (daily 9.30am–5pm; $8; ⓦwww.crmm.org), whose several galleries illustrate different facets of the region's nautical history. The collection begins in the large main hall, which contains models and mock-ups of old boats, either sitting on the floor or perched against the wall with careful rigging. Of the galleries that follow, one of the more interesting is the "Sailing Vessels" section, with its melodramatic ships' figureheads and fancy sideboard retrieved from the nearby wreck of a British ship, the *Peter Iredale* (see p.150). The "Fishing, Tanneries and Whaling" display holds a fascinating collection of old Astoria photographs, as well as several walrus-tusk Inuit sculptures – notably that of a cribbage board – sold as scrimshaw souvenirs to visiting sailors. "Navigation and Marine Safety" focuses on the treacherous sand bar that broke the back of many a ship as it pushed into the Columbia River from the Pacific. With its combination of strong currents, shifting bars, breakers, frequent fog, and stormy weather, the mouth of the Columbia was extraordinarily difficult to negotiate and around two-thousand ships are known to have sunk there. Dredgers, automated buoys, and a pair of gigantic moles have made navigation much easier today,

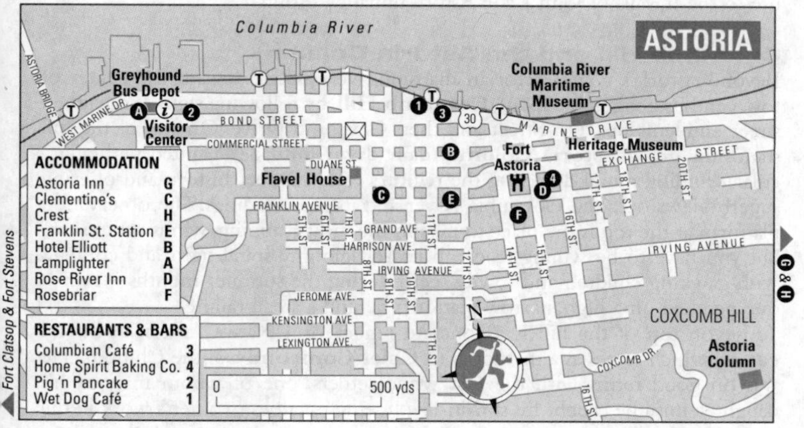

but ships still require the services of Astoria's pilots, whose powerful little boats are often to be seen bobbing about the river. The buoys were installed in 1979, replacing the red-hulled *Columbia* lightship, which is now part of – and moored outside – the museum, though its cramped interior quarters don't really allow for ease of visitation.

Flavel House and the uptown mansions

The most impressive of Astoria's **mansions**, the 1880s **Flavel House**, at 441 8th St and Duane (daily 10am–5pm, summer 11am–4pm; $5; ⓦwww.clatsophistoricalsociety.org), has been restored and refurnished in the manner of its first owner, Captain George Flavel, the house's cresting balconies, shingles, angular tower, wrapround verandas, and hipped roofs are a fine example of the Queen Anne style. Flavel began by piloting ships across the Columbia River bar, but he grew rich as a ship owner and a razor-sharp entrepreneur who trained a beady eye on his property from the telescope he placed in his mansion's tower. While the main rooms are set up as dioramas featuring period furniture and decor, more interesting is the ungainly display of local castoffs like bank-teller windows, farm tools, and horse carriages hiding in the basement. The newly constructed annex, too, has a hodgepodge of interesting items, including relics from the nautical era and photographs of old Astoria.

Entry into the Flavel House also gets you access to a pair of less compelling museums around town – the **Heritage Museum**, 1618 Exchange St (same hours as mansion; $3), and the **Uppertown Firefighters Museum**, Marine Drive at 30th (Wed–Sat 11am–2pm; $3) – though these are fairly provincial and not as well put together as the mansion. Nonetheless, to really understand local history – with all of its rowdy port antics, commercial canning and logging, multi-ethnic workers, and various fires – the Heritage Museum's wall displays and town relics are a useful place to begin.

From Marine Drive, numbered streets climb towards the uptown area, where the wealthy of the late nineteenth century built their elegant mansions well away from the noise of the port. Handsomely restored, with contrasting pastel shades picking up the delicacy of the carving, these appealing timber homes are distinguished by their fanciful verandas, attractive bay windows, and high gables; some of the most enjoyable are concentrated on Exchange, Franklin, and Grand avenues between 11th and 17th streets. Here also, at 15th Street and Exchange, you'll find a replica timber bastion of **Fort Astoria**, a modest tribute to the travails of John Jacob Astor's unhappy group.

Coxcomb Hill and the Astoria Column

Beyond Astoria's fancy Victorian mansions, you ascend toward the center of town and its geographic focus, **Coxcomb Hill**, by following signs and painted street emblems up 16th Street and then Coxcomb Drive. On top of the hill stands the grand **Astoria Column** (daily dawn–dusk; $2), painted with a circular, winding mural depicting the region's early pioneer history and offering superb views over the Columbia River and its surroundings. The observation platform at the top is the place to take in the most stunning, windswept views, but you have to be willing to climb its 164 gloomy spiral stairs and contend with gawking children and rowdy teens during the summer months – everyone perched on a high, narrow platform behind a small railing.

Also on top of the hill is a concrete replica of a Native American **burial canoe**, which serves as a memorial to **Chief Comcomly** of the Chinook. He was on good terms with the first white settlers, one of whom married his daughter, until he caught his son-in-law hoeing potatoes (women's work in the chief's opinion). Comcomly's son, on the other hand, is said to have proposed to **Jane Barnes**, a barmaid from Portsmouth who arrived on an English ship in 1814 to become, Astorians claim, the first white woman in the Northwest. Jane turned him down, which wrought havoc with local race relations. There's nothing inside today's concrete canoe, but the original would have been crammed with tools and weapons to help the spirit of the body in the afterlife.

Eating and drinking

Downtown has several good places to **eat**. *Columbian Café*, 1114 Marine Drive (Ⓣ503/325-2233), has gourmet seafood and vegetarian meals, and offers evening jams by regional musicians in its *Voodoo Room* (Thurs–Sun; $5); and the *Home Spirit Baking Company*, 1585 Exchange (Ⓣ503/325-6846), serves home-made sourdough bread and ice cream in a lovely Victorian home. If all else fails, make like the locals and head to *Pig 'n Pancake*, unavoidable at 146 W Bond St (Ⓣ503/325-3144), where you can get your fill of delightfully greasy, gut-busting breakfasts. For **drinking**, the *Wet Dog Café*, on the waterfront at 144 11th St (Ⓣ503/325-6975), is a prominent hangout with tasty bar food, decent microbrews, and live music.

Fort Clatsop National Memorial

Having finally arrived at the mouth of the Columbia River in November 1805, the explorers **Meriwether Lewis** and **William Clark** needed a winter base before the long trudge back east. Beside a tributary a few miles south and across the bay from current Astoria, they built **FORT CLATSOP** (daily 9am–5pm, summer 8am–6pm; $5; Ⓦwww.nps.gov/focl) and had a thoroughly miserable time there. It rained on all but 12 of their 106 days, and most of the party was infested with fleas. Morale must also have been deflated by the leaders' insistence that the men keep away from native women – no matter how Lewis dressed it up in his *Journals*: "[A group of Chinook women] have formed a camp near the fort and seem determined to lay close siege to us, but I believe, notwithstanding every effort of their winning graces, the men have preserved their constancy to their vow of celibacy."

Lewis and Clark's winter fort, a straightforward log stockade, has been reconstructed here as a national memorial and although it's hardly impressive, the setting is delightful – deep in the forest not far from the water's edge. The **visitor center** nearby has an outstanding display on the explorers' expedition, explaining its historical background as well as providing details of the journey itself. In the summer, docents in pioneer costumes give exhibitions on shooting flintlock muskets, pouring molten bullets, and making beef-tallow candles.

Fort Clatsop is located south of Astoria and is most easily reached via US-101: from downtown Astoria just follow the highway over Youngs Bay bridge and watch for the signs. The fort is about three miles east of US-101. Keep in mind that ongoing renovations in preparation for the explorers' 2005-2006 bicentennial in the area may keep some areas off-limits to the public, and don't be surprised if you're prevented entry altogether during the months leading up to it.

Fort Stevens State Park

Ten miles west of Astoria, and also signposted from US-101 beyond Youngs Bay Bridge, is **FORT STEVENS STATE PARK**, a large recreational area that occupies the tapering sandspit that nudges into the mouth of the Columbia River. Hundreds come here to wander the bike and hiking trails,

Staying at the beach

It's a lucky traveler who finds anything but the most spartan **accommodation** along the Oregon Coast without booking ahead in July and August, though fortunately one- or two-days' advance notice will normally suffice for all but the most popular hotels, inns, and motels. You will also find that prices can rise steeply at peak times, when some places may also insist on a minimum of two-night's stay. In addition, about one-third of the sixty-odd state parks that dot the coast have **campgrounds** (the others are day-use only) for $15–21 per night, and fifteen parks offer novel accommodation in the form of **yurts**. These domed circular tents with wooden floors, electricity, and lockable doors, come equipped with bunk beds that sleep up to eight people; they cost $27 per night regardless of how many you have staying there. Another interesting option, though available at just a few sites, is that of **cabins**, basic wooden structures with many of the same features as yurts, though with a somewhat sturdier construction; these go for $35 per night. Recently, the park system has been rolling out more elaborate yurts and cabins around the state, including ones sporting bathrooms, kitchenettes, and the like, for an additional charge of $8–40, depending on the size. Yurts, cabins, and many campgrounds can be reserved on the **State Park Campground Reservation Line** (Ⓣ1-800/452-5687, Ⓦwww.reserveamerica.com) no less than 48 hours before arrival.

go freshwater swimming, and stroll miles of beach before **camping** (tent sites $18–21, yurts $27–35; Ⓣ1-800/452-5687) for the night. There's also some historical interest a mile to the west of the campground in the beached and rusting wreck of the **Peter Iredale**, a British schooner that got caught out by high winds in 1906, which is slowly sinking into the sand, but remains enough of a marvel to clamber over at low tide. In the "Historical Area" to the north of the campground, an array of **military ruins** spreads out over the park. Fortifications were first constructed here to guard against Confederate raiders during the Civil War, and the army continued to use the site until the end of World War II. Fort Stevens was shelled one night by a passing Japanese submarine, which makes it, incredibly, the only military installation on the mainland US to have been fired on by a foreign government since 1812. You can wander the ruins to your heart's content – and a self-guided walking tour leaflet is available – but it's not overly interesting unless you're into scrambling around old gun batteries.

South to Oswald West State Park

South of Astoria along US-101 and directly at the northwestern end of the most direct coastal route from Portland, US-26, **Seaside** and **Cannon Beach** are used more by outsiders and urban day-trippers than native beach-lovers. Indeed, the two places seem to belie what you may have heard about the Oregon Coast being an idyllic treasure – what you get here instead is street after street of vendors selling souvenirs, salt-water taffy, and T-shirts, while all around great hordes embark on (rather limited) sightseeing expeditions. If this is your idea of what a trip to the beach should be like – and for many, unquestionably, it is – then you'll feel right at home here. For others, your best bet will be to avoid both towns and motor toward the unspoiled state parks found in abundance further south, most prominently around **Hug Point** and **Oswald West** parks.

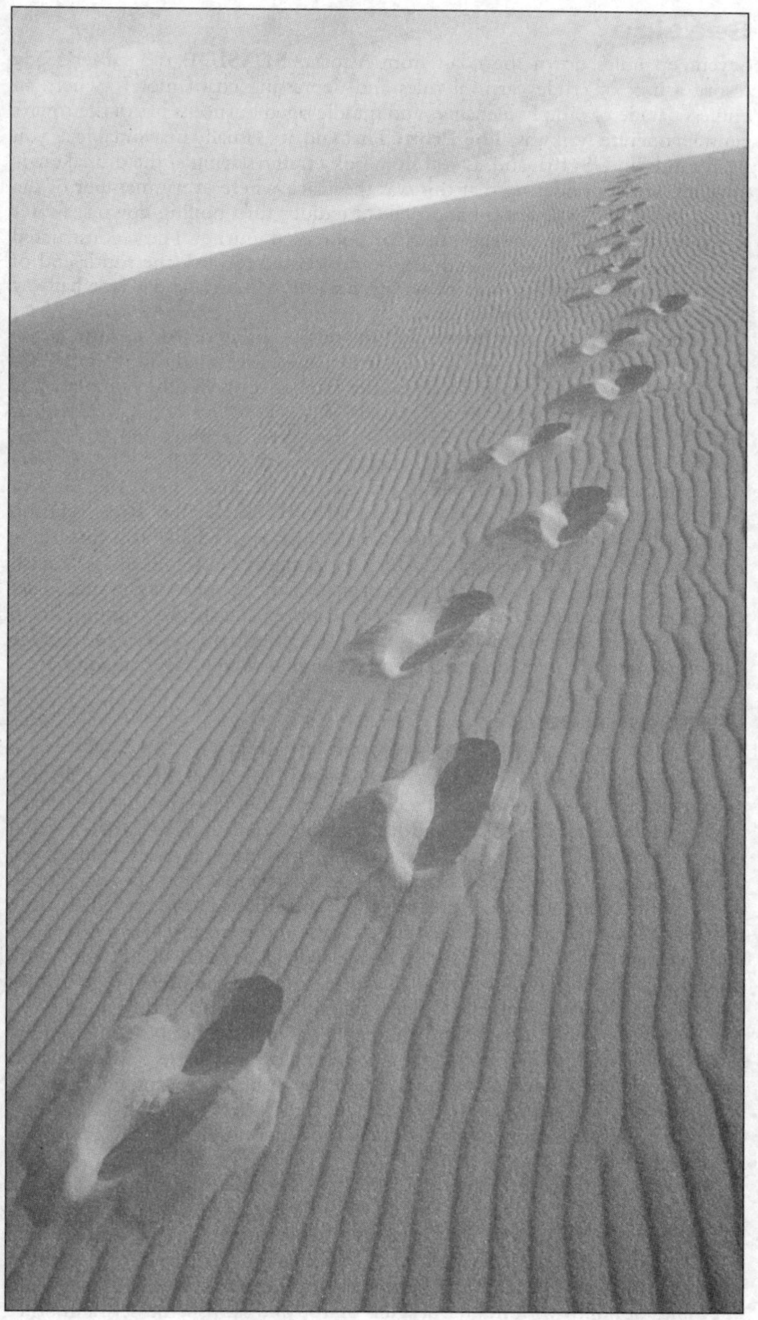

△ Oregon Dunes National Recreation Area

Seaside

Seventeen miles down the coast from Astoria, **SEASIDE** is a rather seedy resort, a mix of crude carnival rides and depressing chain motels, where an endless parade of pimply teenagers and middle-aged burnouts patrol the town's central concrete walkway, **The Prom**. That said, it's visually unavoidable as you head south on US-101, and, as you sit in poky traffic staring at the dismal environs, it's worth pondering that this was the place where every member of the Lewis and Clark expedition had to take a tedious turn boiling down seawater to make salt – vital to preserve meat for the return journey. The reconstructed salt works – a few boulders and pans – are located towards the south end of The Prom, and there's a commemorative statue of Lewis and Clark halfway along The Prom at the traffic circle.

Seaside has lots of dreary **hotels** and **motels**, and the **visitor center**, at the junction of Hwy-101 – here Roosevelt Drive – and Broadway (Ⓣ503/738-6391 or 1-800/444-6740, Ⓦwww.seasidechamber.com) has the complete list. If you have to stay here, try the ten comely Victorian rooms of the 1893 *Gilbert Inn*, 341 Beach Drive (Ⓣ503/738-9770, Ⓦwww.gilbertinn.com; ❺), or the *HI-Seaside Hostel*, 930 N Holladay Drive (Ⓣ503/738-7911, Ⓦwww.2oregonhostels.com; dorms $20, private rooms $39), also the site of **Greyhound** arrivals. The hostel is located a few blocks north of Broadway and a stone's throw from the Necanicum River, which runs parallel to – and a few blocks from – the beach. Another option is Sunset Empire Transit (Ⓣ503/325-0563, Ⓦwww.ridethebus.org), which operates a limited daily service from Astoria to Seaside and on to Cannon Beach ($2), running from Marine Drive in Astoria south along US-101. Other than grabbing a roadside burger, you're well advised not to spend too much money here **eating**.

Cannon Beach

Nine miles south of Seaside, **CANNON BEACH** is a somewhat more upmarket place. The town, which takes its name from several cannons washed onto the beach from the wreck of a USS warship, the *Shark*, in 1846, sees itself as a refined and cultured place, and has building regulations to match – neon signs are banished and there are certainly no concrete high-rises. Painters sell their work from weathered cedar galleries and Portlanders wander from bookshop to bistro, reinforcing the tiny town center's sedate and moneyed air. Still, after wandering the tourist-choked streets for an hour or so, it's hard not to get the impression that this is basically a spruced-up Seaside, albeit with more appealing scenery around it. The quaint little stores sell the usual beach bric-a-brac, the "chic" galleries peddle the likes of marble seagulls and driftwood elves, and there's little in the way of a dining or cultural scene. Nonetheless, the town's one big, justified attraction is its annual **Sandcastle Competition** (Ⓦwww.cannon-beach.net/cbsandcastle), a free, one-day event held around Memorial Day and starting when the tide permits, where you're apt to see anything from dinosaurs and sphinxes to mermaids and monkeys to Elvis and Jesus carved out of sand.

Although the town of Cannon Beach leaves something to be desired, its **beaches** are some of the most beautiful around any town on the Oregon coast, beginning with the wide strip of sand that backs onto the town center at the mouth of Ecola Creek. They continue – about a mile to the south – with a narrower strand that's dominated by the 240-ft **Haystack Rock**, a craggy and imposing monolith with nesting seagulls on top and starfish, mussels, and other shellfish in the rock pools at the bottom – while accessible at low tide, it's definitely not climbable. More remote and less visited beaches are within a few miles of Cannon Beach, too – the highlight being **Ecola State Park**, a couple of miles north of town, where dense conifer forests decorate the basaltic cliffs of Tillamook Head with sea stack-studded beaches down below. A hiking trail runs through the forest along the nine miles of coast within the park and there's a primitive, hikers-only campground about halfway along the trail – the park's only facilities. As a useful alternative, the smaller **Arcadia Beach** on the south side of town is a good choice for picnicking or strolling, with fewer tourists than elsewhere in the area.

Practicalities

Sunset Empire Transit's limited daily **bus** service from Astoria and Seaside to Cannon Beach is right in the center of town within fifty feet of the **visitor center** ($2; Ⓣ503/436-2623, Ⓦwww.cannonbeach.org) at second and Spruce streets. The best way to see Cannon Beach is on **foot**, but if you're after exploring the local coastline it's a good idea to rent a **bike** from Mike's Bike Shop, downtown at 248 N Spruce St (Ⓣ503/436-1266).

There's a wide range of **accommodation** to choose from, but things still get very tight over the summer and impossible during the sandcastle competition. Furthermore, the inns, motels, and hotels along the coast south of the center tend to lack charm, and you're much better off paying a little more to stay downtown. Excellent oceanfront options here include the modern, cedar-shingled *Schooners Cove Inn*, 188 N Larch St (Ⓣ503/436-2300 or 1-800/843-0128, Ⓦwww.schoonerscove.com; ❻), a smart and well-equipped establishment where most of the rooms have sea-facing balconies; the *Waves Motel*, 188 W 2nd St (Ⓣ503/436-2205 or 1-800/822-2468, Ⓦwww.thewavesmotel.com; ❹–❽), another dapper, modern place right on the oceanfront, with a range of studios and suites; and the pricier, but equally well-sited *Webb's Scenic Surf Motel*, 255 N Larch St (Ⓣ503/436-2706 or 1-800/374-9322, Ⓦwww.webbsscenicsurf.com; ❼), a more modest option that you may have to take if rooms are in short supply. There are cheaper alternatives south of the town center near Haystack Rock – try *Cannon Beach Hotel*, 1116 S Hemlock St (Ⓣ503/436-1392, Ⓦwww.cannonbeachhotel.com; ❹), which has a pleasant boarding-house atmosphere that's a big improvement over many of its motel-style rivals.

For **food**, the town center is the best bet with a string of reasonable choices dotted along the main drag, N Hemlock Street. Among them, the informal *Lazy Susan Café* (Ⓣ503/436-2816), next to the Coaster Theater at no. 126, does excellent health food and breakfasts; *Osburn's*, no. 240 (Ⓣ503/436-2578), has decent ice cream and a good deli selection with sidewalk benches; the *Bistro*, at no. 263 (Ⓣ503/436-2661), has tasty seafood and an intimate bar; and *Midtown Café*, 1235 S Hemlock St (Ⓣ503/436-1016), offers the best breakfast in town. *Bill's Tavern & Brewhouse*, 188 N Hemlock St (Ⓣ503/436-2202), is the town's busiest **bar**, offering bar food along with their own handcrafted brews.

Hug Point and Oswald West state parks

South of Cannon Beach, Highway 101 threads through the wooded hills that overlook the ocean and provides some very eye-opening views of the rocky headlands and majestic sweep of the landscape. Many tourists simply blow through this part of 101 on their way down to the cheese factories in Tillamook, but if you're interested in good hiking, there are a number of fine spots in the vicinity. Just a few miles south of Ecola State Park – and accessible via the beach if you've got the legs for it – is the turnoff for **HUG POINT**

Food foraging along the coast

With patience, the region's beaches can yield a **hearty meal**, though there are often limits on the numbers of shellfish and crabs you're allowed to catch, so check for local restrictions – tourist offices, for one, can usually oblige. Be aware also that pollution has made it unsafe to catch anything at all on certain parts of the coast – again ask locally or call the Oregon State Dept of Agriculture (☎503/986-4720). And you do, of course, need to know what you're looking for. There are several sorts of **clams**: razor clams are the hardest to catch, moving through the sand remarkably quickly, but others are easier game. **Gapers**, found at a depth of 14 to 16 inches, and **softshells**, found 8 to 14 inches deep in firmer mud flats, both have meaty and rather phallic-looking "necks"; **cockles** don't have these (a decided advantage if you're at all squeamish) and are also the easiest to dig, lying just below the surface. You may also hear the term **geoduck** ("gooey-duck") in the area, a giant, long-necked specimen that acts as the grail for local clam-diggers and is notoriously difficult to catch. Arm yourself with bucket and spade and find a beach where other people are already digging – obviously a likely spot.

Cleaning and cooking gapers and softshells is not for the faint-hearted. To do so, immerse them in fresh warm water until the neck lengthens so the outer skin will slip off easily. Then prize the entire clam out of its shell with a sharp knife, peel off the outer skin from the neck, and slit lengthwise. Split open the stomach, remove all the cark material and gelatinous rod, and cook as preferred – steamed, fried, battered, or dunked into a chunky chowder soup. Cockle clams are much less messy; you just steam them in fresh or salt water until their shells open – some people prefer them almost raw.

For **crabbing**, you'll need to get hold of a crab ring (often rentable) and scrounge a piece of fish for bait. You lower the ring to the bottom of the bay from a boat, pier, or dock – and wait. The best time to crab is an hour before or an hour after low and high tides; you're not allowed to keep babies (less than 5.75 inches across) or females (identified by a broad round flap on the underside – the male flap is narrow). To cook a crab, boil it in water for twenty minutes, then crack it, holding its base in one hand, putting your thumb under the shell at midpoint, and pulling off its back. Turn the crab over to remove the leaf-like gills and "butter" from its center – then pick the meat from its limbs.

STATE PARK. This romantic-sounding place is nice for sunsets and such, but the name derives from the late-nineteenth-century reaction to the narrow road built around the promontory near beach level. The coach route literally "hugged" the base of the cliff as it made its away around it, no doubt a rather nauseating trip for those facing hours of such transport. Impressively enough, a small stretch of this road is still visible at the place marked **Hug Point**, on a trail leading a half-mile north from the parking lot, and even today you can see the wagon-wheel ruts that were deeply cut into the rock surface, and journey around the point on foot at low tide.

A few miles further south is **OSWALD WEST STATE PARK**, named after the pioneering governor responsible for protecting much of the state's shoreline in the 1910s (see p.141). The park is easily accessible from both sides of the highway, and offers a rugged and densely forested chunk of seashore that incorporates two headlands. The first is **Cape Falcon**, the second the 1660-foot **Neah-Kah-Nie Mountain**, meaning "place of fire" in reference to the local Tillamook tribe's habit of burning the mountain forest to provide better grazing for the deer and elk it relied upon. Neah-Kah-Nie has also been linked with buried treasure ever since white settlers first heard a Tillamook tale of an enormous canoe – presumed to be a Spanish galleon – swept onto the shore with its great white wings flapping in the wind. The Spaniards, so the story went, stashed their valuables in a hole in the mountainside and rounded off the enterprise by slitting the throat of a crew member before burying his body on top of the treasure – which, if nothing else, should have given the Tillamook a clue as to the treatment they might expect from Europeans. Some support has been given to the legend by the discovery hereabouts of a handful of Spanish artifacts and several tons of beeswax – a favorite Spanish trade item – but the treasure has never been discovered, though many people have attempted to dig it up.

In between the two headlands at the mouth of Short Sand Creek, Oswald West State Park has a beach that's good for surfing, a picnic area, and a small and simple **campground** (mid-March to Oct $10, Nov to mid–March $14) with tables, fireplaces, drinking water, and flush toilets. It is a wonderful spot, popular with young surfers with wetsuits; however, it's only accessible on foot, a quick third-of-a-mile hike down the hillside from US-101, where one of the parking lots is for campers only, with plastic wheelbarrows provided to help lug in equipment. It's clearly signed – the other parking lots are for day-users. From the campground, there's a choice of two short **hikes**: either the stiff, four-mile climb south to a vantage point near the top of Neah-Kah-Nie Mountain, or the easier two-and-a-half-mile hike north to the tip of Cape Falcon, weaving through patches of old-growth sitka spruce before reaching some superb coastal views.

Nehalem Bay to Tillamook Bay

Just past Neah-Kah-Nie Mountain, Highway 101 begins a circuitous section that encompasses a string of small beach- or bayside communities that continues down to **Tillamook**. Weaving around the bays of **Nehalem** and Tillamook, with a run past the ocean in between, the road has a number of good stopping points where you can take snapshots of ocean cliffs falling down to rocky shores, rusty skiffs at the waterside, or seagulls perching on old dock pilings. It's a compelling landscape, with its mix of natural wonders and antique hamlets, but you're not apt to find too much to do here beyond hiking and beach-strolling – which can be magnificent in places.

Nehalem Bay and around

A mile or two south of Neah-Kah-Nie Mountain, the highway takes a sweeping turn inland toward a trio of small towns built around **NEHALEM BAY**, a pleasant inlet with fishing boats, sea birds, and little else. At the north end of the bay, the first place of any size is the burg of **Manzanita**, rarely a major sight on the coastal tour route but is a big draw for vacationing Portlanders, who set up shop here in the summer months and wile away the days. Although the locals tout their "**seven mile beach**" as something special, the sands here aren't anything you haven't seen before; still, the place does have a few **restaurants** worth a visit if you're famished for decent chow. *Marzano's,* a block from the beach at 60 Laneda Ave (Ⓣ503/368-3663), has better pizzas and calzones than you'd expect to find at the beach, while *Blue Sky Café*, 154 Laneda Ave (Ⓣ503/368-5712), has a well-deserved reputation as one of the better spots to eat on the coast, with American favorites mixed with Northwest Cuisine – pumpkin bread pudding, seared pork chops, and so on. You can **stay** at **Zen Garden B&B**, near the end of Carey Road (Ⓣ503/368.6697, Ⓦwww.neahkahnie.net/zengarden; ❻), which sports two modest but agreeable rooms and is pleasantly isolated from the main part of town. The B&B is conveniently adjacent to **Nehalem Bay State Park** (day-use fee $3), which occupies the tip of a southward-pointing spit covering the entrance to the bay and provides good **camping** (tent sites $16, yurts $27; reserve at ⓣ1-800/452-5687). With its prime ocean views and relaxing nature strolls, the park is a quiet highlight of the journey around the bay, also offering canoeing, fishing, clamming, and horseback riding – though it does put you at some remove from the rest of it further east along Hwy-101.

Returning to the route will send you twisting around the flanks of the coastal mountains before reaching the village of **Nehalem**. A much older, but rather inferior, neighbor to Manzanita, the town offers little reason to stop aside from some creaky antique stores and knickknack shops. It does, however, feature the *Nehalem Dock*, 35815 Highway 101 (ⓣ503/368-5557), a solid **dining** choice for surf 'n' turf, along with more unusual fare like salmon glazed in mango teriyaki sauce. Indeed, the Oregon Coast often sports small towns such as these, which have almost no conventional sights, but do strangely offer a fine restaurant or two, often run by chefs fleeing the hubbub of the big city. The next town around the Nehalem Bay bend, **Wheeler**, is another such example, a one-horse town oddly featuring a classy eatery. In this case it's the *Nehalem River Inn*, a mile east off Hwy-101 at 34910 Hwy-53 (ⓣ1-800/368-6499), another spot that draws out visiting urbanites for its gourmet offerings of duck, lamb, steak, and seafood presented with color and dash – such as halibut fillet with wildwood fiddleheads and crushed filberts. Keep in mind that if you're not into fancy dining, these towns are well worth skipping.

Eastward from the bay, as Highway 53 and its offshoot Foss Road curve inland, the **Tillamook State Forest** stretches vast and green, having recovered from the forest fires of 1933 and 1945 which devoured over five hundred square miles of premium logging land. In the first fire, a week-long blaze started when a wire rope in a remote lumber camp sawed across – and set fire to – a dead tree. The scorched area, known widely as the **Tillamook Burn**, meant hard times for local logging communities, but it was the second fire, possibly started by a Japanese balloon bomb (see p.231), that really threatened the area's economy: seed sources will survive one conflagration, but not two. To stave off ruin, the timber companies and the state authorities combined to replant the Tillamook Forest in a colossal undertaking that took thirty years to complete – the genesis of Oregon's state-managed forestry.

Tillamook Bay and around

US-101 leaves Nehalem Bay with an abrupt ninety-degree turn to the south and makes a beeline for the dreary sprawl of **Rockaway Beach**, about twenty miles south of Cannon Beach. Perhaps the ugliest of the very small towns on the coast, Rockaway is all linear development and few ocean views. It wouldn't matter – the beach is long, straight, and bland along here anyway – except that the town seems to go on for mile after mile of endless, 25mph traffic. At the southern end of this tedious expanse, the highway veers east round **TILLAMOOK BAY**, once called "Murderer's Harbor" after natives killed a sailor from Gray's expedition here in 1788. On the north side of the bay, **Garibaldi,** named after the 1870 unifier of Italy, is one of the most strangely fetching of the state's declining industrial towns. With a huge disused smokestack announcing the former mill town's presence, Garibaldi has a smattering of evocative ruins, though increasingly these are disappearing as development begins to encroach on the hamlet's old character. For a whiff of the good old days, drop by the modest confines of **Lumberman's Park**, right off 101, and poke around an old steam engine and various industrial-age odds and ends.

A few miles south, Highway 101 rounds the northeast end of the bay to travel its broad eastern side. Along the way, **Bay City** is another small town that offers few sights but does, like those towns arrayed around Nehalem Bay, feature a decent restaurant in the *Artspace Restaurant and Gallery*, Hwy-101 at Fifth Street (Ⓣ503/377-2782), where you can dine on tasty soups, salads, and seafood while taking a peek at the work of regional artists – some of it a bit better than you'll find to the north in Cannon Beach.

From here the highway suddenly veers inland away from the bay and across the wide, green valley that announces **Tillamook**. This plain dairy town is best known for its two cheese-making factories, which are – oddly enough – among the region's most popular tourist attractions. In a bright and cheerful building on the north side of town beside US-101 is the **Tillamook Cheese Factory** (daily 8am–6pm; free; Ⓦwww.tillamookcheese.com), where the self-guided tour provides glimpses of hair-netted workers beside conveyor belts and bent over large, milky vats of cheddar and Monterey Jack. But the factory plays second fiddle to the gift shop, which sells every type of bovine souvenir imaginable. It also offers free samples of cheese, though you have to be fiendishly skillful with a cocktail stick to spear a sizable portion – the frenzied hordes love this place, especially in the summer, when the company's oversized offerings of ice cream are devoured by equally oversized customers. The other factory, the **Blue Heron French Cheese Company** (daily 9am–5pm; free; Ⓦwww.blueheronoregon.com), signposted off US-101 less than a mile south, specializes in locally produced French-style cheeses and has a cheese- and Oregon wine-tasting area. Here you can sample the company's savory pepper-encrusted brie, among others, before heading out back to have a close encounter with a goat, mule, or rooster in a quasi-petting zoo.

Cape Meares to Otter Rock

Heading south from Tillamook on US-101, it's a humdrum forty-five-mile trip along a series of inland valleys – but there's a much more enjoyable, and time-consuming, coastal alternative. By taking Bayocean Road northwest from central Tillamook, you meander through dairy country and bucolic farmsteads until you reach the southern spit of **Bayocean**, which guards Tillamook Bay, and nearby **Cape Meares**. From here the road turns southward and leads you on a lengthy, circuitous trip, lurching around long bays and around jagged promontories, across lowlands and around hillsides, until it merges with Highway 101 west of the coastal **Siuslaw National Forest**. After negotiating the ugliness of **Lincoln City**, you once again find yourself edging a long, straight stretch of Oregon coastline and a variety of natural features and state parks leading to the little town of **Otter Rock**.

Three Capes Scenic Loop

Named after capes Meares, Lookout, and Kiwanda, the clearly signposted **THREE CAPES SCENIC LOOP** is a 38-mile detour from Hwy-101 that begins where Bayocean Road crosses from Tillamook Bay over to the Pacific Ocean. From here you reach the short turnoff for **Cape Meares Lighthouse** (May–Oct daily 11am–4pm; free; Ⓦwww.capemeareslighthouse.org). A late- nineteenth-century structure of sheet iron lined with brick, the lighthouse boasts gorgeous views out along the rough and rocky shoreline. While you're here, take a look also at the so-called "octopus tree," an oddly shaped Sitka spruce a couple of hundred yards from the parking lot. The cape is also a good place to take your binoculars and peer out at the expanse of the **Oregon Islands National Wildlife Refuge**, which is off-limits to human interlopers. Some of the waterfowl you can expect to see here include puffins, murres, and cormorants in the spring, pelicans and terns in the summer and autumn, and loons and grebes in the winter. Amid all the winged creatures is also a smattering of aquatic mammals, which you can see throughout the coastal zone, among them seals and sea lions, dolphins, and whales.

Two and a half miles further along the Cape Meares Loop Road, **Oceanside** is an agreeable little place that spreads along the seashore and up the steep, wooded hill behind. There are fine views of the offshore **Three Arch Rocks**, a favorite with nesting seabirds, especially the tufted puffin, and a long sandy beach. There are also a couple of places to **stay**. Down near the seashore is the simple modern motel *Oceanside Inn*, 1440 Pacific St NW (ⓣ503/842-2961 or 1-800/347-2972; ❸), and up above, high on the hill with great views, is the more appealing *House on the Hill Motel*, 1816 Maxwell Mountain Rd (ⓣ503/842-6030, ⓦwww.houseonthehillmotel.com; ❺), a timber, pastel-painted place where the sea-facing rooms have balconies.

Pushing on down the coast from Oceanside, the shallows of **Netarts Bay** are almost entirely enclosed by a sandspit that protrudes from the bay's south shore. At the base of the spit behind the beach are the picnic area, **campground** and **yurts** (pitch $16–20, yurts $27; ⓣ503/842-4981 or 1-800/452-6949) of **Cape Lookout State Park**, which is named after – and also incorporates – the forested headland immediately to the south. From the campground area, you can stroll out onto the spit and go clamming and crabbing in the sheltered waters of the bay. However, around where Jackson Creek and the entry road meet the sand, the beach is built along a series of sand dunes, and around these dunes lies a helter-skelter array of huge spruce logs that have been jostled around by wind and waves until they've formed into a thick, huge wooden matrix. To the south, it's a brief drive – or a stiff two-and-a-half-mile walk up – from the campground to the trailhead and parking lot ($3) of the Cape Lookout Trail. This is a mildly strenuous and very popular two-and-a-half-mile jaunt to the tip of **Cape Lookout** as it pokes a precipitous finger out into the Pacific.

From the base of Cape Lookout the road jockeys around the small inlet of Sand Lake, around where the **Clay Myers Natural Area** protects an estuary home to many sea birds, salmon, deer, and otter. This carefully conserved zone is one of the state's newest natural preserves, and is accessible to the public during daylight hours. Just south of here, the road reaches the third and final cape on the scenic loop, **Cape Kiwanda**, a sandstone promontory that's trimmed by sand dunes and partly protected by a monolithic mound of basalt, **Haystack Rock** (not to be confused with the same-named rock in Cannon Beach). The headland is near the tiny town of **Pacific City**, which is hidden away near the mouth of the Nestucca River and sheltered from the sea by another sandspit. The fishermen here are known for their ability to launch their fishing dories straight from the seashore into the oncoming surf – a real skill even though outboard motors long ago replaced oars.

If you'd like to **stay** in the vicinity of Cape Kiwanda, a pair of B&Bs offer that opportunity. Closest to the quiet streets of Pacific City, just a few miles outside town, the *Eagles View*, 37975 Brooten Rd (ⓣ1-888/846-3292,

Ⓦwww.eaglesviewbb.com; ❻), is a friendly modern place amid unspoiled terrain, featuring five stylish units with separate baths and an outdoor porch and hot tub. A bit farther inland off Hwy-101 in the town of Cloverdale, the *Sandlake Country Inn*, 8505 Galloway Rd (Ⓣ503/965-6745, Ⓦwww.sandlakecountryinn.com; ❻), has four modest rooms in a century-old farmhouse decorated in Victorian furnishings, with private baths and Jacuzzis.

Cascade Head to Devil's Lake

From Pacific City, it's about four miles back to US-101 and then around fifteen miles south to the enticing natural preserve of **CASCADE HEAD**, protecting nearly ten thousand acres on a coastal promontory rising to 1800ft. Although there are ample opportunities for exploration here, the area's varying topography and stunning views are best taken in on a five-and-a-half mile loop trail that's aimed at hardy outdoor adventurers. To reach it, travel south on 101 a little over three miles past the tiny town of Neskowin and take a gravel road west four miles until it ends. As you hike past ravines and over hillsides, you'll pass an eye-opening display of rugged natural beauty, from a stand of old-growth Sitka spruce to the craggy watery reaches of Hart's Cove to one of the last remaining sections of coastal grasslands in the state.

By dramatic contrast, south of Cascade Head the highway reaches what is easily the ugliest town on the Oregon coast, **Lincoln City**, actually the merged version of five small beach towns, run together in 1965. The amalgamation rattles along the highway for seven congested, motel-lined miles with precious little to entice you to stop. If you're marooned, there are plenty of inexpensive motels to choose from – the **visitor center**, 801 SW US-101 (Ⓣ541/996-2152, Ⓦwww.lincolncity.org) has the complete list. One of Greyhound's Portland–San Francisco **bus** routes reaches the Oregon coast at Lincoln City, shooting through here as it heads south, dropping off at 1410 SE Hwy-101; details at Ⓣ1-800/231-2222.

Your best bet – if you really want immediate access to Cascade Head – is to avoid the city itself and **stay** a few miles east of town in a **campground** at **DEVIL'S LAKE**. As the first of four Satan-themed natural areas along the coast, Devil's Lake is by far the most benign, a fetching summer playground on the eastern edge of Lincoln City that has tent sites and yurts (pitch $18–21, yurts $29; reserve at Ⓣ1-800/452-5687), with opportunities for boating and fishing, too. Conveniently, its main access route, Devil's Lake Road, also provides an alternate route around the massive eyesore of Lincoln City, which you must otherwise traverse at a glacial pace for up to a half-hour by car.

Boiler Bay to Otter Rock

Beyond Lincoln City, US-101 skirts Siletz Bay before slicing down a few miles south to **BOILER BAY**, a heaving, basalt-rimmed inlet where the surf pounds relentlessly and makes for a dramatic sight during winter storms. Named after the boiler of a ship that crashed here in 1910, the nautical relic can actually, some claim, be spotted at low tide – though it's usually more fruitful to explore the accessible tide pools along here, which are as rich and diverse as any place along the coast. Immediately to the south, **Depoe Bay** is an unassuming coastal settlement straddling the tiniest of harbors. The town basically lies along the highway itself, and most of what you'll see are low-end eateries and trinket shops. There's nothing too appealing here, although the redoubtable, gut-stuffing diner *The Sea Hag* (Ⓣ541/765-2734) does have its fans, perhaps more for irony than anything else.

South of here, the highway climbs up towards the forested mass of **Cape Foulweather**, discovered and named by a jaded Captain Cook, whose historic expedition up the Pacific Coast had nearly been dispatched to a watery grave by a sudden Northwest storm – the winds hereabouts can gust at 100mph. A short and narrow side road leads off US-101 to the cape's lookout, from where there are stirring coastal views – but be prepared to negotiate some hair-raising switchbacks on the way.

Returning to US-101, it's just a couple of miles further south to an easier turnoff at **OTTER ROCK**, a tiny town at a bend in the highway that nonetheless hosts one of the coast's most impressive sights, less than a mile west on the coast. Here, **Devil's Punchbowl** is a sandstone cave whose roof has fallen in, and is a well-named cauldron during the winter months, when the sea heaves and churns at high tide, throwing up huge dollops of sea spray and thunderous waves. Luckily, at low tide the waters recede to reveal a lattice of rock pools, which you can explore on a pleasant beachside trail. Directly on the upper lip of the Punchbowl, you can **eat** at *Mo's Otter Rock* (May–Oct; ⓣ541/765-2442), part of a chain of seaside diners, which is little more than a oceanside shack here, but does dole out the thick and delicious seafood slurry known as "slumgullion." A bit further south along Hwy-101, you can **stay** at the elongated sands of **Beverly Beach**, part of which is designated a state park with picnic facilities, yurts, and a large and well-equipped **campground** (pitch $18–21, yurts $29; ⓣ541/265-9278 or 1-800/452-5687).

Newport

With a population of just nine thousand, **NEWPORT** occupies the seashore at the mouth of Yaquina Bay, about 25 miles south of Lincoln City. It's one of several Oregon fishing ports laboring to turn itself into a resort – and here it works really well, with the bits and pieces of the old fishing port decorated by the occasional mural and imaginatively set against more recent development. Although sometimes associated in tourist brochures with Lincoln City, the town has very little in common with that bulging mass, and while there's plenty of (over-) commercial development along Highway 101, Newport has more than enough sights and scenery to hold your interest for a day or two.

Arrival and information

Newport's **Greyhound** depot is at 956 SW 10th St, just north of the Yaquina Bay bridge, off the main drag of US-101 (ⓣ1-800/231-2222). The **visitor center**, nearby at 555 SW Coast Hwy (Mon–Fri 9am–5pm; ⓣ541/265-8801 or 1-800/262-7844, ⓦwww.newportchamber.org), issues maps and brochures on the town and its environs, advises about agate hunting, and has complete motel and campground listings. There are no buses within the town limits, which can be a bit of a pain if you don't have a vehicle – the visitor center is a good mile from both the harbor to the south and Nye Beach to the north.

Accommodation

Newport offers a wide range of **accommodation**, including distinctive **B&Bs** (online listings at ⓦwww.moriah.com/npbba) around Nye Beach, and fairly modern **hotels** which line the bluff above the beach on Elizabeth

Street. Less appealing, drab **motels** are dotted along US-101, where it's less the roar of the sea than the roar of the motor car. There's also a popular **campground** (and yurts) in Beverly Beach State Park seven miles north of town (see opposite), and another – not as well appointed – in **South Beach State Park** (pitches $18–21, yurts $29; ⓣ541/867-4715), a mile or so south of the Yaquina Bay bridge.

Beach House 107 SW Coast St ⓣ541/265-9141 or 1-866/215-6486, ⓦwww.beachhousebb.com. One of the better B&B choices, with three spacious, well-furnished units in a scenic location. ⑤

Elizabeth Street Inn 232 Elizabeth St ⓣ541/265-9400 or 1-877/265-9400, ⓦwww.elizabethstreetinn.com. Particularly large and modern, with sizable rooms having kitchenettes and sea-facing balconies. ⑥

Nye Beach 219 NW Cliff St ⓣ541/265-3334, ⓦwww.nyebeach.com. Much less pompous than its *Sylvia Beach* neighbor, and offering six great oceanfront rooms featuring stove heating, balconies, and hot tubs. The onsite restaurant, though, is a bit less appealing. ⑤

Oar House 520 SW 2nd St ⓣ541/265-9571 or 1-800/252-2538, ⓦwww.oarhouse-bed-breakfast.com. Has five plush, en-suite rooms in a handsome old house that comes complete with a lovely garden and a tower offering sea views; the gourmet breakfasts here are first rate, too. ⑥

Sea Cliff 749 NW 3rd St ⓣ541/265-6664 or 1-888/858-6660. One of the more affordable choices around, a dinky little B&B a few blocks from Nye Beach, with two neat bedrooms. Contains *April's* restaurant (see p.164). ⑤

Sylvia Beach 267 NW Cliff St ⓣ541/265-5428 or 1-888/795-8422, ⓦwww.sylviabeachhotel.com. Overlooking Nye Beach, a renowned three-story hotel that some outsiders love for its literary character – each of the twenty rooms is named after a famous writer – and others dislike for its thick air of pretension. Every evening, mulled wine is served in the upstairs library, where you can look studious with other guests posing as intellectuals. ④–⑥

Vikings Cottages 729 NW Coast St ⓣ541/265-2477 or 1-800/480-2477, ⓦwww.vikingsoregoncoast.com. Pleasingly old-fashioned option on Nye Beach, renovated 1920s units with simple furnishings and private baths, along with more modern, less romantic condominiums. Cottages ⑤, condos ⑥

The Town

Most of Newport lies on the grand curve of **Yaquina Bay**, the outlet of the Yaquina River, with the majority of sights on the bay's north side. Unfortunately, unless you're here for several days, the three main areas of town – the Historic Bayfront and Nye Beach near the center, Yaquina Head and Agate Beach to the north, and the Oregon Coast Aquarium across the bay to the south – are not readily accessible on foot in relation to one another. Even the town's main campground at South Beach (see above) is in a less-than-inviting location on the far side of two jetties and a highway bridge. Unless you have a car, then, you'll be spending most of your time in Newport walking around.

The Historic Bayfront and Nye Beach

Unquestionably, for the great mass of visitors the **Historic Bayfront** along Bay Boulevard, just to the northeast of the 101 highway bridge, is the obvious first stop for many – a breezy collection of souvenir shops, seafood diners, and hordes of sea lions wallowing on the wharves. This lively, often ad hoc mixture can be seen in a quick half-hour-long jaunt along the docks, peeking at the rusty trawlers floating nearby and perhaps taking a bite of fresh clam chowder in a bayside setting. Worth avoiding, though, are the scattered tourist traps such as "Undersea Gardens," outmoded sights that offer a 1960s-era view of the deep blue sea in creaky old confines.

Away from the docks less than two miles to the west, and across US-101, Newport reveals another side of its character among the old and peeling timber

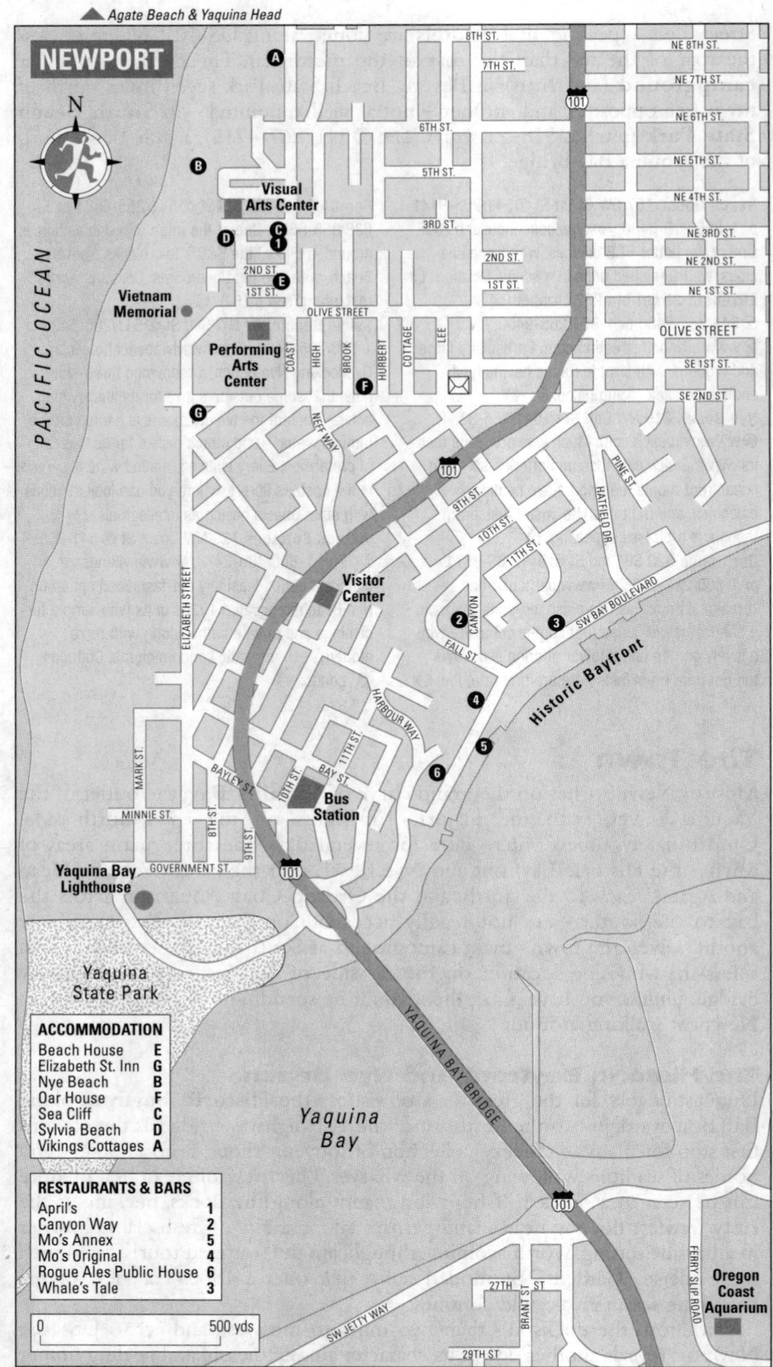
Agate Beach & Yaquina Head
NEWPORT
N
PACIFIC OCEAN
8TH ST.
7TH ST.
6TH ST.
5TH ST.
3RD ST.
2ND ST.
1ST ST.
NE 8TH ST.
NE 7TH ST.
NE 6TH ST.
NE 5TH ST.
NE 4TH ST.
NE 3RD ST.
NE 2ND ST.
NE 1ST ST.
OLIVE STREET
SE 1ST ST.
SE 2ND ST.
101
Visual Arts Center
Vietnam Memorial
Performing Arts Center
COAST
HIGH
BROOK
HURBERT
COTTAGE
LEE
NEFF WAY
PINE ST.
HATFIELD DR.
9TH ST.
10TH ST.
11TH ST.
Visitor Center
CANYON
FALL ST.
SW BAY BOULEVARD
Historic Bayfront
ELIZABETH STREET
HARBOUR WAY
MARK ST.
BAYLEY ST.
BAY ST.
10TH ST.
11TH ST.
Bus Station
MINNIE ST.
8TH ST.
9TH ST.
GOVERNMENT ST.
Yaquina Bay Lighthouse
Yaquina State Park
YAQUINA BAY BRIDGE
Yaquina Bay
ACCOMMODATION
Beach House E
Elizabeth St. Inn G
Nye Beach B
Oar House F
Sea Cliff C
Sylvia Beach D
Vikings Cottages A
RESTAURANTS & BARS
April's 1
Canyon Way 2
Mo's Annex 5
Mo's Original 4
Rogue Ales Public House 6
Whale's Tale 3
0 500 yds
SW JETTY WAY
27TH ST
BRANT ST
29TH ST
FERRY SLIP ROAD
Oregon Coast Aquarium
South Beach State Park

houses that ramble along the oceanfront north of Yaquina Bay. From NW Second Street to around 10th Street, immediately behind the long and uncrowded sands of **Nye Beach**, the hippies of yesteryear have bequeathed a friendly air and arty atmosphere, manifest in a pair of **arts centers** – one for performing arts, at 777 W Olive St and SW Coast Street (Ⓣ541/265-9231, Ⓦwww.coastarts.org), the other for visual arts, at 839 NW Beach Drive (Tues–Sun 11am–6pm; Ⓣ541/265-6540). Apart from this, there are few official sights other than a deserted, modern **Vietnam War Memorial** on a nearby bluff, but the beach itself makes for an excellent stroll, and the seaside development is a bit more restrained than elsewhere in town. South of SW Second Street – but still north of Yaquina Bay – the Nye Beach district gives way to the shiny oceanfront hotels of **SW Elizabeth Street** and the commercial center of town, an uninspiring modern sprawl along US-101, which doubles as the main drag.

Yaquina Head and Agate Beach

Built on a basalt headland three miles north of town, the stately white column of the **Yaquina Head Lighthouse** (tours daily noon–4pm), has been incorporated into the **Yaquina Head Outstanding Natural Area** (daily dawn to dusk; $5 entry), an appropriately named centerpiece of environmental protection – one of the best on the coast. The area's visitor center (daily: June–Sept 10am–6pm; rest of year 10am–4pm) has displays on local flora and fauna and the geology behind this rocky cape, but even better are the unsurpassed views of the coastline, especially from a high path leading over the bluffs, and of whales migrating out at sea during the winter. Other sights include seals, otters, and seabirds gathered on the offshore rocks – nicely viewed at the bottom of a wooden stairway below the lighthouse bluffs. Here, on a beach of rounded (and slippery) dark rocks, you can get a closer view of these creatures than practically anywhere else they exist in their natural environment. Further east, accessed by a special driveway, **Quarry Cove** sits in an oceanside depression formed by a rock quarry. That, however, is long gone, and in its place are a series of **tide pools** inhabited by purple sea urchins, sea stars, hermit crabs, and anemones. However, despite the heroic effort that went into reclaiming this land, the manmade pools can get rather dank and ugly at low tide and you're better off inspecting the same creatures below the bluffs near the lighthouse.

Returning towards Newport, in between Yaquina Head and Nye Beach lies the wide sweep of **Agate Beach**, where winter storms toss up agates from gravelly beds under the sea – though many locals prefer to rock hound at Seal Rock State Park, ten miles south of Newport on US-101. If you walk along either beach towards the sun on an outgoing tide, the agates (after a winter storm, at least) sparkle up at you: moonstone agates are clear, carnelians are bright red and transparent, and ribbon agates have colored layers. Newport's visitor center (see p.160) provides further information.

Yaquina Bay and the Oregon Coast Aquarium

Back in Newport, standing amid the manicured greenery of a tiny state park at the foot of Elizabeth Street, near the bridge over Yaquina Bay, the **Yaquina Bay Lighthouse** (daily 11am–5pm; donation suggested) is one of the coast's more interesting late-nineteenth-century lighthouses. Far from huge, the forty-foot tower sits attached to the old keeper's house, a pleasant timber building constructed in the Cape Cod style and complete with period furnishings. Actually, it's surprising the lighthouse has survived: it was only in operation for

Ocean adventures around Newport

Newport is a good place to try your hand at **deep-sea fishing**: Newport Tradewinds, down by the harbor at 653 SW Bay Blvd (⊕541/265-2101 or 1-800/676-7819, ⊛www.newporttradewinds.com), offers a variety of trips from year-round halibut and sea-bottom fishing – for sea bass, rock cod, sea trout, etc – to seasonal salmon and tuna fishing. A five-hour excursion costs $60 per person, $150 for twelve hours. From March to October, **whale-watching** excursions are possible here, too, with the two-hour cruises of Marine Discovery Tours, 345 SW Bay Blvd ($25; ⊕541/265-6200 or 1-800/903-2628, ⊛www.marinediscovery.com) one option among several operators.

three years during the 1870s while the Yaquina Head Lighthouse – a much larger, and now fully automated edition – was built.

To cross to the south side of the bay, you traverse over the majestic 1938 span of the **Yaquina Bay Bridge**, perhaps the finest bridge on the coast among several contenders. The southern portion of town is considerably removed from its counterpart, and really only holds one sight of any prominence, the large and impressive **Oregon Coast Aquarium** (daily summer 9am–6pm; rest of year 10am–5pm; $10.75; ⊛www.aquarium.org), signposted off US-101 at 2820 SE Ferry Slip Rd. Home to marine mammals like the sea otter and seal, seabirds like the tufted puffin, and a whopping octopus in a glass-framed sea grotto, the aquarium used to be best known for harboring the killer whale Keiko ("Free Willy" from the movies) in his own massive tank. Keiko, however, died in an Icelandic sea pen in 2003 after an illness and his tank is now occupied by *Passages of the Deep*, a shark-oriented underwater tunnel. There are also mock-ups of rocky and sandy shores, wetlands, and coastal waters where the jellyfish steal the show. It's all very professionally done and predictably attracts tourists in the droves.

Eating and drinking

Seafood cafés and other **restaurants** line up along the Historic Bayfront's SW Bay Boulevard, the obvious first choice for dining. Unfortunately, aside from the unappetizing dining and fast-food chains along Hwy-101, there are few other choices around town. Even Nye Beach, so thick with decent accommodation, has limited choices for dining – in some cases not much better than found along the highway.

April's 749 NW 3rd St ⊕541/265-6855. Near the major hotels on Nye Beach, a spot that offers fine Continental cuisine on a changing menu – the town's best restaurant by default.

Canyon Way Restaurant and Bookstore 1216 SW Canyon Way ⊕541/265-8319. Just up from the harbor, a pleasant, pink-painted spot with a wide range of seafood. Dungeness crabs are the specialty, though it's hard to beat the seafood bouillabaisse.

Mo's Original 622 SW Bay Blvd ⊕541/265-2979. Along with *Mo's Annex*, no. 657 (⊕541/265-7512), two decent seafood restaurants in a local chain that have solid, rib-stuffing favorites (clam chowder, fish 'n' chips, etc.) and are always thick with tourist families.

Rogue Ales Public House 748 SW Bay Blvd ⊕541/265-3188. Local brewer serving up the best microbrews in town, everything from light ales like Oregon Golden to the dark and tangy oatmeal Shakespeare Stout to more experimental brews like Yellow Snow Ale and Mocha Porter. Also with solid pizzas, fish 'n' chips, and the like.

Whale's Tale 452 SW Bay Blvd ⊕541/265-8660. Easily the top choice along the Historic Bayfront, offering delicious seafood at affordable prices in cozy, vaguely nautical surroundings.

Seal Rock to Heceta Head

US-101 sticks close to the seashore south of Newport, bobbing past a series of state park beaches such as **Ona Beach** – lying at the mouth of a pretty little creek with places to swim and fish – until it reaches **Seal Rock**, an unassuming little town that was once the terminus of the first coastal stage route linked to the Willamette Valley in the 1860s. Nowadays it's not much, but the eponymous state park here is an attractive spot with dramatic basalt and sandstone sea stacks framing a sandy beach. Western gulls, black oystercatchers, and guillemots are among the many types of seabirds that gather here; there are tide pools to ferret around in, and it's a good spot for clam-digging. Looming over the entire scene is the gnarled dark mass of **Elephant Rock**, a pile of basalt that vaguely resembles a pachyderm, which was stranded in the ocean when the surrounding softer rock eroded away over the course of millions of years. Further south, the highway works its way to **Heceta Head** with as many inspiring seaward vistas and compelling parks as found further north, but with an ever-decreasing stream of tourists – making the striking surroundings that much more evocative.

Waldport to Yachats

From Seal Rock, it's five miles south to the unexciting little town of **WALDPORT**, which straddles the mouth of **Alsea Bay** with the aid of the grand **Alsea Bay Bridge**, whose main arch is frequently photographed in picture postcards of the coast. On the south side of the bridge below its pilings, you can explore more about the heroic days of creating the coastal bridges and highway at the **historical interpretive center** (open daily; information at Ⓣ541/563-2002), or get your feet wet a mile down the road at **Governor Patterson State Park**, providing relaxing walks along the sands and the shoals at the mouth of the bay. Within two miles of here south on 101, drop in at the appropriately named **Beachside State Park**, whose main appeal is being one of the two coastal parks (with Cape Lookout; see p.158) where, along with the requisite hiking and clamming, you can literally **camp** on the sands. This feature, unfortunately, makes the place very popular throughout the year, so you'll have to reserve long in advance (pitches $17–21, yurts $29; reserve at Ⓣ1-800/452-5687).

Continuing south, the green flanks of the Siuslaw National Forest close in around the highway as it zips down to **YACHATS** – pronounced YAH-hots, not the touristy YOCK-its – a low-slung seaside village whose ribbon of cottages and town lanes is at its prettiest round the mouth of the Yachats River. There's nothing too exciting about the place, but the next few miles of coast are startlingly beautiful and the town is a good base if you're keen to explore its nooks and crannies. One of the more enticing places to **stay** is the pretty, well-tended but rather spartan *Rock Park Cottages*, 431 W 2nd St (Ⓣ541/547-3214; ❸), which nonetheless have kitchenettes in many units. Another good choice, the *Shamrock Lodgettes*, south of town at 105 US-101 (Ⓣ541/547-3312 or 1-800/845-5028; ❹), offers comfortable and pleasantly old-fashioned log cabins with fireplaces, kitchenettes, and some with Jacuzzis, along with more conventional motel accommodation. Six miles south of Yachats, you can stay in one of two suites in the four-story pyramid called the *Ziggurat*, 95330 Hwy-101 (Ⓣ541/547-3925, Ⓦwww.newportnet.com/ziggurat; ❼), which boasts colorful modern furnishings, full amenities like kitchenettes and Jacuzzis, and a private sauna, library, and close beach access for each unit. For **food** in Yachats,

La Serre (Ⓣ541/547-3420), by the river at Second and Beach, serves fine steaks and seafood, while the *Drift Inn*, 124 Hwy-101 (Ⓣ541/547-4477), has decent fish tacos, burritos, and burgers.

Cape Perpetua and Devil's Churn

Heading out of Yachats, US-101 winds its way up the densely forested edge of **CAPE PERPETUA**, a colossal mound formed by volcanic action that, at eight hundred feet, is one of the most scenic peaks on the coast. The cape is latticed by hiking trails and the first place to go is the tiny **interpretive center** (Ⓣ541/547-3289), two and a half miles from Yachats, where you can pick up a map with trail descriptions. Of the ten **hikes** to choose from, perhaps the most impressive is the strenuous three-mile return trip along the **St Perpetua Trail**, running from the center to the viewpoint at the cape's summit, a thickly wooded trek with plenty of steep switchbacks, opening up to eye-popping views of the coastal scenery along the way. Once you reach the top, the views over the coast are even better – though you may feel a little resentful to see cars parked up there. If you feel like avoiding the hike but still want the view, take US-101 north from the interpretive center, turn down Forest Road 55 and then take Forest Road 5553. This climbs up to the parking lot and from here you can take a straightforward, ten-minute stroll – on the **Whispering Spruce Trail** – to the viewpoint. Other short but steep trails beginning at the interpretive center snake down to the seashore – either to tide pools or the beach.

Along the oceanside, the **DEVIL'S CHURN** may in many ways be the most compelling, dramatic, and frightening of all the various "Devil's" scenery on the coast – a deep and narrow basalt gash on the shore, where the ocean relentlessly comes in, pounding the rocks hard and sending columns of salt spray and tumultuous waves high in the air. If you get too close, you can easily get pelted, and at worst might well get swept into the whirlpool and crushed on the rocks. Unnervingly, there are no rails or barriers to keep you from meeting this grim fate. In a much safer location, the US Forest Service operates a small **campground** (May to mid-Sept; $12–14) beside a creek in the shadow of the cape: it's signposted from US-101 just north of the interpretive center, down Forest Road 55. Note also that in the summertime the cape's parking lots fill up fast, so try to arrive early.

Heceta Head and around

Beyond Cape Perpetua, the drive along US-101 is incredibly scenic, with dense forests climbing above and the anything-but-pacific surf crashing against the rocks below. After eleven miles, you reach the idyllic **Heceta Head Lighthouse State Park** (day-use only; entry $3), where the slender arc of **Devil's Elbow** beach – much less wicked than its neighbor to the north – lies at the back of a charming cove. This quiet beachside spot is surprisingly photogenic, with a rocky promontory curving up to the north, while the elegant **Cape Creek Bridge** – designed by Oregon bridge master-builder Conde McCullough in 1932 – crosses a little stream to the south with great style.

From the beach, it's a short and easy walk to the old lighthouse keeper's **Heceta House**, an 1893 Queen Anne-style structure you can spot on the headland before you, which has been converted into a graceful **B&B** (Ⓣ541/547-3696, Ⓦwww.hecetalighthouse.com; ❼), offering six rooms (four with private bath), a solid seven-course breakfast, and nighttime visits to the nearby **lighthouse** a short stroll away. You can also tour the facility without staying at the B&B (lighthouse tours June–Aug Thurs–Sun 11am–3pm; donation), and get a close-up view of its classic 1894 beacon – old-time fresnel lens and all – and from there go wandering on some winding trails around the cape, catching excellent views of the scenery along the way. To **stay** in the area without paying a bundle, drop in at **Washburne State Park**, three miles north of – and accessible by loop trail from – Heceta Head, a spot that offers tidepools, fishing, and hiking opportunities as well as **camping** (pitches $17–21; reserve at ⓣ1-800/452-5687).

A mile further on from Heceta Head, the overly hyped and privately owned **Sea Lion Caves** (daily 9am–dusk; $7; ⓦwww.sealioncaves.com) possess an elevator that shoots down through the cliffs to a winding path that leads down the cliffside to an observation point into a dark, cavernous sea cave. However, the Steller sea lions – when they are there – are too far away to be impressive and seem to spend a fair bit of time asleep. All in all, it's much better to save your money and catch sight of them at several points along the seashore elsewhere.

Finally, less than four miles south of the caves comes one of the coast's most bizarre and fascinating attractions, **Darlingtonia Wayside** (daily dawn–dusk; free), right off Highway 101 and accessed by a short trail. This officially protected natural site – laden with explanatory signs – harbors a small collection of unusual **cobra lilies**, carnivorous plants that devour insects by luring them into their gaping leaves, slick with hairs pointing down into their digestive chambers. The curious, boggy landscape and rare plants make for a rather unexpected scene, yet one well worth examining in May and June, when the hungry and deadly lilies are in full bloom.

The South Coast

In any number of ways, the **South Coast** of Oregon is considerably different from its northern counterpart, even though both have large stretches of protected natural habitat, countless state parks, and the linear presence of Highway 101. The most obvious distinction is that this part of the coast, starting south of **Florence** and continuing to the California border, is much less developed and more rugged than in the north, with far fewer visitors and a great number of beauteous parks strung together almost without interruption. The scenery in them, too, is a bit different, with an abundance of sand dunes, beach grass, and especially colossal sea stacks. Indeed, these geological castaways – isolated from the rest of the coastal cliffs – do much to give the area its distinctive topography, and in some places make the edge of the shoreline seem like it's breaking apart into huge basaltic chunks.

The highway provides immediate access to all the beaches and coastal parks, and rarely strays inland as it does further north. The towns along the route are for the most part not destinations in themselves, but little more than way stations or stopovers, if even that. Indeed, the workaday character and industrial visage of these towns, especially **Coos Bay** and **North Bend**, gives them a character out of keeping with the gung-ho pursuit of sightseers embraced

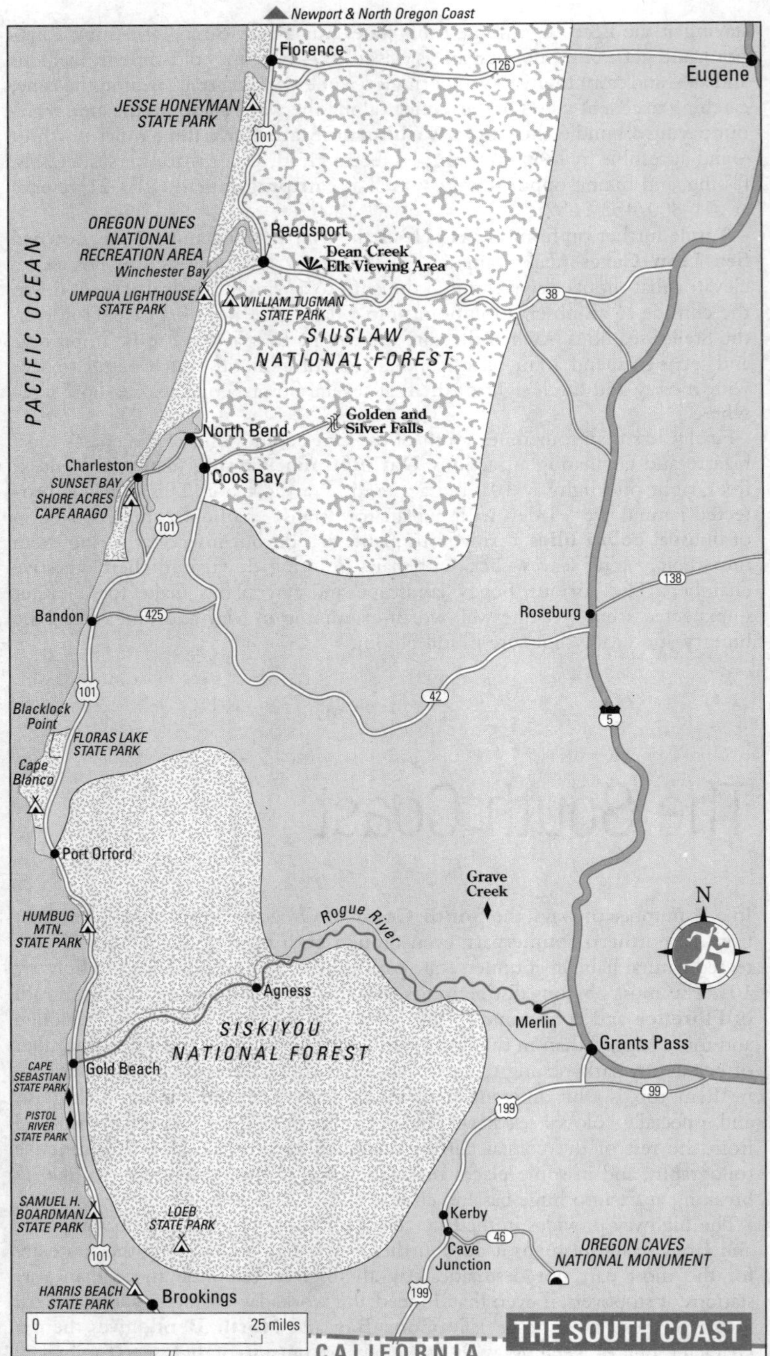
Newport & North Oregon Coast
Florence
Eugene
JESSE HONEYMAN STATE PARK
OREGON DUNES NATIONAL RECREATION AREA
Winchester Bay
Reedsport
Dean Creek Elk Viewing Area
UMPQUA LIGHTHOUSE STATE PARK
WILLIAM TUGMAN STATE PARK
PACIFIC OCEAN
SIUSLAW NATIONAL FOREST
North Bend
Golden and Silver Falls
Charleston
SUNSET BAY
SHORE ACRES
CAPE ARAGO
Coos Bay
Bandon
Roseburg
Blacklock Point
FLORAS LAKE STATE PARK
Cape Blanco
Port Orford
Grave Creek
HUMBUG MTN. STATE PARK
Rogue River
Agness
Merlin
SISKIYOU NATIONAL FOREST
Grants Pass
CAPE SEBASTIAN STATE PARK
Gold Beach
PISTOL RIVER STATE PARK
Ashland
SAMUEL H. BOARDMAN STATE PARK
LOEB STATE PARK
Kerby
Cave Junction
OREGON CAVES NATIONAL MONUMENT
HARRIS BEACH STATE PARK
Brookings
0
25 miles
CALIFORNIA
THE SOUTH COAST
Crescent City, California

elsewhere along the coast. If much of the South Coast, then, is not exactly ready for prime-time tourism, it's all for the better: the rocky beachside scenery, proudly working-class small towns, and absence of gawking shutterbugs give the place a palpable authenticity, and one not likely to be forgotten by anyone interested in exploring sights and having experiences off the beaten path.

Florence and around

Sitting on the north bank of the Siuslaw River, **FLORENCE** was founded in the 1850s as a timber port, but it was never more than a minor player in the lumber business and would probably be struggling today were it not for its proximity to the Oregon Dunes National Recreation Area (see overleaf). It was tourism that saddled the town's main drag (US-101) with its string of routine motels, but the developers did much better down by the river in the **Old Town**, a pint-sized affair whose sturdy early-twentieth-century architecture has been revamped to accommodate cafés, boutiques, and gift shops. With the exception of its striking 1930s Art Deco **Siuslaw River Bridge**, Florence has no sights as such, but the **Old Town** does have an amiable, cheerful air – despite its excessive popularity on sunny summer weekends.

Greyhound **buses** zip through Florence on US-101, dropping off at 1856 37th St – call ⓣ1-800/231-2222 for details. The **visitor center**, just north of the bridge at 270 Hwy-101 (ⓣ541/997-3128, ⓦwww.florencechamber.com), has information on the town, including a long list of accommodation. It also carries bits and pieces on the Oregon Dunes National Recreation Area.

If you decide to **stay** in Florence, it's worth paying a few dollars more to stay in Old Town instead of the colorless motels on Hwy-101. Good **B&B** options include the smart, seven-room *Edwin K*, 1155 Bay St (ⓣ541/997-8360 or 1-800/833-9465, ⓦwww.edwink.com; ⑥), which occupies an attractive two-story timber house at the foot of the riverside bluff; the *Johnson House*, 216 Maple St and 1st St (ⓣ541/997-8000; ④), offering five rooms in an 1892

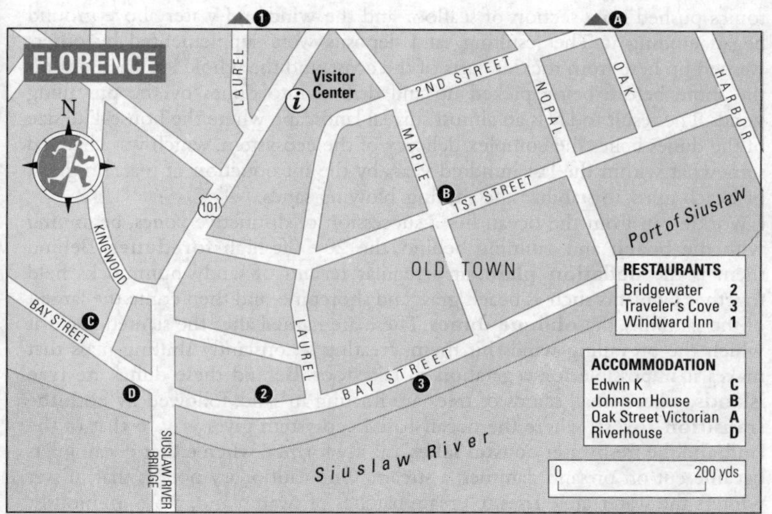

Victorian farmhouse one block from the river; and the comfortable and cottage-like *Oak St Victorian*, 394 Oak St (Ⓣ541/997-4000 or 1-800/853-4005; ❺), four units tucked away beside a wooded bluff at the end of Oak and with a pretty veranda and garden. Alternatively, the *Riverhouse Motel*, 1202 Bay St (Ⓣ541/997-3933 or 1-877/997-3933; ❹), has an appealing setting right down by the river underneath the bridge – and from here you can see a huge sand dune piled up against the opposite river bank. There are several **campgrounds** in the vicinity of Florence, both to the north back along US-101 and in the national recreation area to the south. With two hundred tent sites and a few yurts, **Jesse M. Honeyman Memorial State Park**, three miles south on US-101 (pitch $18–21, yurts $27; reserve at Ⓣ1-800/452-5687), has a freshwater lake on one side for swimming and boating, and dunes on the other.

Old Town's **cafés** and **restaurants** are geared for day-trippers, emphasizing speed rather than quality. Two of the better places are the *Bridgewater*, 1297 Bay St (Ⓣ541/997-9405), for hearty seafood, and the *Traveler's Cove*, 1362 Bay St (Ⓣ541/997-6845), a café with a riverside patio offering sandwiches and salads. West of Old Town, the *Windward Inn*, 3757 US-101 (Ⓣ541/997-8243), has tasty steaks and seafood at reasonable prices.

The Oregon Dunes National Recreation Area

Beginning at Florence, **sand dunes** dominate the coast (though are rarely visible on Hwy-101) as far south as Coos Bay: 45 miles of shifting hills up to an incredible 180-feet high, punctuated with pockets of forest and lake. Mostly lying along the Pacific shoreline up to two and a half miles inland, there are 32,000 acres of dunes, about half of them accessible to the public in the **OREGON DUNES NATIONAL RECREATION AREA**, (part of the Siuslaw National Forest; see Ⓦwww.fs.fed.us/r6/siuslaw). They were formed by the crumbling of sandstone some twelve millions years ago, when plate tectonics pushed up a section of seafloor and the wind and water above ground began eroding it. The resulting sand deposits were supplemented by others washed up here from rockier parts of the coast, and the whole lot dried out on the shore before being picked up and drifted into dunes by the prevailing winds. The result today is an almost surreal landscape where the house-like size of the dunes belies the complex delicacy of the ecosystem, which was changed somewhat within the last hundred years by the introduction of marram grass, or beach grass, to stabilize the shifting, blowing sands.

Working in from the ocean lies a succession of distinctive zones, beginning with the **beach** and, running behind, the 20–30ft high **foredunes**. Behind them is the **deflation plain**, an irregular terrain of sandy hummocks held together by plants such as beach grass and shorepine, and then come the largest of the sandhills, the **oblique dunes**. These are named after the slanted angle at which the prevailing winds hit them, creating a constantly shifting mass that makes it impossible for vegetation to take root. Behind these dunes are **tree islands**, where small stands of trees are floating in sand, followed by both the **transition forest**, where the ocean-based ecosystem gives way to that of the land, and the freshwater **coastal lakes**, mostly formed when either ocean inlets became cut off or sand dammed a stream. One cautionary note is that in wet winters the water table rises to create patches of swamp and, more ominously,

quicksand – watch out for pools of water on the sand in low, unvegetated areas between the dunes.

Park practicalities

Florence and North Bend bracket the dunes on the north and south respectively, and you can reach the dunes from the I-5 freeway in the southern Willamette Valley via highways 126 and 38 – there's no other access over the coastal mountains. The dunes themselves have suffered from the ill effects of ATVs (all-terrain vehicles) and ORVs (off-road vehicles), though their use is now confined to certain parts of the dunes, and in the future it's likely they will be restricted even further – preferably in favor of more environmentally sensitive tourism. The US Forest Service, which manages the dunes, maintains eight **hiking trail** areas that are, for the most part, free of motor vehicles. These are described on the USFS website (see above) or in a free booklet – *Hiking Trails in the Oregon Dunes* – available from local visitor centers and the **Oregon Dunes National Recreation Area Visitor Center**, 855 Highway Ave (Mon–Fri 8am–4.30pm, summer daily; ⓣ541/271-3611), at the junction of US-101 and Hwy-38, twenty miles south of Florence in Reedsport. Indeed, the visitor center carries a veritable raft of free information, and when the office is closed the most useful leaflets are available from the rack outside.

Of the eight hiking trail areas, one of the most enjoyable is the **Oregon Dunes Overlook**, ten miles south of Florence on US-101. Here, the observation platform offers smashing views over the dunes to the sea and acts as the trailhead for a couple of short and fairly easy hiking trails to the beach – the one-mile **Overlook Beach Trail** and the two-and-a-half-mile **Tahkenitch Creek Loop**. There are slightly longer trails a mile to the south on US-101 at **Tahkenitch Creek**, where you can also **camp** at any one of thirteen USFS campgrounds in the area ($5 permit; reserve at ⓣ1-877/444-6777, ⓦwww.reserveusa.com). You can, if you must, hire an ATV or ORV from a long list of rental companies. Charges are around $35 an hour plus deposit. Sandland Adventures, about a mile south of Florence on US-101 (ⓣ541/997-8087, ⓦwww.sandland.com), and Sand Dunes Frontier (ⓣ541/997-5363, ⓦwww.sanddunesfrontier.com), about three miles further south on US-101, are as good as any.

Reedsport to Cape Arago State Park

It's easy to get distracted by the dunes and pay attention to little else as you zip down to the towns of North Bend and Coos Bay, and beyond them the pleasant resort of Bandon. However, there are a number of good spots worth exploring in the vicinity if you have the time, some of which make excellent stops – and visual interludes – in between your travels on the sands. Roughly in the middle of the dunes, the little burg of **REEDSPORT** is a spot that built its existence on the fishing and lumber trades. There's not much to it for visitors, except for the charming neighboring port of **Winchester Bay**, also known as Salmon Harbor, supposedly the largest public harbor in Oregon and a good spot to watch the old-time trawlers and more modern fishing vessels drift by – or if you have the equipment, to go fishing or crabbing yourself. Three miles east of Reedsport on Hwy-138, wildlife enthusiasts won't want to miss the **Dean Creek Elk Viewing Area**, where you can spot a herd of up to a hundred Roosevelt Elk eating, playing, and rutting; the majestic beasts are most visible during the summer mating season, especially around September. Although Reedsport is hardly a place to hang out, if you're hungry there are seafood **diners** dotted along the mouth of the Umpqua River, and of these *Ungers Landing*, 345 River Front Way (☎541/271-3328), is one of several safe and affordable choices.

Just south of Winchester Bay, off Salmon Harbor Drive, lighthouse enthusiasts will enjoy a stop at **Umpqua Lighthouse State Park**, whose main feature, along with a relaxing lakeside trail, is its splendid red-and-white beacon (tours May–Sept; free; ☎541/271-4631), located on a small bluff. The park also has great **camping** for beach and dune trekkers with a full complement of tent sites ($16–20), a pair of cabins ($35), and yurts ($27) – even including a few deluxe models with bathrooms and kitchenettes ($45–65); reserve any of these at ☎1-800/452-5687. A few miles south and on the east side of Hwy-101, **William Tugman State Park** – named after another champion of the state parks system – is one camping alternative (pitch $12–16, yurts $27). Built around freshwater **Eel Lake**, the park offers fine opportunities for bass, trout, and salmon fishing, and for spotting birds like eagles, osprey, and hawks, and mammals like bear, elk, otters, and even cougars. For twelve miles south of here it's all dunes along Highway 101 until you reach the huge, curving mouth of the Coos River.

At the end of the dunes, another fine Conde McCullough bridge spans Coos Bay, a deep natural harbor which groups around its shabby shoreline the merged industrial towns of **North Bend** and **Coos Bay**. There's no mistaking the purpose here, with the main road lined by wood-chip mountains and stacks of cut timber, and it's all very unappealing. The obvious thing to do is to drive straight through on US-101 and head directly to Bandon, about 25 miles to the south, but if you've a couple of hours to spare, there are two enjoyable detours you can take. The first leads you 24 miles northeast of Coos Bay along the winding concourse of Coos River Highway (accessible from 101 at the southern end of the town and Coos Bay itself), up to the gorgeous surroundings of **Golden and Silver Falls** – one of the best attractions in the coastal mountains. Not to be confused with the equally appealing Silver Falls near Salem (see p.192), this park features a pair of striking waterfalls that cascade a hundred feet over basalt cliffs onto wet, rounded boulders. The sheer rock walls and rugged trees of the forest setting are quite impressive, which you can explore on a number of hiking trails leading up to the heights of the falls and past excellent vistas of the mountains and fauna such as hawks and herons.

The other detour from Coos Bay takes you southwest along the coast to a trio of state parks within a mile or so of each other. To get there from US-101 in North Bend/Coos Bay, follow the signs for **Charleston**, a small, workaday sportfishing town about nine miles away. From here, it's about three miles further to **Sunset Bay State Park**, a popular spot on account of its pretty sheltered bay, sandy beach, safe swimming, and **campground** (pitch $16–20, yurts $27; reserve at ☎1-800/452-5687).

The next park along, **Shore Acres** (daily 8am–dusk; $3), is, however, far more diverting and much less crowded. Green and lush, it was once the estate of a shipping tycoon and lumber magnate, one Louis Simpson. Although his palatial mansion was demolished in the 1940s, the formal gardens have survived, planted with exotic species as well as azaleas, rhododendrons, roses, and dahlias. The park also offers seasonal displays of brightly colored foliage in the winter holidays and at other times of the year, drawing even more visitors. The site of the mansion now accommodates an observation shelter, perched on a bluff above the jagged rocks of the seashore, and a footpath leads down through the woods to a secluded cove. It's one of the most delightful parks on the coast and it's also just a mile from **Cape Arago State Park**, a wild and windswept headland where you'll usually be able to spy Steller sea lions, elephant seals, and harbor seals on the offshore rocks in their protected habitat.

The cape is at the end of the road and on the return journey, rather than going all the way back to the US-101 in Coos Bay, you can – in Charleston – take the signposted turning along **Seven Devils Road**. This is a meandering country road which slowly and pleasingly twists its way south to US-101 near Bandon.

Bandon to Brookings

The most southerly section of the Oregon coast from **Bandon** to **Brookings** is in some ways similar to the rest of the South Coast – the close beach access from Hwy-101, the striking scenery of beachside hills and monumental sea stacks, and the presence of small working towns that don't merit much more than a stopover. However, there is one key difference: once you drive south of Bandon you cannot easily cross over to the Oregon interior and I-5 until you reach Crescent City, California. For much of the journey there are almost no roads (other than the occasional winding logging route) that breach this impressively rugged, undeveloped topography, and from Gold Beach onward the interior is inviolate, comprising such huge preserves as the Kalmiopsis Wilderness that barely even have hiking trails, let alone driving routes. Therefore, considering that it may require dropping down into Northern California and returning to the Rogue River Valley (see p.212) on Hwy-199 via the Oregon Caves, a trip to the southern end of the Oregon Coast demands a serious commitment of time and energy.

Bandon

Perhaps the one really appealing little town on this stretch of the Oregon Coast, easygoing and likeable **BANDON** lies 25 miles from Coos Bay at the mouth of the Coquille River. Known as "Bandon-by-the-Sea" in tourist brochures, the place boasts a beguiling combination of old-town restoration and New Age style. Indeed, it's one of the nicest places to stay on the whole of the coast, having shed its blue-collar roots as a logging and fishing port to become something of an arts and crafts center. It's been so since former denizens of Haight Ashbury and Venice Beach moved up here in the late 1960s from California, claiming that Bandon stood directly on a ley-line going from the Bering Sea to the Bahamas, making it one of the earth's top "acupuncture points."

Neither do the vibes end there: Bandon was originally a Native American settlement and when the local Coquille were swept aside in the middle of the nineteenth century, they are supposed to have cursed the town to burn down three times. It's happened twice so far, in 1914 and 1936, and the superstitious are still waiting for the curse to run its course. Memories of these troubled times stirred when townsfolk recently dynamited **Tupper Rock**, a sacred tribal site on Jetty Road, to improve the sea wall, much to the irritation of the remaining Coquille.

Arrival and accommodation

Greyhound **buses** pull in beside the *Sea Star Guest House* (see overleaf), in the town center at First Street and Delaware, a couple of minutes' walk from the **visitor center** at 300 2nd St and Chicago St (daily: June–Oct 10am–5pm;

Nov–May 10am–4pm; ⓣ541/347-9616, ⓦwww.bandon.com). The latter issues free town maps and their daily – except Sunday – newssheet lists local news and activities. As for **accommodation**, there are a number of solid **B&B** and **hostel** options, but if rooms are tight – as they often are in the summer – try the routine modern **motels** dotted south of the center along US-101, which runs inland from – and parallel to – Beach Loop Drive. **Camping** is another option at Bullards Beach State Park (sites $16–20, yurts $27; ⓣ541/347-2209, reserve at ⓣ1-800/452-5687), north of the town center and across the river.

Lighthouse B&B 650 Jetty Rd ⓣ541/347-9316, ⓦwww.lighthouselodging.com. Just west of the town center, along First Street, this comfortable, five-room establishment occupies an old and attractive timber building overlooking the harbor. ❼
Sea Star Guest House 370 1st St ⓣ541/347-9632, ⓦseastarbandon.com. Lively and agreeable spot that has just four rooms (❸) and is attached to the *HI Sea Star Hostel*, 375 Second St (same number), where there are dorm beds ($13–16) and family rooms (❶), self-catering facilities, and a laundry. At both, advance booking is strongly recommended.

Sunset Motel about a mile from town at 1865 Beach Loop Drive ⓣ541/347-2453 or 1-800/842-2407, ⓦwww.sunsetmotel.com. Outstanding waterside option that comprises motel rooms, condos, and, best of all, several older seafront cabins with fabulous views along the coast – it's well worth paying the extra. ❸–❼
Windermere Motel 3250 Beach Loop Drive ⓣ541/347-3710. Modest choice two miles from town that has small but affordable chalet-huts, with fireplaces and kitchenettes in some units. ❹

The Town

More than anything else, Bandon's rugged **seashore** is its real treat, with several miles of sea stack-studded beach stretching south of town beneath pine-pricked cliffs and in view of Beach Loop Drive, which runs past the northern end of **Bandon State Park**. The coast here is especially magnificent in stormy weather, when giant tree stumps are tossed up out of the ocean like matchsticks, and in calmer conditions you can stroll along the beach for hours. Footpaths lead down to the beach from most of the inns and resorts lining Beach Loop Drive, and there's also access from the state park. Toward the north end of the drive, and signposted here and there, you can spot a number of expressive-looking sea stacks with monikers like "Cat and Kittens," "Elephant," and "Five Foot," but the most distinctive is simply known as **Face Rock**, supposedly the basalt visage of a native princess poking her huge rocky head out from the waves and gazing at the sky longingly. Combined with the stories of the sea stacks around it, Face Rock's imagery is complicated enough to require a written explanation behind the legend, on display at the rock's own official state scenic viewpoint.

Bandon's **town center** is itself no more than a cluster of unassuming timber buildings in between US-101 and the Coquille River, but it does have a real sense of place as well as one of the best bookshops on the coast – Winter River, 170 SE Second St (ⓣ541/347-4111). The town's history is on display at the **Coquille River Museum**, 270 Fillmore St and US-101 (daily 10am–4pm; $2; ⓦwww.bandonhistoricalmuseum.org), which has a good section on the fire of 1936 and a large sample of old photographs. There's also a pleasing hodgepodge of wooden shacks and fishing buildings along First Street as it runs west from the center to the mouth of the Coquille.

On the other (north) side of the river, the **Coquille River Lighthouse** (summer tours daily 10am–4pm; donation) is a squat white cylinder that cuts a romantic silhouette even though its beacon has been extinguished since the 1930s. However, its keeper's quarters – almost two-thirds as tall as the lighthouse itself – is now used for a mildly interesting **museum** (same hours) laying out the story of the building and its checkered past. The lighthouse marks the

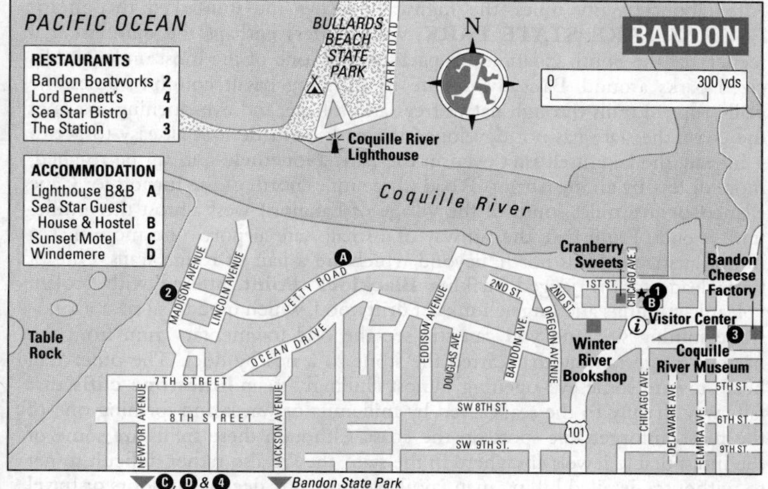

start of **Bullards Beach State Park**, a long stretch of pristine beach and sand dunes knee-deep in contorted piles of driftwood. To get there, take US-101 north over the river and watch for the turnoff on the left. And, as if all that weren't enough, the mud-flats of the Coquille estuary are perfect for **clamming** and **crabbing** from the town's jetties.

The town's biggest shindig is the **Cranberry Festival**, held over three days in the middle of September with a parade, live music, and all sorts of food stalls. Cranberries are big business in Bandon, and there are even tours of the bogs where they grow. Located a few miles east of town off Hwy-42, **Faber Farms** offers such visits during the autumn harvest season and sells the fruit for as little as $1 per pound (information at ⓣ1-866-347-1166, ⓦwww.oregoncranberry.com). You can also pick up these famously tangy treats – mixed with nuts, chocolate, and the like – at Cranberry Sweets, First Street at Chicago SE (ⓣ541/347-9475); if such berries aren't your thing, Bandon is also well known for its Bandon Cheese Factory, 680 E Second St (ⓣ541/347-2456), not exactly a factory tour but a good spot to sample handfuls of free cheese and curds – though the facility is now owned by the Tillamook Cheese company, itself located on the North Coast (see p.157).

Eating

If you haven't already filled up on cranberries and cheese, Bandon has a fair supply of good **cafés** and **restaurants**. The *Sea Star Bistro*, for one, in the hostel, does an excellent range of meals from just $10. Not far away, *The Station*, 635 Second St at Fillmore (ⓣ541/347-9615), is a family-style place that's a popular spot for an all-American breakfast. More upmarket options include two restaurants noted for their seafood, the *Bandon Boatworks* (ⓣ541/347-2111), west of the town center by the river at the end of Jetty Road, and the smart *Lord Bennett's*, about a mile south of the center at 1695 Beach Loop Drive (ⓣ541/347-3663).

Floras Lake State Park

Towns become fewer and farther between as you travel south from Bandon, with Hwy-101 staying a few miles inland as it careens through forested hills.

After about twenty miles, the highway reaches the unmarked turnoff for **FLORAS LAKE STATE PARK**, which offers perhaps the quintessential scenery of the South Coast and is paradoxically one of the most under-publicized parks around. Basically, despite its stunning basalt columns, limestone walls, rugged trails through native trees and foliage, and eye-opening views of the coast, the state has not developed the park or made it at all easy to get to – indeed, the lake itself isn't even in the park. Nonetheless, it can be reached, more or less, by taking Airport Road (three miles north of the turnoff for Cape Blanco, or five miles south of the village of Langlois) west almost three miles until it ends. From here the runway of a small state airport – no more than a minor airstrip – leads north, beyond which are a pair of rough trails. One of these leads to the jagged, striking **Blacklock Point**, littered with broken volcanic columns and huge chunks of driftwood, which used to sit near a sandstone mining site, and you can still see the odd fragmentary ruin from the narrow-gauge railway that carted the stone to a nearby dock. The other trail heads toward some eye-opening, almost chillingly steep **limestone cliffs** that fall away sharply to the sea, carved by millennia of waves and forming one of the most unforgettable spots on the coast. Although these sights are some of the indisputable jewels anywhere in the state, they're also rather difficult to get to without a detailed hiking map (available from any decent outdoors or travel bookshop, or call Oregon State Parks at ⓣ503/378-4168). Lacking this, you're risking getting lost by venturing too far out here, and could find yourself tumbling down a cliff face if you're not careful. Ultimately, take precautions as you would in any true wilderness zone – day-trippers need not apply.

Cape Blanco State Park

Much more user-friendly, and almost as visually appealing, **CAPE BLANCO STATE PARK** lies a short distance south of Floras Lake (though isn't accessible from it) and fills out a bumpy, triangular headland marked by a Victorian **lighthouse** (April–Oct Thurs–Mon 10am–3.30pm; donation suggested), perched high on a clifftop some five miles west of Hwy-101. Signs of the early homesteaders who colonized the coast are rare, but here in the park, in a lovely tranquil spot overlooking the river, is the solitary, shingle-clad **Hughes House** (same hours as lighthouse; donation), a sturdy two-story structure built in the 1890s and now refurnished in period style. The surrounding farmland has been left pretty much untouched, too, and nearby are the scant remnants of a pioneer cemetery. Among several **hikes**, one short trail leads to the coast from the boat ramp near the house, while another winds down from the lighthouse promontory to the craggy beachhead, where you can sometimes see the eerie remains of recent shipwrecks – the cape is still one of the most dangerous areas of the coast for boaters, especially during storms. The **campground**, with its excellent set of cabins (pitch $12–16, cabins $35; ⓣ541/332-6774, reserve at ⓣ1-800/452-5687), sits in the woods on a bluff behind the seashore.

Port Orford

Back on US-101, it's four miles more to **PORT ORFORD**, a casual little fishing port whose main attraction is **Battle Rock**, a large, chunky outcrop that was the site of an 1851 struggle between white settlers, in the form of the crew of the steamship *Sea Gull*, and a band of local Rogue natives. The Rogue lived on the seashore and tried to resist the landing of the whites – with predictably disastrous consequences. The rock pokes up above the seashore beside US-101 on the south side of town, and is a huge enough to climb up if you have good hiking boots; from the wooded crest are fine views of the sea and the town, as well as a precipitous drop from the north face – and a handful of nineteenth-century graves. Next door to the rock is a seasonal **visitor center** (Mon–Fri 10am–5pm; ⓣ541/332-8055, ⓦwww.portorfordoregon.com). Perhaps more appealing than the rock, though, is the **port** itself (signposted throughout town), which unlike most coastal harbors is actually a **dry dock** – a crane hoists every boat from the water and deposits it on the wharves. Thus, walking amid these crusty trawlers is an intriguing and unexpected experience, given that you rarely get to see the underside of such craft or their full size. If sufficiently impressed, you can take **lunch** here at *Dock Tackle* (ⓣ541/332-8985), munching on ultra-fresh crab meat and fish 'n' chips – as good as any meal in town.

Greyhound **buses** shoot through Port Orford on US-101 – call ⓣ1-800/231-2222 for drop-off details. If you break your journey here, you can choose from the cozy **B&B** *Home by the Sea*, 444 Jackson at 5th St (ⓣ541/332-2855, ⓦwww.homebythesea.com; ❺), which offers pleasant views over the coast and has just three guestrooms and, less appealing, several run-of-the-mill **motels** (❸).

Gold Beach and around

Five miles south of Port Orford, US-101 makes a rare and brief turn inland to loop around **Humbug Mountain State Park**, comprising a mighty coastal headland whose 1756-foot summit is reached from the highway along a three-mile switchback-laden hiking trail – making for a strenuous six-mile round trip. The first-come-first-served **campground** (information at ⓣ541/332-6774; $12–16) is down by the river, beside the main road beneath the mountain.

Beyond the park, US-101 sticks close to the coastline in the shadow of forested mountains which sweep smoothly down to the sea. These mountains mark the western limit of the **Siskiyou National Forest**, a vast slab of remote wilderness that is most easily explored by boat along the turbulent **Rogue River** from **GOLD BEACH**, at the river mouth 23 miles from Humbug Mountain. Gold Beach has always been dependent on the Rogue River: in the 1850s the town prospered from the gold the river had washed into its dark sands and later the Rogue fed its salmon canneries. Nowadays, the town – just a long ribbon of modern development strung along US-101, unexciting with the exception of the handsome 1930s bridge – is largely devoted to packing visitors off on **jet boats**, up canyons and through the Rogue's roaring rapids. Among several boat operators, the pick are Mail Boat Hydro-Jets (ⓣ541/247-7033 or 1-800/458-3511, ⓦwww.mailboat.com), whose wharf is on the north side of the river, and Jerry's Rogue Jets (ⓣ541/247-4571 or 1-800/451-3645, ⓦwww.roguejets.com), on the south bank. There are daily jet-boat trips from May to mid-October and charges begin at about $34 per person for six hours through to $75 for an eight-hour excursion. There's a two-hour break for lunch at a riverside lodge, but food isn't included in the price; reservations are strongly advised.

Greyhound **buses** drop off and pick up at 29770 Colvin St, a block east of Hwy-101(ⓣ1-800/231-2222). There are many modern **motels** south of the river along 101; one of the more appealing is the simple and well-kept *Ireland's Rustic Lodges*, 29330 Ellensburg Ave at 11th Street (ⓣ541/247-7718, ⓦwww.irelandsrusticlodges.com; ❸), which has a number of quaint wooden chalets. Although you'll probably not want to linger in town for a fancy **meal** – there are plenty of gut-stuffing seafood diners and fast-food joints to sate your baser appetite – there is one unexpectedly good choice for Northwest Cuisine in *Chives*, 29212 Hwy-101 (ⓣ541/247-4121), a swanky spot serving up tasty cioppino, rock shrimp risotto, and assorted salmon and steak entrees.

Rogue River National Recreation Trail

Exciting though jet boating is, it's easier to concentrate on the scenery around the Rogue River on foot. The forty-mile **Rogue River National Recreation Trail** (also see p.206) begins at Grave Creek, thirty-odd miles to the northwest of Grants Pass (see p.206) – which, of course, you cannot access from here by road without taking a huge, day-long detour around the mountains. In any case, it's much better to negotiate the trail heading downriver and downhill – your best bet is to travel upriver by boat and then hike down. None of the Gold Beach boats get anywhere near Grave Creek, but they do travel far enough upriver to provide a good long hike on the journey back. There are regular first-come-first-served campgrounds ($12–20) along the trail, as well as a series of strategically placed lodges on its lower half, each a day's hike from the other. For detailed advice, visit Gold Beach's **Siskiyou National Forest Ranger Station**, just south of the Rogue River on US-101 at 29279 Ellensburg Ave (Mon–Fri 8am–5pm; ⓣ541/247-3600, ⓦwww.fs.fed.us/r6/siskiyou). The adjacent **visitor center** (ⓣ541/247-7526 or 1-800/525-2334, ⓦwww.goldbeach.org) has details of all the local jet-boat operators.

South to Brookings

Down towards the California border is Oregon's "banana belt," warmed by drifting thermal troughs from the north California coast and unusually sunny (often over 60°F in January), making it popular with retirees though largely undiscovered by the outside world. Starting seven miles south of Gold Beach are a trio of appealing state parks that offer a pleasant landscape in these toasty environs. The first in the succession, **Cape Sebastian**, has a fine viewpoint perched two hundred feet above the surging waves, as well as trails through flowery meadows and ocean bluffs; the second park, just to the south, **Pistol River**, is set among sprawling sand dunes but is best known for its fabulous collection of sea stacks – monstrous, gnarled rocky behemoths scattered amid the waters, providing a dramatic backdrop for the frequent **windsurfing** competitions held here in the summer. Just a few miles beyond Pistol River, **Samuel H. Boardman State Park** is a twelve-mile coastal strip of parkland

Exploring the redwoods

The quickest way to reach the Rogue River Valley from Brookings is to continue south on **US-101** into California. Twenty miles beyond the border, US-101 meets **US-199**, which weaves northeast through the Siskiyou Mountains toward Cave Junction (see p.211), negotiating inhospitable mountain passes and curving around plunging gorges, key features of the landscape's surly beauty. A few miles east of the juncture on US-199 lies **Jedediah Smith Redwoods State Park**, where mighty **redwoods**, colossal trees up to 350 feet tall, crowd in on the highway as it wriggles up toward Oregon, passing the trailhead for the Simpson-Reed Trail, a short and easy stroll through some of the grandest trees. Just past the park, the **Redwood National Park Information Center** (ⓣ707/464-6101 ext 5265, ⓦwww.nps.gov/redw) supplies maps and has cycling and hiking trail details for the series of parks that stretch forty miles along the California coast, protecting groves of the ancient redwoods.

whose viewpoints, picnic areas, and footpaths – from the bluffs down to the beach – are all accessed via US-101. Among several sandy coves, **Whalehead Cove** is one of the most scenic spots, while there are plenty of other striking landscapes as well – sheer cliff walls, chunky basalt monoliths, old mining sites, and three-hundred-year-old stands of Sitka spruce. Especially memorable is the sizable Native American **midden** – a huge pile of ancient discarded seashells and animal bones that's an officially protected artifact.

BROOKINGS, 29 miles south of Gold Beach, is the capital of the banana belt, though the local industry is the genteel art of flower growing. Most of North America's Easter lilies are grown here, and some of the local azaleas are over twenty feet high and three hundred years old, inspiring the annual **Azalea Festival** on Memorial Day weekend at the end of May. Greyhound **buses** pass through town (information at Ⓣ1-800/231-2222) and there's a **visitor center** (Mon–Fri 9am–5pm; Ⓣ541/469-3181, Ⓦwww.brookingsor.com) down by the harbor, but the town is much too glum to keep you from the rugged seashore surrounding it. To **stay** in the area, avoid the dreary motels and venture to the north end of town to **Harris Beach State Park**, right off Hwy-101 (pitch $17–21, yurts $29; information at Ⓣ1-800/551-6949, reserve at Ⓣ1-800/452-5687), which has much of the same compelling scenery found in the above parks, but with the added draw of a national wildlife sanctuary, **Goat Island**, harboring tufted puffins. Alternatively, if you head ten miles northeast of town along North Bank Road, you can swim, boat, and camp at **Loeb State Park** (pitch $12–16, cabins $35; reserve as above), whose major attractions are its stately groves of redwood and myrtlewood trees.

There isn't anything to detain you between Brookings and California, but just over the border lie the mighty redwoods of **Redwood National Park** and **Jedediah Smith Redwoods State Park** (see opposite) and beyond this you can take US-199 over the Siskiyou Mountains to make the loop to the Oregon Caves and Grants Pass (see p.206) – the first highway back to the Oregon interior after more than a hundred miles.

The Willamette and Rogue River valleys

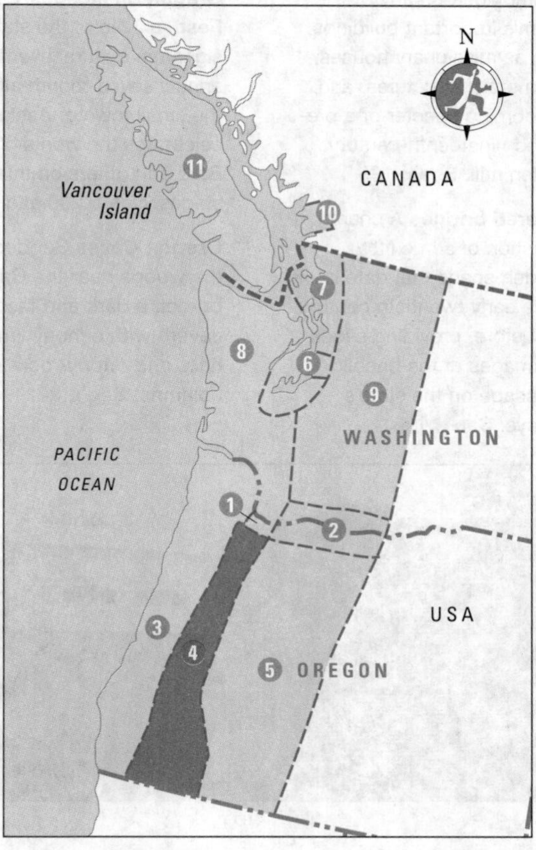

CHAPTER 4

Highlights

* **Silver Falls State Park** Justifiably the most popular park in the state, a beautiful assortment of waterfalls you can traverse on a leafy loop, the highlight of which is the towering cascade of South Falls. See p.192

* **Mission Mill Village** Visit this assemblage of many of Salem's important buildings, such as missionary houses, commercial structures, and the looming specter of a preserved nineteenth-century woolen mill. See p.195

* **Covered bridges** A charming collection of some fifty wooden spans that date back to the early twentieth century and before, providing evocative images of the bucolic landscape on the state's byways. See p.196

* **Eugene Saturday Market** A colorful and frenetic weekly festival of hippie-flavored arts and crafts, buzzing with all kinds of visitors and vendors peddling the likes of beeswax candles, herb soaps, and glass pipes for smoking "tobacco". See p.200

* **Oregon Shakespeare Festival** One of the state's signature cultural events, an annual seven-month affair in the small town of Ashland that celebrates the works of the Bard and others on three stages. See p.209 and p.211

* **Oregon Caves** Set deep in the woods near the California border, a dark and fascinating cavern with echoey limestone halls and drippy rock columns. See p.212

△ Covered bridge

4

The Willamette and Rogue River valleys

Running north-south from Portland (see p.75) almost to the California border, the **Willamette** and **Rogue River valleys** are home to most Oregonians – unlike their neighbors in Washington, who mostly cluster along the coast or inland bays. Host to the state's four largest cities (along with Portland and its suburbs), these valleys may not have quite the natural appeal of the Cascades or the coast, but they make up for it with a number of interesting cultural attractions, historic sites, and colorful festivals and fairs. More importantly, the valleys are immediately accessible along the busy four-lane route of Interstate 5, which leads many to dub the entire area the **I-5 Corridor** – a fast and generally straight route within the valleys, but a hilly, winding concourse in between them. Indeed, this middle section – roughly from **Cottage Grove** to **Grants Pass** – offers some fine views of mountain landscapes and an appealing small town or two, but not much else.

As with Portland, the most engaging towns along the route – such as **Eugene**, **Ashland**, and **Jacksonville** – either have **urban-growth boundaries** or stringent planning and development guidelines. Moreover, their downtown cores typically lie some distance from the freeway, built around historic structures or train depots more than off-ramps and overpasses. Those cities that do little to control development – mainly **Medford** and **Roseburg** – are uninspiring amalgamations of strip malls and office complexes built up along the highway, with hardly any attractions. Note that a second longstanding route, **Highway 99**, provides alternative access, in some places on a pair of highways marked East and West (in relation to I-5); these slower-paced, two-lane roads were the main route up and down the state before the freeway was finished in the 1960s. Even today, many outstanding parks, viewpoints, and historic sites are scattered along Hwy-99, and anyone interested in traveling the backroads will become familiar with it rather quickly.

Geographically the valleys lie roughly an equal distance between the Oregon Cascades and coast, and numerous trans-mountain and -coastal side roads provide decent two-lane access. You will, of course, find immediate **Greyhound** and **Amtrak** access along I-5 (see "Basics," p.32 and p.31). In the case of the latter, the Willamette Valley is served by the **Coast Starlight** line from California, while the Eugene-to-Portland section is serviced by the **Cascades** line – both names having little to do with the Oregon geography through which the trains pass.

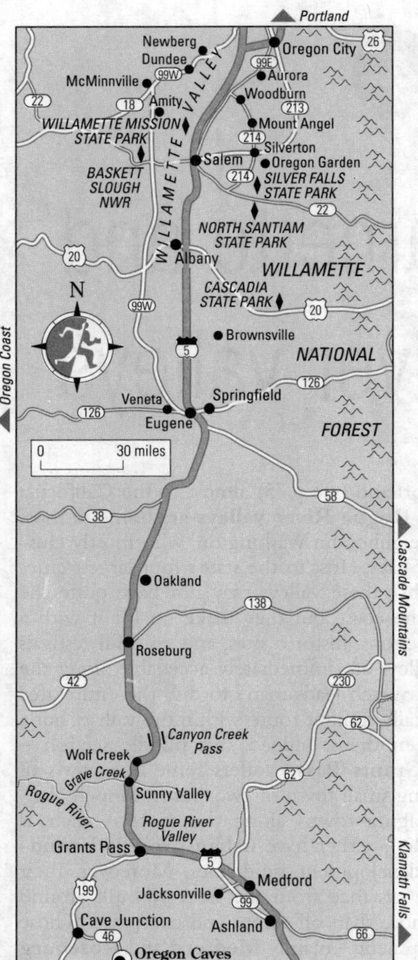

Some history

As both valleys grew up near their eponymous rivers – the **Willamette** flowing northward up to Portland, the **Rogue River** wending east-west from the mountains to the coast – it's not surprising that agriculture and logging were the central occupations in the nineteenth and early twentieth centuries, along with mining in the hills. Boasting rich and fertile soils (in the case of the Willamette Valley, thanks to the monumental Bretz Floods; see box p.122), these valleys were long home to native tribes, along with itinerant white explorers, but it wasn't until the rise of the **Oregon Trail** (see box, p.186) that both areas experienced considerable settlement. The main route of the trail ended in the Willamette Valley, but the Rogue River Valley, too, attracted migrants on the alternate **Applegate Trail** (p.205). These heady pioneer days are still recalled in the minds of many old-time Oregonians with a tall tale that explains their mild disdain for their California neighbors. A legendary **fork** on the Oregon Trail once showed two routes: the one to California was marked by a cairn of shimmering quartz, the other by a marker stating "To Oregon". The pioneers who could read (and were therefore respectable and hardworking) came to Oregon; the greedy rabble went south.

In these early days the region's newcomers, selling the produce from the farms and forests, spawned a handful of trading centers, bustling townships such as Oregon City, Salem, Eugene, and Portland, from where ships left for Europe and the East Coast laden with raw materials. The lack of safe anchorage along the storm-battered coast inspired the success of Portland, and through its burgeoning docks the other Willamette Valley towns gained access to the Pacific via the Columbia River. It was, however, a different sort of natural resource that boosted the pioneer economy sky-high. In 1852, **gold** was unearthed on the Rogue River, and during the subsequent gold rush the prospectors' colony of Jacksonville was even touted as the state capital. However, the gold gave out in the 1880s, and the region, while fueled by the injection of cash, resumed its more pedestrian agricultural progress.

For the next eighty years the commerce from agriculture and the timber trade largely defined the valleys, with all the towns except Portland staying pleasantly small and well preserved. By the 1970s, though, the rise of the **environmental movement** and the demise of many old-growth forests limited the activities of the major logging companies, until by 2003 no significant timber enterprises were based in the state. That said, logging still occurs erratically throughout the western forests, and agriculture is still going strong. Largely because of its liberal politics and considerable farm lobby, the state has some of the most rigid and tightly enforced **land-use planning** codes in the nation, and the widespread development seen along I-5 in California and Washington simply doesn't exist in Oregon. In many ways the valleys represent a slice of preserved social history, a collection of mostly small-acreage farms and rangelands harkening back to the days of the early pioneers (though with modern equipment, of course), and run by descendants of some of the original nineteenth-century trailblazers as well. Moreover, the minimal roadside billboards and many state parks and natural preserves in the region give it the feel of a charming anachronism: rural and small-town America largely free of the excesses of modern development, and kept that way by law.

The Willamette Valley

Running 120 miles parallel to and an hour's drive from the coast, the flat, green **Willamette Valley** was the home of Oregon's first settlements and towns, and the valley (pronounced "wah-LAM-it") is still at the heart of the state's social, political, and cultural existence. Most of Oregon's population is concentrated here, either in the cities strung along the **Willamette River** or in the hinterland of rural villages, and many remain dependent on agriculture even today. Among the more diverting of the valley towns are **Oregon City**, on the periphery of Portland and of historic interest as the settlement at the end of the Oregon Trail; the state capital, **Salem**, which has a handful of historic curiosities, along with its legislative campus; and fun and friendly **Eugene**, a buoyant, lively college town with a New Age feel. Other scattered points of interest include the pleasant **vineyards** on the northwest side of the valley, the giant Howard Hughes airplane, the **Spruce Goose,** in **McMinnville**, and the curious ethnic and religious enclaves of **Aurora** and **Mount Angel**.

Public transportation along the Willamette Valley is excellent, with regular Greyhound **buses** running from Portland to Eugene and beyond, and Amtrak operating two **train** lines. Portland's transit system, Tri-Met, covers Oregon City. Beyond the I-5 corridor, you may have more trouble accessing the various towns and parks, though some city bus systems – notably Eugene's LTD – are excellent and can take you all over their areas.

Oregon City

Set beside the confluence of the Willamette and Clackamas rivers, about thirteen miles south of downtown Portland, **OREGON CITY** is, in a sense, where the state began. This was the end of the Oregon Trail and the **first capital** of the Oregon Territory – though ironically founded by the British-owned Hudson's Bay Company. The company's local agent, **John McLoughlin**, built an early lumber mill here in 1829, when American settlement of the region was largely fanciful and even the term "Northwest" referred to places like Ohio and Michigan, not Oregon. Today, the historic core of this split-level town sits along Highway 99E and consists of an unappetizing modern section down by the river, along with an uptown area of old wooden houses set on a bluff, which you can ascend via steep roads, stairways, and a free elevator at 7th Street and Railroad Avenue.

Among a series of nineteenth-century clapboard houses located on the compact, gridiron upper level is the restored **McLoughlin House**, 713 Center St (Wed–Sat 10am–4pm, Sun 1–4pm; $4; ⓦ www.mcloughlinhouse.org), which was moved up from the riverfront around 1900. It was once the home of John

The Great Migration

Perhaps more than any other early American leader, **Thomas Jefferson** realized the opportunities presented by the vast lands west of the Mississippi, and, after he became president in 1801, he was in a position to act upon his expansionist vision, though with caution. The French held the **Louisiana Territory** between the Mississippi and the Rockies, and the British claimed the land from the Rockies to the Pacific – a vast wilderness known as the **Oregon Country**, buffered by Russian Alaska and Spanish California. Consequently, when Jefferson began organizing an American overland expedition to the Pacific he was careful to define its purpose solely in terms of trade and commerce.

Luckily, the European powers were embroiled in the Napoleonic Wars, and, with the French keen to raise cash, Napoleon sold the Louisiana Territory to the Americans in 1803. And so, when the **Lewis and Clark Expedition** left St Louis for the Pacific in 1804, it had as much to do with taking stock of the country's new possessions as the long-term strategy of contesting British influence. In the event, Anglo-American territorial rivalry dragged on until 1846, but by this time the British claim to the region south of the 49th Parallel (present-day Washington and Oregon) had become academic. Their stake to the land had been swept away by the rising tide of overland immigration launched by pioneer farmers, the majority of whom came from just east of the Mississippi.

The detailed reports emanating from the Lewis and Clark expedition catalyzed the migration west, but the migrants – or **movers**, as they're often called – were much more inspired by the missionaries who went west to Christianize the "heathen" native tribes in the 1830s. After all, Lewis and Clark traveled by canoe, but the missionaries headed out in simple covered wagons encumbered by farming equipment and livestock – precisely as the pioneers had to do. The missionaries also sent back glowing and widely circulated reports of the Oregon Country's mild climate, fertile soil, and absence of malaria, and confirmed crucially that the lands of the West Coast were well forested. Mid-nineteenth-century American farmers judged the fertility of land by the size of the trees it supported, quite wrong from a modern agricultural view, but it explains why they ignored the treeless prairie that barred their route just beyond the Mississippi, commonly calling it the "Great American Desert" – and leaving it to a later generation of farmers.

McLoughlin, who ignored both political antagonisms and the instructions of his employers in providing the Americans who survived the Oregon Trail (see box below) with food, seed, and periodic rescue from hostile native tribes. His main base was north of here in Vancouver on the Columbia River, but he retired to Oregon City in 1846 confident that his cordial relationship with – and generosity to – the American pioneers would stand him in good stead. He was wrong, underestimating the nationalistic prejudices of his American neighbors, and the local administration stripped him of his Oregon City landholdings, leaving McLoughlin an embittered man. His two-story house has been re-furnished in period style, with a good scattering of McLoughlin's own possessions.

Of somewhat lesser interest, the 1845 **Ermatinger House**, 619 6th St (Fri–Sun 11am–3pm; $3; ⓣ503/650-1851), was where the name of neighboring Portland was chosen on the flip of a coin – with "Boston" as the alternative. Call about the house's "living history" tours, in which docents put on period garb and put on the airs of old-time pioneers. Just down the street at no. 603, the **Stevens Crawford House** (Feb–Dec Wed–Fri 10am–4pm, Sat & Sun 1–4pm; $4) is a historic 1908 home, restored to something of its original appearance, with various antiques and decor from the late-Victorian era.

In the spring of 1843, one thousand movers gathered at Independence and Westport on the banks of the Missouri to prepare for the **Great Migration**. The pioneers were a remarkably homogeneous bunch, nearly all experienced farmers, traveling in family groups with ordinary ox-pulled farm wagons with flimsy canvas roofs, often walking alongside their vehicles, instead of riding and adding extra weight to them. Only too aware of the difficulties of the journey, the movers voted in wagon-train leaders after the first hundred miles and established camp rules to govern everything from the grazing of livestock to the collection of fuel (usually buffalo dung).

Traversing almost two thousand miles of modern-day Kansas, Nebraska, Wyoming, and Idaho, they cajoled their wagons across rivers, struggled over mountain passes, endured the burning heat of the plains, chopped their way through forests, and paused at the occasional frontier fort or missionary station to recuperate. They also bartered supplies with various tribes in return for rafts and knowledge of the outback. Finally, after six months on the trail, they arrived at what is now **The Dalles** (see p.135). From here the group had a difficult choice to make before reaching the lush Willamette Valley. Some people built rafts and risked the treacherous currents of the Columbia River, while others took the Barlow Road (see box, p.133) around Mount Hood, notorious for its swiftly changing weather and steep hills, many of which had to be crossed through the use of heavy ropes to lower the wagons down the slopes. Their arrival doubled Oregon's American population, and pushed the US government toward the creation of the **Oregon Territory** just five years later.

Over the next thirty years, further waves of settlers followed the Oregon Trail, along with an offshoot that populated the Rogue River Valley, the **Applegate Trail**. Other amateur adventurers whittled away at the time it took by blazing short cuts across the mountains and finding hitherto unfamiliar passages. Overall, they swelled the population of the Willamette Valley by some 53,000, and only with the coming of the railroad in the 1880s did the trail fall into disuse. Precious little survives today to remember the pioneers by, but out in eastern Oregon a few scattered hillsides still show the deep ruts made by the wheels of their wagons, and there are several interpretive centers along the way.

The Stevens Crawford House is associated with the **Museum of the Oregon Territory**, right off Hwy-99E at 211 Tumwater Drive (Wed–Fri 10am–4pm, Sat & Sun noon–4pm; $4), which has mildly interesting pioneer relics and native artifacts. However, for a more engaging, if not quite as authentic, taste of local history, head to the northern edge of the lower part of town, to the **End of The Oregon Trail Interpretive Center**, 1726 Washington St (March–Oct: Mon–Sat 9.30am–5pm, Sun 10.30am–5pm; Nov–Feb: Wed–Sat 11am–4pm, Sun noon–4pm; $6.50; Ⓦwww.endoftheoregontrail.org). As a gallant attempt to give the flavor of the pioneer's difficult and dangerous trek westward, the center is housed in a trio of giant, imitation covered-wagon buildings, which certainly makes it distinctive. Although the actual artifacts are thin on the ground – basically a series of dioramas, replica antiques, and documentary films – the costumed staff give the lowdown with great gusto as you tour through the facility.

Oregon City has little in the way of hotels or restaurants worth seeking out, so your best bet is visiting on a day-trip from Portland. Tri-Met **buses** #32 and #33, color-coded green, run from downtown Portland (see p.78) to various points in Oregon City, including the upper town.

The northern valley

South and west of Oregon City, the **northern section** of the Willamette Valley is pleasantly bucolic, with nice, rolling green hills, small farmsteads, and rippling creeks, which you can explore on two-lane roads that often trace the routes of nineteenth-century trails. There are fine **wineries** in the area, little European **ethnic** and **religious colonies** in a few spots, and assorted **architectural curiosities** like a monastery library built by Alvar Aalto and a tourable modern house designed by Frank Lloyd Wright. Keep in mind, though, that you'll probably need a **car** to access these sites, and even with that, may find yourself stymied by the lack of bridges across the Willamette River (there's even a ferry here and there). Thus, it's best to choose one side of the valley at a time to explore unless you plan on crossing the river near Newberg or Salem.

West of the river

On the opposite side of I-5 from Oregon City, the land **west** of the Willamette River is a lovely terrain of low valleys and stands of second-growth trees, crossed by narrow two-lane roads that lead by flowing streams, old barns, and plots set aside for growing berries, grasses, and grapes. The latter fruit is particularly propitious, as this is the heart of Oregon's **wine country**, with the hillsides rich with vineyards and many wineries open to the public for tours and tastings. The most direct route into the area is along **Highway 99 West**, which accesses more than two dozen acclaimed wineries, most of which pour superb Pinot Noirs, Chardonnays, and Rieslings. Pick up a wine-country tour map from any local visitor center (or from Ⓦwww.oregonwine.org), and expect the odd traffic delay in little burgs like **Dundee**, now a well-known draw for vino.

Newberg, McMinnville, and Amity

Forty minutes southwest of Portland along Hwy-99W, the historic crossroads of **NEWBERG** boasts a number of fine old structures, some dating to pioneer days. Although none is particularly distinctive (except for the boyhood home of president Herbert Hoover, at 115 River St), the homes do make for a pleasant walking tour. Drop by the **visitor center**, 115 N Washington St (Mon–Fri 9am–5pm, Sat & Sun 9am–2pm; ⓣ503/538-2014, ⓦwww.newberg.org), for a brochure to aid you on your wanderings.

Fifteen miles further southwest, the town of **MCMINNVILLE** dates from the 1840s and is the seat of the oldest county, Yamhill, in the state. Its age is reflected in the town's late-Victorian architecture along **3rd Street** – though the newer structures along the Hwy-99W business route are all fairly drab. What really brings curious visitors out here, though, is the legendary Howard Hughes flying machine **The Spruce Goose**, which until the 1990s was housed in its own dome in Long Beach, California. Nowadays, it sits in the sizable confines of the **Evergreen Aviation Museum**, 3685 NE Three Mile Lane, a mile east of downtown on Hwy-18 (daily 9am–5pm; $11; ⓣ503/434-4180, ⓦwww.sprucegoose.org). Officially, and appropriately, known as the "Hughes Flying Boat," this giant craft is supposedly the largest airplane ever built, and was constructed of laminated wood (more birch than spruce) and achieved a moment of dubious fame when it made a minute-long flight in 1947. More a testament to the towering ego of its creator than an aeronautic milestone, the plane is nonetheless an interesting artifact of the postwar era. Though it can't be toured, it sits amid a slew of fighters, passenger crafts, spyplanes, and other curiosities, making the museum an essential stop for aviation buffs.

About seven miles south of McMinnville on Hwy-99W lies the small village of **AMITY**, home to a **monastery** of Brigittine monks, at 23300 Walker Lane (ⓣ503/835-8080, ⓦwww.brigittine.org), one of several in the Willamette Valley. The facility itself is simple and straightforward, but what brings curious interlopers out here (call or see the website for directions) is the stunning quality of the monks' home-made **fudge** – about as unexpected a delight as you'll find in the Northwest. Indeed, for such a holy place these sweets are amazingly decadent: the likes of amaretto fudge and "cherry nut fudge royale," all freshly prepared on the premises.

Baskett Slough National Wildlife Refuge and Willamette Mission State Park

Ten miles south from Amity on 99W is the striking **BASKETT SLOUGH NATIONAL WILDLIFE REFUGE** (Oct–April dawn–dusk; ⓣ503/623-2749), which occupies nearly 2500 acres and provides winter habitat for a variety of birds, but particularly waterfowl. Here you can spot such majestic creatures as herons, hawks, and Canada geese, along with many types of mammals and reptiles. Another enjoyable natural attraction can be found about seven miles east of Amity, directly on a bend in the Willamette River just past Hwy-221, where **WILLAMETTE MISSION STATE PARK** ($3 day-use fee) commemorates the site where Methodist preacher Jason Lee founded a mission in 1834 to try to convert the native tribes. He wasn't terribly successful in this endeavor (and, in any case, his efforts are better examined in Salem's Mission Mill Village; see p.195), but there is a memorial here to him, along with countless trails for horseback riding, hiking, and cycling, plus a summer **campground** (group sites $40–60). Even better, the park features the site of the region's first river ferry for covered wagons, the **Wheatland Ferry**, which began running in 1844 and is amazingly still in operation, though in a more modern form designed for automobiles (daily 5.30am–9.45pm; vehicles $1.35; bicycles free; ⓣ503/588-7979, ⓦwww.wheatlandferry.com).

Practicalities

Although the area directly west of the Willamette is hardly prime turf for **accommodation** and **eating**, there are several possibilities if you're really into the rural vineyard scene. In Newberg the grand old estate of *Springbrook Hazelnut Farm*, 30295 N Highway 99W (Ⓣ503/538-4606 or 1-800/793-8528, Ⓦwww.nutfarm.com; ❻), is a 1912 restored farmhouse with two additional dwellings that makes for a fine stay among orchards and vineyards; the rooms are thick with both modern furniture and copious antiques. A bit more lively, the *Hotel Oregon*, 310 Evans St in McMinnville (Ⓣ1-888/472-8427, Ⓦwww.hoteloregon.com; ❺), is a refurbished, stately old 1905 pile in this town's smallish downtown core, which used to be a lodge, dance hall, telegraph office, and bus depot, among other things, before it was converted back into a hotel. It now features a microbrew pub with a good selection of beers, free blues and folk concerts three times a week, quirky artwork, and pleasantly renovated rooms and suites (the former cheaper with shared bath). Its restaurant has a serviceable menu of dishes like burgers and pasta, but for tastier fare, head a few miles east, just off Hwy-99 between McMinnville and Newberg on Hwy-18. Here, the tiny hamlet of Dayton is mainly known as the site of the grand Colonial Revival estate of the *Joel Palmer House*, 600 Ferry St (Ⓣ503/864-2995, Ⓦwww.joelpalmerhouse.com). This historic 1853 structure is a nationally renowned restaurant to which Portland urbanites make special trips for its delicious, if expensive, Northwest Cuisine – the likes of escargot with chanterelle mushrooms and roasted loin of elk – so make sure to reserve ahead.

East of the river

To reach the area **east** of the river, you'll soon find that bridges are in very short supply between Oregon City and Salem, potentially leaving you driving around in circles as you hunt for a crossing point. Other than a single overpass on I-5 at the Portland suburb of Wilsonville and the Wheatland Ferry (see p.189), the sole way to traverse the river is a highway bridge a mile south of Newberg on Hwy-219.

Robert Newell House

After crossing, your first (eastbound) left will take you to the agreeable, if uneventful, grounds of **Champoeg State Park** (locally pronounced CHAM-poo-ey) and the **ROBERT NEWELL HOUSE** (Feb–Nov Sat & Sun 1–4.30pm; $2). This 1959 reconstruction of an early Oregon pioneer's house is loaded with antiques from different periods in US history. It also houses a second-floor display of the gowns of the wives of Oregon governors – more interesting than it sounds – providing a colorful look at the changing styles of provincial fashion. The most compelling part of the house is the depiction of Newell himself, who, unlike the typical stoic Protestant pioneer, was a true "mountain man" – an explorer of the West, local town founder, and larger-than-life character who operated various businesses here until an 1861 flood wiped out his enterprises. Since his first wife, of three, was the daughter of a Nez Perce chief, it's not surprising that when tragedy struck, "Doc" Newell hit the road once more, living among the tribe in Idaho for the rest of his life.

Aurora

From Champoeg, it's just a few miles further east along well-signposted country lanes, passing under the I-5 freeway, to the German colony of **AURORA**. After relocating from Bethel, Missouri, the immigrants who started the town in 1857 founded it as a odd mix of Christian spiritual refuge and Marxist commune, with residents sharing goods between themselves and subsisting on the fruits of their farm labor. Although the former part of the equation lasted longer than the latter (the temptations of American capitalism were abundantly on display up the road in Oregon City), Aurora nonetheless held on as an ethnic enclave until well into the twentieth century. Even today it sports a great number of **antique stores**, quaint clapboard houses dating from the nineteenth century, and a small, walkable scale and lack of over-development that gives a good impression of what the place may have been like in the old days. You can find out more about all these things, and pick up a walking-tour brochure of the town's dwellings, at the engaging **Old Aurora Colony Museum**, 2nd Street at Liberty (April–Oct Tues–Sat 10am–4pm, Sun noon–4pm; Nov–Dec & March Fri–Sat 10am–4pm, Sun noon–4pm; donation; ⓦwww.auroracolonymuseum.com), which is stuffed with the furniture, quilts, farm tools, books, and bric-a-brac of the colony, including the simple clothing worn by the residents – many garments sporting hook-and-eye closures, the villagers considering buttons to be a cheap and frivolous adornment.

Woodburn and Mount Angel

The town of **WOODBURN**, about five miles south of Aurora on Hwy-99E, is rapidly developing and visually burying much of its history as an agricultural hamlet. Its main sights are a downtown section off Hwy-214, which buzzes with cheap stores and diners catering to Russian and Mexican immigrants, and the grandly opulent **Settlemier House**, Settlemier Avenue at Garfield (Dec Sun 1–4pm, or by appointment at ⓣ503/982-1897; $3). As one of the valley's most prominent dwellings, this 1892 Queen Anne mansion features a wraparound veranda, conical tower, and an almost Neoclassical portico. As a stylish manor giving a hint of the aspirations of its owner, the town founder and an early horticulturist in the valley, the house is only open once a week during the winter holiday season, but is well worth touring by appointment at other times.

Looping six miles to the southeast on Hwy-214, the small burg of **MOUNT ANGEL** is mainly associated with one thing in the minds of Oregonians – **Oktoberfest**. This annual month-long spectacle is celebrated here with sprightly ethnic displays, copious amounts of beer, and the usual gut-busting German cuisine. Indeed, the place was named after the Swiss city where the town founder received his religious education, Engelberg, and it's been home to German immigrants since the turn of the last century.

Moreover, the town hosts a Benedictine **abbey** atop one of its hills that's open to the public. Late July is a good time to show up, when the monks put on a compelling **Bach Festival** ($40; tickets at ⓣ503/845-3321, ⓦwww.mtangel.edu), employing a grand pipe organ and including a dinner meal in the ticket. Additionally, fans of high-modern architecture won't want to miss the abbey's striking **library**, designed in 1970 by Alvar Aalto and freely tourable with the aid of a helpful brochure. As one of Oregon's few nationally important buildings outside of Portland, the library is a curving, asymmetrical design spread over two floors, with light flooding through hillside windows and skylights, and light-wood paneling giving the space a warm, inviting feel.

For representative **dining** in town during the festival or any time of the year, check out the *Mount Angel Brewing Company*, 210 Monroe St (ⓣ503/845-9624), whose microbrews are a bit lighter than some of the heavy drafts on tap at the local bars, though the sausages and barbecue dishes are plenty filling. Alternately, *Angel's Table*, 415 S Main St (ⓣ503/845-9289), has flavorful Teutonic selections like breaded pork wienerschnitzel and savory chicken breast with spinach and blue cheese.

The Gordon House and Silver Falls State Park

If you're inspired to take in more modern architecture, you won't want to miss the **Oregon Garden**, five miles south of Mount Angel in **Silverton** at 879 W Main St (daily 9am–3pm, summer closes 6pm; $7; ⓦwww.oregongarden.org), where, beyond the predictable array of local foliage, the main attraction is Frank Lloyd Wright's elegant **GORDON HOUSE** (daily 10am–2pm, summer closes 5pm; extra $2), which was moved here from its original location, 25 miles north along the banks of the Willamette, after being saved from demolition. Although intended as mass housing for the middle class, today such "Usonian" homes – with their cantilevered roofs, horizontal layouts, and narrow windows – are curious artifacts from a time when high-class design wasn't solely the province of the elite behind high, guarded walls. The Gordon House is particularly interesting as it features a number of idiosyncratic Wright experiments – hot water piped through a concrete floor for internal heating, a towering skylight over the kitchen (which Wright called the "work space"), an absence of 90-degree angles throughout the structure, and a frame built of concrete block and western red cedar. You can wander the main floor yourself or venture upstairs on a **public tour** for an additional $3 (adding up to $12 per person – an unfortunate case of nickel-and-diming for which the Oregon Garden is notorious). However, these upper spaces, with their low ceilings and ungainly geometry, may make you question Wright's overall judgment and taste.

In a more remote section of the valley, ten miles to the southeast, the lush, green confines of **SILVER FALLS STATE PARK** (ⓣ503/873-8681, ⓦwww.oregonstateparks.org), in part, justify the park as the state's most popular. What really makes the place so enticing, however, are its array of large and small **waterfalls**, which are collectively tourable on a hiking trail that you can pick up at the North or South Falls. One of the best hikes in the state, it takes you past huge stands of trees and verdant native foliage, over hills and across ravines, and along the banks of gently flowing Silver Creek. The undeniable highlight, though, are the two waterfalls that bracket the park – **North Falls**, a precipitous spray of mist you can approach on a narrow trail, and **South Falls**, a huge and spellbinding tower of crashing water that you can actually walk behind on a rocky basaltic ledge, hearing its thundering roar from just a few feet away.

While in the area, you can **stay** at the pleasant 1890 Victorian manor of the *Water Street Inn*, in Silverton at 421 N Water St (ⓣ503/873-3344 or 1-866/873-3344, ⓦwww.thewaterstreetinn.com; ❻), whose five lovely rooms and suites offer tasteful decor with minimal chintz. Another option is **camping** at Silver Falls for $18–21 (or minimally furnished cabins for $35), but you'll have to reserve many weeks or even months in advance to have any chance at getting a spot. Beyond the inn or the park, you're best off trying accommodations in Salem, 26 miles west of Silver Falls via highways 22 and 214. Outside of Oktoberfest and the German diners in Mount Angel, you'll find few distinctive eateries in the immediate area. Either head into town or west of the Willamette River for a meal.

Salem

Despite recently becoming the secondmost populous city in Oregon, **SALEM**, located fifty miles south of Portland, has often proven an elusive attraction for regional visitors. Not only does the modern sprawl of the town defy a sense of cohesiveness (and the visitor's navigation skills), but the build-up of motels and fast-food chains that greet you off the I-5 freeway give the place a strong air of dreariness. There are, not surprisingly, plenty of valid historical attractions here (some among the best in the state), but the city itself doesn't yet have the feeling of a true destination, and after poking around for a day or so, you'll probably be itching to move on to Eugene or Portland.

Arrival and accommodation

Easy to reach along the I-5 corridor, Salem can be visited on a day-trip from Portland or, better, on the way south towards Eugene and Ashland. The Greyhound **bus** station is located conveniently downtown at 450 Church St NE and Center Street, and so is the Amtrak **train** station, at 13th Street SE and Oak. The **visitor center** is part of the Mission Mill Museum, off 12th Street at 1313 Mill St SE (Ⓣ503/581-4325 or 1-800/874-7012, Ⓦwww.scva.org).

Salem has more than its share of modern, budget **motels**, but most of the more enticing places are a little way out from the center. Among them, one good option is the comfortable *Phoenix Inn Suites*, south of downtown at 4370 Commercial St SE (Ⓣ503/588-9220, Ⓦwww.phoenixinn.com; ④), which has around ninety spacious rooms, plus a pool and Jacuzzi. A bit more central is the

serviceable chain lodging at the *Red Lion*, north of the capitol at 3301 Market St NE (Ⓣ503/370-7888 or 1-800/RED-LION, Ⓦwww.redlion.com; ❺), while the *Marquee House*, 333 Wyatt Court NE (Ⓣ503/391-0837 or 1-800/949-0837, Ⓦwww.marqueehouse.com; ❹), is a stately Colonial Revival **B&B** close to downtown, with five rooms elegantly furnished with antiques and fetching gardens surrounding the place.

The City

Salem is not a very user-friendly place for newcomers, and unless you have a state map with a wide, sprawling view of the city, you may well get lost (our map provides a view of the central downtown area, the main area worth seeing). The advent of much new construction around the I-5 corridor and the city suburbs has only made the situation worse, and in the last few years highway exits and interchanges have shifted around with alarming regularity. Perhaps the easiest and most predictable access to downtown is to go westbound on Highway 22 to 17th Street, from where you turn north and go six blocks to State Street, which leads directly to the capitol – used as a starting point for the text below.

The capitol campus and Willamette University

Lying along State Street is the **state capitol campus** and the city's unmistakable centerpiece, the tall, white, Vermont-marble **State Capitol**, main entrance a block away at 900 Court St NE (Mon–Fri 7.30am–5pm; free; Ⓦwww.leg.state.or.us), whose cupola is topped by a large gold-leaf pioneer, axe in hand, eyes to the West. Finished in 1938 in a style dubbed "modern Greek" but actually more along the lines of late-Moderne, the building sports a marble carving at its entrance of Lewis and Clark processing regally towards (presumably) the Willamette Valley. Its caption – "Westward the Star of Empire Takes its Way" – is an odd sort of motto, considering the amount of blood and treasure expended getting rid of the British only a few years before they set off. Inside murals celebrate the state's beginnings and on the floor, under the wings of a bald eagle, there's a large bronze take on the state seal, in which wheat, a covered wagon, and trading ships symbolize Oregon's acceptance into the union in 1859. There are also hourly historical **tours** of the building and its tower for groups of ten or more (9am–3pm; free; reserve at Ⓣ503/986-1388), beginning at the information desk inside the rotunda. Back outside, manicured gardens surround the building, with statues of Salem's founder, Jason Lee, and John McLoughlin on the east side.

Next to the Capitol, south across State Street, leafy **Willamette University** is the oldest university in the West, originally a mission school set up by Lee. Its only real highlight for visitors is the **Hallie Ford Museum of Art**, 700 State St (Tues–Sat 10am–5pm; $3; Ⓦwww.willamette.edu/museum_of_art), which features compelling native baskets and handicrafts, plus assorted antiquities like ancient Greek vases and Egyptian funeral masks, and a handful of original prints by William Hogarth and Auguste Rodin.

The historic downtown core

Downtown Salem has a compact collection of nineteenth-century, low-slung red-brick commercial buildings, which were declared a National Historic District in 2001. Lying just west of the capital on State Street, with most of its key structures concentrated on Liberty and Commercial streets between

Chemeketa and Ferry, the district has as its showpiece the 1869 **Reed Opera House**, Court Street at Liberty, an Italianate 1869 structure that was once the nexus of local cultural activity and is now a trim little shopping mall. Opera houses like this sprang up all over the Northwest in the second half of the nineteenth century – "opera" in the broadest sense, as these boisterous establishments showed pretty much anything that was touring, from Sophocles to dancing dogs.

The old operatic and vaudeville entertainment, though, gave way in the early twentieth century to sparkling movie palaces; the town's best remaining example, the grand **Elsinore Theatre**, three blocks away at 170 High St, is a charming 1926 Neo-Gothic gem that narrowly escaped being razed a decade ago and is now a performing arts center (Ⓣ503/375-3574 or Ⓦwww.elsinoretheatre.com for details). It also shows monthly silent movies (Oct–May Wed 7pm; $5) and employs a Wurlitzer organ to add period atmosphere. Built in a medieval English style, with a name referring to Hamlet's castle, the Elsinore is among Oregon's best and most fascinating old cinemas, with ornate decoration throughout and stained-glass windows showcasing some of the Bard's most famous dramatis personae.

Mission Mill Village and Marion County Historical Society Museum

Methodist missionary Jason Lee's wooden, two-story former dwelling now sits on the grounds of **Mission Mill Village**, just east of the downtown core and Willamette University at 1313 Mill St SE (Mon–Sat 10am–5pm; $7; Ⓦwww.missionmill.org), along with other restored structures of the early pioneers and a looming industrial relic. Volunteers recount the complicated history (see box, overleaf) of Lee's endeavors in great detail as they lead tours at the village, which take you from the simple old houses of Lee and his followers to the huge, somewhat ominous mill facility nearby. As you poke around the array of giant picking, carding, weaving, and drying machines (with some demonstrating their actions at the press of a button), it's hard to imagine the level of dangerous, repetitive work required to produce woolen wear in the high American industrial age, though old photographs try to tell some of the story. In any case, by the later twentieth century the factory was antiquated by modern standards and closed its doors – though its descendants did go on to found the mighty, and still active, Pendleton Woolen Mills out in Eastern Oregon.

Around the back, the separate **Marion County Historical Society Museum**, 260 12th St SE (Wed–Fri noon–4pm, Sat 10am–4pm; $3; Ⓦwww.marionhistory.org), is a modest institution with a main exhibit on the Kalapuyan, who lived in the Willamette Valley until a combination of white settlers, the Klickitat tribe, and disease drove them out. As much as ninety percent of the native population were killed by a nineteenth-century malaria epidemic. The museum's pride and joy is a rickety and rare 125-year-old **canoe**, hollowed out, in the traditional manner, by hot coals.

Deepwood Estate and Bush House

About seven blocks south of the capitol campus are a pair of historic residences that are worth touring if you're spending more than a day in town. The first, **Deepwood Estate**, 1116 Mission St SE (May–Sept Sun–Fri noon–5pm, Oct–April Tues–Sat noon–5pm; $4; Ⓣ503/363-1825, Ⓦwww.oregonlink.com/deepwood), is a spacious, three-level Queen Anne home from 1894 that features pleasant English-style gardens, handsome

The legacy of Jason Lee

When Jason Lee set up Oregon's first US mission north of Salem in 1834 in what is now Willamette Mission State Park (see p.189), he originally intended to convert the area Native Americans. He soon found that his sermons went down better with the white fur-traders who had retired to farm in the area, and, deciding white settlement was the best way to further the cause, requested more recruits. The Methodist Missionary Board in New York sent a shipload of pioneers, and, usefully, the machinery for a grist- and sawmill, which Lee set up by a dam in Salem.

Times, however, became quite difficult due to harsh weather and lack of provisions, and plenty of pioneers perished in the severe conditions, including Lee's first wife and son, and then his second wife a few years later. Lee himself grew ill in 1843, was fired by the Missionary Board a year later, and died in Canada soon after. His ideal of a self-sufficient Willamette farming community, however, lived on and was advanced when an enterprising herder managed to drive a flock of high-grade sheep over the Oregon Trail in 1848 – no mean feat in itself. The woolen mills that came later, worked mostly by local women, sprang the rural valley into the industrial age – and Salem became established as an influential example for other upstart mill towns in the region.

oak-paneled walls, stained-glass windows, and an original adjoining carriage house. As you might expect, the estate is loaded with antiques and Victorian furnishings, and additionally has a quaint little gazebo that was first used in Portland's Lewis and Clark Exposition in 1905, and relocated here 44 years later.

Five blocks west, the **Bush House**, 600 Mission St SE (May–Sept Tues–Sun noon–5pm, Oct–April Tues–Sun 2–5pm; $4; Ⓦwww.salemart.org), has little to do with the line of US presidents, but was the residence of an early newspaper publisher who had a hand in crafting the state constitution. The 1878 house itself is a generally tasteful affair, with a reserved mid-Victorian-era facade and rooms decorated with period furnishings and minor nineteenth-century art. The highlight is the collection of ten Italian **marble fireplaces**, beautiful and ornate creations that seem too elegant to have ever housed burning logs and falling ash. Elsewhere on the grounds, the **pasture park** has a nice selection of rose gardens, orchards, flowerbeds, and a conservatory, while an **art center** sits in the estate's former barn and displays a decent array of modern artworks from regional artists.

Eating and drinking

For **food**, the area around the university is not the busy scene you might expect, and you're best off downtown. Here, the *Dairy Lunch Café*, 347 Court St (Ⓣ503/363-6433), is a classic 1960s diner with primo burgers; *Jonathan's Oyster Bar,* 445 State St (Ⓣ503/362-7219), serves fresh seafood, Cajun, and Southwestern cuisine; the pleasant *Arbor Café*, 345 High St NE (Ⓣ503/588-2353), has an imaginative range of pasta, sandwiches, and salads; and *Da Vinci's*, 180 High St SE (Ⓣ503/399-1413), offers authentic Italian cuisine and pizzas fired in a wood-burning oven.

Although Salem has the usual range of frat-oriented sports bars and grim, divey holes, one notable exception for **drinking** is the terrific *Boon's Treasury*, 888 Liberty St NE (Ⓣ503/399-9062), which offers nightly rock and blues jams (Wed–Sat) and a good array of burgers and microbrews. Even better, the bar is located in a classic old building from 1860, which once housed the state's first treasury.

Moving on from Salem

Unlike the terrain between Portland and Salem, the area between Salem and Eugene is fairly uninspired and mainline attractions are thin on the ground. There are cross-coastal routes, including highways 20 and 22, and same-numbered roads that lead you east into the Cascades, but there are few interesting sights directly off I-5, except for a handful, at best. The standout state parks include **North Santiam**, some twenty miles east of I-5 on Hwy-22, and **Cascadia**, about thirty miles east of I-5 on Hwy-20. Both offer excellent swimming, fishing, and hiking, and the latter has **camping** as well (March–Oct; $10–14; reserve at ⓣ1-800/551-6949, ⓦwww.oregonstateparks.org).

While the major towns off I-5 in this region are largely (and fairly accurately) dismissed by Oregonians not living there – Corvallis as a dull college town, Albany as a smelly industrial burg – the one exception to the dreariness is the quaint hamlet of **Brownsville**, easily accessible four miles east of I-5 on Hwy-228, about twenty miles north of Eugene. Much of the townscape was used in the filming of the movie *Stand By Me*, convincingly doubling as a rural community seen through the haze of a twisted nostalgia, and you may recognize some of the old structures as you lope along Brownsville Road or Kirk Avenue. The **Linn County Historical Museum**, 101 Park Ave (Mon–Sat 11am–4pm, Sun 1–5pm; free; ⓦwww.co.linn.or.us/museum), can give you the lowdown on the town's history (it basically grew up around a woolen mill), but for a closer peek, check out the stately **Moyer House** one block south (same hours and website as museum; free). This two-story 1881 Italianate home not only overflows with wooden gingerbread detailing, finely carved eaves, and ornamental decor, it also sports a rooftop tower, considerable oak and walnut woodworking and panels, and hand-painted nature scenes above the interior windows. If you're anywhere near the area, and have even a passing interest in historic buildings, this fascinating architectural curiosity is not to be missed.

Covered bridges

Homesteaders in the Willamette Valley put roofs over their **bridges** to protect the wooden trusses from the Oregon rain, lengthening the bridge's life-span from ten to up to eighty years or so – a tradition which continued until fairly recently, though many of the bridges have since been preserved by state law. The privacy they afforded earned them the nickname of "kissing bridges." There are no less than fifty covered bridges in the state, and although it's unlikely you'll want to see them all, a good cluster of them can be visited between Salem and Eugene, roughly on or around highways 20, 126, and 34. Since many of them look pretty similar, differing only by color, roof style, support walls and columns, or type of wood used, your best bet is to pick up or order the excellent brochure, *Oregon's Covered Bridges*, which details the exact location of all the Willamette Valley's covered spans. It's available from any major visitor center hereabouts, but especially from the **Willamette Valley Visitors Association** (ⓣ1-800/526-2256, ⓦwww.willamettevalley.org).

Eugene

Some 65 miles south of Salem on I-5, **EUGENE** dominates the southern end of the Willamette Valley. Unlike its industrial annex Springfield, just across the Willamette River, it's a lively social mix of students, professionals, graying hippies, and blue-collar workers. The city takes its name from one **Eugene Skinner**, the first person to build a homestead here in 1846, his success based on his abundant supply of timber rather than the ferry service he ran for local farmers – sunken logs and gravel bars were a constant hazard. Other settlers followed Skinner's tree-cutting example and Eugene soon developed as a supply center for the local agricultural communities, and boomed from the 1870s when the California–Eugene–Portland railroad was completed. The city's role as a cultural focus began with the traveling theater groups that stopped here on their way between Portland and San Francisco in the late nineteenth century. More recently in the late 1960s, Eugene saw Ken Kesey and some of the Merry Pranksters come to live in the woods after tiring of the Bay Area; the famous Nike running shoe, with its sole made on a waffle iron, was first invented by University of Oregon track coach Bill Bowerman and tested by his student athletes; and, in the late 1970s, much of the movie *Animal House* was filmed on campus.

Arrival, information, and city transportation

Eugene is easy to get to by public transit: Greyhound **buses** link the city with Portland and the towns of the Willamette Valley to the north, Ashland and California to the south, and Klamath Falls to the southeast. Amtrak's Coast Starlight and Cascades **trains** connect Eugene to LA, Portland, Seattle, and Vancouver, BC. Both the train and bus **terminals** are both handily located downtown, with Greyhound pulling in at 987 Pearl St at Tenth Avenue, and Amtrak at Fourth Avenue and Willamette Street. For information, there's a useful **visitor center** downtown at 115 W 8th Ave (Mon–Fri 8.30am–5pm, Sat 10am–4pm; Ⓣ541/484-5307 or 1-800/547-5445, Ⓦwww.visitlanecounty.org), which has a full list of local accommodation and leaflets on Eugene and surrounding Lane County, which stretches from the Cascades to the coast. Of specific interest are those brochures detailing driving tours of the area's covered bridges (see box, p.197) and regional wineries – many of which offer free tours and tastings. The visitor center also has myriad maps of **cycling** and **walking** trails, both in the city center and along leafy river banks. You can rent both mountain and street bikes from Paul's Bicycle Way of Life, 152 W 5th Ave (Ⓣ541/344-4105, Ⓦwww.bicycleway.com), or from Pedal Power, 535 High St (Ⓣ541/687-1775); expect to pay around $5 per hour, or $20 per day. Hiking **maps** of the forested hills east of Eugene are available at the **Willamette National Forest Office**, in the Federal Building, downtown at 211 E 7th Ave at Pearl Street (Mon–Fri 8am–4.30pm; Ⓣ541/465-6521, Ⓦwww.fs.fed.us/r6/willamette).

Eugene is best explored on **foot** – it only takes about ten minutes to walk from one side of downtown to the other, or less than twenty minutes from downtown to the campus of the University of Oregon. Named streets run north–south and numbered avenues east–west; the avenues are prefixed "east" and "west," changing from one to the other at their intersection with Willamette Street. Eugene has a terrific **bus system**, the LTD ($1.25; Ⓣ541/687-5555, Ⓦwww.ltd.org), offering day passes for $2.50, and 25¢ rides on the "Breeze" shuttle linking downtown, the university, and local malls. The main bus station and information center are at Willamette and 11th avenues, where free transit maps, timetables, and route-planning advice are available.

Accommodation

To get the flavor of Eugene, it's best to **stay** either downtown or in one of the **inns** or **B&Bs** located on the outskirts of the university or a short distance away. In addition, there is a cluster of reasonably priced chain **motels** on and around Franklin Boulevard, near the university off I-5 (Exit 192), and north of town beside I-5 (Exit 195A). Note also that the rudimentary hotels clustered around W 6th and 7th avenues, just west of Lincoln, are in the town's seediest area and are probably best avoided. **Campers** can access forested campgrounds in the Willamette National Forest (see p.236), the nearest being an hour's drive east of town on Highway 126.

Campbell House 252 Pearl St at E 3rd Ave ⓣ541/343-1119 or 1-800/264-2519, ⓦwww.campbellhouse.com. A fine old B&B built in 1892 and offering lovely gardens, gracious public rooms, and a handsome veranda. Each of the eighteen guestrooms is decorated in period style – lots of tartans and warm colors – as they are in the adjacent carriage house. The inn is well placed on the slopes of a wooded hill with the town center just a few minutes' walk away. The vantage point of Skinner Butte Park is a short, steep walk up above. 5

Doubletree 3280 Gateway St, Springfield ⓣ541/726-8181 or 1-800/222-8733, ⓦwww.doubletreeeugene.com. If you must stay right off I-5 (Exit 195A), this is the pick: a self-contained complex with a restaurant, bar, pool, and decent rooms. 4

Eugene Hilton 66 E 6th Ave ⓣ541/342-2000 or 1-800/937-6660, ⓦwww.eugene.hilton.com. Right in the center of town, next door to the Hult Center for the Performing Arts, this is an excellent downtown option – a sturdy modern tower block with a tasteful, if spartan, interior and many rooms with superb valley views. ❻

Eugene International Hostel 2352 Willamette St ⓣ541/349-0589. Offers twenty clean and comfortable dorm beds for $19 per person; a bit removed from the center, but still worth it for the price, and predictably thick with backpackers and other adventurers.

Excelsior Inn 754 E 13th Ave ⓣ541/342-6963 or 1-800/321-6963, ⓦwww.excelsiorinn.com. In the middle of the university quarter, and handy for its cafés and bars, this small hotel has fourteen rooms and suites named after classical composers (though the modern decor undercuts any real connection). Some units offer VCRs and Jacuzzis as well. ❻

The City

Whereas Salem offers plenty of historic, "official" attractions, though little in the way of a lively entertainment scene, Eugene is the opposite. Its old homes and main commercial architecture aren't quite up to the level of Salem, except in isolated pockets, but its local dining and cultural atmosphere is quite energetic and appealing. You won't necessarily be touring too many classic mansions while you're here, but you can easily spend a week or more eating out, enjoying concerts, and touring the back roads and byways of the excellent surrounding mountain scenery. Although the downtown and campus core of Eugene is fairly centralized – roughly a one-by-two-mile, east-west grid – the larger city area is fairly sprawling, especially as the entire metropolitan area lies several miles west of I-5. Luckily, though, most of the key sights are close together, and there are only a few good reasons to go venturing out any further – mainly Spencer's Butte and Mount Pisgah.

Downtown and around

While short on specific sights, Eugene's homely, rather intimate **downtown** of modern shopping malls and offices is clean and almost devoid of high-rise development. Clustered around the main north–south axis of **Willamette Street**, you'll find many of the town's best restaurants and cafés. Eugene puts on a vivid display at its excellent **Saturday Market**, Eighth Avenue and Oak Street (April–Dec 10am–5pm; ⓦwww.eugenesaturdaymarket.org), a thirty-year-old institution and something of a neo-hippie carnival, with live folk music and street performers. Tie-dye and wholefoods set the tone, but rastas, skateboarders, and students join in, too. **Fifth Street Market**, north at E 5th Avenue and High Street, is blander and more orthodox, three levels of shops built around a brick inner courtyard – actually a converted chicken-processing plant.

From here it's about 600 yards up High Street – over the railway tracks – to **Skinner Butte Park**, whose grassy lower portion trails along the banks of the Willamette River. This was where Eugene Skinner had his initial landholding, as commemorated by a tiny **log cabin**. Up above you'll find the wooded butte that gives the park its name, and you can drive or walk to the top for views of the town and river. On the lower part of the south slope, though, and not to be missed, is the **Shelton-McMurphey-Johnson House**, 303 Willamette St (Tues–Fri 10am–1pm, Sat & Sun 1–4pm; $3; ⓣ541/484-0808, ⓦwww.smjhouse.org), an intriguing 1888 Queen Anne mansion that has long loomed over this part of downtown. Widely known as the "Castle on the Hill," it looks suitably dark and spooky in its decayed condition in the late-twentieth-century, though it has since been restored to some degree. Although not quite as elaborate as it once was, and considerably changed through the centuries from fires and alterations, the house is nonetheless worth a close-up look. Its lurching corner tower, red-and-green color scheme, and wraparound veranda are among its most striking features, giving it the odd, somewhat eerie appearance of a colorfully restored haunted house lurking in the woods.

For information on other historic structures, and the social and political background of the area, the one noteworthy attraction south of downtown is the **Lane County Historical Museum**, 740 W 13th Ave at Monroe (Wed–Fri 10am–4pm & Sat noon–4pm; $2; ⓦwww.lchmuseum.org), hosting exhibits on logging and the Oregon Trail, including an original covered wagon – one of just a handful to survive.

The University of Oregon campus

Simply put, the campus of the **University of Oregon**, a mile southeast of downtown, is the only college in the state that merits a visit for outsiders. Although much of its architecture is built in exhausted 1960s and 1980s High-Modernism and Postmodernism, a few stately old buildings survive from the late nineteenth century. The two oldest, **Deady** and **Villard halls** sit near the northwest corner of campus, and were the place around which the university originally grew, in 1876 and 1885, respectively.

A short distance south of here, the **quadrangle**, though dominated by the ghastly, quasi-corporate **PLC Tower**, is the social nexus of campus (though just a block from its western edge). It's highlighted by Frisbee and hacky-sack players, summer sunbathers, and all manner of joggers and outdoor enthusiasts. Moreover, it's also adjacent to two of the university's key sights. The first, the college's **Museum of Art**, near the southeast corner, plans to reopen in late 2004 after a major renovation, and will presumably present its stock of regional Native American and Asian art, modern artists from the Pacific Northwest, and small clutch of Rodin sculptures (check ⓣ541/346-3024 or ⓦuoma.uoregon.edu for details). The second, the **Philip Knight Library**, on the south end of the quadrangle (hours vary, generally daily 11am–8pm; ⓦlibweb.uoregon.edu), was renamed after the Nike founder and university graduate gave a small fortune for its renovation and reconstruction. The relationship soured a few years ago, though, when the university affiliated itself with a political group investigating the company's alleged worker abuses in East Asian factories. After much uproar in the press, and following Knight's threat to withdraw his remaining endowment, the university smoothed things over with an embarrassing retreat. Naturally, you'll find no mention of this at the library (unless you search old news files). You will, however, see the slick results of the corporate largesse – a modern glass staircase, local artworks made of native wood and stone, and a high-tech computer system to inventory the giant selection of books available.

Just to the west, beyond the official campus boundary, **13th Street** is a two-block-long amalgamation of student-friendly bars, bike shops, book- and record stores, cafés, and boutiques. Although this isn't necessarily the best place to eat or drink in town, it's plenty vivacious, and the mix of students here is more likely to be of the progressive, independent-minded bent. On the other side of campus, the university's estimable **Museum of Natural History**, 1680 E 15th Ave (Tues–Sun noon–5pm; free; ⓦnatural-history.uoregon.edu), covers Oregon's geology, archeology, and anthropology in an engaging style, with plenty of artifacts and relics from over the centuries and epochs. Since the museum will be renovating into a new design and layout in 2004, check the website for details on its closure and reopening.

Spencer's Butte and Mount Pisgah

Although the Eugene area offers plenty of good trails for cycling and hiking – which you can further explore at the visitors center (see p.198) – the highlight, though, is the steep trip to the top of 2000ft-tall **Spencer's Butte**. This towering outcropping of basalt looms over the south part of town, but is largely hidden behind a veil of second-growth trees. To really take it all in, start from the parking lot off Willamette Street (LTD bus #73 can get you within a mile; ask driver for details) and hike two miles up the butte's winding concourse, past the lower stands of imposing trees to the thinner shrubbery of the middle slope, until you finally reach the craggy peaks and rocky boulders at the top. When it's not raining or foggy, the views from the crest of the butte are truly impressive – and somewhat surprising, given that you're only five miles from downtown.

A bit less jaw-dropping in height, but almost as appealing in views, are the slopes of **Mount Pisgah Arboretum**, fifteen miles south of Eugene at 34901 Frank Parrish Rd, east of I-5 and the Willamette River (dawn–dusk; ⓣ541/747-3817, ⓦwww.efn.org/~mtpisgah). The squat mountain features seven miles of trails spread over widely varied terrain, and a nature center providing background on the geology, flora, and fauna of the site. Although you'll probably need a car to access this 200-acre arboretum, it's well worth a trip as the place is a quiet and scenic natural preserve that feels much further from the city than it actually is.

Eating and drinking

With thousands of students to feed and water, Eugene is well supplied with **bars**, **cafés** and **restaurants**, the pick of which are clustered downtown, mostly between Broadway and 5th Avenue in the vicinity of Willamette Street.

Ambrosia 174 E Broadway at Pearl St ⓣ541/342-4141. This large and popular restaurant is one of Eugene's best Italian restaurants and the food is reasonably priced to boot. The pizzas, baked in an oak-fired oven, are first-rate, the pasta is fresh, and the daily specials are great value. Excellent range of Oregon wines and occasional live music, too.

Café Navarro 454 Willamette St at E 5th Ave ⓣ541/344-0943. World-music sounds reinforce the diversity of the Caribbean and Latin cuisine on offer at this tastefully decorated, informal café. A reasonably priced and imaginative menu makes this one of Eugene's better bets.

Café Zenon 898 Pearl St at E Broadway ⓣ541/343-3005. An upbeat café-cum-bistro with marble-topped tables, tile floors, and an eclectic menu ranging from pasta to curry. Don't let the dour setting put you off.

Chanterelle 207 E Fifth Ave ⓣ541/484-4065. An intimate French bistro, one of the more expensive places to eat in town, and also one of the best. Good for its pasta and salmon, but especially for its eponymous mushrooms, when in season.

Euphoria Chocolate 6 W 17th Ave ⓣ541/343-9223, ⓦwww.euphoriachocolate.com. Unbelievably delicious sweets and chocolate truffles – for many Oregonians, reason alone to make a trip to Eugene.

Morning Glory Café 450 Willamette St ⓣ541/687-0709. Footsteps from the train station, this simple café, with its unreconstructed hippie air, may not be to everyone's taste, but it does offer bargain-basement home-made meals for breakfast or lunch.

Oregon Electric Station 27 E 5th Ave at Willamette ⓣ541/485-4444. Housed in a refurbished train station and railway cars, and featuring live music on weekends, this fashionable spot offers delicious, top-quality bar food, from prime rib to pasta. The restaurant menu is similar, but a tad overpriced and fairly formal by Eugene standards.

Steelhead Brewery 199 E 5th Ave at Pearl ⓣ541/686-2739. Resembles a West Coast version of an English pub, with microbrewed beer and decent sandwiches, burgers, and pizzas. Look out for the delicious wheat beers, one or two of which are jazzed up with local fruit such as raspberries.

Wild Duck Brewpub 169 W 6th Ave at Olive ⓣ541/485-3825. Large and casual restaurant with hardwood floors and steel furniture, which serves bar-food standbys and more ambitious meals with local ingredients. One of the flagship beers is the copper-colored Glen's Bitter, but some of the rotating oddball selections include Rasta Organic Hemp Ale and Yeti-Brau.

Nightlife and entertainment

For **nightlife**, countless cafés and bars have **live music** on one or two nights of the week, but the city's **entertainment** showpiece is the **Hult Center for the Performing Arts**, 7th Avenue and Willamette (Ⓣ541/682-5000, Ⓦwww.hultcenter.org). This sleek complex showcases everything from opera to blues and musicals, with performances by touring companies of international standing as well as the city's symphony and ballet company. The center is also the prime venue for Eugene's prestigious annual Oregon Bach Festival (see below). Elsewhere, the older WOW Hall, 291 W 8th Ave at Lincoln (Ⓣ541/687-2746, Ⓦwww.wowhall.org), was once a meeting hall for the Industrial Workers of the World or "Wobblies", but now features up-and-coming rockers and punks, among other musicians. For different musical styles, *Jo Federigo's*, 259 E Fifth Ave (Ⓣ541/343-8488, Ⓦwww.jofeds.com), serves solid Italian cuisine and has nightly jazz, as does the *Oregon Electric Station* (see above) on the weekends.

To catch a **movie**, there are few distinctive modern facilities, but for second-run and arthouse showings, it's hard to beat the Bijou, four blocks from campus at 492 E 13th Ave (Ⓣ541/686-2458, Ⓦwww.bijou-cinemas.com). Housed in a converted Spanish Mission-style church built in 1925, the cinema often makes for a surreal scene, with sexually explicit or gratuitously violent images displayed on the walls of the former nave and rectory. For details of upcoming movie showings, musical events, and other gigs, pick up a copy of the free *Eugene Weekly*, available downtown and at the visitor center.

South from Eugene: Oakland and Roseburg

If you're heading **south from Eugene** into southern Oregon, you can leave most of the traffic far behind by traveling southeast along **Highway 58** through the southern reaches of the Willamette National Forest and over the

Summer festivals around Eugene

Eugene's biggest annual event is the **Oregon Country Fair**, a big hippie festival of music, arts, food, and dancing held during the second weekend in July in **Noti**, which is just west of Veneta, itself ten miles west of Eugene on US-126. Traffic is heavy, so even if you have a car it's easier to travel there by free **shuttle bus**, leaving from downtown Eugene at 10th and Olive streets (10am–7.30pm, every 10–15min). Note that fair tickets must be purchased before you get there ($12–15 per day; Ⓣ541/343-4298, Ⓦwww.oregoncountryfair.org).

Held in late June and early July at the Hult Center, the **Oregon Bach Festival** draws musicians from all over the world (tickets $22–49; Ⓣ1-800/457-1486, Ⓦwww.bachfest.uoregon.edu) to play the music of Johann Sebastian Bach, among a sprinkling of other classical composers. The artists and conductors are a varied and impressive lot, highlighted by the likes of Helmuth Rilling and Krzysztof Penderecki, and drawing plenty of adoring crowds.

Lastly, there's another big summer festival at **Cottage Grove**, twenty miles south of Eugene on I-5. This, the **Bohemia Mining Days** (Ⓦwww.bohemiaminingdays.org), in the third week of July, recalls the nineteenth-century gold strike of one James Bohemia Johnson, and involves a family-oriented carnival scene with gold-panning demonstrations, musical concerts, characters in period costume, and vendors selling food and mining-related trinkets – though the mountaintop burg of Bohemia itself, fifty miles southeast of Eugene, is now an eerie ghost town, and only accessible on perilous roads full of dangerous switchbacks.

crest of Willamette Pass to Crater Lake (see p.227). An alternate route, for the Cascades or the coast, is **Highway 126**. The most obvious – and certainly the quickest – route south from Eugene is along I-5, with the road passing pleasant but easily missable towns like Creswell and Cottage Grove, and leaving the Willamette Valley to thump through vast tracts of mountain forest.

Fifty uneventful miles south from Eugene and two miles east of I-5, tiny **OAKLAND** is good for a pit-stop on the long journey south – or north if you're coming from California. It was settled in the 1840s and soon became the center of a flourishing agricultural district, producing grain, hops, prunes, and eventually prize-winning turkeys. It was also a major stopping point on the stagecoach line from Sacramento to Portland, and its future seemed secure when the railroad came in 1872. Neither were the locals unduly flustered when a series of fires destroyed almost all the original wooden buildings: for one thing, fires were commonplace in Oregon's early timber-built settlements, and for another the townsfolk took the opportunity to replace the old with new stone and brick buildings graced by cast-iron trimmings. But their confidence was misplaced: within the space of twenty years, a rapidly expanding Eugene had stripped the town of its commercial importance and Oakland simply faded away. Today, it's a quiet rural hamlet whose halcyon days are recalled by the neon-free, antique storefronts of **Locust Street**, the main drag. Here, at no. 130, you'll find the pioneer displays of the **Oakland Museum** (daily 1–4pm; donation), housed in the former grocery store and post office, while neighboring City Hall has street plans and walking tips, pointing out what happened where and when among the various red-brick buildings (alternatively, you can check out Ⓦwww.makewebs.com/oakland). While you're in town, don't miss a stop at *Tolly's*, 115 Locust St (Ⓣ541/459-3796), which features an old-fashioned ice-cream parlor, gift shop, and candy counter downstairs, and a acceptable restaurant up above.

Less than twenty miles further south on I-5, **ROSEBURG** is a colorless, conservative enclave with nothing much to offer beyond strip malls, chain stores, and a few middling historical sites. Luckily, its downtown is located away a mile or so from the freeway, so you'll probably only be troubled by the place if you have to stop for gas.

The Rogue River Valley

In contrast to its Willamette counterpart a few hours' drive north, the **Rogue River Valley** is fairly well removed, both geographically and culturally, from the mainstream life of the state. While it certainly has plenty to offer – nicely preserved nineteenth-century architecture and classic theater festivals, for example – the valley is its own distinct entity, a pocket of mostly small towns hemmed in by three mountain ranges (the coastal, Cascade, and Siskiyou ranges) and possessing an odd mix of political and social elements. On the one hand, the only big town in the area (and the one place definitely worth a miss), **Medford**, is a staunchly conservative turf of shopping malls, tract homes, and chain retailers, while just a few miles down the road, **Ashland** is a delightfully progressive little town best known for hosting the Oregon Shakespeare Festival. Apart from these cultural extremes, and lying within a short distance of the I-5 freeway as it makes its sixty-mile journey through the valley from northwest to southeast, are **Wolf Creek**, site of a historic tavern and former stagecoach stop; workaday **Grants Pass**, a popular base for whitewater rafting along the Rogue River; and **Jacksonville**, a lovely preserved pioneer hamlet in the foothills. As one major alternative route, US-199 sneaks southwest through the remote and rugged **Siskiyou Mountains** which stretch over the border behind the California coast, leading through the dark forests, deep ravines, and wild coastal mountains that span this part of the Oregon–California border, and past the strange and fascinating chambers of the **Oregon Caves**.

Traveling the I-5 by Greyhound **bus** is a straightforward affair, with daily services linking Eugene with, among other places, Grants Pass and Ashland. There are also regular services from Eugene to Klamath Falls, but none to Crater Lake in the Cascades. Amtrak **trains** are not so useful, though you can debark from the Seattle-to-California service, the **Coast Starlight**, at Klamath Falls and make your way to the valley by bus.

Canyon Creek to Grants Pass

Some thirty miles south of Roseburg along I-5, the area around **Canyon Creek** tells one of the central parts of the story of the settling of Rogue River Valley – though it's located some 25 miles before you actually get to the valley itself. In 1843 the surveyor and abolitionist **Jesse Applegate** made his way into the Willamette Valley via the Oregon Trail, though he was best known for writing a farm-oriented news column called "A Day with the Cow." An outspoken individualist who espoused of all kinds of causes, Applegate was also a bit of a crank, and he took it upon himself to devise a new trail that would take a more southerly route to fill up the underpopulated Rogue River Valley. This pathway, known as the **Applegate Trail**, opened in 1846 and cut through land previously trekked by fur traders, native tribes, and few others. Applegate's surveying skills were put to the test, as he created a truly arduous, frequently precipitous circuit that ran up and down canyons, along steep cliffs, and across myriad streams and creeks. The most frightening part of the journey was along the gorge at Canyon Creek, a few miles beyond modern-day Canyonville, where the pioneer wagons were forced to make a sudden 1300-ft descent, and their accompanying families were expected to keep them from rolling out of control and smashing down the hillsides. Needless to say, many of these early trekkers met with disaster, leaving a different kind of trail – one of broken and battered wagons, crushed wheels, dead livestock, and lost and abandoned belongings – and were beset by hostile native tribes determined to keep white trespassers out of their land. Even some of the pioneers themselves, such as 16-year-old Martha Crowley, met with an untimely demise, and were buried in the vicinity (see overleaf). Ultimately, the Applegate Trail did bring a small but steady stream of migrants, though many others were no doubt dissuaded by the tales of hardship, as many Oregon Trail pioneers figured their own slog was difficult enough as it was.

Wolf Creek

The first actual sight near the northern edge of the Rogue River Valley, about fifteen miles south of Canyon Creek Pass on I-5, is **WOLF CREEK**, a small burg that's best known for its **Wolf Creek Tavern**, which began as a stagecoach stop in the 1850s and emerged as a hotel within thirty years. The tavern was constructed of rough-hewn boards and planks cut from area trees, but despite its modest early furnishings, the place hosted Republican presidents like Ulysses S. Grant and Rutherford Hayes, as well as writers such as Sinclair Lewis and Hollywood actors like Clark Gable. Its most important visitor, though, was the author and roustabout **Jack London**, who worked on one of his novels while residing here. Nowadays, the tavern-hotel is a protected state-park facility that still offers solid food and drink – mostly steak, seafood, ribs, and chicken – and hosts visitors from around the world. As you might expect, the rooms are cozy but quaint, with some antique decor and a handful of larger suites (reserve at Ⓣ541/866-2474, Ⓦwww.rogueweb.com/wolfcreekinn; ❹).

Sunny Valley and around

As you make your way further toward the Rogue River Valley, five miles from Wolf Creek is the town of **Sunny Valley**, which isn't much in itself, but does sit near some sites relevant to nineteenth-century history. The first, **Grave Creek**, was originally the name of the town (the current version no doubt compensating for its grim earlier moniker) and the place where little Martha Crowley, a typhoid victim, was buried – literally, in this case, under the modern roadway. The creek is crossed, not far from I-5 on a country lane, by a **covered bridge** that dates from 1920 and features small Neo-Gothic windows across its span. In close vicinity, the area saw the worst of the various wars in the 1850s between native tribes and federal soldiers, who were based nearby and the long-gone Fort Leland. A larger look at this period is on display in town at the **Applegate Trail Interpretive Center**, near the center at 500 Sunny Valley Loop, (daily 10am–5pm, Nov–March Thurs–Sun; donation suggested; Ⓣ541/472-8545 or 1-888/411-1846, Ⓦwww.rogueweb.com/interpretive), which itself resembles a two-story wooden frontier outpost. Here you can check out a museum stuffed with old trail artifacts and photos, pioneer relics and letters, and informative exhibits related to Jesse Applegate, Martha Crowley, and the other significant names from the period.

Rogue River National Recreation Trail

If you'd rather focus on the scenery around the Rogue River, the forty-mile **Rogue River National Recreation Trail** (information at Ⓦwww.fs.fed.us/r6/siskiyou/wildroge) begins at Grave Creek. The trail nudges through dense groves of hemlock, Douglas fir, and oak and traverses bare canyon walls with the river far below – altogether providing some wonderfully wild hiking. It's a sweaty walk in summer, and muddy to the point of impassability in winter, but in spring or fall it's an excellent trek for serious hikers, and there are regular first-come-first-served campsites on the way. A series of strategically placed lodges on the lower half of the trail – each a day's hike from the other – makes a rather more comfortable option, and if this appeals your best bet is to start at Gold Beach (see p.177) on the coast, traveling upriver by boat and then hiking down. If all this sounds too daunting, Rogue Wilderness (see below) organizes four- and five-day guided Rogue River hikes for $500–700. The Grants Pass visitor center has a useful range of leaflets on the Rogue River, too.

Grants Pass

Ten miles south of Sunny Valley, **GRANTS PASS** is the first sizable community in the Rogue River Valley, an old sawmill town straddling the Rogue

River as it tumbles from the Cascades to the Siskiyou National Forest. There's not much to the place, but it does have a fine, scenic setting and a tiny, central **historic district** of fetching late-nineteenth- and early-twentieth-century buildings, on and around G Street west of 6th Street. To get to the center from I-5, it's easiest to take Exit 58 and then follow 6th Street (Hwy-99) south. G Street is just beyond the railway tracks, and the Rogue River, with its assortment of logging mills, is a few blocks further. Indeed, the main reason for a visit is the river.

Grants Pass earns much of its living by strapping visitors into bright orange life-jackets, and packing them into rafts or jet boats to bounce over the Rogue's **whitewater rapids**. A half-day tour costs around $50, a full day $70, and $30 and $50 respectively for jet-boat trips; there are longer, overnight excursions, too, and the season lasts from May to early October. Two of the more reliable operators are Hellgate Jetboat Excursions (Ⓣ541/479-7204 or 1-800/648-4874, Ⓦwww.hellgate.com), whose river trips leave from the foot of 6th Street, and the whitewater rafting- and fishing-tour specialists Rogue Wilderness (Ⓣ541/479-9554 or 1-800/336-1647, Ⓦwww.wildrogue.com), based in the hamlet of Merlin, about ten miles northwest of Grants Pass.

Practicalities

The **visitor center**, which is close to – and clearly signed from – I-5 Exit 58, at 1995 NW Vine St (Mon–Fri 9am–5pm, June–Sept also Sat & Sun; Ⓣ541/476-7717 or 1-800/547-5927, Ⓦwww.visitgrantspass.org), has the details of the many licensed companies operating river excursions. If you decide to use Grants Pass as a base, you'll find the bulk of the town's budget **accommodation** on Hwy-99 (7th Street northbound and 6th southbound) between the river and I-5 (Exit 58). Two useful options here are the functional *Super 8 Motel*, 1949 NE 7th St (Ⓣ541/474-0888 or 1-800/800-8000, Ⓦwww.super8.com; ❸), and the rather more pleasant rooms and suites of the *Riverside Inn*, a modern place down by the Rogue River at 971 SE 6th St (Ⓣ541/476-6873 or 1-800/334-4567, Ⓦwww.riverside-inn.com; ❹). There are a number of good **B&Bs** in the area, too, including *Pine Meadow Inn*, 1000 Crow Rd (Ⓣ541/471-6277 or 1-800/554-0806, Ⓦwww.pinemeadowinn.com; ❺), with its cozy rooms and somewhat basic furnishings; and the more spacious and modern *Flery Manor*, 2000 Jump Off Creek Rd (Ⓣ541/476-3591, Ⓦwww.flerymanor.com; ❺), with more lush appointments; both B&Bs offer four rooms and serve up tasty gourmet breakfasts. The best **places to eat** are *The Laughing Clam*, 121 G St (Ⓣ541/479-1110), with excellent seafood dishes and regional wines, and the *Wild River Brewing & Pizza Co* (Ⓣ541/471-7487), specializing in wood-fired pizzas and excellent beers.

From Grants Pass, US-199 leads southwest to the Oregon Caves and into the California redwoods (see p.178), while I-5 veers southeast for Medford, Jacksonville, and, best of all, Ashland.

Jacksonville and Ashland

Heading inland on I-5, it's a quick 25-mile journey from Grants Pass to **Medford**, the Rogue River Valley's urban center – an industrial sprawl squatting among huge paper mills. There's little to divert you here, and most visitors dodge the place altogether, often missing out on the more appealing **Jacksonville**, just five miles west of Medford on Hwy-238, and **Ashland**, whose downtown core is a few miles west of I-5 on Hwy-99. These two towns are easily the most diverting south of Eugene on the freeway, and while Jacksonville makes for an interesting day-trip, Ashland can keep you going with food and drink, nature trails, and of course, Shakespearean plays, for a day or two.

Jacksonville

Once the largest of Oregon's gold rush towns, a flourishing and boisterous prospectors' supply center, **JACKSONVILLE** had its improbable beginnings after a gold-panner's mule kicked up a nugget here in 1851. No sooner had the miners arrived, however, than they were involved in the savage **Rogue River Indian Wars** of 1853–1856, which saw the natives defeated and deported or confined to reservations (see also Grave Creek, p.206). The prospectors on both sides of the Oregon–California border also spent a fair bit of energy trying to secede from their respective states and create their own – variously "Jackson Territory," "Siskiyou", and "Shasta." Initially, the movement was prompted by the region's isolation from the main sources of state power, but later there was a more ominous twist after large numbers of ex-Confederate soldiers migrated here. In any event, the secessionists faded away and then Jacksonville's fortunes took a nose-dive when the gold boom ended in the 1880s; thereafter it crumbled, quietly, until it was old enough to attract tourists.

It only takes an hour or two to fully explore Jacksonville's small **town center**, whose attractively restored late-nineteenth-century buildings roughly cluster around the main intersection of California and Oregon streets. Overall, it's an agreeable ensemble, all false-fronts and symmetrical brickwork, and a particular architectural highlight is the sturdy **US Hotel** of 1880, at California and Third streets, now remodeled into the souvenir-oriented **History Store** (Wed–Sat 10am–5pm, Sun 1–5pm; free). Also worth a glance is the **C.C. Beekman House**, California and Laurelwood streets (Wed–Sun 1–5pm; $3), the period-furnished residence of an early-twentieth-century banker, who, along with his family members, is portrayed by an actor in historic dress when you take the tour.

If this is a bit too cheesy for you, the **Jacksonville Museum of Southern Oregon History**, housed in the glum-looking County Courthouse of 1883, at 206 N 5th St and E C Street (Wed–Sat 10am–5pm & Sun noon–5pm; $2), offers a straightforward presentation of the town's background (with the usual artifacts, tools, and bric-a-brac), highlighted by a selection of compelling early photographs. They are the work of the talented **Peter Britt**, who came to Oregon on an ox cart in the 1850s and spent almost fifty years photographing it. Britt's house burnt down years ago, but the grounds, located a short walk up California from Oregon Street, are now used for the **Britt Festival** (tickets $13–44; ⓣ541/773-6077 or 1-800/882-7488, ⓦwww.brittfest.org), a major outdoor music and performing-arts shindig that takes place from June to August. Classical, jazz, blues, R&B, bluegrass, pop, and folk music are all featured, played by some of the biggest international names around. The grounds have a maximum capacity of 2200, and although the bench-style seats are often booked up months in advance, some of the lawn space is allocated on a first-come-first-served basis.

Practicalities

There are no long-distance **buses** to Jacksonville (the nearest you'll get is Medford), but the Rogue Valley Transportation District (RVTD; $1 per ride; ⓣ541/779-2877, ⓦwww.rvtd.org) provides a bus service (Route #30) to the town from 200 S Main St in Medford, roughly every hour or so. Jacksonville's tiny **visitor center** (ⓣ541/889-8118, ⓦwww.jacksonvilleoregon.org), at N

Oregon and C streets, can give you the lowdown on the main historic buildings and has a complete list of accommodation. Note that it's virtually impossible to find somewhere to stay during the Britt Festival, when it's a good idea to contact the Southern Oregon Reservation Center (Ⓣ1-800/547-8052, Ⓦwww.sorc.com), which books festival tickets and accommodation.

Festival aside, there's no particular reason to hang around Jacksonville once you've finished with the center, though the town does have a limited supply of quaint **B&Bs** in restored old houses. Two of the most appealing are the centrally located *Orth House*, 105 W Main St (Ⓣ541/899-8665 or 1-800/700-7301, Ⓦwww.orthbnb.com; ❻), a two-story brick Victorian manor from 1880, with four rooms with balconies (three with private baths); and the more formal and elegant 1861 *Jacksonville Inn*, 175 E California St (Ⓣ541/899-1900 or 1-800/321-9344, Ⓦwww.jacksonvilleinn.com; ❽), with twelve stately rooms, some of which feature Jacuzzis and fireplaces, though pricier cottages are available. The latter inn provides a swanky **restaurant** where you can indulge in steak, lamb, or seafood, or imbibe various wines from the region. For a cheaper bite to eat, though, *MacLevin's*, in the center at 150 W California St (Ⓣ541/899-1251), has a fine range of light meals and snacks; it bills itself as "The Unconventional Jewish Deli" – with every justification.

Ashland

Throughout Oregon, the small town of **ASHLAND**, twelve miles south of Medford on Hwy-99, is identified with the works of William Shakespeare – a curious cultural anomaly among the workaday timber and farming towns straddling the California border. The idea of an **Oregon Shakespeare Festival** came to a local teacher, **Angus Bowmer**, fifty years ago, and now – from mid-February to the end of October – the town is dominated by all things theatrical. Among several stages (including the functional **Bowmer** and small **New** theaters), the most unusual is the open-air **Elizabethan Theatre**, a delightful half-timbered replica of sixteenth-century London's Fortune Theatre dropped into the middle of town. It may sound a bit contrived, but Ashland is nowhere near as tacky as Shakespeare's real birthplace, and in some ways has the distinct edge: its setting, between the Cascades and the Siskiyou mountains, is magnificent and there's good skiing in the winter and river-rafting in summer. What's more, performance standards are high and there's some excellent contemporary fringe theatre – not to mention pleasant cafés and a young, lively atmosphere.

Arrival, information, and outdoor activities

Ashland is on the main Greyhound line from Portland to San Francisco, but **buses** only pause on the outskirts of town, a couple of miles northwest of the center at I-5 (Exit 19) – dial Ⓣ1-800/231-2222 for drop-off details. The Rogue Valley Transportation District (RVTD; $1 per ride; Ⓣ541/779-2877, Ⓦwww.rvtd.org) provides a limited local bus service between Ashland, Talent, Medford, and Jacksonville; take Route #10 for Ashland. The **visitor center** is downtown at 110 E Main St (Mon–Fri 9am–5pm; Ⓣ541/482-3486, Ⓦwww.ashlandchamber.com), and there's also a seasonal **information kiosk** – with longer hours – nearby, on the plaza at the entrance to Lithia Park. Both issue town maps and brochures, have details of local lodging, and provide information on the festival. They also have lists of recommended **whitewater rafting** companies, most of whom organize trips on the Rogue River, though the Klamath and Umpqua rivers are featured, too. Arguably the most reliable operator is Noah's River Adventures, on Ashland's main plaza at 53 N Main St (Ⓣ541/488-

2811 or 1-800/858-2811, ⓦwww.noahsrafting.com), which runs half-day ($59–75), one-day ($109–135), and two-day campout ($349) whitewater rafting trips daily from mid-May to October. There's also **skiing** and **snowboarding** at the **Mount Ashland Ski Area** (ⓣ541/482-2897, ⓦwww.mtashland.com), high in the Siskiyou Mountains some twenty miles south of town. It's a comparatively small ski area, with four chairlifts and 25 runs – many of them, sure enough, named after Shakespearean plays and characters – and it's open from early November to mid-April. A one-day lift pass costs $34 (slightly more on the weekend), with night skiing for $20; additionally, skis ($19 per day) and snowboards ($28) can be rented on arrival. The ski area is located eight miles west of – and clearly signposted from – I-5 (exit 6). For the latest snow report, telephone ⓣ541/482-2SKI. For details of special **buses** from Ashland to the ski area, ask at Ashland visitor center.

Accommodation

Ashland has many plush **B&Bs**, but they are much in demand and advance booking is pretty much essential – either independently or via an information service such as Ashland B&B Network (ⓣ1-800/944-0329, ⓦwww.abbnet.com) or Southern Oregon Reservation Center (ⓣ541/488-1011 or 1-800/547-8052, ⓦwww.sorc.com), with whom you can also book theater tickets. There is more chance of a vacancy at one of the town's basic **motels**, and these line up along Siskiyou Boulevard east of the center.

Ashland Hostel 150 N Main St ⓣ541/482-9217, ⓦwww.ashlandhostel.com. Friendly, clean, and well-placed budget option near the center of the action, with dorm beds for $20 and private rooms for $46.50.

Ashland Springs 212 E Main St ⓣ541/488-1700, ⓦwww.ashlandspringshotel.com. The best and most prominent hotel downtown, a grand 1925 edifice visible for miles around. This renovated hotel has a charming two-story lobby, day spa, afternoon tea, and nicely appointed rooms. ❺

Coolidge House 137 N Main St ⓣ541/482-4721 or 1-800/655-5522, ⓦwww.abbnet.com/coolidgehouse. Central B&B offering six luxurious en-suite rooms and gourmet breakfasts from its attractively refurbished Victorian premises. ❺

Cowslip's Belle 159 N Main St ⓣ541/488-2901 or 1-800/888-6819, ⓦwww.cowslip.com. Just four en-suite B&B rooms here in this overly precious, but wonderfully comfortable, early-twentieth-century bungalow and carriage house. ❻

Mount Ashland Inn 550 Mt Ashland Ski Rd ⓣ541/482-8707 or 1-800/830-8707, ⓦwww.mtashlandinn.com. Lovely log lodge, perched high up on the wooded slopes of Mt Ashland, with five well-decorated suites featuring antique furniture, fireplaces, and spa tubs. It's just a short drive up to Mt Ashland Ski Area and about twenty minutes to Ashland in the valley below. Mountain bikes and, in winter, snowshoes are available at no extra charge. Inn is located six miles west of I-5 (exit 6). ❼

Palm Motel 1065 Siskiyou Blvd ⓣ541/482-2636 or 1-877/482-2635, ⓦwww.palmmotel.com. Standard-issue motel to the east of the town center, its thirteen plain but perfectly adequate rooms make it the best choice in this category. ❸

Winchester Inn 35 S 2nd St ⓣ541/488-1113 or 1-800/972-4991, ⓦwww.winchesterinn.com. Attractive inn with eighteen en-suite rooms and attractive gardens, plus a pleasant setting just three blocks from the main plaza. ❻

The Town

As the town has no major museums or other attractions of note, the festival is Ashland's one and only claim to fame, but the tiny, café-flanked **plaza** that forms the heart of the town – just around the corner from the Elizabethan Theatre – is a pleasant spot to loiter, especially as it's beside the entrance to leafy **Lithia Park**. This one-hundred-acre park was designed by John McLaren (of Golden Gate Park fame), its shrubs, trails, brooks, and spreading trees reminders of Ashland's pre-festival incarnation as a spa town, a project of New York advertising mogul, Jesse Winburne. He overestimated the appeal of the nasty-tasting local Lithia Springs water, though, and the spa idea failed, but it did lodge the germ of Ashland's potential as a center for tourism.

Eating and drinking

With its ready supply of well-heeled tourists, not to mention its local college students, Ashland has lots of appealing places to **eat** and **drink**. Conveniently,

Seeing the plays in Ashland

The world-renowned **Oregon Shakespeare Festival** runs from February to October. The works of Shakespeare and other Elizabethan and Jacobean dramatists are performed at the **Elizabethan Theatre**, on the edge of Lithia Park, while the adjacent **Angus Bowmer Theatre**, stages both Shakespearean and more recent works and the austere **New Theatre** has a mostly modern repertoire. The trio of theaters share the same box office, at 15 S Pioneer St (ⓣ541/482-4331, ⓦwww.orshakes.org), with **tickets** averaging around $35 (with standing room at the Elizabethan Theatre for $10), and summer prices being $10–15 more expensive.

For a further helping of contemporary drama, the lively **Oregon Cabaret Theater** performs in a renovated church at 1st and Hargadine streets (tickets $18–24; ⓣ541/488-2902, ⓦwww.oregoncabaret.com), while the **Actors' Theater** lies three miles north of town in the tiny village of **Talent**, at Main Street and Talent Avenue ($15–17; ⓣ541/535-5250, ⓦwww.attalent.org).

the best are clustered in and around the plaza, which is flanked – rather confusingly to newcomers – by both North and East Main streets.

Alex's Plaza 35 N Main St ⓣ541/482-8818. Smart and proficient restaurant offering traditional American dishes with a flourish. A popular spot where the specialty is the New Zealand lamb.
Ashland Bakery Café 38 E Main St. Laid-back, slightly arty café where the breakfasts, sandwiches, and pastries are delicious and inexpensive.
Chateaulin 50 E Main St ⓣ541/482-2264. One of the classiest restaurants in town, a formal, attractively decorated place serving up first-rate French cuisine, but only for dinner. Reckon on $25 per person, excluding wine.

Firefly 23 N Main St ⓣ541/488-3212. Eclectic and tasty entrees at this quality restaurant, which include a mix of Northwest Cuisine and more continental dishes – the likes of fresh salmon, spicy prawns, and "cinnamon seared rock hen."
Greenleaf 49 N Main St ⓣ541/482-2808. On the central plaza, this enjoyable, inexpensive eatery has tasty staples like pasta, burgers, salads, and seafood, nicely crafted with fresh local ingredients. Also with al fresco dining on a pleasant riverside terrace.

The Oregon Caves National Monument

Back at Grants Pass, US-199 leaves I-5 (exit 55) to wander down the Illinois River Valley towards the Northern Californian coast (the only practical access to Oregon beach towns on the south coast). It's an enjoyable journey, with forested hills to either side, and after about thirty miles you reach the straggling roadside burg of **Cave Junction**, where Hwy-46 branches off east for the narrow and twisting, twenty-mile trip to the **OREGON CAVES NATIONAL MONUMENT** (tours daily March–Nov: hours vary, often 9am–5pm; 75min trip; ⓣ541/592-2100, ⓦwww.nps.gov/orca), tucked away in a canyon in the Siskiyou Mountains. The caves were discovered in 1874, when a deer-hunter's dog chased a bear into a hole in the mountainside, but they only became famous when the poet Joaquin Miller described his 1909 visit in such ringing phrases as "the marble halls of Oregon" – only then were they preserved as a national monument.

Inside, the caves – actually, one enormous cavern with smaller passages leading off from it – are the stuff of geological fascination. The marble walls were created by the centuries-long compression of mucky lime, mud, and lava, then slowly carved out by subterranean water. Thereafter long years of steady dripping created elaborate formations from the limestone-laden water: clinging stalactites hang from the ceiling, some met by stalagmites to form columns, while rippled flows of rock run from the walls. The caves are open year round, and are wet and slippery, so good shoes or boots are required, as is warm clothing – underground it's a constant 42°F (6°C). You have to go in with the hour-long **tour** ($7.50), but note that although these leave regularly, you can still face a long wait in the summer, when it's wise to turn up early in the day. The monument grounds also contain a couple of **hiking trails** into the surrounding mountains, with the three-mile loop of the Big Tree Trail giving sight of a whopping Douglas fir that's more than a thousand years old.

Easily the best **accommodation** hereabouts is the *Oregon Caves Chateau,* 2000 Caves Highway (mid-May to Sept; ⓣ541/592-3400; ❺), an attractive, rustic affair of high gables and timber walls dating from the 1930s – and a stone's throw from the caves. The lodge, with its comfortable furnishings and fittings, has real character and the restaurant serves good food, too; it's not surprising, therefore, that reservations are pretty much essential. Alternatively, there are drab lodgings in Cave Junction – try the *Holiday Motel*, 24810 Redwood Highway (ⓣ541/592-3003; ❸) – or several **campgrounds** along Hwy-46, with *Grayback* and *Cave Creek* being the closest to the monument ($10–16; ⓣ541/592-2166 for reservations).

5

The Oregon Cascades

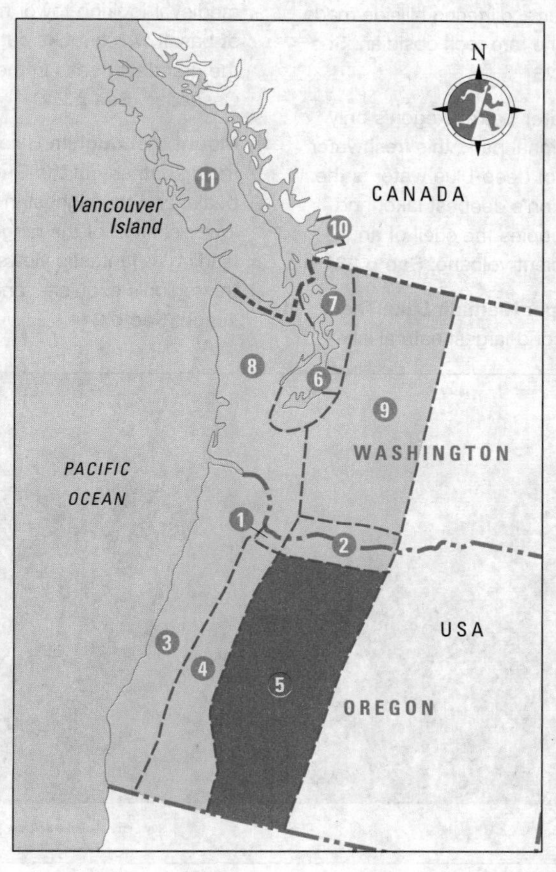

CHAPTER 5

Highlights

* **Smith Rock** Deep gashes in the lava rock in this fascinating state park have created a lovely gorge that's perfect for cycling, horseback riding, and hiking. See p.220

* **Big Obsidian Flow** Monumental outpouring of glassy lava that has formed a bizarre, glittering hillside made of the rare rock obsidian. See p.226

* **Crater Lake** Oregon's only national park, this freshwater pit of deep-blue water is the nation's deepest lake, and occupies the shell of an ancient volcano. See p.227

* **Upper Klamath Lake** The second-largest natural lake west of the Rockies, its excellent National Wildlife Refuge is a seasonal stopover for countless birds from pelicans to herons to swans. See p.233

* **Dee Wright Observatory** Sitting in the middle of an astounding 65 square miles of frozen lava, a rough-hewn, medieval-looking tower made of basalt which looks out at the grandest peaks in the Cascades. See p.240

* **Mount McLoughlin** Hike this most southerly of the Oregon peaks and the highest in the lower section of the range, leading to fantastic views of the region's exquisite landscape. See p.244

△ Newberry National Volcanic Monument

5

The Oregon Cascades

For many outdoor adventurers, the **Oregon Cascades** are the highlight of any trip to the Pacific Northwest. Although generally lower in elevation than Washington's five Cascade peaks, Oregon's members of this 700-mile long volcanic chain are much more closely concentrated and numerous – seventeen major peaks in all, running along a north-south axis from Mount Hood near the Columbia Gorge down to Mount McLoughlin near the California border. These mountains, while not stratospheric in height, are undeniably stunning in appearance, a snowy necklace of radiant white jewels arrayed across the central Oregon landscape. The mountains are also quite varied in appearance, from archetypal volcanoes like mounts **Jefferson** and **Bachelor**, to low-slung calderas like **Newberry**, to exploded peaks-turned-freshwater pits like **Crater Lake**, to strange and gnarled fragments like **Broken Top** and **Mount Thielsen**.

Not surprisingly, almost all the region's highlights are geologic, including expansive lava fields, preserved fossil beds, and deeply set lakes and ravines. With the decline in the lumber trade, most of the region's towns now embrace the rise in outdoors-oriented tourism, such as hiking, skiing, and fishing. High culture, although not quite non-existent, is rarely in evidence, historic preservation is weak and irregular compared to the western valleys, and there's little in the way of eye-opening festivals or hoedowns, or any sense of free-spirited cultural chaos.

There are several major routes to the Cascades from the cities of the west. **Highway 26** begins in Portland, skirts the southern foothills of Mount Hood (see pp.132–133) and a hundred miles later reaches the focus of the Cascades, the vibrant, fashionable town of **Bend**. Well worth a day or two's visit, the town lies within close distance of the wonderful scenery of the ski resort of **Mount Bachelor**. Northeast from Bend, the main axis of the Cascades, **US-97**, passes by the three sites that constitute the **John Day Fossil Beds**, whose remarkable geology – replete with reminders of a tumultuous volcanic past – is brimming with all manner of prehistoric plant and animal skeletons. A short distance southwest of Bend along this route, there's evidence of more volcanic disturbance in **Newberry National Volcanic Monument**, where a sprinkling of cinder cones, lava fields, and a massive caldera are found not far from the highway. Perhaps the most extraordinary sight of all is **Crater Lake**,

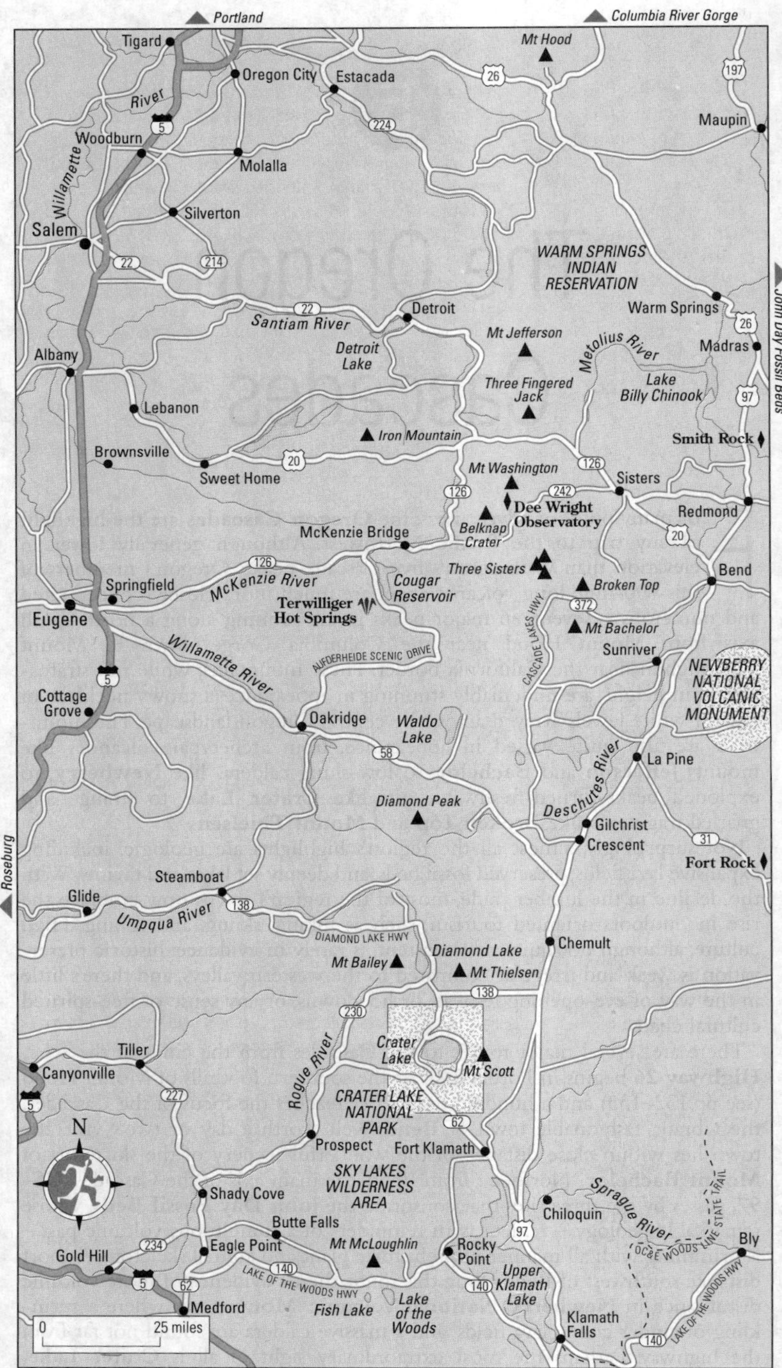
Portland
Columbia River Gorge
Tigard
Oregon City
Estacada
Mt Hood
26
197
224
Maupin
River
5
Woodburn
Molalla
Willamette
Silverton
Salem
22
214
WARM SPRINGS
INDIAN
RESERVATION
John Day Fossil Beds
22
Detroit
Warm Springs
Santiam River
26
Mt Jefferson
Metolius River
Madras
Albany
Detroit
Lake
Lake
Billy Chinook
Three Fingered
Jack
97
Lebanon
Iron Mountain
Smith Rock
Brownsville
20
Sweet Home
Mt Washington
126
Sisters
126
242
Dee Wright
Observatory
Redmond
Belknap
Crater
McKenzie Bridge
20
126
Three Sisters
Bend
McKenzie River
Cougar
Reservoir
Broken Top
Springfield
Terwilliger
Hot Springs
372
Eugene
CASCADE LAKES HWY
Mt Bachelor
Willamette River
AUFDERHEIDE SCENIC DRIVE
Sunriver
NEWBERRY
NATIONAL
VOLCANIC
MONUMENT
5
Cottage
Grove
Oakridge
Waldo
Lake
58
La Pine
Deschutes River
Diamond Peak
Gilchrist
Crescent
31
Fort Rock
Roseburg
Steamboat
Glide
138
Umpqua River
DIAMOND LAKE HWY
Chemult
Diamond Lake
Mt Bailey
Mt Thielsen
138
230
Rogue River
Crater
Lake
Tiller
Mt Scott
Canyonville
227
5
CRATER LAKE
NATIONAL
PARK
62
N
Prospect
Fort Klamath
SKY LAKES
WILDERNESS
AREA
Sprague River
OC&E WOODS LINE STATE TRAIL
Shady Cove
Chiloquin
Butte Falls
97
Bly
234
Eagle Point
Mt McLoughlin
Rocky
Point
Gold Hill
140
5
LAKE OF THE WOODS HWY
62
140
Upper
Klamath
Lake
LAKE OF THE WOODS HWY
Medford
Fish Lake
Lake
of the
Woods
Klamath
Falls
0
25 miles
140
California

The rise of the Cascades

As the only active volcanic chain in the continental US, the **Cascades** are a line of majestic peaks that run from Mount Baker in Washington to Mount Lassen in California. Although Oregon has the greatest number of the larger-sized mountains – 17 of the 27 – the number of recently active volcanoes in the state, seven, is about the same as its neighbors. These mountains all experienced eruptions within the last several thousand years, with **Mount St Helens** (see p.402) erupting in 1980, and Oregon's **Mount Hood** emitting a steam belch in 1865. While it's easy enough to trace the north-south progression of the chain, the Cascades are actually rather complicated geologically, and extend well beyond the twenty-to-thirty mile, east-west zone where the major peaks can be found.

Even in the depths of geologic time, the Cascades are quite old, beginning their rise some forty million years ago when the process of **continental drift** forced the oceanic Juan de Fuca plate to crash into the North American plate. This plate-tectonic pile-up not only caused the uplift of the coastal mountains – as the upper layer of oceanic crust was scraped off – but it propelled the Juan de Fuca plate into the magma below the earth's crust and melt. At the point of melting, around 120 miles inland from the coast and far underground, boiling steam forced the layers of magma to rise, where it either sat below the surface in massive "plutons" or erupted as runny lava or explosive ash. However, this reaction – which occurred from forty up to five million years ago – only created the first incarnation of the Cascades, known as the **Western Cascades**. These once-grand peaks are roughly located between the current volcanoes and the I-5 freeway, but if you go hunting for them, all you're likely to find are severely eroded stumps and rocky nubs, with the highest – **Iron Mountain** – only half the size of the tallest of the modern peaks. Dormant for millions of years, these "old" Cascades ended their days of volcanic glory when faulting caused the entire range to tilt to the east, making for a smoother slope from the west and a more precipitous drop-off on the east – a tectonic shift that helped create the current "rain shadow" in the desert of eastern Oregon.

Some three to four million years ago, this faulting, along with still-mysterious actions in the earth's interior, resulted in a shift of thirty to fifty miles as the range of Cascade volcanic action jumped to the east. In a short time (at least geologically), dozens of new mountains were formed along this great arc, now known as the **High Cascades** – the tallest of which are mounts Rainier (14,410ft) in Washington and Shasta (14,162ft) in Northern California. As with most of the big-name peaks in the region, the latter two are **stratovolcanoes**, or the familiar conical peaks that dominate the landscape and are most people's idea of what a volcano is supposed to look like. However, another type of volcano, the **shield** variety, can be just as explosive and dangerous. Shield volcanoes have a much flatter, rounded appearance that makes them a bit less appealing to outdoors adventurers, skiers, and hikers, not to mention the postcard photographers who advertise the region's image around the world.

Oregon's recently active volcanoes (within the last eight thousand years) include mounts Hood, Jefferson, Bachelor, and the South Sister, the craters of former mounts Mazama and Newberry, and the Belknap shield volcano (aka Belknap Crater). The state's ten other peaks have been inactive for much longer, and many of these have silhouettes that have been fractured, scoured, or split by glaciers. This is even more true of the Western Cascades. Although hard to image nowadays, the irregular rocky stumps and basaltic nubs of these forgotten giants once dominated the landscape for 35 millions years, producing six times the volcanic output of lava, ash, and rock of today's High Cascades – a sobering thought when exploring these invincible-looking titans.

another hour south on US-97, the deep-blue remnant of an ancient volcano that is the state's only national park and well deserves a few days to explore its hiking trails or admire its glimmering surface up close on a boat ride. Also on US-97, the lake is within an hour's drive of **Klamath Falls**, a curious little town with two enjoyable museums, and access to the splendid **Upper Klamath National Wildlife Refuge**.

While US-97 is clearly the best way to explore the vastness of the Cascades, alternate routes are available from the Willamette and Rogue River valleys. From Salem **Highway 22** leads past such vacation centers as **Detroit Lake** and the rocky, wooded **Western Cascades** (see p.233). To the south, Eugene has several routes into the mountains: due east on **Highway 126**, which leads into the forests and lava fields of **High Cascades**, threading past the rugged hamlet of **Sisters** and a bevy of spiky peaks like **Broken Top** and **Three Sisters**; and southeast along **Highway 58** over the verdant crest of Willamette Pass. In southern Oregon **highways 138** and **62** lead toward Crater Lake from Roseburg and Medford, but also compelling is Highway 140, or the **Lake of the Woods Highway**, branching off from Hwy-62 and taking you to the graceful setting of **Mount McLoughlin**.

Getting around

If you're camping, a **car** is pretty much essential – as it is if you're intending to do anything more than hop from town to town, and even that can be difficult by **public transit**. While local bus services are negligible, Greyhound **buses** (Ⓣ1-800/231-2222, Ⓦwww.greyhound.com) run east from Portland and dip through the mountains to Bend, which is linked with Seattle to the north and Klamath Falls to the south. Amtrak **trains** enter from California near Klamath Falls, and proceed diagonally through the south side of the Cascades until they reach Eugene. Unfortunately, the only station in between them – and actually in the mountains itself – is the colorless burg of Chemult on US-97, a good distance from any major sights.

Northeast of the Cascades

Traveling on **US-26** southeast from Portland, many day-trippers only make it as far as the northern reaches of the Oregon Cascades and Mount Hood (see p.132), and in many ways this mountain is more associated with Portland itself and the Columbia Gorge than it is with the heart of central Oregon. Indeed, after the highway skirts the mountain's southern flank it begins a rather tedious trek through dry scrublands and canyons **northeast** of the Cascades, an area that looks more like a parched and isolated desert landscape than the forested peaks and valleys of the mountains. The highlights – especially compared with what's to come – are few and far between, though the Warm Springs Indian reservation draws some for its touristy resort of **Kah-Nee-Tah** (Ⓣ1-800/554-4SUN, Ⓦwww.kah-nee-taresort.com), which, amid the usual golf and gambling elements, offers some rather pricey, but compelling packages ($118–300) for taking a dip in its toasty mineral waters and getting a Swedish massage. Beyond this, the dusty burgs of **Madras** and **Redmond** are two major crossroads into eastern Oregon, though not particularly appealing in themselves. Off US-97 from Madras, however, there are a number of fascinating side trips: either to the brilliant hues of the **John Day Fossil Beds National Monument** or the excellent state parks at **The Cove Palisades** and **Smith Rock**.

When you're in the area, you may take note that Redmond marks the start of an area much favored by "rockhounds," or amateur excavators, who come here to find such trophies as jasper thundereggs, obsidian, and agates. Local visitor centers have details of where you can dig and what for, and shops sell the rocks by the truckload. East of Redmond, Hwy-126 cuts across sagebrush flatlands on its way to uneventful **Prineville**, where it joins US-26 just before it wriggles over the green band of the **Ochoco Mountains**, whose ponderosa and lodgepole pines stand over tightly bunched hills studded with canyons, meadows, and volcanic plugs.

John Day Fossil Beds National Monument

On the eastern side of the Ochoco Mountains are three separate sites – sandcastle-like hills collectively known as the **JOHN DAY FOSSIL BEDS NATIONAL MONUMENT** (Mon–Fri 9am–5pm; free; ⓣ541/987-2333, ⓦwww.nps.gov/joda). Named, like several other features in the immediate area, after a member of the ill-fated Astor expedition of 1811 (see box, p.145), these strangely colored rock formations have been excavated to reveal an amazing assortment of fossils. Dating from the period just after the extinction of the dinosaurs and before the Cascade Mountains raised their rain-blocking peaks to the west, the fossils provide clues of a time when a subtropical rainforest covered this land in a dense jungle of palms, ferns, and tropical fruits. The forest was then inhabited by creatures that predate the evolution of current species – Hpertragulus, a tiny, mouse-sized deer, Diceratherium, a cow-sized rhinoceros, and Miohippus, a small, three-toed horse, to name but three. As the Western Cascades sputtered into being, volcanic ash poured down on the forest, mixing with the rain to make a thick, muddy poultice that fossilized bits of the leaves and fruit and then the bones and teeth of the animals. Consequently, paleontologists, who first visited the area in the 1860s, have been able to put together an epic of evolution and extinction. At all three fossil beds, short **trails** wind through barren hills over crumbly textured earth, and information sheets or plaques are available at key trailheads to point out various geological and paleontological curiosities.

Approaching from the west on US-26, the first of the three sites is the **Painted Hills Unit**, almost eighty miles from Bend (and a couple of miles west of the one-horse town of Mitchell) down a signposted six-mile turnoff north off US-26. The Painted Hills are mainly famous for the color of the rocks rather than the fossils embedded in them: striped in shades of rust and brown, their smooth surface is quilted with rivulets worn by draining water. Close up, the hills are frail, their clay and shale cracked by dryness. The colors grow brighter when it rains and the pores in the earth close up, and are at their most mellifluent in the late afternoon.

Returning to US-26, it's just a mile or so east to the turnoff for the second fossil beds, the **Clarno Unit**, where ash-laden mud flows have inundated a dense prehistoric forest. But this site is a long way north, a tiring backroad drive of some seventy miles, and you'd have to be a real fossil fanatic to make the effort.

Much more accessible – a further 25 miles to the east, just off US-26 – the **Sheep Rock Unit** takes its name from the volcanic capstone that looms like the Matterhorn over the John Day River Valley. At the foot of the capstone, **Cant Ranch** (see above for hours) is a sheep rancher's house from 1917 that has displays and videos on the area's complex geology and a few fossils, but the **Condon Paleontology Center** (Mon–Fri 8.30am–4.30pm) is larger and more elaborate. It's also just two miles south of the **Blue Basin** canyon, where the rock is more of a pale, greenish color, with occasional dark red flashes. Of four short hiking trails, the one-mile **Island in Time** trail takes you into the Blue Basin – a rock-enclosed natural amphitheater – past fossil replicas, including a tortoise that hurtled to its death millions of years ago and a saber-toothed cat.

The Cove Palisades and Smith Rock

About fifteen miles southwest of Madras off US-97, or some 85 miles west of the fossil beds, **THE COVE PALISADES** is perhaps the best state **campground** in the Cascades ($3 day-use, $13–21 pitch or electric, cabins $48–69; reserve at ⓣ1-800/452-5687), an ideal spot for hiking, fishing, boating, and kayaking abutted next to **Lake Billy Chinook**, a 1960s manmade reservoir. The high rocky walls of the park are truly eye-opening with their towering rutted columns, as is the signature **Petroglyph Rock**, a huge boulder carved with mysterious designs.

The Cove makes a good day-trip with **SMITH ROCK**, about fifteen miles southeast or nine miles north of Redmond off US-97 ($3 day-use, $4 primitive camping). A prime geologic field trip for many in the region and a mecca for rock-climbers, Smith Rock's where towering basalt cliffs and overhangs draw thousands of urbanites to practice their skills climbing and rapelling. These craggy, colorful giants were first formed some twelve million years ago when a great outpouring of lava – the Deschutes Formation – overwhelmed the ancient riverbed. Consequently, the Crooked River took a new path that has cut a deep gorge in the park today, making perfect conditions for horseback riding, cycling, and hiking – though not all the trails are easy. In fact, **Asterisk Pass** is a so-called "rock scramble," meaning you get to scamper over piles of chunky lava rocks and try to avoid twisting your ankle. A few miles west from the park across the highway, **Ogden Viewpoint** is another good stop, providing a striking view of a deep rocky gorge created in much the same manner as Smith Rock.

Bend and around

Some 160 miles southeast of Portland, the area **around Bend** appeals foremost for its splendid natural setting and access to some of the best attractions in the Cascades, while the city itself has a lively, easygoing air, with several fine restaurants and charming B&Bs. The surrounding region beyond is excellent for a number of sights – the green, alpine scenery surrounding imposing Cascade peaks, among them the ski haven of **Mount Bachelor**; the stark cones and lava flows of **Newberry National Volcanic Monument** and the superb nearby **High Desert Museum**; and the strange and austere natural sites of **Fort Rock** and **Hole-in-the-Ground**. Unfortunately, public transportation in the region is almost non-existent: there are no **trains** and the only town well served by Greyhound **bus** is Bend, which you can reach from Portland, Klamath Falls, and Seattle via Biggs on the Columbia River.

Bend

A booming resort town, **BEND** benefits economically from an explosion of interest in outdoor pursuits, with cross-country and alpine skiers gathering

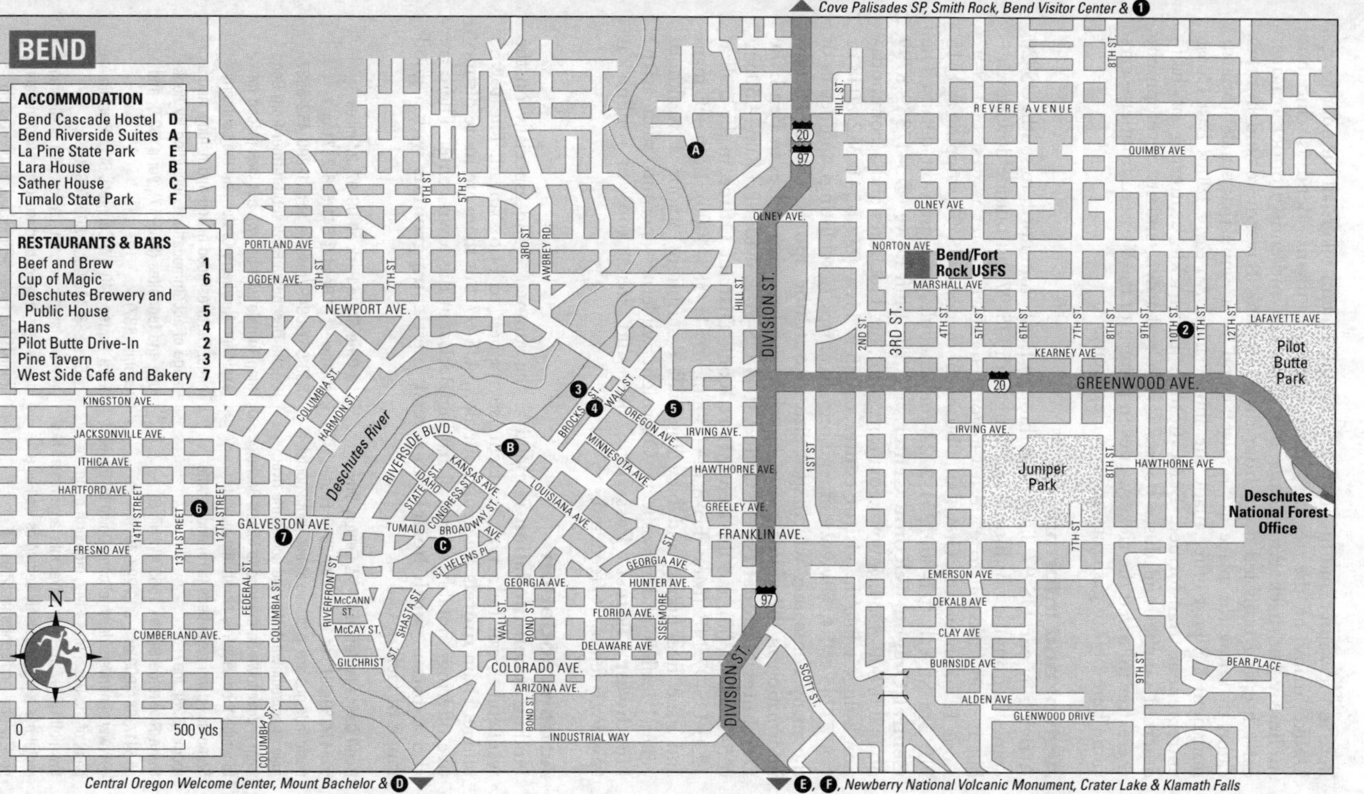
BEND
ACCOMMODATION
Bend Cascade Hostel D
Bend Riverside Suites A
La Pine State Park E
Lara House B
Sather House C
Tumalo State Park F
RESTAURANTS & BARS
Beef and Brew 1
Cup of Magic 6
Deschutes Brewery and Public House 5
Hans 4
Pilot Butte Drive-In 2
Pine Tavern 3
West Side Café and Bakery 7
Cove Palisades SP, Smith Rock, Bend Visitor Center & 1
Central Oregon Welcome Center, Mount Bachelor & D
E, F, Newberry National Volcanic Monument, Crater Lake & Klamath Falls
Bend/Fort Rock USFS
Pilot Butte Park
Juniper Park
Deschutes National Forest Office
Deschutes River
DIVISION ST.
GREENWOOD AVE.
3RD ST.
NEWPORT AVE.
GALVESTON AVE.
FRANKLIN AVE.
COLORADO AVE.
RIVERSIDE BLVD.
INDUSTRIAL WAY
REVERE AVENUE
QUIMBY AVE
OLNEY AVE
NORTON AVE
MARSHALL AVE
LAFAYETTE AVE
KEARNEY AVE
IRVING AVE.
HAWTHORNE AVE
GREELEY AVE.
EMERSON AVE
DEKALB AVE
CLAY AVE
BURNSIDE AVE
ALDEN AVE
GLENWOOD DRIVE
BEAR PLACE
SCOTT ST.
PORTLAND AVE
OGDEN AVE.
KINGSTON AVE.
JACKSONVILLE AVE.
ITHICA AVE.
HARTFORD AVE.
FRESNO AVE
CUMBERLAND AVE.
14TH STREET
13TH STREET
12TH STREET
FEDERAL ST.
COLUMBIA ST.
HARMON ST.
RIVERFRONT ST.
McCANN ST.
McCAY ST.
GILCHRIST ST.
SHASTA ST.
TUMALO AVE.
BROADWAY ST.
CONGRESS ST.
STATE ST.
IDAHO ST.
KANSAS AVE.
ST HELENS PL
LOUISIANA AVE.
MINNESOTA AVE.
OREGON AVE.
WALL ST.
BROCKS ST.
GEORGIA AVE.
HUNTER AVE.
FLORIDA AVE.
DELAWARE AVE
SISEMORE
BOND ST.
ARIZONA AVE.
HILL ST.
1ST ST
2ND ST.
4TH ST.
5TH ST.
6TH ST.
7TH ST.
8TH ST.
9TH ST.
10TH ST.
11TH ST.
12TH ST.
AWBREY RD.
0
500 yds
N

here in the winter, and hikers, rafters, and mountain bikers all summer long. Unlike many of the region's little cowpoke towns, Bend is chic but studiously laid-back. An urbane mix belies its authentic frontier origins: early hunting trails led away from the Deschutes River here, and hunters came to know the place as "farewell bend" – a name that stuck until an impatient US post office made the abbreviation. An early 1900s East Coast entrepreneur transformed Bend from a ramshackle scattering of half-deserted ranches and dusty houses into a real town, and its development thereafter followed the rickety, uneven pattern of the Western frontier – cars came here before gaslights or even electricity.

Arrival and information

Arriving by **car**, US-97 slices right through Bend from north to south; US-20 comes in from the north too – merging with US-97 just outside downtown – but it soon forks off to eastern Oregon. The town center is west of US-97 along Franklin Avenue. Greyhound **buses** shoot along US-97, stopping at 1315 NE 3rd St; call ⓣ1-800/231-2222 for schedules and drop-off details. The **Central Oregon Welcome Center**, 572 SW Bluff Drive (ⓣ541/389-8799 or 1-800/800-8334, ⓦwww.covisitors.com), has brochures and accommodation listings, while the **visitor center**, 63085 N Hwy-97 (ⓣ541/382-8048 or 1-877/245-8484, ⓦwww.visitbend.org), has maps, hotel listings, and details of the many companies which specialize in **outdoor sports**. The USFS puts information in the visitor center, but they also have two offices in Bend, the **Deschutes National Forest Office**, 1645 US-20 E (Mon–Fri 8am–4.30pm; ⓣ541/383-5300), and the **Bend/Fort Rock District Office**, in the mall at 1230 US-97 NE (Mon–Fri 8am–4.30pm; ⓣ541/383-4000). Both sell maps and issue free hiking and bicycling trail descriptions among a wealth of general leaflets and newssheets. Overnight wilderness permits, such as the **Northwest Forest Pass** ($5), are sold here, too, or online at ⓦwww.fs.fed.us/r6/feedemo.

Accommodation

Finding **accommodation** in Bend in the summer – and especially on the weekend – can be a real headache, so it's best to book ahead. The town's budget chain **motels** are strung out along US-97, but there are more distinctive offerings, notably several charming **B&Bs**, in the town center. There are also a spartan **youth hostel** and several forest **campgrounds** with a good range of facilities.

Bend Cascade Hostel 19 SW Century Drive ⓣ541/389-3813 or 1-800/299-3813. Frugal, basic lodgings are available at this youth hostel, a mile or so southwest of – and across the river from – downtown on the road to Mount Bachelor, to which there is a free ski shuttle in winter. Same-sex dorm room beds ($15) and private rooms ($28), too.

Bend Riverside Suites 1565 NW Hill St ⓣ541/388-4000 or 1-800/228-4019, ⓦwww.bendriversidemotel.com. Down by the east bank of the Deschutes River, but north of downtown off US-97 at Revere Ave, this large resort-like motel has a pleasant leafy setting as well as a pool, sauna, and sports facilities. ④

La Pine State Park off US-97, 27 miles southwest of Bend ⓣ541/536-2071 or 1-800/551-6949, reserve at ⓣ1-800-452-5687. On the Deschutes River a bit further from Bend than Tumalo (see below), but well placed for exploring Newberry Crater and the southerly sites. Features good hiking and fishing, and a range of accommodations, including RV hook-ups and tent sites ($13–17), yurts ($27), and cabins ($37).

Lara House 640 NW Congress St at Franklin Ave ⓣ541/388-4064 or 1-800/766-4064, ⓦwww.larahouse.com. Lavish B&B occupying a handsome, high-gabled wooden mansion dating from 1910. Great setting, too, among big old houses near the river and two blocks from downtown. Has six large and comfortable en-suite guestrooms. ❺

Sather House 7 NW Tumalo Ave at Broadway ⓣ541/388-1065 or 1-888/388-1065, ⓦwww.satherhouse.com. Fine B&B with four guestrooms housed in a good-looking Edwardian mansion near both the river and downtown. Antique furnishings, an elegant veranda, and delicious breakfasts add to the charm. ❹

Tumalo State Park 62976 O.B. Riley Rd ⓣ541/388-6055 or 1-800/452-5687, ⓦwww.oregonstateparks .org. The nearest campground to Bend, boasting a lovely setting in a wooded dell shaded by ponderosa pine, junipers, and alders beside the Deschutes River. There are RV hookups and tent sites (both $17–21), and seven yurts ($29) and even two replica, canvas-covered tepees ($29). Located five miles to the northwest of Bend off US-20/97.

The Town

First impressions of Bend are disappointing, and unfortunately, despite being a good base for exploring the Cascades, the city itself has few real attractions. As one exception, the old **town center**, with its unassuming 1930–40s architecture, is a dapper and convivial place tucked against the leafy east bank of the Deschutes River. It only takes a few minutes to stroll from one end of downtown to the other – turn west off US-97 down Franklin Avenue to get there. Afterwards there are panoramic views over Bend from **Pilot Butte**, the remains of a small volcano a mile east of downtown off US-20; you can drive or walk to the top.

There's whitewater rafting and canoeing on the Deschutes and McKenzie rivers, plus horseback riding, climbing, mountain biking, fishing, snowboarding, snowshoeing, and skiing. In particular, Sun Country Tours, 531 SW 13th St (ⓣ541/382-6277 or 1-800/770-2161, ⓦwww.suncountrytours.com), offers first-rate **rafting** trips on the Deschutes and McKenzie rivers from June to September, with one- to four-and-a-half-hour excursions costing $40–115. Wanderlust Tours, 143 SW Cleveland Ave (ⓣ541/389-8359 or 1-800/962-2862, ⓦwww.wanderlusttours.com), has an imaginative range of guided **half-day trips** – summer canoeing, spelunking through caves, or clambering over volcanoes, all for $32–40 per person. Equipment **rental** is widely available, too – again the visitor center has the complete list – but for skis, snowboards, and mountain bikes Bend Ski & Sport, 1009 NW Galveston Ave (ⓣ541/389-4667, ⓦwww.bendskiandboard.com), has equipment for $20–45 per day.

Eating and drinking

Bend is a great place to **eat** and **drink**. There are cafés with an easygoing feel, Western-style diners, brewpubs, chic restaurants, and everything in between – and keen competition keeps prices down to affordable levels.

Beef & Brew 3194 N US-97 ⓣ541/388-4646. Serves superb, well-priced steaks that are the best in town. Don't be deterred by the dreary roadside location – north of the US-20/97 confluence, not far from the visitor center.

Cup of Magic 1304 NW Galveston Ave ⓣ541/330-5539. On the west side of the river across from downtown, this inexpensive, laid-back café with a New Age feel serves great coffees, baked goods, and snacks with a healthfood slant.

Deschutes Brewery and Public House 1044 NW Bond St at Greenwood Ave ⓣ541/385-8606. Downtown brewpub offering good bar food and a wide selection of microbrewed ales and stouts. Among these are Bachelor Bitter, a tangy British-style beer, Cascade Golden Ale, an approachable lager-like ale, and Black Butter Porter, one of the Northwest's most prominent beers.

Hans 915 NW Wall St ⓣ541/389-9700. Smart but informal restaurant dabbling with a wide-ranging menu, but best for its Italian and Southwest cuisine.

Pilot Butte Drive-In 917 NE Greenwood Ave/US-20 and 10th St ⓣ541/382-2972. Folksy, friendly diner that serves up the last word in hamburgers – though its enormous 18oz version looks big enough to amble off the table. Also doles out cheeseburgers topped with the likes of roasted garlic and guacamole, among other odd choices.

Pine Tavern 967 NW Brooks St ⓣ541/382-5581. Serves up microbrewed ales and stouts and offers solid burgers, sandwiches, and the like.

West Side Café & Bakery 1005 NW Galveston Ave ⓣ541/382-3426. Filling all-American breakfasts and a decent range of baked goods, not far from downtown.

Mount Bachelor and the Cascade Lakes Highway

Bend owes a good amount of its success to the development of one of the Northwest's largest ski resorts, **MOUNT BACHELOR**, a 9060ft volcanic peak 22 miles west-southwest of town in the **Deschutes National Forest**, a great slab of forested wilderness that occupies a one-hundred-mile strip on the western side of the High Cascades, tipped by brownish-black lava fields at its highest elevations to the south and west of town. The mountain is reached along a short spur road off the scenic, hundred-mile Cascade Lakes Highway (also known as Hwy-372 or Century Drive Highway closer to Bend). The skiing season runs from around mid-November to as late as June, snowfall permitting (snow reports on ⓣ541/382-7888), and you can rent cross-country and downhill skis as well as snowboards, or attend a well-respected ski school (details at ⓣ541/382-2442 or 1-800/829-2442, ⓦwww.mtbachelor.com). There are thirteen ski lifts on the mountain and no less than seventy runs for snowboarders and downhill and cross-country skiers, covering all levels of difficulty. A one-day ski-lift pass costs $44 and there's a park-and-ride bus shuttle from Bend to the slopes in the winter season. The bus leaves four times daily from the Park & Ride at Colorado and Simpson, about half a mile west of the river.

Beyond Mount Bachelor, the **CASCADE LAKES HIGHWAY** pushes on west before turning south to weave along the slopes of the Cascades, winding through dense forests past deep-blue lakes, crumbly lava flows, and craggy peaks. It's a pleasant enough drive – though it's closed beyond Mount Bachelor during the winter – but the magnificence of the scenery is best appreciated along one of the many **hiking trails** that begin beside the highway. The USFS offices in Bend (see p.222) have all the trail details and will advise as to which of them have been affected by recent wildfires. One of the most enjoyable is the popular **Green Lakes Trail**, whose roadside trailhead is about twenty-five miles out from town. This moderately difficult trail climbs north up gurgling Fall Creek to reach, in a little over four miles, the meadows and lava field beside the three little basin lakes, with the white-capped triple peaks of the **Three Sisters** stretching away to the north. From the lakes you can press on deeper into the wilderness or vary your return via either **Devils Lake** or **Todd Lake**, where there's a backcountry **campground** (free with $5 Northwest Forest Pass; information on all Deschutes forest camping at ⓣ541/383-5300, ⓦwww.fs.fed.us/r6/feedemo). Beyond this, as the highway continues southward it pushes on past sparkling lakes and reservoirs, grand buttes, and idyllic meadows, until it reaches a fork. The west branch leads to Highway 58, which leads back to Eugene over the Willamette Pass, while the east branch takes you to US-97, on which you can either return to Bend or proceed south to Crater Lake.

The High Desert Museum

The diverting **HIGH DESERT MUSEUM**, 59800 US-97 (daily 9am–5pm; $8.50; ⓦwww.highdesert.org), four miles south of Bend on US-97, comprises a fascinating collection of artifacts from Native American and pioneer history, along with displays of regional flora and fauna, and a reconstructed pioneer homestead and sawmill out back. As much a zoo as a museum, its account of life in the arid desert of southeast Oregon parades its best exhibits along an outdoor path, where pens and pools of creatures – river otters, porcupines, and so forth – are interspersed with displays of trees and shrubs, and historical exhibits. A log cabin and a shepherd's wagon stand as testaments to an isolated nineteenth-century life spent guarding the animals against natural perils – and the sheep certainly tested the resourcefulness of their herders. Apart from animal predators, rustlers, and extreme weather conditions, there were poisonous weeds, scabies, liver flukes, and foot rot to contend with, prompting all manner of ingenious treatments. The shepherds dipped their animals in a solution of sulfur, hot water, and black leaf, which was nicotine squeezed from tobacco. Inside, the museum has several well-organized display areas including the **Spirit of the West Gallery**, which takes visitors through a sequence of historical scenes presented as dioramas, and the **Hall of Plateau Indians**, examining the culture of the region's indigenous population.

Newberry National Volcanic Monument

The so-called "**lava lands**" cover a huge area of central Oregon, stretching roughly from Redmond down south to Crater Lake, with the greatest concentration of sizable lava formations in the Bend area. Characterized by curious shapes of hardened basalt, **NEWBERRY NATIONAL VOLCANIC MONUMENT** ($5 parking passes, valid for all of the monument for up to five days; Ⓦwww.fs.fed.us/r6/centraloregon) occupies a narrow slice of the Deschutes National Forest to either side of US-97 just a few miles south of Bend. The monument's volcanic forms – neat conical cones, obsidian deposits, ropy lava and pumice fields, craggy caves, and rocky molds of tree trunks – date back more than seven thousand years to the eruptions of mounts Newberry and Mazama (today's Crater Lake; see p.227), which dumped enormous quantities of ash and pumice across the region. The process is depicted in video re-creations – with various types of volcanic rock on display – at the mildly enjoyable **Lava Lands Visitor Center**, just eleven miles from Bend on US-97 (April–Oct daily 9am–5pm; Ⓣ541/593-2421), also a useful source of maps and practical information on the Newberry monument. Of more immediate interest is the adjacent **Lava Butte**, a colossal, dark cinder cone side-breached by a gush of molten lava that spilled over the surrounding land. Two short trails lead from the visitor center through the cracked moonscape of the lava flow, and you can drive the 1.5 miles to the top of the butte, taking in a wide view of dark green pine forest interrupted by chocolate-colored lava. The butte is cratered at the top, the basin-like hole tinged red where steam once oxidized the iron in the rock; it's also the site of a forest **look-out station**, where distant mountains are visible throughout the year, and in late summer, sometimes ablaze.

A mile or so south of the visitor center, just east off US-97, the **Lava River Cave** (summer daily 9am–5pm; $3, plus $2 for a lamp) leads down a subterranean passage into the chilly volcanic underworld. The cave was created during the last Ice Age by a rush of molten lava, most of which eventually cooled and hardened around the hottest, still-molten center of the flow. When this drained away, it left an empty lava-tube over a mile long, discovered only when part of the roof fell in. There are supposedly all kinds of formations along the cave, but even with a lantern it's hard to see much beyond the next few steps, and it's cold at a constant 42°F (5°C) – wear extra clothes and sturdy shoes.

From the cave, it's about three miles south on US-97 and a further nine miles east along rough, unpaved Forest Road 9720 to the **Lava Cast Forest**. This contains the tree molds – easily seen on a one-mile loop trail from the parking lot – formed centuries ago when lava poured into a forest of ponderosa pines, leaving empty shells when the trees burned to charcoal and ash. The lava here came from what was once the volcano of Mount Newberry, whose multiple eruptions deluged its surroundings for hundreds of years. Finally, worn out by the effort, the mountain collapsed to create **Newberry Crater**, a five-mile-wide caldera that's approached along – and traversed by – a narrow and tortuous 18-mile side road that cuts east off US-97 about 24 miles south of Bend. (Note that this road is closed by snow in winter from about November to May.) The crater is a classic example of a volcanic landscape, featuring **Paulina Peak**, an 8000ft remnant of the original mountain, standing sentinel over two little lochs, **Paulina** and **East lakes**, whose deep, clear waters are popular with fishermen for their regularly stocked trout and salmon. A puncture in the side of the crater provides an outlet for Paulina Lake in the form of the 80ft **Paulina Falls**, while the volcano's most recent eruption – about 1300 years ago – created the **Big Obsidian Flow**, huge hills of volcanic black glass that native tribes throughout the Northwest once quarried to make arrowheads. Crossed by a short hiking trail, the flow is one of the more surreal sights you're ever likely to see, giant mounds of the glassy dark material looming over you, in forms ranging from sheer walls to chunky blocks to glistening crumbs. As the rock is still quite sharp and brittle – and especially rare – you're strongly advised not to take home any geological souvenirs. Beginning at the roadside, **hiking trails** reach every feature of Newberry Crater, ranging from easy half-mile strolls to the obsidian flow and the waterfall, through to the strenuous haul up Paulina Peak. The crater is easily visited on a day-trip from Bend, but there are several seasonal **campgrounds** here, too – reservations and details from Lava Lands visitor center or the USFS offices back in Bend.

Fort Rock and Hole-in-the-Ground

If you haven't the time or inclination to explore Oregon's arid southeast, you can get the flavor of it by visiting **FORT ROCK**, a monumental plateau of volcanic tuff located some seventy miles south of Bend – turn off US-97 a few miles beyond the Newberry crater turnoff to follow Hwy-31 for roughly 30 miles. The rock is interesting in itself as an unusual geological formation, created when billows of steam and rivers of molten rock came into contact with an Ice Age lake; thousands of years later the huge solidified table rock dominated the landscape as it rose above an expansive lakebed, whose various levels are still visible in horizontal "wave cuts" on the rock's exterior walls. Native tribes used to row canoes over these waters to decamp at the rock – their ancient presence later discovered in the 1930s with a pair of nine-thousand-year-old moccasins, one of 75 pairs from the same period found here. Although the old lake has vanished into the dust of a pancake-flat bed of earth, the rock's cliffs are still imposing, up to 325 feet high and overlooking the sagebrush desert as it stretches towards the horizon in all its sun-scorched beauty. To **climb** the rock, contact First Ascent, 975 NE Smith Rock Way, at that state park (Ⓣ541/548-5137 or 1-800/325-5462, Ⓦwww.goclimbing.com), which organizes regular guided climbs. Less than a mile west sits the unmarked entrance to **Fort Rock Cave**, an eerie underground expanse you can only explore through an official 90min state-guided tour (April–Oct twice monthly; reserve at least three days in advance at Ⓣ541/536-2428).

Head back to Bend on Hwy-31, just a few miles to the northwest, for the turnoff for **HOLE-IN-THE-GROUND**, accessed via an unimproved road over crumbly rockfall. One of the more bizarre and lesser-known geological oddities in the region, this mile-wide depression is about three hundred feet deep, with a short, pleasant hiking trail leading to the nadir. Although some theorized that the colossal cavity came from a meteor, more logical explanations credit an ancient volcanic burst from below the ground, which occurred when magma rose to the surface and violently collided with groundwater. This isn't the only curious artifact in the area; less than two miles north, back along Hwy-31, lies another great void known as **Big Hole**, and beyond this the area is littered with rocky buttes and ice caves too numerous to mention. Contact the ranger stations in Bend if you want to try to explore them all.

Crater Lake National Park

Further south on US-97, sitting high up in the Cascades about 120 miles southwest from Bend, **CRATER LAKE NATIONAL PARK** (seven-day access fee $10; Ⓦwww.nps.gov/crla) conserves the Pacific Northwest's grandest volcanic crater, where the jagged shell of **Mount Mazama** holds impossibly blue and resoundingly beautiful **Crater Lake**, the deepest in the US and seventh deepest in the world.

Arriving from the south on Hwy-62, the park's headquarters are at the **Steel Visitor Center** (May–Oct 9am–5pm, rest of year 10am–4pm; Ⓣ541/594-3100, Ⓦwww.crater.lake.national-park.com), located three miles short of Crater Lake, which has details of guided walks and a comprehensive range of maps and information. Its services are a little better than the **Rim Village Visitor Center** (June–Sept daily 9.30am–5pm), perched on the lake's southern rim.

Getting there

Crater Lake National Park does take time to get to, but it's well worth the effort. If journeying from Bend, the trip occupies several hours and requires a westward turn onto highways 138 or 62. If travelling from Eugene, you can take Hwy-58 and then US-97 to either of these access roads. Of the two, the **northern entrance** off Hwy-138 is the more exciting, with a narrow park road emerging from the forests to cut across a bleak pumice desert before arriving at Crater Lake's precipitous northern rim. This road is, however, closed by snow from mid-October to late June, sometimes longer, and attracts more than its share of fog, which can turn what should be a magnificent drive into a white-knuckle endurance test. The **southern entrance** off Hwy-62 is kept open all year, an easier route that creeps up Mazama's wooded flanks to reach the lake at its southern rim. The 33-mile "**Rim Drive**" wriggles right round the crater's edge, linking the two access roads and providing the most magnificent of views – but be aware that it too is only open in summer. On the northern side of the lake, Rim Drive connects with the steep, mile-long **Cleetwood Cove Trail**, the one and only way to reach the lakeshore. From the bottom of the trail, pleasure boats make regular **cruises** of the lake (late-June to mid-Sept daily 10am–4pm; 1hr 45min; $19.25). In late June and from early to mid-September there are four cruises daily, nine daily in July and August; tickets are sold in the parking lot at the Cleetwood Cove trailhead and at the *Crater Lake Lodge* (see below).

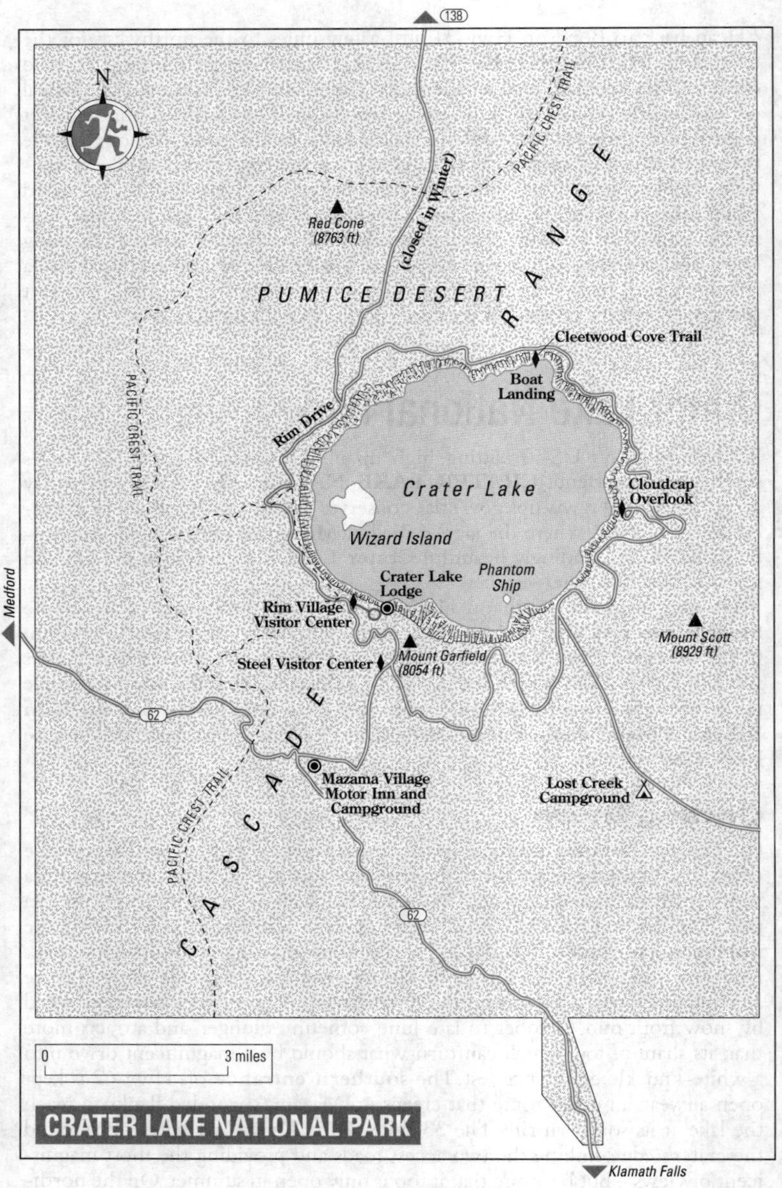

The Park

For half a million years, Mount Mazama sent out periodic sprays of ash, cinder, and pumice, later watched apprehensively by the Klamath tribe, who saw in them signs of a war between two gods, Llao and Skell, and kept well clear. Eventually, the mountain burst, blowing its peak over eight states and three

Canadian provinces in an explosion measured 62 times greater than the recent Mount St Helens blast (see p.402). Conic mini-volcanoes soon began to sprout again within the hollowed-out mountain, but when it cooled and became dormant the basin was filled by springs and melted snow. This new lake eventually submerged all but one of the volcanic outcrops, a cinder cone known as **Wizard Island**, which now pokes a wizened head above the placid waters. In its splendid isolation, Crater Lake is awe-inspiring, especially in summer, when wildflowers bloom and wildlife (deer, squirrels, chipmunks, elks, foxes, porcupines) emerges from hibernation. The lake itself has a small population of rainbow trout and kokanee (landlocked) salmon, but these were introduced in the early 1900s.

There are a number of short **hiking trails** in the park, detailed at the Steel Visitor Center (see p.227), most of which climb the mountainous slopes surrounding Crater Lake. The most popular, though still strenuous, hike is up **Garfield Peak**, an 8054ft mountain that offers a tremendous view of the lake and is particularly striking – and harder to reach – during winter. More intrepid hikers can explore the marginally better views offered by the park's tallest outcrop, **Mount Scott**, rising to almost nine thousand feet. One particularly good route travels along the lake's western rim, a wonderful hike with great views across the caldera. From this trail, two further trails climb up to the **Pacific Crest Trail** (see p.238), which runs right across the national park on its way from Mexico to Canada, though this particular stretch isn't very exciting. The park's higher hiking trails are, of course, snow-covered for most of the year, when they are favored by cross-country skiers.

Practicalities

One of the manmade highlights in the park is the splendid **Crater Lake Lodge** (mid-May to mid-Oct; ⓣ541/830-8700, ⓦwww.craterlakelodges.com; ❻), a fully refurbished 1915 hotel on the lake's south side. The lodge has a magnificent Great Hall, complete with Art Deco flourishes, and pleasant rooms – get either a corner room or at least one overlooking the lake. Advance reservations are pretty much essential, as they are at the lodge's **restaurant**, an expensive establishment whose straightforward food does not quite live up to its setting. There are less expensive lodgings in the modern, shingle-roofed chalets of the *Mazama Village Motor Inn*, on the main access road seven miles south of the lodge (early June to mid-Oct; ⓣ541/830-8700; ❺). Next door is the large *Mazama Village* **campground** (early June to mid-Oct; $10; also ⓣ541/830-8700) in a quiet wooded setting. The park's other campgrounds are the sizable *Mazama* ($10) and the tiny *Lost Creek* (July to mid-Sept; $14.75), down a spur road off Rim Drive southeast of Crater Lake, where there are a dozen basic plots. Beyond the *Crater Lake Lodge*, there's not much decent eats around except rudimentary foodstuffs, so you'll either have to bring your own grub or venture to Bend or Klamath Falls to stock up on supplies.

Klamath Falls and around

On the southern flank of the Cascades, sixty-odd miles from Crater Lake at the south end of Oregon's section of US-97, remote **KLAMATH FALLS** was once a bustling logging town and railway junction as well as a key staging point on the route to the Pacific Coast. It lost most of its early importance years ago, and now records high levels of unemployment, occasionally making the news

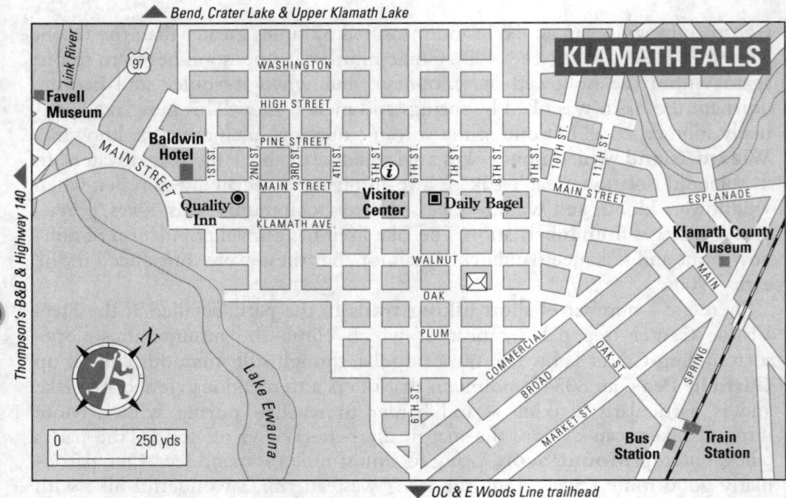

as the site of water wars between local farmers and the federal government. Despite being considered the epitome of dullness by urbanites on the other side of the state, the town still manages to rustle up a couple of diverting museums – good enough even to justify a day-trip, particularly from Crater Lake if the wet and foggy weather proves inhospitable there. Indeed, warm and sunny "K Falls," as residents call it, occupies an interesting geographical location as well, at the southern tip of enormous **Upper Klamath Lake**, the second-largest lake west of the Rockies and part of the pancake-flat **Klamath Basin**. With marshes and reedy lakes spread over the Oregon–California border, marking the transition from the forested mountains of the west to the Great Basin desert lying to the east, the basin is quite active geothermally – much of downtown Klamath Falls is heated by naturally hot water – and seismically unstable, prone to occasional earthquakes.

Arrival and accommodation

Connecting with Portland and Bend, the Greyhound **bus station** is at 445 S Spring St, off Hwy-39. Amtrak **trains** on the Coast Starlight route, linking Seattle with LA (and closer, Eugene), pull in on the eastern edge of downtown at the foot of Oak Street. The **visitor center**, 507 Main St (daily 9am–4.30pm; ⓣ541/445-6728, ⓦklamathcounty.net), issues free town maps and has details of local accommodation.

Once you've visited the museums and wandered along Main Street, it's unlikely you'll want to **stay** the night, but if you're stranded Klamath Falls does have a clutch of mundane motels strung out along 6th Street (Hwy-39) on the south side of town. There are also several bargain-basement places in the center, though note that some of these cater to itinerant fieldhands rather than tourists. Easily the best downtown bet is the *Quality Inn*, 100 Main St (ⓣ541/882-4666 or 1-888/726-2466, ⓦwww.qualityinn.com; ❹), a solid chain motel with clean rooms, though *Thompson's B&B*, 1420 Wild Plum Court (ⓣ541/882-7938, ⓦwww.thompsonsbandb.com; ❹), provides four basic bed-and-breakfast rooms near an expansive city park and the south shore of Upper Klamath Lake.

Captain Jack and the Modoc War

When white settlers reached the Klamath Basin in considerable numbers in the 1850s, they rushed to drain the marshes for pasture land, dispossessing the local natives – the **Modocs** from around Tule Lake on the Oregon–California border, and their traditional rivals, the **Klamath**, to the immediate north – with violent gusto. To justify their actions, the pioneers boasted of their ability to cultivate the land to better advantage, but this merely provided the gloss to a savage cocktail of racism mixed with social and economic ambition. It stands in shameful comparison to the puzzled innocence of the Modoc leader Kientpoos (aka **Captain Jack**) who declared "I have always told the white man to come and settle in my country; that it was his country and Captain Jack's country. That they could come and live there with me and that I was not mad with them." The settlers, of course, didn't see it that way. In 1864, keen to legitimize their new landholdings, they brought in federal treaty commissioners to persuade the Modocs to formally sign away their homeland in return for a reservation beside Upper Klamath Lake.

For the Modocs, signing the treaty brought no respite: they had endless problems with the rival Klamaths, who shared the same reservation, and the Indian agent failed to provide the supplies they had been promised. In desperation, Captain Jack led three hundred of his people back to their old hunting grounds, precipitating the so-called **Modoc War**, whose pathetic finale of 1873 had Captain Jack and his remaining followers holed up in the maze-like lava beds south of Tule Lake. In the event, the US Army found it extremely difficult to smoke out the Modocs, despite their howitzers and a huge numerical advantage – 1000 against 150 – but smoke them out they did. The captured Modocs were then transferred to Oklahoma, with the exception of Captain Jack and three of his followers, who were hanged in Fort Klamath – though even that was not quite enough: Captain Jack's body was dug up, embalmed, and taken East to be exhibited in a freak show.

The Town

The Modoc War (see box above) is detailed at the **Klamath County Museum**, 1451 Main St at Spring (Tues–Sat 10am–5pm; $2), but it's the haunting photographs of the captured Modocs that are memorable rather than the military details. Dusty and cavernous, the museum has an austere character, and even though some of the displays hardly enhance the exhibits, there are several interesting sections on, for instance, the wildlife of the Klamath Basin, local pioneer life, and early steamship travel on Upper Klamath Lake. There's also a tiny exhibit on one of World War II's forgotten episodes – **Japan's balloon bomb attack** on the US. In the spring of 1945, the Japanese released around a thousand gas-filled balloons armed with anti-personnel and incendiary bombs, hoping that Pacific air currents would carry the balloons to the West Coast, where they would cause massive forest fires and force the Americans to withdraw some battalions from the front. This was not (quite) as absurd as it sounds, but in any case the Japanese got the timing wrong and most of the balloons that made it crashed harmlessly into the snow-covered mountains. However, a handful did drop on Klamath County and one exploded on an unsuspecting party of picnickers, killing six of them – the only people killed by enemy action on the North American mainland in World War II.

The Klamath County Museum stands on the northeast edge of the elongated town center, a simple gridiron focused on Main Street and Klamath Avenue. With its faded and fancy early-twentieth-century red-brick facades, **Main Street** has an old-fashioned flavor and is highlighted by the **Baldwin Hotel**,

31 Main St (tours June–Sept Tues–Sat 10am–4pm; reserve at ⓣ541/883-4207), which began life as a 1906 hardware store before turning into accommodation five years later. These days you can't stay here, but can visit the renovated facility on guided tours, and check out a hodgepodge of intriguing antiques and assorted castoffs from the decades.

Main Street runs beyond the hotel past a US-97 slip road before reaching the Link River and the fascinating **Favell Museum**, 125 W Main St (Wed–Sat 9.30am–5.30pm; $5; ⓦwww.favellmuseum.com). Housed in a good-looking modern building, the museum is stuffed with all manner of Western US Native American artifacts, representing the lifelong enthusiasm of Gene Favell and his family. In particular, there's a breathtaking collection of Columbia Gorge pieces, notably hundreds of agate gem points – or arrowheads – all sorts of tools, an intriguing collection of trade goods, and a sample of the three-dimensional rock reliefs for which the gorge tribes are well known. Another display area concentrates on the Modocs and Klamaths, whose stone sculptures feature animal and human figures imbued with spiritual significance – as in the *henwas* used in fertility rites. The museum also features a sizeable collection of twentieth-century paintings about the West, though for the most part these big and breezy canvases adopt a sort of latter-day Custer approach – wild, lean natives and tough, weather-beaten Bluecoats – at its most outlandish with the epic canvases of Mort Kunstler.

Eating

There's nothing fancy in the way of **food** in Klamath Falls, and what there is closes early at night – try the *Daily Bagel*, 636 Main St (ⓣ541/850-0744), a simple café selling filling meals and snacks. If you're looking for something more substantial, *Molatore's*, located in the *Quality Inn* (same phone), has serviceable Italian fare, while *Red's Backwoods BBQ*, 3435 Washburn Way (ⓣ541/883-2175), doles out slabs of country ribs and chops.

OC&E Woods Line State Trail

Although the hale and hardy conservative burg of Klamath Falls seems an unlikely spot for it, the town is nonetheless the embarkation point for one of the best examples of recreational conservation in the state, the **OC&E WOODS LINE STATE TRAIL**. While admittedly a mouthful to speak, the trail is actually a simple concept – a hundred-mile-long former railway bed that has been, in the last ten years, converted into an excellent path for cycling, hiking, and horseback riding, with all manner of stunning vistas and varying topography. Beginning just south of town, just before Washburne Way crosses Hwy-140, the trail occupies the old Oregon, California & Eastern (hence OC&E) railroad – at one time a major carrier for the lumber industry – as it snakes south and then to the far northeast of the **Winema** and **Fremont national forests**. Along the way the trail crosses from paved to gravel to dirt surfaces, parallels pristine streams, climbs over lava buttes and down forested valleys, and crosses hair-raising train trestles and archaic steel bridges before it ends in the tiny village of **Bly** – way out in the middle of nowhere, roughly halfway between Klamath Falls and Lakeview, Oregon, near Hwy-140. Thus, if you want to get back to your departure point, the trail is actually a 200-mile trek, which can seem like an endless slog if you don't have the stamina for it. Nonetheless, there are assorted waysides and **campgrounds** ($10–14) along the path, though you'll need plenty of supplies and a detailed map to find your way to the nearest town should you want to quit in mid-journey. For further details on making this fascinating expedition, or to request a brochure, contact the Klamath Rails-to-Trails Group (Ⓣ541/884-3050, Ⓦwww.u-r-here.com/OCE) or the State Parks Department (Ⓣ1-800/551-6949, Ⓦwww.oregonstateparks.org).

The Klamath Basin National Wildlife Refuges

Most of the Klamath Basin has been drained and turned into either cattle-grazing pasture or potato and onion farmland, but there remain six widely dispersed but broadly similar **NATIONAL WILDLIFE REFUGES** – three each on either side of the Oregon–California border. These refuges are mainly devoted to waterfowl – pelicans, cormorants, herons, ducks, geese, and swans – along with the raptors they attract and a substantial population of bald eagles. They are best visited in spring or fall when hundreds of thousands of birds stop in the basin during their annual migration. The most accessible is the **Upper Klamath Lake National Wildlife Refuge**, situated just north of Klamath Falls off US-97. For detailed advice about the best **bird-watching** sites and maps of the network of rough gravel roads that lattice this and the other refuges, contact either the Klamath Falls visitor center (see above), or the Klamath Wildlife Area Office, Oregon Department of Fish and Wildlife, 1850 Miller Island Rd, West Klamath Falls, 97603 (Ⓣ541/883-5732).

The trans-Cascade roads

Whereas US-97 leads you along a "greatest hits" collection of the High Cascades, from Smith Rock to Crater Lake, the lower-slung **Western Cascades** some thirty to fifty miles away are better explored on the several **trans-Cascade roads** that lead east across the peaks and valleys. Starting in cities along I-5 like Salem, Eugene, Roseburg, and Medford, these state highways are not as straight and purely functional as US-97, and frequently meander up hillsides, down switchbacks, alongside riverbeds, and below mountain flanks. Moreover, the peaks such roads pass are not the big names of the Cascades – such as Hood, Bachelor, and Newberry – but the lesser-known ones, each with its own distinctive silhouette and often only accessible on hiking trails. Venturing into the mountains this way will no doubt closely acquaint you with the area's lakes, hot springs, lava fields, forest glades, and waterfalls, but you may need a detailed hiking or topography map (available at bookstores or forest offices) to find your way through some of the thornier mountain passes and confusing geography. If wandering off the major roads, a sturdy four-wheel-drive vehicle can be a necessity, and make sure to equip yourself with the necessary supplies if embarking on a serious trek through the woods – it's all too easy to get lost in these parts and find your only companion is the icy gaze of a dormant volcano.

Salem to Santiam Junction

Predictably, the most popular east-west route into the heart of the Cascades is **Highway 22** from Salem (see p.192), which day-trippers from Portland use for a quick dip into the mountains. For the first forty miles east the route is fairly uneventful, though it does pass the fine North Santiam State Park (see p.197), about halfway along this first leg. Only when the highway reaches the

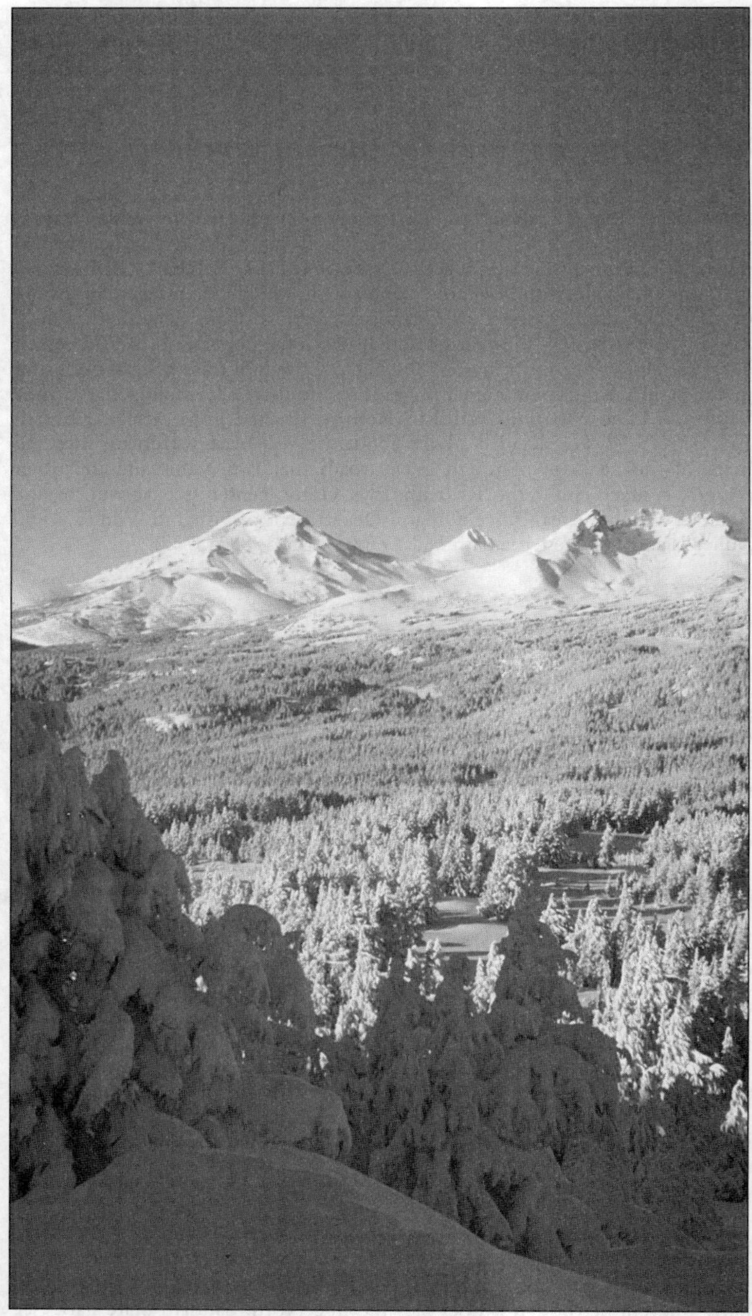

△ Broken Top Mountain

recreational center of **Detroit Lake**, 45 miles from Salem (March–Nov; $3 day-use), does it really spring to life. This eponymous state park is unquestionably a favorite among Oregonians, primarily for its excellent boating, swimming, and fishing, though a walk along its shoreline is also rather pleasant. You can **camp** at the park's lakeshore sites ($16–20; reserve at ⓣ1-800/452-5687), or, if you feel up to it, take a boat and make the journey out to **Piety Knob Island** in the middle of the lake to stay at one of its twelve rudimentary campsites. Keep in mind there are no facilities on the island, though, including water. For maps and information on how to best explore the lake, drop by the **Detroit Ranger Station**, two miles east of the lake in Mill City (Mon–Fri 8am–4.30pm; ⓣ503/854-3366).

Ten miles north of Detroit Lake along Breitenbush Road, is the enticing **Breitenbush Hot Springs** (ⓣ503/854-3320, ⓦwww.breitenbush.com), a New Age resort boasting a collection of three toasty mineral pools, four hot tubs, and a sauna, along with an imitation Native American sweat lodge. There are both basic cabins (❸) and tent sites ($40-50), but you'll have to stay here, and reserve in advance, to use the facilities. Travel another four miles along the road to reach Forest Road 4685, which, after a mile, leads to trailheads for the **South Breitenbush Gorge**, a National Scenic Trail that takes you on a five-mile trek along a river rushing through a steep-walled basalt canyon and back. A Northwest Forest Pass ($5; see p.222) is required to park here, though, available at area ranger stations. To embark on another brisk hike into the woods, continue north on Breitenbush Road for another eight miles and follow the signs for the "**Olallie Lakes Scenic Area**," and you'll soon find yourself at a trailhead with access to dozens of appealingly isolated mountain lakes, best known for their fishing.

Back on Hwy-22, twelve miles east of the town of Detroit is the turnoff for Pamelia Road, which leads after three miles to a trailhead. From here, a path leads you through stately groves of old-growth forest along a creekside until you reach **Pamelia Lake**, another sparkling mountain jewel, which is also good for fishing and acts as a base for trips into the rugged landscape beyond. This spot is so popular that during the summer a free **wilderness permit** is required to visit the lake and its trails, which is only available at the Detroit Ranger Station. Of immediate interest is the ten-mile loop up and around **Grizzly Peak**, a nearly 6000-foot mountain of the Western Cascades that affords excellent views of its High Cascades counterparts – Mount Jefferson, Three Fingered Jack, and in the distance, the Three Sisters. The 10,500-foot **Mount Jefferson** is the closest of the peaks, and adventurous visitors with proper equipment can make a climb for the summit. There are nine primitive **campgrounds** ($5–10) in the area around the mountain, nearly two hundred miles of trails, five glaciers, and 150 lakes of varying size. Again, you'll need a detailed forest map and plenty of planning; contact the Detroit Ranger Station or Willamette National Forest office in Eugene (see p.198) for more information.

Also in the vicinity are a number of good fishing lakes – among them **Marion** and **Lava lakes** – and some fifteen miles south of **Marion Forks** (noted mainly for its fish hatchery), highways 22 and 126 intersect at **Santiam Junction**, sitting in the center of a group of snow parks and winter recreation areas (see p.238).

From Santiam Junction, you can either continue eastbound on Hwy-126 (see p.237) or return west on Hwy-20 to the sleepy Willamette Valley towns of Sweet Home and Albany. The first diverting sight along this latter route, **Sawyer's Ice Caves**, a mile and a half west of the junction, is accessed via an unmarked parking lot. Nonetheless, the site is easy enough to find, and offers a fascinating series of subterranean chambers that remain frozen for much of the year. Around 3500 years old, these lava tubes formed as the conduits for outpouring magma, and more recently were used by pioneer residents to store meat and perishables to keep them from spoiling. Another ten miles west of the Hwy-126 junction, just past the Tombstone campground area, Forest Road 2000-035 leads a short distance north of the highway to the trailhead for **Iron Mountain**. This three-and-a-half mile loop leads to one of central Oregon's prime habitats for **wildflowers**, with some three hundred different varieties visible in the spring or summer, and some excellent views of distant mountains and valleys. At the top is a fire lookout (open summer daily) built atop the mountain's spiky basaltic summit, around 5400ft high, that is one of many local remnants of the ancient Western Cascade chain – the predecessors of today's High Cascades. Visit the **Sweet Home Ranger Station**, at 3225 Hwy-20S (Mon–Fri 8am–4.30pm; ⓣ541/367-5168), for maps and more information on exploring this and other peaks in the Western Cascades.

East from Eugene

Although all of the trans-Cascade routes have their own charm, for many the most inspiring attractions are to be found **east from Eugene** (see p.198) along a trio of state roads: **Hwy-126**, which leads into the central core of the mountains and is one of Oregon's finest drives; **Hwy-242**, a seasonal route that is unlike any stretch in the Pacific Northwest for eerie and bizarre beauty; and **Hwy-58**, heading southeast in the general direction of Crater Lake. Any of these roads, or a combination thereof, would be more than enough to acquaint you with the region's most distinctive and alluring mountain scenery, and must be regarded as the first option for those serious about exploring the Western or the High Cascades.

Practicalities

Most of the routes from Eugene lead into the **Willamette National Forest**, part of the larger **Deschutes National Forest** (see p.224). For **information** on approaching this expansive terrain, the Willamette National Forest Office, in downtown Eugene at 211 E 7th Ave and Pearl (Mon–Fri 8am–4.30pm; ⓣ541/465-6521, ⓦwww.fs.fed.us/r6/willamette), carries a full range of maps, trail details, and information, and can provide Northwest Forest Passes ($5) for many off-road areas. It does not, however, provide the free Limited Access Permits that are designed to control public access to key areas (such as Pamelia Lake, see p.235) in peak months; these you'll need to get from local ranger stations in each forest district. Within the national forest, parts of the McKenzie River offer excellent **whitewater rafting** and **boating**. Several Eugene- and Bend-based companies organize excursions – contact the nearest visitor center or try Rapid River Rafters, 1151 SE Centennial Court #5, Bend (ⓣ541/382-1514 or 1-800/962-3327, ⓦwww.rapidriverrafters.com), or Oregon Whitewater Adventures Inc, 39620 Deerhorn Rd, just east of Eugene in Springfield (ⓣ541/746-5422 or 1-800/820-7238, ⓦwww.oregonwhitewater.com).

As far as public transit is concerned, Lane Transit District runs a regular #91 **bus** (Mon–Fri 4 daily, Sat & Sun 2 daily; $1.25) out of Eugene along Hwy-126 as far as the McKenzie Bridge Ranger Station – the journey takes about an hour and a half. However, although you're dropped close to the foot of the McKenzie River National Recreation Trail (see below), it's a stiff uphill hike from here – much better to start at the top and work down.

Highway 126

In many ways, **HIGHWAY 126** can be considered the Main Street of the Cascades, a resplendent stretch that connects many of the region's iconic peaks and valleys into one eye-opening concourse, along the way passing glittering lakes, secret ice caves, stark lava beds, and countless rugged hiking trails. These last, not surprisingly, comprise some of the best treks in the state, all the way from simple, lovely riverside routes to gut-wrenching trips past cliff walls and rockslides. The truly gung-ho can even take a chance scaling a mountain – though you'll need plenty of preparation and fearlessness for this. Contact area ranger stations for details on maps, outfitters, and any requirements.

McKenzie River Valley to Clear Lake

Of the several roads into Willamette National Forest, Highway 126 is one of the most enjoyable options, as it heads east from Eugene to track along the **MCKENZIE RIVER VALLEY**, passing through miles of fruit and nut orchards before arriving at **Aufderheide Scenic Drive**, with the turnoff 41 miles east of Eugene. This byway is among the most visually appealing in the Cascades, a twisting, verdant concourse through thickly forested glades and around canyons and lakeshores, following the path of the south McKenzie and Willamette rivers. For 57 miles the drive snakes bewitchingly through this fetching topography, ultimately reaching Highway 58 near Oakridge, and provides good opportunities for hiking and cycling as well. Initially, though, its most popular sight is **Cougar Reservoir**, a monumental dammed-up lake high in a mountain canyon that is best known for its **Terwilliger Hot Springs** (also known as Cougar Hot Springs; eleven miles south of the turnoff from Hwy-126), a free, day-use only set of seven hot and warm pools, which range from scalding to tepid the further you descend along the hillside. Along with Rooster Rock on the Columbia River (see p.126), this is one of the state's most renowned **clothing-optional** recreation sites, and there are always plenty of graying hippies and college students around to keep you company. Just make sure to wait to get to the pools before disrobing – they're located a half-mile from the parking lot, and accessed by a narrow dirt path. About twenty miles further along the Scenic Drive, just past Roaring River campground, you come to the highest point on the drive at **Box Canyon**, featuring a series of meadows grazed by deer and elk, along with the occasional bear or mountain lion. There's a horse camp nearby, along with a number of stunning trails leading past waterfalls, mountain ridges, and the source of several state rivers.

As you return to Hwy-126, heading east you soon come to the village of **McKenzie Bridge**, just beyond which are the McKenzie Bridge Ranger Station (late–May to early–Oct daily 8am–4.30pm; ⓣ541/822-3381) and the medium-sized and very popular **Paradise campground** (ⓣ541/822-3381; $10–16), pleasantly tucked away among dense forest close to the river. One mile further on there's a fork in the road and Hwy-242 (see below) splits off to the east, leaving Hwy-126 to wend its way north, climbing steeply as it follows the course of the McKenzie River, passing roadside parking lots that serve as trailheads for a number of good hikes. The first main commercially developed sight, though, is **Belknap Hot Springs** (ⓣ541/822-3512; ❹), a simple motel with several pools of heated mineral water and six of the rooms offering in-room hot-spring water. Of course, the surrounding forest has several isolated sites hosting hot springs for no charge, but you'll have to do a bit of research through the ranger stations, and have a detailed hiking map, to find them. Seven miles north on Hwy-126 is the access road to **Koosah Falls**, a 70-ft waterfall flowing off a lava ridge, which is connected by a short path to **Sahalie Falls**, a higher and grander version of the same thing.

Edged by lava flows another mile or so further north, the delightful **Cold Water Cove campground** (ⓣ541/822-3381; $12–16), overlooks the beautiful blue-green **CLEAR LAKE**, the source of the McKenzie River, which was dammed by onrushing lava some three thousand years ago. Even today, its glimmering waters cloak a submerged forest valley, and if you look hard enough you may even see the skeletons of ancient drowned trees. Two miles north, you can find the handiest place to start hiking (or cycling) the **McKenzie River National Recreation Trail**, a clearly marked, 26-mile route that heads downstream along the McKenzie River Valley, threading through patches of old-growth forest and past thundering waterfalls on its way back to the McKenzie Bridge Ranger Station. The trail is a fine introduction to the local scenery and, as the footpath also runs near Hwy-126, you can reach and walk the more manageable portions relatively easily.

The Santiam Pass to Black Butte

Highway 126 takes a turn to the east after two more miles and merges with Hwy-20. A short distance from here, Hwy-22 leads back to Salem (see p.192), while the Hwy-126/20 combination rises up to the **SANTIAM PASS**, crossing through the heart of the Cascades at nearly five thousand feet. Splendid mountain scenery dominates all vistas, with the gnarled rocky claws of **Three-Fingered Jack** rising to the north just a few thousand feet above the pass, and the spiky crest of **Mount Washington** looming over the road's southern flank. Not surprisingly, there are a wealth of fine hiking trails and outdoor adventures to be had in the area, whether boating on pristine lakes or scaling rocky cliffs; for more information contact the Deschutes National Forest center in Bend, 1645 Hwy-20E (ⓣ541/383-5300). More prominently visible, though, are the number of ski centers and "sno-parks" scattered along this portion of Hwy-126/20; you can give any of them a go – many offer options for downhill or cross-country skiing, snowboarding, and the like. The biggest name is **Hoodoo Ski Bowl** (lift tickets $29–38; ⓣ541/822-3799, ⓦwww.hoodoo.com), unmissable just west of Santiam Pass, with its two lodges, five chair lifts, and forty or so runs, some of them with oddball names like "Frank's Flight" and "Art's Alley."

Less than a mile from the ski bowl you pass over the high ridgeline that marks the perpendicular route of the **Pacific Crest Trail**, connecting a broad swath of the mountains along the West Coast (see "Basics," p.55, for more details). Just beyond lie a pair of glacially carved lakes of very different character: **Suttle Lake**, a shallow, rectangular body of water popular for trout fishing, boating, and swimming, and the much more interesting **Blue Lake**, a small, deep freshwater pit that has only a fifth the surface area of its neighbor, but six times the depth. Indeed, this 300ft-deep bowl is richly blue in color, sitting serenely in the shadow of Mount Washington. It owes its origin to a massive geothermal blowout, which cut this deep chasm and gave meltwater the chance to fill it in – for good reason, then, many refer to this as a Crater Lake in miniature. A few miles beyond these lakes, the highway cruises past the idyllic headwaters of the **Metolius River** – another good area for fishing, hiking, and the like, flowing through the little recreational town of **Camp Sherman** – and past the resort of **BLACK BUTTE** (ⓣ1-800/452-7455, ⓦwww.blackbutteranch.com; ❺–❽ by season), a favorite spot for vacationing urbanites, though a bit overpriced for the outdoors enthusiast. Still, the basic condos for rent here can be quite affordable if you arrive during the winter low season – just as long as golf, tennis, and horseback riding are your focus.

Sisters

About eight miles southeast of Black Butte, Hwy-126 wends its way to the mountain hamlet of **SISTERS**, which sits in close proximity to many of the major sights in the central Cascades, with US-97 less than twenty miles further east. With that in mind, this pleasant little town is a good stopover if you need a break from camping or want to avoid larger-scaled Bend to the southeast. Featuring false-fronted, Wild West-styled businesses in a vaguely similar manner to its Washington Cascades counterpart of Winthrop (see p.382), Sisters has a bit less charm and feels a bit uneasy in its new, tourist-friendly guise. It began as a logging town built in the shadow of looming Cascade mountains, and took its name from the Three Sisters peaks southwest of town. However, after several fires immolated the place and the timber trade met its demise, the town had to find a new purpose – namely drawing the overspill of summer visitors from nearby Bend.

These days it sports a few gussied-up old buildings, dating from the early twentieth century, along **East Cascade Avenue**, on which you can find some serviceable **restaurants**. These include *Bronco Billy's*, no. 190 (Ⓣ541/549-0361), serving up solid steaks, seafood, and barbecue in the former Sisters Hotel, a renovated 1912 relic that is the town's most historic structure. The nearby *Sisters Bakery*, no. 251 (Ⓣ541/549-0361), is also good for its donuts, pastries, breads, and espresso, and is based in the shell of a 1925 general store. There are a few decent places to **stay** in town, including *Conklin's Guest House*, 69013 Camp Polk Rd (Ⓣ541/549-0123 or 1-800/549-4262, Ⓦwww.conklinsguesthouse.com; ❺), with five cozy, quaintly decorated rooms and a swimming pool, and the *Australian Outback Country Lodge*, 68733 Junipine Lane (Ⓣ541/549-4312, Ⓦwww.sisterslodging.com; ❻), whose five curious rooms are stuffed with a hodgepodge of antiques and furnishings from the local region as well as Down Under. If you just want the basics, try the *Best Western Ponderosa Lodge*, 500 Hwy-20W (Ⓣ541/549-1234 or 1-800/893-5354, Ⓦwww.bestwestern.com; ❹), which offers standard rooms with fridges and microwaves, and an onsite pool and hot tub.

Highway 242

Although appearing on maps as a handy, 36-mile shortcut from McKenzie Bridge west to Sisters, **HIGHWAY 242** is in reality one of the state's most twisting and grindingly slow routes – but also one of its most austere and strangely beautiful. Not even publicly accessible between November and March, when steady snowfall make it impassable, the highway has countless waysides for rugged mountain hikes, awe-inspiring vistas of many of the peaks in the central Cascades, and, most of all, the stunning topography of volcanoes run amok. Up to just a few thousand years ago, this area was for millions of years the scene of violent geological upheavals. Nearby mountains belched up towers of smoke and ash, sent bombs of pumice and basalt hurtling through the air, and covered the landscape with rivers of free-flowing lava – which left many square miles of the terrain covered in jagged black hillocks and rutted craters, best seen from such vantages as the **Dee Wright Observatory** and **Black Crater**. You don't have to go far off the road to see this eye-opening world, either, as many great views can be had from the highway itself. That said, a trip along Hwy-242 almost demands a closer look on foot, and luckily there are plenty of places to go exploring.

Proxy Falls to the McKenzie Pass

Starting from the western junction where Hwy-126 turns north, Hwy-242 leads east eight miles toward the turnoff for **PROXY FALLS**. This pair of waterfalls, reached on an easy mile-and-a-half loop trail, is one of the more unusual you'll see: divided into upper and lower sections with drops of 125 and 200 feet, the water tumbles over the rocky ledge only to seemingly disappear at the bottom. This odd effect – a bit different than the typical roar and splash – occurs as the water literally vanishes into thousands of tiny holes in the porous lava rock. Less than two miles east on Hwy-242 lies the striking and serene landscape of **Linton Lake**, where a three-mile trail leads you to a curious mountain lake and its waterfall, sitting amid a forest and meadow into which chunks of broken lava have abruptly, but not completely, intruded. Less than five miles away, as the highway begins to turn sharply through dips and switchbacks, sometimes narrowing to sixteen feet or so, you reach **Scott Lake**, a pristine setting with a pleasant **campground** ($10–16).

The stark lava terrain begins in earnest about three miles east at **Belknap Crater**, an ominous-looking cinder cone whose shield volcano was responsible in large part for this torrential flood of basalt you begin to see everywhere along the road, estimated to be less than three thousand years old. The effect is even more clear a few miles further east – a 65-square-mile landscape of nothing but solidified lava, broken into its own strange jagged swirl of mounds, hills, troughs, and ridges. This is the site of the 5300-foot **MCKENZIE PASS**, the road's highest and most striking plateau. Undoubtedly, the best place to view the dark lunar topography is at the **Dee Wright Observatory**, a 1930s tower just off Hwy-242 which is itself built of chunky lava rocks, making it look as if it simply rose up out of the mottled landscape. Inside the structure, crude windows offer startling views of the many peaks in the region, and just beyond it, a half-mile path leads you around this rough, jagged world, which 1960s astronauts used as an imitation moonscape to practice walking in their spacesuits. In the 1860s, this godawful surface was somehow used for a leg of the **Deschutes Wagon Road** – a fact that may leave you gaping as much as the lava itself.

The Three Sisters Wilderness

As the road continues to the east you go deeper into the harsh land of the **THREE SISTERS WILDERNESS**, and the grand monuments of the **Three Sisters** and **Broken Top** make a clearer appearance to the south. The former peaks – also known as "Faith, Hope, and Charity" – are in various states of geological activity, with the South Sister being the most recently active. By contrast, Broken Top is clearly dormant, and looks as though it's fought a losing battle with the glaciers that have scoured and ruined its summit. Nowadays it's more of a rough bowl with a high ridgeline, but its does make for an interesting hiking excursion if you have a good map to get there; contact the Deschutes National Forest office in Bend for more details (see p.222). There are many serious and worthy treks in the area, but if you pick only one, consider the 7.5-mile jaunt up **Black Crater** ($5 Northwest Forest Pass required), with its trailhead about four miles east of the observatory. While there are no facilities en route and the lengthy slog demands great stamina, the views from the crest of this 7300-foot former volcano are truly awe-inspiring, with a panoply of mountain peaks stretching far into the distance – with the craggy, glacier-damaged face of **North Sister** as the peak's closest and most imposing neighbor. Moreover, the crater itself atop the mountain is the bleak and fascinating high point of the trip – the dark, exploded remnant of a once-proud mountain, from which rivers of lava and columns of ash once issued unmercifully.

The drama of Highway 242 lessens considerably on the last ten miles toward the town of Sisters (see p.239), as you return to alpine meadows, pleasant lakes, and an altogether less threatening landscape. Should want to spend the night here, just off the roadside, the **Cold Springs Campground** ($12), four miles from town, provides 23 sites in the shadow of the mountains. Less than a mile east, a more unexpected attraction can be found at the edge of private **Patterson Ranch**, where crowds of llamas and elk can be observed first-hand from a wayside along the highway.

Highway 58

For those who want their sightseeing to be a bit more sedate, **HIGHWAY 58** east from Eugene to US-97 may have just the appeal. Although it lacks the truly eye-opening spectacle of highways 126 or 242, it still manages to offer quite a few compelling attractions that are well worth your time if you're on your way to Crater Lake or southern Oregon. Dipping down almost due southeast, the road travels 86 miles and crosses the crest of the Cascades at 5100-foot **Willamette Pass**. Well before it gets there, however, it passes by a number of thin, angular lakes carved into shape by glaciers from the last Ice Age and earlier, as well as numerous campgrounds, hiking trails, and gorgeous mountain vistas.

Elijah Bristow State Park, seventeen miles from Eugene, while not necessarily in the thick of the mountains, is still a great spot for horseback riding, fishing, and exploring the scenery on ten miles of trails. The park's forests and wetlands are home to any number of species, but especially for the seasonal displays of bald eagles, osprey, and herons. For the next ten miles there are long, spindly reservoirs along the highway visible at **Dexter** and **Lookout Point**, but for camping in the outback try **Fall Creek**, 27 miles southeast of Eugene on Hwy-58 ($3 day-use, $11–16 campsites), whose 47 primitive sites sit at the western edge of **Willamette National Forest** (see p.236). Back on the highway, it's just seven miles to the burg of **Westfir**, which features the **Office Covered Bridge**, the state's longest such span at 180 feet, looking like a long, thin ranch house plunked across a river. From town, you can take a sharp left northward to access Aufderheide Scenic Drive (see p.237) up to Hwy-126, or continue a few miles east to the workaday town of **Oakridge**, really just a place to gas up and get a snack.

Twenty miles past Oakridge lie a pair of terrific attractions that are the highlight of the journey, both within about two miles of each other. **Salt Creek Falls**, at 286 feet the second-highest waterfall in the state, makes for an excellent two-and-a-half mile trek around its high basaltic cliffs; there are also other, smaller falls nearby worth a look. The second major sight in the vicinity is just a few miles north of Hwy-58 and sits on the east side of the Pacific Crest Trail – **Waldo Lake**, the second-deepest undammed lake in the state at 420 feet. The wonderfully pristine waters and shoreline make a fine spot for cycling, horseback riding, canoeing, or **camping** in any of five Forest Service sites ($12–14). Especially good is the lakeside hiking circuit, which runs 21 miles through varying terrain from idyllic mountain meadows to jagged lava cliffs. Back on Highway 58, you soon cross over the Willamette Pass and near the recreational heart of the area, where the striking **Odell** and **Crescent lakes** sit near the road and offer prime fishing, camping, and hiking opportunities. Immediately north of the road, the **Willamette Pass Ski Area** (Nov–April; lift tickets $35; ⓣ541/345-SNOW, ⓦwww.willamettepass.com) draws winter adventurers for its four chairlifts and 25 or so runs.

From here, continue another five miles to the northbound turnoff for the **Cascade Lakes Highway** (see p.224) back up to Mount Bachelor and Bend, reach US-97 another ten miles past the turnoff, or venture south of Highway

58 to explore the wilderness around **Diamond Peak**. At 8700 feet, this is one of the smaller of the High Cascades, but is still the only major peak along Hwy-58, a dormant shield volcano that sits amid a cluster of smaller volcanoes and offers a number of good trails and **campgrounds** (contact the Deschutes National Forest office in Bend, at 1645 US-20 E (Mon–Fri 8am–4.30pm; ⓣ541/383-5300).

The Diamond Lake Highway

Although the trans-Cascade routes from Salem and Eugene are deservedly the most popular access roads across the mountains, the southerly routes across the Cascades also have a number of decent options for exploring the forested outback. One of the best routes is unquestionably the **DIAMOND LAKE HIGHWAY**, which links Roseburg to Mount Thielsen, and beyond that, Crater Lake (see p.227). Following the curving banks of the nationally recognized "Wild and Scenic" **Umpqua River**, this route, also known as **Highway 138**, provides a wonderful trip through beguiling forest and volcanic scenery, and has countless places to explore. Waterfalls, campgrounds, hiking trails, whitewater rapids, hidden caves, rocky chasms, and even a few hot springs can all be found just off the road. Your first option to orient yourself with the area should be to drop by the **Umpqua National Forest office**, in Roseburg at 2900 NW Stewart Pkwy (ⓣ541/672-6601, ⓦwww.fs.fed.us/r6/umpqua), or the **ranger stations** in Glide, 16 miles east at 18782 Hwy-138 (ⓣ541/496-3532), or nearby Idleyld Park, 2020 Toketee Ranger Station Rd (ⓣ541/498-2531).

In the tiny town of Glide, the North Umpqua and the Little rivers meet appropriately at **Colliding Rivers**, an excellent spot for a picnic in the face of the dramatic, onrushing waters. Just a few miles east of town, signs mark the beginning of the 77-mile **North Umpqua Trail**, which follows the river up to Lemolo Falls, and offers stunning views of lava flows, rocky cliffs, violent river rapids, and numerous meadows, glades, and forests along the way. If you're interested in the full journey – or the exhaustive 155-mile round-trip – make sure to pick up a trail map at the forest office and be prepared to **camp** ($10–16; $5 Northwest Forest Pass required) along the way at the mostly primitive campgrounds en route. **Job's Garden Geological Area** and its appealingly chunky columns of lava rock in gnarled formation lie eight miles further east along the highway, while fifteen miles beyond this are a collection of basalt columns peppering the roadside. The most well known of these is **Eagle Rock**, a mottled rocky tower that developed long ago as a volcanic plug – a big knob of magma that has protruded upward and has been stripped and revealed by erosion. Six and eight miles further along short trails, you reach two of southern Oregon's best waterfalls – **Toketee**, a thin spire of water 135 feet high, and **Watson**, twice as high and the tallest waterfall in the region. Between these lies the turnoff for Toketee Reservoir, north of which Thorn Prairie Road leads to the pleasantly isolated setting of **Umpqua Hot Springs** (day-use only; free), a small tub on a steep hillside that features 106°F (41°C)-degree water flowing through it.

Back on Hwy-138, over the next twenty miles the road takes a sharp turn to the south and eventually leads up toward the slopes of Crater Lake. Most tourists lose sight of everything else and make a final charge up to it, but if you can resist the temptation there is a trio of worthy sights in the fifteen miles before you reach the crater rim. Just before the junction of Highway 230, which leads southwest to Hwy-62 and the south side of Crater Lake, you pass the eastern edge of **Diamond Lake**, a recreational complex highlighted by the **Diamond Lake Resort** (Ⓣ1-800/733-7593, Ⓦwww.diamondlake.net), which offers kayaking, boating, canoeing, cycling, skiing, and so forth. There are a few serviceable, if unsurprising, all-American **restaurants** here, and several options for **lodging**: basic motel rooms (④), more spacious cabins (⑥), and access to some four hundred Forest Service **campsites** ($12–16) around the lake – though you don't need to stay at the resort to use them.

Perhaps more interesting than the traditional attractions at the lake, though, are the two grand mountains rising on each side of it, about equal distance from each other on both sides of Highway 138. To the west, **Mount Bailey** looms 8300 feet above the lake and is accessible on forest roads beginning southwest from its shoreline. From here you can take a strenuous, ten-mile jaunt up and down its slopes and check out the fractured ridge-rock around its summit. On the other side of Hwy-138 lies the trailhead leading to **Mount Thielsen**, a 9200-foot dormant volcano with a distinctly splintered silhouette, rising up to a jagged, razorlike peak that is only ten feet wide – the result of some three-hundred-thousand years of erosion and glacial damage. Nonetheless, experienced hikers and climbers can make it up the slope on an eight-mile round-trip trek, though for the last push to the pinnacle you're forced to scramble over spiky boulders and shattered chunks of lava rock. For more information on climbing either of these mountains, contact the Umpqua National Forest office in Roseburg or the ranger stations east of town (see opposite).

Highway 62

The fast and direct route to Crater Lake from Medford, **HIGHWAY 62**, has many charms that are overlooked by gung-ho vacationers speeding up to that blown-out mountaintop. However, the major attractions don't really begin until you first trudge some thirty miles north from Medford, past its ever-expanding sprawl, and start to travel alongside the upper reaches of the **Rogue River**. Indeed, this is the general area where you can access trailheads for the lovely and curving **Rogue River Trail**. Like other sights in this wilderness, you can find more about it at the Rogue River National Forest Office, 333 W 8th St in Medford (Mon–Fri 8am–4.30pm; Ⓣ541/858-2200, Ⓦwww.fs.fed.us/r6/rogue), or the Prospect Ranger Station, 47201 Hwy-62 in Prospect (same hours; Ⓣ541/560-3400). About ten miles before you get to the ranger station, though, you can **camp** (Ⓣ1-800/551-6949; $12–16) at one of the better state parks in the region, **Joseph H. Stewart**, located 35 miles north of Medford next to the Lost Creek Reservoir. The angling and hiking here are both appealing enough, but you may not want to linger with more engaging sights to the northeast along the highway. At the little town of **Prospect**, there are two options: continue north toward Crater Lake on Hwy-62, or make a sharp turn to the southeast, following a series of forest roads into the **Sky Lakes Wilderness**. Here, in this vast terrain of 113,000 acres, you can explore no less than two hundred lakes of varying size, peppered throughout the forest, with only a network of rough trails (or the odd unimproved road) connecting them. Cut into the rock during the last Ice Age by retreating glaciers, the pools, ponds, and lakes make a perfectly inviting setting for camping ($5 Northwest Forest Pass required; see p.222) amid a lovely and glistening landscape. You can find out much more about them by heading south from town along Butte Falls-Prospect Road to the little town of **Butte Falls**, where a ranger station, at 800 Laurel St (Mon–Fri 8am–4.30pm; Ⓣ541/865-2700), can tell you everything you need to know.

Traveling north nine miles from Prospect on Hwy-62, one of the top draws around is the **Natural Bridge**, a curious geological phenomenon in which the Rogue River is channeled along a narrow rocky gorge until it disappears into an ancient lava tube, over which lies the striking bridge itself. A two-and-a-half mile trek leads you around the area for a closer look at this odd sight. A few miles north, **Union Creek** marks the place where Hwy-62 splits from Hwy-230, which leads 25 miles north through a seemingly unending, hypnotic stand of Douglas fir trees to reach Diamond Lake (see p.243). Hwy-62, however, takes a turn to the east and then the south as it passes by the lower edge of Crater Lake. Seventeen miles from the turnoff you reach **Fort Klamath**, the former federal military base dating from 1863, where Captain Jack and three other Modoc natives were hanged in one of the area's most shameful episodes (see box, p.231). Now the site of a park and **museum** (Wed–Mon 10am–6pm; free), the fort's buildings are all replicas of the original wooden log structures, in chilling contrast to the authentic graves of murdered natives nearby.

From here it's ten miles to the beginning of the lakeshore marking **Agency** and **Upper Klamath lakes**, huge and beautiful preserves lined by several National Wildlife Refuges (see p.233). After merging with US-97, you finally reach the town of Klamath Falls (see p.229) at the latter lake's southern edge.

Lake of the Woods Highway

Traversing the southern edge of the Oregon Cascades, almost to the northern flank of the Klamath Mountains, is **Highway 140**, or the **LAKE OF THE WOODS HIGHWAY**. Although a much more direct route between Medford and Klamath Falls than Hwy-62, this road has plenty of scenic splendor along its 79 miles, though it starts unimpressively just north of the sprawling town of Medford. In the Rogue River National Forest office in that town (see p.243), or at the ranger station up in the village of Butte Falls (p.243), you can get information on the highway and find out about its topography and various campgrounds, hiking trails, and so on. Basically, though, the really distinctive places along the way are right in the middle, about halfway between Klamath Falls and Medford. The first of these is **Fish Lake**, at the junction of the road from Butte Falls 35 miles east of Medford, which sits in a volcanic landscape amid scattered chunks of lava rock, and, not surprisingly, offers excellent fishing ($2 day-use). You can also **camp** here ($17), as you can a few miles east at **Lake of the Woods** (☎1-866/201-4194), a high mountain resort with sparkling waters and plenty of recreational activities.

On the north side of the highway, though, lies the real reason for driving out this far – **Mount McLoughlin**. With a trailhead reached by Forest Road 3650, located between the two lakes, the mountain is the tallest in southern Oregon at 9500 feet, cuts a dashing silhouette against the thick forests and volcanic scenery, and best of all is eminently climbable. Looking more like an impressive alpine peak and less like a frazzled, glacier-cut ruin (such as Mount Thielsen), this mountain's summit is reached on an 11.5-mile loop trail, which intersects with and crosses the Pacific Crest Trail near its base. Higher up, though, the mountain's frame gets more daunting, as you rise past the treeline to encounter rough blocks of andesite or basalt and the hardscrabble remnants of icy moraines. Near the summit it's necessary to scramble over the jagged terrain with nimble footwork, but the view from the top is well worth it – a stunning vista of the magnificent Cascade range, a line of snowy peaks stretching from California's Shasta to Mount Jefferson, just visible at the edge of this great volcanic horizon.

6

Seattle

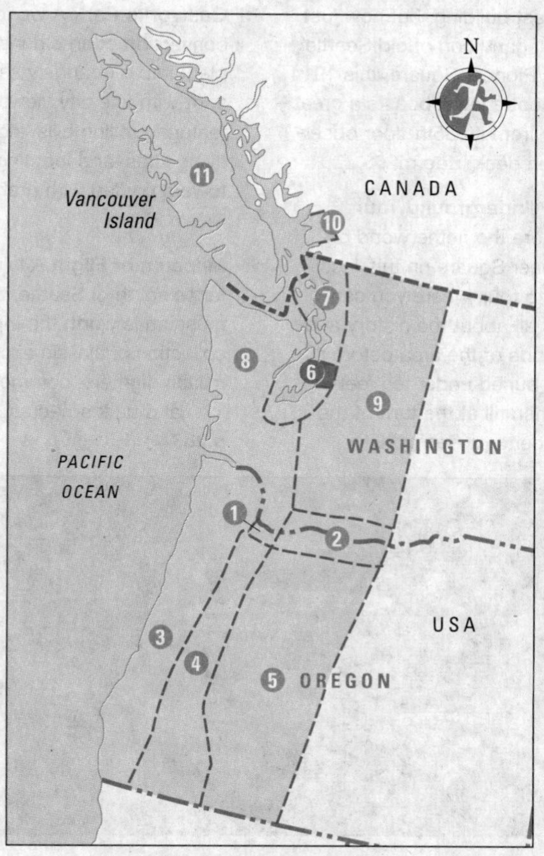
N
CANADA
Vancouver Island
PACIFIC OCEAN
WASHINGTON
OREGON
USA
1
2
3
4
5
6
7
8
9
10
11

CHAPTER 6

Highlights

* **Pike Place Market** Check out this frenetic urban scene loaded with fish vendors, produce stalls, fancy restaurants, underground book and record stores, and just about anything else you can think of. See p.259

* **Smith Tower** Once the city's highest building, but now just an elegant icon of old Seattle near Pioneer Square, this 1914 terracotta jewel boasts a great view from its 35th-floor observation deck. See p.263

* **The Underground Tour** Explore the netherworld of Pioneer Square on this fascinating tour, where you can hear all about the history and legends of the area before it was buried under ten feet of earthen fill at the turn of the last century. See p.264

* **Seattle Center** The former site of the 1962 World's Fair, and now home to museums, athletic arenas, concert stages, a newly reconstructed opera house, and of course, the city's redoubtable icon, The Space Needle. See p.269

* **Gasworks Park** A wondrous conversion of an old industrial plant into a strangely serene spot with fine city views, and featuring rolling hills, kids flying kites, and looming gas towers riddled with graffiti. See p.277

* **Museum of Flight** A fair distance south of Seattle, the museum is worth the trip for its collection of classic aircraft, military fighters, commercial jets, and dark spy-craft. See p.283

△ The Museum of Flight

6

Seattle

The commercial and cultural capital of the state of Washington, **SEATTLE** sits along the curving shore of Elliott Bay, with Lake Washington behind and the snowy peak of Mount Rainier hovering faintly in the distance. The beautiful natural setting plays host to shimmering glass skyscrapers, scenic winding streets, excellent restaurants, colorful nightlife, and a flourishing performing-arts scene, all making for a refreshing and compelling urban experience. Even its old central core, narrowly saved from the wrecking ball by popular outcry, has been restored as a distinctive series of historic districts, which also hold the city's best arts, shopping, and evening diversions.

For all its arriviste character, though, Seattle is not an overly dynamic place or a 24-hr party zone; those expecting the throbbing pulse of a New York or Tokyo will definitely be underwhelmed. While its museums are respectable, its theater scene vibrant, and its café culture unmatched in the US – offering social centers where coffee-drinking, avant-garde decor, and lively performance meld in one artsy pot – the overall mood of the city is decidedly low-key and takes time to fully appreciate. In fact, like much of the Pacific Northwest, it's best experienced on an itinerary that puts as much emphasis on nature hikes, neighborhood strolls, and ferry rides as it does on gung-ho sightseeing and untamed nights out.

Seattle tourist authorities proudly note that the town ranks 44th among US cities as far as **rainfall** goes, somewhat belying its reputation as the rain capital of the US. Still, the reputation is mostly deserved: it's not necessarily the quantity of the rain, but its regularity – in the fall and winter, drizzly days can pile upon one another endlessly, and when it's not raining, it's often overcast. Despite this, Seattle is never really that cold, even in the middle of winter. Summers are lovely – the average monthly rainfall in July and August hovers around just one inch, and the skies are often sunny, but almost never scorching.

Some history

Considering its pre-eminent standing in the economic and cultural life of the Pacific Northwest, Seattle's early **history** was inauspiciously muddy. Flooded out of its initial site on **Alki Beach**, the small logging community replanted along the more desirables shores of Elliott Bay in the 1850s, building its houses on stilts over the soggy ground of what's now Pioneer Square. The early settlement was named "Seattle" in honor of regional tribal leader Chief Sealth (see p.324), who helped arrange treaties in lieu of armed fighting when white

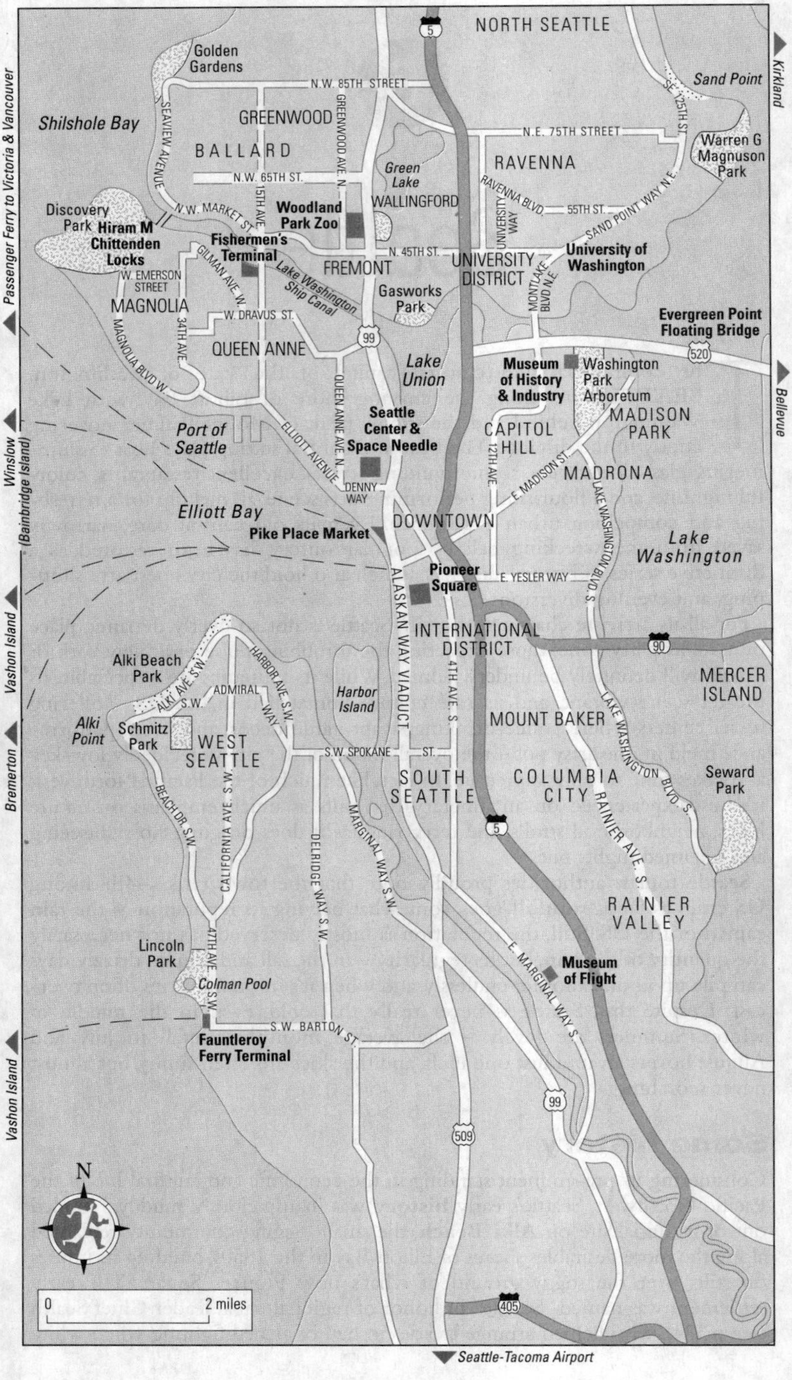

NORTH SEATTLE
Golden Gardens
Sand Point
Kirkland
N.W. 85TH STREET
Shilshole Bay
GREENWOOD
SEAVIEW AVENUE
GREENWOOD AVE N.
N.E. 75TH STREET
NE 125TH ST.
Warren G Magnuson Park
BALLARD
RAVENNA
Green Lake
N.W. 65TH ST.
RAVENNA BLVD.
WALLINGFORD
55TH ST.
Discovery Park
Hiram M Chittenden Locks
N.W. MARKET ST.
15TH AVE
Woodland Park Zoo
UNIVERSITY WAY
SAND POINT WAY N.E.
Fishermen's Terminal
N. 45TH ST.
University of Washington
W. EMERSON STREET
GILMAN AVE. W.
FREMONT
UNIVERSITY DISTRICT
Lake Washington Ship Canal
Gasworks Park
MONTLAKE BLVD N.E.
MAGNOLIA
34TH AVE.
W. DRAVUS ST.
Evergreen Point Floating Bridge
99
520
QUEEN ANNE
Lake Union
Museum of History & Industry
Washington Park Arboretum
MAGNOLIA BLVD W.
QUEEN ANNE AVE. N.
Bellevue
Seattle Center & Space Needle
MADISON PARK
Port of Seattle
ELLIOTT AVENUE
CAPITOL HILL
12TH AVE.
Winslow (Bainbridge Island)
E. MADISON ST.
MADRONA
DENNY WAY
Elliott Bay
DOWNTOWN
LAKE WASHINGTON BLVD. S.
Pike Place Market
Lake Washington
Pioneer Square
E. YESLER WAY
ALASKAN WAY VIADUCT
Vashon Island
INTERNATIONAL DISTRICT
90
HARBOR AVE. S.W.
Alki Beach Park
ALKI AVE. S.W.
MERCER ISLAND
ADMIRAL WAY
Harbor Island
4TH AVE. S.
S.W.
Alki Point
Schmitz Park
MOUNT BAKER
LAKE WASHINGTON BLVD. S.
WEST SEATTLE
S.W. SPOKANE ST.
Bremerton
Seward Park
SOUTH SEATTLE
COLUMBIA CITY
BEACH DR. S.W.
CALIFORNIA AVE. S.W.
DELRIDGE WAY S.W.
MARGINAL WAY S.W.
RAINIER AVE. S.
5
RAINIER VALLEY
Lincoln Park
47TH AVE. S.W.
E. MARGINAL WAY S.
Museum of Flight
Colman Pool
S.W. BARTON ST.
Fauntleroy Ferry Terminal
Vashon Island
Passenger Ferry to Victoria & Vancouver
99
509
N
0
2 miles
405
Seattle-Tacoma Airport

arrivals began to claim some of the most desirable land. Clashes could not be staved off indefinitely, though both moniker and settlement survived the skirmishes and ambushes of the **Puget Sound War** of 1855–56, a conflict that resulted in local natives being consigned to reservations. Sealth himself was living on a reservation when he died of a heart attack in 1866.

As the surrounding forest was gradually felled and shipped abroad, Seattle became an emerging timber town and port, but it wasn't until the **Klondike Gold Rush** of 1897 that Seattle was put firmly on the national map, boosting its trade in shipbuilding and sales of goods and mining equipment to prospectors heading north. Its rise as a major Pacific Coast port sparked its development as a large industrial center, one that to this day holds a significant place in US labor history. With so many residents employed in shipping and manufacturing (particularly timber), trade unions grew strong and the Industrial Workers of the World, or "Wobblies," made Seattle a main base, coordinating the country's first general strike in 1919 (see box, p.544).

World War II brought even more growth through the rise of the defense industry, and the following decades saw Seattle thrive as the economic center of the Pacific Northwest, highlighted by the **Century 21 Exposition** of 1962: the World's Fair that gave the city even greater prominence, along with its most familiar icon, the Space Needle. By the 1990s, Seattle was among the most prosperous cities in the US. Its thriving high-tech industries – spearheaded by nearby software monolith Microsoft – along with increased Pacific Rim trade, underpinned the development of new museums, a healthy performing-arts scene, and countless small businesses. The good times came to an end in 2000, though, when the **high-tech bubble burst**, and countless Seattle firms went out of business or suffered through some of the toughest years they had ever experienced. What was a national recession became something closer to a regional depression for some industries here, ultimately making Washington and Oregon the national leaders in unemployment.

The February 2001 **earthquake** only made things more dismal, adding to the dreary outlook with a slew of damaged or closed businesses. In combination with the weakened local economy, the decrease in public revenue through reduced taxes and slash-and-burn ballot measures caused **widespread cutbacks** in state funding for the arts, parks, social programs, and business development.

Nowadays the region's economic fortunes are largely tied to the presence of aerospace giant **Boeing**, whose area plants employ tens of thousands of workers – but recent cutbacks have taken their toll there, too. In 2004, it looks highly unlikely that Seattle will soon recover the economic dynamism it possessed only a few years before. Despite this, it still retains the museums, technology, parks, and people that it gained during the last boom, and continues to remain one of the most appealing, and affordable, destinations for visitors from around the globe.

Arrival

Unless you happen to live on the West Coast, the quickest and best way of getting to Seattle is **by plane**. While alternatives certainly exist – motoring up the freeway, enjoying a scenic train ride – there's little question that for most people, their first view of the Emerald City will be from above. A distant second to flying is **rail travel**, with few options save for Amtrak, the ailing US train system. The cheapest and most cost-effective way is to go by **bus**, but it's also the least comfortable and the most time-consuming. Similarly lengthy, a **car** ride to Seattle will most assuredly devour your travel time unless you live nearby.

By air

Seattle-Tacoma International Airport, almost always known as **Sea-Tac** (Ⓣ206/433-5388 or 1-800/544-1965, Ⓦwww.portseattle.org/seatac), is fourteen miles south of downtown Seattle and features four large concourses and two satellite terminals connected to the main terminal via swift underground trains. There's a small **visitor information booth** (summer daily 9am–7pm, winter daily 9am–6pm) in front of baggage carousel 8. Keep in mind that through 2005, considerable demolition and expansion work will be ongoing, so be sure to budget a little extra time to account for it.

The **Gray Line Airport Express** bus (5.20am–11.20pm every 30min; $8.50, $14 round-trip; Ⓣ206/626-6088 or 1-800/426-7532, Ⓦwww.graylineofseattle.com) drops off at seven major hotels Downtown, with connector services to other locations in the area from 5.30am to 9pm for $2.50 extra; reserve at least one hour in advance. A bit further away from the terminal along the same road, **Metro bus** #194 ($1.25, $2 during peak hours Mon–Fri 6–9am & 3–6pm) makes a 35-minute trip into the Downtown underground bus-tunnel terminal (depositing riders at the Convention Center), while the slower #174 runs down to 4th Avenue. Major **car rental** firms have airport branches, and Alamo, Avis, Budget, Hertz, and National have counters in the baggage-claim area and car pick-up and drop-off zones on the first floor of the garage across from the Main Terminal. Other companies with off-airport branches provide courtesy van service to their pickup points. Once you're behind the wheel, Hwy-99, the Pacific Highway, leads into town; it's also easy to get onto I-5, which may be more convenient if you're going to a neighborhood other than Downtown.

By car

If you're **driving**, you'll probably approach Seattle on **I-5**, the main north–south highway between Canada and California. Major north- and southbound exits include Seneca Street (for central Downtown), Mercer Street (Seattle Center), and Dearborn/James streets (Capitol Hill). Coming in from the east, you'll likely arrive via **I-90**, which runs from Seattle to central Washington. I-90's Downtown exits (164–167) come quickly from both sides of the freeway; keep alert for off-ramps onto Stewart or Union streets for Downtown.

By train and bus

Trains pull in at the **Amtrak** terminal in King Street Station, Third Avenue and Jackson Street, near the International District (Ⓣ206/382-4125 or 1-800/872-7245, Ⓦwww.amtrak.com), about a dozen blocks from the city center.

The area code for Seattle is Ⓣ206.

Greyhound buses (ⓣ206/628-5526 or 1-800/231-2222, ⓦwww.greyhound.com) arrive at Eighth Avenue and Stewart Street, on the eastern edge of Downtown, as well as at King Street Station, at Third Avenue and Jackson Street, near the International District.

By ferry

Puget Sound **ferries** (ⓣ206/464-6400 or 1-800/84-FERRY; ⓦwww.wsdot.wa.gov/ferries) dock at Pier 52 (Colman Dock) on Downtown's waterfront, with a couple of passenger-only routes using Pier 50. Long-distance services from British Columbia dock at Pier 69, and other ferry routes connect at Fauntleroy in West Seattle (for a list of routes, see box in "Puget Sound" chapter, p.320).

Information

In addition to Sea-Tac's visitor information booth (see opposite), the **Seattle-King County Visitor's Bureau**, inside the Washington State Convention Center at 7th Avenue and Pike Street (year-round Mon–Fri 8.30am–5pm, April–Oct also Sat 10am–4pm, June–Aug Sun 10am–4pm; ⓣ206/461-8304, ⓦwww.seeseattle.org), has racks of brochures on Seattle and Washington State, plus handy free maps and local bus timetables. From June through September, an additional branch operates daily from 10am to 6pm in Pioneer Square at Occidental and S Main Street.

City transportation

For **getting around** Seattle, there are a number of options, though Downtown is easy enough to cover by walking alone. Beyond this, the buses are frequent and well run by US standards, and most of the more interesting neighborhoods are pretty close to one another. There are, however, substantial drawbacks: steep hills challenge weak knees both Downtown and elsewhere, and some areas are not well served by public transportation, especially at night. Thus, although traffic can be horrendous at peak hours, for some places you may well need to take a car or, in some cases, even a ferry.

Metro

Seattle's mass transit system, known as the **Metro** (ⓣ206/553-3000, ⓦwww.metrokc.gov/kcdot or transit.metrokc.gov), runs bus routes

Major bus routes

From Downtown

#1, 2, 3, and **4** Seattle Center and Queen Anne

#5, 26 and **28** Fremont

#10, 12 Capitol Hill

#15, 18 Ballard, via Seattle Center and Queen Anne

#16, 26 Wallingford

#17 Ballard and the Hiram M. Chittenden Locks

#19, 24, and **33** Magnolia and Discovery Park

#25 University District

#37 Alki Beach, West Seattle

#43, 71, 72, and **73** University District

#261, 550 Bellevue

Other routes

#7, 9 University District to Capitol Hill

#31 Magnolia to University District, via Fremont and Wallingford

#167 University District to Bellevue

#174 and **194** Sea-Tac Airport to Downtown (Museum of Flight en route)

throughout the city and King County, extending into the Eastside suburbs across Lake Washington, and south to the airport. **Customer service stations** are available in the Metro Tunnel at Westlake Station, under Pine Street between Third and Sixth avenues (Mon–Fri 9.30am–5pm) and at King Street Station, 201 S Jackson St (Mon–Fri 8am–5pm); both offer maps and schedules, and are the most reliable places to buy daily passes on weekdays. The Metro's best feature is its **Downtown Ride Free Area**, bounded by Battery Street, S Jackson Street, 6th Avenue, and the waterfront. From 6am to 7pm daily, bus trips beginning and ending within this zone are free; cross out of the free zone – to the University District, for example – and you pay the driver as you get off; come back in and you pay as you enter.

Outside of the Ride Free Area, **fares** are $1.25 off-peak, $1.50 peak (Mon–Fri 6–9am & 3–6pm) for adults and a mere 50¢ for kids under 18; if you're taking a "two-zone" ride that takes you outside the city limits (for instance, from Downtown to the airport), the peak price rises to $2. **Transfers** are valid for about one hour after they're issued. **Day passes** for $2.50 are available for weekends and holidays only; you can buy them from the driver. For daily passes during the week, you'll have to visit a customer service center and pay $5. Bus **maps** or **schedules** are available at the visitor's bureau, libraries, shopping centers, and Metro Tunnel stations. The customer service offices also dispense free copies of the large *Metro Transit System Map*, although this is such a densely packed grid that you're better off picking up the pocket-sized schedules of the routes you plan to travel frequently.

The monorail and waterfront streetcar

Built for the World's Fair in the early 1960s, the **Seattle monorail** (every ten minutes Mon–Fri 7.30am–11pm, Sat–Sun 9am–11pm; one-way fares $3, kids $1.50; Ⓦ www.seattlemonorail.com) connects Seattle Center with the Westlake Center shopping mall and is not of much use unless you need to get from Downtown to Seattle Center. Those gearing up for a thrilling or particularly scenic high-tech ride will surely be disappointed: with no stops on the route, the uneventful journey takes just two minutes or so from start to finish.

Built in 1927, the charming **waterfront streetcar** (daily 6.30am–7pm; $1.25, $1.50 peak, seniors 25¢, kids 50¢; Ⓣ 206/553-3000, Ⓦ www.transit.metrokc.gov) begins its twenty-minute route at Jackson Street in the International District, proceeds through Pioneer Square and then runs

City tours

Seattle offers a few dozen walking, boating, flying, and biking **tours** of the region, sometimes organized according to a specific theme. While not exactly a tour, the **Seattle CityPass** ($35, kids $21.50; good for nine days; Ⓦwww.citypass.net) can act as a useful sort of "self-guided" option. It covers admission to the Seattle Aquarium, Pacific Science Center, Space Needle, Museum of Flight, and Woodland Park Zoo, and includes a harbor tour as well, costing half of what it would to visit all six attractions at regular prices. The CityPass can be purchased at any participating attraction.

Argosy Cruises Ⓣ206/623-4252, Ⓦwww.argosycruises.com. Offering April–Dec tours through most local waters, including a Harbor Cruise of Elliott Bay (1hr; $12.75, $16 summer), Lake Cruise in Lake Washington and Lake Union (2hr; $20.25, $25 summer), and Locks Cruise (2hr 30min; $23, $29 summer). Good with use of a CityPass (see above).

Gray Line Ⓣ206/626-5208 or 1-800/426-7532, Ⓦwww.graylineofseattle.com. Three-hour narrated tours of Seattle's most well-known attractions ($29); also offers a six-hour Grand City Tour ($39), and is on offer daily at 10am from late April to late September. Also has trips to the Boeing plant ($39) and Mt Rainier ($54).

Seattle Seaplanes Ⓣ206/329-9638 or 1-800/637-5553, Ⓦwww.seattleseaplanes.com. Twenty-minute flights of various routes over Seattle, for $67.50 per person, including pricier options for floatplane and dinner flights.

See Seattle Ⓣ425/226-7641, Ⓦwww.see-seattle.com. Half-day walking tours of Downtown for $20, strolling by the major sights from Pike Place Market to the International District, as well as specialized tours for prearranged groups.

Victoria Clipper Ⓣ206/448-5000, Ⓦwww.victoriaclipper.com. Featuring eye-opening trips to Friday Harbor on San Juan Island ($38 one-way, $59 round-trip) or to Vancouver Island in Canada ($59–79 one-way, $99–142 round-trip), leaving on the high-speed, passenger-only *Victoria Clipper* from Seattle's Pier 69.

Viewpoints Ⓣ206/667-9186, Ⓦwww.seattlearchitectural.org. Walking tours through the architectural highlights of several Seattle neighborhoods on selected Wednesday lunch hours, and on Saturday mornings for 2–3 hours. April–Oct only; $10 Wed tours, $20 Sat tours.

up Alaskan Way from Pier 48 to Pier 70/Broad Street. Also known as Metro route 99, the streetcar runs three times an hour and, while not exactly speedy, makes for a touristy indulgence worth enjoying at least once.

Accommodation

In most of its neighborhoods, Seattle has plenty of choices for **accommodation**; the problem is not so much getting a room as finding good mid-range deals, achieving a balance between decent amenities and affordable rates. Seattle's **hotels** are mostly geared toward the business traveler, with many four-star accommodations Downtown that easily run $150 or more a night. There are few good mid-level options, and if you want a room for under $60 a night, the level of service and cleanliness tend to drop dramatically, as does the desirability of the location. Bear in mind that Seattle imposes a steep **hotel room**

tax of 15.6 percent. The Seattle Convention and Visitors' Bureau's **Seattle Hotel Hotline** makes reservations at local hotels (April–Oct Mon–Fri 8.30am–5pm; ⓣ206/461-5881 or 1-800/535-7071, ⓦwww.seeseattle.org); the rest of the year (Nov–March), the service has additional weekend hours (Sat–Sun 10am–2pm) and specializes in offseason discount deals. Further out, the chain **motels** on Aurora Avenue (Highway 99) and around Sea-Tac airport are all rather bland, grungy, or otherwise inhospitable.

Seattle's **B&Bs** typically offer a good balance of comfort and value: the often-stylish rooms are almost always bigger and nicer than hotel units that go for the same rates, and many are in converted early-twentieth-century mansions – mostly grand old **Capitol Hill** homes – with period decor and antique furnishings. There are usually fewer than ten rooms in each, making reservations a necessity during peak travel times; there's also often a two-night minimum stay. For **booking assistance**, call A Pacific Reservation Service (ⓣ206/439-7677 or 1-800/684-2932, ⓦwww.seattlebedandbreakfast.com), which makes reservations in Washington and has an inexpensive list of guest homes available. Another company, A Travelers' Reservation Service (ⓣ206/364-5900), can put you in touch with B&Bs throughout the Northwest, as can the Seattle Bed and Breakfast Association (ⓣ206/547-1020 or 1-800/348-5630, ⓦwww.seattlebandbs.com).

Hostels, unsurprisingly, offer the best deals for the budget traveler, with dorm beds going for around $17 a night, along with inexpensive private rooms for which you should always call ahead. **Campsites** are predictably few and far between in the city, but are in abundance in the outlying areas around Puget Sound.

Seattle's **hostels** are generally close to the center of Downtown. Memberships are also useful in a few of them for procuring space or getting reduced rates, but are not necessary to qualify for a bed in most cases. There's usually a limit to the number of consecutive days you can stay, though at the private hostels these rules are sometimes relaxed during the offseason. Most hostels offer **private rooms** for couples and single travelers, although you'll be paying about two or three times the dorm rate. Regardless of the standard you choose, don't take a vacancy for granted; there's no harm in calling ahead.

Hotels and motels

Downtown

Edgewater Inn Pier 67, 2411 Alaskan Way ⓣ206/728-7000 or 1-800/624-0670, ⓦwww.noblehousehotels.com/edgewater. Seattle's top waterfront hotel has a central location and nice rooms, the best of which have windows right on the bay – though for those you'll need to both pay about $30 more and reserve well in advance. All rooms have fireplaces and there are some nice extras, like complimentary use of bicycles and onsite athletic facilities. ❼

Grand Hyatt Seattle 721 Pine St ⓣ206/774-1234, ⓦwww.grandseattle.hyatt.com. Ultra-chic and modern digs not far from I-5. Excellent for business and upscale travelers, with great views from rooms and suites stuffed with pricey designer furnishings. There's also plenty of onsite dining, a health club, and big-ticket contemporary art in the public spaces. ❾

Inn at Harbor Steps 1221 1st Ave at University St ⓣ206/748-0793 or 1-888/728-8910, ⓦwww.foursisters.com/inns/innatharborsteps. Upscale accommodations in a 20-room hotel, a very short walk from both Pike Place Market and the art museum. Each room has a fireplace, refrigerator with complimentary beverages, and a balcony overlooking an interior garden courtyard; some have spa tubs. ❼

Pacific Plaza 400 Spring St at 4th Ave ⓣ206/623-3900 or 1-800/426-1165, ⓦwww.pacificplazahotel.com. Renovated hotel in a restored 1928 building near the middle of the

Financial District, with clean and comfortable doubles. Halfway between Pike Place Market and Pioneer Square. ❻

Pioneer Square Hotel 77 Yesler Way between 1st Ave and Alaskan Way ⓣ206/340-1234 or 1-800/800-5514, ⓦwww.pioneersquare.com. A restored 1914 brick hotel, built by Seattle founding father Henry Yesler. The best (if the only) choice in Pioneer Square for mid-price hotel accommodation, with a good level of comfort, and a saloon and juice bar on the lobby floor. ❺

Hotel Vintage Park 1100 5th Ave ⓣ206/624-8000, ⓦwww.hotelvintagepark.com. Offering upscale decor without the accompanying attitude (or astronomical prices), a stylish boutique hotel with rooms themed around wine-drinking and vineyards, and amenities including fireplaces, Jacuzzis, and of course, nightly tastings of vino. ❼

W Seattle 1112 4th Ave ⓣ206/264-6000, ⓦwww.whotels.com. Stylish modern tower in the Financial District, with a staff of beautiful people and smart, cozy rooms with standard luxury amenities. Chic lobby bar has often-packed "cocktail couches" downstairs, and an adjoining Northwest Cuisine restaurant, *Earth and Ocean* (see p.286), is one of the city's best. ❾

Westin Seattle 1900 Fifth Ave ⓣ206/728-1000 or 1-800/WESTIN-1, ⓦwww.westin.com. Expansive, gorgeous views from the higher of the 865 rooms in these twin cylinder towers – one from 1969, the other from the 1980s – with spacious rooms and good amenities including indoor swimming pool, health club, and spa. ❾

Belltown

Ace 2423 1st Ave at Wall St ⓣ206/448-4721, ⓦwww.theacehotel.com. Slightly arty, modern rooms in a hotel above the *Cyclops* restaurant, in the heart of Belltown. Hardwood floors, lofty ceilings, and shared bathrooms in the rooms, while more comfortable and well-appointed suites start at around $50 more. ❺

Claremont 2000 4th Ave ⓣ206/448-8600 or 1-800/448-8601, ⓦwww.claremonthotel.com. Intimate, European-style hotel with nicely appointed rooms and suites. Weekend rates for basic rooms significantly lower than weekday rates for suites. Complimentary continental breakfast included. ❼

Commodore 2013 2nd Ave between Virginia and Lenora sts ⓣ206/448-8868, ⓦwww.commodorehotel.com. Functional but unexciting rooms and some suites on the border between Belltown and Downtown. The "European" rooms with shared baths, for $14 less, offer the best overall value. ❸

Moore 1926 2nd Ave at Virginia St ⓣ206/448-4851 or 1-800/421-5508, ⓦwww.moorehotel.com. Ancient-feeling 1908 structure (part of a theater building) with drab decor and bland rooms, though it's well placed to take advantage of Downtown sightseeing and Belltown nightlife; the *Nite Lite* lounge has a decent selection of beer from Seattle microbreweries, and offers some pretty strong cocktails, too. ❹

Wall Street Inn 2507 1st Ave ⓣ206/448-0125 or 1-800/624-1117, ⓦwww.wallstreetinn.com. Former merchant-marine quarters now converted into a boutique hotel, where the rooms have smart, stylish furnishings and a free continental breakfast with fresh pastries from local bakeries. Rates dip considerably for single occupancy. ❼

Seattle Center and Queen Anne

Inn at Queen Anne, 505 1st Ave N at N Republican St ⓣ206/282-7357 or 1-800/952-5043, ⓦwww.innatqueenanne.com. Small but comfortable lodging on the edge of Seattle Center, with rooms offering queen-sized beds, kitchenettes, and microwaves, plus complimentary breakfast and Downtown shuttle service. ❺

MarQueen 600 Queen Ave N ⓣ206/282-7407 or 1-800/445-3076, ⓦwww.marqueen.com. More expensive than most Seattle Center accommodations, but also swankier: a refurbished, classically styled 1918 building with 56 rooms and suites, featuring period antiques and amenities like hardwood floors, kitchenettes, microwaves, and fridges, as well as an onsite spa. ❼

Capitol Hill

Eastlake Inn 2215 Eastlake Ave E ⓣ206/322-7726. Average motor lodge, but more conveniently situated than most – it's a few blocks from Lake Union's houseboats – and cheaper than the ones around Seattle Center; some units are mini-suites with kitchens. ❸

Silver Cloud Inn 1150 Fairview Ave N ⓣ206/447-9500, ⓦwww.scinns.com. A few blocks west of I-5 near Lake Union, with simple, clean, and modern rooms; amenities include fridges and microwaves, and most rooms feature a view of the lake as well. There's another location near the University of Washington at 5036 25th Ave NE (ⓣ206/526-5200 or 1-800/205-6940). ❻

Sorrento 900 Madison St ⓣ206/622-4400 or 1-800/426-1265, ⓦwww.hotelsorrento.com. Just east of the I-5 freeway in First Hill, a modernized, 76-room edifice with a European flair, stylish decor, and posh onsite restaurant *The Hunt Club*. The regal 1908 exterior surrounds a circular courtyard with palm trees; some rooms have views of Puget Sound. ⑨

University District

University Inn, 4140 Roosevelt Way NE at NE 42nd St ⓣ206/632-5055 or 1-800/733-3855, ⓦwww.universityinnseattle.com. Average-looking business-oriented hotel off University Way. Some rooms have kitchens, and your stay comes with complimentary continental breakfast; there's also an onsite pool and spa. ⑤

University Tower 4507 Brooklyn Ave NE ⓣ206/634-2000 or 1-800/899-0251, ⓦwww.meany.com. Located near the main action on University Way; a little more attractive than some of the other big hotels in the U District, with rooms in bright retro-Art Deco motifs and fine views of the city and campus. ⑥

The suburbs

Bellevue Club 11200 SE 6th Ave, Bellevue ⓣ425/454-4424, ⓦwww.bellevueclubhotel.com. Maximum-chic spa hotel with in-room soaking tubs, copious elegant decor, fitness complex, swimming pool, basketball and tennis courts, and a guest list of well-bronzed yuppies with perfect teeth. ⑨

Woodmark 1200 Carillon Point, Kirkland ⓣ206/822-3700 or 1-800/822-3700, ⓦwww.thewoodmark.com. Located in the wealthy suburb of Kirkland, seven miles east of Downtown on the shores of Lake Washington, this splendid modern hotel is the height of luxury for its swanky furnishings, but it's only worth the price if you're in one of the lakeside rooms (or suites), which typically run $50 more. ⑨

Bed-and-breakfasts

Amaranth Inn 1451 S Main St, near the International District ⓣ206/720-7161 or 1-800/720-7161, ⓦwww.amaranthinn.com. Overflowing with ornamental antiques and fancy rugs, with quaint late-Victorian furnishings and rooms with flowery decor, some with hot tubs and fireplaces. Located east of I-5 near a Buddhist temple. ⑤

Bacon Mansion 959 Broadway E, Capitol Hill ⓣ206/329-1864 or 1-800/240-1864, ⓦwww.baconmansion.com. Eleven elegant rooms and spacious suites in a grand 1909 Tudor Revival structure, just north of Broadway's main drag. The least expensive rooms are fairly cheap for the area, although the price doubles at the high end. ④

Gaslight Inn 1727 15th Ave, Capitol Hill ⓣ206/325-3654, ⓦwww.gaslight-inn.com. Fifteen rooms with large common areas, some units with fireplaces and decks, and more expensive suites for longer-term stays. Home-made scones, swimming pool, hot tub, and a prime location – not to mention the contemporary decor and colorful modern art on view – make this a unique, compelling option. ⑤

Green Gables 1503 2nd Ave W, Queen Anne ⓣ206/282-6863 or 1-800/400-1503, ⓦwww.greengablesseattle.com. Sizable 1904 estate near Highland Drive, where most of the hill's great mansions are located, offering four rooms (three with private baths), antique beds, stained glass, and hardwood floors throughout. ⑤

Pensione Nichols 1923 1st Ave, Belltown ⓣ206/441-7125. This elegant little B&B is a great deal, with small but clean rooms, shared baths, and simple, tasteful decor in a classic 1904 building. Suites with kitchenettes add about $75 to the total, but they can be shared by four people. ⑤

Salisbury House 750 16th Ave E, Capitol Hill ⓣ206/328-8682, ⓦwww.salisburyhouse.com. Four doubles in this grand maple-floored, high-ceilinged 1904 mansion at a quiet yet convenient location. Ask for the "Blue Room" if you want morning sun, or the "Lavender Room" if you want the biggest space. ⑤

Shafer-Baillie Mansion 907 14th Ave E, Capitol Hill ⓣ206/322-4654, ⓦwww.shaferbaillie.com. Always a popular site for weddings and receptions, this mansion's oak-paneled walls and late-Victorian decor echo its 1914 construction, and it also offers a range of period-furnished rooms, from cramped "servants' quarters" to more spacious suites with antique tubs and refrigerators. ⑥

Hostels

Bigfoot Backpackers 126 Broadway Ave E between E Olive Way and E Denny St ⓣ206/720-2965 or 1-800/600-2965. Reached via an alley near the busiest corner in Capitol Hill, a good choice if you don't want a Downtown base. Forty-five beds include four-to-a-room dorms ($15–17) and a few private rooms ($35 single, $45 double). No curfew and lots of extras: free breakfast, Downtown pick-up, Internet access, and parking. It also runs a tour of the graves of Jimi Hendrix and, nearby in Capitol Hill's Lakeview Cemetery, Bruce and Brandon Lee, also stopping at Kurt Cobain's former house.

Green Tortoise 1525 2nd Ave between Pike and Pine sts, Downtown ⓣ206/340-1222 or 1-888/424-6783, ⓦwww.greentortoise.net. The best budget Downtown deal, with a great location a block away from Pike Place Market. Has old-style hotel digs now functioning as four-to-the-room dorms for $21, or private doubles for $42. Free Downtown pick-up and Internet access; also offers summer walking tours of the city.

Hosteling International Seattle 84 Union St between 1st and Western aves, Downtown ⓣ206/622-5443 or 1-888/622-5443, ⓦwww.hiseattle.org. For location this is hard to beat, just a block from Pike Place Market, with Pioneer Square minutes away. Modern, comfortable dorms, with about two hundred beds ($22, or $25 for non-members), though reservations are still advisable in the summer. Private rooms with shared baths cost $54, while hotel-type units with private bathrooms and kitchens cost up to $100. Free pick-up from bus and train stations.

YWCA 1118 5th Ave at Spring St, Downtown ⓣ206/461-4888. Open to women only, the ambience here is more functional than colorful, but it's safe and clean, a reasonable choice for women visitors on a budget. Twenty-one rooms in all; $35–60 (the higher-priced rooms include a private bath).

The City

Seattle has roughly an hourglass shape, quite skinny in its central section and widening to the north and south, with **Elliott Bay** – an extension of Puget Sound – providing Downtown's western border. The city is separated from its eastern suburbs by **Lake Washington**, which is connected to the sound by the **Lake Washington Ship Canal**, a narrow waterway that, at various points, widens into Portage Bay, Union Bay, and **Lake Union**. Boats – and salmon – exit the canal into Puget Sound through the Ballard Locks, at the western edge of Salmon Bay.

Downtown contains a predictable collection of tall office blocks, but also many of the city's top attractions, particularly Pike Place Market, a busy, crowded agora of stalls and cafés; the waterfront, where ferries depart for destinations throughout the Sound; and the worthwhile Seattle Art Museum. Just south of Downtown is **Pioneer Square**, Seattle's oldest area, where the restored red-brick buildings are lined with taverns, and the **International District**, aka Chinatown, which is also home to significant numbers of Japanese and Vietnamese immigrants. North of Downtown lies the upscale neighborhood of **Belltown**, with the vestiges of a hip edge, and the nearby **Seattle Center**, a large complex of theaters, sports arenas, and museums, dominated by the futuristic, flying-saucer-topped tower of the Space Needle. Further northwest are the quaint neighborhoods of **Queen Anne** and **Magnolia**, the latter holding one of the finest expanses of urban greenery in the US, **Discovery Park**. Across the canal north from the district, industrial **Ballard** is known primarily for its locks and a strip of historic architecture, old-time diners, and rocking taverns. To the southeast, the Woodland Park Zoo makes for an excellent family outing, while further east is **Fremont**, the city's most unpretentiously bohemian corner, highlighted by excellent public artwork. Neighboring **Wallingford** is home to a liberal, middle-class air and the curious industrial playground of Gasworks

Navigating the city

Whatever your mode of transportation, it's essential to familiarize yourself with a few basics of Seattle's confusing streetplan. To begin with, most addresses are preceded or followed by a direction (eg, NW 67th Street, or 13th Avenue E). These tags do not indicate the directional position of an address *on* a street, as they do in many American cities, but rather the position the *entire street* holds in relationship to the city's plan. Consequently, 2nd Avenue W and 2nd Avenue S are two different streets, and the location of something on 2nd Avenue W might be a good five miles or so from an address on 2nd Avenue S.

Think of Downtown as the center of a compass used to plot out the city's coordinates. Thoroughfares running east–west are usually designated as streets, with the section of the city in which it lies placed at the beginning of the address (eg, 500 N 36th St, since this part of 36th Street is north of Downtown), while those running north–south are usually designated avenues, with the section of the city in which it lies following the address (eg, 5000 22nd Ave NE, since this part of 22nd Avenue is northeast of Downtown). Be careful when you ask directions, too: natives have a habit of casually referring to a street address without directionals, so the 15th Avenue address you were heading to in Capitol Hill may actually be in the University District, depending on if it's 15th Avenue E or 15th Avenue NE.

Park. Across the I-5 lies the **University District**, dominated by the campus of the University of Washington and its main thoroughfare of student life, University Way, or "the Ave". Bridges across the ship canal lead back toward Downtown and **Capitol Hill**, the nexus of Seattle's best cafés, shops, and nightlife.

On the eastern side of Lake Washington are the bulk of Seattle's suburbs, notably **Bellevue**, home to a few scattered but worthwhile sights. South of Seattle is the first-rate **Museum of Flight**, charting the development of air travel, while historic **Alki Beach** is in West Seattle, separated from Downtown by the industrial zone of Elliott Bay's Harbor Island.

Downtown

Downtown Seattle is the unquestioned commercial and financial hub of the Pacific Northwest and one of the West Coast's densest urban cores. Not surprisingly, it's the place where most tourists drop anchor (either by boat or freeway) upon arriving in town, even though it's not Seattle's most exciting quarter. Much is functional and drab, with the same proliferation of chain department stores and fast-food vendors you find everywhere else in the US. Downtown does, however, present a formidable **skyline** that is best appreciated from the water, and the cityscape is nicely romanticized by views of Puget Sound and its steady traffic of ferries, pleasure boats, and commercial vessels.

The sizable **Seattle Art Museum** and **Benaroya Hall** (home to the Seattle Symphony) has bolstered the city's cultural reputation considerably, while the old favorite **Pike Place Market** alone merits a trip Downtown, as do the **waterfront**'s scattered museums and nautical attractions. Elsewhere, the staid **Business District** holds scattered appeal only for architecture enthusiasts, mainly for its 76-story **Bank of America Tower**, the Northwest's tallest building.

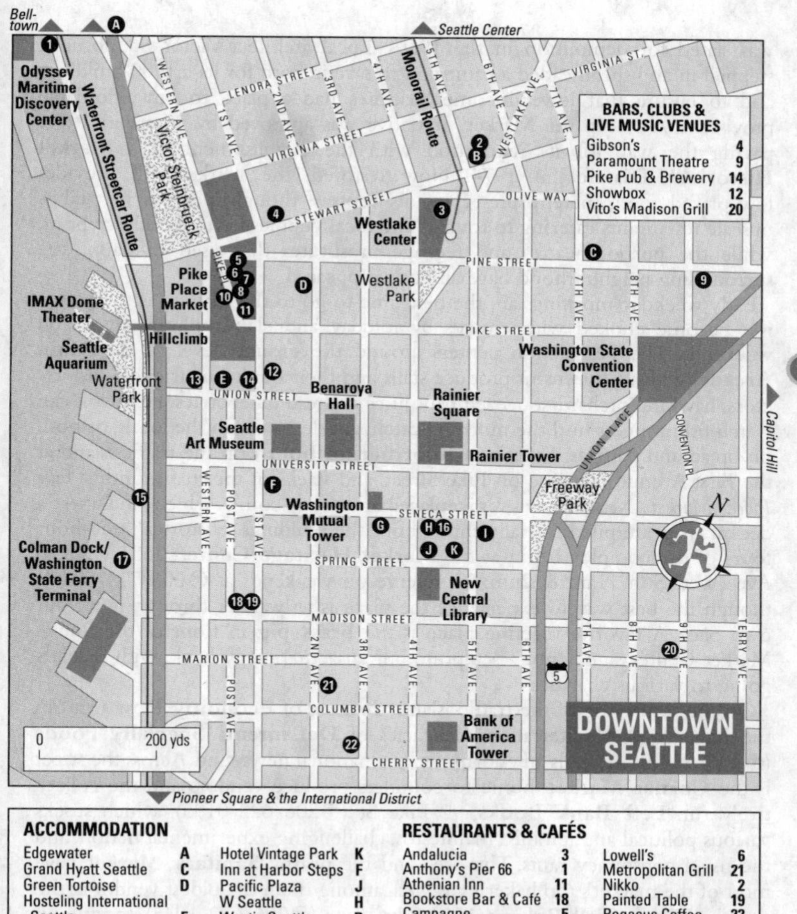

Pike Place Market

The hectic center of Downtown Seattle's pedestrian life, **Pike Place Market** (Mon–Sat 10am–6pm, Sun 11am–5pm; ⓣ206/682-7453, ⓦwww.pikeplacemarket.org) is a vibrant bazaar whose splendid retro-neon clock and sign make it one of the most recognizable places in America. The market is within easy reach of most buses passing through Downtown (with its official entrance at First Avenue and Pike Street), and is still owned, managed, and patronized by locals. It's also huge – with thirteen buildings on a triangular lot covering nine acres and encompassing three hundred produce and fish vendors, bakeries, craft stalls, and small retailers, many of whom grow or make what they sell.

It's actually a miracle Pike Place Market exists at all. Established in 1907 as a way for local farmers to sell their products directly to the city's consumers, it was slated for demolition in the 1960s. Local architect Victor Steinbrueck stepped in and spearheaded a campaign to save it, both for its c.1900 buildings and to ensure that lower-income Seattlites had a place to buy affordable provisions. A "Keep the Market" initiative was approved by voters in 1971, paving the way for its renovation with the establishment of a **Market Historical District** in 1974. Now restored, the market still provides low-priced food, thereby preserving its roots – though, perhaps inevitably, upscale restaurants catering to tourists and local yuppies have recently crept in, while the porno theatres and teenage prostitutes that used to haunt the surrounding neighborhood have all but disappeared.

Early weekday mornings are the best time to go to the market, as the premises become choked with crowds by midday, and claustrophobically so on weekends. The best action centers around the ground level of the **Main Arcade**, with its dozens of produce stalls and their frank-but-friendly proprietors, hawking orchard-squeezed fruit juice or fresh blueberries. Here you can watch fishmongers hurl the morning catch, guzzle java with the locals, or nosh on bread and pastries. There's an **information booth** on the traffic island at the First Avenue entrance on Pike Street, and stacks of the free monthly *Pike Place Market News* (Ⓦwww.pikeplacemarketnews.com), which includes a decent map, are piled liberally throughout the buildings. Historical, one-hour tours of the complex begin at the **Market Heritage Center**, 1531 Western Ave (Wed–Sun 11am & 2pm; $7; reserve on weekends at Ⓣ206/774-5249), though the best way to experience the place is to wander through it at your own pace. A favorite meeting place is the **brass pig** in front of the Public Market Center sign – not a sculpture but an actual piggy bank, with receipts going to various charities.

On the south side of the traffic island, the aisle of **Economy Row** features the Italian and Mediterranean delicacies of **DeLaurenti Specialty Foods** (Ⓣ206/622-0141), plus an enormous international newsstand. Across the street is the **Corner Market**, home to countless produce vendors and the collectively run **Left Bank Books**, 92 Pike St (Ⓣ206/622-0195), which stocks various political and feminist manifestos, challenging experimental fiction, and the usual conspiracy rants. This area and the nearby **Sanitary Market** have most of the market's top bakeries as well, among them the oldest vendor at the site, the **Three Girls Bakery**, 1514 Pike Place (Ⓣ206/622-1045), serving up baked goodies since 1912. Another notable Sanitary Market retailer is the ironically tiny **Sub Pop Megamart** record shop (Ⓣ206/652-4356, Ⓦwww.subpop.com), the relocated outpost of the most famous Seattle alternative rock label. The crowds can get particularly dense as you head to the narrower, arts and crafts-dominated **North Arcade**, thick with dealers in jewelry, silk-screened shirts, and wooden carvings, while directly across Pike Place, at no. 1912 in the **Stewart House** building, you'll find the original seed of the *Starbucks* chain (Ⓣ206/448-8762). Just northwest of the market, **Victor Steinbrueck Park** is worth a look for its pleasantly modest, hilly patches overlooking Puget Sound, which are jammed on sunny days with tourists, office workers, and transients.

The waterfront

Heading west from the market's brass pig, you descend the **Hillclimb**, a formidable staircase that leads down from the market's lower levels past several levels of cafés and shops and under the Alaskan Way Viaduct, a towering mass of concrete looming over a shadowy no-man's-land that's best avoided at night.

The steep array of steps terminates at the **waterfront**, where the harbor's no longer deep enough for modern commercial freighters and container ships, and the old wooden jetties have been colonized by tourism, offering a busy stretch of ferry landings, trinket stalls, and hotels. Almost opposite the Hillclimb, **Pier 59** now houses Seattle's **Aquarium** (daily Memorial Day–Labor Day 10am–7pm; rest of year 10am–5pm; $11, kids $7; ⓣ206/386-4320, ⓦwww.seattleaquarium.org), with around four hundred species of fish, birds, plants, and marine mammals in a reasonably spacious, easily navigable layout, part of which is actually outdoors near the waterfront shore. Opposite the Aquarium, Pier 59 also houses the **IMAX Dome Theatre** (daily starting at 10am; $7, $2 for each additional movie; ⓣ206/622-1868 for films and show-times, ⓦwww.seattleimaxdome.com), with a 100-foot curved, domed screen and six-channel sound system, often alternating the engaging *Eruption of Mount St Helens* documentary with other short features. If you're also planning to visit the Aquarium, you can save a few bucks with a **combined ticket** ($16.50, kids $11.75).

South of Pier 59, the waterfront is lined with souvenir shops, restaurants, and fish-and-chip stands, of which the most famous is *Ivar's Acres of Clams*, at Pier 54 (ⓣ206/624-6852, ⓦwww.ivars.net), well deserving of its own special stop ("Clam Central Station") on the **waterfront streetcar** (see p.252). South of *Ivar's* at Pier 52, **Colman Dock** is the terminal for Washington State Ferries (see p.320), taking you to spots like West Seattle and Bainbridge Island; Pier 50, further south, handles foot passengers between Seattle and Vashon Island.

Retrace your steps toward the northern part of the waterfront, where the platform above Pier 66 offers good bay watching, with free telescopes for up-close views of the ships cruising the water. At Pier 66 itself, also known as Bell Street Pier, the **Odyssey Maritime Discovery Center** (Tues–Sat 10am–5pm, Sun noon–5pm; $7, kids $5; ⓣ206/374-4000, ⓦwww.ody.org), presents nearly fifty interactive exhibits devoted to trade and transport in Puget Sound, and heavy on celebratory displays of maritime equipment. Although kids might get a kick out of a simulated sea kayak journey, the working models of shipping boats and propellers, or the computer game that lets you play crane operator, most adults will find the experience interminable.

A bit north of the last streetcar stop along the waterfront sits the developing 8.5-acre **Olympic Sculpture Park** (ⓦwww.seattleartmuseum.org/visit/OSP/visitOSP.asp), an ongoing project by the Seattle Art Museum highlighted by Alexander Calder's 39-foot *Eagle*, a jagged array of red steel arcs. The rest of the sculptures will arrive when the park is officially opened in 2004. Extending north from the OSP is **Myrtle Edwards Park**, with bike and pedestrian paths winding along the shore for a couple of miles and continuing through the adjoining Elliott Bay Park before terminating near the Magnolia Bridge.

Seattle Art Museum

Close to Pike Place Market along First Avenue, the **Seattle Art Museum** (Tues–Sun 10am–5pm, Thurs until 9pm; $10, free first Thurs of month; ⓣ206/654-3100, ⓦwww.seattleartmuseum.org), is one of the top cultural institutions in the Pacific Northwest. Designed by Robert Venturi, the museum is visually unmistakable for the giant, inset letters on its facade. It's also well known for artist Jonathan Borofsky's **Hammering Man** kinetic sculpture, a 48-foot black-steel and aluminum marvel pounding away in front of the entrance.

Inside the four-story building, a grand staircase leads from the lobby to the upper galleries, under the watchful eye of Chinese sculptures of camels, rams, and guards. The second level is given over to temporary exhibitions, which cover everything from Asian porcelain, European modernist painting, and twentieth-century American photography to works by Frida Kahlo and Diego Rivera. The third floor, however, is the most diverting, featuring a variety of **international art**, including traditional and modern works from Japan, China, the Koreas, Indonesia, the Andes, and the Near East. An especially large section is devoted to indigenous art from the Northwest Coast – highlighted by rattles and clappers, canoes, prow ornaments, dancing masks, and enormous totem poles from British Columbia. The fourth floor traces the development of art in Europe and the United States, with small, unimpressive selections of eighteenth- and nineteenth-century works, as well as pockets of Baroque, medieval, Renaissance, and ancient Mediterranean pieces. But the main attractions are the **twentieth-century works**: Andy Warhol's *Double Elvis*, the sixteen photographic tunnels of Gilbert & George's *Coloured Shouting*, Bruce Nauman's neon wall piece *Double Poke in the Eye II*, Roy Lichtenstein's *Study for Vicki!*, and Robert Arneson's provocative *John With Art* – a crude visual pun.

The museum also holds a full schedule of concerts, films, lectures, and other special programs, detailed in the quarterly guides available in the lobby, while the fine-art bookshop just inside the entrance offers quality browsing. If used within a week, tickets are also good for entrance to the Seattle Asian Art Museum (p.280), and presumably the museum's Olympic Sculpture Park (p.261), once it opens in 2004.

The Business District

Between Second and Seventh avenues, most of Downtown is dominated by the steel-and-glass office towers of Seattle's **Business District**. While some large, local enterprises do have their flagship stores here, including Eddie Bauer, REI and Nordstrom, and there are the usual array of enclosed malls, the resident cultural attractions are mostly limited to a few arts complexes and a handful of distinctive buildings.

The heart of the commercial center is the giant **Westlake Center**, 400 Pine St (daily 10am–9pm; ⓣ206/287-0762), a multi-story enclosed mall that offers the standard retail experience, but is most notable for being the southern terminus of the 1.3-mile **monorail** (see p.252). Departing every ten minutes from the loading point on the mall's top floor, a two-minute journey onboard, replete with plenty of wide-eyed tourists to keep you company, will take you to the Seattle Center. The adjacent, diagonal **Westlake Park**, on Fourth Avenue between Pike and Pine, hosts occasional lunchtime concerts and the odd political rally near its distinctive water-wall fountain. Two blocks south of the mall, at Fifth Avenue and University, the **Rainier Tower** is a familiar presence on any list of big-name Seattle skyscrapers, notable for its narrowly tapering base, which gives the structure an uneasy, top-heavy appearance.

A block west, **Benaroya Hall**, the home of the **Seattle Symphony** (see p.298), occupies an entire city block. The hall's massive, curving glass-curtain wall in the Grand Lobby affords views of Elliott Bay, while the curious Robert Rauschenberg mural and chandeliers by glass titan Dale Chihuly are just a few of the decorative highlights. Heading south are a handful of the city's most noteworthy pieces of modern architecture, starting with the postmodern

Washington Mutual Tower, 1201 3rd Ave, a 1988 landmark presenting an array of glittering, convex glass paneling and gradual setbacks, and rising up to a striped triangular roof. Seattle's highest building is the darkly looming **Bank of America Tower**, further south at 701 Fifth Ave, with three concave walls that give the structure an oddly curving silhouette. Nearly a thousand feet high, the tower is the biggest by number of stories west of the Mississippi – 76. As you might expect, the **observation deck** (Mon–Fri 8.30am–4.30pm; $5, kids $3) on the 73rd floor provides a superb panoramic view of the surrounding area.

Much more visually appealing, though, at the edge of the Business District, is Seattle's first major skyscraper, the white terracotta-trimmed **Smith Tower**, Yesler Way and 2nd Avenue. Built in 1914 by the New York gun and typewriter mogul, L.C. Smith, the 42-floor tower was long the tallest building west of the Mississippi. If you're passing by, it's worth looking in on the elegant lobby, decked out with marble and carved Native American busts. Eight old-fashioned brass elevators, still manually operated after nearly ninety years, serve the 35th-floor **observation deck** (Sat–Sun 11am–4pm; $5), and the building is home to scads of modern, renovated offices – though some of the high-flying dot-coms that called the place home in the 1990s have since gone bankrupt.

Pioneer Square and around

Smith Tower sits on the boundary of Seattle's oldest district, **Pioneer Square**, whose rough-hewn, stone-clad architecture harkens back to the glory days of Romanesque Revival design in the 1890s. Unlike the sanitized historical zones of some cities, Seattle's variety hasn't lost all its old-time grime and squalor, making it more authentic than the usual array of chain retailers hiding behind Victorian storefronts. **Occidental Park** and tours of the **Seattle Underground** draw a steady stream of visitors, while at night, rock music spills out from a group of lively taverns (see "Nightlife," p.292), with blues, rock, and jazz bands on the bill at a handful of top-notch clubs.

The Great Seattle Fire

The **Great Seattle Fire**, which caused more than $15 million worth of damage to Downtown, was in many ways an unexpected blessing: the city was forced to rebuild the area with a safer infrastructure, which helped to modernize its business district and give rise to many of the Romanesque Revival buildings that give Pioneer Square its historic character today. The fire occurred June 6, 1889, when one **John Back** was melting glue on a stove in a basement carpentry shop. The glue pot overheated, starting a blaze that quickly spread to the streets and ignited about fifty tons of ammunition in nearby hardware stores. More than ninety percent of the buildings in the central business district were wooden – with both streets and buildings on stilts to keep them out of the mud – and, though no lives were lost, much of Seattle was wiped out overnight. In rebuilding the area, businesses operated from makeshift tents, the wooden structures were replaced by brick ones, streets were straightened and widened to make them friendlier for commerce, and Seattle gained 17,000 residents over the next year alone.

For an informative exhibit on the fire, visit the Museum of History and Industry, p.281.

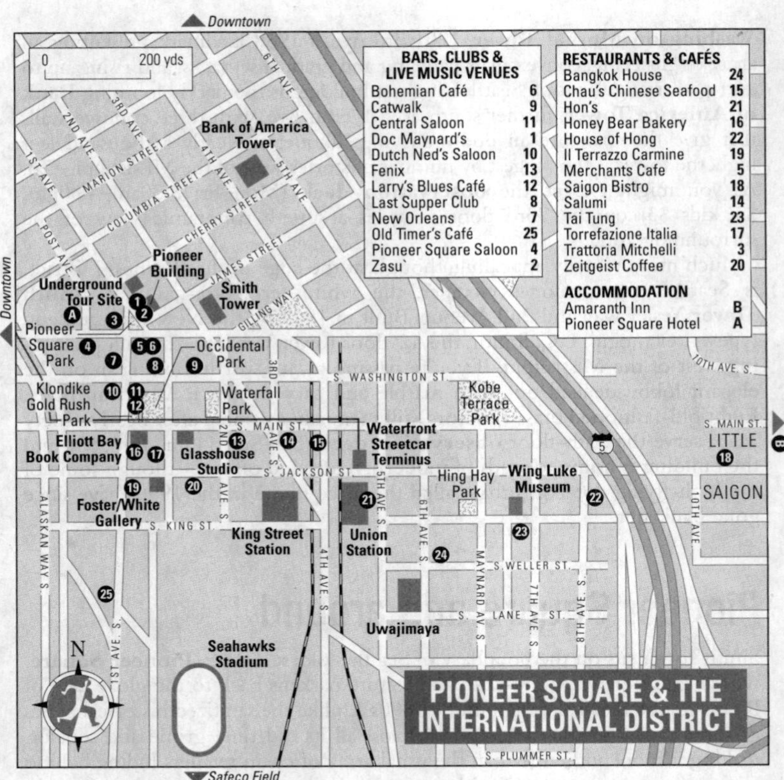

Pioneer Square Park

A good place to start your explorations is at the triangular block of **Pioneer Square Park**, between James Street and First Avenue, which marks the place where Henry Yesler's **sawmill** first processed logs in the 1850s. Decades later, the site was to come under the shadow of the adjacent **Pioneer Building**, a massive pile of stone cladding, chunky columns, and rough-hewn arches and towers, highlighted inside by an elegant atrium and vintage gated elevators. Outside the building, at First and Yesler, a glass and iron **pergola** has long been a local landmark (and a national one since 1977), where businessmen and transients hide from the rain, architects and designers admire the elegant form and detail, and history buffs can imagine the grand marble bathrooms that once could be accessed below ground. Nearby, another officially designated national landmark, the **Tlingit totem pole**, was acquired in 1899, after local members of the Chamber of Commerce broke into an Alaskan Indian village and stole it without apology or recompense. Although the men were fined $500 for their actions by a judge, the city was allowed to keep its booty.

The Seattle Underground

Adjacent to the park, and promising "Dirt!…Corruption!…Sewers!…Scandal!", **Bill Speidel's Underground Tour** (hours vary by month, usually leaving daily on the hour 11am–4pm or 6pm; $9, kids $5; ⓣ206/682-4646, ⓦwww.undergroundtour.com) is the most popular way of touring the **Seattle Underground**, though a few other places provide more limited access to it as well (notably an antique mall in the basement of the Pioneer Building). Departing from *Doc Maynard's* pub, 610 1st Ave, the tour offers a bewitching ninety-minute look at the subterranean history of the former streets of Pioneer Square. After rising tides repeatedly backed up sewage drains and caused flooding, street levels were elevated by an entire story (ten feet) in the 1890s, and the original storefronts soon became underground businesses in several ways. Operating amid narrow passageways, creaky ladders, and dark stairways, the legitimate merchants continued to hawk their wares until the subsurface zone was officially closed in 1907, even as some truly "underground" businesses like speakeasies, burlesque joints, and brothels were still accessible via subterranean corridors well into the twentieth century.

Klondike Gold Rush National Park and Elliott Bay Book Company

A few blocks south from Pioneer Square Park, at 117 S Main St, **Klondike Gold Rush National Park** (daily 9am–5pm; free) is not a park at all, but rather a simple but informative museum where free films and a few artifacts portray the 1897 rush, kick-started by the discovery of the precious ore in the Klondike region of Canada. As soon as the first ship carrying Klondike gold docked in the city, Seattle's sharp-eyed capitalists envisioned massive trading potential in selling groceries, clothing, sledges, and even ships to the gold-seekers. Hastily they launched a formidable publicity campaign, bombarding inland cities with propaganda billing Seattle above all other ports as the gateway to Yukon gold. It worked: prospectors streamed in, merchants (and con men) scented easy profit, the population escalated, and traders made a quick fortune.

A block west of Klondike Park, at First and Main, one of the neighborhood's other top attractions is the famed **Elliott Bay Book Company**, 101 S Main St (Mon–Fri 9.30am–10pm, Sat 10am–10pm, Sun 11am–7pm; ⓣ1-800/962-5311, ⓦwww.elliottbaybook.com), with a selection of 150,000 volumes on three levels. The store is an essential spot for browsing, meeting other literary-minded friends, or listening to a nightly reading downstairs in the underground section.

Occidental Park and around

Just north of the bookstore, the 1889 **Grand Central Arcade** is a prime location for restaurants and boutiques, its glassy, subterranean arcade leading to **Occidental Park**, a cobblestoned plaza lined with trees and featuring a pergola and assorted boutiques and coffeehouses, but also home to some of the city's most down-and-out residents. A block east on Main is the **Waterfall Garden**, whose 22-foot cascade was built in 1907 with rough boulders and surrounding foliage, commemorating the delivery company UPS, which first operated here in the early twentieth century.

South of Occidental Park, the pedestrian **Occidental Avenue** holds the greatest concentration of Seattle's **galleries**. The most noteworthy among them, the Foster/White Gallery, 123 S Jackson St (Mon–Sat 10am–5.30pm, Sun noon–5pm; ⓣ206/622-2833, ⓦfosterwhite.com), showcases contemporary artists from the Pacific Northwest working in a variety of media, among them local glass-blowing heavyweight Dale Chihuly. Nearby at the Glasshouse

Studio, 311 Occidental S (Mon–Sat 10am–5pm, Sun 11am–4pm; Ⓣ206/682-9939, Ⓦwww.glasshouse-studio.com), you can watch less-heralded, but no less appealing, artists busy with their own creations.

The International District

Like many neighborhoods named by municipal bureaucracies, the so-called **International District** is a charmless moniker for what is in fact a broad collection of thriving Asian communities (see Ⓦwww.internationaldistrict.org for the official perspective). Once known by the now-inaccurate term Chinatown (erroneous given the great influx of other minorities), this vivacious urban zone just southeast of Pioneer Square has in recent years welcomed immigrants from the Philippines, Laos, South Korea, and especially Vietnam. The International District, called the ID in some quarters, is not so much a place to visit official museums and exemplary architecture as it is to casually hang out in the parks, diners, and bars favored by the locals, getting an unvarnished sense of the place and perhaps sampling the dim sum or the neighborhood theater while you're at it.

Bordered by Second and Twelfth avenues (west–east) and Washington and Weller streets (north–south), the dozen or so blocks that comprise the district can be covered by foot in a few hours. The most active local scene can be found between Fifth and Eighth avenues on Jackson and King streets. One great place to sample the district's flavor is at the huge pan-Asian supermarket/variety store **Uwajimaya**, 519 6th Ave (daily 9am–10pm; Ⓣ1-800/889-1928, Ⓦwww.uwajimaya.com). Acting as much a busy community center as a retail outlet, it offers not only a giant array of foodstuffs from spicy seasonings to the prized geoduck ("gooey-duck") clam, but also a wide range of Asian gifts and hand-crafted items, scented candles, and origami paper, and even classes on making sushi.

At the southern edge of the International District lies impressive **Safeco Field**, home to the Seattle's major league baseball team, the Mariners, and a bit further north, **Seahawks Stadium**, home to the eponymous professional football team (see p.300.)

Union and King Street stations

Beginning on the west side of the International District, the unmistakable focal point is a pair of rail centers that, at one time or another, served as the city's transportation hubs. The first, **Union Station**, Fourth Avenue at Jackson Street, is Seattle's once-dilapidated, recently restored showpiece for historic preservation, a sparkling complex that has maintained the allure of old-fashioned railroad transit while changing step for a new era. Originally built by a Union Pacific subsidiary in 1911, the building's splendid centerpiece is the **Great Hall**, a barrel-vaulted Beaux Arts jewel whose ceiling rises to eighty feet and whose walls feature ornate glass windows and *trompe l'oeil* detailing that gives the impression of classical stone construction.

Built in 1911, Union Station competed directly with **King Street Station**, a mere block to the west at 303 S Jackson St, the Northern Pacific Railroad's 1906 entry into the rail transit scene. Now servicing Amtrak trains (see p.250), the dreary and somewhat dilapidated King Street interior isn't much to look at, especially compared with Union Station. However, the old-fashioned building is a classic fixture of the cityscape as you approach from the south, and renovation plans have slowly developed over the last few years; in any case, it's worth a look at both stations – renovated or not – to get a glimpse of the proud old stables that were once home to the Iron Horse.

Wing Luke Asian Museum

Three blocks east of Union Station, the main cultural institution of note in the International District is the **Wing Luke Asian Museum**, 407 Seventh Ave S (Tues–Fri 11am–4.30pm, Sat–Sun noon–4pm; $4, $2 kids; ⓣ206/623-5124, ⓦwww.wingluke.org), whose namesake was the first Asian-American elected official in the Northwest when he won a seat on the Seattle City Council in 1962. Portraying two hundred years of Asian and Pacific Island immigration, from the first Hawaiian settlers to more recent newcomers from Southeast Asia, its several small rooms are easily covered within an hour or two. The museum holds old photographs, ceremonial garments, oral and written histories of individual immigrants, and various intriguing artifacts, the most eye-catching of which are the hand-painted kites that hang from the rafters.

Hing Hay and Kobe Terrace parks

Just across from the museum, **Hing Hay Park**, at the corner of King and Maynard streets, is the nominal center of the International District, with its ornate pagoda made in Taiwan and its large, somewhat faded dragon mural. Although it's pleasant enough, you're better off heading three blocks north, taking a steep hike up to the top of Washington Street to enter the far greener **Kobe Terrace Park**, named after Seattle's Japanese sister city, where a two-hundred-year-old, eight-thousand-pound stone lantern graces the entrance. Narrow paths wind down through community gardens built into the park's slope, quaint cherry trees add to the splendor, and the sweeping views of the region can be inspiring when it's not raining – even though the rush of traffic on nearby I-5 does prove to be something of a distraction to one's reverie.

Belltown

Starting just above Pike Place Market and extending a mile north toward Seattle Center, **Belltown** (also known as **Denny Regrade**) has been through more changes in the last century than any other part of the city. From decaying inner-city wasteland to the desired address of would-be hipsters, Belltown's transformation has been remarkable – though not always necessarily for the better. Shiny high-rise housing sits next to funky brick flophouses, upscale restaurants meet low-rent diners, grungy thrift stores compete with overpriced boutiques for visitors' attention and wallets, and the downtrodden presence of the homeless receives scant eye contact from self-styled fashion mavens in knockoff designer-wear.

Belltown became a focus of Seattle's music and arts scene in the latter part of the 1980s, with **Sub Pop Records** (see p.269) famously promoting the alternative-rock scene. Nowadays, the hip core of Belltown is confined to a three-block area of **Second Avenue** between Lenora and Battery streets, where the strip's remaining cafés, bars, secondhand clothing outlets, record stores, and offbeat galleries cater to those local students and artists who haven't yet moved on to less-gentrified turf in Capitol Hill and Fremont. For a glimpse of the remaining color and quirkiness of the area, visit the **Crocodile Café**,

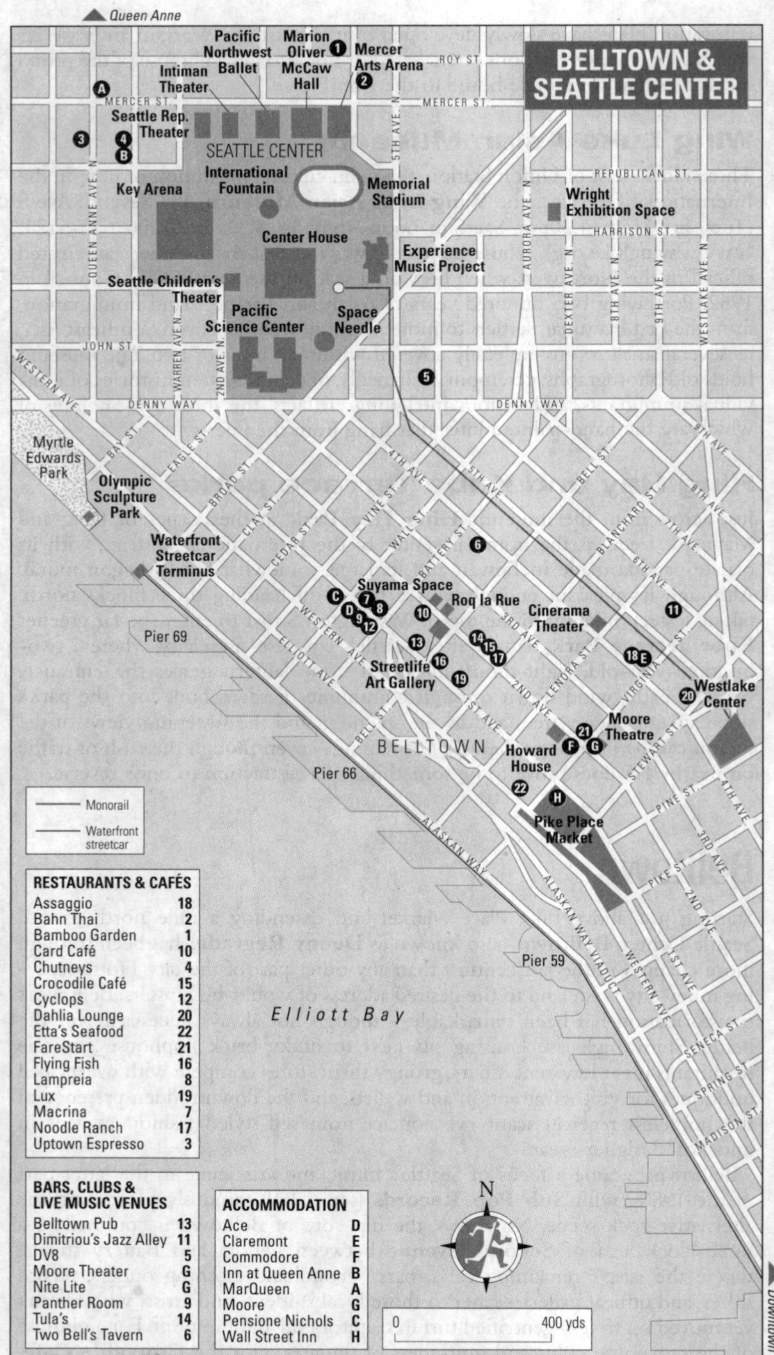

BELLTOWN & SEATTLE CENTER
Queen Anne
Pacific Northwest Ballet
Marion Oliver McCaw Hall
Mercer Arts Arena
Intiman Theater
Seattle Rep. Theater
SEATTLE CENTER
International Fountain
Memorial Stadium
Key Arena
Center House
Experience Music Project
Seattle Children's Theater
Pacific Science Center
Space Needle
Wright Exhibition Space
ROY ST.
MERCER ST.
REPUBLICAN ST.
HARRISON ST.
JOHN ST.
DENNY WAY
QUEEN ANNE AVE. N.
WARREN AVE. N.
2ND AVE. N.
5TH AVE. N.
AURORA AVE. N.
DEXTER AVE. N.
8TH AVE. N.
9TH AVE. N.
WESTLAKE AVE. N.
WESTERN AVE.
BAY ST.
EAGLE ST.
BROAD ST.
CLAY ST.
CEDAR ST.
VINE ST.
WALL ST.
BATTERY ST.
BELL ST.
BLANCHARD ST.
LENORA ST.
VIRGINIA ST.
STEWART ST.
PINE ST.
PIKE ST.
SENECA ST.
SPRING ST.
MADISON ST.
ELLIOTT AVE.
ALASKAN WAY
ALASKAN WAY VIADUCT
1ST AVE.
2ND AVE.
3RD AVE.
4TH AVE.
5TH AVE.
6TH AVE.
7TH AVE.
8TH AVE.
9TH AVE.
Myrtle Edwards Park
Olympic Sculpture Park
Waterfront Streetcar Terminus
Pier 69
Pier 66
Pier 59
Suyama Space
Roq la Rue
Cinerama Theater
Streetlife Art Gallery
Westlake Center
Moore Theatre
Howard House
BELLTOWN
Pike Place Market
Elliott Bay
Downtown
Monorail
Waterfront streetcar
RESTAURANTS & CAFÉS
Assaggio 18
Bahn Thai 2
Bamboo Garden 1
Card Café 10
Chutneys 4
Crocodile Café 15
Cyclops 12
Dahlia Lounge 20
Etta's Seafood 22
FareStart 21
Flying Fish 16
Lampreia 8
Lux 19
Macrina 7
Noodle Ranch 17
Uptown Espresso 3
BARS, CLUBS & LIVE MUSIC VENUES
Belltown Pub 13
Dimitriou's Jazz Alley 11
DV8 5
Moore Theater G
Nite Lite G
Panther Room 9
Tula's 14
Two Bell's Tavern 6
ACCOMMODATION
Ace D
Claremont E
Commodore F
Inn at Queen Anne B
MarQueen A
Moore G
Pensione Nichols C
Wall Street Inn H
N
0 400 yds

Sub Pop Records

No Seattle label has had a greater impact upon rock music and popular culture than **Sub Pop Records**, which grew out of DJ, rock critic, and record-store owner Bruce Pavitt's fanzine on the burgeoning Seattle alternative rock scene in the early 1980s. By mid-decade, local musician and club booker Jonathan Poneman had joined the Sub Pop team, and the label quickly became recognized for recording and promoting a distinct style of music that fused punk with metal. Characterized by sludgy guitars, dirge-like riffs, and an attitude, particularly evident in the lyrics, that was even more sour and cynical than either metal or punk, this sometimes-incendiary mix became loosely known as **grunge** – though it was also inspired by such non-grunge artists as The Pixies, Sonic Youth, and My Bloody Valentine. Green River, Tad, Mudhoney, Soundgarden, and Nirvana, all Sub Pop labelmates, were some of the leaders of the movement, and their album covers were as easily recognized as their sound for their viciously satirical graphics. Though Nirvana left for major label Geffen before *Nevermind* propelled them to stardom, Sub Pop managed to garner a small percentage of the profits from that album's sales as part of Geffen's contract buy-out deal with the band, helping to keep the financially troubled label afloat in the early 1990s. A few years later, Sub Pop sold off part ownership to Warner Brothers for a reported $20 million, though its heyday had already passed.

2200 Second Ave (Ⓣ206/441-5611, Ⓦwww.thecrocodile.com), presenting both unknowns and underground-rock royalty, along with poetry, theater, art, and "circus side shows."

The hub of Belltown's **gallery scene** can be found along a similar stretch of Second Avenue. Integrating the local underclass into the art world is the unusual **Streetlife Art Gallery** at 2301 Second Ave (daily 10am–8pm; free; Ⓣ206/956-8046, Ⓦwww.realchangenews.org/StreetLife/), where all the artists are or were homeless, the space providing them with basic necessities as well as a venue for their art. Nearby, another gallery, **Suyama Space**, no. 2324 (Mon–Fri 9am–5pm; Ⓣ206/256-0809), is well regarded for its challenging avant-garde and conceptual installations, while much lighter-hearted is the close-by **Roq La Rue**, no. 2316 (Tues–Fri 2–6pm, Sat noon–4pm; free; Ⓣ206/374-8977, Ⓦwww.roqlarue.com), presenting a flashy parade of brightly colored, often-bizarre works with themes taken from pop culture and mass entertainment. Finally, a little further down Second, the **Howard House**, no. 2017 (Tues–Sat 11am–6pm; free; Ⓣ206/256-6399, Ⓦwww.howardhouse.net), combines the usual media like painting and photography with sculptural work in ceramics, glass, and metal, all of it with a strong avant-garde or conceptual bent.

The Seattle Center

The **Seattle Center** campus (Ⓦwww.seattlecenter.com) grew out of 1962's World's Fair, along with the **monorail** route that leads to it (see p.252). Since then, it's transformed itself into a busy sports and culture hub, highlighted by such varied institutions as the **Pacific Science Center**, the **Children's Museum**, the **Experience Music Project**, and, of course, the **Space Needle**. In addition, it features public plazas, and venues for opera, dance, and drama. For sports fans, **Key Arena** is the home of pro basketball and minor-league hockey teams (see p.300 for ticket info), and the other large on-site facilities, **Memorial Stadium** and **Mural Amphitheatre**, are mainly used for amateur sports and concert events, respectively. The Amphitheatre often features some of the Northwest's largest festivals (see p.299).

The Space Needle

The most prominent relic of the World's Fair is the **Space Needle** (daily 9am–11pm, Sat–Sun closes at midnight; $12, kids $10, two trips in 24 hrs $18; ⓣ206/905-2100, ⓦwww.spaceneedle.com). With a shaft rising 605ft to support the familiar flying-saucer-shaped floors near its crown, the tower was built to symbolize the future – though it more resembles an oversized prop from a vintage sci-fi flick. Nonetheless, whatever its architectural value, the Needle has become so inextricably linked to the skyline of the city that it now personifies the official face of Seattle, becoming its one indelible icon to the rest of the world. The 43-second elevator ride to the **observation deck** is a pricey but obligatory experience for the first-time visitor to Seattle. Any cynicism sparked by the mobs of tourists and overpriced admission tends to disappear upon arriving at the top: the striking panorama of the surrounding region encompasses neighboring lakes, the Downtown skyline, Puget Sound, Queen Anne, and distant peaks like Mt Rainier – provided the skies are clear, of course.

The Children's Museum

Near the base of the Space Needle, the bland mall of the **Center House** is the unlikely home of the first-rate **Children's Museum** (Mon–Fri 10am–5pm, Sat–Sun 10am–6pm; all ages $6; ⓣ206/441-1768, ⓦwww.thechildrensmuseum.org), which emphasizes interactive activities scaled down to make things inviting for those under four feet tall. Inside, the **Global Village** section simulates a visit to a tailor shop in Ghana, travelling around the Philippines on a tricycle, and so on, while the wilderness exhibit has an **artificial mountain forest** that lets kids crawl through logs or simulate a rock climb. Those herding a group can try the "If I Had a Hammer" construction zone, which lets kids collaborate on building an eight-by-eleven-foot home (reservations recommended).

Pacific Science Center

Close by, the ever-popular **Pacific Science Center** (daily 10am–5pm, Sat–Sun closes at 6pm, summer daily 10am–6pm; $9, kids $6.50; ⓣ206/443-2001, ⓦwww.pacsci.org) is easily recognizable by its modernist white arches and shallow, stagnant "lake." Comprising five large interconnected buildings, the center's emphasis is firmly on hands-on interactive exhibits, some computer-oriented, but most simple enough for pre-adolescents to operate. It makes for a lively environment, full of bright, innovative, and often noisy exhibits, from robotic dinosaurs to machines that let you measure your grip strength, peripheral vision, sense of smell, and other traits in a highly tactile manner that's more akin to operating pinball machines than getting tested at the doctor's office. Fans of giant-screen, nature-oriented **IMAX films** have a chance to see such curiosities (provided they haven't already visited the IMAX Dome on the waterfront, p.261) for the price of a combination museum/film ticket ($14.50, kids $12; IMAX only $7.50).

The Experience Music Project

Northeast of the Pacific Science Center is the looming metallic shell of the Experience Music Project – or EMP, as it's known by locals (daily 10am–5pm, Sat–Sun closes at 9pm; $20, kids $15; concert tickets at ⓣ206/770-2702,

Ⓦwww.emplive.com). The controversial design by world-famous architect **Frank Gehry** – of Guggenheim Bilbao and Disney Hall fame – has not one single right angle in its swooping contortions of metal, though it does allow for the passage of the monorail through its southern section. Along with Cleveland's Rock and Roll Hall of Fame, it's one of the two largest museums in the world devoted to popular music. Largely funded by Microsoft co-founder and billionaire Paul Allen, the EMP was originally intended as a museum for Seattle native Jimi Hendrix before Allen and the Hendrix estate had a falling out. The final product still includes a fair amount of Hendrix memorabilia, but its focus has become much broader, with interactive exhibits drawing from a collection of nearly 80,000 rock and pop artifacts.

The visit begins on level two, where you'll be handed a bulky **Museum Exhibit Guide**, a device carried like a shoulder bag with attached headphones. There's also a remote control unit with a built-in text screen, which, when pointed at displays in the museum, dictates the content of the images on the screen as well as the automated narration by the likes of Robbie Robertson and Bob Dylan. Of the major permanent exhibits, standouts include the **Hendrix Gallery**, which traces Jimi's career from his days as a sideman with the Isley Brothers to his short-lived psychedelic funk group Bands of Gypsies. Nearby, the **Guitar Gallery** displays dozens of acoustic and electric guitar and bass models, such as the intriguing 1933 Dobro all-electric (with built-in speakers) and the 1957 Gibson "Flying V," while **Northwest Passage** traces the local rock scene from instrumental guitar pioneers the Ventures through grunge to modern-day rockers like Sleater-Kinney, with an entire case devoted to the regional rock anthem, *Louie Louie*.

On the third level, the **Milestones** gallery covers many of the music styles that have influenced rock or been spawned from it, including New Orleans R&B; punk, rap, and country. Standout displays include Bo Diddley's trademark square guitar, the turntables used by Grandmaster Flash to DJ in the early 1980s, and a chance to hear Bill Haley's 1952 single *Rock the Joint*, the prototype for his much more famous *Rock Around the Clock*. Across from Milestones, the large **Sound Lab** enables visitors to play electric guitars, basses, keyboards, drums, and DJ turntables, with a bit of help from the staff and interactive computer terminals; there are rooms for jamming, a chance to mix on a professional console, and an entire corner of effects pedals.

Queen Anne

Spreading out northwest from the Seattle Center is the charming, well-heeled hillside district of **Queen Anne**. Originally sited a fair distance from Seattle's nineteenth-century city center, the upscale citizens of "Queen Anne Town" lived in a different world than the rest of their neighbors, a rarefied place where historic-revival mansions towered above the city and the only neighborhood access, other than walking, was by streetcars tugged by counterweights up a steep incline.

The best route into the neighborhood is still by the steeply sloped Queen Anne Avenue, which heads northwest from the Seattle Center and connects the commercially oriented **Lower Queen Anne**, home to many decent bars and nightspots to the loftier precinct of **Upper Queen Anne**, where the main activity takes place between Galer and McGraw streets, a six-block strip of fancy eateries and yuppie-oriented coffeehouses. Running east-west between the upper and lower parts of the district, **Highland Drive** features multimillion-dollar estates and somewhat smaller mansions, most with awe-inspiring views of the metropolis and Puget Sound. Amid this collection of Neoclassical, Georgian, Italianate, and Colonial Revival dwellings is an excellent spot to get a wondrous view of the city, **Kerry Park**, Highland at Second Avenue W, where the Space Needle and Business District are well placed for shutterbugs and the entire city spreads out before your eyes.

Magnolia and Discovery Park

Even though it's only a few miles along the curve of Elliott Bay northwest from Downtown, affluent **Magnolia** feels much further away, with pleasant tree-lined slopes and an aura of isolation. The neighborhood is most notable for Seattle's hidden jewel, **Discovery Park**. With more than five hundred acres of meadows, rustic fields, woods, and walking trails, it's that rare urban park that, on its best days, feels like a genuine slice of wilderness. The **visitor center** (daily 8.30am–5pm; ⓣ206/386-4236), just inside the east entrance at 36th Avenue W and W Government Way, organizes weekend walks spotlighting the park's abundant bird and plant life – from herons and owls to wildflowers. A 2.8-mile **loop trail** can be entered here that winds among much of the park's most densely forested regions. It's better to head for the **south entrance** on W Emerson Street near Magnolia Boulevard, however, and take a trail across the windswept meadows between the parking lot and the nearby bluffs, where the view – taking in Puget Sound ships, Bainbridge Island, and on a clear day the snow-capped Olympic Mountains – is one of the city's grandest, especially at sunset. In the park's southwestern corner, there are still vestiges of the military's presence in the old buildings of **Fort Lawton** (daily 4am–11.30pm; free), where the **history tours** (information at ⓣ206/684-4075) take you inside the guard house where drunk or misbehaving soldiers were jailed in three solitary confinement cells, each measuring just four feet by eight feet.

The Lake Washington Ship Canal

Eight miles long, the **Lake Washington Ship Canal** separates the town proper from the northern districts and connects Elliott Bay to **Lake Union** and further east to the larger **Lake Washington**. Built around 1900 to carry ships to safe harbors on the inland lakes, the canal was used during World War I to safeguard battleships from exposure to attack in the open sea. These days, along with a sizable – and locally famous – community of **houseboats** along Lake Union's eastern shore, there are a few sights along the canal that are among the city's top tourist attractions. If you want to get a look at this part of Lake Union from the water, hourly **Sunday cruises** on the *Fremont Avenue* ferry depart nearby from under the Aurora Bridge, 801 N Northlake Way (on the hour 11am–4pm; $7, kids $4; ⓣ206-713-8446, ⓦwww.seattleferryservice.com), and include close-up perspectives on Seattle's canals and lakes, views of noteworthy houseboats, and a glimpse at Dale Chihuly's waterside studio.

If you have an hour to spare, the procession of boats passing from salt water to fresh through the **Hiram M. Chittenden Locks** (daily 7am–9pm; ⓣ206/783-7059, ⓦwww.nws.usace.army.mil/opdiv/lwsc), near the mouth of the canal, makes pleasant viewing (bus #17 from Downtown). Migrating salmon bypass the locks via the **fish ladder**, a sort of piscine staircase laid out with viewing windows. In peak migrating season (late summer for salmon) the water behind the locks is full of huge, surging fish. The visitor center (Oct–April Thurs–Mon 10am–4pm, summer daily 10am–6pm; free), between the parking lot and the locks, has interesting exhibits on the history of the canal and the locks' construction, and free guided **tours** of the locks leave from here (mid-May to mid-Sept Mon–Fri 1pm & 3pm, Sat–Sun 11am, 1pm & 3pm; mid-Sept to Nov & mid-March to May Thurs–Mon 2pm; reserve at ⓣ206/783-7059). East of the locks spreads Salmon Bay, on the south side of which, beside the Ballard Bridge at 15th Avenue NW, lies **Fishermen's Terminal**, 3919 18th Ave W (daily 7am–4.30pm; ⓣ206/728-3395, ⓦwww.portseattle.org/harbor), a leading homeport for West Coast commercial fishing, providing moorage for about seven hundred vessels. Ranging in length from a few dozen feet to a few hundred, many of these trawlers are on view at the dock by the parking lot; during weekdays, you may catch their operators unloading their crab and salmon hauls.

Ballard

Positioned at the mouth of the ship canal, north of Magnolia, the blue-collar neighborhood of **Ballard** has become a surprisingly hip scene in places, loaded with rugged, early-twentieth-century buildings housing grass-roots galleries, alternative clubs, old-style dive bars, and scruffy diners. Begin your exploration on and around **Ballard Avenue** between 17th and 22nd avenues NW. The highlight is the old **Fire House no. 18**, 5429 Russell Ave NW (ⓣ206/784-3516), an eye-catching brick structure from 1911 with wooden roof brackets, looming tower, and quaint red gates that used to open for the station's horse-drawn fire engines. Decommissioned in 1974, it's since become home to a rock and alternative music club called, naturally, the *Ballard Firehouse* (see p.294). One of several notable venues in the area, the club offers a taste of everything from folk and bluegrass to pop and rockabilly. However, if the tunes don't grab you, visit on the second Saturday night of the month for one of the district's groovy **Art Walks** (7–10pm), where you can immerse yourself in the trendy local art scene at the late-closing galleries.

For a hint of Ballard's old-time character, the **Nordic Heritage Museum**, 3014 NW 67th St (daily 10am–4pm, Sun opens at noon; $4, kids $2; ⓦwww.nordicmuseum.com), takes you through the immigrant experience from 1840 to 1920, spotlighting the Scandinavian-American communities of the region. The **Ballard Story** display re-creates these early days of the community in old photographs and historical narratives, while the second floor has artifacts from five Nordic groups, including traditional clothing, tapestries, and household items decorated with folk art, such as a Danish flax beater and a Finnish birdhouse designed to look like a church.

Woodland Park Zoo

East of central Ballard, off Aurora Avenue, more than 250 species reside in the **Woodland Park Zoo**, N 55th Street and Phinney Avenue N (daily 9.30am–4pm, summer closes at 6pm; $10, kids $7.50; ⓣ206/684-4026), a sleek facility whose spacious layout, humane exhibits, and botanical garden-quality trees and plants make it attractive to anyone with a love of rare animals. The diversity is impressive, including such exotic species as lion-tailed macaques, pygmy marmosets (the smallest monkey species in the world), black-and-white colobus monkeys with lustrous white tails, porcupines, Sumatran tigers, and a Malayan sun bear – the smallest species of bear in the world.

Be sure to check out the indoor **Day and Night** section, where you creep along in near-darkness so as not to disturb an assortment of nocturnal birds and reptiles that slither in and out of sight. Nearby are gorillas almost close enough to touch, and more than close enough to examine their puzzled facial expressions, albeit behind protective glass. You can also get within a few feet of the elephants in the **Tropical Asia** section, though you'll have to be content to see the zebras and giraffes from a much greater distance: they're allowed to roam uncaged through the large field of the **African Savanna** – about as accurate as a North American facsimile can get. Don't leave before taking a peek at the tiny, burrowing prairie dog (tucked into an easily missed corner behind the Pony Ring), one of several species on display like snow leopards, Komodo dragons, and penguins that don't fit into any easily defined categories.

Fremont and Wallingford

Just like Belltown in the early 1990s, the northern Seattle districts of **Fremont** and **Wallingford** are vigorous, spirited communities that, thanks to their quirky appeal and unpretentious bohemian vibe, are being forced to cope with an influx of newcomers and a potential tidal wave of new development. What makes these places so engaging has little to do with their location (isolated from much of the city) or their conventional attractions (few in number), but their laid-back attitudes and preservation of a certain old-fashioned Seattle style, before the city exploded with the high-tech boom and changed its character from a mellow, slightly oddball place to one obsessed with its international image and the bottom line. Today, even with the new condos sprouting here and there, Fremont and Wallingford retain their eccentric liberal charm and easygoing lifestyles.

Fremont

As you cross into the hub of Fremont from Ballard along Leary Way NW, or from Queen Anne via the Fremont Bridge over the ship canal, signs proclaim "Welcome to Fremont, Center of the Universe. Turn your watch back 5 minutes." Another reads, "Welcome to Fremont, Center of the Universe. Throw your watch away." Both offer fair warning that the self-described **Artists Republic of Fremont** is not for those who take themselves too seriously. The district's core is the stretch of **Fremont Avenue N** that runs from the comparatively tiny Fremont Bridge at N 34th Street to N 37th Street, an array of coffeehouses, restaurants, used bookstores, and secondhand boutiques. One of the quirkier local merchants is **Deluxe Junk**, 3518 Fremont Place N, which for the last quarter-century has been showcasing a strange assortment of antiques, memorabilia, and flat-out junk in its (former) funeral-parlor setting, including vintage cameras, clothing and jewelry, space-age cocktail shakers, and mod furniture. Along with hunting for vintage or worn-out collectibles, a trip into central Fremont is also good for simply hanging out with the locals, drinking coffee, munching on desserts, or drinking your troubles away. Amid everything else, though, downtown Fremont is best regarded for its eye-catching, often outlandish, public art (see box).

Public art in Fremont

Fremont's indigenous **public art** embodies its playful sense of surrealism, and tourists are encouraged to wander the area by visiting one sculpted or painted curiosity after another. Start your tour of the art scene by picking up the free *Walking Guide to Fremont* at the kiosk of the **Rocket at the Center of the Universe**, a 53-ft monument at the corner of N 35th Street and Evanston Avenue that looks more like a giant toy model than a space-traveling vessel, even though it's alleged to be an actual rocket fuselage taken from the facade of an Army surplus store. Whatever the case, as the "Story of the Rocket" placard at the bottom deadpans, this was originally intended as a monument to commemorate the discovery of the center of the universe in Fremont in 1991.

A block north, at the triangular corner of 36th and Fremont Place, another oddity is almost as eye-catching, or at least jaw-dropping: a colossal statue of **Vladimir Lenin** stands thrusting forth toward passing motorists, surrounded by blocky flames. This sculpture from Poprad, Slovakia, by Slavic artist Emil Venkov, is the only representation of Lenin "surrounded by guns and flames instead of holding a book or waving a hat" claims the adjoining placard. One Lewis Carpenter found it in Slovakia after it was toppled in the 1989 Velvet Revolution, and mortgaged his home to bring it back to Issaquah, a small town near Seattle. It's situated "temporarily" at this busy corner, on sale for a mere $150,000 – ironically, offers to buy the Communist Party stalwart are now entertained by the Fremont Chamber of Commerce (Ⓣ206/632-1500, Ⓦwww.fremontseattle.com).

Down the road at N 34th Street, a much less aggressive artwork can be seen just east of Fremont Bridge, Richard Beyer's brilliant late-1970s sculpture **Waiting for the Interurban**, lifelike aluminum statues of five dour commuters waiting for the bus – supplemented by a small child and a dog – regularly adorned with football helmets, Hawaiian leis, and other offbeat accoutrements by locals.

The undeniable highlight of the entire district, though, is the huge **Fremont Troll** that lurks underneath Aurora Bridge, a five-minute walk from the *Interurban* at N 36th Street and Aurora Avenue N. Note how the left hand of the eighteen-foot, ferroconcrete ghoul is eternally crushing a real Volkswagen Bug, then walk back a block or so down the hill to view the Troll at a respectful distance. Under the steel lid of Aurora Avenue and between the concrete bridge pilings, the beast really does seem to preside over his own gloomy lair. The sculpture also serves as an inspiration for Fremont's Luminary Procession on October 31, dubbed "**Trolloween.**" Starting here, this parade of costumed masqueraders – some wearing jester outfits and wielding torches – moves through Fremont, with lively street performances and cacophonous music throughout.

Wallingford

Often tagged by Seattlites as "the next Fremont" – with all the concordant implications of higher rents and new development that label carries with it – **Wallingford** is in fact different in several key ways. For one, an assertively bohemian atmosphere is largely lacking here; in its place is a friendlier, more relaxed vibe, making Wallingford a comfortable neighborhood largely free of poseurs and black-clad hipsters, though still with an excellent assortment of restaurants, bars, antique stores, vintage clothing dealers, and cinemas.

The axis of Wallingford lies along **North 45th Street** from Woodlawn to Bagley avenues, the neighborhood's five-block main drag and a fine place to dine on Asian or Mexican cuisine, shop for books or secondhand clothing, and sip on coffee or knock back a beer. Among the more notable merchants here is **Open Books**, no. 2414 (Ⓣ206/633-0811, Ⓦwww.openpoetrybooks.com), a

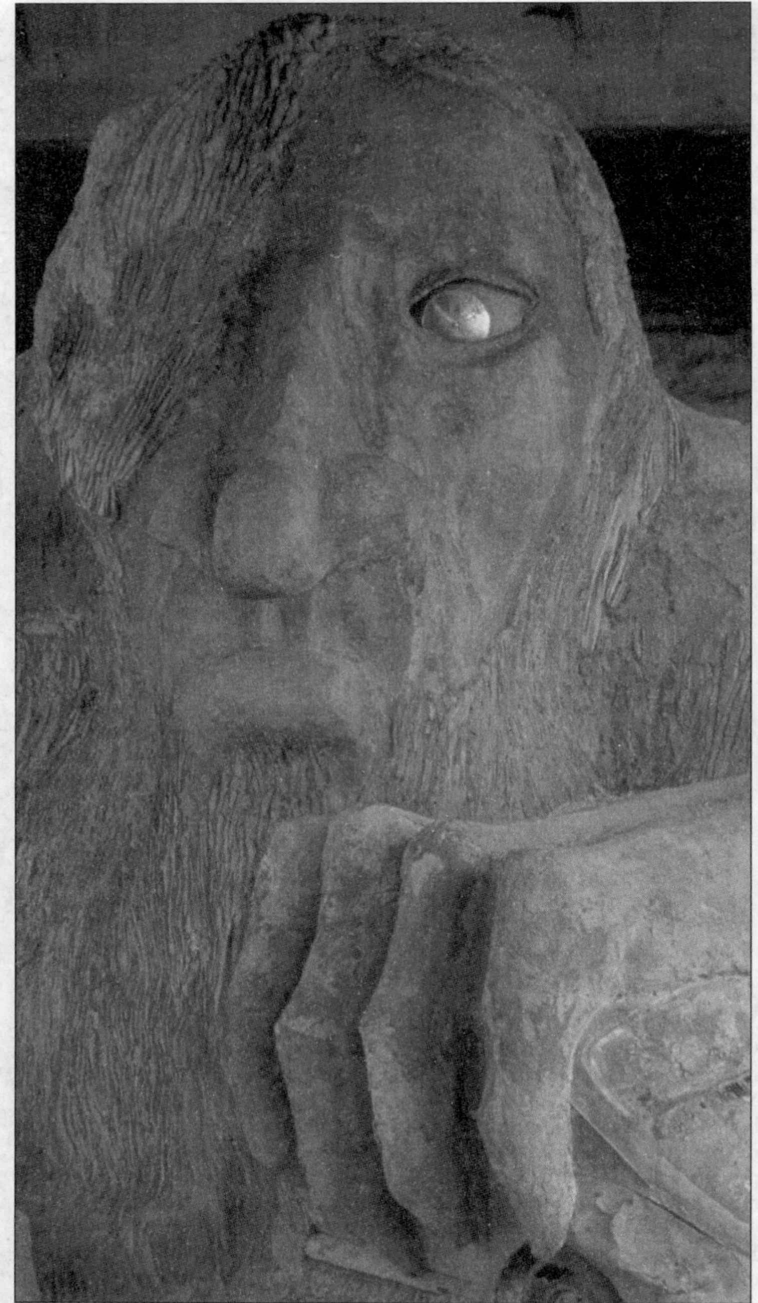

△ The Fremont Troll

self-described "poem emporium" located below a wine bar, flush with mainstream and alternative poetry and periodically hosting readings by notable local and national authors. The excellent pair of movie theaters known collectively as the **Guild 45th**, no. 2115 (Ⓣ206/633-3353, Ⓦwww.landmarktheatres.com), is also a draw for its mainstream and independent fare presented in two distinct cinemas, while the bland-looking **Wallingford Center**, no. 1815 (Ⓣ206/547-7246), has the usual variety of boutiques and restaurants in a three-story former school building. Across the street, the very center of the strip, or of the entire area, is marked with giant capital letters atop a supermarket at no. 1801, spelling out "WALLINGFORD" in eye-catching blue-and-white neon.

Gasworks Park

On the southern edge of Wallingford, along the shores of **Lake Union**, is one of the best and most bizarre places to get an expansive view of the city, **Gasworks Park**, 2101 N Northlake Way (daily 4.30am–11.30pm, parking lot open 6am–9pm; Ⓣ206/684-4075). The park's grounds were, until the mid-1950s, occupied by the **Seattle Gas Company**, whose massive industrial plant converted coal and oil into gas. Several gigantic, ugly brown oxygen gas-generator towers still remain, the clash between the rotting dark structures and the surrounding green hills lending the site a strangely artistic dissonance – although the fences enclosing these relics haven't been able to prevent locals from splattering the monoliths with all sorts of imaginative graffiti. Remodeled into a twenty-acre park, its small hills and windy location on the banks of the lake make it a favorite spot for kite flyers, and its location makes it Seattle's prime vantage point for Fourth of July fireworks, with Downtown and the Space Needle looming to the southwest.

The University District

East of I-5 sits the **University** or **"U" District**, centered on the **University of Washington**, home to 35,000 or so students. The 639-acred campus houses the **Henry Art Gallery**, one of the finest art museums in the city, and the **Burke Memorial Museum**, rich in its exhibits on Native Americans in the Pacific Northwest. But as with Capitol Hill, the U District's chief draw is its main drag, **University Way**, known as **"The Ave,"** with its dozen or so blocks of student-centric establishments that stretch northwards from NE 41st Street. It's always jam-packed with students and shoppers, who frequent the strip's cheap restaurants (particularly Asian ones), secondhand music stores, and funky and vintage clothing boutiques.

The University of Washington campus

The **University of Washington** (Ⓣ206/543-9198, Ⓦwww.washington.edu) – or UW (pronounced U-dub), as it's known – is the most prominent educational institution in the Northwest, with sixteen schools and colleges. Before your wanderings, stop in at the **Visitors Information Center**, 4014 University Way NE (Mon–Fri 8am–5pm, Ⓣ206/543-9198, Ⓦdepts.washington.edu/visitors), to pick up the free *Campus Walk* booklet, a self-guided tour of the university's highlights. Foremost among them is the **medicinal herb garden** near Benson Hall (Mon–Fri 8am–5pm; free; tours May–Oct second Sun of month at noon; Ⓣ206/543-1126, Ⓦnnlm.gov/pnr/uwmhg), one of the largest of its kind in the US, hosting everything from familiar plants like poppies, goldenrod, and foxglove, to rarer and more bizarre curiosities like monkeyflower, devil's tongue, panther lily, and Bible-leaf. Further along, the Gothic Revival **Suzzallo Library** (Mon–Thurs 7.30am–10pm, Fri 7.30am–6pm, Sat 9am–5pm, Sun noon–10pm; ⓣ206/543-0242, ⓦwww.lib.washington.edu/Suzzallo), has a reading room resembling the nave of a medieval church, and faces **Central Plaza**, dubbed "Red Square" for its red bricks, a major student hotspot for socializing. At the edge of Union Bay, the **Waterfront Activities Center** (daily 10am–dusk, except holidays and Dec winter break; ⓣ206/543-9433, ⓦwww.depts.washington.edu/ima/IMA.wac) rents rowboats or canoes for $6.50 an hour, a great way to take in the nearby lakes.

Henry Art Gallery

The University's **Henry Art Gallery**, west of Central Plaza at 15th Avenue NE at NE 41st Street (Tues–Sun 11am–5pm, Thurs closes at 8pm; $6, all students free; ⓣ206/543-2280, ⓦwww.henryart.org), presents some of the most imaginative exhibits found in any of Seattle's art museums, though the exhibits in each gallery change about three or four times a year, so what you see is likely to be totally different from one visit to the next. Selections from the Henry's **permanent collection** include late-nineteenth- and early-twentieth-century landscapes by Winslow Homer and Ralph Blakelock, figurative paintings by Jacob Lawrence, prints by Rembrandt and Whistler, and photographs by Ansel Adams and Imogen Cunningham. By contrast, the **lower level** is devoted to changing contemporary exhibits, with three galleries largely devoted to risk-taking art, sometimes incorporating multiscreen projections and high technology, as well as barn-sized installations combining sculpture, sound design, and architecture.

The Burke Museum

A few blocks north of the Henry Art Gallery, the **Burke Museum**, 17th Avenue NE at NE 45th Street (daily 10am–5pm; $6.50, non-UW students $3, UW students free; ⓣ206/543-5590, ⓦwww.washington.edu/burkemuseum), is UW's other top cultural attraction, focusing mostly on the natural and cultural history of Washington, the Pacific Northwest, and the Pacific Rim. Holding the US's largest collection of Native American art and artifacts west of the Mississippi, it has been remodeled to showcase two large permanent exhibitions. On the upper floor, the **Life and Times of Washington State** is a kid-oriented timeline of geological history offering the likes of volcanic crystals, a 140 million-year-old allosaurus, and a giant Ice Age-era sloth – found during construction of a Sea-Tac airport runway. On the lower floor, **Pacific Voices** is a broad series of exhibits covering the cultures of Pacific Island and coastal communities, highlighted by an assemblage of masks used in the potlatch ceremonies of the Kwakwaka'wakw tribe of the Northwest Coast – including ones that change from one creature into another at the pull of a string.

Capitol Hill and around

South across Portage Bay from the U District lies **Capitol Hill**, one of Seattle's best-loved residential neighborhoods, both for its easy going vibe and its liberal atmosphere, as well as its location not far from the city center. The area is fairly mixed by class – the well-preserved homes share space with apartment

RESTAURANTS & CAFÉS

611 Supreme	18
Aurafice	23
B&O Espresso	12
Bauhaus Books & Coffee	22
Byzantion	4
Café Dilettante	7
Café Flora	5
Café Septième	11
Capitol Hill Café	10
Coffee Messiah	14
Ezo Noodle Café	9
Globe Café	27
Gravity Bar	8
Kingfish Café	3
Machiavelli	20
Online Coffee Company	17
Piecora's	28
Siam on Broadway	2
Teapot	16
Victrola Coffee and Art	13
Vivace Espresso	15

BARS, CLUBS & LIVE MUSIC VENUES

Bad Juju Lounge	24
Baltic Room	21
Century Ballroom	30
Chop Suey	29
Comet Tavern	25
Eastlake Zoo	1
Hop Vine Pub	6
Linda's Tavern	19
Vogue	26

buildings both smart and funky, if not quite seedy. It has also, since the Sixties, been a center for the city's left-leaning political and cultural forces, an influence apparent in the area's alternative-minded shops and nightlife, its political canvassers who hawk petitions on the street corners, and its status as the undisputed center of the **gay and lesbian community**. Never is that more in evidence than during the annual Gay Pride parade down **Broadway** on the last Sunday in June, which has now become one of the city's most popular celebrations.

Volunteer Park

The northern end of the Capitol Hill district radiates old money, complete with gold-rush-era mansions sitting sedately around the shrubs and trees of **Volunteer Park**, 1247 15th Ave (daily 6am–11pm; Ⓣ206/684-4075), named in honor of those who volunteered for the Spanish-American War of 1898. The lovely 1912 glass **Conservatory** here (daily summer 10am–7pm; rest of year 10am–4pm; free) is divided into galleries simulating different climates (jungle, desert, rainforest, etc). There's also a wealth of ferns and cacti, plus olive trees, orchids, and yuccas, along with bromeliads (look for the silver, confetti-like tillandsias) that crawl over rocks, shrubs, and trees.

Also located within the park is the **Seattle Asian Art Museum** (Tues–Wed & Fri–Sun 10am–5pm, Thurs 10am–9pm; Ⓦwww.seattleartmuseum.org; $3), home to one of the most extensive collections of Asian art outside of that continent. Its exhibits encompass Japanese, Korean, Vietnamese, and Chinese art, and are richest in ceramics and sculpture. Also in the park, the old **water tower** is, at 75ft, Capitol Hill's highest structure. At the top is the budget alternative to the Space Needle's observation deck: a free panoramic view of Seattle, although the wire mesh covering the small windows may well remind you why it's free.

Broadway and around

Despite recent commercialization, **Broadway** remains *the* place to hang out in Capitol Hill, whether you're browsing for trinkets, taking in the scene at a bar or club, popping into one of the many boutiques, or sitting at one of the sidewalk cafés watching the crowds. Taking up an entire block between Republican and Harrison streets, **Broadway Market**, no. 401 (Mon–Sat 10am–9pm, Sun noon–6pm; Ⓣ206/322-1610, Ⓦwww.thebroadwaymarket.com), is a multistory hodgepodge of mildly trendy shops, fast-food joints, chain clothiers, coffeehouses, and fitness and beauty centers.

Many Capitol Hill attractions are located on streets just off Broadway, such as **Olive Way**, offering a good concentration of cafés, or further south around **Pike** and **Pine streets**, featuring funky clubs, coffeehouses, record stores, and tattoo and piercing parlors. Back on Broadway, just north of Pine, the striking, life-size statue of **Jimi Hendrix** was modeled on his famous pose from the 1967 Monterey Pop Festival, in which the guitar wizard kneeled down before the crowd to set his axe ablaze.

A few blocks south is the campus of Seattle University, meriting a visit only for the unusual **Chapel of St Ignatius**, next to the parking lot at Marion and 12th (Mon–Thurs 7am–10pm, Fri 7am–7pm, Sat 9am–5pm, Sun 9am–10pm; Ⓣ206/296-6000 Ⓦwww.seattleu.edu/chapel), whose interior offers hanging baffles and multihued windows, many of them thin rectangular slits, which combine to cast moving patterns of colored light throughout the church, each hue representing a different sacrament or theme.

Frye Art Museum and CoCA

Southwest of Capitol Hill, the **Frye Art Museum**, 704 Terry Ave (Tues–Sat 10am–5pm, Sun noon–5pm, Thurs closes at 8pm; free; ⓣ206/622-9250, ⓦfryeart.org), is the most traditional of Seattle's major art museums, devoted to figurative Western painting from the last two centuries. The spacious, dimly lit galleries include works by Winslow Homer, John Singer Sargent, Thomas Eakins, and a few (anti)modern artists like Andrew Wyeth. The building also holds one of the most important concentrations of the **Munich school** of painting in the US, focusing on the Belle Epoque between 1870 and 1900, when Munich was one of Europe's foremost cultural centers.

Art of a more unconventional sort is on view down the street at the **Center on Contemporary Art**, or **CoCA**, north of Seattle University at 1420 11th Ave (Tues–Thurs 2–8pm, Fri–Sun noon–5pm; $5 suggested donation; ⓣ206/728-1980, ⓦwww.cocaseattle.org), whose small space is given over to rotating exhibits of work that's more risqué than what you'll see in the Seattle Art Museum's contemporary galleries. Nam June Paik, Survival Research Laboratories, and Lydia Lunch are some of the artists who received their first major exposure in the Northwest through these eye-opening exhibits.

Museum of History and Industry

Northeast of Capitol Hill, across Montlake Bridge from the university, the **Museum of History and Industry**, 2700 24th Ave E (daily 10am–5pm, Thurs closes at 8pm; $7, kids $5; ⓣ206/324-1126, ⓦwww.seattlehistory.org), provides a detailed history of the Puget Sound region, including displays on cannery work, the timber industry, Klondike Gold Rush, aviation pioneers, nautical life, and discarded neon signs. The museum's highlight is the well-executed **Great Seattle Fire** exhibit in the basement, with an interactive terminal featuring graphics that let you see how the fire started (see p.263) and engulfed Downtown; nearby is the small glue pot believed to have started the blaze.

The permanent displays include a full-scale replica of a Seattle street in the 1880s and a section devoted to the salmon industry, but better are the temporary exhibits covering a wide range of subjects, from intricate dollhouses to experimental hydroplanes.

Washington Park Arboretum

With 230 acres and more than five thousand kinds of plants, the **Washington Park Arboretum** (daily 7am–dusk; free; ⓣ206/543-8800, ⓦdepts.washington.edu/wpa) is a lush showcase for regional vegetation, and a beautiful place to stroll – best on uncrowded weekdays – and observe the magnolias, camellias, witch hazels, and more exotic specimens. The **Graham visitors center**, at the north end of Arboretum Drive near Foster Island Road (daily 10am–4pm), has a free trail map and can also inform you about the numerous walks and activities held on the grounds, such as the free tours that leave from the center every Saturday and Sunday at 1pm. The most popular destination is the **Japanese Garden**, just off the large parking lot on Lake Washington Boulevard near the Madison Street entrance (March–Nov daily 10am–dusk; $3; ⓣ206/684-4725, ⓦwww.seattlejapanesegarden.org). Constructed with more than five hundred granite boulders taken from the Cascade Mountains, it's a lovely, well-landscaped spot, particularly at the bridges near Emperor's Gate, where exotically colored carp swim in the pond and terrapins sun themselves on nearby Turtle Island.

Along Lake Washington Boulevard

East of Capitol Hill and south of the Washington Park Arboretum, **Lake Washington Boulevard** meanders through the ritzy confines of the Madison Park district for a mile or so before reaching the shores of **Lake Washington**, where it hugs the water's edge for another five miles. It's Seattle's most scenic drive, passing some of the city's more elegant neighborhoods in the north, and then through the middle-class, but extremely pleasant, Mount Baker and Rainier Valley districts before terminating at **Seward Park** to the south.

Highlights along the way include the stone-walled former **residence of Kurt Cobain**, at 171 Lake Washington Blvd E, sitting next to cozy **Viretta Park** (daily 4am–11.30pm) and best viewed from that vantage point; in April 1994 the house became the site of Cobain's suicide. Further south, **Leschi Park** (daily 7am–11.30pm; ⓣ206/684-4075) is a one-time amusement-park site that now features pleasant nature walks amid trees and flower gardens. The adjacent **Frink Park** (daily 7am–11.30pm) offers wooded hiking terrain built around a steep ravine and the curve of the boulevard.

After another ten blocks, Lake Washington Boulevard passes over the tunnel section of I-90 and soon reaches **Colman Park** (daily 6am–10pm), where swimmers will have the water practically to themselves. From here the boulevard continues on its winding, lakeside route through **Mount Baker Park** (daily 6am–10pm) and down to **Seward Park**. The entire three-mile stretch is set up as a linear parkway, and it's best on the occasional weekend days (May–Sept second Sat & third Sun 10am–6pm) when it's closed to traffic and its tree-lined concourse fills with cyclists and joggers.

At the southern terminus of Lake Washington Boulevard, peninsular Seward Park (daily 4am–11.30pm; ⓦwww.sewardpark.net) is a serene turnaround point for cyclists, pedestrians, and rollerbladers. Encircled by a two-and-a-half-mile loop path, the park offers an even more secluded forest preserve at its hilly center, replete with stately trees and is home to a fish hatchery, Greek amphitheater, and bathhouse. A couple miles south of Seward Park is **Kubota Garden**, at Renton Avenue and 55th Avenue S (daily dawn–dusk; free; ⓣ206/684-4584, ⓦwww.kubota.org), a quaint and less-prominent alternative to Washington Park's Japanese Garden. Established in 1927 by landscaper Fukitaro Kubota, this garden – traversed by paths constructed to simulate a miniature mountain walk on a 65-foot hillside – has twenty acres of tranquil ponds, pines, cypresses, bamboos, carved stones, open lawn space, and a waterfall.

The Seattle suburbs

Until it was bridged, Lake Washington isolated the city from the countryside and small farms to the east. Ferries laden with farm produce made slow progress across the water, and the lake became a sort of tradesmen's entrance to the city while the center of Seattle looked towards the big commercial ships docking in Elliott Bay. All this changed when two long, floating bridges, one built in the 1940s, the second in the 1960s, turned the one-time rural towns of **Bellevue**, **Kirkland**, and **Redmond** into affluent **city suburbs**. Redmond became the world headquarters of software giant Microsoft; Kirkland built plush businesses and accommodations along its waterfront; and Bellevue – the only one of the three now worth visiting – quickly outgrew its suburban status to become the state's fourth largest city with its own smart business district and shopping area. Elsewhere, the handful of appealing sights in the Seattle outskirts are few and far between, even though some of them – notably the **Museum of Flight** – more than merit the trip. Other diverting destinations include the **Boeing** airplane-assembly tours in northerly Everett and the city's original townsite of **Alki Beach** in West Seattle.

Bellevue

Complete with Downtown skyscrapers and thriving local businesses, **Bellevue** is one of the hottest real-estate markets in the US. Its city center is dominated by **Bellevue Square** (daily 9.30am–9.30pm; ⓣ425/454-8096, ⓦwww.bellevuesquare.com), a several-square block shopping plaza that holds two hundred-plus shops and restaurants as well as the newly relocated **Bellevue Art Museum**, 510 Bellevue Way NE (Tues–Sat 10am–5pm, Thurs closes at 8pm, Sun noon–5pm; $6, students $4; ⓣ425/519-0770, ⓦwww.bellevueart.org). Often spotlighting Pacific Northwest artists, it's devoted exclusively to rotating exhibits of contemporary work and has far more cutting-edge stuff than you'd expect from its suburban location: there's conceptual art, comic-book and pop-art designs, postmodern puppetry, inflatable pieces, and even a bizarre "public aviary" using two hundred thongs stretched across the gallery.

A few blocks north, the unusual **Museum of Doll Art**, 1116 108th Ave NE (Mon–Sat 10am–5pm, Sun 1–5pm; $7; ⓣ425/455-1116, ⓦwww.dollart.com), is surprisingly worthwhile and tastefully executed, with appeal for both adults and children. The large, modern facility's two floors contain more than 1200 dolls of all sizes and nationalities from the last few centuries; among the most intriguing are Peruvian burial dolls, African fertility dolls, and Mexican Day of the Dead ceremonial figures. There are also exquisitely crafted miniatures – look for the Japanese boy made from ground oyster shells – and unexpected tableaux like a seventeenth-century Russian Orthodox wedding.

About a mile east past the 405 freeway, another appealing detour can be found at the **Bellevue Botanical Garden**, 12001 Main St (daily dawn–dusk; free; ⓣ425/451-3755, ⓦwww.bellevuebotanical.org), located in Wilburton Hill Park and featuring a nice range of variously themed sections on almost forty acres, including plots devoted to a Japanese Garden, a spacious site for perennials, a water-conservation zone filled with hardy specimens, and an Alpine Rock Garden that features an array of imported plants from northern elevations.

The Museum of Flight

The biggest of Seattle's museums – and one of the best – the **Museum of Flight**, 9404 E Marginal Way (daily 10am–5pm; $11, kids $6.50; ⓣ206/764-5720, ⓦwww.museumofflight.org), more than makes up for the twenty-minute bus ride (#174) south from Downtown through the port's dreary industrial hinterland. Its collection includes more than 130 military and civilian aircraft and several large complementary exhibits, although only those with an abiding fascination for aviation history need the entire day to see it.

The museum's centerpiece is the hangar-like **Great Gallery**, which displays more than fifty full-size vintage aircraft, many of which are suspended from the steel-and-glass roof. The first presidential jet (used by Eisenhower in 1959) is here, as well as some early commercial planes and bizarre manifestations of aviation design such as the *Aerocar III*, a flying red sportscar that can be converted from automobile to aircraft in ten minutes. There are conventional bombers too, but more interesting are the early airmail planes and wacky home-built designs. Among these are the transcontinental gliders such as the *Aerosonde*, a robotic flier that took more than one day and less than two gallons of gas to cross the Atlantic, and the *Gossamer Albatross II*, whose propellers were connected through a series of gears to a constantly pedaling pilot. In another wing of the museum, the 1909 **Red Barn** was Boeing's original manufacturing plant and now offers a serious-minded, text-heavy spread of relics from the early days of flight.

The achievements of the Wright Brothers get their due, but the displays go back even further than 1900 to the ambitious designs of dreamers without the technology to enact their fantasies, and include European pioneers like the French who helped develop manned flight in the early 1900s (such as the crossing of the English Channel in Louis Bleriot's *Model XI* in 1909). The impact of World War I and the early years of commercial flight are also traced; check out the nearly decrepit 1914 *Caproni Ca* 20, the world's first fighter plane.

Everett and the Boeing Tour Center

Thirty miles north of Seattle, the last major suburb along I-5, **Everett**, is home to the manufacturing plant for **Boeing**, a huge corporation with about 170,000 employees worldwide, a somewhat smaller number of workers after the company cut 35,000 jobs in 2002-03 – half of them in the Seattle area alone. One item it didn't cut was its ever-popular program of hour-long tours at the **Boeing Tour Center**, entrance on Hwy-526, a few miles west of exit 189 off I-5 (Mon–Fri 9am–3pm on the hour, except noon; $5 for same-day tickets, $10 in advance; tickets and info at Ⓣ1-800/464-1476, Ⓦwww.boeing.com/companyoffices/aboutus/tours). It's a good idea to arrive early, as the first-come-first-serve tickets (from the counter just inside the center) often run out quickly, with waits of an hour or more not uncommon once you've gotten your time slot. Not surprisingly, the tour is a smoothly executed PR exercise, focusing on Boeing's impressive technological accomplishments, including the 98-acre **factory** that's listed in the *Guinness Book of World Records* as the largest building in the world by volume (472 million cubic feet). Overhead platforms afford views of much of the floor space, cluttered by new planes in various phases of gestation, and the tour concludes with a bus ride on the "flight line," where finished 747, 767, and 777 models are tested, giving you a glimpse of some of the newest jets about to hit the skies.

West Seattle and Alki Beach

The isolated neighborhood of **West Seattle**, separated from Downtown by the industrial piers and waterways of Harbor Island, is technically within the city limits, though it feels as much like a suburb as Bellevue does. There are few attractions here other than the narrow strip of **Alki Beach** (daily dawn–dusk; Ⓣ206/684-4075), located on the peninsula's northwestern edge and around its northern tip of Duwamish Head. It once featured a turn-of-the-century amusement park and ferry service across Elliott Bay to Downtown, but both the thrill rides and the transit boats are long gone. Still, it's the city's most popular beach, crowded on warm days with bathers, volleyball players, and other recreants, and the view across the bay is impressive, taking in the Space Needle, Magnolia, and Queen Anne.

Alki Beach: A Pacific Northwest Plymouth

Alki Beach is where the first party of Seattle's white settlers landed in November 1851. Ten adults and twelve children were met by advance scout and fellow pioneer **David Denny**, who helped them ashore in the midst of heavy rain. The settlement – comprising a mere four cabins – was optimistically named New York in honor of settler Charles Terry's home state. This was quickly amended with the addition of the Chinook slang word "alki" to the sardonic New York-Alki, which roughly translates to "New York eventually" or "New York by and by." The settlers soon determined that the deep-water harbor further north in Elliott Bay would be far more suitable for settlement, especially as ships could not dock at Alki, and the pioneers began staking claims around the area where Pioneer Square is now sited.

Near 63rd and Alki avenues, a small **commemorative column** in Alki Beach Park, inscribed with the names of the settlers, identifies the spot of the 1851 landing, and its base also features a stone from an even more famous landing site – Plymouth Rock in Massachusetts. Two blocks inland, the whole tale is recounted in depth at the **Log House Museum**, 3003 61st Ave SW (Thurs noon–6pm, Fri 10am–3pm, Sat & Sun noon–3pm; $2; ⓣ206/938-5293, ⓦwww.loghousemuseum.org), which serves as the headquarters of the SW Seattle Historical Society and has plenty of exhibits about the settlement of the early city, history of Native Americans in the region, and the less interesting development of West Seattle. As for the house itself, it's not one of the original Alki cabins, but is rather the renovated carriage house of a local soap magnate, built around 1903 in an agreeable Arts and Crafts style.

If you're out this way in a car, it's worth taking a few extra minutes to follow Alki Avenue as it curves south around Alki Point and turns into **Beach Drive**, a scenic coastal route with views of the Puget Sound and the Olympic Mountains. A few miles south down the road, **Lincoln Park** (daily 4am–11.30pm) offers a narrow beach with a paved promenade, picnic tables, and the onsite **Colman Pool**, 8603 Fauntleroy Way SW (daily mid-June–Aug; ⓣ206/684-7494), a heated outdoor saltwater swimming pool. True park lovers and avid hikers might also want to wander through the rugged and nearly deserted **Schmitz Park** (daily 4am–11.30pm; ⓦwww.schmitzpark.org), about ten blocks from Alki Point (enter at SW Admiral Way and SW Stevens Street), a fifty-acre old growth forest with Douglas fir, Western red cedar, and Western hemlock.

Eating

Seattle's **restaurants** are surprisingly broad in scope and encompass a wide range of international foodways, styles of cooking, and regional twists on familiar flavors. The term "**Northwest Cuisine**" is bandied about quite a bit in Seattle, and is basically a regional variation on California Cuisine, namely a wide array of flavors, gastronomic experiments, and often exotic-sounding dishes made using local ingredients, available in season and not out of cans or freezers. Locally caught **seafood** is, not surprisingly, of a high standard, especially the salmon. The International District has countless inexpensive East Asian spots, particularly strong on **Chinese**, **Japanese**, and **Vietnamese** offerings, while **pan-Asian** food, which fuses different kinds of Asian dishes into the same menu, or mixes Asian and North American styles, has become trendy here in recent years throughout the West Coast. Although there are several quality **steakhouses** in town, **vegetarians** will not have a problem in Seattle, which is approaching coastal California standards in providing a wealth of meatless alternatives.

With its broad assortment of low-end diners, chic eateries, and chain restaurants, **Downtown**'s eating choices are as numerous as anywhere in the city, and, since the majority of visitors are based here, are often packed during peak hours – whether or not their cuisine merits the attention. Elsewhere, options at **Capitol Hill** include ethnic gems and the occasional exclusive bistro, while the **University District** is synonymous with bargain-basement dining.

Pike Place Market

Athenian Inn main floor of Main Arcade ☎206/624-7166. A good place to check out views of Puget Sound and do a bit of people watching. Try the seafood platter if you're coming for a proper meal. Breakfast (especially the hash) is popular, and the lengthy menu is matched by an extensive beer list.

Campagne 1600 Post Alley at Pine St ☎206/728-2800. The top restaurant in the market area, offering delicacies like potato-wrapped striped bass filet and foie gras parfait in a puff pastry with shallots and turnips. Heaviest on seafood specialties, though there's an excellent vegetarian ravioli with garlic and carrot puree. There's also a less expensive café for breakfast, lunch, and Sunday brunch.

Copacabana Triangle Building ☎206/622-6359. A Bolivian restaurant that's one of Pike Place's most offbeat eateries, with a concentration on stuffed pies (such as *huminta*, or corn pie) and fish soups. The outdoor balcony seating has a good view of the foot traffic on Pike Place below.

Lowell's main floor of Main Arcade ☎206/622-2036. Along with the *Athenian Inn*, the most popular of the Pike Place restaurants with waterfront views, renowned for its breakfasts, coffee, and seafood – try the oysters. There is sometimes a lengthy wait to get a seat on the upper floor.

Place Pigalle on the staircase behind *Pike Place Fish*, Main Arcade ☎206/624-1756. Tucked so unobtrusively in a market alley that it's easily missed, a French bistro boasting high-quality seafood like mussels and regionally caught sturgeon. Patio open in warm weather. Closed Sun.

Saigon 1916 Pike Place, on ground floor of Soames-Dunn Building in Pike Place Market ☎206/448-1089. One of the best inexpensive places to eat in Pike Place, with a menu of Vietnamese seafood and vegetarian dishes featuring some sweat-inducing curries; try the curry tofu soup or the lemon-grass squid.

Three Girls Bakery lower floor of Sanitary Market ☎206/622-1045. Endure the long lines at this well-loved haunt for the large, tasty sandwiches, like herb focaccia with hummus, available at either the takeout counter or the small adjoining café.

Waterfront and Business District

Andaluca 407 Olive Way in the *Mayflower Park* hotel ☎206/382-6999. An elegant slice of Art Nouveau design in a top Spanish restaurant, affordable for its breakfasts of citrus pancakes and salmon scrambles, but better for its delicious dinners of old-style paella, beef tenderloin, spicy lamb chops, and cherry duck breast.

Anthony's Pier 66 2201 Alaskan Way ☎206/448-6688. Good seafood, like shellfish, mahi mahi, and oysters, served in a waterfront restaurant with the best view of the Puget Sound in town. There's a less expensive lunch menu, and the restaurant also runs the even cheaper takeout-oriented *Anthony's Fish Bar* in the same building.

Earth & Ocean 1112 4th Ave, in the *W Seattle* hotel ☎206/264-6060. A marvelous, top-shelf spot for Northwest Cuisine, highlighted by the likes of ahi tuna and salmon fillets, but best for its risk-taking Menu Sauvage, in which you can expect to chow down on anything from wild boar ravioli to elk steak, depending on the season and the mood of the chef.

Elliott's Oyster House 1201 Alaskan Way ☎206/623-4340. As the name suggests, succulent bivalves and other seafood dishes like crab and lobster are the main attraction at this popular waterfront spot, contained in a dark, handsome interior with nice views of the bay.

Metropolitan Grill 820 2nd Ave between Columbia and Marion sts ⓣ206/624-3287. The beef-lover's best bet in town, with a good choice of top cuts of steak, in a place that's heavy on power suits and has one of the longest bars in Seattle. Open for lunch and dinner weekdays, dinner only weekends.

Nikko 1900 5th Ave at Stewart St, in the *Westin* hotel ⓣ206/322-4641. Top-notch Japanese restaurant with an extensive sushi bar and many grilled dishes. The complete sushi menu is not offered at lunchtime, but there is a smaller lunch menu with an all-you-can-eat sushi special.

Painted Table 1st Ave and Madison St, in the *Alexis* hotel ⓣ206/624-3646. Serving dishes like three-clam linguini, incorporating produce fresh from Pike Place Market and served on hand-painted plates. For dessert, try the updated "S'mores" – warm chocolate ganache with vanilla-bean meringue and home-made Graham-cracker crust.

Wild Ginger 1400 Western Ave at Union ⓣ206/623-4450. Ever-popular pan-Asian restaurant with extensive daily specials to supplement a lengthy and ambitious menu. Best to stick with dishes that don't try to do too much at once, like the tuna manada (yellowfin tuna fried in spicy Indonesian sauce). Good, if a bit overpriced.

Pioneer Square

Honey Bear Bakery 1st Ave S and S Main St ⓣ206/682-6664. Café in the basement of Elliott Bay Book Company that serves a good assortment of moderately priced, wholefood-oriented soups, salads, quiches, and the like. Newspapers and weatherbeaten hardcover books are available for perusal while you eat.

Il Terrazzo Carmine 411 1st Ave S ⓣ206/467-7797. The height of Italian chic in the area, perhaps the entire city, offering splendid risottos, rack of lamb, gnocchi, and a fine range of pastas for exquisitely steep prices.

Merchants Cafe 109 Yesler Way ⓣ206/624-1515. Local landmark from 1890, the oldest restaurant on the West Coast and still enjoyable for its colorful clientele, warm, dark ambience, hearty dishes like beef stews and chicken sandwiches, and stomach-stuffing steak-and-egg breakfasts.

Salumi 309 3rd Ave S ⓣ206/621-8772. Sausages made the old-fashioned way, served in cheap, delicious sandwiches with home-made bread, and issued piping hot at this local institution, where hogs are made the most of and the heavy and succulent ingredients include the likes of oxtail, prosciutto, and lamb.

Trattoria Mitchelli 84 Yesler Way ⓣ206/623-3883. Another fine Italian eatery in Pioneer Square, though much cheaper than *Il Terrazzo Carmine*, and offering a succulent range of thin-crust pizzas and filling portions of pasta. Open until the wee hours to accommodate late-night revelers.

International District

Bangkok House 606 S Weller St ⓣ206/382-9888. Straightforward Thai restaurant with lightning-fast service. Anything with peanut sauce here is succulent, and the *pad Thai* is worth a try.

Chau's Chinese Seafood 310 4th Ave S ⓣ206/621-0006. Well-regarded Chinese place on the Downtown–International District border does mostly seafood dishes – though it's also a good place for duck – and has weekday lunch specials for around $5–7.

Hon's 416 5th Ave S ⓣ206/623-4470. Cheap and filling Chinese, Szechuan, and Vietnamese cuisine served right across from the International District Metro Tunnel.

House of Hong 409 8th Ave S ⓣ206/622-7997. Tasty and simple Chinese food in a large restaurant open relatively late on weekends, making it a good option for dining after events in the Pioneer Square/Safeco Field area. Also offering supreme dim sum until 5pm daily.

Saigon Bistro 1032 S Jackson St ⓣ206/329-4939. Old-fashioned Vietnamese favorites – including hot soups, spicy salads, rice pancakes, and various noodle dishes – well-made for a mixed crowd of locals and outsiders.

Tai Tung 659 S King St ⓣ206/622-7372. One of the district's oldest Cantonese restaurants, which has an incredibly extensive menu of traditional staples, some better than others; to get a dose of a few things at once, opt for one of the combo meals, which run around $8.

Belltown

Assaggio 2010 4th Ave between Leonora and Virginia sts ⓣ206/441-1399. Good Italian restaurant that sprinkles in some unexpected items, like fusilli with currants and pinenuts in cream sauce, among the typical moderately priced pizzas, pastas, and veal.

Crocodile Café 2200 2nd Ave ⓣ206/448-2114. Best known as one of Belltown's prime haunts for alternative music, and an affable diner by day, serving the biggest breakfasts in the city. Enjoy dishes like the *chilliques* (eggs or tofu with veggies, cheddar cheese, black beans, and salsa) under the gaze of stuffed animals, papier-mâché sculptures, and cheesy thrift-store album sleeves.

Cyclops 2421 1st Ave ⓣ206/441-1677. Bohemian though not too cheap, displaying jagged modern artwork overlooking the diner-style booths, where patrons munch on well-prepared dishes like pecan-crusted catfish and chile relleno with roasted squash, peppers, and pinenuts.

Dahlia Lounge 1904 4th Ave between Stewart and Virginia sts ⓣ206/682-4142. One of Seattle's most established upscale restaurants, and most famed for its seafood, of which the crabcakes are a specialty. Other main courses can imaginatively include squash tamales and apricot chicken.

FareStart 1902 2nd Ave between Stewart and Virginia sts ⓣ206/448-6422. Roomy restaurant dedicated to providing job training to the homeless, and serving up decent $7 lunch buffets of American staples, plus good desserts. On Thursday nights (by reservation, 4.30–8pm), guest chefs from upscale restaurants around town provide something more elaborate for around $15. Eight blocks away, at 2326 6th Ave, the *FareStart Café* offers soups, salads, and sandwiches (ⓣ206/374-8897).

Flying Fish 2234 1st Ave ⓣ206/728-8595. Though lacking the eponymous fish on the menu, this is a fine choice for all other kinds of seafood, serving up anything from familiar fare like ahi tuna to more adventurous entrees like monkfish and escolar.

Lampreia 2400 1st Ave at Battery St ⓣ206/443-3301. Very pricey Northwest Cuisine spot specializing in beef and fish, augmented with über-trendy ingredients like grilled organic polenta and white truffle mushrooms. Expect plenty of attitude if you're not wearing the right clothes.

Noodle Ranch 2228 2nd Ave between Blanchard and Bell sts ⓣ206/728-0463. Delicious pan-Asian cuisine starting at $10, offering imaginative noodle-based dishes and other creations in a casual atmosphere. The green curry is the chef's specialty and packs quite a punch.

Seattle Center and Queen Anne

The 5 Spot 1502 Queen Anne Ave N ⓣ206/285-SPOT. The most colorful of Queen Anne's cheap eateries, a Southern-style diner with specialties like the Tennessee Mountain Pone platter of corn-vegetable patties, the Truck Stop Pork Chop sandwich, and Coca-Cola cake – all good old-fashioned gut-busters.

Bahn Thai 409 Roy St ⓣ206/283-0444. Relaxed Thai spot with a decorous atmosphere and a long menu of well-spiced dishes – the seafood selection is especially varied and good, with imaginative salmon and squid options.

Bamboo Garden 364 Roy St ⓣ206/282-6616. Look at the menu here and you might expect the standard Chinese dishes, but everything is in fact made from vegetable-protein and 100-percent vegetable oil. Though fake meat may not be your thing, it's all pretty good, best topped with a peanut pudding (actually peanut soup) dessert.

Chinoise 12 Boston St ⓣ206/219-6911. Popular pan-Asian eatery with an eclectic range of choices, from *pad Thai* to tempura platters and *udon* noodles, though best for its sushi and sashimi. Adventurous diners might try a bite of *unaju* – broiled eel to the uninitiated. One of several citywide branches.

Chutneys 519 1st Ave N ⓣ206/284-6799. The best place in town for a sit-down Indian meal, and equally adept at meat tandooris and vegetarian curries; there's also a cheap, all-you-can-eat lunch buffet, plus locations in Capitol Hill, 605 15th Ave E (ⓣ206/726-1000), and in Wallingford Center, 1815 N 45th St (ⓣ206/634-1000).

Capitol Hill

611 Supreme 611 E Pine St ⓣ206/328-0292. French creperie with many savory and sweet crepes, the best of which are the *saumon-chèvre*, with smoked salmon and goat cheese, and the *épinard*, with spinach, roasted peppers, cambozola, and walnuts.

Byzantion 601 E Broadway at E Mercer St ⓣ206/325-7580. The best Greek food in town, reasonably priced, and served with enough pita bread to make the prospect of dessert unthinkable; notably good spinach pie and souvlaki.

Café Flora 2901 E Madison St at 29th Ave E ⓣ206/325-9100. Offers creatively crafted soups, salads, and entrees like wild mushroom curry and grilled seitan fish; the white-chocolate raspberry cheesecake is amazing. While the prices are expensive, the setting is pleasant, especially the stone patio wing, complete with trees and a fountain under a pyramid skylight.

Ezo Noodle Café 408 Broadway E ⓣ206/861-0222. Continental America's only taste of a compelling Japanese chain based in Tokyo, doling out delicious ramens (the dark shoyu with fish or the BBQ pork are both excellent), along with gyoza, teriyaki, and curry rice. The key words here are simple, traditional, and cheap.

Globe Cafe 1531 14th Ave between Pine and Pike sts ⓣ206/324-8815. Hard to beat for a Seattle food experience, with a tasty all-vegan menu of full meals, drinks, and desserts, and an unpretentiously goofy decor of globes, oddly shaped, painted salt shakers, and blackboards for patrons to doodle on. Also hosts evening poetry events Sundays and Tuesdays after closing time.

Gravity Bar first floor of Broadway Market, 401 Broadway E at Thomas ☎ 206/325-7186. The last word in postmodern vegetarian cuisine and decor, serving delicious rice-and-veggie dishes, meatless pizza, and more complex dishes as well, all in modernist surroundings; there's also a juice bar.

Kingfish Cafe 602 19th Ave E between E Mercer and E Roy sts ☎ 206/320-8757. Affordable Southern-styled food like griddle cakes and beans and rice, with terrific vintage soul and R&B music playing as you munch beneath large sepia-toned photos. The grilled catfish and shrimp can almost rival New Orleans fare.

Machiavelli 1215 Pine St at 12th Ave ☎ 206/621-7941. Despite the name, no scheming behind this place, just good Italian food, served in somewhat small portions and featuring tangy and creative pasta sauces. Try the penne with roasted red pepper pesto, sun-dried tomatoes, walnuts, and cream.

Piecora's 1401 E Madison St at E Pike St ☎ 206/322-9411. The best pizza parlor in a city not known for its pizza joints, with satisfyingly rich, flavorful and gooey pies and a friendly neighborhood atmosphere.

Siam on Broadway 616 Broadway E at E Roy St ☎ 206/324-0892. Perennially crowded and reasonably priced, an open-kitchen Thai restaurant with both counter and table seating; good for digging into familiar noodle and curry dishes that rank among the spiciest in the city.

Teapot 125 15th Ave E between E John St and E Denny Way ☎ 206/325-1010. Delicious all-vegan, mostly Asian food, with dozens of soups, curries, "hot pots," and "sizzling platters." Some of the house specialties, such as tofu prawns in tomato sauce, mimic the flavor and textures of seafood and meat dishes.

The University District

Araya's 4732 University Way NE between NE 47th and NE 50th sts ☎ 206/524-4332. Quality Thai restaurant presenting the usual staples, but the real reason to come here is for the $7 all-you-can-eat vegetarian buffet lunch.

Flowers 4247 University Way NE between NE 42nd and NE 43rd sts ☎ 206/633-1903. A bar and restaurant most notable for its lunchtime vegan buffet; choose from about twenty items, including good pasta dishes, for about $8.

Saigon Deli 4142 Brooklyn Ave NE between NE 41st and NE 42nd sts ☎ 206/634-2866. Hole-in-the-wall diner whips out fine Vietnamese dishes for eat-in or takeout. Most of the dishes are under $5; you won't go away hungry.

Silence Heart Nest 5247 University Way NE between NE 52nd and NE 55th sts ☎ 206/524-4008. Indian-leaning vegetarian menu, with daily specials and a rotating selection of desserts, served in a placid New-Age atmosphere. Dishes like veggie meatloaf are available, but it's better to stick with the Indian favorites, especially the *masala dosai* – crepes stuffed with spicy potatoes.

Tandoor 5024 University Way NE between NE 50th and NE 52nd sts ☎ 206/523-7477. Amid numerous Indian joints offering all-you-can-eat buffet lunches, an eatery standing out for having the lowest prices, though the food (mostly standards like curry, tandoori, and vindaloo dishes) is as tasty as that available at the pricier spots.

Magnolia

Chinook's 1900 W Nickerson St ☎ 206/283-HOOK. Popular both for its fresh seafood and its floor-to-ceiling view of the boats in Fishermen's Terminal. Vast menu encompasses many dishes beyond fish, but it's still worth checking out dishes like "Baked Salmon Chinook," cooked with sun-dried tomato-basil butter. *Little Chinook's*, next door, is a much less expensive fish bar.

Kinnaree 3311 W McGraw St ☎ 206/285-4460. Fine Thai restaurant whose menu allows you to order any item in vegetarian, meat, or seafood versions. The green coconut milk curry is particularly tasty.

Szmania's 3321 W McGraw St ☎ 206/284-7305. One of the finest neighborhood restaurants in the city, mixing German, Continental, and Northwest Cuisine on a menu that changes according to the season, with many inventive and tasty entrees – everything from German pork cutlets to butternut-squash ravioli.

Ballard

Hattie's Hat 5231 Ballard Ave NW ☎ 206/784-0175. Longstanding favorite for its hefty slabs of meatloaf and hamburgers, 2am nightly bar closing time, and colorful mix of hard-bitten old-timers and grungy hipsters.

Madame K's 5327 Ballard Ave NW ☎ 206/783-9710. Onetime bordello-turned-pizza joint, dishing out deep-dish meat pies and pastas with hefty portions and rich flavors. Not subtle, but worth it after a day prowling the antique stores.

Ray's Cafe 6049 Seaview Ave ☎ 206/789-4130. Always-popular seafood haunt that offers high-priced cuisine in its *Boathouse* downstairs, and more affordable items like salmon skewers and coconut prawns in the café above. Great waterside views add to the appeal.

Fremont and Wallingford

Asteroid Café 1605 N 45th St, Wallingford ⓣ206/547-2514. Humble coffee bar by day, groovy Italian spot by night, dishing out primo panini and pasta, as well as more unexpected items like calamari steak and grilled quail.
El Camino 607 N 35th St, Fremont ⓣ206/632-7303. Regional and affordable Mexican cuisine with a nouvelle twist, offering a tasty assortment of elaborately prepared dishes and home-made sodas. The rock shrimp quesadilla, with a margarita, is a nice start; the tamarind-glazed salmon and chili-flavored seared scallops are also worth a try.
Jitterbug 2114 N 45th St, Wallingford ⓣ206/547-6313. A hot spot for breakfast, with friendly waiters and adventurous wild-mushroom or "cactus cooker" (avocado, grilled squash, onion, and cheese) omelettes; get here early for weekend "blunch," when the small diner quickly reaches capacity.
Kabul 2301 N 45th St, Wallingford ⓣ206/545-9000. One of the more offbeat ethnic restaurant choices in town, an Afghan establishment with a menu of moderately priced kebabs and both veggie and meat entrees, as well as live sitar music on Tuesdays and Thursdays. Try the *qorma-i tarkari*, an Indian-like stew of cauliflower, carrots, potatoes, and rice.
Longshoreman's Daughter 3510 Fremont Place N, Fremont ⓣ206/633-5169. Valued not so much for its diner food – hearty, familiar fare like waffles, sandwiches, and eggs – as its funky vibe, with counter seating and heart-shaped chairs, which make it one of the best places to hang out in central Fremont.
Pontevecchio 710 N 34th St, Fremont ⓣ206/633-3989. Dark, cozy eight-tabled Italian bistro near the Fremont Bridge serving light but authentic meals of panini and pasta, served with exuberance. Occasional guitar and flamenco dance performances. Moderately priced.

The Seattle suburbs

Herbfarm 14590 NE 145th St, Woodinville ⓣ206/784-2222. Internationally renowned eatery specializing in elaborate dinners made with fresh ingredients and herbs of the Northwest. Each day's menu is finalized just hours before the meal, but seafood figures prominently in these nine-course, five-hour affairs. The prix-fixe menu ranges from $159 to $189/person.
I Love Sushi 11818 NE Eighth St, Bellevue ⓣ425/454-5706. You'll share the sentiment of this place's name after you finish dining on its wide range of affordable Japanese delicacies, among them fresh salmon, eel, mussels, quail eggs, and geoduck clams.
Waters Lakeside Bistro 1200 Carillon Point, Kirkland ⓣ425/803-5595. Inside the luxury *Woodmark* hotel, a top-notch restaurant with a superb lakeside setting, patio seating, and excellent Northwest Cuisine – predominantly seafood-based, with main plates like Dungeness crab cakes and seafood paella.

Cafés

Seattle is famed as a city in which **coffee** is consumed in vaster quantities, and with more enthusiasm, than any other metropolis in North America. It's not necessary to be an espresso connoisseur, however, to enjoy the friendly, funky ambience of its numerous **cafés**, which function as much as local pubs or bars as centers for low-key unwinding. As a hotbed of activity for both cutting-edge technology and the arts, Seattle provides a proliferation of cafés which are in effect multimedia spaces, offering Internet terminals, poetry readings, galleries, alternative music – even laundry facilities – along with the expected coffee, tea, snacks, and light meals. Whatever your preference – solitude, art, socializing, or a strong buzz – in Seattle there's a café to suit every taste and mood.

The best spot to begin your sampling of café culture is unquestionably **Capitol Hill**, but there are alternatives: for a taste of the bohemian scene, check out the cafés in **Fremont**; for a mix of alternative-chic and yuppie smugness, **Belltown**; for boisterous chat, the **University District**; for a blend of hipsters and the working class, **Pioneer Square**.

Downtown and Pioneer Square

Bookstore Bar & Cafe 1007 1st Ave ☎206/582-1506. Off the lobby of the *Alexis* hotel, a cozy, upscale spot for light lunches and dinners, but most notable for its books, international magazines, and newspapers for browsing, as well as its bourbons, ports, cognacs, and malt scotches – and rash of cigar-smokers.

Pegasus Coffee 711 3rd Ave at Cherry St ☎206/682-3113. In the lobby of the Dexter Horton Building, a more relaxing place to imbibe the java than the usual coffee bar, with brews of Pegasus beans.

Torrefazione Italia 320 Occidental Ave S at S Jackson St ☎206/624-5847. Pioneer Square espresso bar, with top-notch roast coffees in an Old World-styled setting, heightened by the outdoor seating area on the pedestrian section of Occidental Ave; it also sells fine Italian ceramics. Part of a chain with numerous other city branches.

Zeitgeist Art and Coffee 171 S Jackson St ☎206/583-0497. Mostly coffee, a few sandwiches and pastries, and modern art at this haunt at the heart of Pioneer Square's gallery scene. Also offers periodic showings of local and independent films. Another similarly artsy location is in Capitol Hill at 609 Summit Ave E (☎206/323-7841).

Belltown

Card Café 2321 2nd Ave ☎206/269-0662. Offers not only the usual bagels, coffee, and pastries, but also a large selection of funky cards, magnets, candles, and jigsaw puzzles.

Lux 2226 1st Ave ☎206/443-0962. Dark, moody coffeehouse with curious art and antiques – somewhere between high art and a thrift shop – with coffee drinks that are tasty and thoughtfully prepared. The ambience is just right for the student crowd, but far too hip for the burgeoning yuppie clientele.

Macrina 2408 1st Ave ☎206/448-4032. Café in the heart of the action on First Avenue, with both coffee and a bakery serving goodies like banana ginger muffins and squash harvest bread.

Seattle Center and Queen Anne

El Diablo Coffee Company 1811 Queen Anne Ave N ☎206/285-0693. Famed for its colorful artwork and furnishings, and for its powerful, eye-opening blends of Cuban-roasted java, but equally regarded for its savory sandwiches and pastries, and delicious fruit and chocolate desserts.

Uptown Espresso 525 Queen Anne Ave N ☎206/285-3757. Despite the name, located in Lower Queen Anne, catering to a loyal crowd of bleary-eyed morning regulars and late-night revelers – Seattle Center visitors in the know come here to knock back quality javas and munch on succulent pastries while the tourists head to *Starbucks*.

Capitol Hill

Bauhaus Books & Coffee 301 E Pine at Melrose Ave E ☎206/625-1600. Busy hangout for the dressed-in-black crowd, dispensing coffee and some teas in a self-consciously somber atmosphere (its name alluding to early-modernist architecture), with high chairs at the windowside counter. The small, artsy used-book section is largely devoted to architecture volumes.

Café Dilettante 416 E Broadway ☎206/329-6463. Though this pleasant café on the busiest stretch of Broadway in Capitol Hill does serve coffee, people come here more for the chocolate treats, the best in town. Does a big business in both takeout and eat-in service.

Capitol Hill Café 219 Broadway E ☎206/860-6858. The best of Seattle's virtual cafés dispenses muffins and espresso, but the chief attraction is the Web browsing, graphic design, computer games, and other high-tech activities, available on ten computers for ten cents a minute in a pleasant low-key, two-tiered lofty space.

Coffee Messiah 1554 E Olive Way at E Denny Way ☎206/860-7377. One of the most irreverent bohemian outposts in town, with its kitschy crucifixes, odd images of Christ, and a spark-emitting windup nun. They have coffee, too (albeit featuring a "Blood of Christ" blend of coffee beans), as well as chai, herbal tea, cider, juice, and occasional free live music.

Online Coffee Company 1720 E Olive Way ☎206/328-3731. Spacious and relaxed Internet café with coffee, beer, wine, and baked goods to go along with the $6/hr high-speed Internet access; the outside patio has a view of Puget Sound.

Victrola Coffee and Art 411 15th Ave E ☎206/325-6520. Another good choice for browsing at modern art, taking in a spoken-word or musical performance, and imbibing in rich brews and devouring a range of healthy snacks and light fare, some with a vegan slant.

Vivace Espresso 901 E Denny Way at Broadway ☎206/860-5869. Large-sized haunt for Capitol Hill's most serious coffee drinkers, run by self-proclaimed "espresso roasting and preparation specialists."

University District

Allegro Espresso Bar 4214 University Way NE ☎206/633-3030. One of the favorite haunts of those who take their coffee seriously, and something of a hangout for the university's more intellectual and international element. There are also computer terminals with Internet access (available only if you're also having something at the café).

Grand Illusion Espresso and Pastry 1405 NE 50th St at University Way ☎206/523-3935. The homiest of the U District cafés, with a living-room feel and good snacks, as well as basic light meals and some outdoor seating, and a great place to peruse a newspaper or book for a couple of hours. Adjoins the Grand Illusion cinema.

Fremont and Wallingford

Still Life In Fremont 709 N 35th St ☎206/547-9850. One of Fremont's best hangouts has breakfast specials, sandwiches, quiches, and the offbeat dishes like corn tortilla pie. Its big draws, though, are the large wooden tables and benches, popular for reading and studying. Quirky art and occasional free live music also make this a unique, appealing spot.

Zoka 2200 N 56th St ☎206/545-4277. Classic Wallingford coffeehouse in a comfortable setting, with weekend jazz and country-music performers; not as weird as the ones in the hippier districts, but fine for brews and relaxation.

Drinking and nightlife

When you consider the city's hip reputation, Seattle's low-key **nightlife** can seem pretty provincial at times, with the usual AOR cover bands and lounge crooners you find in most other cities. Nonetheless, there's plenty going on here most nights, and the scene is only sleepy in comparison to those of the biggest American cities. The drinking scene is spirited and (usually) non-threatening, music and dancing are staged in friendly and comfortable settings, cover charges are low, and dress codes only enforced in snooty, self-important places that aren't worth entering to begin with.

Bars

Although Seattle's cafés are noticeably more popular than its **bars**, you still don't need to look far to find a watering hole in any neighborhood. There are plenty of typically raucous, hell-for-leather joints and sedate local hangouts, but the bar scene here is generally quite varied. The most interesting bars are typically found in the more bohemian or culturally diverse zones, such as **Pioneer Square**, **Capitol Hill**, and **Fremont**. Some Seattle bars bear at least a passing resemblance to British pubs, or cafés that serve alcohol, complete with singer-songwriters, art displays, and DJs on occasion. Others cater to discriminating palates by specializing in cigars, wines, whiskeys, or bourbons. **Microbreweries**, defined as operations that produce less than 15,000 barrels a year, are big in the Northwest, and some of them run their own onsite bars, including a few which are listed in this chapter. In Washington State, you must be 21 or older to drink legally and bars generally close around 2am.

Downtown

Kells Irish Pub 1916 Post Alley, Pike Place Market ☎206/728-1916. Free-spirited Irish bar and restaurant in a central location, with patio seating and nightly performances by Irish-oriented folk and rock groups.

Pike Pub & Brewery 1415 1st Ave ☎206/622-6044. Small craft brewery serving its own respectable beers and numerous bottled brands; also offers a large wine list and extensive fish- and pizza-oriented menu. The sprawling multileveled, nonsmoking premises are slick but unpretentious.

Vito's Madison Grill 927 Ninth Ave ☎206/682-2695. Old-style Italian bar, with kitschy decor (red vinyl and lush carpet), a gregarious crowd of graying regulars, and double-barreled drinks that may leave you gasping for air. Later on, a more youthful contingent takes over, bringing with it karaoke, techno, and retro-disco tunes.

Pioneer Square

Central Saloon 207 1st Ave S at S Washington St ☎206/622-0209. Bills itself as "Seattle's oldest saloon" (established 1892), and consistently crowded owing to its location at the epicenter of the tourist district.

Doc Maynard's 610 1st Ave between Cherry and James ☎206/682-4649. The meeting point for Bill Speidel's Underground Tours (p.265) is also a good 1900s-style bar, but is only open to the larger public on weekend nights. Not the place to go if you want to avoid hordes of tourists, but still worthwhile for its boozy, libertine atmosphere and pile-driving rock bands.

Dutch Ned's Saloon 206 1st Ave S at S Washington St ☎206/340-8859. Hosts the "Seattle Slam" poetry competition/event every Wednesday night at 9pm for $3. If you'd rather chug a brewski than wax eloquent, it has 32 beers on tap.

Pioneer Square Saloon 73 Yesler Way ☎206/628-6444. Part of a restored 1914 brick hotel, a classic watering hole featuring fifteen microbrews, an amiable crowd of boozy regulars, and poetry-slam nights as well.

Belltown

Belltown Pub 2322 1st Ave ☎206/728-4311. Set in the heart of Belltown's rapidly gentrifying First Avenue, a high-ceilinged spot in an 1880s building with eighteen microbrews on tap and above-average, Italian-oriented bar food.

Nite Lite 1926 2nd Ave ☎206/443-0899. An essential nexus for young and old, where grizzled regulars rub shoulders with black-clad newbies, amid decor like vinyl walls and neon lights that look at least thirty years out of date. The main attraction, of course, is the liquor – strong, dark, and authentic.

Panther Room 2421 1st Ave ☎206/441-1677. Attached to the *Cyclops* restaurant, a swinging lounge with excellent, quirky drinks like the appropriately potent Latin Fireball and Dragon Mary, and even good bar food like *saltimbocca* chicken and pistachio-crusted brie.

Two Bells Tavern 2313 4th Ave between Bell and Battery ☎206/441-3050. A Belltown institution, drawing artistic and literary types as well as overflow from the Downtown business crowd. Occasional free live music.

Capitol Hill

Bad Juju Lounge 1518 11th Ave ☎206/709-9951. Dark, swirling techno beats and eerie artworks (nerve-jangling portraits and snake skeletons) are the main draws to this stylish, often-packed hangout, which attracts both slummers and scenesters for its hip ambience and bracing cocktails.

Comet Tavern 922 E Pike St just off Broadway ☎206/323-9853. The oldest bar in Capitol Hill: a smoky dive and rocker's hangout. While the drinks are nothing special, the grunge atmosphere is, with authentic axe-wielders and bleary-eyed burnouts mixing with youthful hangers-on. An offshoot, the *Satellite Lounge*, 1118 E Pike St (daily 11.30am–2am; ☎206/324-4019), also offers live music, but better food and cleaner surroundings.

Linda's Tavern 707 E Pike St at Harvard Ave E ☎206/325-1220. One of Capitol Hill's most happening bars attracts an alternative/underground rock crowd that gets more crowded and intense as the night wears on. DJs spin two or three nights a week (no cover); blues and soul nights are recommended.

University District

Big Time Brewery and Alehouse 4133 University Way NE ☎206/545-4509. Longstanding microbrewery whose ales are the stock in trade – try the Bhagwan's Best IPA – but featuring other drinks as well, such as the potent Old Wooly barley wine, all served in a large space with hardwood decor and a shuffleboard in the back room.

Blue Moon Tavern 712 NE 45th St ☎206/633-6267. A well-loved dive with a literary reputation: Dylan Thomas, Allen Ginsberg, and Jack Kerouac are some of the celebrities who passed through its doors. It retains a loose bohemian atmosphere and hosts occasional readings and musical performances. Wide range of local beers.

Ballard

Hale's Ales 4301 Leary Way NW ☎206/782-0737. Handcrafted English-styled ales from the third-oldest microbrewery in the Northwest, highlighted by the hearty Dublin Style Stout, as well as a decent menu of pub-styled food. The gracefully designed, spacious interior is highlighted by a bar with porcelain tap fixtures.

People's Pub 5429 Ballard Ave NW ☎206/783-6521. Belt-breaking German cuisine mixed with belly-filling draughts straight out of Deutschland, including the likes of Schlenkerla Rauchbier – a smoked beer with an almost overwhelming flavor – plus wine, scotch, and curious bar fare like deep-fried pickles.

Fremont and Wallingford

Dad Watson's 3601 Fremont Ave N ☎206/632-6505. Seattle outpost of an Oregon microbrewery chain, featuring excellent craft beers like Hammerhead and Terminator Stout. Other branches are *Six Arms* in Capitol Hill, 300 E Pike St (☎206/223-1698), and *McMenamins Queen Anne Hill*, 300 Roy St #105 (☎206/285-4722).

Murphy's 1928 N 45th St at Meridian Ave N, Wallingford ☎206/634-2110. Often featuring live Irish music on Friday and Saturday nights for around a $3 cover. They pour a nice Guinness, the Irish coffee is good, and there's a wide selection of Northwest beers.

Triangle Lounge 3507 Fremont Place N ☎206/632-0880. So-named because of the small, triangular outdoor seating area, Fremont's best tavern is a relaxed affair that serves grilled fish and salads along with microbrews and pear cider. The outdoor tables are great for people watching on sunny days.

Live music

Seattle's **live music** scene got a lot of notice in the early 1990s, particularly when grunge gained national attention due to Nirvana's rise and the influence of Sub Pop Records (see p.269), but today you'll rarely find a gig by the few remnants of that scene. There's still plenty of **alternative rock** to see, however, and the best spots are concentrated Downtown and still in Belltown – though gentrification has undercut the underground band scene there to a large degree. Pioneer Square is the place for **blues** and, to a lesser extent, **jazz**. The Pioneer Square **joint cover night** scheme allows you into a bunch of bars and clubs – *Bohemian Café*, *Central Saloon*, *Doc Maynard's*, *Fenix*, *Larry's Blues Café*, *New Orleans*, *Old Timer's Café*, and *Zasu* – for one blanket fee ($5 weekdays, $10 weekends). **Folk** and **acoustic** singer-songwriters are easy to find throughout the city in cafés and the more genteel bars. **Reggae** and **world music** bands play with less frequency, but are scattered here and there.

Rock and pop

Ballard Firehouse 5429 Russell Ave NW ☎206/784-3516. Nightly live music, mostly rock and blues, with a large dance floor. There are occasional reggae, dance, and hip-hop nights, and the odd big-name mainstream act, though most of these are way past their prime. Prices vary from seven-bands-for-$10 deals to $30 advance tickets.

Crocodile Café 2200 2nd Ave, Belltown ☎206/441-5611. By day a diner (p.287), by night a hip and intimate rock club, one of the best Seattle spots to see most any kind of music, from jazz, rock, and R&B to poetry readings and grunge. One of the hippiest places in town, albeit a bit short on space. Usual cover $6–10.

Fenix 315 2nd Ave S, Pioneer Square ☎206/467-1111. A venue where it's hard to predict what you'll see, from rockabilly and swing to world beat and 1980s cover bands. There's also a dance club, *Fenix Underground*, on the same premises.

Gibson's 116 Stewart St, Downtown ☎206/448-6369. Straightforward bar and grill near Pike Place Market, presenting some of the most cacophonous and chaotic live shows you'll likely ever hear (Thurs–Sat), by completely unknown rock and punk groups with something to prove and plenty of testosterone to spare. $3–6.

Moore Theater 1932 2nd Ave, Belltown ☎206/443-1744. 1907 former vaudeville auditorium seats nearly 1500 and sometimes hosts exciting, up-and-coming rock and pop bands. $25–40.

Paramount 911 Pine St, Downtown ☎206/682-1414. On the eastern edge of Downtown, a large movie palace, built in 1928 for vaudeville shows and silent films, now seating around three thousand and hosting musicals, comedy, rock- and pop-concerts, silent film retrospectives, and other events. $25–90.

Showbox 1426 1st Ave, Downtown ☎206/628-3151. With a capacity of a thousand, a space near Pike Place Market that's the best place to catch touring acts yet to make the leap to bigger arenas, along with well-regarded regional bands, usually with an indie slant. Grab a drink in the venue's adjacent *Green Room* bar before the show. $5–20.

Jazz

Dimitriou's Jazz Alley 2033 6th Ave, Belltown ⓣ206/441-9729. The best of the primary jazz venues in Seattle, if a bit mainstream, presenting a steady march of notable out-of-towners. Heavy on established veterans, who often headline for a week or so, with the occasional blues or R&B act. $15–35.

Tula's 2214 2nd Ave, Belltown ⓣ206/443-4221. Jazz of all stripes every evening, mostly from regional unknowns, with jam sessions Sunday nights and live vocal jams some Monday evenings. Also open for food and drink starting at 3pm. $5–12.

Zasu 608 1st Ave, Pioneer Square ⓣ206/682-1200. Featuring funk and disco on Fridays and Saturdays, this restaurant otherwise offers mellow, easygoing jazz tunes, and is a part of the joint cover night deal for the district (see opposite).

Blues and folk

Hop Vine Pub 507 15th Ave E, Capitol Hill ⓣ206/328-3120. Mostly local live acts, with an emphasis on mellow acoustic folk, blues, and jazz – with the occasional open-mike event – for little or no cover and best accompanied by the pub's quality variety of microbrews.

Larry's Blues Café 209 1st Ave S, Pioneer Square ⓣ206/624-7665. Regional blues performers, along with R&B and funk musicians. Like the two listings below, part of the area's joint cover night deal (see opposite).

New Orleans 114 1st Ave S at Yesler Way, Pioneer Square ⓣ206/622-2563. A compelling attraction for hearing roots rock, blues, jazz, and Cajun tunes, best when zydeco is featured. The Cajun cuisine isn't bad, either. $5–15.

Old Timer's Café 620 1st Ave S, Pioneer Square ⓣ206/623-9800. A crowded tavern where blues and R&B are featured on Tuesday and Wednesday, karaoke on Monday and Tuesday, and frenetic live salsa on the weekends. $5–10, occasional free shows.

World-beat and reggae

Bohemian Café 111 Yesler Ave, Pioneer Square ⓣ206/447-1514. Far from the most bohemian place in town, though it does feature decent reggae and world music, including the occasional big name. $5–25.

Century Ballroom 915 E Pine, 2nd Floor, Downtown ⓣ206/324-7263. Major world-music acts from all over the globe swing through this spacious ballroom with a huge wooden dance floor. It also offers swing nights (Sun & Wed 9pm; $5) and salsa nights (Thurs 9pm, $5; and Sat 8.30pm, $7), as well as infrequent tango nights on Fridays (9.30pm; $7). Concerts $10–30.

Tractor Tavern 5213 Ballard Ave NW, Ballard ⓣ206/789-3599. Zydeco, Irish, and bluegrass, with the occasional high-profile international act. Sometimes a better alternative than similar spots in Pioneer Square. $7–15.

Clubs

Compared to its bars and cafés, Seattle's **clubs** are few in number. Still, the majority are very relaxed, with nonexistent dress codes, and all musical tastes and sexual orientations welcomed. Almost all of the noteworthy clubs are situated in Pioneer Square or Capitol Hill, specializing in varied music and/or DJs on a nightly basis, and it's not at all unusual for the same venue to feature gothic-industrial, 1980s New Wave, and electronica in the same week. With these possibilities, not to mention the way some clubs will mix in live music, comedy, or poetry readings, consulting the entertainment listings in the *Seattle Weekly* or *The Stranger* is essential. (See box for gay-oriented clubs.) **Cover charges** are usually in the $5-12 range, with prices varying according to the night of the week. Additionally, some clubs have regular free or ultra-cheap nights, and the cover can vary according to the time of the night; early in the evening it may be free, after 9pm $5, and ultimately $10 that same night for the peak crowd.

Baltic Room 1207 Pine St, Capitol Hill ⓣ206/625-4444. Divided into bar, music, and balcony sections, with a view of the Space Needle from the front window. It has more live music (of an eclectic, alternative variety) than most DJ-oriented clubs do.

Catwalk 172 S Washington St, Pioneer Square ⓣ206/622-1863. Best known as a goth hangout, but also an energetic, sometimes eye-opening, dance club and live-music spot where you can hear anything from metal to techno to rock to industrial.

Gay and lesbian Seattle

Gay and lesbian culture in Seattle centers around **Capitol Hill** – unsurprising given the neighborhood's history of progressive politics. In fact, many gays and lesbians have moved to Seattle from other parts of the Pacific Northwest (and indeed the US) due to the city's longstanding liberalism and increasingly cosmopolitan character. The main **publication** for the gay community is the weekly *Seattle Gay News* (25¢; ⓦwww.sgn.org), available at newsstands and larger bookshops throughout the city. It includes an events calendar and coverage of both political and arts activity. Meanwhile, *Beyond the Closet*, 518 E Pike St, Capitol Hill (ⓣ206/322-4609, ⓦwww.beyondthecloset.com), is the best-stocked gay & lesbian **bookstore** in the Pacific Northwest; it's also a good source of information for local and regional events and news. Columbia Funmaps (ⓦwww.funmaps.com) publishes a handy map of gay Seattle for tourists, and the biannual *Lesbian & Gay Pink Pages Northwest* (free; ⓦwww.lesgaypinkpages.com/seattle), available at various cafés and shops throughout town, lists companies supportive of the gay and lesbian community and includes a comprehensive resource directory. On the last Sunday in June, Seattle's gay and lesbian **Pride Parade and Freedom Rally** takes over a dozen blocks on Capitol Hill's main strip, Broadway; it's one of the city's most exuberant events, drawing some 75,000 participants and spectators.

Bars and clubs

Manray 514 E Pine St, Capitol Hill ⓣ206/568-0750. Low-key, upscale "video bar" with retro-60s futuristic decor and 1980s music videos, plus an outdoor patio with wooden deck and fountain. No dancing, but some live entertainment.

Neighbours 1509 Broadway E, Capitol Hill ⓣ206/324-5358. Broadway's most popular gay nightclub, and the place to go if you want to dance yourself into delirium to loud, throbbing beats. Not too musically adventurous, though daily variety is ensured by drag, disco, and 1980s nights. Increasingly straight in recent years.

Re-Bar 1114 Howell St, First Hill ⓣ206/233-9873. Seattle's hottest dance spot, with an ever-shifting nightly focus that encompasses acid jazz, hip-hop, funk, soul, and Latin. Long-running Queer Disco Night happens every Thursday at 9pm. Also some live music, as well as occasional theater.

Thumper's 1500 E Madison St, Capitol Hill ⓣ206/328-3800. Combination bar/restaurant serving Northwest Cuisine and attracting a friendly professional crowd, with occasional cabaret performances; rustic, wood-paneled setting with a fireplace lounge, patio, and views over Downtown.

Timberline Spirits 2015 Boren Ave, Downtown ⓣ206/883-0242. Looking a bit like a ski chalet, a country-and-western line-dancing club with occasional live music, drawing gay men, lesbians, and straights to its large wooden dance floor. Line-dancing and two-stepping lessons from 7.30 to 9pm on Tuesdays, with the proper dancing starting immediately afterward. Colorful Monday karaoke (9pm–1am) is also worth a try.

Wild Rose 1021 E Pike St, Capitol Hill ⓣ206/324-9210. Seattle's most popular lesbian bar, and a comfortable mixing point for having a bite (the menu has a pretty wide selection), playing pool or darts, or just hanging out. If you want something livelier, Thursday through Saturday evenings are dance nights.

Chop Suey 1325 E Madison St, Capitol Hill ⓣ206/324-8000. Intentionally kitschy dance club and live-music venue decorated with leopard-print designs and Chinese lanterns, presenting an array of DJs on some nights (hip-hop, house, funk), dance bands on others, and a chaotic mix of instruments and turntables on occasion.

DV8 131 Taylor N ⓣ206/448-0888. A few blocks east of the Seattle Center, a converted roller rink that plays host to a nice range of beats, from house and garage to hip-hop and jungle, and periodically offers live shows by rock and dance bands. All ages.

Last Supper Club 124 S Washington St, Pioneer Square ⓣ206/748-9975. Two dance floors with computerized lighting effects at a chic spot that varies the DJ attack from night to night, from trance to a "jungle femme fatale invasion" to acid house, Latin, and salsa.

Vogue 1516 11th Ave, Capitol Hill ⓣ206/324-5778. One of the older Seattle club scene institutions, and still packing in youthful, edgy crowds to sounds that vary from new wave and gothic to the more industrial-oriented, ever-popular Sunday Fetish Night, and kinkier fare like a vamp drag show and talent contest. $3–5.

Performing arts and film

Seattle's **performing arts** scene is relatively sophisticated, particularly in the realm of **theater**. A dozen or so bright and innovative theatrical companies rework the classics and devise contemporary plays, and the city's a magnet for hopeful young actors, many of whom are marking time behind the craft stalls in Pike Place Market. There's also a fair demand for art and classic **movies**, shown in a fine collection of small, atmospheric cinemas.

Two alternative weeklies, the *Seattle Weekly* and *The Stranger*, are free from boxes on the streets and numerous cafés and stores, and are good for arts **listings**. The Friday edition of the *Seattle Post Intelligencer* contains live music and entertainment details, as does the "Ticket" supplement in the Friday edition of the *Seattle Times*. For **tickets** to the shows and various goings-on around town, TicketMaster (ⓦwww.ticketmaster.com) is the main vendor; otherwise, check with the relevant venue. Ticket Window (ⓣ206/325-6500 or 206/324-2744, ⓦwww.ticketwindowonline.com) runs the Ticket Ticket service, which sells day-of-show theater and concert tickets at half-price. Outlets are at the Pike Place Market information booth, First Avenue and Pike Street (Tues–Sun noon–6pm), and Broadway Market, second level, 401 Broadway E, Capitol Hill (Tues–Sat noon–7pm, Sun noon–6pm); tickets go on sale daily at noon, and are walk-up-only and cash-only.

Classical music, dance, and opera

Seattle's main options for **classical music**, **dance**, and **opera** are all worthwhile institutions that often put on compelling productions. They mostly revolve around venues located in the **Seattle Center**, though a few alternative sites can be found scattered throughout the city. **Ticket prices** are all over the place; as a rule, Benaroya Hall and Seattle Center performances cost the most, running anywhere from $15–100, while alternative performances anywhere else often cost a fraction of this.

Classical music and opera

Meany Theatre near the intersection of 15th Ave NE and NE 40th St ⓣ206/543-4880 or 1-800/859-5342, ⓦwww.meany.org. On the University of Washington campus, the 1200-seat theater stages classical music, world dance, opera, world music, and theatrical events, many featuring performers of international repute.

Northwest Chamber Orchestra ⓣ206/343-0445, ⓦwww.nwco.org. This thirty-year-old company presents concerts at Benaroya Hall, whose acoustics are rated as among the finest in the world (see p.262), as well as the Seattle Art Museum and Volunteer Park, with a wide repertoire ranging from Bach to Shostakovich to brand-new pieces.

Seattle Opera ⓣ206/389-7676, ⓦwww.seattleopera.org. The opera has brand-new digs at Marion Oliver McCaw Hall, whose dramatic modernist design and enhanced acoustics provide quite the spectacle. The operatic fare, however, is less surprising – mainly the usual Italian and German heavyweights, with more unfamiliar pieces thrown in only rarely.

Seattle Symphony at Benaroya Hall ⓣ206/215-4747, ⓦwww.seattlesymphony.org. Under the direction of conductor Gerard Schwarz and hosting concerts by the likes of pianist Van Cliburn and the Kronos Quartet, with the requisite light pops fare.

Dance

On the Boards 100 W Roy St, Queen Anne ⓣ206/217-9888, ⓦwww.ontheboards.org. In addition to its theater program (see below), stages cutting-edge dance events, often of a multidisciplinary nature.

Pacific Northwest Ballet ⓣ206/441-2424, ⓦwww.pnb.org. When not touring internationally, the Ballet puts on around seven programs from September to June, with the most popular being a December staging of Tchaikovsky's *Nutcracker*.

Spectrum Dance Theater at Madrona Dance Studio, 800 Lake Washington Blvd ⓣ206/325–4161, ⓦwww.Spectrumdance.org. One of the more prominent jazz-dance companies in the US, with a wide-ranging repertoire.

Theater

Theater is one of Seattle's strongest suits, and there's never a shortage of dramatic options, from sweeping reinterpretations of the classics and big-budget musical spectaculars to tiny experimental works. **Tickets** for prestigious performances at venues in the Seattle Center can cost more than $40, whereas many smaller shows around town often cost $10 or less. The scene is at its most adventurous during the **Seattle Fringe Festival** (late–Sept to early–Oct, ⓣ206/526-1959, ⓦwww.seattlefringe.org), which stages events in more than half a dozen Capitol Hill locations; tickets are usually in the $6–20 range.

A Contemporary Theatre (ACT) Kreielsheimer Place, 700 Union St, Downtown ⓣ206/292-7676, ⓦwww.acttheatre.org. A bit mainstream for a purported contemporary drama company, but it has put on world premieres of risk-taking productions as well as adventurous new interpretations of classic works. Check ahead, as the theater has recently flirted with bankruptcy due to cuts in arts grants from the state. Sept–May. Ticket prices can be as low as $5, or more than $40 for good seats.

Consolidated Works 500 Boren Ave N, Downtown ⓣ206/860-5245, ⓦwww.conworks.org. Hip arts center whose theatrical shows often involve multimedia – mainly film, music, and the visual arts – with the aesthetic emphasis strongly on the quirky, conceptual, and alternative. Prices vary.

Fifth Avenue Theatre 1308 5th Ave, Downtown ⓣ206/625-1418, ⓦwww.5thavenuetheatre.org. Seattle theater at its glitziest, located in a gigantic 1926 vaudeville house that replicates the throne room of China's Forbidden City, presenting mainstream musicals with big-name stars. $25–50.

Intiman Theatre Seattle Center ⓣ206/269-1900, ⓦwww.intiman.org. Classics and premieres of bolder new works, along with the occasional surprise like a Spalding Gray monologue. $25–45.

Northwest Actors Studio 1100 E Pike St, Capitol Hill ⓣ206/324-6328, ⓦwww.nwactorsstudio.org. A theater-arts center that, in addition to offering acting courses, puts on a performance calendar with a wide scope: comedy, Shakespeare, and the ultra-avant-garde are all fair game. Tickets are usually $10 or less.

On the Boards 100 W Roy St, Queen Anne ⓣ206/217-9888, ⓦwww.ontheboards.org. In addition to its contemporary dance program, challenging contemporary theater is also performed, often mixing dance and drama in the same production. Prices vary.

Open Circle 429 Boren Ave N, Downtown ⓣ206/382-4250, ⓦwww.opencircletheater.org. A fifty-seater that's one of the city's more intimate

Seattle Festivals

Seattle has several outstanding **festivals**, many of them based at the Seattle Center. For four days at the beginning of September, **Bumbershoot** (Ⓣ206/281-7788, Ⓦwww.bumbershoot.org) presents a mammoth multi-event extravaganza that's one of the city's best parties. Musical acts range from the famous to the obscure, with plenty of film, comedy, and theater, too. All in all, some five hundred acts perform at twenty different venues around town. Less well-known outside of Seattle, but just as popular, the **Northwest Folk Festival** (Ⓣ206/684-7300, Ⓦwww.nwfolklife.org), on Memorial Day weekend, attracts 200,000 visitors and six thousand participants for all types of traditional music, including bluegrass, Celtic, and world music, along with crafts, ethnic food, dance, and storytelling. **Seafair** (Ⓣ206/728-0123, Ⓦwww.seafair.com), in July and August, is a three-week celebration of Northwest maritime culture, held at various locations and including maneuvers by the Navy's Blue Angels squad, hydroplane races on Lake Washington, and milk-carton races on Green Lake. Finally, the **Fremont Fair & Solstice Parade** (Ⓣ206/633-4409, Ⓦwww.fremontfair.com), in late June, is Seattle's most enjoyable neighborhood celebration, with hundreds of food stalls and arts vendors, plus a parade allowing only human-powered floats and costumes, and followed by a pageant at the end of the route in Gasworks Park.

playhouses; its own company gives several shows and workshop performances each year, with content from Jean Genet to rock musicals. Around $15.

Seattle Children's Theatre Charlotte Martin Theatre, Seattle Center Ⓣ206/441-3322, Ⓦwww.sct.org. Half a dozen mainstage productions each year from a company that also tours Seattle schools. Sept–June; $15–20.

Seattle Repertory Company 155 Mercer St, Seattle Center Ⓣ206/443-2222. Oldest and most established company in town, performing popular contemporary material, with a dash of the classics, at Bagley Wright Theatre. A second stage in the same facility, Leo K. Theatre, has smaller-scaled works. Oct–May; tickets $10–45.

Film

Seattle has enough quality **movie** venues that you can enjoy foreign art-films, oddball independent cinema, or mainstream Hollywood blockbusters in a variety of different settings. The most interesting and atmospheric are the **repertory theaters** in Capitol Hill and the U District, many of which are housed in classic buildings that are either comfortably dilapidated or spruced up with recent renovations. There are also several **film festivals** in Seattle, highlighted by the Seattle International Film Festival in the spring (Ⓣ206/464-5830, Ⓦwww.seattlefilm.com).

Admiral Twin 2347 California Ave SW, West Seattle Ⓣ206/938-3456. 1938 Streamline Moderne charmer with a nautical theme: boatlike motifs on the facade, interior designs of whales and etched-in-glass seahorses, and two auditoriums called Port 1 and Port 2. *Rocky Horror Picture Show* on the first Saturday of the month (11.30pm).

Cinerama 2100 4th Ave, Belltown Ⓣ206/441-3080, Ⓦwww.seattlecinerama.com. Massive facility with state-of-the-art sound and picture quality. Features a modern 70mm screen for showing the latest blockbusters and a 90-by-30-foot screen with two thousand vertical panels for experiencing epics old and new.

Egyptian 801 E Pine St, Capitol Hill Ⓣ206/323-4978. Housed in an old Masonic Temple, the Art Deco headquarters of the annual Seattle International Film Festival.

Grand Illusion 1403 NE 50th St, University District Ⓣ206/523-3935, Ⓦwww.wigglyworld.org. Seattle's best repertory house, a small venue holding seventy seats and featuring an archival projection booth. The programming is challenging and first-rate: director retrospectives, little-seen foreign films, and independents.

Harvard Exit 807 E Roy St, Capitol Hill ⓣ206/323-8986. Well-worn building at the northern edge of Broadway shows a consistent program of left-of-center current releases and festival films.

Little Theatre 608 19th Ave E at E Mercer St ⓣ206/675-2055, ⓦwww.wigglyworld.org. Indeed little, holding only about fifty seats, this non-profit cinema puts on an eclectic, often daring selection of independent and foreign films, as well as some overlooked nuggets from the past.

Seven Gables 911 NE 50th St at Roosevelt Way ⓣ206/632-8820. Very cozy and attractive 1925 two-story home and former dance hall at the edge of the U District, showing mainly independent fare.

Varsity 4329 University Way NE, University District ⓣ206/632-3131. A trio of theaters from 1940, running one or two art-house movies every day, including old classics, documentaries, foreign films, and newly released independents.

Sports and outdoor activities

With temperatures that seldom dip below freezing and a close proximity to some of the most scenic mountains and waterways of North America, Seattle is well suited for year-round **outdoor activities**. The ubiquitous rain hardly stops the pace of hiking, climbing, and biking during the colder months, and most weekend campers and sailors find plenty of opportunities to explore the outdoors, regardless of the weather.

Major **sports franchises** didn't arrive here until the 1960s and 1970s, and were slow to catch on. Now, buoyed by the recent addition of two of the best venues in all of sports, the city has embraced its professional sports teams with fervent enthusiasm.

Spectator sports

Seattle's successful and widely popular major league **baseball** team, the Mariners, play at Safeco Field, which hosted its first game in July 1999 (tickets at ⓣ206/622-HITS, ⓦseattle.mariners.mlb.com). Tickets range from $6 for the cheapest seats (in the centerfield bleachers) to $45 for the most expensive (the lower box section).

When there's not a game going on, baseball aficionados may find it enjoyable to take the hour-long tours of the stadium (April–Oct usually daily 10.30am & 12.30pm, Nov–March Tues–Sat 12.30 & 2.30pm; $7, kids $3), which admit visitors into some otherwise off-limits areas, including the dugouts, the clubhouse, and the press box.

Basketball's SuperSonics (or just "Sonics") play at Key Arena in the Seattle Center (ⓣ206/283-DUNK, ⓦwww.nba.com/sonics); the range of prices is almost ridiculous, running $11–325.

The resident professional **football** team, the Seattle Seahawks (ⓣ1-888/NFL-HAWK, ⓦwww.seahawks.com), plays at the new Seahawks Stadium (800 Occidental Ave S; tickets at ⓣ1-888/NFL—HAWK, ⓦwww.seahawks.com); tickets range from $20 to $280. For an up-close, behind-the-scenes look at this glorious $425 million, 67,000-seat facility for an improving pigskin squad, 90-minute tours of the stadium are available to the public (Thurs–Mon 12.30 & 2.30pm; $7, kids $5; reserve at ⓣ206/381-7582).

The University of Washington's football team, the Huskies, play at Husky Stadium on campus, near Lake Washington; tickets (ⓣ206/543-2200,

Ⓦwww.gohuskies.com) cost $32–36 for reserved seats, $16–18 for general admission to the bleachers.

Biking

Despite its rainy climate, hilly topography, and crowded roads, Seattle has a great number of **bicyclists** and once you spend a bit of time in the city it becomes clear why: there are about thirty miles of bike/pedestrian trails and nearly one hundred miles of marked bike routes. Although you'll have a hard time finding level routes unless you stick close to the lakes, the semi-mountainous terrain guarantees a good workout, and the scenery is often magnificent.

The most popular route is the twelve-mile **Burke-Gilman Trail**, which starts near Eighth Avenue NW and NW 43rd Street in Ballard and follows the banks of the Lake Washington Ship Canal, Lake Union, and western Lake Washington, passing through such areas as central Fremont, Gasworks Park, and the U District. The path is also open to joggers and walkers; at its northern end, it connects to the ten-mile Sammamish River Trail, which brings riders over to Redmond in the Eastside.

Another good route is the stretch of **Lake Washington Boulevard** that starts at the Arboretum (see p.281) and skirts the lake's edge for a few miles before terminating at Seward Park, passing through such attractive districts as Madison Park, Madrona, and Mount Baker. Even better, the southern end of the route is closed to automotive traffic from 10am to 6pm on the second Saturday and third Sunday of the month between May and September.

Far more challenging, and quite stunning, is **Magnolia Boulevard**, which climbs a steep hill from the Magnolia Bridge to Discovery Park, passing gorgeous cliffside views of Puget Sound en route. For more rural terrain, there's great biking in **Vashon Island** (p.320) and **Lopez Island** (p.331).

Bikes can be **rented** at Blazing Saddles, 1230 Western Ave, Downtown (Ⓣ206/341-9994); Gregg's, 7007 Woodlawn Ave NE, Green Lake (Ⓣ206/523-1822 Ⓦwww.greggscycles.com); Bicycle Center, 4529 Sandpoint Way NE, Sand Point (Ⓣ206/523-8300); and Al Young Bike & Ski, 3615 NE 45th St, University District (Ⓣ206/524-2642). Rental rates tend to fluctuate from $5–12 per hour, or $20–45 per day, depending on the proximity of the bike shop to major attractions. If you're planning on doing a lot of cycling while you're in the area, call the bicycle division of the city's transportation department at Ⓣ206/684-7583; leave your name and address (or fill out an online request form at Ⓦwww.cityofseattle.net/transportation/bikemaps), and they'll send you the free and very handy *Seattle Bicycling Map*, which outlines bicycle routes and lists cycling regulations. Other transportation department maps offer detailed views of the Burke-Gilman Trail, as well as routes in the U District and Downtown, among other places.

Running

Running is big in Seattle in all kinds of weather, and every lunch break finds the waterfront populated with office workers who have changed into athletic gear to take in a few miles of jogging along Puget Sound. Seattle's numerous parks and waterside lanes offer many choices for the fitness enthusiast, and some of the better routes are multipurpose biking/running/walking paths, such as the Burke-Gilman Trail (see above) and routes along Green Lake, Lake Washington, the Washington Park Arboretum, and Myrtle Edwards Park; Discovery Park has a challenging 2.8-mile loop trail that goes through dense forest and along bluffs with great views of Puget Sound. For more on the various footpaths and jogging routes through the city's parks, the Department of Parks and Recreation offers online info, as well as brochures you can order through the mail or download (ⓣ206/684-4075, ⓦwww.cityofseattle.net/parks/parkguide).

Competitive **races** are held in town throughout the year, highlighted by late November's Seattle Marathon/Half-Marathon (ⓣ206/729-3660 or 729-3661, ⓦwww.seattlemarathon.org), partly following attractive Lake Washington Boulevard and featuring an option to do the full 26.2-mile route or just half of it. *Northwest Runner* (ⓦwww.nwrunner.com), a local periodical available at sporting goods outlets, has a calendar of races in Seattle and the entire Northwest.

Hiking and climbing

Hiking is integral to the Northwest lifestyle, with the best places being a few hours outside of town at **Mount Rainier** and the **Cascade Mountains** (see Chapter 9, p.375). A closer option is **Mount Si**, only about a half-hour's drive east of Seattle, near Snoqualmie Falls. Here, a four-mile climb ascends about 4000 feet to take in glorious panoramas of the surrounding mountains; see p.389 for further details.

Within the urban boundaries, your options are considerably fewer, with most parks simply not designed to provide a vigorous hike; one of the exceptions is **Frink Park**, off Lake Washington Boulevard in Madrona (daily 7am–11.30pm; ⓣ206/684-4075), which offers nicely wooded terrain built around a steep ravine.

Trail maps are found in all good bookstores and outdoors shops; in Seattle, though, particularly good **travel bookstores** include Metzker Maps, 702 First Ave, Pioneer Square (ⓣ206/623-8747, ⓦwww.metskers.com), Wide World Books & Maps, 4411 Wallingford Ave N, Wallingford (ⓣ206/634-3453, ⓦwww.travelbooksandmaps.com), and The Mountaineers, 300 Third Ave W, Queen Anne (ⓣ206/284-6310, ⓦwww.mountaineersbooks.org), as well as the outdoors superstore REI, 222 Yale Ave N (ⓣ206/223-1944, ⓦwww.rei.com/stores/seattle).

REI is also a good place to get hiking and camping gear, or to practice your **climbing** on their 65-ft indoor rock "pinnacle," which you can ascend with guidance from the store staff ($8, or free for REI members; climb usually limited to one route or 15 minutes; hours Mon 10am–6pm, Wed–Fri 10am–9pm, Sat–Sun 10am–7pm). More serious – and more expensive – climbs are offered by Vertical World, 2123 W Elmore St in Fishermen's Terminal (ⓣ206/283-4497, ⓦwww.verticalworld.com), which has almost 15,000 square feet of space and more than a hundred routes of various degrees of difficulty (Mon & Fri 10am–10pm, Tues–Thurs 6am–11pm, Sat–Sun 10am–7pm; day pass $15).

Water activities

Watching boats sail through the Hiram M. Chittenden Locks in Ballard is a popular spectator sport, and there are several inexpensive **water activities** centers in Seattle that enable you to get in on the action as well. Foremost among these is the **Waterfront Activities Center** on the UW campus (daily 10am–dusk, except holidays and winter break; ⓣ206/543-9433), which rents rowboats or canoes for $6.50 an hour with a valid ID; on weekdays there's rarely a wait, and the marshes of Foster Island are just a few minutes of rowing away. The **Center for Wooden Boats**, on Lake Union at 1010 Valley St (daily 11am–5pm in summer, rest of year Wed–Mon 11am–5pm; free; ⓣ206/382-2628, ⓦwww.cwb.org), rents sailboats and rowboats for $12.50–46/hr, depending upon the size of the boat and day of the week. Located between Mount Baker and Seward Park, the small peninsula of Stan Sayres Park, 3808 Lake Washington Blvd S, holds a **Rowing and Sailing Center** (summer Mon–Thurs 5.30am–9pm, Fri 5.30am–6pm, Sat 7am–4pm, Sun noon–7pm; ⓣ206/386-1913), from which you can launch anything from a dinghy to a sailboat and take classes on kayaking, canoeing, or general sailing.

Back on **Lake Union**, the Northwest Outdoor Center, 2100 Westlake Ave N (ⓣ206/281-9694 or 1-800/683-0637, ⓦwww.nwoc.com), rents kayaks by the hour ($10 single, $15 double) and the day ($50 single, $70 double). The same hourly rates are also offered by the Agua Verde Paddle Club, on Lake Union's Portage Bay at 1303 NE Boat St (ⓣ206/545-8570 ⓦwww.aguaverde.com), which has a slightly cheaper daily price ($45 single, $60 double) but is only open March through October. Lastly, Urban Surf, 2100 N Northlake Way (May–Sept Mon–Fri 10am–7pm, Sat 10am–5pm, Sun 11am–5pm; ⓣ206/545-9463, ⓦwww.urbansurf.com), rents **windsurfers** for $45/day, on weekdays only.

Outdoor swimming is usually not a comfortable proposition in Seattle without a wetsuit, but the hardy do take to the waves at the city's two most popular beaches, **Alki Beach** (p.284) and **Ballard's Golden Gardens** (p.284) – although the water temperatures are actually warmer, and the crowds thinner, around **Lake Washington**. Alternatively, the city has eight **indoor swimming pools** where you can take a dip for a modest fee, the most conveniently located of these being Queen Anne Pool at 1920 First Ave W, Queen Anne (ⓣ206/386-4282), and Evans Pool on the edge of Green Lake at 7201 E Green Lake Drive N (ⓣ206/684-4961). There's also the heated outdoor Colman Pool, in West Seattle's Lincoln Park, 8603 Fauntleroy Way SW (daily mid-June through Aug; ⓣ206/684-7494).

Fitness centers

Working out at the gym is not a huge part of the social scene in Seattle, but the frequent rain can make indoor exercise an attractive option. There are several dozen **fitness centers** in town, many of them conveniently located Downtown, and with daily or weekly rates often available. Athletic clubs with **day-passes** include The Vault, 808 Second Ave, Pioneer Square ($15; ⓣ206/224-9000, ⓦwww.vaultfitness.com); 24 Hour Fitness, off I-5 at 1827 Yale St, Downtown (free ten-day passes; ⓣ206/624-0651, ⓦwww.24hourfitness.com); Gold's Gym, 825 Pike St in the Convention Center ($10; ⓣ206/583-0640, ⓦwww.goldsgym.com); and Gateway Athletic Club, 700 Fifth Ave, 14th Floor, Downtown ($10; ⓣ206/343-4692, ⓦwww.gatewayathletic.com). Further out are Pro-Robics, 1530 Queen Anne Ave N, Queen Anne ($12; ⓣ206/283-2303, ⓦwww.prorobics.com), and University Fitness, 4511 Roosevelt Way NE, University District ($10; ⓣ206/632-3460), which has the added bonus of being open around the clock.

Listings

Air tours Kenmore Air schedules five flights daily from Downtown Seattle on Lake Union to Victoria (ⓣ1-800/543-9595; $116 one-way, $177–198 round-trip; ⓦwww.kenmoreair.com), as well as six flights to the San Juan Islands ($98 one-way, $163–194 round-trip).

Airlines Air Canada ⓣ1-800/247-2262, ⓦwww.aircanada.ca; Alaska Air ⓣ1-800/426-0333, ⓦwww.alaska-air.com; American ⓣ1-800/433-7300, ⓦwww.americanairlines.com; British Airways ⓣ1-800/247-9297, ⓦwww.british-airways.com; Continental ⓣ1-800/525-0280, ⓦwww.continental.com; Delta ⓣ1-800/221-1212, ⓦwww.delta.com; Jet Blue ⓣ1-800/JETBLUE, ⓦwww.jetblue.com; Northwest ⓣ1-800/225-2525, ⓦwww.nwa.com; Southwest ⓣ1-800/435-9792, ⓦwww.iflyswa.com; United ⓣ1-800/241-6522, ⓦwww.ual.com; US Airways ⓣ1-800/428-4322, ⓦwww.usair.com.

Banks Central Downtown branches: Bank Of America, 701 Second Ave ⓣ206/358-0500, ⓦwww.bankofamerica.com; Keybank, 700 Fifth Ave ⓣ206/684-6507, ⓦwww.keybank.com; Union Bank of California, 910 Fourth Ave ⓣ206/587-6100, ⓦwww.uboc.com; US Bank, 1301 Fifth Ave ⓣ206/344-2395, ⓦwww.usbank.com; Washington Mutual, 1201 Third Ave ⓣ206/461-6475, ⓦwww.washingtonmutual.com; Wells Fargo, Westlake Center, 1620 Fourth Ave ⓣ206/287-0039, ⓦwww.wellsfargo.com. Most banks are open at least Mon–Fri 10am–4pm.

Bike rental Bikes can be rented at Blazing Saddles, 1230 Western Ave, Downtown (ⓣ206/341-9994), Gregg's, 7007 Woodlawn Ave NE, Green Lake (ⓣ206/523-1822 ⓦwww.greggscycles.com), Bicycle Center, 4529 Sandpoint Way NE, Sand Point (ⓣ206/523-8300, ⓦwww.bicyclecenterseattle.com), and Al Young Bike & Ski, 3615 NE 45th St, University District (ⓣ206/524-2642); rates tend to fluctuate from $5-12 per hour, $20–45 per day.

Bookstores University Bookstore, 4326 University Way, University District (ⓣ206/634-3400, ⓦwww.bookstore.washington.edu), and Elliott Bay Book Company, 101 S Main St, Pioneer Square (ⓣ206/624-6600, ⓦwww.elliottbaybook.com), are the city's biggest booksellers. Metsker Maps, 702 1st Ave, Pioneer Square (ⓣ206/623-8747, ⓦwww.metskers.com), has a comprehensive selection of local and regional maps; and Wide World Books and Maps, 4411 Wallingford Ave N, Wallingford (ⓣ206/634-3453, ⓦwww.travelbooksandmaps.com), features a wide assortment of travel guides and literature. Twice Sold Tales, 905 E John St, Capitol Hill (ⓣ206/324-2421, ⓦwww.twicesoldtales.com), is Seattle's best secondhand bookshop, one in a chain of three local stores. The collectively run Left Bank Books, Pike Place Market at 92 Pike St (ⓣ206/622-1095, ⓦwww.leftbankbooks.com), is a formidable left-wing bookshop.

Car rental Advantage ⓣ1-800/777-5500, ⓦwww.arac.com; Alamo ⓣ1-800/462-5266, ⓦwww.goalamo.com; Avis ⓣ1-800/331-1212, ⓦwww.avis.com; Budget ⓣ1-800/527-0700, ⓦwww.budgetrentacar.com; Dollar ⓣ1-800/800-4000, ⓦwww.dollar.com; Enterprise ⓣ1-800/325-8007, ⓦwww.enterprise.com; Hertz ⓣ1-800/654-3131, ⓦwww.hertz.com; National ⓣ1-800/328-4567, ⓦwww.nationalcar.com; Payless ⓣ1-800/729-5377, ⓦwww.paylesscarrental.com; Thrifty ⓣ1-800/847-4389, ⓦwww.thrifty.com.

Consulates Australia, 401 Andover Park East ⓣ206/575-7446; Canada, 600 Stewart St #412 ⓣ206/443-1777; New Zealand, 6810 51st Ave NE ⓣ206/525-0271; UK, 900 Fourth Ave ⓣ206/622-9255.

Currency exchange Most large Downtown banks will change foreign currency and travelers' checks. American Express checks should be cashed at their Downtown office, 600 Stewart St (Mon–Fri 8.30am–5.30pm; ⓣ206/441-8622, ⓦtravel.americanexpress.com). Thomas Cook (ⓣ1-800/287-7362, ⓦwww.us.thomascook.com) changes money at Sea-Tac Airport (daily 6am–8pm; ⓣ206/248-0401), Downtown in Westlake Center, Level Three, 400 Pine St (Mon–Sat 9.30am–6pm, Sun 11am–5pm; ⓣ206/682-4525), and in Bellevue at 10630 NE Eighth St (Mon–Fri 8.30am–5pm, Sat 10am–2pm; ⓣ425/462-8225).

Dentist The Seattle/King County Dental Society, 2201 Sixth Ave, Suite 1306 (ⓣ206/443-7607 ⓦwww.skcds.org), provides a referral service to low-cost dental clinics around town.

Emergencies ⓣ911.

Hospital The best overall choice is Northwest Hospital, 1550 N 115th St (ⓣ206/364-0500, ⓦwww.nwhospital.org); for minor injuries try Country Doctor Community Clinic, 500 19th Ave E (ⓣ206/461-4503). Women can also use the Aradia Women's Health Center, 1300 Spring St (ⓣ206/323-9388, ⓦwww.aradia.org).

Internet access Some hotels have terminals for guests to use (for a steep fee), plenty of cafés have at least one or two computers, and cyber-cafés even more, for around $6 per hour. For the latter, the most reliable choices include Aurafice, 616 E Pine St, Capitol Hill (ⓣ 206/860-9977 ⓦ www.aurafice.com), Capitol Hill Café, 219 Broadway E (ⓣ 206/860-6858 ⓦ www.capitolhill.net), Hotwire, 4410 California Ave SW, West Seattle (ⓣ 206/935-1510 ⓦ www.hotwirecoffee.com), and Online Coffee Company, 1720 E Olive Way, Capitol Hill (ⓣ 206/328-3731 ⓦ www.onlinecoffeeco.com).

Laundromats 12th Ave Laundry, 1807 12th Ave, Capitol Hill ⓣ 206/328-4610; Fremont Avenue Laundromat, 4237 Fremont Ave N, Fremont ⓣ 206/632-8924; Lost Sock Laundry, 5020 Roosevelt Way NE, University District ⓣ 206/524-7855.

Left luggage You can leave luggage at Sea-Tac Airport at Ken's Baggage, under the escalator between baggage-claim carousels 9 and 12 (daily 5.30am–12.30am; ⓣ 206/433-5333), or in storage lockers at Greyhound, 811 Stewart St (ⓣ 206/628-5508), for up to 24 hours.

Legal advice Seattle King County Bar Association Lawyer Referral & Information Service ⓣ 206/623-2551, ⓦ www.kcba.org.

Library The main, newly rebuilt branch of the Seattle Public Library is Downtown at 1000 Fourth Ave (Mon–Wed 10am–8pm, Thurs–Sat 10am–6pm, Sun 1–5pm; ⓣ 206/386-4636, ⓦ www.spl.org). The same phone number is also a handy general information line.

Police stations West Precinct, 610 Third Ave ⓣ 206/684-8917; East Precinct, 1519 12th Ave ⓣ 206/684-4300; North Precinct, 10049 College Way N ⓣ 206/684-0850; South Precinct, 3001 S Myrtle St ⓣ 206/386-1850.

Post office The main post office is Downtown at 301 Union St (Mon–Fri 7.30am–5.30pm; ⓣ 206/748-5417 or 1-800/275-8777).

Rape Crisis Line 24hr ⓣ 206/632-7273.

Tax Sales tax in Seattle is 8.8 percent, applied to everything except groceries, though a Food & Beverage Tax (mainly for restaurants) bumps the total up to 8.93 percent; it's similar throughout the rest of the metropolitan area. There's also a steep hotel tax of 16 percent.

Taxis The more reliable companies include Graytop Cab (ⓣ 206/282-8222) and Yellow Cab (ⓣ 206/622-6500). Fares for the big outfits have standardized at $1.80 for the meter drop, and $1.80 for each mile or 50¢ per minute.

Telephones Public phones are plentiful throughout the city; local calls cost 50¢, and considerably more (often at least $1 per call) in major hotels.

Traveler's Aid 909 Fourth Ave, Suite 630, Downtown (Mon–Fri 9am–4pm; ⓣ 206/461-3888).

Weather 24-hr report provided by the *Seattle Times* (ⓣ 206/464-2000, ext. 9902).

Women's resources The Women's Information Center at University of Washington, Imogen Cunningham Hall AJ50 (ⓣ 206/685-1090, ⓦ depts.washington.edu/womenctr), has information and referral services for a variety of needs; the Seattle Women's Commission (ⓣ 206/684-4537, ⓦ www.cityofseattle.net/womenscommission) maintains a large online list of women-oriented social and civic organizations; and Planned Parenthood of Western Washington, 2211 E Madison, Capitol Hill (ⓣ 206/328-7700, ⓦ www.ppww.org), has clinical services and reproductive health education.

Puget Sound

N
CANADA
Vancouver Island
PACIFIC OCEAN
WASHINGTON
OREGON
USA

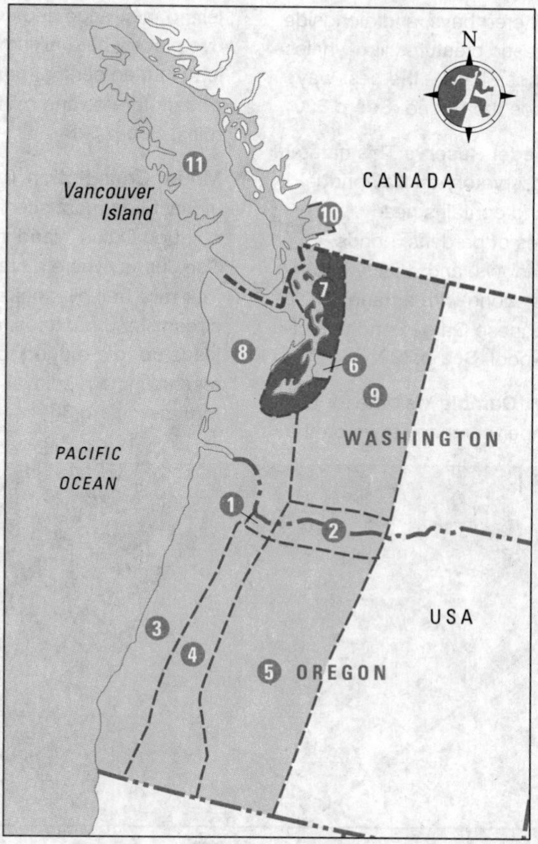

CHAPTER 7 **Highlights**

* **Museum of Glass** In downtown Tacoma, a sparkling new institution devoted to the art of glass, with the work of favorite son Dale Chihuly prominently on display. See p.314

* **Puget Sound ferry rides** Sail past small islands, around sheltered bays, and alongside majestic creatures like whales and sea lions – the best way to see the Sound. See p.320

* **Bloedel Reserve** This natural conservatory on Bainbridge Island contains nearly 150 acres of gardens, ponds, meadows, and wildlife habitats, along with a tranquil Japanese Garden and reflecting pool. See p.322

* **Port Gamble** Visit the former lumber-company town on the edge of the Kitsap Peninsula that resembles a slice of New England – white clapboard houses, elm trees, quaint churches – transported to the Pacific Northwest. See p.324

* **Fort Ebey State Park** Located on massive Whidbey Island, a strange and evocative place where hiking trails lead into an eerie atmosphere of dark forests and military ruins. See p.328

* **Mount Constitution** The highest and most scenic point on Orcas Island in the San Juans, where a steep four-mile trail overlooks streams and pastures, and leads up to a rugged tower resembling a medieval stone fortress. See p.334

△ The Museum of Glass

7

Puget Sound

Measuring about a hundred miles from north to south, the grand waterway of **PUGET SOUND** is the most prominent geographical feature of western Washington. Lined with some of the state's major cities and dotted by hundreds of islands ranging in size from the largest in the continental US to tiny, remote refuges, the Sound offers a wide variety of inviting locales. Heading south on I-5 from Seattle – itself situated on the inlet of Elliott Bay – the notable cities of **Tacoma** and **Olympia** together boast renovated historical architecture, engaging museums, and untrammeled parks. West of Seattle, ferries provide easy access to two of the most popular, and easily reached, of the Sound's islands: **Vashon** and **Bainbridge**, both offering a handful of sights along with appealing cycling routes and hiking trails. From Bainbridge Island, it's a quick trip over the Sound to the sizeable **Kitsap Peninsula** where villages like **Suquamish** and **Port Gamble** stand out for their rich heritage and historic architecture. Further north along the waterway, **Whidbey Island** is a gargantuan stretch of land worth exploring for its pleasant townships, verdant state parks, and preserved military ruins. Along the mainland coast east of Whidbey, artsy **La Conner** makes for an enjoyable waterside diversion. The most distant – and perhaps the most spectacular – American destinations in the Sound are the idyllic **San Juan Islands**, home to striking vistas, tranquil countryside, and the appealing burg of **Friday Harbor**. Finally, nestled in a bay along the Sound just below the Canadian border, **Bellingham**, rewards a visit north with its nicely preserved Victorian buildings and lively college-town atmosphere.

South of Seattle

Located adjacent to the Sound thirty and sixty miles **south of Seattle**, respectively, **Tacoma** and **Olympia** are independent cities – in theory, anyway. Both have been almost completely enveloped by metropolitan sprawl, which has made its way south from Seattle along the interstate Highway 5 corridor. As a result, the entire stretch now resembles one long, linear suburb. If you're in Seattle for a week or so, the cities together merit at least a

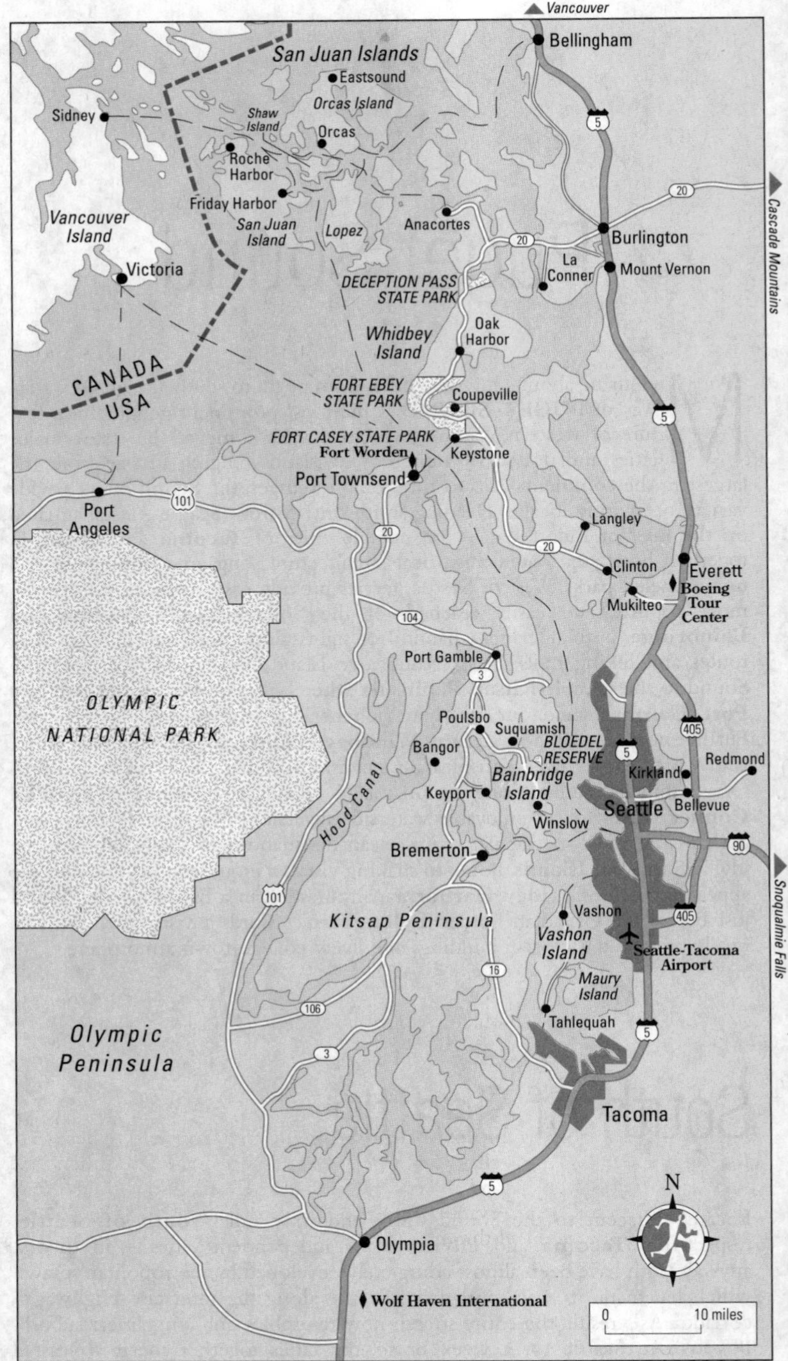
Vancouver
Bellingham
San Juan Islands
Eastsound
Orcas Island
Sidney
Shaw Island
Orcas
Roche Harbor
Friday Harbor
San Juan Island
Lopez
Anacortes
Cascade Mountains
Burlington
Vancouver Island
Victoria
La Conner
Mount Vernon
DECEPTION PASS STATE PARK
Whidbey Island
Oak Harbor
CANADA
USA
FORT EBEY STATE PARK
Coupeville
FORT CASEY STATE PARK
Fort Worden
Keystone
Port Townsend
Port Angeles
Langley
Clinton
Everett
Boeing Tour Center
Mukilteo
Port Gamble
OLYMPIC NATIONAL PARK
Poulsbo
Suquamish
BLOEDEL RESERVE
Bangor
Redmond
Kirkland
Bainbridge Island
Keyport
Hood Canal
Seattle
Bellevue
Winslow
Bremerton
Snoqualmie Falls
Vashon
Kitsap Peninsula
Vashon Island
Seattle-Tacoma Airport
Maury Island
Tahlequah
Olympic Peninsula
Tacoma
N
Olympia
Wolf Haven International
0
10 miles
Mt St Helens
5
20
101
104
3
405
90
16
106

day-trip, though there's little else in the vicinity to distract you, aside from the curious preserve of **Wolf Haven International**. South of Olympia, I-5 chugs through one of the less remarkable stretches of the state, on the way down to Portland, while northbound from town, Highway 101 begins its lengthy route around the edge of the Olympic Peninsula (see p.349). Near the beginning of this journey, the Kitsap Peninsula (see p.323) is within reach along Route 3 – though its most compelling attractions are on its north end, and best accessed from Bainbridge Island.

Tacoma

Long a workaday mill town with a notably foul stench and not much else to speak of, **TACOMA** has never been a top attraction. Nowadays, Tacoma's putrid reputation has changed dramatically, as all but one of its odorous pulp mills have closed, and an influx of middle-class families, young people, artists, and inspired city planning has rejuvenated this once tired industrial center. In fact, Washington's second largest city has undergone such an extensive revitalization that it has now actually become something of a tourist magnet – to the shock and amazement of Northwesterners.

Arrival and information

Coming in on I-5 from the north, you'll pass the enormous blue-gray roof of the **Tacoma Dome** (2727 East D St; information at ⓣ253/272-3663, ⓦwww.tacomadome.org) sports and concert venue, on your way to the city center. The downtown area is perched above Puget Sound at **Commencement Bay**, a deep harbor whose geographical appeal helped Tacoma be chosen over Seattle as the western terminus for the Northern Pacific Railroad's transcontinental route in 1873.

Tacoma is easily accessed by local and regional **mass transit**: Amtrak (ⓣ1-800/USA-RAIL, ⓦwww.amtrak.com) pulls in at Freighthouse Square, 1001 Puyallup Ave; Pierce Transit (ⓣ253/581-8000, ⓦwww.ptbus.pierce.wa.us) runs frequent Seattle Express bus service between the two cities, as well as local routes, while Sound Transit (ⓣ1-800/201-4900, ⓦwww.soundtransit.org) offers Seattle-bound express buses and the Sounder commuter rail (from a station at the Tacoma Dome).

The small **Tacoma-Pierce County Visitors Center**, 1001 Pacific Ave, Suite 400 (Mon–Fri 8.30am–5pm, ⓣ253/627-2836, ⓦwww.tpctourism.org), has maps and literature about the attractions of the area, along with walking guides to the various sights.

Accommodation

The city's better choices for **accommodation** are unfortunately rather scattered. Typically, the usual chain hotels can be found downtown, functional motels just off the freeway, and an array of interesting **B&Bs** in rather far-flung locations. A Travelers' Reservation Service (ⓣ206/364-5900), can put you in touch with B&Bs here and throughout the Northwest.

Devoe Mansion 203 133rd St East ⓣ253/539-3991, ⓦwww.devoemansion.com. Four elegant B&B rooms in a 1911 Colonial Revival estate named after a locally famous women's-rights pioneer, with savory breakfasts and several park-like acres of grounds. Located just south of downtown Tacoma. ❻

Motel 6 1811 S 76th St, near exit 129 off I-5 ⓣ253/473-7100 or 1-800/466-8356, ⓦwww.motel6.com About five miles south of downtown, this chain hotel has an outdoor pool and 120 rooms at the cheapest rates you're likely to find in the city. ❷

Sheraton Tacoma 1320 Broadway Plaza, between 13th and 15th ⓣ253/572-3200 or 1-800/845-9466, ⓦwww.sheratontacoma.com. One of the plushest hotels in town, next to an enormous convention center. Ask for a room with a view over Commencement Bay. Suites with parlors also available for a bit more money. ❼, suites ❾.

The Villa 705 N 5th St ⓣ253/572-1157 or 1-888/572-1157, ⓦwww.villabb.com. About a mile northeast of downtown, this Renaissance Revival mansion, surrounded by luxurious gardens, has been converted into a B&B with plenty of creature comforts. Some of the rooms (named after Italian towns) have private verandas with views of Commencement Bay and the Olympic Mountains. ❼

The City

Tacoma is an easy city to get around, with many of its chief sights either lying on **Pacific Avenue** or around the renovated **Theater District**. A venture further north takes you takes you to pleasant **Wright Park**, while the extensive acreage of **Point Defiance Park** marks the northern end of the city's worthwhile destinations. From here, the state ferry service can take you to Vashon Island, and from there on to the rest of the Sound.

Pacific Avenue

From the freeway, Exit 133 leads toward **Pacific Avenue**, the main cultural drag of downtown Tacoma and the axis of the city's recent rejuvenation. Here, on the west end of the bridge across the 705 freeway, the earliest and most visible example of Tacoma's rebirth is **Union Station**, 1717 Pacific Ave (Mon–Fri 10am–4pm; ⓣ253/572-9310), a 1911 Baroque Revival treasure with a copper dome and marble lobby. Graced with world-renowned artist and native son Dale Chihuly's colorful glassworks, this elegant old station hasn't hosted an arriving train in twenty years. Instead, after being renovated inside and out for $57 million, it has been reborn as a federal courthouse. More of Chihuly's vibrant works are on display at the adjacent **Tacoma Art Museum**, 1701 Pacific Ave (Tues–Wed & Fri–Sun 10am–5pm, Thurs 10am–8pm; $6.50; ⓣ253/272-4258, ⓦwww.tacomaartmuseum.org), which, like the other contemporary works here by Northwest-based artists, are the highlights of the museum's collection. While the minor pieces on display by Picasso, Degas, Renoir, and Frederic Remington aren't too inspiring, the building itself is quite a marvel – a gleaming new, steel-and-glass creation by Antoine Predock that opened in May 2003.

Along with Union Station, another vivid example of historic preservation lies across Pacific Avenue at the **University of Washington Tacoma** (ⓦwww.tacoma.washington.edu), which showcases a handful of old grain and grocery warehouses that have been cleverly converted into classrooms and offices. On the south side of Union Station, the excellent **Washington State History Museum**, 1911 Pacific Ave (Mon–Wed & Fri–Sat 10am–5pm, Thurs 10am–8pm, Sun noon–5pm; $7, free Thurs 5–8pm; ⓣ253/272-3500, ⓦwww.wshs.org/wshm), has a huge array of exhibits on regional history. Large galleries nicely re-create the milieu of frontier towns and early logging industries. The museum doesn't shy away from controversial topics either, with exhibits on alcoholism among Native Americans and the 1919 General Strike in Seattle (see p.544).

Finally, the most prominent attractions lie over the 705 and across from Union Station. The first, the **Chihuly Bridge of Glass**

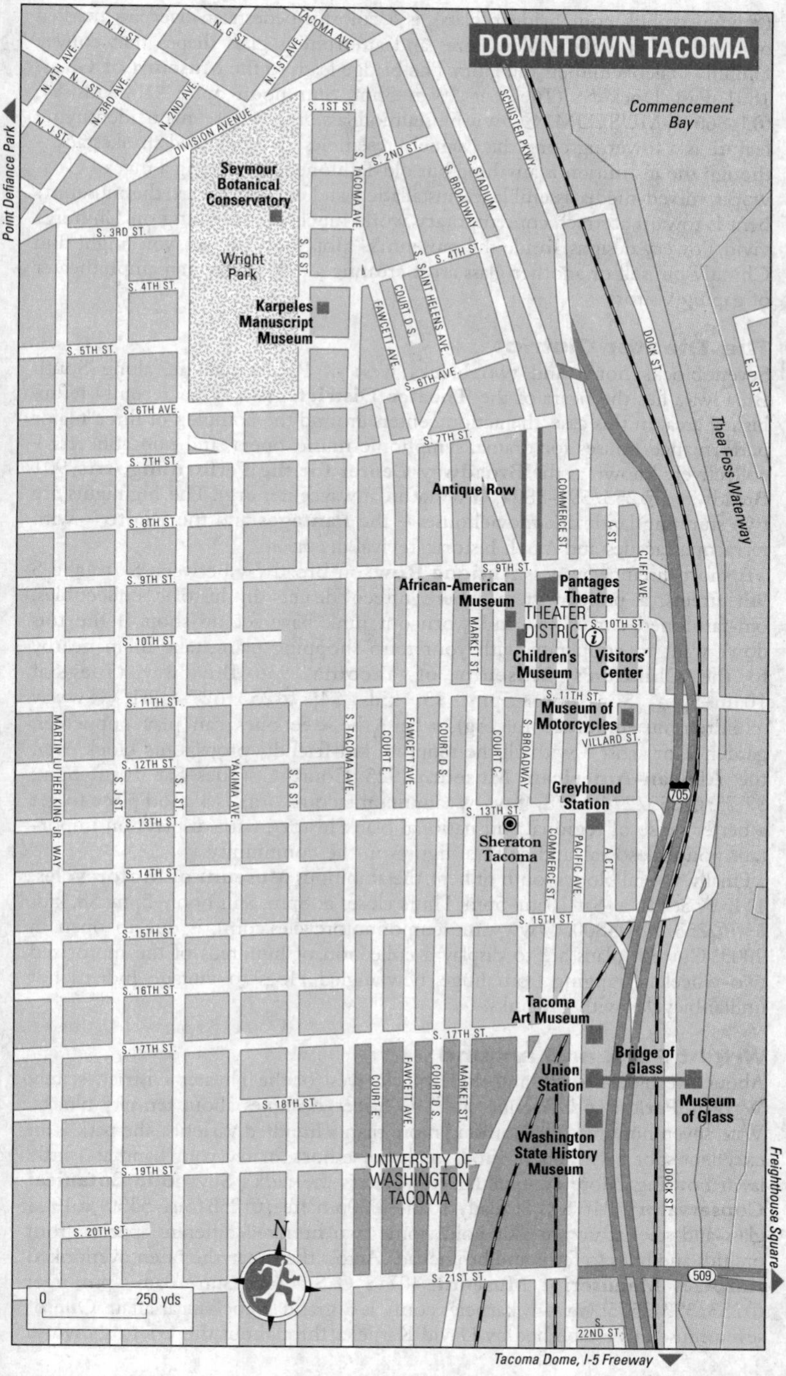

DOWNTOWN TACOMA

Commencement Bay

Seymour Botanical Conservatory

Wright Park

Karpeles Manuscript Museum

Antique Row

African-American Museum

Pantages Theatre

THEATER DISTRICT

Children's Museum

Visitors' Center

Museum of Motorcycles

Greyhound Station

Sheraton Tacoma

Tacoma Art Museum

Union Station

Bridge of Glass

Museum of Glass

Washington State History Museum

UNIVERSITY OF WASHINGTON TACOMA

Thea Foss Waterway

N. H ST.
N. G ST.
TACOMA AVE.
N. 4TH AVE.
N. I ST.
N. 3RD AVE.
N. 2ND AVE.
N. 1ST AVE.
N. J ST.
DIVISION AVENUE
S. 1ST ST.
S. 2ND ST.
S. 3RD ST.
S. 4TH ST.
S. 5TH ST.
S. 6TH AVE.
S. 6TH AVE.
S. 7TH ST.
S. 8TH ST.
S. 9TH ST.
S. 10TH ST.
S. 11TH ST.
S. 12TH ST.
S. 13TH ST.
S. 14TH ST.
S. 15TH ST.
S. 16TH ST.
S. 17TH ST.
S. 18TH ST.
S. 19TH ST.
S. 20TH ST.
S. 21ST ST.
S. 22ND ST.
VILLARD ST.
S. TACOMA AVE.
S. G ST.
S. BROADWAY
S. STADIUM
SCHUSTER PKWY.
DOCK ST.
E. D ST.
COURT D S.
FAWCETT AVE.
SAINT HELENS AVE.
COMMERCE ST.
A ST.
CLIFF AVE.
MARKET ST.
COURT E
COURT C
PACIFIC AVE.
A CT.
MARTIN LUTHER KING JR. WAY
S. J ST.
S. I ST.
YAKIMA AVE.

705
509

Point Defiance Park

Freighthouse Square

Tacoma Dome, I-5 Freeway

N

0 250 yds

(Ⓦ www.chihuly.com/bridgeofglass), is a colorful pedestrian overpass marked by a pair of crystalline blue spires and amorphous glass shapes that convey Chihuly's talents in their full glory. The bridge leads to the **Museum of Glass**, 1801 East Dock St (Tues–Sat 10am–5pm, Sun noon–5pm; $10, kids $4; Ⓣ 1-866/4-MUSEUM, Ⓦ www.museumofglass.org), whose main identifying feature is a towering cone that vaguely resembles an antiquated smokestack – though the institution is anything but old-fashioned. Presenting a mix of glass-works, mixed-media assemblages, installation and conceptual art, the museum's bent is toward abstract, contemporary work, much of it focusing on Chihuly's vivid, flowery designs. Inside the museum's "Hot Shop," in fact, you might find Chihuly himself or another glass artist creating a piece before an amphitheater of gaping visitors.

The Theater District

Seven blocks north and two blocks west of Pacific Avenue, along South Broadway, lies the heart of the **Theater District**, yet another recently refurbished area. In this case, the action centers around the complex of three major performance houses for drama, symphonic music, opera, and pop concerts – collectively known as the **Broadway Center for the Performing Arts**, 901 Broadway (Ⓣ 253/591-5894, Ⓦ www.broadwaycenter.org). The highlights are two stunning landmark moviehouses – the **Pantages** and the **Rialto** – with terracotta facades and much historic-revival decor.

A short distance away is **Antique Row**, on Broadway between S 7th and S 9th streets, a popular strip where fifteen dealers in historic collectibles, old-fashioned curiosities, and worn-out junk have set up shop. If the tots don't want to cooperate with your retro shopping plans, take them nearby to the **Children's Museum of Tacoma**, 936 Broadway (Tues–Sat 10am–5pm, Sun noon–5pm; $3, kids $4; Ⓣ 253/627-6031, Ⓦ www.childrensmuseumoft.acoma.org), where the wee ones can play puppeteer, gardener, or artist – with all the requisite kid-friendly props. One block over, the **African-American Museum**, 925 Court C (Tues–Sat 10am–5pm; $2.75; Ⓣ 253/274-1278, Ⓦ www.aamuseumtacoma.org), is a good place to get a better sense of regional and national black history, with displays on important political, social, and cultural figures in the community.

Finally, several blocks south of here, the ambitious **Museum of Motorcycles**, 1113 A St (Tues–Sat 10am–5pm, Thurs closes at 8pm, Sun noon–5pm; $8, kids $3; Ⓣ 253/779-4800, Ⓦ www.museumofmotorcycles.com), is due to open in 2005. Current plans are to display a collection of hundreds of the motorized two-wheelers, ranging from huge, newfangled Hogs to vintage Indians not unlike bicycles with gas tanks.

Wright Park and around

About five blocks north and three blocks west of the Theater District, stately **Wright Park**, at 6th Avenue and S G Street, occupies about ten city blocks. With seven hundred plants among more than a hundred varieties, the park is an excellent spot in which to stroll, pitch horseshoes, or try your hand at a little lawn bowling. More compelling, however, is the park's **Seymour Botanical Conservatory**, 316 S G St (daily 10am–4.30pm; free; Ⓣ 253/591-5330), a 1908 glass-and-steel structure that holds some two hundred different species, from orchids and lilies to ferns and bromeliads. Across the street, the often overlooked **Karpeles Manuscript Museum**, 407 S G St (Tues–Sun 10am–4pm; free; Ⓣ 253/383-2575, Ⓦ www.karpeles.com), is a grand Neoclassical affair. One of seven museums established by David Karpeles throughout the US to showcase his immense collection of manuscripts, among its holdings are the concluding page of Darwin's *Origin of Species* and a study page for Karl Marx's *Das Kapital.*

Point Defiance Park

About four miles north of downtown, at Pearl Street off Ruston Way, lies picturesque **Point Defiance Park**. At 700 acres, it's one of the largest urban parks in the USA. Its **Five-Mile-Drive** loop has fine vistas of Puget Sound and various points from which you can lose yourself on the numerous trails that weave their way through the park. Signs along the drive direct you to **Fort Nisqually** (April–May Wed–Sun 11am–5pm; June–Aug daily 11am–6pm; Sept–March Wed–Sun 11am–4pm; $3 March–Oct, rest of year $2; ⓣ253/591-5339, ⓦwww.fortnisqually.org), a reconstruction of the fur-trading post Hudson's Bay Company set up in 1833. Near the fort, on the southern boundary of the park, **Camp Six** museum (Feb–May & Oct Wed–Sun & holidays 10am–4pm; June–Sept Wed–Fri 10am–4pm, weekends & holidays 10am–7pm; free; ⓣ253/752-0047, ⓦwww.camp-6-museum.org), is a reconstructed logging camp with bunkhouses, period logging equipment, and a restored, fully functional steam engine (rides $3). There's also a worthwhile **zoo** and **aquarium** in the park at 5400 N Pearl St (hours vary, generally daily 9.30am–5pm; $7.75; ⓣ253/404-3636, ⓦwww.pdza.org), with displays of arctic creatures like polar bears, plus red wolves, sharks, and a beluga whale.

Eating and drinking

While **dining** out in Tacoma is not, by and large, a terribly adventurous culinary experience, there are several dependable options to be found.

Antique Sandwich Company 5102 N Pearl St ⓣ253/752-4069. Serviceable budget food and an inviting ambience are both on offer here, a good place to catch an acoustic concert by a local performer or listen to self-styled singers take part in Open Mic Night.

Engine House No. 9 611 N Pine St ⓣ253/272-3435. Jovial tavern with fire-station decor, a good place for drinking and live music as well as eating. Pizza dominates the menu – about as good as it gets in Tacoma.

Luciano's Ristorante 3327 Ruston Way ⓣ253/756-5611. Quality upscale dining with the usual Italian pasta staples at a waterfront restaurant (and casino), whose deck has good views of Puget Sound and the Olympic Mountains.

Shakabrah Java 2618 6th Ave ⓣ253/572-4369. In Seattle this would be just another coffeehouse; here it stands out for offering decent java and some interesting live music.

Spar Tavern 2121 North 30th St ⓣ253/627-8215. Classic brick diner and watering hole near the waterfront in Old Town Tacoma, serving up burgers, seafood, and brewskis, plus blues on Sunday nights.

Olympia

Thirty miles southwest of Tacoma on I-5, **OLYMPIA** was chosen as Washington's territorial capital in 1853 – a decade after the first white settlers reached the area – in the hope that what was then no more than a muddy little logging community would turn into a major metropolis. While that became Seattle's fate, Olympia did earn the title of the state's **capital** in 1889 when Washington finally entered the Union, nearly three decades after Oregon.

Even as Tacoma has recently experienced a steady upswing of good times, Olympia has endured a spate of misfortune. The 2001 earthquake, whose epicenter was a mere eleven miles away in Nisqually, dramatically shook the city. Severe state budget cuts further rocked the capital, and then, to make matters worse, one of its most popular attractions, the **Olympia Brewery** in nearby Tumwater, closed in 2003. Still, the city retains its small-town charm despite the recent setbacks, and is a good spot for a brief visit if you're spending a few days around Tacoma.

Very much unlike the rather staid environment of Oregon's state capital of Salem (see p.192), Olympia, somewhat surprisingly perhaps, has a bit of an eccentric streak. Cartoonists Matt Groening (creator of *The Simpsons*) and Lynda Barry spent their college years here, as did Sub Pop Records co-founder Bruce Pavitt and numerous indie rockers. Kurt Cobain even lived in Olympia for several years before his rise to fame in Nirvana.

Arrival, information, and getting around

Olympia is on I-5 and easily accessible by **car** or bus. Greyhound is located in the town center at 107 7th Ave SE (ⓣ360/357-5541, ⓦwww.greyhound.com), just north of the Capitol Campus, and runs **buses** from Seattle to Olympia several times a day (2hrs). Intercity Transit (ⓣ360/786-1881, ⓦwww.intercitytransit.com), serves the Olympia area (75¢ per bus ride, $1.50 for daily pass). The State Capitol **visitor center**, Capitol Way at 14th Avenue (Mon–Fri 8am–5pm, ⓣ360/586-3460), is stocked with maps and brochures to set you on your way.

Accommodation

For **accommodation**, the standard assortment of chain motels are typically clean and comfortable, and as with Tacoma, there are interesting B&Bs to be found if you look hard enough.

Best Western Aladdin Motor Inn 900 Capitol Way ⓣ360/352-7200 or 1-800/367-7771, ⓦwww.bestwestern.com. Predictably clean motor lodge with outdoor pool near Olympia's center. ❹

Harbinger Inn 1136 E Bay Drive NE ⓣ360/754-0389. The best of Olympia's limited number of B&Bs is a five-room 1910 block mansion with balconies and Puget Sound views. ❹

Millersylvania State Park Tilley Rd ⓣ360/753-1519, ⓦwww.parks.wa.gov. Ten miles south of Olympia, this 840-acre campground has 135 tent sites, 52 RV hook-ups, and four primitive sites near a beach, with rugged facilities designed during the New Deal era. ❶

Phoenix Inn 415 Capitol Way ⓣ360/570-0555, ⓦwww.phoenixinnsuites.com. Perhaps the best choice overall for affordable luxury and convenience, with fridges and microwaves in each room, and onsite pool, Jacuzzi, and gym. ❻

Swantown Inn 1431 11th Ave SE ⓣ1-360/753-9123, ⓦwww.olywa.net/swantown. Four pleasant, if a bit precious, B&B rooms in a remodeled 1889 Victorian structure. Offers onsite gardens and gazebo, fairly affordable prices, and a location not far from the city center. ❺

The City

Olympia sits at the very southern tip of Puget Sound, along the waterway of Budd Inlet, which sits just above **Capitol Lake**. These two bodies of water form the western boundary for the city's most appealing sights – basically meaning the downtown core and, farther south, the **Capitol Campus**. While the place spreads out further to the south and east, you'll most likely be spending the majority of your time in the easily walkable city center, and may not even need a car to get around.

Downtown and Capitol Lake

Downtown Olympia stretches along the east bank of Budd Inlet in the shadow of the state capital buildings. Comprising a decent but unexceptional selection of restaurants, cafés, and the odd offbeat shop, the area is mainly worth visiting for its **Old Capitol Building**, Washington at 7th Avenue (Mon–Fri 8am–5pm; free; ⓣ360/586-3460). Erected in 1892, this jewel with Gothic turrets and arched windows, which overlooks the pleasant green square of **Sylvester Park**, now houses various administrative offices. Beyond this, there are few other notable attractions downtown except for the **Yashiro Japanese Garden**, 9th Avenue at Plum Street (daily dawn–dusk; free; ⓣ360/753-8447), a small refuge with a pagoda, fish pond, and waterfall. Just west of downtown lies **Capitol Lake**, where you'll find the waterfront **Olympia Farmers Market**, 700 N Capitol Way (April–Oct Thurs–Sun 10am–3pm; Nov–Dec Sat & Sun only; ⓣ360/352-9096, ⓦwww.farmers-market.org), and a hearty selection of fruits, vegetables, herbs, pastries, and other baked goods, and handcrafted items like soaps and puzzles.

The Capitol Campus

Just south of downtown lies over thirty acres of Olympia's impressive **Capitol Campus** and its unequivocal focal point, the grand **Legislative Building**. Constructed as an imposing Romanesque Revival edifice, it was finally completed in 1928, after 34 years in the making, and, at 287ft, is the tallest all-masonry domed building in the US, and the sixth-tallest in the world. Not to be outdone, the unabashedly opulent interior is highlighted by the Rotunda's Tiffany chandelier, six bronze entry-doors weighing five tons each, and the base of the large circular Russian Circassioan Walnut table in the State Reception Room – carved from a single tree trunk in the shape of eagles' legs. Epic **murals** were originally planned for the interior – and the *Twelve Labors of Hercules* by Michael Spafford is indeed up on a governmental chamber's walls, but Washington's pious legislators were apparently so shocked by the "pornographic" images of the painting that their immediate reaction was to spend $15,000 covering it up with hardboard and curtains. Mercifully, these have now been removed, but all these treasures are currently off-limits to the public due to an ongoing, $100-million construction project to repair damage from the 2001 earthquake – which unfortunately marred many of the building's features that had been renovated only a few years before. You can try back in November 2004, when the building is due to re-open to the public, or call ⓣ360/586-3460 or visit ⓦwww.ga.wa.gov/visitor to see if the repair schedule has changed.

Elsewhere at the site, the **Hall of Justice**, directly across from the Capitol (Mon–Fri 8am–5pm; same information as above), is the Neoclassical home of the state supreme court, with a colonnade clad in sandstone. Next door to the Capitol, is the **Governor's Mansion** (Wed only, by reservation at ⓣ360/586-8687, ⓦwww.governor.wa.gov/bios/tour) a red-brick Georgian house that was erected as a temporary site in 1908 and slated for demolition soon after. Surprisingly enough, it has lasted nearly a century and even been renovated and expanded several times. On the northern side of the campus, the **Capitol Conservatory and Gardens**, 11th Avenue at Water Street (Mon–Fri 8am–3pm; free; ⓣ360/586-TOUR), is noteworthy for its eclectic selection of plants from tropical to northern regions, many of which are grown and used to decorate the various other gardens on the campus site.

A few blocks further south, the **State Capitol Museum**, 211 W 21st Ave (Tues–Fri 10am–4pm, Sat–Sun noon–4pm; $2; ⓣ360/753-2580, ⓦwww.wshs.org/wscm), occupies the Renaissance Revival-styled 1920s mansion of the wealthy Lord family. The building is actually more enticing than its displays, which feature a detailed but dry trawl through the history of Olympia on the ground floor and a few Native American bygones up above.

Eating

There is a nice – if albeit small – mix of worthwhile **dining** options in Olympia, with most centered just north of downtown.

Otto's 111 N Washington St NE ⓣ360/352-8640. Popular and reliable bagel bakery that offers cheap and healthy breakfast and lunch dishes.

Saigon Rendezvous 117 5th Ave SW ⓣ360/352-1989. Good mix of Chinese and Vietnamese food – favorites like pad Thai, pho soups, and curry dishes – that's reasonably priced and well portioned, right in the city center.

Santosh 116 4th Ave W ⓣ360/943-3442. Extensive menu of decent Indian dishes with straightforward subcontinental decor, and an all-you-can-eat lunchtime buffet for around $8.

Spar Café 114 4th Ave E ⓣ360/357-6444. Old-time American diner cuisine in a funky 1935-era setting, with long, curving counter, old photos of Olympia on the wall, and backroom lounge for smokers and drinkers.

Urban Onion 116 Legion Way ⓣ360/943-9242. Café that serves up delicious burgers for the vegetarian and carnivore alike.

Entertainment

As for **entertainment**, Olympia is home to one of the Northwest's better indie-rock scenes, spawning acts such as Beat Happening, Lois, and Sleater-Kinney (named for an I-5 off-ramp further north), most of whom play a mixture of punk, rock, and grunge, with a smattering of folk thrown in. To dive into the scene, check local listings or drop by the **Capitol Theater**, 206 5th Ave E (ⓣ360/754-5378, ⓦwww.olyfilm.org), an art cinema that often stages rock shows, including Yoyo a Go Go, a multi-day extravaganza of regional and international bands held every two or three years since 1994. If rock isn't your thing, check out the **Washington Center for the Performing Arts**, 512 Washington St SE (ⓣ360/753-8586, ⓦwww.washingtoncenter.org), which has a full schedule of classical and world music, drama, and ballet.

Wolf Haven International

About ten miles south of Olympia, following Capitol Way as it turns into Old Highway 99, a left turn on Offut Lake Road leads to **Wolf Haven International** (May–Sept daily 10am–5pm; April & Oct Mon & Wed–Sun daily 10am–4pm; March, Nov & Dec Sat–Sun 10am–4pm; $6; ⓦwww.wolfhaven.org). Established in 1982 to provide a safe breeding ground for the threatened North American timberwolf, and a sanctuary and open-air hospital for wolves shot or poisoned by livestock ranchers, Wolf Haven has grown into an 80-acre facility that's now home to more than forty of these surprisingly affectionate, sociable creatures.

On the hourly guided tours (last tour one hour before closing), you can walk within yards of the unexpectedly friendly animals. Be sure to steady yourself if your tour guide happens to let loose with full-throated imitation wolf howls – encouraging a blood-curdling frenzy of mournful braying among the resident lupines. The institute also hosts affordable group presentations for ten or more people (May–Aug hours vary; $8), which you must reserve two weeks in advance, focusing on wolves from different parts of

The legend of D.B. Cooper

Before the airlines clamped down on security in the 1970s, plane hijackings, or **skyjackings**, were surprisingly common – there were no fewer than 150 between 1967 and 1972. Unlike the modern image of fanatical terrorists armed with box-cutters, though, skyjackers sometimes played the part of dashing rogues and colorful rascals. Few caught the popular imagination as much as **D.B. Cooper**, who boarded a Portland-to-Seattle flight on Thanksgiving evening in 1971. As soon as the plane had taken off, Dan Cooper – or at least the man who had bought his ticket under that name – gave a stewardess a note saying he was carrying a bomb. The stewardess actually thought he was trying to chat her up, so she pocketed the note without examining it, obliging him to ask her to read it. After this initial hurdle, Cooper forced the plane to land in Seattle and, in return for releasing all the other passengers, was given four parachutes and $200,000. Airborne again and flying south, he ordered all the crew into the cockpit, opened the rear exit and jumped out – in the midst of a storm – never to be seen again. He was likely killed by the freezing cold and/or by landing amid the dense forests east of the Washington city of Vancouver, but neither his body nor his parachutes have ever been discovered, fueling speculation that he was an expert survivalist and army veteran who survived to live a wealthy life abroad. The FBI looked for him for years without success, the only find being the discovery of one bag of his loot on the banks of the Columbia River in 1980.

the world, and the current challenges these creatures face from human predation. The best time to come, though, is for the Saturday night "**Howl-Ins**" (June–Sept Sat 6–8.30pm; $10; reserve tickets at ⓣ360/264-4695), when storytellers evoke various wolf-related myths and legends, especially those of the Native Americans. When darkness falls, a sort of call-and-response kicks off between the audience and the nearby wolves, baying to the rising moon.

West of Seattle

Accessed by ferry, the sylvan islands **west of Seattle** provide a favorite weekend getaway for that city's denizens, and are consequently home to sizable elite country estates and a smattering of the types of businesses you find everywhere in the Emerald City – coffeehouses, boutiques, bike-rental shops. From Downtown and West Seattle, regular ferry routes take visitors on a quick trip over Puget Sound to sample the windswept, bucolic scenery of these preserves. **Vashon Island** and adjacent **Maury Island**, best suited for unhurried biking and hiking, are less developed than **Bainbridge Island**, which has a few more sights worth closer inspection – notably the elegant grounds of the **Bloedel Reserve** and the quaint shops in the island's main hamlet of **Winslow**. From here, you can return by water to Seattle or take a highway bridge across to the main attractions of the **Kitsap Peninsula**, which offers its own historic appeal in places like **Suquamish** and **Port Gamble**.

Puget Sound ferries

If you do any traveling outside of the city during your visit, particularly into Puget Sound, you'll likely be using **ferries** quite often; access points are listed where applicable throughout this guide. Most routes are run by Washington State Ferries (ⓣ206/464-6400 or 1-800/84-FERRY; ⓦwww.wsdot.wa.gov/ferries); tickets are available on the Seattle's Downtown waterfront from Pier 52, Colman Dock, along with Fauntleroy in West Seattle. Timetables and fares vary by season, and sailing times differ between weekdays and weekends, so it's best to pick up sailing/fare schedules before making plans. Note that **fares** have been increasing annually, so the fees below should only be considered minimum rates, with fee hikes usually planned for late spring.

Anacortes to San Juan Islands To Lopez (45–55min), Orcas (1hr 5min–1hr 25min), and Friday Harbor on San Juan Island (1hr 5min–2hr 5min). Fares are $8.80 for foot passengers, $10.60 peak. With car: mid-May to mid-Oct $29.75 to Lopez, $35.25 to Orcas, $39.50 to San Juan Island; mid-Oct to mid-May $22 to Lopez, $26 to Orcas, $29.25 to San Juan Island. There's a $4 surcharge for bicycles, and fares are free for interisland passenger trips ($11.25 for cars, $14.25 peak season).

Downtown Seattle to Bainbridge Island Departs from Pier 52 approximately hourly from 5.30am to 1.35am; 35min journey length; foot passengers $5.40 round-trip, vehicle and driver $9.50 round-trip, $12 peak season.

Downtown Seattle to Bremerton (Kitsap Peninsula) 14 sailings daily 6am–12.50am; 60min; foot passengers $5.40, vehicle and driver $ 9.50, $12 peak season.

Downtown Seattle to Vashon Island (passenger only) Eight per day Mon–Fri 6.10am–8.35pm, no weekend service; 25min; $7.40 round-trip.

Fauntleroy (West Seattle) to Vashon Island Around 35 sailings daily 5.30am–2am; 15min; foot passengers $3.50 round-trip, vehicle and driver $12.25 round-trip, $15.50 peak season.

Mukilteo to Clinton, Whidbey Island Departs Mukilteo, about thirty miles north of Seattle; weekdays 5am–9pm every half-hour, 9pm–1am hourly; weekends 6am–8am hourly, 8am–9pm every half-hour, 9pm–1am hourly; 20min; foot passengers $3.20 round-trip, vehicle and driver $5.75 round-trip, $7.25 peak season.

Point Defiance to Tahlequah (Tacoma to Vashon Island) Around 20 sailings daily 6am–10pm; 15min; foot passengers $3.50 round-trip, vehicle and driver $12.25 round-trip, $15.50 peak season.

Port Townsend to Keystone, Whidbey Island Ten sailings daily, 6.30am–8.30pm; 30min; foot passengers $2.10 round-trip, vehicle and driver $7.50 round-trip, $9.50 peak season.

Vashon and Maury islands

Only 25 minutes from Seattle by ferry, **Vashon Island** lures visitors with its sizable parks, open fields, rocky beaches, and bike-friendly country roads. The main route, **Vashon Highway**, runs completely across the narrow island, while a sliver of sandbar and fill connect it to **Maury Island**, less than half the size of its neighbor, with much of the same scenery found on the larger island.

The ferry from Seattle arrives on the north tip of the island at Vashon Point, while from Tacoma it pulls in at Tahquelah on the southern end. While you can bring over a car via West Seattle's Fauntleroy ferry terminal, the best way to explore **Vashon Island** is to take a **bike** over from the Downtown Seattle terminal – though you should note that only ten bicycles are permitted on the passenger-only ferry that serves Vashon from Downtown. Alternatively, on the island you can rent bikes at Vashon Island Bicycles, 9925 SW 178th St (ⓣ206/463-6225) – they go for $5 an hour, $25 a day, and $50 for a three-day weekend. For an entirely different view of the two islands, you can rent a

kayak at Puget Sound Kayak, near Vashon Island's center at 8900 SW Harbor Drive (Ⓣ206/463-9257), and explore the beaches and coves in a single- or double-seat kayak ($12-20 per hour, $40-65 per day).

On the whole, there are few actual "sights," and the tranquil inland parks, hills and valleys, attractive vistas, and low-key atmosphere of the two islands are their main appeal. Worth seeking out, as much for its wide, striking views of Downtown Seattle and Mt Rainier as anything else, is the beachside setting of the **Point Robinson Lighthouse**, on the eastern end of **Maury Island** off Point Robinson Road (tours by reservation at Ⓣ206/463-9602), a tiny beacon whose lens has been shining for almost ninety years.

Elsewhere, Vashon Island's main town of **Vashon**, a sleepy hamlet for most of its history, has become more popular recently with Seattle yuppies, who locals say you can count by the increasing number of Mercedes and Jaguars loading onto the ferries. Although companies like the ski-manufacturer K2 have their headquarters here, Vashon is mainly useful to visitors as a base for exploring the rest of the islands. If you do happen to be here during mid-July, though, check out the annual **Strawberry Festival**, which showcases natural foods and features spirited parades, upbeat music, and locals garbed in all manner of colorful costumes.

If you'd rather not return directly to Seattle when departing the island, carry on to Tahlequah at Vashon's southern tip. From here Washington State Ferries sail every hour or so to Point Defiance on the northern outskirts of Tacoma (see opposite). Incidentally, you only have to pay to get to the island – leaving is free.

Practicalities

Vashon has several predictable **B&Bs** (details from Castle Hill Reservation Service at Ⓣ206/463-5491), including *Artist's Studio Loft* 16592 91st Ave SW (Ⓣ206/463-2583, Ⓦwww.asl-bnb.com; ❻), which offers four swanky rooms and cottages with tasteful modern furnishings, fireplaces, and kitchenettes, as well as onsite gardens and a hot tub. *Lavender Duck*, 16503 Vashon Hwy SW (Ⓣ206/463-2592, Ⓦwww.vashonhostel.com/ldmain; ❸) is Vashon's most affordable B&B, though it actually doesn't serve breakfast, but does deliver on the crucial "bed" part, offering four serviceable, if rather basic, rooms in an 1986 farmhouse. *Swallow's Nest Guest Cottages*, 6030 SW 248th St (Ⓣ206/463-2646, Ⓦwww.vashonislandcottages.com; ❺–❽), has eight cottage units themed after birds, featuring varying amenities (from utilitarian to elegant Victorian decor), and located in four separate sites throughout Vashon. Finally, the *Vashon Island Hostel (AYH)*, 12119 SW Cove Rd (May–Oct; Ⓣ206/463-2592, Ⓦwww.vashonhostel.com; reservations advised; ❶–❷), is a good six miles from the ferry dock; to get there head down the main island road and take the signposted turnoff on the right, or you can call ahead for a free pick-up. Surrounded by forest, the hostel's covered wagons and tepees provide family accommodation, as well as rooms for couples; a log cabin is used as a dorm, with rates starting at $10 for members ($13 non-members). Free bicycles are provided.

As for **food**, *Casa Bonita*, 17623 100th Ave SW (Ⓣ206/463-6452), is a good Mexican restaurant – a rarity in the area – with large portions of enchiladas, fajitas, and the like. *Express Cuisine*, 17629 Vashon Hwy SW (Ⓣ206/463-6626), has a very informal setting, with large shared tables, and delicious, filling dishes, dominated by seafood. *Island Crossroads*, 20312 Vashon Hwy SW (Ⓣ206/463-3565), has straightforward sandwiches, salads, and pastries in an agreeable setting, while *Rock Island Pizza*, 17322 Vashon Hwy SW (Ⓣ206/463-6814), provides solid gourmet pizzas and microbrews.

Bainbridge Island

The ferry ride to green and rural **BAINBRIDGE ISLAND**, gliding by the Magnolia bluffs on the outward journey across Elliott Bay and offering a panoramic view of the Seattle skyline upon the return, is so delightful that for many the island itself is simply an excuse for the trip. That said, there are enough worthwhile diversions on Bainbridge Island to reward you for stepping off the ferry.

Washington State Ferries leave about every hour from Pier 52 in Downtown Seattle and land in the island's main town of **Winslow**. While a car is necessary to reach Bainbridge Island's best-known attraction, **Bloedel Reserve** (see below), an alternative is to cycle the island's narrow country roads – Bainbridge is only ten miles from top to bottom – and **camp** in Fay Bainbridge State Park (see below). Bainbridge Island's **visitor center** is located in Winslow at 590 Winslow Way E (ⓣ206/842-3700, ⓦwww.bainbridgechamber.com).

Accommodation

Cedar Meadow 10411 NE Old Creosote Hill Rd ⓣ206/842-5291. Relaxed B&B with five simple units in a modern cedar home. Located in a wooded space across the harbor from Winslow, it offers a free pick-up from the ferry if you call ahead. ❺

Fay Bainbridge State Park off Sunrise Drive NE ⓣ206/842-3931, ⓦwww.parks.wa.gov. Seventeen-acre campground on the northeast tip of Bainbridge Island, with 36 very basic sites and a beach with good views of the surrounding area. Closed mid-Oct to mid-April (but open for day use year-round). Camp sites $15–21.

Furin-Oka 12580 Vista Drive NE, 3mi north of Winslow ⓣ206/842-4916, ⓦwww.futonandbreakfast.com. Stylish Japanese guest-house with traditional Japanese amenities like soaking tub, kimonos, and shoji screens, located in a bamboo grove. Japanese or American breakfasts available. ❼

Island Country Inn 920 Hildebrand Lane NE, just north of Winslow ⓣ206/842-6861, ⓦwww.nwcountryinns.com. Bainbridge's only hotel, a worthwhile choice with 46 rooms, all with queen- or king-size beds; there's also a pool and Jacuzzi. Suites available with microwaves and fridges for about $30 more a night. ❻

Mary's Farmhouse 5129 McDonald Rd NE ⓣ206/842-4952. The most affordable B&B on Bainbridge, near the south side of the harbor, across the water from Winslow; two simple guestrooms with shared bathrooms in a remodeled 1904 farmhouse on five acres of pastured land. ❹

The Island

Bainbridge's only noteworthy town, **Winslow**, features pleasant restaurants and boutiques on Winslow Way and Madison Avenue. On the plaza behind City Hall (on Madison Avenue), the **farmers' market** sells produce and crafts on Saturday mornings from Easter to October. Meanwhile, **Bainbridge Arts and Crafts**, 151 Winslow Way E (ⓣ206/842-3132, ⓦwww.bainbridgeartscrafts.org), displays occasionally inventive work by local artists. **Eagle Harbor Books**, next door at 157, is a fine small bookstore featuring local authors such as David Guterson.

The island's undisputed gem is **Bloedel Reserve**, 7571 NE Dolphin Drive, off the Agatewood Road exit of Hwy-305 (Wed–Sun 10am–4pm; $6; by reservation only at ⓣ206/842-7631, ⓦwww.bloedelreserve.org), a natural conservatory containing nearly 150 acres of gardens, ponds, meadows, and wildlife habitats, including 84 acres of second-growth forest and more than 15,000 cyclamen plants. It's often blissfully serene except for the birds – there's also a refuge with swans, blue herons, and more – and the geometric Japanese garden and forest-enclosed reflecting pool add to the ethereal aura.

To sample the more woodsy essence of Bainbridge Island, however, try strolling through the whimsically named "**Grand Forest**," a 240-acre park with second-growth forests and wetlands. Park on the roadside near the signs on Miller Road, just south of Koura Road.

Eating and drinking

Café Nola 101 Winslow Way ☎206/842.3822. A popular bistro – open for lunch and dinner – whose frequent turnover of owners has cost it some local fans, but it still manages to be worthwhile for its tasty pastries, vegetarian fare, and agreeable Sunday brunch.

Pegasus Coffee House 131 Parfitt Way SW ☎206/842-6725. Brick-and-ivy coffee joint with a fine selection of brews and convivial atmosphere. An area fixture for 25 years.

Ruby's on Bainbridge 4738 Lynwood Center Rd, on the south side of the island ☎206/780-9303. Provincial French-leaning eatery with tasty (and somewhat unusual) pastas and entrees, like wild mushroom fettuccini, hazelnut pork medallions, and bread pudding with caramel and rum sauce.

Sawatdy Thai Cuisine 8770 Fletcher Bay Rd NE ☎206/780-2429. On the opposite side of the island from Winslow, an excellent Thai restaurant; try its traditional staples like spicy soup and noodle dishes.

Winslow Way Café 122 Winslow Way, Winslow ☎206/842-0517. One of the pricier local restaurants, but also the best; worth it for the gourmet pizza, pasta, and seafood.

The Kitsap Peninsula

Lurking behind Bainbridge Island, and sprawling jaggedly into the middle of Puget Sound, the **KITSAP PENINSULA** bristles with high-budgeted defense projects for the US arsenal: a nuclear submarine base at **Bangor**, a torpedo-testing station in **Keyport**, and colossal shipyards at **Bremerton**. All of these add up to a formidable dollop of military might, and understandably worth avoiding, but luckily the peninsula has more inviting areas, too. These are spread out along **Hwy-305**, which merges into Hwy-3 to form the handiest route from Seattle to the Olympic Peninsula (see p.349). You can get to the peninsula from the northern end of Bainbridge Island by taking Agate Passage Bridge, on the Kitsap side of which is Port Madison Indian Reservation.

Suquamish and around

The tiny burg of **SUQUAMISH** offers little in the way of atmosphere by itself, though it does sit among some of the more compelling historical sights on the peninsula. Just beyond the Agate Passage Bridge, a signed right turn leads a couple of miles off the highway to quiet **St Peter's Churchyard**, 7076 NE South St (daily, dawn–dusk), which holds the **grave of Chief Sealth**, Seattle's namesake, who was the tribal leader of the Suquamish people when the first whites arrived. Two painted canoes stand above the headstone and the plaque proclaims him "The firm friend of the whites" – something of a dubious accolade, considering how things turned out (see below). Nearby, surrounded by modern housing, poky **Old Man House State Park** marks the site of the tribe's cedar longhouse, which stretched along the seashore for five hundred feet: the government had it burnt down in 1870 to eliminate communal living, that great enemy of private property. Today, the park is a pleasant little spot that provides a nice respite and good views of the sound.

Back on Hwy-305, it's a couple of minutes' drive to the turnoff which twists down to the **Suquamish Museum**, 15838 Sandy Hook Rd (May–Sept daily 10am–5pm; Oct–April Fri–Sun 11am–4pm; $4; Ⓦwww.suquamish.nsn.us/museum). The museum traces the history of the Suquamish, who occupied much of the Kitsap Peninsula until American settlers arrived. Chief Sealth chose to avoid conflict with his new neighbors, but it didn't do much good, and his people received an appallingly bad deal from the carving-up of their land. Formerly based throughout Puget Sound, they have, since that 1855 treaty (followed by the brief Puget Sound War between the settlers and about fifteen tribes), been stuck on the 7500-acre **Port Madison Indian Reservation**. The museum, however, celebrates Native American culture more than it laments injustices, interspersing exhibits of craftwork, canoes, games, folk art, and photographs with quotations from tribal elders, whose recorded voices also overlay a slide show that portrays the lifestyle of present generations, caught between traditional values and Western hegemony.

Poulsbo and around

Further north on Hwy-305, **POULSBO** makes a gallant bid for the tourist trade. Founded by Norwegians, it has exploited its heritage by revamping the cafés and souvenir shops along its main route, **Front Street**, in "little Norway" kitsch. It's all rather daft but endearing nonetheless, and locals take every opportunity to dress up in fancy Nordic duds, especially during mid-May's **Viking Fest** (Ⓣ360/779-3378, Ⓦwww.vikingfest.org). The rest of the year, traditional Norwegian food is served up all over the place, and the *Poulsbohemian Coffeehouse*, 19003 Front St (Ⓣ360/779-9199), offers strong java, music, and poetry readings – but otherwise there's not much to keep you here for very long.

North from Poulsbo, you can keep to the main road (highways 305 and 3) as it cuts a mundane course towards the Olympic Peninsula, or you can turn right off Hwy-305 just north of town along Hwy-307 and, after about four hundred yards, take a left down **Big Valley Road**. Drifting through a river valley of antique wooden farmhouses, rolling farmland, and forested hills, this lovely country lane passes by the delightful **Manor Farm Inn**, 26069 Big Valley Rd (Ⓣ360/779-4628, Ⓦwww.manorfarminn.com; ❻). Here, a working farm surrounds a charming picket-fenced farmhouse of 1890 that's been tastefully converted into a plush hotel. Reservations are advised; the restaurant is excellent, too, with a full meal costing around $40. Heading north along Big Valley Road, you soon rejoin the main road – Hwy-3 – about three miles west of the **Hood Canal Floating Bridge**, which crosses over to the Olympic Peninsula (see p.349). More than a mile in length, the bridge used to be billed as an engineering miracle – until a chunk of it floated out to sea during a violent storm in 1979. It was more than three years before the bridge was reopened, with engineers' assurances that it had been reinforced.

Port Gamble

Draped above a tiny bay just a mile or so beyond the Hood Canal Floating Bridge is the Kitsap's prettiest settlement, **PORT GAMBLE**, a pocket-sized hamlet whose entrepreneurial founders, Pope and Talbot, made a killing in Puget Sound timber. They also satisfied a sentimental attachment to their hometown, East Machias, Maine, by shipping out East Coast elm trees to overhang quaint, New-England-style clapboard houses, many built in the 1850s and all owned by the company and rented to the employees of the town sawmill. Pope and Talbot carefully maintained the port's late-nineteenth-century appearance, and all might have been well if they hadn't closed the mill down in 1995. As a result, Port Gamble is presently a very pretty town, but one without much of a purpose.

In this tranquil, leafy setting, the **Port Gamble Historical Museum**, directly facing the bay (May–Oct daily 10.30am–5pm; $2.50; ⓣ360/297-8074, ⓦwww.ptgamble.com), traces the development of the town and its lumber trade, and is well worth a quick look along with the adjoining **General Store**, whose cast-iron pillars and wooden floors accommodate a collection of seashells on the upper floor. Not far away sits the charming, Carpenter Gothic-styled **St Paul's Episcopal Church.** Up the hill, the old **cemetery** holds the grave of one Gustave Engelbrecht, who was killed by local natives in 1856, the first US sailor to die in action on the Pacific Coast. Glorious it was not: he took a potshot at a native and, eager to check his kill, jumped up from behind the log which provided his cover, only to be promptly shot himself.

At the moment, there's nowhere **to stay** in Port Gamble, but there are vague plans to establish a B&B – for an update, call or drop by the Kitsap Peninsula Visitor and Convention Bureau, in town at 2 Rainier Ave (ⓣ360/297-8200, ⓦwww.visitkitsap.com).

Keyport and Bremerton

Military enthusiasts will be keen to visit **KEYPORT**, south of Poulsbo, site of the **Naval Undersea Museum**, just east of Hwy-3 on Hwy-308 (June–Sept daily 10am–4pm; Oct–May closed Tues; free; ⓦnum.kpt.nuwc.navy.mil). Operated by the US Navy, it displays an imposing array of nautical weaponry, from torpedoes to depth charges to aquatic mines and various other bombs and destructive gadgets – though it avoids mentioning too many details about the local presence of nuclear submarines in nearby Bangor (see box).

Nuclear weapons in Washington State

While the town of **Bangor** hardly ranks on the list of major Washington tourist attractions, it is the only site harboring active **nuclear weapons** in the Pacific Northwest. Being one of two US naval bases hosting the country's formidable fleet of **Ballistic Missile Submarines**, unlikely little Bangor is a prime target in the event of a nuclear war. Armed with approximately half of all the warheads in the American arsenal, these "Submarine Launched Ballistic Missiles" form one leg of America's triad of nuclear weapons systems, the others being long-range bombers and ICBMs, and are poised at the ready on the eighteen **Trident** subs that patrol the world's oceans. Less than ten submarines are therefore based out of Bangor, but according to some estimates, each carries two dozen missiles fitted with eight warheads, making for some 1700 hydrogen-based bombs here, with a destructive power of 800 megatons – enough to destroy life on Earth several times over.

Needless to say, you can forget about taking a tour of one of these high-powered underwater ships. While the US Navy is happy to have you look over the array of outmoded Civil War mines and disused warships in Bremerton, it has no patience with interlopers who might want to sneak a peek at something they saw in a movie like *Crimson Tide*, or read about in a Tom Clancy novel. Trespassing at the base will surely get you a harsh interrogation and even jail time, so be sure to stick to the more anodyne martial attractions found elsewhere on the peninsula.

Ten miles south along Hwy-3, **BREMERTON** is a rough-edged shipyard town that's home to the **Bremerton Naval Museum**, 130 Washington Ave (summer Mon–Sat 10am–5pm, Sun 1–5pm; donation; ⓣ360/479-SHIP), which presents an unsurprising, but mildly interesting, assortment of historic weaponry and model ships. If you're still in need of a military fix, you can tour the warship **USS Turner Joy**, 300 Washington Beach Ave (summer daily 10am–5pm; $7; ⓣ360/792-2457). This 1959 destroyer is most notable for being involved in the 1965 Gulf of Tonkin incident, which became President Lyndon Johnson's main excuse for Congress to escalate the war in Vietnam dramatically. Finally, for a waterside look at the "Mothball Fleet," a handful of warships held in readiness just offshore (and off-limits to the public), Kitsap Harbor Tours (ⓣ360/377-8924) offers daily, hour-long boat trips ($8.50) round the warships from mid-May to September.

Whidbey Island

The longest island in the continental US, **WHIDBEY ISLAND** is the first spot in Puget Sound to feel like a world unto itself. Nearly fifty miles in length, its narrow country roads wind through farmland and small villages. A land of sheer cliffs and craggy outcrops, rocky beaches, and prairie countryside, Whidbey's flat glacial moraine and bucolic landscape make it ideal cycling country. Not easily seen on a short ferry trip, it requires at least a full day – probably more – to appreciate its diverse qualities. Its small towns of **Langley** and **Coupeville** are both pleasant getaways, while **Fort Casey**, **Fort Ebey**, and **Deception Pass state parks** are more enticing with their remote wooded trails and stark cliffside vistas – certainly preferable to Oak Harbor, Whidbey's largest (and dullest) town, with a slew of drab motels. Once considered a key stronghold in the defense of the Sound, the island also carries martial relics from various eras: nineteenth-century blockhouses built against Native American attack, concrete bunkers from World War II, and a large naval base housing modern air and naval defense systems.

Arrival and information

If you're heading north to the San Juan Islands, it's much more pleasant to meander through Whidbey than dash up I-5 from Downtown Seattle. Coming from town, the quickest route onto Whidbey Island is via the Mukilteo **ferry** (see box, p.320, for schedule and fares), about thirty miles north of Seattle, adjacent to Everett. The twenty-minute ride terminates at **Clinton**, a tiny town near Whidbey's southern edge. From here Hwy-525 snakes through the middle of the island to Deception Pass at the top, turning into Hwy-20 halfway into the journey. A second ferry leaves Port Townsend on the Olympic Peninsula for the half-hour trip to Whidbey's Keystone, halfway up the island just south of Coupeville, the main town. Bringing a car is advisable, although Island Transit has a free **bus service** serving the length of the island on eleven different routes (daily except Sun; ⓣ360/678-7771, 360/321-6688 or 1-800/240-8747,

Ⓦ www.islandtransit.org). Velocity Bikes, 5603 S Bayview Rd in Langley (Ⓣ 360/321-5040), rents **bikes** for around $22 per day.

The Central Whidbey Chamber of Commerce runs a **Visitor Information Center** in Coupeville, 107 S Main St (Mon–Fri 10am–5pm; Ⓣ 360/678-5434, Ⓦ www.centralwhidbeychamber.com), with all the requisite brochures, though a free visitor's guide, with a detailed map of the island, can also be picked up on the ferry.

Accommodation

For **accommodation**, Whidbey isn't much for fancy hotels, and its Oak Harbor motels are fairly unexceptional. However, many of the island's old villas, especially in Coupeville, have been turned into lavish (and sometimes quite expensive) **B&Bs**. The visitor center has brochures about many of them, you can try the online visitor's guide at Ⓦ www.whidbey.net/visitor/visitors.

Camping is another option with 250 tent sites as well as primitive grounds at **Deception Pass State Park** 5175 N Hwy-20 ($10–21; Ⓣ 360/657-2417 Ⓦ www.parks.wa.gov), one of the most popular state parks in the US. Still, it fills up quickly in the summer months, so call ahead. Smaller **Fort Ebey State Park** Hill Valley Drive, Coupeville ($10–21; Ⓣ 360/678-4636 Ⓦ www.parks.wa.gov), is built around an old defense battery, with good hiking trails, and offers fifty tent sites and three primitive sites (without a vehicle).

Captain Whidbey Inn 2072 W Captain Whidbey Inn Rd, Coupeville Ⓣ 360/678-4097 or 1-800/366-4097, Ⓦ www.captainwhidbey.com. Out of the way but worth it, with quiet rooms overlooking Penn Cove, cottages and chalets in the forest, and a restaurant renowned for its seafood (see p.329). Four-to-six-day package trips include cruises on the Inn's *Cutty Sark* ship ($1950 and up). 5–9

Country Cottage of Langley 215 Sixth St, Langley Ⓣ 360/221-8709 or 1-800/718-3860 Ⓦ www.acountrycottage.com. Five rooms in a restored 1920s farmhouse, on a bluff above Langley and Puget Sound. All rooms have CD players and fridges, while higher-end suites have Jacuzzi tubs and fireplaces. 7

Drake's Landing 203 Wharf St, Langley Ⓣ 360/221-3999. The least expensive of Langley's B&Bs, it's still quite acceptable, with bathrooms in each room and decent views of the harbor. 4

Fort Casey Inn three miles south of Coupeville at 1124 S Engle Rd Ⓣ 360/678-8792. Charming establishment where duplex accommodation is available in a row of renovated officers' houses on the edge of the state park. 5

The Inn at Langley 400 First St, Langley Ⓣ 360/221-3033 Ⓦ www.innatlangley.com. One of the poshest stopovers on Puget Sound, built into a bluff overlooking the water; starting around $225, all 24 rooms have porches with waterfront views, with suites and private cottages costing about two and three times as much. 9

Langley and Coupeville

The Mukilteo ferry lands at sleepy, unexceptional **Clinton**, but a more interesting first stop is **LANGLEY**, a well-heeled seaside village just a few miles away off Hwy-525, with an old-West-style stretch of wooden storefronts set on a picturesque bluff overlooking the water. Quaint and appealing, **First Street** is lined with antique stores and galleries such as the **Artists Cooperative of Whidbey Island**, no. 314 (Ⓣ 360/221-76750), and the various artisans at the **Hellebore Glass Studio**, no. 308 (Ⓣ 360/221-2067, Ⓦ www.helleboreglass.com), where you can pick up handmade art and craftworks, including some interesting and detailed glass pieces.

In the island's center, **COUPEVILLE** is Washington's second-oldest city and home to Whidbey's most historic district, with several dozen buildings dating back to the late nineteenth and early twentieth centuries, and neighborhoods dotted with vintage Victorian homes – leftovers from its days as a flourishing seaport. It was settled back in the 1850s by sea captains and merchants attracted by the protected harbor in **Penn Cove**, and by the plentiful oak and pine trees. The several blocks of waterfront on **Front Street**, between Main Street and the pier, feature most of Coupeville's top shops and eateries, while the area around **Main Street** offers a selection of attractive homes and other classic structures along a half-mile south from the shoreline. The 1886 **Loers House**, Eighth Street at Grace Street, is especially worth a look for its mix of traditional Victorian architecture with an inexplicable onion-domed turret.

The **Island County Historical Museum**, 908 NW Alexander St (daily 10am–4pm, summer closes at 5pm; donation suggested; ⓣ360/678-3310, ⓦwww.islandhistory.org), gives thirty-minute guided historical **walking tours** of Front Street (June–Sept weekends 11am; $2), though the most historically interesting building in town, **Alexander's Blockhouse**, just outside the museum, can be seen on its own for free. This small wooden structure was built by settlers in 1855 to defend themselves from possible attack by the local Skagit Indians – which never occurred.

Fort Casey and Fort Ebey state parks

Coupeville is actually part of **Ebey's Landing National Historical Reserve** (ⓣ360/678-3310, ⓦwww.nps.gov/ebla), an officially protected series of farms, forests, and privately owned land named after one of the island's first white settlers, **Colonel Isaac Ebey**. In 1851 the colonel penned a letter to his brother describing his new home as "almost a paradise of nature . . . I think I could live and die here content." Ebey did get part of his wish: in 1857 he was slain by Alaskan Tlingit in revenge for the killing of one of the tribe's chieftains.

On the western side of the island are the reserve's two state parks, each of which have several miles of shoreline on the Strait of Juan de Fuca. The smaller of the two, **FORT CASEY STATE PARK** (daily 8am–dusk), is three miles south of Coupeville off Hwy-20. Built at the beginning of the twentieth century to guard the entrance to Puget Sound, the fort was obsolete by the 1950s. Check out the grim cluster of dark **gun batteries**, whose World War II-era artillery emplacements can be freely explored, and the squat but charming **Admiralty Head Lighthouse** (summer tours by reservation at ⓣ360/679-7391), one of several lighthouses around the long, irregularly shaped island. A half-mile southeast of Fort Casey, the **Keystone ferry landing** allows you to make the short trip to Port Townsend (see p.350), just across Admiralty Inlet to the southwest.

Seven miles north along the beach from Fort Casey, the aesthetically pleasing **FORT EBEY STATE PARK** (summer 6.30am–dusk, winter 8am–dusk; ⓣ360/678-4636), reachable by car by turning left on Libby Road four miles northwest of Coupeville, offers an attractive shoreline and plenty of opportunities for hiking, biking, and fishing. An abandoned gun and bunker emplacement, built in 1942 to defend against a possible attack from the Pacific, remains in a remote location within the park amid dense forest cover and makes for an eerie visit. If time or energy don't permit the beachside trek to the park, a small parking area between the forts at Ebey's Landing (at the southern end of Ebey Road) puts you right next to a gorgeous trail. Rising and dipping for a mile or two along a ridge that overlooks the bluff and Admiralty Inlet, it yields some of the most striking views to be found anywhere on Puget Sound.

Deception Pass State Park

Beyond Ebey's Reserve, contemporary military matters dominate the economy of **Oak Harbor**, Whidbey's largest – and most unappealing – town. The nearby Naval Air Station, built in 1941, is home to the navy's tactical electronic-warfare squadrons, and the town's ugly suburban sprawl is best passed straight through. You'd do much better to continue north to **DECEPTION PASS STATE PARK**, 5175 N Hwy-20 (daily 8am–dusk; ⓣ360/675-2417), where a steel bridge arches gracefully over the narrow Deception Pass gorge between Whidbey and Fidalgo Island, a connecting-point (via Anacortes) for the San Juan Islands. With excellent hiking trails and campsites, the park occupies land on both islands. The turbulent waters in between were originally thought to have been a small bay when charted by the Spanish. Even the intrepid George Vancouver was wary of them, initially deceived (hence the name) into believing he had charted part of the Whidbey "peninsula," rather than the strait that makes it an island.

Grab a map from the Whidbey-side park office and head to the **Lighthouse Point Trail** that begins near the **Civilian Conservation Corps Interpretive Center** (summer only during park hours), meanders along beach and forest for nearly a mile, and eventually leads to rocky bluffs with good views of the pass. The center has a small but interesting exhibit and video on the creation and history of the CCC, one of the programs initiated by President Franklin Roosevelt in the 1930s to create employment, at the same time helping to conserve the nation's natural resources. Most of the two-and-a-half million men that enrolled were young, hungry, and in need of the steady meals (and $30/month pay) the organization provided. In Washington State, the CCC built most of the structures in about a dozen state parks, including the trails and facilities in the park itself.

Eating and drinking

As you might expect, most of the good **eating** and **drinking** options on Whidbey Island are located in either Coupeville or Langley.

Captain Whidbey Inn 2072 W Captain Whidbey Inn Rd, Coupeville ⓣ360/678-4097 or 1-800/366-4097. The restaurant of one of the island's top B&Bs (see p.327). Serves fine seafood, including locally harvested mussels, and fresh herbs and vegetables from its gardens. Reservations essential.

Christopher's Front Street Café 23 Front St, Coupeville ⓣ360/678-5480. Decent lunches, dinners, and microbrews that strike a balance between basic diner food and ritzier eating.

Knead & Feed 4 Front St, Coupeville ⓣ360/678-5431. Scrumptious home-made bread, pies, and cinnamon rolls at its bakery, as well as sit-down lunches, and weekend breakfasts and dinners.

Langley Village Bakery 221 2nd St #1, Langley ⓣ360/221-3525. Great baked goods, pizza, and soup, either to go or to eat-in.

Neil's Clover Patch Cafe 2850 Hwy-525, Langley ⓣ360/321-4120. Buffet spot with gut-busting weekly specials of fish 'n' chips (Mon) and ribs (Tues nights), and hefty staples like steak 'n' eggs the rest of the time.

Toby's Tavern 8 Front St, Coupeville ⓣ360/678-4222. Basic wharfside joint with serviceable seafood, burgers, and microbrews.

The San Juan Islands

Northwest of Whidbey Island, midway between the Washington coast and Canada, the **San Juan Islands** scatter across the eastern reaches of the Strait of Juan de Fuca and, for many people, entirely upstage the rest of Puget Sound. Tailor-made for strolling, cycling, and nature-watching, the idyllic San Juans act as breeding grounds of rare birds and sea creatures: white-headed bald eagles circle over treetops, and Orca ("killer") whale pods pass close to shore. A convoluted maze of green islands, with myriad bluffs and bays, the archipelago has 743 islands, but only about 170 of them are actually visible during high tide, and only sixty of those are populated. The best of them are exceptionally scenic getaways, but unless you've got your own boat or quite a bit of money, your visits will be restricted to the three major islands served by Washington State Ferries – **San Juan**, **Orcas**, and **Lopez**. San Juan, by far the largest island, offers historic state parks and a thriving port, **Friday Harbor**; Orcas is the most scenic, especially in the mountainous interior of **Moran State Park**; while Lopez is the most sedate, its flat and largely empty roads a haven for bicyclists.

The islands were first spotted by Europeans in 1592 when explorer **Juan de Fuca**, now believed to be a Greek sailing for the Spanish, claimed to have

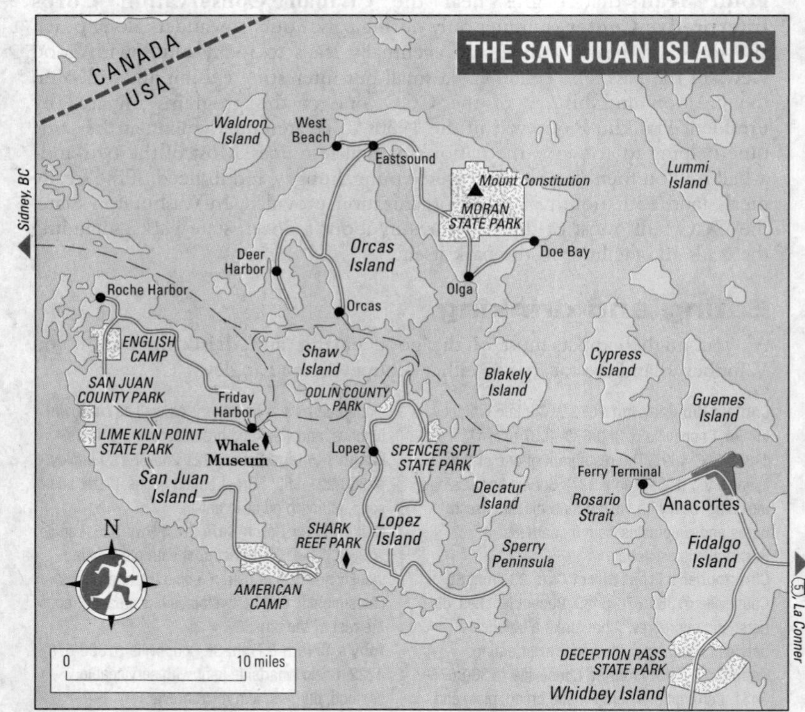

found an inlet at 47 degrees north latitude while searching for the mythical northwest passage connecting the Pacific and Atlantic. This discovery went unacknowledged until 1787, when Englishman **Charles Barkley** found a strait at the approximate location and named it in honor of de Fuca. It was the Spanish, though, who first fully explored the strait in 1790 under **Manuel Quimper**, accounting for the Spanish names that grace several of the islands today. However, the days when the islands were simple rustic retreats are long gone and nowadays the islands' farming and fishing communities are jostled by escapees from the cities. Indeed, in summer there are more visitors than the islands can accommodate, and you'll definitely need to book somewhere to stay in advance: during high-season weekends dozens of disappointed travelers end up spending the night at the ferry terminal, something all the tourist authorities work hard to avoid. However, even in July and August, peaceful corners away from the crowds are easy to find.

Getting to the islands

Washington State Ferries (ⓣ206/464-6400 or 1-888/808-7977, ⓦwww.wsdot.wa.gov/ferries), departs for the San Juans from the terminal complex about four miles west of the unassuming port of **Anacortes**, just west of La Conner (see p.339) on Hwy-20, reachable from the convention center in Downtown Seattle by Gray Line **bus** (daily 6am; $23 one-way; 1hr 30min; ⓣ206/626-5208 or 1-800/426-7505, ⓦwww.graylineofseattle.com). As way-stations go, Anacortes isn't bad, with a few decent places to stock up on snacks and sandwiches before getting on the boat. Try *Geppetto's*, 3320 Commercial Ave, for good Italian takeout **food** and baked goods, or *La Vie en Rose*, 418 Commercial Ave, which serves tasty deli sandwiches, desserts, and breads. If you plan to stay overnight to catch a crack-of-dawn ferry, Commercial Avenue is lined with numerous budget **hotels**, the least generic of which is the *Islands Inn*, no. 3401 (ⓣ360/293-4644, ⓦwww.islandsinn.com; ❹), offering bayside views and fireplaces, while the *Majestic Hotel*, no. 419 (ⓣ360/293-3355; ❺), is a nicely renovated grand hotel from 1889, with old-fashioned decor and a good onsite restaurant and bar.

There are about a dozen Washington State ferries daily, the earliest of which leaves around 6am (see box on p.320 for schedule and prices). If you're bringing a vehicle, you should come early – ideally two hours in advance – as the lines at the port can be long. A passenger-only alternative is the **Victoria Clipper** (ⓣ360/448-5000 or 1-800/888-2535, ⓦwww.victoriaclipper.com), which runs from Pier 69 in Seattle to San Juan's Friday Harbor ($38 one-way, $59 return) and, with a four-hour layover in Friday Harbor, to Orcas's Rosario ($45 one-way, $69 return). Boats leave once daily from mid-May to mid-September, and weekends to Friday Harbor only April to mid-May; you can save about $10 by booking a round-trip seven days in advance.

Lopez Island

The first stop on the ferry route, which runs through the Rosario Strait east of the islands, is usually **LOPEZ ISLAND**, a quiet, pastoral retreat where country lanes lace rolling hills and gentle farmland that once supplied much of western Washington with meat and fruit. Although today it's not the agricultural power it was, there are still plenty of orchards and cattle around, if little else. In as much as the island has a base, it's the little roadstop of **Lopez Village**. Still, while there isn't much to do, the island is a cyclist's paradise, which is a large part of its appeal: Lopez never gets as crowded as its larger neighbors and is virtually undeveloped, with a population of fewer than two thousand souls. Accordingly, the locals do not entirely welcome the recent construction of an opulent summer home for Microsoft billionaire Paul Allen on **Sperry Peninsula**, the most remote part of the island – an estate that you will most assuredly be prevented from seeing, much less touring.

Arrival and information

The best way to explore small, mostly flat Lopez is by **bicycle**. Rentals are available in Lopez Village – from The Bike Shop on Lopez (ⓣ360/468-3497), or further south at 2847 Fisherman Bay Rd, from Lopez Bicycle Works (ⓣ360/468-2847, ⓦwww.lopezbicycleworks.com); both will deliver bikes anywhere on Lopez, and charge around $5 per hour or $25 a day. At the latter location, Lopez Kayaks (May–Oct only; ⓣ360/468-2847, ⓦwww.lopezkayaks.com), also arranges **sea trips** ($35/2hr tour, $75/ 3hr 30min tour) and rents **kayaks** ($12 to 35/hr).

Accommodation

For such an untrammeled island, Lopez does offer a nice range of **places to stay**, both in price and type.

Hotels and B&Bs

Blue Fjord Cabins 862 Elliott Rd ⓣ1-888/633-0401, ⓦwww.interisland.net/bluefjord. A quiet retreat in the woods, offering two cozy, secluded cabins at reasonable rates. ❺

Inn at Swifts Bay 856 Port Stanley Rd ⓣ360/468-3636, ⓦwww.swiftsbay.com. The most luxurious B&B on Lopez, nestled at the bottom of a little-traveled road near the ferry; turn left one mile south of the dock, and it's on the right, just past the fire station. Only a few minutes' walk from the beach, the *Inn* has five units (three of them suites) with hot tubs, fireplaces, and an onsite sauna. ❺–❽

Lopez Islander 2847 Fisherman Bay Rd ⓣ360/468-2233 or 1-800/736-3434, ⓦwww.lopezislander.com. The only luxury hotel on Lopez has thirty spacious rooms (most with sunset views), swimming pool, and hot tub; Lopez Bicycle Works and Lopez Kayaks are also located here. ❻–❼

Campgrounds

Lopez Farm Cottages & Camping Fisherman Bay Rd south of Military Rd ⓣ1-800/440-3556, ⓦwww.lopezfarmcottages.com. For about twice the price of the more basic campgrounds on Lopez (see below), these campsites have a few more modern amenities, for $33 (open May–Oct 1). Comfortable cottages – each with fireplace, porch, and deck – are available year-round, varying from $100–150 according to season.

Odlin County Park North side of Lopez, south of Upright Head ⓣ360/378-1842, ⓦwww.co.san-juan.wa.us/parks. By the beach, just a mile from the ferry; charges $16 for campsites ($19 for premium sites on the beach), or $11 for those without a vehicle; lower rates Nov–March.

Spencer Spit State Park Baker View Rd ⓣ360/468-2251, ⓦwww.parks.wa.gov. Thirty-four tent sites (along with three primitive ones w/o vehicle) at an isolated park with good hiking and clamming nearby. The best place to camp on Lopez, so reserve ahead in peak season. Closed Nov–Feb 1. Campsites $15–21.

The Island

In Lopez Village, there are few actual sights except for the **Lopez Island Historical Museum**, 28 Washburn Place (May, June & Sept Fri–Sat noon–4pm, July & Aug also open Wed & Thurs; donation; ⓣ360/468-2049, ⓦwww.rockisland.com/~lopezmuseum), which will give you an adequate introduction to the native tribes and early pioneers who populated the place, but is mainly useful as the place where you can pick up a useful map of a **driving tour** of the area's historic sites and homes.

Lopez's top destination is **Shark Reef Park** (daily 7am–10pm; free; ⓣ360/378-8420), at the island's southwest tip on Shark Reef Road, accessible via Fisherman Bay and Airport roads. A ten- to fifteen-minute walk through dense forest is rewarded by beautiful vistas at the water's edge, from where you can spot the occasional sea lion past the tidepools. Inland, there's fishing at **Hummel Lake**, and on the island's northeast coast, **Spencer Spit State Park**, in addition to its campsites (see "Accommodation," above), offers good hiking among the trees, beach walking, and clamming.

Eating and drinking

Almost by default, the island's best **eating** and **drinking** options can be found in Lopez Village.

Bay Cafe 9 Old Post Rd, Lopez Village ⓣ360/468-3700. The only spot in Lopez for elegant dining, and the eclectic entrees – the likes of seafood tapas and risotto cakes - in the $17–20 range are worth it. Reserve in advance; live jazz on Sunday nights.

Holly B's Bakery 165 Cherry Tree Lane, Lopez Village ⓣ360/468-2133. Small but worthwhile stop for buns, breads, pastries, and light snacks.

Isabel's Espresso Village House Building, Lopez Village ⓣ360/468-4114. One of the better spots to have your coffee in town, with juice drinks, tea, sweets, and some lunch items, too. A good place to fuel up on espresso or cool down with herbal tea.

Orcas Island

The most alluring destination in the San Juans for striking scenery, horseshoe-shaped **ORCAS ISLAND** teems with rugged hills and leafy timber that tower over its leisurely roads, craggy beaches, and abundant wildlife. It's not only the island's fairly rustic topography that keeps the hordes away, but also that it hasn't been fully exploited as a tourist destination. You can literally come here and easily find a quiet cove or tranquil setting and peaceably spend the day. Nonetheless, while not completely overridden with outsiders, its enviable qualities have not escaped the notice of the larger world, either: though there are only 3500 full-time island residents, there are three times as many property owners. Yet, despite being much busier than Lopez, Orcas's holiday resorts are so well tucked into distant coves that the island's peace and quiet is hardly disturbed.

Arrival and information

Ferries dock in tiny **Orcas**, and down the main road of Horseshoe Highway is the slightly larger town of **Eastsound**. Maps and island **information** are available at the **Chamber of Commerce**, N Beach Road in Eastsound (ⓣ360/376-2273, ⓦwww.orcasisland.org), next to *Bilbo's Festivo* restaurant (see below). You can rent **bikes** (for $30 per day) in Orcas from Dolphin Bay Bicycles, just up from the dock (ⓣ360/376-3093, ⓦwww.rockisland .com/~dolphin), or in Eastsound from Wildlife Cycles, 350 N Beach Rd at A Street (ⓣ360/376-4708, ⓦwww.wildlifecycles.com), and cycle north through the island's fetching farm country – the onetime heart of the state's apple orchards, until Eastern Washington was irrigated and commercialized.

Accommodation

Accommodation choices on Orcas Island are plentiful, but, as with the other major San Juan islands, advance **reservations** are advised, especially when visiting during summer months.

Hotels and B&Bs

Beach Haven Resort 684 Beach Haven Rd ⓣ360/376-2288, ⓦwww.beach-haven.com. An appealing refuge three miles west of Eastsound, where fifty-year-old beachfront log cabins line up along a densely wooded, sunset-facing cove. In summer the cabins are only available by the week, with reservations recommended a year in advance, but out of season they can be rented on a nightly basis. ⑤

Orcas Hotel at the ferry landing in Orcas ⓣ360/376-4300, ⓦwww.orcashotel.com. A restored Victorian inn whose plushest rooms have Jacuzzis, balconies, and harbor views; the rooms on the sides and in the back don't, though they're considerably less expensive. ⑤–⑧

Outlook Inn 171 Main St, Eastsound ⓣ360/376-2200, ⓦwww.outlook-inn.com. Pleasant late-Victorian complex offering waterside rooms and suites with hot tubs, fire-places, and balconies, plus onsite restaurant and lounge. ⑥

Rosario Resort & Spa 1 Rosario Way ⓣ1-800/562-8820, ⓦwww.rosario-resort.com. Former Seattle mayor and wealthy shipbuilder Robert Moran built this elegant waterside mansion that now serves as a (newly renovated) luxury resort; it's expensive even by San Juan Islands standards. ⑨

Campgrounds

Doe Bay Village & Resort Doe Bay Rd ⓣ360/376-2291, ⓦwww.doebay.com. Reachable by turning right at the sign for Doe Bay Natural Foods Cafe & General Store, this establishment has six hostel dorm beds for $35 per night, plus yurts and various types of cabins for about two to three times as much. Hot tub and sauna use included (except for hostelers); $35 campsites cover a single tent (for two persons).

Moran State Park off Horseshoe Hwy southeast of Eastsound ⓣ1-800/452-5687, ⓦwww.orcasisle.com/~elc or www.parks.wa.gov. Nicely rugged park with plenty of wooded terrain, lakes, and thirty miles of hiking trails, and topped by the imposing sight of Mount Constitution. Campsites $15–21.

The Island

While **Orcas** will most likely be your first stop on the island, it's really just a street with a few simple shops. **Eastsound**, ten miles in on the main road, is a slightly larger town which offers more, including a handful of decent restaurants. Here, amid a rather pedestrian array of modern buildings, you can find the **Orcas Island Historical Society & Museum**, 181 N Beach Rd (Tues–Sun 1–4pm, Fri closes at 7pm; free; ⓣ360/376-4849, ⓦwww.orcasisland.org/~history), which illuminates the island's Native American and pioneer backgrounds. The museum is most noteworthy, however, for its layout – spread over six interconnected log cabins from the 1880s and 1890s, it was originally constructed by homesteaders carving out a space on the isolated terrain.

Past Eastsound, it's a few miles to the gates of **Moran State Park** (camping reservations at ⓣ1-800/452-5687, ⓦwww.orcasisle.com/~elc), five thousand acres of forest and lakes and thirty miles of trails. Overlooking the expanse is **Mount Constitution**, at 2409ft the highest point on the San Juans. A tough but exhilarating four-mile trail leads from Cascade Lake on the Horseshoe Highway to the top (also accessible by car via a five-mile paved road). The steep path twists around creeks, fields, and thick foliage, and there's a fair chance of spotting some of the nearly two hundred species of birds on Orcas. At the summit, the stone **Mount Constitution Tower** has an intriguingly rugged design – resembling a medieval fortress from the

Crusades. The panoramic views here are as good as you'd expect, looking out as far as Vancouver Island, and back towards snow-capped mounts Baker and Rainier.

Whether you need to recover from the strenuous hike or just unwind, the best place to accomplish both is at **Doe Bay Village & Resort** (see "Accommodation" above), even if you're not staying there. Nestled around on the east side of the island, it's about as far from the ferry as you can get. To reach it, keep to the main road round the park, turn left at the intersection of Olga and Doe Bay, and turn right three miles later at the sign for Doe Bay Natural Foods Cafe & General Store. Perched at one of the calmest spots in the San Juans, it's a lovely place, built on a secluded bay, with echoes of its previous incarnation as a New Age-flavored "human potential center" still hanging meditatively around its cabins, cottages, and hostel dorms. Its open-air, mineral spring-fed hot tubs are available for day use by non-guests ($8). A more adventurous dip into the water is provided by Shearwater Adventures, on kayak trips that leave from Doe Bay, Deer Harbor Marina, and *Rosario Resort* ($49 half-day, $85 full; ⓣ360/376-4699, ⓦwww.shearwaterkayaks.com), yielding closer views of the island's cache of bald eagles, seals, and whales.

Eating and drinking

When it comes to **eating** and **drinking**, the challenge in Orcas is hunting down the best spots throughout the island. While serviceable food is available in most places, finding distinctive eating requires more effort.

Bilbo's Festivo North Beach Rd and A St, Eastsound ⓣ360/376-4728. Reasonably good Mexican food, dished out in an affable setting. It's a popular spot, so reservations are advised.

Café Olga corner of Olga Rd and Doe Bay Rd, on the eastern side of the island ⓣ360/376-5098. Former strawberry cannery now doling out meals and pies served either indoors or on an outdoor porch, with an adjoining art gallery. Especially tasty are the home-made cinnamon rolls and blackberry pies.

The Kitchen 249 Prune Alley, off Horseshoe Hwy north of Orcas ⓣ360/376-6958. Appetizing pan-Asian fare, such as seared salmon, chicken teriyaki, and spring-roll wraps; most everything's cheap and tasty.

Portofino Pizzeria A St, Eastsound ⓣ360/376-2085. Handcrafted pizza and calzones, made mostly with thin crusts and using fresh local ingredients, including sun-dried tomatoes, mushrooms, and the like.

San Juan Island

The ever-popular **SAN JUAN ISLAND** holds the San Juans' only incorporated town, **Friday Harbor**, whose wharfside blocks seem more commercially active than the rest of the islands put together. That said, the rest of San Juan Island is rural and sparsely populated, with plenty of good scenery, hiking, and even a few cultural sights – most notably, a **whale museum** and two national historic parks, **American Camp** and **English Camp**, which were military bases during a land dispute in the mid-1800s.

Arrival and information

Ferries arrive at **Friday Harbor**, where San Juan Transit maintains a **visitors center** in the Cannery Building, next to the terminal at 91 Front St (Mon–Fri 9am–4.30pm; ⓣ360/378-8887) – it's a good place to pick up information and a **map** of the island's irregular main roads. The main office of the **San Juan**

Island National Historical Park, First and Spring streets (Mon–Fri 8.30am–4.30pm; ⓣ360/378-2240, ⓦwww.nps.gov/sajh), is not a visitors center per se, but will be happy to answer questions about the island.

A **car** is the best way to check out the scattered points of interest on San Juan; you can either bring one over by ferry or rent one in Friday Harbor. M&W, 725 Spring St (ⓣ1-800/323-6037), is a local outfit renting vehicles for $30–50 a day, depending on the season. From April–September, though, the **San Juan Shuttle** stops at most of the island's principal attractions ($4/one-way, $7/round-trip, $10/day-pass, $17/two-day-pass, or $18/25-min guided bus tours; ⓣ360/378-8887 or 1-800/887-8387, ⓦwww.sanjuantransit.com). **Bikes** ($30/day) and **scooters** ($50/day) can be rented at Island Bicycles, 380 Argyle St (Thurs–Sat only; ⓣ360/378-4941, ⓦwww.islandbicycles.com), while **mopeds** are available from Susie's Mopeds, corner of First and A streets, across from the ferry departure lanes ($17/hour or $51/day; ⓣ360/378-5244 or 1-800/532-0087, ⓦwww.susiesmopeds.com).

To get on the water, San Juan Safaris (ⓣ360/378-1323 or 1-800/450-6858, ⓦwww.sanjuansafaris.com) runs **sea kayak treks** and **whale-watching cruises** ($49 each) from Friday and Roche harbors. Crystal Seas Kayaking (ⓣ360/378-7899, ⓦwww.crystalseas.com) and Sea Quest Kayak Expeditions (ⓣ360/378-5767, ⓦwww.sea-quest-kayak.com) run more elaborate multi-day kayak tours (starting at $250–280), while Island Dive & Watersports (ⓣ360/378-2772, ⓦwww.divesanjuan.com) has half-day scuba-diving charters ($75 per person).

Accommodation

The most prevalent form of **accommodation** on the island is from **bed and breakfasts**, though it also holds the odd hotel and a range of worthwhile **campgrounds** – with none, unfortunately, sited in the national parks. It's essential to book ahead in summer for rooms in Friday Harbor, especially during the popular **San Juan Island Jazz Festival** (ⓣ360/378-5509), held the last weekend in July.

Hotels and B&Bs

Blair House 345 Blair Ave, Friday Harbor ⓣ360/378-5907 or 1-800/899-3030, ⓦwww.fridayharborlodging.com. Up from the ferry off Spring Street, one of the island's less pretentious B&Bs, with three units nearly enclosed by trees, and a big front porch and hot tub. ❻

Friday's 35 First St, Friday Harbor ⓣ360/378-5848 or 1-800/352-2632, ⓦwww.friday-harbor.com/lodging. Renovated 1891 hotel, convenient to the ferry, with agreeable ambience and a range of rooms from economy to suites. ❺–❾

Hotel de Haro 248 Reuben Memorial Drive, Roche Harbor ⓣ360/378-2155 or 1-800/451-8910, ⓦwww.rocheharbor.com. Located in the Roche Harbor Village, an elegant 1886 complex with standard rooms, but more upscale suites and quaint cottages with some antique decor. ❺–❼

Wharfside slip K-13, port of Friday Harbor ⓣ360/378-5661, ⓦwww.slowseason.com. Two private staterooms on a 60-ft sailboat in the harbor make for an interesting change of pace from the usual B&B. Offers morning breakfast cruises around the harbor in summer (though at substantially higher seasonal rates). ❼–❾

Wildwood Manor 5335 Roche Harbor Rd, Roche Harbor ⓣ360/378-3447 or 1-877/298-1144, ⓦwww.wildwoodmanor.com. Old-fashioned Victorian estate with three rooms – Pink, Blue, and French – offering the standard B&B amenities, but in an appealing forested location with fine views of the island and strait. ❼

Campgrounds and hostels

Lakedale Resort 4313 Roche Harbor Rd, between Roche Harbor and Friday Harbor ⓣ360/378-0944 or 1-800/617-2267, ⓦwww.lakedale.com. Offering guest-only lake activities with swimming, fishing, and kayaking, and a range of accommodation, including simple campsites ($21–26), tasteful lodge rooms ($120–195), and individual log cabins ($160–265).

Pedal Inn 1300 False Bay Drive, five miles from the Friday Harbor ferry dock ⓣ360/378-3049. Hiker- and cyclist-oriented camp with onsite showers and laundromat, for only $5 per person. April–Oct only.

San Juan County Park 380 West Side Rd ⓣ360/378-1842, ⓦwww.co.san-juan.wa.us/parks/sanjuan. Located on the western edge of the island, appealing for its rugged bluffs and rocky beaches, offering campsites with fire rings and picnic tables, and an onsite boat launch. $23–25.

Wayfarer's Rest 35 Malcolm St, Friday Harbor ⓣ360/378-6428, ⓦwww.rockisland.com/~wayfarersrest. The island's only hostel, reachable on foot from the ferry, with just ten beds in bunk rooms, for $20/night. Full kitchen facilities and herb garden; advance booking is advised.

Friday Harbor

When **FRIDAY HARBOR** became the county seat in 1873, it had a population of no more than three. Thanks in part to a protected harbor and good anchorage, by the turn of the century the town's residents numbered up to four hundred, and it continued to grow through the first half of the 1900s, until a postwar decline refocused the town toward tourism and real estate. Now, with a population of nearly two thousand, Friday Harbor is by far the biggest town in the San Juans.

With its numerous cafés and restaurants, the **waterfront** area is the inevitable place to eat before touring the island, though the cafés of the commercial district are all fairly unexceptional. The area's main highlight is the modest but enjoyable **Whale Museum**, 62 First St N (daily June–Aug 10am–5pm, rest of year noon–5pm; $5; ⓣ1-800/946-7227, ⓦwww.whalemuseum.org), which has a small collection of whale skeletons and displays explaining their migration and growth cycles, as well as a listening booth for seven different kinds of whale songs, along with walrus, seal, and dolphin soundtracks. Short documentaries detail research expeditions, and the museum also monitors whale activities on a "whale hotline" (ⓣ1-800/562-8832), to which you can report any sightings. The local Orca whales are protected by a ban on their capture, which was instituted in 1976, but they're still threatened by pollution. The museum promotes an "Adopt an Orca" program as there are, apparently, ninety or so left in Puget Sound; about twenty of them remain in the Sound year-round, while the others only return to the Sound for about four or five months, starting in May.

One good place to spot them is at **Lime Kiln Point State Park**, known to some as "Whale-Watcher Park," on the island's western side at 6158 Lighthouse Rd. Named after the site's former lime quarry, this is where orcas come in summer to gorge on migrating salmon, and there's usually at least one sighting a day. If you're really interested in seeing the whales up-close, San Juan Safaris (see opposite) runs good cetacean-oriented tours.

American Camp and English Camp

At San Juan's southern tip is **AMERICAN CAMP** (dawn–11pm; free; ⓣ360/378-2902, ⓦwww.nps.gov/sajh), a national park that played a role in the infamous Pig War (see box). Morale among the US troops once stationed here was quite low, and it's not hard to see why: the windswept, rabbit hole-strewn fields are bleak and largely shorn of vegetation. A self-guided, one-mile **trail** begins from the parking lot, passing the camp's few remaining buildings and what's left of a gun emplacement.

On the island's western side is **ENGLISH CAMP** (same information as American Camp), the site of the only foreign flag officially flown by itself on

The Pig War

Both English Camp and American Camp were established on San Juan Island as a result of the **Pig War**, a dispute in which not a single shot was fired at a human being, the lone casualty being a swine that belonged to the British. Its death, however, ultimately sparked the resolution of a long-simmering border conflict between the US and the UK (which still ruled Canada).

The **Oregon Treaty of 1846** had given the United States possession of the Pacific Northwest south of the 49th parallel, extending the boundary "to the middle of the channel which separates the continent from Vancouver's Island." As there were two channels – Haro and Rosario straits – between Vancouver Island and the mainland, and San Juan Island lay between them, both the British and the Americans claimed the island and began settling it in the 1850s.

In 1859, short-tempered American settler **Lyman Cutlar** shot a wayward British-owned pig that was munching on his garden vegetables. When the British threatened to arrest him, 66 American troops were sent in; the governor of British Columbia responded by sending three warships. Eventually, US President James Buchanan sent Winfield Scott, commanding general of the US Army, to cool things down. An agreement was reached allowing for joint occupation of the island until the dispute could be settled (or more importantly in the case of the US, until the Civil War came to an end). This co-ownership ultimately lasted for twelve years, until the dispute was finally referred to Kaiser Wilhelm I of Germany in 1871, who ruled in favor of the US the following year.

American soil. Here, forests line pleasant green fields and big-leafed maple trees dot the shoreline, where four military buildings from the 1860s and a small formal garden have been restored. A slideshow in the barracks (summer daily 10am–6pm; free) explains the Pig War – a tale that you will no doubt have fully memorized over the course of your visit. From here you can hike an easy loop to **Bell Point**, a promontory with expansive waterside views, or retreat to the parking lot to mount the short but steep one-mile wooded trail to **Young Hill**, passing the small **cemetery** on the way. The 650-ft summit has views over much of the island, and looks out to the shore of British Columbia, not more than ten miles away. Costumed volunteers re-enact life in both camps during the summer; drop in at the **visitor center** for details (summer daily 8.30am–5pm, rest of year Thurs–Sun 8.30am–4.30pm; free).

Roche Harbor

At San Juan's northwest tip is **ROCHE HARBOR**, established in the 1880s around the limestone trade, and highlighted by the gracious, white **Hotel de Haro** (see "Accommodation," p.336), built over the harbor in 1886 to house visiting lime-buyers. The hotel's now part of the *Roche Harbor Resort*, and unless you're staying here, it's only worth a quick peek at the building and a stroll around the minuscule wharf and general area.

When you head back up to Roche Harbor Road, veer off to the left just before the arch welcoming visitors to town, and then park at the small lot near the cemetery marked "Mausoleum Parking." A few yards further down the road, you'll find a small footpath leading into the **Roche Harbor Cemetery** (daily dawn–dusk); signs from here lead you to the haunting mausoleum of **John Stafford McMillin**, founder of the Hotel de Haro. Set far back from the street in the woods, with seven crumbling pillars surrounding a chipped round-table and chairs honoring various members of the McMillin clan, one half-expects the howling of wolves to break the eerie silence. For an explanation of all the weird, complicated Masonic symbolism behind the design of the site, check out Ⓦwww.rocheharbor.com/walkingtour.

Eating and drinking

Most appealing **eating** and **drinking** options on the island can be found in Friday Harbor, and while this isn't exactly prime dining turf, there are enough decent entries to make a culinary stop worthwhile.

Bella Luna 175 First St, Friday Harbor ⓣ360/378-4118. Hefty Italian and American fare, best for pizzas, pastas, and breakfasts, which include frittatas and English muffins smothered with veggies, eggs, and hollandaise sauce.

Cannery House 174 First St, Friday Harbor ⓣ360/378-2500. Interesting menu of assorted fresh seafoods, soups, sandwiches, and home-made breads; good views of the harbor, too.

Friday Harbor House 130 West St, Friday Harbor ⓣ360/378-8455. Swank, elegant spot for dining on Northwest Cuisine, but particularly good for its sizable wine list, hard ciders, and well-made cocktails.

Garden Path Café 232 A St, Friday Harbor ⓣ360/378-6255. Simple, straightforward breakfasts and lunches – the big bonus is the view of the harbor, with both indoor and patio seating.

Roche Harbor Restaurant 248 Reuben Memorial Drive, Roche Harbor ⓣ360/378-5757. Not too surprising with its steak and seafood entrees, but enjoyable nonetheless and offers pleasing water-side vistas; it's one of the few decent places to eat in Roche Harbor.

San Juan Donut Shop 209 Spring St, Friday Harbor ⓣ360/378-5059. The most popular breakfast place in town (and not just for donuts but for eggs, muffins, and so on); open early to serve diners on their way to the crowded morning ferries.

Thai Kitchen 42 First St, Friday Harbor ⓣ360/378-1917. Reasonable Thai food, mainly familiar but tasty staples like spring rolls and pad Thai. Located on the main drag, near the Whale Museum.

North of Seattle

North of Seattle, the urban sprawl drifts up the coast on either side of I-5, sweeping round Everett to stretch out towards the pancake-flat floodplain of the Skagit River, whose waters are straddled by the twin towns of Mount Vernon and Burlington. There's precious little here to catch the eye – the exception being the attractive town of **La Conner**, near the mouth of the Skagit – though both US-2 and (the more appealing) Hwy-20 fork east off I-5 for the splendid 450-mile Cascade Loop, which travels through some of Washington's finest mountain scenery (see p.378). North of here, further along I-5, is **Bellingham**, part bustling student town, part outdoor base, from where it's just a short hop over the border to Vancouver (see p.409).

La Conner

Located near the Skagit Bay section of Puget Sound, across from the north-eastern corner of Whidbey Island, quaint **LA CONNER** offers touristy, yet amiable, souvenir shops and cafés. Its downtown is situated along the bumpy waterfront of the **Swinomish Channel**, a sheltered inlet between the San Juan Islands and Puget Sound. Before the area was diked and drained, the surrounding landscape of the **Skagit delta** was a marshy morass prone to flooding; the original trading post here was built on a hill to avoid the soggier ground, and named by the town's leading landowner after his wife L(ouisa) A(nn) Conner. When the railroads reached the Pacific Northwest in the 1880s, La Conner was all but abandoned – though in the 1930s, the artist Morris Graves became attracted by its isolation, cheap land, and romantic lighting of its scenic landscapes. Kindred spirits – such as fellow painter Guy Anderson – followed, and the backwater town became both an artists' colony and the hang-out of oddballs and counterculture types. Since the 1970s, though, when the waterfront was spruced up with new shops and amenities, the town has traded on its offbeat reputation to pull in the tourist dollar. As such, it's hard nowadays to get a glimpse of anything vaguely "alternative," unless you count the town's several **art galleries**, though even they offer mostly unadventurous pieces aimed at visiting urbanites.

Arrival and accommodation

La Conner is located about an hour's drive north of Seattle off Hwy-20, or by bridge from Whidbey Island along the same highway. La Conner's **visitor center**, a short walk from the waterfront at Morris and Fifth streets (Mon–Fri 10am–4pm, Sat–Sun 11am–4pm; T 360/466-4778, W www.laconnerchamber.com), issues free maps and has a comprehensive list of local **accommodation**. Lodgings can get scarce during the month-long **Skagit Valley Tulip Festival** (W www.tulipfestival.org) in April, when it's best to book ahead.

Hotel Planter 715 S First St T 360/466-4710 or 1-800/488-5409. Plush, modern doubles within a remodeled century-old inn. 5

Katy's Inn 503 S Third St T 360/466-3366 or 1-800/914-7767. Attractive old B&B with wraparound porch, antique pump organ, two standard rooms, and two slightly more expensive suites. 5–6

La Conner Channel Lodge 205 N First St T 360/466-1500, W www.laconnerlodging.com. Lavish waterside doubles featuring an adjacent dock; 6–9. Also operates the *La Conner Country Inn*, 107 S Second St (T 1-888/466-4113), offering 28 basic rooms at cheaper rates; 5 for these.

Wild Iris Inn 121 Maple Ave T 360/466-1400 or 1-800/477-1400, W www.wildiris.com. Twelve fancy suites with hot tubs, fireplaces, and decks, along with six smaller rooms which sport fewer amenities. 5–6

The Town

Although lined by pleasant boutiques and eateries, the highlight of La Conner's attractive waterfront is the excellent **Museum of Northwest Art** (**MoNA**), 121 S First St (Tues–Sun 10am–5pm; $4; T 360/466-4666, W www.museumofnwart.org), which showcases the work of the region's painters. The first floor is given over to temporary displays, while the second holds the permanent collection – a bold and challenging sampling of modern art in which the forceful paintings of Guy Anderson are of particular note for their naked human figures adrift against somber regional landscapes.

A few blocks away, at 703 S 2nd St, the Gaches Mansion – the MoNA's former home – now holds the **La Conner Quilt Museum** (Wed–Sat 11am–4pm, Sun noon–4pm, closed Dec–Jan; $4; T 360/466-4288, W www.laconnerquilts.com), which presents a rotating display of quilts from around the world. If anything, the museum's grand edifice is just as interesting as its collection, an odd mix of Eastlake and other Victorian architecture styles, with a touch of Tudor Revival in its half-timbered dormers and fairy-tale tower.

Eating and drinking

Being a rather small place, La Conner is not a hotspot for **eating** and **drinking**, though the occasional culinary experiment – helmed by a European expat chef, perhaps – may open with fanfare, then close a month later. In any case, it's best to stick with a few reliable choices.

Calico Cupboard Café and Bakery 720 S First St ⓣ360/466-4451. Affordable breakfasts and lunches in a tearoom-like atmosphere. Try the banana-walnut pancakes, or an apricot bar from the takeout bakery.

La Conner Brewing Company 117 S First St ⓣ360/466-1415. Located next door to the art museum, functional spot offering a wide range of tempting beers and tasty pizzas.

La Conner Seafood & Prime Rib House 614 S First St ⓣ360/466-4014. Good seafood, burgers, and steak are the focus of the menu here, with outdoor seating and nice waterside vistas.

Bellingham

A successful blend of industry, Victorian architecture and college-town liveliness, **BELLINGHAM** runs ten miles along a broad curve of wedge-shaped Bellingham Bay, 85 miles north of Seattle and just eighteen miles south of the Canadian border. It's actually the sum of four smaller communities, whose separate street patterns make a disjointed, hard-to-navigate whole – though orientation isn't too difficult if you use I-5 to get your bearings.

Arrival and information

Greyhound **buses** and Amtrak **trains** pull in at the **Bellingham Cruise Terminal** (ⓦwww.portofbellingham.com) in the Fairhaven district, which is also the starting point of the Alaska Marine Highway (see box overleaf). Victoria-San Juan Cruises (ⓣ360/738-8099 or 1-800/443-4552, ⓦwww.whales.com) operates a passenger-only summer service to San Juan Island and Victoria in British Columbia ($69 one-way, $79 round-trip), though it's primarily aimed at whale-watchers. Other companies based at the terminal operate agreeable sightseeing and whale-watching cruises. Local Whatcom Transit **buses** (ⓣ360/676-RIDE, ⓦwww.ridewta.com) ply thirty routes for a fare of 50¢, with the **transit center** at E Magnolia and Railroad Avenue. The **visitor center** is at 904 Potter St, off I-5 exit 253 (ⓣ360/671-3990 or 1-800/487-2032, ⓦwww.bellingham.org), and provides maps and information on the town as well as the surrounding Whatcom County.

Accommodation

From the Cruise Terminal, it's only five hundred yards to the center of Fairhaven along Harris Avenue, where you'll find several good places to **stay**, including pleasant **B&Bs** and reasonable hotel chains. The town's chain **motels** are strung along Lakeway Drive, off I-5 at exit 253. Peppered with idyllic lakes and beachside coves, **Larrabee State Park**, seven miles south of Bellingham on Hwy-11 ($15–21; Feb–Nov only; ⓣ1-888/226-7688, ⓦwww.parks.wa.gov), is the best place to **camp** in the vicinity, though there are other campgrounds along the road heading eastbound to Mount Baker as well.

Bellwether near Roeder Ave and F Street ⓣ1-877/411-1200, ⓦwww.hotelbellwether.com. Large resort, looking oddly like a big, fancy motel, that has the usual range of upscale amenities: spacious suites with modern furnishings, onsite spa, gym, and salon, and private boat dock for your finest yacht. ⑧

Fairhaven 1714 12th St at Chuckanut Drive ⓣ360/734-7243 or 1-888/734-7243, ⓦwww.fairhavenbandb.com. Cozy B&B with the standard Victorian antiques and decor, with one room and a more elegant suite, plus an onsite hot tub. ❹

HI-Bellingham Hostel in Fairhaven Park, 107 Chuckanut Drive ⓣ360/671-1750. A tiny cabin-like affair next to a rose garden, a short walk south of the center of Fairhaven, where you can get a dorm room for $16.

North Garden Inn 1014 N Garden St ⓣ360/671-7828 or 1-800/922-6414, ⓦwww.northgardeninn.com. The best rooms in town, eight quaint units in a beautifully gabled Victorian mansion-turned-B&B. Near downtown and just off I-5, with first-class breakfasts and a great view of the bay. ❹

The Town

The late-nineteenth-century brick and sandstone buildings that comprise central **Fairhaven** – the most southerly (and easily the most diverting) of the town's districts – occupy a four-block square between 10th and 12th streets to either side of Harris Avenue. These commercial structures witnessed two brief booms – the first in the 1870s when the town was touted as the Pacific terminus of the Great Northern Railroad, the second twenty years later during the Klondike Gold Rush. Nowadays, Fairhaven is noted for its laid-back cafés and bars, which have an arty flavor that's very refreshing, especially if you've been hiking the great outdoors. Moving north on I-5, Exit 252 accesses the hillside campus of **Western Washington University** and Exit 253 leads **downtown**, where a routine gridiron of high-rises congregates on the bluff above the industrial harbor. There's nothing too inspiring here, though you could drop by the old **City Hall**, a grandiose 1892 red-brick building that is now the main part of the **Whatcom County Museum of History and Art**, 121 Prospect St (Tues–Sun noon–5pm; $3; ⓦwww.whatcommuseum.org), displaying Victorian antiques, clothing, and a fair smattering of doodads and trinkets. In an annex across the street, there's more Victoriana on view, including period dioramas with quaint clothing and furniture, plus exhibits touching on aspects of Native American history and culture.

Beyond all this, however, Bellingham's chief attraction is its access to a wide range of excellent **parks**, set among the bluffs and forests in and around the city, with myriad hiking trails and inspiring vistas. **Sehome Hill Arboretum**, off McDonald Parkway (daily dawn–dusk; free), is a splendid 165-acre preserve that overlooks the city (and includes an observation tower for this purpose),

The Alaska Marine Highway

The **Alaska Marine Highway** (ⓣ360/676-0212 recorded schedule information, ⓣ360/676-8445 administrative office, ⓦwww.akmhs.com; winter $270, summer $296) is a three-day ferry ride that winds between wooded islands and hard, craggy coast from Washington's **Bellingham** to Alaska's **Skagway**, with stops along the way at Ketchikan, Wrangell, Petersburg, Juneau, and Haines. A similar, parallel service starts further north at Canada's Prince Rupert. Ferries leave the Bellingham Cruise Terminal every Friday early in the evening from May to September (less frequently in the winter) and arrive in Skagway the following Monday night. The round-trip takes about a week. Vehicles and cabins have to be reserved months in advance and even walk-on passage requires at least a couple of weeks notice. You can, however, try at the Bellingham terminal on the day of departure – but don't bank on success. For further details, contact Alaska Marine Highway, PO Box 25535, Juneau, Alaska 99802-5535, or Alaska Ferry Adventures, 4667 Homer Spit Rd, Suite 1, Homer, AK 99603.

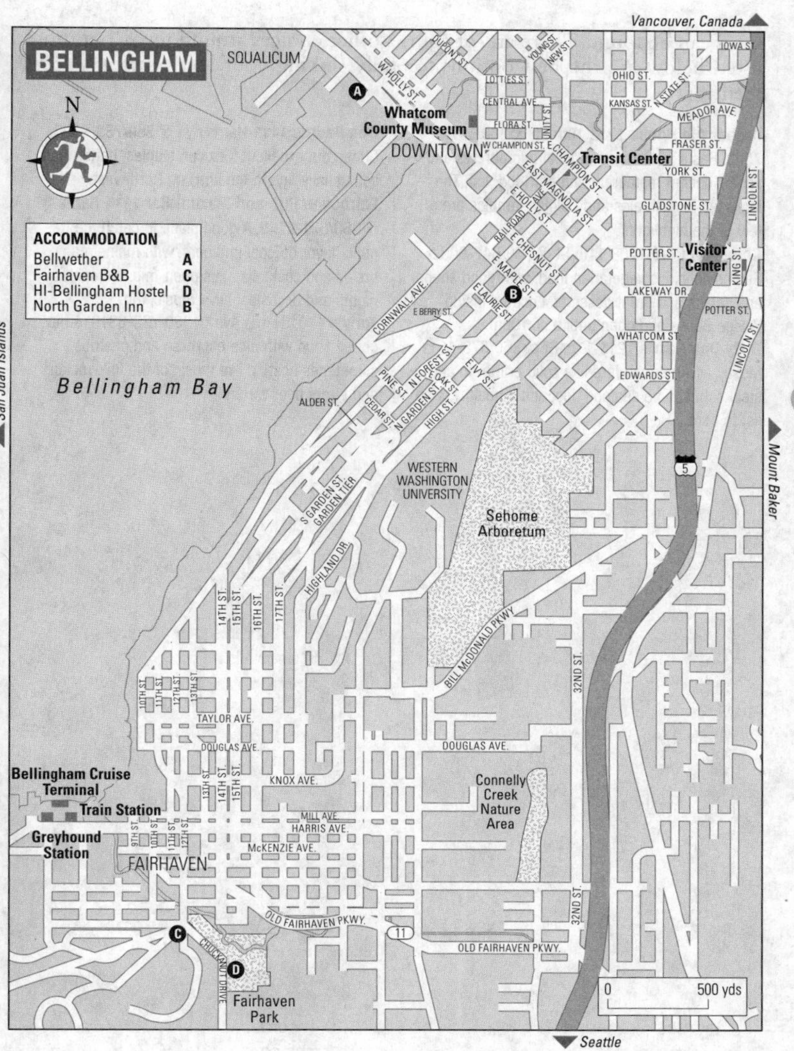

but is best for its six miles of nature walks and abundant views of wildlife such as native birds, deer, and even the odd mountain lion. Also worthwhile is **Connelly Creek Nature Corridor**, Donovan Avenue at 30th Street, where you can pick up an easy, half-hour-long trail that leads around varied natural scenery like forest groves, meadows, and a swamp, and is mostly aimed at casual sightseers of nature.

Eating and drinking

If you've come to Bellingham to **eat** and **drink**, you're probably going to end up in **Fairhaven**, where most of the notable restaurants, bars, and other night spots can be found. There are, of course, other choices around town, but those listed below are the best options for fully sinking your teeth into the local scene.

Archer Ale House 1212 10th St, ⓣ360/647-7002. Has a wide range of local microbrews and serves decent restaurant and bar food, too. The imported English ales and Belgian lambics are a few of the highlights.
Colophon Café 1208 11th St ⓣ360/647-0092. Serves delicious vegetarian food, with good soups and salads and great desserts. Located inside Village Books and open until 9 or 10pm.
Dirty Dan Harris 1211 11th St ⓣ360/676-1011. Mostly all-American fare like solid prime rib and steaks, but some seafood, too, and a healthy wine list to boot.
Dos Padres 1111 Harris Ave ⓣ360/733-9900. Cheap but excellent Mexican staples, better than you usually find in the outlying Northwest.
Fairhaven Pub and Martini Bar 1114 Harris ⓣ360/671-6745. A good place to catch the frenetic flavor of local imbibers, with mainstream brews and cocktails, plus open-mic and comedy nights and occasional live music, too.
Tony's 1101 Harris Ave ⓣ360/733-6319. A hip coffee shop with nice espresso and pastries, sometimes hosting live music of the folk-rocker and street poet variety .

The Olympic Peninsula and SW Washington

CANADA
Vancouver Island
PACIFIC OCEAN
WASHINGTON
USA
OREGON

CHAPTER 8

Highlights

* **Port Townsend** See the September Wooden Boat Festival in this nicely preserved Victorian hamlet from the late nineteenth century, peppered with elegant mansions, quaint restaurants, charming boutiques. See p.350

* **Dungeness National Wildlife Refuge** Littered with weirdly shaped driftwood, this fetching wilderness preserve hosts countless waterfowl in the winter, and shorebirds arriving in the thousands during the spring and fall. See p.356

* **Hurricane Ridge** Rugged stretch of cliffs and precipices, piercing peaks and glistening glaciers in the Olympic Mountains, where the snow-capped peak of Mount Olympus rises before you. See p.362

* **Sol Duc Hot Springs** Relax at this peaceful spot in the Olympic range, in which mineral water bubbles out of the earth to be channeled into three pools. See p.363

* **Quinault Rainforest** The most accessible and beautiful of the rainforests of the Olympic Peninsula, home to dark green foliage surrounding the deep blue waters of Quinault Lake. See p.365

* **Cape Disappointment** At this dangerous, striking promontory where the mouth of the Columbia River meets the Pacific Ocean, more than two hundred ships have been wrecked. See p.369

△ Hurricane Ridge

8

The Olympic Peninsula and SW Washington

West of Seattle, rugged peaks dominate the core of the **Olympic Peninsula**, rising high above the lush mountain vegetation, which gives way to the tangled rainforests of the western valleys, and the sea-lashed wilderness beaches on the Pacific edge. Fringed with logging communities and encircled by US-101, the peninsula's most magnificent parts are protected within **Olympic National Park**, complete with scores of superb hiking trails and numerous campsites, and several fine old lodges. You can also stay just outside of it in **Sequim**, the most likable of the surrounding towns, not least because it's in the rain shadow of the Olympic Mountains. Closer to Puget Sound, **Port Townsend** serves as another possible base for visiting the national park, though this lively little town is well worth a visit in itself for its fancy Victorian architecture and sociable nightlife.

The sheltered bays that punctuate the **southwest corner** of the state along the **Pacific Coast** are protected from the open sea by elongated sand spits. While the shoreline stretches out for miles, the scenery is mostly flat and monotonous, and even though resorts like Ocean Shores and Long Beach are popular, they're often characterized by dreary seaside chalets and RV parks. Moreover, powerful undertows and drifting logs make swimming dangerous and the beaches are minimally protected by law, so people drive all over them – in contrast to the Oregon Coast (see p.139), where vehicles are rarely allowed. It's best to head for the scenic pleasures – if not the military remains – of **Cape Disappointment State Park** at the mouth of the Columbia River in the very southwest tip of the state. As an alternative, further east you can access I-5 south of Olympia (see p.315) to reach Washington's own **Vancouver**, site of a reconstructed Hudson's Bay Company fur-trapping colony. Beyond is Portland, Oregon, one hundred and seventy miles from Seattle.

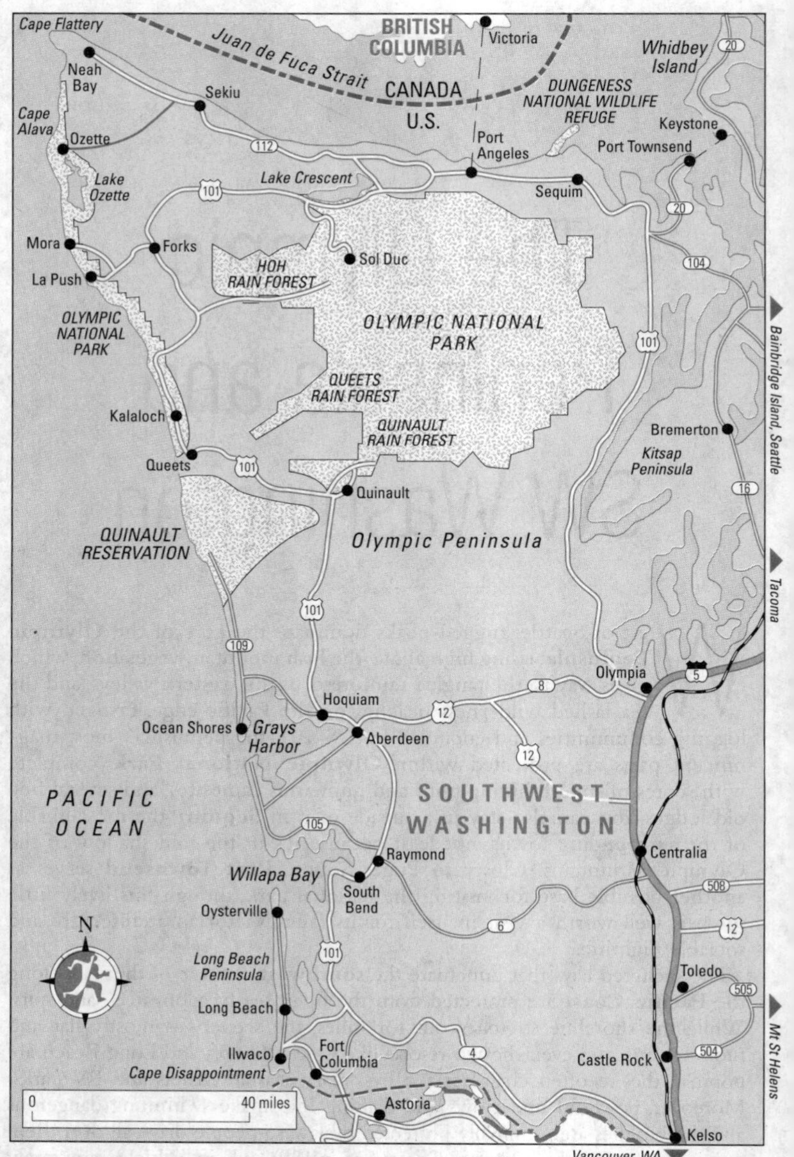

The Olympic Peninsula

Projecting west from Puget Sound, the **OLYMPIC PENINSULA** is a broad mass where dense temperate rainforests nestle between imposing, glacier-draped mountains and the rocky and remote Pacific coastline. Small towns sprinkle the peninsula's edges, but at its center the mighty Olympic Mountains thrust upwards, shredding clouds as they drift in from the Pacific, causing the peninsula's western side to be constantly drenched by rain. These moist conditions have led to the peninsula being carpeted with a thick blanket of forest, and, in the western river valleys, the dense vegetation thickens into **temperate rainforest**, primarily composed of Sitka spruce, Western hemlock, Douglas fir, alder, and maple – a rare and remarkable environment. The peninsula's wild and lonely Pacific shore is not quite so unique, but it offers extraordinary scenery, and both the forests and the coast provide habitats for a huge variety of wildlife and seabirds.

It was partly to ensure the survival of a rare elk subspecies that Franklin D. Roosevelt created **Olympic National Park** here in 1939, where, appropriately, the largest herd of Roosevelt elk in the US roams. The park also protects the heart of the peninsula, but large tracts of forest surrounding it are heavily logged. The issue of economy versus ecology is debated with particular intensity here, since it was the timber trade that lured settlers in the first place, and the logging industry still provides many local jobs. Environmentalists reluctantly favor tourism as the lesser ecological evil, and the number of visitors is gradually increasing.

Graced by its charming waterside setting and ornate old mansions, northerly **Port Townsend** is easily the most appealing town on the peninsula and, handily enough, it's the logical first stop if you're arriving from the east: ferries arrive here from Keystone on Whidbey Island (see p.326), and a short drive will get you here from Seattle via Bainbridge Island (see p.322). The rest of the peninsula's settlements are, however, rather nondescript: only **Sequim**, a pleasant little town in the rain shadow of the Olympic Mountains, offers much incentive to hang around, though industrial **Port Angeles** is useful for its ferry links with Victoria in Canada and as the location of the Olympic National Park Visitor Center. Otherwise, you're well advised to make straight for the wilderness, either to camp at or stay in one of the national park's excellent lodges.

Getting around

The peninsula's main highway, **US-101**, loops around the coast, but no roads run across the peninsula's mountainous core. However, several paved and/or gravel-topped arteries do nudge into the interior, exploring the peripheries of the national park. Two local **bus** companies provide a limited and slow Monday-through-Saturday service across the northern part of the peninsula. Clallam Transit buses (75¢–$1.50; ⓣ360/452-4511 or 1-800/858-3747, ⓦwww.clallamtransit.com), go west from Port Angeles around the peninsula to Lake Crescent, Neah Bay, and Forks, and east to Sequim – from there connecting with Jefferson Transit (50¢–$1; ⓣ360/385-4777, ⓦwww.jeffersontransit.com) buses to Port Townsend. That said, if you want to do any walking, you'll have problems reaching trailheads without your own vehicle – and a **car** is by far the best bet: on a **bike**, you're most likely to get soaked time and again, and sharp corners and hurtling logging trucks represent rather considerable hazards.

Port Townsend and around

Located at the tip of the Quimper Peninsula, a stumpy northeast adjunct to the adjoining mass of the Olympic Peninsula, **PORT TOWNSEND**, with its brightly painted Victorian mansions, convivial cafés, and vigorous cultural (and countercultural) scene, has always had aspirations beyond its small-time logging roots. A would-be San Francisco since the mid-nineteenth century, it was poised for local supremacy in the 1890s, when confident predictions of a railway terminus lured rich settlers, who set about building extravagant Neo-Gothic homes on the bluff above the port. Unfortunately for the investors, the railway petered out before it reached Port Townsend, the hoped-for boom never happened, and the town was left with a glut of stylish residences and a very small business district.

Much to the surprise of many, this combination turned out to be Port Townsend's salvation. Ever since the old mansions were bought up and restored in the 1960s, the town has mellowed into an artsy community with hippie undertones and a good degree of charm. Tourists in search of Victoriana fill plush B&Bs, while jazz and blues fans flock to the annual music festivals, and nearby, nineteenth-century **Fort Worden** provides ample camping and youth hostel facilities.

Arrival and information

Port Townsend is easy to reach, either by a half-hour **ferry** ride from Keystone on Whidbey Island, or by **road** either over the Hood Canal Bridge from the Kitsap Peninsula or up along US-101 from Olympia. By **bus**, things get a bit more complicated: from the Bremerton ferry terminal, pick up the Kitsap Transit bus ($1; ⓣ360/373-2877 or 1-800/501-RIDE, ⓦwww.kitsaptransit .org) to Poulsbo for the onward connection with

Jefferson Transit (50¢–$1; ⓣ360/385-4777, ⓦwww.jeffersontransit.com) to Port Townsend. On weekdays, there are three services daily between Bremerton and Port Townsend, and one daily on the weekend; the whole trip takes up to five hours. The town can also be reached by passenger **boat** from Friday Harbor, on San Juan Island, with PS Express (May–Sept 1 daily; 3.5hr; $34.50 one-way, $52.50 return; ⓣ360/385-5288, ⓦwww.pugetsoundexpress.com).

Port Townsend's compact center occupies a triangle of land jutting out into the sea. The **ferry terminal** is downtown, just off the main drag, Water Street, which is dotted with stops for the Jefferson Transit bus (50¢ per ride, $1.50 day pass). Pick up information at the helpful **visitor center**, 2437 E Sims Way (daily 9am–5pm; ⓣ360/385-2722, ⓦwww.ptguide.com), half a mile south of the center on Hwy-20. To get around, **rent a bike** from PT Cyclery, by the waterfront at 100 Tyler St (Mon–Sat 9am–6pm; ⓣ360/385-6470).

Accommodation

Port Townsend is Washington's **B&B** capital, with more than a dozen moderately expensive establishments sprinkled among the old villas of the uptown area. At B&Bs, advance **reservations** are strongly advised throughout the summer; prices fluctuate considerably with demand and with the room – some B&Bs have smaller rooms for as little as $60, as well as suites for upwards of $200. A few miles north of town, the old military compound at **Fort Worden State Park** has two **campsites** (Fort Worden, off Cherry Street. ⓣ360/385-4730, ⓦwww.olympus.net/ftworden/camping; $15-21): one's near the conference center, while the other's in a more enticing location by the seashore; it also offers vacation units, dorms, and a youth hostel (see below).

Ann Starrett Mansion 744 Clay St at Adams ⓣ360/385-3205 or 1-800/321-0644, ⓦwww.starrettmansion.com. With its high gables and precocious tower, this 1889 Queen Anne is one of the town's most imposing Victorian mansions. The antique-filled interior features ceiling frescoes, a splendid spiral staircase, and ornate and extremely comfortable doubles. ❺

Fort Worden State Park Housing 200 Battery Way, Fort Worden ⓣ360/344-4434, ⓦwww.olympus.net/ftworden/accommod.html. Thirty-three old officers' lodgings have been refurbished as fully furnished houses, with fireplaces and kitchens, starting at $102 for a double and rising to $273 for six people. Also on the compound, spartan dorms with wood and linoleum floors house one to eight people for $36. Two daily meals are served from $14. Advance reservations essential. ❻

Holly Hill House 611 Polk St at Clay ⓣ360/385-5619 or 1-800/435-1454, ⓦwww.hollyhillhouse.com. Enticing, well-run B&B in an appealing late-nineteenth-century structure with high gables, a nice garden, and a relaxing veranda. Each of the four guestrooms – all with private baths – is adorned with lavish period decor. ❺

James House 1238 Washington St at Harrison ⓣ360/385-1238 or 1-800/385-1238, ⓦwww.jameshouse.com. Appealing old pile on the edge of the bluff overlooking the harbor with high brick chimneys and a handsome front terrace. Eleven tastefully decorated rooms, ten en suite, plus a private bungalow for $60 more. ❻

Manresa Castle 7th and Sheridan sts ⓣ360/385-5750 or 1-800/732-1281, ⓦwww.manresacastle.com. Quasi-French castle from 1892 that's now an elegant hotel with thirty rooms that range from cozy single units to swanky suites in the tower. ❺–❽

Old Consulate Inn 313 Walker St at Washington ⓣ360/385-6753 or 1-800/300-6753, ⓦwww.oldconsulateinn.com. This elegant 1889 villa, with its spiky tower and wraparound veranda, has seven plush suites (plus one rather small room), as well as a grand piano and an old organ. It takes its name from the days when the German consul lodged here. Suites ❼, room ❻

Olympic Youth Hostel 272 Battery Way, Fort Worden State Park ⓣ360/385-0655. Up the hill from the Parade Ground, this HI-affiliated hostel has dorm beds as well as private rooms ($25) and a kitchen. Beds $14 for members, $17 non-members. Check-in 5–10pm; checkout 9.30am. Access by Jefferson Transit bus #5 from downtown.

Palace Hotel 1004 Water St at Tyler ⓣ360/385-0773 or 1-800/962-0741, ⓦwww.palacehotelpt.com. In the middle of the town center by the harbor, this small hotel in a century-old brick building features high arched windows. The spacious rooms have high ceilings and are decorated in a mix of styles, though the general flavor is vaguely Victorian. Cheapest units share a bath; another $39 gets you a private bath and kitchenette. ❸

Point Hudson Resort 103 Hudson St ⓣ360/385-2828 or 1-800/826-3854, ⓕ360/385-7331. Unusual motel occupying the hospital block of the old Coast Guard Training Station at Point Hudson. Spartan rooms have a certain military flavor, but are well kept and oddly charming. The cheapest double rooms, with shared baths, come in at $59 – add $20 for en suite and $40 for a second-floor room with a harbor view. ❹

Port Townsend Inn 2020 Washington St ⓣ360/385-2211 or 1-800/216-4985, ⓦwww.porttownsendinn.com. Comfortable motel at south end of town center, with continental breakfast, microwaves, and fridges in the rooms, indoor heated pool, and spa. ❹

Quimper Inn 1306 Franklin St at Harrison ⓣ360/385-1060 or 1-800/557-1060, ⓦwww.olympus.net/quimper. Delightful 1888 B&B in old Colonial Revival house, with lovely double porches on the first two floors set beneath tidy gables and dormers of the third. Immaculately restored and furnished in period style, the house has five guestrooms (three en suite), each of which is extremely comfortable; the breakfasts are delicious. Check-in 4–6pm. ❺–❼

The Town

Port Townsend's physical split – half on a bluff, half at sea-level – reflects Victorian-era social divisions, when wealthy merchants built their homes uptown, and the working class were stuck amid the noise and ruckus of the port below. Nowadays, though, both sections have their appealing sights. It's simple enough to reach the town from the rest of the peninsula: Highway 20 comes in from the southwest and turns into the main drag of **Water Street** by the Sound; from downtown, **Cherry Street** leads north into Fort Worden State Park.

Downtown

Occupying the area below the bluff and still the commercial center of town, **downtown** sports an attractive medley of 1890s brick and stonework buildings centered on **Water Street**. To the business folk of the late nineteenth century, these structures were important status symbols: timber is the obvious building material in the area, so a sizable brick building was quite a coup in a pioneer town. Today, many of these structures are occupied by stylish restaurants, boutiques, and especially, **art galleries**. The latter are particularly concentrated on Water and the parallel Washington street, from Quincy to Tyler streets, and sell all manner of locally crafted items – from the masks, dolls, and textiles of native tribes (at Pacific Traditions; 637 Water St; ⓣ360/385-4770) to cedar and myrtlewood sculptures and carvings (Forest Gems; 807 Washington St; ⓣ360/379-1713) to colorful, hand-blown glass bowls and vases (Old World Glass Studio; 1005 Water St; ⓣ360/379-9568). The most prominent edifice in the area, though, is the **City Hall**, at Water and Madison streets, a robust red-brick assertion of civic dignity that manages to incorporate a baffling mixture of architectural styles – with Gothic, Romanesque, and even Neoclassical features. The functional interior, which held the firehouse and courthouse, has survived intact, making the **Jefferson County Historical Society Museum** (Mon–Sat 11am–4pm, Sun 1–4pm; $4; ⓣ360/385-1003, ⓦwww.jchsmuseum.org), which now occupies part of the premises, one of the more interesting museums in the state. On the ground floor, look out for the photographer's chair draped with bear and buffalo skins, which were intended to add luster to the picture-portraits so popular in the late nineteenth century, and the unusual late-nineteenth- and early-twentieth-century two-necked harp guitars by local musician and instrument-builder Chris Knutsen. Prison cells that were actually used as the city jail occupy part of the basement, where there's also an excellent section devoted to the history of local prostitution and VD, a common hazard in port towns a hundred years ago, with countless euphemisms to describe it.

From the museum, it's just a short walk northeast to the waterfront bluff of **Chetzemoka Park**, named after a native chief who was extremely helpful to the first white settlers. It's a particularly pretty park with banks of rhododendrons, pine trees, manicured lawns, a trim bandstand, and a narrow slice of beach.

The upper town

Chetzemoka Park is at the foot of Blaine Street, which you can follow west as far as Adams, where a left turn brings you among the big old wooden mansions of the **upper town**. The 1889 icon of Port Townsend's boom period, the **Ann Starrett Mansion** (see "Accommodation", p.351), at Adams and Clay streets, swarms with gables and boasts an octagonal tower and an impressively ornate elliptical staircase that has to be seen to be believed. By contrast, the 1868 **Rothschild House**, at nearby Franklin and Taylor streets (May–Sept daily 10am–5pm; $2; ⓣ360/385-1003), predates the high times, its plankboard frame and simple columns resembling a sedate Colonial Revival farmhouse. The house was built for a local merchant, one D.C.H. Rothschild, a German immigrant who was related to the famous banking family – as he put it, "enough to get the name, but not the money." More impressive than either house, though – or practically anything else in town – is the grand **Jefferson County Courthouse**, Walker and Jefferson streets (Mon–Fri 9am–5pm; ⓦwww.co.jefferson.wa.us), a towering red Romanesque Revival edifice with a clock tower that looks like a medieval Italian version of Big Ben.

Eating, drinking, and entertainment

Port Townsend has a good supply of plain, inexpensive **cafés**, many of which offer light meals and snacks with a vegetarian or healthfood slant, and pricier **restaurants** serving a wider than expected mix of cuisines. Uptown, Aldrich's, at Lawrence and Tyler (ⓣ360/385-0500, ⓦwww.aldrichs.com), is a pleasantly traditional general store with great coffee and sandwiches, and supposedly the oldest business in town. Nearby, the hippie-oriented Food Co-op, 414 Kearney St (ⓣ360/385-2883), sells organic products and local produce, and has recently been expanded to larger digs.

Belmont 925 Water St ⓣ360/385-3007. A smart, bistro-style restaurant featuring a range of delicious entrees, mostly steaks, seafood, and salads, with main courses averaging $20.

Fountain Café 920 Washington St ⓣ360/385-1364. Seafood and pasta specialties like oyster stew and wild mushroom risotto in a small spot a short distance from the waterfront.

Landfall 412 Water St ⓣ360/385-5814. Pleasant dining on the Point Hudson waterfront, with an imaginative menu of seafood and vegetarian dishes, as well as fresh salmon for summer barbecue specials.

Maxwell's Brewery 126 Quincy St at Water ⓣ360/379-6438. Funky live-music joint showcasing blues and rock bands, and boasting a wonderful old wooden bar with an enormous mirror to boot.

Salal Café 634 Water at Taylor ⓣ360/385-6532. Renowned for its breakfasts – blintzes, omelets, frittatas, and crepes – and also good for its solid lunchtime burgers and pastas. Serves up a mean tofu stroganoff, too.

Sentosa Sushi 218 Polk St ⓣ360/385-2378. A wide variety of sushi, as well as tasty pan-Asian noodle dishes.

Silverwater Café 237 Taylor St ⓣ360/385-6448. Renowned for its seafood dishes – such as northwest floribunda and ahi tuna with lavender pepper – the café also has decent pasta and vegetarian selections.

Sweet Laurette Patisserie 1029 Lawrence St ⓣ360/385-4886. One of the best bets for French-style baked goods in town, with elaborate (and expensive) cakes that resemble artworks, and more affordable scones, pies, and pastries with a range of fresh local ingredients.

Outdoor activities

For **outdoor activities**, Port Townsend is a major launching point for **kayaking** in Puget Sound. Kayak Port Townsend, 435 Water Street (ⓣ1-800/853-2252, ⓦwww.kayakpt.com), organizes a varied program of **sea-kayaking** excursions, from a two-hour paddle along the waterfront ($30) to overnight trips in the surrounding bays ($239) and four-day expeditions to the San Juan Islands ($429). They offer kayak rental, too – a single kayak costs $40 per day, $55 for a double. PT Outdoors, 1071 Water St at Tyler (ⓣ360/379-3608, ⓦwww.ptoutdoors.com), also offers competitive kayak rentals and harbor tours.

Fort Worden

FORT WORDEN, two miles north of downtown Port Townsend (Jefferson Transit bus #5 from Water Street; ⓣ360/344-4400, ⓦwww.olympus.net/ftworden), was part of a trio of coastal fortifications built at the beginning of the twentieth century, designed to protect Puget Sound from attack by the new breeds of steam-powered battleships then being developed by all the great powers. Used by the army until 1953, then converted into a juvenile detention center for the next twenty years, Worden is now designated as a 443-acre state park. Just beyond the main gates is the large, green **Parade Ground** where soldiers marched, lined on one side by the barracks, a series of plain wooden buildings that are rented as vacation accommodation (see p.351) – the *Olympic Youth Hostel* and the **visitor center**, 200 Battery Way (summer daily 10am–4pm, rest of year Sat & Sun only; ⓣ360/344-4458), are also found here. Another barracks contains the **Coastal Artillery Museum** (March–Oct daily noon–4pm; $2), which gives the military lowdown on the site and has a scale model of the Kinzie Battery (see below). Lining the south side of the Parade Ground is the century-old **Officers' Row**, which culminates in the sedate **Commanding Officer's House** (June–Aug daily 10am–5pm; March–May & Sept–Oct Sat & Sun noon–4pm; $2), a 1904 Colonial Revival home whose interior has been carefully decked out in full Victorian style.

Beyond the Parade Ground, old bunkers and gun batteries radiate out across the park – though the most diverting are down along the seashore, where you can scramble around the massive concrete gun emplacements of the 1890s **Kinzie Battery**. Also along the shore – but much nearer to the Parade Ground, at the end of the wharf – the small **Marine Science Center**, 532 Battery Way (call for opening hours; $2; ⓣ360/385-5582, ⓦwww.ptmsc.org),

Port Townsend festivals

Port Townsend puts on several big **music festivals** throughout the year, most notably the **Blues and Heritage Festival** at the end of June, the **Festival of American Fiddle Tunes** in early July, and the **Jazz Port Townsend Festival** in late July. The programs are organized by a nonprofit arts organization, Centrum, based in Fort Worden (ⓣ360/385-5320 or 1-800/733-3608, ⓦwww.centrum.org). Perhaps the town's most celebrated festival, however, is the annual **Wooden Boat Festival** (ⓣ360/385-4742, ⓦwww.woodenboat.org), a three-day weekend event in September put on by the prestigious **Wooden Boat Foundation** at Point Hudson, with more than 150 wooden boats of all shapes and vintages on display.

has large tanks in which you can touch tidepool creatures and observe local animals and plants, and review a timeline of Puget Sound natural history.

Don't leave the area before you've had a chance to see one of Port Townsend's visual icons, the **Point Wilson Lighthouse**, a 1913 column at the end of Quimper Peninsula off Harbor Defense Way, just beyond Fort Worden (grounds tours Wed 11am–4pm; donation suggested). Even today, the isolated beacon guides ships through the Admiralty Inlet of Puget Sound, giving you a sense of the rugged maritime atmosphere of a century ago – even though the light's been automated for forty years.

Along the northern coast

South of Port Townsend, Hwy-20 rounds Discovery Bay to meet **US-101** at the start of its journey west along the **northern Olympic peninsula**'s narrow coastal plain, with the national park on one side and the **Juan de Fuca Strait** on the other. The most immediate sights are **Sequim** and the **Dungeness National Wildlife Refuge**, and just beyond, the Olympic National Park gateway of **Port Angeles**. Further west, though, the major attractions are much fewer and farther between, until you reach the remote and windswept settlement of **Neah Bay** at the very northwestern tip of the peninsula – and of the continental US.

Sequim

Eighteen miles from the junction of Hwy-20 and US-101 lies **SEQUIM** (pronounced "Skwim"), the only town on the rain-soaked peninsula to hold an annual irrigation festival (early May; ⓦwww.irrigationfestival.com). While drenching everything else, the Olympic Mountains cast a rain shadow over this area (depositing just seventeen inches of rainfall per year), and the sunshine has attracted senior citizens in droves to live here. The result is a cozy little town whose neat bungalows align either side of the long main drag, **Washington Avenue**, which runs just to the north of the US-101 bypass – and divides into West and East at Sequim Avenue, the town's main intersection. There's nothing remarkable here, but it's close enough to Olympic National Park to use as a base. For a quick glimpse at local heritage – ancient and modern – drop by the **Museum and Arts Center**, 175 Cedar St (Tues–Sat 8am–4pm; donation suggested; ⓦwww.sequimmuseum.org), whose collection encompasses an

The Juan de Fuca Strait and Plate

The **Juan de Fuca Strait**, linking the Pacific Ocean with Puget Sound, was once thought to be the fabled **Northwest Passage** on the basis of a chance meeting, famous among early-seventeenth-century mariners, between an English merchant and one **Apostolos Valerianos** in Venice in 1596. The Greek Valerianos claimed to be an exiled Spanish sea captain by the name of Juan de Fuca and, for good measure, added that he had sailed from the Pacific to the Arctic Ocean via the strait that bears his (assumed) name. The gullible explorers sought to follow in his nautical footsteps, and the name stuck to the strait. More recently it has also, curiously enough, been appended by geologists to the triangular crustal plate just to the west, which, thanks to continental drift, has been colliding with the North American Plate for many millions of years. In helping build up the mountains in western Washington, the **Juan de Fuca Plate** is also known to trigger the occasional earthquake in the Pacific Northwest as well – a rather impressive legacy for a minor historical charlatan.

assortment of regional antiques, early automobiles and buggies, and even the bones of Ice Age-era mastodons.

Sequim's **visitor center**, on the east edge of town at 1192 E Washington Rd (Mon–Sat 9am–5pm & Sun 10am–4pm; ⓣ360/683-6197, ⓦwww.visitsun.com), has free local maps and a list of all the available accommodation. Several comfortable **motels** are strung out along W Washington Avenue, among them the garish *Red Ranch Inn*, at no. 830 (ⓣ360/683-4195 or 1-800/777-4195, ⓦwww.redranch.com; ❸), and the serviceable *Econo Lodge*, no. 801 (ⓣ360/683-7113 or 1-800/488-7113, ⓦwww.sequimeconolodge.com; ❸). Beyond this, there are a handful of predictably Victorian **B&Bs**, though the best is the more rustic, wooden digs of the *Dungeness Lodge*, 1330 Jamestown Rd (ⓣ1-877/294-0173, ⓦwww.dungenesslodge.com; ❻), which offers five spacious units with handsome modern decor, waterside views, and a minimum of chintz.

For a small town, Sequim has a surprisingly good range of inexpensive all-American **restaurants**: there's delicious home-style cooking at *Gwennie's*, 701 E Washington near Sequim Avenue (ⓣ360/683-4157), while the *Highway 101 Diner*, 392 W Washington (ⓣ360/683-3388), serves up tasty burgers in strikingly kitschy Fifties surroundings, and the quaint *Oak Table Café*, one block south of the highway at 292 W Bell and S 3rd Avenue (ⓣ360/683-2179), offers excellent gourmet breakfasts and lunches – try the baked apple pancakes or the '49ers flap-jacks. **Dungeness crabs**, perhaps the ultimate in crabmeat, are a local specialty: a good place to try them is the *Three Crabs*, 11 Three Crabs Rd (ⓣ360/683-4264), located on the coast about five miles north of Sequim. To get there, turn off Washington Avenue along Sequim Avenue and keep going – you'll see the signs.

Monday through Saturday, Jefferson Transit (50¢–$1; ⓣ360/385-4777, ⓦwww.jeffersontransit.com) runs several **buses** daily from Port Townsend to Sequim, and Clallam Transit (75¢–$1.50; ⓣ360/452-4511 or 1-800/858-3747, ⓦwww.clallamtransit.com) links Sequim with Port Angeles. Sequim's main **bus stop** and transfer point is one block north of Washington at N 2nd Avenue and W Cedar Street.

Dungeness National Wildlife Refuge

The triangular chunk of farmland north of Sequim ends with **Dungeness Spit**, a long and slender sand bar that curves out into the Juan de Fuca Strait for almost six miles. On its exposed northern edge, the surf-pounded stretch is littered with rocks and weirdly shaped driftwood, but its sheltered side – where the attached Graveyard Spit cuts back towards the shore providing even more protection – is entirely different. Here, among the rich tidal flats waterfowl rest and feed during winter, and shorebirds – typically the likes of murres, oyster-catchers, and shovelers - arrive in the thousands during spring and fall migrations, with fewer numbers of threatened or endangered species such as snowy plovers, marbeled murrelets, and bald eagles. The area is now protected as **DUNGENESS NATIONAL WILDLIFE REFUGE** (daily dawn–dusk; $3; ⓦwww.dungeness.com/refuge). Although sections – including the Graveyard Spit – are not open to the public, a lovely hiking trail leads from the parking lot at the base of Dungeness Spit, through a patch of coastal forest to a bluff, and then out along the beach to the squat historic **lighthouse** built in 1857– a round-trip of ten miles. Although the hike isn't difficult – you can easily complete it in a day – be sure to take provisions and enough drinking water.

There are several ways to reach the refuge, but the most straightforward is to head west out of Sequim along US-101 and then – four miles from the town center – take the signposted right turn along Kitchen Dick Lane. From the turn, follow the signs for the five-mile drive to the parking lot. Incidentally, don't get confused by the separate Dungeness Recreation Area, which you drive through as you near your destination.

Port Angeles

Founded by the Spanish in 1791, and named "Puerto de Nuestra Senora de los Angeles" until confused postal clerks insisted one Los Angeles on the West Coast was enough, **PORT ANGELES**, seventeen miles west of Sequim, is the peninsula's main town and the most popular point of entry for those heading for Olympic National Park. Although a recent uplift has encouraged the growth of new small businesses – from quaint boutiques to trinket shops – the place is still mostly a working town; its main strip of motels and commercial buildings – on Front and First streets – is a bit too drab to attract visitors by itself alone. Although the surrounding scenery and ferry connections with Victoria, BC, do bring in the tourists, it's timber that's Port Angeles' real preoccupation.

Arrival and information

Port Angeles has the peninsula's best transportation connections and the ferry and bus terminals are close together; the **bus depot** is beside the waterfront at W Front and Oak streets and from there it's a couple of minutes' walk to the main **ferry terminal**. Olympic Bus Lines (ⓣ360/452-3858, ⓦwww.olympicbuslines.com) offers daily trips to Seattle ($29) and Sea-Tac Airport ($43), while Clallam Transit buses (75¢–$1.50; ⓣ360/452-4511 or 1-800/858-3747, ⓦwww.clallamtransit.com) go west from Port Angeles around the peninsula to Lake Crescent, Neah Bay, and Forks, and east to Sequim – from there connecting with Jefferson Transit (50¢–$1; ⓣ360/385-4777, ⓦwww.jeffersontransit.com) buses to Port Townsend.

Black Ball Transport (ⓣ360/457-4491, ⓦwww.cohoferry.com) **car ferries** arrive from – and shuttle over to – Victoria in Canada (March–Dec 2–4 daily; 1 hr 45min-trip; one-way fares $9 walk-on, $33.50 per car), but note that peak-season delays are commonplace for those taking a vehicle and reservations are not accepted. Arriving at a neighboring pier at the foot of Lincoln Street, the **passenger ferries** of Victoria Express (ⓣ360/452-8088 or 1-800/633-1589, ⓦwww.victoriaexpress.com) operate a faster service (2–3 daily) for $25 round-trip. Finally, local **car rental** firms offer reasonable rates for one- and two-day rentals; you'll see their billboards all over the ferry dock. Budget, 111 E Front St (ⓣ360/452-4774 or 1-800/345-8038, ⓦwww.budgetofportangeles.com), is as competitive as any.

The town's **visitor center**, right by the main ferry terminal at 121 E Railroad Ave (summer daily 7am–6pm; rest of year Mon–Fri 10am–4pm; ⓣ360/452-2363, ⓦwww.portangeles.org), has information on the entire peninsula and can put you in touch with local river-rafting and sea-kayaking operators. Port Angeles also houses the **Olympic National Park Visitor Center**, 600 E Park Ave (daily 9am–4pm, summer closes 8pm; ⓣ360/452-0330 or 565-3100, ⓦwww.nps.gov/olym), an excellent source of the maps and information you'll need if you're planning any hiking. Next door, the **Wilderness Information Center**, 3002 Mount Angeles Rd (April–May daily 8am–4.30pm, May–June daily 7.30am–6pm, July Sun–Thurs 7.30am–6pm and Fri–Sat 7.30am–8pm), specializes in backcountry hiking and camping.

The Town

The harbor has its own gritty beauty: sheltered by the long arm of the Ediz Hook sandspit, mammoth freighters are backdropped by mountains, and out in the bay cormorants hover over the fishing boats. You can spend a few minutes wandering the compact downtown core, just behind the waterfront between Oak and Chase streets, where there's a smattering of old and good-looking brick buildings highlighted by the stately Federal-style pile of the **Clallam County Courthouse**, 223 E Fourth St at Lincoln (Mon–Fri 9am–noon & 1–4pm; ⓣ360/417-2279), a little slice of the East Coast dropped into the Pacific Northwest. A few blocks north, the **Feiro Marine Life Center**, 315 N Lincoln St (June–Sept Tues–Sun 10am–6pm, Oct–May Sat & Sun noon–4pm; $2.50; ⓦwww.olypen.com/feirolab), has the usual marine-biology exhibits and a "touch tank" enabling you to take a poke at helpless tidepool creatures, but more compelling is the **Port Angeles Fine Arts Center**, 1203 E Lauridsen Blvd (Tues–Sun 11am–5pm; free; ⓦwww.portangelesartscenter.com), a cut above the typical provincial art gallery thanks to its curious **Webster's Woods Art Park**. Here, amid a five-acre outdoor setting, some 75 sculptures are arrayed on the grounds, hiding in the trees and in the foliage, making for a nice blend of art and nature. There's no mistaking town's real attraction, however: its closeness to Olympic National Park (see p.360), and even with the town's various minor attractions, that's probably the main place you'll want to go.

Port Angeles is a good place to get properly equipped: Sound Bikes and Kayaks, 120 E Front St (ⓣ360/457-1240), rents **mountain bikes** and organizes **kayak trips**, while Olympic Mountaineering, 140 W Front St at Oak (ⓣ360/452-0240, ⓦwww.olymtn.com), hires out climbing, camping, and hiking tackle, though its specialty is guided mountaineering trips. The most popular excursion is a day-long climb to the 7965-ft summit of Mount Olympus, which costs $295 per person.

Practicalities

Although it's preferable to stay inside the national park, Port Angeles has a number of inexpensive chain **motels** near its uninspiring one-way main drags, First Street and Front Street. These include the *Best Western Olympic Lodge,* 140 Del Guzzi Dr (ⓣ1-800/600-2993, ⓦwww.portangeleshotelmotel.com; ❹), and *Traveler's Motel,* 1133 E First St (ⓣ360/452-2303, ⓦwww.travelersmotel.net; ❷), but for more upscale accommodation, try *Domaine Madeleine,* 146 Wildflower Lane (ⓣ360/457-4174, ⓦwww.domainemadeleine.com; ❻–❽), an elegant B&B with art-themed rooms and a lovely five-acre garden, or *The 5 Seasuns*, 1006 S Lincoln (ⓣ360/452-8248, ⓦwww.seasuns.com; ❺), which occupies a handsome 1920s villa amid extensive gardens and offers four guestrooms. If you're staying inside the park, at any of the sixteen excellent **campgrounds** ($8–16; ⓣ360/565-3130, ⓦwww.nps.gov/olym), you'll need your own vehicle. Try **Heart o' the Hills**, six miles south of Port Angeles, along Hurricane Ridge Road (see p.362), or further west, **Elwah** and **Altaire** (closed in winter), which are equally good with access to the numerous hiking trails; these three campgrounds are all $10 per night.

For **breakfast** or **lunch**, head for the tiny *First Street Haven*, 107 E First St and Laurel (ⓣ360/457-0352), for its seafood, sandwiches, and pasta; for **dinner**, the upscale *Bella Italia,* 118 E First St (ⓣ360/457-5442), has decent seafood and traditional Italian cuisine, while *Thai Peppers*, 222 N Lincoln St (ⓣ360/452-4995), offers surprisingly good Thai staples.

Neah Bay and Cape Alava

West of Port Angeles, US-101 cuts inland to begin its circuitous journey round the flanks of Olympic National Park. This is the obvious route to follow, but it's also possible to take **Hwy-112** right along the coast, a seventy-mile drive that becomes increasingly solitary the further you go. Eventually, the road passes the graveled turnoff that bumps down to Lake Ozette before clinging precariously to the cliffs as it approaches end-of-the-world **NEAH BAY**, the small and rundown last village of the **Makah** tribe. At the northern corner of the Makah Reservation is **Cape Flattery**, the continental US's northwesternmost point, a remote headland accessible on an unpaved road from Neah Bay. A half-mile hike from the road through the rainforest leads to the cape that once "flattered" Captain Cook with the hope of finding a harbor. Below the cape, the waves have worn caves into the sheer rock of the cliff face, while opposite, on **Tatoosh Island**, the Coast Guard runs a remote lighthouse (closed to public view).

The Makah's bitter history is typical of the area: a seagoing tribe, it once lived by fishing and hunting whales and seals, moving from camp to camp across the western part of the peninsula. Like most Native Americans, they were happy to trade with passing European ships, and even when the Spanish built a stockade here in 1792 (abandoned four months later) the relationship remained cordial and mutually beneficial. However, when whites began to settle in the 1840s, bringing smallpox with them, Makah social structures were decimated by an epidemic of savage proportions. Samuel Hancock, who had built a trading post at Neah Bay in 1850, recorded the tragedy: "The beach for a distance of eight miles was literally strewn with the dead bodies . . . still they continue to die in such numbers that I finally hauled them down the beach at low tide, so they would drift away." Other indignities were to follow: treaties restricted their freedom of movement, white settlers were given vast chunks of their land, and they were forced to speak English at white-run schools, as missionaries set about changing their religion.

The Makah's tenuous grip on their culture received an unexpected boost in 1970, when a mudslide at an old village site on **CAPE ALAVA**, several miles south of their present reservation, revealed part of their ancient settlement – buried, Pompeii-like, by a previous mudslide some five hundred years before and perfectly preserved. The first people to uncover the remains encountered bizarre scenes of instantaneous aging – green alder leaves, lying on the floor where they fell centuries ago, shriveled almost as soon as they were exposed – but more important were the archeological finds. After eleven years of careful excavation, the **Ozette Dig** revealed thousands of artifacts, everything from harpoons for whale hunts, intricately carved seal clubs, watertight boxes made without metal, strangely designed bowls, and toys all belonging to a period before trade began with Europeans. Rather than being carted off to the depths of the Smithsonian, these artifacts have remained in Makah hands, and a number are now displayed at Neah Bay's **Makah Cultural and Research Center**, Hwy-112 at Bayview Avenue (daily summer 10am–5pm, rest of year Wed–Sun only; $4; Ⓦwww.makah.com/museum.htm), a well-curated museum displaying marine dioramas, dugout cedar canoes, fishing gear, a life-size replica of a fifteenth-century longhouse, and some poignant nineteenth-century photographs of the Makah people. The site of the ancient village was, however, reburied in 1981 to preserve it.

You can get to Neah Bay on Clallam Transit (see p.357), though there are few good options for **accommodation**. Given the area's drab motels, to find anything special you'll have to head seventeen miles east to **Sekiu**, a sports fishing town, to reach *Van Riper's Resort,* 280 Front St (Ⓣ360/963-2334, Ⓦwww.vanripersresort.com; ❸–❻), which has a range of simple motel rooms and campsites, and more elaborate lodge units and waterfront suites, along with beach access and boat rentals.

Olympic National Park

Magnificent **OLYMPIC NATIONAL PARK** (ⓣ360/452-0330, ⓦwww.nps.gov/olym), consisting of the colossal Olympic Mountains in the heart of the peninsula plus a separate sixty-mile strip of Pacific coast further west, is one of Washington's prime wilderness destinations, with boundless opportunities for spectacular hiking and wildlife watching. Although the park is best known as the location of the only **temperate rainforests** in North America, the special conditions responsible for producing such zones only prevail at lower altitudes, and into its one-and-a-half million acres are crammed an extraordinarily diverse assortment of landscapes and climates. About sixty percent of the park – the areas between two and four thousand feet – is **montane forest**, dominated by Pacific silver and Douglas firs. At higher elevations, these trees give way to a **subalpine forest** of mountain hemlock, Alaska cedar, and fir, broken up by intermittent forest and lush meadow. Higher up still, the mountain slopes and summits constitute a forbidding **alpine zone** where windborne ice crystals can feel like flying shards of glass, the hiking trails are only free of snow for about two months a year (late June–Aug), and hardy mosses and lichens are nearly the only vegetation. The **coast** is different again, for here the wild and lonely Pacific beaches that stretch down the peninsula's west side are studded with black rocks that point dramatically out of a gray sea, inhabited mostly by loons, grebes, puffins, and cormorants – and federally protected as **Flattery Rocks National Wildlife Refuge**.

No roads cross the central segment of the park from one side to the other, but many run into it from separate directions, and only parts of the coastal strip are accessible by road. The text which follows reflects the most logical itinerary, working **counterclockwise on US-101** around the park and making forays into different sections from the access points along the way. As noted, some parts of the park can only be reached on gravel-topped roads and should be approached with caution (if at all) in an ordinary vehicle, particularly in wet or foggy weather. If you're planning to do a lot of backcountry driving, equip

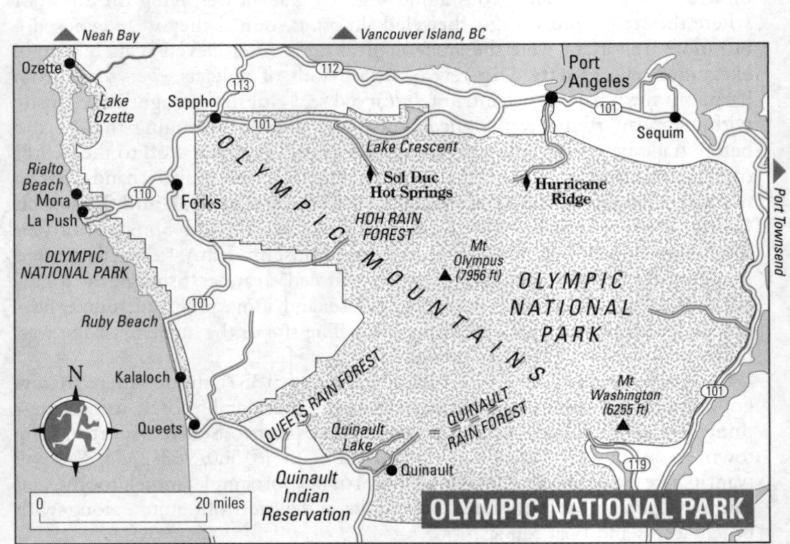

yourself with a four-wheel-drive and carry the necessary equipment in case of emergency.

Park practicalities

Before heading into the park, load up on information at the **Olympic National Park Visitor Center** and the **Wilderness Information Center**, both back in Port Angeles (see p.357). There are other, smaller NPS visitor centers at **Hurricane Ridge** and **Hoh Rainforest**, and these main services are supplemented by a string of seasonal **ranger stations** – at Lake Crescent, Ozette, Mora, Kalaloch, Queets, Lake Quinault, and elsewhere – as well as the occasional US Forest Service station in the adjoining Olympic National Forest. Most have a wealth of literature, including free maps and visitors' guides – though not always the detailed maps needed by hikers. Most NPS centers and stations will issue backcountry permits ($5 to register, $2 per person to camp, both good for fourteen days), but don't assume this to be the case, and always ring ahead. **Entrance** to the park costs $10 per vehicle, $5 for cyclists and pedestrians; the ticket is valid for seven consecutive days' admission.

More than six hundred miles of **hiking trails** course through the park, ranging from the gentlest of Sunday strolls to lung-wrenching torture treks. The usual backcountry rules apply: treat the water before drinking it, store food out of the reach of bears, avoid defecating near water sources, and get a backcountry permit if you're venturing beyond the park's established campgrounds to stay overnight. Naturally, the weather on the west (rainforest) side of the park is incredibly wet – 140 inches is an average annual precipitation, the highest level in the Pacific Northwest – and though the eastern slopes are considerably drier, rain is frequent here, too. That said, summer days can be hot and sunny, and even the heaviest rain clouds are often swept away by the prevailing westerlies. On the coast, strong currents, cold water, and hidden rocks make the **beaches** unsuitable for swimming (especially as floating logs present a real hazard), but the hiking can be magnificent, if very strenuous – the coastal headlands hereabouts are often extremely difficult to negotiate. Also, you do hear the odd horror story about hikers cut off by the tide, so carry a tide table, printed in the *Peninsula Daily News* (Ⓦwww.peninsuladailynews.com), or copy down such times at a ranger station or visitor center, and err on the side of caution. Lastly, wherever you go, don't forget the insect repellent.

The one-horse communities dotting the park's perimeter offer **motel** accommodation, but, generally speaking, you're better off inside it. Here you can either **camp** – there are sixteen established campgrounds ($11–16), ten open all year and operating on a first-come-first-served basis, and around ninety backcountry sites ($2) – or stay in one of the **lodges** (❹–❼), among which there are three of note: at Lake Crescent, Lake Quinault, and Kalaloch. The *Sol Duc Hot Springs Resort* (see p.363), deep within the park, is another excellent choice. At all four establishments, book your room well in advance.

The park is best accessed by car, but Clallam Transit of Port Angeles (see p.357) does provide a reasonably frequent weekday **bus** service to *Lake Crescent Lodge* and Forks (#14 line), where you can change for La Push (#15). Alternatively, Royal Tours offers a bus line from the Port Angeles ferry dock (linking by ferry to its tour of Victoria, BC), to Hurricane Ridge for $21 (Ⓣ360/417-8006 or 1-888/381-1800, Ⓦwww.royaltours.bc.ca).

Hurricane Ridge and the Olympic Mountains

On the southern edge of Port Angeles, the Olympic National Park Visitor Center (see p.361) is the starting point for the seventeen-mile haul up to

HURRICANE RIDGE – passing (after about five miles) the **Heart O' the Hills** campground. It's a formidable drive, as the road wraps itself around cliffs and precipices until the piercing peaks and glistening glaciers of the **OLYMPIC MOUNTAINS** spread out before you, a huge, thick band of snow-capped peaks with mighty Mount Olympus the tallest of all at nearly eight thousand feet. A **day lodge** on the ridge (May–Oct) has tourist facilities and information, and **hiking trails** lead off to more isolated spots, through meadows filled with wildflowers in early summer.

The most popular trek is the **Hurricane Hill Trail**, a three-mile round-trip to the top of a neighboring hill, where there are great views out across the Juan de Fuca Strait. Longer alternatives include the strenuous eight-mile hike west, over the mountains through classic alpine and sub-alpine scenery, to **Lake Mills**, where there's a backcountry campground. East from Hurricane Ridge, a difficult and steep nine-mile dirt road heads off to **Obstruction Peak**, noted for its views of Mount Olympus; several trails venture from the end of the road into the valley beyond, with one leading to the campground at **Deer Park**.

Lake Crescent and the Sol Duc River Valley

West of Port Angeles, US-101 slips through low-lying forest on its fifteen-mile journey to glacier-cut **LAKE CRESCENT**, a handsome fishing lake known throughout the region for its fine Beardslee trout. Just off the highway, beside the lake's southern shore, the 1930s *Lake Crescent Lodge* (May–Oct; ⓣ360/928-3211, ⓦwww.lakecrescentlodge.com; ❹–❼), occupies a beautiful, densely wooded headland, offering simple rooms to more elegant cottages. Nearby, the one-mile **Marymere Falls Trail** leads through old-growth forest to a ninety-foot waterfall, and continues up the forested mountain slope, as the two-mile Mount Storm King Trail, to Happy Lake Ridge, where there are magnificent views back over the lake. If you're staying at the lodge, they're only too pleased to provide further hiking (and boating) suggestions.

The temperate rainforests of Olympic National Park

Extraordinary as it may seem in cool Washington, a nearly unique combination of climatic factors in the river valleys on the western side of the Olympic Peninsula produces an environment akin to a jungle. **Temperate rainforests** are extremely rare – the only others are located in Patagonia and New Zealand – but here an average annual rainfall of 140 inches, mixing with river-water running down from the mountains, creates conditions wet enough to produce a density of foliage normally associated with much warmer climes. Sitka spruce and maple flourish, all but overwhelmed by the thick, trailing tendrils of club mosses and lichens, epiphytes whose roots gather nourishment from the drizzly air. On the ground, some three hundred species of plants jostle for space to grow, crowding the ground with ferns, mushrooms, and wood sorrel oozing out of the dense, moist soil. The rainforests intermingle with the montane forests of Western hemlock and Douglas fir, among which are the park's largest trees – in fact the world's biggest Douglas fir stretches skyward in the Queets Valley.

Several rainforest areas can be visited, notably those in the valleys of the Hoh and Quinault rivers. The only way to get through the rainforest is on the specially cleared, and in places paved, **trails**, though these tend to get slippery as moss grows back again – wear boots or shoes that grip well. You'll need a **vehicle** to reach any of the trailheads, but there are **campgrounds** in both valleys and lodging beside Quinault Lake.

Just beyond the western tip of Lake Crescent, a paved turnoff branches south off US-101 to thread up through the densely forested **SOL DUC RIVER VALLEY**, a fascinating part of the transitional zone between the rainforests to the west and the drier lowland forest to the east. After twelve miles the road reaches the *Sol Duc Hot Springs Resort* (mid-May to late–Sept; ⓣ360/327-3583, ⓦwww.northolympic.com/solduc; ❻). First impressions are not especially favorable – the resort's modern timber chalets sit unceremoniously in a forest clearing – but the units are perfectly adequate, if rather spartan. The restaurant, though, is outstanding, serving fine Northwest Cuisine, and splendid hiking trails nudge into the surrounding mountains. What's more, bathing in the resort's **hot springs** (summer daily 9am–9pm; April to mid-May & Oct Fri–Sun 9am–7pm) is extraordinarily relaxing, with the mineral water bubbling out of the earth to be channeled into three outside pools – from 100 to 108°F (38 to 42°C). Overnight guests can use the heated pools for free, but visitors – including those using the resort's **campground** ($20) – have to pay $10.

From the end of the road, a couple of miles beyond the resort, you can hike further along the river to **Sol Duc Falls**, from where a steep path heads off south along Canyon Creek up into the mountains to the **Seven Lakes Basin**. More ambitious souls can hike across the Bogachiel Peak, past Hoh Lake and down into the Hoh River Valley – the site of one of the most visited rainforest areas (see overleaf).

Forks

Back on US-101, it's about fourteen miles west from the Sol Duc turnoff to Hwy-113, which cuts off north for the lengthy journey to Neah Bay (see p.359), and another fourteen miles to the small blue-collar burg of **FORKS**, located between the main mountainous section and the coastal portion of Olympic National Park. Despite half-hearted attempts to catch the peninsula's growing tourist trade, Forks remains very much a timber town, and it's been hit hard by the gradual decline of the industry. Nonetheless, heavy trucks still trickle through Forks, unloading logs at local sawmills and hauling sawn lumber away to be shipped out of Port Angeles or Grays Harbor.

If you're sufficiently inspired by the timber trade, the history of logging is on display at the **Forks Timber Museum**, about a mile south of town on US-101 (mid-April to Oct daily 10am–4pm; donation). Various exhibits depict life in the lumber camps of the 1920s and 1930s, when men were based in the forest, sleeping in bunkhouses and hitting the towns for only a few days each month. Inexpensive road-building ended the camps after World War II and in recent years mechanized devices (some on display) have also made logging less hazardous, though it remains a dangerous occupation.

If you're not interested in catching the flavor of the Northwest lumber scene, and have little interest in the town's world-class river fishing – which you can investigate at the town's **visitors center** at 1411 S Forks Ave (ⓣ360/374-2531 or 1-800/44-FORKS, ⓦwww.forkswa.com) – there's little reason to visit the place, except as a base for touring the mountains. Decent **accommodation** is available at *Miller Tree Inn*, 654 E Division St (ⓣ360/374-6806, ⓦwww.millertreeinn.com; ❹–❻), with Victorian-styled suites and pleasant guestrooms, and at *Olympic Suites*, 800 Olympic Drive (ⓣ360/374-5400 or 1-800/262-3433, ⓦwww.olympicsuitesinn.com; ❸), with spacious one- and two-bedroom units. Clallam Transit (see p.357) runs **buses** from Port Angeles to Forks, with connections on to the coast at La Push. For **eating**, the *Forks Coffee Shop* (ⓣ360/374-6769), is the place to go for decent all-American burgers and sandwiches for lunch, and more expensive steaks and seafood for dinner, while good old-fashioned *Sully's Drive-In*, 220 N Forks Ave (ⓣ360/374-5075), whips up burgers, pizza, and fountain favorites like sundaes and banana splits.

The Pacific coastline

A couple of miles north of Forks, Hwy-110 cuts west off US-101 for the half-hour drive west to the park's **coastline**. About eight miles along the turnoff the road splits into two branches – one above, the other below the Quillayute River: the southern branch meanders round to the down-at-heel village of **La Push**, on the small Quillayute Indian Reservation, while the northern fork continues on into the national park's coastal strip at **Mora**, site of an attractive **campground** ($10) sitting amid old-growth forest, and a ranger station (ⓣ360/374-5460). Close by, a mile or two further down the road, lies **Rialto Beach**, a driftwood-cluttered strand from where it's possible to hike north along the shoreline, passing beneath the wooded bluffs to the sound of the booming surf. Most visitors are content with a manageable hike along the coast, but others opt for the longer, extremely arduous, twenty-mile trek north to **Ozette**, where the ranger station (ⓣ360/963-2725) and **campground** ($10) are a little inland beside Lake Ozette. This longer hike takes three to four days, and you should arrange transportation at both ends; as always, take good care not to get cut off by the tide and be prepared for strenuous climbs over steep coastal headlands. A comparatively easy 3.3-mile trail – part of the Indian Village Nature Trail – runs from Ozette Ranger Station to the coast at Cape Alava, the site of the **Ozette Dig**, a prehistoric Makah village revealed (and subsequently reburied) after a 1970 mudslide (see p.359).

South of Forks beyond the Hoh turnoff (see below), US-101 dips down to the park's wild **southern beaches**, where black rocks jut out of the tumultuous sea, and the strong undertow, floating tree trunks, and dramatic tides make the waters striking to watch, if rather unsuitable for swimming. The hiking can be magnificent, though, and a series of short, appealing trails head down to and along the seashore – **Ruby Beach**, named for its red-and-black-pebbled sand, is the unmistakable highlight. Near the end of the park's coastal stretch, **Kalaloch** has a few **campgrounds** ($12–16; reserve at ⓣ1-800/365-CAMP), while the impressive *Kalaloch Lodge* (ⓣ360/962-2271, ⓦwww.visitkalaloch.com), has basic lodge rooms (❹–❻) and more upscale cabins (❺–❼), as well as a good onsite restaurant. The **ranger station** here also provides information and suggestions for hiking trips (ⓣ360/962-2283).

The Hoh and Queets rainforests

South of Forks, US-101 threads through logging country to pass, after about fourteen miles, the paved turnoff that leads deep into the **HOH RAINFOREST**. This is the most popular of the Olympic rainforests, principally because of the excellent **visitor center**, located nineteen miles from US-101 (daily 9am–4pm, summer closes 6.30pm; ⓣ360/374-6925), where you can examine various displays on the unusual habitat and pick up all sorts of explanatory pamphlets. Afterwards, you can explore the rainforest along two short trails, the three-quarter-mile **Hall of Mosses Trail** or the slightly longer **Spruce Trail**, which reaches the Hoh River on a circuit through the forest. More energetic hikers can follow the 36-mile round-trip **Hoh River Trail** right up to the base of Mount Olympus; climbing the ice-covered peak is a major undertaking, but even if you just want to camp out along the route, be sure to check in with the rangers and get a backcountry permit. There's also a ninety-site **campground**

($12–16) next to the visitor center, but keep in mind that cougars and other beasts are very much present in the park, and in winter Roosevelt elk from higher elevations gather here.

Further to the southwest, the next rainforest over is only accessible via US-101 south of the park's southern beaches (see above). Here, just beyond Kalaloch, the highway loops awkwardly inland to skirt the sizable **Quinault Indian Reservation**, an infertile chunk of wilderness wedged against the shoreline. It's home to several Salish-speaking tribes who were stuck here in the 1850s during the aggressive treaty-making period that followed Washington's incorporation as a US territory. The highway runs along the northern edge of the reservation, passing, after about ten miles, the fourteen-mile-long dirt road which heads inland to the **QUEETS RAINFOREST**, the least visited of the three main rainforest areas, but worthwhile for its rustic, accessible trails, which take you through a rare coniferous rainforest populated by the likes of Western hemlock and cedar trees. It's also the site of the world's **largest Douglas fir** – 220 feet tall and 45 feet around.

Quinault Lake and Rainforest

Further inland from the turnoff to the Queets Rainforest, US-101 reaches, in short succession, the two side roads that lead the couple of miles off the highway to **QUINAULT LAKE**, whose dark blue waters are surrounded by the deep greens of the **QUINAULT RAINFOREST**, the most accessible and perhaps the most beautiful of all the peninsula's rainforests. The lake was already a popular resort area when Teddy Roosevelt visited in the 1900s and proclaimed it part of an expanded Olympic National Park: you only have to glimpse the lake and its idyllic setting to see why Roosevelt was so impressed.

Of the two **access roads** leading off US-101, one travels the length of the lake's north shore, the other the south, but they don't connect until you're well past the lake and further up the river valley – a thirty-mile loop. Dense overgrowth crimps the narrow road as it enters the deeper recesses of the forest, but it perseveres (as a rough gravel track), and the loop is negotiable by vehicle – though you should check conditions before you set off: floods have on occasion wrecked the more remote portions of the road.

A variety of **hiking trails** lead off from the road; the longer and more strenuous is through the rainforest of the **Quinault River Valley** and on up to the alpine meadows and glaciated peaks at the center of the national park. Others serve as easy introductions to the rainforest: the half-mile **Maple Glade Trail** is one of the best short hikes, clambering along a small stream through signature rainforest vegetation, while the four-mile **Quinault Loop Trail** snakes through a wonderful old-growth forest dominated by colossal Douglas firs that keep out the light, turning the undergrowth into a dark land of mystery. Backcountry permits, hiking maps, weather forecasts, details of all the trails, and information on the five **campgrounds** ($11–16) dotted around the lakeshore are available at the **ranger station** at 353 S Shore Rd (Mon–Fri 8am–4.30pm, Sat & Sun 9am–4pm; ⓣ360/288-2525, ⓦwww.olympus.net/onf). A few yards away, occupying a fine lakeshore location, the high timber gables and stone chimneys of **Lake Quinault Lodge** (ⓣ360/288-2900 or 1-800/562-6672, ⓦwww.visitlakequinault.com; woodside rooms ❻, lakeside ❼) date from the 1920s, though the interior has been revamped in a comfortable modern style. It's a justifiably popular spot, so reservations are essential. There's less expensive accommodation in the vicinity, too – try the **Lochaerie Resort**, 638 North Shore Rd (ⓣ360/288-2215, ⓦwww.lochaerie.com; ❺), which has five comfortable cabins also dating from the 1920s.

Southwest Washington

Compared to the glories of Seattle, Puget Sound, and the Olympic Peninsula, **southwest Washington**'s offerings are rather thin on the ground. Although the state's southern coast is popular for many regional visitors, and the southern stretch of I-5 almost unavoidable heading down to Portland, visitors from outside the area may find little here that can't be found in bigger, glossier, and more scenic form elsewhere in western Washington or northwestern Oregon. That said, there are a number of scattered points of interest that are comparable in historic and cultural value to other spots in the state, and a handful of decent choices for accommodation. And clearly, if you want to get a true sense of the region, and appreciate the region's nineteenth-century commercial and pioneer background, you can't miss historic spots like **Grays Harbor**, **Cape Disappointment**, and **Fort Vancouver**. Nonetheless, with almost nothing of interest between **Vancouver**, at the state's southern edge, and **Centralia**, midway between Portland and Seattle, it's perhaps not surprising that transit links to the region – except of course along the I-5 corridor, an essential route for Amtrak **trains** and Greyhound **buses** – are spotty at best.

The southern Pacific coast

As you leave the Olympic Peninsula's western half for the state's **southern Pacific coast**, the scenery gradually grows tamer and the national forests are replaced by privately owned timber land, gashed by bald patches of clear cutting. The coastline cuts deeply into the mainland at two points: the bay of **Grays Harbor**, at the apex of which lie the twin industrial cities of Hoquiam and **Aberdeen**, and muddy **Willapa Bay**, dotted with oyster beds and wildlife sanctuaries. The sand spit sheltering Willapa Bay – **Long Beach Peninsula** – was formed from sediment carried here by the ocean from the churning mouth of the Columbia River near its base. The beach is extraordinarily long, but visitors are allowed to drive on almost all of it and the straggling resorts behind it are scrawny, modern places without much appeal. The lower coast's saving grace is right at its southern tip just beyond tiny **Ilwaco**, where the ruggedly handsome headland that pokes out into the mouth of the Columbia River is protected as **Cape Disappointment State Park** – and here you can camp or stay in the old lighthouse-keeper's quarters.

Grays Harbor and Aberdeen

South of Olympic National Park's Quinault rainforest (see p.365), US-101 cuts across logging country, whizzing through the forested hills until it hits gritty Hoquiam, beside the bay of **GRAYS HARBOR**, which takes a big bite out of the coastline. The loggers who settled here in the mid-nineteenth century originally meant to stay only until the dense forest within easy reach of the waterfront had been cut down and the area was "logged out." But railways soon made it possible to transport lumber from deeper in the forest, and a combination of this and the plentiful fishing – canneries soon joined the sawmills along the waterfront – led to the development of Hoquiam and its larger neighbor **ABERDEEN** – grunge icon Kurt Cobain's reviled hometown. Now hit by a seemingly endless recession in both the fishing and forestry industries, these twin towns are not obvious places for a visit, though Aberdeen is making a plucky attempt at catching passing tourists with its **Grays Harbor Historical Seaport** (Ⓣ360/532-8611 or 1-800/200-2359, Ⓦwww.ladywashington.org). In these unpromising surroundings, this harbor reinvigoration project has painstakingly reconstructed the *Lady Washington*, the eighteenth-century sailing ship of Captain Robert Gray, the American trader who discovered Grays Harbor. Built to conform both to original designs and modern Coast Guard safety regulations, the ship is now a floating museum with a crew dressed in period costume. There are guided tours ($3) plus three-hour sailing trips for $40 per person – call for schedules and reservations, as the ship sometimes sails to different ports for months at a time.

US-101 cuts through Aberdeen's town center, located on the north bank of the Chehalis River as it flows into the bay. The historical seaport is just to the east across the Wishkah River, a tributary of the Chehalis – just follow the signs. In the unlikely event you want to **stay** in Aberdeen, the Grays Harbor **visitor center**, off US-101 at 506 Duffy St (Ⓣ360/532-1924, Ⓦwww.graysharbor.org), is on the strip connecting Hoquiam and Aberdeen, and has a comprehensive list of local lodgings.

Willapa National Wildlife Refuge and Ilwaco

US-101 leads south out of Aberdeen over the hills to **Raymond**, a pocket-sized lumber town where the highway turns west to skirt the flat and tedious shoreline of **Willapa Bay**. Too shallow to be used as a commercial port, Willapa Bay is much less developed than Grays Harbor, and its muddy depths support a profitable underworld of oysters – you'll spot the bivalve beds from the highway. Several parts of the bay have been incorporated into the 11,000-acre **WILLAPA NATIONAL WILDLIFE REFUGE**, whose various dunes, forests, marshes, and mudflats shelter some two hundred species of migrating shorebirds. Most of the refuge is only accessible by boat, but one of its sections – Leadbetter Point at the tip of Long Beach Peninsula – can be reached by car. Advice on what wildlife to see and where can be obtained from the refuge **visitor center** (Ⓣ360/484-3482, Ⓦwillapa.fws.gov), beside US-101 across from Willapa Bay's Long Island, about 35 miles south of Raymond.

Named after a Chinook chief, the fishing port of **ILWACO**, ten miles southwest of Willapa Bay, achieved some notoriety at the start of the twentieth century when competition between fishermen with nets and those with traps broke into a series of street battles, the **gillnet wars**, fought with knives and rifles – and only finally resolved when fishtraps were banned on the Columbia in 1935. Nowadays, Ilwaco is an unassuming little place, where everyone knows the times of the tides and where to dig for clams. There's nothing much to see, though you could take a **sea-fishing trip** – there are several operators down along the harborfront – or drop by the **Heritage Museum**, 115 SE Lake St (Mon–Sat 9am–4pm; till 5pm & Sun noon–4pm in summer; $3; Ⓦwww.ilwacoheritagemuseum.org), which has displays on Chinook culture, pioneer artifacts, and the myths and realities of the Lewis and Clark expedition.

There are more interesting places to stay nearby – in Cape Disappointment and Fort Columbia state parks (see p.369) – but Ilwaco does have a reasonable supply of **accommodation**. The pick of the bunch is the *Inn at Ilwaco*, 120 Williams Ave NE (Ⓣ360/642-8686 or 1-888/244-2523; ❻), whose nine comfortable rooms occupy the renovated parsonage and vestry of the Presbyterian church on a wooded rise just above the town. The *Shaman Motel*, 115 3rd St SW (Ⓣ360/642-3714 or 1-800/753-3750, Ⓦshamanmotel.com; ❹), is a second, much cheaper choice, offering some units equipped with kitchenettes and fireplaces.

Long Beach Peninsula

Lined by 28 miles of uninterrupted beach, and less prone to fog than other parts of Washington's coast, the **LONG BEACH PENINSULA**, separating

The Chinook

Although there's not much evidence of it today, the area around the mouth of the **Columbia River** was once populated by the **Chinook** people. Their "Chinook jargon," an Esperanto-style mix of their own language with French and English, was widely used for trading, and later, for treaty-making. By all accounts, it was extremely easy to learn: Paul Kane, an Irish-Canadian explorer and painter who passed this way in the mid-1840s, wrote that it only took a few days before he could "converse with most of the chiefs with tolerable ease; their common salutation is *Clak-hoh-ah-yah*, originating . . . in their having heard in the early days of the fur trade . . . *Clark, how are you?*"

The Chinook also caught nineteenth-century white imaginations with their supposedly **flattened skulls**, as depicted in careful sketches brought back to a curious East by both Kane and explorers Lewis and Clark, who spent the winter of 1805–6 quartered at Fort Clatsop, on the south side of the river (see p.149). The skull-flattening was achieved by pressing a piece of bark firmly to a baby's (padded) forehead every time it went to bed for about a year, the end result being seen as a sign of noble distinction.

Although this practice died out by the twentieth century, and the Chinook had to deal with threats from white encroachment and exploitation, the tribe has survived on its ancestral lands and puts on festivals, craftwork displays, and other events several times a year around the southwest Washington region. To get a sense of tribal culture, check out Ⓦwww.chinooknation.org, which provides information on the remaining Chinook's various festivities and details their history, lore, and legends, as well as offering a photographic glimpse of what people looked like with their skulls flattened.

the Pacific Ocean and Willapa Bay, has been a holiday destination since steamboats ferried vacationing Portlanders here in the 1890s. Today it's something of a low-rent resort area, offering little more than chain motels and a smattering of tourists, who come to browse the kite shops, gnaw on salt-water taffy, and pick up tacky souvenirs. One of the peninsula's few attractions, the **Pacific Coast Cranberry Museum**, 2907 Pioneer Rd in the town of Long Beach (Ⓣ360/642-5553, Ⓦwww.cranberrymuseum.com), gives you the opportunity to wander through a cranberry bog and pick up berry-flavored treats.

The best reason to visit the peninsula, though, is to drive up toward the northern tip to **Oysterville**, about sixteen miles north of Ilwaco on Hwy-103, which made a killing in the 1860s and 1870s by shipping oysters to San Francisco and selling them to the big names of the gold rush, at up to $40 a plate. Then, in an all-too-familiar pattern, increasing demand fueled over-harvesting; with the oysters soon decimated, the town slipped into a long decline, leaving little more than the tiny **historic district** of today, with its Victorian houses of shingles and scrollwork set behind trim picket fences. Once you've strolled around town, there's nothing much to do, though you can sample the local delicacy at the bayside **Oysterville Sea Farms** (Ⓣ360/665-6585), recognizable by its bayside piles of discarded shells and worth a trip for its freshly packaged oysters ($5 per pound). The other attractions at the north tip of the peninsula are the dunes and marshes of **Leadbetter Point**, which form one section of the Willapa National Wildlife Refuge (see p.367). Several vague footpaths meander over the point, but wet conditions soon flood them out and there are no set hiking trails. Before you set out, get advice from the refuge's headquarters.

Cape Disappointment State Park

A few miles southwest of Ilwaco, a heavily forested promontory pokes out into the mouth of the Columbia River, sheltering the town from the full force of the Pacific. Scenic **CAPE DISAPPOINTMENT STATE PARK** (daily summer 6.30am–10pm, rest of year closes 4pm; Ⓦ www.parks.wa.gov), covers the whole of the headland, based around the fortifications constructed here in the 1860s. **Fort Canby** was one of a chain of military installations whose batteries guarded the Pacific Coast (and here, the river mouth) from the middle of the nineteenth century through both world wars. Little remains of the fort today – just a few weather-beaten gun emplacements – but there are two interesting lighthouses. The first – reached down a short side road as you approach the park – is **North Head Lighthouse** (tours summer daily 11am–3pm; $1), built in 1898 in a magnificent spot high above Dead Man's Hollow, named after the unfortunate victims of an earlier shipwreck.

Doubling back, the main park road pushes on to the **Lewis and Clark Interpretive Center** (daily 10am–5pm; $2), where the displays dealing with the hazards of navigating the Columbia River mouth are a good deal more compelling than the attempt to outline the expedition's journey to the Pacific; if you're interested in the explorers, head instead for the better displays at Fort Clatsop, outside Astoria (see p.149). From the center, a steep, three-quarter-mile trail leads down to the more southerly of the two beacons, **Cape Disappointment Lighthouse** (no public access), perched on **Cape Disappointment** itself, a short finger of land stuck at a right angle to the rest of the promontory. The cape got its name when a British fur trader, John Meares, failed to sail his ship over the dangerous sandbar at the river's entrance in 1788. In fact, Meares was lucky – more than two hundred ships were later wrecked on the sandbar, and although dredges, automated lights, and a pair of long jetties have now made the river mouth much safer, the Coast Guard still trains off the cape; you can sometimes see their small boats facing massive waves.

There's a large **campground** ($15–21) in the park between the Interpretive Center and North Head Lighthouse. Even better, two old North Head **lighthouse-keeper's houses** have been revamped to accommodate tourists, with three bedrooms, living room, kitchen, and dining room in each. Although one house is a bit larger, they both hold a maximum of six people, and the cost is $230 and $325 per night per each in the summer, with discounts of up to half off during weekdays in the offseason (Nov–May); reservations at Ⓣ 1-888/226-7688.

Fort Columbia State Park

Heading east from Ilwaco on Hwy-101, it's eight miles to **FORT COLUMBIA STATE PARK** (daily summer 6.30am–9.30pm, rest of year 8am–5pm; Ⓦ www.parks.wa.gov), which occupies a hilly, wooded headland that was purchased from the Chinook in 1867. The headland was developed as a military installation in the 1890s, acting as a second line of nautical defense behind forts Canby (see above) and Stevens (see p.149). Several gun emplacements dot the park: grim concrete affairs built largely underground with their seaward-facing sides flush to the land to mitigate the effects of incoming shells – which they never encountered. Behind, just up the hill, are several rows of regulation army houses, with wide verandas and neat columns. One of them, the former enlisted men's barracks, houses an **Interpretive Center** (April–Sept 10am–5pm; $2, includes museum) with several period rooms, and the former commander's quarters – Columbia

House – holds a modest **museum** (April–Sept 11am–4pm) with yet more of them.

The park itself has a fine seashore setting, and you can stay here either in the former hospital, now **Scarborough House**, which accommodates up to twelve and costs $350 per night, or in the **Steward's House**, which has two bedrooms and costs $143 per night. Each has a kitchen and living room, linen is provided, and there's a minimum stay of two nights from April to September and on winter weekends. As with the houses at Cape Disappointment, there's a discount of up to half off during the offseason. Reservations are strongly recommended at Ⓣ1-800/360-4240.

From Fort Columbia, it's two miles to the huge, four-mile 1966 bridge that spans the Columbia River over to Oregon's Astoria (see p.144).

South on I-5: Centralia to Vancouver

The only other places of interest in southwest Washington are peppered along **I-5 south** from Olympia, from where it only takes about ninety minutes to cover the one hundred miles to Portland. For the most part, there's precious little to detain you, though the workaday lumber town of **CENTRALIA**, 23 miles from Olympia, is of passing interest as the site of one of the nastiest incidents in the history of Washington's Wobblies (see p.544). During the Armistice Day parade of 1919, several members of the American Legion attacked the town's union building (807 N Tower St) and, in the fight that followed, four Legionnaires were shot. Local Wobblies were promptly rounded up and thrown into jail, but vigilantes broke in that night to seize, mutilate, and then lynch one of their number, a certain Wesley Everest. To make sure the others took the point, the police laid the body out on the jail floor.

Beyond this bit of history, a few odd visitors stop here to drop in on the **Olympic Club** (Ⓣ360/736-5164, Ⓦwww.mcmenamins.com; ❸), a restored hotel, restaurant, and brewpub in the McMenamins chain, which showcases nightly movies, quirky artwork, and tasty microbrewed beer – in an Art Nouveau-styled room with antique chandeliers. The hotel once operated as a union stronghold, speakeasy (repeatedly raided by federal "revenuers"), and hangout for all kinds of unsavory characters, some of whom are commemorated with pictures in the hotel's affordable rooms (with shared bath), including assorted thugs with names like Tacoma Iron Mike and One-Eyed Tony. The Club has the advantage of being a mere block from the **Amtrak** station at 210 Railroad Ave, making it a convenient stopover on train journeys between Seattle and Portland.

A bit further south on I-5, the most obvious detour is east to **Mount St Helens** (see p.400), where the scarred, volcanic landscape, witness to the massive eruption of 1980, constitutes one of the region's most remarkable attractions. Several turnoffs lead to the volcano, but the easiest (and busiest) is located about halfway between Olympia and Portland: coming from the north, turn down Hwy-505 near Toledo, or approaching from the south, take Hwy-504 at Castle Rock; Hwy-505 joins Hwy-504 about fifteen miles east of I-5.

Vancouver

At the southern edge of the state, Washington's **VANCOUVER**, much more modest than its Canadian counterpart, lies just across the Columbia River from Portland, Oregon. Dwarfed by its larger and more prosperous neighbor, Vancouver is a drab sort of place – half bedroom community, half small town. The only real sight worth detaining you, **Fort Vancouver National Historic**

Site (daily 9am–4pm; $3; Ⓦ www.nps.gov/fova), serves as a credible reconstruction of the Pacific Northwest's first substantial European settlement, located just east of I-5 (Exit 1C, Mill Plain Boulevard). Dating from the 1820s, this stockaded outpost of the British-owned Hudson's Bay Company was, for more than twenty years, a remote but prosperous station dedicated to the fur trade. Its early occupation was part of the case the British made for including present-day Washington in their empire, but, as American colonists poured into the Willamette Valley, the British claim lost all weight. At last, when the 49th Parallel became the official border between the US and Canada, Fort Vancouver was left stranded in US territory. By 1860, the Hudson's Bay Company had moved out, and the fort and buildings disappeared, only to be mapped and rebuilt by archeologists in the 1960s.

These days, rangers give interpretive tours throughout the day, and the site – five one-story log structures protected within a rectangular palisade – certainly merits a look, as does nearby Officers' Row, elegant villas built for US Army personnel between 1850 and 1906. If you're here on Independence Day, try to drop in on the formidable display of **fireworks**, supposedly the biggest such spectacle in the Pacific Northwest, on the West Coast, or west of the Mississippi, depending on whom you ask. Whatever the case, it's a remarkably popular affair, with the crowds arriving as early as dawn to stake out favorable seating and the colorful explosions even getting telecast on local TV.

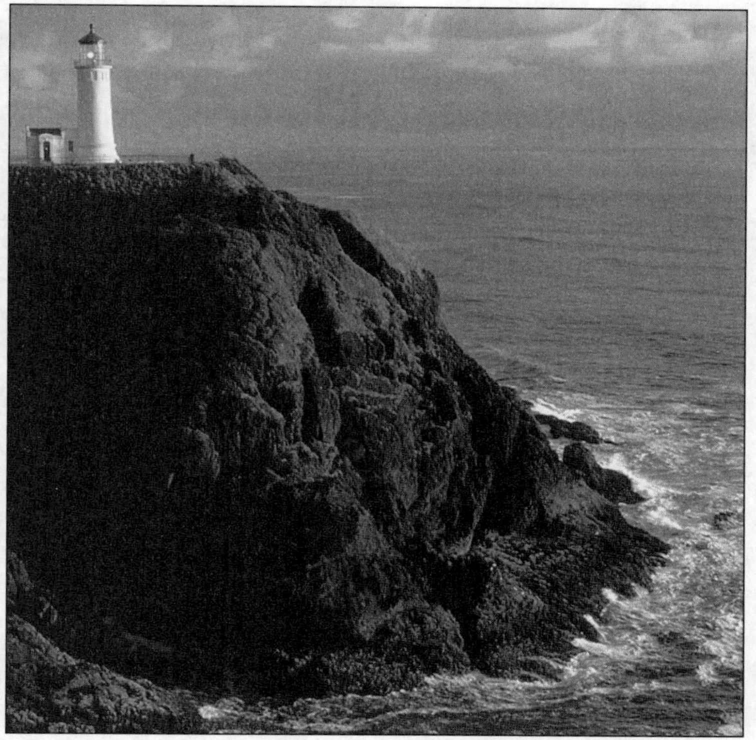

△ The lighthouse at Cape Disappointment

9

The Washington Cascades

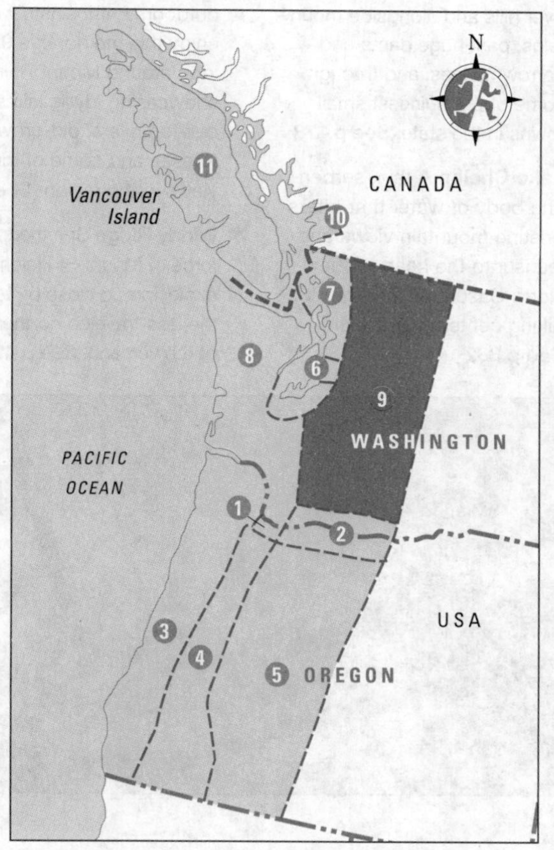

CHAPTER 9

Highlights

* **Mount Baker** Climb up and ski down this grand snowy peak offering pristine slopes about a hour's drive east of Bellingham. See p.377

* **The Cascade Loop** Perhaps the best driving circuit in the Pacific Northwest, a 350-mile roundabout that sends you over hills and alongside mountains, past huge dams and narrow ravines, and through some of the quirkiest small towns in the state. See p.378

* **Lake Chelan** A thin, serpentine body of water that offers pristine mountain views and leads into the heart of the North Cascades and the hiking center of Stehekin. See p.382

* **Snoqualmie Falls** A 270-ft waterfall that flows from the heights of a solid-bedrock gorge, located near the opulent wooden Salish Lodge – both sights familiar from the cult TV show Twin Peaks. See p.389

* **Wonderland Trail** Hardcore outdoors enthusiasts will enjoy this memorable 93-mile loop around Mount Rainier, showcasing idyllic lakes, glacier-fed rivers, old-growth forests, and some of the best views in the region. See p.398

* **Windy Ridge** See the true force of Mount St Helens' 1980 explosion up close by taking the less-traveled northeast side of the volcano. See p.404

△ Windy Ridge

9

The Washington Cascades

Separating the wet, forested regions of western Washington from the parched prairies and canyonlands of the east, the snow-capped and pine-covered **Washington Cascades** extend north-south across the state toward Oregon, where they are gashed by the mighty Columbia River. Although these snowy peaks, which provide an idyllic backdrop for countless Washington postcards, appear as the image of serenity, they still conceal a colossal and dangerous geothermal power – as Mount St Helens proved when it exploded in 1980, annihilating wildlife over a massive area and covering the region with ash. Protected by a series of national parks and national forests stretching across the state, the Washington Cascades feature mile upon mile of dense wilderness, traversed by a skein of beautiful trails.

Best accessed by state highways from the populous communities lining Puget Sound, these Cascades sit along a rough axis stretching from Canada to Oregon, part of a volcanic chain that continues down to northern California. From north to south, the first of the major peaks is **Mount Baker**, a short drive east from Bellingham along Highway 542 and a lovely destination often overshadowed by the state's other big mountains. Further south, the **North Cascades** and the **Cascade Loop**, reached by several eastbound freeways from Mount Vernon to Seattle, are a remote but fascinating array of rugged peaks, glacial lakes, sheltered valleys, and small resort towns – the most agreeable of which are **Chelan** and **Leavenworth** – that eagerly await summer tourist traffic.

Another eastbound route, Highway 90, leads from Seattle past the incomparable spray of **Snoqualmie Falls** and over the mountains into dusty towns on the edge of eastern Washington like **Ellensburg** and **Toppenish**, likable little places with a handful of attractions, before finally continuing south, via US-97, toward the Columbia Gorge (see p.119). South on I-5 from Seattle, several exits lead toward the two most prominent mountains in the entire Cascade chain – **Mount Rainier**, an imposing peak set in its own national park and readily accessible from Tacoma and Olympia, and the blasted terrain of **Mount St Helens**, a National Volcanic Monument that offers a dramatically scarred landscape, fascinating and forbidding in equal measure. The last major peak, **Mount Adams**, on the same longitude as St Helens but forty miles further east, is more remote and less visited, but has its own charm for hikers and outdoors enthusiasts.

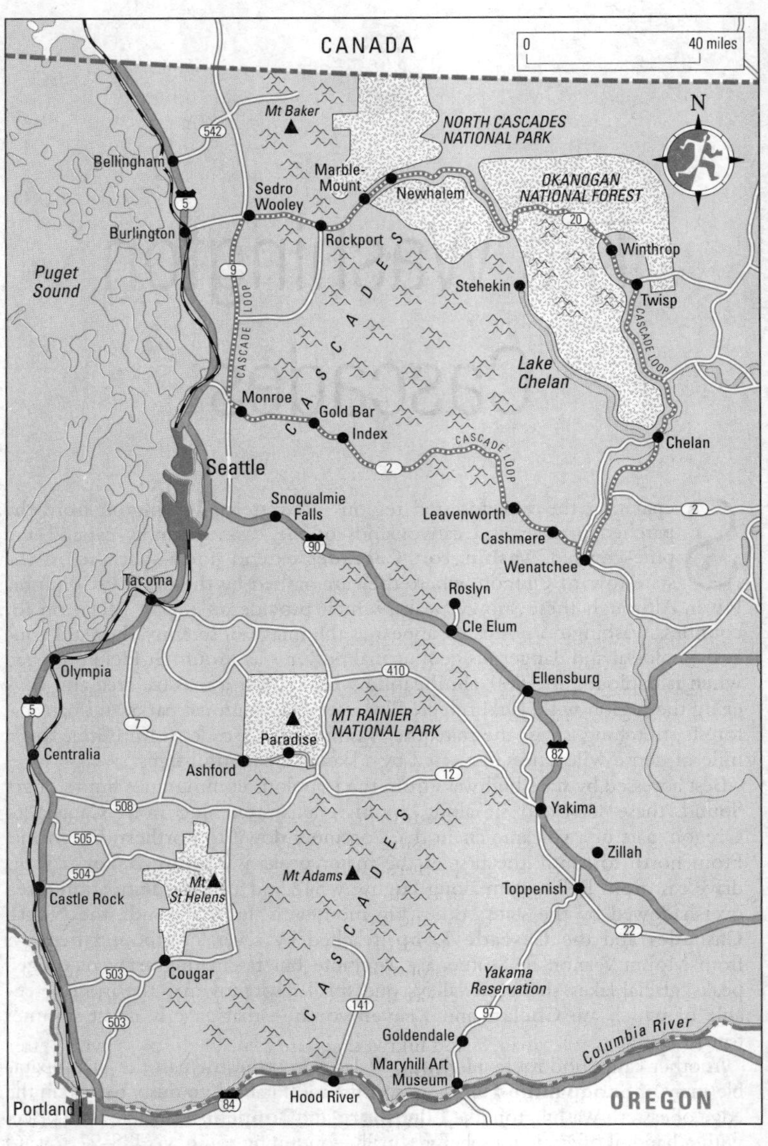

Despite claims of the tourist authorities, the **climate** here, as elsewhere in western Washington, is either wet or snowy for much of the year, with just a brief respite in July and August. Don't let this put you off, though: even seen through a haze of fine gray drizzle, the scenery is incredibly beautiful, and you should try to tackle at least a few hiking trails, which are well laid-out and come in manageably short varieties.

Getting around

Public transportation throughout the region is fairly rudimentary. There's a reasonable range of bus services further west, but almost nothing at all to the three leading attractions, the North Cascades and mounts Rainier and St Helens. **Greyhound buses** (Ⓣ1-800/231-2222, Ⓦwww.greyhound.com) run east from Seattle along I-90 to Ellensburg, Yakima, Toppenish, and down to Oregon, while from Seattle, Northwestern Trailways (Ⓣ1-800/366-3830, Ⓦuser.nwadv.com/northw) runs across the mountains on US-2 to Leavenworth, Cashmere, and Wenatchee. Amtrak **trains** (Ⓣ1-800/872-7245, Ⓦwww.amtrak.com) connect Portland to Seattle, and Vancouver to eastern Washington. **Local buses** are rare, but the LINK network (Ⓣ1-800/851-LINK, Ⓦwww.linktransit.com) connects some of the towns of the eastern foothills in the vicinity of Chelan, Leavenworth, and Wenatchee.

Mount Baker and around

With snow lasting from early November to mid-May, **MOUNT BAKER**, sixty-odd miles east of Bellingham (see p.341), has become one of Washington's premier resorts (daily lift tickets $36 on weekends, $28 midweek; Ⓣ360/734-6771, ski reports on Ⓣ360/671-0211, Ⓦwww.mtbaker.us). With a seven-month ski season, its lifts and runs are dotted over several lower slopes in the shadow of the great mountain itself. At 10,778 feet, Mount Baker is the highest peak for miles around, a volcanic behemoth that hisses great clouds of steam during periods of geothermal activity – the last significant time was in 1975. Not surprisingly, it has played a leading role in native folklore: the local Lummi saw it as a sort of Ararat, the one peak that survived the Great Flood to provide sanctuary for a Lummi "Noah" in his giant canoe. It was also here in 1947 that a USAF pilot saw the unidentified flying objects that he creatively christened "flying saucers."

The main approach road from Bellingham, Hwy-542, loops round the mountain's northern foothills, passing three USFS **campgrounds** ($10–16) beyond the village of **Glacier**, before a final, nail-biting fling up through the ski area to **Artist Point**, where you can get an appropriately painterly and evocative view of Mount Baker and the rest of the region. From here, a stiff 1.5-mile trail leads up lava cliffs to flat-topped Table Mountain, with Baker soaring high above. There are lots of other trails, but this is the basic starter with several possible extensions, such as the difficult trek south along Ptarmigan Ridge to Coleman Pinnacle.

In Bellingham, information and hiking maps are available in the town's better bookshops and at the **Glacier Public Service Center** (mid-June to mid-Oct daily 8.30am–4.30pm; rest of year Sat & Sun 8.30am–4.30pm; Ⓣ360/599-2714, Ⓦwww.fs.fed.us/r6/mbs), in tiny Glacier, about 25 miles from the mountain. **Ski equipment** can be rented at the resort ski shop and in Bellingham at – among several places – Fairhaven Bike and Mountain Sports, 1103 11th St (Ⓣ360/733-4433, Ⓦfairhavenbike.com).

Also in Bellingham, the **American Alpine Institute**, 1515 12th St (Ⓣ360/671-1505, Ⓦwww.mtnguide.com), offers a variety of hiking and climbing programs for Mount Baker and the North Cascades from May to October, covering everything from simple, two-day treks in the hills to gut-wrenching, two-week alpine ice climbs. Naturally, the cost varies widely depending on the number of days for your outing, level of training required, and the skills you need to learn; prices range from $185 to $990, though costlier programs are given (in the $2500 range) for training expedition leaders in the wilderness.

The Cascade Loop

When Hwy-20 opened up the rugged **North Cascades** in 1972, the towns of the eastern foothills got together and came up with the 350-mile **CASCADE LOOP** (information at ⓣ509/662-3888, ⓦwww.cascadeloop.com), which channels tourist traffic from the highway through **North Cascades National Park** and several small villages before sending it south along Hwy-97 and finally back west over US-2. There's no denying it's a magnificent trip, with long stretches of the road shadowed by the wet western forests and, at higher elevations, jagged, glacier-studded mountains, but unless you've three or four days to spare – maybe more – it all becomes something of a motorized gallop. With less time, you're better off focusing on the pick of the scenery, which straddles Hwy-20, and **camping** in the mountains, or at least staying as near to the mountains as you can: **Marblemount**, on the west side of the range, is the handiest spot, though it only has a handful of inns and motels.

The towns of the eastern foothills offer much more choice of accommodation, the most amenable being **Chelan**, an easygoing, lakeshore resort that's the starting point for boat (or seaplane) trips up Lake Chelan to the remote village of **Stehekin**, at the heart of good hiking country. Two other towns have made heroic efforts to rise from the ruins of their industrial past, with **Winthrop** dressing itself up in Wild West regalia, and **Leavenworth** in ersatz Bavarian.

The Cascade Loop is only feasible during the summer, as snow closes the mountain passes and completely covers the hiking trails for several months of the year – usually from mid-November to mid-April. For the latest details, contact the Winter Mountain Pass Report agency (ⓣ1-888/766-4636). There's no **bus** service over Hwy-20, but Northwestern Trailways (ⓣ1-800/366-3830, ⓦwww.user.nwadv.com/northw) runs across the mountains on US-2 from Seattle to Leavenworth (for Spokane) and LINK (ⓣ1-800/851-LINK, ⓦwww.linktransit.com) provides a frequent minibus service between the towns of the eastern foothills, including Chelan, Wenatchee, and Leavenworth.

East on Highway 20

The north side of the Cascade Loop is traversed by eastbound **HIGHWAY 20**, which leaves I-5 (Exit 230) about sixty miles north of Seattle at Burlington, traveling from the flat, tulip-growing farmlands of the Skagit Valley on to the road's southward curve around **Winthrop**. From there it continues on a circuitous course to eastern Washington, while at tiny **Twisp**, Highway 153 merges with Highway 97 and continues the loop on its eastern side.

North Cascades National Park

The North Cascades are crossed by several hundred miles of **hiking trails**, offering everything from short and easy strolls to arduous treks up steep slopes, around glaciers and over high mountain passes, and there are plenty of first-come-first-serve **campgrounds** to choose from, too. **Information** on the trails and campgrounds is available from a baffling assortment of government agencies,

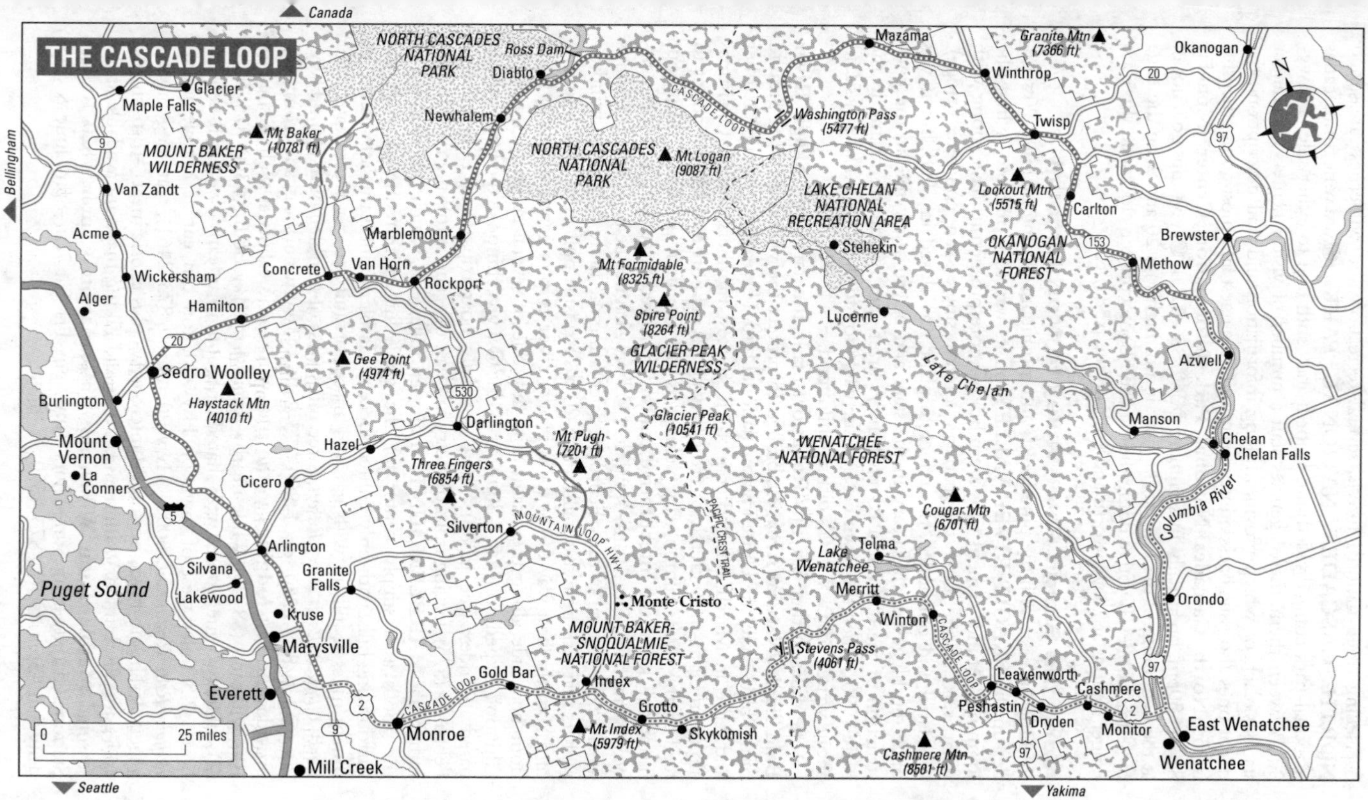

THE CASCADE LOOP

overseeing three national forests, several recreation and wilderness areas, and **NORTH CASCADES NATIONAL PARK** (Ⓦwww.north.cascades.national-park.com), divided into a north and south unit to either side of Hwy-20. Between them, these agencies staff a number of visitor centers and ranger stations, each of which provides hiking information and trail descriptions; the major ones also issue backcountry permits. The biggest and most comprehensive is the **North Cascades National Park Information Center** (Mon–Fri 8am–4.30pm, open daily in summer; Ⓣ360/856-5700, Ⓦwww.nps.gov/noca), at the beginning of the loop at the junction of highways 20 and 9, on the edge of Sedro Woolley. If you're doing the Cascade Loop counter-clockwise, there are ranger stations at Leavenworth and Chelan (see p.383).

Along the Skagit River Valley to Marblemount

Pushing on east, with the pine forests and mountains closing in, Hwy-20 scuttles up the **SKAGIT RIVER VALLEY** on its way to **Concrete**, where the looming, defunct cement silos are relics of more prosperous days (along with what was at one time the nation's longest single-span concrete bridge). Outdated and outmoded, the concrete plant was closed in 1968, but it was once the biggest such factory in the state and played a key role in the construction of the Columbia River dams. A brief glint of attention came in the early 1990s, when the town became the backdrop to the movie *This Boy's Life*, about writer Tobias Wolffe's dismal childhood.

Nine miles further east, tiny **Rockport** marks the start of the **Skagit River Bald Eagle Natural Area**, established to protect the winter hunting ground of the bald eagle, the United States' national bird. The eagles arrive in October and leave in March, but gather in their greatest numbers around Christmas along an eight-mile stretch of river between Rockport and Marblemount to feed on the river's salmon, easy pickings as they die after spawning. To find out more, check out the **interpretive center**, on Alfred Street south of the highway (winter Fri–Sun 10am–4pm; free; Ⓦwww.skagiteagle.org), which mounts a bald eagle festival in early February, celebrating the more than three hundred raptors that visit here seasonally. Hwy-20 has roadside pull-ins to watch for the birds, but the best way to see them is on a **river trip**, a gentle three- to four-hour boat ride along the Skagit with any one of several companies, notably Chinook Expeditions (Ⓣ1-800/241-3451, Ⓦwww.chinookexpeditions.com), based in Index (see p.388). There are daily boat trips from December to February ($75), leaving from the jetty just east of – and across the river from – minuscule **MARBLEMOUNT**, about ten miles east, which was founded in the 1860s as a supply center for the gold diggers ferreting through the surrounding hills, with only limited success. Marblemount is the last chance for ninety miles to fill up with gas, and an opportunity to get a roof over your head. *Clark's Skagit River Resort*, three miles west of Marblemount along Hwy-20 (Ⓣ360/873-2250 or 1-800/273-2606, Ⓦwww.northcascades.com; ❹), provides the best **lodgings** in the area, with rustic cabins as well as sites for RVs and tents ($8–20), while nearby *Salmonberry Way B&B* (Ⓣ360/873-4016; ❸), offers two guestrooms with shared bathroom in an early-twentieth-century house 2.5 miles west of town on Hwy-20. You can **eat** at Marblemount's *Buffalo Run Restaurant*, 60084 Hwy-20 (Ⓣ360/873-2461), featuring organic vegetables, home-made bread, and microbrews plus exotic meats – ostrich, elk, and, naturally, buffalo. Wilderness permits and hiking maps are available at the seasonal **Marblemount Wilderness Information Center**, 7820 Ranger Station Rd (July–Aug Sun–Thurs 7am–6pm, Fri–Sat 7am–8pm; June & Sept daily 8am–5pm; Ⓣ360/873-4500).

Ross Lake National Recreation Area

Just beyond Marblemount, Hwy-20 enters **ROSS LAKE NATIONAL RECREATION AREA**, a narrow, elongated slice of river valley that divides North Cascades National Park into two sections. The first town you reach is **Newhalem**, owned by Seattle City Light, whose electrical generators lie a little to the east in a chain of three dams spanning the Skagit River. Unfortunately, with the company's recent financial misadventures, jobs are being slashed across the board and some fear the place becoming a ghost town before long. Nevertheless, the town is the site of a useful **North Cascades National Park Information Center**, milepost 120 on Hwy-20 (May–Oct daily 8.30am–5pm, plus some winter weekends; ⓣ206/386-4495). From Newhalem, it's about three miles to the first dam, the **Gorge**, and a few more to the second, **Diablo**, built at a dangerous bend in the river called "Devil's Corner," its name translated into Spanish so as not to offend local sensibilities. Here the highway offers views across the dam and its little blue-green lake; the dam's parking lot is where you catch the water taxi to *Ross Lake Resort* (see below).

A couple of miles east of Diablo Dam on Hwy-20 lies the first-come-first-served **Colonial Creek campground** (mid-May to mid-Oct; $12; ⓣ360/856-5700, ext. 515). Boasting an attractive location along the lakeshore, the campground serves as the starting point for several particularly fine hikes; a few minutes away are the fabulous mountain views of the overlook for **Diablo Lake**, which is tourable by boat through Seattle City Light (June–Sept; 2hr 30min trip; $17; reserve at ⓣ206/684-3030, ext. 1). More imposing, **Ross Dam** is the largest dam of the three and the one that created **Ross Lake** (ⓦwww.nps.gov/rola), which stretches north for twenty-five pine-rimmed miles into Canada, flanked by hiking trails and campgrounds - but no roads. Reached by boat ($10 round-trip) from Diablo Dam and then by truck ($6 round-trip), or along a two-mile hiking trail from Ross Dam, the *Ross Lake Resort* (mid-June to Oct; ⓣ206/386-4437, ⓦwww.rosslakeresort.com) provides some of the region's most distinctive lodgings. Built for City Light workers, the resort literally floats on its log supports and has various **cabins** with simple 1950s designs (❺), modern, en-suite types (❻), bunkhouse versions holding up to ten guests (❼), and a chic, two-story model with full amenities, for up to ten people (❽). The resort has no telephones in the cabins and you have to bring your own food, but it does operate a water-taxi service to the remote trailheads further up Ross Lake.

Okanogan National Forest

Hwy-20 bypasses Ross Lake, veering southeast after Ross Dam to leave the national park for the remote wilds of the 1.7-million-acre **OKANOGAN NATIONAL FOREST**, running up Ruby and Granite creeks to **Rainy Pass**, where it crosses the Pacific Crest Trail (see p.55). To the north the long-distance trail heads off into the depths of the Okanogan, while to the south it slips along Bridge Creek and curves round the flanks of McGregor Mountain to meet the rough dirt road that leads onto Stehekin at the tip of Lake Chelan (see p.382). Beyond Rainy Pass, Hwy-20 has an abundance of stopping-points, each providing remarkable views over the Cascades. One of the most magnificent is at **Washington Pass Overlook**, about thirty miles east of Ross Dam, where a short paved trail from the roadside parking lot leads to a spectacular mountain panorama featuring the craggy, rocky peak of **Liberty Bell Mountain**. After, there's a final flurry of mountain scenery before the road reaches the tamer landscapes of the **Methow Valley** and descends to Winthrop.

Winthrop

Beyond the mountains Hwy-20 turns south, leading into **WINTHROP**, where wooden false fronts, boardwalks, swinging saloon doors, and other western trappings bedeck the main drag of **Riverside Avenue**. Winthrop was actually founded by an East Coast entrepreneur, Guy Waring, who turned up in 1891 with a wagonload of merchandise and diplomatically named the settlement he founded after John Winthrop, the Puritan governor of his native Massachusetts – the state that provided his backing. Waring was visited by an old Harvard classmate, Owen Wister, whose *The Virginian*, widely acclaimed as the first Western novel, was clearly (in the town's opinion) based on Winthrop. Waring's log-cabin home, set on a hill behind the main street at 285 Castle Ave, is now part of the **Shafer Museum** (summer Thurs–Mon 10am–5pm; donation suggested), whose assortment of old buildings – such as a print shop, milliners, and assay office – is crammed with pioneer antiques. It is, however, Waring's cabin, with its heavy-duty logs, that most catches the eye – just as it was meant to: he labored away for months building this structure to entice his wife out west, away from the more familiar creature comforts of New England.

Winthrop's handy **visitor center**, 202 Riverside Ave (late April–Sept daily 10am–5pm; ⓣ509/996-2125, ⓦwww.winthropwashington.com), is well stocked with brochures on outdoor activities from horse riding and whitewater rafting to fishing – both in the valley and the neighboring mountains; there's a seasonal USFS **ranger station** (ⓣ509/996-4000, ⓦwww.fs.fed.us/r6/oka) downtown on Hwy-20, too.

Winthrop has a reasonable range of **accommodation**, including a clutch of serviceable motels. Try the *Hotel Rio Vista*, 285 Riverside Ave (ⓣ509/996-3535 or 1-800/398-0911, ⓦwww.hotelriovista.com; ❸–❼), whose facade resembles something out of an old Hollywood Western, but offers nice suites with hot tubs, kitchenettes, and DVD players; or the more basic lodging at the *Best Western Cascade Inn*, 960 Hwy-20 (ⓣ509/996-3100 or 1-800/468-6754, ⓦwww.winthropwa.com; ❹). The luxurious *Sun Mountain Lodge* (ⓣ509/996-2211 or 1-800/572-0493, ⓦwww.sunmountainlodge.com; ❺–❾) has rustic cabins and lodge rooms in a grand setting on the edge of the Cascades, nine miles southwest of town along Twin Lakes and then Patterson Lake Road. As for **eating** options, the *Duck Brand Cantina*, 248 Riverside Ave (ⓣ509/996-2192, ⓦwww.methownet.com/duck), serves up cheap and tasty Mexican fare, and has six simple, Western-themed rooms in its onsite B&B (❸), and *Winthrop Brewing Co*, 155 Riverside Ave (ⓣ509/996-3183), offers solid microbrews like the excellent Outlaw Pale Ale.

Continuing south along the Methow Valley, it's eleven miles to drab little **Twisp**, where Hwy-20 begins its long and circuitous journey through the remote national forests that fill out the northeastern corner of Washington, while Highway 153, merging with 97, forms the eastern edge of the Cascade Loop, then moves on for the lengthy trip down to the Columbia River Gorge (see p.119).

Lake Chelan and around

Highway 97 follows the Columbia River as it curves south to the short turnoff (US-97Alt) that leads over the hills to glacially carved **LAKE CHELAN**. Framed by wooded hills and mountains, the long, thin lake's southern reaches are laced with fine **hiking trails**, many of which are fairly easy to reach from the town of **Chelan** along a patchwork of rutted forest roads. Alternatively, several of Chelan's sports shops rent out transport like mountain bikes and kayaks – but be aware of the sudden squalls on the lake. If you have time, a ferry trip to the lake's remote northern outpost of **Stehekin** can be a fun excursion, though not quite a necessity if you're taking the full, lengthy circuit of the Cascade Loop.

Chelan

Tucked in between the lake's southeastern shore and the Chelan River is the pocket-sized resort of **CHELAN**, not much more than a simple grid of modest buildings. Local apple growers drop by to pick up supplies, but mainly Chelan is quite happy just to house and feed those hundreds of visitors who come here intent on exploring the lake and its mountainous surroundings.

Your first stop should be the **visitor center**, near the waterfront at 102 E Johnson Ave (Mon–Fri 9am–5pm, Sat 10am–4pm; summer open longer hours & Sun; ⓣ509/682-3503 or 1-800/4-CHELAN, ⓦwww.lakechelan.com), which has free information about the region and can provide maps and general hiking advice. For more detailed trail guidance, the **ranger station** is a five-minute walk over the bridge and along the waterfront from the visitor center, at 428 W Woodin Ave (daily 7.30am–4.30pm; ⓣ509/682-2576). Monday through Saturday, local LINK (ⓣ1-800/851-LINK, ⓦwww.linktransit.com) **buses** connect Chelan with several nearby towns, including Leavenworth.

Chelan has lots of **places to stay**, but in the height of the summer rooms can still be hard to find, so book ahead. The town's premier hotel, *Campbell's Resort*, 104 W Woodin Ave (ⓣ509/682-2561 or 1-800/553-8225, ⓦwww.campbellsresort.com; ❹–❽), is the most appealing for its range of lakeside rooms and suites – some of which come with fireplaces, kitchenettes, and balconies – though rates vary widely by season. Other reliable options include

Lake Chelan ferries

The Lake Chelan Boat Company, 1418 W Woodin Ave (ⓣ509/682-2224 info, ⓣ509/682-4584 reservations, ⓦwww.ladyofthelake.com), provides one of the area's highlights in the form of its **Lady of the Lake** passenger ferry. Sailing the 55 miles from Chelan up the lake to Stehekin, the ferry usually stops at Lucerne, where it drops supplies for **Holden**, a Lutheran retreat that occupies the site of an old copper mine in a remote valley to the west, where the spiritually inclined can find inspiration in the rugged mountain environment (information at ⓦwww.holdenvillage.org). The scenery becomes even more impressive the further you go, with the forested hills of the south giving way to the austere, glaciated peaks that circle in on the furthest part of the lake, lying at the very heart of the North Cascades.

Leaving from the jetty a mile west of town along Woodin Avenue, the ferry makes the four-hour trip once daily (May–Oct leaves 8.30am, returns by 6pm; $16.50 one-way, $26 round-trip) with a ninety-minute stopover at Stehekin. The faster **Lady Express** (May–Oct $28.50 one-way, $45 round-trip; Nov–April $26 round-trip) departs at 8.30am or 10am and takes just over two hours to complete the same trip. Quicker still is the **Lady Cat**, a high-speed catamaran that can get from Chelan to Stehekin in an hour and fifteen minutes (June–Sept only; $57 one-way, $90 round-trip). You can go up on one boat and return on another, and if you juggle with the schedule you can give yourself several hours in Stehekin. If taking a bicycle, it'll cost you an additional $8 each way.

Finally, if you're flush, you can take a **seaplane** to Stehekin on Chelan Airways ($80 one-way, $120 round-trip; ⓣ509/682-5555, ⓦwww.chelanairways.com), which is also available for airborne **tours** of the region ($80–169).

the lakeshore *Caravel Resort*, just across the bridge at 322 W Woodin Ave (ⓣ509/682-2582 or 1-800/962-8723, ⓦwww.caravelresort.com; ❸), which offers rooms with fireplaces, and a heated pool and hot tub; and the rather precious *Mary Kay's Romantic Whaley Mansion*, 415 3rd St (ⓣ509/682-5735 or 1-800/729-2408; ❺), a Victorian B&B whose six en-suite guestrooms occupy an attractive older house a five-minutes' walk from the town center. A less expensive choice is the straightforward *Apple Inn Motel*, 1002 E Woodin Ave (ⓣ509/682-4044; ❸). The best **restaurant** in town is at *Campbell's Resort*, known for its steak, pasta, and salmon, as well as its extensive array of single-malt scotches. For something more informal, and less expensive, head off to *Peter B's Bar & Grill*, 116 E Woodin Ave (ⓣ509/682-1031), and *Deepwater Brewing & Public House*, 225 Hwy-20 (ⓣ509/682-2720), which has burgers, salads, and steaks, as well as its own microbrews.

Stehekin

Accessible only by trail, seaplane, or boat, **STEHEKIN**, at Lake Chelan's mountainous northern tip, makes an excellent base for hiking in the North Cascades. In every direction, trails strike into the mountains, nudging up along bubbling creeks through the thinning alpine forest, with easier trails along the lakeshore. In the village, a few yards from the jetty, the *North Cascades Stehekin Lodge* (see below) rents bikes and boats and also runs daily bus trips up to **Rainbow Falls**, a mist-shrouded, 312-ft waterfall flanked by red cedars just four miles north of the village; times of departure are fixed to coincide with the arrival of the ferry. Alternatively, Stehekin's **Golden West Visitor Center** (April–Oct daily 8am–5pm; ⓣ360/856-5700, ⓦwww.nps.gov/noca), also a short walk from the jetty, operates a seasonal **shuttle bus** that travels up along the Stehekin River Valley on a 23-mile dirt road – an exhilarating trip through landscapes that accesses trailheads and campgrounds and follows a small portion of the Pacific Crest Trail; advance booking is advised.

The pleasant *North Cascades Stehekin Lodge* (ⓣ509/682-4494, ⓦwww.stehekin.com; ❹–❻), where the lakeside rooms are a bit pricier than standard units, is the only **place to stay** in the village and reservations here are usually necessary, as they are for the handful of cabin-lodges further up the Stehekin Valley. Campground details, hiking advice, and wilderness permits are available at the Golden West Visitor Center, or better yet, get advice before you leave Chelan.

Wenatchee

South of Chelan, the Columbia River weaves its way through prime apple-growing country, tracked by US-97 on its east and US-97Alt on its west bank. Both roads lead the forty-odd miles to **WENATCHEE**, which straddles the Columbia River and has long been Washington's **apple capital**, the center of an industry that fills the valleys of the eastern foothills with orchards, and grows nearly half the country's supply. Despite increased competition from China, fruit is still big business here, and apple stalls dot the roadsides in the fall, piled mostly with sweet, outsized Red Delicious, the most popular kind in the US, as well as the enormous Golden Delicious, red Winesap, and tart green Granny Smith.

The town has a rather drab, workaday air, and it's unlikely you'll want to hang around long. However, apple fanatics can learn about the history of the industry at the **Wenatchee Valley Museum**, 127 S Mission St (Tues–Sat 10am–4pm; $3; ⓦwww.wenatcheevalleymuseum.com), and there's more information at the **Washington Apple Commission Visitor Center**, on the northern edge of town at 2900 Euclid Ave (May–Dec Mon–Fri 8am–5pm; free; Ⓦwww.bestapples.com), where you can munch away on various varieties and guzzle apple juice as well. Fittingly, Wenatchee's big annual celebration, the ten-day all-American **Apple Blossom Festival** (Ⓦwww.appleblossom.org), features carnival floats and marching bands in late April.

Wenatchee's Columbia Station, downtown at Wenatchee Avenue and Kittitas Street, is something of a public **transit** hub for the immediate area. Northwestern Trailways **buses** (Ⓣ1-800/366-3830, Ⓦwww.user.nwadv.com/northw) pull in here, bound for Seattle or Spokane, and so do Amtrak **trains** (Ⓣ1-800/872-7245, Ⓦwww.amtrak.com) connecting Wenatchee with Portland, Seattle, Leavenworth, and Spokane. In addition, local – and free – LINK buses (Ⓣ1-800/851-LINK, Ⓦwww.linktransit.com) depart Wenatchee (Mon–Sat) for several nearby towns – most usefully Chelan and Leavenworth.

West on Highway 2

Heading **west on Highway 2** from Wenatchee, the last, southerly section of the Cascade Loop (if proceeding clockwise around it) provides a good access route into the Washington Cascades from Seattle, and is peppered with worthwhile campgrounds, hikes, and mountain lakes. Undoubtedly, the highlights along this stretch include the Bavarian theme town of **Leavenworth** and the lovely preserve of the **Alpine Lakes Wilderness**.

At the practical end of the Cascade Loop, you reach **Monroe**, a neon-lit sprawl heralding Seattle, just thirty miles away. Alternatively, you can continue north onto Highway 9 to access yet another interesting circuit, The **Mountain Loop Highway** (see box p.386) – basically a smaller route contained within the bounds of the Cascade Loop, and compelling for its intriguing blend of rustic scenery and historic ruins.

Cashmere

Just north of Wenatchee, Highway 2, in combination with US-97, heads west into the mountains towards the themed village of **CASHMERE**. Showcasing a tasteful late-nineteenth-century main street and a small, outdoor **Pioneer Village**, the town comprises about twenty restored and relocated buildings such as a school, hotel, saddle shop, and general store. These architectural antiques form part of the **Chelan County Museum** (March–Dec daily 9.30am–5pm; $4), whose main building holds a large and wide-ranging collection focused on the Northwest. Among the Native American artifacts displayed on the upper floor are archeological treasures such as petroglyphs and early tools, as well as baskets and headdresses, weapons, and Hudson's Bay Company trading trinkets. Cashmere is also famous, at least locally, for its sugary "aplets" and "cotlets" (as in apricot) – available at **Liberty Orchards**, 117 Mission St (April–Dec Mon–Fri 8am–5.30pm, Sat & Sun 10am–4pm; Jan–March Mon–Fri 8.30am–4.30pm; free). Made of boiled-down fruit juices and walnuts coated with corn starch and powdered sugar, these popular confections were launched by two immigrant Armenian farmers at the beginning of the twentieth century to dispose of the fruit they could not sell. Naturally, it made them a fortune.

Leavenworth

Brace yourself as you head further west towards **LEAVENWORTH**, a former timber and railroad town that warded off economic death thirty years ago by going Bavarian. Local motels and stores now sport steeply roofed half-timbered, ski chalet-style facades, complete with wooden balconies and quaint window-boxes. Wiener schnitzel, sauerkraut, and strudel feature on local menus and gift shops sell musical boxes that play "alpine" folk music. This can be fun if you're in the right mood, and even if you're not, you can always escape into the surrounding gorgeous mountain scenery.

No longer combined with US-97 (which darts south toward the Columbia River Gorge), Hwy-2 heads westbound into Leavenworth and forms the northern perimeter of the town center, which slopes south to fill out a small loop in the Wenatchee River. Leavenworth's main drag, **Front Street**, runs parallel to – and one block south of – Hwy-2, and Northwestern Trailways **buses** (ⓣ1-800/366-3830, ⓦwww.user.nwadv.com/northw) from Seattle and Spokane stop a five-minute walk from downtown. The municipal **visitor center**, 894 Hwy-2 (ⓣ509/548-5807, ⓦwww.leavenworth.org), has copious listings of places to stay and eat, though you're still advised to book ahead in summer. They also have details of the many local companies that organize **outdoor activities** – everything from horse-drawn wagon rides, treks on snowmobiles and snowshoes, and dog sledding to skiing, whitewater rafting, fishing,

The Mountain Loop Highway

Although hardly one of the best-known routes into the Cascades, the **Mountain Loop Highway** represents one of the better day-trips from the north Seattle area, a hundred-mile "**National Scenic Byway**" taking you through some striking landscapes and past the preserved ruins of the region's early-twentieth-century heyday. To access the route, take Hwy-2 east from I-5 in the suburb of Everett, then pick up highways 204 and 9 (both northbound) until you reach Hwy-92. Continue on 92 for some ten miles until the road ends in the little burg of **Granite Falls** – the start of the Mountain Loop Highway. The town itself is a quaint holdover from the late nineteenth century, with a few old-fashioned storefronts recalling glory days when it served as the western terminus of a mining railroad that transported gold from the area around the **Stillaguamish River** canyon.

The railroad eventually closed in 1936 due to various persistent obstacles, one of which was the river's frequent **flooding**, whose impact is vividly on display six miles from Granite Falls along the three-mile **Old Robe Trail** (watch for turnout signs on the highway). The hike itself is one of the most striking in the Cascades, a winding concourse along the long-disused rock cuts of the railbed, down narrow switchbacks and passes, and through two large tunnels carved out of the hillsides. Most conspicuous, though, is the presence of the Stillaguamish alongside, in winter a heaving churn of dark gray current notorious for spilling over its banks, tearing out trees, and causing massive rockslides – the second of which leads to the trail's abrupt end.

At mile 12 on the highway, a right-side turnout leads you seven miles up the slope of **Mount Pilchuck**, once the site of a popular winter resort. Although there's no more skiing (unless you want to carry your gear up and risk a hell-for-leather trip down), the mountain offers a fine but difficult three-mile hike up to an accessible fire lookout at the top, a 2200-foot rise that affords great views of the surrounding terrain in the North Cascades.

The ski area and the nearby mining operation (with its ruined dam at mile 14 and filled-in tunnels at miles 19 and 21) were not the only conspicuous failures on this section of the Mountain Loop Highway. Indeed, three miles beyond tiny Silverton (itself at mile 22), you reach the former site of the **Big Four** resort, which operated in grand fashion here with a golf course, cabins, and tennis courts from 1921 to 1949, when a mysterious fire closed it for good. Nowadays, all that remains are and hunting. The town also has a **ranger station**, off the highway at 600 Sherbourne St (daily 7.45am–4.30pm; ⓣ509/782-1413), where you can pick up hiking maps and trail descriptions. Leavenworth Mountain Sports, 940 Hwy-2 at Icicle Rd (ⓣ509/548-7864), rents out skis, canoes, mountain bikes, and climbing gear.

Practicalities

Downtown **accommodation** includes the excellent *Hotel Pension Anna*, 926 Commercial St (ⓣ509/548-6273 or 1-800/509-2662, ⓦwww.pensionanna.com; ④–⑥), a psuedo-Austrian lodge that also has some suites in the onion-domed chapel across the street, and *Mrs Anderson's Lodging House*, 917 Commercial St (ⓣ509/548-6173 or 1-800/253-8990, ⓦwww.quiltersheaven.com; ③), offering ten comfortable rooms with antique furnishings in the style of Grandma Moses – there's even an onsite quilt shop. Another mock-Teutonic spot, the *Enzian Motor Inn*, just west of the center at 590 Hwy-2 (ⓣ509/548-5269 or 1-800/223-8511, ⓦwww.enzianinn.com; ⑤), is a grand motel-lodge with commodious rooms done out in full Alpine style – and offers regular alphorn concerts.

sidewalks leading nowhere and the vestiges of a grand fireplace. You can, however, take an easy, one-mile hike to the area's popular **ice caves**, created when the winter's runoff collects in caves and forms frozen columns and the like. Keep in mind, though, that the site is only officially open in the late summer and autumn – when there's no snow – so you'll be taking a risk (and disobeying the rather ominous signs) if you venture inside during the colder months, when rock and ice-falls have injured more than a few unwary visitors.

The highway at, or even well before, Big Four is usually closed in the winter, and may only be accessible from April to October. If it's open, you can head another five miles (to mile 30) to reach **Barlow Pass**. From here, a closed section of roadway – which you'll need to travel on foot or a bike – leads some four miles away to the centerpiece of the area, the ghost town of **Monte Cristo**, which was formerly the eastern terminus of the mining railway and subsquently a small-time resort from the 1920s to the 60s. These days, little remains from either heyday, aside from a few rusty old tools, cabins, and pieces of antiquated machinery. However, the site is a great place to hike or mountain bike, and the scenery is filled with unkempt paths and road cuts, boarded-up mine entrances, and overgrown foliage.

The Mountain Loop Highway continues past Monte Cristo for another seventy miles as it travels down the pleasant route of the Sauk River and reaches the hamlet of **Index** (see overleaf), before connecting on the Cascade Loop to highways 2 and 9 back to Lake Stevens. All in all, it's a nice enough journey, even though most of the highlights are densely packed into the first thirty miles of the mountain loop, and you won't miss too much simply by turning around at Barlow Pass and returning through Granite Falls.

As for **lodging**, the main place to stop is the basic motel of the *Mountain View Inn*, 32005 Mountain Loop Highway, around mile 10 (ⓣ206/691-6668; ④), which also provides the best of a very limited selection of **restaurants** in the area – in this case, serving up steaks, seafood, and burgers, highlighted by a nice rainbow trout. If you'd prefer to rough it and **camp**, there are plenty of options on this scenic byway, (most $8–16): Mount Pilchuck and Monte Cristo offer some of the most scenic choices. Finally, if you're intending to **hike**, a $5 Northwest Forest Pass is required at a number of sites along the road. Order online or pick one up at a local ranger station; check ⓦwww.fs.fed.us/r6/mbs/passes for details.

Leavenworth has more than its share of undistinguished **restaurants** geared up for the passing tourist trade, but you can still find some tasty surprises. *Los Camperos*, upstairs on The Alley at 200 8th St (ⓣ509/548-3314), dishes up surprisingly decent Mexican fare; *Andreas Keller*, 829 Front St (ⓣ509/548-6000), doles out hefty helpings of gut-busting German cuisine; and *King Ludwig's*, 921 Front St (ⓣ509/548-6625), also features lively Bavarian dancing, hearty pork schnitzel, and beer-bearing barmaids – bring your Tyrolean hat.

Alpine Lakes Wilderness

The real point of visiting Leavenworth is to **hike** the surrounding mountains, a small portion of the colossal Wenatchee National Forest, which extends north as far as Lake Chelan and south to I-90. Among these striking wilderness areas, the **ALPINE LAKES WILDERNESS**, west of Leavenworth, boasts some of the region's finest scenery, with plunging valleys and scores of crystal-clear mountain lakes set beneath a string of spiraling peaks.

From Leavenworth, the most straightforward approach into the Alpine Lakes is along **Icicle Road**, which weaves south then west through thick forest and past cascading waterfalls to a series of trailheads and busy **campgrounds** ($5–10; Northwest Forest Pass required; see p.387). The nine-mile-long **Enchantment Lake Trail** is a particularly popular route, with hikers heading south up Mountaineer Creek for the beautiful lakes that pepper the mountains above; the trailhead is about eight miles out of town. For something less strenuous, stick to the forested footpath running beside Icicle Road. For more **information** on the area, contact the ranger station in Leavenworth or inquire at ⓣ509/674-4411, ⓦwww.fs.fed.us/r6/wenatchee/cle-elum-wilderness.

West from Leavenworth

Heading **west from Leavenworth** toward Puget Sound, Hwy-2 scrambles over the Cascade Mountains at **Stevens Pass**, named after the Great Northern Railroad's surveyor John Stevens, who chose to route trains this way in 1892. Beyond, the highway loops down to the Skykomish River Valley, where tiny **Index**, an old mining and quarrying settlement a mile or so from the highway, is worth a pit-stop for its antique **general store**, selling everything from sandwiches to fertilizer. The sheer, four-hundred-foot granite cliff towering over Index, the so-called **Town Wall**, is a favorite with Seattle rock climbers. More importantly, Index is a key access point for reaching the best sites along the **Mountain Loop Highway** to the north (see box).

Eight miles further west lies **Gold Bar,** one of the last sights of any interest before the Cascade Loop reaches its end at Monroe. Once a hard-edged mining town and railroad settlement where, as anti-Chinese sentiment reached a boiling point in the 1890s, a railway engineer shipped terrified Chinese locals out in purpose-built "coffins," Gold Bar is best known today for its proximity to **Wallace Falls State Park** (closed winter Mon & Tues; ⓦwww.parks.wa.gov). Two miles northeast of town, the pleasant park boasts **campgrounds** ($15–21) and two trails – one three, the other four miles long – leading to a 265-ft waterfall.

East from Seattle

The drive **east from Seattle** – through the mountains on I-90 and then along their eastern flank on I-82/US-97 – is one of the prime escape routes for urbanites, and, in the other direction, for tourists headed to the Emerald City. Not surprisingly, it is also among the least engaging ways to see the Washington Cascades, with a smattering of major attractions here and there, and a steady stream of SUVs and RVs to crowd your path. Although **Snoqualmie Falls** is one of the most prominent sites, the others further east are altogether more incongruous – the Wild West trappings of **Ellensburg**, the vineyards around **Yakima**, and the murals of **Toppenish**. With such a grab bag of attractions, it's perhaps not surprising that this section of central Washington is as much a gateway to the desert and scrubland of the east as it is an access point for the snowy peaks and verdant lakes of the Cascades.

East on I-90

The major arterial of **Interstate 90** will quickly become familiar to you if you're approaching Puget Sound from the east, and while many dismiss it as just a traffic corridor, there are a handful of sights worth checking out if you're using the road. The first big one, **Snoqualmie Falls**, is one of the state's best, but beyond this the highway meanders past a few serpentine lakes and rugged mountain passes, but doesn't hit any other considerable towns until the dusty, but likeable, cowtown of **Ellensburg**.

Snoqualmie Falls and Pass

As the lowest and most traversible of the Cascade crossings, **SNOQUALMIE PASS** was long the regular route of traders, trappers, and Native Americans. Upon reaching the area, some twenty-five miles outside Seattle, turn off at Exit 31 for the five-mile detour north through North Bend along Hwy-202 to **SNOQUALMIE FALLS** (Ⓣ425/831-5784, Ⓦwww.snoqualmiefalls.com), the dreamlike vision pictured in the opening sequence of David Lynch's cult TV show *Twin Peaks*, which exceeds Niagara Falls in height by a hundred feet. The flow, actually controlled by the local power company, cascades 270ft from the heights of a solid-bedrock gorge, and spews out a dense, almost choking mist in places. Unfortunately, instead of a slow, eerie soundtrack by Angelo Badalamenti, you'll most likely hear the incessant chatter of hundreds of tourists. The **observation platform** is just across from the parking lot, but for an equally dramatic and less crowded viewpoint, take the half-mile **River Trail**, which leads from the platform to the bottom of the falls. Between the platform and the waterfall is the **Salish Lodge** (Ⓣ425/888-2556 or 1-800/826-6124, Ⓦwww.salishlodge.com; ⑨), the grand wooden structure that featured in many *Twin Peaks* episodes, but is better to visit casually than to stay in unless you've got a spare $350 to part with.

Those who've never seen the show may be more interested in hiking some of the nearby trails; the steep four-mile climb up **Mount Si**, which starts on Mount Si Road in North Bend, is the most popular, with summit views of the surrounding mountains and Mount Rainier. Towering trees shade the trail most of the way to the stony area near the 4000-ft peak, but the hair-raising walk to the top of the nearby "Haystack" outcropping is not advised for casual day-trippers.

Mount Baker-Snoqualmie National Forest

From Snoqualmie Falls, I-90 dips, rises, and curves around the topography of the southern side of **MOUNT BAKER-SNOQUALMIE NATIONAL FOREST**, which has agreeable hiking trails along the way. Among them is the trans-continental Pacific Crest Trail (see p.55), which crosses the summits of

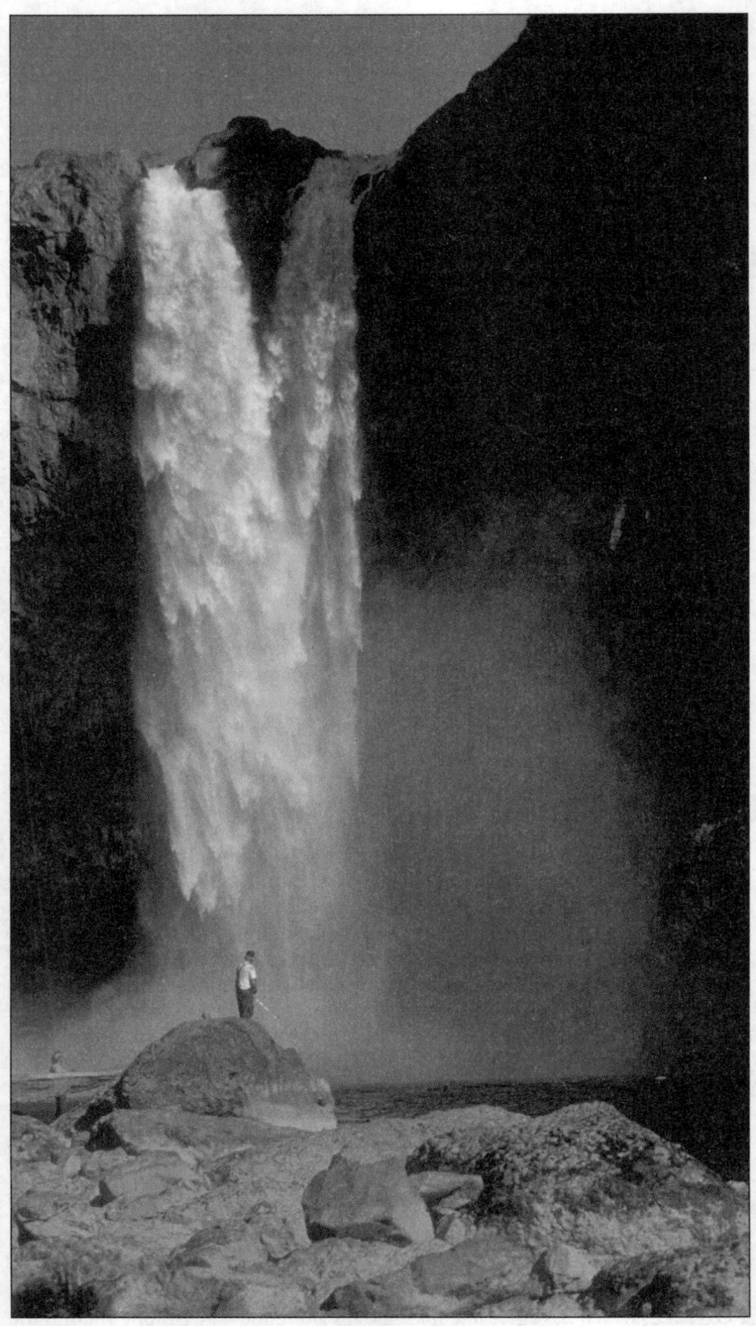

△ Snoqualmie Falls

Red Mountain and Silver around a severe clockwise hairpin in the highway. A few miles beyond this, the road passes a trio of glacially carved finger lakes – **Keechelus**, **Kachess**, and **Cle Elum** – surrounded by handsome mountain scenery and lined with a number of **campgrounds** ($10–21). For more information on exploring this striking landscape, visit the **ranger station** back in North Bend, 42404 SE North Bend Way (Mon–Fri 8am–4.15pm; Ⓣ425/888-1421, Ⓦwww.fs.fed.us/r6/mbs).

Just to the southeast of Cle Elum Lake, you reach drab **Cle Elum** ("Swift Water" in Salish), and can stock up on fresh bread and cinnamon rolls at the Cle Elum Bakery, 501 E 1st St (Ⓣ509/674-2233). The main draw is, however, the town's neighbor, **Roslyn**, a five-minute drive from the lakeshore on Hwy-903, an Appalachian look-alike of old timber houses in a forest pocked with slag heaps, reminders of the collieries that once produced two million tons of coal a year – the last one closed in 1963. Every inch a company town, no one seemed bothered about Roslyn until TV "discovered" its unreconstructed appearance as the set for *Northern Exposure*. With its fame have come the sightseers (now much fewer since the show's been cancelled), but it's still an odd, mournful sort of place. To get the lowdown on the town's history and see memorabilia from the TV show, check out the **Roslyn Museum**, 203 Pennsylvania Ave (daily 1–4pm; Ⓣ509/649-2776). Next door, the *Roslyn Café* (Ⓣ509/649-2763) serves delicious burgers and bagels.

Ellensburg

On the eastern side of the Cascade Mountains from Seattle, I-90 reaches the country town of **ELLENSBURG**, sitting in the middle of the wide and fertile Kittitas Valley. The town began when a couple of white traders set up shop here in the 1860s, making a tidy profit from the steady stream of settlers and drovers heading over Snoqualmie Pass. As a joke, the partners called their trading post "Robbers' Roost," and the name stuck until a Seattle merchant bought them out and renamed the settlement "Ellensburg" after his wife. The Northern Pacific Railroad reached the site in 1886, and the town boomed, its boosters even arguing it should become the state capital when the matter was put to the vote in 1889, the year of statehood. When Olympia, the old territorial capital, won, the editor of the local newspaper thundered "Capital or no capital, Ellensburg will get there. No grass in her streets, no flies on her back, no lard on her tail. Whoop her up again, boys!"

Despite such marked enthusiasm, that same year Ellensburg suffered the fate of many frontier towns when its early timber buildings were razed by fire, but there was enough money – and confidence – to pay for it to be rebuilt in brick and stone. Many of these commercial buildings have survived and several are worth a closer look, especially the imposing 1911 **Land Title Building**, 5th Avenue and Pearl Street, with its Neoclassical pillars and columns and fetching sandstone trimmings. Another, the horseshoe-arched **Cadwell Building**, 114 E 3rd Ave at Pine Street, is home to the **Kittitas County Museum** (May–Sept Mon–Sat 10am–4pm, Oct–April Tues–Sat 11am–3pm; donation suggested), which is the proud possessor of – among a hodgepodge of pioneer and native artifacts – a six-pound hunk of the locally unique Ellensburg blue agate. More diverting is the **Clymer Museum of Art**, 416 N Pearl St at 4th Avenue (Mon–Fri 10am–5pm, Sat & Sun noon–5pm; $3; Ⓦwww.clymermuseum.com), named after John Ford Clymer, a diligent painter of historical Western scenes and a talented illustrator, who was responsible for no less than eighty *Saturday Evening Post* covers. Born in Ellensburg, Clymer loved the West and traveled the region extensively, painting a long series of bold, sweeping historical pictures

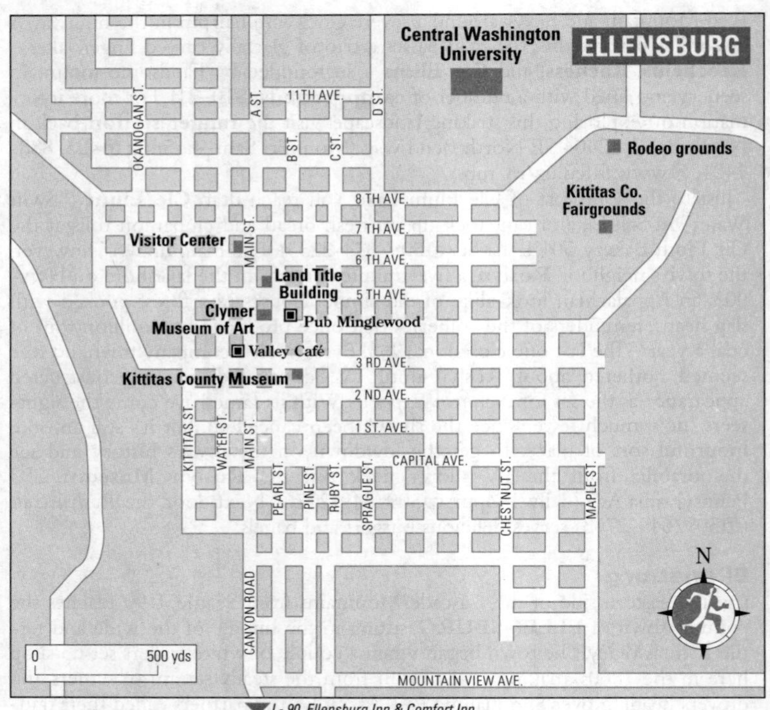

with titles like *John Colter Visits the Crows 1807*, *Salute to the Old West*, and *Whiskey, Whiskey*. The museum details Clymer's life and displays many of his historical paintings and illustrations alongside a solid program of temporary exhibitions focused on the West – everything from patchwork quilts and wheat weaving to cowboy poetry.

In keeping true to the town's identity, the main event hereabouts is appropriately linked to the Old West. The annual **Ellensburg Rodeo**, held over Labor Day weekend, fills the town with Stetson-wearing cowboys and cowgirls, who rope steers, ride bulls, and hold onto bucking broncos, accompanied by much pageantry and unfurling of star-spangled banners. For tickets, call the Rodeo Ticket Office (Ⓣ509/962-7831 or 1-800/637-2444, Ⓦwww.ellensburgrodeo.com): prices start at around $10, and include admission to the **Kittitas County Fair** (Ⓦwww.somepig.org), an odd combination of penned livestock and showy carnival rides that takes place at the same time.

Practicalities

Connecting Seattle as well as Spokane, Greyhound **buses** stop in Ellensburg at 1512 Hwy-97. In the downtown area, north of the highway, the **visitor center**, 609 N Main St (Mon–Fri 8am–6pm, Sat 10am–4pm, Sun 10am–2pm; Ⓣ509/925-3137, Ⓦwww.ellensburg-chamber.com), provides maps and has a list of local **accommodation**. Chain motels string along Canyon Road, the main access road into town, and among them the pick are the *Ellensburg Inn*, no. 1700 (Ⓣ509/925-9801 or 1-800/321-8791; ④), offering comfortable rooms plus an indoor pool and a sauna, and the new *Comfort Inn*, no. 1722 (T 509/925-7037 or 1-800/228-5150, W www.comfortinn.com; 4), also with an indoor pool. Needless to say, if you're here to see the rodeo, you should book accommodation well ahead of time. As for **eating**, the Art Deco *Valley Café*, 103 W 3rd Ave at Main (T 509/925-3050), has a wide-ranging and imaginative menu, and is by far the nicest place in town for any meal. Two other options are the reasonably priced *Pub Minglewood*, 402 N Pearl at 4th Avenue (evenings only, closed Sun; T 509/962-2260), where the local specialty – Ellensburg lamb – is a real treat, and the Mexican cuisine of *Casa de Blanca*, 1318 Canyon Rd at Ruby (T 509/925-1693).

The Yakima River Valley

South of Ellensburg, I-82/US-97 splits from I-90 (which heads into eastern Washington) and dips down into the **YAKIMA RIVER VALLEY**, via mildly interesting spots like **Yakima** and **Toppenish**, before finally reaching the Columbia Gorge at the esteemed Maryhill Museum of Art (see p.136).

Yakima

The Yakima River cuts free of its canyon setting and eases out into a wide valley to absorb the Naches River, where the sprawling **YAKIMA**, the region's urban hub, has a fairly drab, plodding air. It is, however, one of the region's most successful towns, a busy trading center with a huge agricultural hinterland and a population of more than sixty thousand. Since the 1940s, much of the local farm labor has been provided by migrant Mexican workers, and today Hispanic-Americans form a sizable minority in the valley.

Yakima's initial prosperity was due to the railroad, though initially in 1884 the Northern Pacific decided to bypass the town, plunking its vital tracks a few miles north. The decision saved the railroad money – as empty prairie was a good deal cheaper than developed land – and although the townsfolk were infuriated, there was nothing they could do except move. Thus, they rolled the better houses on logs to the new site to establish what the local paper called a "Messiah of Commerce."

Yakima has tried to brighten up its **downtown** – take I-82's Exit 33 if coming from Ellensburg – though the only appealing section is among the brightly painted railroad cars of **Track 29**, Yakima Ave at N First Street (T 509/542-4879), a mall that houses a collection of shops and food vendors. Other than that, the **visitor center**, downtown at 10 N 8th St at Yakima Avenue (Mon–Fri 8.30am–5pm, also summer weekends 9am–4pm; T 509/575-3010 or 1-800/221-0751, W www.visityakima.com), has details of wine tastings and tours amongst the many vineyards of the Yakima Valley (see box overleaf).

If you want to **stay the night**, decent options include a standard-issue *Travelodge*, 110 S Naches Ave at E Chestnut Avenue (T 509/453-7151 or 1-800/255-3050, W www.travelodge.com; 3), and the *Red Apple Motel*, 416 N 1st St at D Street (T 509/248-7150; 3), distinguished by is its apple-shaped outdoor pool. More distinctively, *Birchfield Manor B&B*, 2018 Birchfield Rd (T 509/452-1960, W www.birchfieldmanor.com; 6), occupies an attractively revamped 1880s house set in its own grounds just two miles east of town off Hwy-24; they have five en-suite guestrooms and six cottage units for slightly more money. There's also **camping** across the Yakima River on Hwy-24 at **Sportsman State Park** ($15–21; T 509/575-2774 or 1-800/562-0990).

Yakima Valley vineyards

Southeast of its namesake town, the **Yakima Valley** turns into fruit- and vine-growing country, where apples, cherries, pears, peaches, apricots, and grapes grow prolifically in what was once sagebrush desert. Although the valley's volcanic soil is naturally rich and the sun shines about three hundred days of the year, copious irrigation has made the land fertile, and intricate systems of reservoirs, canals, and ditches divert water from the Yakima River around the orchards and vineyards.

There have been **vineyards** in the Yakima Valley since the 1930s, but it was not until the introduction of classic European vinifera vines thirty years later that the foundation of today's industry was laid. Organized by a group of Washington vintners, the introduction of the precious vine was actually something of a gamble: many experts thought the state's winters would be too harsh for them to survive, but the plants flourished, and nowadays the Yakima Valley is Washington's premier grape-growing region, regularly producing vintages of international standing. Acidity is the key to the individuality of the valley's wines. The intense cold of winter stresses the vines and concentrates the flavor of the fruit, while in summer the days are boiling hot and the nights comparatively cold, giving valley wine its characteristic crispness.

The **Yakima Valley Wine Growers Association** (Ⓣ1-800/258-7270, Ⓦwww.yakimavalleywine.com) helps monitor the quality of every bottle sporting the region's appellation and has information on the area's vintages on its website. About twenty valley wineries offer **tours** and **tastings**, and all the region's visitor centers can provide detailed directions and opening hours. A particularly good one, thanks to its lovely tasting room and fine wines, is the **Covey Run Winery** (daily April–Oct 10am–5pm, Nov–March 11am–4pm; Ⓣ509/829-6235, Ⓦwww.coveyrun.com), located at 1500 Vintage Rd, about four miles north of Zillah, itself some twenty miles from Yakima.

For **food**, *Santiago's*, 111 E Yakima Ave at N 1st Street (Ⓣ509/453-1644), serves excellent, inexpensive Mexican dishes and has a convivial atmosphere, as does *Grant's Brewery Pub*, 32 N Front St (Ⓣ509/575-2922), which serves hand-crafted ales and tasty pub food. *Birchfield Manor* (see above; dinner only, closed Sun) offers a classy, imaginative menu of Continental and Northwest cuisine and excellent local wines – main courses around $20 – and finally *Gasparetti's*, a few blocks north of the center at 1013 N 1st St at I Street (dinners only, closed Sun; Ⓣ509/248-0628), is the best of Yakima's Italian restaurants, and reasonably priced, too.

Toppenish

US-97 cuts a quiet, pleasant route to the south of the Yakima River and, after about twenty miles, reaches **TOPPENISH**, easily the best base for exploring the valley. In true Western style, the town started out as a telegraph office and water tower beside the Northern Pacific Railroad. The railway employees were soon joined by horse traders, who made a handsome profit buying wild horses from the adjacent Yakama Indian Reservation and selling the animals in New York. Fortuitously, just when the horse trade began to fizzle out, a sugar company moved in, building a sugar-beet processing plant here in 1918. When the plant closed in 1980, locals looked around for an alternative money-maker and hit upon something genuinely inventive. Coining a promotional cliché, "The City Where the West Still Lives," they set about commissioning sixty high-quality **murals** focusing on local characters and events. More than forty of these bright and breezy paintings now adorn the tiny town center, focused on Toppenish Avenue, and although some are rather hackneyed (cowboys-by-the-light-of-the-moon), others tell intriguing tales or set the scene perfectly, as in the historic buildings and peoples depicted in *The Palace Hotel, Toppenish*, and *Indians' Winter Encampment*.

The **visitor center**, downtown at 5A Toppenish Ave (April–Oct daily 10am–4pm, Nov–March daily 11am–3pm; ⓣ509/865-3262 or 1-800/569-3982), provides a free guide to the murals, with each painting described in detail. It only takes an hour or two to walk around them all, but there are **guided tours** by covered wagon and stagecoach from April to mid-November (daily every two hrs 10am–4pm; 90min ride; $10), while the annual **Mural-in-a-Day** extravaganza, usually held in early June, sees Toppenish stuffed with tourists who come to watch a team of artists put up a brand new mural. The town's other festival is the four-day **Toppenish Pow Wow and Rodeo** (tickets from $10; ⓦwww.toppenishrodeo.com), held every Fourth of July weekend. Finally, just as the larger Yakima Valley is known for growing vines for wine, Toppenish itself is known for raising hops for beer, and the **American Hop Museum**, 22 South B St (May–Sept 11am–4pm; donation suggested; ⓦwww.americanhopmuseum.com), offers a mildly diverting selection of old photos and antiques to illustrate the agricultural history of this overlooked vine.

Toppenish has a small supply of **motels**, among which the *Best Western Lincoln Inn*, 515 S Elm St (ⓣ509/865-7444 or 1-800/222-3161; ❸), is the most comfortable with its indoor pool, though the plain but adequate *Oxbow Motor Inn*, nearby at 511 S Elm St (ⓣ509/865-5800; ❷), is a second possibility. There is a smattering of good **restaurants** in the area, notably *Snipes Mountain Brewery & Restaurant,* 905 Yakima Valley Hwy in nearby Sunnyside (ⓣ509/837-BREW), which serves great regional food – the likes of pork tenderloin, baked brie, and King salmon – along with, handcrafted microbrews and local wines.

Yakama Nation Cultural Center

For some thirty miles from Yakima, the Yakima River marks the northern boundary of the **Yakama Indian Reservation** – the tribal council having changed the "i" to an "a" – a great slab of dry and rugged land that stretches down towards the Columbia River. Here, set beside US-97 just northwest of Toppenish, the large **YAKAMA NATION CULTURAL CENTER**, holds a variety of community facilities and, in a 76-foot-tall replica wigwam, a **museum** (daily 9am–5pm; $4; ⓣ509/865-2800) outlining Yakama traditions by means of dioramas and wall displays. One of the most unusual exhibits is a time-ball, a sort of macramé diary kept by married women as a record of their lives; in old age, major events were recalled by unraveling the sequence of knots and beads. Several exhibits are devoted to Yakama religious practices involving **Spilyay** – the local version of the god-like coyote figure that crops up in many Native American legends – and to the series of brutal skirmishes in the 1850s known as the **Yakima War**, in which the tribe was forcibly ejected from its traditional lands along the Columbia and Yakima rivers and consigned to this largely infertile reservation. You can find out more about this grim chapter in local history, in a somewhat sanitized version, at **Fort Simcoe**, a state park inside the reservation, west of Toppenish via Fort Road. Here, an **interpretative center** (April–Sept Wed–Sun 9.30am–4.30pm; ⓣ509/874-2372) provides an overview of white-native relations in that troubled era and features five original military buildings (amid other modern replicas) used by the government to keep its thumb on the tribe.

Mount Rainier National Park

Set in its own national park ninety miles southeast of Seattle, glacier-clad **MOUNT RAINIER** is, at 14,410ft, the tallest and most accessible of the Cascade peaks, and a major Washington landmark. To Native Americans living in its shadow, it spawned a complex mythology, appearing as a jealous wife who was magically metamorphosed into a giant mountain vengefully protective of its higher ridges and peaks. On no account would local **Klickitats** venture up the slopes into this hostile spirit country, where the hazards were inscrutable to human eyes – apt considering the summit is wreathed in clouds much of the time. The Klickitat called the mountain *Tahoma* ("Snowiest Peak"), and there have been moves to revive the original appellation if for no other reason than to end the dire puns about the name describing the weather (though the mountain's name is actually pronounced "ray-NEER"). In a much less grand fashion, the mountain acquired its current moniker after explorer George Vancouver named it after one of his cronies, eighteenth-century British rear admiral, **Peter Rainier**, who never even saw it.

The long winter season sees heavy snowfall and a steady stream of visitors who mostly come here to go **snowboarding** and **cross-country skiing** from mid-December to early April. As spring takes hold, the snowline creeps up the mountain, unblocking roads and revealing a web of **hiking trails**, though the

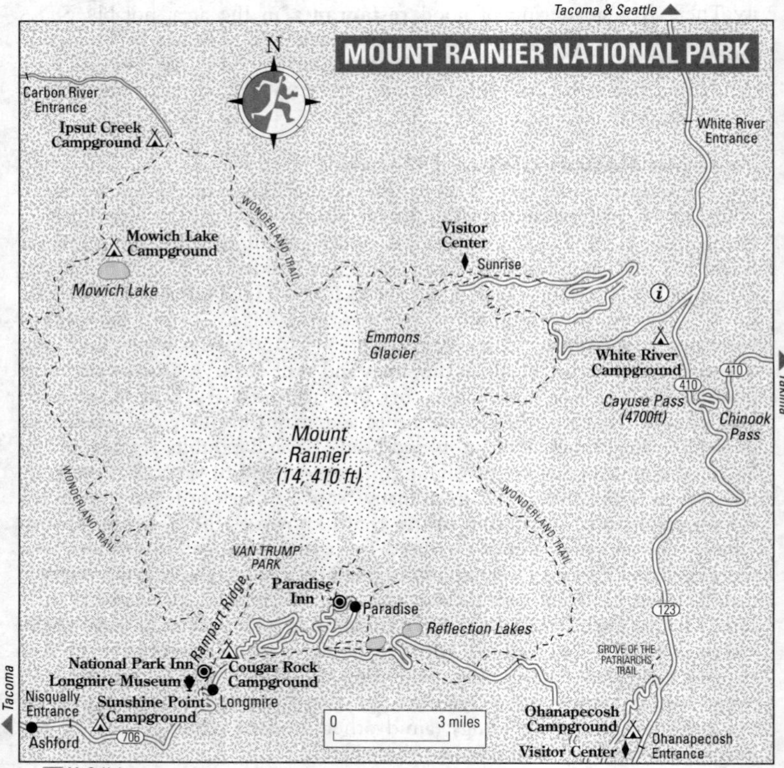

ones at higher elevations are rarely clear before mid-June. July and August are the sunniest months, and it's then that the mountain makes for some perfect hiking: the air is crisp and clear, meadows sprout alpine flowers, and wildlife emerges, with deer, elk, and mountain goats at the forest edges and small furry marmots scuttling between their burrows.

Arrival and information

Mount Rainier National Park is roughly square in shape, with an entrance at each corner; the nearest to Seattle, **Nisqually**, lies at the park's southwest corner. Other than this main entrance, there are two entrances on the park's eastern flank, **Ohanapecosh** to the south and **White River** in the north. **Carbon River**, the fourth and least-visited entrance, can be found in the park's more remote northwest corner; visitor center information for each of these is provided on the following pages.

If you're coming in by car, head south on I-5, taking Exit 127 onto Hwy-512 east, and after a few miles follow Hwy-7 south to Hwy-706, where you'll enter the park just short of Longmire, a small cluster of buildings that includes the **Longmire Museum** (daily 9am–4pm, summer 8.30am–4.30pm; ⓣ360/569-2211, ext. 3314). The museum offers information on area wildlife and the mountain and sells **park permits** – $10 per vehicle, or $5 each for those on foot, bike, or motorcycle. Be aware that road access depends on weather conditions, so unless you're traveling in the height of summer, call ahead to the National Park Service (ⓣ360/569-2211, ⓦwww.nps.gov/mora) for details. Next door to the Longmire Museum, the **Wilderness Information Center** (late May–Sept Mon–Fri 8am–6.30pm, Sat–Sun 7.30am–7pm; closed in winter when services are transferred to the museum; ⓣ360/569-HIKE) has plenty of information on the park's network of **trails**, over three hundred miles in all, ranging from easy walks through the forests of the lower slopes to steep treks to Rainier's summit. Longmire's *National Park Inn* (see "Accommodation," below) is the only place in the park to rent **skis** and **snowshoes** in winter, starting at $15 and $12 per day, respectively.

Rainier Shuttle (ⓣ360/569-2331, ⓦwww.rainiershuttle.com) runs a daily, three-hour trip from Sea-Tac Airport to Paradise, a small town on the southern side of the park (May–Oct; $46 one-way), and **Gray Line** operates daily, ten-hour-long round-trips (May–Sept; $54; ⓣ360/624-5077 or 1-800/426-7505, ⓦwww.graylineseattle.com). In both cases reservations are required.

Accommodation

It's possible to stay in the park at either of the two national park **lodges** in Longmire and Paradise (see below), and there are plenty of wilderness and six serviced **campgrounds** ($10–15). Of the latter, two are near the southwest entrance and there's one each at the other three; the final campground is a walk-in-only affair at Mowich Lake, about five miles from the Carbon River entrance. Serviced campgrounds operate on a first-come-first-served basis and are – with the exception of the Sunshine Point campground in the southwest and the one at Ipsut Creek in the northeast – only open in the summer. If all else fails, there's also a range of fairly standard accommodation in **Ashford**, just outside the park's Nisqually entrance.

Mountain Meadows Inn 28912 SR 706 East, Ashford ⓣ360/569-2788, ⓦwww.mountainmeadowsinn.com. Six cozy, antique-laden rooms with various historic themes (early Colonial, Native American, etc), some detached from the main house and offering kitchenettes and claw-foot tubs. Onsite hot tub also available for use by all guests. ❼

Mounthaven 38210 SR 706 East, Ashford ⓣ360/569-2594 or 1-800/456-9380, ⓦwww.mounthaven.com. Ten cabins, some with fireplaces, kitchenettes, fridges, and porches, on six acres lying between two mountain creeks. Hot tub (for a fee) and playground; minimum two-day stay on weekends. Also seventeen full-hook-up RV sites for $20. ❺

National Park Inn at Longmire in Mount Rainier National Park ⓣ360/569-2275, ⓦwww.guestservices.com/rainier. Comfortable, modern accommodations in a classically rustic lodge, with 25 guestrooms and a restaurant. Cross-country skiing and snowshoe rentals available. Open year-round, though with complimentary breakfast in winter and spring; reservations essential. ❹

Paradise Inn at Paradise in Mount Rainier National Park ⓣ360/569-2275, ⓦwww.guestservices.com/rainier. Stately 1917 timber hotel whose bedrooms vary in quality and price (if you want a room with bath, for example, it's an extra $28), but have great views from more than 5000 feet above sea level; offers a spacious, historic dining hall as well. Open mid-May to Sept only; reservations essential. ❹

Whittaker's Bunkhouse 30205 SR 706 E, Ashford ⓣ360/569-2439, ⓦwww.welcometoashford.com. A favorite among local climbers and hikers, this old loggers' bunkhouse offers both dorm beds and double rooms, with private baths. Located next door to Rainier Shuttle stop. ❶–❹

Nisqually entrance trails

After passing through the **Nisqually entrance**, and beginning at Longmire, the **Trail of the Shadows** is a popular half-hour stroll around the alpine meadow where James Longmire, a local farmer, built a now-defunct mineral-springs resort at the end of the nineteenth century. Although it's no match for the higher, steeper, and more inaccessible trails, it's still a pleasant walk through meadow and forest in the shadow of mountain peaks, passing an early homestead cabin along the way. Leading off from this loop are more strenuous hikes, such as the five-mile **Rampart Ridge Trail**, which takes you on a climb through thick trees to the ridge – created by an ancient lava flow – from where you'll have a good view of the mountain.

The Trail of the Shadows loop also intersects with the 93-mile **Wonderland Trail**, which encircles the mountain and is an essential route for serious nature enthusiasts in excellent physical condition; hiking the length of it will take you ten to fourteen days. A hardy but manageable hike branching off from the trail (four to five hours one-way) begins back in Longmire near the Wilderness Information Center (see p.397). From there, head two miles northeast through old-growth forest to the Cougar Rock campground; as the trail meanders to Reflection Lakes, five miles east, it crosses over the Nisqually River – with its muddy-gray, glacier-fed waters – then follows Paradise River by some lovely waterfalls.

Keep in mind that, although trails around Longmire are free from snow earlier than those at higher elevations, in midsummer you'll probably want to drive further up the mountain, where much of the snow, still many feet deep even in June, will have melted enough to allow passage that's impossible at other times of the year.

Trails from Paradise

From Longmire, it's just eleven miles through the thinning forest, past waterfalls of glacial snowmelt, to **Paradise**, where a **visitor center** (May to mid-Oct daily 9am–7pm; Nov–April Sat–Sun 10am–5pm; ⓣ360/569-2211 ext. 2328) shows films and exhibits on natural history and offers a circular observation room for viewing the mountain. From Paradise, both the 1.2-mile **Nisqually Vista Trail** loop and the five-mile **Skyline Trail** climb the mountain, providing gorgeous views of its craggy peak and glistening glaciers. The park rangers also offer a summer program of **guided walks**, and from late December to early April, two-hour guided snowshoe walks leave from the visitor center (weekends only 10.30am & 2.30pm; limited to 25 people on a first-come-first-served basis; $1 for snowshoe rental, or bring your own).

Paradise is the starting point for **climbing Mount Rainier**, a serious endeavor involving ice axes, crampons, and some degree of danger. It usually takes two days to get to the summit – with its twin craters rimmed with ice-caves – and back. On the first day climbers aim for the base camp at **Camp Muir**, ready for the strenuous final assault and the descent to Paradise on the second. Unless you're very experienced (and even then, you have to register with the rangers), the way to do it is with the Rainier Mountaineering guide service in Paradise (Ⓣ360/569-2227, Ⓦwww.rmiguides.com), which offers three-day courses – one day's practice, then the two-day climb – from May to mid-October for $771. Specialist equipment rental (lug-sole climbing boots, ice axes) costs extra, and reservations with advance payment in full are required.

Other entrances

In summer, it's possible to drive about an hour from Paradise along rugged **Stevens Canyon Road** to the park's southeast corner, cruising around hillside ridges on a winding concourse with plenty of switchbacks. Here, the **Ohanapecosh entrance** and **visitor center** (mid-June to Sept daily 9am–6pm; Ⓣ360/569-6046) is set in deep forest near the gurgling Ohanapecosh River. Among several trails in the area, one of the most enjoyable is the **Grove of the Patriarchs**, a 1.5-mile loop along a river islet, where there are ancient groves of giant Douglas fir, Western hemlock, and red cedar trees.

North from Ohanapecosh, in the park's northeast corner, is the **White River entrance** and the **White River Wilderness Information Center** (June–Sept Sun–Thurs 8am–4.30pm, Fri–Sat 7am–7pm; Ⓣ360/569-6046), which gives out backpacking and climbing permits as well as trail information. Six miles west at the White River campground, you can reach any number of trails leading around mountain ridges and the lower reaches of glaciers, or pick up the **Wonderland Trail**, which leads around the dramatic Shadow and Frozen lakes and offers astounding views of the volcanic terrain. Eleven miles further up the mountain, on another winding route full of switchbacks, the **Sunrise visitor center** (July–Sept daily 9am–6pm; Ⓣ360/663-2425) affords wonderful views of **Emmons Glacier**, a huge tongue of ice on the mountain's northeastern side, and of the mountain summit.

The last and least frequently visited of the national park's four entrances, the **Carbon River entrance** lies in the northwest corner of the park, and isn't linked by road to the other three. Hwy-165, the paved approach road, runs as far as the ranger station, which serves as the trailhead for the short and easy **Carbon River Rainforest Trail**, which nudges into Mount Rainier's one and only chunk of temperate rainforest. As visually evocative as the forest's moss-covered spruces and canopies of greenery are, it's a long way to go for a trail that's just a third of a mile long. More rugged types should consider the seven-mile round-trip **Carbon Glacier Trail**, beginning at the Ipsut Creek campground (four miles east of the Carbon River park entrance), highlighted by a suspension bridge that crosses a river below the mouth of the dirty, crumbling Carbon Glacier – the glacier of lowest elevation in the US outside of Alaska, and the source for the Carbon River itself.

Mount St Helens National Volcanic Monument

The native Klickitat knew **MOUNT ST HELENS** as *Tahonelatclah* or "Fire Mountain" – and, true to its name, in May of 1980 the mountain erupted, leaving a blasted landscape and scenes of almost total destruction for many miles around. Slowly but surely, though, second-growth forests are emerging, and the ash is disappearing beneath new vegetation. That said, much of the land continues to bear witness to the incredible force of the eruption, with once-pristine valleys sheared by mudflows, mangled trees ripped from their roots, and entire mountainsides resembling a post-nuclear wasteland.

Arrival and information

Designated a National Volcanic Monument, Mount St Helens has understandably become a major attraction in the region, making a feasible **day-trip** of around two hundred miles from Olympia. While it's only half that distance from Portland, the approach from the south passes slopes that bear few traces of the eruption – the most dramatic views are almost entirely confined to its northwest side. Thus, most tourists head for the two **visitor centers** – **Coldwater Ridge** and the smaller **Johnston Ridge Observatory** – that overlook the blast area from the northwest. These are reached, traveling north on I-5, by turning off at Hwy-504 (or traveling south, via its main feeder road, Hwy-505) roughly halfway between Olympia and Portland. The other main approach road is the quieter Hwy-503, which runs to the mountain's steep and densely forested southern slopes. During the summer, the east side of the mountain can also be reached along paved forest roads from US-12 to the north and Hwy-14 in the south. These eastern access roads are connected to Hwy-503, which means it's possible to drive across the mountain's south and east flanks, though this is a time-consuming and occasionally nerve-jangling business.

Since the mountain's forest roads are often damaged by winter flooding, you can check conditions ahead of time (and for general information) by calling the **Mount St Helens National Volcanic Monument Headquarters**, outside Amboy on Hwy-503 (daily 8am–5pm; ⓣ360/247-3900, ⓦwww.fs.fed.us/gpnf/mshnvm). The one-day **Monument Pass** ($6) allows entry to everything in the monument area, while the **Site Day Pass** ($3) is good only for the Coldwater Ridge and Mount St Helens visitor centers, the Johnston Ridge Observatory, and Ape Cave. Confusingly, there is also the **Northwest Forest Pass**, a per vehicle charge of $5 per day required at many of the area's viewpoints and trailheads.

A network of **hiking trails** radiates out from the access roads as they near the mountain, exploring its every nook and volcanic cranny, but unless you're indifferent to clouds of dust and ash, a morning or afternoon hike is really enough. For those interested in **climbing** the mountain above 4800ft, **permits** are necessary (lower-level routes don't require them), and only one hundred of them are issued per day from mid-May to October. The majority are booked far ahead of time, but forty are set aside for distribution by **lottery** one day in advance. To enter the lottery, you have to be at *Jack's Restaurant and Store* (ⓣ360/231-4276), five miles west of Cougar, a lakeside settlement on Hwy-503, at 6pm; the restaurant is also where all prospective climbers have to register before they set out. The rest of the year, things ease

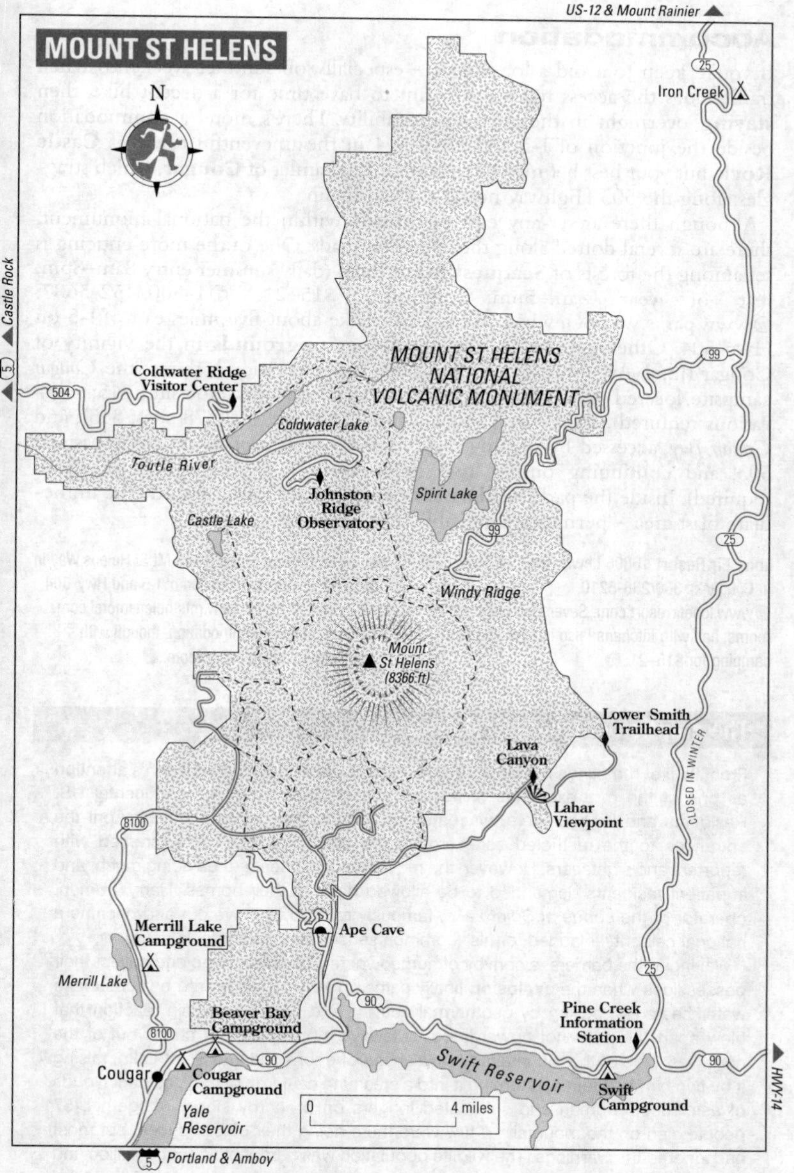

up, though all prospective climbers still have to register at *Jack's* before they go. The climbing route begins at the Climbers' Bivouac, at the end of a hair-raising road high up the mountain, and the round-trip takes between seven and twelve hours. The climb takes you to the crater rim, but the crater itself – a jagged cauldron of rock and steam – is out of bounds (though geologists and other scientists are allowed to visit it by helicopter).

Accommodation

If you're keen to avoid a long drive – especially on summer weekends when traffic clogs the access roads – or want to have time for a decent hike, then **staying** overnight in the area is a possibility. There's motel accommodation beside the junction of I-5 and Hwy-504 in the uneventful town of **Castle Rock**, but your best bet may be to aim for the hamlet of **Cougar**, which straggles along the 503 Highway nearer the mountain.

Although there aren't any **campgrounds** within the national monument, there are several dotted along the approach roads. One of the more enticing is set among the forests of **Seaquest State Park** (daily summer entry 8am–8pm, rest of year 8am–5pm; campsites \$15–21; ⓣ1-800/452-5687, ⓦwww.parks.wa.gov), which abuts Silver Lake about five miles east of I-5 on Hwy-504. Other options are the **private campgrounds** in the vicinity of Cougar (June–Aug only; ⓣ503/813-6666 for reservations): there's the *Cougar* campsite, located on Yale Reservoir just north of the village (60 sites; \$15; reservations required), *Beaver Bay*, about a mile north on 503 (78 sites; \$15), and *Cresap Bay*, accessed by turning right at *Jack's Restaurant* while going east on 503, and continuing on for two miles south (73 sites; \$15; reservations required). Inside the park, **wilderness camping** is allowed outside the immediate blast area – permits are available from any visitor center.

Lone Fir Resort 16806 Lewis River Rd (Hwy-503) in Cougar ⓣ360/238-5210, ⓦwww.lonefirresort.com. Seventeen basic motel rooms, half with kitchens; also has RV and tent camping for \$15–21. ③

Mount St Helens Motel 1340 Mt St Helens Way in Castle Rock, near the junction of I-5 and Hwy-504 ⓣ360/274-7721, ⓦwww.mtsthelensmotel.com. Standard motel accommodation, though with queen-sized beds in every room. ③

The eruption of Mount St Helens

From its first rumblings in March 1980, **Mount St Helens** drew the nation's attention as one of the rare examples of (recent) volcanic activity in the continental US. Residents and loggers were evacuated and roads were closed, but by April the entrances to the restricted zone around the steaming peak were jammed with reporters and sightseers. However, the mountain didn't seem to be doing much, and impatient residents demanded to be allowed back to their homes. Harry Truman, operator of the *Lodge at Spirit Lake*, famously refused to move out and became a national celebrity – lauded for his "common sense" by Washington's governor.

Waiting at the barriers, a convoy of homeowners was about to go and collect their possessions when the **explosion** finally came on May 18 – powered by subsurface water heated to boiling by geothermal activity, and causing a chain reaction that blew apart the peak not upwards but sideways, ripping a great chunk out of the northwest side of the mountain. An avalanche of debris slid into Spirit Lake, raising it by two hundred feet and turning it into a steaming cauldron of mud, as dark clouds of ash buried Truman and suffocated loggers on a nearby slope. Altogether, 57 people died on the mountain: a few were there doing their official duties, but most had ignored the warnings. The wildlife population was harder hit: about a million and a half animals – deer, elk, mountain goats, cougars, and bears – were killed, and thousands of fish were boiled alive in sediment-filled rivers. There were dire economic effects, too, as falling ash devastated the land, and millions of feet of timber were lost. These days, the volcanic result is still visible, and not just up-close on the mountain roads – looking north from Portland, you can't help but notice the unmistakable silhouette of a ruined gray mound looming over the horizon, the remains of what was once a lively and romantic winter playground.

Silver Lake Motel & Resort Hwy-504 six miles east of I-5 in Silver Lake ⓣ360/274-6141, ⓦwww.silverlake-resort.com. Convenient for mountain access and for bass fishing – you can even cast a line from your balcony. Clean, comfortable motel rooms and cabin sites (both ⑤), which both offer kitchenettes, with RV and campsites ($24) also available.

Coldwater Ridge and Johnston Ridge Observatory

Heading east from I-5, Hwy-504 runs through dark-green forests, past **Silver Lake** and **Toutle River Valley** until bald, spiky trees signal a sudden change: beyond, thousands of gray tree-shards still lie in uniform rows, knocked flat in different directions back in 1980 when blast waves bounced off the hillsides. It's a weird and disconcerting landscape, the matchstick-like flattened forest left to rot to regenerate the soil and provide cover for small animals and insects. There are several good vantage points as you progress up the road – notably at **Hoffstadt Bluffs**, where you can make out the path taken by the avalanche of debris that swept down the valley – to the **COLDWATER RIDGE visitor center** (daily 10am–6pm; ⓣ360/274-2131), which has exhibits, interpretive programs, and a film detailing the eruption. Eight miles further along Hwy-504, the low-slung **JOHNSTON RIDGE OBSERVATORY** (May–Sept daily 10am–6pm; ⓣ360/274-2140) is as close as you'll get to the mountain by car; the views here, over the still-steaming lava dome and pumice plain, are quite extraordinary. Again, interpretive displays, a video, and a fifteen-minute film give the background. Outside the center, the half-mile paved **Eruption Trail** leads to slightly higher viewpoints marked with interpretive displays; there's also a short, dusty, and in places steep hiking trail that takes you toward **Spirit Lake**, with much longer and more strenuous side trails leading up towards the edge of the crater peak.

The south and east slopes

I-5 intersects Hwy-503 twice before it reaches Portland, and either exit will do for the journey to both **Cougar**, where there's a motel and a campground, and nearby **Beaver Bay**, which just has a campground. Beyond Cougar, around the **south slope** of Mount St Helens, it's ten miles further to **Ape Cave**, a tube-like lava cavern – the longest in the continental US – channeled two thousand years ago by the rushing molten lava of an ancient eruption. Despite the compelling name, there are no oversized primates lurking inside – the place was named after the St Helens Apes, an outdoors group for local youth. There are two subterranean routes to choose from: the three-quarter-mile lower trail, where you have to return to the entrance to get out, and the much more difficult one-and-a-half-mile upper trail which emerges higher up the mountain. For a less strenuous jaunt, the quarter-mile **Trail of Two Forests** boardwalk, off the road shortly before Ape Cave, has a 55-foot crawl through a lava tunnel; bring a flashlight. Ranger-led **tours** (late–June to early–Sept daily on the hour 10.30am–4.30pm), which point out all kinds of geological oddities you'd otherwise miss, leave from **Apes' Headquarters** (late–June to early–Sept daily 10am–5.30pm) beside the cave. Lanterns can be rented until 4pm for $3.50 at headquarters, or from *Jack's Restaurant* back in Cougar, for $10, plus a $20 deposit. Also, keep in mind that it's much colder in the cave than outside, so bring extra clothing.

Back on Forest Road #83, it's a few miles more to the turnoff that threads its way up to several **hiking trails** that traverse the mountain's higher slopes.

The most popular climbing route begins at the Climbers' Bivouac trail base, at the end of Road 83's hair-raising journey high up the mountain, taking you to the crater rim and back in seven to twelve hours. Climbing is hedged with restrictions, though (see p.400 for details): wind, rain, fog, and snow can arrive quickly and unpredictably here, with the temperature at the volcano rim regularly twenty to thirty degrees colder than in the valley – so take detailed advice from Apes' Headquarters before you set out on all but the shortest of hikes. Remember to pack plenty of water, too. Beyond this, **Lava Canyon**, eight miles past Ape Cave, has a trail leading past striking waterfalls to dramatic, mudflow-scoured landscapes from earlier eruptions. Shortly before you get there, **Lahar Viewpoint** gives you a good look at how the south side of the mountain was changed by these ancient mudflows.

In the summer, you can drive east from Cougar along the mountain's southern slopes to **Pine Creek Information Station** (summer daily 9am–6pm) and then head twenty-five miles north along Forest Road 25, traveling on the mountain's **east slope** for the final push up Forest Road 99 to **Windy Ridge**, a rocky outcrop with breathtaking views of the crater from the northeast. A short hike from here also leads to the long, circular trail around the summit and the easier walk down past Spirit Lake to Johnston Ridge (see above). On the ridge, tourists are much fewer in evidence, and the devastation wrought by the 1980 eruption even more vivid than elsewhere: entire slopes denuded of foliage, colossal tree husks scattered like twigs, and huge dead zones where anything alive was simply vaporized.

Windy Ridge can also be accessed from the north from **Randle** along USFS-25 and -99, which provides access to what remains of Spirit Lake and passes through lava flows with numerous viewpoints en route.

Mount Adams

A mere forty miles east of Mount St Helens, but inaccessible from it by road, the 12,276-ft **MOUNT ADAMS** is one of the less-heralded peaks in the Washington Cascades which nevertheless attracts its own devoted flock of outdoor adventurers. Although the Yakama Indian Reservation (see p.395) stretches to its eastern flanks, the mountain is best approached via Washington Hwy-14 in the Columbia Gorge, with a northbound turn onto Hwy-141 around Oregon's Hood River. Although about a thousand feet taller than its southern neighbor Mount Hood (see p.132) on the opposite side of the gorge, Mount Adams has a less distinctive presence in the region, no doubt because of its smoother, more rounded summit and the sloping topography of the land. Nonetheless, the mountain offers a fascinating topography with its surrounding landscape of broken lava beds, cinder cones, and basaltic buttes – highlighted by the **Ice Cave** (May–Nov, daily dawn–dusk); located where Hwy- 141 turns west and then becomes southbound Route 24. A 650-ft long lava tube whose stalactites and stalagmites are coated in ice and frost much of the year, it is especially dramatic in autumn, when the cave is a strange and chilly world of frosty domes, sparkling walls, and spiky ice crystals. The ice on the floors and rails can be hazardous, though, so make sure to bring along a flashlight, and don't get too enthralled by the natural spectacle and take a tumble onto the beautiful, but unforgiving, rocks.

Around the bend on Highway 141, Route 80 leads north toward the upper slopes of Mount Adams, but in branching off into the narrower Route 8040, stops at the trailhead at **Cold Springs**. In this area there are countless rugged hikes and paths around natural bridges, waterfalls, and the like, but if you want to aim for the summit, you'll need a **climbing pass** ($10 weekdays, $15 weekends) and the requisite gear. This hike is expressly not for casual lovers of the outdoors. It is, however, quite a stunning jaunt, taking you up the slope once traversed by mules, when the crest of the mountain was used for sulfur mining, and over the upper reaches of **Suksdorf Ridge** leading to the false summit of Pikers Peak, and then the actual summit. The mountain is not just for climbing per se, and attracts a small but fervent crowd of **skiers** during the spring and summer. If you're expecting Mount Hood-style chairlifts and color-coded runs, you'll be sadly mistaken – all gear must be carried up the slopes **on foot**, and the mountainside runs are for serious schussing, gliding over steep canyon walls, across ice fields and around glaciers, and other challenging elements.

For **information** on the many excellent trails around the mountain, or for attaining climbing passes, maps, and other materials, contact the official site for **Gifford Pinchot National Forest**, of which Mount Adams is a part (Ⓣ509/395-3400, Ⓦwww.fs.fed.us/gpnf).

10

Vancouver and around

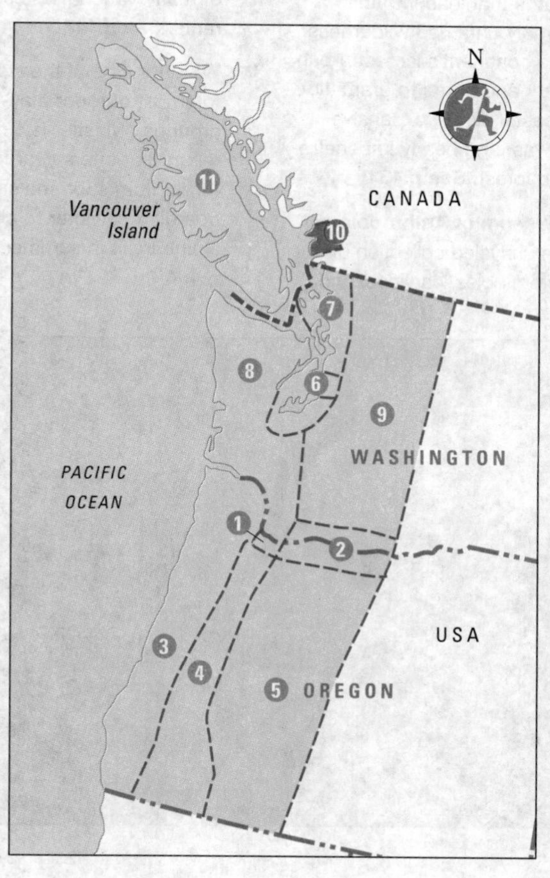

CHAPTER 10

Highlights

- **Canada Place** Stroll by day or night around the walkways of this striking convention center, hotel and cruise-ship terminal for wonderful views of Vancouver's port. See p.423
- **Stanley Park** Stroll myriad paths that lead into this largely untamed wilderness, the continent's largest urban park and home to dramatic coastal views, expansive lawns, and nearly impenetrable forest. See p.431
- **Museum of Anthropology** An unrivaled collection of totem poles, carvings, and other Native Ameican artifacts make this award-winning museum Vancouver's most compelling. See p.437
- **Pacific Rim Cuisine** Sample the inspired fusion of Far-Eastern, Italian, and West Coast cooking, a mainstay of many Vancouver restaurants. See p.447
- **Whistler** One of the world's foremost outdoor playgrounds, Whistler is a rare resort that offers year-round thrills, from supreme snowboarding in winter to classic alpine treks in summer. See p.464

△ Grouse Mountain Skyride

10

Vancouver and around

Cradled between the Pacific and snowcapped peaks, **Vancouver**'s dazzling Downtown district fills a narrow peninsula bounded by Burrard Inlet to the north, English Bay to the west, and False Creek to the south, with greater Vancouver sprawling south to the Fraser River. Edged around Downtown's idyllic waterfront are fine beaches, a dynamic port, and a magnificent swath of green – Stanley Park – not to mention the mirror-fronted ranks of skyscrapers that look across Burrard Inlet and its busy harbor to the residential districts of North and West Vancouver (or North Shore). Beyond these comfortable suburbs, the Coast Mountains rise in steep, forested slopes to form a dramatic counterpoint to the Downtown skyline and the most stunning of the city's many outdoor playgrounds.

Vancouver serves as an ideal base for excursions to Victoria (see Chapter 11) as well as the 150-km **Sunshine Coast**, the only stretch of accessible coastline on mainland British Columbia, and a possible springboard to Vancouver Island. Also within striking distance of Vancouver, the famous world-class ski resort of **Whistler** is well worth visiting at any time of the year, with winter an obviously busy time and summer almost equally popular, thanks to the area's many outdoor activities.

Vancouver

Though it doesn't demand relentless sightseeing, Vancouver's breathtaking physical beauty makes it a place where often it's enough just to wander and watch the world go by – "the sort of town," as Welsh writer Jan Morris noted, "nearly everyone would want to live in." In summer, you'll probably end up doing what the locals do, if not actually sailing, hiking, skiing, fishing, or whatever, then certainly going to the beach, lounging in one of the parks, or spending time in waterfront cafés.

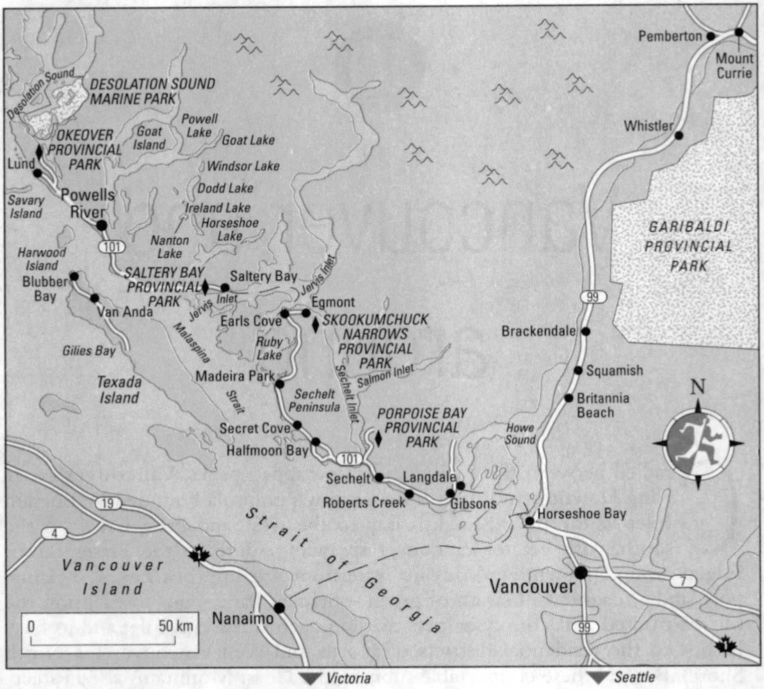

In addition to the myriad leisure activities, however, there are a handful of sights that make worthwhile viewing by any standards. Vancouver's nearly two million residents exploit its spectacular natural setting to the hilt, and when they tire of the immediate region can travel a short distance to the unimaginably vast wilderness of the British Columbia interior. No wonder, given its superb natural heritage and outdoor facilities, that, in 2003, the city completed a successful bid to stage the 2010 Winter Olympics. The city also has plenty that contributes to a cultured atmosphere: top-notch museums, superb restaurants – arguably the best in North America after New York and San Francisco – countless cafés, great parks and gardens, and any number of hip bars and clubs. Vancouver claims a world-class symphony orchestra, as well as opera, theater, and dance companies at the cutting edge of contemporary arts. Festivals proliferate throughout its mild, if occasionally rain-soaked summer, and numerous music venues provide a hotbed for up-and-coming rock bands and a burgeoning jazz scene.

Business growth continues apace in Canada's third largest city, much of its prosperity stemming from a **port** that handles more dry tonnage than Seattle, Tacoma, Portland, San Francisco, and San Diego together. The port owes its prominence to Vancouver's much-trumpeted position as a **gateway to the Far East**, and its increasingly pivotal role in the new global market of the Pacific Rim. This lucrative realignment is strengthened by a two-way flow in traffic: in the past decade Vancouver has been inundated with Hong Kong Chinese (the so-called "yacht people"), an influx that has pushed up property prices and slightly strained the city's reputation as an ethnically integrated metropolis.

Much of the city's earlier immigration focused on Vancouver's extraordinary **Chinatown**, just one of a number of ethnic enclaves – Italian, Greek, Indian, and Japanese in particular – which lend the city a refreshingly gritty quality that belies its sleek, modern reputation. Low rents and Vancouver's cosmopolitan young have also nurtured an unexpected **counterculture**, at least for the time being, distinguished by varied restaurants, secondhand shops, avant-garde galleries, clubs, and bars – spots where you'll probably have more fun than in many a Canadian city

Some history

Vancouver, in the modern sense, has existed for a little over 110 years. Over the course of the previous nine thousand years the Fraser Valley was home to the **Tsawwassen**, **Musqueam**, and another twenty or so native tribes, who made up the **Stó:lo Nation**, or "people of the river." The fish, particularly salmon, of this river were the Stó:lo lifeblood. Venturing relatively little over the millennia into the mountainous interior, the Stó:lo inhabited about ten villages on the shores of Vancouver's Burrard Inlet before the coming of the Europeans. A highly developed culture, the Stó:lo were skilled carpenters, canoe-makers, and artists, though little in the present city – outside its museums – pays anything but lip service to their existence; Vancouver Island is the best bet if you're in search of latter-day tokens of aboriginal culture.

Europeans first appeared on the scene in notable numbers in the eighteenth century, when **Spanish** explorers charted the waters along what is now southwestern British Columbia. In 1778, **Captain James Cook** reached nearby Nootka Sound while searching for the Northwest Passage, sparking off immediate British interest in the area. In 1791, José Maria Narvaez, a Spanish pilot and surveyor, glimpsed the mouth of the Fraser from his ship, the *Santa Saturnia*. His appearance led to wrangles between the British and Spanish, disputes quickly settled in Britain's favor when Spain became domestically embroiled in the aftermath of the French Revolution. **Captain George Vancouver** officially claimed the land for Britain in 1792, but, after studying the Fraser from a small boat, decided that it seemed too shallow to be of practical use. Instead, he rounded a headland to the north, sailing into a deep natural port – the future site of Vancouver – which he named Burrard after one of his fellow seafarers. He then traded briefly with several Squamish tribespeople at X'ay'xi, a village on the inlet's forested headland – the future Stanley Park. Afterwards the Squamish named the spot Whul-whul-Lay-ton, or "place of the white man." Vancouver sailed on, having spent just a day in the region – scant homage to an area that was to be named after him a century later.

Vancouver's error over the Fraser was uncovered in 1808, when Scottish-born **Simon Fraser** made an epic 1368-kilometre journey down the river from the Rockies to the sea. In 1827, the Hudson's Bay Company set up a fur-trading post at **Fort Langley**, 48km east of the present city, bartering not only furs but also salmon from the Stó:lo, the latter being salted and then packed off to company forts across Canada. The fort was kept free of homesteaders, despite being the area's first major white settlement, their presence deemed detrimental to the fur trade. Major colonization of the area only came after the Fraser River and Cariboo gold rushes in 1858, when **New Westminster** bustled

The telephone code for Vancouver is ☎604.

with the arrival of as many as 25,000 hopefuls, many of whom were refugees from the 1849 Californian rush. Many also drifted in from the US, underlining the fragility of the national border and the precarious nature of British claims to the region. These claims were consolidated when British Columbia was declared a crown colony, with New Westminster as its capital. Both were superseded by **Fort Victoria** in 1868, by which time the gold rush had dwindled almost to nothing.

In 1862, meanwhile, three British prospectors, unable to find gold in the interior, bought a strip of land on the southern shore of Burrard Inlet and – shortsightedly, given the amount of lumber around – started a brickworks. This soon gave way to the Hastings Sawmill and a shantytown of bars which by 1867 had taken the name of **Gastown**, after "Gassy" – as in loquacious – **Jack Leighton**, proprietor of the site's first saloon. Two years later, Gastown became incorporated as the town of **Granville** and prospered on the back of its timber and small coal deposits. The birth of the present city dates to 1884, when the **Canadian Pacific Railway** decided to make it the terminus of its transcontinental railway. In 1886, on a whim of the CPR president, Granville was renamed Vancouver, only to be destroyed on June 13 that year when fire razed all but half a dozen buildings. The setback proved short-lived, and, since the arrival of the first train from Montréal in 1887, the city has never looked back.

Arrival

Linked to almost every major city in the world, **Vancouver's International Airport** receives 13 million visitors a year, making it the second busiest in Canada (after Toronto). The city's **bus and train station**, Pacific Central, is located southeast of Downtown and links it to many Canadian and a few American cities. Those arriving in **by car** will find Vancouver's network of one-way streets provides ample challenge, and the city rather congested, especially at rush hours.

By air

Vancouver International Airport (Ⓣ604/207-7077, Ⓦwww.yvr.ca) is situated on Sea Island, 13km south of Downtown. International flights arrive at the majestic new main terminal; domestic flights at the smaller and linked old Main Terminal. If you're an international passenger, you'll find a **tourist information** desk (daily 7am–midnight; Ⓣ604/688-5515) as you exit customs and immigration, and before entering the terminal's public spaces. On the left, before you exit to the public spaces, are desks for direct bus services from the airport to Victoria (Pacific Coach Lines) and Whistler (there are also services for Bellingham Airport (Seattle) and Sea-Tac Airport in the US available outside Arrivals: see below). Domestic passengers also have a tourist information desk just before the terminal exit.

The best way to get into Vancouver is on the private **Airporter bus** (6.45am–1.10am; $12, $18 round-trip; Ⓣ604/946-8866 or 1-800/668-3141, Ⓦwww.yvrairporter.com), which leaves every fifteen minutes; domestic arrivals can walk here if you need visitor information or wait at the domestic arrivals pick-up outside the terminal. Note that if you're headed straight for the bus depot (see below) on route #3 you need to transfer to another Airporter service closer to Downtown: the driver will tell you all you need to know.

Departure tax

All passengers departing from Vancouver International Airport must pay an **Airport Improvement Fee** – $5 if traveling within BC, $10 within North America (including Mexico and Hawaii) and $15 outside North America. The tax is levied as you pass through to the gates and must be paid on the spot with cash or credit. Save time by pre-paying at the automatic machines dotted around the various check-in areas.

Returning to the airport, buses run round the same pick-up points, including the bus depot.

Taxis into town cost about $25–30, limos $41.73. **Public transport** is cheaper but slower and involves a change of bus – take the BC Metro Transit bus #100 to the corner of 70th Street and Granville (it leaves the domestic terminal roughly every 30min), then change to the #20 or #21 which drops off Downtown on Granville Street. Tickets cost $3 during rush hour, $2 off-peak (weekdays after 6.30pm, Sat & Sun and all public holidays), and exact change is required to buy tickets on board. Make sure you get a transfer if the driver doesn't automatically give you one (see "City transportation" overleaf for more on peak and off-peak times and transfers).

You can pick up direct **buses to Victoria** from the airport. Ask for details at the bus desk in international arrivals, or head straight to the hotel shuttle bus stop outside the international terminal. Pacific Coach Lines (Ⓣ604/662-8074 or 1-800/661-1725, Ⓦwww.pacificcoach.com) runs between one and three daily direct services from the airport to Victoria depending on the time of year (1–3 daily year-round; 2–4 daily mid-May to late June and early Sept to Oct; 7 daily late June to early Sept; $36 single, $71 return).

By bus

Vancouver's main **bus terminal** at 1150 Station St is used by Pacific Coach Lines (Ⓣ604/662-7575, Ⓦwww.pacificcoach.com) for Victoria; Maverick Coach Lines (Ⓣ604/940-2332, Ⓦwww.maverickcoachlines.bc.ca) for Whistler, the Sunshine Coast, and Nanaimo; and all Greyhound services (Ⓣ604/482-8747, Ⓦwww.greyhound.ca). It's too far to walk to Downtown from here, so bear left from the station through a small park, to the Science World–Main St SkyTrain station and it's a couple of stops to the city center. Take the train marked "Waterfront"; tickets ($2) are available from platform machines. Alternatively, you can take a taxi Downtown from the station for about $6–8. There are **left-luggage** facilities here and a useful **hotel board**, whose freephone line connects to some of the city's genuine cheapies (but check locations) – some of whom will deduct the taxi fare from the terminal from your first night's bill.

By train

The skeletal **VIA Rail** services operate out of Pacific Central Station (Ⓣ604/640-3741 or 1-800/561-8630, Ⓦwww.viarail.ca); they run to and from Jasper (3 weekly), where there are connections for Prince George and Prince Rupert, and on to Edmonton and the east (3 weekly). VIA–Amtrak (Ⓣ253/931-8917 or 1-800/872-7245, Ⓦwww.amtrak.com) operates one train a day between Vancouver and Seattle.

Information

The excellent **Tourist InfoCentre** (mid-May–Sept daily 8am–6pm; Sept–May Mon–Sat 8.30am–5pm; Ⓣ604/683-2000 or 1-800/663-6000, Ⓦwww.tourismvancouver.com) can be found almost opposite Canada Place (see p.423) in the Waterfront Centre, 200 Burrard St at the corner of Canada Place Way. Besides information on the city and much of southeastern British Columbia, the office provides **foreign exchange** facilities, BC TransLink (transit or public transport) tickets and information, and tickets to sports and entertainment events through a separate Ticketmaster booth. Same-day tickets for events are also often available at a discount. It also has one of the most comprehensive **accommodation services**, backed up by bulging photo albums of hotel rooms and B&Bs: the booking service is free. Smaller kiosks open in the summer (July & Aug) in a variety of locations, usually including Stanley Park and close to the Vancouver Art Gallery on the corner of Georgia and Granville (daily 9.30am–5.30pm, Thurs & Fri till 9pm).

City transportation

Vancouver's **public transport** system is an efficient, integrated network of bus, light-rail (SkyTrain), SeaBus, and ferry services, which are operated by **TransLink** (daily 6.30am–11.30pm; Ⓣ604/953-3333 or customer relations Ⓣ604/953-3040, Ⓦwww.translink.bc.ca).

Tickets are valid across the system for bus, SkyTrain, and SeaBus. Generally they cost $2 for journeys in the large, central Zone 1 and $3 or $4 for longer two- and three-zone journeys – though you're unlikely to go out of Zone 1 unless you're travelling to the airport from Downtown which involves crossing from Zone 1 to 2. These regular fares apply Monday to Friday from start of service until 6.30pm. After 6.30pm and all day Saturday, Sunday, and public holidays, a flat $2 fare applies across all three zones.

Tickets are valid for **transfers** throughout the system for ninety minutes from the time of issue; on buses you should ask for a transfer ticket if the driver doesn't automatically give you one. Otherwise, you can buy tickets individually (or in books of ten for $18 for Zone 1) at station offices or machines, 7-Eleven, Safeway, and London Drugs stores, or any other shop or newsstand displaying a blue TransLink sticker (so-called "FareDealer" outlets). You must carry tickets with you as proof of payment. Probably the simplest and cheapest deal if you're going to be making three or more journeys in a day is to buy a **DayPass** ($8), valid all day across all three zones; Zone 1 monthly passes are $63. If you buy these over the counter at stores or elsewhere (not in machines) they're "Scratch & Ride" – you scratch out the day and month before travel. If you lose anything on the transport system go to the **lost property** office at the SkyTrain Stadium Station (Mon–Fri 8.30am–5pm; Ⓣ604/682-7887 or 985-7777 for items left on West Van buses).

If you don't wish to use public transport, **car and bicycle rental** and **taxis** are easy to come by – see "Listings" on p.458 for details.

Buses

The useful *Transit Route Map & Guide* ($1.95) is available from the infocentre and FareDealer shops, while free **bus** timetables can be found at the

Bus routes

Major routes

#1 Gastown–English Bay loop.

#3 and #8 Gastown–Downtown Robson at Granville–Marine Drive at Main.

#4 UBC and #10 UBC Granville Street–University of British Columbia–Museum of Anthropology.

#17 and #20 Downtown–Marine Drive; transfer to #100 for the airport at Granville and 70th Street.

#19 Pender Street (Downtown)–Stanley Park (Stanley Park Loop).

#23, #35, #123 and #135 Downtown (Pender and Burrard)–Stanley Park.

#50 Gastown – False Creek–Broadway.

#51 SeaBus Terminal–Downtown–Granville Island.

#236 Lonsdale Quay terminal (North Vancouver)–Capilano Suspension Bridge–Grouse Mountain.

Scenic routes

#52 "Around the Park" service takes 30min through Stanley Park (April–Oct Sat, Sun & holidays only); board at Stanley Park Loop (connections from #23, #35, or #135) or Denman Street (connections from #1, #3, or #8).

#210 Pender Street–Phibbs Exchange; change there for the #211 (mountain route) or #212 (ocean views) to Deep Cove.

#250 Georgia Street (Downtown)–North Vancouver–West Vancouver–Horseshoe Bay.

#351 Howe Street–White Rock–Crescent Beach (1hr each way).

infocentre, 7-Eleven stores, and the central library. You can buy tickets on the bus, but make sure you have the right change (they don't carry any); be sure to ask specially if you want a transfer ticket. Normal buses stop running around midnight, when a rather patchy "Night Owl" service comes into effect on major routes until about 4am. Note that blue **West Van** buses (Ⓣ604/985-7777) also operate (usually to North and West Vancouver destinations, including the BC Ferries terminal at Horseshoe Bay) in the city and BC Transit tickets are valid on these buses as well. The box above shows some of Vancouver's more useful routes.

SeaBuses and ferries

SeaBuses ply between Downtown and Lonsdale Quay in North Vancouver, and they're a ride definitely worth taking for its own sake: the views of the mountains across Burrard Inlet, the port, and the Downtown skyline are superb. The **Downtown terminal** is Waterfront Station in the old Canadian Pacific station buildings at the foot of Granville Street. There is no ticket office, only a ticket machine, but you can get a ticket from the small newsagent immediately on your left as you face the long gallery that takes you to the boats. Two 400-seat catamarans make the thirteen-minute crossing every fifteen to thirty minutes (6.30am–12.30am). Arrival in North Vancouver is at Lonsdale Quay, where a bus terminal offers connections to Grouse Mountain and other North Vancouver destinations. Bicycles can be carried onboard.

The city also has a variety of small **ferries** – glorified bathtubs – run over similar routes by two rival companies: Aquabus (Ⓣ604/689-5858, Ⓦwww.aquabus.bc.ca) and False Creek Ferries (Ⓣ604/684-7781,

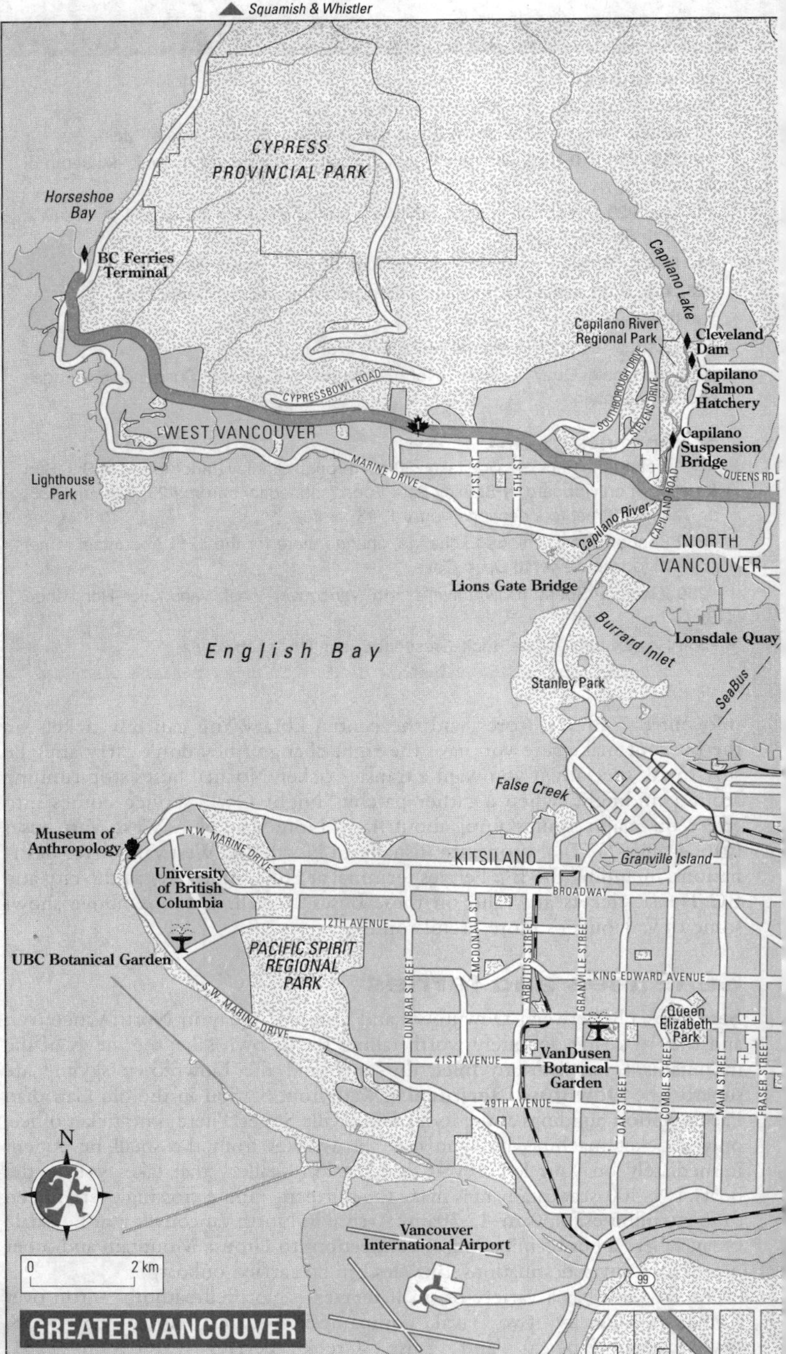

Squamish & Whistler
CYPRESS PROVINCIAL PARK
Horseshoe Bay
BC Ferries Terminal
Capilano Lake
Capilano River Regional Park
Cleveland Dam
Capilano Salmon Hatchery
Capilano Suspension Bridge
CYPRESSBOWL ROAD
SOUTHBOROUGH DRIVE
STEVENS DRIVE
WEST VANCOUVER
MARINE DRIVE
21ST ST
15TH ST
QUEENS RD
CAPILANO ROAD
Capilano River
Lighthouse Park
NORTH VANCOUVER
Lions Gate Bridge
Burrard Inlet
Lonsdale Quay
English Bay
Stanley Park
SeaBus
False Creek
Museum of Anthropology
N.W. MARINE DRIVE
KITSILANO
Granville Island
University of British Columbia
BROADWAY
12TH AVENUE
MCDONALD ST
ARBUTUS STREET
GRANVILLE STREET
UBC Botanical Garden
PACIFIC SPIRIT REGIONAL PARK
KING EDWARD AVENUE
DUNBAR STREET
S.W. MARINE DRIVE
Queen Elizabeth Park
41ST AVENUE
VanDusen Botanical Garden
49TH AVENUE
OAK STREET
COMBIE STREET
MAIN STREET
FRASER STREET
N
Vancouver International Airport
0
2 km
99
GREATER VANCOUVER
Tsawwassen Ferry Terminal

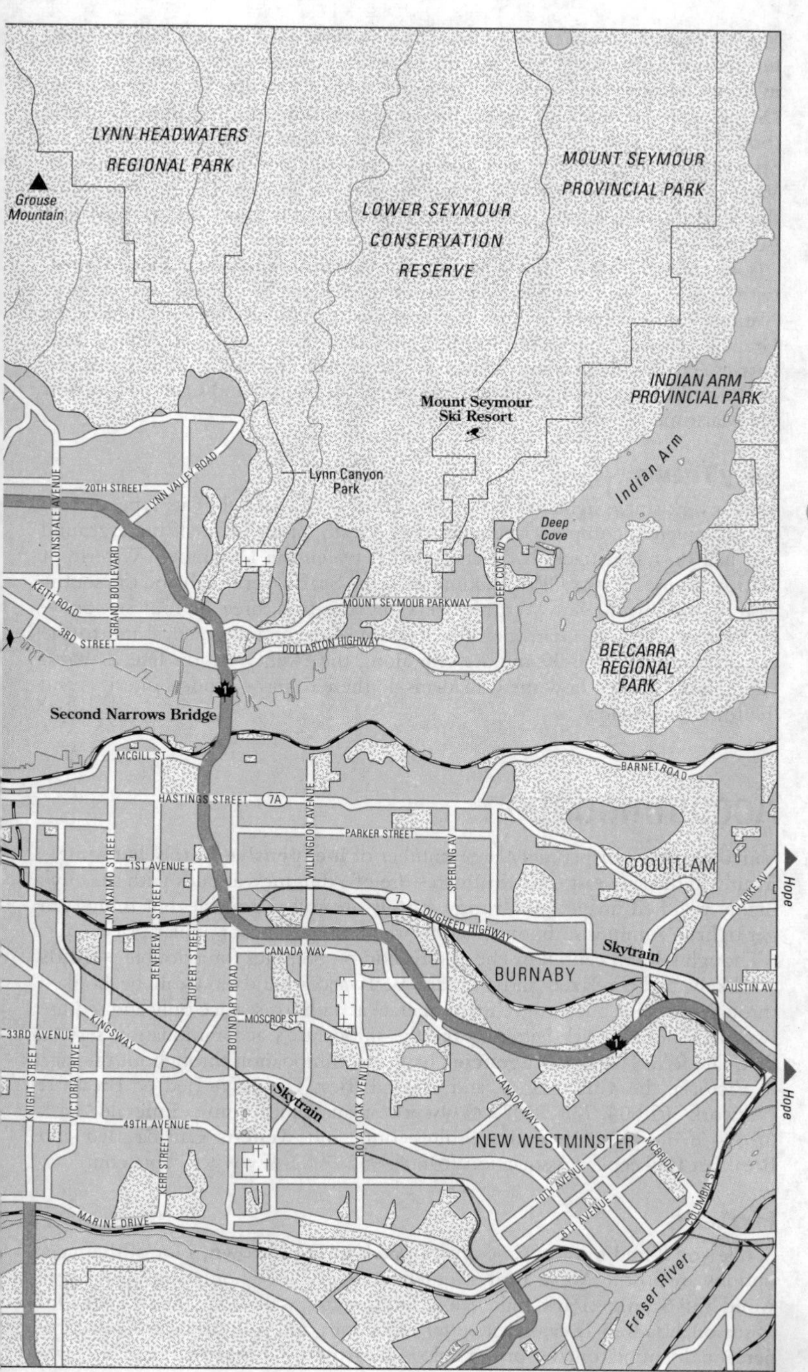
LYNN HEADWATERS REGIONAL PARK
Grouse Mountain
LOWER SEYMOUR CONSERVATION RESERVE
MOUNT SEYMOUR PROVINCIAL PARK
INDIAN ARM PROVINCIAL PARK
Mount Seymour Ski Resort
Indian Arm
Lynn Canyon Park
Deep Cove
20TH STREET
LYNN VALLEY ROAD
LONSDALE AVENUE
GRAND BOULEVARD
KEITH ROAD
3RD STREET
MOUNT SEYMOUR PARKWAY
DEEP COVE RD
DOLLARTON HIGHWAY
BELCARRA REGIONAL PARK
Second Narrows Bridge
MCGILL ST
BARNET ROAD
HASTINGS STREET
7A
WILLINGDON AVENUE
PARKER STREET
SPERLING AV
COQUITLAM
Hope
NANAIMO STREET
1ST AVENUE E
RENFREW STREET
RUPERT STREET
7
LOUGHEED HIGHWAY
CLARKE AV
Skytrain
CANADA WAY
BURNABY
AUSTIN AV
BOUNDARY ROAD
MOSCROP ST
33RD AVENUE
KINGSWAY
KNIGHT STREET
VICTORIA DRIVE
ROYAL OAK AVENUE
CANADA WAY
Skytrain
Hope
49TH AVENUE
NEW WESTMINSTER
MCBRIDE AV
KERR STREET
10TH AVENUE
COLUMBIA ST
6TH AVENUE
MARINE DRIVE
Fraser River

Ⓦ www.granvilleislandferries.bc.ca). These provide a useful, very frequent, and fun service daily 7am–10.30pm (until 8.30pm in winter). Aquabus runs boats in a continuous circular shuttle from the foot of Hornby Street to the Fish Docks on the seawalk to Vanier Park and the museums, to Granville Island (both $2), and to the Yaletown dock by the road loop at the east foot of Davie Street ($3). False Creek Ferries also runs to Granville Island ($2), and also to Vanier Park ($3 from Granville Island, $2 from the Aquatic Centre) just below the Maritime Museum – a good way of getting to the park and its museums (see p.436).

Both companies also offer what amount to **mini-cruises up False Creek**, with connections from Granville Island to Science World and the Plaza of Nations. You can pick up the Aquabus boat at the Arts Club Theatre on Granville Island, the foot of Hornby Street Downtown or – with False Creek Ferries – below the Aquatic Centre at the foot of Thurlow and northern end of Burrard Bridge, on Granville Island or below the spit and small harbor near the Maritime Museum in Vanier Park.

SkyTrain

Vancouver's single light-rail line – **SkyTrain** – is a model of its type: driverless, completely computerized, and magnetically propelled, half underground and half on raised track. It covers 28km between the Downtown Waterfront Station (housed in the CPR building with the SeaBus terminal) and the southeastern suburb of New Westminster. Only the first three or four stations – Waterfront, Burrard, Granville, and Stadium – are of any practical use to the casual visitor, but the 39-minute trip along the twenty-station line is worth taking if only to see how the Canadians do these things – spotless interiors and Teutonic punctuality.

Accommodation

Vancouver has a surprisingly large number of **inexpensive hotels**, but some – mainly in the area east of Downtown – are of a dinginess at odds with the city's highly polished image. **Mid-range hotels** are still reasonable, but things can get tight in summer so book ahead for the best and most popular places.

Though seldom central or cheap – reckon on $80 plus for a double – **B&Bs** are likely to be relaxed and friendly. B&B accommodation can be booked through agencies, but most of them operate as a phone service only and require two-days' notice – it's better to try the infocentre's accommodation service first. The following **B&B agencies** have accommodation throughout the city, in Victoria, the Gulf Islands, and beyond: Best Canadian Bed & Breakfast Network (Ⓣ 604/738-7207, Ⓦ www.bestcanadianbb.com); Emerald Park (Ⓣ 604/878-1328, Ⓦ www.travelsuites.com); and Western Canada Bed and Breakfast Innkeepers' Association (Ⓣ 604/952-0982, Ⓦ www.wcbbia.com).

Hotels

While you'll find most of Vancouver's hotels in **Downtown**, a lot of the nicer options are in the **West End**, a quiet residential area bordering Vancouver's wonderful **Stanley Park**, only five or ten minutes' walk from Downtown. Out of season, hotels in all categories offer reductions, and you can reckon on thirty percent discounts on the prices below. **Gastown**, **Chinatown**, and the area between them hold the cheaper places, often on top of a bar where live bands and late-night drinking will keep you awake till the small hours. These areas are not safe for women at night, and everyone needs to avoid the backstreets.

Downtown

Barclay Hotel 1348 Robson St at Jervis ⓣ604/688-8850, ⓦwww.barclayhotel.com. This is one of the nicer of several hotels at the north end of Robson (see also the *Greenbriar* and *Robsonstrasse* below), about halfway between Stanley Park and the Vancouver Art Gallery. It features ninety rooms in several price categories (low-season rates are available) and a rather chintzy French rustic ambience in places. Given its rooms and facilities, which include a/c, a restaurant, and a licensed lounge, it's something of a bargain. ❹

Bosman's Hotel 1060 Howe St between Nelson and Helmcken ⓣ604/682-3171 or 1-888/267-6267, ⓦwww.bosmanshotel.com. As long as you don't want too many frills, this is a well-located hotel with free parking, restaurant, and lounge just two blocks from Robson. It has 102 modern, air-conditioned rooms (all with TVs) at a range of prices, but some look on to Howe, one of the city's busier streets, so even with double-glazing, traffic may be an issue here. There is, however, an outdoor swimming pool for use in summer. ❺

Burrard Motor Inn 1100 Burrard St near Helmcken ⓣ604/681-2331 or 1-800/663-0366, ⓦwww.vancouver-bc.com/burrardmotorinn. A pleasantly dated motel with standard fittings: eighteen of the seventy rooms have kitchen facilities for self-catering (you'll pay an extra $5 for these), making this a good bet for families; some rooms look onto a charming garden courtyard. The general location isn't as convenient as some Downtown hotels, but you are still just four blocks from Robson Street and from Yaletown to the east. Rooms have phone and TV; other facilities include a restaurant and free parking. ❹

Comfort Inn Downtown 654 Nelson St ⓣ604/605-4333 or 1-888/605-5333, ⓦwww.comfortinnDowntown.com. There have been lodgings of sorts in this heritage building for years, but after a 1950s retro-inspired refit, complete with lots of black and white photographs and period neon – this boutique hotel now has a hip and stylish look. Rooms all come with high-speed Internet access, voicemail, dataports, and a/c. The room price includes a continental breakfast in *Doolin's Irish Pub*, and a pass to three clubs (*Roxy*, *BaBaLu*, and *Fred's Uptown Tavern*) owned by the same management. The location is convenient for the restaurant and clubs of both Yaletown and the lower end of Granville St. ❺

Dufferin Hotel 900 Seymour St ⓣ604/683-4251 or 1-877/683-5522, ⓦwww.dufferinhotel.com. Not far from the preferable *Kingston* (see below), the *Dufferin* tends to pick up its overflow. It's not as calm, cheap, or pleasant as its rival, but does offer free parking, dining room, and a choice of family rooms, and rooms with and without private bathrooms. Noise and late-night bustle can be an issue here, as there is a (predominantly gay, but straight-friendly) pub on the premises. ❹

The Fairmont Hotel Vancouver 900 W Georgia St at Burrard ⓣ604/684-3131 or 1-800/441-1414, ⓦwww.fairmont.com. This venerable but thoroughly renovated 1939 hotel is Vancouver's most famous and prestigious. It is the one to go for if money's no object and you want more traditional old-world style than some of the city's world-class hotels, a Downtown location, and all the refinements (spa, fitness center, pool, and so on) and attention to detail you'd expect in a hotel of this class. Doubles range from around $269 to $589, but low-season rates (down to about $190) are available. ❾

The Fairmont Waterfront 900 Canada Place Way ⓣ604/691-1991 or 1-800/441-1414, ⓦwww.fairmont.com. This fabulous 489-room, multistory affair on the dazzling Downtown waterfront boasts an unbeatable location, especially if you have a room with a view. As in the Vancouver, the open-to-the-lobby restaurant and bar is a good place to eat or drink even if you're not staying here. Guests can use the health center or third-floor heated outdoor pool, fringed by a herb garden whose produce is used in the hotel's restaurant, distinguished by huge floor-to-ceiling windows looking out over Coal Harbour. Doubles range from $295 to $625, with low-season rates available. ❽

Greenbriar Hotel 1393 Robson St at Broughton ⓣ604/683-4558 or 1-888/355-5888, ⓦwww.greenbriarhotel.com. The *Greenbriar* stands on a pleasant city block between Stanley Park and the heart of Downtown. Though nothing great to look at, the interior of this former apartment block has been nicely transformed into a variety of 32 one-bed and family suites with neat, modern decor and the option of fully equipped kitchens. Many rooms have sea and mountain views, and there's free parking, but Robson is busy day and night, so this isn't the most tranquil of locations. There's a $40 range from the cheapest to most expensive double. ❻

Kingston Hotel 757 Richards St at Robson ☎604/684-9024 or 1-888/713-3304, ⓦwww.kingstonhotelvancouver.com. One of Vancouver's best-known bargains, the *Kingston* is well run, clean, safe, and handily situated on the eastern edge of Downtown. Its well-decorated interior successfully affects the warm and comfortable look and feel of a European-style hotel, though its 55 rooms are fairly small and standard in appearance. Nine have private bathrooms and TVs, while the rest have a phone (no TV), washbasin, and share good bathrooms at the end of each corridor. There's also a coin laundry and a modest but free breakfast to start the day. Off-street parking is available half a block away from $10 a day. Book well ahead. ❸

Riviera Hotel 431 Robson St at Nicola ☎604/685-1301 or 1-888/699-5222, ⓦwww.rivieraonrobson.com. More towards the Stanley Park than Vancouver Art Gallery end of Robson, the *Riviera* started life in the 1960s as an apartment building, but has been converted into a hotel with thirteen large studios and 27 twin-room/one-bedroom suites. All have well-equipped kitchens and balconies, with great harbor and mountain views from the rear (north-facing) side of the building. ❻

Robsonstrasse City Motor Inn 1394 Robson St at Broughton ☎604/687-1674 or 1-888/667-8877, ⓦwww.robsonstrassehotel.com. Like the nearby *Greenbriar*, this hotel, midway between Stanley Park and the center of Downtown, has a variety of double rooms and suites with kitchenettes at a wide range of prices. It's also air-conditioned, and offers free parking and a guest laundry. ❺

Sandman Hotel Downtown 180 W Georgia at Homer ☎604/681-2211 or 1-800/726-3626, ⓦwww.sandman.ca. This large hotel is the flagship of a reliable mid-price chain with hotels all over western Canada, and is well placed at the eastern edge of Downtown. The renovated rooms are bland but comfortable in the manner of chain hotels, and are well equipped and rather spacious: all have a/c and some have kitchenettes. Underground parking is available and residents have access to an indoor swimming pool, whirlpool, and health club. The ground floor hosts the popular *Shark Club Bar & Grill* (see p.451). Low-season rates are available. ❹

Gastown and Chinatown

Budget Inn-Patricia Hotel 403 E Hastings St at Dunlevy Ave ☎604/255-4301 or 1-888/926-1017, ⓦwww.budgetpathotel.bc.ca. This 92-room hotel is well known among backpackers and budget travelers, and is widely advertised across Vancouver. However, the six-story building is located a long way from Downtown in the heart of Chinatown (certainly too far to walk comfortably). The hotel itself is clean, well run, in relatively good condition, and the best of the many generally awful places in this district. Rooms are available in several price categories, and rates include a good breakfast at a nearby café. Free parking is available. ❸

Dominion Hotel 210 Abbott St ☎604/681-6666 or 1-877/681-1666, ⓦwww.dominionhotel.bc.ca. This is a nice, well-kept old hotel on the edge of Gastown, but it forms part of a popular pub and restaurant. Rooms come with phones (no TVs) and shared or private bathrooms, and if possible you should request one of the more recently renovated rooms with private bathroom well away from the live music. ❸

Victorian Hotel 514 Homer St on the corner of Pender ☎604/681-6369 or 1-877/681-6369, ⓦwww.victorianhotel.com. The family-run *Victorian* is situated about as far east as you'd want, but remains within easy walking distance of Gastown and the rest of Downtown. It was built in 1898 as one of the city's first guest-houses, and has been carefully restored, and many of its rooms have high ceilings, hardwood floors, elegant bathrooms, and period features such as original fireplaces and moldings. Prices vary by up to $60 between double rooms, depending on whether they have private bathrooms and/or kitchenettes. All rooms have phones and small TVs; continental breakfast is included. ❹

Stanley Park and the West End

Buchan Hotel 1906 Haro St at Robson and Denman ☎604/685-5354 or 1-800/668-6654, ⓦwww.buchanhotel.com. Some of the 61 rooms in this 1926 three-story building are smallish and only half boast private bathrooms, but all are clean and priced accordingly (there's a $60 range from top to bottom for rooms of differing standards here). Try for rooms on the east side, which are brighter and overlook a small park, or the four "executive" front-corner rooms, which are well furnished and the best in the house. On a quiet tree-lined West End, the hotel is not convenient for walking to Downtown; pick-up and drop-off for the airport shuttle (see p.412) is a five-minute walk away. Facilities include a laundry and in-house bike and ski storage, and rooms have TV but no phones. Children under 12 stay free in their parents' room. ❸.

Shato Inn Hotel at Stanley Park 1825 Comox St between Denman and Gilford ⓣ604/681-8920. If you can't get into the *Sylvia* (see below), then the *Shato* lies just a block to the northeast. It's a quiet, family-run place convenient to Stanley Park and the beach. All rooms have phones and TVs, and some have balconies and/or kitchen units. Underground parking is available. ❺

Sylvia Hotel 1154 Gilford St ⓣ604/681-9321, ⓦwww.sylviahotel.com. Located in a 1912 greystone, the *Sylvia* is an ivy-covered local landmark that stands on English Bay virtually on the beach two blocks from Stanley Park, and its snug bar, quiet, friendly service, restaurant (with outdoor terrace for summer dining), old-world charm, and sea views make it one of Vancouver's best in its price range. It's also a perennially popular place, making reservations for one of its 119 rooms essential. If you can, angle for one of the more expensive south- or southwest-facing rooms – they have the best views of English Bay and the sunset. Low-season rates are available between October and May. ❹–❼

Hostels

Vancouver has three good Hostelling International **hostels**, plus a handful of other reasonable privately run hostels. Be warned, though, that there are a rash of dreadful "hotels," "hostels," and "rooming houses" (dirty, badly run, and occasionally dangerous), particularly on Hastings Street a few blocks either side of Main Street: don't be tempted into these on any account.

Cambie International Hostel Gastown 300 Cambie St at Cordova ⓣ604/684-6466 or 1-888/395-5335, ⓦwww.cambiehostels.com. Just off Gastown's main streets, the *Cambie* has a much nicer and more central position than many of the city's hostels. Beds are arranged in two-, four- or six-bed bunkrooms and there are laundry, luggage-storage, and bike-storage (but no cooking) facilities. There's a deservedly popular and inexpensive bar-grill with good patio downstairs, so aim for beds away from this area if you want a relatively peaceful night's sleep. No curfew. $20 per person in a dorm room ($17.50 Oct–April); private, double, or quad rooms $22.50 person ($20 offseason). Weekly rates available.

Vancouver Central Hostel (HI) 1025 Granville St ⓣ604/685-5335 or 1-888/203-8333, ⓦwww.hihostels.ca. Vancouver's newest and smartest HI hostel offers 226 beds in private double rooms with TV and en-suite bathrooms, four-bed dorms, and a/c in most rooms. Family rooms are also available. Facilities include a kitchen, pub, reading lounge, and shuttle runs to the other city HI hostels and the Pacific Central Station. Check-in is at noon and checkout 11am. Dorm beds start at $20 for members and $24 for non-members. Private doubles start at $57.

Vancouver Downtown Hostel (HI) 1114 Burnaby St at the corner of Thurlow ⓣ604/684-4565 or 1-888/203-4302, ⓦwww.hihostels.ca. There are 223 beds here, split up between shared and private rooms (maximum of four per room). Bike rental and storage as well as laundry, kitchen, Internet access, and storage lockers are available. A free shuttle operates between this hostel, the *Jericho Beach Hostel* (see below), and the Pacific Central railway and bus terminal; if there's no bus, call the hostel to find when the next one is due. No curfew. Check-in 24 hours a day; reservations essential. Beds cost $20 for members ($24 for non-members), private doubles $55 for members, $64 for non-members.

Vancouver Jericho Beach Hostel (HI) 1515 Discovery St off MW Marine Drive ⓣ604/224-3208 or 1-888/203-4852, ⓦwww.hihostels.ca. The 286-bed hostel fills up quickly, occasionally leading to a three-day limit in summer. There are dorm beds and ten private rooms (sleep up to six), which go quickly, with reductions for members and free bunks occasionally offered in return for a couple of hours' work. Family rooms are available. Facilities include kitchen, licensed café (April–Oct), bike rental and storage, storage lockers, Internet access, and an excellent cafeteria. There is no curfew, but a "quiet time" is encouraged between 11pm and 7am. Check-in 24 hours a day. Dorm beds cost $18 for members, $22 for non-members. Doubles are $51 for members, $61 for non-members.

YWCA Hotel-Residence 733 Beatty St between Georgia and Robson ⓣ604/895-5830 or 1-800/663-1424, ⓦwww.ywcahotel.com. Vancouver's excellent 'Y' offers the best inexpensive accommodation in the city. The nearest SkyTrain station is Stadium, a five-minute walk. There are no dorm beds. TVs come with most rooms, plus there are sports and cooking facilities, Internet access, lounges, a/c, laundry rooms as well as a cheap cafeteria and rooms with mini-kitchens. Open to men, women, couples and families. Check-in is 3pm, checkout by 11am. Singles cost $49 (mid-Oct–April), $51 (May) and $57 (June–mid-Oct); doubles ($56, $64, and $69 with shared bathroom, $75, $98, and $113 with private bathroom). If you are in a group, or family, four-person rooms (two double beds) are also available from $84, $113, and $132, plus $5 for each additional adult.

Campsites

Vancouver is not a camper's city – the majority of the in-city **campsites** are for RVs only and will turn you away if you've only got a tent. We've listed the few places that won't.

Burnaby Cariboo RV Park 8765 Cariboo Place, Burnaby ⓣ 604/420-1722, ⓦ www.bcrvpark.com. This 237-pitch site about 16km east of the city center has luxurious facilities (indoor pool, Jacuzzi, laundry, free showers, and convenience store) and a separate tenting area away from the RVs (for which there are full hook-up facilities). Take the Gaglardi Way exit (#37) from Hwy-1, turn right at the traffic light, then immediately left. The next right is Cariboo Place. Open year-round. $25–39.50 per site.

Capilano RV Park 295 Tomahawk Ave, North Vancouver ⓣ 604/987-4722, ⓦ www.capilanorvpark.com. This is a pretty unattractive place but it is the city's most central site for trailers and tents, located beneath the north foot of the Lions Gate Bridge and a short walk from the Park Royal Shopping Centre: exit Capilano Rd S or Hwy-99 exit off Lions Gate Bridge. There are full RV facilities and hook-ups, plus swimming pool, free showers, washrooms and laundry, ice and water. Reservations (with deposit) essential June to August. $29.68–40.28 per site.

Park Canada Recreational Vehicles Inn 4799 Hwy-17, Delta ⓣ 604/943-5811 or 1-877/943-0685, ⓦ www.parkcanada.com. Convenient for the Tsawwassen ferry terminal to the southwest, this 145-pitch site has partial and three-way hook-ups for RVs and – despite the name – some separate tent sites. There are free showers, washrooms, laundry, heated pool, grocery store, and, if this is your thing, the site's right next to a waterslide and golf course. Tent sites $18.50, RV sites $21–27.50.

Peace Arch RV Park 14601-40 Ave, Surrey ⓣ 604/594-7009, ⓦ www.peacearchrvpark.com. Calling this a city campsite is a bit of a stretch as it's in Surrey about 30km southeast of Downtown near the junctions of Hwy-99 and the King George Highway. However, it's a good place to pause before hitting Vancouver if you've driven up from the US. There are 250 tent and RV sites with full hook-ups, a games room, and a swimming pool. $18.50–27.50 per site.

Richmond RV Park and Campground 6200 River Rd at Hollybridge and River Rd, Richmond ⓣ 604/270-7878, ⓦ www.richmondrvpark.com. Best of the RV outfits in terms of location, with the usual facilities (including free showers), but there are also tent sites; 14km from Downtown – take Hwy-99 N to the Westminster Hwy exit (#36) and follow the signs. April–Oct. $17–27 per site.

The City

You'll inevitably spend a good deal of time in the **Downtown** area and its Victorian-era neighbor, **Gastown**, now a renovated and less than convincing pastiche of its past. **Chinatown**, too, could easily absorb a morning, and contains more than its share of interesting shops, restaurants, and bustling streets. For a taste of the city's sensual side, hit **Stanley Park**, a huge area of semi-wild parkland and beaches that crowns the northern tip of the Downtown Peninsula. Take a walk or a bike ride here and follow it up with a stroll to the **beach**. Be certain to spend a morning on **Granville Island**, by far the city's most alluring spot for wandering and people watching. If you prefer a cultural slant, hit the formidable **Museum of Anthropology**, on the University of British Columbia campus, or the museums of the **Vanier Park** complex, easily accessible from Granville Island.

Trips across Burrard Inlet to **North Vancouver**, worth making for the views from the SeaBus ferry alone, lend a different panoramic perspective of the city, and lead into the mountains and forests that give Vancouver its tremendous setting. The most popular destinations here are the Capilano Suspension Bridge, something of a triumph of PR over substance, and the more worthwhile cable-car trip up **Grouse Mountain** for staggering views of the city.

Downtown

You soon get the hang of Vancouver's **Downtown**, an area of streets and shopping malls centered on **Robson Street**. On hot summer evenings it's a dynamic meeting place crammed with bars, restaurants, late-night stores, with preening bronzed youths ostentatiously cruising in open-topped cars. At other times, a more sedate class hangs out on the steps of the Vancouver Art Gallery or glides in and out of local department stores. Downtown's other principal thoroughfares are **Burrard Street** – all smart shops, hotels, and offices – and **Granville Street**, partly pedestrianized with plenty of shops and cinemas but seedy in places, especially at its southern end near the Granville Street Bridge. New development, however, is taking Downtown's reach farther east, and at some point in your stay you should take in the 1995 **public library**, at 350 W Georgia St, a focus of this growth and a striking piece of modern architecture to boot.

For the best introduction to Vancouver, stroll down to the waterfront and **Canada Place** (walkways open daily 24 hours; free; ⓣ604/775-7200, ⓦwww.canadaplace.ca). The Canadian pavilion for Expo '86, the huge world exhibition held in the city, this architectural tour de force houses a luxury hotel, a cruise-ship terminal, and two glitzy convention centers. It makes a superb viewpoint, with stunning vistas of the port, mountains, sea, helicopters, and float planes; the port activity, especially, is mesmerizing. Vancouver's port began by exporting timber in 1864 in the shape of fence pickets to Australia but today is one of North America's busiest, handling seventy million tons of cargo annually, turning over $40 billion in trade, and processing 3000 ships a year from almost a hundred countries. Canada Place's design and the manner in which it juts into the port are meant to suggest a ship, a nod to the vital role of the city's port both past and present. This visual allusion is reinforced by the building's most distinctive feature, the five great 27-metre-high Teflon-coated fabric "sails" that make up its roof, a motif continued by the vast hotel and convention center – the "mast" – which rises above the complex. Inside are expensive shops, an unexceptional restaurant, and an IMAX cinema ($9–16; ⓣ604/682-4629, 682-2384 or 1-800/582-4629, ⓦwww.imax.com/vancouver); unfortunately, most of the films shown – often on boats, rock concerts, and obscure wildlife – are a waste of a good screen.

An alternative to Canada Place's vantage point, the nearby **Harbour Centre Tower**, at 555 W Hastings St, (daily May–Sept 8.30am–10.30pm; Oct–April 9am–9pm; The Lookout! $10; ⓣ689-0421, ⓦwww.vancouverlookout.com), is one of the city's tallest structures. Opened by the first man on the moon, Neil Armstrong in 1977, it was the city's tallest building for a long time and known by locals as the "hamburger," after its bulging upper storys. On a fine day, it's definitely worth paying to ride the stomach-churning, all-glass, SkyLift elevators that run up the side of the tower – 167m in a minute – to the fortieth-story observation deck. This deck is known as "The Lookout!" and provides a glorious 360° view: free tours lasting between 25 and 45 minutes pointing out the city landmarks below are available every hour on the hour. Note that admission is valid all day so you can return and look out over the bright lights of Vancouver at night.

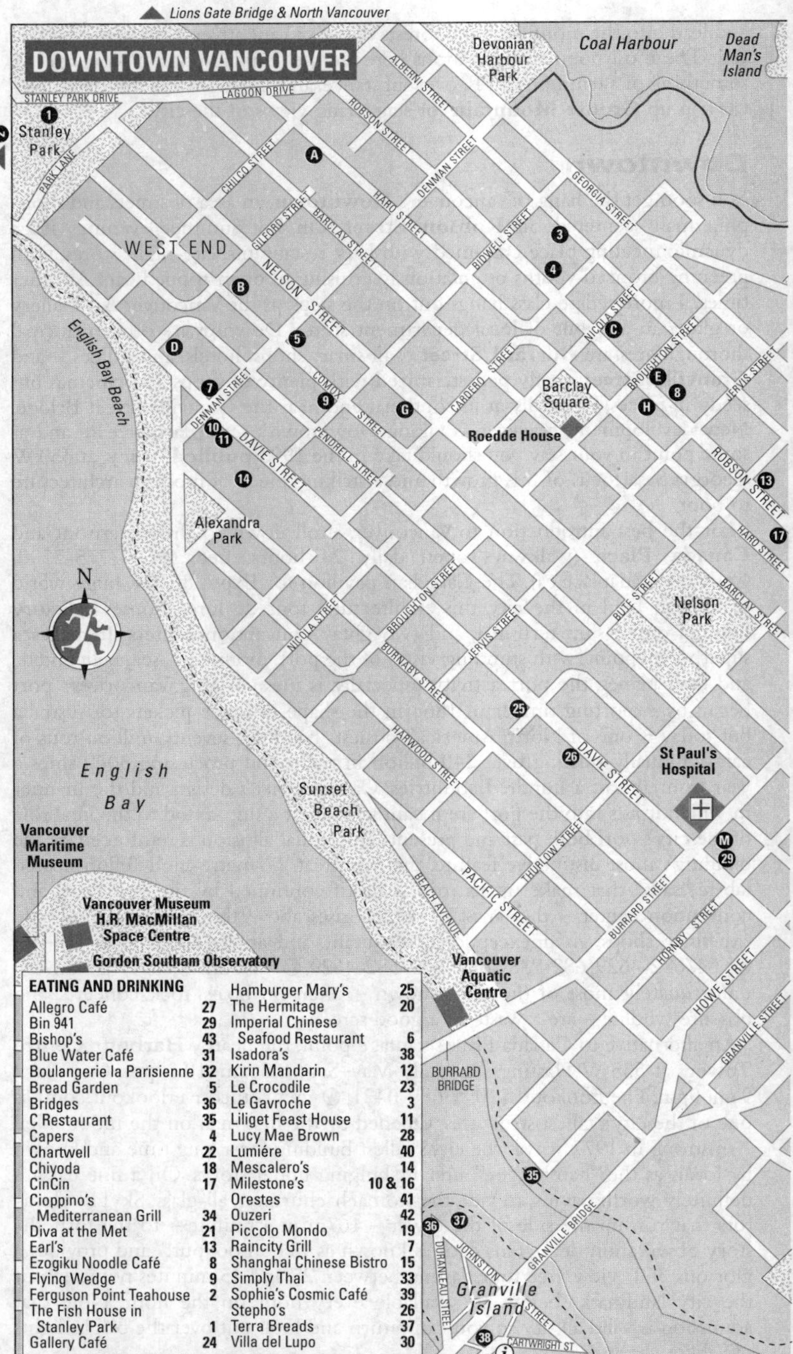

Lions Gate Bridge & North Vancouver
DOWNTOWN VANCOUVER
Stanley Park
Devonian Harbour Park
Coal Harbour
Dead Man's Island
STANLEY PARK DRIVE
LAGOON DRIVE
PARK LANE
ALBERNI STREET
ROBSON STREET
CHILCO STREET
DENMAN STREET
GEORGIA STREET
HARO STREET
GILFORD STREET
BARCLAY STREET
BIDWELL STREET
WEST END
NELSON STREET
NICOLA STREET
BROUGHTON STREET
JERVIS STREET
CARDERO STREET
COMOX STREET
Barclay Square
Roedde House
English Bay Beach
DAVIE STREET
PENDRELL STREET
Alexandra Park
BUTE STREET
Nelson Park
BURNABY STREET
HARWOOD STREET
St Paul's Hospital
English Bay
Sunset Beach Park
THURLOW STREET
PACIFIC STREET
BEACH AVENUE
BURRARD STREET
HORNBY STREET
HOWE STREET
GRANVILLE STREET
Vancouver Maritime Museum
Vancouver Museum
H.R. MacMillan Space Centre
Gordon Southam Observatory
Vancouver Aquatic Centre
BURRARD BRIDGE
GRANVILLE BRIDGE
DURANLEAU STREET
JOHNSTON STREET
Granville Island
CARTWRIGHT ST
39, 40, 41, 42, 43 & South Vancouver
EATING AND DRINKING
Allegro Café 27
Bin 941 29
Bishop's 43
Blue Water Café 31
Boulangerie la Parisienne 32
Bread Garden 5
Bridges 36
C Restaurant 35
Capers 4
Chartwell 22
Chiyoda 18
CinCin 17
Cioppino's Mediterranean Grill 34
Diva at the Met 21
Earl's 13
Ezogiku Noodle Café 8
Flying Wedge 9
Ferguson Point Teahouse 2
The Fish House in Stanley Park 1
Gallery Café 24
Hamburger Mary's 25
The Hermitage 20
Imperial Chinese Seafood Restaurant 6
Isadora's 38
Kirin Mandarin 12
Le Crocodile 23
Le Gavroche 3
Liliget Feast House 11
Lucy Mae Brown 28
Lumiére 40
Mescalero's 14
Milestone's 10 & 16
Orestes 41
Ouzeri 42
Piccolo Mondo 19
Raincity Grill 7
Shanghai Chinese Bistro 15
Simply Thai 33
Sophie's Cosmic Café 39
Stepho's 26
Terra Breads 37
Villa del Lupo 30

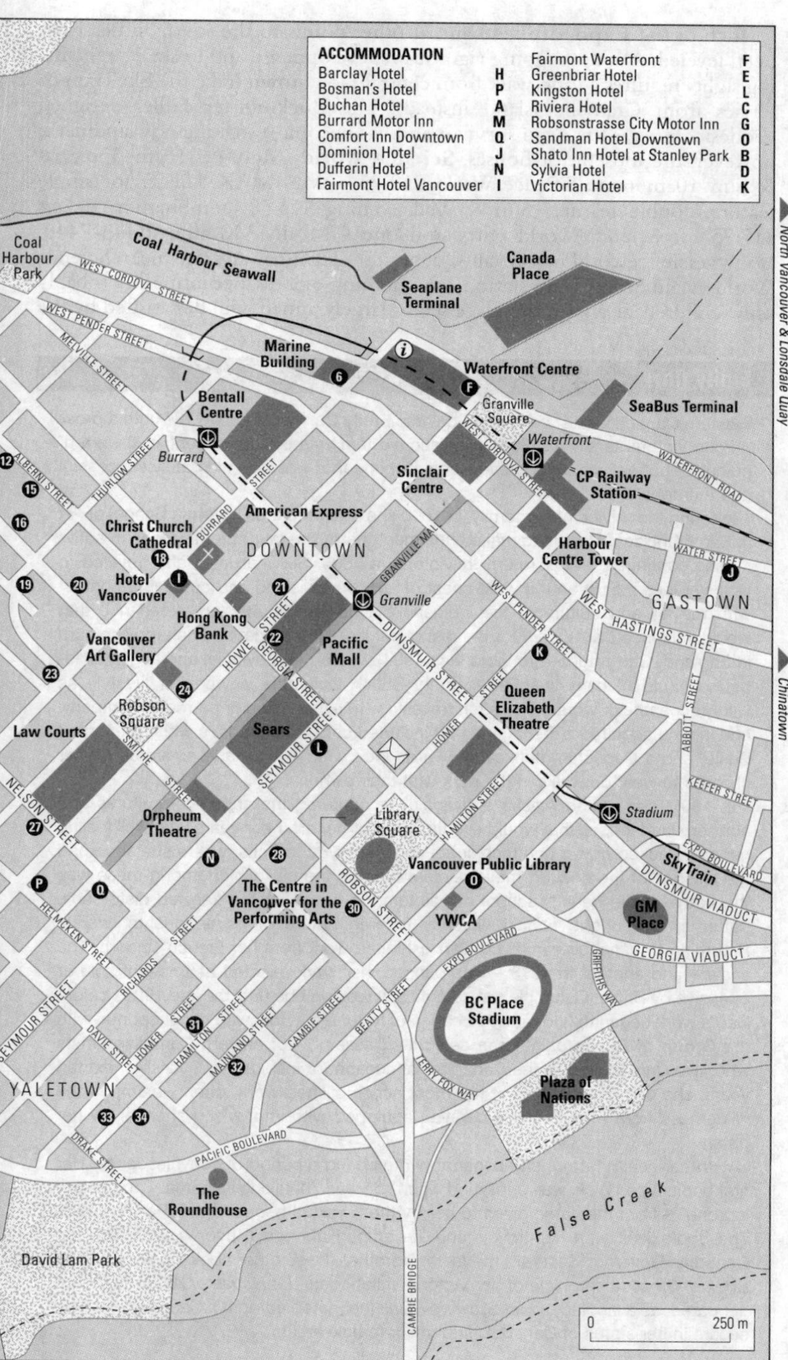
ACCOMMODATION
Barclay Hotel H
Bosman's Hotel P
Buchan Hotel A
Burrard Motor Inn M
Comfort Inn Downtown Q
Dominion Hotel J
Dufferin Hotel N
Fairmont Hotel Vancouver I
Fairmont Waterfront F
Greenbriar Hotel E
Kingston Hotel L
Riviera Hotel C
Robsonstrasse City Motor Inn G
Sandman Hotel Downtown O
Shato Inn Hotel at Stanley Park B
Sylvia Hotel D
Victorian Hotel K
Coal Harbour Park
Coal Harbour Seawall
West Cordova Street
West Pender Street
Melville Street
Canada Place
Seaplane Terminal
Marine Building
Waterfront Centre
Bentall Centre
Burrard
Granville Square
Waterfront
SeaBus Terminal
North Vancouver & Lonsdale Quay
Waterfront Road
CP Railway Station
Sinclair Centre
Thurlow Street
Alberni Street
Burrard Street
American Express
Christ Church Cathedral
DOWNTOWN
Granville Mall
Harbour Centre Tower
Water Street
GASTOWN
West Hastings Street
Hotel Vancouver
Granville
Hong Kong Bank
West Pender Street
Howe Street
Dunsmuir Street
Vancouver Art Gallery
Georgia Street
Pacific Mall
Chinatown
Robson Square
Law Courts
Smithe Street
Sears
Seymour Street
Homer Street
Queen Elizabeth Theatre
Abbott Street
Nelson Street
Keefer Street
Hamilton Street
Stadium
Orpheum Theatre
Library Square
Expo Boulevard
SkyTrain
Vancouver Public Library
Dunsmuir Viaduct
The Centre in Vancouver for the Performing Arts
Robson Street
YWCA
GM Place
Helmcken Street
Georgia Viaduct
Griffiths Way
Richards Street
Seymour Street
Davie Street
Homer Street
Hamilton Street
Mainland Street
Cambie Street
Beatty Street
BC Place Stadium
Terry Fox Way
Plaza of Nations
YALETOWN
Drake Street
Pacific Boulevard
The Roundhouse
False Creek
David Lam Park
Cambie Bridge
0
250 m
South Vancouver

Much of the **Expo site** here and at other points to the south and east has been leveled or is undergoing rigorous redevelopment, and to see its remaining sights requires a long walk from central Downtown (take the SkyTrain or ferries from Granville Island instead). The Buckminster Fuller–designed geodesic dome is the main survivor and has become a striking city landmark; however, the museum it houses, **Science World** (Mon–Fri 10am–5pm, Sat & Sun 10am–6pm; Science World $12.75, OMNIMAX $11.25 for single feature, double features Sun & Wed evening $13.50; combination tickets $17.75 for Science World entry and one OMNIMAX film; ⓣ443-7440, ⓦwww.scienceworld.bc.ca), at Québec St–Terminal Avenue near Science World–Main St SkyTrain station, is something of a disappointment. Probably only children, at whom the place seems largely aimed, will be satisfied by the

Emily Carr

Western Canada's most celebrated painter, **Emily Carr** was born in 1871into a prosperous Victoria family and led an artistic life that was by turn eccentric, thwarted, ridiculed, bohemian, and impoverished, but one that was also ultimately successful and triumphant.

Ignoring the advice of her family, in 1890 she attended the California School of Art in San Francisco. Unable to make ends meet there, she taught for a living, an activity she continued on her return to Victoria in 1893. Six year later, she traveled to Ucluelet (see p.518) on the west coast of Vancouver Island and came into contact with the art and culture of the indigenous **Nuu-chah-nulth**, an experience that would influence Carr's work for the rest of her life. After a brief and unhappy sojourn in England, Carr returned to Victoria in 1904, where the provincial and largely hidebound world of early-twentieth-century British Columbia viewed her lifestyle as wildly eccentric or worse. She often traveled with either a dog or parrot for company, and in time acquired a menagerie that included cats, cockatoos, a white rat named Susie, and a Capuchin monkey known as Woo. Carr even made pinafores for her charges to wear on walks in the park with their owner.

In 1907, she visited Alaska and again encountered the aboriginal cultures and northern landscapes that would eventually color her art. Four years later, still feeling her work lacked power and technique, she journeyed to Paris, where she absorbed the lessons of the new art movements sweeping the city. Chief among these was the **Fauve** ("wild beast") school of painters, so called for the frenzied distortions, patterns, and bright, almost violently colored nature of its exponents' works. Returning to Vancouver in 1911, Carr exhibited work from her French sojourn. The show – and another in 1913 – was panned, her work rejected as impenetrable or offensive by British Columbia's staid critics. It wouldn't be until the late 1920s before Carr's work began to find fame, a change of fortune that followed her encounter with the **Group of Seven** painters, a celebrated assembly of eastern Canadian artists who, like Carr, looked to the Canadian landscape for inspiration. Over the next ten years, she completed some of her most accomplished work, often working in the wilderness from a ramshackle caravan equipped with improvised shelters for her pets.

With her health failing, she began to write during a period of convalescence. Her first book, *Klee Wyck*, was published when she was 70, taking its name – "the laughing one" – from the name given to her by the Kwakiutl people of the Pacific coast. The book dealt with her travels and life among aboriginal people, and won the Canadian Governor General's medal for literature. Three other books followed – *The Book of Small* (a chronicle of her Victoria childhood), *The House of All Sorts* (about her career as a landlady), and *Growing Pains* (her autobiography). Carr died in 1945, secure in her status of Canada's first major female artist.

various high-tech, hands-on displays, which include the opportunity to make thunderous amounts of noise on electronic instruments and drum machines. Galleries deal with all manner of science-related themes, but probably the best things here if you're an adult are the building itself and the vast screen of the OMNIMAX Cinema at the top of the dome – though as with the similar screen at Canada Place, only a limited range of quality movies have been produced to suit the format.

The Vancouver Art Gallery

Centrally located in the imposing old city courthouse is the rather exorbitantly priced **Vancouver Art Gallery**, at the corner of Howe and Robson streets (late April to mid-Oct Mon–Wed & Fri–Sun 10am–5.30pm, Thurs 10am–9pm; mid-Oct to mid-April Tues–Wed & Fri–Sun 10am–5.30pm, Thurs 10am–9pm; Ⓣ662-4700, recorded information Ⓣ662-4719, Ⓦwww.vanartgallery.bc.ca; $12.50). While the permanent collection comprises over 80,000 works and is valued at over $100 million, the only part of the collection you can be sure of seeing is the Emily Carr section on the top floor. The other three floors are given over to (admittedly excellent) touring shows and rotating displays from the permanent collection, which features a rather sparse international collection with some of the lesser works of Warhol and Lichtenstein, as well as Italian, Flemish, and British paintings spanning the sixteenth to the twentieth centuries.

In recent years, though, the gallery has made a determined effort to concentrate on contemporary works – videos, sculptures, installations, and, in particular, photo-based and photo-conceptual art. In the last area, the gallery boasts the largest such collection in North America, including wonderful pieces by Cindy Sherman (notably her "self" portraits), Jeff Wall, Rachel Whitread, Jenny Holzer, and magnificent monumental photographs by Andreas Gursky.

Yet what ultimately redeems the place are its temporary exhibitions and the powerful works of Emily Carr (see box opposite). Characterized by deep greens and blues, they evoke something of the scale and intensity of the West Coast and its native peoples. The *Gallery Café* (see p.444) is also excellent, with a sun-trap of a terrace if you want to sit outside.

Gastown

An easy walk east of Downtown – five minutes from Canada Place and concentrated largely on Water Street – **Gastown** is a determined piece of city rejuvenation aimed fair and square at the tourist, distinguished by new cobblestones, fake gas lamps, *Ye Olde English Tea Room*-type cafés, and a generally over-polished patina. The name derives from "Gassy" Jack Leighton, a retired sailor turned publican and self-proclaimed "mayor," who arrived on site by canoe with his native wife and a mangy yellow dog in 1867, quickly opening a bar to service the nearby lumber mills, whose bosses banned drinking on or near the yards. Leighton's statue stands in **Maple Tree Square**, Gastown's heart, focus of its main streets, and reputed site of this first tavern. Trade was brisk, and a second bar opened, soon followed by a village of sorts – "Gassy's Town" – which, though swept away by fire in 1886, formed in effect the birthplace of modern Vancouver. Over the years, the Downtown focus moved west and something of Gastown's boozy beginnings returned to haunt it, as its cheap hotels and warehouses turned into a skid row for junkies and alcoholics. By the 1970s, the area was declared a historic site – the

GASTOWN & CHINATOWN

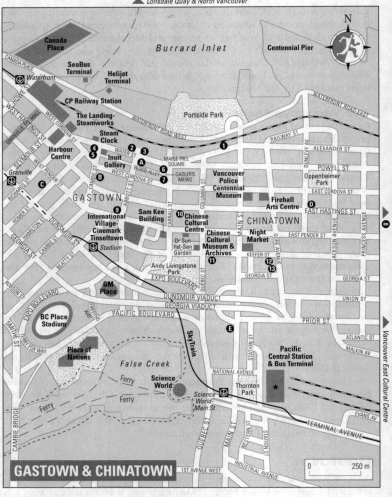

ACCOMMODATION		EATING AND DRINKING					
Budget Inn-Patricia Hotel	D	Alibi Room	1	Hon's Wun-Tun House	12	The Only Café	10
Cambie International Hostel Gastown	B	Bavaria	6	The Irish Heather	7	Phnom-Penh	13
C&N Backpackers Hostel	E	Blake's	6	La Luna Café	2	Pink Pearl	8
Dominion Hotel	A	Cordova Café	5	The Old Spaghetti Factory	3	Water Street Café	4
Victorian	C	Floata Sea Food Restaurant	11			Wild Rice	9

buildings are the city's oldest – and an enthusiastic beautification program was set in motion.

The end product never quite became the dynamic, city-integrated spot the planners had hoped, but Gastown is certainly worth a stroll for its buskers, Sunday crowds, and occasional points of interest. These do not include the hype-laden two-ton **steam-powered clock**, the world's first and hopefully last, at the west end of Water Street. It's invariably surrounded by tourists armed with cocked cameras, all awaiting the miniature Big Ben toots and whistles every fifteen minutes, and bellowing performances on the hour that seem to presage imminent explosion.

Probably the most surprising aspect of Gastown, however, is the contrast between its manicured pavements and the down-at-heel streets immediately to the south and east. The area between Gastown and Chinatown is both a thoroughly unpleasant skid row yet, nearer Gastown, a haven for secondhand clothes shops, bookshops, galleries, new designers, and cheap five-and-dimes. In places, however, this area recalls Gastown's bad old days: unpleasantly seedy, pocked with the dingiest of dingy bars and hotels, and inhabited by characters to match.

Lurking between Gastown and Chinatown, Vancouver's **Police Centennial Museum** (May–Aug Mon–Sat 10am–3pm; Sept–April Mon–Fri 9am–3pm; $6; ⓣ665-3346, ⓦwww.city.vancouver.bc.ca/police/museum) at 240 E Cordova St, is a bizarre and fascinating little museum. The museum is housed in the city's old Coroner's Court Building and takes its name from the fact that it was established in 1986 to celebrate the centennial of the Vancouver police force.

The building has its own place in Vancouver folklore, not least for the fact that it was here that the actor **Errol Flynn** was brought after he died in Vancouver in 1959. Flynn arrived in the city in October 1959 with his best acting days well behind him. With him was his "personal assistant," a 17-year-old blonde girl not known for her secretarial skills. Within two days, Flynn had dropped dead in his rented West End apartment. The body was brought to the Coroner's Court, where the pathologist conducting the autopsy is said to have removed a piece of Flynn's penis and placed it in formaldehyde to keep as a souvenir. The horrified chief coroner Glen McDonald, a rather more fastidious operator, is said to have pulled rank and reattached the missing piece of member to the corpse with sticky tape. The body was then dispatched to Los Angeles for burial. This was not the end of the story, for it emerged that somewhere between the West End and the morgue, a key to a Swiss safety-deposit box that Flynn wore round his neck had disappeared. When Flynn's lawyers opened the box three years later, the stock certificates and half a million dollars in cash they had expected to find were nowhere to be seen.

The **autopsy room** is still there, together with a suitably macabre selection of mangled and preserved body parts arranged around the walls. Check out the morgue's cooler, penultimate resting place of many over the years. Other rooms include a forensics lab, a simulated autopsy room, police cell, and radio room, while a variety of thematic displays include sections on notorious local criminals, weapons seized from criminals (some pretty unusual), crime-scene reconstructions, gambling, uniforms, counterfeit money, and a sizeable collection of firearms. Among the more light-hearted exhibits is a collection of model police cars from around the world.

To get here by public transport, take buses #10, #16, #20, #23, #35 or #150 along Hastings Street to Main then walk one block north to E Cordova.

Chinatown

Vancouver's vibrant **Chinatown** – clustered mainly on Pender Street from Carrall to Gore and on Keefer Street from Main to Gore (buses #22 or #19 east from Pender, or #22 north from Burrard) – is a city apart. Vancouver's 100,000-plus Chinese, the vast majority of whom live in the area, make up one of the largest Chinese communities outside the Far East – on a par with those of New York and San Francisco – and are the city's oldest and largest ethnic group after the British-descended majority. Many crossed the Pacific in 1858 to join the Fraser Valley gold rush; others followed under contract to help build the Canadian Pacific Railway. Most stayed and found themselves treated appallingly, seeking safety and familiarity in a ghetto of their own, where clan associations and societies provided for new arrivals and helped build the distinctive houses of recessed balconies and ornamental roofs that have made the area a protected historic site.

Unlike Gastown's gimmickry, Chinatown is genuine – shops, hotels, markets, tiny restaurants, and dim alleys vie for attention amidst an incessant hustle of jammed pavements and the buzz of Chinese conversation. Virtually every building replicates an Eastern model without a trace of self-consciousness, and written Chinese characters feature everywhere in preference to English. Striking and unexpected after Downtown's high-rise glitz, the district brings you face to face with Vancouver's oft-touted multiculturalism, and helps explain why Hong Kong immigrants continue to be attracted to the city. It is, however, a district with a distinct edge, and visitors should avoid the area's dingier streets at night and parts of East Hastings near Main Street just about any time.

Apart from the obvious culinary temptations (see "Eating and drinking," p.443), Chinatown's main points of reference are its **shops**. Some of the best boast fearsome butchery displays and such edibles as live eels, flattened ducks, hundred-year-old eggs, and other stuff you'll be happy not to identify. Check out the open-air **night market** at Main and Keefer streets (summer 6pm–midnight), a wonderful medley of sights. Keefer Street is **bakery** row, with lots of tempting stickies on offer like moon cakes and *bao*, steamed buns with a meat or sweet-bean filling. On the corner of Keefer and Main, the Ten Ren Tea and Ginseng Company offers a vast range of teas, many promising cures for a variety of ailments (free tastings). It's also worth dropping into one of the local **herbalists** to browse among their panaceas: snakeskins, reindeer antlers, buffalo tongues, dried sea horses, and bears' testicles are all available if you're feeling under the weather. Most people also flock dutifully to the 1913 **Sam Kee Building**, on the corner of Carrall and Pender streets; at just 1.8m across, it's officially the world's narrowest building.

Chinatown's chief cultural attraction is the small **Dr Sun Yat-Sen Garden** (May–mid-June daily 10am–6pm; mid-June to Aug daily 9.30am–7pm; Sept daily 10am–6pm; Oct daily 10am–4.30pm; Nov–April Tues–Sun 10am–4.30mpm; $8.25; ⓣ662-3207, ⓦwww.vancouverchinesegarden.com) at 578 Carrall St near Pender Street. Named after the founder of the first Chinese Republic, who was a frequent visitor to Vancouver, the park was created for the Expo '86 and cost $5.3 million, $500,000 of which came from the People's Republic accompanied by 52 artisans and 950 crates of materials. The whole thing is based on classical gardens developed in the city of Suzhou during the Ming Dynasty (1368–1644). China's horticultural emissaries, following traditional methods that didn't allow use of a single power tool, spent thirteen months in the city replicating a Suzhou Ming garden to achieve a subtle balance of Yin and Yang: small and large, soft and hard, flowing and immovable, light and dark. Free forty-five-minute **guided tours** are given on the half-hour and explain other elements of the Taoist philosophy behind the carefully placed elements. At first glance it all seems a touch small and austere, and isn't helped by a preponderance of sponsors' nameplates and the glimpses of the road, pub, and high-rise building outside the walls. After a time, though, the chances are you'll find the garden working its calm and peaceful spell.

Alongside the entrance to the gardens, the **Chinese Cultural Centre Museum & Archives** (Tues–Sun 11am–5pm; $3; ⓣ604/658-8880), Chinatown's community focus and sponsor of its New Year festivities, offers classes and hosts changing exhibitions. It also has a museum that focuses on early Chinese pioneers and Chinese veterans who served Canada in the two world wars. Next to the gardens and center is a small and slightly threadbare Dr Sun Yat-Sen Park (free), which, though less developed than the Dr Sun Yat-Sen Garden, is still a pleasant place to take time out from Chinatown. Hours are the same as for the garden, and there's an alternative entrance on Columbia Street and Keefer.

Stanley Park

At nearly 1000 acres, **Stanley Park**, Vancouver's green heart, is the largest urban park in North America, less a tame collection of lawns and elms than a semi-wilderness of dense rainforest, marshland, and beaches. Ocean surrounds it on three sides, with a road and parallel cycleway/pedestrian promenade following the seawall all the way round the peninsula for a total of 10.5km. From here, views of the city and across the water to the mountains are particularly spectacular. Away from the coastal trail network and main draw – Vancouver Aquarium Marine Science Centre – the interior is nearly impenetrable scrub and forest, with few paths and few people. At the same time there are plenty of open, wooded, or flower-decorated spaces to picnic or watch the world go by.

The park is a simple though rather dull **walk** from most of Downtown, if a fairly lengthy one from the eastern districts. Beach Avenue to the south and Georgia to the north are the best approaches if you're on foot, leading to the southern and northern starts of the seawall respectively. Walking all the way round the seawall path takes about two hours at a brisk lick. Perhaps a better approach is to take a Stanley Park **bus** #23, #35 or #135 from the corner of Burrard and Pender streets Downtown, which drop you near the so-called Stanley Park Loop just inside the park by Lost Lagoon and in summer continue deeper into the park to the Stanley Park Loop.

To rent a bike, go to the corner of Denman and Georgia streets, where there's a cluster of **bike rental** outlets. Spokes, 1798 W Georgia St (ⓣ604/688-5141, ⓦwww.vancouverbikerentals.com), is a big, busy place that's been in business since 1938 (from $3.75 an hour for a wide variety of bikes, including children's bikes and tandems with child trailers). You need to leave ID, and a cash, Visa, or MasterCard deposit. If this place looks too frenetic you might be better advised to walk a few metres up the street, where Bikes 'n' Blades (ⓣ604/602-9899) is smaller, less busy, and rents **rollerblades** as well. Directly opposite at 745 Denman St is Bayshore Bicycle & Rollerblade Rentals (ⓣ604/688-2453, ⓦwww.bayshorebike.ca). From Denman it's just a minute's pedaling to the park.

If you don't want to walk, cycle, or skate, then there's a free TransLink "Stanley Park Shuttle" **bus service**, which runs on a 15-minute schedule in summer only (daily June–Aug/early Sept 9/10am–6.30pm; information ⓣ257-8400). It makes fourteen stops at the most popular sights around the park. You can transfer to the service from the #1 and #5 buses on Denman or the #23, #35, and #135 at Stanley Park Loop: both Denman and the Loop are a few moments' walk from the shuttle's stops at Stanley Park Entrance, Pipeline

Road, or the Vancouver Rowing Club. Driving a **car** here is foolish, especially at weekends, when parking is just about impossible.

The Park

The first thing you see is the **Lost Lagoon**, a fair-sized lake that started life as a tidal inlet, and got its name because its water all but disappeared at low tide. Dozens of waterfowl species inhabit its shoreline. Just east are the pretty Rose Garden and Vancouver Rowing Club, before which stands a statue of Scottish poet Robbie Burns. From here you can follow the seawall path all the way, or make a more modest loop past the **totem poles** and round Brockton Point.

Moving around the seawall anticlockwise, odd little sights dot the promenade, all signed and explained, the most famous being the *Girl in a Wetsuit* statue, a rather lascivious update of Copenhagen's *Little Mermaid*. If you want a more focused walk, the **Cathedral Trail**, northwest of the Lost Lagoon, takes you past some big first-growth cedars. **Beaver Lake**, carpeted green with water lilies, is a peaceful spot for a sleep or a stroll. **Lumberman's Arch**, near the aquarium (see below) was raised in 1952 to honor those in the lumber industry – an odd memorial given that the industry in question would probably give its eyeteeth to fell the trees in Stanley Park. Its meadow surroundings are a favorite for families and those looking for a good napping spot. **Prospect Point**, on the park's northern tip, is a busy spot but worth braving for its beautiful view of the city and the mountains rising behind West Vancouver across the water. There's a café-restaurant here, popular for its outdoor deck and sweeping views. West of here lies **Siwash Rock**, an outcrop which has defied the weather for centuries, attracting numerous native legends in the process, and which is distinguished by its solitary tree (not visible from the road, but quickly reached by path). Further around the wall there are various places to eat and drink, the best being the *Teahouse Restaurant* at Ferguson Point, about a kilometre beyond Siwash Rock.

Though people do swim in the sea at beaches around the park's western fringes, most bathers prefer the **swimming pool** next to Second Beach (see box opposite). Facilities of all sorts – cafés, playgrounds, golf, outdoor dancing – proliferate near the Downtown margins.

Vancouver Aquarium Marine Science Centre

Stanley Park zoo and its all too obviously distressed animals has thankfully closed, leaving the **Vancouver Aquarium Marine Science Centre** as the park's most popular destination (daily July to early Sept 9.30am–7pm; early Sept to June 10am–5.30pm; $15.95; Ⓣ604/659-3474, Ⓦwww.vanaqua.org). At its entrance at 845 Avison Way stands a vast killer whale in bronze, the work of celebrated Haida artist Bill Reid, whose famous *Raven and the Beast* sculpture forms the centerpiece of the Museum of Anthropology (see p.437). The aquarium is ranked among North America's best, and, with over a million visitors a year, claims to be the most-visited sight in Canada west of Toronto's CN Tower. It contains over 8000 living exhibits representing some 600 different species, though in truth this is a relatively modest summation of the eighty percent of the world's creatures that live in water. Like the zoo before it, the complex has been targeted by animal-rights campaigners for its treatment of performing beluga and killer whales, not to mention cooped-up seals and otters. Given the aquarium's reputation as a tourist attraction and claims as a research center, however, the campaigners have a long, uphill battle. The whales in particular are huge draws, but you can't help but feel they

Vancouver's beaches

Vancouver, it's rather surprising to find, has **beaches**. All are clean and well kept: the clarity of the water is remarkable given the size of the city's port – and the majority have lifeguards during the summer months. The best face each other across False Creek and English Bay, starting with Stanley Park's three adjacent beaches: **English Bay Beach**, ranged along Beach Avenue; **Second Beach**, to the north, which also features a shallow onshore swimming pool (mid-May or mid-June Mon–Fri noon–8.45pm, Sat–Sun 10am–8.45pm; mid-June to mid-Sept daily 10am–8.45pm; $4; ⓣ604/257-8371); and **Third Beach**, further north still, least crowded of the three and the one with the best views of West Vancouver and the mountains. English Bay at the southern end of Denman is the most readily accessible, and easily visited after seeing Stanley Park.

Across the water to the south and west of the Burrard Bridge, **Kitsilano Beach**, or "Kits," is named – like the district behind it – after Chief Khahtsahlano, a Squamish chieftain of a band who once owned the area. Walk here from Vanier Park and the museums (30min) on the coast path or, from Downtown, take a #22 **bus** southbound on Burrard Street. Kits is a city favorite and the busiest and most self-conscious of the beaches. It's especially popular with the university, volleyball, and rippling torso crowds, and the more well-heeled locals. Vancouver's largest and most popular outdoor heated pool is the **lido** at Yew and Cornwall (mid-May to mid-June Mon–Fri noon–8.45pm, Sat–Sun 10am–8.45pm; mid-June to mid-Sept Mon–Fri 7am–8.45pm, Sat–Sun 10am–8.45pm; $4; ⓣ604/731-0011), while the **shoreline path** is a lovely place for an evening stroll, cycle, or time out on a bench to watch the streetlife. Follow the path all the way east and it takes you to Granville Island by way of Vanier Park and the museums.

Jericho Beach, west of Kits and handy for the youth hostel, is a touch quieter and serves as a hangout for the windsurfing crowd. Still further west, Jericho blurs into **Locarno Beach** and **Spanish Banks**, progressively less crowded, and the start of a fringe of sand and parkland that continues round to the University of British Columbia campus. Locals rate Spanish Banks the most relaxed of the city's beaches, while Locarno is one of its most spectacular, especially at low tide, when the sand seems to stretch for ever. You can rent canoes from Ecomarine Ocean Kayak 1668 Duranleau St (ⓣ604/689-7575 or 1-888/425-2925, ⓦwww.ecomarine.com). It also has an office at the Jericho Sailing Centre at 1300 Discovery St on Jericho Beach itself.

At low tide the more athletically inclined could walk all the way round to UBC (otherwise take the bus as for the Museum of Anthropology; see p.437), where the clothing-optional **Wreck Beach** (see p.439) lies just off the campus area below NW Marine Drive – ask any student to point you towards the half-hidden access paths. The atmosphere is generally laid-back – though women have been known to complain of voyeurs – and nude peddlers are often on hand to sell you anything from pizza and illegal smokeables to (bona fide) massage and hair-braiding. Finally, **Ambleside**, west of the Park Royal Mall along Marine Drive (turn south at 13th Street W), is the most accessible beach if you're in North or West Vancouver.

should really be in the sea, for all the hoopla surrounding their $14-million marine-mammal area.

The aquarium has several key areas to see. The **Arctic Canada** section concerns itself with the surprisingly fragile world of the Canadian north, with a chance to see whales face to face through glass and hear the sounds of whales, walruses, seals, and other creatures in this icy domain. The **Amazon Gallery** displays the vegetation, fishes, iguanas, sloths, and other creatures of the rainforest in a climate-controlled environment, while the **Pacific Northwest**

△ Indigenous totem poles

Habitat performs a similar role for otters, beavers, and other creatures of the waters of BC. The **BC Waters Gallery** and **Ducks Unlimited Wetlands** displays are fairly self-explanatory.

Granville Island

Huddled under the Granville Street Bridge south of Downtown, **Granville Island** is the city's most enticing "people's place" – the title it likes for itself – and pretty much lives up to its claim to be the "heart of Vancouver." Friendly, easygoing, and popular, its shops, markets, galleries, marina, and open spaces are juxtaposed with a light-industrial setting whose faint whiff of warehouse squalor saves the area from accusations of pretentiousness. The island was reclaimed from swampland in 1917 as an ironworks and shipbuilding center, but by the 1960s the yards were derelict and the place had become a rat-infested dumping ground for the city's rubbish. In 1972, the federal government bankrolled a program of residential, commercial, and industrial redevelopment that retained the old false-fronted buildings, tin-shack homes, sea wall, and rail sidings. The best part of the job had been finished by 1979 – and was immediately successful – but work continues unobtrusively today, the various building projects only adding to the area's sense of change and dynamism. Most people come here during the day, but there are some good restaurants, bars, and the Arts Club Theatre, which are all enough to keep the place buzzing at night.

The most direct approach is to take **bus** #50 from Gastown or Granville Street. The walk down Granville Street and across the bridge is deceptively long and not terribly salubrious. Alternatively and more fun, private **ferries** ($2, pay on board) ply back and forth almost continuously between the island and little quays at the foot of Hornby Street or the Aquatic Centre at the foot of Thurlow Street (see "Seabuses and Ferries," p.415). They also connect from Granville Island to Science World (hourly) and to Vanier Park (half-hourly), a much nicer way than bus to get to the park's Vancouver Museum, Maritime Museum, and Space Centre (see p.437). A logical and satisfying day's **itinerary** from Downtown, therefore, would take you to Granville Island, to the museums and back by ferry. You might also choose to **walk** from the island along the False Creek sea wall (east) or west to Vanier Park (see overleaf) and Kits Beach.

There's a good **infocentre** at the heart of the island for Island-related information only (Ⓣ604/666-5784, Ⓦwww.granvilleisland.bc.ca). Note that many of the island's shops and businesses close on Mondays, and that if you want a **bus back** to Downtown you should *not* take the #51 from the stop opposite the infocentre (it will take you in the wrong direction): walk out of the island complex's only road entrance and the #50 stop is immediately on your right at the junction.

Virtually the first building you see on the island walking from the bus stop augurs well: the **Granville Island Brewery**, 1441 Cartwright St (tours June–Sept Mon–Fri on the hour noon–5pm, Sat & Sun on the half-hour 11.30am–5pm; $7; Ⓣ604/687-2739), a small concern that, despite having no formal pub, offers guided tours that include tastings of its fine additive-free beers. Dominant amongst the maze of shops, galleries, and businesses, the **Granville Island Public Market** (daily 9am–6pm; closed Mon in winter) is the island's undisputed highlight. On summer weekends, it's where people go to see and be seen and it throngs with arts-and-crafts types, and a phalanx of dreadful, but harmless buskers. The quality and variety of **food** is staggering, with dozens of kiosks and cafés selling ready-made titbits and potential picnic ingredients. Nearby parks, patios, and walkways furnish lively areas to eat and take everything in. Other spots to look out for include Blackberry Books, the Water Park and Kids Only Market (a playground with hoses to repel adult intruders). You can also rent **canoes** for safe and straightforward paddling in False Creek and English Bay from Ecomarine Ocean Kayak on the island at 1688 Duranleau St (Ⓣ604/689-7575). See box, p.433 for more on canoe rentals.

The island also has a trio of small, linked **museums** almost opposite the brewery at 1502 Duranleau St (all daily 10am–5.30pm; $6.50 – ticket gives admission to all three museums; Ⓣ604/683-1939): these are the self-explanatory Granville Island Model Trains Museum, Model Ships Museum, and Sport Fishing museum. These will probably appeal only to children and to model or fishing enthusiasts. The Model Trains Museum claims to contain the largest collection of toy trains in the world on public display.

The Vanier Park museum complex

A little to the west of Granville Island, **Vanier Park** conveniently collects most of the city's main museums: the **Vancouver Museum**, the **Maritime Museum**, and the **H.R. MacMillan Space Centre** (the last combines the old planetarium and observatory). The complex sits on the waterfront at the west end of the Burrard Bridge, near Kitsilano Beach and the residential-entertainment centers of **Kitsilano** and West 4th Avenue, and Vanier Park itself is a fine spot to while away a summer afternoon. You could easily incorporate a visit to the museums with a trip to Granville Island using the **ferry** (see overleaf), which docks just below the Maritime Museum. Coming from Downtown, take the #22 Macdonald **bus** south from anywhere on Burrard or West Pender – get off at the first stop after the bridge and walk down Chester Street to the park. The park's pleasant but open – there's little shade – and has a few nice patches of sandy beach on its fringes if you don't want to trek all the way to Kits and Jericho beaches (see box, p.433).

The Vancouver Museum

The **Vancouver Museum**, 1100 Chestnut St (Mon–Wed & Fri–Sun 10am–5pm, Thurs 10am–9pm; $10; Ⓣ604/736-4431, Ⓦwww.vanmuseum.bc.ca), traces the history of the city and the lower British Columbian mainland. It invokes the area's past with its flying-saucer shape, a nod to the conical cedar-bark hats of the Northwest Coast natives, former inhabitants of the area. The **fountain** outside, looking like a crab on a bidet, recalls the animal of native legend that guards the port entrance.

Though it's the main focus of interest at Vanier Park, the museum is not as captivating as you'd expect from a city like Vancouver. It claims 300,000 exhibits, but it's hard to know where they all are, and a visit needn't take more than an hour or so. A patchy collection of baskets, tools, clothes, and miscellaneous artifacts of aboriginal peoples – including a huge whaling canoe, the only example in a museum – homes in on the 8000 years before the coming of white settlers. After that, the main collection, weaving in and out of Vancouver's history up to World War I, is full of offbeat and occasionally memorable insights if you have the patience to read the material – notably the accounts of early explorers' often extraordinary exploits, the immigration section (which re-creates what it felt like to travel steerage), and the forestry displays. The twentieth-century section is disappointing, most of the time looking more like an antique shop than a museum.

The H.R. MacMillan Space Centre

The **H. R. MacMillan Space Centre**, also known as the Pacific Space Centre (July–Aug daily 10am–5pm, Sept–June Tues–Sun 10am–5pm; evening laser shows at varying times Thurs–Sun; Space Centre $13.50, additional Virtual Voyage rides $6; evening laser shows $9.35; Ⓣ604 738-7827, Ⓦwww.hrmacmillanspacecentre .com), incorporates the MacMillan Planetarium and a range of space-related displays and shows. Like the Vancouver Museum – to which it is close – it lies in Vanier Park and can be accessed at 1100 Crescent St or from the small ferry landing in the park. Its main draws are its star shows – the standard planetarium fare – and very loud, very brash evening laser and music extravaganzas. These are held in the H. R. MacMillan Star Theatre – there's an extra charge for the evening shows, but the 40-minute star shows (held several times daily, usually in the afternoon) are included in the general admission. The evening shows are very popular, so arrive in good time or make reservations.

Many of the center's exhibits are high-tech and hands-on, especially in the Cosmic Courtyard, where interactive displays allow you to battle an alien, design a spaceship, guide a lunar robot, or plan a voyage to Mars. Many displays also involve lots of impressive computer and other audiovisual effects, notably the Virtual Voyages Simulator, a flight simulator complete with the "motion" you might encounter during space travel and other journeys. The "rides" on the simulator last about five minutes (entrance is included with admission) and experiences range from collisions with a comet to trips on a roller-coaster and simulated space flights to the planets. The GroundStation Canada Theatre shows 20-minute films on various aspects of space roughly hourly from mid-morning.

The **Gordon Southam Observatory**, the small domed building close to the Space Centre, has a telescope that is usually available for public stargazing on clear weekend nights (call Space Centre or Ⓣ604 736-2655 for current times); astronomers are on hand to show you the ropes and help you position your camera for a "Shoot the Moon" photography session of the heavens ($10).

The Maritime Museum

After the space-age look and high-tech displays of the Space Centre, the rather dated appearance of Vancouver's **Maritime Museum** (May–Sept daily 10am–5pm, Oct–April Tues–Sat 10am–5pm, Sun noon–5pm; $8; Ⓣ604 257-8300, Ⓦwww.vmm.bc.ca) is likely to come as a disappointing jolt. That said, it features lovely early photographs evoking c.1900 Vancouver, though the rest of the presentation doesn't quite do justice to the status of the city as one of the world's leading ports. The less-arresting displays, however, are redeemed by the renovated *St Roch*, a two-masted schooner that was the first vessel to navigate the famed Northwest Passage in a single season; it now sits impressively in its own wing of the museum, where it can be viewed by guided tour only. Special summer shows spice things up a little, as do the recent Pirates' Cove and Children's Maritime Discovery Centre, both aimed at making the museum more attractive to children. Outside, just below the museum on **Heritage Harbour** (quay for ferries to and from Granville Island), you can admire, free of charge, more restored old-fashioned vessels.

The Museum of Anthropology

Well out of Downtown on the University of British Columbia campus, the superlative **Museum of Anthropology** (mid-May to early Sept Mon & Wed–Sun 10am–5pm, Tues 10am–9pm; early Sept to mid-May Tues

11am–9pm, Wed–Sun 11am–5pm; $9, free Tues 5–9pm; ⓣ604/822-5087, ⓦwww.moa.ubc.ca), at 6393 NW Marine Drive, emphasizes the art and culture of the natives of the region, and the Haida in particular. Its collection of carvings, totem poles, and artifacts is unequalled in North America.

To get there by bus, catch the #10 or #4 bus south from Granville Street and stay on until the end of the line. The campus is huge and can be disorienting – to find the museum, turn right from the bus stop, walk along the tree-lined East Mall to the very bottom (10min), then turn left on NW Marine Drive and walk till you see the museum on the right (another 5min). In the foyer pick up a free mini-guide or the cheap larger booklet – a worthwhile investment, given the exhibits' almost total lack of labeling, but still pretty thin.

Much is made of the museum's award-winning layout, a cool and spacious collection of halls designed by Arthur Erickson, the eminent architect also responsible for converting the Vancouver Art Gallery. Particularly outstanding is the huge **Great Hall**, inspired by native cedar houses, which makes as perfect an artificial setting for its thirty-odd **totem poles** as you could ask for. Huge windows look out to more poles and Haida houses, which you're free to wander around, backed by views of Burrard Inlet and the distant mountains. Most of the poles and monolithic carvings, indoors and out, are taken from the coastal tribes of the Haida, Salish, Tsimshian, and Kwakiutl, all of which share cultural elements. The suspicion – though it's never confessed – is that scholars really don't know terribly much of the arcane mythology behind the carvings, but the best guess as to their meaning is that the various animals correspond to different clans or the creatures after which the clans were named. To delve deeper into the complexities, it's worth joining an hour-long, all-year **guided walk**.

One of the museum's great virtues is that none of its displays are hidden away in basements or back rooms; rather, they're jammed in overwhelming numbers into drawers and cases in the galleries to the right of the Great Hall. Most of the permanent collection revolves around **Canadian Pacific** cultures, but the **Inuit** and **Far North** exhibits are equally outstanding. So, too, are the jewelery, masks, and baskets of Northwest native tribes, all markedly delicate after the blunt-nosed carvings of the Great Hall. Look out especially for the argillite sculptures, made from a jet-black slate found only on BC's Haida Gwaii or Queen Charlotte Islands. The **African** and **Asian** collections are also pretty comprehensive, if smaller, but appear as something of an afterthought alongside the indigenous artifacts. A small, technical archeological section rounds off the smaller galleries, along with a new three-gallery wing designed to house the Koerner Collection, an assortment of six hundred European ceramics dating from the fifteenth century onwards.

The museum saves its best for last. Housed in a separate rotunda, **The Raven and the Beast**, a modern sculpture designed by Haida artist Bill Reid, is the museum's pride and joy and has achieved almost iconographic status in the city. Carved from a 4.5-ton block of cedar and requiring the attention of five people over three years, it describes the Haida legend of human evolution with stunning virtuosity, depicting terrified figures squirming from a half-open clam shell, overseen by an enormous and stern-faced raven. Beautiful as the work is, however, its rotunda setting makes it seem oddly out of place.

Around the museum

There are any number of odds and ends dotted around the museum, but they amount to little of real interest. For the exception, turn right out the front entrance and a five-minute walk leads to the **Nitobe Memorial Garden** (daily mid-March–mid-May & Sept–mid-Oct 10am–5pm; mid-May–Aug 10am–6pm; mid-Oct–mid-March Mon–Fri 10am–2.30pm; $3 or $6 with the Botanical Garden, free mid-Oct–mid-March; Ⓣ604/822-6038, Ⓦwww.nitobe.org), a small Japanese garden near Gate 4, Memorial Rd, off West Mall that is good for a few minutes of peace and floral admiration. Considered the world's most authentic Japanese garden outside Japan (despite its use of many non-Japanese species), it is full of gently curving paths, trickling streams, and waterfalls, as well as numerous rocks, trees, and shrubs placed with traditional precision.

Almost directly opposite the Nitobe Garden, at 16th Avenue and 6804 SW Marine Drive, the larger **UBC Botanical Garden** (daily mid-March–mid-Oct 10am–6pm; rest of the year 10am–3pm; $4.50 or $6 with Nitobe Garden; Ⓣ822-4208, Ⓦwww.ubcbotanicalgarden.org), was established in 1916 and is Canada's oldest botanical garden. It claims some 10,000 different plants, shrubs, and trees and consists of eight separate gardens – Alpine, Arbour, Asian, British Columbian Native, Contemporary, Food, Perennial Border, and Physic. If you're more curious or green-fingered, you'll take time to look at all five component parts of the garden. The Asian Garden is cradled amidst a swath of second-growth forest of fir, cedar, and hemlock, home to 400 varieties of rhododendrons, roses, flowering vines, and floral rarities such as blue Himalayan poppy and giant Himalayan lily. The BC Native Garden shelters some 3500 plants and flowers found across British Columbia in a variety of bog, marsh, and other habitats, while the Alpine Garden conjures rare alpine varieties from five continents at around 2000m lower than their preferred altitude. The Food Garden produces a cornucopia of fruit and vegetables from a remarkably restricted area, the entire crop being donated to the Salvation Army.

While you're out at the university, you might also take advantage of the **University Endowment Lands**, on the opposite, west side of the museum. A huge tract of wild parkland – as large as Stanley Park, but used by a fraction of the number of people – the endowment lands boast 48km of trails and abundant wildlife (blacktail deer, otters, foxes, and bald eagles). Best of all, there are few human touches – no benches or snack bars, and only the occasional signpost.

Wreck Beach

About a kilometre south of the Nitobe garden, **Wreck Beach** is well known for its pristine patch of sand, where you can strip off as many clothes as you like. These days, the nudity is pretty much accepted and attitudes are fairly relaxed. The beach becomes pretty crowded and commercialized in summer, but there are plenty of driftwood logs and fallen tree trunks on the sand which allow you to lay claim to a private patch of sand.

Access is from SW Marine Drive near Gate 6 at the foot of University Boulevard. The beach can be a little tricky to find, but plenty of well-worn tracks, including numbered trails #3, #4, and #6, lead down the steep slopes above the beach, and just about any student on the campus will be able to point you in the right direction. On a busy summer day, you won't be able to miss the access, for parked cars are jammed bumper to bumper on SW Marine Drive above the trails to the beach.

Trail #4 leads down to Tower Beach to the north of Wreck Beach from Gate 4 a short distance south of the museum and before the Nitobe Garden. The best of the Wreck Beach sand is below trail #6, the trailhead for which you'll find just beyond the Nitobe Garden heading away from the Museum of Anthropology. To the south of this is the North Arm breakwater, separating the beach from log-booming grounds farther to the south and east. The trailhead for #7, farther round S W Marine Drive, leads to the Old Wreck Beach Trail, which runs south and west round the peninsula for a look at the uncommercialized section of the beach.

North Vancouver

Perhaps the most compelling reason to visit **North Vancouver** (known colloquially as North Van) is the trip itself – preferably by SeaBus – which affords views of not only the Downtown skyline but also the teeming port area, a side of the city easily missed. Most of North Van itself is residential, as is the neighboring **West Vancouver** (West Van), but you'll probably cross to the north shore less for leafy suburbs than to sample the outstanding areas of natural beauty here – **Lynn Canyon**, **Grouse Mountain**, **Capilano Gorge** (the most popular excursion), **Mount Seymour Provincial Park**, **Lighthouse Park**, and the **Lower Seymour Conservation Reserve**. All are found in the mountains that rear up dramatically almost from the waterfront, the proximity of Vancouver's residential areas to genuine wilderness being one of the city's most remarkable aspects. Your best bet if you wish to **hike**, and want the wildest scenery close to Downtown, is Mount Seymour (see p.442).

Most of North Vancouver is within a single bus ride of **Lonsdale Quay**, the north shore's SeaBus terminal. **Buses** to all points leave from two parallel bays immediately in front of you as you leave the boat – blue West Van buses are run by an independent company but accept BC Transit tickets. If you've bought a ticket to come over on the SeaBus, remember you have ninety minutes of transfer time to ride buses from the time of purchase, which should be long enough to get you to most of the destinations below.

Grouse Mountain

The trip to **Grouse Mountain**, named by hikers in 1894 who stumbled across a blue grouse, is popular largely because of the Swiss-built **cable cars** – North America's largest – which run from the 290-metre base station at 6400 Nancy Greene Way to the mountain's 1250-metre summit (daily 9am–10pm; $24.95; ⓣ980-9311, ⓦwww.grousemountain.com). A favorite among people learning to ski or **snowboard** after work, the mountain's brightly illuminated slopes and dozen or so runs are a North Vancouver landmark on winter evenings. A day-pass costs $39: for more information call ⓣ984-0661 or visit the website (see above). In summer, the cable car is an expensive way of getting to the top, yet it's possible to walk up on the aptly named Grouse Grind Trail from the base station. However, it's not a great hike, so settle instead into the inevitable line for the ticket office (get here early if you can). After two stomach-churning lurches over the cables' twin towers you reach the summit, which, with its restaurants and allied tourist paraphernalia, is anything but wild. The views, though, are stunning, sometimes stretching as far as the San Juan Islands 160km away in Washington State. Have a quick look at the interpretative center off to the right when you leave the cable car. A 3-D quality film is shown in the theater downstairs (admission is included in your cable-car ticket) and there are a couple of cafés and a smarter restaurant if you need fortifying after your ascent. The first of the cafés, *Altitudes Bistro*, has panoramic views and serves contemporary West Coast food, but it fills up quickly; otherwise try *The Observatory* restaurant (see above). Ask at the interpretative center, or the small information desk just beyond the center, about easy **guided walks** (summer daily 11am–5pm): the

Tribute to the Forest (30min) leaves on the hour, the similar Walk in the Woods every hour on the half-hour (35min).

Walk up the paved paths away from the center for about five minutes – you can't get lost – and you pass a cabin office offering guided "gravity assisted" (read downhill) **bike tours** from the summit (May–Oct 3 daily; 20km trips cost from around $85, 30km $95 including cable-car fee): behind the office you can sign up for expensive helicopter tours. On the left up the path lies the scene of the "Logging Sports" shows (twice daily; free), involving various crowd-pleasing sawing and wood-chopping displays. Just beyond this is the **Peak Chairlift** (also included in your ticket), which judders upwards for another eight minutes to the mountain's summit: views of the city and Fraser delta are even better, only slightly spoilt by the worn paths and odd buildings immediately below you. Check with the office at the lower cable-car base station for details of long **hikes** – many are down below rather than up at the summit proper. The best easy stroll is to **Blue Grouse Lake** (15min); the Goat Ridge Trail is for experienced hikers. More rugged paths lead into the mountains of the West Coast Range, but for these you'll need maps.

To get directly to the base station of the cable car from Lonsdale Quay, take the special #236 Grouse Mountain **bus** from Bay 8 to the left of the SeaBus terminal. You can also take a #246 Highland bus from Bay 7 and change to the #232 Grouse Mountain at Edgemount Village.

Capilano River Regional Park

Lying just off the approach road to Grouse Mountain, **Capilano River Regional Park**'s (daily May–Labour Day 8am–9pm, rest of the year 8am–5pm or dusk, whichever is later; ⓣ604/224-5739 or 432-6350, ⓦwww.gvrd.bc.ca), most publicized attraction is the inexplicably popular seventy-metre-high and 137-metre-long **suspension bridge**. Built in 1956, the world's longest pedestrian suspension bridge crosses the vertiginous Capilano Gorge (daily mid-May–Aug 8.30am–8pm, early May & Sept–mid-Oct 9am–7.30pm, late Oct & mid-March–mid-April 9am–6pm, late April 9am–6.30am, Nov–mid-March 9am–5pm; $14.95 May–Oct, $10.25 Nov–April; prices exclude GST; ⓣ604/985-7474, ⓦwww.capbridge.com). Stick to the paths elsewhere in the park and avoid the pedestrian toll, which buys you miscellaneous tours, forestry exhibits, and trails, and a visit to a native carving center. Frankly they don't amount to much, especially when you can have much the same sort of scenery for free up the road. Far more interesting, the **salmon hatchery** just upstream (open daily June–Aug 8am–8pm, May & Sept 8am–7pm, April & Oct 8am–6pm, Nov–March 8am–6pm; free; ⓣ604/666-1790, ⓦwww.heb.pac.dfo-mpo.gc.ca), is a provincial operation dating from 1977 designed to help salmon spawn and thus combat declining stocks: it nurtures some two million fish a year, and was the first of many similar schemes across the province. The building is well designed and the information plaques interesting, but it's a prime stop on city coach tours, so the place can often be packed.

Capilano is probably best visited on the way back from Grouse Mountain – from the cable-car station it's an easy downhill walk (1km) to the north end of the park, below the Cleveland Reservoir, source of Vancouver's often disconcertingly brown drinking water. From there, marked trails – notably the **Capilano Pacific Trail** – follow the eastern side of the gorge to the hatchery for about two kilometers. The area below the hatchery is worth exploring, especially the Dog's Leg Pool (1km), which is along a swirling reach of the Capilano River, and if you really want to stretch your legs you could follow the river the full 7km to its mouth on the Burrard Inlet. Alternatively, you could ride the #236 Grouse Mountain bus to the Cleveland Dam or the main park entrance – the hatchery is quickly reached via a side road (or the Pipeline Trail) from the signed main entrance left off Nancy Greene Way. This comes not far after the busy roadside entrance to the Capilano Suspension Bridge (on the bus, ring the bell for the stop after the bridge).

Lynn Canyon Park

Among the easiest targets for a quick taste of backwoods Vancouver is **Lynn Canyon Park** (7am–dusk; free), a quiet, forested area with a modest ravine and suspension bridge, which, unlike the more popular Capilano Suspension Bridge (see below), you don't have to pay to cross. Several walks of up to ninety minutes take you through fine scenery – cliffs, rapids, waterfalls, and, naturally, the eighty-metre-high, bridge over Lynn Creek – all just twenty minutes from Lonsdale Quay. Take bus #228 from the quay to its penultimate stop at Peters Street, from where it's a ten-minute walk to the gorge; alternatively, take the less-frequent #229 Westlynn bus from Lonsdale Quay, which drops you about five minutes closer. Before entering the gorge, it's worth popping into the **Ecology Centre**, 3663 Park Rd, off Peters Road (June–Aug daily 10am–5pm; Oct–Feb Mon–Fri 10am–5pm, Sat & Sun and holidays noon–4pm; donation suggested; ⓣ604/981-3103 or 987-5922, ⓦwww.dnv.org), a friendly and informative place where you can pick up maps and pamphlets on park trails and wildlife.

Mount Seymour Provincial Park

At 3508 hectares, **Mount Seymour Provincial Park** (always open; free; ⓣ604/924-2200, ⓦwww.gov.bc.ca/bcparks) is the largest of the North Vancouver parks, the most easterly and the one that comes closest to the flavor of high-mountain scenery. It's 16km north of Vancouver and named after the short-serving BC provincial governor, Frederick Seymour (1864–69). To get there by **bus**, take the #239 from Lonsdale Quay to Phibbs Exchange and then the #215 to the Mount Seymour Parkway (1hr) – from there you'll have to walk or cycle up the thirteen-kilometre road to the heart of the park. The road climbs to over 1000m and ends at a parking lot where boards spell out clearly the trails and mountaineering options available. Views are superb on good days, particularly from the popular **Vancouver Lookout** on the parkway approach road, where a map identifies the city landmarks below. In winter this is the most popular family and learners' **ski area** near Vancouver (call ⓣ986-2261 or visit ⓦwww.mountseymour.com for information; passes cost $33 daily).

There are four major **trails** here, manageable in a day though you should be aware that conditions can change rapidly and snow lingers as late as June. The easiest hikes go out to Goldie Lake, a half-hour stroll, and to Dog Mountain, an hour from the parking area (one-way), with great views of the city below. Still better views, requiring more effort, can be had on the trails to First and Second Pump. The wildest and most demanding hike bypasses Mount Seymour's summit and runs by way of an intermittently marked trail to the forest- and mountain-circled Elsay Lake.

Adjacent to the park to the northwest is the **Lower Seymour Conservation Reserve** (daily 8am–dusk or 9pm in summer; ⓣ604/987-1273, ⓦwww.gvrd.bc.ca/lscr), a 14,000-acre area of mostly temperate rainforest, nestled in the lower part of a glacier-carved valley. It's situated at the northern end of Lillooet Road and, if going by public transport, you need to take the #229 Lynn Valley bus to Dempsey Road and Lynn Valley Road. From here it's a ten-minute walk over Lynn Creek via the bridge on Rice Lake Road. You're far better off, however, coming up here on a bike, for the 40km of trails in the area offer some of the best **mountain biking** close to Downtown. Forestry education is the area's chief concern, as the area's name suggests, and you can follow various sixty- and ninety-minute marked **hiking trails** that will top up your general knowledge about local trees, soils, fish, and wildlife.

Cypress Provincial Park

Cypress Provincial Park (always open; free; ⓣ604/926-6007, ⓦwww.gov.bc.ca/bcparks) is the most westerly of the big parks that part-cover the dramatic mountains and forest visible from Vancouver's Downtown. It's also among British Columbia's most visited day-use parks and probably the most popular of the North Shore's protected areas. This is partly to do with its scenic diversity, but also its wilderness. The 3012-hectare park divides into northern and southern sections joined by a narrow corridor of land. The southern section (first designated in 1975) has road access in the shape of the **Cyprus Access Road** (or Cypress Parkway), some developed facilities, accessible trails, and lots of rugged backcountry. The northern section (protected in 1982) is considerably wilder and can only be approached via the 29-kilometre Howe Sound Crest Trail from the southern section or by tracks from Hwy-99 and Howe Sound to the west.

To get here you really need a car or bike: the heart of the park, main parking lot, Alpine ski area and principal trailheads in the southern section are at **Cypress Bowl** at the end of the access road, 15km north of Exit #8 of Hwy 1-99 (the Upper Levels Highway) at Cypress Bowl Road. Note that as you follow the road you'll pass a turn after 13km to the right for the **Hollyburn** Nordic skiing area, only really relevant if you are here in winter (see below) or wish to tackle one or both of the trails that start from this area. To get within striking distance using public transport, take the #253 Caulfield/Park Royal or the #257 Horseshoe Bay Express **bus** from the Park Royal interchange. The Cypress Access Road, the main approach, has great **views** over the city and as far as Mount Baker in Washington State.

Lighthouse Park

The 75-hectare **Lighthouse Park** (always open; free), just west of Cypress, offers a seascape semi-wilderness at the extreme western tip of the north shore, 8km from the Lions Gate Bridge. Smooth granite rocks and low cliffs line the shore, backed by huge Douglas firs up to 1500 years old, some of the best virgin forest in southern BC. The rocks make fine sun beds, though the water out here is colder than around the city beaches. A map at the parking lot shows the two trails to the 1912 Point Atkinson **lighthouse** itself – you can take one out and the other back, a return trip of about 5km which involves about two-hours' walking. Although the park has its secluded corners (no camping allowed), it can be disconcertingly busy during summer weekends. For more **information** on the park, contact the infocentre or call ⓣ925-7200 or 925-7000. The West Van #250 **bus** makes the journey all the way from Georgia Street in Downtown.

Eating and drinking

Vancouver's restaurants are some of Canada's finest, and span the price spectrum from budget to blowout. As you'd expect, the city also offers a wide range of ethnic cuisines. **Chinese** and **Japanese** restaurants have the highest profile, followed by **Italian**, **Greek**, and other European imports. **Vietnamese** and **Thai** are more recent arrivals and can often provide the best starting points – cafés and the ubiquitous fast-food chains aside – if you're on a tight budget. Specialist **seafood** restaurants are surprisingly thin on the ground, but those that exist are of high quality and often remarkably cheap. In any case, seafood does crop up on most menus and salmon is heavily featured. **Vegetarians** are well served by a number of specialist places.

The city also has a commendable assortment of **bars**, many a cut above the functional dives and sham pubs found elsewhere in BC. Note, however, that the definitions of bar, café, restaurant, and nightclub can be considerably blurred: food in some form – usually substantial – is available in most places, while day-time cafés and restaurants also operate happily as night-time bars.

Cafés

Countless **cafés** are found mainly around the beaches, in parks, along Downtown streets, and especially on Granville Island. Many sell light meals as well as the coffee and snack staples. **Little Italy**, the area around Commercial Drive (between Venables and Broadway), is good for cheap, cheerful, and downright trendy cafés and restaurants, though new waves of immigrants from other locales are slowly filling Little Italy. The heavily residential **West End**, notably around Denman and Davie streets – Vancouver's "gay village" – is also booming, having gained a selection of interesting shops and restaurants.

Bavaria 203 Carrall St, Gastown (no phone). A simple, small, and no-frills place with a couple of tables outside on Maple Tree Square almost in front of Gassy Jack's statue. Its inexpensive all-day breakfast is great value.

Blake's 221 Carrall St, Gastown ⓣ604/899-3354. One of several relaxed places on this short Gastown stretch of Carrall Street to drop by for a coffee, sandwich, or snack and the chance to while away an hour writing a postcard or reading the newspaper.

Boulangerie la Parisienne 1076 Mainland St, Yaletown ⓣ604/ 684-2499. A café and bakery with a striking and very pretty all-blue interior that – true to its name – opens up French-style onto the pavement in summer.

Bread Garden 1040 Denman St at Comox St, West End ⓣ604/685-2996. Locals love to moan about the slow service, but food in these hyper-trendy deli-cafés is among the best – and best-looking – in the city. Great for people watching. Also in Kitsilano at 1880 W 1st Ave at Cypress, and 812 Bute St, Downtown, off Robson.

Capers 1675 Robson St, Downtown ⓣ604/687-5299. *Capers* is a three-branch chain of pristine supermarkets selling natural and organic foods, many of which can be bought as sandwiches and snacks in the onsite cafés. There is also a branch at 2285 West 4th Ave (ⓣ739-6676).

Flying Wedge 3499 Cambie St, Downtown ⓣ604/874-8284, ⓦwww.flyingwedge.com. If you want good, cheap pizza this is the place; thin-crust pizza by the slice (but no alcohol) and take-away at various outlets throughout the city.

Gallery Café Vancouver Art Gallery 750 Hornby St, Downtown ⓣ604/ 688-2233. Relaxed, stylish, and pleasantly arty place at the heart of Downtown for coffee, good lunches, and healthy, high-quality snack food and light meals (especially good desserts); also has a popular summer patio.

Hamburger Mary's 1202 Davie St and Bute, West End ⓣ604/687-1293. These may well be the best burgers in the city (though by no means the cheapest), but there are plenty of other things on the menu. Lots of people end the evening for a snack at this former West End diner. Outside tables when the weather is fine. Open very late (usually 3am).

La Luna Café 117 Water St, Gastown ⓣ604/687-5862. One of only a couple of places for coffee, muffins, and snacks on Gastown's main street that has the character – helped by a warm and welcoming, yellow-painted interior – to raise it above the usual tourist-oriented cafés in this part of the city.

The Only Café 20 E Hastings and Carrall St, Chinatown ⓣ604/ 681-6546. One of Vancouver's most famous institutions, founded in 1912, and worth the trip to a less than salubrious part of town to sample some of the best seafood in town and the old-world atmosphere. That said, this tiny greasy spoon (just 17 counter seats and two booths) has little more than seafood and potatoes on its menu; no toilets, no credit cards, no license, and no messing with the service. Closed Sun.

Sophie's Cosmic Café 2095 W 4th Ave, South Vancouver ☎604/ 732-6810. This 1950s-style diner is a Kits institution, packed for weekend breakfast and weekday lunch. It is renowned for its vast, spicy burgers, mussels, milkshakes, good vegetarian options, and whopping breakfasts. Some may find its self-conscious kitsch a little too contrived.

Terra Breads Granville Island Public Market and branches ☎604/ 685-3102. Tremendous rustic, grainy, and fresh-baked breads are the speciality here, with black olive, rosemary, focaccia, cheese, onion, rye, raisin, grape, pine nut, and other variations also available. You can also pick up the odd accompaniment and sandwich to combine with a drink from elsewhere.

Restaurants

Restaurants are spread around the city – check locations carefully if you don't want to travel too far from Downtown – though are naturally thinner on the ground in North and West Vancouver. Places in Gastown are generally tourist-oriented, with some notable exceptions, in marked contrast to Chinatown's bewildering plethora of genuine and reasonably priced options. Downtown also offers plenty of chains and huge choice, particularly with top-dollar places and fast-food fare, and the old warehouse district of **Yaletown**, is a key – and still developing – eating and nightlife area. Similar places line Fourth Avenue in Kitsilano and neighbouring West Broadway, though these require something of a special journey if you're based in or around Downtown.

Chinese

Floata Seafood Restaurant 400–180 Keefer St, Chinatown ☎604/ 602-0368. You can eat dim sum in many Vancouver Chinese restaurants but one of the most popular places to indulge is *Floata*, currently Canada's largest Chinese restaurant. Despite its size – the main dining area is nearly the length of a city block – it is not easy to find: it's on the third floor of a mall close to the Dr Sun Yat-Sen Garden. Dim sum is popular – and cheap – at lunch (choose from the carts being wheeled around by countless waitresses), but in the evening menu items become more adventurous and more expensive: shark-fin and bird's-nest soups, Peking duck and so forth.

Hon's Wun-Tun House 108–268 Keefer St at Gore St, Chinatown ☎604/ 688-0871. This canteen-like Cantonese spot started life more than twenty years ago as an inexpensive, basic, and popular place known for the house specialities, "potstickers" – fried meat-filled dumplings – home-made noodles (go for those with shrimp, meat, dumplings, or the spicy oyster, ginger, and green onion) and ninety-odd soups (including fish ball and pig's feet). It's invariably packed and hectic, but the service is efficient. Dim sum is available and there's a separate vegetarian menu. Also at 1339 Robson St.

Imperial Chinese Seafood Restaurant 355 Burrard St, Downtown ☎604/688-8191. A grand and opulent spot in the old Marine Building that serves fine, but pricey, Cantonese food (good dim sum, fresh egg noodles, delicious lobster in black bean sauce, pan-fried black cod, and more) and looks nothing like the standard Chinese restaurant: the long dining room has white walls, smart royal-blue carpet, and crisp, white table linen; windows run down one side, offering good city views.

Kirin Mandarin 1166 Alberni St near Bute St, Downtown ☎604/ 682-8833. This was among the first of the city's smart Chinese restaurants when it opened in 1987, with a big business clientele and elegant, postmodern decor – green pastel walls, pink table linen, and lots of black lacquer – that put it a world away from the more traditional and basic canteens of old-fashioned Chinatown. The expensive, superior food covers several Chinese regions: Cantonese (good scallops in black-bean sauce), Shanghai, and the spicier dishes of Szechuan (try the hot chilli fish). Prices are high, but you're repaid with good food and great views of the mountains.

Pink Pearl 1132 E Hastings St near Glen Drive, Chinatown ☎604/ 253-4316. This Vancouver institution is a big, fun, bustling, and old-fashioned place with an unpretentious and highly authentic feel – but it's in a dingy part of town and ten blocks east of the main part of Chinatown. The inexpensive food has a Cantonese slant, strong on seafood and great for dim sum (served daily): good bets are clams in black-bean sauce, spicy prawns, or other fish and seafood options (crab, shrimp, scallops, oysters, rock cod, and more) scooped from big glass tanks near the entrance.

Shanghai Chinese Bistro 1128 Alberni St, Downtown ☎604/ 683-8222. A modern-looking but less ostentatious and more reasonably priced alternative to the *Imperial* if you want to eat Chinese Downtown. The handmade noodles are a must – there's also a daily noodle-making demonstration for the curious. Dim sum is available, but fresh seafood is the speciality. Open till around 2 or 3am.

Wild Rice 117 West Pender St, Gastown ☎604/642-2882. A western take on Chinese food from a former chef at *Bin 941* (see p.449), with moderate dishes and ingredients from across China refined and reworked for Canadian consumption. Go for the bite-size tasters or platters to share and don't worry too much about cost – this is high-quality food at reasonable prices. Dishes might include wild boar with jasmine rice and plantain, rabbit wontons, winter melon salad, crispy fried duck, and warm rice pudding with chocolate and ginger. There is a good, short wine list and a choice of teas and martinis.

French

Cioppino's Mediterranean Grill 1133 Hamilton St, Yaletown ☎604/688-7466. This is an attractive and convenient place if you are in this part of town – the name comes from San Francisco's *cioppino* fish stew, but some food is French-influenced, other dishes are Italian. Perhaps the best thing to do is sample a little of almost everything with the tasting menu. If the food seems too expensive, make instead for the *Cioppino* wine bar next door for a drink.

The Hermitage 115–1025 Robson St near Thurlow St, Downtown ☎604/689-3237. Warm brick walls, a big fireplace, crisp linen, antique furnishing, French-speaking waiters, and a courtyard setting give this central and very highly rated Downtown restaurant a cozy almost European feel. The chef here once cooked for King Leopold of Belgium – the onion soup is unbeatable. You can also go for classic calorie-laden French food, such as duck Magret with an Armagnac sauce or veal tenderloin with a wild mushroom sauce. Lunch Mon–Fri, dinner daily.

Le Crocodile 100–909 Burrard St, entrance on Smithe St, Downtown ☎604/669-4298. This plush, French-Alsace upmarket bistro pushes *Bishop's* (see opposite) for the title of the city's best restaurant. The punchy decor – bright yellow walls – conjure up a suitable Parisian feel, while the menu offers something for traditionalists and the more adventurous alike – anything from classic steak tartare, onion tarte, Dover sole, and calf's liver to more outré dishes involving non-Gallic staples of the Pacific Rim. A memorable meal is guaranteed – but check your credit limit first. Lunch Mon–Fri, dinner daily.

Le Gavroche 1616 Alberni St, Downtown ☎604/685-3924. *Le Crocodile* may take the culinary plaudits, but this top French restaurant (with a West Coast twist) is not far behind. It's a formal but amiable place located in an old West End townhouse, and while the food is excellent – with particularly fine sea bass with white beans or veal tenderloin with lobster sauce – it's the highly romantic setting that really sets this place apart. The dining room is wonderfully cozy thanks to dark-painted walls and a big open fireplace, grand mirrors and old paintings. Lunch Mon–Fri, dinner daily.

Lucy Mae Brown 862 Richards St, Downtown ☎604/899-9199. This intimate restaurant is one of the most popular in the city, and takes its name from the owner of a former brothel and boarding-house on the site. Food changes regularly with the seasons, but is always lusty (lamb shanks or ahi tuna with capers) without forgetting its sophisticated French and West Coast inspirations. Downstairs is a secret, club-like little bar that opens late and has a simplified menu. Dinner only Mon–Sat.

Lumière 2551 W Broadway near Trafalgar St, South Vancouver ☎604/739-8185. This is in the first rank of Vancouver's restaurants. Cooking here is "contemporary French", a bit lighter than what you might expect to find at its rivals (see above), but no less pricey. A good option is to take one of the two set-price "tasting" menus offered each evening; one vegetarian, the other meat, fish, and fowl. You'll need to book, for the simple, tasteful dining room accommodates just fifty diners. Closed Mon.

Greek

Orestes 3116 W Broadway between Trutch and Balaclava sts, South Vancouver ☎604/738-1941. Good, basic food in one of the city's oldest Greek restaurants. Belly dancers shake their stuff Thursday to Saturday and there's live music on Sunday.

Ouzeri 3189 W Broadway at Trutch St, South Vancouver ☎604/739-9995. A friendly and fairly priced restaurant on a part of the strip with several other good restaurants and cafés. You'll find all the Greek standards here, but the vegetable moussaka is a standout, as are the chicken livers and the prawns with ouzo and mushrooms.

Stepho's 1124 Davie St between Thurlow and Bute sts, West End ⓣ604/683-2555. This central restaurant has simple interior, fine food, big portions, low prices, efficient service, and is very popular (expect lines). The daily specials are always a good bet (go for the baby back ribs if they are available): otherwise, avgolemono soup (a chicken broth with lemon and egg) is good, as are staples such as chicken, lamb, or beef pita (with fries and tzatziki garlic sauce), or meat brochettes (souvlaki) accompanied by potatoes, rice pilaf, or Greek salad.

Italian

Allegro Café 1G–888 Nelson St, Downtown ⓣ604/683-8485. The inexpensive to moderate Italian and Mediterranean food here is excellent and good value for Downtown. Try the great soups (roast garlic a standout), exotic pastas (cappelli with scallops, leeks, and Roma tomatoes), or ambitious mains (pan-seared halibut medallions in apple fennel butter sauce with celery-root chips). Puddings are also good: go for Cajun bread pudding or peanut butter pie, the latter courtesy of chef Barbara Reese, of the Reese Peanut Butter Cup dynasty.

CinCin 1154 Robson St, Downtown ⓣ604/688-7338. Plenty of fashion, politics, arts and media luminaries frequent the place, but it's never precious or showy. The refined Italian food merits the highish prices and includes top-grade home-made pastas, pizzas, and desserts. Some of the best dishes, notably chicken and game, are cooked over the alderwood-fired open grill. The restaurant also boasts one of the best wine lists in this or any other city, with plenty of wines by the glass. In summer, try to book an outside table on the terrace. Lunch Mon–Sat, dinner daily.

The Old Spaghetti Factory 55 Water St, Gastown ⓣ604/ 684-1288. Part of a chain and hardly *alta cucina*, but a standby if you're in Gastown and better than the tourist trap it appears from the outside, with its spacious 1920s Tiffany interior and a good range of pastas, chicken, and other meat and fish dishes. A good place to go with children as prices are low, there's plenty of room, the atmosphere is informal, and the simple Italian food is likely to appeal.

Piccolo Mondo 850 Thurlow St and Smithe St, Downtown ⓣ604/688-1633. A nicely restrained dining room, just off Robson Street, that's not as formal as the austere red-brick facade, plain white walls, and wooden floors first make it appear. The *osso bucco* is excellent, as are the veal loin and rather un-Italian starter of sweet-and-sour prawns; other good bets include *zuppa di pesce* or ravioli with salmon and ricotta. The wine list is also superb, drawing from a cellar of over 4000 bottles. Lunch Mon–Fri, dinner daily.

Villa del Lupo 869 Hamilton St, Downtown ⓣ604/ 688-7436. Authentic, high-quality food in a renovated, unfussy and elegant Victorian-era "country" house on the eastern edge of Downtown. There's not a better *osso bucco* in Vancouver if you want to eat traditional Italian, though more sophisticated dishes include tuna loin with cracked black-pepper crust or sweetcorn broth with ricotta and spinach gnocchi.

Seafood and West Coast cuisine

Bishop's 2183 W 4th St near Yew Ave ⓣ604/738-2025. *Bishop's* is consistently ranked as one of Vancouver's best restaurants. Although there's a frequent film-star and VIP presence, the welcome's as warm for everyone. The light and refined "contemporary home cooking" – Italy meets the Pacific Rim – commands high prices but is worth it. Menus change three or four times a year according to season: if in doubt, the daily special is invariably a winner. Booking days (sometimes weeks) ahead is essential.

Blue Water Café 1095 Hamilton St, Yaletown ⓣ604/688-8078. This big restaurant has quickly become one of Yaletown's most popular fixtures, thanks to its sushi, fish, and seafood, and to the attractive terrace and long interior, the last a dark, comfortable space of exposed beams and brick originally used as ballast in 1890s ships. There's an open kitchen for the fish and seafood staples (great halibut dishes, BC sablefish or salmon with pumpkin seed gnocchi), plus Eastern and Western bars (for sushi or ceviche, caviar and other treats receptively).

Bridges 1696 Duranleau St, Granville Island ⓣ604/687-4400. This is an unmissable big, yellow restaurant upstairs; pub and informal bistro (the best option) downstairs, with a large outdoor deck. A reliable and very popular choice on Granville Island for a drink, snack (good nachos), or fuller meal of predictable pasta, fish, and meat options.

C Restaurant 2-1600 Howe St near Pacific Blvd, Downtown ⓣ604/ 681-1164. There are those that claim this is the best fish restaurant in Canada. The lengthy menu, which shows plenty of Southeast Asian influences, might include a choice from the "raw bar" – say a *tartare* trio of scallop, wasabi salmon, and smoked chilli tuna – and fish such as Alaskan Arctic char. The taster of starters might include salmon gravlax cured in Saskatoon-

berry tea, grilled garlic squid, abalone tempura, and artichoke carpaccio – though the Skeena River sockeye terrine is unbeatable. Main courses might feature *Maui hai* tuna sashimi with 50-year-old balsamic vinegar or octopus bacon wrapping diver scallops with seared Québec fois gras. Views from the dining room are almost as good as the food.

Chartwell *Four Seasons Hotel*, 791 W Georgia St, Downtown ⓣ604/844-6715. Don't let the fact that this is a hotel dining room put you off: the gracious, almost gentleman's club-like ambience is good if you want to dress up or have an indulgent lunch, and fine service, a great wine list, and progressive Pacific Rim-influenced food make this one of the top restaurants in Vancouver. Ingredients are invariably organic and lavished on dishes that might include oxtail *confit* and sublime puddings such as white chocolate and lime mousse.

Diva at the Met Metropolitan Hotel, 645 Howe St, Downtown ⓣ604/602-7788. Like the *Chartwell* (see above), *Diva* has carved out a character completely separate to the hotel with which it's associated (a vast glass wall separates restaurant and hotel). The food is punchy and imaginative and the dining rooms are modern and clean-lined. The popular tasting menu is the best way to sample the food, albeit at some of Vancouver's highest prices. A great place for a treat or full-on brunch.

Earl's 1185 Robson St, corner of Bute St, Downtown ⓣ604/ 669-0020. Come here first if you don't want to mess around scouring Downtown for somewhere to eat. The mid-priced, and often innovative, high-quality food is as eclectic as you please – everything from North American burgers to Far Eastern stir-fry and all points in between – and is served in a big, buzzy, open, and casual-to-a-fault dining area. You can eat on the outside terrace in summer. Inexpensive.

Ferguson Point Teahouse Ferguson Point, Stanley Park ⓣ604/669-3281. The best place for a lunch or brunch during a walk or ride round the park. The food here embraces most West Coast and French–Italian staples (fine carrot soup, good seafood, and excellent steaks), though between 2.30 and 5pm daily the tearoom and patio serve simple light snacks and refreshments. Book a table on the terrace a day or so in advance.

The Fish House in Stanley Park 8901 Stanley Park Drive ⓣ604/681-7275. The leafy setting is pretty, the restaurant is housed in an attractive white-clapboard building, and the seafood is among the city's best. Inside, the three club-like dining rooms are painted in rich greens and whites offset by lots of dark wood. Indulge at the Oyster Bar, order any available fish baked, broiled, steamed, or grilled, or check out the daily specials. Obvious choices such as fish-cakes don't disappoint, but here it pays to be more adventurous: how about prawns flambéed with ouzo or ahi tuna with green-pepper sauce or – as one of several excellent vegetable accompaniments – red cabbage with fennel and buttermilk mash.

Isadora's 1540 Old Bridge St, Granville Island ⓣ604/681-8816. A popular choice for a beer or a straightforward meal, *Isadora's* offers fine breakfasts, weekend brunches, and light meals (with plenty of good vegetarian and wholefood options) and a menu that covers most North American bases. There's lots of outdoor seating, but expect lines and slower service at weekends, particularly Sunday brunch. Closed for dinner Mon Sept–May.

Liliget Feast House 1724 Davie St, West End ⓣ604/681-7044. This aboriginal restaurant – the only one of its kind in Vancouver – serves types of food you'll get nowhere else in the city: things like seaweed, steamed ferns, roast caribou, and barbecued juniper duck. However, the cedar tables and benches inside, designed to resemble those of a Coast Salish longhouse, make the dining room a mite austere.

Milestone's 1145 Robson St, Downtown ⓣ604/682-4477; 1210 Denman St ⓣ604/ 662-3431; Yaletown at 1109 Hamilton St at Helmcken ⓣ604/ 684-9112. Three popular mid-market chain restaurants with cheap drinks and standard but well-prepared and occasionally innovative North American food (especially good breakfasts) in very generous portions.

Raincity Grill 1193 Denman St, West End ⓣ604/685-7337. The candles and a position near Davie St overlooking English Bay make for a romantic dining experience, but it is the food and wine, both of which make the most of British Columbian and Pacific Northwest ingredients (more than 100 varieties of Northwest and Californian wines by the glass are available) which are the main attraction. The regional menu changes regularly, but you can always be sure to find salmon, seafood, and other locally produced food (much of it organic) and at least four vegetarian options. Dinner daily, brunch Sat & Sun.

Water Street Café 300 Water St, Gastown ⓣ604/689-2832. The café-restaurant of choice if you wind up in Gastown. The dining rooms (one downstairs, two upstairs) are pretty and relaxed, but in summer try to book an outside table. The menu at lunch and dinner is short and well planned, and mixes cuisines, but with a bias towards modern Italian-influenced cooking – salmon with soy sauce and balsamic vinegar, pasta with chicken, and dishes with Parmesan *gratinée*.

Other ethnic restaurants

Bin 941 941 Davie Street, West End ☎604/ 683-1246. *Bin 941* and its sister outlet at 1521 West Broadway in South Vancouver (☎734-9421) are tiny, on the slightly crazy side of funky, and packed long and late with people drawn by the up-tempo bars (the West Broadway location is marginally more subdued) and some of the city's best – and best-value – bite-size food. The menu's "tapatizers" include great fries ($3 for a mountain of hand-cut Yukon Gold potato fries), jumbo scallops, tiger-prawn tournedos, crabcakes, charred *bok choy*, and many more. Open for dinner daily until 2am.

Chiyoda 1050 Alberni St at Burrard St, Downtown ☎604/ 688-5050. Chic but convivial – the emphasis is on *robata* (grilled food) bar rather than sushi – *Chiyoda* draws Japanese visitors and business people at lunch and the fashionable in the evenings. The day's produce is laid out on ice on the wooden counter in front of the grills – choose from around thirty different items (fish, prawns, oysters, and so forth) and then have your choice of food grilled, seasoned, and returned to you on long paddles.

Ezogiku Noodle Café 1329 Robson St at Jervis St, Downtown ☎604/685-8608. This tiny 70-seat Japanese ramen noodle house (with sister outlets in Tokyo and Honolulu) is a perfect place for quick, good food Downtown. The lines may be off-putting, but the turnover's speedy. Cash only and no alcohol.

Mescalero's 1215 Bidwell St, West End ☎604/669-2399. Very popular Mexican restaurant with fine, if predictable food: what draws people here are the fair prices, very lively atmosphere, and the chance to eyeball the other fit and young.

The Naam 2724 W 4th Ave near Stephens St, South Vancouver ☎604/ 738-7151. The oldest and most popular health-food and vegetarian restaurant in the city. The ambience is comfortable and friendly – as you'd expect from a place with Kits's hippie-era origins – with live folk and other music as well as outside eating some evenings. Open 24hr.

Phnom-Penh 244 E Georgia St near Gore St, Chinatown ☎604/ 682-5777; 955 W Broadway near Oak St, South Vancouver ☎604/734-8988. Excellent Vietnamese and Cambodian cuisine, with some Chinese dishes, are served in this pair of friendly, family-oriented restaurants. Seafood is a strength, with a renowned spicy garlic crab, plus delicious garlic and pepper prawns (in season). Also try the *bank xeo*, a Vietnamese pancake filled with prawns and bean sprouts.

Pho Hoang 3610 Main St at 20th Ave, Chinatown ☎604/874-0810; 238 E Georgia St, Chinatown ☎604/682-5666. Choose from thirty soup varieties with herbs, chillis, and lime at plate-side as added seasoning. Open for breakfast, lunch, and dinner. The more recent Chinatown branch is right by the *Phnom-Penh* (see above).

Simply Thai 1211 Hamilton St at Davie St, Yaletown ☎604/642-0123. This plain, modern but inviting Yaletown restaurant is packed at lunch (11.30am–3pm) and dinner, thanks to the keen prices as well as the good and very authentic food – the chefs are all from Bangkok.

Tojo's 777 W Broadway at Willow St, South Vancouver ☎604/872-8050. Quite simply the best Japanese food in the city. Well worth the journey from Downtown,– anything on the menu involving tuna is superb, but you should sample some of the many more unusual (such as shrimp dumplings with hot mustard sauce) or standards such as lobster claws, crab, and herring roe. This is sushi close to perfection – but at prices which make sure you savor every mouthful. Dinner only Mon–Sat.

Topanga Café 2904 W 4th Ave near Macdonald St, South Vancouver ☎604/733-3713. A small but extremely popular Cal-Mex restaurant that's become a Vancouver institution. Prices are low and helpings large, a combination that has drawn hungry diners here for over twenty years and makes this a good place for people traveling with children. There are just forty places, so arrive before 6pm or after 8pm to avoid the worst of the waiting in line. Closed Sun.

Vij's 1480 W 11th Ave at Granville St, South Vancouver ☎604/736-6664. *Vij's* East Indian cooking has deservedly won just about every award going in Vancouver for Best Ethnic Cuisine. At the time of writing you still couldn't make reservations – you simply line up with other hopefuls and enjoy the free tea and *poppadoms* while you wait. The menus change roughly monthly, but never let go of old faithfuls such as curried-vegetable rice pilaf with cilantro cream sauce or Indian lentils with naan and yoghurt-mint sauce. The vegetarian options are excellent. Dinner only. Moderate.

Bars

In this section we've highlighted **bars** whose main emphasis is food and drink; entertainment venues are listed in the next section. Note, too, that Vancouver has a handful of places that stay open all night or until the small hours; a selection of these is listed below.

Alibi Room 157 Alexander St between Columbia and Main ☎604/623-3383. Various movie makers and shakers put money into this unashamedly hip and happening bar-restaurant – and the result is a crowd that is trendy, but not to the extent that it spoils this as a good place for drinks and – perhaps – dinner. Excellent and eclectic food is served upstairs, with a short, modern menu and surprisingly reasonable prices; downstairs you can drink and venture onto the small dancefloor.

The Arts Club 1585 Johnston St, Granville Island ☎604/687-1354. The Arts Club's popular *Backstage Bar and Grill*, part of its theater complex, has seating with a waterfront view on Granville Island beneath the bridge, easygoing atmosphere, decent food, and blues, jazz, and other live music Friday and Saturday evenings. It's especially well known for its 50-plus selection of whiskies.

Bar None 1222 Hamilton St ☎604/689-7000. A busy and reasonably smart under-forty-something Yaletown bar and club with brick and wooden beam interior where you can eat, drink, watch TV, smoke cigars (there's a walk-in humidor), play backgammon, or shoot pool and listen to live music. A house band plays Mondays and Tuesdays, with a DJ the rest of the week, though patrons are generally a touch too cool to make fools of themselves on the small dancefloor. Closed Sun.

Blarney Stone 216 Carrall St ☎604/687-4322. This lively pub and restaurant, in Gastown features nightly live Irish music from house band and dancefloor. If it looks a bit rough and ready, or just too plain rowdy, try *The Irish Heather* almost opposite across the street (see opposite). Closed Sun.

Bridges 1696 Duranleau St, Granville Island ☎604/687-4400. You can eat here (see p.447), but when the sun's shining it's hard to choose between the busy patio here and the *Dockside Brewing Company* (see below) as to which is the nicest place to have a waterside drink on Granville Island: *Bridges* is more central and thus more convenient.

The Cambie 300 Cambie St ☎604/684-6466. An obvious place to drink if you're staying at the linked hostel (see p.421), but the roomy (and invariably crowded) outdoor area and cheap pitchers of beer bring in a fair number of locals. Inside, it's all smoke, pool tables, and down-to-earth drinking.

Cardero's Marine Pub 1583 Coal Harbour Quay on Cardero St ☎604/669-7666. The location of this pub-restaurant is neither one thing nor the other, around midway between Stanley Park and Burrard, but the waterfront location and patio (heated on cooler evenings) at the northern end of Cardero St offers great views of the park, moored boats, Burrard Inlet, and the North Shore.

Cloud Nine *Empire Landmark Hotel*, 1400 Robson St at Nicola St ☎604/687-0511. Vancouver has several bars with a view – notably the lounge in the *Sylvia* (see opposite) and *Bridges* on Granville Island (see p.448) – but none that can match the panorama from this super-sleek lounge bar on the 42nd floor of the *Empire Landmark Hotel*. The bar rotates, so your view changes by six degrees every sixty seconds. There's a modest cover charge for entry on Fri and Sat, but it's worth paying for the panorama.

Darby D. Dawes 2001 Macdonald St and West 4th Ave ☎604/731-0617. Relatively handy for the youth hostel and Kits Beach. People often start the evening here with a beer or game of darts – meals are served 11.30am–7pm, snacks till 10pm – and then move on to the *Fairview* for live blues (see p.453). Live music (a mixture of jazz, blues, and rock) in the pub is generally only played on Friday and Saturday evenings with jam sessions on Saturday afternoons.

Dockside Brewing Company 1253 Johnston St, Granville Island ☎604/685-7070. Beer buffs should try this sylish lounge in the *Granville Island Hotel* to sample some of the establishment's on-site microbrewery's ales. The atmosphere is relaxed and the generally well-heeled crowd thirty-something. Things tend to be more lively early in the evening, and in summer there's a fine outdoor patio.

Gerard Lounge 845 Burrard St between Robson and Smithe ☎604/682-5511. A smooth wood-panelled 25-seat lounge and piano bar in the smart *Sutton Place Hotel*, that re-creates the look and atmosphere of an English gentleman's club, complete with leather chairs, tapestries, old oil paintings, and wall-mounted stuffed animals. It all makes for elegant and rather distinctive Downtown drinking. This is also, at least until fashions change, one of the places to spot the stars currently filming in town – plus plenty of the wannabes.

The Irish Heather 217 Carrall St ⓣ604/688-9779. This charming Gastown place is a definite cut above the usual mock-Irish pub, with an intimate bar, varied clientele – anything from students to local gallery owners – lots of nooks and crannies, live Irish music some nights, and good Guinness (apparently it sells the second largest number of pints of the stuff in Canada).

La Bodega 1277 Howe St near Davie St ⓣ604/684-8815. This place towards the south of Downtown recreates a Spanish bar that could almost be in Spain. As a result, it's one of the city's best and most popular places to drink, with fine tapas (great *chorizo*) and excellent main courses to mop up the alcohol (including sangria and other Spanish drinks). Food aside, though, it's chiefly dedicated to lively drinking. It's packed later on, especially on Friday and Saturday, so try to arrive before 8pm. Closed Sun.

Shark Club Bar & Grill *The Sandman Hotel*, 180 W Georgia St ⓣ604/687-4275. This is currently the best and busiest of several sports bars in the city. This being Canada, ice hockey is popular, but you'll also catch basketball, baseball, soccer, and American and Canadian football (especially the last, as it's close to BC Place, home to the local team). There are thirty screens, a 180-seat oak bar, more than twenty beers on tap, Italian food from the kitchen, and lots of testosterone, though the place is by no means confined to rowdy jocks.

Sylvia Hotel 1154 Gilford St and Beach Ave ⓣ604/688-8865. There doesn't seem much here at first glance in this nondescript, easygoing hotel bar, but it is popular for quiet drinks and superlative waterfront views, and makes a very pleasant retreat after a stroll in Stanley Park and/or English Bay Beach.

Yaletown Brewing Company 1111 Mainland St at Helmcken ⓣ604/681-2739. There's no danger of missing this extremely large, modern bar and restaurant with its own six-beer onsite brewery. It's very popular, and one of the long-established leaders in the funky Yaletown revival. All the beers are excellent, as are the snacks and Italian and West Coast food in the restaurant. The patio is good in summer, and if the weather's bad you can retreat to several cozy indoor rooms.

Nightlife and entertainment

Vancouver gives you plenty to do come sunset, laying on a varied and cosmopolitan blend of both **live and dance music**. Clubs are more adventurous than in most Canadian cities, particularly the fly-by-night alternative dives on and around Main Street and Commercial Drive, and in the backstreets of Gastown and Chinatown. There's also a choice of smarter and more conventional clubs, a handful of discos, and a selection of **gay** and **lesbian** clubs and bars. Summer nightlife often takes to the streets in West Coast fashion, with outdoor bars and (to a certain extent) beaches becoming venues in their own right.

The most comprehensive **listings** guide to all the goings-on is *Georgia Straight* (ⓦwww.straight.com), a free weekly published on Thursday and available in larger stores and street boxes around the city. Many other free magazines devoted to different musical genres and activities are available at the same points, but they come and go quickly. Selected **club listings** can also be found by visiting ⓦwww.clubvibes.com, while ⓦwww.vancouverjazz.com/directory offers a list of **jazz venues**.

Tickets for many major events are sold through Ticketmaster, with forty outlets round the city (ⓣ604/280-3311 for general tickets or 604/280-4444 for rock concerts, ⓦwww.ticketmaster.ca); they'll sometimes unload discounted tickets for midweek and matinee performances. Half-price and last-minute same-day tickets are available via "Tickets Tonight" (ⓦwww.ticketstonight.ca) at participating venues, or through the outlet at the main TouristInfo visitor center at 200 Burrard St (see p.414).

Live music and clubs

Vancouver's live-music venues showcase a variety of musical styles, but mainstream **rock** groups are the most common bill of fare; the city is also a fertile breeding ground for **punk** bands, with particularly vocal fans. **Jazz** is generally hot news in Vancouver, with a dozen spots specializing in the genre (ring the Jazz Hot Line at ⓣ682-0706 for current and upcoming events).

Many venues also double as **clubs and discos**, and as in any city with a healthy alternative scene there are also plenty of fun, one-off clubs that have an irritating habit of cropping up and disappearing at speed. Cover charges are usually nominal, and tickets are often available (sometimes free) at record shops. At the other end of the spectrum, the 60,000-seat Pacific Coliseum is on the touring itinerary of most international acts.

Rock

The Cave Plaza of Nations, 750 Pacific Blvd and Cambie St ⓣ604/603-8597. A loud and young, progressive dance and live-music club with a big1000-plus capacity. It's blessed with five bars, a staggeringly loud sound system, and a huge and invariably packed dancefloor – think warehouse or aircraft hangar.

Commodore Ballroom 868 Granville St and Smithe St ⓣ 604/280-4444 or 739-7469. The city's best mid-sized venue (there's room for 990 people) benefited from a $1 million face-lift after being empty for three years, a makeover that to general rejoicing retained its renowned 1929 dancefloor and Art Deco patina. There is an adventurous music policy that embraces many different types of band (rock, pop, jazz, and blues), and they feature a new DJ every two to three weeks.

Piccadilly Pub 620 West Pender near Granville ⓣ604/682-3221. The "Pic" is a long-established pub with a guarantee of raucous music of some description (garage, rock, punk, rockabilly) most nights, usually Thursday to Saturday. It's a laid-back, non-poseur sort of place aimed at those who simply want beer, music, and a good time.

Railway Club 579 Dunsmuir St and Seymour St ⓣ604/681-1625. This is one of the city's best small –the place is tiny – venues, a long-established favorite with excellent bookings, casual atmosphere, and a wide range of live music (folk, blues, jazz, and rock). It's also a good place just for a drink and a game of darts – the upstairs pub is quieter and more relaxed than the stage bar downstairs. There's a separate "conversation" lounge where it's more peaceful, so it's ideal if you don't just want to come here for the music. If you arrive before 10pm at weekends be prepared to pay a nominal "private-club" membership fee.

Roxy 932 Granville and Nelson St ⓣ604/331-7999. The *Roxy* – "where life is like a beer commercial" – has been around for a while, providing a successful, casual, and fun place for the city's UBC college crowd and people in from the 'burbs. Four bars feature slick bartenders showing off their moves and there are live bands most nights – often the two very competent "house" bands – with an emphasis on 1950s to 1970s music. Also has theme dance nights and karaoke sessions.

Sonar 66 Water St and Abbott St ⓣ604/683-6695. This is one of central Vancouver's best and most heavily patronized music venues, largely by virtue of its cool, funky vibe and convenient mid-Gastown location. The live music nightly often seems something of a distraction – the place is also a good dance club and known as something of a pick-up spot. The clientele is mainly a casual bunch of 19- to 24-year-olds, and the music anything from jazz, reggae, trance, and soul to rock, hip-hop, techno, and progressive house. Bar food and piano lounge until 9pm, when the band strikes up and the more serious dancing and partying begin.

Jazz and blues

Arts Club Theatre Backstage Lounge 1585 Johnston St, Granville Island ⓣ604/687-1354. The lounge is a nice spot to hear R&B, jazz, and blues, or watch the boats and sunset on False Creek.

Capone's 1141 Hamilton St ⓣ604/684-7900. *Capone's* is one of the better fixtures that has opened up in burgeoning Yaletown. On the face of it, the place is primarily a restaurant – mostly pizza and pasta – but it also takes its jazz seriously, and there's a stage for nightly live performances. The restaurant's layout is oddly long and narrow, however, so arrive early or book a table near the stage if you want a decent view of what's going on.

Cellar Restaurant & Jazz Club 3611 West Broadway ⓣ 604/738-1959,

Ⓦ www.cellarjazz.com. Kitsilano has only recently acquired clubs, and this tiny 70-seat red-walled basement with black booths and low tables is one of the most popular, frequently offering the best live jazz in the city four or more nights a week (generally Wed–Sat). Join the enthusiastic crowd for top local outfits or big international names.

Fairview 898 W Broadway at the Ramada Inn Ⓣ 604/872-1262. Good local blues and 1950s rock'n'roll in something resembling a pub atmosphere – fans seem unperturbed by the hotel setting – which means there's generally a lively buzz but precious little room to move on the small dancefloor. Snacks are served during the day and good-value meals in the evening. Live music nightly from Monday to Saturday, with a cover charge at weekends depending on the band.

Purple Onion 15 Water St Ⓣ 604/602-9442, Ⓦ www.purpleonion.com. Casual club right in the heart of Gastown: top-notch jazz and live Latin music upstairs, dancefloor, cigars, oysters, and cabaret downstairs. Currently a very popular choice, so expect to wait in line on Friday and Saturday.

Yale 1300 Granville St and Drake St Ⓣ 604/681-9253. An outstanding venue: *the* place in the city to hear hardcore blues and R & B. Relaxed air, big dancefloor, and occasional outstanding international names. Often jam sessions with up to 50 players at once, on Saturday (3–8pm) and Sunday (3pm–midnight). Recommended. Closed Mon & Tues.

Discos and clubs

Au Bar 674 Seymour St Ⓣ 604/648-2227. Downtown club for suits and mini-skirts, with martinis the (expensive) drink of choice. Strict dress code and vetting on the door (you'll spot the Seymour Street lines from afar), but the exclusive air is what attracts punters. If you get in, people watching may prove the most entertaining part of your evening. Three bars and small dancefloor with safe Top 40, hip-hop, and R & B.

Atlantis 1320 Richards St Ⓣ 604/662-7707, Ⓦ www.atlantisclub.net. This newly renovated club has cutting edge music, lights, and dancefloor, and a sharp clientele to match. There's plenty of room at the rear bar for a drink and a break from the music, with hip-hop currently on Saturdays and a wide range of sounds on theme nights the rest of the week.

Plaza Club 881 Granville St Ⓣ 604/646-0064, Ⓦ www.plazaclub.net. A popular, no-nonsense dance club with great sound and lighting in a former cinema in central Granville St location. Music has a strong British bias, but there are also theme nights. Saturday is very popular, so expect to wait in line.

Richard's on Richards 1036 Richards St and Nelson St Ⓣ 604/687-6794, Ⓦ www.richardsonrichards.com. A well-known club and disco, but pretentious and aimed at the BMW set. Long waits and dress code. Open Thurs–Sat.

Shine 363 Water Street Ⓣ 604/408-4321. Happening Gastown club that attracts some of the city's top DJs, notably Dicky Doo. Understated decor, with comfortable retro 1960s couches and all-white color scheme provide a sophisticated setting for house, reggae, soul, R & B, hip-hop, and other sounds. Dress up a touch, or you'll feel out of place.

Voda *Westin Grand Hotel*, 783 Homer St Ⓣ 604/684-3003, Ⓦ www.voda.com. Arrive early in this very roomy hotel lounge near the central library and chances are it'll be empty. Come later and you'll find it heaving. The sleek look and fittings – wood panelling, back-lit bar, lots of candles, waterfalls, rocks, angled beams – are offset by the generally very elegant and fashion-conscious clientele. Don't wear your jeans. Music for the smallish dancefloor covers most bases, from R & B and funk to electro and old-school house. Closed Sunday and Monday.

Performing arts and cinema

Vancouver serves up enough highbrow culture to suit the whole spectrum of its cosmopolitan population, with plenty of unusual and avant-garde performances to spice up the more mainstream fare you'd expect of a major North American city. The main focus for the city's performing arts is the **Queen Elizabeth Theatre** (Ⓣ 604/299-9000, Ⓦ www.city.vancouver.bc.ca/theatres) at 600 Hamilton St at Georgia, which plays host to a steady procession of visiting theater, opera, and dance troupes, and even the occasional big rock band. It was joined in 1996 by the **Centre in Vancouver for**

the Performing Arts opposite the central library at 777 Homer St (Ⓣ604/602-0616, Ⓦwww.centreinvancouver.com). The refurbished **Orpheum Theatre**, 884 Granville at Smithe (Ⓣ604/665-3050, Ⓦwww.city.vancouver.bc.ca/theatres), is Vancouver's oldest theater and headquarters of the Vancouver Symphony Orchestra. Further afield, the **Chan Centre for the Performing Arts**, 6265 Crescent Rd, University of British Columbia (Ⓣ604/822-2697, Ⓦwww.chancentre.com) has the 1400-seat Chan Shun Concert Hall, the main space of the three-hall UBC performance complex. It has the best acoustics in the city, and hosts shows by outside and university music, drama, and other groups, as well as fashion shows, world-music, and other events. The UBC has a smaller Recital Hall at Gate 4, 6361 Memorial Rd. **Tickets** can be obtained from box offices or through the Ticketmaster agency (see p.451).

The western capital of Canada's film industry, Vancouver is increasingly favored by Hollywood studios in their pursuit of cheaper locations and production deals. It's therefore no surprise that the spread of **cinemas** is good. Home-produced and Hollywood first-run films play in the Downtown cinemas on "Theater Row" – the two blocks of Granville between Robson and Nelson streets – and other big complexes, and there's no shortage of cinemas for more esoteric productions.

Classical music

Early Music Vancouver 1254 West 7th Ave Ⓣ604/732-1610, Ⓦwww.earlymusic.bc.ca. Early music with original instruments where possible; concerts all over the city, and at the UBC during the Early Music Festival in July and August (see p.456).

Festival Concert Society The Vancouver Academy of Music, 1270 Chestnut St at Kits Point in Vanier Park Ⓣ604/736-3737. The society often organizes cheap Sunday morning concerts (jazz, folk, or classical) at the Queen Elizabeth Playhouse.

Music-in-the-Morning Concert Society 1270 Chestnut, Vanier Park Ⓣ604/873-4612, Ⓦwww.musicinthemorning.org. This began modestly in someone's front room over a decade ago but now organizes innovative and respected concerts of old and new music with local and visiting musicians.

University of British Columbia School of Music Recital Hall, Gate 4, 6361 Memorial Rd Ⓣ604/822-5574, Ⓦwww.music.ubc.ca. The UBC presents around eight major and many smaller performances during January and February and between September and November. Many of the concerts are free.

Vancouver Bach Choir 805-235 Keith Rd, West Vancouver Ⓣ604/921-8012, Ⓦwww.vancouverbachchoir.com. The city's top amateur choir performs three major concerts yearly at the Orpheum Theatre.

Vancouver Cantata Singers 5115 Keith Rd Ⓣ604/921-8588, Ⓦwww.cantata.org. Various locations are used by this 40-strong, semi-professional choir for performances of traditional and contemporary choral music.

Vancouver Chamber Choir 1254 W 7th Ave Ⓣ604/738-6822, Ⓦwww.vancouverchamberchoir.com. One of two professional, internationally renowned choirs in the city. They perform at the Orpheum and on some Sunday afternoons at the *Hotel Vancouver*.

Vancouver New Music Society 837 Davie St Ⓣ604/663-0861, Ⓦwww.newmusic.org. Responsible for several annual concerts of cutting-edge twentieth-century music, usually at the East Cultural Centre (see "Drama" below).

Vancouver Opera 500-845 Cambie St Ⓣ604/638-0222, Ⓦwww.vanopera.bc.ca. Four operas are produced annually at the Queen Elizabeth Theatre and productions currently enjoy an excellent reputation.

Vancouver Recital Society 304-873 Beatty St Ⓣ604/736-0363, Ⓦwww.vanrecital.com. Hosts two of the best and most popular cycles in the city: the summer Chamber Music Festival (at St George's School) and the main Vancouver Playhouse recitals (Sept–April). Catches up-and-coming performers plus a few major international names each year.

Vancouver Symphony Orchestra 601 Smithe St Ⓣ604/876-3434, Ⓦwww.vancouversymphony.ca. Presents most concerts at the Orpheum or new Chan Shun Hall on Crescent Rd off NW Marine Drive, but also sometimes gives free recitals in the summer at beaches and parks, culminating in a concert on the summit of Whistler Mountain.

Drama

Arts Club Theatre 1585 Johnston St, Granville Island ⓣ604/687-1644, ⓦwww.artsclub.com. A leading light in the city's drama scene, performing at three venues: the main stage, at 1585 Johnston St on Granville Island, offers mainstream drama, comedies, and musicals; the next-door bar presents small-scale revues and cabarets; and a third stage, at 1181 Seymour and Davie streets, focuses on avant-garde plays and Canadian dramatists – a launching pad for the likes of Michael J. Fox.

Firehall Arts Centre 280 E Cordova St and Gore St ⓣ604/689-0926, ⓦwww.firehall.org. The leader of Vancouver's community and avant-garde pack, presenting mime, music, video, and visual arts.

Theatre Under the Stars Malkin Bowl, Stanley Park ⓣ604/687-0174 or 257-0366, ⓦwww.tuts.bc.ca. Summer productions here are fun, but can suffer from being staged in one of Canada's rainiest cities.

Vancouver East Cultural Centre1895 Venables St and Victoria Drive t604/251-1363, wwww.vecc.bc.ca. Renowned performance space housed in an old church, used by a highly eclectic mix of drama, dance, mime, and musical groups.

Vancouver Playhouse Theatre Company Hamilton St at Dunsmuir St ⓣ604/665-3050. One of western Canada's biggest companies. It usually presents six top-quality shows with some of the region's premier performers and designers during its October to May season.

Waterfront Theatre 1411 Cartwright St, Granville Island ⓣ604/685-6217. Home to three resident companies that also hold workshops and readings.

Dance

Anna Wyman Dance Theatre 707-207 West Hastings St ⓣ604/685-5699, ⓦwww.annawyman.com. Although their repertoire is wide, this group specializes in contemporary dance. As well as standard shows, they occasionally put on free outdoor performances at Granville Island and at Robson Square.

Ballet British Columbia 1101 West Broadway ⓣ604/732-5003, ⓦwww.balletbc.com. The province's top company performs – along with major visiting companies – at the Queen Elizabeth Theatre.

EDAM Western Front Lodge, 303 East 8th Ave ⓣ604/876-9559, ⓦwww.edamdance.org. Experimental Dance and Music present modern mixes of dance, film, music, and art.

Karen Jamieson Dance Company 4036 W 19th Ave ⓣ604/893-8807. Award-winning company and choreographer that often use Canadian composers and artists, and incorporates native cultural themes.

Scotiabank Dance Centre 677 Davie St ⓣ604/689-0926. This new dance center provides studio and rehearsal space for around 30 companies, and is open to the public for workshops, classes, exhibitions, and other events. It also houses the Vancouver Dance Centre, a major source of information on dance in Vancouver and beyond (ⓣ604/606-6400, ⓦwww.thedancecentre.ca). Contact it for details of the major Dancing on the Edge Festival in July.

Film

Capitol 6 820 Granville Mall ⓣ604/669-6000. This complex is one of the biggest first-run venues in the center of the city, and – as it's bang in the middle of Downtown and shows all the new releases – the main 1000-seat screen makes a good first choice if you want to see the movies of the moment. Screens in the upstairs theatres are much smaller.

Denman Cinema 1737 Comox St at Denman ⓣ604/683-2201. A good choice in the West End if you need a break after Stanley Park or want to catch a movie before or after hitting the cafés and bars on Denman Street. Expect second-run or near first-run films at good prices.

Fifth Avenue Cinemas 2110 Burrard St at W 5th Ave ⓣ604/734-7469. Fiveplex cinema in south Vancouver run by the founder of the Vancouver Film Festival. It is one of the better in the city for art-house or more arty first-run films.

Hollywood 3123 West Broadway between Tutch and Barclay sts ⓣ604/738-3211, ⓦwww.hollywoodtheatre.ca. A Kitsilano repertory cinema which can also always be relied on for good (and good-value) double bills and second-run (or just over first-run) movies.

Pacific Cinémathèque 1131 Howe St near Helmcken St ⓣ604/688-3456, ⓦwww.cinematheque.bc.ca). The non-profit film society that runs this screen is devoted to furthering the understanding of cinema and contemporary visual arts. As part of its brief, it shows a good range of arthouse, overseas, and experimental films. All of which makes it the best nonmainstream cinema in the city. The programs can be hit or miss, but any film buff will find something to tempt them.

Ridge Theatre 3131 Arbutus St at West 15th Ave ⓣ604/738-6311, ⓦwww.ridgetheatre.com. A great neighborhood place for second-run, classic, and other films. Look out for its provocatively

Festivals in Vancouver

Warm summers, outdoor venues, and a culture-hungry population combine to make Vancouver an important festival city. To learn more about events and shows, contact Tourism Vancouver (ⓣ604/683-2000, ⓦwww.tourismvancouver.com), or pick up *The Vancouver Book*, an annually updated listing of festivals and general information available free from the Tourist InfoCentre (see p.414). Other listings can be found by visiting ⓦwww.foundlocally.com/vancouver or ⓦwww.bcpassport.com/festivals.

Among the major festivals is the annual **Du Maurier International Jazz Festival** (late June to early July) organized by the Coastal Jazz and Blues Society (ⓣ604/872-5200, ⓦwww.coastaljazz.ca). Some 800 international musicians congregate annually, many offering workshops and free concerts in addition to paid-admission events.

Other music festivals include the **Vancouver International Folk Music Festival** (ⓣ604/602-9798 or 1-800/985-8363, ⓦwww.thefestival.bc.ca), a bevy of international acts centered on Jericho Park and the Centennial Theatre for several days during the third week of July. In July, Vancouver loses its collective head over the **Sea Festival** (ⓣ604/684-3378) – nautical fun and excellent fireworks around English Bay. In Whistler (see p.464), there's a **Country & Bluegrass Festival** held in mid-July.

Theater festivals come thick and fast, particularly in the summer. The chief event is the **Fringe Festival** (ⓣ604/257-0350 or 257-0366, ⓦwww.vancouverfringe.com), modeled on the Edinburgh equivalent. It currently runs to more than 550 shows, staged by some ninety companies at ten venues. There's also an annual **Bard on the Beach Shakespeare Festival** (ⓣ604/739-0559, ⓦwww.bardonthebeach.org; June–Aug) in Vanier Park and an International Comedy Festival (ⓣ604/683-0883, ⓦwww.comedyfest.com) in early August on Granville Island. Many of the city's art-house cinemas join forces to host the **Vancouver International Film Festival** (ⓣ604/685-0260, ⓦwww.viff.org), an annual showcase for more than 150 films running from late September to mid-October.

paired double bills and late-lunch (1.30pm) "Movies for Mommies" screenings. Built in 1950, it's virtually unchanged – there's even an enclosed "crying room" for parents with boisterous children or howling infants.

The Blinding Light! 36 Powell St ⓣ604/684-8288, ⓦwww.blindinglight.com. A great 100-seat Gastown venue for diehard film buffs who watch all manner of experimental and plain crazy films (sample title: *Jesus Christ Vampire Hunter*), as well as home movies and crazed animation. It helps host the Vancouver Underground Film Festival and presents theme nights such as "bring-your-own-movie" sessions.

Gay and lesbian Vancouver

Vancouver may not have the profile or élan of San Francisco, but it enjoys the same laid-back West Coast attitudes and joie de vivre. There is a large, vibrant, and unabashed **gay and lesbian community** here, much of which is culturally and politically active and aware. There's also a lively and diverse nightlife scene, with plenty of clubs – theme nights are a popular phenomenon – drag shows, and up-to-the-minute discos.

Davie Village, which runs from Burrard along Davie to Denman, is where you will find the highest concentration of long-established gay clubs, pubs, and stores, though there are plenty of other venues throughout the city; lesbians, for their part, have traditionally chosen to live on or around Commercial Drive (The Drive). Most clubs are late-night opening, usually until 4am, a relatively new freedom following the relaxation of licensing laws.

While there are no vast **events or festivals** in the manner of Sydney's Mardi Gras, there are plenty of one-off and occasional events that have become, or are becoming, permanent fixtures. The main draw in Vancouver's gay calendar is **Pride**, which celebrated 25 years in 2003. It usually takes place over three days during the first long weekend in August. Special events are held in clubs across the city, while the traditional parade along Denman and Beach has, by general consent, become bigger and better each year, with ever-more exuberant floats. For further information contact Vancouver Pride Society (ⓣ604/687-0955 or 737-7433, ⓦwww.vanpride.bc.ca).

The **Queer Film and Video Festival** (ⓦwww.outonscreen.com) takes over the city's movie theaters shortly after Gay Pride in August. Other note-worthy events include the **Gay Ski Week** (ⓣ604/899-6209, ⓦwww.outontheslopes.com), which has attracted thousands every year since its inception in 1991. Event organizers also now have a summer event, with riding, biking, and rafting among warmer-weather activities.

For detailed information on **gay and lesbian** events, check out (*X-xtra* ⓣ604/684-XTRA, ⓦwww.xtra.ca) a regular free magazine aimed specifically at the gay and lesbian community, which is available at clubs, bookshops, and many of the *Georgia Straight* distribution points. Also useful is the monthly *Outlooks* (ⓦwww.outlooks.ca) magazine.

Other general contacts include the **Gay & Lesbian Centre Help Line** (ⓣ604/684-6869) and the **Gay & Lesbian Business Association** (ⓣ604/253-4307 or 739-4522), the latter being a source for gay- and lesbian-friendly businesses in the city. The **Gay Lesbian Transgendered Bisexual Community Centre** – The Centre for short – has a good library at 1170 Bute (ⓣ604/684-5307). Little Sister's Book and Art Emporium at 1238 Davie St (ⓣ604/669-1753) sells everything from dildos to greetings cards, and also has a comprehensive noticeboard. It also sells tickets for various events, as does GayMart at 1148 Davie (ⓣ604/681-3262). BiVancouver (ⓣ604/787-4330, ⓔbivancouver@hotmail.com) is for **bi-sexual** and bi-friendly people of all ages.

Bars, pubs, and restaurants

Café Luxy 1235 Davie St ⓣ604/669-5899. Davie Village and the West End have no shortage of gay-friendly places to eat and drink, but this stands out by virtue of its fresh, home-made pastas and jazz-groove DJ nights, currently every Tuesday.

Dufferin 900 Seymour St and Smithe St ⓣ604/683-4251, ⓦwww.dufferinhotel.com. This is one of the city's key places for gay men to shake their stuff on the dancefloor, but it also hosts a lot of drag-nights – the Buff at the Duff drag shows (Mon–Thurs) are an institution – as well as providing strippers, go-go boys (Fri and Sun), and karaoke.

Fountainhead Pub 1025 Davie ⓣ604/687-2222, ⓦwww.thefountainheadpub.com. A popular and pleasantly buzzing place at the heart of Davie Village for good food, drink (including microbrewed beers), and a large, heated patio from which to spy on all the street action. Also has a pool table, darts, and multiple TV screens. Tends to attract a slightly older, more mellow crowd.

Global Beat 1249 Howe St ⓣ604/689-2444. A gay-owned restaurant and lounge with billiard tables that makes a good place for an inexpensive meal (fine Italian-influenced food) or a drink – there's no heavy cruising – to start the evening, especially if you're heading to *Odyssey*, a club which stands right next door (see overleaf).

Oasis 1240 Thurlow ⓣ604/685-1724, ⓦwww.theoasispub.com. Vancouver's only gay piano bar. Comfortable upstairs place for people who want to be heard above the music. Long list of martinis and a tapas menu, with daily specials and a roof-top patio. Open 9pm until late daily.

Pump Jack Pub 1167 Davie ⓣ604/685-3417, ⓦwww.pumpjackpub.com. A spacious spot and Vancouver's leather bar of choice: it's favored by

Western Canada Leather Pride and the so-called BC Bears, a gay affiliation for those with a penchant for the hairy and/or bearded. Arrive early to guarantee a cruisey window-side bar stool to watch the men go by. There are pool tables and uniform nights.

Sugar Daddy's 1262 Davie St ⓣ604/632-1646. Another West End gay rendezvous of some standing, thanks to video sports, big-screen TVs, and good burgers and margaritas.

Clubs

Club 23 23 West Cordova ⓣ604/662-3277. A cool, dark split-level club, perfect for the various theme nights held here, such as the naked parties held by the Pacific Canadian Association of Nudists (ⓣ684-9872 ext 2026, ⓦwww.p-can.org), "Lesbians on the loose" and "Sin City" fetish nights.

Heritage House Hotel 455 Abbott St ⓣ604/685-7777. The three bars here host a number of gay and lesbian nights: *Charlie's Bar and Grill* on the main floor fills up with women only on Saturdays and *Chuck's Pub* has "Guys in Disguise" on Fridays and men-only on Saturdays; call for latest details. The *Lotus Sound Lounge* downstairs has a women-only dance club (Fri) and a lesbian hangout every Wednesday to Saturday at the Lick Bar. There are some mixed nights and occasional fetish and other theme nights. Call before you go for latest permutations and times.

Lava Lounge 1180 Granville St ⓣ604/605-6136. This is a gay and lesbian club with different theme nights several times a week: "Sexy Friday" has go-go boys, while "Soirée la Femme" is a girls-only night every third Sunday of the month.

Numbers 1042 Davie St and Burrard St ⓣ604/685-4077. This is a cruisy multilevel venue which has been in business for over twenty years, with a gay disco, kitsch mirrored dancefloor, movies, and pool tables upstairs, men and women downstairs – but with very few women. Tends to attract a slightly more mature crowd. As with virtually all other clubs listed here, there is a wide variety of theme nights.

Octane 1188 Davie ⓣ604/688-0677. A hip club and bar with DJs and a happening, youngish crowd. Best of the spinning is at the late-night event on Sundays. There's currently live jazz on Saturdays.

Odyssey 1251 Howe St near Davie St ⓣ604/689-5256, ⓦwww.theodysseynightclub.com. A young gay and bisexual club with house and techno disco and theme shows on most nights. Expect to wait on Fridays and Saturdays as it currently has the reputation as the hippest and wildest place in town.

Sublime 816 Granville St ⓔsublimenightclub@hotmail.com A good place to wind up in the small hours if you're still raring to go at the weekend: the after-hours dance club runs from 1 to 6am on Fridays and Saturdays.

Listings

Airlines Air Canada (ⓣ604/688-5515, 1-888/247-2262 or 1-800/661-3936); American Airlines (ⓣ604/222-2532 or 1-800/433-7300); Baxter: float-plane services to Victoria's Inner Harbour (ⓣ604/688-5136); British Airways (ⓣ604/270-8131 or 1-800/247-9297); Continental (ⓣ1-800/525-0280); Delta (ⓣ1-800/241-4141); Harbour Air Seaplanes: services to Victoria Inner Harbour (ⓣ604/274-1277 or 1-800/665-0212); Helijet Airways: helicopter service to Victoria (ⓣ604/273-1414 or 1-800/665-4354); KLM (ⓣ604/303-3666); United (ⓣ1-800/241-6522); West Coast Air: seaplane services to Victoria and Gulf Islands (ⓣ604/688-9115, 606-6888 or 1-800/347-2222); Whistler Air: direct flights to Whistler from Vancouver Harbour Air Terminal by *Pan Pacific Hotel* (ⓣ604/932-6615 or 1-888/806-2299).

BC Parks ⓣ604/924-2200, ⓦwww.gov.bc.ca/bcparks.

Bike rental Bayshore Bicycles & Rollerblade Rentals, 745 Denman St (ⓣ604/688-2453); Harbour Air, Harbour Air Terminal at the waterfront one block west of Canada Place and the foot of Burrard St (ⓣ604/688-1277) – also rents blades and motorcycles; Spokes, 1798 Georgia at Denman (ⓣ604/688-5141).

Buses Airporter (ⓣ604/946-8866 or 1-800/668-3141, ⓦwww.yvrairporter.com) for shuttle from Vancouver Airport to bus depot and Downtown; BC Transit for city buses, SeaBus, and SkyTrain (ⓣ604/953-3333, ⓦwww.translink.bc.ca); Greyhound (ⓣ604/662-3222 or 1-800/661-8747, ⓦwww.greyhound.ca) for BC, Alberta, Yukon, and long-haul destinations including Seattle and the US; Malaspina Coach Lines (ⓣ1-877/227-8287) for the Sunshine Coast, Powell River, Whistler, Pemberton, and Nanaimo on Vancouver Island; Pacific Coach Lines (ⓣ604/662-8074 or 1-800/661-1725, ⓦwww.pacificcoach.com) for

Victoria, Vancouver Island; Perimeter (Ⓣ604/266-5386 or 905-0041, Ⓦwww.perimeterbus.com) for services between Whistler and Vancouver Airport; Quick Shuttle (Ⓣ604/940-4428 or 1-800/665-2122, Ⓦwww.quickcoach.com) for Bellingham Airport, Downtown Seattle, and SeaTac Airport.
Car rental Budget, airport, 501 W Georgia St and 1705 Burrard St (Ⓣ604/668-7000 or 1-800/268-8900 in Canada, 1-800/527-0700 in US); Hertz, 1128 Seymour St (Ⓣ604/688-2411 or 1-800/263-0600); Lo-Cost, 1835 Marine Drive (Ⓣ604/986-1266); National (Ⓣ1-800/227-7368), airport (Ⓣ604/207-3730) and 1130 W Georgia at Thurlow (Ⓣ604/609-7150); Rent-a-Wreck, 1349 Hornby St (Ⓣ604/688-0001).
Consulates Australia, 1225–Suite 888 Dunsmuir St (Ⓣ604/684-1177); Ireland, 1400–100 W Pender St (Ⓣ604/683-8440); New Zealand, 1200–Suite 888 Dunsmuir (Ⓣ604/684-7388); UK, 800–1111 Melville St (Ⓣ604/683-4421); US, 1095 W Pender (Ⓣ604/685-4311).
Directory enquiries Ⓣ411.
Doctors The College of Physicians can provide names of three doctors near you (Ⓣ604/733-7758). Drop-in service at Bentall Centre Rexall Drugstore, Suite 400, Bental 4, 1055 Dunsmuir (Ⓣ604/684-8204, Ⓦwww.rexall.ca).
Emergency services (police, fire, and ambulance) Ⓣ911.
Ferries BC Ferries (Ⓣ1-888/223-3779 in BC or 250/386-3431 outside the province, Ⓦwww.bcferries.com) for services to Vancouver Island, the Gulf Islands, the Sunshine Coast, Prince Rupert, the Inside Passage, Bella Coola, and the Haida-Gwaii-Queen Charlotte Islands. Aquabus (Ⓣ604/689-5858, Ⓦwww.aquabus.bc.ca) and False Creek Ferries (Ⓣ604/684-7781, Ⓦwww.granvilleislandferries.bc.ca) for services between Downtown, Granville Island, and Vanier Park.
Hospitals St Paul's Hospital is the closest to Downtown at 1081 Burrard St near Davie St (Ⓣ604/682-2344). The city hospital is Vancouver General at 855 W 12th near Oak, south of Broadway (Ⓣ604/875-4111).
Left luggage At the bus station ($2 per 24hr).
Lost property BC Transit (Ⓣ604/682-7887); West Vancouver Transit (Ⓣ604/985-7777); police (Ⓣ604/665-2232); airport (Ⓣ604/276-6104).
Police Non-emergency 24-hr (Ⓣ604/717-3321); RCMP (Ⓣ604/264-3111); Vancouver City Police (Ⓣ604/665-3535).
Post office Main office at 349 W Georgia and Homer (Mon–Fri 8am–5.30pm; Ⓣ604/662-5722). Post-office information (Ⓣ1-800/267-1177).
Taxis Black Top (Ⓣ604/731-1111 or 681-2181); Vancouver Taxi (Ⓣ604/255-5111 or 604/874-5111); Yellow Cab (Ⓣ604/681-3311 or 604/681-1111).
Train inquiries VIA Rail (Ⓣ604/669-3050 or toll-free in Canada only Ⓣ1-800/561-8630, 1-800/561-3949 in the US, Ⓦwww.viarail.ca); Amtrak (Ⓣ1-800/872-7245, Ⓦwww.amtrak.com); Rocky Mountain Railtours (Ⓣ604/606-7200 or 1-800/665-7245) for expensive rail tours through the Rockies.
Weather Ⓣ604/664-9010.

The Sunshine Coast and Whistler

From Vancouver the 150-kilometre **Sunshine Coast**, the only stretch of accessible coastline on mainland British Columbia, is easily accessible. Ferries depart from Powell River, the coast's largest town, to Comox on Vancouver Island. From here you can explore the north of Vancouver Island, or head west to enjoy the sublime seascapes of the Pacific Rim National Park. Another, and far more tempting, trip is the inland route to **Garibaldi Provincial Park**, which contains by far the best scenery and hiking country within striking distance of Vancouver, and the world-class ski resort of **Whistler**. En route to Whistler you'll pass through **Squamish**, rapidly emerging as one of North America's premier destinations for windsurfing, climbing, and – in season – eagle watching.

The Sunshine Coast

A mild-weathered stretch of sandy beaches, rugged headlands, and quiet lagoons running northwest of Vancouver, the **Sunshine Coast** is heavily promoted, though the scenic rewards are slim compared to the grandeur of the BC interior. Even as a taste of the province's mountain scenery it leaves much to be desired, and the best that can be said of the region is that in summer it offers some of western Canada's best diving, boating, and fishing. If you are just coming out for the day, the best parts of the trip are the various **ferry crossings** en route: the first is from Horseshoe Bay at the western extreme of West Vancouver to Langdale and Gibson's Landing, where you pick up Highway 101 for the 79-kilometre run along the coast to Earl's Cove and the beautiful (and slightly longer) crossing to Saltery Bay, where the boat provides views of some fine maritime landscapes. The road then continues 35km to Powell River before coming to an abrupt conclusion 23km later at the village of Lund.

Highway 101 runs almost the length of the coast from Gibsons Landing, just 5km from the ferry terminal at Langdale for boats coming from **Horseshoe Bay** at the end of Marine Drive and western edge of West Vancouver. You can reach the ferry terminal here from the city by taking bus #250 or the #257 express westbound from points on West Georgia Street Downtown. Given that the coast is hardly worth full-scale exploration by car, and that the two ferry crossings provide two of the trip's highlights, you might consider saving the price of a rental and go by **bus**; it's perfectly feasible to get to **Powell River** in a day. Malaspina Coachlines (Ⓣ604/485-5030 or 1-888/227-8287) runs two buses daily to Powell River, currently at 8.30am and 6.30pm (5hr; $37.50 one-way). Returns leave at 8.30am and 2.30pm.

Along Highway 101

Soon reached and well signposted from North Vancouver, **Horseshoe Bay** is the departure point for the first of the Hwy-101 **ferry** crossings, an almost 40-minute passage through the islands of fjord-like Howe Sound. There are regular sailings year-round, and tickets ($8.25 adults, $28.75 cars, $2.50 bikes) cost a little less outside the late-June to early-September peak period. Note that each ticket is valid for one of Horseshoe Bay-Langdale (return), Earl's Cove-Saltery Bay (return), or single journeys on both the Horseshoe Bay-Langdale and Earl's Cove-Saltery Bay crossings. Ferries ($10 per adult, $34.75 for cars, though less offseason) also ply from here to Nanaimo (see p.502) on Vancouver Island, with hourly sailings in summer and every other hour offseason. For information on these services, contact BC Ferries (Ⓣ604/669-1211 or 1-888/223-3779, Ⓦwww.bcferries.com), or pick up a timetable from the Vancouver infocentre.

Gibsons, the terminal on the other side of Howe Sound, is a scrappy place spread widely over a wooded hillside. The town's two modest museums: the **Sunshine Coast Maritime Museum** (June–Aug Tues–Sat 10.30am–4pm; free) on Molly's Lane and the **Elphinstone Pioneer Museum** (May–Sept Thurs–Sat 10.30am–4.30pm; free) at 716 Winn Rd, contain predictable displays of maritime and frontier memorabilia. For more on the town and details of local trails, beaches, and swimming areas, visit the **infocentre** at 1177 Stewart Rd (daily 9am–6pm; Ⓣ604/886-2325, Ⓦwww.gibsonschamber.com).

Further west on Hwy-101, Pender Harbour is a string of small coastal communities, of which **Madeira Park** is the most substantial; whales occasionally pass this section of coast – which, sadly, is the source of many of the whales in the world's aquariums – but the main draws are fishing and boating. **Earl's Cove** is nothing but the departure ramp of the second ferry hop – a longer crossing (45min) that again offers fantastic views, including an immense waterfall that drops off a "Lost World"-type plateau into the sea.

From Jervis Bay, the opposite landing stage, it's a couple of kilometres up the road to the best of all the provincial parks in this region, **Saltery Bay Provincial Park**. Everything here is discreetly hidden in the trees between the road and the coast, and the campsites ($12) – beautifully situated – are connected by short trails to a couple of swimming beaches. Further along on the main road, various **campsites** give onto the sea, notably the big *Oceanside Resort Motel* site, which has eleven cabins, 7km short of Powell River, and sits on a superb piece of shoreline (Ⓣ604/485-2435 or 1-888/889-2435, Ⓦwww.oceansidepark.com; sites $16 per two persons; ❸).

Powell River and beyond

Despite being on the seafront, **POWELL RIVER**'s unfocused sprawl and nearby sawmill dampen its appeal. If you're catching the **ferry** to Courtenay on Vancouver Island (4 daily; 75min), you might not see the town site, as the terminal is 2km to the east at Westview, and some of the **buses** from Vancouver are timed to coincide with the boats. If your bus doesn't connect, you can either walk from the town center or bus terminal or call a taxi (Ⓣ604/483-3666). The local **infocentre** (daily 9am–5pm; Ⓣ604/485-4701 or 1-877/817-8669, Ⓦwww.discoverpowellriver.com), immediately at the end of the wooden ferry pier at 4690 Marine Ave, can furnish a visitors' map showing the many trails leading inland from the coast hereabouts. They can also advise on boat trips on Powell Lake, immediately inland, and tours to Desolation Sound farther up the coast. The most central of several **campsites** is the 81-site *Willingdon Beach Municipal Campground* on the seafront off Marine Avenue at 6910 Duncan St (Ⓣ604/485-2242; $15–20).

The northern end-point of Hwy-101 is the hamlet of **Lund**, 28km up the coast from Powell River. **Desolation Sound Marine Provincial Park**, about 10km north of Lund, offers some of Canada's best boating and scuba diving, plus fishing, canoeing, and kayaking. There's no road access to the park, but a number of outfitters in Powell River run tours to it and can hire all the equipment you could possibly need – try Westview Live Bait Ltd, 4527 Marine Ave, for **canoes**; Coulter's Diving, 4557 Willingdon Ave, for **scuba gear**; and Spokes, 4710 Marine Drive, for **bicycles**. The more modest **Okeover Provincial Park**, immediately north of Lund, has an unserviced campsite ($14).

The Sea to Sky Highway

A fancy name for Hwy-99 between North Vancouver and Whistler, the **SEA TO SKY HIGHWAY** has a slightly better reputation than it deserves, mainly because Vancouver's weekend hordes need to reassure themselves of the grandeur of the scenery at their doorstep. It undoubtedly scores in its early coastal stretch, where the road clings perilously to an almost sheer cliff and mountains come dramatically into view on both sides of Howe Sound. Views here are better than along the Sunshine Coast, though plenty of campsites, motels, and minor roadside distractions fill the route until the mountains of the Coast Range rear up beyond **Squamish** for the rest of the way to Whistler.

You're better off driving the highway only as far as **Garibaldi Provincial Park** – the section between Pemberton and Lillooet, the Duffy Lake Road, is very slow going and often impassable in winter, though the drive is a stunner with wonderful views of lakes and glaciers. Regular buses (see Perimeter bus details on p.464) connect Vancouver and Whistler (some continue to Pemberton), which you can easily manage as a day-trip (it's 2hr 30min one-way to Whistler from Vancouver by bus).

Britannia Beach

Road and rail lines meet with some squalor at tiny **BRITANNIA BEACH**, 53km from Vancouver, whose **BC Museum of Mining** is the first reason to take time out from admiring the views (early May to early Sept daily 9am–4.30pm; $12.95; Ⓣ604/688-8735, Ⓦwww.bcmuseumofmining.org). Centering on what was, in the 1930s, the largest producer of copper in the British Empire – 56 million tons of ore were extracted here before the mine closed in 1974 – the museum is housed in a huge, derelict-looking building on the hillside and is chock-full of hands-on displays, original working machinery, a 235-ton monster mine truck, and archive photographs. You can also take guided underground tours (every 30min) around about 350m of the mine's galleries on small electric trains.

Beyond Britannia Beach lie several small coastal reserves, the most striking of which is **Shannon Falls Provincial Park**, 7km beyond Britannia Beach, signed right off the road and worth a stop for its spectacular 335-metre **waterfall**. Six times the height of Niagara, it can be seen from the road, but it's not five minutes walk to the viewing area at the base, where the proximity of the road, plus a campsite and diner, detract from the effect.

Squamish

The sea views and coastal drama end 11km beyond Britannia Beach at **SQUAMISH**, whose houses spread out over a flat plain amidst warehouses, logging waste, and old machinery. However, if you want to climb, windsurf, or mountain bike, there's almost nowhere better in Canada to do so. At a glance, all the town has by way of fame is the vast granite rock overshadowing it, "The Stawamus Chief," which looms into view to the east just beyond Shannon Falls and is claimed to be the world's "second-biggest free-standing rock" (after Gibraltar, apparently). The town rates as one of Canada's top spots for **rock climbing**, and the area recently earned provincial park status. Around 200,000 climbers from around the world come here annually, swarming over more than four hundred routes over the 625-metre monolith: the University Wall and its culmination, the Dance Platform, is rated Canada's toughest climb.

The rock is sacred to the local Squamish, whose ancient tribal name – meaning "place where the wind blows" – gives a clue as to the town's second big activity: **windsurfing**. There are strong, consistent winds to suit all abilities, but the water is cold, so a wetsuit's a good idea (there are rental outlets around town). Most people head for the artificial **Squamish Spit**, a dike separating the waters of the Howe Sound from the Squamish River, a park area run by the Squamish Windsurfing Society (Ⓣ604/926-WIND or 892-2235). It's around 3km from town and a small fee is payable to the Society to cover rescue boats, insurance, and washroom facilities.

Rounding out Squamish's outdoor activities is the tremendous **mountain biking** terrain – there are 63 trails in the area ranging from gnarly single-track trails to readily accessible deactivated forestry roads – and the growing trend of

bouldering, which involves clambering (very slowly and without ropes) over large boulders.

The town has one more unexpected treat, for the Squamish River, and the tiny hamlet of Brackendale in particular (10km to the north on Hwy-99), is – literally – the world's **bald eagle** capital. In winter around 2000 eagles congregate here, attracted by the migrating salmon. The best place to see them is the so-called Eagle Run just south of the center of Brackendale, and on the river in the 550-hectare Brackendale Eagles Provincial Park. For more information, and for another good viewing spot, visit the Brackendale Art Gallery on Government Road north of Depot Road (Ⓣ898-3333, Ⓦwww.brackendaleartgallery.com).

Practicalities

Most of the relevant parts of the town are concentrated on Cleveland Avenue, off Hwy-99, including the **Greyhound** bus drop and pick-up (6 buses daily to and from Vancouver, 4 to and from Pemberton), **infocentre** (May–Sept daily 9am–5pm; Oct–April Mon–Fri 9am–5pm, Sat & Sun 10am–2pm; Ⓣ604/892-9244, Ⓦwww.squamishchamber.bc.ca), a big supermarket and the most central **accommodation** if you're not at the hostel (see below), the *August Jack Motor Inn* opposite the infocentre (Ⓣ604/892-3504; ❸) or cheap 30-room *Garibaldi Budget Inn*, 38012 3rd Ave (Ⓣ604/892-5204 or 1-888/313-9299, Ⓔmotorinn@shaw.ca; ❷). The superlative *Squamish Hostel* on Buckley Avenue (Ⓣ604/892-9240 or 1-800/449-8614, Ⓦwww.hostels.com/squamish; ❶) is clean and friendly, with a kitchen, common room, and 18 beds including two private rooms. Beds are $15 a night (three nights cost $40) and private rooms are $30. The owners are set to open a larger 60-bed hostel nearby at Mamquam Blind Channel on Hwy-99. The best **hotel** accommodation is the *Howe Sound Inn & Brewing Company*, 37801 Cleveland Ave (Ⓣ892-2603, Ⓦwww.howesound.com; ❺), in the center off Hwy-99 at the end of Cleveland Avenue. It has a pub, restaurants, climbing wall, sauna, and twenty spacious rooms.

If you're looking into **renting equipment**, Vertical Reality Sports Centre at 38154 2nd Ave (Ⓣ604/892-8248) rents climbing shoes ($10 a day) and mountain bikes ($15–40 a day), whilst Slipstream Rock & Ice (Ⓣ604/898-4891 or 1-800/616-1325, Ⓦwww.slipstreamadventures.com) offers rock- and ice-climbing guiding and instruction. Most of its tours are for two days and start from about $160 and they teach all abilities. For **mountain bike hire**, contact Tantalus (Ⓣ604/898-2588), by the Greyhound depot at 40446 Government Rd, or Corsa Cycles (Ⓣ604/892-3331, Ⓦwww.corsacycles.com) at Hunter Place: rates for both sart at about $20 for a half-day hire.

Garibaldi Provincial Park

Unless you're skiing, **GARIBALDI PROVINCIAL PARK** is the main incentive for heading this way. It's a huge and unspoilt area that combines all the usual breathtaking ingredients of lakes, rivers, forests, glaciers, and the peaks of the Coast Mountains (Wedge Mountain, at 2891m, is the park's highest point). Four rough roads access the park from points along the highway between Squamish and Whistler, but you'll need transport to reach the trailheads at the end of them. Other than camping, the only accommodation close to the park is at Whistler.

There are five main areas with trails, of which the **Black Tusk/Garibaldi Lake** region is the most popular and probably most beautiful. Further trails fan out from Garibaldi Lake, including one to the huge basalt outcrop of **Black Tusk** (2316m), a rare opportunity to reach an alpine summit without any rock climbing. The other hiking areas from south to north are **Diamond Head**, **Cheakamus Lake**, **Singing Pass**, and **Wedgemount Lake**. Outside these small and defined areas, however, the park is untrammeled wilderness. For more **information**, visit Ⓦwww.garibaldipark.com or pick the dedicated BC Parks pamphlet from infocentres in Vancouver and elsewhere.

Whistler

WHISTLER, 56km beyond Squamish, is Canada's finest four-season resort, and frequently ranks among most world top-five winter ski resort lists. Skiing and snowboarding are clearly the main activities here, but all manner of other winter sports are possible, and in summer the lifts keep running to provide supreme highline hiking and other outdoor activities (not to mention North America's finest summer skiing). It is a busy place – over two million lift tickets are sold here every winter, more than any other North American resort. Fortunately it also has one of the continent's largest ski areas, so the crowds are spread thinly over the resort's 200-plus trails and twelve Alpine bowls.

The resort consists of two adjacent but separate mountains – **Whistler** (2182m) and **Blackcomb** (2284m) – each with its own extensive lift and chair systems, and each covered in a multitude of runs. Both are operated by the same company, Intrawest (Ⓣ604/932-3434 or 1-800/766-0449), whose excellent website contains full details of virtually all you need to know (Ⓦwww.whistler-blackcomb.com). The two mountains are accessed from a total of five bases, including lift systems to both from the resort's heart, the purpose-built and largely pedestrianized **Whistler Village**, the tight-clustered focus of many hotels, shops, restaurants, and après-ski activity. Around this core are two other "village" complexes, **Upper Village Blackcomb** about a kilometre to the northeast and the recently completed **Village North** about 700m to the north. Around 6km to the south of Whistler Village is **Whistler Creekside** (also with a gondola and lift base), which has typically been a cheaper alternative but is now undergoing a $50 million redevelopment that will see its accommodation and local services duplicating those of its famous neighbor.

Arrival, getting around, and information

There are several ways of **getting to** Whistler. If you're driving from Vancouver, allow about two hours or so for the 125-kilometre run north on the highway. Perimeter (Ⓣ604/266-5386 or 1-877/317-7788, Ⓦwww.perimeterbus.com) runs a shuttle **bus** from Vancouver airport and various Vancouver hotels to Whistler. Reservations are required for the service, with prepayment by credit card and cancellations allowed up to noon one day prior to travel (May–Nov 7 daily, 3 of which are express services and do not stop at Vancouver hotels – there are 8 southbound departures including 3 express runs; Dec–April 11 daily, including 5 express services; 2hr 30min–3hr; $58 plus tax one-way). Note that winter schedules can be affected by bad weather on the Sea to Sky Highway.

Maverick/Greyhound (Ⓣ604/662-8051 in Vancouver, Ⓣ604/932-5031 in Whistler or 1-800/661-TRIP from anywhere in North America, Ⓦwww.greyhound.ca) runs six daily bus services from Vancouver's bus depot (see p.413) to

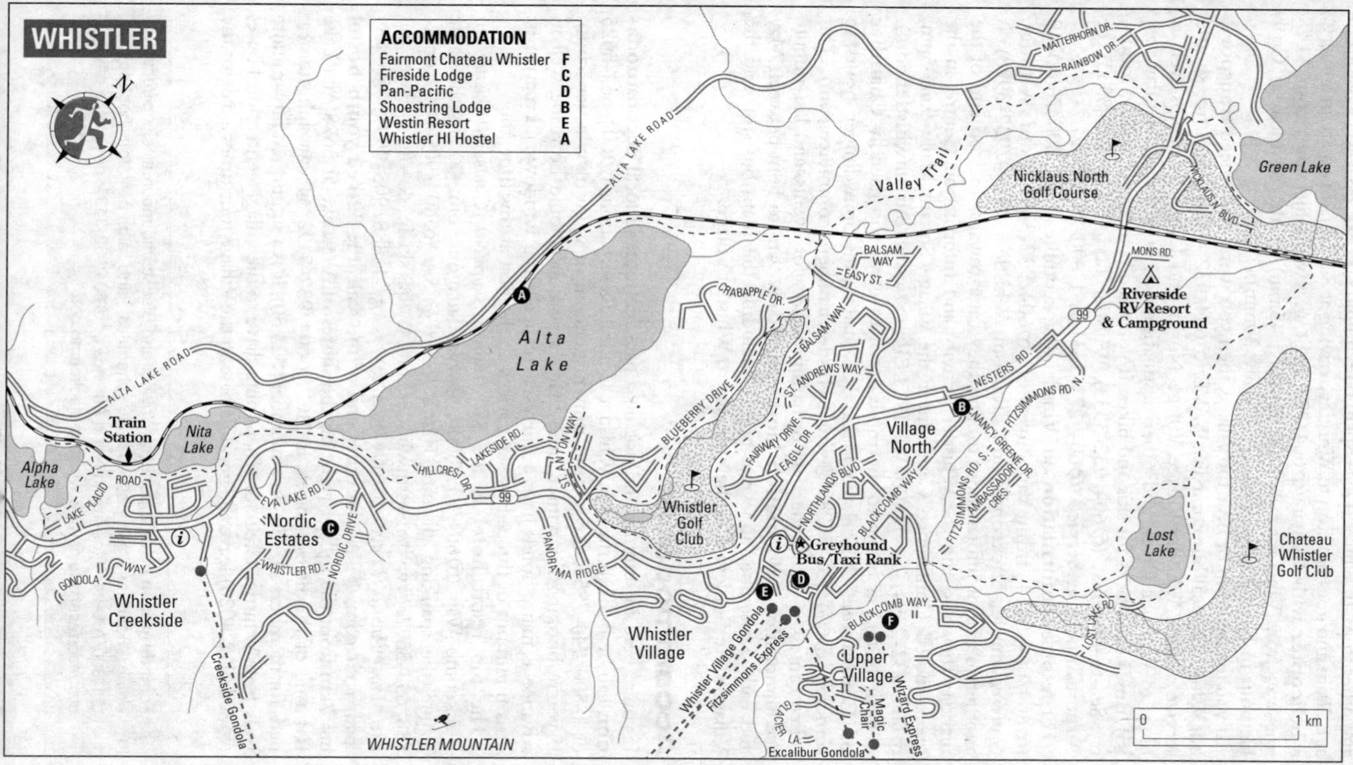

WHISTLER

ACCOMMODATION

Fairmont Chateau Whistler	F
Fireside Lodge	C
Pan-Pacific	D
Shoestring Lodge	B
Westin Resort	E
Whistler HI Hostel	A

N
Alta Lake Road
Alta Lake
Alpha Lake
Nita Lake
Train Station
Lake Placid Road
Gondola Way
Whistler Creekside
Creekside Gondola
Nordic Estates
Eva Lake Rd.
Nordic Drive
Whistler Rd.
Hillcrest Dr.
Lakeside Rd.
St. Anton Way
Panorama Ridge
99
Whistler Mountain
Whistler Golf Club
Blueberry Drive
Crabapple Dr.
Balsam Way
Easy St.
St. Andrews Way
Fairway Drive
Eagle Dr.
Northlands Blvd
Blackcomb Way
Greyhound Bus/Taxi Rank
Whistler Village
Whistler Village Gondola
Fitzsimmons Express
Upper Village
Magic Chair
Wizard Express
Glacier La.
Excalibur Gondola
Village North
Nesters Rd.
Nancy Greene Dr.
Fitzsimmons Rd. N.
Fitzsimmons Rd. S.
Ambassador Cres.
Valley Trail
Nicklaus North Golf Course
Matterhorn Dr.
Rainbow Dr.
Nicklaus N. Blvd
Green Lake
Mons Rd.
Riverside RV Resort & Campground
Lost Lake
Lost Lake Rd.
Chateau Whistler Golf Club
0 — 1 km

the Village (2hr 30min; $21.50 one-way) via Britannia Beach, Whistler Creek, and other stops. In winter (Dec–April) Greyhound's ski express leaves Vancouver at 6.30am and goes nonstop to Whistler arriving at 8.30am. If you are in a hurry, a **helicopter** with Helijet (Ⓣ604/273-1414, Ⓦwww.helijet.com) costs $147 one-way from Vancouver Airport (2 daily; 45min) or the terminal at Coal Harbour in Downtown Vancouver (2 daily; 30min).

If you're staying in or near the Village, then you won't really need **transport**, but Whistler's local bus company, WAVE (Ⓣ604/932-4040) runs a free shuttle service around Whistler Village, Village North, and Upper Village as well as buses to Whistler Creek and other destinations ($1.50 flat fare, five-day pass $5). Buses have racks for skis and bikes. If you need taxis to get around locally, try Sea-to-Sky Taxi (Ⓣ604/932-3333), Whistler Taxi (Ⓣ604/938-3333), or Airport Limousine Service (Ⓣ604/273-1331 or 1-800/278-8742).

For recorded **information** on Whistler-Blackcomb call Ⓣ1-800/766-0449 (Ⓣ604/664-5614 from Vancouver or Ⓣ604/932-3434 from Whistler, Ⓦwww.whistler-blackcomb.com). Tourism Whistler (Ⓣ604/932-3928) is another source of information, though they cater towards the top end of the market; they also run the Whistler Activity and Information Centre, in the green-roofed Conference Centre near the Village Square (daily 9am–5pm; Ⓣ604/932-2394 or 1-800/WHISTLER, Ⓦwww.tourismwhistler.com). Whistler Creek is home to the more down-to-earth and friendly **Chamber of Commerce**, 2097 Lake Placid Rd (daily 9am–5pm, longer hours in summer; Ⓣ604/932-5528, Ⓦwww.whistlerchamberofcommerce.com). This office can assist with general information, tickets for events, and last-minute accommodation. **Information kiosks** open daily 9am to 5pm between May and early September at several points, including the main bus stop and the Village Gate Boulevard at the entrance to Whistler Village.

Accommodation

If you're here in summer and not on a package tour, all local **accommodation** can be booked through Whistler Central Reservations (Ⓣ604/664-5625 or 1-800/944-7853, Ⓦwww.tourismwhistler.com or www.mywhistler .com). If you're booking for winter, note that reservations should be made well in advance as many hotels have a thirty-day cancellation window and may insist on a minimum of three-days' stay; prices are highest at this time, too.

The top resort **hotel** is the $75-million *Fairmont Chateau Whistler* on Blackcomb Way (Ⓣ604/938-8000; Ⓦwww.fairmont.com; ⑨). In the same league, the spanking all-suite *Westin Resort & Spa* (Ⓣ604/905-5000 or 1-888/634-5577, Ⓦwww.westinwhistler.com; ⑨) has ski-in, ski-out facilities and the *Pan Pacific Lodge* (Ⓣ604/905-2999 or 1-888/905-9995, Ⓦwww .panpacific.com; ⑨). At the other end of the scale, the 32-bed **youth hostel** lies 7km from the Village right on the shores of Alta Lake at 5678 Alta Lake Rd, one of the nicest hostels in BC (Ⓣ604/932-5492, Ⓦwww.hihostels.ca; beds for members $19.50, non-members $23.50). It is a signposted fifty-minute walk from Whistler Creek or ten-minute drive to the village center; local buses (Ⓣ604/932-4020) leave the gondola base in the Village four times a day for the

For **information** on all aspects of Whistler and Blackcomb mountains, including skiing, boarding, ski passes, lift schedules, and summer activities call Ⓣ1-800/766-0449 toll-free in North America or Ⓣ604/932-3434; or visit the official resort website Ⓦwww.whistler-blackcomb.com.

On the slopes

The **skiing and snowboarding season** for Whistler and Blackcomb begins in late November, weather permitting. While the snowfall varies from year to year, the yearly average is a whopping ten metres. Blackcomb closes at the end of April, while Whistler stays open until early June. Then the mountains switch places, as Whistler closes and Blackcomb reopens in early June for glacier skiing and snowboarding (lift passes for summer skiing cost $42 a day for adults), staying open until late July. The lifts are open daily 8.30am–3pm, and until 4pm after January.

Lift tickets give you full use of both Whistler and Blackcomb mountains, and it will take days for even the most advanced skiier or snowboarder to cover all the terrain. Tickets are available from the lift base in Whistler Village, but the lines can be horrendous. Instead, plan ahead and purchase your tickets online from ⓦwww.whistler.net. Your hotel can often set you up with tickets if you pre-book far enough in advance. **Prices** increase in peak season – over Christmas and New Year and from mid-February to mid-March – and lift tickets are subject to a seven-percent tax. Regular/peak season tickets: $65/69 adults. You can save money by purchasing your lift pass before the end of September or, if you plan to ski regularly at Whistler, by purchasing an **Express Card**. These cost $79 for adults, $67 for youths, and $39 for seniors, and are valid all season – scan it each time you ski and it automatically charges your credit card. Your first day skiing is free and then you pay a discounted rate of $35–53 depending on the season; call ⓣ1-800/766-0449 for more details.

Intermediate and expert skiers can join the **free tours** of the mountains that leave at 10.30am and 1pm daily. The Whistler All-Mountain tour departs from the Guest Satisfaction Centre at the top of the Whistler Village gondola. The Blackcomb All-Mountain tour meets at the Mountain Tour Centre, top of the Solar Coaster Express, or at the *Glacier Creek Lodge*. To explore Blackcomb's glaciers join the tour at the *Glacier Creek Lodge*, weather permitting.

For **snow conditions** call ⓣ604/932-4211 in Whistler or ⓣ604/687-7507 from Vancouver.

hostel 15min; $1.50). As it's popular year-round, reserve ahead. Check-in is between 4 and 10pm.

The *Shoestring Lodge*, with an often-rowdy adjacent pub, is an equally popular alternative. It has private rooms with small bathrooms – aim to be as far from the bar as possible – as well as dorms and is a ten-minute walk north of Whistler Village on Nancy Greene Drive (ⓣ604/932-3338). Another reasonable choice is the *Fireside Lodge*, 2117 Nordic Drive (ⓣ604/932-4545; ❷) at Nordic Estates, 3km south of the village.

Best of the **campsites** is the *Riverside RV Resort and Campground* (ⓣ604/905-5533 or 1-877/905-5533, ⓦwww.whistlercamping.com), 1.8km north of Whistler Village at 8018 Mons Rd, which has 14 five-person log cabins for $125–205 and 107 RV/tent sites for $25 per two persons in winter, $30 in summer.

Whistler Village

WHISTLER VILLAGE is the center of the resort, a newish and rather characterless and pastel-shaded conglomeration of hotels, restaurants, mountain-gear shops, and more loud people in fluorescent clothes than are healthy in one place at the same time. Its name is said to derive either from the distinctive shriek of the marmot (a rather chubby rodent), or else the sound of the wind whistling through Singing Pass up in the mountains. Whatever its origins, huge amounts of money have been invested in the area since the resort opened in 1980, and the investments have paid off well; the resort's services, lifts, and general overall polish are almost faultless, and those of its nearby satellites are not far behind. Whistler's challenge is now turning towards being able to rein in development before it spoils the scenery, killing the goose that laid the golden egg.

Whistler and Blackcomb mountains

Winter-sports enthusiasts can argue long and late over the relative merits of **WHISTLER MOUNTAIN** and its rival, Blackcomb Mountain, both accessed from Whistler Village's lifts. Both are great mountains, and both offer top-notch skiing and boarding, as evidenced by world-class events like the Snowboard FIS World Cup in December and the World Ski and Snowboard Festival in April – both held on Whistler. Each mountain has a distinctive character, however, at least for the time being, for major injections of money are on the way to upgrade Whistler Mountain's already impressive facilities.

Traditionally Whistler has been seen as the more intimate and homely of the two mountains, somewhere you can ski or board for days on end and never have to retrace your steps. There are over a hundred marked **trails** and seven

Whistler activities

Outdoor activities aside, there's not a lot else to do in Whistler save sit in the cafés and watch the world go by. In summer, though, chances are you'll be here to walk or mountain bike. If you're **walking**, remember you can ride the ski lifts up onto both mountains for tremendous views and easy access to high-altitude trails (July to early Sept daily 10am–8pm; early Sept to late Sept daily 10am–5pm, late Sept to mid-Oct Sat & Sun 10am–5pm; adults $23, youth and seniors $19). **Mountain bikers** can also take bikes up and ride down, for an additional $4 charge for the bike. You must have a helmet and the bike undergoes a safety inspection.

If you're going it alone, pick up the duplicated sheet of biking and hiking trails from the infocentres (see p.466), or better yet buy the 1:50,000 *Whistler and Garibaldi Region* **map**. The two most popular shorter walks are the **Rainbow Falls** and the six-hour **Singing Pass** trails. Other good choices are the four-kilometre trail to Cheakamus Lake or any of the high-alpine hikes accessed from the Upper Gondola station (1837m) on Whistler Mountain or the Seventh Heaven lift on Blackcomb: you can, of course, come here simply for the view. Among the eight walks from Whistler Mountain gondola station, consider the **Glacier Trail** (2.5km round-trip; 85m ascent; 1hr) for views of the snow and ice in Glacier Bowl. Or go for the slightly more challenging **Little Whistler Trail** (3.8km round-trip; 265m ascent; 1hr 30min–2hr), which takes you to the summit of Little Whistler Peak (2115m) and gives grand views of Black Tusk in Garibaldi Provincial Park. Remember to time your hike to get back to the gondola station for the last ride down (times vary according to season).

Snowshoe rental and tours are available to get you across some of the safer snow fields in summer. For **snowshoe tours** for novices contact Outdoor Adventures (ⓣ604/932-0647, ⓦwww.adventureswhistler.com; from $39 for 90 minutes) or Whistler Cross Country Ski & Hike (ⓣ604/932-7711 or 1-888/771-2382, ⓦwww.whistlerhikingcentre.com).

If the high-level hiking seems too daunting (it shouldn't be – the trails are good and less than 4km, save the Musical Bumps trail at 19km) – then there are plenty of trails (some surfaced) for bikers, walkers, and in-line skating around the Village. The **Valley Trail** system starts on the west side of Hwy-99 by the Whistler Park Gold major bowls. **Lifts** include two high-speed gondolas, six high-speed quads, two triple and one double chairlift, and five surface lifts. Snowboarders are blessed with a half-pipe and park. Total vertical drop is 1530m and the longest run is 11km.

BLACKCOMB MOUNTAIN, the "Mile-High Mountain," is a ski area laden with superlatives: the most modern resort in Canada, North America's finest summer skiing (on Horstman Glacier), the continent's longest unbroken fall-line skiing, and the longest *and* second longest lift-serviced vertical falls in North America (1609m and 1530m).

Blackcomb is slightly smaller than Whistler, at 3341 acres, but has a similar breakdown of **terrain** (fifteen percent beginner, fifty-five percent intermediate, and thirty percent expert). **Lifts** are one high-speed gondola, six express quads, three triple chairlifts, and seven surface lifts. There are over a hundred marked trails, two glaciers and five bowls along with two half-pipes and a park for snowboarders. Even if you're not skiing, come up here (summer or winter) on the ski lifts to walk, enjoy the **view** from the top of the mountain, or to eat in the restaurants like *Rendezvous* or *Glacier Creek*. If you want some **cross-country skiing** locally, the best spots are 22km of groomed trails around Lost Lake and the *Chateau Whistler* golf course, all easily accessible from Whistler Village.

Course and takes you through parks, golf courses, and peaceful residential areas: the 30km of trails on and around **Lost Lake**, entered by the northern end of the Day Skier parking lot at Blackcomb Mountain, wend through cedar forest and past lakes and creeks; the eponymous lake is just over a kilometre from the main trailhead.

There are also numerous operators offering guided walks and bike rides to suit all abilities, as well as **rental outlets** for bikes, blades, and other equipment around the Village. **All-Terrain Vehicles (ATVs)** can be rented from Canadian All Terrain Adventures (Ⓣ1-877/938-1616, Ⓦwww.cdn-snowmobile.com) for guided tours that include splurges through mud-pits. If you want to go **riding**, contact Edgewater Outdoor Centre (Ⓣ604/932-3389), The Adventure Ranch (Ⓣ604/932-5078), or Cougar Mountain (Ⓣ604/932-4086).

Between May and September, Whistler River Adventures (Ⓣ604/932-3532, Ⓦwww.whistlerriver.com; from $75 for one-hour cruise to $135 for six-hour trip) has **jet boating** on the Green River to below the Nairn Falls, with a good chance of spotting wildlife such as moose and bears. It also has rafting trips from $65 for two-hour trips and $140 for full-day tours: beginners are taken to the Green River, while experts can plump for the Class-IV thrills of the Elaho or Squamish River rapids.

You can play tennis at several public courts, or ask at the visitor center for details of hotels which allow drop-in players to use their courts and provide racquet rental (from $10 an hour); or play squash or **swim** at the Meadow Park Sports Centre (Ⓣ604/938-7275).

If you're a **golfer** the area has four great courses, including one designed by Jack Nicklaus. Despite a recent upgrade, the Whistler Golf Club course remains the cheapest course to play at between about $70 and $150 (Ⓣ604/932-4544 or 1-800/376-1777), while the others, including Nicklaus North (Ⓣ604/938-9898), all cost from about $125 at low season to $205 at peak season in July and August. After any of these activities there are umpteen **spas** for massage, mud baths, and treatments that soothe all aches and pains – try Whistler Body Wrap (Ⓣ604/932-4710) at next to The Keg in the Village at 210 St Andrew's House or for utter luxury the top-of-the-range spa at the *Fairmont Chateau Whistler* (Ⓣ604/938-2086).

Eating and drinking

When it comes to **food and drink**, Whistler Village and its satellites are loaded with cafés and around a hundred restaurants, though none really have an "address" as such. These can come and go at an alarming rate, but one top-rated restaurant of long standing is *Araxi's Restaurant and Antipasto Bar* in Village Square (☎604/932-4540), which serves up expensive West Coast-style food and inventive pasta dishes – try the amazing mussels in chilli, vermouth, and lemongrass followed by a perfect *crème brûlée* for dessert. Equally fine, the *Rim Rock Café & Oyster Bar* at 2117 Whistler Rd (☎604/932-5565) is excellent for seafood. Other more down-to-earth places to try are *Trattoria di Umberto* (☎604/932-5858) in the *Mountainside Lodge*, beside the *Pan Pacific*, for a cozy Italian meal; *Black's Dining Room* (☎604/932-6408) in Mountain Square for pizza and pasta and a snug bar, *Black's Pub*, upstairs; the simple *Amsterdam Café* (☎604/932-8334) for reliable pub food; and *Citta's Bistro* (☎604/932-4177), a modern American-style bistro. At the foot of the Whistler Village Gondola, the *Garibaldi Lift Co Bar & Grill* (☎604/905-2220) has a deck and terrace that's popular with people just off the slopes, and with others who come later for dinner.

Nightlife

Winter or summer Whistler enjoys a lot of **nightlife** and après-ski activity, with visitors being bolstered by the large seasonal workforce – among which a vocal antipodean presence figures large. If you want relative peace and quiet, the key spot is one of the smartish bars in the *Fairmont Chateau Whistler* hotel. If you're just off Whistler Mountain, the après-ski haunt is the sports-crazy *Longhorn Saloon and Grill* (☎604/932-5999) in the Village at the base of the gondolas with the lively beer-heavy *Merlin's* (☎604/938-7700) in the *Blackcomb Lodge* performing the same function for Blackcomb. As evening draws on, make for the *Dubh Linn Gate* Irish pub (☎604/905-4047) at 4320 Sundial Crescent or *Buffalo Bill's Bar & Grill* (☎604/932-6613) across from the Whistler gondola at the *Timberline Lodge*, a thirty-something bar/club with comedy nights, hypnosis shows, video screens, a huge dancefloor, and live music.

A younger set, snowboarding hipsters among them, makes for **clubs** in both the Village and North Village. These include *Tommy Africa's* (☎604/932-6090); the musically adventurous *Maxx Fish* (☎604/932-1904), home to hip-hop and house DJs; and the lively *Moe Joe's* (☎604/935-1152), where locals hang out to catch DJs and live music. Locals tend to make for the *Boot Pub*, away from the center of things at the *Shoestring Lodge* on Nancy Greene Way: the beer's cheap and there's occasional live music. In Village North, the *Brewhouse Pub & Restaurant* near Blackcomb Way is the drinking and people-watching bar of choice.

11

Vancouver Island

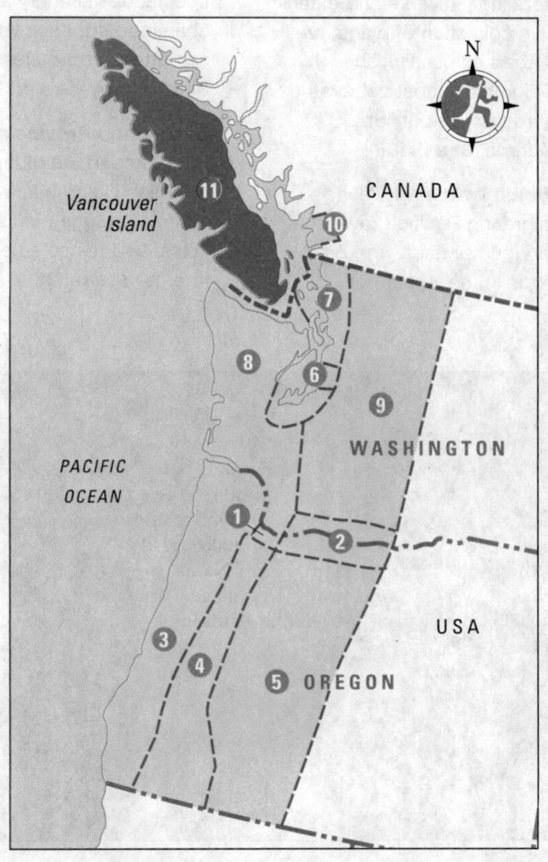

CHAPTER 11 **Highlights**

* **The Royal British Columbia Museum** Victoria's showcase museum mixes fascinating historical displays with stunning natural history dioramas. See p.481

* **Butchart Gardens** A dazzlingly diverse and extensive collection of plants are spread across British Columbia's most celebrated gardens just outside of Victoria. See p.486

* **Whale watching** View migrating Pacific grays, solitary humpbacks, and orca pods in the whale-rich waters off the island's coast, from Victoria to Port Hardy. See p.487

* **West Coast Trail** A grueling, but immensely rewarding, long-distance trek skirting the Pacific Coast, offering spectacular scenery and a chance to spot sea lions, sea otters, and majestic birds of prey. See p.521

* **Strathcona Provincial Park** Hike through the oldest park in British Columbia, a rugged realm of craggy peaks, icy lakes, and dense emerald forests. See p.526

△ Victoria's Inner Harbour

11

Vancouver Island

VANCOUVER ISLAND's proximity to Vancouver makes it one of the Pacific Northwest's premier travel destinations, though its popularity is slightly out of proportion to what is, in most cases, a pale shadow of the scenery on offer in the Northwest's major mountain regions. The largest of North America's West Coast islands, it stretches almost 500km from north to south, but has a population of around only 500,000, mostly concentrated around **Victoria**, whose small-town feel belies its role as British Columbia's provincial capital and second metropolis. While Victoria makes a convenient base for touring the island – and, thanks to a superlative museum, merits a couple of days in its own right – most of the island's other sizeable towns don't justify an overnight stop.

For most visitors, Vancouver Island's main attraction is the great outdoors. **Whale-watching** opportunities abound – from Victoria to **Tofino**, **Ucluelet**, and several other places up and down the coast – and are among the best in the world. The scenery is a mosaic of landscapes, principally defined by a central spine of snow-capped mountains that divide it decisively between the rugged and sparsely populated wilderness of the west coast and the more sheltered lowlands of the east. Rippling hills characterize the northern and southern tips, and few areas are free of the lush forest mantle that supports one of BC's most lucrative logging industries. Apart from three minor east–west roads, all the urban centers are linked by a good highway running along almost the entire length of the east coast. Note that if you don't have time for a full-blown tour of the island, then the **Southern Gulf Islands** – a sprinkling of lovely islets in the waters between Vancouver and Vancouver Island – offer a taste of what you are missing.

Once beyond the southern east coast towns of **Duncan** and **Nanaimo**, the northern two-thirds of Vancouver Island is distinctly underpopulated. Despite this, the beaches at **Parksville** and **Qualicum** manage to lure a huge number of locals and tourists alike. West on Highway 4 past **Port Alberni** lies the stunning seascapes of the unmissable **Pacific Rim National Park,** which lines the perennially misty central coast, while further north rugged **Strathcona Provincial Park** embraces the heart of the island's mountain fastness. Both of these parks offer the usual panoply of outdoor activities, with hikers being particularly well served by the national park's **West Coast Trail**, a tough and popular long-distance trek. A newer, but less dramatic (and less busy) trail, the **Juan de Fuca Trail** runs to the south of the park and ends in the town of **Port Renfrew**.

The telephone code for Victoria and Vancouver Island is ☎250.

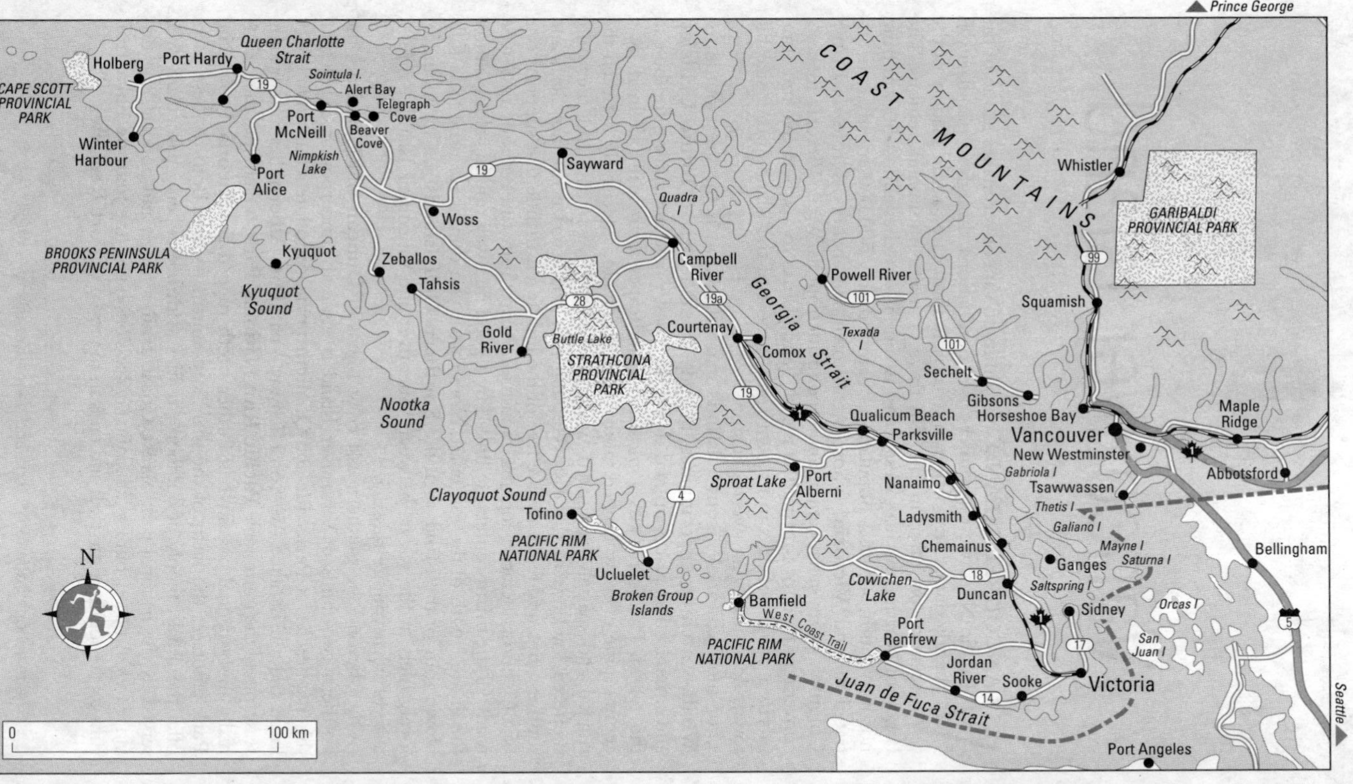
Prince George
Seattle
COAST MOUNTAINS
GARIBALDI PROVINCIAL PARK
Whistler
Squamish
99
Powell River
101
Texada I
Sechelt
Gibsons
Horseshoe Bay
Vancouver
New Westminster
Maple Ridge
Abbotsford
Bellingham
5
Tsawwassen
Gabriola I
Thetis I
Galiano I
Mayne I
Saturna I
Saltspring I
Ganges
Orcas I
San Juan I
Sidney
17
Victoria
Port Angeles
Juan de Fuca Strait
Sooke
14
Jordan River
Port Renfrew
Duncan
18
Chemainus
Ladysmith
Nanaimo
Cowichen Lake
Parksville
Qualicum Beach
Port Alberni
Sproat Lake
Bamfield
West Coast Trail
PACIFIC RIM NATIONAL PARK
Broken Group Islands
Ucluelet
Tofino
Clayoquot Sound
4
Georgia Strait
Comox
Courtenay
19a
19
Campbell River
Quadra I
STRATHCONA PROVINCIAL PARK
Buttle Lake
28
Gold River
Nootka Sound
Tahsis
Zeballos
Woss
Sayward
Kyuquot
Kyuquot Sound
BROOKS PENINSULA PROVINCIAL PARK
Port Alice
Nimpkish Lake
Port McNeill
Beaver Cove
Telegraph Cove
Alert Bay
Sointula I.
Queen Charlotte Strait
Port Hardy
Holberg
Winter Harbour
CAPE SCOTT PROVINCIAL PARK
N
0
100 km

An inland boat trip on a small working vessel from the tiny northern settlement of **Gold River** is becoming increasingly popular and is a charming primer for the ferry that follows the so-called **Inside Passage**. This breathtaking trip up the British Columbia coast to Prince Rupert lures thousands annually who embark at **Port Hardy**, linked by bus from Victoria, at the island's northern tip.

Victoria

VICTORIA is not named after a queen and an era for nothing. Much of the waterfront area has an undeniably quaint and likeable English feel – "Brighton Pavilion with the Himalayas for a backdrop," said Rudyard Kipling – and Victoria has more British-born residents than anywhere in Canada. However, its tourist offerings are exploited chiefly by American visitors, and are served up with lashings of fake Victoriana and chintzy commercialism, with ersatz echoes of empire at every turn. Despite the seasonal influx, and the sometimes atrociously tacky attractions designed to part tourists from their money, it's a small, relaxed, and pleasantly sophisticated place, worth lingering in if only for its inspirational museum. It also serves as a base for a range of outdoor activities and slightly more far-flung attractions, chief of these being whale watching, with a plethora of companies on hand to take you out to the teeming waters around the city (see p.487). As a final lure, the weather here – though often damp – is extremely mild: Victoria's meteorological station is the only one in Canada to record a winter in which the temperature never fell below freezing.

Some history

Victoria's site was originally inhabited by **Salish natives**, and in particular by the Lekwammen, who had a string of some ten villages in the area. Here they cultivated camas bulbs – vital to their diet and trade – and applied their advanced salmon-fishing methods to the shoals of migrating salmon in net-strung reefs offshore. In 1792 Captain George Vancouver, who was mapping the North American coast and apparently unaware of the aboriginal presence, described his feelings on first glimpsing this part of Vancouver Island: "The serenity of the climate, the innumerable pleasing landscapes, and the abundant fertility that nature puts forth, require only to be enriched by the industry of man with villages, mansions, cottages and other buildings, to render it the most lovely country that can be imagined."

The first step in this process began in 1842 when Victoria received some of its earliest **white visitors**, notably Hudson's Bay Company representative James Douglas, who disembarked at present-day Clover Point during a search for a new local headquarters for the Hudson's Bay Company. One look at the natural harbor and its surroundings was enough: this, he declared, was a "perfect Eden," a feeling only reinforced by the friendliness of the indigenous population, who helped him build Fort Camouson, named after an important aboriginal landmark (the name was later changed to Fort Victoria).

The aboriginal peoples from up and down the island settled near the fort, attracted by the new trading opportunities it offered. Soon they were joined by British pioneers, brought in to settle the land by a Bay subsidiary, the Puget Sound Agricultural Company, which quickly built several large company farms to accommodate settlers. In time, the harbor became the busiest West Coast

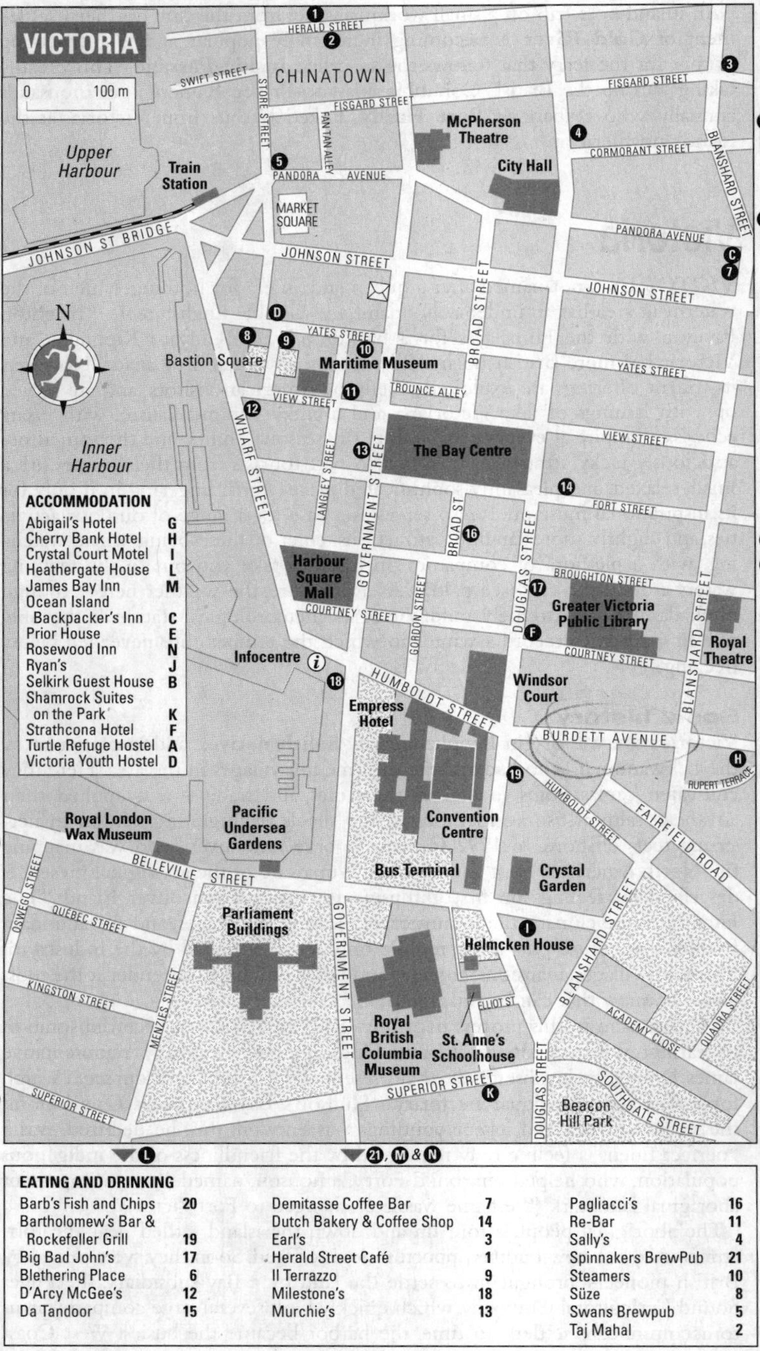

VICTORIA

ACCOMMODATION

Abigail's Hotel	G
Cherry Bank Hotel	H
Crystal Court Motel	I
Heathergate House	L
James Bay Inn	M
Ocean Island Backpacker's Inn	C
Prior House	E
Rosewood Inn	N
Ryan's	J
Selkirk Guest House	B
Shamrock Suites on the Park	K
Strathcona Hotel	F
Turtle Refuge Hostel	A
Victoria Youth Hostel	D

EATING AND DRINKING

Barb's Fish and Chips	20
Bartholomew's Bar & Rockefeller Grill	19
Big Bad John's	17
Blethering Place	6
D'Arcy McGee's	12
Da Tandoor	15
Demitasse Coffee Bar	7
Dutch Bakery & Coffee Shop	14
Earl's	3
Herald Street Café	1
Il Terrazzo	9
Milestone's	18
Murchie's	13
Pagliacci's	16
Re-Bar	11
Sally's	4
Spinnakers BrewPub	21
Steamers	10
Süze	8
Swans Brewpub	5
Taj Mahal	2

port north of San Francisco and a **major base** for the British navy's Pacific fleet, a role it currently fulfills for the bulk of Canada's present navy.

Boom time came in the 1850s following the **mainland gold strikes**, when Victoria's port became an essential stop-off and supplies depot for prospectors heading across the water and into the interior. Military and bureaucratic personnel moved in to ensure order, bringing the morals and manners of Victorian England with them. Alongside there grew a rumbustious shantytown of shops, bars, and brothels, one bar run by "Gassy" Jack Leighton, who was soon to become one of Vancouver's founders.

Though the gold rush was predictably short-lived, Victoria carried on as a military, economic, and political center, becoming the **capital** of the newly created British Columbia in 1866 – years before the founding of Vancouver. In 1908 the Canadian Pacific Railway built the *Empress Hotel* in place of a proposed railway link that never came into being. Victoria's intended role as Canada's western rail terminus was surrendered to Vancouver, and with it any chance of realistic growth or industrial development. These days the town survives quite well almost entirely on the backs of tourists, the civil-service bureaucracy, and retirees in search of a mild-weathered retreat. Its population today is around 350,000, almost exactly double what it was just thirty years ago.

Getting there

There are two ways to reach Victoria – by **ferry** or **air**. Most people traveling under their own steam from Vancouver use the first means, which is a simple matter of buying an all-inclusive through-ticket from Vancouver's bus terminal (see below) to Victoria's bus depot. By far the quickest approach, however, is to take a seaplane from Vancouver's port: this approach takes just 25 minutes – as opposed to 3hr 30min by bus and ferry – and drops you right in Victoria's Inner Harbour; however, it works out around three times as expensive.

You can also reach Victoria directly from Vancouver Airport by inclusive coach and ferry arrangements: ask for details at the bus desk in international arrivals of Pacific Coach Lines bus services (7 daily; $36 single, $71 return). Journey time is about 3hr 30min.

By ferry from Vancouver

If you're without your own transport, the most painless way to Victoria from Vancouver is by **bus and ferry**. Pacific Coach Lines (Ⓣ604/662-8074 or 1-800/661-1725, Ⓦwww.pacificcoach.com) picked up at the Vancouver bus terminal at 1150 Station St, takes you, inclusive of the ferry crossing and journeys to and from ferry terminals at both ends, to Victoria's central bus station at 700 Douglas St. Buses leave hourly in the summer, every two hours in the winter: total journey time is about 3hr 30min and a single ticket costs $29 ($56 return). No bookings are necessary: overflow passengers are simply put on another coach. Be sure to keep your ticket stub for reboarding the bus after the crossing.

If you are traveling by **car**, BC Ferries operates four routes to Vancouver Island across the Georgia Strait from mainland British Columbia (Ⓣ1-888/223-3779 from anywhere in BC; otherwise Ⓣ604/444-2890 or 250/386-3431 in Vancouver, Victoria, or outside BC, Ⓦwww.bcferries.com). Reservations are essential in summer if you want to avoid long waits. The route used by most Victoria–Vancouver passengers is the **Tsawwassen–Swartz Bay connection**, also the route used by Pacific Coach Lines' buses. Ferries ply the route almost continuously from 7am to 10pm (sixteen sailings daily in summer, minimum of eight daily in winter). Car tickets cost $34.75 at weekends (noon Fri to last sailing on Sun) and $32.75 on weekdays in high season from late June to early Sept ($31.50/29.75 in shoulder season from mid-March to mid-June and early Sept to Oct); $2.50 year-round to bring a bicycle. Fares do not include driver or passenger fares, which are $10 per person daily in peak season and $9.50 daily in the shoulder season.

By ferry from the United States

Washington State Ferries, 2499 Ocean Ave, Sidney (in Victoria ⓣ250/381-1551 or 656-1531 in Sidney, in Seattle ⓣ206/464-6400 or 1-888/808-7977 in Washington only; ⓦwww.wsdot.wa.gov/choices/ferries.cfm) runs ferries from Anacortes, ninety minutes north of Seattle, to Sidney, thirty minutes (and 30km) north of Victoria (summer 2 daily in each direction, winter 1 daily; 3hr–3hr 30min), with one of the two summer departures traveling via Orcas Island and Friday Harbor on the San Juan Islands. Passenger fares for the full trip are around US$13.10 (a little less in winter), a car and driver US$44.25. Car reservations are required from Orcas and Friday Harbor and can be made by calling at least a day in advance (ⓣ360/378-4777 in Friday Harbor).

Black Ball Transport, 430 Belleville St, Victoria (in BC ⓣ250/386-2202 or 1/800-972-6509, in Washington ⓣ360/457-4491 or 1-800/833-6388; ⓦwww.cohoferry.com) operates a ferry across the Juan de Fuca Strait between Port Angeles on Washington's Olympic Peninsula right to Victoria's Inner Harbour (1–4 daily; 95min). Passenger fares are US$8.50 and US$32.50 for cars. Reservations are not accepted. Car drivers should call ahead in summer to have some idea of how long they'll have to wait. Crossing time is 95 minutes.

For foot passengers, and day-trippers in particular, a speedier option is **Victoria Express**'s service from Port Angeles (2 daily late May to late June & Sept to mid-Oct; late June to Aug 3 daily; 55min) to Victoria's Inner Harbour. The fare is US$12.50 one-way, US$25 return; bicycles cost $3 one-way or return. Ferries run only from mid-May to mid-Oct (ⓣ250/361-9144 in BC, ⓣ360/452-8088 in Port Angeles, or ⓣ1-800/633-1589 across the US; ⓦwww.victoriaexpress.com).

Alternatively, the 300-passenger-only *Victoria Clipper* **catamaran** travels between Pier 69 in Downtown Seattle and Victoria's Inner Harbour in three hours or two hours if you take the quicker "Turbojet" departures (250 Bellevue St, Victoria; ⓣ250/382-8100 in Victoria, ⓣ206/448-5000 in Seattle or 1-800/888-2535 outside Seattle and BC; ⓦwww.victoriaclipper.com). There is one sailing daily in each direction from January to March and mid-September to December; two sailings daily in the first half of May and second half of September; and four sailings daily from mid-May to mid-September. Tickets prices vary according to season – US$62 single, US$103 return offseason, US$68/113 for three-hour crossings and US$77/129 for the Turbojet in summer.

By air

Flying into Victoria from Vancouver airport is an expensive option. Open return fares from Vancouver typically run to around $150, excursion fares (tickets have restrictions) around $100. If you are going to fly, however, it's more fun and more direct to travel from **Vancouver's Burrard Inlet to Victoria's Inner Harbour** by helicopter or float plane: Harbour Air and West Coast Air fly from the Tradewinds Marina just west of Canada Place in Vancouver (see below for details) for a one-way price of $99. Helijet Airways (ⓣ604/273-1414) flies from the helipad to the east or from Vancouver Airport for $140 one-way, less if you book in advance.

Arrival, information, and transportation

Victoria International Airport (ⓣ250/953-7500, ⓦwww.cyyj.ca or ⓦwww.victoriaairport.com) is 26km north of Downtown on Hwy-17 near the Sidney ferry terminal. Hwy-17 runs south and takes you to the city outskirts, where it becomes Douglas Street, which runs to the heart of Downtown. The Akal Airporter shuttle bus heads Downtown (where it stops at major hotels) every half-hour between about 4.30am and 1am; a single fare for the 45-minute journey is $13 (ⓣ250/386-2525, 386-2526 or 1-877/386-2525, ⓦwww.akalairporter.travel.bc.ca). They can also arrange pick-ups to the airport. Otherwise contact Harbour Air (ⓣ250/384-2215 or 1-800/665-0212, ⓦwww.harbour-air.com) or West Coast Air (ⓣ250/388-4521 or 1-800/347-2222, ⓦwww.westcoastair.com), which operate efficient and quick float planes between Vancouver's port and Victoria's Downtown Inner Harbour: both companies share terminals in both cities ($99 single; planes leave about every hour; crossing time is 35 minutes). Helijet Airways (ⓣ604/273-1414, ⓦwww.helijet.com) flies from Vancouver airport or a terminal east of Canada Place in Downtown to Victoria's Inner Harbour from $140 single.

Victoria's **bus terminal** is Downtown at 700 Douglas St and Belleville Street, close to the Royal British Columbia Museum. Pacific Coach Lines' buses from Vancouver or Vancouver airport will drop you here, and it is the base for onward connections on Vancouver Island provided by Laidlaw Coach Lines (ⓣ250/385-4411, ⓦwww.grayline.ca/victoria).

Victoria's busy **infocentre** is at 812 Wharf St, in front of the *Empress Hotel* on the harbor (daily May–Sept 8.30am–6.30pm; Oct–April 9am–5pm; ⓣ250/953-2033, for accommodation reservations 1-800/663-3883, ⓦwww.tourismvictoria.com). The staff can help you book whale-watching and other tours (see box, p.487), and provide a huge range of general information.

The most enjoyable means of **transportion** around Victoria are the tiny Inner Harbour **ferries** that sail around the harbor. Stops include Fisherman's Wharf, Ocean Pointe Resort, and West Bay Marina, but they're worth taking just for the ride: try an evening mini-cruise around the harbor (buy $3 tickets on ferries in the Inner Harbour or book at the infocentre). You're unlikely to need to take a local **bus** if you stick to the Downtown area, but if you do venture out, most services run from the corner of Douglas and Yates streets. The fare within the large central zone is $1.75 – tickets and the DayPass ($5.50) are sold at the infocentre, 7-Eleven stores, and other marked outlets, or you can pay on board if you have the exact fare. For 24-hour recorded information on city transport, call the Busline (ⓣ250/382-6161, lost property ⓣ250/995-5637, ⓦwww.bctransit.com).

Accommodation

Victoria fills up quickly in the summer, and most of its budget **accommodation** is well known and heavily patronized. Top-price hotels cluster around the Inner Harbour area; **hostels** and more downmarket alternatives are scattered all over, though the largest concentration of cheap **hotels** and **motels** is around the Gorge Road and Douglas Street areas northwest of Downtown. Reservations are virtually obligatory in all categories, though the infocentre's accommodation service will root out a room if you're stuck

(Ⓣ1-800/663-3883 in North America, 250/953-2033 outside North America). They are more than likely to offer you **B&B** accommodation, of which the town has a vast selection, though prices for many are surprisingly elevated; many owners of the more far-flung places will pick you up from Downtown.

Victoria's commercial **campsites** are full to bursting in summer, with most space given over to RVs. Few of these are convenient for Downtown – given that you'll have to travel, you might as well head for one of the more scenic provincial park sites. Most are on the Trans-Canada Highway to the north, or on Hwy-14 east of Victoria.

Hotels and bed and breakfasts

Abigail's Hotel 960 McClure St Ⓣ250/388-5363 or 1-800/561-6565, Ⓦwww.abigailshotel.com. A very classy, small hotel in a fine building with log fires, voluminous duvets, Jacuzzis, and a good breakfast. If you want to treat yourself, this is the place. All rooms are nonsmoking. Situated on the corner of Quadra St, a block east of Blanshard St and within easy walking distance of the city center. 8–9.

Cherry Bank Hotel 825 Burdett Ave Ⓣ250/385-5380 or 1-800/998-6688, Ⓦwww.bctravel.com/cherrybankhotel. Reservations are essential at this deservedly popular and pleasantly eccentric 26-room budget hotel (note the rooftop rotating mermaid), which has excellent rooms and breakfast included. First choice in this price range. 3

Crystal Court Motel 701 Belleville St Ⓣ250/384-0551, Ⓦwww.crystalcourtmotel.supersites.ca. This is a large, functional, and fairly priced motel well located just one block from the Inner Harbour, though it fronts a fairly busy road. 4

Heathergate House 122 Simcoe St Ⓣ250/383-0068 or 1-888/683-0068, Ⓦwww.heathergatebb.com. This small B&B offers three en-suite rooms plus a separate two-bed cottage within walking distance of the Inner Harbour and the sights. There's a private floor for guests with a lounge and TV room. 5

James Bay Inn 270 Government St at Toronto St Ⓣ250/384-7151 or 1-800/836-2649, Ⓦwww.jamesbayinn.bc.ca. This 45-room hotel vies with the *Cherry Bank* as Victoria's best reasonably priced option, though rates have climbed in the last couple of years. The Edwardian building was the home of painter Emily Carr. Simple rooms at varying prices, with a restaurant and pub. Two blocks south of the Parliament Buildings. 6

Prior House 620 St Charles St Ⓣ592-8847 or 1-877/924-3300, Ⓦwww.priorhouse.com. A stylish five-room B&B; once the home of Victoria's lieutenant governor – ask for his suite, complete with bathroom with chandelier. About 2.5km east of Downtown, so it's better if you have transport. 7

Rosewood Inn 595 Michigan St near Government St Ⓣ250/384-6644 or 1-866-986-2222, Ⓦwww.rosewoodvictoria.com. A comfortable, smart, small hotel a couple of blocks south of the Royal BC Museum. 6–7.

Ryan's 224 Superior St Ⓣ389-0012 or 1-877/389-0012, Ⓦwww.ryansbb.com. A very pretty 1892 heritage building south of the Royal BC Museum and a five-minute walk to Downtown; all seven rooms are nicely decorated and have private bathrooms. 7

Selkirk Guest House 934 Selkirk Ave Ⓣ250/389-1213 or 1/800-974-6638, Ⓦwww.selkirkguesthouse.com. Fine historic waterfront home dating from 1909, northwest of the Inner Harbour. It's well placed for bike and walking trails (it's on the Galloping Goose Trail; see p.496) and you can rent boats and canoes. A bed in a dorm room costs $20 and there's a choice of four other good double rooms $75–90 with breakfast at $5. Take bus #14 from Douglas St (to within two blocks) 4

Shamrock Suites on the Park 675 Superior St at the corner of Douglas Ⓣ250/385-8768 or 1-800/294-5544. The *Shamrock* lies a block from the Royal BC Museums close to Beacon Hill Park and has just sixteen units. Prices have gone up, but the studios and one-bedroom suites are roomy and come with kitchenettes at no extra cost: some rooms have park views. A continental breakfast is included in the rates between July and September. 5

Strathcona Hotel 919 Douglas St Ⓣ250/383-7137 or 1-800/663-7476, Ⓦwww.strathconahotel.com. Large, modern hotel where rooms include baths and TVs. There's a British-style pub and restaurant downstairs with booming DJ and live music which may not be to all tastes. 3

Hostels

Ocean Island Backpacker's Inn 791 Pandora Ave at Blanshard St Ⓣ250/385-1788 or

1-888/888-4180, Ⓦ www.oceanisland.com. A good, reasonably central location in the northeast corner of Downtown. The restored 1893 heritage building has a wide variety of dorms and rooms (singles and doubles with and without bathroom. Facilities include private and shared rooms, Internet access, a music room with instruments, no curfew, free morning coffee, laundry room, free bike storage, linen and towels provided, and limited parking at $4 a day. The following prices are Fri and Sat rates and assume you do not have an HI card (subtract $1-3 if you do): dorm beds cost $17.75 from mid-Oct to mid-March up to $23 in July and Aug. Private doubles cost from $40 to $55.

Turtle Refuge Hostel 1608 Quadra St at corner of Pandora Ⓣ 250/386-4471, Ⓔ turtlerefuge@hotmail.com. Central residential home (also known as the *Backpackers' Lodge*) with 25 dorm beds, two doubles and two four-bed family rooms. There's a communal kitchen, laundry, no curfew, parking, luggage storage, and free morning coffee. Dorm beds cost $13 ($12 Nov–April), doubles $40 ($30) plus $10 for each extra person.

Victoria Youth Hostel (HI) 516 Yates and Wharf streets. Mon–Thurs 7.30am to midnight, Fri–Sun 7am–2am; Ⓣ 250/385-4511 or 1-888/883-0099, Ⓦ www.hihostels.ca. Large, modern, welcoming, and extremely well-run place just a few blocks north of the Inner Harbour. The bunk rooms, though, can be noisy: the reception, rather ominously, sells earplugs. The noticeboards are packed with useful information on the city. Members $16–20 nonmembers $17–24. A handful of private doubles are available at $38 for members, $48 for nonmembers.

Campsites

Fort Victoria RV and Park Campground 340 Island Hwy-1A Ⓣ 250/479-8112,, Ⓦ www.fortvicrv.com. Closest site to Downtown, 6km north of Victoria off the Trans-Canada Hwy. Take bus #14 (for Craigflower) from the city center: it stops right by the gate. Large 300-pitch site mainly for RVs but with a few tent sites; free hot showers. $29 per two persons.

Goldstream Provincial Park 2930 Trans-Canada Hwy Ⓣ 604/689-9025 or 1-800/689-9025, Ⓦ www.discovercamping.ca. Bus #50 from Douglas St from Downtown. Although 20km north of the city off Hwy-1, this site is set in old-growth forests of cedar and Douglas fir and is Victoria's best camping option. Flush toilets and free hot showers, with plenty of hiking, swimming, and fishing opportunities nearby. $22 per site.

Thetis Lake 1938 Trans-Canada Hwy at 1938 West Park Lane Ⓣ 250/478-3845, Ⓔ thetislake@shaw.ca. Runs a close second to *Goldstream Provincial Park's* campsites for the pleasantness of its setting, and is only 10km north of Downtown. Family-oriented, with 147 sites, as well as laundry and coin-operated showers. $16 per two persons.

The Inner Harbour

The Victoria that merits close inspection is very small: almost everything worth seeing, as well as the best shops and restaurants, is within walking distance of the **Inner Harbour**, the heart of which runs for around 300m from the Parliament Buildings in the south to the infocentre in the north. On summer evenings this area is alive with strollers and buskers, and a pleasure to wander as the sun drops over the water. Foremost among the daytime diversions are the enthralling **Royal British Columbia Museum** and the immense **Empress Hotel**. Most of the other trumpeted attractions – like the Royal London Wax Museum – are dreadful, and many charge entry fees out of all proportion to what's on show. If you're tempted, details are available from the infocentre.

The Royal British Columbia Museum

The **Royal British Columbia Museum** (daily 9am–5pm; National Geographic IMAX Theatre: daily 9am–8pm; museum $9.75, IMAX Theatre only $9.75, combined ticket $16.25, IMAX double feature $15; museum Ⓣ 250/356-7226 or 1-888/447-7977, Ⓦ www.rbcm.gov.bc.ca) is a short stroll along the waterfront from the infocentre at 675 Belleville St. Founded in 1886, it is arguably the best museum in Canada. All conceivable aspects of the province are examined, but the **aboriginal peoples** section is probably the definitive collection of a much-covered genre, while the natural history sections – huge re-creations of natural habitats, complete with sights, sounds, and smells – are mind-boggling in scope and imagination. Allow at least two trips to take it all in.

From the first thing you see as you enter the display area – a huge stuffed **mammoth** – you can tell that thought, wit, and a lot of money have gone into the museum. Much of the cash must have been sunk into its most popular display, the **Open Ocean**, a self-contained, in-depth look at the sea and the deep-level ocean. Groups of ten are admitted into a series of tunnels, dark rooms, elevators, and mock-ups of submarines at thirty-minute intervals. You take a time-coded ticket and wait your turn, so either arrive early or reckon on seeing the rest of the museum first. Though rather heavy-handed in its "we're-all-part-of-the-cosmic-soup" message, it's still an object lesson in presentation and state-of-the-art museum dynamics. It's also designed to be dark and enclosed, so stay out if you suffer even a twinge of claustrophobia.

The first floor contains **dioramas**, full-scale reconstructions of some of the many natural habitats found in British Columbia. The idea of re-creating shorelines, coastal rainforests, and Fraser Delta landscapes may sound far-fetched, yet all are incredibly realistic, down to dripping water and cool, dank atmospheres. Audiovisual displays and a tumult of information accompany the exhibits (the beaver film is worth hunting down), most of which focus attention on the province's 25,600km of coastline, a side of British Columbia usually overlooked in favor of its interior forests and mountains.

The mother of all the tiny museums of bric-a-brac and pioneer memorabilia in BC can be found on the second floor. Arranged eccentrically from the present day backwards, it explores every aspect of the province's **social history** over two centuries in nitpicking detail. Prominently featured are part of an early-twentieth-century town, complete with cinema and silent films, plus comprehensive displays on logging, mining, the gold rush, farming, fishing, and lesser domestic details: all the artifacts and accompanying information being presented with impeccable finesse.

Up on the third floor, a superb collection of **aboriginal peoples' art, culture, and history** is presented in gloomy light against muted wood walls and brown carpet, creating a solemn atmosphere in keeping with the tragic nature of many of the displays. The whole collection takes you to the point where smallpox virtually wiped out in one year a culture that was eight millennia in the making. A section on land and reservations is left for last – the issues are contentious even today – and even if you're succumbing to museum fatigue, the arrogance and duplicity of the documents on display will shock you. The highlights in this section are many, but try to make a point of seeing the short film *In the Land of the War Canoes* (1914), the **Bighouse** (a facsimile of a meeting hall) and its chants, and the audiovisual display on aboriginal myths and superstition. The **National Geographic Theatre** in the museum plays host to a huge IMAX screen and a changing program of special-format films.

Helmcken House

Built in 1825, the **Helmcken House** (daily May–Oct 10am–5pm, Thurs–Mon 11am–4pm; $5; ⓣ250/361-0021) stands strangely isolated off Belleville Street, directly adjacent to the museum. The oldest house in BC still on its original site, it is a predictable heritage offering that showcases the home, furnishings, and embroidery talents of the Helmcken family. Dr John Helmcken was Fort Victoria's doctor and local political bigwig (he married the daughter of the governor Sir James Douglas), and his house is a typical monument to stolid Victoria values. Upstairs it contains various attic treasures and some of the good doctor's fearsome-looking medical tools. If you visit, pick up the free guided tapes and hear "voices from history" (those of actors and actresses) that give a more personalized slant on the building: listen, for example, to "Aunt Dolly" as she tells why she left the good doctor's room untouched as a shrine after his death.

Just behind the house there's another old white-wood building, the **St Anne's Pioneer Schoolhouse** (interior closed to the public), originally purchased by a Bishop Demers for four sisters of the Order of St Anne, who in 1858 took it upon themselves to leave their Québec home to come and teach in Victoria. Built between 1843 and 1858, it's believed to be the oldest building in Victoria still in use.

The Parliament Buildings

The huge Victorian complex of the **Parliament Buildings** (daily June to early Sept 9am–5pm; early Sept to May 9am–4pm; free) one block west of the museum at 501 Belleville St is old and imposing in the manner of a large and particularly grand British town hall. Beautifully lit at night by some three hundred tiny bulbs (though locals grumble about the cost), the domed building is fronted by the sea and well-kept gardens – a pleasant enough ensemble, though it doesn't really warrant the manic enthusiasm visited on it by hordes of summer tourists. You're more likely to find yourself taking time out on the front lawns, distinguished by a perky statue of Queen Victoria and a giant sequoia, a gift from the state of California. Designed by Francis Rattenbury, also responsible for the nearby *Empress Hotel*, the building was completed in 1897, in time for Queen Victoria's jubilee. Figures from Victoria's grey bureaucratic past are duly celebrated, the main door guarded by statues of Sir James Douglas, who chose the site of the city, and Sir Matthew Baillie Begbie (aka the "Hanging Judge"), responsible for law and order during the heady days of gold fever. Sir George Vancouver keeps an eye on proceedings from the top of the dome.

Free guided tours (every 20–30min Oct–April, booked tours only the rest of the year Mon–Fri hourly 9am–3pm plus one public tour at 4pm; Ⓣ250/387-3046 or 1-800/663-7867 in BC) start to the right of the main steps and are led by chirpy guides full of anecdotes. Look out for the dagger that killed Captain Cook, and the gold-plated dome, painted with scenes from Canadian history.

Crystal Garden

Modeled after London's Crystal Palace, **Crystal Garden** (daily mid-March to mid-June & mid-Sept to Oct 9am–6pm; mid-June to mid-Sept 9am–8pm; Nov–mid-March 10am–4.30pm; $9; Ⓣ250/381-1213, Ⓦwww.bcpcc.com/crystal), behind the bus terminal at 713 Douglas St, was billed, on opening in 1925, as housing the "Largest Saltwater Swimming Pool in the British Empire." Much restored, the greenhouse – filled with flora, monkeys, and birds – makes for an unaccountably popular tourist spot; only the exterior has any claims to architectural sophistication, and much of its effect is spoilt by the souvenir and other shops on its ground-floor arcade. Once the meeting place of the town's tea-sipping elite, it still plays host to events such as the "Jive and Ballroom Dance Club" and the "People Meeting People Dance." The daytime draws are the conservatory-type tearoom and tropical gardens. Inhumanely enclosed birds, butterflies, and monkeys, though, are liable to put you off your scones.

The Empress Hotel

A town is usually in desperate shape when one of its key attractions is a hotel, but in the case of Victoria, the **Empress Hotel** is so physically overbearing and plays such a part in the town's tourist appeal that it demands attention. Worth a visit alone just to wander through the huge lobbies and palatial dining areas for a glimpse of well-restored colonial splendor. In a couple of lounges there's a fairly limp "Smart Casual" dress code – no dirty jeans, running shoes, short shorts, or backpacks – but elsewhere you can wander freely. If you want to **take tea**, which is why most casual visitors are here, enter the **Tea Lounge** by the hotel's side entrance (the right, or south side): there you can enjoy scones, biscuits, cakes, and, of course, tea over six courses but you have to abide by the dress code and be prepared for an enormous outlay. In other lounges, you can ask for just tea and scones.

The hotel's **Crystal Lounge** and its lovely Tiffany-glass dome form the most opulent part of the hotel on view, but the marginally less ornate entrance lounge is *the* place for the charade of afternoon tea, and indulging can be a bit of a laugh. There's also a reasonably priced bar and restaurant downstairs, **Kipling's**, and the attractive **Bengal Lounge**, complete with tiger-skin over the fireplace, where you can have a curry and all the trimmings for about $15. For a bigger treat, take dinner amidst the Edwardian splendor of *the Empress Dining Room*.

The Old Town

Adjacent to the Inner Harbour to the north, **the Old Town**, unsurprisingly, is Victoria's oldest district. Within it lies the city's historical focal point, **Bastion Square**, the original site of Fort Victoria. These days, Bastion Square's former saloons, brothels, and warehouses have been spruced up and turned into offices, cafés, and galleries. The modest **Maritime Museum** at 28 Bastion Square (daily 9.30am–4.30pm; $6; ⓣ250/385-4222, ⓦwww.mmbc.bc.ca) is of interest mainly for the lovely chocolate-and-vanilla-coloured building in which it's housed, the former provincial courthouse. Displays embrace old charts, uniforms, ships' bells, old photographs, lots of models, and a new BC Ferries section on the second floor. Note the old open elevator built to reach the restored vice-admiralty courtroom, commissioned by Chief Justice Davie in 1901, supposedly because he was too portly to manage the stairs.

Two blocks to the north of the square lies the attractive **Market Square**, the old heart of Victoria but now a collection of some 65 speciality shops and cafés around a central courtyard (bounded by Pandora Avenue and Store and Johnson streets). This area boomed in 1858 following the gold rush, providing houses, saloons, opium dens, stores, and various salacious entertainment for thousands of chancers and would-be immigrants. On the Pandora Avenue side of the area was a ravine, marked by the current sunken courtyard, beyond which lay **Chinatown** (now centered slightly further north on Fisgard Street), the oldest on North America's west coast. Here, among other things, 23 factories processed 90,000 pounds of opium a year for what was then a legitimate trade and – until the twentieth century – one of BC's biggest industries.

As for the **shopping streets**, it's worth looking out for E A Morris, a wonderful old cigar and tobacco shop next to *Murchie's* coffee shop at 1110 Government St, and Roger's Chocolates, 913 Government St, whose whopping Victoria creams (among other things), are regularly dispatched to Buckingham Palace for royal consumption.

Beyond the city center

Outside the Inner Harbour and the Old Town, Victoria and its outlying area have a scattering of attractions that don't fit into any logical tour, the more compelling of which are **Craigdarroch Castle** and its lofty perch and the floral exuberance of the **Butchart Gardens**.

Beacon Hill Park

The best park within walking distance of the city center is **Beacon Hill Park**, south of the Inner Harbour and a few minutes' walk up the road behind the Royal British Columbia Museum. Victoria's biggest green space, it has lots of paths, ponds, big trees, and quiet corners, and plenty of views over the Juan de Fuca Strait to the distant Olympic Mountains of Washington State (especially on the park's southern side).

The gardens in the park are by turns well tended and wonderfully wild and unkempt. Some of the trees are massive old-growth timbers that you'd normally only see on the island's unlogged west coast. Come here in spring and you'll catch swaths of daffodils and blue camas, the latter a floral monument to Victoria's earliest aboriginal inhabitants, who cultivated it for its edible bulb. Some 30,000 other flowers are planted in the gardens annually. The park, a favored retreat of celebrated Victorian artist, Emily Carr, also claim's the world's tallest totem pole at 48m, as well as the "Mile Zero" marker of the Trans-Canada Highway.

Emily Carr House

Only ten rooms are open to the public at **Emily Carr House** (daily 10am–5pm; $5.35; ⓣ250/383-5843), two blocks from the Inner Harbour at 207 Government St. This was the early home of British Columbia's best-known artist, born here during a blizzard in 1871 in the old wooden bed still visible in what would become her bedroom. The fine Victorian building was constructed in 1864, and has been painstakingly restored to its former state with an almost neurotic attention to detail. Fans of the artist may want to pay homage, but don't expect much by way of original art - the works on the walls are copies. For originals, be sure to see her collection at the Art Gallery of Victoria (see below).

Craigdarroch Castle and the Art Gallery of Victoria

Perched on a hilltop at 1050 Joan Crescent in Rockland, one of Victoria's more prestigious neighborhoods **Craigdarroch Castle** (mid-June to early Sept 9am–7pm; early Sept to mid-June 10am–4.30pm; $10; ⓣ250/592-5323, ⓦwww.craigdarrochcastle.com) was built by Robert Dunsmuir, a caricature of a Victorian politician, strike-breaker, robber baron, and coal tycoon, who was forced to put up this gaunt Gothic pastiche to lure his wife away from Scotland. The fact, though, that he chose the highest point in the city for its construction was less out of concern for her than a by-product of his megalomania. Only the best was good enough, from the marble, granite, and sandstone of the superstructure to the intricately handworked panels of the ceilings over the main hall and staircase. Dunsmuir never enjoyed his creation – he died in 1889, two years after the castle was begun and a year before it was finished. Among the 39 rooms there's the usual clutter of Victoriana and period detail, in particular some impressive woodwork and stained and leaded glass. To get here by **bus** take the #11-University or #14-University from Downtown to the foot of Joan Crescent, two minutes' walk from the castle. If you decide to walk the whole way, allow 45 minutes from the Inner Harbour.

The **Art Gallery of Greater Victoria** (Mon–Sat 10am–5pm, Thurs until 9pm, Sun 1–5pm; $5; ⓣ250/384-4101, ⓦwww.aggv.bc.ca) is near Craigdarroch Castle at 1040 Moss St, just off Fort Street. is of little interest unless you're partial to contemporary Canadian paintings and the country's best collection of Japanese art: the building, housed in the 1890 Spencer Mansion, boasts what the gallery claims is the only complete Shinto shrine outside Japan. It does, however, have a small permanent collection of Emily Carr's work as well as a temporary exhibition, usually interesting, that changes every six weeks. To get here by **bus**, take the #10-Haultain, #11-Uplands/Beacon Hill or #14-University from Downtown.

Point Ellice House and Gardens

The 1861 Victorian-Italianate **Point Ellice House and Gardens** (guided tours mid-May to mid-Sept daily noon–5pm; $5.35; ⓣ250/387-4697) at 2616 Pleasant St is magnificently recreated but less enticing than Craigdarroch Castle because of its slightly shabby surroundings. These can be overlooked, however, if you make a point of arriving by sea, taking one of the little Harbour Ferry services to the house (10min; $14 as part of 45-minute tour) from the Inner Harbour. Ferry staff issue tokens which allow you to get on and off at various points for your $14. The restored Victorian-style gardens here are a delight on a summer afternoon. The interior retains its largely Victorian appearance thanks partly to the reduced circumstances of the O'Reilly family, whose genteel slide into relative poverty over several generations (they lived here from 1861 to 1974) meant that many furnishings were simply not replaced. Tea, inevitably, is served on the lawns in the summer: it's a good idea to book ahead. **Bus** #14-University will get you here from Downtown if you don't fancy the approach by water.

The Butchart Gardens

If you're into things horticultural, make a trek out to the celebrated **Butchart Gardens**, 21km north of Victoria at 800 Benvenuto Ave, Brentwood Bay on Hwy-17 towards the Swartz Bay ferry terminal (daily mid-June to Aug 9am–10.30pm, first two weeks of Sept & Dec 9am–9pm; rest of the year 9am–sunset; $10.50 in early Jan, then on a sliding scale through year to $20 between mid-June and Sept; ⓣ250/652-4422 or 652-5256, ⓦwww.butchartgardens.com). The gardens were started in 1904 by Jenny Butchart, wife of a mine owner whose initial aim was to landscape one of her husband's quarries; the garden now covers fifty breathtaking acres, comprising rose, Japanese, and Italian gardens, and lots of decorative details. About half a million visitors a year tramp through the foliage, which includes over a million plants and seven hundred different species. At the same time, the amount of space actually given over to gardens may strike you as slightly disproportionate to the space allotted to the parking lot, gift shop, and restaurant.

The gardens are also renowned amongst visitors and locals alike for the stunning **firework displays** that usually take place each Saturday evening in July and August. During the late-evening hours between mid-June and the end of September the gardens are illuminated. There is also a restaurant and various other commercial enterprises, with musical entertainments well to the fore.

To get here by public transport take **bus** #75 for "Central Saanich" from Downtown. Otherwise, there are regular summer **shuttles** (May–Oct daily, hourly in the morning, half-hourly in the afternoon; ⓣ250/388-5248) from the main bus terminal, where tickets ($4) are obtainable not from the main ticket office but a separate Gray Lines desk.

Eating, drinking, and nightlife

Victoria has a plethora of **restaurants**, some extremely good, offering greater variety – and higher prices – than you'll find anywhere else on the island. **Pubs** tend to be plastic imitations of their British equivalents, with one or two

Whale-watching trips

The waters around Victoria are not as whale-rich as those around Tofino on the west coast of Vancouver Island (see p.513), but there's still a very good chance of spotting the creatures. Three pods of orcas (killer whales) live in the seas around southern Vancouver Island, about a hundred in all, so you may see these, though minke are the most commonly spotted whale, with occasional greys and humpbacks also visible. Few outfits guarantee sightings, and many cover themselves by letting you know that if you don't see whales you stand a good chance of seeing harbor or Dall's porpoises, harbor or elephant seals, and California and Steller sea lions.

While there are many outfits to choose from, they offer almost identical trips at the same prices, typically around $60 to $90 for a three-hour outing. There's usually a naturalist, or at least a knowledgeable crewmember, to fill you in on what you're seeing (or not). The only real variables are the **boats** used, so you need to decide whether you want rigid-hull cruisers (covered or uncovered), which are more comfortable and sedate (and usually the most expensive at around $90), a catamaran ($75–90), or the high-speed aluminium-hull inflatables known as "zodiacs" ($60–90), which are infinitely more exhilarating, but can offer a fast and sometimes bumpy ride that makes them unsuitable for pregnant women, young children, or people with back problems. They won't have toilets on board either. The two companies below have been around longer than most; the infocentre (p.479) will have details on other options.

Seacoast Expeditions 146 Kingston Street, behind the Harbourside Hotel (Ⓣ250/383-2254 or 1-800/386-1525, Ⓦwww.seacoastexpeditions.com), is Victoria's founding whale-watching company, offering one three-hour trip daily in April and October, four trips daily in May, June, and September, and five daily in July and August ($79). It also offers a guaranteed sighting deal (May–Aug only), whereby you carry a "WhaleAlert" pager that instructs you to turn up at the office for a tour only when killer whales have been spotted. All tours are guided by a naturalist and are in one of the company's three 12-passenger zodiacs.

Five Star Charters at 706 Douglas St (Ⓣ250/388-7223 or 1-800/634-9617, Ⓦwww.5starwhales.com), has claimed the highest percentage of whale sightings out of all the tour operators (thanks to spotter boats and a good network of contacts). It runs three daily three-hour trips from mid-April through September ($79) and two daily two-hour trips from October to mid-April ($60). Trips are in 12-passenger open cruiser or 40-person "Supercat" boat.

worthy exceptions, as do the numerous **cafés** that pander to Victoria's self-conscious afternoon-tea ritual.

Nocturnal diversions in Victoria are for the most part tame: highbrow tastes, though, are surprisingly well-catered for, and there's a smattering of **bars**, as well as **live music** venues and **clubs** to keep you happy for the limited time you're likely to spend in the city. **Jazz** is particularly popular – for information on the city's jazz underground, contact the Victoria Jazz Society, 250-727 Johnson St (Ⓣ250/388-4423, Ⓦwww.vicjazz.bc.ca).

Listings appear in the main daily newspaper, the *Times-Colonist* and in a variety of free magazines (titles change from year to year) you can pick up in shops, cafés, and hotels: the latest is the excellent *Monday* magazine (Ⓦwww.mondaymag.com), published every Thursday. **Tickets** for most offerings are available from the McPherson Playhouse, 3 Centennial Square, Pandora and Government streets (Ⓣ250/386-6121 or 1-888/717-6121, Ⓦwww.rmts.bc.ca).

Cafés, tea, and snacks

Barb's Fish and Chips 310 St Lawrence St, Fisherman's Wharf, off Kingston St ⓣ250/384-6515. A much-loved floating shack that offers classic home-cut chips, fish straight off the boat, and oyster burgers and chowder to boot: the bathtub-size ferries from the Inner Harbour drop you close by.

Blethering Place 2250 Oak Bay Ave ⓣ250/598-1413 or 1-888/598-1413. Along with the *Empress Hotel*, this is known as a place to indulge in the tea-taking custom. Scones, cakes, and dainty sandwiches are served up against the background of hundreds of Toby jugs and royal-family memorabilia – perhaps a tad overrated.

Demitasse Coffee Bar 320 Blanshard St near Pandora Ave ⓣ250/386-4442. A popular, elegantly laid-back hole-in-the-wall café with excellent coffee, salads, bagels, lunch-time snacks, and an open fire in season.

Dutch Bakery & Coffee Shop 718 Fort St ⓣ250/385-1052. A Victoria institution serving pastries and chocolate to take away. You can also eat in the popular, if plain, coffee shop at the back.

Empress Hotel 721 Government St ⓣ250/348-8111. Try tea in the lobby, with tourists and locals alike on their best behaviour amidst the chintz and potted plants. A strict dress code allows no dirty jeans, anoraks, or sportswear.

Murchie's 1110 Government St ⓣ250/381-5451. The best central place for basic tea, coffee, and cakes, thanks to the quality of its products and convenient location in the center of Victoria's shopping streets.

Re-Bar 50 Bastion Square at Langley St ⓣ250/360-2401. A great place that serves teas, coffees (charcoal-filtered water), and health food at lunch (usually organically grown), but most remarkable for its extraordinary range of freshly squeezed juices in strange combinations, smoothies, "power tonics" and frighteningly healthy wheatgrass drinks ("Astro Turf": a blend of carrot, beet, garlic, and wheatgrass).

Sally's 714 Cormorant St near Douglas St ⓣ250/381-1431. Funky little café that's very popular with locals and office workers despite its location on the northern edge of Downtown.

Restaurants

Da Tandoor 1010 Fort St ⓣ250/384-6333. Tandoori specialist that is, along with the *Taj Mahal*, the best of Victoria's half-dozen or so Indian restaurants offering good food and a definitely over-the-top interior.

Earl's 1703 Blanshard St and Fisgard St ⓣ250/386-4323. You'll find an *Earl's* in many Canadian towns, but the restaurants are none the worse for being part of a chain: good – not fast – food, with a lively, pleasant interior and friendly service.

Herald Street Café 546 Herald St ⓣ250/381-1441. An excellent and stylish old favorite for Italian-influenced food. Pricey, but good value, along with a relaxed atmosphere and lots of art on the walls. Well worth the walk from the Inner Harbour.

Il Terrazzo 555 Johnson St, Waddington Alley ⓣ250/361-0028. Smooth, laid-back ambience with lots of red brick and plants and a summer patio that provides the setting for good North American versions of Italian food. With *Pagliacci's* (see below), this is the best place in town for Italian food.

Milestone's 812 Wharf St ⓣ250/381-2244. Popular mid-priced place for burgers, pastas, steaks, and the like, slap-bang on the Inner Harbour beneath the infocentre, so expect lots of bustle, passing trade, and good views.

Pagliacci's 1011 Broad St between Fort and Broughton ⓣ250/386-1662. The best restaurant in Victoria if you want a fast, furious atmosphere, live music, good Italian food, and excellent desserts. A rowdy throng begins to line up almost from the moment the doors are open.

Süze 515 Yates St ⓣ250/383-2829. The eclectic menu ranges from Asian cuisine to steak, pasta, chicken, and seafood, which you can take either at tables up on the tiny mezzanine or in the cozy dining room through the velvet curtains to the right. This is a great place for an early- or late-evening drink, thanks to its snug, informal, and vaguely exotic feel, and to its wonderful broad bar.

Taj Mahal 679 Herald St ⓣ250/383-4662. Housed in a mini Taj Mahal and a bit of a walk from the center, this restaurant serves good Indian food with chicken, lamb, and tandoori specialities.

Bars

Bartholomew's Bar and Rockefeller Grill *Executive House Hotel*, 777 Douglas St ⓣ250/388-5111. This is an upbeat pub with a steady diet of local bands.

Big Bad John's 919 Douglas St ⓣ250/383-7137. Next to the *Strathcona Hotel* this is Victoria's most atmospheric bar by far with bare boards, a fog of smoke, and authentic old banknotes and IOUs pasted to the walls. It also hosts occasional live bands and singers, usually of a country-music persuasion.

D'Arcy McGee's 1127 Wharf St ⓣ250/380-1322. It was only a matter of time before Victoria acquired an "Irish pub." This one has a prime site on the edge of Bastion Square, offers predictable food and beer, and has excellent occasional live Irish music.

Spinnakers BrewPub 308 Catherine St near Esquimalt Rd. ⓣ250/384-6613. Thirty-eight beers, including several home-brewed options, a restaurant, live music, occasional tours of the brewery, and good harbor views draw a mixed and relaxed clientele. Take bus #23 to Esquimalt Rd.

Steamers 570 Yates St. In the same vein as *Bartholomew's*, here you'll catch enthusiastic local bands most nights, and most types of music from reggae to Celtic.

Swans Brewpub 506 Pandora Ave at Store St ⓣ250/361-3310. This pretty and highly popular hotel-café-brewery, housed in a 1913 warehouse, is the place to watch Victoria's young professionals at play. Several foreign and six home-brewed beers on tap, with the *Neptune Soundbar* nightclub in the basement.

Clubs and live music

Esquimalt Inn 856 Esquimalt Rd ⓣ250/382-7161. A long-established venue with country bands most nights and occasional jam sessions. Take bus #23.

Evolution 502 Discovery St ⓣ250/388-3000. One of Victoria's more interesting clubs and discos, thanks to plenty of techno, rave, and alternative sounds.

Hermann's Jazz Club 753 View St ⓣ250/388-9166. Dimly lit club thick with 1950s-atmosphere that specializes in Dixieland but has occasional excursions into fusion and blues.

Legends 919 Douglas St ⓣ250/383-7137. The biggest, best, and noisiest of the live-music venues, this club occupies the garish, neon-lit basement of the *Strathcona Hotel*. Varied live bands, including the occasional big name, and dancing nightly.

Neptune Soundbar 1605 Store St at Pandora Ave ⓣ250/360-9098. You may well have to line up to join the thirty-something crew who frequent the basement disco of *Swans Brewpub*. 1960s and 1970s classics generally rule as well as current Top 40 fodder, but there's also a sprinkling of hip-hop and more modern offerings.

Festivals and outdoor events in Victoria

Free entertainment above and beyond the buskers clustered around James Bay, Market Square, and Beacon Hill in summer is not too hard to come by in Victoria; the city has a nice range of **festivals** and **outdoor events** on offer throughout the year. Annual highlights, listed chronologically, include:

TerrifVic Jazz Party, April ⓣ250/953-2011. A showcase for about a dozen top international bands held over four days.

Jazz Fest, June ⓣ250/386-6121, ⓦwww.vicjazz.bc.ca. More than a hundred assorted lesser-known bands perform in Market Square.

Canada Day, July 1. Celebration of Canada's national day concentrated in and around the Inner Harbour and includes fireworks, food, music, and other cultural events.

Victoria International Festival, July and August ⓣ736-2119. Victoria's largest general arts jamboree.

Folk Fest, last week of July ⓣ250/388-4728. Multicultural arts extravaganza.

First People's Festival, early August ⓣ250/384-3211. Celebration of the cultures of Canada's aboriginal peoples.

Victoria Dragon Boat Festival, mid-August ⓦwww.victoriadragonboat.com. Over 100 international teams take part in dragon-boat races on the Inner Harbour.

Classic Boat Festival, August 30–September 1 ⓣ250/385-7766. Dozens of wooden antique boats on display.

Royal Victoria Marathon, early October ⓣ250/658-0951, ⓦwww.royalvictoriamarathon.com. Marathon and half-marathon around the city streets and surroundings held on the Canadian Thanksgiving weekend.

Fringe Festival, September ⓣ250/383-2663. Avant-garde performances of all kinds.

The Great Canadian Beer Festival, second week of November ⓣ250/952-0360, ⓦwww.gcbf.com. Selections of beer from some of the province's best micro-breweries can be tasted at the Victoria Conference Centre, 720 Douglas St.

Merrython Fun Run, mid-December ⓣ250/953-2033. A 10-kilometre run through Downtown Victoria.

Listings

Bike rental Cycle Victoria Rentals, 950 Wharf St (☎250/885-2453 or 1-877/869-0039, ⓦwww.cyclevictoriarentals.com); Harbour Rentals, 811 Wharf St (☎250/995-1661 or 1-877-733-6722), rent a big range of bikes (from $6 an hour, $19 daily) plus five types of scooter (from $12 per hour, $45 daily); also kayaks, rowing boats, motor boats, and motor bikes.

Car rental Avis, 62B-1001 Douglas St (☎250/386-8468 or 1-800/879-2847) and Victoria Airport (☎250/656-6033); Budget, 757 Douglas St (☎250/953-5300 or 1-800/268-8900); National, 767 Douglas St (☎250/386-1213 or 1-800/227-7368).

Doctor and dentist Most hotels have a doctor or dentist on call. Otherwise contact Cresta Dental Centre in the Tillicum Street Mall at 3170 Tillicum Rd, Burnside St (☎250/384-7711). The Tillicum Mall Medical Clinic at the same address (☎381-8112) accepts walk-in patients.

Hospital Victoria General Hospital, 35 Helmcken Rd (☎727-4212).

Outdoor equipment rental Sports Rent, 1950 Government St at Discovery (☎250/385-7368, ⓦwww.sportsrentbc.com). Rents a colossal range of equipment, including bikes, rollerblades, all camping, hiking, climbing, and diving gear.

Post office Main office, 714 Yates St at Douglas (☎250/953-1352, 1-800/267-1177 in Canada). Mon–Fri 8.30am–5pm.

Taxis Blue Bird Cabs (☎250/382-4235); Empress Cabs (☎250/381-2222); Victoria Taxi (☎250/383-7111).

Weather Victoria Environment Canada Weatherline (☎250/656-3978).

The Southern Gulf Islands

Scattered between Vancouver Island and the mainland lie several hundred tiny islands, most no more than lumps of rock, a few large enough to hold permanent populations and warrant a regular ferry service. Two main clusters are accessible from Victoria: the **Southern Gulf Islands** and the San Juan Islands, both part of the same archipelago, except that the San Juan group (see p.330) belongs to the United States.

You get a good look at the Southern Gulf Islands on the seaplanes from Vancouver (see p.479) or on the ferry from Tsawwassen – twisting and threading through their coves and channels, the ride sometimes seems even a little too close for comfort. The coastline makes for superb **sailing**, and an armada of small boats crisscrosses between the islands whatever the weather allows. Hikers and campers are also well served, and **fishing**, too, is good, with some of the world's biggest salmon having met their doom in the surrounding waters. With its abundance of marine wildlife (sea lions, orcas, seals, bald eagles, herons, cormorants), the Gulf Islands have become the idyll of many people from Washington State and BC. For full details of what they're all up to, grab a copy of the local listings, the *Gulf Islander* (published annually), distributed on the islands and the ferries or the *Gulf Islands Driftwood*, published every Wednesday.

Salt Spring Island

SALT SPRING is the biggest (20 by 10km), most populated (9500), and most visited of the Southern Gulf Islands – its population triples in summer. If you're without transport, though, think twice about coming here on a day-trip as getting around is pretty tough. It's served by Harbour Air seaplanes from Vancouver (see p.479) and three ferry terminals (see opposite): **Fulford Harbour** in the south, **Vesuvius Bay** in the northwest, and **Long Harbour** midway down the east coast. The last is also the main terminal for inter-island travel.

In the past the Salt Spring Island Bus service has connected the ferry terminals with **Ganges**, the island's main village on the east coast 5km from Long

Gulf Islands ferries

BC Ferries (Ⓣ250/386-3431 or 1-800/223-3779, Ⓦwww.bcferries.com) charges a wide range of fares for the many connections between the Gulf Islands, many of which have more than one ferry terminal, and ferry terminals on Vancouver Island and the mainland. These fares are further complicated by the fact that rates are generally lower **offseason**, which most years means **early September to late June**. One or two routes also involve cheaper fares midweek. Detailed here are high-season and low-season fares, and the rates for foot passengers and cars, though note that larger vehicles incur higher fares.

Buckley Bay to Denman and Horby Islands Sixteen sailings daily, 10min; $5/$4.75 return for foot passengers, $12.25/$10.50 return for a car)

Campbell River to Quadra Island Up to 17 daily, 10 min; foot passengers $5/$4.75 return, cars $12.50/$11.

Crofton to Salt Spring Island (Vesuvius Bay) Thirteen sailings daily; 20min; foot passengers $6.25/6 return, cars $20/$17.25.

Nainamo to Gabriola Island There are about fifteen daily crossings to Gabriola Island (6km, 20min; foot passengers $5.50/$5.25, cars $14/$12.50)

Tsawwassen to Galiano Island (Sturdies Bay) Two per day, 50 min; foot passengers $10/$9.75 return, cars $36.50.

Tsawwassen to Mayne Island one-way tickets from Tsawwassen via Galiano/Montague Harbour in high season cost foot passengers $10, cars cost $36.50.

Tsawwassen to North Pender Two sailings daily; 2hr 10min; foot passengers $10/$9.75 one-way, less off-peak; cars $36.50/$31.50.

Tsawwassen to Salt Spring Island (Long Harbour) Up to three sailings daily, three hours; foot passengers $10/$9.75 return, cars $36.50.

Tsawwassen to Saturna One to two sailings daily, with transfer at Mayne and stop at Galiano; 2hr; foot passengers $10.25/$10 return, cars $38/$32.50.

Victoria to Galiano Island (Montague Harbour) Four sailings daily, 65 min; foot passengers $6.50/$6.25 return, cars $22.25/$19.50.

Victoria to North Pender Up to seven daily; 40min direct or 2hr via Galiano and/Mayne; foot passengers $6.50/$6.25 return, cars $22.25/$19.50.

Victoria to Salt Spring Island (Fulford Harbor) Ten sailings daily, more in summer, 35 min; foot passengers $6.25/6 return, cars $20/$17.25.

Victoria to Saturna 2–3 daily; $6.25 return for foot passengers, vehicles $21.50.

Harbour, but check with the Victoria or local infocentre (see below) for the latest. For more complicated journeys, call up the Silver Shadow Taxi (Ⓣ250/537-3030) or consider **renting a bike** from the Salt Spring Kayaking & Cycling, 2923 Fulford-Ganges Rd, Fulford Harbour (Ⓣ250/653-4222, Ⓦwww.saltspring.com/sskayak). Rates start at $5 hourly, $25 for 24hrs, and $35 for two days. Kayak rentals are $12 hourly ($20 for a double kayak) and $45 daily ($80). If necessary the company will deliver bikes or kayaks to where you are staying on the island for $15. You can also rent a scooter, kayak, or car from Salt Spring Island Marina (Ⓣ1-800/334-6629, Ⓦwww.mobyspub.com), one of several rental places near *Moby's Marine Pub* (Ⓣ250/537-5559) – a popular local hangout for drinks, meals, and occasional live music in Ganges at 124 Upper Ganges Rd.

Most enjoyment on Salt Spring, as with the other Gulf Islands, is to be had from sinking back into its laid-back approach to life: grabbing a coffee at a café overlooking the water, browsing galleries, cycling the backroads, hiking the odd easy trail, and so on. If you're here to slum it on a **beach**, the best strips are on the island's more sheltered east side: Beddis Beach in particular, off the Fulford to Ganges road, Vesuvius Bay in the northwest, and at Drummond Park near Fulford in the south. Beddis can be seen en route to one of the best parks in the Gulf Islands, the **Ruckle Provincial Park**, 486 hectares of lovely forest, field, and maritime scenery tucked in the island's southeast corner 10km east of Fulford Harbour. Most of its 15km-worth of trails set off from trailheads at Beaver Point, the rocky headland that marks the end of the access road – the best path marches north from here along the coast of tiny coves and rocky headlands to Yeo Point. The park also has an outstanding campsite at the end of the access road (see below), but note that there are no reservations - it is first-come-first-served. The island's other main park is **Mount Maxwell Provincial Park** midway up the west coast: the eponymous mountain provides a tremendous 588-metre viewpoint. The park is accessed on Cranberry Road, which strikes west midway down the island off the main road.

Ganges, close to Long Harbour on the east coast, is armed with a small **infocentre** (see below) and a rapidly proliferating assortment of galleries, tourist shops, and holiday homes. Community spirits reach a climax during the annual **Artcraft** (late June to mid-Sept), a summer crafts fair in Ganges' Mahon Hall that displays the talents of the island's many dab-handed creatives. The other main focus for cultural events is ArtSpring, 100 Jackson, Ganges (ⓣ250/537-2102 or 1-866/537-2102, ⓦwww.artspring.ca), a summer festival of the performing arts (July–Aug). Between April and October, head for the Saturday Market (Sat 8.30am–3pm) in Ganges' Centennial Park for food and crafts.

Practicalities

Ganges' infocentre at 121 Lower Ganges Rd (daily 10am–4pm; ⓣ250/537-5252 or 537-4223, ⓦwww.saltspringtoday.com) is the place to check out the island's relatively plentiful **accommodation**. A lot of independent travelers are lured here by the prospect of the HI-affiliated **youth hostel**, the lovely *Salt Spring Island Hostel*, set amidst ten peaceful acres on the eastern side of the island (5km south of Ganges and just over a kilometre from Beddis Beach) at 640 Cusheon Lake Rd (ⓣ250/537-4149; a/c; closed Nov–mid-March; check-in 5–8pm). Under your own steam from Victoria, take the #70 Pat Bay Hwy bus ($2.50) to the Swartz Bay ferry terminal. Catch the ferry to Fulford Harbour ($6.25 return) and ask car drivers disembarking the ferry if they're headed past the hostel on Cusheon Lake Road: if they're locals, and en route for Ganges, most say yes. You can choose between dorm rooms in a cedar lodge ($17 for members, $21 for non-members), three tepees, two adult and family tree houses (be sure to book these and be prepared to pay around $65), and private family room ($40–70) – 35 beds in all. Note, however, that's there's no camping, but you can rent bikes and scooters.

Otherwise you can choose from the hundred or more (but often rather exorbitant) B&B options (owners can arrange to pick you up from the ferry) or one of the so-called "resorts" dotted round the island – usually a handful of houses with camping, a few rooms to rent, and little else. Each of the ferry terminals also has a range of mid-price motels. Some of the more reasonable include the twelve-unit *Beachcomber Motel* at 770 Vesuvius Bay Rd at Vesuvius Bay 7km from Ganges (ⓣ250/537-5415 or 1-866/537-5415; ④) – some rooms have sea views and others have kitchenettes; the *Harbour House Hotel*, 121 Upper Ganges Rd, Ganges (ⓣ250/537-5571 or 1-888/799-5571, ⓔharbourhouse@saltspring.com; ④) with waterfront dining, and the 28-unit *Seabreeze Inn* in an attractive park-like setting above

Gulf Islands Water Taxi

The **Gulf Islands Water Taxi** (Ⓣ250/537-2510, Ⓦwww.saltspring.com/watertaxi) has been a feature of island life since 1978, complementing the BC Ferries service and carrying visitors, schoolchildren, fishermen, and others on two scheduled routes from the Visitors' Dock below the *Oystercatcher Bar* in Ganges: Salt Spring (Ganges Harbour)-Galiano (Sturdies Bay)–Mayne Island (Miners Bay); currently two daily Sept–June 6.45am & 3.45pm from Salt Spring; $20 round-trip between any two points, $15 one-way, no extra charge for bicycles.

Prices and departure details are the same on the second route: Salt Spring (Ganges Harbour)-Saturna (Lyall Harbour)-Horton Bay-Pender (Port Washington). A third "Island Hopping" route operates in summer (Wed & Sat 9am & 3pm from Ganges) calling at Galiano and Mayne. Reservations are recommended for all services which are arranged so that you can realistically make short sightseeing trips to other islands from Salt Spring.

Ganges Harbour at 101 Bittancourt Rd (Ⓣ250/537-4145 or 1-800/434-4112, Ⓦwww.seabreezeinns.com; ❺).

The island's best **campsite** lies within Ruckle Provincial Park. The magnificent 78-pitch site ($14 in summer, $9 in winter; day-use parking $3) lines Swanson Channel at Beaver Point and is accessible by following Beaver Point Road from the Fulford Harbour ferry terminal (10km).

One of the island's best places to **eat** is *The Vesuvius Inn* (Ⓣ250/537-2312) alongside the ferry at 805 Vesuvius Bay Rd, blessed with live music nightly and a great **bar** deck overlooking the harbor where you can dine on expensive seafood and the usual range of pastas, chickens, and salads. In Ganges, there are numerous cafés and coffee shops for high-quality sandwiches: for something more ambitious, try the appealing *Treehouse Café-Restaurant*, 106 Purvis Lane (Ⓣ250/537-5379), which serves breakfast, lunch, and dinner and has places to sit outside and low-key live (often acoustic) music most nights of the week. For a treat, the place to go is *House Piccolo*, 108 Hereford Ave, Ganges (Ⓣ250/537—1844, dinner only), which has won *Wine Spectator* magazine awards and serves high-quality European and Scandinavian food.

Galiano Island

North of Salt Spring, long and finger-shaped, **GALIANO** is just 27km from north to south and barely five kilometres wide, but it remains one of the more promising and less-developed islands to visit if you want variety and a realistic chance of finding somewhere to stay. There are two ferry terminals: **Sturdies Bay** in the southeast, which takes boats from the mainland, and **Montague Harbour** on the west coast, which handles the Vancouver Island crossings from Swartz Bay. You can also get here with the Gulf Islands Water Taxi and there are inter-island BC Ferries connections (1–4 daily) from Salt Spring via Pender and Mayne. Go Galiano Island Shuttle (Ⓣ250/539-0202) provides a taxi service.

The calm waters, cliffs, and coves off the island's west coast make for excellent **kayaking**. You can rent kayaks or join guided kayak tours at Galiano Island Kayaking at the marina at Montague Harbour (Ⓣ250/539-2442, Ⓦwww.seakayak.ca). For a chance to explore Galiano's bucolic environs by **bike**, rentals can be had at Galiano Bicycle Rental at 36 Burrill Rd in Sturdies Bay (Ⓣ250/539-9906; four hours $23, day $28). **Hikers** can walk almost the entire length of the east coast, or climb Mount Sutil (323m) or Mount Galiano

(342m) for views of the mainland mountains. To reach the trailhead for the latter, take Burrill south from the ferry at Sturdies Bay and along Bluff Road through the forest of Bluffs Park. A left fork, Active Pass Drive, takes you to the trailhead (a total of 5km from the ferry).

The locals' favorite **beach** is at Coon Bay at the island's northern tip, but there are excellent marine landscapes and beaches elsewhere, notably at **Montague Harbour Provincial Marine Park**, 10km from the Sturdies Bay ferry terminal on the west side of the island (and immediately in and around the Montague Harbour terminal). The park has stretches of shell and pebble foreshore, a waterfront trail to Gray Peninsula (though you can easily forge you own shore walks), and a glorious provincial campsite ($17 in summer, $9 in winter; 15 walk-in reservable tent sites, and 25 drive-in sites, of which eight are reservable). Booking is essential in summer: see p.43 for details of provincial park campsite reservations.

Practicalities

The island's **infocentre** is a booth at 2590 Sturdies Bay Rd (July–Aug daily 9am–5/6pm; Ⓣ250/539-2233 or 1-866/539-2233 or 539-2507 offseason, Ⓦwww.galianoisland.com). For **food and drink** – and to meet locals – the island's main pub, the *Hummingbird Inn* (Ⓣ250/539-5472) is about 2km away from Sturdies Bay at 47 Sturdies Bay Rd. The inn's good regional cooking is inexpensive, likewise at French-influenced *La Bérengerie*, about the same distance from Montague Harbour on the corner of Montague and Clanton roads (Ⓣ250/539-5392; ❸), a genteel restaurant that usually rents three good B&B rooms upstairs.

For a comfortable **stay** in peaceful and elegant surroundings close to Montague Harbour Provincial Marine Park, try the excellent but pricey 12-room *Woodstone Country Inn* (Ⓣ250/539-2022 or 1-888/339-2022, Ⓔwoodstone@gulfislands.com; ❺) on Georgeson Bay Road, 4km from the ferry: breakfast and afternoon tea are included in the price. Right at Sturdies Bay is the very pleasant but expensive 10-room *Galiano Inn*, 134 Madronna Drive (Ⓣ250/539-3388, Ⓦwww.galianoinn.com; ❼), though rates include gourmet breakfast in the downstairs restaurant. For a lovely and romantic stay, head for one of the three rooms at the *Bellhouse Inn*, 29 Farmhouse Rd (Ⓣ1-800/970-7464, Ⓦwww.bellhouseinn.com; ❻), an historic waterfront farmhouse set in beautiful grounds with sandy beach and great ocean views; breakfast is included in the room rate. A good choice on the island's quieter northern end are the seven log cabins of the *Bodega Resort*, at 120 Monastee Rd off Porlier Pass Drive and Cook Drive (Ⓣ250/539-2677, Ⓦwww.cedarplace.com/bodega; ❸), complete with kitchens and wood-burning stoves and set in acres of woods and meadows with sea views.

North and South Pender

The somnolent bridge-linked islands of **NORTH** and **SOUTH PENDER,** south of Galiano Island, occupy just 24 square km and muster about a two thousand people between them, many of who will try to entice you into their studios to buy local arts and crafts. Otherwise you are likely here to swim, snooze, or walk on one of the many tiny **beaches** – there's public ocean access at some twenty points around the island. Two of the best are Hamilton Beach near Browning Beach on the east coast of North Pender and Mortimer Spit just south of the bridge that links the two islands. The latter spot is also the place to pick up trails to Mount Norman and Beaumont Provincial Marine Park.

Ferries arrive from Swartz Bay and Tsawwassen. The **infocentre** booth is just east up the hill from the ferry terminal in **Otter Bay** on the island's west coast at 2332 Otter Bay Rd (daily mid-May to early Sept 9am–6pm; ⓣ250/629-6541) on North Pender, home to the Otter Bay Marina, where you can rent **bikes** and buy maps for a tour of the islands' hilly interior.

Accommodation-wise there are a handful of B&Bs, most of which open and close with a good deal of regularity, and a small wooded **campsite** at Prior Centennial Provincial Park, 6km south of the Otter Bay ferry terminal (March–Sept; $14). For the only **hotel**-type rooms, as opposed to B&Bs, try the 12-room *Inn on Pender Island* prettily situated in 7.5 acres of wooded country near Prior Park at 4709 Canal Rd, North Pender (ⓣ250/629-3353 or 1-800/550-0172, ⓦwww.innonpender.com; ❹); or the newly refurbished *Poets Cove at Bedwell Harbour*, a plush resort at 9801 Spalding Rd, South Pender (ⓣ250/629-3212 or 1-888/512-7638, ⓦwww.poetscove.com; ❼), which has a pool, marina, bistro-pub, restaurant, store, tennis, harbor views, canoe, boat and bike rentals, and a choice of rooms or cabins; or the three fully equipped self-catering cottages 500m sharp left from the ferry at *Arcadia by the Sea*, 1325 MacKinnon Rd, North Pender (ⓣ250/629-3221 or 1-877-470-8439, ⓦwww.arcadiabythesea.com; ❺; mid-April–Oct), with tennis court, outdoor pool, and private decks.

Mayne and Saturna islands

MAYNE is the first island to your left (Galiano is on your right) if you're crossing from Tsawwassen to Swartz Bay – which is perhaps as close as you'll get, since it's the quietest and most difficult to reach of the islands served by ferries. That may be as good a reason as any for heading out here, however, particularly if you have a bike to explore the quiet country roads which snake the island's 21 square km. Mayne also has few places to stay, so, as ever in the Gulf Islands, aim to fix up accommodation before you arrive.

Best of several **beaches** is Bennett Bay, a sheltered strip with warm water and good sand. It's reached by heading east from the island's principal community at Miner's Bay (5min from the ferry terminal at Village Bay on the west coast) to the end of Fernhill Road and then turning left onto Wilks Road. If you want a small **hike**, try the 45-minute climb up Mount Parke in the eponymous regional park: it starts near the Fernhill Center on Montrose Road.

Village Bay – don't be fooled by the name: there's no village – has a summer-only **infocentre** booth (daily 9am–6pm; no phone, ⓦwww.mayneislandchamber.ca) which should be able to fill you in on the limited (currently seven) but expanding number of **B&B** possibilities – though the island is small enough to explore as a day-trip. Try the *Blue Vista Cottages*, eight fully equipped cabins overlooking Bennett Bay at 563 Arbutus Drive 6km from the ferry terminal (ⓣ250/539-2463 or 1-877/535-2424, ⓦwww.bluevistaresort.com; ❸), with ferry pick-up, handy sandy beach, park-like setting, and bike, canoe, and kayak rental. The *Tinkerer's B&B* on Miner's Bay at 417 Sunset Place off Georgina Point Road (ⓣ539-2280; ❹; April to Oct), 2.4km from the Village Bay ferry terminal, is nicely offbeat: it rents bikes, provides hammocks, and offers "demonstrations of medicinal herb and flower gardens." For a real treat, the best **food** around (good fish and seafood) is to be found at the waterfront *Oceanwood Country Inn*, 2km south of the ferry at 630 Dinner Bay Rd (ⓣ250/539-5074, ⓦwww.oceanwood.com; ❼; March–Nov), which also has twelve smart rooms, sauna, oceanfront hot tub, and a superb, quiet garden setting.

SATURNA, to the south, boasts some good **beaches**, the best being at Russell Reef and Winter Cove Marine Park (no campsite) on its northwest tip. There's walking, wildlife, and good views to the mainland from Mount Warburton Pike (497m) and on Brown Bridge in the southwest of the island.

The island is another **B&B** hideaway: try the three-room waterfront *Lyall Harbour B&B* (Ⓣ250/539-5577 or 1-877/473-9343; ❺), 500m from the ferry at 121 East Point Rd in Saturna Point, home to a shop and modest **infocentre** (May–Sept daily 8am–6pm; no phone, Ⓦwww.saturnatourism.bc.ca). Another option is the *East Point Resort*, East Point Road (Ⓣ250/539-2975; ❺), situated in a park-like setting near a gradually sloping sandy beach; its six cabins are fully equipped and you can choose between one- and two-bedroom units – note that in July and August there's generally a one-week minimum stay (no credit cards). There are no campgrounds and only one or two places to eat, notably the pub-restaurant at the modern, waterfront *Saturna Lodge,* 130 Payne Rd (Ⓣ250/539-2254, Ⓦwww.saturna-island.bc.ca; ❻; May–Oct), which also has seven rooms to rent; rates include breakfast.

Gabriola Island

Most northern of the southern Gulf Islands, **GABRIOLA ISLAND** is a quiet place off the coast of Nainamo and is home to about 2000 people, many of them artists and writers. Author Malcolm Lowry, he of *Under the Volcano* fame, immortalized the island in a story entitled *October Ferry to Gabriola Island* (characters in the tale never actually reach the island). Gabriola also offers several **beaches** – the best are Gabriola Sands' Twin Beaches at the island's northwest end and Drumbeg Provincial Park – and lots of scope for scuba diving, birdwatching (eagles and sea birds), beachcombing, and easy walking, plus the added curiosity of the **Malaspina Galleries**, a series of caves and bluffs near Gabriola Sands sculpted by wind, frost, and surf.

Gabriola has numerous **B&Bs**, including the *Hummingbird Lodge*, 1597 Starbuck Lane (Ⓣ250/247-9300; ❺), a vast cedar lodge set in seven acres of grounds. For more accommodation information, check with the Nanaimo infocentre or Gabriola's own office at 575 North Rd (July & Aug daily 9am–6pm, mid-May–June & Sept–mid-Oct Sat & Sun 9am–5pm; closed the rest of the year; Ⓣ250/247-9332, Ⓦwww.gabriolaisland.org).

Highway 14: Victoria to Port Renfrew

Highway 14 runs 107km west from **Victoria** to **Port Renfrew** and is lined with numerous beaches and provincial parks, most – especially those close to the city – heavily populated during the summer months. The route is covered in summer by the West Coast Trail Bus (see box on p.498), a private service originally for hikers walking the West Coast Trail (see p.521) and Juan de Fuca Trail (see opposite) but also popular for the ride alone. Victoria city buses go as far as **Sooke** (38km; take #50 to Western Exchange and transfer to a #61). Keen walkers or cyclists should note that you can also come here on the Galloping Goose hiking and biking trail, a 55-kilometre former railway line (visit Ⓦwww.crd.bc.ca/parks for more on the trail).

Sooke and around

The village of **SOOKE** is best known for its excellent art galleries, notably the Sooke Fine Art Gallery, 6703a Westcoast Rd (Ⓣ250/642-6411) and the South Shore Gallery, 2050 Otter Point Rd (Ⓣ642-2058), a clutch of good restaurants, and **All Sooke Day** in mid-July, when lumberjacks from all over the island compete in various tests of forestry expertise. The **infocentre** lies across the Sooke River Bridge at 2070 Phillips and Sooke streets (daily 9/10am–6pm; Ⓣ250/642-6351, Ⓦwww.sooke.museum.bc.ca). Check out the small **Sooke Regional Museum**, (daily July–Aug 9am–6pm; Sept–June 9am–5pm; donation suggested) in the same building if you want to bone up on the largely logging-dominated local history.

The town is the last place of any size, so stock up on supplies if you're continuing west. It also has a surfeit of **accommodation**, with a bias towards comfortable B&Bs, if you're caught short (most Victoria locals come here for the day). Quite a few people make the trip here just for the **food** at *Sooke Harbour House*, 1528 Whiffen Spit (Ⓣ250/642-3421, Ⓦwww.sookeharbourhouse.com, ❾), one of the finest restaurants on the West Coast; it's expensive, but has a surprisingly casual atmosphere and, of course, sublime food. Dishes might include grilled rock sole with prune, plum, ginger sauce and flowering fennel oil, blue Salt Spring Island mussels and shrimp tossed with nugget potatoes and corn, or firewood honey and lavender parfait with walnut cream and Alpine strawberry-day lily sauce. It also has 28 top-notch **rooms**, but prices range from a prohibitive $299 to $555, though rates are lower offseason. A far less expensive place to eat in the village center is the homely *Mom's* at 2036 Shields Rd for the usual coffee, snacks, and light meals.

The mostly empty beaches beyond Sooke are largely grey pebble and driftwood, but none the worse for that, the first key stop being **French Beach Provincial Park** (day-use parking $3) 20km beyond Sooke. There's good walking on the fairly wild and windswept beach, and a 69-pitch provincial park campsite (summer $14, winter $10) on the grass immediately away from the shore. Three kilometres beyond, the 25 log cabins of *Point No Point*, 1505 West Coast Rd (Ⓣ250/646-2020, Ⓦwww.pointnopointresort.com, ❻) make a tremendous place to overnight near the water.

Sandy, signposted trails lead off the road to beaches over the next 9km, including **Jordan River**, a one-shop, one-hamburger-stall (*Shakies*) logging community known for its good surf, which you can admire from the waterfront *Breakers* café. Just beyond is the best beach along this coast, in part of **China Beach Provincial Park** (no camping) reached after a fifteen-minute walk from the road through rainforest. The West Coast Trail Bus makes stops at all these parks and beaches on request.

Port Renfrew

The road is partly gravel from China Beach on – past Mystic and Sombrio beaches to **PORT RENFREW**, a logging community that's gained from being the eastern starting point of the **West Coast Trail**. A second trail, the **Juan de Fuca Marine Trail**, also starts near Port Renfrew, running east towards Victoria for about 50km. This does not have the complicated booking procedure of the West Coast Trail, but the scenery is also less striking and the going far easier for the less experienced or more safety-conscious walker. The Juan de Fuca trailhead is 6km south of the village on a logging road at **Botanical Beach**, a sandstone shelf and tidal-pool area that reveals a wealth of marine life at low tide. Parking lots and highway

West Coast Trail Bus

The **West Coast Trail Bus**, or West Coast Trail Express (ⓣ250/477-8700 or 1-888/999-2288, ⓦwww.trailbus.com), provides an invaluable complement to the limited scheduled bus services on Vancouver Island. It offers a shuttle service between May and September only (days vary: call for details) from Victoria to Gordon River ($35), Port Renfrew ($35), Pachena Bay ($55), and Bamfield ($55), thus providing access to the trailheads of the West Coast Trail and to points in the Pacific Rim National Park, such as Bamfield, otherwise difficult to reach without your own transport. It also provides inter-town shuttles between most combinations of these destinations and others such as Nanaimo (connections to Pachena Bay and Bamfield; $55) and Port Alberni (to Pachena Bay and Bamfield; $35).

Departure points are as follows: Victoria (700 Douglas St); Nanaimo (Departure Bay ferry terminal); Port Alberni (7-11 Store on 3rd Street); Pachena Bay (trailhead parking lot); Bamfield (*Trails Motel*); Gordon River (trailhead office); Port Renfrew (Parkinson Road).

Another service runs from Victoria to Port Renfrew ($35) along Hwy-14 with stops at Sooke, French Beach ($25), Jordan River ($30), China Beach ($30), Sombrio Beach ($30), and Parkinson Creek ($30). Reservations are highly recommended for all services.

access points are also dotted along the trail's length, allowing you to enjoy strolls or day-hikes. Beyond China Beach is the start of the **Juan de Fuca Provincial Park**, designed to protect the beaches and coastal rainforest strip explored by the trail (day-use parking $5, frontcountry camping $14, back-country camping $5).

Accommodation in town is still pretty limited: try the four cottages on the San Juan River at *Gallaugher's West Coast Fish Camp* off Beach Road at 5222 Heritage Drive (ⓣ250/647-5535, ⓔgallaughers@shaw.ca; ❹; May–Oct); the five beachfront rooms of the *Arbutus Beach Lodge*, 5 Queesto Drive (ⓣ250/647-5458, arbutus@sookenet.com; ❸–❹); the *West Coast Trail Motel*, Parkinson Road (ⓣ250/647-5565, ⓦwww.westcoasttrailmotel.com; ❸); and the *Trailhead Resort* on Parkinson Road (ⓣ250/647-5468, ⓦwww.trailhead-resort.com; ❹), which has six rooms.

If you're driving and don't want to retrace your steps, think about taking the gravel logging roads from the village on the north side of the San Juan River to either Shawnigan Lake or the Cowichan Valley (see p.501). They're marked on most maps, but it's worth picking up the detailed map of local roads put out by the Sooke Combined Fire Organization (ask at the Victoria infocentre); heed all warnings about logging trucks.

Highway 1: Victoria to Nanaimo

If you leave Victoria with high hopes of seeing Vancouver Island's lauded scenery, **Hwy-1** will come as a disappointing introduction to what you can expect along most of the island's southeast coast. After a lengthy sprawl of suburbs, the landscape becomes suddenly wooded and immensely lush; unfor-tunately the beauty is constantly interrupted by bursts of dismal motels and other highway junk. **Buses** operated by Laidlaw make the trip between Victoria and Nanaimo (up to 6 daily). One **train** a day (more in summer) covers this route, and beyond to Courtenay, but it's a usually a single-carriage job and gets booked solid in summer; it stops at every stump. For more information from Via Rail (Ⓣ1/800-561-8630, Ⓦwww.viarail.ca).

Goldstream Provincial Park

Pretty **GOLDSTREAM PROVINCIAL PARK**, 20km from Victoria's center, is home to an ancient forest of Douglas fir and Western red cedar, a large provincial park **campsite** with good facilities, and a visitor center (day-use parking $3, summer frontcountry camping $22, winter $9). There's also a network of marked **trails** to hilltops and waterfalls designed for anything between five minutes' and a few hours' walking. Try the paths towards Mount Finlayson (three-hour's hard walk all the way to the summit) for views of the ocean – views you also get if you carry on up the highway, which soon meets Saanich Inlet, a bay with a lovely panorama of wooded ridges across the water. Look out for the Malahat Summit (31km from Victoria) and Gulf Islands (33km) viewpoints. If you need a place to **stay**, the small *Malahat Oceanview Motel* (Ⓣ250/478-9231, Ⓔoceanview@coastnet.com; ❸), 35km north of Victoria, is best situated to catch the sea and island vistas.

A scenic diversion off the main road (Hwy-1) takes you 7km to **Shawnigan Lake**, fringed by a couple of provincial parks: West Shawnigan Park on the lake's northwest side has a safe beach and swimming possibilities. If you're biking or are prepared to tackle pretty rough roads, note the logging road that links the north end of the lake to Port Renfrew on the west coast (check access restrictions at the Victoria infocentre).

Duncan and around

DUNCAN, 60km north of Victoria, begins inauspiciously, with a particularly scrappy section of highway spoiling what would otherwise be an exquisitely pastoral patch of country. Still, the town's aboriginal center – the **Quw'utsun Cultural Centre** – merits a brief stop, unlike the Glass Castle, a messy affair made from glass bottles off the road to the south, and the even sillier "World's Largest Hockey Stick," arranged as a triumphal arch into the town center.

Duncan's **infocentre** is at 381A Trans-Canada Hwy opposite the supermarket on the main road (mid-April to mid-Oct Mon–Fri 8.30am–5pm, longer hours July & Aug; Ⓣ250/746-4636, Ⓦwww.duncancc.bc.ca), close to the **bus station**, which has up to six daily connections to and from Victoria (1hr 10min). Duncan is not a place you should even consider staying in, but for **meals** you could try the excellent *Arbutus Café*, 195 Kenneth St, at Jubilee (Ⓣ250/746-5443), much-frequented by locals keen for the usual Italian- and Pacific Rim-influenced food. You can also visit one of several local vineyards: one of the best is the **Vigneti Zenatta Winery**, 5039 Marshall Rd, Glenora (call for tour details on Ⓣ250/748-2338), which has been in business for over forty years; as well as their wine, you can also buy meals at the lovely but expensive restaurant.

Quw'utsun Cultural Centre

The first real reason to pull over along Hwy-1 out of Victoria is Duncan's **Quw'utsun Cultural Centre**, 200 Cowichan Way (May–early Sept Mon–Fri 9am–6pm, Sat & Sun 9am–9pm; rest of the year closes at 5/6pm daily; $11; Ⓣ250/746-8119, Ⓦwww.quwutsun.ca), on your left off the highway in the unmissable wooden buildings next to Malaspina College. Duncan has long been the self-proclaimed "City of Totems," reference to a rather paltry collection of poles – arranged mostly alongside the main road – that belong to the local Cowichan tribes, historically British Columbia's largest aboriginal group. The tribes, about 3000 strong locally, still preserve certain traditions, and it's been their energy – along with cash from the civic authorities, attuned as ever to potentially lucrative tourist attractions – that has put up the poles and pulled the project together. Much of the heavily worked commercial emphasis is on shifting aboriginal crafts, especially the ubiquitous lumpy sweaters for which the area is famous, but there is a good 20-minute film and tour of the center (included in the price) and you can usually expect to find historical displays and demonstrations of dancing, knitting, carving, weaving, and native cooking.

British Columbia Forestry Discovery Centre

Vancouver Island is one of the most heavily logged areas in Canada, and the **BC Forest Discovery Centre**, 1km north of town on Hwy-1 (early May to Sept daily 10am–6pm; ⓣ250/715-1113, ⓦwww.bcforestmuseum.com; $9, children 5–12 $5), preserves artifacts from its lumbering heritage; but with industry bigwigs as museum trustees, you can't help feeling it's designed to be something of a palliative in the increasingly ferocious controversy between loggers and environmentalists. Nonetheless, it does a thorough job on trees, and if the forestry displays in Victoria's museum have whetted your appetite, you'll have a good couple of hours rounding off your arboreal education. The entrance is marked by a small black steam engine and a massive piece of yellow logging machinery.

Old-growth forests: going, going, gone

While Vancouver Island isn't the only place in North America where environmentalists and the forestry industry are at loggerheads, some of the most bitter and high-profile confrontations have taken place here. The island's wet climate is particularly favourable to the growth of thick **temperate rainforest**, part of a belt that once stretched from Alaska to Northern California. The most productive ecosystem on the planet, **old-growth** virgin Pacific rainforest contains up to ten times more biomass per acre than its more famous tropical counterpart – and, though it covers a much smaller area, it is being felled at a greater rate and with considerably less media outrage. Environmentalists estimate that British Columbia's portion of the Pacific rainforest has already been reduced by two-thirds and predict all significant areas will have been felled within about ten or fifteen years. Conversely, the powerful logging industry claims two-thirds survive, but even the Canadian government – largely in thrall to, and supportive of, the industry – concedes that only a small percentage of the BC rainforest is currently protected.

The controversy over logging often pits neighbor against neighbor, for some 250,000 in the province depend directly or indirectly on the industry, and big multinationals dominate the scene. **Employment** is a major rallying cry here, and the prospect of job losses through industry regulation is usually enough to override objections. The trend towards **automation** only adds fuel to the argument: by volume of wood cut, the BC forestry industry provides only half as many jobs as in the rest of Canada, which means, in effect, that twice as many trees have to be cut down in BC to provide the same number of jobs.

In the meantime, ninety percent of timber is still lifted from the rainforest instead of from managed stands, clear-cutting of old-growth timber is blithely described by the vast McMillan company as "a form of harvesting," and independent audits suggest that companies are failing to observe either their cutting or replanting quotas. The provincial government has pledged to improve forestry practices, but only a tiny percentage of BC lies within reserves with a degree of environmental protection.

Ranged over a hundred-acre site next to a scenic lake, the well-presented displays tell everything you want to know about trees and how to cut them down. The narrow-gauge steam train round the park is a bit gimmicky (10am–5.30pm only), but a good way of getting around; check out the forest dioramas and the artifacts and archive material in the **Log Museum** in particular. There's also the usual array of working blacksmiths, sawmills, a farmstead, an old logging camp, and a few as-yet-underforested patches where you can take time out.

The Cowichan Valley

Striking west into the hills off Hwy-1 north of Duncan, Hwy-18 enters the **COWICHAN VALLEY** and fetches up at the 32-kilometre long **Lake Cowichan**, the largest freshwater lake on the island. A road, rough in parts, circles the lake (its 75km round the lake by road – allow 2hr) and offers access to a gamut of outdoor pursuits, most notably fishing – the area is touted, with typical smalltown hyperbole, as the "Fly-Fishing Capital of the World." The water gets warm enough for summer swimming (the aboriginal name for the area – Kaatza – means the 'land warmed by the sun'), and there's also ample hiking in the wilder country above. At Youbou on the north shore you can visit the **Heritage Mill**, a working sawmill (tours May–Sept): this area boasts some of the most "productive" forest in Canada, thanks to the lake's mild microclimate, and lumber is the obvious mainstay of the local economy. On the road up to the lake from Duncan you pass the **Valley Demonstration Forest**, another link in the industry's public-relations weaponry, with signs and scenic lookouts explaining the intricacies of forest management.

For details of the area's many tours, trails, and outfitters contact the **infocentre** at Lake Cowichan village, 125 South Shore Rd (Mon–Sat 9am–4pm, Sun 1–4pm; ⓣ250/749-3244 or 749-6772, ⓦwww.cowichanlakecc.ca). Good, cheap **campsites** line the shore, which despite minimal facilities can be quite busy in summer – don't expect to have the place to yourself. There's a municipal site, *Lakeview Park*, 3km west of the village at 885 Lakeview Rd (May–Sept; ⓣ250/749-6681, ⓦwww.town.lakecowichan.bc.ca; $17), but the biggest and best is at *Gordon Bay Provincial Park* (day-use parking $3, summer camping $22, winter $9) on the south shore 14km from Lake Cowichan Village on South Shore Road, a popular family place but with a quiet atmosphere and a good sandy **beach**.

Chemainus

CHEMAINUS is the "Little Town That Did," as billboards for miles around never stop telling you. Its mysterious achievement was the creation of its own tourist attraction, realized when the closure of the local antiquated sawmill in 1982 – once among the world's largest – threatened the place with almost overnight extinction, despite the opening of a modern, more efficient mill. In 1983, the town's worthies commissioned an artist to paint a huge **mural** – *Steam Donkey at Work* – recording the area's local history. This proved so successful that some 35 panels quickly followed, drawing 350,000 (and rising) visitors annually to admire the artwork and tempting them to spend money in local businesses as they did. As murals go, these are surprisingly good, and if you're driving it's worth the short, well-signed diversion off Hwy-1. You might also want to drop in on the **Chemainus Valley Museum**, 9799 Waterwheel Crescent (March–May & Nov–Dec Wed–Sun 10am–3pm; June–Oct daily 10am–6pm; donation suggested), a community-run museum with displays on logging and pioneer life. Ironically, the opening of the modern sawmill has done nothing to deter the influx of resident painters and craftspeople attracted by the murals, a knock-on effect that has done much to enliven the village's pleasant – if occasionally over-quaint – community feel.

Buses also detour here on the run up to Nanaimo, and the train drops you slap-bang next to a mural. You can also pick up a ferry from the obvious jetty in Chemainus to the small islands of **Kuper** and **Thetis** (both $5 for foot passengers, $12.75 for cars). Chemainus Tours (Ⓣ250/381-5109 in Victoria or 246-5055 in Chemainus) will bring you to the town for the day from Victoria for $49 plus GST. There's a **infocentre** in town at 9796 Willow St (daily June–Aug 9am–5pm, rest of the year Mon–Fri 10am–4pm; Ⓣ250/246-3944, Ⓦwww.chemainus.bc.ca).

If you **stay** – the village's waterside setting is nicer than either Duncan or Nanaimo – it's worth booking ahead, as the village's increasing popularity means the local **hotel** and half a dozen or so **B&Bs** are in heavy demand in summer. For motel accommodation, try the *Fuller Lake Chemainus Motel*, 9300 Trans-Canada Hwy (Ⓣ250/246-3282 or 1-888/246-3255, Ⓦwww.chemainus-fullerlakemotel.com; ❸). The best B&B is the pretty *Bird Song & Castlebury Cottage*, 9909 Maple St (Ⓣ250/246-9910, Ⓔbirdsong@island.net; ❺). The choice of **campsites** is between the *Chemainus Gardens RV Park*, 3042 River Rd, 1km east of Hwy-1, set in 37 acres of natural forest with separate tenting area, laundry, and showers (Ⓣ250/246-3569; $18–25), or the larger *Country Maples RV Resort*, 9010 Trans-Canada Hwy (Ⓣ250/246-2078, Ⓦwww.holidaytrailsresorts.com; $26–33; April–Oct) in sixty acres of open and treed parkland 16km north of Duncan above the Chemainus River with showers, laundry, and pool. About 5km south of the village on the river is the quiet *Bald Eagle Campground*, 8705 Chemainus Rd (Ⓣ250/246-9457 or 1-800/246-9457; $16–22). All manner of dinky little cafés, shops, and tearooms have sprung up across the village: for **food**, try the *Willow Street Café*, 9749 Willow St in the newer part of town, with cheap, varied snacks, or the *Waterford* for full meals five minutes north of the village center at 9875 Maple St (Ⓣ250/246-1046).

Nanaimo and around

With a population of about 75,000, **NANAIMO**, 113km from Victoria, is Vancouver Island's second biggest city, the terminal for ferries from Horseshoe Bay and Tsawwassen on the mainland, and a watershed between the island's populated southeastern tip and its wilder, more sparsely inhabited countryside to the north and west. The town itself is unexceptional, though the setting, as ever in BC, is eye-catching – particularly around the harbor, which bobs with yachts and rusty fishing boats and, if you've come from Victoria, affords the first views across to the big mountains on the mainland. If you are going to stop here, more than likely it'll be for **Petroglyph Park** or the town's increasingly famous **bungee-jumping** zone. If not, the Nanaimo Parkway provides a 21-kilometre bypass around the town.

Coal first brought white settlers to the region, many of whom made their fortunes here, including the Victorian magnate **Robert Dunsmuir**, who was given £750,000 and almost half the island in return for building the Victoria–Nanaimo railway – an indication of the benefits that could accrue from the British government to those with the pioneering spirit. Five bands of Salish natives originally lived on the site, which they called **Sney-ne-mous**, or "meeting place," from which the present name derives. It was they who innocently showed the local black rock to Hudson's Bay agents in 1852. The old mines are now closed, and the town's pockets are padded today by forestry, deep-sea fishing, tourism, and – most notably – by six deep-water docks and a booming port.

Arrival and information

Nanaimo's **bus terminal** (Ⓣ250/753-4371) is some way from the harbor on the corner of Comox and Terminal, with six daily Laidlaw runs to Victoria, two to Port Hardy, and three or four to Port Alberni, for connections to Tofino and Ucluelet. **BC Ferries** (Ⓣ250/386-3431 or 1-888/223-3779, Ⓦwww.bcferries.bc.ca) sail to and from Departure Bay (Ⓣ250/753-1261), 2km north of downtown, to Horseshoe Bay on the mainland north of Vancouver (summer hourly 7am–9pm; offseason every 2hr; foot passengers $10 one-way, cars $34.75; cheaper in low season and midweek). To reach downtown take the Seaporter shuttle (Ⓣ250/753-2118; $14.98) or Hammond Bay bus #2 to the north end of Stewart Avenue. Another newer and more convenient terminal, Duke Point (Ⓣ250/722-0181), handles ferries from Tsawwassen (south of Vancouver) and operates just to the south of the town.

The town lies on the Victoria–Courtenay line and sees two trains daily, northbound around 11am and southbound at 3pm: the **station** is a little west of the center of downtown off Selby and near the corner of Fitzwilliam: turn left from the station and take the latter (and Bastion) to reach the heart of downtown. The Nanaimo-Collishaw **airport** is 15km south of downtown on Hwy-19 and is connected by regular shuttle buses to the town center. Seaplane connections to Vancouver with Harbour Air (see p.479) land close to downtown below Front Street on the harborfront.

You'll find a typically overstocked **infocentre** north of the center off the main highway in Beban Park at Beban House, 2290 Bowen Rd (May–Sept daily 8am–8pm; Oct–April Mon–Fri 9am–5pm; Ⓣ250/756-0106 or 1-800/663-7337, Ⓦwww.tourism.nanaimo.com). They'll phone around and help with **accommodation** referrals, and shower you with pamphlets on the town and the island as a whole. There are also details of the many boat rides and tours you can make to local sawmills, canneries, nature reserves, and fishing research stations.

Accommodation

For **hotels**, try *Fairwinds Schooner Cove Resort Hotel and Marina*, 3521 Dolphin Drive Ⓣ250/468-7691 or 1-800/663-7060, Ⓦwww.fairwinds.ca; ⑤), a busy, upmarket resort hotel 26km north of town near Nanoose Bay or *Howard Johnson Harbourside Hotel*, at 1 Terminal Ave Ⓣ250/753-2241 or 1-800/663-7322, Ⓦwww.hojonanaimo.com; ④), a good chain hotel conveniently near the bus terminal. Nanaimo's most central **hostel** is *Cambie International Hostel* at 63 Victoria Crescent (Ⓣ250/754-5323), featuring accommodation for fifty in small dorm rooms. It has a very cheap café, bakery, and bar, and charges $22.50 for dorm beds; $45 for a private double. The *Nicol Street Hostel*, at 65 Nicol St (Ⓣ250/753-1188, Ⓦwww.nanaimohostel.com), is older and a bit cheaper than the *Cambie*, It offers dorm beds and a handful of camping spots on the lawn (with ocean views). Bike rentals, laundry facilities, and kitchen and internet access are available, and the hostel charges $19 for the dorm beds, $9 for camping sites. By far the best choice of the local **camping** options, *Newcastle Island Provincial Park* has the only pitches (18 in all so arrive early) apart from the *Nicol Street Hostel*; they charge $14 in summer, $9 in winter.

The Town

In downtown Nanaimo itself, only two other sights warrant the considerable amount of energy used to promote them. The **Nanaimo District Museum**, just off the main harbor area at 100 Cameron St by the Harbour Park Mall (May–early Sept daily 10am–5pm, Oct–Dec, Feb–April Tues–Sat 10am–5pm; $2; ⓣ250/753-1821), houses a collection that runs the usual historical gamut of pioneer, logging, mining, native peoples, and natural history displays. The best features are the reconstructed coal mine and the interesting insights into the town's cosmopolitan population – a mix of Polish, Chinese, aboriginal peoples, and British citizens – who all see themselves today as some of the island's "friendliest folk." The **Bastion**, two blocks north at the corner of Bastion and Front streets, is a wood-planked tower built by the Hudson's Bay Company in 1853 as a store and a stronghold against native attack, though it was never used during such an attack. It's the oldest (perhaps the only) such building in the West. These days it houses a small **museum** of Hudson's Bay memorabilia (summer only Wed–Sun 10am–4pm; $1); its silly tourist stunt, without which no BC town would be complete, is "the only ceremonial cannon firing west of Ontario" (summer only, daily at noon). This is marginally more impressive than the town's claim to have the most retail shopping space per capita in the country.

Like any self-respecting BC town, Nanaimo also lays on a fair few **festivals**, best known of which is the annual **Bathtub Race**, in which bathtubs (souped-up, mind you) are raced (and sunk, mostly) around a looping course in the Georgia Strait. The winner receives the silver Plunger Trophy from the Loyal Nanaimo Bathtub Society. It's all part of the four-day **Marine Festival** held over the third weekend of July. More highbrow is the late May to early June **Nanaimo Festival**, a cultural jamboree that takes place in and around Malaspina College, 900 Fifth St. The town's other minor claim to fame is the **Nanaimo bar**, a glutinous chocolate confection made to varying recipes and on sale everywhere.

Big efforts are being made to spruce Nainaimo up, not least in the town's 25 or so gardens and small parks. Many of these hug the shore, perfectly aligned for a seafront breath of air. The **Harbourfront Walkway** allows you to stroll 3km along the seafront. Also popular for swimming, snoozing, and its picnic area, the Swyalana Lagoon is an artificial tidal lake built on a renovated stretch of the downtown harbor in Maffeo Sutton Park. For **beaches** you could head

Nanaimo: bungee-jumping pioneer

Nanaimo's major claim to fame is as home to North America's first legal public bungee-jumping site. The **Bungy Zone Adrenalin Centre** is 13km south of the town at 35 Nanaimo River Rd (daily 11.30am–6/8pm; ⓣ250/753-5867 or 1-800/668-7771 and 1-888/668-7874, ⓦwww.bungyzone.com; jumps from $95): look out for the signed turn off Hwy-1. To date it has played host to around almost 100,000 safe bungee jumps, including night jumps. It's become so popular that various variations have been added to the standard 42-metre plunge off the bridge, all slightly less terrifying than the bungee jump. The "Flying Fox" is a line to which you are fixed extending in a deep arc along the canyon – expect to hit speeds of 100kph; "Rap Jumping" involves a rapid mountaineering rappel straight down from the bridge; while the "Ultimate Swing" lets you jump off the bridge and swing in a big arc at speeds of up to 140kph. There is provision for **camping** here (with showers, laundry, and tents for rent), and if you call in advance you can book free shuttles from Victoria and Nanaimo.

for **Departure Bay**, again north of the center off Stewart Avenue. Plenty of local shops rent out a range of marine gear, as well as bikes and boats.

Eating

Where **eating** is concerned, get your obligatory Nanaimo bar, or other cheap edibles, at the food stands in the **Public Market**, which is near the ferry terminal on Stewart Avenue (daily 9am–9pm). The big Overwaitea supermarket is 2km north of town on Hwy-19. For meals try *Gina's*, a left turn off the north end of Front Street at 47 Skinner St (☎250/753-5411) – it's an unmissable Mexican outfit perched on the edge of a cliff and painted bright pink with an electric-blue roof. The town's best **seafood** choice is the *Bluenose Chowder House*, 1340 Stewart Ave (☎250/754-6611; closed Mon), also party to a nice outside terrace. Front Street has a choice of places, most with the benefit of terraces or patios looking out to sea: at the plaza at 90 Front St is *Javawocky* (☎250/753-1688), a good little café, while for fuller snacks or steaks and seafood you should try the *Globe Bar & Grille*, 25 Front St (☎250/754-4910).

Beyond the town

For the wildest of the local parks, head due west of town to **Westwood Lake Park**, good for a couple of hours' lonely hiking and some fine swimming. Tongue-twisting **Petroglyph Provincial Park**, off Hwy-1 3km south of downtown, showcases aboriginal peoples' carvings of the sort found all over BC (particularly along coastal waterways), many of them thousands of years old. Often their meaning is vague, but they appear to record important rituals and events. There are plenty of figures – real and mythological – carved into the local sandstone here, though their potential to inspire wonder is somewhat spoilt by more recent graffiti, traffic noise, and the first thin edge of Nanaimo's urban sprawl.

Another escape from town, and barely a stone's throw offshore, is **Newcastle Island**. Ferries (☎250/391-2300, Ⓦwww.scenicferries.com) make the 10-minuute crossing to Newcastle every hour on the hour (10am–7pm; foot passengers $5 one-way) from Maffeo Sutton Park (the wharf behind the Civic Arena) to **Newcastle Island Provincial Park**, which has a fine stretch of sand, tame wildlife, no cars, and lots of walking (18km of trails in all) and picnic possibilities. It'll take a couple of hours to walk the 7.5-kilometre trail that encircles the island. You can buy snacks on Newcastle from various concessions, but if camping take supplies.

From Nanaimo to Port Alberni

North of Nanaimo Hwy-1 is replaced by **Hwy-19**, a messy stretch of road spotted with billboards and a rash of motels, marinas, and clapboard houses. Almost every last centimetre of the coast is privately owned, this being the chosen site of what appears to be every British Columbian's dream holiday home. Don't expect to weave through the houses, wooden huts, and boat launches to reach the tempting beaches that flash past below the highway. For sea and sand you have to hang on for **Parksville**, 37km north of Nanaimo, and its quieter near-neighbour **Qualicum Beach**.

Parksville marks a major parting of the ways: while Hwy-19 continues up the eastern coast to Port Hardy, **Hwy-4**, the principal trans-island route, pushes west to **Port Alberni** and on through the tremendously scenic Mackenzie

Mountains to the Pacific Rim National Park. Laidlaw runs up to three **buses** daily from Nanaimo to Port Alberni, where there are connecting services for Ucluelet and Tofino in the national park.

Parksville and Qualicum Beach

The approach to **PARKSVILLE** from the south is promising, taking you through lovely wooded dunes, with lanes striking off eastwards to hidden beaches and a half-dozen secluded **campsites**. Four kilometres on is the best of the area beaches, stretched along 2km of **Rathtrevor Beach Provincial Park** (the tide goes out a kilometre here to reveal vast swathes of sand). In summer there's more beach action here than just about anywhere in the country – and if you want to lay claim to some of the park's **camping** space (summer $22, winter $9; day-use parking $5) expect to start lining up first thing in the morning or take advantage of the provincial park reservations service (see p.43).

The dross starts beyond the bridge into Parksville and its eight blocks of motels and garages. The worst of the development has been kept off the promenade, however, which fronts **Parksville Beach**, whose annual **Sandfest** draws 30,000 visitors a day in July to watch the World Sandcastle Competition. The beach offers lovely views across to the mainland and boasts Canada's warmest seawater – up to 21°C (70°F) in summer. Though busy, it's as immaculately kept as the rest of the town – a tidiness that bears witness to the civic pride of Parksville's largely retired permanent population. You'll see some of these worthy burghers at play during August, when the town hosts the World Croquet Championships.

For local **information**, Parksville's Chamber of Commerce is clearly signed off the highway in downtown at 1275 E Island Hwy (June–early Sept daily 8am–8pm; rest of the year Mon–Fri 9am–5pm; Ⓣ250/248-3613, Ⓦwww.chamber.parksville.bc.ca). Ask especially for details of the many **hiking** areas and other nearby refuges from the beaches' summer maelstrom, and **fishing**, another of the region's big draws.

If you're staying overnight, camping offers the best locations. There are a multitude of cheapish Identikit **motels** in town and "resort complexes" out along the beaches, though summer vacancies are few and far between. South of Rathtrevor Beach Provincial Park, try a pair of cottage resorts that look onto the sea: the big *Tigh-Na-Mara Resort Hotel*, 1095 E Island Hwy (Ⓣ250/248-2072 or 1-800/663-7373, Ⓦwww.tigh-na-mara.com; ⑥), with log cottages and oceanfront apartments, forest setting, beach, indoor pool, and self-catering units; or the smaller and slightly cheaper *Gray Crest Seaside Resort*, 1115 E Island Hwy (Ⓣ250/248-6513 or 1-800/663-2636, Ⓦwww.graycrest.com; ⑥), which has considerably lower rates offseason. The *Sea Edge Motel*, 209 W Island Hwy (Ⓣ250/248-8377 or 1-800/667-3382, Ⓦwww.seaedge.com; ⑤), with its own stretch of beach, is cheaper.

A few kilometres north of Parksville on 19A, **QUALICUM BEACH**, claims its Chamber of Commerce, "is to the artist of today what Stratford-on-Avon was to the era of Shakespeare" – a bohemian enclave of West Coast artists and writers that has also been dubbed the "Carmel of the North" after the town in California. Obviously both estimations pitch things ridiculously high, but compared to Parksville the area has more greenery and charm, and it's infinitely less commercialized, though its beaches probably draw just as many summer visitors.

More a collection of dispersed houses than a town, at least near the water, Qualicum's seafront is correspondingly wilder and more picturesque, skirted by the road and interrupted only by an **infocentre** at 2711 W Island Hwy, the obvious white building midway on the strand (daily 9am–6pm, open longer in summer; Ⓣ250/752-9532, Ⓦwww.qualicum.bc.ca), and a couple of well-situated **hotels**: the *Sand Pebbles Inn* (Ⓣ250/752-6974 or 1-877/556-2326, Ⓦwww.spebbles.com; ④) and the small *Captain's Inn* (Ⓣ250/752-6743, Ⓦwww.captains-inn.com; ③). A cluster of **motels** also sit at its northern end, where the road swings inland. There's plenty of other local accommodation and B&Bs and campsites: contact the infocentre for details. Keep heading north and the road becomes quieter and edged with occasional **campsites**.

Highway 4 to Port Alberni

If you've not yet ventured off the coastal road from Victoria, the short stretch heading west from near Parksville on **Hwy-4 to Port Alberni** offers the first real taste of the island's beauty. The first worthwhile stop is **Englishman River Falls Provincial Park**, 3km west of Parksville (exit at Errington Road) and then another 8km south off the highway. Named after an early immigrant who drowned here, the park wraps around the Englishman River, which tumbles over two main sets of waterfalls. A thirty-minute trail takes in both falls, with plenty of swimming and fishing pools en route. The popular year-round provincial park **campsite** (summer $17, winter $9; day-use parking $3) is on the left off the approach road before the river, secreted amongst cedars, dogwoods – BC's official tree – and lush ferns.

Back on the main highway, a further 8km brings you to the **Little Qualicum Hatchery**, given over to chum, trout, and chinook salmon, and just beyond it turn right for the **Little Qualicum Falls Provincial Park**, on the north side of Hwy-4 19km west of Parksville, which some claim is the island's loveliest small park. A magnificent forest trail follows the river as it drops several hundred metres through a series of gorges and foaming waterfalls. A half-hour stroll gives you views of the main falls, but for a longer **hike** try the five-hour Wesley Ridge Trail. There's a sheltered provincial park **campsite** (summer $17, winter $9; day-use parking $3) by the river and a designated **swimming area** on the river at its southern end.

Midway to Port Alberni, the road passes **Cameron Lake** and then an imperious belt of old-growth forest. At the lake's western end, it's well worth walking ten minutes into **McMillan Provincial Park** (no campsite) to reach the famous **Cathedral Grove**, a beautiful group of huge Douglas firs, some of them reaching 70m tall, 2m thick, and up to a thousand years old. The park is the gift of the large McMillan timber concern, whose agents have been responsible for felling similar trees with no compunction over the years. Wandering the grove will take only a few minutes, but just to the east, at the Cameron Lake picnic site, is the start of the area's main **hike**. The well-maintained trail was marked out by railway crews in 1908 and climbs to the summit of **Mount Arrowsmith** (1817m), a long, gentle twenty-kilometre pull through alpine meadows that takes between six and nine hours. The mountain is also one of the island's newer and fast-developing ski areas. To stay locally, head for the *Cameron Lake Resort* (Ⓣ250/752-6707, Ⓦwww.cameronlakeresort.com; ④; April–Oct), based in a park-like setting on the lake at 1313 Chalet Rd: it has a cottage and a campsite ($19–25).

Port Alberni and around

Self-proclaimed "Gateway to the Pacific" and – along with half of Vancouver Island – "Salmon Capital of the World," **PORT ALBERNI** is a dispersed town more or less dominated by the sights and smells of its huge lumber mills. Despite its relative ugliness, it's also an increasingly popular site for exploring the center and west coast of the island, and a busy fishing port, situated at the end of the impressive fjord-like Alberni Inlet, Vancouver Island's longest inlet. Various logging and pulp-mill tours are available, but the town's main interest to travelers is as a forward base for the Pacific Rim National Park. If you've ever wanted to hook a salmon, though, this is probably one of the easier places to do so and there are a number of boats and guides ready to help out.

The town's only conventional sight, the **Alberni Valley Museum**, 4255 Wallace St and 10th Avenue (summer Tues–Sat 10am–5pm, Thurs until 8pm; donation suggested; ⓣ250/723-2181), is home to a predictable but above-average logging and aboriginal peoples collection, a waterwheel and small steam engine. Alternatively, check out the industry-backed **Forestry Visitor Center** (summer daily 9.30am–5.30pm, rest of the year Fri–Sun 11am–4pm; ⓣ250/720-2108) on the colourful harbor quay where in summer a small steam train runs from the old train station at the corner of Kingsway and Argyle for about 30 minutes along the waterfront to the **McLean Mill National Historic Site** (site open daily year-round; mill building and steam train mid-June–early Sept Wed–Thurs 10am–5pm; site donation suggested; mill $6.50; train $22 round-trip, including mill admission; ⓣ250/723-1376, ⓦwww.alberniheritage.com), an old steam-operated mill at 5633 Smith Rd, also reachable by bike or on foot on the twenty-kilometre Log Trail from the infocentre.

For hot-weather swimming, locals head out to **Sproat Lake Provincial Park**, 8km north of town on Hwy-4. It's a hectic scene in summer, thanks to a fine beach, picnic area, and a pair of good campsites ($15; April–Oct), one on the lake, the other north of the highway about 1km away. Of peripheral interest, you can take a guided tour of the world's largest fire-fighting planes or follow the short trails that lead to a few ancient petroglyphs on the park's eastern tip. Sproat Lake marks the start of the superb scenery that unfolds over the 100km of Hwy-4 west of the town. Only heavily logged areas detract from the grandeur of the Mackenzie Range and the majestic interplay of trees and water. Go prepared, however, as there's no fuel or shops for about two hours of driving.

Practicalities

Laidlaw runs five **buses** daily to and from Nanaimo, with the terminal on Victoria Quay at 5065 Southgate (though the bus company is based at 4541 Margaret St). Jump off at the 7-Eleven, one stop earlier, to be nearer the center of town. The same company runs connections from here on to Ucluelet and Tofino in Pacific Rim National Park. Western Bus Lines (ⓣ250/723-3341) run two services weekly to Bamfield (Mon & Fri; $17 one-way) as does the Pacheenaht First Nation Bus Service (ⓣ250/647-5521). Several other companies from Victoria (see p.479) make connections to Bamfield for the West Coast Trail (see p.521). For help and information on fishing charters, hiking options, or tours of the two local pulp mills, call in at the **infocentre**, unmissable as you come into town at 2533 Redford St, RR2, Site 215 Comp 10 (July & Aug Mon–Fri 8am–6pm, Sat & Sun 9am–5pm; rest of the year Mon–Fri 9am–5pm, Sat & Sun 10am–2/4pm; ⓣ250/724-6535, ⓦwww.avcoc.com) off Hwy-4 east of town – look out for the big yellow mural.

If you're in town for the 8am departure of the MV *Lady Rose* (see opposite), there's a good chance you may have to stay overnight in the town. For **accommodation** there are the usual motel choices – the closest to the quay, and thus

The MV Lady Rose

The thing you'll probably most want to do in Port Alberni is to leave it, preferably on the **MV Lady Rose**, a small, fifty-year-old Scottish-built freighter that plies between Kildonan, Bamfield, Ucluelet, and the Broken Group Islands (see p.519). Primarily a conduit for freight and mail, it also takes up to a hundred passengers, many of whom use it as a drop-off for canoe trips or the West Coast Trail at Bamfield. You could easily ride it simply for the exceptional scenery – huge cliffs and tree-covered mountains – and for the abundant wildlife (sea lions, whales, eagles, depending on the time of year). Such is the boat's popularity that another has been added to the "fleet" – the 200-passenger MV *Frances Barkley* – and reservations for trips are now virtually essential. Remember to take a sweater and jacket and wear sensible shoes, for these are still primarily working boats, and creature comforts are few.

The basic year-round **schedule** is as follows: the boat leaves at 8am from the Argyle Pier, 5425 Argyle St at the Alberni Harbour Quay (year-round Tues, Thurs & Sat). It arrives in **Bamfield** ($23 one-way, $45 return) via Kildonan ($12/$24), at 12.30pm and starts its return journey an hour later, reaching Port Alberni again at 5.30pm. From October to May the boat stops on request in advance at the Broken Group Islands.

From June to mid-September, there are additional sailings on Monday, Wednesday, and Friday to **Ucluelet** and the Broken Group Islands, departing 8am and arriving at Ucluelet at 12.30pm via the islands, where the boat docks at 11am at Sechart ($23/$45), site of the *Sechart Whaling Station Lodge* (Ⓣ250/723-8313, Ⓦwww.ladyrosemarine.com), the only place to stay if you're not wilderness camping on the archipelago. Cost per night is $100 per person, $155 for two people, including meals, slightly less per night if you stay two or more days. The return journey starts from Ucluelet at 2pm, calling at Sechart again (3.30pm) before arriving back at Port Alberni (7pm).

From July 6 to August 31 only, there is an additional sailing on Sundays on the route from Port Alberni (8am) to Bamfield (1.30pm) and return with an outbound stop at Sechart at 11am.

Contact Lady Rose Marine Services, 5425 Argyle St, Port Alberni, for information and reservations (Ⓣ250/723-8313 year-round or 1-800/663-7192 April–Sept, Ⓦwww.ladyrosemarine.com; April–Sept only). They also offer canoe and kayak rentals and transportation of the same to the Broken Group Islands (canoe and single-kayak rental $35, double kayak $50 daily including lifejackets, paddles, pumps, and spray skirts). Note that smaller boats running more irregular services to the same destinations can occasionally be picked up from Tofino and Ucluelet.

the MV *Lady Rose*, is the *Bluebird*, 3755 3rd Ave (Ⓣ250/723-1153, Ⓦwww.bluebirdmotel.net; ❸), but it only has fifteen rooms, so be sure to book ahead. For a more memorable central hotel you will be better off with the *Coast Hospitality Inn*, 3835 Redford St (Ⓣ723-8111 or 1-800/663-1144, Ⓦwww.coasthotels.com; ❻), not cheap, but probably the town's best bet. *The Best Western Barclay*, 4277 Stamp Ave (Ⓣ250/724-7171 or 1-800/563-6590, Ⓦwww.bestwesternbarclay.com; ❻), with outdoor pool and the smaller *Somass Motel & RV*, 5279 River Rd (Ⓣ250/724-3236 or 1-800/927-2217, Ⓦwww.somass-motel.ca; ❸), are also both reliable choices. The infocentre has a list of the constantly changing **B&Bs**: an excellent first choice is the *Edelweiss B&B*, 2610-12th Ave (Ⓣ250/723-5940; ❸), which is not particularly central, but does have very welcoming hosts. For **camping**, best options are on Sproat Lake (see above). Further afield is the bigger 250-site *China Creek Marina and Campground*, 2011 Bamfield Road (Ⓣ250/723-2657; $16–25; May–Sept), 15km south of the town on Alberni Inlet, which has a wooded, waterside location, and sandy, log-strewn beach. Camping at Sproat Lake (see p.508) is excellent, but busy in the summer.

Eating possibilities are numerous. For coffee, good breakfasts, and snacks down by the dock before jumping aboard the MV *Lady Rose*, try the *Blue Door Café* at 5415 Argyle St, an old-fashioned place much-patronized by locals. For lunch, make for the *Swale Rock Café*, 5328 Argyle St (☎250/723-0777), which has good light meals, or if you're on a tighter budget try the snacks at the *Paradise Café*, 4505 Gertrude St (☎250/724-5050), or one of several deli-bakeries. For **seafood** check out the waterfront *Clockworks*, Harbour Quay (☎723-8862), while *The Canal*, 5093 Johnson St (☎250/724-6555), serves good Greek food.

Pacific Rim National Park

The single best reason to visit Vancouver Island, the **PACIFIC RIM NATIONAL PARK** is a stunning amalgam of mountains, coastal rainforest, wild beaches, and unkempt marine landscapes that stretches intermittently for 130km between the towns of Tofino in the north and Port Renfrew to the south. It is comprised of three distinct areas: **Long Beach**, which is the most popular; the **Broken Group Islands**, hundreds of islets only really accessible to sailors and canoeists; and the **West Coast Trail**, a tough but popular long-distance footpath. The whole area has also become a magnet for **surfing** and **whale-watching** enthusiasts, and dozens of small companies run charters to view the migrating mammals. By taking the MV *Lady Rose* from Port Alberni (see box above) to Bamfield or Ucluelet, and combining this with shuttle buses or Laidlaw buses from Victoria, Port Alberni, and Nanaimo, a wonderfully varied combination of itineraries is possible around the region.

Lying at the north end of Long Beach, **Tofino**, once essentially a fishing village, is now changing in the face of tourism, but with its natural charm, scenic position, and plentiful accommodation, the town still makes the best base for area exploration. **Ucluelet**, to the south of Long Beach, is comparatively less attractive, but almost equally geared to providing tours and accommodating the park's 800,000 or so annual visitors. **Bamfield**, a tiny and picturesque community with a limited amount of in-demand accommodation, lies still further south and is known mainly as the northern trailhead of the West Coast Trail and a fishing, marine research, and whale-watching center. Unless you fly in, you enter the park on Hwy-4 from Port Alberni, which means the first part you'll see is Long Beach (Hwy-4 follows its length en route for Tofino), so if you're dashing in by car for a day-trip, cut straight to the section dealing with this area on opposite page. Long Beach, rather than Tofino, is also the site of the park's main **information center** and the nearby Wickaninnish Centre, an interpretive center. There is a **park fee** of $10 per vehicle per day.

Weather in the park is an important consideration, because it has a well-deserved reputation for being appallingly wet, cold, and windy – and that's the good days. An average of 300cm of rain falls annually, and in some places it buckets down almost 700cm, well over ten times what falls on Victoria. So don't count on doing much sunbathing (though surfing's a possibility): think more in terms of spending your time admiring crashing Pacific breakers, hiking the backcountry, and maybe doing a spot of beachcombing. Time your visit to coincide with the worst of the weather offseason – **storm watching** is an increasingly popular park pastime.

Spotting whales off the coast

The Pacific Rim National Park is among the world's best areas for **whale watching**, thanks to its location on the main migration routes, food-rich waters, and numerous sheltered bays. People come from all over for the spectacle, and it's easy to find a boat going out from Tofino, Ucluelet, or Bamfield, most charging around $60–80 a head for the trip depending on duration (usually 2–3hr). Regulations prohibit approaching within 100m of an animal but, though few locals will admit it, there's no doubt that the recent huge upsurge in boat tours has begun to disrupt the **migrations**. The whales' 8000-kilometre journey – the longest known migration of any mammal – takes them from their breeding and calving lagoons in Baja, Mexico, to summer feeding grounds in the Bering and Chukchi seas off Siberia. The northbound migration takes from February to May, with the peak period of passage between March and April. A few dozen animals occasionally abort their trip and stop off the Canadian coast for summer feeding (notably at Maquinna Marine Park, 20min by boat from Tofino). The return journey starts in August, hitting Tofino and Ucluelet in late September and early October. Even if you don't take a boat trip, you stand a faint chance of seeing whales from the coast as they dive, when you can locate their tails, or during fluking, when the animals surface and "blow" three or four times before making another five-minute dive. There are telescopes at various points along Long Beach, the best known viewpoints being Schooner Cove, Radar Hill, Quistis Point, and Combers Beach near Sea Lion Rocks.

Long Beach and around

The most accessible of the park's components, **LONG BEACH** is just what it says: a long tract of wild, windswept sand, and rocky points stretching for about 30km from Tofino to Ucluelet. Around 19km can be hiked unbroken from Schooner Bay in the west to Half Moon Bay in the east. The snow-covered peaks of the Mackenzie Range rise up over 1200m as a scenic backdrop, and behind the beach grows a thick, lush canopy of coastal rainforest. The white-packed sand itself is the sort of primal seascape that is all but extinct in much of the world, scattered with beautiful, sea-sculpted driftwood, smashed by surf, broken by crags, and dotted with islets and rock pools oozing with marine life. Note that Long Beach, while a distinct beach in itself, also loosely refers to several other **beaches** to either side, the relative merits of which are outlined below.

Scenery aside, Long Beach is noted for its **wildlife**, the BC coastline reputedly having more marine species than any other temperate area in the world. As well as the smaller organisms in tidal pools – sea stars, anemones, snails, sponges, and suchlike – there are large mammals like whales and sea lions, as well as thousands of migrating birds (especially in October and November), notably pintails, mallards, black brants, and Canada geese. Better weather brings out lots of beachcombers (Japanese glass fishing floats are highly coveted), clam diggers, anglers, surfers, canoeists, windsurfers, and divers, though the water is usually too cold to venture in without a wetsuit, and rip currents and rogue lumps of driftwood crashed around by the waves can make swimming dangerous. Resist the temptation to pick up shells as souvenirs – it's against park regulations.

The beaches

As this is a national park, some of Long Beach and its flanking stretches of coastline have been very slightly tamed for human consumption, but in a most discreet and tasteful manner. The best way to get a taste of the area is to walk the beaches or forested shorelines themselves – there are plenty of hidden coves – or to follow any of nine very easy and well-maintained **hiking trails** (see box, below). If you're driving or biking along Hwy-4, which backs the beaches all the way, there are distinct areas to look out for. Moving west, the first of these is the five-kilometre **Florencia Beach** (1.5km from the Hwy: access by trails 1, 2, 3, and 5; see box), also known as Wreck Beach and formerly the home of hippie beach dwellers in driftwood shacks before the park's formation. This is something of a local favorite, with relatively few people and good rock pools.

Around 8km beyond the Long Beach Road turnoff is the entrance to the *Green Point* park **campsite** and further access to Long Beach, while 4km beyond that lies the turnoff on the right to Tofino's small airstrip. Around here the peninsula narrows, with **Grice Bay** coming close to the road on the right (north side), a shallow inlet known in winter for its countless wildfowl. Beyond

Long Beach walks

While various trails drop to the beach from the main Hwy-4 road to Tofino, there are nine official ones, most of them short and very easy. All the paths are clearly marked from Hwy-4, but it's still worth picking up a *Hiker's Guide* from the infocentre. From east to west you can choose from the following. The linked trails **1** and **2**, the **Willowbrae Trail** (2.8km round-trip), are accessed by turning left at the main Hwy-4 junction and driving or biking 2km towards Ucluelet. A level wooded trail then leads from the trailhead towards the beach, following the steps of early pioneers who used this route before the building of roads between Tofino and Ucluelet. Just before the sea it divides, dropping steeply via steps and ramps, to either the tiny Half Moon Bay or the larger, neighboring Florencia Bay to the north.

All other walks are accessed off Hwy-4 to Tofino, turning right (north) at the main Hwy-4 junction. The gentle **3 Gold Mine Trail** (3km round-trip), signed left off the road, leads along Lost Shoe Creek, a former gold-mining area (look out for debris), to Florencia Beach. For walks **4**, **5**, and **6**, take the turn left off the highway for the Wickaninnish Centre. The **4 South Beach Trail** (1.5km round-trip) leaves from behind the center, leading above forest-fringed shores and coves before climbing to the headlands for a view of the coast and a chance to climb down to South Beach, famous for its big rock-crashing breakers and the sound of the water ripping noisily through the beach pebbles. The **5 Wickaninnish Trail** (5km) follows the South Beach Trail for a while and then at the top of the first hill is signed left, passing through rainforest – once again this is the route of the old pioneer trail – before ending at the parking area above Florencia Beach to the east. The **6 Shorepine Bog Trail** (800m) is a wheelchair-accessible boardwalk trail (accessed on the left on the access road to the center) that wends through the fascinating stunted bog vegetation; trees which are just a metre or so tall here can be hundreds of years old.

Moving further west towards Tofino along Hwy-4, the **7 Rain Forest Trails** are two small loops (1km each round-trip), one on each side of the road, that follow a boardwalk through virgin temperate rainforest: each has interpretive boards detailing forest life cycle and forest "inhabitants" respectively. Further down the road on the right at the Combers Beach parking area, a road gives access to the gentle **8 Spruce Fringe Trail** (1.5km loop). This graphically illustrates the effects of the elements on spruce forest, following a log-strewn beach fringe-edged with bent and bowed trees before entering more robust forest further from the effects of wind and salt spray. It also crosses willow and crab-apple swamp to a glacial terrace, the site of a former shoreline, past the airport turnoff. The final walk, the **9 Schooner Beach Trail** (1km one-way), leads left off the road to an extremely scenic beach at Schooner Cove. This might be the end of the official trails, but don't fail to climb to the viewpoint on **Radar Hill** off to the right as you get closer to Tofino.

the airstrip turnoff comes a trail to Schooner Cove (see box, opposite) and 3.5km beyond that a 1.5-kilometre turnoff to Kap'yong, or **Radar Hill** (96m), the panoramic site of a wartime radar station. By now Tofino is getting close, and 4.5km further on (and a couple of kilometres outside the park boundary) you come to **Cox Bay Beach**, **Chesterman Beach**, and **Mackenzie Beach**, all accessed from Hwy-4. Cox and Chesterman are known for their breakers; Mackenzie for its relative warmth if you want to chance a dip.

Practicalities

Long Beach's **Pacific Rim National Park Information Centre** is just off Hwy-4, 3km north of the T-junction for Tofino and Ucluelet. After paying a **park fee** of $10 per vehicle, be sure to make full use of the wealth of material the center provides on all aspects of the park. In summer the staff offer guided walks and interpretive programs ((daily mid-March to mid-June 10.30am–6pm, mid-June–Aug 8am–8pm, Sept–mid-Oct 10am–6pm; ⓣ250/726-4212, ⓦwww.parkscanada.gc.ca). For year-round information, call the Park Administration Office (ⓣ250/726-7721). For more Long Beach information, viewing decks with telescopes, and lots of well-presented displays, head for the **Wickaninnish Centre**, Long Beach Road (mid-March to early Oct daily 10.30am–6pm; ⓣ250/726-4701) on a headland at the start of Long Beach. The center is the departure point for several trails (see box opposite), has telescopes for whale-spotting and a variety of films, displays, and exhibits relating to the park and ocean..

There is one park **campsite**, the *Green Point*, set on a lovely bluff overlooking the beach ($20 for the 94 drive in sites; washrooms but no showers; 20 primitive walk-in sites $14). However, it's likely to be full every day in July and August, and it's first-come first-served for the walk-in sites (reservations are taken up to three months in advance for the drive-in sites), so you may have to turn up for several days before getting a spot. There's usually a waiting-list system, however, whereby you're given a number and instructions as to when you should be able to return. The nearest commercial sites and conventional accommodation are in Tofino (see overleaf) and Ucluelet (see p.518).

Tofino and around

TOFINO, most travelers' target base in the park, is showing the adverse effects of its ever-increasing tourist influx, but locals are keeping development to a minimum, clearly realizing they have a vested interest in preserving the salty, waterfront charm that brought them – and visitors – here in the first place. Crowning a narrow spit, the fishing village has a superb situation, bounded on three sides by tree-covered islands and water, a location that graces it with magnificent views and plenty of what the tourist literature refers to as "aquaculture." As a service center it fulfills most functions, offering food, accommodation, and a wide variety of boat and sea-plane tours, most of which have a **whale-watching**, **surfing** (Canada's best surf is close at hand), and **fishing** angle or provide a means to travel out to **islands and hot springs** close by (see p.517). Sleepy in offseason, the place erupts into a commercial frenzy during the summer, though there's little to do in town other than walk its few streets, enjoy the views, and soak up the casual atmosphere.

Arrival and information

Tofino's easily reached by Laidlaw **bus** (ⓣ250/385-4411 or 1-800/318-0818) from Port Alberni (2 daily; 3hr) and Nanaimo (1 daily; 4hr 30min), with a single early-morning connection from Victoria, changing at Nanaimo (6hr 30min). The bus depot is on 1st Street near the junction with Neil Street. There is also a daily mini-bus shuttle, the Tofino Bus, 564 Campbell St (Ⓣ250/725-2871 or 1-866/986-3466, Ⓦwww.tofinobus.com), from Victoria or Nanaimo (connecting with ferry from Horseshoe Bay, Vancouver). The smaller Pacific Rim 5-Star shuttle (Ⓣ250/954-8702 or 1-800/697-1114, Ⓦwww.prshuttle.ca) runs daily to Nanaimo or Comox ($85) and Victoria ($170) from Tofino and Ucluelet.

More small airlines have added Tofino to their schedules as the destination's popularity increases. Best is the excellent North Vancouver Air (Ⓣ250/604/278-1608 or 1-800/228-6608, Ⓦwww.northvanair.com), which operates to here once or twice daily from Vancouver (1hr flight; $175 one-way, $75 standby) and Victoria (45min; $200 one-way). The tiny airport is close to the northern end of Long Beach: there are no shuttle connections to Tofino, but taxis are generally available.

The **infocentre** at 121 Third St at the corner of Campbell Street (April–Sept daily 9am–8/9pm, Oct–March Mon–Fri 9am–4pm; Ⓣ250/725-3414, Ⓦwww.tofinobc.org or www.island.net) can give you the exhaustive lowdown on all the logistics of boat and plane tours.

Accommodation

There are two main concentrations of **accommodation** options: in Tofino itself or a couple of kilometres out of town to the east en route for Long Beach on or near Lynn Road, which overlooks Chesterman Beach. Bed-and-breakfast options, in particular, tend to be out of town near Chesterman Beach; an extensive listing can be found at Ⓦwww.island.net/~tofino/tcbb. Note that out of town but across the water (access by water taxi) there's also the desirable but expensive self-contained units at the *Hot Springs Lodge* (Ⓣ250/724-8570; ⑥), the main accommodation at Hot Springs Cove (see p.517), but book early.

Otherwise you can try one of the near-town **campsites** (don't forget that there is a park campsite at Long Beach; see overleaf) or the **private hostels** that now seem to spring up overnight here and disappear just as quickly. Note that some of these places can be home to a sprinkling of the untrustworthy sort of beach-bum year-round drifters who give travelers a bad name.

Hotels and bed and breakfasts

Brimar 1375 Thornberg Crescent Ⓣ250/725-3410 or 1-800/714-9373, Ⓦwww.brimarbb.com. At the south end of Chesterman Beach, off Lynn Rd, these three rooms have good Pacific Ocean views and come with a full breakfast. ⑥

Dolphin Motel 1190 Pacific Rim Hwy Ⓣ250/725-3377, Ⓦwww.dolphinmotel.ca. Rooms with coffee-maker and fridge or self-catering units 3km south of town; 5min walk to Chesterman Beach. ③

Duffin Cove and Resort 215 Campbell St Ⓣ250/725-3448 or 1-888/629-2903, Ⓦwww.duffin-cove-resort.com. Thirteen nice cabins and suites (for one to eight people) with kitchens and sea-view balconies just south of the *Cable Cove Inn* at the western edge of town overlooking the Clayoquot Sound. ⑥

Gull Cottage 1254 Lynn Rd Ⓣ250/725-3177, Ⓦwww.gullcottagetofino.com. A few minutes' walk to the beach, at the west end of Lynn Rd, this Victorian-era home has three rooms (private bathrooms) and a hot tub in the woods. ⑤

Maquinna Lodge 120 1st St Ⓣ250/725-3261 or 1-800/665-3199. Central town location at the corner of Main and 1st St, containing 32 renovated rooms, some overlooking Tofino Harbour and Meares Island. ⑤

Middle Beach Lodge 400 Mackenzie Beach Ⓣ250/725-2900, Ⓦwww.middlebeach.com. Extremely nice, secluded place south of town and west of Chesterman Beach with big stone fireplace, deep old chairs, and the gentle splash of waves on tiny Templar Beach to lull you to sleep. ⑤

Penny's Place 565 Campbell St Ⓣ250/725-3457. A choice of rooms on the east edge of the small downtown with and without private bathrooms offering a full breakfast but nonsmoking. 5

Schooner Motel 311 Campbell St ⓣ250/725-3478, ⓦwww.schoonermotel.net. Overlooking Tofino Inlet and Meares Island in the town center, this motel has some rooms complete with kitchen. 6

Tofino by the Beach 1277 Lynn Rd ⓣ250/725-2441, ⓦwww.tofinobythebeach.com. Away from the center of Tofino on Chesterman Beach at its northern end. Rooms have private bathrooms; continental breakfast included. 6

Tofino Motel 542 Campbell St ⓣ250/725-2055, ⓦwww.tofinomotel.com. A small motel on the eastern edge of town including rooms with balconies offering views of the sea and neighboring islands. 6

Tofino Swell Lodge 341 Olsen Rd ⓣ250/725-3274. On the eastern edge of town near Crab Dock, this excellent lodge on the waterfront looking out to Meares Island has kitchen or plain sleeping units. 4

Village Gallery B&B 321 Main St ⓣ250/725-4229. Quiet upper room and living room in a heritage building in the center of town with good ocean view and full breakfast. 5

Wickaninnish Inn Osprey Lane at Chesterman Beach ⓣ250/725-3100 or 1-800/333-4604, ⓦwww.wickinn.com. If you're feeling like a splurge (rooms start at $380, less offseason), shell out for this superb $8.5-million 45-room inn, situated on a rocky promontory at the western end of Chesterman Beach. All rooms are large and have ocean views, fireplaces, and baths big enough for two. As well as the obvious local attractions, storm watching here is a growing wintertime activity. 8

Wilp Gybuu 311 Leighton Way ⓣ250/725-2330, ⓦwww.tofinobedandbreakfast.com. Three rooms in walking distance south of town close to *The Tide's Inn*. Sea views, good breakfast, and private en-suite bathroom. 5

Campsites and hostels

Bella Pacifica Campground Pacific Rim Hwy ⓣ250/725-3400, ⓦwww.bellapacifica.com. Sites with hot showers, flush toilets, and laundry 2km south of town, with wilderness and oceanfront sites, private nature trails to Templar Beach, and walk-on access to Mackenzie Beach. Reservations recommended. March–Oct. $28–40.

Crystal Cove Beach Resort Mackenzie Beach ⓣ250/725-4213, ⓦwww.crystalcove.cc. Sites with flush toilets, laundry, and showers and some cabins; 3km south of town in a pretty secluded cove and also 1km from Mackenzie Beach with one- and two-bedroom smart log cabins with kitchens and ocean views. Reservations recommended. $30–50; cabins 6

Hummingbird International Hostel at Ahousaht on Flores Island, ⓣ250/670-6979, ⓦwww.hummingbird-hostel.com. A stay here offers a good chance of seeing whales, bald eagles, and sea otters (as well as hummingbirds), with the opportunity to hike trails and bathe in natural sulfur springs. Dorm beds from $20, private doubles from $70, plus cost of 35-minute water-taxi or boat connection; from $14 each way; departures from First St dock at 10.30am & 4pm, returning 8.30am & 1pm.

Mackenzie Beach Resort 1101 Pacific Rim Hwy ⓣ250/725-3439, ⓦwww.mackenziebeach.com. Located on a fine sandy beach 2km south of Tofino and 10min walk from Long Beach; indoor pool, Jacuzzi, hot showers, and kayak rentals. Some walk-in beachfront tent sites. $35–45.

Whalers on the Point 81 West St ⓣ250/725-3443, ⓦwww.tofinohostel.com. Near the west end of Main Street with fabulous ocean views Hostelling International-affiliated *Whalers* is the best of the local hostels. Facilities include kitchen, games room, sauna, bike rental and storage, surf and wetsuit lockers, and a shuttle service to Long Beach. Reservations are essential. Beds are $22 per person ($24 for non-members) in high season (May–Sept) – $2 less the rest of the year. Private doubles are available for $66–75 ($70–80 for non-members), $40–45 in low season. All prices exclude 15 percent room taxes and $2 for one-night stays from mid-June to mid-Sept.

WindRider Retreat for Women 231 Main St ⓣ250/725-3240 or 1-877/725-3240, ⓔinfo@windride.org. A good option for women travelers, this women-only central house offers shared rooms with two or three beds ($25) and private doubles/twins ($60/$65).

The Town

Drop into the small **Whale Center** at 411 Campbell St (March–Oct daily 9am–8pm; free; ⓣ250/725-2132), one of many places to book whale-watching tours, but also home to exhibits and artifacts devoted to local seafaring and trading history, whales and aboriginal peoples' culture. Repaying closer inspection is the **Eagle Aerie Gallery**, 350 Campbell St at the corner of Second Street

(Ⓣ250/725-3235 or 1-800/663-0669, Ⓦwww.royhenryvickers.com), belonging to (and exhibiting many paintings by) the noted Tsimshian artist Roy Henry Vickers and housed in a traditional longhouse-style building with a beautiful cedar interior. Two blocks east is the **Rainforest Interpretive Centre**, at 451 Main St at the corner of Fourth Street (Ⓣ250/725-2560; free), which offers background on the ecosystems of the Pacific temperate rainforest.

Two fine beaches also lie within walking distance to the southeast of the town: **Mackenzie Beach** and **Chesterman's Beach** (for access to the latter take Lynn Road right just beyond the *Dolphin Motel* as you leave town), the former one of the warmer spots locally, the latter home to a fair number of out-of-town accommodation possibilities (see p.515).

Eating and drinking

Alley Way Café 305 Campbell and First St, behind the bank, Ⓣ250/725-3105. A friendly and long-established locals' type of place which sells the usual coffee, teas, pastries, and snacks.

Common Loaf Bake Shop 180 1st St, behind the bank, Ⓣ250/725-3915. Just about everyone in town clusters around the heaving tables; deservedly the most popular choice for coffee and snacks. In the evening the home-made dough is turned into excellent pizzas instead of bread and rolls.

Maquinna Lodge 120 First St Ⓣ250/725–3261. The lodge's downstairs pub is Tofino's best choice for a beer and dancing and the place to be on Friday and Saturday nights.

Café Pamplona 1084 Pacific Hwy Ⓣ250/725-1237. Located in the Tofino Botanical Gardens on the main highway into town (which becomes Campbell St), a good spot for coffee and snacks.

The Pointe Restaurant at the *Wickaninnish Inn* Ⓣ250/725-3100; see hotel listings overleaf. Just out of town, the area's best upmarket restaurant, on account of both its food and its views and you will pay for it – expect to drop over $150 for a full gourmet nine-course special with wine.

RainCoast Café 101-120 Fourth St Ⓣ250/725-2215. Intimate and sleek, offering excellent Pacific Rim fusion food, dinner only. Good fish and seafood, with great halibut dishes and soups.

Schooner 331 Campbell St Ⓣ250/725-3444. An award-winning romantic locale set in pretty gardens with tremendous views of the Tofino Inlet, with elevated cuisine (mainly fish and seafood).

Sea Shanty 300 Main St Ⓣ250/725-2902. With outdoor dining overlooking the harbor, this restaurant serves fine fish and seafood, and offers some of the best views in town and a chance to see some tremendous sunsets on fine evenings.

Activities

Ucluelet to the south may claim to be "whale-watching capital of the world," but **whales** – the main reason a lot of people are here – are just as easily seen from Tofino. As in Victoria, you have plenty of operators to choose from, most costing about the same and offering similar **excursions**: all you have to do is decide what sort of boat you want to go out on – zodiacs (inflatables), which are more thrilling and potentially wetter, or rigid-hull cruisers (covered or uncovered), which are more sedate. See the box on p.511 for more whale-watching tips. Remember that if you take tours to Meares Islands, Hot Springs Cove, and elsewhere, especially in spring or autumn (best times to see whales), you stand a good chance of seeing whales en route anyway – some operators try to combine whale watching and excursions. Reckon on spending from around $65 for a two- or three-hour trip in a Zodiac and $85 on a rigid-hull.

Operators to try include: Cypre Prince Tours midway down the main street at 430 Campbell St (Ⓣ250/725-2202 or 1-800/787-2202, Ⓦwww.tofinooutdoors.com); Chinook Charters, 450 Campbell St (Ⓣ250/725-3431 or 1-800/665-3646), which offers trips (2hr 30min) on rigid or Zodiac boats; and the Jamie's Whaling Station, 606 Campbell St (Ⓣ250/725-3919 or 1-800/667-9913, Ⓦwww.jamies.com), established in 1982 (the first such venture in Tofino), which also offers a choice of Zodiac or the twenty-metre *Lady Selkirk*, which comes with heated cabin, no small consideration on cold days, of which Tofino has a few. If you don't see whales, Jamie's offers a voucher which can used on another trip. See "Whales" box, p.511, for more general information.

Many of these companies double up as **fishing** charters, though for a more long-established specialist operator contact Bruce's Smiley Seas Charters, based at 210 Campbell St (May–Sept; ⓣ250/725-2557), which is quite happy to have novices aboard. Still on the water, Tofino is quickly becoming the **surfing** capital of Canada, thanks to some enormous Pacific waves, though floating driftwood and big lumps of lumber caught up in the waves can be a hazard. For information, board rental, and all other equipment, contact Live to Surf well east of the town center at 1180 Tofino Hwy (ⓣ250/725-4464, ⓦwww.livetosurf.com). Established in 1984, it rents boards from $25 and many other items, as well as offering lessons from $45 for two hours. If you want to go out in a **kayak** (no experience required) contact Tofino Sea Kayaking, 320 Main St (ⓣ250/725-4222 or 1-800/863-4664, ⓦwww.tofino-kayaking.com), which offers day-trips or longer **tours** with lodge accommodation or wilderness camping.

Trips from Tofino

Once they've wandered Tofino's handful of streets, most people head south to explore Long Beach, or put themselves at the mercy of the many boat and plane operators. Their playground is the stretch of ocean and landscapes around Tofino known as **Clayoquot Sound**, where there are five main destinations for boat and float-plane trips. The nearest is **Meares Island**, easily visible to the east of Tofino and just fifteen minutes away by boat. A beautiful island swathed in lush temperate rainforest, this was one of the areas earmarked for the lumberjack's chainsaw, despite its designation as a Nuu-chah-nulth tribal park in 1985. At present its ancient cedars and hemlock are safe, and visible on the Meares Island Big Cedar Trail (3km), which meanders among some of the biggest trees you'll ever see, many of them more than a thousand years old and up to 6m across – big enough to put a tunnel through. **Vargas Island**, the nearest target, lies just 5km from Tofino to the north, and is visited for its beauty, beaches, kayaking, and swimming possibilities. **Flores Island**, 20km to the northwest, is accessed by boat or plane and, like Vargas Island, is partly protected by partial provincial park status. At the aboriginal peoples' community of Ahousaht you can pick up the Ahousaht Wild Side Heritage Trail ($20 fee unless staying at the *Hummingbird* hostel on the island; see p.515), which runs for 16km through idyllic beach and forest scenery to the Mount Flores viewpoint (886m). This is also a chance to encounter aboriginal culture and people at first hand, with **tours** accompanied by local guides available: see the Tofino infocentre or call ⓣ250/725-3309 for details and information on trail conditions.

Perhaps the best, and certainly one of the most popular trips from Tofino, is the 37-kilometre boat or plane ride to **Hot Springs Cove**, site of one of only a handful of hot springs on Vancouver Island. This takes an hour by water-taxi (ⓣ250/726-8631; from $65) and 15 minutes by float plane with Tofino Air (ⓣ250/725-4454, ⓦwww.tofinoair.ca; from $85), though the most cost-effective way of seeing the island is to take a day tour with one of Tofino's many operators, most of which also offer whale watching en route (from $85). A thirty-minute trek from the landing stage brings you to the springs, which emerge at a piping 43°C (109°F) and run, as a creek, to the sea via a small waterfall and four pools, becoming progressively cooler. Be prepared for something of a crowd in summer when swimming costumes can be optional. An expensive hotel, the *Hot Springs Lodge* – a way to beat other punters by getting in an early-morning or late-night dip – sits on the cove near the landing stage (see "Accommodation" on p.514). Finally, a forty-kilometre trip north takes you to **Hesquiat Peninsula**, where you land at or near Refuge Cove, site of a Hesquiat aboriginal village. Locals offer tours here and some lodgings: ask for the latest details at the Tofino infocentre. The infocentre is also the place to pick up information on **tours**: otherwise, contact Seaside Adventures, 300 Main St (ⓣ250/725-2292 or 1-888/332-4252), Chinook Charters, 450 Campbell St (ⓣ250/725-3431 or 1-800/665-3646), or the whale-watching companies listed under "Activities" on p.516, most of whom also offer boat tours to the above destinations.

Ucluelet and around

UCLUELET, 8km south of the main Hwy-4 Port Alberni junction, means "People of the Sheltered Bay," from the aboriginal word *ucluth* – "wind blowing in from the bay." It was named by the Nuu-chah-nulth, who lived here for centuries before the arrival of whites who exploited some of the world's richest fishing grounds immediately offshore. Today the port is the third largest in BC by volume of fish landed, a trade that gives the town a slightly dispersed appearance and an industrial fringe – mainly lumber and canning concerns – and makes it a less appealing, if nonetheless popular base for anglers, whale watchers, water-sports enthusiasts, and tourists headed for Long Beach to the north.

Buses and **boats** call at Ucluelet from Port Alberni and Tofino – a local transit bus generally makes the road trip twice a day en route to and from Tofino and/or Port Alberni, with one Laidlaw connection daily from Port Alberni to Nanaimo and Victoria. Boats from Port Alberni usually dock here three days a week (see p.509). A car or bike is useful here, as there's relatively little in the small central area, though location isn't vital unless you want to be near the sea. For full details, plus information on the many whale-watching, fishing, and other tours, visit the **infocentre** at the main junction of Hwy-4 (daily mid-May to early Sept daily 10am–6pm, ⓣ250/726-7289, ⓦwww.uclueletinfo.com).

Practicalities

The most unusual **hotel** in town is the popular *Canadian Princess Resort* (ⓣ250/726-7771 or 1-800/ 663-7090, ⓦwww.canadianprincess.com; ❺–❽; March–Sept) at 1943 Peninsula Rd just west of the center, a hotel with on-shore rooms or good-value one- to six-berth cabins (the smallest rooms share bathrooms) in a 175-metre 1932 West-Coast steamer moored in the harbor. You can also book upmarket whale-watching and fishing trips here in big, comfortable cabin cruisers, and it has a restaurant and bar open to nonresidents. The two key inexpensive central choices are the *Pacific Rim Motel*, 1755 Peninsula Rd (ⓣ250/726-7728, ⓔdcorlazz@island.net; ❹), a place between the harbor and small center near the corner of Bay Street, and the *Peninsula Motor Inn*, a short way east across the road at 1648 Peninsula Rd (ⓣ250/726-7751 or 1-888/368-5593; ❹). Another well-located option is the *Island West Fishing Resort* overlooking the boat basin and marina at 160 Hemlock St (ⓣ250/726-4624, ⓦwww.islandwestresort.com; ❹): it has a pub on site for drinks and food and also organizes fishing charters and tours. Right at the end of Peninsula Road up by the lighthouse are two good **B&B** options: *Spring Cove B&B*, 963 Peninsula Rd (ⓣ250/726-2955, ⓦwww.springbeach.com; ❹–❼), a quiet oceanfront place with three rooms at varying prices (shared bathroom), and *Ocean's Edge B&B*, 855 Barkley Crescent (ⓣ250/726-7099, ⓦwww.oceansedge.bc.ca; ❺), a three-room place in old-growth forest with views and private entrance and bathroom.

The **public campsite** (ⓣ250/726-4355, ⓦwww.islandwestresort.com; $18–30; April–Oct) overlooks the harbor at 260 Seaplane Base Rd (first right off Peninsula Road after the *Canadian Princess*) to the west of the center and has washroom and shower facilities. The central *Island West Fishing Resort* (see above) also has an RV campsite. It is also the base for a wide range of tour and charter operators.

Seafood here is as fresh as it comes, and is best sampled at *Smiley's* just a little west from the *Canadian Princess* at 1992 Peninsula Rd (ⓣ250/726-4213): a no-frills, no-decor diner popular with locals (eat in or take out), and to work off the meal there's five-pin bowling and billiards here as well. For coffee and snacks head for *Blueberries Café* (ⓣ250/726-7707) on the strip in town at 1627 Peninsula Rd. It also serves breakfast, lunch, and dinner, is licensed, and has an outdoor patio with sea views. Other popular spots are the pub-restaurant at the *Canadian Princess* and the *Peninsula Restaurant* (ⓣ250/726-7751) by the *Peninsula Motor Inn* (see above) for inexpensive Chinese and Canadian food.

Activities

Just outside of town, the scenic **Wild Pacific Trail** opened in 1999, though then it consisted of just 2.7km of path. Planned in seven phases, only phases three and four have currently been completed, running along the jagged cliffs and shoreline northwest of the town. When the trail is finished it will stretch 14km and link with Halfmoon Bay near Florencia Bay and Long Beach in the national park. The trailhead is located at the end of Coast Guard Road, passing the nearby Amphirite Point Lighthouse (great views of the ocean and perfect for storm watching) and the He-Tin-Kis Park, where a boardwalk enables you to complete this first section as a loop. Other completed phases have pushed the track from Big Beach Park to the bike path just outside Ucluelet itself.

Many companies are on hand to offer whale-watching, fishing, and sightseeing **tours**. The longest-established outfit in the region is here, Subtidal Adventures, 1950 Peninsula Rd at the corner of Norah Road (ⓣ250/726-7336). They run all the usual boat trips in Zodiacs or a ten-metre former coast-guard rescue vessel, and do a nature tour to the Broken Group Islands with a beach stop.

The Broken Group Islands

The only way for the ordinary traveler to approach the hundred or so **BROKEN GROUP ISLANDS**, speckled across Barkley Sound between Ucluelet and Bamfield, is by sea plane, chartered boat, or boat tours from Port Alberni or Ucluelet (see p.509 and opposite); boats dock at Sechart, where you can stay at the former whaling station (see below). Immensely wild and beautiful, the islands have the reputation for tremendous wildlife (seals, sea lions, and whales especially), the best **canoeing** in North America, and some of the continent's finest **scuba diving**. You can hire canoes and gear – contact the *Lady Rose* office in Port Alberni or Sea Kayaking at 320 Main St, Tofino (ⓣ250/725-4222), and then take them on board the *Lady Rose* to be dropped

Nuu-chah-nulth whale hunts

All the peoples of the Northwest coast are famed for their skilfully constructed canoes, but only the **Nuu-chah-nulth** – whose name translates roughly as "all along the mountains" – used their fragile cedar crafts to pursue whales, an activity once accompanied by elaborate ritual. Before embarking on a whaling expedition the whalers had to not only be trained in the art of capturing these mighty animals but also required purification through a rigorous program of fasting, sexual abstinence, and bathing. Whalers also visited forest shrines made up of a whale image surrounded by human skulls or corpses and carved wooden representations of deceased whalers – the dead were thought to aid the novice in his task and to bring about the beaching of dead whales near the village.

When the whaler was on the chase, his wife would lie motionless in her bed; it was hoped that the whale would become equally docile. His crew propelled the canoe in total silence until the moment of the harpooning, whereupon they frantically back-paddled to escape the animal's violent death throes as it attempted to dive, only to be thwarted by a long line of floats made from inflated sea-lion skins. After exhausting itself, the floating whale was finally killed and boated back to the village, where its meat would be eaten and its blubber processed for its highly prized oil.

off en route (check current arrangements). It's imperative that you know what you're doing, however, as there's plenty of dangerous water, and you should pick up the marine chart *Canadian Hydrographic Service Chart: Broken Group* 3670, available locally or from the CHS in Sidney (☎250/363-6358). Divers can choose from among fifty shipwrecks claimed by the reefs, rough waters, and heavy fogs that beset the aptly named islands. Because of the sheer number of people now visiting the islands, measures are being considered to introduce a quota system: contact the park information center for details (see p.513).

The *Sechart Whaling Station Lodge* (book by calling ☎250/723-8313 or 1-800/663-7192; ⑤) is a potentially magical base for exploring and the only place to **stay** if you're not wilderness camping on the archipelago. Access is via the MV *Lady Rose*, which docks nearby (see p.509 for detailed schedule to the islands). Seven rough **campsites** also serve the group, but water is hard to come by; pick up the park leaflet on camping and freshwater locations.

Bamfield

BAMFIELD is a quaint spot, half-raised above the ocean on a wooden boardwalk, accessible by unpaved road from Port Alberni 102km to the northeast, by boat – the MV *Lady Rose* – or gravel road from Lake Cowichan 113km to the east. Shuttle **buses** run along the Port Alberni road route if you're without transport and don't want to take the boat: for details, see p.508. The village is best known as the northern starting point of this trail (the trailhead is 5km away at Pachena Bay), but its population jumps to well over 2000 in the summer with the arrival of divers, canoeists, kayakers, and fishermen, the last attracted by its suitability as a base for salmon fishing in the waters of Alberni Inlet and Barkley Sound. Plenty of services have sprung up in the more downbeat part of the village away from the boardwalk to meet visitors' demands, with lots of tours, fishing charters, stores, and galleries, but only relatively limited accommodation (see opposite).

However, the village retains its charm, with the boardwalk accessing one side of Bamfield Inlet (the open sea, the other), so that the bay below the boardwalk is a constant hum of activity as boats ply across the water. Trails lead down from the boardwalk to a series of nice small beaches. For a short stroll, wander to **Brady's Beach** or the Cape Beale Lighthouse and Keeha and Tapaltos beaches some way beyond. And if you just want to tackle the stage to the trailhead of the West Coast Trail and return to Bamfield in a day, you can walk the 10km (round-trip) to the **Pachena Lighthouse**, starting from the Ross Bible Camp on the Ohiaht First Nation campsite at Pachena Beach. After that, the route becomes the real thing.

Practicalities

Bamfield's **infocentre** booth is in Centennial Park (Ⓣ250/728-3006, Ⓦwww.bamfieldcommunity.com or www.bamfieldchamber.com), but is open daily (9am–7/8pm) only in July and August. The village has only limited and mainly expensive **accommodation**. If you think you'll need a bed, definitely make reservations, especially at the small *Seabeam Fishing Resort and Campground* overlooking Grappler Inlet, which runs as a campsite and a small hostel-like hotel with eight rooms (Ⓣ250/728-3286; ❶, tent and RV sites $18–20; May–Oct) and phone for directions or for a taxi pick-up. The setting is tranquil, and the resort has a small kitchen, common room with open fire, and sixteen beds arranged as one-, two-, or three-bed dorms. Price is $30 per person.

Otherwise try the *Bamfield Inn*, Customs House Lane, a **lodge** built in 1923 overlooking Bamfield Harbour, Barkley Sound, and the islands (Ⓣ250/728-3354; ❻; Feb–Oct): annex rooms are available at a slightly lower price. The modest *McKay Bay Lodge* (Ⓣ250/728-3323; ❹; May–Oct) also overlooks the harbor and is good for families and fishing enthusiasts. Another option is the excellent *Woods End Landing Cottages*, 168 Wild Duck Rd, which has six secluded and high-quality self-contained log cottages sleeping up to four people on a two-acre waterfront site with great opportunities for outdoor activities, birdwatching, scuba diving, and kayaking (Ⓣ250/728-3383; ❼). **B&B** options open and close each year – currently there are four: first choices for location and pretty setting are *Marie's*, 468 Pachena Rd (Ⓣ250/728-3091 or 728-2000; ❹; no credit cards), just a stroll from the center, and *West Coast Magic*, 286 Brady's Beach Trail (Ⓣ250/728-3132, Ⓦwww.westcoastmagic.com; ❺), a 15-minute walk from the village in the rainforest on a bluff overlooking the ocean.

If you're **camping**, try the *Ohiaht First Nation Pachena Bay* campsite (Ⓣ250/728-1287, Ⓔpachena@island.net; call for reservations, which are essential, and for latest prices) at Pachena Beach. You can also camp at *Centennial Park* (Ⓣ250/728-3006) and at the *Seabeam Fishing Resort* (Ⓣ250/728-3286, Ⓔseabeamcanada@hotmail.com; $18–20; May–Sept), just on the edge of Bamfield on Tower Road.

The West Coast Trail

One of North America's classic treks, the **West Coast Trail** starts 5km south of Bamfield and traverses exceptional coastal scenery for 77km to Port Renfrew. It's no leisurely stroll, and though now quite popular – quotas operate to restrict numbers – it still requires experience of longer hikes, proper equipment, and a fair degree of fitness. Many people, however, do the first easy stage as a day-trip from Bamfield. Count on five to eight days for the full trip; carry all your own food, camp where you can, and be prepared for rain, treacherous stretches, thick soaking forest, and almost utter isolation.

As originally conceived, the trail had nothing to do with promoting the great outdoors. Mariners long ago dubbed this area of coastline the "graveyard of the Pacific," and when the SS *Valencia* went down with all hands here in 1906 the government was persuaded that constructing a trail would at least give stranded sailors a chance to walk to safety along the coast (trying to penetrate the interior's rainforest was out of the question). Many thousands now make the trip annually, and the numbers, so far as quotas allow, are rising (see below). The trail passes through the land of the Pacheenaht First Nation near Port Renfrew, passing through Ditidaht First Nation country before ending at Bamfield in the traditional territory of the Ohiaht First Nation. Wardens from each of these tribes work in association with Parks Canada to oversee the trail's management and the care of traditional native villages and fishing areas.

Weather is a key factor in planning any trip; the trail is really only passable between June and September (July is the driest month), which is also the only period when it's patrolled by wardens and the only time locals are on hand to ferry you (for a fee) across some of the wider rivers en route. However, you should be prepared for dreadful weather and poor trail conditions at all times.

Practicalities

Pre-planning is essential if you wish to walk the trail, as Parks Canada have a **quota system** and reservation-registration-orientation procedure to protect the environment. Numbers are limited to around 8000 a year while the path is open (mid-April/May to end Sept). A total of 52 people are allowed onto the trail each day: 26 starting at Port Renfrew center (Gordon River trailhead is 5km north of the town; trailhead infocentre ⓣ250/647-5434; daily in season 9am–6pm), 26 at Bamfield-Pachena Bay (trail starts 5km south of Bamfield; infocentre ⓣ250/728-3234, daily in season 9am–6pm), and eight from Nitinat Village. These are the *only* allowed entrance and exit points from the trail except in exceptional circumstances.

Note that the quota system does not apply in the shoulder season (May–mid-June & last two weeks of Sept), as Parks Canada found the quotas were not being taken up. However, it still makes sense to reserve the necessary West Coast Trail (WTC) Overnight Use Permit – effectively your passport to the trail and its ferry crossings – in these periods.

Reservations can made from April of the year you wish to walk for June departures, May 1 for July departures, June 1 for August departures, and July 1 for September walks. The phones start ringing on the first of the month, so move fast. To make bookings, call ⓣ250/387-1642 or 1-800/435-5622 (Mon–Fri 7am–9pm). Be ready to nominate the location from which you wish to start, the date of departure, two alternative start dates, credit card details, and the number in your party. July and August are clearly the most popular months.

It **costs** $25 to make a reservation (payment by Visa or MasterCard). This is nonrefundable, though you may change your date of departure if spaces are available on another day. Another $90 per person is payable as a user fee, paid in person at the beginning of the trail. Allow another $14 to pay for each of the two ferry crossings (at Gordon River and Nitinat narrows) along the route (paid at the WCT centers at the orientation sesssion – see below: the WTC Overnight Permit is your receipt for these crossings), bringing the total to $143. Standby hikers pay the same rates minus the booking fee, a total of $118. You must then register in person at the park center at Bamfield or Port Renfrew between 9am and 12.30pm on the day you have booked to start your walk. (You may want to arrive the night before – if so, be sure to book accommodation in Bamfield if you're starting there: see below.) If you miss this deadline your place is forfeited and will be given to someone on the **waiting list**.

Of the 52 places available each day at Pachena Bay and Gordon River, a minimum of ten (five at each departure point) are available on a first-come-first-served basis. Unless you're very lucky this still doesn't mean you can just turn up and expect to start walking. You must first register in person at either the Port Renfrew or Bamfield center. Here you'll be given a waiting-list number and told when to come back, which could be anything between two and ten days.

Finally, you need to attend compulsory 90-minute **orientation** sessions at the trailhead infocentre, where you will receive your permit and a briefing on conditions, safety issues, and so forth. Gordon River sessions are at 9.30am, noon, 1.30pm, and 3.30pm; at Pachena Bay they take place at 9.30am, 1.30pm, and 3.30pm. Reservations are not required.

Further **information** regarding the trail, path conditions, and preplanning can be obtained from the Parks Canada offices near Port Renfrew at the trailhead (Ⓣ250/647-5434), or from the infocentres in Tofino, Ucluelet, Long Beach, or Port Alberni. Updated details are also given at Ⓦwww.parkscanada.gc.ca. An increasing amount of literature and **route guides** are appearing on the trail every year, available directly or by mail order from most BC bookshops. Two of the best are *The West Coast Trail* by Tim Leaden (Douglas and McIntyre; $12.95) and the more irreverent *Blisters and Bliss: A Trekker's Guide to the West Coast Trail* by Foster, Aiteken and Dewey (B&B Publishing Victoria; $10.95). The recommended **trail map** is the 1:50,000 *West Coast Trail, Port Renfrew–Bamfield*, complete with useful hints for walking the trail, available locally or direct from the Ministry of the Environment, 553 Superior St, Victoria (Ⓣ250/387-1441).

Access to and from the trailheads is also an important consideration. Several small shuttle-bus companies have sprung up to run people to the trailheads, mostly from Victoria to Bamfield via Nanaimo, not all of which are likely to survive (consult the Victoria infocentre for latest updates). For the northern trailhead at Bamfield, the most exhilarating and reliable access is via the MV *Lady Rose* or other boats from Port Alberni (see p.509 for full details). Otherwise the West Coast Trail Express, (see box, p.498) 3954 Bow Rd, Victoria (May to early Oct; Ⓣ250/477-8700) runs a daily shuttle bus in each direction between Victoria and Pachena Bay/Bamfield via Duncan, Nanaimo; to Port Renfrew and back from Victoria; and between Bamfield and Port Renfrew (see p.534 for details). Pick-ups are possible from these points, but reservations are essential to secure a seat from any departure point. They also have a daily service to Port Renfrew. Western Bus Lines, 4521 10th Ave, Port Alberni (Ⓣ250/723-3341), also runs a service on Monday and Friday along the 100-kilometre gravel road from Port Alberni to the Bamfield.

Northern Vancouver Island

It's a moot point where **northern Vancouver Island** starts, but if you're traveling on Hwy-19 the landscape's sudden lurch into more unspoilt wilderness after Qualicum Beach makes as good a watershed as any. The scenery north of Qualicum Beach is uneventful but restful, and graced with ever-improving views of the mainland. Few of the towns along Hwy-19 amount to much, and you could bus, drive, or hitch the length ofVancouver Island to Port Hardy and take the **Inside Passage** ferry up to Prince Rupert – the obvious and most tantalizing itinerary – without missing a lot. Alternatively, you could follow the main highway only as far as Courtenay, and from there catch a ferry across to the mainland. If you have the means, however, try to get into the wild, central interior, much of it contained within **Strathcona Provincial Park**.

Denman and Hornby islands

North along Hwy-19 from Qualicum Beach is the hamlet of Buckley Bay, which consists of little more than a ferry terminal to **DENMAN** and **HORNBY** islands. These two outposts have been described, with some justification, as the "undiscovered Gulf Islands". Big-name celebrities have recently bought property here, complementing a population made up of artists, craftspeople, and a laid-back (if wary) mishmash of alternative types.

Ferries drop you on Denman on the west coast a few moments' walk from Denman Village: to get to Hornby you need to head 11km across Denman on Denman Road to another terminal at Gravelly Bay, where a fifteen-minute crossing ($5/$4.75 return for foot passengers, $12.25/$10.50 return for a car) drops you at Hornby's Shingle Spit dock. Most of what happens on Hornby, however, happens at **Tribune Bay** on the far side of the island, 10km away – try hitching a lift from a car coming off the ferry if you're without transport. There's no public transport on either island, so you'll need a car or bike to explore.

Highlights on Denman, the less retrogressive of the islands, are the beaches of the **Sandy Island Provincial Marine Park**, an island off the northwest tip (take Northwest Road from the village), and the 800-metre loop trail of Boyle Point Park at the southernmost tip (just beyond the Gravelly Bay ferry terminal) to the Chrome Island Lighthouse. A left turn off Denman Road about 4km, or a third of the way to the terminal, brings you to Fillongley Provincial Park, where there's a provincial campsite (see below), forest trails, and a pretty stretch of coastline.

On sleepy Hornby you'll want to explore the **Helliwell Bay Provincial Park** at the island's southern tip (take Helliwell Road from Tribune Bay) and its trails, the best a six-kilometre (1hr–1hr 30min) loop to Helliwell Bluffs, offering plenty of opportunities to see eagles, herons, spring wild flowers, and lots of aquatic wildlife. Whaling Station Bay and Tribune Bay Provincial Park have very good beaches (and there's a nudist beach at Little Tribune Bay just to the south of the latter), with a campsite (see below) at Tribune Bay..

Practicalities

Accommodation is in short supply on both islands, and it's virtually essential in summer to have prebooked rooms. On Denman the main options are the *Sea Canary Bed & Breakfast*, 3305 Kirk Road (Ⓣ250/335-2949; ❺), close to the ferry terminal (turn left on Northwest Rd then left again on Kirk) with three **guestrooms**, and the *Hawthorn House Bed and Breakfast*, 3375 Kirk Rd (Ⓣ250/335-0905; ❹), a restored 1904 heritage building also with three rooms. There's a small (10-site), rural provincial park **campsite** at Fillongley Provincial Park, close to old-growth forest and pebbly beach 4km across the island from the ferry on the east shore facing the Lambert Channel (summer $17, winter $9).

Hornby has more **rooms** and **campsites**: *Sea Breeze Lodge*, Big Tree 3–2, Fowler Road (Ⓣ250/335-2321, Ⓦwww.seabreezelodge.com; ❺), with fifteen waterfront cottages with sea views; *Hornby Island Resort*, Shingle Spit Road (Ⓣ250/335-0136; ❸, tents $19), with four waterfront cabins and nine camp sites, tennis court, boat rental, pub, waterfront restaurant – a good place to **eat** – and sandy beach; *Days Gone By at Bradsdadsland Campsite*, 1980 Shingle Spit Rd (Ⓣ250/335-0757, Ⓦwww.daysgoneby.org; tents $23–36; May–Oct), 3.3km from the ferry terminal; *Ford's Cove Marina* at Ford's Cove, 12km from the ferry at Government Wharf (Ⓣ335-2169; cottages generally let weekly, tents $18–24), with six fully equipped cottages, grocery store, and camp and RV sites; and the big *Tribune Bay Campsite*, Shields Road (Ⓣ250/335-2359, Ⓦwww.tribunebay.com; $18–25; April–Oct), a treed site close to a sandy beach and with hot showers, restaurant, and bike rental.

Eating places on Denman are concentrated near the ferry, the best being the *Denman Island Store and Café*. At the ferry dock on Hornby is *The Thatch*, a tourist-oriented restaurant, pub, and deli with great views. Across at Tribune Bay the Co-op (no street address) is the hub of island life, with virtually everything you'll need in the way of food and supplies (Ⓣ250/335-1121). There's a café, *Jan's*, and a bike-rental outlet here, the Off-Road Bike Shop, which rents bikes in summer. For further **information** on Hornby, including accommodation, call Ⓣ250/335-0506 or visit Ⓦwww.hornbyisland.com.

Campbell River

Another of the hundred or so Canadian towns that claim to be "Salmon Capital of the World," **CAMPBELL RIVER**, is probably the one that comes closest to justifying the boast. Fish and fishing dominate the place to a ludicrous degree, and you'll soon be heartily sick of pictures of grinning anglers holding impossibly huge chinook salmon. Massive shoals of these monsters are forced into the three-kilometre channel between the town and the mainland, making the job of catching them little more than a formality. More than half of all the town's visitors come to dangle a line in the water. Others come for the scuba diving, while for the casual visitor the place serves as the main road access to the wilds of Strathcona Provincial Park (see overleaf) or an overnight stop en route for the morning departures of the MV *Uchuck III* from Gold River (see p.528).

If you want to **fish**, hundreds of shops and guides are on hand to help out and hire equipment. It'll cost about $25 a day for the full kit, and about $60 and upwards for a morning's guidance. Huge numbers of people, however, fish ($2 plus license) from the 182-metre **Discovery Pier**, Canada's first saltwater fishing pier. If you want to learn about salmon before they end up on a plate, visit the **Quinsam Salmon Hatchery**, 5km west of town on the road to Gold River (daily 8am–4pm).

Campbell River's well-stocked **infocentre** is at 1235 Shopper's Row (daily 9am–6pm; Ⓣ250/287-4636, Ⓦwww.campbellriverchamber.ca). Four Laidlaw **buses** run daily to Victoria, but there's only one, occasionally two, a day north to Port Hardy and towns en route. Airlines big and small also **fly** here (see Vancouver "Listings" on p.458 for details). The **bus terminal** is on the corner of Cedar and 13th near the Royal Bank (Ⓣ250/287-7151). **Accommodation** is no problem, with numerous motels, Campbell River being a resort first and foremost: try the *Super 8 Motel*, 340 S Island Hwy, on the main road south of town (Ⓣ250/286-6622 or 1-800/800-8000, Ⓦwww.super8.com; ❹), or the carving-stuffed *Campbell River Lodge and Fishing Resort,* a kilometre north of the town center at 1760 N Island Hwy (Ⓣ250/287-7446 or 1-800/663-7212, Ⓦwww.campbellriverinns.com; ❹). You won't be able to escape the fishing clutter common to all hotels unless you head for a **B&B**. Contact the infocentre for listings, or try *Pier House B&B*, 670 Island Hwy (Ⓣ250/287-2943,

Ⓔpierhse@island.net; ❹), a three-room 1920s antique-filled heritage home in downtown right by the fishing pier. The place to **camp** locally lies 5km west of town at the *Parkside Campground*, 6301 Gold River Hwy (Ⓣ250/830-1428; $16-22; May–Oct).

Cheap **places to eat** abound, mainly of the fast-food variety, and in the pricier restaurants there's no prize for spotting the main culinary emphasis.

Quadra Island

QUADRA ISLAND and its fine beaches and museum are fifteen minutes away from Campbell River and make a nice respite from the fish, though the famous fishing lodge here has been host to such big-name fisherfolk over the years as John Wayne, Kevin Costner, and Julie Andrews. The main excuse for the crossing is the **Kwagiulth Museum and Cultural Centre**, in Cape Mudge Village south of the terminal near the island's southern tip (take Cape Mudge Road). The island's other, and main community, Heriot Bay, is on the east coast. The center is home to one of the country's most noted collections of aboriginal regalia (closed for renovation; call for latest opening information Ⓣ250/285-3733). As elsewhere in Canada, the masks, costumes, and ritual objects were confiscated by the government in 1922 in an attempt to stamp out one of the natives' most potent ceremonies; they only came back in the 1980s on condition they would be locked up in a museum. The museum has around three hundred articles, and you should also ask directions to the petroglyphs in the small park across the road.

While on the island you could also laze on its beaches, walk its **trails** – Mortle Lake (5km loop) and Newton Lake from Granite Bay (8km round-trip) – or climb Chinese Mountain (3km round-trip) in its rugged northern reaches for some cracking views. There's swimming in a warm, sheltered bay off a rocky beach at **Rebecca Spit Provincial Park**, a 1.5-kilometre spit near Drew Harbour 8km east of the ferry terminal, but the water's warmer still and a trifle sandier at the more distant **Village Bay Park**. Pick up trail **maps**, information, and **bike rentals** at Island Cycle (Ⓣ250/285-3627, Ⓦwww.kayak-adventures.com) in Heriot Bay at 651 Taku Rd, part of the main center for tours, hikes, kayaking, and other outdoor activities on the island.

Around seven places offer **accommodation**, including the *Heriot Bay Inn & Marina* on Heriot Bay Road (Ⓣ250/285-3322, Ⓦwww.heriotbayinn.com; ❹–❻, camping from $14–20), which has cottages, camping, and RV sites, and the superb *Tsa-Kwa-Luten Lodge*, 1 Lighthouse Rd (Ⓣ250/285-2042 or 1-800/665-7745, Ⓦwww.capemudgeresort.bc.ca; ❺), a waterfront lodge by the Cape Mudge Lighthouse. Based on a longhouse, and with a predominantly aboriginal decorative scheme and design, it was built by local aboriginal people amid 440ha of forest on high bluffs overlooking Discovery Passage. There is a restaurant, cottage and lodge units, and many facilities including sauna, Jacuzzi, laundry, and access to numerous tours and outdoor activities. The island's only official **campsite** is at the *Heriot Bay Inn* (see above).

Strathcona Provincial Park

Vancouver Island's largest protected area (250,000 hectacres), and the oldest park in British Columbia, **STRATHCONA PROVINCIAL PARK** (established in 1911) is one of the few places on the island where the scenery approaches the grandeur of the mainland mountains. The island's highest point,

Golden Hinde (2220m) is here, and it's also a place where there's a good chance of seeing indigenous wildlife (the Roosevelt elk, marmot, and black-tailed deer are the most notable examples). Only two areas have any sort of facilities for the visitor – **Forbidden Plateau** on the park's eastern side, approached from Courtenay, and the more popular **Buttle Lake** region, accessible from Campbell River via Hwy-28. The rest of the park is unsullied wilderness, but fully open to backpackers and hardy walkers. Be sure to pick up the blue *BC Parks* pamphlet (available from the infocentre at Campbell River and elsewhere): it has a good general map and gives lots of information, such as the comforting fact that there are no grizzly bears in the park. You'll see numerous pictures of **Della Falls**, around Campbell River, which (at 440m) are Canada's highest (and amongst the world's highest), though unfortunately it'll take a two-day trek and a canoe passage if you're going to see them.

The approach to the park along Hwy-28 is worth taking for the scenery alone; numerous short trails are signposted from rest stops, most no more than twenty-minutes' stroll from the car. **Elk Falls Provincial Park**, noted for its gorge and waterfall, is the first stop, ten minutes out of Campbell River. It also has a large provincial park **campsite** (summer $14, winter $9; backcountry camping $5). On the access road and lakeshore proper, good **shorter trails** include the 500-metre stroll to Lupin Falls, an impressive cataract; the Karst Creek Trail (2km loop), which runs through a strange limestone landscape of sinkholes and vanishing streams; Bedwell Lake at the lake's southern end, a steep (600-metre ascent) ten-kilometre round-trip trail to the eponymous lake and high meadows (allow 2hr each way); and Upper Myra Falls (3km each way), which climbs from near the end of the road to a viewpoint over the Myra waterfall.

Hiking in Strathcona

Hiking, it hardly needs saying, is superb in Strathcona, with a jaw-dropping scenic combination of jagged mountains – including Golden Hinde (2220m), the island's highest point – lakes, rivers, waterfalls, and all the trees you could possibly want. Seven marked **trails** fan out from the Buttle Lake area, together with six shorter nature walks, most of which are less than 2km long, and among which the Lady Falls and Lupin Falls trails stand out for their waterfall and forest views (see main text). All the longer trails can be tramped in a day, though the most popular, the **Elk River Trail** (10km), which starts from Drum Lake on Hwy-28, lends itself to an overnight stop. Popular with backpackers because of its gentle grade, the path ends up at Landslide Lake, an idyllic camping spot. The other highly regarded trail is the **Flower Ridge** walk, a steep 14-kilometre round-trip (extendable by 10km) that starts at the southern end of Buttle Lake and involves a stiff 1250-metre elevation gain. The same lung-busting ascent is called for on the **Crest Mountain Trail** (10km round trip), a trail into high mountain country accessed from Hwy-28 at the park's western edge.

In the Forbidden Plateau area, named after a native legend that claimed evil spirits lay in wait to devour women and children who entered its precincts, the most popular trip is the **Forbidden Plateau Skyride** to the summit of Wood Mountain where there's a two-kilometre trail to a viewpoint over Boston Canyon. Backcountry camping is allowed throughout the park, and the backpacking is great once you've hauled up onto the summit ridges above the tree line. For serious exploration, buy the relevant topographic maps (1:50,000 -92F/11 *Forbidden Plateau* and -92F/12 *Buttle Lake* at MAPS BC, Ministry of Environment and Parks, Parliament Buildings, Victoria.

Fifteen **information shelters** around the lake provide some trail and wildlife information. Buttle Lake has two provincial **campsites** with basic facilities – one alongside the park center at Buttle Lake, the other at Ralph River (both summer $14, winter $9) on the extreme southern end of Buttle Lake, accessed by the road along the lake's eastern shore. Both have good **swimming** areas nearby. Backcountry camping costs $5.

The park's only commercial **accommodation** is provided by the *Strathcona Park Lodge* (Ⓣ250/286-3122, Ⓦwww.strathcona.bc.ca; ❹–❼), just outside the Buttle Lake entrance, a mixture of hotel and outdoor-pursuits center. You can **rent canoes**, **bikes**, and other outdoor equipment, and sign up for any number of organized tours and activities.

Gold River and around

There's not a lot happening in **GOLD RIVER**, a tiny logging community west of Strathcona – founded in 1965 to service a big pulp mill 12km away at Muchalat Inlet (it closed in 1998). The place only has one hotel and a couple of shops – but the ride over on Hwy-28 is superb, and there's the chance to explore the sublime coastline by boat, the main reason for the settlement's increasing number of visitors.

Accommodation in Gold River is in short supply: the only sizeable place is the *Ridgeview Motor Inn*, in a panoramic spot above the village at 395 Donner Court (Ⓣ250/283-2277 or 1-800/989-3393, Ⓦwww.ridgeview-inn.com; ❹). The *Peppercorn Trail Motel and Campground* on Mill Road (Ⓣ250/283-2443, Ⓦwww.peppercorn.bc.ca) offers ten rooms, as well as a 75-pitch **campsite** ($18–25). There is one **B&B**, the three-room *Shadowlands*, 580 Dogwood Drive (Ⓣ250/283-2513, Ⓔgravesite@telus.net; ❸).

The MV Uchuck III

Year-round, the **MV Uchuck III**, a converted World War II US minesweeper, takes mail, cargo, and passengers to logging camps and settlements up and down the surrounding coast on a variety of routes. For information and **reservations**, contact Nootka Sound Service Ltd (Ⓣ250/283-2325 or 283-2515, Ⓦwww.mvuchuck.com).

There are **three basic routes**, all of them offering wonderful windows onto the wilderness and wildlife (whales, bears, bald eagles, and more) of the region's inlets, islands, and forested mountains. The dock is at the end of Hwy-28, about 15km southwest of Gold River. The **Tahsis Day-Trip** ($45) departs at 9am every Tuesday year-round for the small logging community Tahsis, (arriving at 1pm), returning after a one-hour stopover to Gold River at 6pm. The shorter **Nootka Sound Day-Trip** ($40) leaves Gold River every Wednesday at 10am July to mid-September only (returning at 4.30pm), with longer stops at Resolution Sound and Kyuquot (the native word for "Friendly Cove"), the latter involving a $9 landing fee, proceeds from which go to the Mowachaht Band for the redevelopment of the aboriginal site. During the ninety-minute halt aboriginal guides offer a guided tour around their ancestral home. The previous stop, at Friendly Cove, is equally historic, for it was here that Captain Cook made his first-known landing on the West Coast in 1778, from which, among other things, was to spring the important sea-otter fur trade. Whites named the area and people here "Nootka" – though locals today say *nootka* was merely a word of warning to Cook and his crew, meaning "circle around" to avoid hitting offshore rocks. If you're equipped with provisions and wish to stay over, there are **cabins** and a **campsite** here, but call first to confirm arrangements (Ⓣ250/283-2054). The third trip, the **Kyuquot Adventure** ($195 single, $310 double), is a two-day overnight cruise, departing every Thursday year-round (April–Oct 7am; Nov–March 6am). It takes you much further north up the coast, returning to Gold River at 4 or 5pm on Friday afternoon: accommodation is included, as is breakfast – though you make it yourself from food supplied – and you can buy Thursday's evening meal on board or onshore at Kyuquot. A 25 percent **deposit** is required for these trips, refundable in full up until two weeks before departure. People on all trips should bring warm and waterproof clothing. There's a coffee shop on board for drinks and hot snacks. **Kayakers** should note that they can be deposited by lift into the sea at most points en route by prior arrangement.

Boat aside, the area has two natural attractions that lure visitors from afar in their own right. The first is **Quatsino Cave**, the deepest vertical cave in North America, parts of which are open to the public. For details ask at the **infocentre** at the corner of Hwy-28 and Scout Lake Road (daily 9.30am–4/5pm mid-May to mid-Sept; Ⓣ250/283-2418 or 283-7500, Ⓦwww.village.goldriver.bc.ca). The other draw is the **Big Drop**, a class IV stretch of Gold River white water known to kayakers worldwide.

Telegraph Cove

North from Gold River and 8km south of Port McNeill, tiny **TELEGRAPH COVE**, reached by a rough side road, is a likeable place, though not quite the best of BC's so-called "boardwalk villages." Its growing popularity, and the fact that it is now pretty much owned by a single company, has given it a slightly artificial and commercialized air that is not evident in somewhere like Bamfield (see p.520). The whole community is raised on wooden stilts over the water, a sight that's made it rather too popular with tourists for its own good. This is not to take away from its role as one of the island's premier **whale-watching** spots, the main attraction here being the pods of orcas (killer whales) that calve locally. Some nineteen of these families live or visit Robson Bight, 20km down the Johnstone Strait, which was established as an ecological reserve in 1982 (the whales like the gravel beaches, where they come to rub). This is the world's most accessible and predictable spot to see the creatures – around a ninety percent chance in season. The best outfit for a trip to see them is the very popular Stubbs Island Charters at the dock at the end of the boardwalk (Ⓣ250/928-3185, 928-3117 or 1-800/665-3066, Ⓦwww.stubbs-island.com). They run up to five three- or five-hour trips daily (June–Oct; from $65); call well in advance to get a place.

In summer you can buy food at a café, boardwalk pub, and resort (see below), but otherwise the only provision for visitors is an incongruous modern building with shop, ice-cream counter, and coffee bar. The only **accommodation** is the large wooded *Telegraph Cove Resorts* (Ⓣ250/928-3131 or 1-800/200-4665, Ⓦwww.telegraphcoverresort.com; ❻, camping $19–24; May–Oct), a short walk from the village: reservations are essential in summer. It has 17 rooms and 121 RV/tent sites with showers, laundry, restaurant, boat rentals, and access to guides, charters, and whale-watching tours. The *Hidden Cove Lodge* (Ⓣ250/956-3916, Ⓦwww.hiddencovelodge.com; ❺–❼) at Lewis Point, a secluded cove on Johnstone Strait 7km from Telegraph Cove, has eight superb lodge units, but they go very quickly. The big *Alder Bay Campsite* 6km off Hwy-19 en route for Telegraph Cove from Port McNeill provides grassy tent sites with ocean views (Ⓣ250/956-4117, Ⓦwww.alderbayresort.com; reservations recommended; $17–26; May–Sept).

The Inside Passage

The **Inside Passage** aboard BC Ferries' *Queen of the North*, between Port Hardy and Prince Rupert on the British Columbia mainland, is a cheap way of getting what people on the big cruise ships are getting: 274 nautical miles of mountains, islands, waterfalls, glaciers, sea lions, whales, eagles, and some of the grandest coastal scenery on the continent. By linking up with the Greyhound bus network or the VIA Rail terminal at Prince Rupert, it also makes a good leg in any number of convenient itineraries around British Columbia. Some travelers will have come from Washington State, others will want to press on from Prince Rupert to Skagway by boat and then head north into Alaska and the Yukon (see p.342 for details on the Alaska Marine ferries). A lot of people simply treat it as a cruise, and sail north one day and return south to Port Hardy the next.

The boat carries 750 passengers and 160 cars and runs every two days, departing at 7.30am on **even-numbered days** in August, **odd-numbered days** in June, July, September, and the first half of October. Odd and even days swap for the return leg from Prince Rupert. The journey takes around fifteen hours, arriving in Prince Rupert about 10.30pm, sometimes with a stop at McLoughlin Bay and arrival at 11.30pm. Be aware that from about October 15 to May 25 the sailings are less frequent in both directions and are predominantly at night (they leave Port Hardy in the late afternoon), which rather defeats the sightseeing object of the trip. On board there are cafeterias, restaurants, and a shop (among other services).

The cost from mid-June to mid-September (peak) is $102.50 single for a foot passenger; $82 for a Peak Special (mid-May–mid-June and last two weeks of Sept), $54.25 low season (Jan–March) and $75.50 the rest of the year. Taking a car costs $241.50, Peak Special $193, $128 in low season and $170.50 the rest of the year; while taking a bike costs $6.50 year-round. Reservations are **essential** throughout the summer season if you're taking a car or want a cabin. Bookings can be made by phone (ⓣ1-888/223-3779 toll-free anywhere in BC, ⓣ250/386-3431 elsewhere, online at ⓦwww.bcferries.com), or by post to BC Ferry Corporation, 1112 Fort St, Victoria, BC V8V 4V2. Include name and address; number in party; length, height, and type of car; choice of cabin; and preferred date of departure and alternatives. Full payment is required up front. **Day cabins** can be reserved by foot passengers, and range from around $25 for two berths with basin, to $45 on the Promenade with two berths, basin, and toilet. If you are making the return trip only you can rent **cabins overnight**, saving the hassle of finding accommodation in Port Hardy, but if you do you are obliged to take the cabin for the following day's return trip as well. Cabins are not available as an alternative to rooms in town, so don't think you can rent a cabin overnight and then disappear next morning at Prince Rupert. Two-berth overnight cabins cost $50 one-way with basin and toilet only and $60 for shower, basin, and toilet.

If you're making a return trip and want to leave your car behind, there are several supervised lock-ups in Port Hardy. You can leave vehicles at the ferry terminal, but there have been incidents of vandalism in recent years: neither BC Ferries nor the Port Hardy infocentre seem to recommend the practice. Note, again, that it is vital to book accommodation at your final destination before start-

Alert Bay

The breezy fishing village of **ALERT BAY**, on Cormorant Island, is reached by numerous daily ferries from Port McNeill just 8km away (foot passenger ($5.50 return, car $13.75). The fifty-minute crossing in the migrating season provides a good chance of seeing whales en route. Despite the predominance

ing your trip; both Port Hardy and Prince Rupert hotels are very busy on days when the boat arrives.

The Discovery Coast Passage

The huge success of the Inside Passage sailing amongst visitors led BC Ferries to introduce the **Discovery Coast Passage**. The route offers many of the scenic rewards of the Inside Passage, but over a shorter and more circuitous route between Port Hardy and **Bella Coola**, where you pick up the occasionally steep and tortuous road (Hwy-20) through the Coast Mountains to Williams Lake – it goes nowhere else. En route, the boat, the *Queen of Chilliwack*, stops at McLoughlin Bay, Shearwater, Klemtu, and Ocean Falls (in the past the boat has also stopped at Namu as a request stop which must be booked in advance; check with BC Ferries for latest details). If the route takes off as BC Ferries hope, you can expect visitor facilities to mushroom at these places – you can disembark at all of them – but at present the only places to stay overnight are campsites at McLoughlin Bay and a resort, hotels, cabins, and B&B at Shearwater. Bella Coola is better equipped, and will probably become more so as the route becomes better known. BC Ferries is offering inclusive ferry and accommodation **packages** – even renting fishing tackle so you can fish over the side – and these too may mature as the service finds its feet.

Currently there are **departures** roughly every couple of days between late May and the end of September, leaving at 9.30am on Tues and Thurs and 9.30pm on Sat. There's a slight catch, however, for while the early morning departures offer you plenty of scenery, some arrive at McLoughlin Bay at 7.30pm and Bella Coola at 6.30am in the morning, meaning that the very best bit of the trip – along the inlet to Bella Coola – is in the middle of the night. The 9.30am departures are quicker (they don't stop en route) and make Bella Coola the same day, arriving at 10.30pm, so the problem is lessened. Alternatively take the 9.30pm departures and wake at McLoughlin Bay at 7am with a further daylight trip towards Bella Coola, arriving at 7.30am the next morning – read the timetables carefully. Making the trip southbound from Bella Coola gets round the problem, though there are similar staggered departure and arrival times (services currently leave Mon, Wed, and Fri at 7.30 or 8am, arriving Port Hardy 9pm on the Mon departure, 7.45am on Wed sailing and 9am on the Fri boat), with overnight and same-day journeys and a variety of stopping points depending on the day you travel. Unlike the Inside Passage, there are **no cabins**: you sleep in aircraft-style reclining seats and – for the time being – sleeping bags seem OK on the floor: check for the latest on freestanding tents on the decks.

Reservations can be made through BC Ferries (see Inside Passage, opposite, for details). **Prices** for a foot passenger are $106.25 one-way to Bella Coola, $63.75 to all other destinations. If you want to camp or stop over and hop on and off, the boat fares between any two of McLoughlin Bay, Ocean Falls, and Klemtu are $21.50 (except Shearwater to McLoughlin Bay: $5.25) and $39.50 from any of these to Bella Coola. Cars cost $212.50 from Port Hardy to Bella Coola, $135.75 to all other destinations ($43.50 and $77.25 respectively for the single-leg options). To take a **canoe** or **kayak** costs $12.75 stowage from Port Hardy to Bella Coola and between points en route. Taking a bike cost $6.50.

of the non-indigenous industries (mainly fish processing), half the population of the island are aboriginal 'Namgis, and a visit here offers the opportunity to get to grips with something of their history and to meet those who are keeping something of the old traditions alive. Be sure to have pre-booked accommodation (see below) before heading here in high season. The **infocentre** (late June–Aug daily 9am–6pm; rest of the year Mon–Fri 9am–5pm; ⓣ250/974-

5024, ⓦwww.alertbay.bc.ca) is at 116 Fir St to your right as you come off the ferry opposite the unmissable purple building. Also off to the right from the terminal are the totems of a 'Namgis Burial Ground: you're asked to view from a respectful distance.

Bear left from the terminal out of the main part of the village to reach the excellent **U'Mista Cultural Centre** on Front Street (mid-May to early Sept daily 9am–5pm; Oct to mid-May Mon–Fri 9am–5pm; $5.35; ⓣ250/974-5403), a modern building based on old models, which houses a collection of potlatch items and artifacts. It also shows a couple of award-winning films, and you might also come across local kids being taught native languages, songs, and dances. For years the village also claimed the world's tallest fully carved **totem pole** (other contenders, say knowing villagers, are all pole and no carving), though much to local chagrin Victoria raised a pole in 1994 that *The Guinness Book of Records* has recognized as 2.1m taller. Also worth a look is the wildlife and weird swamp habitat at **Gator Gardens** behind the bay, accessible via several trails and boardwalks.

Most people come over for the day, but **accommodation** options include the six-room *Orca Inn*, 291 Fir St, ten-minutes' walk from the ferry terminal (ⓣ250/974-5322 or 1-877/974-5322; ❷), with steak and seafood restaurant and café overlooking Broughton Strait and the sea; the *Ocean View Cabins*, 390 Poplar St, 1km from the ferry terminal overlooking Mitchell Bay (ⓣ250/974-5457; ❸); and the 23-site *Alert Bay Camping and Trailer Park* on Alder Road (ⓣ250/974-5213, ⓦwww.alertbay.com; $10–15).

Port Hardy

Dominated by big-time copper mining, a large fishing fleet, and the usual logging concerns, **PORT HARDY**, a total of 485km from Victoria and 230km from Campbell River, is best known among travelers as the departure point for ships plying one of the more spectacular stretches of the famous **Inside Passage** (see box p.530) to Prince Rupert (and thence to Alaska) and the more recently introduced **Discovery Coast Passage** (see box p.531).

You can **fly** from Vancouver to Port Hardy (the airport is 12km south of the town) with Pacific Coastal Airlines (ⓣ250/273-8666, ⓦwww.pacific-coastal.com) from $148 one-way. If possible, time your arrival to coincide with one of the Inside Passage **sailings** which leave every other day in summer and once or twice weekly in low season. **Bus** services aren't really scheduled to do this for you, with a Laidlaw bus generally timed to meet each *incoming* sailing from Prince Rupert. A Laidlaw bus (ⓣ250/949-7532 in Port Hardy, ⓣ250/385-4411 or 388-5248 in Victoria) also leaves Victoria daily (currently 11.45am), sometimes with a change in Nanaimo, arriving at the Port Hardy ferry terminal in the evening (currently 9.50pm) to connect with the ferry next morning; in summer an extra service departs from Victoria on the morning before ferry sailings. If you stay in town overnight, leave plenty of time to reach the ferry terminal – sailings in summer are usually around 7.30am. North Island Transportation provides a shuttle service between the ferry and the town's airport, main hotels, and the **bus station** at 7210 Market Street just south of Hastings Street and the infocentre, whence it departs ninety minutes before each sailing (ⓣ250/949-6300 for information or to arrange a pick-up from hotel or campsite); otherwise call a **taxi** (ⓣ250/949-8000).

The Port Hardy **ferry terminal** is visible from town but is actually 10km away at Bear Cove, where buses stop before carrying on to terminate opposite the **infocentre**, 7250 Market St (year-round Mon–Fri 9am–5pm; to early June to late Sept 8am–8pm; ⓣ250/949-7622, ⓔchamber @capescott.bc.ca). The infocentre can give you all the details about the immense wilderness of **Cape Scott Provincial Park**, accessible only by foot and which is supposed to have some of the most consistently bad weather in the world (and some of the most voracious biting insects). As a short taster you could follow the forty-minute hike from the small campsite and trailhead at San Josef River to some sandy beaches. Increasingly popular, but demanding (allow eight hours plus), is the historic **Cape Scott Trail**, part of a complex web of trails hacked from the forest by early Danish pioneers. Around 28km has been reclaimed from the forest, opening a trail to the cape itself.

Many travelers to Port Hardy are in RVs, but there's still a huge amount of pressure on hotel **accommodation** in summer, and it's absolutely vital to call ahead if you're not camping or haven't worked your arrival to coincide with one of the ferry sailings. Note that the ferry from Prince Rupert docks around 10.30pm, so you don't want to be hunting out rooms late at night with dozens of others. There are **rooms** at the *North Shore Inn*, 7370 Market St (ⓣ250/949-8500 or 1-877-949-8516; ④), at the end of Hwy-19, where all units have ocean views, and the *Thunderbird Inn*, 7050 Rupert St and Granville (ⓣ250/949-7767 or 1-877-682-0222, ⓦwww.thunderbirdinn .com; ④). The former has nice views of the harbor but sometimes has noisy live music. Five minutes south of town at 4965 Byng Rd, in a park-like setting near the river, is the *Pioneer Inn* (ⓣ250/949-7271 or 1-800/663-8744, ⓔpioneer@island.net; ⑤), which has rooms and RV sites ($17). The *Wildwoods* **campsite** (ⓣ250/949-6753; $7; May–Oct) is a good option, being signed and within walking distance (3km) of the ferry, though it's not too comfy for tenting – or try the *Quatse River Campground* at 5050 Hardy Rd (ⓣ250/949-2395, ⓔquatse@island.net; $14–18), with 62 spruce-shaded sites almost opposite the *Pioneer Inn*, 5km from the ferry dock.

Food here is nothing special, but there's a bevy of budget outlets, so you should be able to fill up for well under $10. Granville and Market streets have the main restaurant concentrations: try the pub/restaurants of the *Glen Lyon* and *Quarterdeck*, both popular, or *Snuggles*, next to the *Pioneer Inn*, which aims at a cozy English pub atmosphere with live music, theater (Friday nights), and steaks, salads, and salmon grilled over an open fire. The cafeteria-coffee shop in the *Pioneer* does filling breakfasts and other snacks.

Contexts

Contexts

A brief history of the Pacific Northwest

Unlike much of the rest of North America, whose residents often seem eager to ignore or pave over the past in their aggressive pursuit of the new and modern, the Pacific Northwest is particularly animated by its **history** in a variety of ways. From the traces of ancient volcanoes, to the artifacts of Native American and European settlement, to the preservation of historic architecture and old-time customs, the region has long kept an eye to its past and interacted with it. Even when this history has been dark or violent – native genocide, racist upheavals, or natural catastrophes – a considerable record often remains of it, whether etched across the land or preserved in memorials and libraries. Unsurprisingly, the region offers plenty of opportunity to tour the routes and concourses of vastly different periods in time, from the military sentinels of Puget Sound to the lava fields of the Cascades, and these are detailed throughout the guide. But for a broad overview of the historical framework of the Pacific Northwest, a short introduction is entirely appropriate and potentially quite useful.

Geological beginnings

Some fifty million years ago, what was the West Coast of the North American landmass (or something that vaguely resembled it) lay just west of the current border with Idaho; the Pacific Northwest, for all practical purposes, simply did not exist. In the coming millennia, however, the actions of **plate tectonics**, through which the earth's crustal plates are forever moving, disappearing, and re-emerging on a geological conveyor belt known as **continental drift**, caused the rupture and eastward drift of an oceanic plate to the immediate west – with profound consequences for the future. In the northern part of the region, this process of drift would cause a volcanic ridge in the Pacific to slam up against the mainland and force the uplift of **Vancouver Island** and other parts of British Columbia and the **Olympic Mountains**. Elsewhere, this great crustal crunch had the effect of crumpling, smashing, and otherwise deforming the lowland that was raised to become the **North Cascades**, while it also moved distant **tropical-island arcs** up toward the expanding edge of North America and welded them too against the coastline. Much of the area, then, became a hodgepodge of discordant layers of land and rock from different eras, with some mountain chains like the **Klamath** in Southern Oregon and California among the oldest, and colossal peaks like today's **High Cascades** among the newest. Indeed, the latter volcanic chain – with most of the region's familiar peaks – is generally less than five million years old, with some mountains only emerging in the last 200,000 years, a blip by geological standards. Other major changes – the demise of the old **Western Cascades**, the lava floods of Central Oregon, and the spectacular formation of the **Columbia River Gorge** – have had an equally impressive effect on the region (discussed further in their respective chapters), and show once more just how substantial the earth's volcanic dynamism has been in shaping the great beauty and sudden violence etched on the landscape.

Native peoples

The ancestors of the **native peoples** of the Pacific Northwest first entered the region from eighteen to twelve thousand years ago, when vast glaciers covered most of the North American continent, keeping the sea level far below that of today. These first human inhabitants to cross the land bridge linking Asia with present-day Alaska were likely **Siberian hunter-nomads** in pursuit of mammoths, hairy rhinos, bison, wild horses, and giant ground sloths, the Ice Age animals that made up their diet. These people left very little evidence of their passing, apart from some simple graves and the grooved, chipped stone spearheads that earned them the name **Fluted Point People**. In successive waves they moved down through North America, across the isthmus of Panama, until they reached the southernmost tip of South America. As they settled, so they slowly developed distinctive cultures and languages.

Numbering perhaps 150,000, the peoples that settled along the Pacific Northwest divided into three main language groups: **Algonquian**, **Athapascan**, and **Inuktitut** (Inuit). Within these linguistic groups there were several commonalities: None had a written language, the wheel was unknown to them, and most were reliant on the canoe, though the plains and plateau peoples east of the coastal mountains used draft animals – the largest of which was initially the dog. Over the centuries, each of the tribes developed techniques that enabled them to cope with the problems of survival posed by their particular environments.

In what is now the Pacific Northwest, the main group comprised **coastal peoples** who took advantage of an agreeable climate and fertile environment to create a sophisticated culture that stretched from southeast Alaska to Oregon. Here, a multitude of groups such as the **Tlingit**, **Nootka**, **Salish**, **Suquamish**, and **Makah** depended on the ocean to provide them with a plentiful supply of food. Living a comparatively settled life, they moved only from established winter villages to summer fishing sites, and occupied giant cedar lodges, clan dwellings dominated by a hereditary chief. There was, however, little cohesion within tribes, and people from different villages – even though of the same tribe – would at times war against each other. Surplus food, especially salmon, was traded and the sizeable profits underpinned a competitive culture revolving around an intricate system of ranks and titles, which culminated in the winter **potlatch**, a giant feast where the generosity of the giver – and the eloquence of the speeches – measured the clan's success. Prestige was also conferred upon clans according to the excellence of their woodcarvings, the most conspicuous manifestation being totem poles.

Other tribes, living south of the northern forests and east of the Pacific Coast, developed cultures in particular response to climatic conditions. The nomadic hunter-gatherers of the inland valleys and prairies, like the **Nez Percé**, foraged for nuts and roots and mixed seasonal fishing with hunting, while the **Modoc** and **Klamath** tribes of the arid basin surrounding today's Upper Klamath Lake in southern Oregon, subsisted on plants and waterfowl and lived in semi-subterranean, earthen-domed lodges. Further inland, the culture of the plateau tribes of the east, such as the **Palouse** and **Spokane**, echoed that of their more famous bison-dependent cousins on the prairies east of the Rockies. In the late seventeenth century, the hunting techniques of these prairie-plateau peoples were transformed by the arrival of the **horse** – which had made its way from Mexico, where it had been introduced by the Spanish *conquistadors*. On the prairies, the horse made the bison easy prey and a ready food supply spawned a militaristic culture centered on the prowess of the tribes' young braves.

The arrival of the Europeans

Europeans first espied the Pacific Northwest coast in 1542, when a Spanish expedition sailing from Mexico dropped anchor at the mouth of the Rogue River in southern Oregon. Stormy weather and treacherous currents prevented a landing, just as adverse conditions were later to hinder a succession of early explorers, most famously **Sir Francis Drake**, whose *Golden Hind* was buffeted up and down the Oregon coast in 1579. The Spaniards, fresh from their conquest of Mexico, were looking to extend their American empire, whereas Drake was searching for the fabled **Northwest Passage** from the Atlantic to the Pacific – and hence the Orient. By finding the passage, the English hoped to break free of the trading restrictions imposed by the Portuguese at the Cape of Good Hope and the Spanish at Cape Horn. There was indeed a Northwest Passage, but it was so blocked by Arctic ice as to be an impossible commercial route; not until the end of the nineteenth century did a (steel-hulled) ship finally manage to sail it. Consequently, the Pacific Northwest coast remained a Spanish preserve well into the eighteenth century, with only the gossip of Mediterranean sea captains remaining to excite English nautical interest. The most famous rumor was put about by **Juan de Fuca**, who insisted he had discovered the (ice-free) Northwest Passage – a shameful lie that ultimately got a strait named after him.

Meanwhile, far to the north, **Russian Cossacks** were moving east across Siberia subjugating the Mongols, just as later eighteenth-century Russians were to conquer the Kamchatka Peninsula and chart the Bering Strait – leading to more traders and navy surveyors charting the Alaskan shore. Rumors of Russian activity prompted the Spaniards in Mexico City to reassess their situation, and in 1769 they launched an invasion of the California coast, establishing a string of Jesuit missions and fortified settlements that were eventually to blossom into cities such as San Francisco and San Diego. In fact, the Russians posed no real threat – unlike the British who, still searching for the Northwest Passage, dispatched the illustrious **Captain Cook** to the Pacific Northwest in 1776. Cook took the easterly route, sailing round the Cape of Good Hope and across the Pacific Ocean to land on Vancouver Island after a year at sea. He hunted in vain for both the Northwest and Northeast (Siberian) Passage, and, while wintering in the Sandwich Islands (present-day Hawaii), was murdered by Polynesians. On the way home, Cook's ships dropped by Canton, where the sailors found, much to their surprise, that the Chinese were keen to buy the **sea otter skins** they had procured from the Native Americans for next to nothing. News of the expedition's fortuitous discovery – and its commercial potential – spread quickly, and by 1790 around thirty merchants from various countries were shuttling back and forth between China and the Pacific Coast.

The British Admiralty were, however, still preoccupied with the Northwest Passage. In 1791, they sent **George Vancouver** out to have another look. Although his ultimate aim was unachievable, Vancouver did chart a long stretch of coastline, including the island that bears his name. He named dozens of other features too, some in honor of bigwigs at home, others after his subordinates – Whidbey, Puget, Baker, and Rainier to name but a few. Vancouver failed to notice the mouth of the Columbia River – a failure remedied by the American **Robert Gray** shortly afterwards.

All this colonial activity did not, however, lead to any fighting, and the competing claims of the three European nations as to sovereignty over the Pacific Northwest coast were temporarily settled by the **Nuu-chah-nulth Convention** of 1790. In this, the British squeezed themselves in between Russian Alaska and Spanish California. Needless to say, no one bothered to consult the indigenous peoples. Although they had benefited by trading furs for metal goods, and relations between them and the newcomers were often cordial, they could hardly have guessed at the catastrophe that was soon to overwhelm them.

British ascendancy

In 1670, Charles II of England established the **Hudson's Bay Company** and gave it control of a million and a half square miles adjacent to Hudson Bay, a vast inland sea about 1500 miles east of the Pacific Coast. His two main objectives were to consolidate the British fur trade and to encircle New France (broadly Québec). Montréal was well established as the center of the French fur trade and it was from here that trappers and traders, the **voyageurs**, launched themselves deep into the interior, venturing as far as the Rockies. Unlike their British counterparts, who waited for the furs to be brought to their stockades, many of the voyageurs adopted native dress, learned aboriginal languages, and took wives from the tribes through which they passed. The pelts they brought back to Montréal were shipped downriver to Québec City, from where they were shipped to France.

In 1760, at the height of the struggle known here as the **French and Indian War** (and in Europe as the Seven Years War), the British captured Montréal, marking the beginning of the end of the French North American empire. But with French knowledge and experience of the interior too valuable to jettison, British merchants employed many of the voyageurs in the newly formed **North West Company**. After Captain Cook's sailors had demonstrated the potential of the Chinese fur trade, the search was on for an easy way to export furs westward across the Pacific, and both companies dispatched long-haul expeditions into the Rockies, with **Alexander Mackenzie** making the first continental crossing north of Mexico in 1793. Decades of rivalry came to an end when the two companies merged to form an enlarged Hudson's Bay Company in 1821.

For the purposes of the Pacific Northwest, the company ruled the region as a virtual fiefdom until almost the middle of the nineteenth century, discouraging immigration in order to protect its fur trade. It did, however, exercise its powers in the name of the British Crown and consequently, after the **War of American Independence**, was used to aggressively counter American territorial aspirations.

American settlement

Under the terms of the **Louisiana Purchase** of 1803, the US paid just $15 million dollars for the French territory that blocked its path west, a huge chunk of land stretching from Canada to Mexico between the Mississippi and the Rockies. Thereby, France obligingly dropped its last major colonial claim

Native Americans in the Pacific Northwest

From the 1830s onwards, the **Native Americans of the Pacific Northwest** were simply overwhelmed by the pace of events and the rise of the United States. Lacking any political or social organization beyond the immediate level of the tribe, they found it difficult to act against the legions of white colonists arriving – though admittedly European-borne diseases did much of the damage, with epidemics of measles and smallpox decimating the region's indigenous population by up to seventy percent.

In the Oregon Country, the **US government** initially tried to move willing tribes onto fairly large reservations, but as more settlers came, the tribes were forced onto smaller and smaller parcels of land. Some groups chose to resist – the **Cayuse** slaughtered the Whitmans, the **Nez Percé** killed a handful of white settlers and, most determined of all, the **Modocs** from the California–Oregon border fought a long-running guerrilla war against the US Army. For the most part, though, the native peoples were simply swept aside by the tide of guns, disease, and immigration. By 1880, the survivors had been consigned to **Indian reservations**, which mostly comprised the infertile land no one else wanted. Further damage was inflicted by the **Dawes Severalty Act** of 1887, which required Native Americans to select individual 160-acre reservation landholdings (lands had traditionally been held communally, and land ownership was an alien concept to most of the tribes) and obliged their children to attend government or mission schools. Deprived of their traditions and independence, many lapsed into poverty, alcoholism, and apathy.

In **Canada**, events followed a similarly depressing course. Herded onto reservations under the authoritarian paternalism of the **Ministry of Indian Affairs**, Canadian native peoples were subjected to a concerted campaign of Europeanization: the potlatch was banned, and they were obliged to send their children to boarding schools for ten months of the year. In the late 1940s, the Canadian academic Frederick Tisdall estimated that no fewer than 65,000 reservation aboriginals were "chronically sick" from starvation. Further north, the Inuit were drawn into increasing dependence on the Hudson's Bay Company, which encouraged them to hunt for furs rather than food, while the twin agencies of the Christian missions and the Royal Canadian Mounted Police worked to integrate them into white culture. As in the States, the settlers brought with them diseases to which the native peoples had no natural immunity; TB, for example, was, right up until the 1960s, fifteen to twenty times more prevalent among the aboriginal population than in the rest of the population.

In recent years, both the Canadian and US governments have (somewhat intermittently) attempted to right historic wrongs, but socio-economic indicators demonstrate that native peoples remain at a significant disadvantage compared to the rest of the population. More positively, native peoples have begun to assert their culture and campaign for self-determination. In Canada "Status Indians" are now represented by the **Assembly of First Nations** (AFN), which has sponsored a number of legal actions over treaty rights. In the US, starting in the1960s, the rise of **ethnic identity** movements (spurred by the civil rights marchers of the 1950s and later Black Power movement) emboldened some native groups to demand more favorable treatment. Nowadays, although some compacts have been re-negotiated with tribes, and the situation isn't quite as dismal as it once was, the future is still troubled. While the so-called Indian casinos have been touted as the solution to the economic malaise of the reservations, other native critics see little potential in a dubious enterprise such as organized gambling to solve entrenched sociopolitical problems.

on the North American continent, leaving the US and Britain to sort matters out between themselves. Perhaps the only US politician to realize the full importance of the purchase was President Thomas Jefferson, who both engineered the deal and bankrolled the **Lewis and Clark expedition** the following year, with the expectation that the two explorers would open up the interior to American fur traders. At that time the tribes of the Missouri basin carried their furs to Hudson's Bay Company posts in Canada, and Jefferson believed, quite rightly, that they would find it far easier to dispatch the pelts downriver to American buyers. Indeed, Jefferson's dream was to displace the British entirely – both in the interior and along the West Coast – thereby securing economic control of a continent whose potential he foresaw. With this in mind, his two protégés were dispatched to the Pacific with instructions to collect every scrap of information they could find.

Setting out on May 14, 1804, the expedition comprised forty-eight men, three boats, four horses, twenty-one bales of trade goods and presents to buy goodwill, and, in case that failed, rifles, a blunderbuss, and a cannon. Lewis and Clark ascended the Missouri, crossed the Rockies, and descended the Columbia River to reach the Pacific eighteen months later. It was a brilliantly led expedition and the two leaders dealt tactfully with the tribes they encountered, hiring local guides wherever possible and dispatching emissaries ahead to reassure the next tribe down the line of their peaceful intentions before they arrived. Ultimately, they steered clear of any real conflict and suffered only one casualty (from appendicitis), though they did endure all sorts of hardships – treacherous whitewater rapids, dangerous trails, and just plain discomfort: they were all, for example, infested with fleas in their winter base on the West Coast, **Fort Clatsop**. They covered about four thousand miles on the outward trip, carefully mapping and describing the country and its people in their **journals** (see p.561), which provide intriguing glimpses of Native American cultures just before they were largely destroyed.

Lewis and Clark also laid the basis for American competition with British fur traders: Clark founded the **Missouri Fur Company** on his return, and **John Jacob Astor** was sufficiently encouraged to base an American fur trading post, Astoria, at the mouth of the Columbia River in 1811. In the next twenty years, several factors combined to accelerate the pace of the American move westward: the opening of the Santa Fe Trail from Missouri to the far southwest (then in Mexican hands); the exploratory probing of the Rocky Mountain Fur Company, among whose employees was Kit Carson; and the dispatch of missionaries – most notably **Dr Marcus Whitman**, who set about Christianizing the Cayuse from his farm near today's Walla Walla. The Whitmans wrote home extolling the virtues of the **Oregon Country** (as both Washington State and Oregon were then known), firing the interest of relatives and friends. Perhaps more importantly, the Whitmans had made their long journey west by ordinary farm wagon: if they could do it, then so, it was argued, could other settler families.

The Oregon Trail

The early explorers, fur traders, and missionaries who traveled west from the Missouri blazed the trails that would lead thousands of American colonists to the Pacific Coast. Indeed, it was Whitman himself who, in 1843, guided the first sizable wagon train (of a thousand souls) along the **Oregon Trail** – a pioneering journey that became known to later generations as the **Great Migration**. The migrants sweated their way across the plains, chopped through forests, and hauled their wagons over fast-flowing streams behind oxen that traveled at around 2mph. It was a long and hard trip, but impressions of the trail varied enormously. To some who encountered hostile natives, grizzlies, cholera, or bitter weather, it was hell on earth; to others it was exhilarating – "a long picnic," wrote one. Each succeeding year a couple of thousand more emigrants followed, and soon American farmers – for the vast majority of migrants heading for the Oregon were precisely that – were crawling all over the **Willamette Valley**, much to the consternation of the Hudson's Bay Company. Later groups forged their own paths, whether settling in the dusty lands of Eastern Oregon or trekking further afield. Most notably, Jesse Applegate led a bedraggled group of settlers down to southern Oregon along the soon-to-be-infamous **Applegate Trail**, sending wagons tumbling down hillsides and pioneers into fits of disease, anger, and frustration. In the end, though, this smaller trail had the same effect as its more famous sibling – despite the hardships, it brought settlers to new lands far from their original homes. The totality of this mass movement made Oregon an American community and was to ensure its future lay within the USA.

Fixing the frontiers

In 1783 the **Treaty of Paris** wrapped up the American War of Independence and recognized the United States's northern and western frontiers with British and French territory as being on the Great Lakes and along the banks of the Mississippi River, respectively. The **Louisiana Purchase** brought America's western border to the Rockies, beyond which was Mexican-governed "California," though the Spaniards quickly modified their territorial claims, withdrawing to the 47th Parallel (the present Oregon/California boundary). This strategic retreat forecast their later relinquishing of independence to onetime colony Mexico; soon after the Mexican-American War ended with the US gaining control of California in 1847. Long before this, Britain and the United States had signed the **Treaty of Ghent** in 1814 to formalize American recognition of the legitimacy of British North America. The latter's border was established along the 49th Parallel west from Lake of the Woods in Ontario to the Rockies. Less conclusive was the arrangement concerning present-day Oregon and Washington: the treaty deferred the issue of sovereignty until the indefinite future, while promising the nationals of both regions free access to the whole area.

Initially, events on the ground went in Britain's favor. Astor was so irritated by the failure of the Americans to trounce the English in the War of 1812 that he lost all interest in Astoria, selling his trading post to the Hudson's Bay Company, who promptly relocated their western headquarters to **Vancouver**, near the mouth of the Columbia River. But soon the dominant position of the Company was undermined by the influx of American farmers along the Oregon Trail. In the presidential campaign of 1844, under the jingoistic slogan of "**54-40 or fight**," James Polk agitated for American control over the region up to central British Columbia – a jarring demand. With Polk's administration soon waging the Mexican-American War, it looked quite possible that the British could be the next target, and a third Anglo-American conflict would inevitably follow. However, in due course the present international frontier was fixed in 1846, following a sensible westward extension of the original 49th Parallel.

The **Oregon Territory** came into being the following year – and Washington was sliced off it in 1853. Oregon's subsequent application for US statehood was, however, delayed by the issue of slavery, with neither the existing free states nor the rival slave states eager to re-fight the drama of California's admission as a free state in 1850. Oregon was finally accepted as a free state in 1859, though with an appalling state constitution that forbade free

The Wobblies

In 1905, enthusiastic delegates to a labor congress in Chicago founded the **Industrial Workers Of The World** (the IWW), the most successful revolutionary labor movement in US history. It was born out of frustration with the dominant union organization of the day, the American Federation of Labor (AFL), both for its failure to organize successful strikes and its ideological conservatism: the AFL had no political strategy and its main objective was to protect the interests of skilled workers. IWW members became known as **Wobblies** as a result of mispronunciation of the movement's acronym by the Chinese immigrants, who constituted a sizeable proportion of its members. Dedicated to the overthrow of capitalism by means of agitation and strikes, their flyers proclaimed "The working class and the employing class have nothing in common." The IWW's goal was to unite the workers of individual industries – such as mining, construction, and logging – within brotherhoods that would eventually be combined into the so-called **One Big Union**.

IWW membership was never large – it reached a peak of around 100,000 in 1912 – but the Wobblies managed to exercise an influence out of all proportion to their numbers. They inspired thousands of workers to actively struggle against harsh anti-strike laws, low pay, and dreadful conditions. The IWW was particularly strong in Washington and Oregon, calling a series of strikes against the lumber companies. The employers frequently resorted to violence to defeat the union's causes, and in 1916, in one of several bloody incidents, seven IWW organizers were shot, and many others drowned when the sheriff of Everett tried to stop them from leaving the steamboat that had brought them from Seattle.

Three years later, a (peaceful) general strike mobilized 60,000 workers and paralyzed Seattle. IWW organizers fed strikers at labor-run cafeterias, handled emergency services, and delivered milk to babies so effectively that many employers feared they were witnessing the beginnings of a Bolshevik-style revolution. But in fact the Wobblies had never devised a coherent political program, nor did they want to seize power, and the strike simply faded away. Indeed, the IWW was by then deeply split between radical revolutionary factions and elements that favored democratic reform. In the 1920s, the IWW began to fragment, its legacy a lasting preference in the US for large industrial unions.

blacks from living there at all; this was rescinded after the Civil War. Thinly populated **Washington** only managed to assemble enough settlers to qualify for statehood in 1889.

Economic booms

In 1848, **gold** was discovered in California's Sierra Nevada mountains. Guessing the effect the news would have in Oregon, a certain **Captain Newell** sailed up the Willamette River buying every spade, pick, and shovel he could get his hands on. He then informed locals of the gold strike, and promptly sold their own tools back to them – with a substantial mark-up. It was quite a scam and, in the ensuing California Gold Rush, over two thirds of able-bodied Oregonians hightailed it south. Yet, despite the exodus, the gold rush turned out to be a boon for Oregon. For the first time, there was a ready market for the farmers of the Willamette Valley – and an even closer one when gold was found at **Jacksonville** in 1850 – while Oregon lumber towns like Ashland and Roseburg boomed supplying building materials, and Portland flourished from the dramatic upturn in trade.

In the early 1860s, the story was repeated when gold was unearthed in the Oregon interior, in the hills around John Day and Baker City. Both strikes had a dramatic impact, opening up the area east of the Cascade Mountains – and displacing the native population, who had previously been assured they'd be allowed to stay there. To feed the miners, thousands of cattle were driven over the mountains and, once they'd reached the interior, drovers found their animals thrived on the meadow grass of the valley bottoms and the plentiful supply of bunchgrass. This marked the beginning of the great **cattle empires** of eastern Oregon, though the ranchers' success was short-lived: the railroad reached the west in the 1880s and at a stroke overturned local economics. Railroad transportation meant that more money could be made from an acre sown than an acre grazed, and the cattle barons soon gave way to farmers.

Washington followed a similar pattern, with the eastern towns of Spokane and Walla Walla prospering as supply depots for the gold and silver mines of Idaho and Montana. Here, too, cattle grazed the rolling grasslands of the interior until the appearance of the railroad (and the savage winter of 1881) precipitated the move over from the livestock industry to grain production. The Washington seaboard got in on the act during the **Klondike Gold Rush** of the 1890s, when Seattle became the jumping-off point for Alaska-bound miners, and grew to rival San Francisco. The town was inundated with fortune-seekers, their dreams fired by tales of those who had found unimaginable wealth up north. The Seattle Chamber of Commerce created a committee for drawing gold diggers to Seattle, placing numerous ads in papers and magazines across the nation extolling the Seattle–Klondike connection. Eventually, even one of Seattle's mayors caught gold fever, quitting his job to take part in the frenzy up north. Few of the fortune hunters who set off from Seattle returned with their pots of gold, but with the massive influx of traffic through the town, business boomed in banks, shops, shipbuilding, and real estate.

Canadian confederation

All this American activity was in contrast to **British North America**, which was still a collection of self-governing colonies, and the discovery of gold beside BC's Fraser River in 1858 fueled British anxiety. In response to the influx of American prospectors, British Columbia was hastily designated a **Crown Colony** – as was the Klondike when gold was struck there in 1895. Yet British North America remained incoherently structured and, as a means of keeping the US at bay, the imperial government encouraged confederation. After three years of colonial debate, the British Parliament passed the **British North America Act** of 1867, which provided for a federal parliament and for each province to retain a regional government and assembly. British Columbia joined the Confederation, which became the **Dominion of Canada**, in 1871.

Two years later, the federal authorities created the Mounties (the North West Mounted Police), who came to perform a vital role in administering the Canadian west, acting both as law enforcement officers and as justices of the peace. From the 1880s, patrols diligently crisscrossed the Canadian Pacific Northwest, their influence reinforced by a knowledge of local conditions accumulated in the exercise of a great range of duties, from delivering the mail to providing crop reports. More than any other organization, the Mounties ensured that these remote provinces were not poached or overrun by American traders and prospectors. They were aided in this respect by the coming of the railroad: in 1886 the first train ran from Montréal to Vancouver, opening up the west and the interior of the country to Canadian settlers.

The twentieth century

At the beginning of the **twentieth century**, the region's economy was largely reliant on primary products, principally timber, grain, and fish, but there were also pockets of manufacturing, especially in and around Seattle and Tacoma. The shipping and timber industries were hit hard by the **Great Depression**, but **World War II** reinvigorated Seattle and Portland, boosting the cities' small black populations as African Americans moved here to work in war-related industries. Simultaneously, though, the **Japanese-American** population, previously the largest minority in Seattle, was persecuted and depleted as a result of President Roosevelt's **Executive Order 9066**, which interned them in **detention camps**.

World War II also accelerated the pace of industrialization and urbanization with the Pacific Northwest playing a prominent part in the war effort – its factories churning out aircraft and munitions, its shipyards building warships, and its huge Columbia River dams supplying the hydropower for aluminum manufacturing. This trend towards industrialization continued after the war, further alleviating dependence on logging, fishing, and farming, but was not enough to insulate the Pacific Northwest from the wearisome cycle of boom and bust, with prices determined by Eastern stock markets far beyond local control.

The talent needed to run the upstart aerospace company **Boeing** – particularly its engineers and technicians – also gave rise to significant scientific research in the area. This marriage of industry and technology was celebrated by the **Century 21 Exposition** (also known as the World's Fair) in 1962, for which Seattle's most recognizable symbol, the **Space Needle**, was built. In short order, though, the political movements sweeping much of America in the 1960s were mirrored here in microcosm. There were the requisite **Vietnam War** protests on the campuses of the universities of Oregon and Washington, and the subsequent trials of radicals such as the so-called **Seattle Seven**. Eugene, Oregon, became something of a hippie center as well, attracting great numbers of people practicing alternate lifestyles, among them writer **Ken Kesey**, who took his "Merry Pranksters" here to escape the chaos of the Bay Area.

Within the next decade, Oregon made headlines for the anti-urban sprawl and pro-environmental policies championed by Governor **Tom McCall**, while Portland too shook off the torpor of its decaying timber-town image and emerged as a leader in the urban "**quality of life**" movement. Guided by progressive mayors like Neil Goldschmidt, the city took such steps as dismantling a waterfront freeway to create a park, closing off traffic lanes to make a newfangled bus mall, and stopping unrestrained development through its own "**urban growth boundary**" – all fairly revolutionary for the time. Seattle, however, showed little interest in such thinking on a smaller scale, and through its business initiatives and aggressive development emerged as the showcase city of the Pacific Northwest – to the chagrin of some old-timers.

The turn of the 1980s was marked by two dramatic events: the colossal **explosion of Mount St Helens** on May 18, 1980, coating the region in ash and blowing apart one of the region's signature postcard images, and the later, rapid emergence of **high-tech companies**, many of whom rooted themselves along the Pacific seaboard, with their prime practitioner – Microsoft – based in Seattle. At the same time, the logging and fishing industries found themselves threatened by federal lawsuits against timber **clear-cutting** and the problems of **overfishing**, respectively, and a region that had once been thoroughly blue collar was suddenly flooded with white-collar computer and service workers. This structural change underpinned the newfound chic that washed over Seattle and, to a lesser extent, Portland and Vancouver in the 1990s: the new IT companies were renowned for laid-back work practices and informal dressing; bars lost out to coffeehouses; and a slew of bright new museums, skyscrapers, and civic institutions rose against the urban horizon. The transformation was also essentially urban, though, as the small resource towns that once characterized the region were firmly excluded. However, while Portland and Seattle could complacently, even smugly, view the struggles of the ports and mill towns with a certain distance, the new millennium brought a fresh understanding of what economic struggle really meant.

A troubled new era

At the end of 2000, the **high-tech bubble** abruptly burst, and the national economy, key to so much local success, soured. Countless firms went out of business or suffered through their toughest years yet. Even Boeing began laying off thousands of workers, moving its corporate headquarters to Chicago in the process, and longstanding resource companies like Willamette and Louisiana-Pacific also packed up shop for good. Ultimately, what started as a national recession became something closer to a regional depression for some industries, ultimately making Washington and Oregon national leaders in **unemployment**.

Washington's February 2001 **earthquake** only made things more dismal, adding to the dreary outlook with a slew of damaged or closed businesses, including many old structures in Pioneer Square. The combination of a weakened local economy, steep decreases in public revenue through reduced taxes, and unconscionable slash-and-burn ballot measures caused **widespread cutbacks** in state funding for health care, education, the arts, parks, social programs, and business development. By 2002, the bloom was officially gone from the region's monumental growth, with Portland soon making national headlines not for its quality of life, but for the state's inability to fund even basic education.

In 2004 it looks highly unlikely that the region will soon recover the economic dynamism it possessed only a few years before. While more jobs and state funding will eventually return, nothing can replace the billions lost when the high-tech economy crumbled, and it's hard to imagine the re-emergence of the same brash attitudes and devil-may-care business plans by local venture capitalists and entrepreneurs. Still, even though the Pacific Northwest has lost its economic edge and gained a measure of fear and caution, it still retains the museums, technology, parks, and people that it gained during the last boom. Moreover, despite the dark financial circumstances, the region – amazingly – continues to draw scads of newcomers, who may not be able to get an affordable house or a decent job, but do find a engaging civic culture, attractively preserved buildings, fetching parks and plazas, and all kinds of funky restaurants, bars, and clubs.

Northwest wildlife

The Pacific Northwest boasts a wide range of natural habitats, from glaciers on Cascade mountainsides to parched deserts in central Oregon. Between these extremes the region's hills, forests, and grasslands support an incredible variety and profusion of wildlife – any brief account can only scratch the surface of what you can expect to see. National, state, and provincial parks offer the best starting points, and we've listed some of the outstanding sites for spotting particular species. Don't expect to see the big attractions like bears and wolves easily, however; despite the enthusiasm of guides and tourist offices, these are encountered only rarely.

The ocean

The **Pacific Ocean** largely determines the climate of the Northwest, keeping the coastal temperatures moderate all year round. In spring and summer, cold nutrient-rich waters rise to the surface, producing banks of cooling fog and abundant phytoplankton (microscopic algae). The algae nourishes creatures such as krill (small shrimps), which provide baby food for juvenile fish. This food chain sustains millions of nesting seabirds, as well as elephant seals, sea lions, and whales.

Gray whales, the most common species of whale spotted from land, were almost hunted to the point of extinction, but have returned to the coast in large numbers. During their southward migration to breeding grounds off Mexico, from December to January, they are easy to spot from prominent headlands all along the coast, and many towns have charter services offering whale-watching tours. On their way back to the Arctic Sea, in February and March, the newborn whale calves can sometimes be seen playfully leaping out of the water, or "breaching." Look for the whale's white-plumed spout – once at the surface, it usually blows several times in succession.

Humpback whales are also frequently seen, largely because they're curious and follow sightseeing boats, but also because of their surface acrobatics. They too were hunted to near-extinction, and though protected by international agreement since 1966 they still number less than ten percent of their former population.

Vancouver Island's inner coast supports one of the world's most concentrated populations of **killer whales** or **orcas**. These are often seen in family groups or "pods" traveling close to shore, usually on the trail of large fish – which on the Northwest coast means salmon. The orca, however, is the only whale whose diet also runs to warm-blooded animals – hence the "killer" tag – and it will gorge on walrus, seal, and even minke, gray, and beluga whales.

Another Northwest resident, **sea otters** differ from most marine mammals in that they keep themselves warm with a thick soft coat of fur rather than with blubber. This brought them to the attention of early Russian and British fur traders, and by the beginning of the twentieth century they were virtually extinct. Found in numbers in Alaska, they were reintroduced in 1969 to the Northwest coast, where they are now breeding successfully at the heart of their original range. With binoculars, it's often easy to spot these charming creatures lolling on their backs, using rocks to crack open sea urchins or mussels and eating them off their stomachs; they often lie bobbing asleep, entwined in kelp to stop them floating away. If all else fails, you can see them in resigned captivity in a space like the Oregon Coast Aquarium in Newport.

Northern **fur seals** are often seen off the British Columbia coast during their migrations. They are "eared seals," and can manage rudimentary shuffling on land thanks to short rear limbs which can be rotated for forward movement. They also swim with strokes from front flippers, as opposed to the slithering, fishlike action of true seals. Another eared seal, the northern **sea lions**, are year-round residents who can be spotted on the rocks and wharves around Newport and various other towns.

Tidepools

The Pacific Northwest's shorelines are composed of three primary ecosystems: **tidepools**, sandy beaches, and estuaries. You can explore tidepools at the twice-daily low tides (consult local newspapers for times), so long as you watch out for freak waves and take care not to get stranded by the incoming tide. You should also tread carefully – there are many small lives underfoot. Of the miles of beaches with tidepools, some of the best are at Pacific Rim National Park on Vancouver Island, or off Yaquina Head on the central Oregon coast. Here you will find sea anemones (which look like green zinnias), hermit crabs, purple and green shore crabs, red sponges, purple sea urchins, starfish ranging from the size of a dime to the size of a hub cap, mussels, abalone, and Chinese-hat limpets – to name a few. Black oystercatchers, noisily heard over the surf, may be seen foraging for an unwary, lips-agape mussel. Gulls and black turnstones are also common and during summer brown pelicans dive for fish just offshore.

The life and soul of the tidepools is the **hermit crab**, which protects its soft and vulnerable hindquarters with scavenged shells, usually those of the aptly named black turban snail. Hermit crabs scurry busily around in search of a detritus snack, or scuffle with other hermit crabs over the ownership of vacant snail shells.

Much of the **seaweed** you see growing from the rocks is edible. As one would expect from a Pacific beachfront, there are also **palms** – sea palms, with 10cm-long rubbery stems and flagella-like fronds. Their thick root-like tethers provide shelter for small crabs. You will also find giant **kelp** washed up on shore – harvested commercially for use in thickening ice cream.

Sandy beaches

Long, golden **sandy beaches** may look sterile from a distance, but observe the margin of sand exposed as a gentle wave recedes, and you will see jetstreams of small bubbles emerge from numerous clams and mole crabs. Small shorebirds called sanderlings race among the waves in search of these morsels, and sand dollars are often easy to find along the high-tide line.

The most unusual shore creatures are the **northern elephant seals**, which will tolerate rocky beaches, but prefer soft sand mattresses for their rotund torsos. The males, or bulls, can reach lengths of over six meters and weigh upwards of four tons; the females, or cows, are petite by comparison – four meters long, and averaging a mere 1000 kilograms in weight. They have large eyes, adapted for catching fish in deep or murky waters; indeed, elephant seals are the deepest diving mammals, capable of staying underwater for up to twenty minutes and reaching depths of more than 1000 meters, where the pressure is ninety times that at the surface. They dive deeply to avoid the attention of the **great white sharks** lurking offshore, for whom they are a favorite meal.

As the otter population was plundered by fur-traders, so the elephant seals were decimated by commercial whalers in the mid-nineteenth century for their blubber and hides. By the late nineteenth century less than a hundred remained, but careful protection has partially restored the population in many of their native Northwest habitats.

Elephant seals emerge from the ocean only to breed or molt; their name comes from the male's long trunk-like **proboscis**, through which they produce a resonant pinging sound that biologists call "trumpeting," which is how they attract a mate. In December and January, the bulls haul themselves out of the water and battle for dominance. The predominant, or alpha, male will do most of the mating, siring as many as fifty young pups (one per mating), in a season. Other males fight it out at the fringes, each managing one or two couplings with the defenseless females. During this time, the beach is a seething mass of blubbery seals – flopping sand over their back to keep cool, squabbling with their neighbors while making rude snoring and belching sounds. The adults depart in March but the weaned pups hang around until May.

Estuaries

Throughout much of the Northwest, especially in the more developed south of the region, many **estuary** or rivermouth habitats have been filled, diked, drained, "improved" with marinas, or contaminated by pollutants. Those that survive consist of a mixture of **mudflats**, exposed only at low tide, and **salt marsh**, together forming a critical wildlife area that provides nurseries for many kinds of invertebrates and fish, and nesting and wintering grounds for many birds. Cordgrass, a dominant wetlands plant, produces five to ten times as much oxygen and nutrients per acre as does wheat.

Many interesting creatures live in the thick organic ooze, including the fat Innkeeper, a revolting-looking pink hot dog of a worm that sociably shares its burrow with a small crab and a fish, polychaete worms, clams, and other such things. Most prominent of estuary birds are the great blue herons and egrets. Estuaries are the best place to see wintering shorebirds such as dunlin, dowitchers, western sandpipers, and yellowlegs. Peregrine falcons and osprey are also found here.

Coastal bluffs

Along the shore, **coastal meadows** are bright with pink and yellow sand verbena, lupins, sea rocket, sea fig, and the bright orange California poppy – which, despite its name, is also found in Washington and Oregon. Slightly inland, the hills are covered with coastal scrub, consisting largely of coyote brush. Coastal canyons contain broadleaf trees such as California laurel (known as myrtlewood in Oregon), alder, buckeye, and oaks, and a tangle of sword ferns, horsetail, and cow parsnip.

Common rainy-season canyon inhabitants include ten-centimeter-long banana slugs and rough-skinned newts. Coastal thickets also provide homes for weasels, bobcats, gray foxes, raccoons, black-tailed deer, quail, and garter snakes, together with the reintroduced **Tule elk**, a once common member of the deer family. You can also spot majestic **Roosevelt elk** in certain viewing corridors just inland from the shore.

River valleys

Like many fertile **river valleys**, the large river systems of the Northwest – near cities at least – have in places been affected by agriculture. Riparian (streamside) vegetation has been logged, wetlands drained, and streams contaminated by agricultural runoff. Despite this, the riparian environment that does remain is a prime wildlife habitat, especially in the mountain parks, where conditions in many respects are still pristine. Wood ducks, kingfishers, swallows, and warblers are common, as are gray foxes, raccoons, and striped skunks. Common winter migrants include Canada geese, green-winged and cinnamon teals, pintail, shovelers and widgeon, and their refuges are well worth visiting. Don't be alarmed by the large numbers of duck-hunters – the term "refuge" is something of a misnomer, although many such areas do have places where hunting is prohibited.

Mountain forests

Mountain forests cover much of the Pacific Northwest and, depending on location and elevation, divide into four types: West Coast, Columbia, montane, and subalpine.

Some of the creatures common to most of these forests include **beavers**, which you may see at dawn or dusk, heads just above the water as they glide across lakes and rivers. Signs of their legendary activity include log jams across streams and ponds, stumps of felled saplings resembling sharpened pencils, and dens which look like domed piles of mud and sticks. Forest **wetlands** also offer refuge for **ducks** and **geese**, with loons, grebes, and songbirds attracted to their undergrowth. Three species of ptarmigan – willow, rock, and white-tailed – are common, and you'll see plenty of big raptors, including the great **gray owl**, the Northwest's largest owl. In certain wilderness preserves, you may even spot grand creatures like the **bald eagle** or a variety of **hawks** and **osprey**, and such rich habitats are often prominently highlighted by local preservation groups.

West Coast forest

The **West Coast forest**'s torrential rainfall, mild maritime climate, deep soils, and long growing season produce the Northwest's most impressive forests and its biggest trees. Swaths of luxuriant temperate **rainforest** cover much of Vancouver Island and the Olympic Peninsula, dominated by Sitka spruce, Western red cedar, Pacific silver fir, Western hemlock, Western yew and, biggest of all, **Douglas fir**, some of which tower 90m and are 1200 years old. However, these conifers make valuable timber, and much of this forest is under severe threat from logging. Some of the best stands – a fraction of the original – have been preserved in Vancouver Island's Pacific Rim National Park.

Below the luxuriant, dripping canopy of the big trees lies an **undergrowth** teeming with life. Shrubs and bushes like salal, huckleberry, bunchberry, salmonberry, and twinberry thrive alongside mosses, ferns, lichens, liverworts, skunk cabbage, and orchids. All sorts of animals can be found here, most notably the **cougar** and its main prey, the Columbian blacktail **deer**, a subspecies of the mule deer. Birds are legion, and include a wealth of woodland species such as the Townsend's warbler, Wilson's warbler, orange-crowned warbler, junco, Swainson's thrush, and golden-crowned kinglet. Rarer birds include the rufous hummingbird, which migrates from its wintering grounds in Mexico to feed on the forest's numerous nectar-bearing flowers.

Columbia forest

The **Columbia forest** covers the lower slopes (400–1400m) of the Cascades and British Columbia's interior mountains. Trees here are similar to those of the warmer and wetter rainforest – Western red cedar, Western hemlock and Douglas fir – with Sitka spruce, which rarely thrives away from the coast, as the notable exception. The undercover, too, is similar, with lots of devil's club (a particularly vicious thorn), azaleas, black and red twinberry, salmonberry, and redberry alder. Mountain lily, columbine, bunchberry, and heart-leaf arnica are among the common flowers.

Few mammals live exclusively in the forests with the exception of the **red squirrel**, which makes a meal of conifer seeds, and is in turn preyed on by hawks, owls, coyotes, and weasels, among others. Bigger predators roam the mountain forest, however, most notably the **brown bear**, a western variant of the ubiquitous black bear. Aside from the coyote, the tough, agile black bear is one of the continent's most successful carnivores and the one you're most likely to see around campgrounds and rubbish dumps. Black bears have adapted to a wide range of habitats and food sources, and their only natural enemies – save wolves, which may attack young cubs – are hunters, who bag some 30,000 annually in North America.

Scarcer but still hunted is the famous **grizzly bear**, a far larger and potentially dangerous creature distinguished by its silver-tipped, brownish fur and the ridged hump on its back. Now extinct in many of its original habitats, the grizzly is largely confined in this region to the remote slopes of the West Coast range, where it feeds mainly on berries and salmon. Like other bears, grizzlies are unpredictable and readily provoked.

Montane forest

Montane forest covers the more southerly and sheltered reaches of Washington, Oregon, and the dry plateaux of interior British Columbia, where spindly Douglas fir, western larch, ponderosa pine, and the **lodgepole pine** predominate. The lodgepole requires intense heat before releasing its seeds, and huge stands of these trees grew in the aftermath of the forest fires that accompanied the building and operation of the railways.

Plentiful voles and small rodents attract **coyotes**, whose yapping – an announcement of territorial claims – you'll often hear at night close to small towns. Few predators have the speed to keep up with coyotes – only the stealthy **cougar**, or wolves hunting in tandem, can successfully bring them down. Cougars are now severely depleted in North America, and the British Columbia interior and Vancouver Island are the only regions where they survive in significant numbers. Among the biggest and most beautiful of the carnivores, they seem to arouse the greatest bloodlust in hunters. **Wolves**, too, have been significantly hunted and are thin on the ground, and your best bet for spotting or hearing them may be to attend a "howl-in" at Wolf Haven International (see p.318) outside Olympia.

Ponderosa and lodgepole pines provide fine cover for **birds** like goshawks, Swainson's hawks and lesser species like ruby-crowned kinglets, warblers, pileated woodpeckers, nuthatches, and chickadees. In the forest's lowest reaches the vegetation and birds are those of the southern prairies – semi-arid regions of sagebrush, prickly pear, and bunch grasses, dotted with lakes full of common ducks like mallard, shoveler, and widgeon. You might also see the cinnamon teal, a red version of the more common green-wing teal, a bird whose limited distribution lures bird-watchers to British Columbia.

Subalpine forest

Subalpine forests cover mountain slopes from 1300m to 2200m throughout the Northwest, supporting lodgepole, whitebark and timber pines, alpine fir, and Engelmann spruce. They also contain a preponderance of alpine larch, a deciduous conifer whose vivid yellows dot the mountainsides in the fall to beautiful effect.

One of the more common animals of this zone is the elk, or **wapiti**, a powerful member of the deer family which can often be seen in large herds above the tree line in the summer. Elk court and mate during the fall, making a thin nasal sound called "bugling." Make sure to respect their privacy, as rutting elk have notoriously unpredictable temperaments.

Small herds of **mule deer** migrate between forests and alpine meadows, using glands between their hooves to leave a scent for other members of the herd to follow. They're named after their distinctive ears, designed to provide early warning of predators. Other smaller animals which are also attracted to the subalpine forest include the golden-mantled ground squirrel, and birds such as Clark's nutcracker – both tame and curious creatures which often gather around campgrounds in search of scraps.

Alpine zones

Alpine zones occur in mountains above the tree line, which in the Northwest means parts of the Cascades and much of British Columbia. Plant and animal life vary hugely between summer and winter, and according to terrain and exposure to the elements.

In spring, alpine meadows are carpeted with breathtaking displays of **wildflowers**: clumps of Parnassus grass, lilies, anemones, Indian paintbrushes, lupins, and a wealth of yellow flowers such as arnica, cinquefoil, glacier lily, and wood betony – especially appealing are the slopes of Iron Mountain in the Western Cascades. Alpine meadows make excellent pasture, attracting **elk** and **mule deer** in summer, as well as full-time residents like **Dall's** and **bighorn sheep**. **Marmots**, resembling hugely overstuffed squirrels, hibernate through the worst of the winter and beyond. In a good year they can sleep for eight months, prey only to grizzly bears, which are strong enough and have the claws to dig down into their dens. In their waking periods they can be tame and friendly, often nibbling contentedly in the sunnier corners of campgrounds. When threatened, however, they produce a piercing and unearthly whistle. (They can also do a lot of damage: some specialize in chewing the radiator hoses of parked cars.) The strange little **pika**, a relative of the rabbit, is more elusive but keeps itself busy throughout the year, living off a miniature haystack of fodder which it accumulates during the summer.

Birds are numerous in summer, and include rosy finches, pipits, and blue grouse, but few manage to live in the alpine zone year-round. One which does is the **white-tailed ptarmigan**, a plump, partridge-like bird which, thanks to its heavily feathered feet and legs, is able to snowshoe around deep drifts of snow; its white winter plumage provides camouflage. Unfortunately, ptarmigans can be as slow-moving and stupid as barnyard chickens, making them easy targets for hunters and predators.

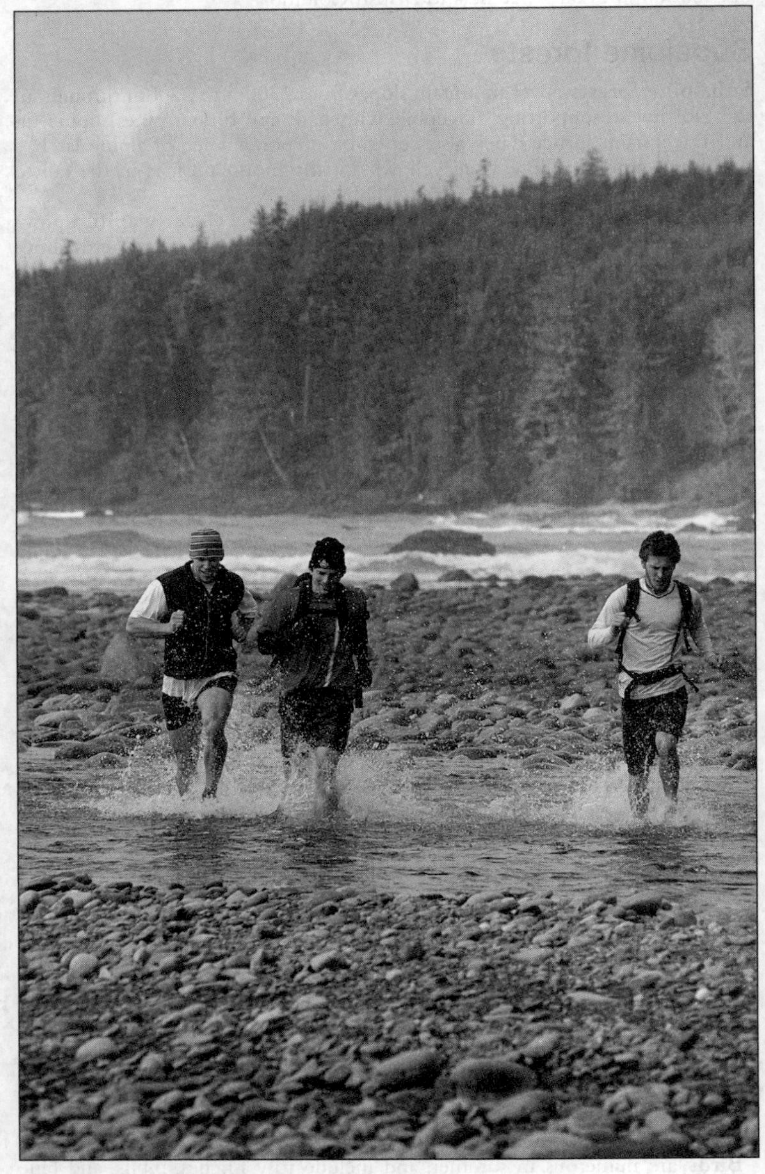

△ The West Coast Trail

The Northwest on film

Despite being one of the most photogenic regions of North America, the Northwest's presence on film is less stellar than you might expect. Hollywood, especially during the first fifty years of its history, often opted for the mountains of its own backyard rather than to trek all the way north. Even a movie as distinctly northwestern as Stanley Donen's boisterous Oregon musical *Seven Brides for Seven Brothers* (1955) was shot on studio lots against backdrops so fake they might as well have been left over from *Bambi*. The situation has improved since then: In the early 1970s the mists and gloomy skies that are a staple of the northwestern climate – the same that had scared off many a film crew in the past – suddenly became popular among the European-influenced auteurs of the American New Wave. Moreover, movies are now regularly filmed on location, directors continue to discover the region's attributes, and there's now an actual homegrown filmmaking industry here to boot.

Portland

Drugstore Cowboy (Gus Van Sant 1989). Grim tale of pharmacy bandits who prowl Portland hunting for prescription-drug highs, starring Matt Dillon in one of his better roles.

Elephant (Gus Van Sant 2003). Stark, desaturated take on the Columbine killings, set in a Portland high school. Well-made, disturbing portrait of teen angst and subsequent violence, though with little empathy for any of the characters.

The Hunted (William Friedkin 2003). Not a particularly good thriller, this formulaic Vietnam vet-turned-psycho-killer plot is enlivened by countless views of the city, including a climactic chase on a fictional train running over the Hawthorne Bridge – which seems to span for endless miles.

Mala Noche (Gus Van Sant 1985). Depressing tale of drugs and street hustlers set in a grim slice of mid-1980s Portland. The film that first won its director his indie acclaim.

My Own Private Idaho (Gus Van Sant 1991). Somewhat overlooked curiosity with River Phoenix and Keanu Reeves portraying a psycho-sexual drama with allusion to the works of Shakespeare.

Western Oregon

Bend of the River (Anthony Mann 1952). Jimmy Stewart adventure set around the Columbia River Gorge, in which reformed lawbreaker Jimmy Stewart's smiling new attitude is severely tested when he's abandoned by a greedy bunch of wagoneers on Mount Hood.

Emperor of the North (Robert Aldrich 1973). Uniquely northwestern Depression-era showdown in which a sadistic Ernest Borgnine battles freeloading hobo Lee Marvin on the railroads of Oregon.

Free Willy (Simon Wincer 1993). Family-oriented flick about a boy and his killer whale. Filmed in Astoria, and the main reason why the orca "Keiko" ended up in the Oregon Coast Aquarium for several years.

One Flew Over the Cuckoo's Nest (Milos Forman 1975). Ken Kesey novel filmed at the Oregon State Hospital in Salem, and memorable for Jack Nicholson being lobotomized and the resident Native American thundering his way to freedom.

Paint Your Wagon (Joshua Logan 1969). Groan-a-minute spectacular filmed in the woods of Oregon that has gold prospectors Lee Marvin and Clint Eastwood belting out a bevy of B-grade show tunes. Often cited as a key reason for the demise of the old-time Hollywood musical.

The Shining (Stanley Kubrick 1980). Liberally changed movie version of the Stephen King novel, with exterior filmed at Mount Hood's *Timberline Lodge*. Unfortunately, the grand horror sets were shot in a British soundstage.

Sometimes a Great Notion (Paul Newman 1971). Quintessential Northwest movie providing a stark look at the fallout from a lumber-mill strike in a small Oregon town. Based on the Ken Kesey book and starring the director.

Stand By Me (Rob Reiner 1986). The director's soft-focus paean to lost youth, with River Phoenix as a bad little boy and based on the Stephen King tale "The Body." Memorably filmed in Brownsville, Oregon.

Seattle

The Far Country (Anthony Mann 1954). Jimmy Stewart drives a herd of cattle from Seattle up to the Yukon during the Gold Rush, with little interest in his civic duty. A few obviously painted mattes notwithstanding, this director's films present the region in all its natural splendor.

House of Games (David Mamet 1987). Modern film noir about a psychologist who gets drawn into a ring of con men, making effective use of dark, gritty Seattle locations.

Hype (Doug Pray 1996). Nostalgic grunge documentary chronicling the old days of the alt-rock scene in places like Seattle's Belltown, which has changed markedly since then. Has interviews with most of the major musicians and scenesters and live footage of all the knowns and unknowns.

It Happened at the World's Fair (Norman Taurog 1963). Typically dispensable Elvis Presley film – flimsy plot, mediocre music, and a spectacular location, in this case the Century 21 Exposition.

The Parallax View (Alan Pakula 1974). Stunning paranoid thriller – the epitome of 1970s conspiracy filmmaking – that begins with a memorable assassination at the top of Seattle's Space Needle.

Singles (Cameron Crowe 1992). Romantic, very early-Nineties look at young Seattlites living in a Capitol Hill apartment building, with cameos by members of Pearl Jam and Soundgarden. Also interesting for Matt Dillon's turn as a goateed grunge wannabe.

Sleepless in Seattle (Nora Ephron 1993). Sappy smash in which a widowed Tom Hanks falls for reporter

Meg Ryan, with help from his son and talk radio. Great location scenes, and a long comic exchange with Rob Reiner in Pike Place Market's *Athenian Inn*.

Streetwise (Martin Bell 1984). Poignant documentary about homeless kids on Seattle's Pike Street, one of the grittiest views of any Northwest city.

Trouble in Mind (Alan Rudolph 1986) Seductive, romantic vision of urban life and melodramatic malaise in which Seattle is aptly re-imagined as "Rain City."

Western Washington

Fire Walk with Me (David Lynch 1992). Less inspired movie prequel to the director's classic TV series *Twin Peaks*, which really put the snowcapped mountains and logging towns of Washington on the media map. You can still visit the Double R Diner (aka the *Mar-T Cafe*) in North Bend and order a damn fine slice of cherry pie.

Five Easy Pieces (Bob Rafelson 1970). Classic "dismal Northwest" piece that takes middle-class piano-prodigy drop-out Jack Nicholson from the sun-baked oilfields of Texas north to visit his family in Washington's San Juan Islands – the change of scenery and climate perfectly conveying his cruel malaise.

McCabe & Mrs Miller (Robert Altman 1971). Perhaps the greatest film ever made about the pioneer history of the Northwest, starring Warren Beatty and Julie Christie. Set in the Washington frontier town of "Presbyterian Church" at the beginning of the twentieth century, where an unexpected three-day blizzard provided Altman with an unforgettable cinematic climax.

An Officer and a Gentleman (Taylor Hackford 1982). Debra Winger and Richard Gere military melodrama filmed in Port Townsend, though Louis Gossett, Jr, has the best role as a tough-as-nails drill sergeant.

This Boy's Life (Michael Caton-Jones 1993). Based on Tobias Wolff's book (see p.567) and set in the small North Cascades town of Concrete, Washington. Stars Leonardo DiCaprio as the victim of abusive patriarch Robert De Niro.

The Vanishing (George Sluizer 1993). American remake of a better Dutch original by the same director. Set in wilderness Washington and involving a particularly eerie and creepy abduction – though this version slaps on a mindless happy ending.

British Columbia

A Child's Garden and the Serious Sea (Stan Brakhage 1991). Experimentally delirious paean to nature and memory by one of the towering figures of the avant-garde, and set in British Columbia.

The Grey Fox (Phillip Borsos 1982). Beautifully evoked slice of British Columbia in which Richard Farnsworth plays an Old West criminal on the run from the modern world.

Stand-ins

Animal House (John Landis 1978). Still the archetypal frat-house movie, with John Belushi and a cast of lesser-knowns as drunken college students in the 1960s, causing all manner of destruction. Eugene's University of Oregon and other Willamette Valley locations pose as the grounds of Faber College on the East Coast.

The Deer Hunter (Michael Cimino 1978). Vietnam War-era epic ostensibly set in the mountains of Pennsylvania, but actually shot three thousand miles across the country in the Cascade Mountains.

Dogfight (Nancy Savoca 1991). Shot on location in Seattle, which is somehow passed off as 1963 San Francisco in this offbeat film about an unlikely romance between a plain folksinger and a serviceman about to go to Vietnam (played by River Phoenix).

The General (Buster Keaton 1927). Undeniably one of the most beautiful of all silent movies, a railroad-chase masterpiece filmed in southwest Oregon, despite the fact that the film was supposed to be taking place two thousand miles away in Civil War–ravaged Georgia.

Roxanne (Fred Schepisi 1987). Steve Martin update of *Cyrano de Bergerac*, seemingly set in Nelson, Washington, but actually filmed in winsome Nelson, BC.

Rumble in the Bronx (Stanley Tong 1996). Hopeless Jackie Chan attempt to make squeaky clean Vancouver, BC, stand in for the rougher edges of New York.

Books on the Northwest

Many, though not all, of these books are readily available in the UK, US, and Canada. Publishers for each title are listed in the form UK/US publisher, unless the book is published in one country only; o/p means out of print. Note that major Canadian bookshops will stock virtually all the listed books published in the US; we've indicated those books only published in Canada. Out of print books can usually be found quite readily on the Internet, and unless truly rare, typically cost the same as or less than their original retail prices. Titles marked with ★ are especially recommended.

Travel

Peter Alden *National Audubon Society Field Guide to the Pacific Northwest* (Knopf, US). Excellent, all-purpose guide to the region covering all the flora and fauna you might see and where you'll see it. Superbly illustrated.

David D. Alt and Donald W. Hyndman *Roadside Geology of Washington*, *Roadside Geology of Oregon* (Mountain Press, US). Excellent volumes in the series, pointing out and analyzing everything from the rock visible at highway roadcuts to the reasons for the area's earthquakes.

David Dunbar *The Outdoor Traveler's Guide to Canada* (Stewart, Tabori & Chang, o/p). Too bulky to be a useful portable guide, but a lavishly illustrated introduction to the outdoor pursuits, wildlife, and geology of the best national and provincial parks.

Ranulph Fiennes *The Headless Valley* (Hodder and Stoughton, o/p). Tales of derring-do from the illustrious explorer, who goes whitewater rafting down the South Nahanni and Fraser rivers of British Columbia and the NWT.

★ **Ralph Friedman** *In Search of Western Oregon* (Caxton, US). Simply put, the travel bible for exploring the western half of the state in depth, loaded with observations and anecdotes about even the smallest of towns and arranged by journeys on major and minor roads.

Ruth Kirk and Carmela Alexander *Exploring Washington's Past: A Road Guide to History* (University of Washington Press, US). Every nook and cranny of the state is explored in detail in this comprehensive book, which has been revised several times. Jam-packed with intriguing information.

★ **Tom Kirkendall and Vicky Spring** *Bicycling the Pacific Coast* (Mountaineers Books, US). Detailed guide to the bike routes all the way along the coast from Mexico up to Canada, with many fine avenues to explore along the Oregon Coast. Also good is the authors' *100 Best Cross-Country Ski Trails in Washington*, from the same publisher.

Cathy McDonald and Stephen R. Whitney *Nature Walks in and Around Seattle* (The Mountaineers, US). Guides to several dozen walks in parks, forests, and wetlands in Seattle and environs, from favorites like the Discovery Park loop trail to obscurities like West Hylebos Wetlands State Park.

John McKinney *Great Walks of North America: the Pacific Northwest*

(Henry Holt, o/p). Lucid introduction to many of the region's best hikes, though the trail descriptions are overly terse and the maps insufficiently detailed.

Marge and Ted Mueller *The San Juan Islands Afoot & Afloat* (The Mountaineers, US). Trails, parks, campgrounds, and water activities in the San Juans, by authors who have done similar guides to the North, Middle, and South Puget Sound areas.

★ **Rhonda and George Ostertag** *100 Hikes in Oregon* (Mountaineer Books, US). Excellent volume with many fine, detailed suggestions for wandering the outback of the state. Used by many outdoor-adventuring locals, it's more specific and focused than other guides with similar-sounding titles.

Chuck Palahniuk *Fugitives and Refugees* (Crown, US). In one of the most offbeat tours of any city you're likely to find, cult-fiction author (see below) directs you to Portland's quirkiest and most disturbing spots – from a vacuum-cleaner museum and a four-story sex club to junk emporia and haunted moviehouses.

Andy Perdue *The Northwest Wine Guide: A Buyer's Handbook* (Sasquatch, US). One of the most current overviews of the major vintners from Oregon and Washington to British Columbia and Idaho, with the history, price range, and character of each of the given wineries.

Betty Pratt-Johnson The author has produced five separate books (Adventure Publishing, Canada) whose 157 canoeing routes provide the definitive account of how and where to canoe the lakes and rivers of British Columbia. Also good is her *101 Dives: from the Mainland of Washington to British Columbia* (Heritage House, o/p).

Robert Schnelle *Valley Walking* (University of Washington Press, US). The author, who lives in the Kittitas Valley, explores its remoter reaches on foot with this book of 33 essays – meditative hikes laced with thought-provoking comments on the environment.

William L. Sullivan *Exploring Oregon's Wild Areas* (Mountaineers Books, US). Detailed guide to backpacking, climbing, rafting, and other outdoor activities across the state. One of several of Sullivan's outdoor guides to Oregon.

Native American

★ **Dee Brown** *Bury My Heart at Wounded Knee* (Vintage/Henry Holt). Seminal 1970 work that played a leading role in the rewriting of Native American history: a grim story that details the brutal campaigns that punctuated the American drive west. Of particular relevance are the chapters on the Nez Percé and the Modoc.

Ella C. Clark *Indian Legends of the Pacific Northwest* (University of California Press, US). Good selection of tales from several tribes, organized into thematic sections and linked by useful critical passages.

Christian F. Feest *Native Arts of North America* (Thames & Hudson, US & UK). Erudite and comprehensive survey of the development of North American native arts with chapters devoted to painting and engraving, textiles, and sculpture. Easily the best book on the subject, it's also lavishly illustrated.

Paula R. Fleming *Native American Photography at the Smithsonian*

(Smithsonian, US). Broad visual overview of the major native groups photographed near the end of an era. The stylized poses don't detract from a plaintive record of a way of life that has all but vanished.

Warren Jefferson *The World of Chief Seattle: How Can One Sell the Air?* (Book Pub. Co., US). Fine historical portrait of the city's namesake and his Suquamish tribe, from the injustice visited on them by white settlers to their modern society and lifestyle.

Alan B. McMillan *Native Peoples and Cultures of Canada* (Douglas & McIntyre, UK). Excellent anthology on Canada's native groups from prehistory to current issues of self-government and land claims. Well-written and illustrated throughout.

★ **Francis Parkman** *The Oregon Trail/The Conspiracy of Pontiac* (Library of America, US). Memorable nineteenth-century studies by one of the country's greatest historians. In these volumes, the author, who spent considerable time among native tribes, argued that the end of the French empire in North America would inevitably lead to British and American domination and the demise of Native Americans.

Explorers

Stephanie Ambrose Tubbs and Clay Jenkinson *The Lewis and Clark Companion: An Encyclopedia Guide to the Voyage of Discovery* (Henry Holt, US). An essential guide to the famous expedition, covering everything from munitions to draft animals to barter, including incisive portraits of the group members. Essential for its incorporation of significant recent scholarship and discussions of conflicting historical perspectives.

Ron Anglin *Forgotten Trails: Historical Sources of the Columbia's Big Bend Country* (University of Washington Press, US). Enjoyable book that brings together samples from the best of early pioneer and explorer travel accounts of the Grand Coulee area, including that of David Thompson and Paul Kane.

Owen Beattie and John Geiger *Frozen in Time* (Greystone, US). An account of the doomed Franklin expedition (1845–48) to find the Northwest Passage and the subsequent discovery of artifacts and bodies frozen in the northern ice; worth buying for the extraordinary photos.

★ **Meriwether Lewis and William Clark** *The Journals of the Lewis and Clark Expedition, 1804–1806* (University of Nebraska, US). Six volumes of meticulous jottings by some of the Northwest's first inland explorers, scrupulously recording every detail of flora, fauna, and native inhabitants. Interesting to dip into, though booklets of extracts sold at historic sites and bookshops across the Northwest are generally of more use to the casual reader. Bernard DeVoto's classic, *The Journals of Lewis & Clark* (Mariner, US), provides a well-edited selection.

Edward W. Nuffield *The Pacific Northwest: Its Discovery and Early Exploration by Sea, Land and River* (Hancock House, US). Lengthy, highly detailed look at every major expedition to the region, up to Astor's establishment of a fur-trading outpost at Astoria in 1811.

Alan Villiers *Captain Cook, the Seamen's Seaman* (MacMillan o/p). Well-written account of the captain's exploratory voyages with a separate chapter on his search for the

Northwest Passage. Interesting too for anecdotes about Cook's progressive treatment of his men and his death in Hawaii.

Natural environment

John Eliot Allen, et al *Cataclysms on the Columbia* (Timber Press, US). Excellent introduction to the colossal Ice Age floods that created the modern landscape of the Columbia River Gorge and the Willamette Valley, and how the floods were discovered through the efforts of a pioneering researcher facing a tidal wave of scientific hostility.

Charles A. Blakeslee *Crater Lake National Park: Wild and Beautiful* (Far Country Press, US). Splendid coffee-table book full of vivid, detailed photos of the magnificent former Mount Mazama, which, since blowing its top, has become the deepest lake in North America.

Rob Carson *Mount St. Helens: The Eruption and Recovery of a Volcano* (Sasquatch, US). Fine historical overview and photographs covering the devastation wrought by the mountain in May 1980, as well as the subsequent rebirth of its surrounding landscape over the next twenty years.

★ **Timothy Egan** *The Good Rain: Across Time and Terrain in the Pacific Northwest* (Vintage, US & UK). One of the key books about the region, focusing on its beleaguered ecology and social and environmental leaders, as well as the industries that have done much to reshape the landscape.

Tim Fitzharris and John Livingston *Canada: A Natural History* (Penguin, UK). The text is prone to purple fits, but the expressive photographs make this a book to savor.

★ **Stephen L. Harris** *Fire Mountains of the West: The Cascade and Mono Lake Volcanoes* (Mountain Press, US). Easily the best introduction to the geology, history, and lore of the Cascades (throwing in a few California volcanoes for good measure), also providing useful information on visiting and climbing these majestic peaks.

Philip Jackson and A. Jon Kimerling *Atlas of the Pacific Northwest* (Oregon State University Press, US). Shows every imaginable aspect of Washington and Oregon in graphs or maps – from geology, history, and land ownership to hunting and fishing. Updated several times since its 1985 debut.

Bruce Obee *The Pacific Rim Explorer* (Whitecap, UK). Good summary of the walks, wildlife, and social history of the Pacific Rim National Park and its nearby towns.

Sallie Tisdale *Stepping Westward: The Long Search for Home in the Pacific Northwest* (Perennial, US). Personal, thoughtful stories and observations of the ongoing conflict between man and nature throughout the region, contrasting the harmony of the natural environment with clear-cut logging, dams, and other human threats.

History

Kurt E. Armbruster *Orphan Road: the Railroad Comes to Seattle 1853-1911* (University of Washington Press, US). History of the long, tortuous process of bringing railways to the region, including the story of how Tacoma was initially chosen as a rail terminus instead of Seattle.

Arthur H. Campbell *Antelope: The Saga of a Western Town* (Maverick o/p). Detailed account of this small and remote Oregon town, where the Indian guru Bhagwan Shree Rajneesh famously set up shop in 1981.

Gordon DeMarco *A Short History of Portland* (Lexicos o/p). Thorough and charmingly written account of the city's development, with a wry tone and pointed perspective missing from booster accounts of the city's history. Well worth seeking out a copy if you can find one.

Robert L. Friedheim *The Seattle General Strike* (University of Washington Press, US). The most complete documentation of this 1919 event, though perhaps a bit dry and detailed for the casual reader.

★ **Stewart Holbrook** *Wildmen, Wobblies & Whistle Punks* (Oregon State University Press, US). Entertaining tales from across Washington and Oregon written by one of the region's most popular journalist-writers. About thirty short stories appear here, a small part of Holbrook's enormous output. Each tale delves into a colorful historical event in a laconic, folkloric style.

Washington Irving *Astoria* (Kegan Paul, UK & US). Originally published in 1839, this account of Oregon's first American fur-trading colony offers fascinating insights into contemporary attitudes to the then still-unsettled Northwest.

★ **Frank McLynn** *Wagons West: The Epic Story of America's Overland Trails* (Grove Press, US). A British writer's grand history of all the great migrations of the 1840s, with particular focus of the travails of the pioneers on the Oregon Trail and troubled expeditions like the Applegate Trail. Likely to become the definitive volume on this important subject.

Dorothy Nafus Morrison *Outpost: John McLoughlin & the Far Northwest* (Graphic Arts Center, o/p). An employee of Canada's Hudson's Bay Company, McLoughlin disobeyed orders and sheltered incoming American settlers reaching the Willamette Valley from the Oregon Trail (see p.542). This book tells the tale, over six hundred informative pages.

National Park Service *The Overland Migrations* (US Dept of the Interior, US). Short but useful guide to the trails that led pioneers west from the Missouri Valley in the middle of the nineteenth century.

Peter C. Newman *Caesars of the Wilderness* (Penguin, o/p). Highly acclaimed and readable three-volume account of the rise and fall of the Hudson's Bay Company.

Carlos Schwantes *The Pacific Northwest: An Interpretive History* (University of Nebraska, US). A leading Northwest historian explores every aspect of Oregon and Washington's history (along with Idaho's), from prehistoric to modern times, in a thoughtful and perceptive manner. Well illustrated and highly recommended.

Janet Thomas *The Battle in Seattle: The Story Behind and Beyond the WTO Demonstrations* (Fulcrum, US). Excellent opinionated analysis of the motives behind the 1999 protests and discussions of some of the key participants – including the author's.

Jean M. Ward and Elaine A. Maveety (eds.) *Pacific Northwest Women 1815–1925; Lives, Memories and Writings* (Oregon State University Press, US). Potent collection of writing from Northwest women of the era, touching on marriage, racism, women's rights, and family life, and highlighted with poems and photographs.

George Woodcock *A Social History of Canada*, aka *Canada and the Canadians* (Viking, o/p). Arguably Canada's finest historian, who wrote perceptively on Canadian literature and poetry. This erudite book explores the social development of Canada from imperial outpost to industrial powerhouse. Essential reading.

Biography

Anahareo *Grey Owl and I: A New Autobiography* (P. Davies, o/p). Written by the Iroquois wife of Grey Owl (see below), this book tells the story of their fight to save the beaver from extinction and of her shock at discovering that her husband was, in fact, an Englishman. Leavened by insights into the changing life of Canada's native peoples.

Walt Crowley *Rites of Passage* (University of Washington Press, US). Memoir of left-wing activism and counterculture in 1960s Seattle by the editor of an underground newspaper, who went on to become one of the city's most renowned journalists.

Lovat Dickson *Wilderness Man* (Pocket Books, UK); *Grey Owl: Man of the Wilderness* (MacMillan, o/p). The fascinating story of Englishman Archie Belaney, who became famous in Canada as his adopted persona, Grey Owl. Written by his English publisher and friend – one of many that did not discover the charade until after his death.

Paul Kane *Wanderings of an Artist among the Indians of North America* (Dover, UK & US). Kane, one of Canada's better-known landscape artists, spent three years traveling the Pacific Coast in the 1840s. His witty account of his journeys makes a delightful read.

James MacKay *Robert Service: Vagabond of Verse* (Traflagar Square, o/p). Not the first, but certainly the most substantial biography discussing this prominent Canadian poet's life and work, among which the *Songs of a Sourdough* collection of 1907 is perhaps the most memorable.

John E. Tuhy *Sam Hill, the Prince of Castle Nowhere* (Timber Press, o/p). Detailed biography of the life and times of the amazingly energetic and eccentric Sam Hill, the tycoon who built Washington's Maryhill Art Museum.

★ **Brent Walth** *Fire at Eden's Gate: Tom McCall and the Oregon Story* (Oregon Historical Society, US). Well-written biography of Oregon's most important politician, a liberal Republican whose favorite causes – beach protection, the bottle bill, anti-sprawl policies – would influence civic planners nationwide. Most famous for posting signs at the state border reading, "You are welcome to visit Oregon, but please don't stay."

Art, music, and architecture

Ginny Allen *Oregon Painters – The First 100 Years, 1859–1959* (Oregon Historical Society, US). Thoroughly researched and well-presented account of its subject, but given the mediocrity of most of the painters concerned, the tome is most useful as a reference guide.

Gideon Bosker and Lena Lencek *Frozen Music: A History of Portland Architecture* (Oregon Historical Society, US). Still the definitive saga of the city's structures and the social landscape that produced them, from Victorian terracotta wonders to modern steel boxes.

James Bush *Encyclopedia of Northwest Music* (Sasquatch, US). Biographical entries and discographies of numerous Northwest musicians of all styles, as well as essays on major regional musical movements.

Kurt Cobain *Journals* (Riverhead Press, US). Controversial reproduction of the diaries of the Nirvana frontman, complete with random thoughts, creative ideas, and various doodles, plus brickbats for more aged rockers like Pete Townsend and other targets.

William Goetzmann *Looking at the Land of Promise: Pioneer Images of the Pacific Northwest* (Washington State University Press, US). Beautiful book covering early artists' and then photographers' impressions of Washington and Oregon. The text is illuminating, though most of the painters are second-rate.

★ **Clark Humphrey** *Loser* (Feral House, US). The definitive account to date of Seattle rock, starting from its pre-rock origins in jazz/R&B, but focusing mainly on the punk and post-punk periods of the last twenty-five years.

Bart King *An Architectural Guidebook to Portland* (Gibbs Smith, US). Long-overdue guide to the city's finest buildings, along with some of its more unfortunate modern debacles.

Jeffrey Carl Ochsner and Dennis Alan Andersen *Distant Corner: Seattle Architects and the Legacy of H.H. Richardson* (University of Washington Press, US). Penetrating look at the architecture of Pioneer Square, and how a brief historical opportunity – rebuilding after a massive fire and the rise of a Romanesque Revivalist – could reshape an entire district in one architect's image, from an entire continent away.

Tina Oldknow *Pilchuck: A Glass School* (University of Washington Press, US). Illustrated history of the founding and evolution of the art institution, overseen by the imposing figure of Dale Chihuly, that has had the most profound effect on art in Washington State over the last 25 years.

Mary Willix *Jimi Hendrix: Voices from Home* (Creative Forces, US). Portraits of the major people and places that played a role in the creative development of the guitar wizard, when he lived in Seattle as a youth.

Sally B. Woodbridge and Roger Montgomery *A Guide to Architecture in Washington State* (University of Washington Press, US). Although published in 1980, still the most useful and handy guide to the region's architecture, which is presented in a manner that's more insightful and less gushing than more current guides.

Fiction and literature

Sherman Alexie *Indian Killer* (Warner). Acclaimed story of a Seattle serial murderer and the community reaction to the crimes. On a broader level it serves as a framework for reflections on interracial relations. One of several fine volumes by this native writer.

Lynda Barry *Cruddy* (Scribner, US). Affecting, sometimes shocking, tale of a teenage girl in early-1970s Seattle, told with copious dark humor and vivid descriptions, enhanced further by the author's own lurid, striking illustrations.

Richard Brautigan *Trout Fishing in America, The Pill Versus the Springhill Mine Disaster* and *In Watermelon Sugar* (Mariner/Houghton Mifflin). Collected work of this Tacoma-born writer and poet. Associated with the West Coast Beat writers of the 1950s and 1960s, his surreal fables at first seem simple and straightforward, but are overlaid with cultural references that question, and often attack, the social and political drift of the US.

Ernest Callenbach *Ecotopia* (Bantam, US). Highly influential fantasy of the Pacific Northwest breaking away from the US and establishing a progressive, ecologically friendly utopia. While not too realistic, the book has served as loose inspiration to countless local nature-lovers and environmental activists.

★ **Raymond Carver** *What We Talk About When We Talk About Love* (Harvill/Vintage); *Cathedral* (Panther/Vintage); *Fires* (Vintage, US); *Elephant* (Harvill, UK); *Where I'm Calling From* (Harvill/Vintage). Northwest-born and -raised writers whose short stories (many set locally) are superbly written, terse, and melancholic tales of everyday life and disintegrating family relationships. Best-known poetry volume is *A New Path to the Waterfall* (Atlantic Monthly Print, US).

Robin Cody *Ricochet River* (Blue Heron, US). Affecting coming-of-age novel set in a declining mill town in the Oregon Cascades, focusing on love and loss and the elusive search for community in the modern age.

Katherine Dunn *Geek Love* (Vintage UK & US). Bizarre, surprisingly influential cult novel set in Portland about a family of traveling circus geeks and sideshow freaks, narrated by a dwarf albino and (very) strangely compelling for its colorful characters and energetic, experimental style.

G.M. Ford *Black River* (Avon/Eos). Gripping thriller about Seattle-based reporter and crime novelist Frank Corso, who becomes immersed in tracking down an evasive and thoroughly dangerous mobster in the Emerald City.

David Guterson *Snow Falling on Cedars* (Bloomsbury/Vintage). Highly regarded, but long-winded and repetitive, tale of life and death on a rural Puget Sound island. The central plot deals with a Japanese-American fisherman accused of murder. Many people swear by the book – as they do by the same author's moody short stories, *Country Ahead of Us, the Country Behind* (Bloomsbury/Vintage).

★ **Ken Kesey** *Sometimes a Great Notion* (Penguin, US). A stark evocation of Oregon's declining timber industry provides the background for a tale of psychological complexity. More famous for his *One Flew Over the Cuckoo's Nest* (Picador/Penguin), where a psychiatric ward serves as a metaphor for a fascistic US culture, though his *Demon Box* (Penguin, US), is an equally compelling selection of quasi-autobiographical short stories.

Craig Lesley *Winterkill* (Picador, US). Nez Percé drifter and failed rodeo star – Danny Kachiak – attempts to reconnect with his son after the death of his wife. The Portland writer returned to similar themes – and the same protagonist – five years later in *River Song* (Picador, US), Another novel, *The*

Sky Fisherman (Picador, US), is set in small-town Oregon and deals with the coming of age of a white youngster in a bigoted society.

Glen A. Love (ed.) *The World Begins Here: An Anthology of Oregon Fiction* (Oregon State University Press, US). No lightweights here (Ken Kesey, Raymond Carver, and Ursula K. Le Guin), but it's the other writers (Molly Gloss, Juan Armando Epple) that bring home the real nature of locality and roots.

Malcolm Lowry *Hear Us O Lord from Heaven thy Dwelling Place* (Penguin, UK). A difficult read to say the least: a fragmentary novella that among other things describes a disturbing sojourn on Canada's wild Pacific Coast. The author spent almost half his writing life (1939–54) in the log cabins and beach houses he built around Vancouver.

Grey Owl *The Adventures of Sajo and the Beaver People* (Stoddart, UK), *Tales of an Empty Cabin* (Key Porter, UK & US). First published in the 1930s, these books romantically describe life in the wilds of Canada at a time when exploitation was changing the land forever. *Sajo* is also published with *Pilgrims of the Wild* and *Men of the Last Frontier* in the recent anthology *Grey Owl: Three Complete and Unabridged Canadian Classics* (Firefly, US).

Chuck Palahniuk Increasingly Portland's signature author, with a huge international cult following. His debut novel *Fight Club* (Vintage/Henry Holt) concerns bare-knuckle, illicit fighting as a metaphor for social and cultural rot; *Invisible Monsters* (Vintage/Norton) deals with a model whose looks are destroyed in a car accident; and the most recent volume, *Diary* (Doubleday, US), is a surreal horror tale set on an island resort.

Robert Service *The Best of Robert Service* (A & C Black/Perigee). Victorian ballads of pioneer and gold-rush life that have a certain charm and capture the essence of the gold-rush era.

Lee Williams *After Nirvana* (Quill, US). Dark portrait of the lives of four homeless street kids living in the Seattle demimonde, where drugs and prostitution are commonplace and a morbid humor often creeps into the grimmest predicaments.

Tobias Wolff *This Boy's Life* (Harper Perennial, US). Set in 1950s Washington State, a mournful, forceful memoir relates a painful, brutal upbringing. A sharp, self-deprecating humor infuses the book as it does Wolff's *In Pharaoh's Army* (Picador/Vintage), culled from his Vietnam War experiences.

Rough Guides

advertiser

THE ROUGH GUIDE TO THE MUSIC OF EGYPT
ypt
ROUGH GUIDE
Cairo to Nubia: the source of Arabic music
THE ROUGH GUIDE TO VENEZUELA
Venezuela
MUSIC ROUGH GUIDE
salsa, gaita, parranda: a kaleidoscope of sounds
THE ROUGH GUIDE TO BRAZILIAN ELECTRONICA
Brazilian Electronica
MUSIC ROUGH GUIDE
evolution & revolution: future sounds of Brazil
THE ROUGH GUIDE TO SALSA COLOMBIA
lsa Colombia
ROUGH GUIDE
THE ROUGH GUIDE TO BOLLYWOOD LEGENDS: ASHA BHOSLE
Asha Bhosle
MUSIC ROUGH GUIDE
ORIGINAL RECORDINGS
Bollywood diva: action, suspense & romance
THE ROUGH GUIDE TO CHICAGO BLUES
Chicago Blues
MUSIC ROUGH GUIDE
mojo working: electric blues in the city

small print and

Index

A Rough Guide to Rough Guides

In the summer of 1981, Mark Ellingham, a recent graduate from Bristol University, was traveling round Greece and couldn't find a guidebook that really met his needs. On the one hand there were the student guides, insistent on saving every last cent, and on the other the heavyweight cultural tomes whose authors seemed to have spent more time in a research library than lounging away the afternoon at a taverna or on the beach.

In a bid to avoid getting a job, Mark and a small group of writers set about creating their own guidebook. It was a guide to Greece that aimed to combine a journalistic approach to description with a thoroughly practical approach to travelers' needs – a guide that would incorporate culture, history, and contemporary insights with a critical edge, together with up-to-date, value-for-money listings. Back in London, Mark and the team finished their Rough Guide, as they called it, and talked Routledge into publishing the book.

That first *Rough Guide to Greece*, published in 1982, was a student scheme that became a publishing phenomenon. The immediate success of the book – with numerous reprints and a Thomas Cook prize shortlisting – spawned a series that rapidly covered dozens of destinations. Rough Guides had a ready market among low-budget backpackers, but soon also acquired a much broader and older readership that relished Rough Guides' wit and inquisitiveness as much as their enthusiastic, critical approach. Everyone wants value for money, but not at any price.

Rough Guides soon began supplementing the "rougher" information about hostels and low-budget listings with the kind of detail on restaurants and quality hotels that independent-minded visitors on any budget might expect, whether on business in New York or trekking in Thailand.

These days the guides – distributed worldwide by the Penguin group – offer recommendations from shoestring to luxury and cover more than 200 destinations around the globe, including almost every country in the Americas and Europe, more than half of Africa, and most of Asia and Australasia. Our ever-growing team of authors and photographers is spread all over the world, particularly in Europe, the USA, and Australia.

In 1994, we published the *Rough Guide to World Music* and *Rough Guide to Classical Music*; and a year later the *Rough Guide to the Internet*. All three books have become benchmark titles in their fields – which encouraged us to expand into other areas of publishing, mainly around popular culture. Rough Guides now publishes:

- Travel guides to more than 200 worldwide destinations
- Dictionary phrasebooks for 22 major languages
- History guides ranging from Ireland to Islam
- Maps printed on rip-proof and waterproof Polyart™ paper
- Music guides running the gamut from Opera to Elvis
- Restaurant guides to London, New York, and San Francisco
- Reference books on topics as diverse as the Weather and Shakespeare
- Sports guides from Formula 1 to Man Utd
- Pop culture books from *Lord of the Rings* to Cult TV
- World Music CDs in association with World Music Network

Visit **www.roughguides.com** to see our latest publications.

Rough Guide credits

Editor: Steven Horak
Layout: Umesh Aggarwal
Cartography: Katie Lloyd-Jones and Ed Wright
Picture research: Jj Luck
Proofreader: Karen Parker
Editorial: **London** Martin Dunford, Kate Berens, Helena Smith, Claire Saunders, Geoff Howard, Ruth Blackmore, Gavin Thomas, Polly Thomas, Richard Lim, Lucy Ratcliffe, Clifton Wilkinson, Alison Murchie, Fran Sandham, Sally Schafer, Alexander Mark Rogers, Karoline Densley, Andy Turner, Ella O'Donnell, Keith Drew, Andrew Lockett, Joe Staines, Duncan Clark, Peter Buckley, Matthew Milton; **New York** Andrew Rosenberg, Richard Koss, Yuki Takagaki, Hunter Slaton, Chris Barsanti, Thomas Kohnstamm, Steven Horak
Design & Layout: **London** Dan May, Diana Jarvis; **Delhi** Madhulita Mohapatra, Umesh Aggarwal, Ajay Verma
Production: Julia Bovis, John McKay, Sophie Hewat
Cartography: **London** Maxine Repath, Ed Wright, Katie Lloyd-Jones, Miles Irving; **Delhi** Manish Chandra, Rajesh Chhibber, Jai Prakesh Mishra, Ashutosh Bharti, Rajesh Mishra, Animesh Pathak
Cover art direction: Louise Boulton
Picture research: Mark Thomas, Jj Luck
Online: **New York** Jennifer Gold, Cree Lawson, Suzanne Welles, Benjamin Ross; **Delhi** Manik Chauhan, Amarjyoti Dutta, Narender Kumar
Marketing & Publicity: **London** Richard Trillo, Niki Smith, David Wearn, Chloë Roberts, Demelza Dallow, Kristina Pentland; **New York** Geoff Colquitt, David Wechsler, Megan Kennedy
Finance: Gary Singh
Manager India: Punita Singh
Series editor: Mark Ellingham
PA to Managing Director: Julie Sanderson
Managing Director: Kevin Fitzgerald

Publishing information

This fourth edition published June 2004 by
Rough Guides Ltd,
80 Strand, London WC2R 0RL
4th Floor, 345 Hudson St,
New York, NY 10014, USA
Distributed by the Penguin Group
Penguin Books Ltd,
80 Strand, London WC2R 0RL
Penguin Putnam, Inc.
375 Hudson Street, NY 10014, USA
Penguin Books Australia Ltd,
487 Maroondah Highway, PO Box 257,
Ringwood, Victoria 3134, Australia
Penguin Books Canada Ltd,
10 Alcorn Avenue, Toronto, Ontario,
Canada M4V 1E4
Penguin Books (NZ) Ltd,
182–190 Wairau Road, Auckland 10,
New Zealand
Typeset in Bembo and Helvetica to an original design by Henry Iles.

Printed in Italy by LegoPrint S.p.A

592pp includes index

A catalogue record for this book is available from the British Library

ISBN 1-84353-285-9

1 3 5 7 9 8 6 4 2

Help us update

We've gone to a lot of effort to ensure that the fifth edition of **The Rough Guide to the Pacific Northwest** is accurate and up to date. However, things change – places get "discovered", opening hours are notoriously fickle, restaurants and rooms raise prices or lower standards. If you feel we've got it wrong or left something out, we'd like to know, and if you can remember the address, the price, the time, the phone number, so much the better.

We'll credit all contributions, and send a copy of the next edition (or any other Rough Guide if you prefer) for the best letters. Everyone who writes to us and isn't already a subscriber will receive a copy of our full-color, thrice-yearly newsletter. Please mark letters: "**Rough Guide to the Pacific Northwest Update**" and send to: Rough Guides, 80 Strand, London WC2R 0RL, or Rough Guides, 4th Floor, 345 Hudson St, New York, NY 10014. Or send an email to **mail@roughguides.com**

Have your questions answered and tell others about your trip at **www.roughguides.atinfopop.com**

Acknowledgments

JD would like to thank Brenna, Elizabeth, and associates in Washington including Art, Charlotte, Charles, Mary, Jose, Lettie, Michael, and David, and all friends, contacts, and assorted characters in Oregon. JD would also like to thank his steadfast editor Steve, who provided a generous amount of verve, diligence, and resolve in guiding this project from beginning to end, adding both style and panache.

Tim would like to thank his editor, Steve; Yuki Takagaki; Lucy Hyslop; James and Vicky Ballentyne; Air Canada; Charlotte Fraser and Fairmont Hotels; Claire Griffin and Four Seasons hotels; and Kathleen Eccles.

The editor would like to thank JD and Tim for their many talents and tireless efforts; Umesh Aggarwal for his patient typesetting; Jj Luck for her spirited picture research; Karen Parker for her assiduous proofreading; Katie Lloyd-Jones and Ed Wright for their mapmaking ingenuity; Richard Koss for his eminently skillful managing; and Andrew Rosenberg for his overall guidance.

Readers' letters

Thanks to all the readers who took the trouble to write in with their comments and suggestions (and apologies to anyone whose name we've misspelt or omitted):

Paul Brians, Stephanie Caldwell, Paula Elliot, Chris Gleeson, John Jackson, Beth Anne Klonoski, Andreas Lober, Carolyn McIntyre, Nathan Reynolds, Darian Weir, Dawn Windley

Photo credits

Cover credits

main front Ecola State Park, Oregon ©Corbis
small front top picture Seattle ©Robert Harding
small front lower picture Mount Hood ©Robert Harding
back top picture Crater Lake National Park ©Robert Harding
back lower picture Kentucky Falls ©Robert Harding

Introduction

Seaplane ©Terry Whitakker/Tavel Ink
Cape Blanco ©Terry W. Eggers/CORBIS
Mt Hood - volcano ©Master File
Moss growing on Hemlock, Vancouver Island ©David Muench/CORBIS
Hood River ©Master File
Clock Tower in Portland ©ZEFA
Ferry leaving Seattle Waterfront ©Joel W. Rogers/CORBIS
John Day Fossil Beds ©Robert Harding
North Cascades Highway ©Michael T. Sedam/CORBIS

Things not to miss

01 Oregon Beaches ©Robert Harding
02 Elk in Olympic National Park ©Kennan Ward/CORBIS
03 Multnomah Falls ©Master File
04 Mount St Helens ©Roger Ressmeyer/CORBIS
05 Butchart Gardens ©Courtesy of The Butchart Gardens Ltd., Victoria,BC, Canada
06 Crater Lake ©Robert Harding
07 Column Millers Chapel, Oregon Caves ©National Park Service Photo
08 Seafood Presentation, Seattle ©Dave Bartruff/CORBIS
09 Wonderland Trail ©Charles Mauzy/CORBIS
10 View from Mount Constitution ©David Muench/CORBIS
11 Rose Festival ©Portland Rose Festival Association
12 Kayaker watching pod of Orcas ©Joel W. Rogers/CORBIS
13 Historic Columbia River Gorge Highway ©Robert Harding
14 Bumbershoot Festival ©Paul A. Souders/CORBIS
15 Snoqualmie Falls ©1999 Jim Heuster/EcoStock
16 "The Raven and the First Men" by Bill Reid (Haida), 1980 Courtesy Museum of Anthropology, Vancouver ©Bill McLennan
17 Lake Chelan ©Pat O'Hara/CORBIS
18 Pioneer Square ©2003 Michael Smith Lewis/EcoStock
19 Pike Place Market ©ALAMY
20 Windsurfer ©Warren Morgan/CORBIS
21 Whistler ©Master File
22 Pink Mansion, Port Townsend ©Pat O'Hara/CORBIS
23 Stanley Park ©Master File
24 Vineyard in Willamette Valley ©Janis Miglavs/CORBIS
25 Shakespeare Festival ©David Cooper
26 Fremont Public Art ©ALAMY
27 Cattle Walking on Road ©Carol Cohen/CORBIS
28 Doorway in Underground Seattle ©Kelly-Mooney Photography/CORBIS

Black and white photos

Pioneer Square ©Dave G. Houser/CORBIS (p.74)
Forest Park ©ALAMY (p.94)
Crown Point Vista House ©Michael T. Sedam/CORBIS (p.120)
Pistol River State Park ©Royalty-Free/CORBIS (p.140)
Oregon Dunes National Recreation Area ©CORBIS (p.151)
Covered Bridge ©Philip James Corwin/CORBIS (p.182)
Obsidian, Newberry Volcano National Monument ©Ric Ergenbright/CORBIS (p.214)
Snowy Forest Below Broken Top Mountain ©Warren Morgan/CORBIS (p.234)
Museum of Flight, gallery panorama ©Museum of Flight (p.246)
The Fremont Troll ©Morton Beebe/CORBIS (p.276)
Hot Shop Cone at the Museum of Glass ©John and Lisa Merrill/CORBIS (p.308)
Hurricane Ridge ©Master File (p.346)
Cape Disappointment with Lighthouse ©Richard A. Cooke/CORBIS (p.371)
Windy Ridge ©Wolfgang Kaehler/CORBIS (p.374)
Snoqualmie Falls ©Mike Zens/CORBIS (p.390)
Grouse Mountain Skyride ©Grouse Mountain Resorts Ltd (p.408)
Totem Poles, Stanley Park © Nick Hanmer (p.434)
Victoria Inner Harbour ©William Gray/Tavel Ink (p.472)
West Coast Trail, Vancouver Island © Noel Hendrickson/Masterfile www.masterfile.com (p.554)

Index

Map entries are in **color**.

I

INDEX

N

O

P

T

U

V

W

Y

Map symbols

Maps are listed in the full index using colored text.

	International boundary		Lighthouse
	Province/territory border		Ruins
	Chapter boundary		Ski area
5	Interstate		Golf course
5	US highway		Gardens
15	Canadian autoroute		Accommodation
1	Trans-Canada highway		Restaurant
5	Province/state highway		Campsite
	Pedestrianized street		Information office
	Unpaved road		Post office
	Path/track		Statue
	Railway		Hospital
	Tram		Bus stop
	Ferry route		Airport
	Waterway		Vancouver SkyTrain
	Place of interest		Museum
	Mountains		Building
	Peak		Church
	Waterfall		Stadium
	Spring		Park
	Gorge		Cemetery
	Cave		Forest
	Castle/fort		Glacier
	Viewpoint		

I

INDEX | Map symbols